Hawaii

a Lonely Planet travel survival kit

Glenda Bendure
Ned Friary

Hawaii

3rd edition

Published by
Lonely Planet Publications
Head Office: PO Box 617, Hawthorn, Vic 3122, Australia
Branches: 155 Filbert St, Suite 251, Oakland, CA 94607, USA
                10 Barley Mow Passage, Chiswick, London W4 4PH, UK
                71 bis rue du Cardinal Lemoine, 75005 Paris, France

Printed by
Colorcraft Ltd, Hong Kong

Photographs by
All photos by Ned Friary & Glenda Bendure except:
Michael Clark (MC)
Erin Reid (ER)
David Russ (DR)

Front cover: Coconut palms at sunset, Waikiki, Oahu (Ned Friary)

First Published
August 1990

This Edition
May 1995

National Library of Australia Cataloguing in Publication Data

Bendure, Glenda
    Hawaii – a travel survival kit

    3rd ed.
    Includes index.
    ISBN 0 86442 262 8.

    1. Hawaii – Guidebooks. I. Friary, Ned. II. Title.
    (Series: Lonely Planet travel survival kit).

919.6904

text & maps © Lonely Planet 1995
photos © photographers as indicated 1995

Glenda Bendure & Ned Friary

Glenda grew up in California's Mojave Desert and first traveled overseas as a high school AFS exchange student to India.

Ned grew up near Boston, studied Social Thought & Political Economy at the University of Massachusetts in Amherst and upon graduating headed west.

They met in Santa Cruz, California, where Glenda was completing her university studies. In 1978, with Lonely Planet's first book *Across Asia on the Cheap* in hand, they took the overland trail from Europe to Nepal. The next six years were spent exploring Asia and the Pacific, with a home base in Japan where Ned taught English and Glenda edited a monthly magazine.

The first of many extended trips to Hawaii was in 1980, when they went straight from Osaka to the green lushness of Kauai, a sight so soothing for concrete-weary eyes that a two-week vacation turned into a four-month sojourn.

Ned and Glenda have a particular fondness for islands and tropical climates. They are also the authors of Lonely Planet's *Micronesia – a travel survival kit* and *Eastern Caribbean – a travel survival kit* and wrote the Norway and Denmark chapters of LP's *Scandinavian & Baltic Europe on a Shoestring*.

They now live on Cape Cod in Massachusetts – at least when they're not on the road.

From the Authors

Many thanks to the people who helped us on this project: State Parks archaeologist Martha Yent; Linda Delaney from the Office of Hawaiian Affairs; Christina Meller, Na Ala Hele Program Manager; Bill Puleloa, aquatic biologist for the Department of Land & Natural Resources; Daniel Kawaiaea, park ranger at Puukohola Heiau National Historic Site; Jean Greenwell of the Kona Historical Society; Jon Giffin of the Division of Forestry & Wildlife; Leon Bruno of the Lyman Museum in Hilo; Roy Damron of the Kona Reefers Dive Club; John P Lockwood, geologist at Hawaiian Volcano Observatory; and to the Hawaii Visitors Bureau.

Thanks also to those friends and travelers who have shared insights and experiences with us along the way. A special acknowledgment to Richard Heinisch, Gareth Kernaghan, Glenn Thering and Ted Brattstrom, who have joined us in exploring many of Hawaii's more remote corners and back trails.

From the Publisher

This third edition of *Hawaii – a travel survival kit* was edited and proofread at the Lonely Planet US office by Carolyn Hubbard, Kim Haglund, Ellen Towell and Jeff Campbell. Carolyn also compiled the index. Scott Summers, Hugh D'Andrade, Alex Guilbert, Julie Bilski, Patti Keelin and Hayden Foell redesigned and corrected the maps. Richard Wilson and Hugh were responsible for the layout and design of the color sections. Hugh and Alex also did illustrations and cover design. David Russ provided editorial guidance.

Thanks also to those travelers who wrote in with information:

Birgit Ahrens (D), Tera & Joseph Antaree (USA), Gabriele Babik (D), Ann Babson (USA), John Barbier, Caroline Barnes (USA), Melika Barnes (UK), Dinah Bear (USA), Robert Butterfield (USA), Carolyn Camburn (USA), Louise Castle (J), Barrie Chaffell (Aus), A Nota & M Clampin (USA), Garth & Norma Cooper (USA), Nancy Cornwall (USA), Kevin Curry, Jan de Weerd (NL), Ellen Dudley (USA), Mike & Annette Endres (USA), Robin Gaffney (USA), Barbara Geissler (USA), Maureen Griffin (J), Margrit & Olivier Guye (CH), Kirby Guyer (USA), Bernard Halliwell (USA), Chuck & Margie Heberle (USA), Marie Hermanson (USA), David Hill (UK), Hal & Dorsey Holappa (USA), Susan Horie, Marilyn Jarvis (Aus), Santija Jonas (USA), Maxine Kamin (USA), Hiro Kelley, Allan Kempe (USA), Marjorie Ketcher, L M Kirsch (D), Elisabeth Kotzinger (A), Nathan Landau (USA), Mary Catherine Lombard (USA), Steve & Lynda Loupe (USA), Claudine Maison (USA), Michael McCoy (USA), Wolfgang Minas (CH), Andrew Moncrieff (J), Barbara Moore-Link (USA), G & J Morse (USA), Luly Nakanishi (USA), Jan Newhouse (USA), Malin Nygren (S), Gavin O'Priscoll (UK), Elke Obermeier (D), David Otake, Vikki Patterson (USA), Frank Pietronigro (USA), Sally Proctor (USA), Peter Rastall (USA), Marvin Reich (USA), Sally Richards (USA), Sally Ringdahl (USA), Dr Gwyn Roberts (UK), Sandra Anna Rocci (I), Daryl Rotta (USA), Carsten Rudolph (D), Rachel Sheffield, Joseph Sidebottom (USA), Darril Smith (Aus), Rosemary Smith (USA), Gail Smith (USA), Chris Solari, Cindy Stainton, Rick & Regina Steinkamp (USA), Leon Strauss (Aus), Alex & Michael Tboring (D), Nick Thow (UK), Michael Tuggle (USA), Ken White (Aus), Maria Wilson (USA), Patrick Winston, Derrick & Pip Woodcock (C)

A – Austria, Aus – Australia, C – Canada, CH – Switzerland, D – Germany, F – France, I – Italy, J – Japan, NL – Netherlands, S – Sweden, UK – United Kingdom, USA – United States of America

Warning & Request

Things change – prices go up, schedules change, good places go bad and bad places go bankrupt – nothing stays the same. So if you find things better or worse, recently opened or now closed, please write and tell us and help make the next edition better.

Your letters will be used to help update future editions and, where possible, important changes will be included in a Stop Press section in reprints.

We greatly appreciate all information that is sent to us by travelers. Back at Lonely Planet we employ a hard-working readers' letters team to sort through the many letters we receive. The best ones will be rewarded with a free copy of the next edition or another Lonely Planet guide if you prefer. We give away lots of books, but, unfortunately, not every letter or postcard receives one.

Contents

HAWAII – THE BIG ISLAND 227

MAUI 353

Map Legend

BOUNDARIES

───────── International Boundary
─·─·─·─·─ Internal Boundary

ROUTES

━━━━━━ Freeway
───────── Major Road
───────── Paved Road
─ ─ ─ ─ ─ Unpaved Road or Track
═════════ Major City Street
═════════ City Street
····+───+···· Railway, Railway Station
················ Foot Trail
───────── Underground Railway
─ ─ ─ ─ ─ Ferry Route

AREA FEATURES

Park
National Park
Built-Up Area
Pedestrian Mall
Beach or Desert
Ancient or City Wall

HYDROGRAPHIC FEATURES

Coastline
River, Creek
Intermittent River
Lake
Swamp
Rapids, Waterfalls

SYMBOLS

✪ NATIONAL CAPITAL
◉ State Capital
░ MAJOR CITY
● City
● Town

■ Hotel, B&B (Place to Stay)
▼ Restaurant (Place to Eat)
🍺 Pub, Bar (Place to Drink)

🏊 Swimming Pool
🏛 Museum
🍷 Winery or Vineyard
🏛 Stately Home
⌂ Observatory
⌒ Cave

✿ Gardens
🐘 Zoo
🌲 Picnic Site
🗿 Monument
■ Tomb
⌂ Hut or Chalet

⊕ Hospital
✈ Airport
✉ Post Office
❶ Tourist Information
◒ Bus Station/Terminal
← One Way Street
✿ Shopping Center
⛺ RV Park
🏌 Golf Course

★ Police Station
✛ Airfield
☎ Telephone
❸ Bank
🅿 Parking
(H1) (86) (99) Route Number
🅖 Gas Station
▲ Campground
🏠 Youth Hostel

▲ Mountain or Hill
🏮 Lighthouse
)(Pass
⌐ Cliff or Escarpment
🐟 Fishing
✝ Church
🗿 Mosque
⊥ Buddhist Temple
∴ Archaeological Site, Ruins, Heiaus

✳ Lookout
✕ Shipwreck
⚲ Spring
⟹ Tunnel
◩ Dive Site/Shop
✝ Cathedral
✿ Synagogue
⚖ Hindu Temple

Note: not all symbols displayed above appear in this book

Introduction

Hawaii's natural beauty is extraordinarily grand. Mark Twain fittingly called Hawaii 'the loveliest fleet of islands that lies anchored in any ocean'. Volcanic in origin, the Hawaiian Islands are high and rugged, lushly green and cut by spectacular gorges and valleys. The beaches are beautiful, ranging from bleached white to jet black. The terrain is amazingly varied, climbing from lowland deserts to alpine mountaintops, with everything from barren lava flows to tropical rainforest found in between.

Hawaii is the world's most isolated archipelago, 2500 miles from the nearest land mass. Its isolation is so great that of the thousands of species of flora & fauna that have evolved here, over 90% exist nowhere else on earth.

Geologically, it's also singularly unique. Hawaii has the world's most active volcano (Kilauea), its largest dormant volcano (Haleakala), its highest mountain when measured from the sea floor (Mauna Kea) and its highest sea cliffs (on Molokai).

As one of the world's leading visitor destinations, Hawaii does have the expected mass tourism, high-rise hotels and crowded beaches. But that's only one side of it.

You can also find scores of untouristed areas and secluded beaches to explore, while your accommodation options include upcountry lodges, isolated resorts, B&B inns and oceanside cottages. And the best the islands have to offer is still free for hikers and backcountry campers.

The islands have some of the world's top

surfing and windsurfing, as well as excellent conditions for snorkeling, swimming, diving, bodysurfing and most other water sports.

Hawaii's climate is unusually pleasant for the tropics, as near-constant trade winds prevail throughout the year. Much of the time the rain falls as short daytime showers that are accompanied by rainbows.

Hawaii's six main islands all have lovely beaches and splendid scenery. Their leeward coasts are sunny, dry and desert-like, with white sands and turquoise waters. The mountainous windward sides have tropical jungles, cascading waterfalls and pounding surf. The uplands are cool and green, with rolling pastures, small farms and ranches.

Oahu is the most crowded and developed of the islands, with Waikiki still providing half the tourist accommodations in Hawaii. Honolulu has all the pluses and minuses of urban life, from good museums and lively nightlife to congested traffic. It has wonderful restaurants, with both inexpensive ethnic foods and gourmet cuisines. Oahu also has the best surf.

Maui is the second largest and second most developed of the islands, although it has plenty of unspoiled places well off the beaten path. The scenic coastal drive to Hana and the sunrise at Haleakala are two of its highlights. Maui is also the best island for watching humpback whales.

The Big Island has two things the others don't: snow and erupting volcanoes. There's room to move, with niches for cowboys, astronomers and traditional fishing villages, as well as alternative communities settling in on the side of lava flows.

Kauai has Hawaii's greenest scenery, a deeply cut canyon resembling a mini-Grand Canyon and the famous razorback cliffs of the Na Pali Coast.

Molokai, the most Hawaiian of the islands, is charmingly rural and slow-paced. Lanai, the smallest island, is undergoing a jolting transition from an economy based on pineapple growing to a new identity as a luxury resort destination.

Hawaii is ethnically diverse with an appealing collage of East, West and Pacific peoples and cultures. While less than 1% of the population is pure Hawaiian, almost a quarter of the islanders boast some Hawaiian ancestry and there's a resurgence of interest in traditional Hawaiian culture among islanders of all races.

Facts about Hawaii

HISTORY

Hawaii is the northern point of the huge triangle of Pacific Ocean islands known as Polynesia. The other two points of the triangle are Easter Island to the southeast and New Zealand to the southwest.

The original settlers of Polynesia, which means 'many islands', apparently followed a long migratory path through Southeast Asia, down through Indonesia and across Melanesia, before settling the Polynesian islands of Tonga and Samoa in about 1000 BC. Over the next 1500 years they migrated to the more distant islands of Polynesia, with Hawaii being one of the last areas settled.

Archaeological evidence indicates the first Polynesians arrived in Hawaii from the Marquesas between 500 and 700 AD.

Among the links are ancient stone statues found on Hawaii's now uninhabited Necker Island which have striking similarities to statues found on the Marquesas.

When the first wave of Tahitians arrived in Hawaii in about 1000 AD they apparently conquered and subjugated the Marquesans, forcing them to build their temples, irrigation ditches and fishponds.

Hawaiian legends of a tribe of little people called *menehune* may well refer to the Marquesans. Indeed, the word 'menehune' is very similar to the Tahitian word for 'outcast'.

Ancient Hawaii

The earliest Hawaiians had simple animistic beliefs. Good fishing, a safe journey and a healthy child were all the result of

Kauai
Princeville
Lihue

Niihau

Oahu
Honolulu

Molokai
Kaunakakai
Kahului

Lanai
Lanai City
Maui

Kahoolawe

PACIFIC
OCEAN

PACIFIC
OCEAN

Hawaii
The Big Island

Kailua-Kona
Hilo

Main Hawaiian Islands

0   150   300 km
0   100   200 miles

being in tune with the spirits of nature. Their offerings to the gods consisted of prayers and a share of the harvest.

Around the 12th century, in a later wave of migration, a powerful Tahitian *kahuna* (priest), Paao, arrived on the Big Island. Convinced that the Hawaiians were too lax in their worship, Paao introduced the offering of human sacrifice to the gods and built the first *luakini heiau,* a type of temple where these sacrifices took place. He also established the *kapu* system of taboos which strictly regulated all social interaction.

The kapus forbade commoners from eating the same food or even walking the same ground as the *alii,* or royalty. A commoner who crossed the shadow of a king could be put to death. Kapus prohibited all women from eating coconuts, bananas, pork and certain varieties of fish.

Paao decided that Hawaii's blueblood was too diluted and summoned the chief Pili from Kahiki (Tahiti) to establish a new royal lineage. With Pili as chief and Paao as high priest, a new ruling house was formed. Their dynasty was to last 700 years.

King Kamehameha the Great, like all the Big Island chiefs, traced his lineage to Pili. Likewise, Kamehameha's *kahuna nui* (high priest) descended from Paao.

Religion In the old Hawaiian religion there were four main gods: Ku, Lono, Kane and Kanaloa.

Ku was the ancestor god for all generations of humankind, past, present and future. He presided over all male gods while his wife, *Hina,* took charge of the females. When the sun rose in the morning, it was said to be Ku; when it set in the evening it was Hina. Like Yin and Yang, they were responsible for heaven and earth.

Ku had many manifestations, one as the benevolent god of fishing, *Ku-ula* (Ku of the abundant seas), and others as the god of forests and farming. People prayed to Ku when the harvest was scarce. At a time of drought or other such disaster, a temple would be built to appease Ku.

One of the most fearful of Ku's manifes-

tations was *Kukailimoku* (Ku, the snatcher of land), the war god that Kamehameha the Great worshipped. The temples built for the worship of Kukailimoku were offered sacrifices not only of food, pigs and chickens but also human beings.

Lono was the god in charge of the elements that brought rain and an abundant harvest. He was also the god of fertility and peace.

Kane created the first man out of the dust of the earth and breathed life into him (the Hawaiian word for man is *kane),* and it was from Kane that the Hawaiian chiefs were said to have descended.

Ku, Lono and Kane together created the earth, the moon, the stars and the ocean.

Kanaloa, the fourth major god, was often pitted in struggles against the other three gods. When heaven and earth separated it was Kanaloa who was placed in charge of the spirits on earth. Forbidden from drinking *kava,* these spirits revolted and along with Kanaloa were driven to the underworld where Kanaloa became the ruler of the dead.

Below the four main gods, there were 40 lesser gods. The best known of them was *Pele,* goddess of volcanoes. Her sister *Laka* was goddess of the hula, and another sister, *Poliahu,* was the goddess of snow.

The Hawaiians had gods for all occupations and natural phenomena. There was a god for the tapa maker and a god for the canoe builder, shark gods and mountain gods.

Heiaus The temples erected in ancient Hawaii, called *heiau,* were built in two basic styles, both of which were constructed of lava rock. One was a simple rectangular enclosure of stone walls built directly on the ground. The other was a more substantial structure built of rocks piled high to form raised terraced platforms. (The remains of both types can still be found throughout the islands today.)

Inside the heiaus were prayer towers, taboo houses and drum houses. These structures were made of ohia wood, thatched with pili grass and tied with cord from the native olona shrub. Tikis, or god images, called *kii*, were carved of wood and placed around the prayer towers.

Heiaus were most commonly dedicated to Lono, the god of harvest, or Ku, the god of war. The heiaus built in honor of Ku were called luakini heiau and were the only ones where human sacrifices took place.

Petroglyphs
The ancient Hawaiians had no written history, although they did cut petroglyphs into smooth lava rock. Many of these carved pictures are stylized stick figures depicting warriors with spears, barking dogs, birds, canoes and other decipherable images. Some are linear marks which may have been made to record important events, or represent calendars or genealogical charts.

The meanings and purposes behind Hawaiian petroglyphs are not well understood. Some may have been intentionally cryptic, while others may just be random graffiti or the carvings of a budding artist.

Most petroglyphs are found along ancient footpaths and may have been clustered at sites thought to have mana.

The Big Island has the greatest concentration of petroglyphs, with several large fields just a few minutes' walk from the road. ■

Heiaus were built in auspicious sites, often perched on cliffs above the coast or in other places thought to have *mana*, or 'spiritual power'. A heiau's significance lay not in the structure itself but focused on the mana of the site. When a heiau's mana was gone, it was abandoned.

The Makahiki

According to legend, the god Lono rode a rainbow down from the heavens to a breadfruit grove above Hiilawe Falls in Waipio Valley where, in a paradise-like setting, he found Kaikilani, a beautiful princess. They fell in love, married and moved across the island to Kealakekua Bay.

When Lono discovered that a chief was lusting after Kaikilani, he became enraged and beat Kaikilani who, as she lay dying, professed her faithful love for Lono alone. In his grief, Lono traveled restlessly around the island challenging every man he met to a wrestling match and other competitions.

After four months, a still disheartened Lono set sail on a canoe with a tall mast hung with sails made of finely woven Niihau mats. The huge canoe was laden with so much food that it took 40 men to carry it down to Kealakekua Bay. Lono promised to return one day on a floating island covered with trees and full of chickens and pigs.

The Hawaiians remembered Lono each year with a harvest festival, called the *makahiki*, which lasted from October to February. Numerous inter-island competitions similar to the Olympics were held, including outrigger canoe races, fishing and surfing tournaments, foot races, wrestling matches and *holua* (sled) racing. Even during wartime, fighting would be suspended for the four months of the makahiki, so that the games and festivities dedicated to Lono could proceed.

Captain Cook

The Hawaiian Islands were the last of the Polynesian islands to be 'discovered' by the West. Early European explorers who entered the Pacific around the tips of either

Hawaiian Sports

Holua racing was ancient Hawaii's most exciting spectator sport. Racers would ride prone on narrow wooden sleds, racing at high speed down steep hills along furrows which had been covered with pili grass or ti leaves to make the surface smooth. Many of the holua slide paths were a mile or two long.

Hawaiians were heavy betters and often wagered on the holua races, as well as on foot races, surfing competitions and many other sports.

Surfing is a Hawaiian creation that was as popular in old Hawaii as it is today. When the waves were up, everyone was out. There were royal surfing grounds and spots for commoners as well. Boards used by commoners were made of breadfruit or *koa* wood and were about six feet long. Only the alii were free to use the long *olo* boards, which were up to 16 feet in length and made of *wiliwili*, the lightest of native woods. The boards were highly prized possessions and were carefully wrapped in tapa cloth and suspended from the ceilings of homes.

Other popular Hawaiian games included *ulu maika*, in which rounded stone discs were rolled between two stakes, somewhat resembling bowling, and *moa pahee*, a similar game using a large wooden dart.

For the more passive, there was *konane*, a strategy game similar to checkers. Indentations were carved into a stone board to hold the pebbles of white coral and black lava that were used as playing pieces. ■

Africa or South America centered their explorations in the southern hemisphere.

Although the English were the first known Western explorers to set foot on Hawaiian shores, there is speculation that the Spanish, whose Manila galleons had been making annual runs between Mexico and the Philippines since 1565, may have stumbled upon Hawaii and kept the discovery a secret.

British explorer Captain James Cook spent the better part of a decade exploring and charting most of the South Pacific before chancing upon Hawaii as he sailed from Tahiti in search of a northwest passage to the Atlantic.

On January 18, 1778, Cook spotted the islands of Oahu, Kauai and Niihau. The winds favored approaching Kauai and on January 19 Cook's ships, the *Discovery* and the *Resolution*, sailed into Kauai's Waimea Bay. Cook named the Hawaiian archipelago the Sandwich Islands in honor of the Earl of Sandwich.

Cook was surprised to find that the islanders had a strong Tahitian influence in their appearance, language and culture. They sailed out in canoes to welcome the ships and were eager to trade fish and sweet potatoes for nails. The islanders were not interested in the useless beads and trinkets that Cook used successfully as barter else-

where in the Pacific. The only thing they cared to exchange anything for was metal, which was totally absent from their islands.

After two weeks of stocking provisions on Kauai and Niihau, Cook's expedition continued its journey north. Failing to find the fabled passages through the Arctic, Cook set sail back to Hawaii where his arrival date virtually coincided with that of his initial visit to the islands the year before.

This time he discovered the remaining Hawaiian islands. On January 17, 1779, Cook sailed into Kealakekua Bay on the Big Island where a thousand canoes came out to greet him.

When Cook went ashore the next day he was met by the high priest and guided to a temple lined with skulls. Everywhere the English captain went people fell face down on the ground in front of him to the chant of 'Lono'.

As fate would have it, Cook had landed during the makahiki festival. The tall masts and white sails of Cook's ships and even the way he had sailed clockwise around the island all fitted the legendary descriptions of how the god Lono would reappear on the scene.

Whether the priests actually believed Cook was the reincarnated Lono or whether they just used his appearance to enhance their power and add a little flair to the festivities is unknown. What is clear is that Cook never realized that both of his arrivals to Hawaii had coincided with the makahiki festivals – he assumed this was the way things were in everyday Hawaii.

There's little wonder Cook had a favorable impression of the islands. The islanders treated his crew with open hospitality. Hawaiian men invited the sailors to boxing matches and other competitions and the women performed dances and readily bedded down with them.

For men who had just spent months roaming inhospitable frozen tundra, this was paradise indeed.

The expedition's skilled artist, John Webber, was allowed to move freely in the villages. Today his detailed drawings of native people, costumes and village life constitute the best visual accounts of old Hawaii.

A few weeks after their arrival the crews

A Man of the Sandwich Islands
by John Webber

had restocked all the supplies needed except firewood. Rather than scour the hillsides for wood, Cook directed his men to haul on board the temple railings and wooden images from the harborside temple dedicated to Lono. As Cook had been passed off as Lono himself, the priests didn't attempt to stop them.

On February 4 the English vessels and their crews headed north out of Kealakekua Bay for Maui. En route they ran into a storm off the northwest coast of the Big Island where the *Resolution* broke a foremast. Uncertain of finding a safe harbor in Maui, Cook decided to go back to Kealakekua to repair the mast – a decision that would prove to be a fatal mistake.

When they arrived at Kealakekua Bay on February 11 the islanders quickly appeared with the usual provisions to barter. The ruling alii, however, seemed upset with the ships' reappearance.

Apparently the makahiki had ended and not only was Cook's timing inauspicious but so were the conditions of his return. This time he had arrived in a counterclockwise direction and with a broken sail.

Thievery became a big problem and after a cutter was stolen, Cook ordered a blockade of Kealakekua Bay and then set off with a party of 11 men to the main village at the northern point of the bay. His intention was to capture the high chief Kalaniopuu and hold him until the cutter was returned. This was a tactic which Cook had used elsewhere in the Pacific and which he saw as reasonable diplomacy.

While Cook was en route to the village, a Hawaiian canoe attempting to sail out of the bay was fired upon by the English sailors. Unknown to Cook's crew, the canoe was transporting a chief, Noekema, who was killed in the musket fire.

In the meantime Cook had reached Kalaniopuu's house and the chief had agreed to go with him. But as they walked down to the shore, Kalaniopuu's wailing wife ran after him and the old chief suddenly balked and attempted to get away. In the midst of it all, word of Noekema's death reached the village where a crowd quickly gathered.

Hoping to prevent bloodshed, Cook let the chief go, but the situation continued to escalate. As Cook was walking towards his boat, he shot at one of the armed Hawaiians who tried to block his way. The pistol misfired and the bullet bounced off the man's chest. The Hawaiians began to throw stones, and Cook ordered his men on shore to fire more shots.

Cook had always assumed, as had been the case on other Pacific islands, that if trouble developed his men could fire a few shots and the natives, upon seeing the blood, would run. Instead the Hawaiians, who were now in an angry frenzy, attacked rather than retreated.

The sailors in the boats fired another round as their captain began to make his way towards them over slippery rocks. Before they could reload, the crowd of Hawaiians moved in and Cook was struck on the head. Stunned by the blow, he staggered into the shallows where the Hawaiians beat and stabbed him, passing the daggers to share in the kill. Four other sailors also died in the battle.

In this freak melee on a shore of the Sandwich Islands, his last discovery, the life of the greatest explorer and navigator of the century came to a bloody end.

Cook's men, shocked by his death, went on a rampage. They burned a village, beheaded two of their victims and rowed across the bay with the heads on poles.

Eventually Kalaniopuu made a truce and returned those parts of Cook's dismembered body he was able to find. The skull was returned but it had been stripped of its skin – a common practice bestowed upon great chiefs.

Cook's remains were buried at sea in a military funeral, at which time the Hawaiians placed a kapu on the bay and also held ceremonies of their own.

A week after Cook's February 14 death the two ships set sail, landing briefly on Oahu, Kauai and Niihau before finally leaving Hawaiian waters on March 15, 1779.

Cook and his crew left the Hawaiians a costly legacy in the iron that was turned

Captain Cook's death,
illustrated by John Webber

into weapons, the introduced diseases that decimated the natives and the birth of the first children of mixed blood. The crews also returned home with charts and maps that would allow others to follow in their wake and in Britain and Europe their stories and drawings were published, stirring the public's sense of adventure.

Some of Cook's crew returned to the Pacific leading their own expeditions. Among them was Captain George Vancouver, who brought the first cattle and horses to Hawaii, and the ill-fated William Bligh who captained the *Bounty*.

Kamehameha the Great

At the time of Cook's arrival in Hawaii in 1778 the islands were divided into separate warring chiefdoms. Kamehameha the Great, who by 1791 had become sole chief of the Big Island, was to become the first to unite all the Hawaiian Islands.

In 1795, after conquering Maui and Molokai, Kamehameha successfully invaded Oahu and established his reign there as well.

Kamehameha made two attempts to invade Kauai, the only island not yet under his control. In 1796 his canoes were caught in a storm at sea and forced to turn back before ever reaching the island. In 1804, while Kamehameha was in Oahu again

Fishponds

The Hawaiians had a well developed aquaculture system with numerous coastal fishponds.

There were essentially two kinds of fishponds. One type was inshore and totally closed off from the sea, although generally close enough to have brackish water. These inshore ponds would be stocked with fry (young fish) and often had varying salinity levels which the Hawaiians took advantage of by cultivating different varieties of fish in different parts of the pond.

The other kind was a shoreline fishpond, created by building a long stone wall that paralleled the beach and curved back to shore at both ends. For these walled ponds the Hawaiians built *makaha*, or 'sluice gates', that allowed young fish to swim through but kept fattened fish from swimming back out. The fish in the pond could be easily netted at any time.

Amaama (mullet) and *awa* (milkfish) were the two varieties of fish most commonly raised in these fishponds. Most fishponds were strictly for the alii, and commoners were not allowed to eat the fish raised in them. ■

preparing for an invasion of Kauai, his warriors were struck by a deadly outbreak of a feverish disease, probably cholera, and the invasion plans were scrapped. The luck of the roll may have been Kauai's at the time, but Kamehameha's power was too obvious to ignore, so in 1810 Kauai agreed by treaty to accept Kamehameha's suzerainty.

The Sandalwood Trade

By the mid-1780s Hawaii was becoming a popular port of call for Yankee traders plying the seas between North America and China.

In the early 1790s American sea captains discovered that Hawaii had great stocks of sandalwood, which were worth a premium in China. When the captains showed interest in it, Hawaiian chiefs readily began bargaining their wood away in exchange for foreign weapons.

A lucrative three-way trade developed. From Hawaii the ships sailed to Canton and traded loads of sandalwood for Chinese silk and porcelain which were then carried back to New England ports and sold at high profit. In New England the ships were reloaded with goods to be traded to the Hawaiians.

Hawaii's forests of sandalwood were so vast at this time that the Chinese name for Hawaii was *Tahn Heong Sahn* – the 'Sandalwood Mountains'.

To try to maintain the resource Kamehameha eventually put a kapu on all sandalwood forests, giving himself total control over the trade. Even under Kamehameha's relatively shrewd management, the bulk of the profits ended up in the sea captains' pockets. Payment for the sandalwood was in overpriced goods, originally cannons and rifles, and later exotic items such as European furniture.

While Kamehameha was careful not to use up all his forests or overburden his subjects, his successor, Liholiho, partially lifted the royal kapu, allowing island chiefs to get in on the action. The chiefs began purchasing foreign luxuries by signing promissory notes to be paid in future shipments of sandalwood.

To pay off the rising 'debts', the *makaainana* (commoners) were forced into virtual servitude. They were used like packhorses to haul the wood, the sandal-

Ancient Crafts

Tapa Weaving In ancient Hawaii, women spent much of their time beating *kapa* (tapa cloth) or preparing *lauhala* for weaving.

Tapa made from the *wauke* (paper mulberry tree) was the favorite. The bark was carefully stripped, then beaten with a stick. The beaters were carved with different patterns which then became the pattern of the tapa. Dyes were made from charcoal, flowers and sea urchins.

Tapa had many uses in addition to clothing, from food containers to burial shrouds. After the missionaries introduced cotton cloth and western clothing, the art of tapa making slowly faded away. These days most of the tapa for sale in Hawaii is from Samoa, with bold designs. Hawaiian tapa was different, with more delicate patterns.

Wooden Bowls The Hawaiians had no pottery and made their containers using either gourds or wood. Wooden food bowls were mostly of kou or milo, two native woods which didn't leave unpleasant tastes.

Hawaiian bowls were free of designs and carvings. Their beauty lay in the natural qualities of the wood and in the shape of the bowl alone. Cracked bowls were often expertly patched with dovetailed pieces of wood. Rather than decrease the value of the bowl, patching suggested heirloom status and such bowls were amongst the most highly prized.

Lauhala Weaving Lauhala weaving uses the *lau* (leaves) of the hala tree. Preparing the leaves for weaving is hard, messy work as there are razor-sharp spines along the leaf edges and down the center.

In old Hawaii, lauhala was woven into mats and floor coverings, but these days smaller items like hats, placemats and baskets are most common.

Featherwork & Leis The Hawaiians were known for their elaborate featherwork. The most impressive were the capes worn by chiefs and kings. The longer the cape, the higher the rank. Those made of the yellow feathers of the now extinct *mamo* bird were the most highly prized.

The mamo was a predominately black bird with a yellow upper tail. An estimated 80,000 mamo birds were caught to create the cape that King Kamehameha wore. It's said that bird catchers would capture the birds, pluck the desired feathers and release them unharmed. Feathers were also used to make helmets and *leis* (garlands).

The *lei palaoa*, a Hawaiian neck-lace traditionally worn by royalty, is made of finely braided human hair hung with a smoothly carved whale tooth pendant shaped like a curved tongue. Before foreign whalers arrived, many of these pendants were made of bone. ∎

wood strapped to their backs with bands of ti leaves. The men who carted the wood were called *kua leho*, literally 'calloused backs' after the thick permanent layer of calluses which they developed. It was not uncommon for them to carry heavy loads 20 miles from the interior to ships waiting on the coast. Missionaries recorded seeing caravans of as many as 3000 men carting wood during the height of the trade.

In a few short years after Kamehameha's death Hawaii's sandalwood forests were exhausted. In a futile attempt to continue the trade, Oahu's Governor Boki, who had heard of vast sandalwood reserves in New Hebrides, set sail in November 1829 with 500 men on an ill-conceived expedition to harvest the trees. Boki's ship was lost at sea and the expedition's other ship, not too surprisingly, received a hostile welcome in New Hebrides.

In August 1830, 20 emaciated survivors sailed back into Honolulu Harbor. Boki had been a popular if troubled leader in a rapidly changing Hawaii. Hawaiians grieved in the streets of Honolulu when they heard of Boki's tragedy, and his death marked the end of the sandalwood trade.

End of the Old Religion

King Kamehameha died in 1819 at his Kamakahonu residence on the Big Island. The crown was passed to his reluctant son, Liholiho, who was proclaimed Kamehameha II. In reality the power was passed to Kaahumanu, who had been the favorite of Kamehameha's 21 wives.

Kaahumanu was an ambitious woman, determined to break down the ancient kapu system of taboos that restricted her powers. Less than six months after Kamehameha's death, Kaahumanu threw a feast for women of royalty at the sacred Kamakahonu compound. Although one of the most sacred taboos strictly forbade men from eating with women, Kaahumanu forcefully persuaded Liholiho to sit beside her and join in the meal.

It was an otherwise uneventful meal; not a single angry god manifested itself. But in that one act the old religion was cast aside, along with 600 years of taboos and restrictions. Hawaiians no longer had to fear being put to death for violating the kapus, and a flurry of temple smashing and idol burning immediately followed.

Those chiefs and kahunas who resisted were easily squelched by Liholiho using the powerful army which Kamehameha had left behind. It was the end of an era.

The Missionaries

On April 19, 1820, the brig *Thaddeus* arrived from Boston with the first of the Christian missionaries to Hawaii. By a twist of fate, they landed in Kailua Bay, a stone's throw from Kamakahonu, where six months earlier Kaahumanu had feasted the overthrow of the old religion.

It was a timely arrival for the missionaries. The loss of their religion and social structure had left the Hawaiians with a spiritual void into which the Christians zealously stepped.

The *Thaddeus* carried 23 Congregationalists, the first of 12 groups to be sent in the

Kamehameha Statue, Kapaau, Big Island

next three decades by the New England-based American Board of Commissioners of Foreign Missions (ABCFM). The leader of this initial group of missionaries was Hiram Bingham.

The missionaries befriended Hawaiian royalty and made their inroads quickly. After Queen Kaahumanu became seriously ill, Sybil Bingham nursed her back to health. Shortly after, Kaahumanu showed her gratitude by passing a law forbidding work and travel on the Sabbath.

Up until this time the Hawaiians had no written language. Using the Roman alphabet the missionaries established a written Hawaiian language that allowed them to translate the Bible. They taught the Hawaiians to read and write and established the first 'American' high school west of the Rocky Mountains.

With encouragement from the missionaries, the Hawaiians quickly took on Western ways, Western clothing and Western laws.

Whaling ship figurehead, Lahaina

Liholiho (Kamehameha II)

With Kaahumanu holding the real power, in November 1823 a floundering Liholiho set sail for England with his favorite wife to pay a royal visit to King George – although he failed to inform anyone in England of his plans.

When Liholiho arrived unannounced in London, misfitted in Western clothing and lacking in royal etiquette, the British press roasted him with racist caricatures. He never met King George. While being prepped in the social graces for their audience with the king, Liholiho and his wife came down with measles. They died in England within a few weeks of each other, in July 1824.

The Whalers

Within a year of the missionaries' arrival, whalers began calling on Hawaiian ports. The first were mostly New England Yankees and a sprinkling of Gay Head Native Americans and African American men. As more ships came on line, men of all nationalities roamed Hawaiian ports. Most were in their teens or twenties, ripe for adventure.

Towns sprung up with shopkeepers catering to the whalers, and saloons, brothels and hotels boomed. Honolulu and Lahaina became bustling ports of call.

From 1825 to 1870 Hawaii was the whaling center of the Pacific. It was a convenient way station for whalers hunting both the Arctic and Japanese whaling grounds. At its peak, between 500 and 600 whaling ships were pulling into Hawaiian ports each year.

Whaling brought big money to Hawaii and the dollars spread beyond the whaling towns. Many Maui farmers got their start supplying the whaling ships with potatoes; Big Island cattle ranches grew with the demand for beef; and even the average Hawaiian could earn a little money by turning in sailors who had jumped ship.

Hawaiians themselves made good whalers, and sea captains gladly paid a $200 bond to the Hawaiian government for each 'kanaka' allowed to join their crew. Kamehameha IV even set up his own fleet of whaling ships which flew under the Hawaiian flag.

Whaling in the Pacific peaked in the mid-

1800s and quickly began to burn itself out. In a few short years all but the most distant whaling grounds were being depleted and whalers were forced to go farther afield to make their kills. By 1860 whale oil prices were dropping as an emerging petroleum industry was beginning to produce a less expensive fuel for lighting.

The last straw for the Pacific whaling industry came in 1871 when an early storm in the Arctic caught more than 30 ships by surprise, trapping them in ice floes above the Bering Strait. Although over 1000 seamen were rescued, half of them Hawaiian, the fleet itself was lost.

Sugar Plantations
Ko, or sugar cane, arrived in Hawaii with the early Polynesian settlers. While the Hawaiians enjoyed chewing the cane for its juices, they never refined sugar.

The first known attempt to produce sugar in Hawaii was in 1802 when a Chinese immigrant in Lanai boiled crushed sugar cane in iron pots. Other Chinese soon set up small sugar mills on the scale of neighborhood bakeries.

In 1835 a young Bostonian, William Hooper, saw a bigger opportunity in sugar and set out to establish Hawaii's first sugar plantation. Hooper convinced Honolulu investors Ladd & Company to put up the money for his venture and then worked out a deal with Kamehameha III to lease 980 acres of land on Kauai for $300. His next step was to negotiate with the alii for the right to use Hawaiian laborers.

In the mid-1830s Hawaii was still largely feudalistic. Commoners were tied into subsistence fishing and agriculture and worked when needed for the alii. Therefore, before Hooper could hire any work hands, he had to first pay the alii a stipend to free the Hawaiians from their traditional work obligations.

The new plantation system, which introduced the concept of growing crops for profit rather than subsistence, marked the advent of capitalism and the introduction of wage labor in Hawaii.

The sugar industry emerged at the same time whalers began arriving in force. Together they formed the root of Hawaii's moneyed economy.

By the 1850s sugar plantations were established on Maui, Oahu and the Big Island, as well as Kauai.

Sugar cane, a giant grass, only flourishes with abundant water, so plantations were limited to the rainier parts of Hawaii and even then were vulnerable to drought. In 1856 an 11-mile irrigation ditch was dug to bring mountain water to Lihue cane fields which were suffering from a drought. While this Kauai ditch was intended as a rescue procedure, its success signaled plantation owners to the possibilities for diverting water to irrigate heretofore unsuitable lands. In the 1870s the 17-mile Hamakua Ditch was dug on Maui, the first of several extensive aqueducts that would carry millions of gallons of water daily from upland rainforests to water-thirsty plantations. These artificial waterways turned dry central plains into drenched cane fields. Today Hawaii is still criss-crossed with hundreds of miles of working ditches and aqueducts built a century ago.

In addition to the irrigation systems, the sugar companies built flumes and railroads to carry the cane from the fields to the mills. For over 100 years, sugar was the backbone of the Hawaiian economy.

Hawaii's Immigrants
As the sugar industry was booming, Hawaii's native population was in decline, largely as the result of diseases introduced by foreigners.

To expand their operations, the plantation owners began to look overseas for a labor supply. They needed immigrants who would be accustomed to working long days in hot weather and for whom the low wages being paid would seem like an opportunity.

In 1852 the plantation owners began recruiting laborers from China. In 1868 they went to Japan and in the 1870s they brought in Portuguese from Madeira and the Azores. After Hawaii's annexation to the USA in 1898 resulted in restrictions on Chinese immigration, plantation owners

Dance & Music

Ancient Hula Perhaps nothing is more uniquely Hawaiian than the hula. There are many different schools of hula, all very disciplined and graceful in their movements. Before Western contact, students spent years training in hula schools, sometimes moving to other islands to enroll with the masters.

Most ancient hula dances expressed historical events, legendary tales and the accomplishments of the great alii. Facial expressions, hand gestures, hip sway and dance steps all conveyed the story. They were performed to rhythmic chants and drum beatings, serving to connect with the world of spirits. Eye movement was very important; if the story was about the sun the eyes would gaze upward, if about the netherworld they would gaze downward.

One school, the *hula ohelo*, was very sensual, with movements suggesting the act of procreation.

Hula dancers wore tapa cloth, not the grass skirts which were introduced from Micronesia only a hundred years ago.

The Christian missionaries thought it all too licentious for their liking and suppressed it. The hula might have been lost forever if not for King Kalakaua, the 'Merrie Monarch', who revived it in the latter half of the 19th century.

Musical Instruments The *pahu hula*, a knee drum carved from a breadfruit or coconut log, with a sharkskin drum head, was used solely at hula performances. Other hula musical instruments include *ke laau* sticks, used to keep the beat for the dancers; *iliili*, stone castanets; *puili*, rattles made from split bamboo; and *uliuli*, gourd rattles decorated with colorful feathers.

The early Hawaiians were a romantic lot. Instruments used for courting included the *ohe*, a nose flute made of bamboo, and the *ukeke*, a musical bow with a couple of strings. ■

turned to Puerto Ricans and Koreans. The Filipinos were the last group of immigrants brought in to work the fields; the first wave came in 1906, the last in 1946.

Although these six ethnic groups made up the bulk of the field hands, South Sea islanders, Scots, Scandinavians, Germans, Galicians, Spaniards and Russians all came in turn.

Each group brought its own culture, food and religion. Chinese clothing styles mixed with Japanese kimonos and European bonnets. A dozen languages filled the air and a unique pidgin English developed as a means for the various groups to communicate with one another.

Conditions varied with the ethnic group and the period. At the turn of the century Japanese contract laborers were being paid $15 a month. After annexation, the contracts were considered indentured servitude and were declared illegal under US law. Still, wages as low as a dollar a day were common up until the 1930s.

In all, approximately 350,000 immigrants came to Hawaii to work on the sugar plantations. A continuous flow of immigrant workers was required to replace those who invariably found better options elsewhere. Although some workers came for a set period to save money and return home, others worked out their contracts and then moved off the plantations to farm their own plots or start their own businesses.

Plantation towns like Koloa, Paia and Honokaa grew up around the mills, with barber shops, fish markets, beer halls and bathhouses catering to the workers.

The major immigrant populations – Japanese, Chinese, Filipino and Western European – came to outnumber the native Hawaiians. Together they created the unique blend of cultures that would continue to characterize Hawaii for generations to come.

Kamehameha III

Kamehameha III, the last son of Kamehameha the Great, ruled for 30 years from 1825 to 1854. In 1840 he introduced Hawaii's first constitution, both to protect his powers and adjust to changing times. The constitution established Hawaii's first national legislature and provided for a Supreme Court.

Kamehameha III was also responsible for passing the Great Mahele land act, establishing religious freedom and giving all male citizens the right to vote.

Hawaii's only 'invasion' by a foreign power occurred during Kamehameha's reign. In 1843, George Paulet, an upstart British commander upset about a petty land deal involving a British subject, sailed into Honolulu commanding the British ship *Carysfort* and seized Oahu for six months. In that short period, he Anglicized street names, seized property and began to collect taxes.

To avoid bloodshed, Kamehameha III stood aside as the British flag was raised and the ship's band played 'God Save the Queen'. Queen Victoria herself wasn't flattered. After catching wind of the incident, she dispatched Admiral Richard Thomas to restore Hawaiian independence. Admiral Thomas re-raised the Hawaiian flag at the site of what is today Honolulu's Thomas Square. As the flag was raised Kamehameha III uttered the words *Ua mau ke ea o ka aina i ka pono*, meaning 'The life of the land is perpetuated in righteousness', which remains Hawaii's motto.

The Great Mahele

The Great Mahele of 1848, which was introduced under the urging of influential missionaries, permanently altered Hawaiian concepts of land ownership. For the first time, land became a commodity that could be bought and sold.

Through the provisions of the Great Mahele, the king, who had previously owned all land, gave up title to the majority of it. Island chiefs were allowed to purchase some of the lands which they had controlled as fiefdoms for the king. Other lands, which were divided into three-acre farm plots called *kuleana*, were made available to all Hawaiians. In order to retain title, chiefs and commoners alike had to pay a tax and register the land.

The chiefs had the option of paying the tax in property and many did so. Commoners had no choice but to pay the taxes in cash. Although the act was intended to turn Hawaii into a country of small farms, in the end only a few thousand Hawaiians carried through with the paperwork and received kuleanas.

In 1850 land purchases were opened to foreigners. Unlike the Hawaiians, the Westerners jumped at the opportunity and before the native islanders could clearly grasp the concept of private land ownership, there was little land left to own.

Within a few decades the Westerners, who were more adept at wheeling and dealing in real estate, owned 80% of all privately held lands. Even many of the Hawaiians who had gone through the process of getting their own kuleana eventually ended up selling it to the *haoles* (Whites).

Contrary to the picture the missionaries had painted for Kamehameha III, the Hawaiians suddenly became a landless people, drifting into ghettos in the larger towns. With a bitter twist, many of the missionaries themselves ended up with sizable tracts of land and more than a few of them left the church to tend their new estates.

Although Hawaiian commoners had no rights to the land prior to the Great Mahele, they were free to move around and work the property of any chief. In return for their personal use of the land they paid the chief in labor or with a percentage of their crops. In this way they lived off the land. After the Great Mahele, they were simply *off* the land.

Kamehameha IV

Kamehameha IV had a short and rather confusing reign that lasted from 1855 to 1863. He tried to give his rule an element of European regality, à la Queen Victoria, and he and his consort, Queen Emma, established a Hawaiian branch of the Anglican Church of England. He also passed a law mandating all children be given a Christian name along with their Hawaiian name. The law stayed on the books until 1967.

Stained glass of Kamehameha IV & Queen Emma at St Andrew's Cathedral, Honolulu

Struggles between those wanting to strengthen the monarchy and those wishing to limit it marked Kamehameha IV's reign.

Kamehameha V

Kamehameha V's (1863-1872) major accomplishment was the establishment of a controversial constitution that gave greater power to the king at the expense of elected officials. It also restricted the right to vote.

Kamehameha V, who suffered a severe bout of unrequited love, was the last king from a royal lineage that dated back to the 12th century. From childhood he was enraptured by Princess Bernice Pauahi who in the end turned down his proposals, opting instead to marry American Charles Bishop. Jolted by the rejection, Kamehameha V never married, yet he also never gave up on the princess. Even on his death bed he offered Princess Bernice his kingdom, which she declined.

As the bachelor king left no heirs, his death in December 1872 brought an end to the Kamehameha dynasty. Future kings would be elected.

Lunalilo

King Lunalilo (1873-1874) had a short reign. His cabinet, made up largely of Americans, was instrumental in paving the way for a treaty of reciprocity with the USA.

Although the USA was the biggest market for Hawaiian sugar, US sugar tariffs ate heavily into profit margins. As a means of eliminating the tariffs, most plantation owners favored the annexation of Hawaii to the USA.

The US Government was cool to the idea of annexation, but it warmed to the possibility of establishing a naval base on Oahu. In 1872 General John Schofield was sent to assess Pearl Harbor's strategic value. He was impressed with what he saw – the largest anchorage in the Pacific – and reported his enthusiasm back to Washington.

Although native Hawaiians protested in the streets and the Royal Troops even staged a little mutiny, there would eventually be a reciprocity agreement that would cede Pearl Harbor to the USA in exchange for duty-free access for Hawaiian sugar.

King Kalakaua

King David Kalakaua (1874-1891) was Hawaii's last king. Although known as the 'Merrie Monarch', he ruled in troubled times.

The first challenge to his reign came on election day. His contender had been the dowager Queen Emma and when the results were announced her followers rioted in the streets, requiring Kalakaua to request aid from US and British warships which happened to be in Honolulu Harbor at the time.

Despite the initial turmoil, Kalakaua went on to become a great Hawaiian revivalist. He brought back the *hula*, turning around decades of missionary repression against the 'heathen dance', and composed the national anthem *Hawaii Ponoi*, which is now the state song. He also tried to ensure some self-rule for native Hawaiians, now a minority in their own land.

When Kalakaua left for his first trip overseas, scores of Hawaiians came to the waterfront weeping. The last king to leave the islands, Kamehameha II, had come back in a coffin.

While in the USA, Kalakaua met with President Ulysses Grant and persuaded him to accept the reciprocity treaty which the US Congress had been resisting. Kalakaua also managed to postpone the ceding of Pearl Harbor for eight years. He returned to Hawaii a hero, to the business community for the treaty and to the Hawaiians for simply making it back alive.

The king became a world traveler, visiting India, Egypt, Europe and Southeast Asia. Kalakaua was well aware that Hawaii's days as an independent Polynesian kingdom were numbered. To counter the Western powers that were gaining hold of Hawaii, he made a futile attempt to establish a Polynesian-Pacific empire. On a visit with the emperor of Japan, he even proposed a royal marriage between his niece Princess Kaiulani and a Japanese prince but the Japanese declined.

Visits with other foreign monarchs gave Kalakaua a taste for royal pageantry. He returned to build Iolani Palace for what the haole business community thought was an extravagant $360,000. To many influential Whites, the king was perceived as a lavish spender who was fond of partying and throwing public luaus.

As Kalakaua incurred debts, he became increasingly less popular with the sugar barons whose businesses were now the backbone of the economy. They formed the Hawaiian League in 1887 and developed their own armies which stood ready to overthrow Kalakaua. The league presented Kalakaua with a list of demands and forced him to accept a new constitution strictly limiting his powers. It also limited suffrage to property owners, which by then excluded the vast majority of Hawaiians.

On July 30, 1889 about 150 Hawaiians attempted to overthrow the new constitution by occupying Iolani Palace. Called the Wilcox Rebellion after its part-Hawaiian leader, it was a confused and futile attempt and the rebels were forced to surrender.

Kalakaua died in San Francisco in 1891.

Statue of Queen Liliuokalani, Honolulu

Queen Liliuokalani

Kalakaua was succeeded by his sister, Liliuokalani, wife of Oahu's governor John Dominis.

Queen Liliuokalani (1891-1893) was even more determined than Kalakaua to strengthen the power of the monarchy. She charged that the 1887 constitution had illegally been forced upon King Kalakaua. The Hawaii Supreme Court upheld her contention.

In January 1893, as Liliuokalani was preparing to proclaim a new constitution to restore royal powers, a group of armed haole businessmen occupied the Supreme Court and declared the monarchy overthrown. They announced a provisional government, led by Sanford Dole, son of a pioneer missionary. A contingent of US sailors came ashore, ostensibly to protect the property of US citizens, but instead of flanking the property they claimed to be protecting, the troops marched on the palace and positioned their guns at the queen's residence. Realizing it was futile to oppose US forces, the queen opted to avoid bloodshed and stepped down.

The provisional government immediately appealed to the USA for annexation, while the queen appealed to the USA to restore the monarchy. To the dismay of Dole's representatives, the timing was to the queen's advantage. Democrat president Grover Cleveland had just replaced a Republican administration and his sentiments clearly favored the queen.

Cleveland sent an envoy, James Blount, to investigate the situation and determine what course of action the US Government should take.

In the meantime he received Queen Liliuokalani's niece, Princess Kaiulani, who, at the time of the coup, had been in London being prepared for the throne. The beautiful 18-year-old princess eloquently pleaded the monarchy's case. She also made a favorable impression with the American press which largely caricatured those involved in the annexation as dour, greedy buffoons.

Cleveland ordered the US flag be taken down and the queen restored to her throne. However the provisional government, now firmly in power, turned a deaf ear, declaring that Cleveland was meddling in 'Hawaiian' affairs.

The new government, with Dole as president, inaugurated itself as the

Republic of Hawaii on July 4, 1894. Although Cleveland initially favored reversing the situation, he also knew the American public's sense of justice was thin and that ousting a government of white Americans and replacing them with native Hawaiians could backlash on his own political future. Consequently his actions were largely limited to rhetoric.

Weary of waiting for outside intervention, in early 1895 a group of Hawaiian royalists attempted a counterrevolution that was easily squashed in a fortnight. Liliuokalani was accused of being a conspirator and placed under arrest.

To humiliate her, she was tried in her own palace and referred to only as Mrs John O Dominis. She was fined $5000 and sentenced to five years of hard labor, later reduced to nine months of house arrest at the palace.

Liliuokalani spent the rest of her life in her husband's residence, Washington Place, one block from the palace. When she died in November 1917, all of Honolulu came out for the funeral procession. To most islanders, Liliuokalani was still their queen.

Annexation

With the Spanish-American War of 1898, Americans acquired a taste for expansionism.

Not only was Hawaii gifted with Pearl Harbor, but it took on a new strategic importance being midway between the USA and its newly acquired possession, the Philippines. Annexation of Hawaii passed in the US Congress on July 7, 1898. Hawaii would enter the 20th century as a territory of the USA.

In just over a century of Western contact the native Hawaiian population had been decimated by foreign diseases to which they had no immunities. It began with the venereal disease introduced by Captain Cook's crew in 1778. The whalers followed with cholera and smallpox, and Chinese immigrants, who came to replace Hawaiian laborers, brought leprosy. By the end of the

19th century, the native Hawaiian population had been reduced from an estimated 300,000 to less than 50,000.

Descendants of the early missionaries had taken over first the land and now the government. Without ever having fought a single battle against a foreign power, Hawaiians had lost their islands to ambitious foreigners. All in all, as far as the native Hawaiians were concerned, the annexation wasn't anything to celebrate.

The Chinese and Japanese were also uneasy. One of the reasons for the initial reluctance of the US Congress to annex Hawaii had been the racial mix of the islands' population. There were already restrictions on Chinese immigration to USA, and restrictions on Japanese immigration were expected to follow.

In a rush to avoid a labor shortage the sugar plantation owners quickly brought 70,000 Japanese immigrants into Hawaii. By the time the immigration wave was over the Japanese accounted for over 40% of Hawaii's population.

In the years since the reciprocity agreement, sugar production had increased tenfold. Those who ruled the land ruled the government and closer bonding with the USA didn't change the formula. In 1900, US President McKinley appointed Sanford Dole the first territorial governor.

WW I

Soon after annexation, the US Navy set up a huge Pacific headquarters at Pearl Harbor and built Schofield Barracks, the largest US army base anywhere. The military quickly became the leading sector of Oahu's economy.

The islands were relatively untouched by WW I, even though the first German prisoners of war 'captured' by the USA were in Hawaii. They were escorted off the German gunboat *Grier* which had the misfortune to be docked at Honolulu Harbor when war broke out.

The war affected people in Hawaii in other ways. Heinrich Hackfeld, a German sea captain long settled in the islands, had established Hawaii's most successful

Pineapple fields, Oahu

merchandise stores, B F Ehler's and Company. He had also developed a real estate empire rooted in sugar, purchasing Lahaina's Pioneer Mill, among other properties. He lost it all during WW I.

Anti-German sentiments forced Hackfeld to liquidate his holdings and American Factors (Amfac) took over his properties, renaming the stores Liberty House.

Pineapple & Planes

In the early 1900s pineapple emerged as Hawaii's second major export crop. James Dole, a cousin of Sanford, purchased the island of Lanai in 1922 and turned it into the world's largest pineapple plantation. Although sugar remained king in export value, the more labor-intensive pineapple eventually surpassed it in terms of employment.

In 1936 Pan American flew the first passenger flights from the US mainland to Hawaii, an aviation milestone which ushered in the transpacific air age. Hawaii was now only hours away from the West Coast.

WW II

On December 7, 1941, a wave of Japanese bombers attacked Pearl Harbor, jolting the USA into WW II. The attack caught the US fleet totally by surprise, even though there had been warnings, some of which were far from subtle.

At 6:40 am the USS *Ward* spotted a submarine conning tower approaching the entrance of Pearl Harbor. The *Ward* immediately attacked with depth charges and sank what turned out to be one of five midget Japanese submarines launched to penetrate the harbor.

At 7:02 am a radar station on the north shore of Oahu reported planes approaching. Even though they were coming from the wrong direction, they were assumed to be US planes from the mainland.

At 7:55 am Pearl Harbor was hit. Within minutes the USS *Arizona* went down in a fiery inferno, trapping 1177 men beneath the surface. Twenty other US ships were sunk or damaged, along with 347 aircraft. More than 2500 people were killed.

It wasn't until 15 minutes after the bombing started that US anti-aircraft guns began to shell the Japanese warplanes. The Japanese lost 29 aircraft in the attack.

Hawaii was placed under martial law and Oahu took on the face of a military camp. Already heavily militarized, vast tracts of Hawaii's land were turned over to the US forces for expanded military bases, training and weapons testing. Much of that land

Hawaii's state flag

would never be returned. Throughout the war, Oahu served as the command post for the USA's Pacific operations.

Following the attack on Pearl Harbor a wave of suspicion landed on the *nisei* (people of Japanese descent) in Hawaii. While sheer numbers prevented the sort of internment practices that took place on the mainland, the Japanese in Hawaii were subject to interrogation and their religious and civic leaders were sent to mainland internment camps.

Japanese language schools were closed and many of the teachers arrested. Posters were hung in restaurants and other public places warning islanders to be careful about speaking carelessly in front of anyone of Japanese ancestry. Nisei were dismissed from posts in the Hawaiian National Guard and prevented from joining the armed services.

Eventually Japanese-Americans were allowed to volunteer for a segregated regiment, although they were kept on the mainland and out of action for much of the war.

During the final stages of the war, when fighting was at its heaviest, the nisei were given the chance to form a combat unit.

Volunteers were called and more than 10,000 nisei signed up, forming two distinguished Japanese-American regiments. One of these, the 442nd Second Regimental Combat Team, which was sent into action on the European front, became the most decorated fighting unit in US history.

The veterans returned to Hawaii with different expectations. Many went on to college using the GI bill and today account for some of Hawaii's most influential lawyers. One of the veterans of the 442nd is Hawaii's senior US senator, Daniel Inouye, who lost an arm in the fighting.

Unionizing Hawaii

The feisty mainland-based International Longshoremen's and Warehousemen's Union (ILWU) began organizing Hawaiian labor in the 1930s.

After WW II, the ILWU organized an intensive campaign against the 'Big Five' – C Brewer, Castle & Cooke, Alexander & Baldwin, Theo Davies and Amfac – Hawaii's biggest businesses and landholders, all with roots in sugar.

The ILWU's six-month waterfront strike

in 1949 virtually halted all shipments to and from Hawaii. The union went on to organize plantation strikes which resulted in Hawaii's sugar and pineapple workers becoming the world's highest paid.

The new union movement helped develop a political opposition to the staunchly Republican big landowners, who had maintained a stronghold on the political scene since annexation.

In the 1950s McCarthyism, the fanatical wave of anti-Communism which swept the mainland, spilled over to Hawaii. In the fallout, the leader of the ILWU in Hawaii, Jack Hall, was tried and convicted of being a Communist.

Post-War Hawaii

WW II brought Hawaii closer to the center stage of American culture and politics.

The prospect of statehood had long been the central topic in Hawaiian political circles. Three decades has passed since Hawaii's first delegate to the US Congress, Prince Jonah Kuhio Kalanianaole, introduced the first statehood bill in 1919. It had received a cool reception in Washington at that time and there were mixed feelings in Hawaii as well. However by the time the war was over, opinion polls showed that two out of three Hawaiian residents favored statehood.

Still, Hawaii was too much of a melting pot for many politicians to support statehood, particularly those from the segregated southern states. To the overwhelmingly White and largely conservative Congress, Hawaii's multiethnic community was too exotic and foreign to be thought of as 'American'.

Congress was also concerned with the success of Hawaiian labor strikes and the growth of membership in the ILWU. It all combined to keep statehood at bay until the end of the 1950s.

Hawaiian Home Lands

In 1920, under the sponsorship of Prince Jonah Kuhio Kalanianaole, the Territory of Hawaii's congressional delegate, the US Congress passed the Hawaiian Homes Commission Act. The act set aside almost 200,000 acres of land for homesteading by native Hawaiians, who were by this time the most landless ethnic group in Hawaii. The land was but a small fraction of the crown lands that were taken from the Kingdom of Hawaii when the USA annexed the islands in 1898.

Under the legislation, people of at least 50% Hawaiian ancestry were eligible to apply for 99-year leases at $1 a year. Originally most of the leases were for 40-acre parcels of agricultural land, although more recently residential lots as small as a quarter of an acre have been allocated.

Hawaii's prime land, already in the hands of the sugar barons, was excluded from the act. Much of what was designated for homesteading was on far more barren turf.

Indeed, the first homesteading village, at Kalanianaole on Molokai, failed when the wells drew brackish waters and destroyed the newly established crops. Still many Hawaiians were able to make a go of it, settling homesteads on Oahu, the Big Island, Kauai, Maui and Molokai. Presently there are about 5000 native Hawaiian families living on 25,000 acres of homestead lands.

Like many acts established to help native Hawaiians, administration of the Hawaiian Home Lands has been riddled with abuse. The majority of the land has not been allocated to native Hawaiians but has been leased out to big business, ostensibly as a means of creating an income for the administration of the program.

Parker Ranch on the Big Island has 32,845 acres of Hawaiian Home Lands under lease at $3.79 an acre. Kekaha Sugar, an Amfac subsidiary, leases the lion's share of Kauai's 18,569 acres of Hawaiian Home Lands, while less than 5% is made available to native Hawaiians.

In addition the federal, state and county governments have illegally, and with little or no compensation, taken large tracts of Hawaiian Home Lands for their own use. The Lualualei Naval Reservation alone constitutes one-fifth of all homestead lands on Oahu, where over 5000 native Hawaiians remain on the waiting list – some for as many as 30 years. ■

Statehood

In March 1959 the US Congress finally passed legislation to make Hawaii a state. On June 27 a plebiscite was held in Hawaii, with more than 90% of the islanders voting for statehood. The island of Niihau was the only precinct to vote against it.

On August 21, 1959, after 61 years of territorial status, Hawaii became the 50th state of the USA.

Hawaiian Sovereignty

A Hawaiian sovereignty movement intent on righting some of the wrongs of the past century has moved into the forefront of political issues in Hawaii. The success of the Protect Kahoolawe movement, growing discontent over the mismanagement of Hawaiian Home Lands, and the heightened consciousness created by the centennial anniversary in 1993 of Queen Liliuokalani's overthrow have all served as rallying points. Things are still in a formative stage and a consensus on what form sovereignty should take has yet to emerge.

The largest of the Hawaiian sovereignty groups, Ka Lahui Hawaii, has adopted a constitution for a Hawaiian nation within the USA, similar to that of 300 Native American groups on the mainland who have their own tribal governments and lands. Ka Lahui Hawaii wants all Hawaiian Home Lands, as well as the title to much of the crown land taken during annexation, turned over to native Hawaiians. These lands include nearly 1¾ million acres that were held by the Hawaiian Kingdom at the time of the 1893 overthrow. On Kauai alone the crown lands represent nearly half of the island, including extensive park lands such as those along the Na Pali Coast.

Other native Hawaiian groups are also calling for self determination. Some favor the restoration of the monarchy, while others focus on monetary reparations, but the majority are looking at some form of a nation-within-a-nation model.

The first of their demands was answered in November 1993 when President Clinton, reversing the hard-line attitude of the Bush Administration, signed a resolution apologizing 'to Native Hawaiians for the overthrow of the Kingdom of Hawaii on January 17, 1893 with participation of agents and citizens of the United States, and the deprivation of the rights of Native Hawaiians to self-determination'. The apology went on to 'acknowledge the ramifications of the overthrow' and expresses a commitment to 'provide a proper foundation for reconciliation'.

The state of Hawaii has since established the Hawaiian Sovereignty Advisory Commission to create a mechanism for native Hawaiians to determine what form sovereignty should take. The commission, whose members represent more than 50 native Hawaiian groups, is conducting voter and sovereignty education programs and has scheduled a November 1995 plebiscite on self-determination. People with any amount of Hawaiian ancestry, age 18 or older, will be allowed to vote.

Although it's an emerging process and attitudes may change as the movement takes shape, recent polls show that 75% of all Hawaii residents support the concept of sovereignty if it's within the framework of a nation-within-a-nation. Interestingly, the

Flying the flag upside down has come to represent the sovereignty movement

support doesn't vary greatly along ethnic lines.

Incidentally the Hawaiian flag, flown upside down as a sign of distress, has come to represent the Hawaiian sovereignty movement.

GEOLOGY

The Hawaiian Islands are the tips of massive mountains, created by a crack in the earth's mantle which has been spewing out molten rock for 25 million years. The hot spot is stationary, but the ocean floor is part of the Pacific Plate which is moving northwest at the rate of about three inches a year. (The eastern edge of this plate is California's San Andreas fault.)

As weak spots in the earth's crust pass over the hot spot, molten lava bursts through as volcanoes, building underwater mountains. Some of them finally emerge above the water as islands.

Each new volcano eventually creeps northward past the hot spot which created it. The farther from the source, the lower the volcanic activity, until the volcano is eventually cut off completely and turns cold.

Once the lava stops it's a downhill battle. The forces of erosion – wind, rain and waves – slowly wash the mountains away. In addition, the settling of the ocean floor causes the land to gradually recede.

Thus the once mountainous Northwestern Hawaiian Islands, the oldest in the Hawaiian chain, are now low flat atolls that in time will be totally submerged.

The Big Island, Hawaii's southernmost island, is still in the birthing process. Its most active volcano, Kilauea, is directly over the hot spot. In its latest eruptive phase, which began in 1983 and still continues, Kilauea has pumped out more than two billion cubic yards of lava, making this the largest known volcanic eruption in Hawaii's history.

Less than 30 miles southeast of the Big Island, a new seamount named Loihi has already built up 15,000 feet on the ocean floor. The growing mounds of lava are expected to break the ocean surface within 10,000 years – however if it were to get hyperactive, it could emerge within a century or two.

In 1987 the Woods Hole Oceanographic Institution explored Loihi with *Alvin*, the same deep-water mini-sub that had discovered the *Titanic* wreck the year before. They measured Loihi's summit to be 3117 feet below the surface of the water.

Hawaii's volcanoes are shield volcanoes which form not by explosion but by a slow build-up of layer upon layer of lava. They rise from the sea with gentle slopes and a relatively smooth surface. It's only after eons of facing the elements that their surfaces become sharply eroded. It's for this reason that the Na Pali cliffs on Kauai, the

---

The Creation Myth

The early Hawaiians were astutely tuned in to geological forces and knew the order in which the islands were created. Their creation story goes something like this:

Pele, the goddess of volcanoes and fire, was born of the marriage of earth and sky. She is both Creator and Destroyer (not unlike the Hindu god Shiva). Her eruptions of molten lava both build the mountains and wreak havoc over everything in their path.

Pele was driven from her home in the northwestern shoals by a jealous older sister, Na Maka O Kahai, goddess of the seas. Pele fled to the southeast and built her home in a crater on Niihau, then on Kauai, then Oahu, and each island in turn. Each time she dug down into the fiery earth deeper than the time before, and each time she was chased away by her sister, the sea.

After being routed from her home on Haleakala on Maui, Pele crossed over to the Big Island. There she built her highest mountains yet and in their volcanic recesses made a home far from the reaches of Na Maka O Kahai.

The sea goddess, however, is still never far from Pele's doorstep. She persistently wears away at Pele's home, her waves taking on the lava, eroding it down and crushing it into sand.

In time Pele will again be forced to move on, but for now she makes her home deep in Kilauea, the most active volcano on earth. ■

Kilauea volcano lava flow, near Kalapana, Big Island

oldest of the main islands, are the most jagged in Hawaii.

Hawaii's active volcanoes are Kilauea and Mauna Loa, both on the Big Island. The Big Island's Mauna Kea and Hualalei and Maui's Haleakala are dormant, with future eruptions possible. The volcanoes on all the other Hawaiian islands are considered extinct.

GEOGRAPHY

The Hawaiian Islands stretch 1523 miles in a line from Kure Atoll in the northwest to the Big Island in the southeast. Ka Lae, on the Big Island, is the southernmost point of the USA.

The equator is 1470 miles south of Honolulu and all the main islands are in the tropic of Cancer. Hawaii shares the same latitude as Hong Kong, Bombay and Mexico's Yucatán Peninsula.

Hawaii's eight major islands are, from largest to smallest, Hawaii (the Big Island), Maui, Oahu, Kauai, Molokai, Lanai, Niihau and Kahoolawe. They have a total land area of 6470 sq miles, which includes 96 small offshore islands with a combined area of less than three sq miles.

The Northwestern Hawaiian Islands lie scattered across a thousand miles of ocean west of Kauai. They consist of 28 islands in nine clusters with a total land area of just under three sq miles.

The Midway Islands, geographically in the Hawaiian archipelago but politically not part of the state of Hawaii, are not included in these figures.

In total, Hawaii is a bit smaller than Fiji and a bit larger than the US state of Connecticut.

Hawaii's highest mountain is Mauna Kea on the Big Island, which is 13,796 feet above sea level. According to the *Guinness Book of Records* it's the world's highest mountain (33,476 feet) when measured from the ocean floor. Mauna Loa, also on the Big Island, is Hawaii's second highest mountain, at 13,679 feet.

CLIMATE

Overall, Hawaii has great weather. It's balmy and warm, with northeasterly trade winds prevailing most of the year.

Average temperatures differ only about 7°F from winter to summer. Near the coast daily temperatures average a high of about 83°F and a low of around 68°F.

The rainiest time of the year is from December to March. Apart from the fact that winter has about twice the rainfall of summer, winter storms can also hang around for days. In summer the rain is more likely to fall as passing showers. This doesn't mean winter is a bad time to go to Hawaii, it just means the weather is more of a gamble.

Pahoehoe and aa lava types at Hawaii
Volcanoes National Park

Rainfall varies even more with location than with season. In places like Kailua-Kona, on the Big Island, you can sunbathe on the beach for all but a few days a year. At the same time you can watch typical afternoon showers pour on the hill slopes just a mile or two inland and know you're well beyond reach.

Hawaii's high volcanic mountains trap the trade winds that blow from the northeast, blocking their moisture-laden clouds and bringing abundant rainfall to the windward side of the islands. Hilo, the rainiest city in the USA with 130 inches annually, is on the windward side of the Big Island.

Conversely, the same mountains block the wind and rain from the southwesterly, or leeward side of the islands, so it's there you'll find the driest, sunniest conditions and the calmest waters. Leeward areas generally receive only 10 to 25 inches of rain a year.

During kona weather the winds blow from the south, a shift from the typical northeast trades. The ocean swell pattern also changes – dive spots suddenly become surfing spots and vice versa. Kona storms usually occur in winter and are very unpredictable.

The summits of Mauna Kea and Mauna Loa on the Big Island receive snow each winter and on some years Haleakala on Maui catches a short-lived snow cover as well. The lowest temperature ever recorded on Mauna Kea, Hawaii's coldest spot, was 11°F, while the highest temperature there was 66°F.

FLORA & FAUNA

The Hawaiian island chain, 2500 miles from the nearest continental land mass, is the most geographically isolated place in the world.

All living things that reached Hawaii's shores were carried across the ocean on the wind or the waves – seeds clinging to a bird's feather, a floating hala plant, or insect eggs in a piece of driftwood. Probably the first to arrive on the newly emerged volcanic islands were fern and moss spores, able to drift thousands of miles in the air.

It's estimated that before human contact a new species managed to take hold in Hawaii only once every 100,000 years. New arrivals found specialized habitats ranging from desert to rainforest and elevations climbing from sea level to nearly 14,000 feet. Each species evolved to fit a specific niche in its new environment.

Over 90% of Hawaii's native flora & fauna are found nowhere else on earth. Some still resemble their ancestors. The *nene*, for instance, looks like its cousin the Canada goose, but its feet have adapted to walking on lava by losing most of their webbing. The majority of Hawaiian birds, however, have evolved so thoroughly that it's not possible to trace them to any continental ancestors.

Many of Hawaii's birds may have evolved from a single species, as is thought to have been the case with over 30 species of native honeycreeper.

At the time of Western contact, Hawaii had 70 native bird species. Of those, 24 are now extinct and an additional 36 are threatened with extinction.

Having evolved with limited competition and few predators, Hawaii's native species generally fare poorly amongst more

Climate Information

Average temperature and rainfall for various island locations by month

The top of the gray bar indicates the average high temperature, the bottom indicates the average low. Temperatures are in °F and °C.

The blue bar indicates the average rainfall in inches and centimeters.

Nene

Hawaiian stilt, or aeo

Black-crowned night heron, or aukuu

Red-crested cardinal

Wild peacock

aggressive introduced flora & fauna. They are also highly sensitive to habitat destruction.

When the first Polynesian settlers arrived, they weren't traveling light. They brought food and medicinal plants, chickens, dogs and pigs.

The pace of introducing exotic species escalated with the arrival of Westerners, starting with Captain Cook who dropped off goats and left some melon and pumpkin seeds. The next Western visitors left cattle and horses.

Prior to human contact, Hawaii had no land mammals at all except for monk seals and hoary bats. The introduction of free-ranging pigs, cattle and goats, who grazed and foraged at will, devastated Hawaii's fragile ecosystems and spelled extinction for many plants.

Released songbirds and game birds spread avian diseases to which native Hawaiian birds had no immunity. Erosion, deforestation and thousands of introduced plants which compete with and choke out native vegetation have all taken their toll.

Today more than 25% of all endangered species in the USA are Hawaiian plants and animals. Of approximately 2400 different native plants, half are either threatened or endangered.

Hawaiian Monk Seal

The Hawaiian monk seal, so named for the cowl-like fold of skin at its neck and for its solitary habits, exists only in Hawaii. The species has remained nearly unchanged for 15 million years but is now in danger of dying out completely. Only about 1000 remain.

Hawaiian monk seals, which are sensitive to human disruption, breed and give birth primarily in the Northwestern Hawaiian Islands. In recent years, however, sightings of seals hauling themselves onto Kauai's beaches have increased.

Of the world's two other monk seal species, the Caribbean monk seal is already extinct and the Mediterranean monk seal numbers only in the hundreds.

Whales

Whales, the largest of the marine cetaceans, are air breathing, warm blooded, placental mammals that lactate and nurse their young. Basically there are two types: toothed whales, which use their teeth to catch and rip apart their prey; and baleen whales, which have rows of a horny elastic material, called baleen or whalebone, that hangs from the upper jaw and acts as a filter to extract food from the water.

Several types of whales frequent Hawaiian waters, though it is the migrating humpback that everyone wants to see. Luckily for whale watchers, humpback whales are coast-huggers, preferring waters with depths of less than 600 feet. Other migratory whales that pass by the islands on occasion include the fin whale, minke whale and right whale. All are baleen whales.

Hawaii's year-round resident whales, which are all toothed whales, include the sperm whale, false killer whale, pigmy killer whale, beaked whale, melon-head whale and, most common of all, the pilot whale. The latter is a small whale which often travels in large pods and, like most whales, prefers deep offshore waters.

Curiously, the early Hawaiians seem to have paid little attention to whales. They are not found in petroglyph drawings and there are virtually no legends about whales.

Humpback Whales Humpbacks are the fifth largest of the great whales. They reach lengths of 45 feet and weigh 40 to 45 tons.

Humpbacks have distinctive long white flippers and knobby heads. They're great performers, known for their acrobatic displays which include arching dives, lobtailing, breaching and fin splashing. In breaching, humpbacks jump almost clear out of the water and then splash down with tremendous force.

They save the best performances for breeding time. Sometimes several bull whales will do a series of crashing breaches to gain the favor of a cow, often bashing into one another, even drawing blood,

Whale Songs

Humpbacks are remarkable not only for their acrobatics but also for their singing. They are the only species of large whales known to do either.

Each member of the herd sings the same set of songs, in the same order. Their songs last anywhere from six to 30 minutes and evolve as the season goes on, with new phrases added and old ones dropped, so that the songs the whales sing when they arrive in Hawaii become different songs by the time they leave.

It's thought that the humpbacks don't sing in their feeding grounds in Alaska. When they return to Hawaii six months later they recall the songs from the last season and begin where they left off. The humpback's complex songs include the full range of frequencies audible to the human ear. ■

before the most impressive emerges the winner.

Once one of the most abundant of the great whales, humpbacks were hunted almost to extinction and are now an endangered species. Around the turn of the century an estimated 15,000 humpbacks remained. They were still being hunted as late as 1966 when the International Whaling Commission enforced a ban on their slaughter.

The entire population of North Pacific humpbacks is now thought to be about 2000. More than half of those winter in Hawaii, while most of the others migrate to Mexico.

Humpbacks feed all summer in the plankton-rich waters off Alaska, developing a layer of blubber which sustains them through the winter. One of the toothless whales, humpbacks gulp in huge quantities of water and then strain it back out through the filter-like baleen in their mouths, trapping krill and small fish. They can eat close to a ton of food a day.

During their romantic winter sojourn in the warm tropical waters off Hawaii, humpbacks mate and give birth. The gestation period is 10 to 12 months.

Mothers stay in shallow waters once their calves are born, apparently as protection from shark attacks. At birth calves are about 12 feet long and weigh 3000 pounds. They are nursed for about six months and can put on 100 pounds a day in the first few weeks. Adults go without eating while in Hawaii.

Humpbacks don't arrive in Hawaii en masse, but start filtering in around November. They can be found throughout the islands, but their most frequented wintering spot is the shallow waters between Maui, Lanai, Molokai and Kahoolawe. The Kona coast of the Big Island is another favored spot, as is the Penguin Bank west of Molokai.

Whales are highly sensitive to human activity and noise and seek out quiet coastal areas. They have abandoned areas where human activities have picked up and seem to have a particular distaste for jet skis.

Humpbacks are protected by US federal law under the Marine Mammal Protection Act and the Endangered Species Act. Approaching within 100 yards of a humpback (300 yards in cow/calf waters) is prohibited and can result in a $25,000 fine. The rules apply to everyone, including swimmers, kayakers and surfers, and are strictly enforced – whether violators are aware of the law or not.

The humpback whale has been designated Hawaii's official marine mammal.

Dolphins

Dolphins, which like whales are marine cetaceans, are common to Hawaii. Spinner, bottlenose, slender-beaked, spotted, striped and rough-toothed varieties are all found in Hawaiian waters.

Dolphins are nocturnal feeders who often come into calm bays during the day to rest. Although it may seem tempting to swim out and join them, approaching the dolphins can apparently disturb their rest; in addition, it will subject swimmers to a hefty fine under the Marine Mammal Protection Act. This is a current controversy in Hawaii, as swimmers who claim that dolphins enjoy playing in the surf with humans are at odds against federal officials bent on enforcing laws against the harassment of marine mammals.

Incidentally, the *mahimahi* or 'dolphin' that you may come across on menus in Hawaii is not the mammal but a fish.

Environmental Groups
Sierra Club Legal Defense Fund The Sierra Club Legal Defense Fund (SCLDF) is in the forefront pressing legal challenges against abuses to Hawaii's fragile environment.

In conjunction with Greenpeace Hawaii, they've forced the state of Hawaii to prohibit jet skis in waters used by endangered humpback whales. On behalf of several environmental groups, the SCLDF filed legal challenges that halted a geothermal energy project on the Big Island which would have carved up one of Hawaii's last remaining lowland rainforests.

In another challenge, SCLDF took on the National Rifle Association and the state to force the removal of introduced mouflon game sheep from the slopes of Mauna Kea. The sheep were found to be the primary cause for the decline of the palila, a native honeycreeper. A landmark case, it was the first time that habitat destruction was successfully defined as the 'taking' (meaning killing, harming or harassing) of an endangered species under the US Endangered Species Act.

On Kauai, the SCLDF is contesting the state's signing of an agreement allowing the US Army to close off half of Polihale State Park's 1700 acres to the public because they are adjacent to a new missile launching site. The site, which launched its first missile in 1993, before SCLDF forced the government to file an environmental impact statement, is part of a 10-year military project related to the Reagan-era Star Wars program.

If you want to learn more about their present struggles, write to the Sierra Club Legal Defense Fund's headquarters at 180 Montgomery St, Suite 1400, San Francisco, CA 94104.

Nature Conservancy The Nature Conservancy of Hawaii is protecting Hawaii's rarest ecosystems by buying up vast tracts of land and working out long-term stewardships with some of Hawaii's biggest landholders.

One project included purchasing the Kipahulu Valley on Maui in conjunction with the state and turning the 11,000 acres over to the federal government to become part of Haleakala National Park. The Oheo Pools south of Hana are part of this land.

On Molokai the Nature Conservancy manages the rainforest at Kamakou and Pelekunu Valley on the island's wet northeast coast and the windswept Moomomi dunes on the dry northwest coast.

They also manage a crater above Hanauma Bay on Oahu, the Waikamoi rainforest on Maui, a native dryland forest in Lanai and a Kauai nesting site for the *ao* (Newell's shearwater), a threatened species once thought extinct.

For more information on guided hikes into Nature Conservancy preserves or to find out more about their projects contact the Nature Conservancy of Hawaii (☎ 537-4508), 1116 Smith St, Honolulu, HI 96817.

Na Ala Hele Of special interest to hikers and naturalists is the work of Na Ala Hele, a group affiliated with Hawaii's Division of Forestry & Wildlife. Na Ala Hele was established in 1988 with the task of documenting public access to trails as part of a movement to preserve Hawaii's natural environment and cultural heritage.

Na Ala Hele has undertaken demonstration trails on each island, the most ambitious of which is a shoreline trail along a 35-mile stretch of the leeward coast of the Big Island. Throughout the state, they've negotiated with private landowners and the military to gain access to previously restricted areas and re-establish abandoned trails.

Tikis, or *kii,* are god images placed around prayer towers

The Na Ala Hele logo signpost is marking an increasing number of trailheads as their work continues. For more information contact: Na Ala Hele (☎ 587-0058), Division of Forestry & Wildlife, 567 S King St, Suite 132, Honolulu, HI 96813.

Other Environmental Groups There are over 150 environmental groups in Hawaii, ranging from chapters of international organizations fighting to save the rainforest to neighborhood groups working to protect local beaches from impending development.

One of the broadest based is the Hawaii chapter of the Sierra Club, which has groups on all the main islands. Its activities range from political activism on local environmental issues to outings to eradicate invasive plants from native forests. The Sierra Club also maintains trails and leads guided hikes. For further information, see the individual island chapters.

GOVERNMENT

Hawaii has three levels of government: federal, state and county. The seat of state government is in Honolulu.

Hawaii has a typical state government with executive power vested in the governor, who is elected to a four-year term. The present governor, Benjamin Cayetano, who took office in December 1994, is the first US state governor of Filipino ancestry.

The state's lawmaking body is a bicameral legislature. The Senate is comprised of 25 members, elected for four-year terms from the state's 25 senatorial districts. The House of Representatives has 51 members, each elected for a two-year term.

The legislature has a typical Hawaiian casualness. The regular legislative session, which convenes on the third Wednesday of January, meets for only 60 days a year. Special sessions of up to 30 days can be convened by the governor, but otherwise that's it.

Hawaii is the only US state to have a public education system run by the state, rather than county or town education boards. Education accounts for approximately one-third of the state budget.

Hawaii is divided into four county governments, but unlike the mainland states, it has no municipal government. The city of Honolulu is part of Honolulu County which governs all of Oahu; Hawaii County governs the Big Island; Kauai County governs Kauai and Niihau; and Maui County governs Maui, Molokai and Lanai.

While the leprosy colony of Kalaupapa on Molokai is called the 'county' of Kalawao, in actuality it has no county government and is under the jurisdiction of the Hawaii State Department of Health.

Each county has a mayor and county council. The counties provide services, such as police and fire protection, that on the mainland are usually assigned to cities. Development issues are usually decided at county level and are the central issue of most mayoral elections.

ECONOMY

Tourism is Hawaii's largest industry and accounts for about one-third of the state's income. Hawaii gets about 6½ million visitors a year. In total they spend almost $10 billion in the state, but not all at the same rate. The four million visiting Americans spend an average of $120 a day, while the 1.4 million Japanese average nearly $350 a day.

The second largest sector in the economy is the US military, pumping out $3 billion annually. Agriculture is a distant third.

Sugar and pineapple, which once formed the backbone of Hawaii's economy, are rapidly losing ground. Pineapple production has ceased on Lanai, which until recently was dubbed the 'Pineapple Island', and in a few years sugar is expected to disappear from the landscape on both the Big Island and Oahu. Currently the two crops account for $225 million in sales, about half of their value a decade earlier.

Meanwhile, diversified crops, defined as all crops except sugar and pineapple, have increased two-fold over the past decade and have a combined sales value of $200 million. Of this, Hawaii's 700 farms and nurseries sold $70 million in flowers, while macadamia nuts brought in another $40 million. Other sizable crops included vegetables ($38 million), fruits ($26 million), coffee and seed corn.

Not all of Hawaii's agricultural endeavors are legal. Although the amount has dropped dramatically in recent years, over a billion dollars worth of marijuana is still grown on the islands, making it the biggest cash crop in Hawaii.

Hawaii is also making advances in the area of high technology. The state is in the forefront of renewable energy research, including ocean thermal energy conversion. It's also home to the world's most powerful and sophisticated astronomical observatories.

Hawaii's former agribusiness-based economy is in the midst of change. Hawaii's 'Big Five' companies – Amfac, Castle & Cooke, C Brewer, Theo Davies and Alexander & Baldwin – all had their origins in sugar, now on the wane. The Big Five hold onto their plantations not so much for what's being produced on them, but for the potential they hold as future golf courses and condo developments – and bit by bit they're being sold off for those purposes. The biggest buyers are Japanese developers; over a third of all Japanese investment in the USA is now in Hawaii.

Throughout the 1980s the islands underwent a major building boom, largely in resort developments and new subdivisions of exclusive housing. The boom was so rapid that island governments are still trying to catch up with it. Some regions that saw their populations nearly double now suffer from insufficiencies in basic infrastructure, including water supplies, hospitals and schools. While economic downturns in Japan and the US mainland have at least temporarily stalled the boom, the number of proposed construction projects remains staggering. In the long run, the construction crane, often said in jest to be Hawaii's state bird, doesn't appear to be endangered.

The cost of living is 20% higher in Honolulu than in the average US mainland city, while wages are 9% lower. For those stuck in service jobs, the most rapidly growing sector of the economy, it's tough to get by.

Native Hawaiians have the lowest median family income in Hawaii and are at the bottom of most health and welfare indicators, including high school drop-out rates, suicide rates and tragic death and major disease statistics. They also make up a disproportionately high percentage of the homeless who live out of their cars on the beach.

The Military Presence

Hawaii is the most militarized state in the nation.

In total, the military has a grip on 265,000 acres of Hawaiian land. The greatest holding is on Oahu, where 25% of the island is controlled by the armed forces and where there are more than 100 installations, from ridge-top radar stations to Waikiki's Fort DeRussy Beach.

Oahu is the hub of the Pacific Command which directs military activities from the west coast of the USA to the east coast of Africa. The navy, which accounts for 40% of Hawaii's military presence, is centered at Pearl Harbor, home of the Pacific Fleet.

Despite the ending of the Cold War the military still spends $3 billion annually in the state. It pays out $500 million in contracted services and employs 19,000 civilians directly. There are 52,500 military personnel and an additional 57,000 military dependents living on the islands.

Hawaii's politicians, while otherwise liberal-leaning, generally embrace the military presence. The Chamber of Commerce of Hawaii even has a special military affairs council that lobbies in Washington DC to draw still more military activity to Hawaii.

About 3000 nuclear weapons, some 10% of the US nuclear arsenal, are stockpiled in Oahu. Pearl Harbor has the most, while other nuclear weapons are based at Schofield Barracks army base and the Kaneohe Marine Corps Air Station.

POPULATION & PEOPLE

The population of Hawaii is 1,160,000. (This figure does not include the 140,000 visitors in Hawaii on an average day.) For the island breakdown, 865,000 people live on Oahu, 130,500 on the Big Island, 99,400 on Maui, 55,100 on Kauai, 6800 on Molokai, 2800 on Lanai and 230 on Niihau.

There is no ethnic majority in Hawaii – everyone belongs to a minority. Some 32% of the population claims 'mixed ethnicity', with a majority of those having some Hawaiian blood. As for the rest, Caucasians and Japanese each account for approximately 22% of the population, followed by Filipinos (12%), Chinese (5%), African Americans, Koreans, Samoans and Puerto Ricans. There are 9200 full-blooded Hawaiians, less than 1% of the population.

Hawaii's people are known for their racial harmony. Race is generally not a factor in marriage. Islanders have a 50/50 chance of marrying someone of a race different than their own and the majority of children born in Hawaii are *hapa*, or mixed blood.

ARTS

Hula

Hula *halaus* (schools) have experienced an influx of new students in recent years. Some practice in public places, such as school grounds and parks, where visitors are welcome to watch. Although many of the halaus rely on tuition fees, others receive sponsorship from hotels and shopping centers and give weekly public performances in return.

There are also numerous island-wide hula competitions; two of the biggest are the Prince Lot Hula Festival held each July in Oahu and the week-long Merrie Monarch Festival which begins on Easter Sunday in Hilo.

Music

Contemporary Hawaiian music gives center stage to the guitar, most prominently the steel guitar, an instrument designed in 1889 by Joseph Kekuku, a native Hawaiian. The steel guitar is one of only two major musical instruments invented in what is now the USA. (The other is the banjo.) The steel guitar is usually played with slack-key tunings and carries the melody throughout the song.

The ukulele, so strongly identified with Hawaiian music, was actually derived from the braginha, a Portuguese instrument introduced to Hawaii in the 1800s. The word 'ukulele' is Hawaiian for 'jumping flea'.

Both the ukulele and the steel guitar were essential to the light-hearted, romantic music popularized in Hawaii from the 1930s to the 1950s. *My Little Grass Shack, Lovely Hula Hands* and *Sweet Leilani* are classic examples. Due in part to the

---

'Agricultural' Golf Courses

In the late 1980s the state passed a controversial bill that allowed golf courses to be built on agriculture-zoned land.

This bill led to the gobbling up of major tracts of farmland by Japanese developers and the eviction of small leasehold farmers. Hawaii is one of the few Pacific island chains where island-grown produce has been relatively abundant and the continued eviction of farmers who have been growing crops on the land for generations will no doubt make the islands more reliant on imported foods. One of the slogans of the resistance movement is: 'No can eat golf balls.'

Currently the state has 70 golf courses, but the proposed courses on the drawing board could more than double that number in the next few years.

Not surprisingly, attempts to control the development of new golf courses is one of the forefront issues confronted by island environmentalists. ■

Kaina Keana'aina Hula Troupe, Big Island

'Hawaii Calls' radio show, which for more than 30 years was broadcast worldwide from the Moana Hotel in Waikiki, this music became instantly recognizable as Hawaiian, conjuring up images of beautiful hula dancers swaying under palm trees in a tropical paradise.

Some of Hawaii's more renowned slack-key guitar players include Raymond Kane, Peter Moon and Atta Isaacs Jr, and the late Gabby Pahinui and Sonny Chillingworth.

One of the current sounds in Hawaii is Jawaiian, a blending of Hawaiian music and Jamaican reggae. Some of the better-known island musicians who incorporate Jawaiian elements include Bruddah Waltah, Willie K, Brother Noland, Kapena and Manao Company. Other popular contemporary Hawaiian musicians include vocalist Henry Kapono; the innovative Peter Moon Band; the rock band Kalapana; and Jerry Santos and Olomana, who blend Hawaiian and folk. One of the finest new groups in Hawaii is Hapa, the duo of Kelii

Kanealii and Barry Flanagan, who fuse folk, rock and traditional Hawaiian elements. For a more traditional Hawaiian sound, there's Makaha Sons of Niihau and the Brothers Cazimero.

Art

Many artists draw inspiration from Hawaii's rich cultural heritage and natural beauty.

Well-known Hawaiian painter Herb Kawainui Kane creates detailed oil paintings focusing on the early Polynesian settlers and King Kamehameha's life. His works are mainly on display in museums and at gallery collections in resorts.

Rocky Kaiouliokahihikoloehu Jensen does wood sculptures and drawings of Hawaiian gods, ancient chiefs and early Hawaiians with the aim of creating sacred art in the tradition of *makaku*, or 'creative artistic mana'. Jensen is the director of Hale Naua III, the Society of Hawaiian Artists.

Pegge Hopper paints traditional

Hawaiian women in relaxed poses using a distinctive graphic design style and bright washes of color. Her work has been widely reproduced on posters and postcards.

Some of Hawaii's most impressive crafts are ceramics, bowls made of native woods and baskets woven of native fibers. The goddess Pele is a source of inspiration for many Big Island artists – some even use molten lava as a sculpting material.

Hawaiian quilting is another unique art form. The concept of patchwork quilting was introduced by the early missionaries but the Hawaiians, who had only recently taken to Western cotton clothing, didn't have a surplus of cloth scraps – and the idea of cutting up new lengths of fabric simply to sew them back together again in small squares seemed absurd. Instead the Hawaiian women created their own designs using larger cloth pieces, typically with stylized tropical flora on a white background.

A more transitory art form is the creation of leis. Although the type of leis most widely worn by visitors are made of fragrant flowers such as plumeria and tuberose, traditional leis of mokihana berries and maile leaves were more commonly worn in old Hawaii. Both types are still made today.

CULTURE

In many ways, contemporary culture in Hawaii resembles contemporary culture in the rest of the USA.

Hawaiians listen to the same pop music and watch the same TV shows as Americans on the mainland. Hawaii has discos and ballroom dancing, rock bands and classical orchestras, junk food and nouvelle cuisine. The wonderful thing about Hawaii, however, is that the mainland influences largely stand beside, rather than engulf, the culture of the islands.

Not only is traditional Hawaiian culture an integral part of the social fabric, but so are the customs of the ethnically diverse immigrants who have made Hawaii their home. Hawaii is more than just a meeting place of East and West; it's also a place

Hawaiian quilt

Lava flow hits the ocean, Hawaii Volcanoes National Park, Big Island where the cultures merge, typically in a manner that brings out the best of both worlds.

The 1970s saw the start of a Hawaiian cultural renaissance that continues today. Hawaiian language classes are thriving and there is a concerted effort to reintroduce Hawaiian words into modern speech. Hula classes concentrate more on the nuances behind hand movements and facial expressions than on the dramatic hip-shaking that sells dance shows. Many Hawaiian artists and craftspeople are returning to traditional mediums and themes.

Certainly the tourist centers have long been overrun with packaged Hawaiiana, from plastic leis to theme-park luaus, that seems almost a parody of island culture. But fortunately for the visitor the growing interest in traditional Hawaiiana is having an impact on the tourist industry and authentic performances by hula students and contemporary Hawaiian musicians are increasingly easier to find.

RELIGION

Hawaii's population is religiously diverse. In addition to the standard Christian denominations, Hawaii has about 100 Buddhist temples, scores of Shinto shrines and two dozen Hindu temples. There are also Taoist, Tenrikyo, Jewish and Muslim houses of worship.

Christianity has the largest following, with Catholicism being the predominant religious denomination in Hawaii. Interestingly, the United Church of Christ, which includes the Congregationalists who initially converted the islands, claim only about half as many members as the Mormons and one-tenth as many as the Catholics.

LANGUAGE

The unifying language of Hawaii is English, although it's liberally peppered with Hawaiian phrases, loan words from the various immigrant languages and pidgin slang.

It's not uncommon to hear islanders speaking in other languages, as the main language spoken in one out of every four homes in Hawaii is a mother tongue other than English.

The Hawaiian language itself is still spoken among family members by about 9000 people. Closely related to other Polynesian languages, Hawaiian is melodic, phonetically simple and full of vowels and repeated syllables.

Some 85% of all place names in Hawaii are in Hawaiian and as often as not they have interesting translations and stories behind them.

The Hawaiians had no written language until the 1820s when Christian missionaries arrived and wrote down the spoken language in roman letters.

Pronunciation

The written Hawaiian language has just 12 letters. Pronunciation is easy and there are few consonant clusters.

Vowel sounds are about the same as in Spanish or Japanese, more or less like this:

a ah, as in 'father' or uh, as in 'above'
e ay, as in 'gay' or eh, as in 'pet'
i ee, as in 'see'
o oh, as in 'go'
u oo, as in 'noon'

Hawaiian has diphthongs, created when two vowels join together to form a single sound. The stress is on the first vowel, although in general if you pronounce each vowel separately, you'll be easily understood.

The consonant *w* is usually pronounced like a soft English *v* when it follows the letters *i* and *e* (the town Haleiwa is pronounced Halei*v*a) and like the English *w* when it follows *u* or *o*. When *w* follows *a* it can be pronounced either *v* or *w* – thus you will hear both Ha*w*aii and Ha*v*aii.

The other consonants – h, k, l, m, n, p – are pronounced about the same as in English.

Glottal Stops & Macrons Written Hawaiian uses both glottal stops and macrons, although in modern print they are often omitted.

The glottal stop (') indicates a break between two vowels producing an effect similar to saying 'oh-oh' in English. A macron, a short straight line over a vowel, stresses the vowel.

Glottal stops and macrons not only affect pronunciation, but can give a word a completely different meaning. For example *ai* can mean 'sexual intercourse' or 'to eat', depending on the pronunciation.

All this takes on greater significance when you learn to speak Hawaiian in depth. If you're using Hawaiian words in an English-language context (this *poi* is *ono*), there shouldn't be much problem.

Compounds Hawaiian may seem more difficult than it is because many proper names are long and look similar. Many begin with *ka*, meaning 'the', which over time simply became attached to the beginning of the word.

When you break each word down into its composite parts, some of which are repeated, it all becomes much easier. For example: *Kamehameha* consists of the three compounds Ka-meha-meha. *Humu-humunukunukuapuaa*, which is Hawaii's state fish, is broken down into humu-humu-nuku-nuku-a-pu-a-a.

Some words are doubled to emphasize their meaning. For example: *wiki* means 'quick', while *wikiwiki* means 'very quick'.

There are some easily recognizable compounds repeatedly found in place names and it can be fun to learn a few. For instance, *wai* means 'freshwater' – Waikiki means 'spouting water', so named for the freshwater springs that were once there. *Kai* means 'seawater' – Kailua means 'two seas'. *Lani* means 'heavenly' – Lanikai means 'heavenly sea'. *Hana* means 'bay' – Hanalei means 'crescent bay'.

Shaka Sign
Islanders greet each other with the shaka sign, which is made by folding down the three middle fingers to the palm and extending the thumb and little finger. The hand is then usually held out and shaken in greeting. It's as common as waving.

Common Hawaiian Vocabulary

Learn these words first: *aloha* and *mahalo*, which are everyday pleasantries; *makai* and *mauka*, commonly used in giving directions; and *kane* and *wahine*, often on bathroom doors. Check the glossary in the back of the book for more useful words.

aina
    land
akamai
    clever
alii
    chief, royalty
aloha
    love, welcome, goodbye
aloha aina
    love of the land
hala
    pandanus
hale
    house
hana
    work; or bay, a compound in place names
haole
    Caucasian
hapa
    half; or person of mixed-blood
hapa haole
    half-white, used for a person, thing or idea
hau
    lowland tree with flowers resembling hibiscus
Hauoli Makahiki Hou
    Happy New Year
haupia
    coconut pudding
Hawaii nei
    all the Hawaiian islands, as distinguished from the Big Island
heiau
    ancient Hawaiian temple
holoholo
    to walk, drive or ramble around for pleasure
holoku
    a long dress similar to the muu-muu, but more fitted and with a yoke
hui
    group, organization
hula
    traditional Hawaiian dance
imu
    underground earthen oven used in traditional luau cooking
kahuna
    wise person in any field, commonly a priest, healer or sorcerer

kalua
    traditional method of baking in an underground oven

kamaaina
    native-born Hawaiian or a long-time resident; literally 'child of the land'

kane
    man

kapu
    taboo, part of strict ancient Hawaiian social system; today often used on signs meaning 'Keep Out'

kaukau
    food

keiki
    child, children

kiawe
    a relative of the mesquite tree introduced to Hawaii in the 1820s, now very common; its branches are covered with sharp thorns

koa
    native hardwood tree often used in woodworking

kokua
    help, cooperation; 'Please Kokua' on a trash can is a gentle way of saying 'don't litter'

kona
    leeward, or a leeward wind

lanai
    veranda

lauhala
    leaves of the hala plant used in weaving

lei
    garland, usually of flowers, but also of leaves or shells

lilikoi
    passion fruit

limu
    seaweed

lolo
    stupid, crazy

lomi
    salmon, raw diced salmon marinated with tomatoes and onions

lomilomi
    massage

luau
    traditional Hawaiian feast

mahalo
    thank you

makai
    towards the sea

malihini
    newcomer, visitor

manini
    convict tang (a reef fish); also used to refer to something small or insignificant

mano
    shark

mauka
    toward the mountains, inland

mele
    song, chant

Mele Kalikimaka
    Merry Christmas

muu-muu
    long, loose-fitting dress introduced by the missionaries

nene
    Hawaii's state bird, a native goose

ohana
    family, extended family

ono
    delicious; also the name of the wahoo fish

pakalolo
    marijuana; literally 'crazy smoke'

pali
    cliff

paniolo
    Hawaiian cowboy

pau
    finished, no more; *pau hana* means quitting time

puka
    any kind of hole or opening

pupu
    snack food, hors d'oeuvres; shells

puu
    hill, cinder cone

tutu
    aunt, older woman

ukulele
    stringed musical instrument

wahine
    woman

wikiwiki
    hurry, quick

Pidgin

Hawaii's early immigrants communicated with each other in pidgin, a simplified, broken form of English. It was a language born of necessity, stripped of all but the most needed words.

Modern pidgin is better defined as local slang. It is extensive, lively and ever-changing. Whole conversations can take place in pidgin, or often just a word or two is dropped into a more conventional English sentence.

Even Shakespeare's *Twelfth Night* has been translated (by local comedian James

Grant Benton) to *Twelf Nite O Wateva*. Malvolio's line 'My masters, are you mad?' becomes 'You buggahs crazy, o wat?'

Short-term visitors will rarely win friends by trying to speak pidgin. It's more like an insider's code that you're allowed to use only after you've lived in Hawaii long enough to understand the nuances.

Some characteristics of pidgin include: a fast staccato rhythm, two-word sentences, dropping the soft 'h' sound from words that start with 'th', use of loan words from many languages (often Hawaiian) and double meanings which trip up the uninitiated.

Some of the more common words and expressions:

blalah
    big Hawaiian fellow
brah
    brother, friend; also used for 'hey you'
broke da mouth
    delicious
buggah
    guy
chicken skin
    goose bumps
coconut wireless
    word of mouth
cockaroach
    steal
da kine
    that kind of thing, whatchamacallit etc; used whenever you can't think of the word you want but you know the listener knows what you mean
geev em
    go for it, beat them
grinds
    food, eat; *ono grinds* is good food.
haolefied
    become like a *haole*
howzit?
    hi, how's it going?
how you stay?
    how are you?
humbug
    a real hassle
like beef?
    wanna fight?
mo' bettah
    much better, the best
slippahs
    flip-flops, thongs

stick
    surfboard
stink eye
    dirty look, evil eye
talk story
    any kind of conversation, gossip, tales
tanks
    thanks. More commonly *tanks brah*.
tree
    three

Official Hawaii
State nickname: The Aloha State
State flower: *pua aloalo* – hibiscus
State tree: *kukui* – candlenut tree
State bird: *nene* – Hawaiian goose
State marine mammal: humpback whale
State fish: *humuhumunukunukuapuaa* – rectangular triggerfish
State motto: *Ua mau ke ea o ka aina i ka pono* – 'The life of the land is perpetuated in righteousness.'
State song: *Hawaii Ponoi* – written by King Kalakaua
State flag: Designed for King Kamehameha I prior to 1816, it has the UK's Union Jack in the upper left-hand corner. Eight stripes of red, white and blue represent the eight largest islands.
State seal: The state seal incorporates the state motto and a heraldic shield flanked by Kamehameha I on one side and the Goddess of Liberty holding the Hawaiian flag on the other. It also has taro and banana leaves, ferns, a phoenix and the statehood year of 1959. ■

Facts for the Visitor

MONEY

Credit Cards

Major credit and charge cards are widely accepted throughout Hawaii, including at car rental agencies and most hotels, restaurants, gas stations, shops and larger grocery stores. Most recreational and tourist activities in Hawaii can also be paid for by credit card. The most commonly accepted cards are Visa, MasterCard and American Express, although JCB, Discover and Diners Club cards are also accepted by a fair number of businesses.

Automatic Teller Machines

Automatic teller machines (ATM) are another plastic alternative. We no longer take any traveler's checks at all when we go to Hawaii, choosing instead to withdraw money from a bank account back home using ATMs. The small service charge works out cheaper than the 1% fee charged for traveler's checks and there's no need to carry a bundle of checks around.

Major banks such as Bank of Hawaii (Bankoh for short), First Hawaiian Bank and Bank of America have extensive ATM networks throughout Hawaii that will give cash advances on major credit cards (including MasterCard, Visa and JCB) and allow cash withdrawals with affiliated ATM cards. Most ATM machines in Hawaii accept bank cards from both the Plus and Cirrus systems, the two largest ATM networks in the USA.

In addition to traditional bank locations, you can also find ATMs at most large grocery stores, in mall-style shopping centers and in a growing number of convenience stores.

Costs

How much money you need for visiting Hawaii depends on your traveling style. Some people get by quite cheaply while others rack up huge balances on their credit cards.

The air fare to Hawaii is usually one of the heftier parts of the budget. Fares vary greatly, particularly from the US mainland, so shop around. (Note that Hawaii stopovers are often thrown in free, or for a nominal charge, on trips between North America and Asian or Pacific countries.)

Flights between Hawaiian islands cost about $50 to $75 one way. Hawaii has only two ferry services, one of which operates between Lanai and Maui and the other between Molokai and Maui; both cost $25 one way.

It can be a challenge to explore the islands without renting a car, except on Oahu where there's a good inexpensive bus system. Renting a car usually costs between $165 and $200 a week.

Camping is an alternative to paying for a hotel. Every island except Lanai has at least one state park with free camping as well as inexpensive county campgrounds. In addition, Maui and the Big Island have excellent national parks with free camping.

Currently each of the four main islands has at least a couple of hostel-style places with dormitory beds for $15 or less and either B&Bs or spartan hotels for around $40. For hotels with more standard middle-class amenities expect to pay nearly double that and if you've got your mind set on a first-class beachfront hotel get ready to pay upwards of $125 a night. For a splurge on a luxury hotel – and Hawaii has some of the world's finest – rates generally begin around $250.

If you're staying awhile, there are ways to cut accommodation costs. Weekly and monthly condo rental rates can beat all but the cheapest hotels. Besides having more space most condos are turn-key, with virtually everything you'll need from towels and beach mats to a kitchen stocked with pots and pans. Being able to prepare your own meals in a condo can save a bundle on your food bill.

Another cost-cutter is to travel in the low

season, generally from April to mid-December, when accommodation rates are often discounted as much as 30%.

Since much of Hawaii's food is shipped in, grocery prices average 25% higher than on the mainland. Because of the shipping costs, bulky items like cereal have the highest mark-ups, while compact items such as canned tuna have the lowest. Food in local neighborhood restaurants is a good value in Hawaii, with prices generally as cheap as you'll find on the mainland.

The good news for visitors is that lots of things in Hawaii are free. There are no parking or entrance fees at any beach or state park for instance, and most of the islands' historical sights can be explored for free.

Tipping

Tipping practices are the same as in the rest of the USA. In restaurants, waiters expect a tip of about 15%, while 10% is generally sufficient for taxi drivers.

Consumer Taxes

Hawaii has a 4.17% state sales tax that is tacked onto virtually everything, including all meals, groceries, car rentals and accommodation. An additional 6% room tax brings the total tax added to all accommodation bills to 10.17%. Another tax targeted at visitors is a $2-a-day 'road use' tax imposed upon all car rentals.

WHEN TO GO

Hawaii is a great place to visit any time of the year.

Although the busiest tourist season is in winter, that has more to do with weather *elsewhere*, as many visitors are snowbirds escaping cold winters back home. Essentially the weather in Hawaii is agreeable all year round. It's a bit rainier in the winter and a bit hotter in the summer but there are no extremes and cooling trade winds modify the heat throughout the year.

In terms of cost, spring through fall can be a bargain, as hotel prices drop significantly around April 1 and most don't climb back up again until mid-December.

Naturally, for certain activities there are peak seasons. If you're a board surfer, you'll find the biggest waves in winter, whereas if you're a windsurfer you'll find the best wind conditions in summer.

WHAT TO BRING

Hawaii has balmy weather and a casual attitude towards dress so, for the most part, packing is a breeze.

At the lower elevations it's summer all year. Shorts, sandals and a T-shirt or cotton shirt are the standard day dress. If you don't intend to spend time at higher elevations, a light jacket or sweater will be the warmest clothing you'll need.

Pack light. You can always pick up something with a floral Hawaiian print when you get there and dress island style.

An aloha shirt and lightweight slacks for men, and a cotton dress for women, is pretty much regarded as 'dressing up' on the islands. Only a few of the most exclusive restaurants require anything dressier.

Hawaii does, however, have highland areas (called upcountry on the islands) as well as mountains, and most people get at least as far as the former. The upcountry can be a good 20°F cooler than the coast and when the fog blows in and the wind picks up, it gets quite nippy. If you intend to spend any time in the upcountry, plan on another layer of clothes.

The temperature on the mountain summits on the Big Island and Maui can dip below freezing. If you're going to be camping at high elevations, you need to be prepared for cold weather; a tent, winter-rated sleeping bag, rain gear and layers of warm clothing, preferably wool, are a must.

Camping on the beach is another matter entirely. A very lightweight cotton bag is the most you'll need. Public campgrounds require tents – and because of mosquitoes they're a good idea anyway. If you don't want to pack camping gear, it can be rented on Oahu, Kauai and the Big Island.

For hiking, bring footwear with good traction. Many people just wear sneakers, although walking on lava can be tough on the ankles. Serious hikers should consider lugging along their hiking boots.

You won't regret bringing binoculars for watching whales and birds, and a flashlight is useful to explore caves. We always carry a snorkel, mask and fins, but you can also buy or rent them there. Actually, you don't need to worry too much about what to bring, as just about anything you forget to pack you can easily buy in Hawaii.

TOURIST OFFICES

The Hawaii Visitors Bureau (HVB) provides free tourist information on the state. On request they'll mail out a little packet containing general statewide tourist information and booklets listing member hotels and restaurants.

The central office (☎ 923-1811; fax 922-8991) is in the Waikiki Business Plaza, Suite 801, 2270 Kalakaua Ave, Honolulu, HI 96815. There are branch offices on Maui, Kauai and the Big Island that can provide information more specific to their

Hawaii Visitors Bureau warrior sign

islands. Information on these offices is in the individual island chapters.

There are also four toll-free numbers that can be called to order tourist information. For a magazine-like booklet on all Hawaii, call (800) 257-2999. For a similar booklet on Maui, call (800) 525-MAUI. For Kauai the number is (800) AH-KAUAI and for the Big Island it's (800) 648-BIG1.

HVB offices on the US mainland include:

180 N Michigan Ave, Suite 2210, Chicago, IL 60601 (☎ (312) 236-0632; fax (312) 236-9781)
Central Plaza, 3440 Wilshire Blvd, Room 610, Los Angeles, CA 90010 (☎ (213) 385-5301; fax (213) 385-2513)
Empire State Building, Suite 808, 350 Fifth Ave, New York, NY 10118 (☎ (212) 947-0717; fax (212) 947-0725)
50 California St, Suite 450, San Francisco, CA 94111 (☎ (415) 392-8173; fax (415) 398-4940)

HVB offices outside the USA are listed in the Facts for the International Visitor section at the end of this chapter.

Brochures and travel information on Molokai are available from the Molokai Visitors Association (☎ 553-3876, (800) 800-6367; fax 553-5288), Box 960, Kaunakakai, HI 96748.

For a free guide to the state parks on all the islands, with a brief description of each park and camping information, contact the Division of State Parks (☎ 587-0300), Box 621, Honolulu, HI 96809.

USEFUL ORGANIZATIONS
Information for Disabled Visitors

The Commission on Persons with Disabilities (☎ 586-8121), 919 Ala Moana Blvd, Room 101, Honolulu, HI 96814, distributes the comprehensive three-part *Aloha Guide to Accessibility,* which contains detailed travel tips for physically disabled people. Part I has general information and covers airport access on the major islands. Part II discusses accessibility to parks, theaters, shopping centers and other visitor attractions. Part III lists hotels with wheelchair access or specially-adapted rooms or

Hawaiian Weddings

Many visitors come to Hawaii not only for their honeymoon, but to make their wedding vows as well.

Getting married in Hawaii is a straightforward process. Hawaii requires that the prospective bride and groom appear in person together before a marriage license agent and pay $25 for a license, which is given out on the spot. Women will need to present a health certificate for rubella screening (or an exemption certificate) from a doctor. There's no waiting period and no residence or citizenship requirements. The legal age for marriage is 18, or 16 with parental consent.

Full information and forms are available from the Department of Health (☎ 586-4544), Marriage License Office, Box 3378, 1250 Punchbowl St, Honolulu, HI 96813. The office is open from 8 am to 4 pm Monday to Friday.

There are numerous companies that provide wedding services. One of these, Affordable Weddings of Hawaii (☎ 923-4876, (800) 942-4554; fax 396-0959), Box 26475, Honolulu, HI 96825, will mail out a brochure with tips on planning your wedding, choosing a location, photography services etc. The amiable Reverend M C Hansen, of Affordable Weddings, can provide a nondenominational service, starting at $55 for a simple weekday ceremony and going up to much more elaborate packages from there.

For something more traditional (or nontraditional, depending on your perspective), Helemano Kauihimalaihi, dressed in a loincloth and carrying a carved staff, performs a ceremony entirely in the Hawaiian language. He's attempted to recreate an ancient ceremony using Hawaiian chants and proverbs, draping of the bride and groom in tapa and the like. For information, call 671-8420 or write to him at 91-1125 Ahona St, Ewa Beach, HI 96706. ■

facilities. All three parts are free if picked up from the commission office. If ordered by mail, Part I will be sent free, while Part II and Part III will cost $4 each to cover postage and handling.

Information for Gay Travelers

The following information sources can help visitors get oriented to Hawaii's gay scene.

Island Lifestyle (☎ 737-6400), 2851A Kihei Place, Honolulu, HI 96816, is a 66-page monthly magazine for Hawaii's gay community. It can be picked up free at various gay clubs in Honolulu. Annual subscriptions cost $24 by first-class mail in the USA, $36 overseas. Lifestyle also sells *The Pages*, a directory of clubs, B&Bs, restaurants and other businesses that are supportive to the gay community.

The *Gay Community News* (☎ 521-6000), Box 37083, Honolulu, HI 96837, a monthly newspaper, is available free around Honolulu or by subscription.

Pacific Ocean Holidays (☎ 923-2400, (800) 735-6600), Box 88245, Honolulu, HI 96830, arranges vacation packages for gay men and women. They also produce a small booklet called *Pocket Guide to Hawaii* which is geared to the gay community and costs $4 when ordered by mail.

BUSINESS HOURS

While there's a variance of half an hour in either direction, the most common office hours in Hawaii are 8:30 am to 4:30 pm Monday to Friday. Shops in central areas and malls, as well as large chain stores, are usually open into the evenings and on weekends, and some grocery stores are open 24 hours.

HOLIDAYS & SPECIAL EVENTS

With its multitude of cultures and good year-round weather, Hawaii has a seemingly endless number and variety of holidays, festivals and sporting events. The two lists that follow – one for cultural events and one for sporting events – include the highlights.

As dates for many events change a bit from year to year, it's best to check activity schedules in local papers or pick up the current-year calendar of events from the Hawaii Visitors Bureau. Water sports particularly are reliant on the weather and the surf, so any schedule is tentative.

January

New Year's Day is a national holiday. Fireworks displays are held in many of the larger towns and resorts on New Year's Eve and firecrackers are shot off nonstop through the night.

Chinese New Year begins at the second new moon after winter solstice (mid-January to mid-February) with lion dances and strings of firecrackers. Honolulu's Chinatown is the center stage.

The *Narcissus Festival*, part of the Chinese New Year celebrations, runs for about five weeks and includes arts & crafts, food booths, a beauty pageant and coronation ball. (Oahu)

Martin Luther King Day is a national holiday observed on the third Monday of the month.

Ka Molokai Makahiki, a modern-day version of the ancient makahiki festival, is held in Kaunakakai in mid-January. The week-long celebration begins with a fishing contest using outrigger canoes and concludes with a tournament of traditional Hawaiian games and sporting events. There's also Hawaiian music and hula on the final day. (Molokai)

February

Presidents' Day, a national holiday, is observed on the third Monday.

Cherry Blossom Festival, which covers the entire month and spills over into March, features a variety of Japanese cultural events including tea ceremonies, mochi pounding and taiko drummers. Most activities occur on Oahu.

March & April

St Patrick's Day, March 17th, is celebrated with a parade down Kalakaua Ave, Waikiki. (Oahu)

Prince Kuhio Day, March 26th, is a state holiday honoring Jonah Kuhio Kalanianaole, Hawaii's first delegate to the US Congress. On his native island of Kauai there's a week-long festival including canoe races, a royal ball, music and dance.

Easter falls in March or April. Many business offices are closed on *Good Friday* as well.

The *Merrie Monarch Festival*, named after King David Kalakaua, is Hawaii's biggest hula competition and Hawaiiana festival. Held in Hilo, it starts on Easter Sunday and lasts for a week. (Big Island)

May

May Day is Lei Day in Hawaii. Everybody dons a lei for this one, held on the first of the month. There are lei-making competitions on several islands and Oahu crowns a lei queen.

Molokai Ka Hula Piko celebrates the birth of the hula, with traditional dance performances, Hawaiian food, cultural demonstrations and visits to sacred sites. It's held on Molokai in mid-month.

Memorial Day, on the last Monday in May, is a national holiday to honor soldiers killed in battle.

June

King Kamehameha Day is a state holiday celebrated on June 11 or the nearest weekend, with events on all islands. On Oahu the statue of Kamehameha is ceremoniously draped with leis and there's a parade from downtown Honolulu to Kapiolani Park. On the Big Island the Kamehameha statue in the king's hometown of Kapaau is also draped with leis.

The *King Kamehameha Hula & Chant Competition*, one of Hawaii's biggest hula contests, is held in Honolulu near the end of the month. (Oahu)

July

The *Puuhonua O Honaunau Cultural Festival* is held at the Puuhonua O Honaunau national historical park on the weekend closest to July 1. The festival includes a 'royal court', a *hukilau* (net fishing with a seine), hula and traditional craft displays. (Big Island)

Independence Day, on the 4th, is a national holiday celebrated with fireworks and festivities on the main islands and a rodeo at Parker Ranch on the Big Island.

The *Prince Lot Hula Festival*, held at Moanalua Gardens on the third Saturday, features hula competitions from Hawaii's major hula schools. (Oahu)

August

Admission Day, a state holiday on the third Friday, observes the anniversary of Hawaiian statehood.

The *Obon* season, which is celebrated around the islands in July and August, is marked by Japanese bon odori dances to honor deceased ancestors. The final event is a floating lantern ceremony at Waikiki's Ala Wai Canal on the evening of August 15.

Hawaiian Slack-Key Guitar Festival features Hawaii's top slack-key guitarists in a free five-hour concert at Ala Moana Beach Park. (Oahu)

Ka Himeni Ana is a contest of old-style Hawaiian singing without amplification. All the songs are pre-WW II numbers that are sung in Hawaiian. It's held at the University of Hawaii in August or September. (Oahu)

September

Aloha Week is a celebration of all things Hawaiian with parades, cultural events, contests, canoe races and Hawaiian music. Festivities are staggered throughout September and October, depending on the island. Oahu has a street fair in downtown Honolulu and a parade in Waikiki.

Labor Day is a national holiday observed on the first Monday.

October

Columbus Day is a national holiday observed on the second Monday of the month.

The *Kona Coffee Cultural Festival*, a two-week event held in Kailua-Kona in late October and early November, features a parade, a coffee-picking contest and cultural events. (Big Island)

November

Election Day, on the second Tuesday of the month, is a state holiday during election years.

Veterans Day, on the 11th, is a national holiday.

The *Hawaii International Film Festival* features about 150 films from Pacific Rim and Asian nations. Films are shown throughout Oahu for a week around mid-November and on the Neighbor Islands the following week. The local papers print the schedules.

Thanksgiving is a national holiday celebrated on the fourth Thursday.

December

Bodhi Day, the Buddhist Day of Enlightenment, is celebrated on the 8th with ceremonies at Buddhist temples.

Christmas Day is a national holiday. Christmas festivals and craft fairs are held on all the islands throughout December.

Sporting Events
January

The *Hula Bowl*, the classic East/West college all-star football game, is held at Aloha Stadium on a Saturday in January. (Oahu)

The *Hawaiian Open Golf Tournament* at Waialae Country Club is a PGA event with a $1

million purse that's held in January or February. (Oahu)

The *Morey Bodyboards Competitions* are held at Honolua Bay in late January or early February, depending upon surf conditions. (Maui)

February

The *NFL Pro Bowl*, the annual all-star game of the National Football League, is held at Aloha Stadium near the beginning of the month. (Oahu)

The *Great Aloha Run* is a popular 8.2-mile fun run from Aloha Tower to Aloha Stadium held on Presidents Day. (Oahu)

At the *Morey Bodyboards Competitions*, held around late February, some of the world's top bodyboarders hit the Banzai Pipeline's towering waves. (Oahu)

Buffalo's Big Board Surfing Classic, held at Makaha Beach, is a surf contest using old-time 12-foot longboards. Held over two weekends in late February or early March. (Oahu)

March

Oahu Kite Festival is a weekend event held early in the month at Kapiolani Park. It includes stunt championships by the pros, with colorful kites dancing against the backdrop of Diamond Head. (Oahu)

The *Hawaii Ski Cup*, a ski race down Mauna Kea, and *Pele's Cup Mauna Loa Cross Country*, the 'world's highest cross country ski race,' are held in March – snow permitting. (Big Island)

April

The *Marui/O'Neill Invitational*, held at Hookipa Beach early in the month, is the world's top international windsurfing competition and has a purse of around $200,000. (Maui)

The *Carole Kai International Bed Race & Parade* is an offbeat wheeled-bed race from Fort DeRussy to Kapiolani Park held in late April. (Oahu)

May

The *Kanaka Ikaika Molokai to Oahu Kayak Race*, held in mid-May, is a 32-mile kayak race across the treacherous Kaiwi Channel, from Kaluakoi Resort, Molokai to Koko Marina, Oahu.

The *Keauhou-Kona Triathlon* is a half-Ironman with a mere 56-mile bike race, 13-mile run and 1.2-mile swim, starting at Keauhou Bay. (Big Island)

June & July

On odd-numbered years sailboats in the *Transpacific Yacht Race* leave southern California on the July 4 weekend and arrive in Honolulu 10 to 14 days later. The race has been held since the turn of the century. (Oahu)

Parker Ranch Rodeo is held at Paniolo Park in Waimea on July 4th. (Big Island)

Makawao Rodeo is an old-fashioned rodeo in Makawao's cowboy country that lasts for a few days around the July 4th holiday. (Maui)

The *TDK/Gotcha Pro* is a professional surf meet for both board surfers and bodysurfers held at Sandy Beach, usually around mid-July. (Oahu)

The *Kilauea Volcano Wilderness Marathon and Rim Runs* at Hawaii Volcanoes National Park includes a 10-mile run around the rim of Kilauea, a 5½-mile race into Kilauea Iki Crater and a 26.2-mile marathon through the Kau Desert. It's held near the end of July and draws an international crowd. (Big Island)

August

The *Hawaiian International Billfish Tournament* is the world's number one marlin tournament. Held in Kailua-Kona, it lasts a week, usually beginning in early August. (Big Island)

The *Haleakala Run to the Sun* is a 36.2-mile marathon that begins at dawn at sea-level Kahului and climbs 10,000 feet to the top of Haleakala. It's held in August or September. (Maui)

September

The *Hana Relay* is a 54-mile relay run from Kahului to Hana. (Maui)

Bankoh Na Wahine O Ke Kai, Hawaii's major annual women's outrigger canoe race, starts at sunrise at Hale O Lono Harbor on Molokai and ends 40 miles later at Waikiki's Fort DeRussy Beach on Oahu. It's held near the end of the month.

October

The *Bankoh Molokai Hoe* is Hawaii's major men's outrigger canoe race, held near mid-month. It starts after sunrise from Hale O Lono Harbor on Molokai and finishes at Fort DeRussy Beach on Oahu about five hours later. Teams from Australia, Tahiti, Germany and the US mainland join Hawaiian teams in this annual competition which was first held in 1952.

The *Ironman Triathlon*, held on a Saturday in mid-October, is considered by many the ultimate endurance race. This is the triathlon that started it all and remains the world's best known. The 2.4-mile swim, 112-mile bike race and 26.2-mile marathon begins and ends at Kailua Pier. (Big Island)

November

The *Morey Bodyboards Championships* take place on the North Shore around early November. (Oahu)

The *Triple Crown of Surfing* consists of three professional competitions that draw the world's top surfers to Oahu's North Shore. The events begin in November and run throughout December, with the exact dates and locations depending on when and where the surf's up.

December

The *Honolulu Marathon*, Hawaii's biggest, is run mid-month along a 26-mile course from the Aloha Tower to Kapiolani Park. (Oahu)

The *Aloha Bowl* is the big collegiate football game held at Aloha Stadium on Christmas Day and televised nationally. (Oahu)

POST & TELECOMMUNICATIONS
Postal Rates

Postage rates for first-class mail within the USA are 32c for letters up to one ounce (23c for each additional ounce) and 20c for postcards. First-class mail between Hawaii and the mainland goes by air and usually takes three to four days.

International airmail rates are 50c for a half-ounce letter and 40c for a postcard to any foreign country with the exception of Canada (40c for a one-ounce letter and 30c for a postcard) and Mexico (35c for a half-ounce letter and 30c for a postcard).

The cost for parcels airmailed anywhere within the USA is $3.00 for two pounds or less, $6.00 for five pounds. For heavier items, rates differ according to the distance mailed.

Receiving Mail

You can have mail sent to you c/o General Delivery at any post office in Hawaii that has its own zip (post) code. An exception is on Oahu, where all general delivery mail sent to Honolulu or Waikiki is delivered to the main post office near the airport.

Telephone

The telephone area code for all of Hawaii is 808. The area code is not used when making calls on the same island, but must be added to all Hawaiian phone numbers when calling from outside the state and when calling from one Hawaiian island to another.

All phone numbers listed in this book beginning with 800 are toll-free numbers from the US mainland, unless otherwise noted. The same numbers are sometimes toll free from Canada as well.

In Hawaii, like the rest of the USA, pay phones can be found in public places such as shopping centers, hotel lobbies and beach parks. Although there are some pay phones that operate on credit cards, by far the most common types are the ones that accept coins only. You can either insert change into them or make collect calls via the operator.

Local calls within Hawaii cost 25c at pay phones, and there's no time limit. Any call made from one point on an island to any other point on that island is a local call. Calls from one island to another are long distance.

To dial direct from one Hawaiian island to another from a pay phone, the rate from 8 am to 5 pm weekdays is $1.60 for the first minute plus 27c for each additional minute. From 5 to 11 pm Sunday to Friday it's $1.46 for the first minute and 18c for each additional minute. At all other times the rate is $1.36 for the first minute and 11c for each additional minute.

Most hotels add on a service charge of 50c to $1 for each local call made from a room phone and most also have hefty surcharges for long-distance calls. Public coin phones, which can be found in most lobbies, are always cheaper. You can pump in quarters, use a phone card issued by your own telephone company or make collect calls from pay phones. In Hawaii you can make 800-number (toll-free) calls from pay phones without inserting any money.

For directory assistance on the same island dial 1-411, for other islands dial 1-(808)-555-1212. To find out if there's an inter-island toll-free number for a business, dial 1-(800)-555-1212.

Information on calling overseas is given in the Facts for the International Visitor section at the end of this chapter.

TIME

Hawaii does not observe daylight-saving time. When it's noon in Hawaii the time in other parts of the world is: 1 pm in Anchorage, 2 pm in Los Angeles, 5 pm in New York, 10 pm in London, 11 pm in Bonn, 7 am the next day in Tokyo, 8 am the next day in Sydney and Melbourne, and 10 am the next day in Auckland.

The time difference is one hour greater during those months when other countries observe daylight saving. For example from April to October when it's noon in Hawaii it's 3 pm in Los Angeles and 6 pm in New York; and from November to March when it's noon in Hawaii it's 9 am in Melbourne and 11 am in Auckland.

Hawaii has about 11 hours of daylight in mid-winter and almost 13½ hours in mid-summer. In mid-winter the sun rises at about 7 am and sets about 6 pm. In mid-summer it rises before 6 am and sets after 7 pm.

And then there's Hawaiian Time, which is a slow-down-the-clock pace or a euphemism for being late.

BOOKS

Hawaii is said to be the most written-about place in the Pacific. There are books on just about every subject you can think of, from the origin of volcanoes to the history of hula. There are even reference books devoted to the books of Hawaii.

People

Keneti by Bob Krauss (University of Hawaii Press, Honolulu, 1988) is a biography of Kenneth 'Keneti' Emory, the esteemed Bishop Museum archaeologist who over the years sailed with writer Jack London, worked with anthropologist

Margaret Mead and surfed with Olympian Duke Kahanamoku. Emory, who died in 1992, spent much of his life uncovering the ruins of villages and temples throughout the Pacific, recording them before they disappeared forever.

Paddling My Own Canoe by Audrey Sutherland (University of Hawaii Press, Honolulu, 1978) details the author's explorations in an inflatable kayak along the rugged and isolated north shore of Molokai. The book helped popularize wilderness kayaking in Hawaii.

Father Damien, the priest who worked in the leprosy colony on Molokai, is the subject of many books including *Holy Man: Father Damien of Molokai* by Gavan Daws (Harper & Row, New York, 1973), *Damien the Leper* by John Farrow (Doubleday & Co, New York, 1954) and others.

Aloha Cowboy by Virginia Cowan-Smith & Bonnie Domrose Stone (University of Hawaii Press, Honolulu, 1988) is an illustrated account of 200 years of *paniolo* life in Hawaii.

History & Politics

Hawaiian Antiquities by David Malo (Bishop Museum Press, Honolulu, 1992), written in 1838, was the first account of Hawaiian culture written by a Hawaiian. It gives an in-depth history of Hawaii before the arrival of the missionaries.

Shoal of Time by Gavan Daws (University of Hawaii Press, Honolulu, 1974) is a comprehensive and colorful history covering the period from Captain Cook's 'discovery' of the islands to statehood.

Hawaii's Story by Hawaii's Queen by Queen Liliuokalani (Mutual Publishing, Honolulu, 1990), written in 1897, is an autobiographical account of Liliuokalani's life and the circumstances surrounding her 1893 overthrow.

The Betrayal of Liliuokalani: Last Queen of Hawaii, 1838-1917 by Helena G Allen (Mutual Publishing, Honolulu, 1990) is an insightful account not only of the queen's life but also of missionary activity and foreign encroachment in Hawaii.

Fragments of Hawaiian History by John Papa Ii (Bishop Museum Press, Honolulu, 1993), translated by Mary Kawena Pukui, is a first-hand account of old Hawaii under the *kapu* system. Ii lived in Kailua-Kona at the time of Kamehameha I.

Kauai, the Separate Kingdom by Edward Joesting (University of Hawaii Press, Honolulu, 1984) is the authoritative history book on Kauai, the only Hawaiian kingdom never conquered in battle.

The Hawaiian Kingdom by Ralph S Kuykendall (University of Hawaii Press, Honolulu) is a three-volume set written from 1938 to 1967. It covers Hawaiian history from 1778 to 1893 and is considered the definitive work on the period.

Six Months in the Sandwich Islands by Isabella Bird Bishop (University of Hawaii Press, Honolulu, 1964) is the personal account of a Victorian lady's travels around Hawaii in 1873.

Natural History

Hawaii: The Islands of Life (Signature Publishing, 1988) has strikingly beautiful photos of the flora & fauna and landscapes of areas being protected by the Nature Conservancy of Hawaii. The text is by respected Pacific author Gavan Daws.

The Many-Splendored Fishes of Hawaii by Gar Goodson (Stanford University Press, 1985) is one of the better of several small, inexpensive fish identification books on the market, and has good descriptions and 170 color drawings.

Hawaii's Fishes: A Guide for Snorkelers, Divers and Aquarists by John P Hoover (Mutual Publishing, Honolulu, 1993) is a more expensive and comprehensive field guide covering over 230 reef and shore fishes of Hawaii. It's fully illustrated with color photographs and gives insights on island dive sites.

Hawaii's Birds (Hawaii Audubon Society, Honolulu, 1993) is the best pocket-sized guide to the birds of Hawaii. It has color photos and descriptions of all the native birds and many of the introduced species.

For something more comprehensive, there's *A Field Guide to the Birds of Ha-*

waii & the Tropical Pacific by H Douglas Pratt, Phillip L Bruner and Delwyn G Berrett (Princeton University Press, New Jersey, 1987). The 409-page book contains 45 pages of color plates.

Mammals in Hawaii by P Quentin Tomich (Bishop Museum Press, Honolulu, 1986) is the authoritative book on the mammals in Hawaii, with interesting stories on how they arrived in the islands. He includes all species of whales and dolphins found in Hawaiian waters.

Trailside Plants of Hawaii's National Parks by Charles H Lamoureux (Hawaii Natural History Association, 1976) covers common trailside plants and trees in some depth. It's a good book to have if you'll be spending time hiking in the national parks.

Similarly, *Hawaiian Forest Plants* by Mark David Merlin (Oriental Publishing Company, Honolulu, 1976) has descriptions and color photos of many of the plants encountered on Hawaii's forest trails.

Plants and Flowers of Hawaii by S H Sohmer & R Gustafson (University of Hawaii Press, Honolulu, 1987) has quality color photos and descriptions of over 130 native plants of Hawaii, including information on their habitat and evolution.

Flowers in Hawaii (Hakubundo, Honolulu), with text in both English and Japanese, is a good picture book of common flowers found in Hawaii.

Practical Folk Medicine of Hawaii by L R McBride (Petroglyph Press, Hilo, 1975) has descriptions of many native medicinal plants and their uses.

Maui – How It Came to Be by Will Kyselka & Ray Lanterman (University of Hawaii Press, Honolulu, 1980) is a readable geology book on the evolution of Maui from volcanic formation to present day.

Hawaiian Culture

The Kumulipo by Martha Beckwith (University of Hawaii Press, Honolulu, 1972) is a translation of the Hawaiian chant of creation. The chant of 2077 lines begins in the darkness of the spirit world and traces the genealogy of an *alii* (royalty) family, said to be the ancestors of humankind.

Hawaiian Mythology by Martha Beckwith (University of Hawaii Press, Honolulu, 1970) has comprehensive translations of Hawaii's old myths and legends.

Nana I Ke Kumu (Look to the Source) by Mary K Pukui, E W Haertig & Catherine A Lee (Hui Hanai, 1972, 2 vols) is a fascinating collection of information on Hawaiian cultural practices, social customs and beliefs.

The Legends and Myths of Hawaii (Charles Tuttle Co, Rutland, Vermont, 1985) is a collection of legends as told by King David Kalakaua. It has a short introduction to Hawaiian culture and history as well.

The Hula by Jerry Hopkins (APA Productions, Hong Kong, 1982) is a history of the hula and the musical instruments used in the dance. It also includes biographical sketches of some of hula's most important people.

Hawaiian Music and Musicians: An Illustrated History by George S Kanahele (University of Hawaii Press, Honolulu, 1979) is a history of the islands' music, including singers and composers and some of their songs and chants.

Niihau Shell Leis by Linda Paik Moriarty (University of Hawaii Press, Honolulu, 1986) explains the development of the unique Hawaiian craft of shell lei making by Niihauans and illustrates the various styles.

Hawaiian Petroglyphs by J Halley Cox (Bishop Museum Press, Honolulu, 1990), lists petroglyph sites and includes extensive photos and illustrations.

Na Wahi Pana O Koolau Poko by Anne Kapulani Landgraf (University of Hawaii Press, Honolulu, 1994) discusses the historical and cultural sites of the Koolau district of Windward Oahu, which was once a major population center for Hawaiians. The book has 82 quality duotone photographs accompanying a Hawaiian/English text.

Fiction

A Hawaiian Reader, edited by A Grove Day & Carl Stroven (Mutual Publishing, Honolulu, 1959), is an excellent anthology with 37 selections, both fiction and nonfiction. It starts with a log entry by Captain James Cook and includes writings from early missionaries as well as Mark Twain, Jack London, Somerset Maugham, David Malo, Isabella Bird, Martha Beckwith and others. If you only have time to read one book about Hawaii this inexpensive paperback is a great choice.

O A Bushnell is one of Hawaii's best-known contemporary authors. The University of Hawaii Press, Honolulu, has published his titles *The Return of Lono* (1971), a historical novel of Captain Cook's final voyage; *Kaaawa* (1972), about Hawaii in the 1850s; *The Stone of Kannon* (1979), about the first group of Japanese contract laborers to arrive in Hawaii, and its sequel *The Water of Kane* (1980).

Stories of Hawaii (Mutual Publishing, Honolulu, 1990) is a collection of 13 of Jack London's yarns about the islands.

Hawaii (Fawcett, New York, 1986) is James Michener's ambitious historical novel of the islands, from their volcanic origins to their emergence as a state. This sweeping saga traces the Polynesian settlers, the arrival of the missionaries and whalers, the emergence of the sugar barons and the development of Hawaii's multi-ethnic society.

Outdoor Activities

Hawaiian Hiking Trails by Craig Chisholm (The Fernglen Press, Lake Oswego, Oregon, 1993) is a good, detailed hiking guide to Hawaii's best known trails. Chisholm illustrates each hike with a USGS map of the route. He also has trail guides to Kauai and the Big Island.

The pocket-sized *Hawaii's Best Hiking Trails* by Robert Smith (Wilderness Press, Berkeley, California, 1991) combines the best trails from hiking guides that Smith has written to each of the main islands.

On the Na Pali Coast by Kathy Valier (University of Hawaii Press, Honolulu, 1988) is a guide for hikers and boaters in Hawaii's most spectacular state park. It has maps and narrative covering both ethnobotany and practical details.

The Beaches of Oahu (1977), *The Beaches of Maui County* (1989), *Beaches of the Big Island* (1985) and *Beaches of Kauai and Niihau* (1990) are by John R K Clark (University of Hawaii Press, Honolulu). These comprehensive books detail each island's coastline and every one of its beaches, including water conditions, shoreline geology and local history. The Maui edition includes Maui, Molokai, Lanai and Kahoolawe. If you're going to be spending a lot of time exploring beaches, these books are the ones to have.

The Divers' Guide to Hawaii by Chuck Thorne & Lou Zitnik (Hawaii Divers' Guide, Kihei, 1984) is a guide to the best shore dives on all the islands. It has comprehensive directions to sites, maps of entry points, what you'll see and hazards to expect, all written in a light and colorful style. Although it's geared for divers it's of some value to snorkelers as well.

Diving and Snorkeling Guide to the Hawaiian Islands by Doug Wallin (Pisces Books, New York, 1991) is a good guide to both diving and snorkeling on the four main islands. It has color photos of sites and fish.

Let's Go Shore Dive'n' on the Kona Coast by Dick Dresie (DPD Associates) is a shore dive guide to the west coast of the Big Island. Dresie gives first-person accounts of his diving experiences in each spot.

Surfer's Guide to Hawaii: Hawaii Gets All the Breaks by Greg Ambrose (Bess Press, Honolulu, 1991) describes the top surfing spots throughout the islands. It's written in an entertaining style and is packed with info on everything you need to know about surfing in Hawaii.

Six Islands on Two Wheels by Tom Koch (Bess Press, Honolulu, 1990) is a comprehensive guide to cycling in Hawaii. Koch encourages you to bring your own bike to Hawaii and tells you how to outfit it, where to ride and what to expect.

Reference

The *Atlas of Hawaii* by the Department of Geography, University of Hawaii (University of Hawaii Press, Honolulu, 1983), is loaded with data, maps and tabulations covering everything from land ownership to seasonal ocean wave patterns. This 238-page atlas is the most comprehensive reference book of Hawaii.

Place Names of Hawaii by Mary Kawena Pukui, Samuel H Elbert & Esther T Mookini (University of Hawaii Press, Honolulu, 1974) is a glossary of 4000 Hawaiian place names. The meaning and background of each name is explained.

Hawaiian Dictionary by Mary Kawena Pukui & Samuel H Elbert (University of Hawaii Press, Honolulu, 1986) is the authoritative work on the Hawaiian language. It's in both Hawaiian-English and English-Hawaiian, with 30,000 entries. They also have a $4.95 pocket-size version with 10,000 Hawaiian words.

There are many other Hawaiian language books on the market including grammar texts, conversational self-study guides and books on pidgin.

Bookstores
The four largest islands all have good bookstores with extensive Hawaiiana sections. Bookstore locations are listed under each island.

Ordering by Mail The following publishers will send catalogs of their books that can be ordered by mail:

Bess Press
    Box 22388, Honolulu, HI 96823 (☎ 734-7159; fax 732-3627)
Bishop Museum Press
    Box 19000-A, Honolulu, HI 96817 (☎ 848-4134)
Mutual Publishing
    1127 11th Ave, Mezz B, Honolulu, HI 96816 (☎ 732-1709; fax 734-4094)
Petroglyph Press
    201 Kinoole St, Hilo, HI 96720 (☎ 935-6006; fax 935-1553)
University of Hawaii Press
    2840 Kolowalu St, Honolulu, HI 96822 (☎ 956-8255, (800) 956-2840; fax 988-6052)

MAPS
If you're renting a car the guide booklets handed out by the rental agencies have simple maps showing the main roads. However, if you really want to explore, a more detailed road map is invaluable.

Rand McNally and Gousha both put out good Oahu street maps, which have detailed Honolulu sections. The American Automobile Association (AAA) puts out a good Honolulu map and an all-Hawaii map which it distributes free to its members.

The University of Hawaii (UH) Press publishes separate relief maps of Oahu, Kauai, Maui, the Big Island and Molokai/Lanai. Overall they're the best general maps for the Neighbor Islands as they not only cover roads but also beaches, historical sites and major hiking trails. UH maps, which cost $3, are available in bookstores and in many shops frequented by tourists.

The United States Geological Survey (USGS) publishes topographical maps of Hawaii. Both full-island and detailed sectional maps are available, and there's also an individual USGS map for Hawaii Volcanoes National Park. Maps can be ordered by mail from the US Geological Survey, Box 25286 Denver Federal Center, Denver, Colorado 80225. Prices per map range from $2.50 to $4.

USGS maps can also be purchased at several places in Hawaii, including on Kauai at the Kauai Museum in Lihue and the Kokee State Park museum; on Oahu at the Pacific Map Center, 250 Ward Ave, Suite 400, Honolulu; and on the Big Island at the Middle Earth Bookshoppe in Kailua-Kona, Basically Books in Hilo and Hawaii Volcanoes National Park.

Nautical charts published by the National Oceanic and Atmospheric Administration can be ordered by mail from the NOAA Distribution Branch, National Ocean Service, Riverdale, Maryland 20737. They can also be ordered by phone (☎ (301) 436-6990) using Visa or MasterCard. Upon request NOAA will send a complete list of charts available and addresses where they can be purchased around the world.

If you're looking for NOAA nautical chart maps after you arrive on the islands, you can find them at the Pacific Map Center in Honolulu, Basically Books in Hilo and a number of the larger marine supply companies.

For those who want to dig a little deeper, the basement of Hamilton Library at the University of Hawaii, Manoa campus, has a great map room with thousands of esoteric maps on Hawaii and other Pacific islands. You can't buy them, but you can photocopy them.

MEDIA
Newspapers
Hawaii's two main daily papers are the *Honolulu Advertiser* which comes out in the morning and the *Honolulu Star-Bulletin* which comes out in the afternoon.

For copies of either paper, contact the Circulation Department (☎ 538-6397), Box 3350, Honolulu, HI 96801. Single copies sent airmail to the US mainland cost $2.85 for a weekday copy and $6.75 for a Sunday copy. Prices vary to other countries.

The Honolulu papers are sold throughout Hawaii but the Neighbor Islands also have their own newspapers. The *Hawaii Tribune-Herald* in Hilo, *West Hawaii Today* in Kailua-Kona, the *Maui News* in Wailuku and the *Garden Island* in Lihue are each published five to six times a week.

Several mainland and international newspapers are also widely available, including *USA Today, Wall Street Journal* and the *Los Angeles Times*. Look for them in the lobbies of larger hotels.

Magazines
Honolulu, Aloha and *Hawaii Magazine* are the largest general interest magazines about Hawaii. *Honolulu* is geared more towards residents and is published monthly by the Honolulu Publishing Co, 36 Merchant St, Honolulu, HI 96813. *Aloha* (Box 469035, Escondido, CA 92046) and *Hawaii Magazine* (Box 485, Mt Morris, IL 61054) have more visitor-oriented feature articles; both are published six times a year.

There are also numerous tourist maga-zines distributed free on the islands which are well worth picking up. They usually have simple maps, a bit of current event information, lots of ads and discount coupons for everything from hamburgers to sunset cruises.

TV & Radio
Hawaii has commercial TV stations representing the three major US networks, and cable network stations which include tourist information and Japanese language channels. Almost anything you can watch on the mainland you can watch in Hawaii.

For some local flavor, the evening news on Channel 2 ends with some fine slack-key guitar music by Keola and Kapono Beamer and clips of people waving the shaka sign.

Hawaii has about 50 AM and FM radio stations. There's a wide variety of programming, including some stations that feature Hawaiian music. More information is given in the individual island chapters.

FILM & PHOTOGRAPHY
Both print and slide film are readily available on all the islands. If you're going to be in Hawaii for any length of time consider having your film developed there as the high temperature and humidity of the tropics greatly accelerate the deterioration of exposed film. The sooner it's developed, the better the results.

Kodak and Fuji have labs in Honolulu, and island drug stores and camera shops usually send in to those labs. Longs Drugs is one of the cheapest places for both purchasing film and having it developed. All the tourist centers have one-hour print processing shops as well; Fox Photo is the largest and reportedly does good work.

Don't leave your camera in direct sun any longer than necessary. A locked car can heat up like an oven in just a few minutes.

Sand and water are intense reflectors and in bright light they'll often leave foreground subjects shadowy. You can try compensating by adjusting your f-stop or attaching a polarizing filter, or both, but the most effective technique is to take photos in the gentler light of early morning and late afternoon.

LAUNDRY

Many hotels, condominiums and hostels have coin-operated washers and dryers. If there's not one where you're staying, you can find commercial coin-operated laundries on all the islands. The average cost is about $1 to wash a load of clothes and another dollar to dry. Laundry locations are listed in each island chapter.

HEALTH

Hawaii is a very healthy place to live and to visit. As it's 2500 miles from the nearest industrial center, there's little air pollution – other than that caused by volcanic activity. Hawaii ranks first of all the 50 US states in life expectancy, which is currently about 76 years for men and 81 years for women.

There are few serious health concerns. The islands have none of the nasties like malaria, cholera or yellow fever and you can drink water directly out of any tap, although all stream water needs to be boiled or treated.

No immunizations are required to enter Hawaii or any other port in the USA.

Be aware that there are many poisonous plants in Hawaii, so you should never taste a plant that you cannot positively identify as edible.

If you're new to the heat and humidity you may find yourself easily fatigued and more susceptible to minor ailments. Acclimatize yourself by slowing down your pace and setting your body clock to the more kicked-back 'Hawaiian Time'. Drink plenty of liquids.

If you're planning on a long outing or anything strenuous, take enough water and don't push yourself.

Predeparture Preparations
Health Insurance Foreign visitors should be warned that health care in the USA is expensive, and while Hawaii is the only one of the 50 states that has an extensive

health insurance program, the coverage is limited to Hawaii residents.

Therefore, a travel insurance policy that covers medical expenses may be a wise idea. There are a wide variety of policies available and your travel agent should have recommendations. While you may find a policy that pays doctors or hospitals direct, be aware that many private doctors and clinics in Hawaii will demand payment at the time of service. If you have to make a claim later be sure you keep all documentation.

Check the small print because some policies exclude 'dangerous activities' like scuba diving, motorcycling, anything to do with parachutes and even trekking.

Medical Kit A small first-aid kit is a sensible thing to carry on your travels to cope with minor health problems or injuries, especially if you plan on camping or hiking into the backcountry.

A basic kit should have things like aspirin or Panadol for pain or fever; an antihistamine (such as Benadryl) for use as a decongestant, to relieve the itch from insect bites or to help prevent motion sickness; an antiseptic and antibiotic ointment or powder for cuts and scratches; calamine lotion to ease the irritation from bites and stings; Band-aids and bandages; scissors, tweezers, insect repellent and sunblock.

Bring adequate supplies of any prescription medicine or contraceptive pills you may already be taking.

Medical Care

Hawaii has 25 acute-care hospitals, 2600 physicians and 1200 dentists. While the rural islands of Molokai and Lanai have limited medical facilities, the other islands have fully-staffed hospitals with modern facilities. Still, for specialized care and serious illnesses, many islanders have more confidence in Honolulu hospitals than in Neighbor Island facilities.

Medical Problems & Treatment
Leptospirosis Visitors to Hawaii should be aware of leptospirosis, a bacterial dis-

ease found in freshwater streams and ponds. The disease is transmitted from animals such as rats, mongoose and wild pigs.

Humans most often pick up the disease by swimming or wading in freshwater contaminated by animal urine. Leptospirosis can exist in any fresh water, including idyllic-looking waterfalls and jungle streams, because the water may have washed down the slopes through animal habitats.

Leptospirosis enters the body through the nose, eyes, mouth or cuts in the skin. Wetland taro farmers, swimmers and backcountry hikers account for the majority of cases.

Symptoms can occur within two to 20 days after exposure and may include fever, chills, sweating, headaches, muscle pains, vomiting and diarrhea. More severe symptoms include blood in the urine and jaundice. Symptoms may last from a few days to several weeks.

There are a few dozen confirmed cases statewide each year. Because symptoms of leptospirosis resemble the flu and hepatitis, other cases probably go unconfirmed. Although deaths have been attributed to the disease they are relatively rare, accounting for half a dozen fatalities in Hawaii since 1982. Leptospirosis is not specific to Hawaii and can be found on the mainland as well.

Some precautions include wearing waterproof *tabis* (reef walkers) when hiking and avoiding unnecessary freshwater crossings, especially if you have open cuts.

Leptospirosis can be serious, yet thousands of people swim in Hawaiian streams without contracting it. The state has posted warnings at many trailheads and freshwater swimming areas. Islanders have differing opinions on leptospirosis – some never swim in fresh water because of it, while others consider it such a long shot that they take no precautions at all.

Sunburn Sunburn is always a concern in the tropics, as the closer you get to the equator the fewer of the sun's rays are blocked by the atmosphere. Don't be fooled by what appears to be a hazy overcast day as those rays still get through.

Sunscreen with an SPF (sun protection factor) of 10 to 15 is recommended if you're not already tanned. If you're going into the water use one that's water-resistant. Snorkelers may want to wear a T-shirt if they plan to be out in the water a long time. You'll not only be protecting against sunburn but potential skin cancer and premature aging of the skin.

Fair-skinned people can get both first and second degree burns in the hot Hawaiian sun and wearing a sun hat for added protection is a good idea. The most severe sun is between 10 am and 2 pm.

Prickly Heat Prickly heat is an itchy rash caused by excessive perspiration trapped under the skin. It usually strikes people who have just arrived in a hot climate and whose pores have not yet opened sufficiently to cope with greater sweating. Keeping cool by bathing often or resorting to air-conditioning may help until you acclimatize.

Heat Exhaustion Dehydration or salt deficiency can cause heat exhaustion. Take time to acclimatize to high temperatures and make sure you get sufficient liquids. Salt deficiency is characterized by fatigue, lethargy, headaches, giddiness and muscle cramps and in this case salt tablets may help. Vomiting or diarrhea can deplete your liquid and salt levels.

Heat Stroke This serious, sometimes fatal, condition can occur if the body's heat-regulating mechanism breaks down and the body temperature rises to dangerous levels. Long, continuous periods of exposure to high temperatures can leave you vulnerable to heat stroke. Avoid strenuous activity in open sun (such as lengthy hikes or bike rides across lava fields) when you first arrive. The symptoms of heat stroke are feeling unwell, not sweating very much or at all and a high body temperature (102°F to 106°F). Where sweating has ceased the skin becomes flushed and red. Severe, throbbing headaches and lack of coordination will also occur, and the sufferer may be confused or aggressive. Eventually the victim may become delirious or convulse. Hospitalization is essential, but meanwhile get patients out of the sun, remove their clothing, cover them with a wet sheet or towel and then fan continually.

Fungal Infections The same climate that produces lush tropical forests also promotes a prolific growth of skin fungi and bacteria. Hot weather fungal infections are most likely to occur between the toes or fingers or in the groin.

Keeping your skin dry and cool and allowing air to circulate is essential. Choose loose cotton clothing rather than synthetics, and sandals rather than shoes. If you do get an infection, wash the infected area daily with a disinfectant or medicated soap. Rinse and dry well and then apply an antifungal powder.

Altitude Sickness On the Big Island, people planning to go to the summits of Mauna Kea or Mauna Loa need to be aware of the possibility of Acute Mountain Sickness (AMS), which occurs at high altitudes due to lack of oxygen and is potentially fatal. While AMS can generally be avoided by making gains in elevation at a slow pace, Hawaii presents an unusual situation as most people who visit Mauna Kea summit do so by car. Many of those visitors drive straight up to nearly 14,000 feet from their hotels on the coast, a mere two-hour ride that offers no time to acclimatize. As a result AMS is a common problem for summit visitors, even though most cases are on the mild side. AMS symptoms include headaches, nausea, dizziness and shortness of breath, while confusion and lack of coordination and balance are real danger signs. With all but the mildest of symptoms, travelers experiencing signs of AMS should immediately descend to a lower elevation. For more information, see Precautions in the Saddle Road/Mauna Kea section in the Big Island chapter.

Motion Sickness Eating lightly before and during a trip will reduce the chances of motion sickness. If you are prone to motion sickness try to find a place that minimizes disturbance – near the wing on aircraft or close to midships on boats. Fresh air usually helps; reading or cigarette smoke doesn't. Commercial antimotion-sickness preparations, which can cause drowsiness, have to be taken before the trip commences; when you're feeling sick it's too late. Ginger is a natural preventative and is available in capsule form.

Cuts & Scratches Cuts and skin punctures are easily infected in Hawaii's hot and humid climate, and infections can be persistent. Keep any cut or open wound clean and treat it with an antiseptic solution. Keep the area protected but, where possible, avoid bandages which can keep wounds wet.

Coral cuts are even more susceptible to infection because tiny pieces of coral can get embedded in the skin. These cuts are notoriously slow to heal as the coral releases a weak venom into the wound.

Pesky Creatures Hawaii has no land snakes but it does have its fair share of annoying mosquitoes as well as centipedes which can give an unpleasant bite. The islands also have bees and groundnesting wasps which, like the centipede, generally pose danger only to those who are allergic to their stings.

This being the tropics, cockroaches are plentiful and although they don't pose much of a health problem they do little for the appetite. Condos with kitchens have the most problems. If you find that the place you're staying is infested you can always call the manager or the front desk and have them spray poisons – which are no doubt more dangerous than the roaches!

While sightings are not terribly common, there are two dangerous arachnids on the islands: the black widow spider and the scorpion.

Black Widow Spiders Found in much of the USA, the black widow is glossy black with a body that's a half-inch in diameter, a leg span of two inches and a characteristic red hourglass mark on its abdomen. It weaves a strong, tangled web close to the ground and inhabits brushpiles, sheds and outdoor privies.

Its bite, which resembles the prick of a pin, can be barely noticeable, however it's followed in about 30 minutes by severe cramping in which the abdominal muscles become boardlike and breathing becomes difficult. Other reactions include vomiting, headaches, sweating, shaking and a tingling sensation in the fingers. In severe cases the bite can be fatal. If you think you've been bitten by a black widow, seek immediate medical help.

Scorpions The scorpion, confined principally to warm dry regions, is capable of inflicting a painful sting by means of its caudal fang. Like the black widow, the venom contains neurotoxins. Severity of the symptoms generally depends on the age of the victim and can even be fatal for very young children. Symptoms are shortness of breath, hives, swelling or vomiting. Apply diluted household ammonia and cold compresses to the area of the sting and seek immediate medical help.

While the odds of encountering a scorpion are quite low in Hawaii, campers should always check inside their hiking boots before putting them on!

Ciguatera Poisoning Ciguatera is a serious illness caused by eating fish affected by ciguatoxin, which herbivorous fish can pick up from marine algae. There is no ready way of detecting ciguatoxin, and it's not diminished by cooking. Symptoms of food poisoning usually occur three to five hours after eating.

Ciguatoxin is most common among reef fish (which are not commonly served in restaurants) and hasn't affected Hawaii's deep-sea fish such as tuna, marlin and mahimahi. The symptoms, if you do eat the wrong fish, can include nausea, stomach cramps, diarrhea, paralysis, tingling and numbness of the face, fingers and toes, and a reversal of temperature feelings so that hot things feel cold and vice versa. Extreme cases can result in unconsciousness and even death. Vomit until your stomach is empty and get immediate medical help.

EMERGENCY

For police, fire and ambulance emergencies dial 911. The inside front cover of island phone books lists other vital service agencies, such as poison control, coast guard rescues and suicide and crisis lines.

If you lose your passport, contact your consulate in Honolulu; a complete list of consulate phone numbers can be found in the telephone book yellow pages.

For refunds on lost or stolen American Express traveler's checks, call (800) 221-7282; for lost MasterCard traveler's checks, dial (800) 223-9920.

WOMEN TRAVELERS

Women travelers are no more likely to encounter problems in Hawaii than anywhere else in the USA. We don't advise women to hitchhike, especially those traveling alone, but if you do, size up the situation carefully and don't hesitate to decline a ride from anyone who makes you feel uncomfortable. If you're camping, select your campground carefully, opting for popular, well-used camping areas, rather than more remote locales where you might be the only camper, as these lesser-used spots sometimes become impromptu drinking hangouts.

DANGERS & ANNOYANCES
Tsunamis

Tsunamis, or tidal waves, are not common in Hawaii but when they do hit they can be severe.

Tsunamis are generated by earthquakes or other natural disasters. The largest to ever hit Hawaii was in 1946, the result of an earthquake in the Aleutian Islands.

Waves reached a height of 55.8 feet, entire villages were washed away and 159 people died. Since that time, Hawaii has installed a modern tsunami warning system which is aired through yellow speakers mounted on telephone poles around the islands. They're tested on the first working day of each month at 11:45 am for about one minute.

Although tsunamis which travel across the Pacific can take hours to arrive, others can be caused by earthquakes or volcanic eruptions within Hawaii. For these there may be little warning. Any earthquake strong enough to cause you to grab onto something to keep from falling is a natural tsunami warning. If you're in a low-lying coastal area when one occurs, immediately head for higher ground.

Tsunami inundation maps in the front of island telephone books show susceptible areas and safety zones.

Ocean Safety

Drowning is the leading cause of accidental death for visitors.

If you're not familiar with water condi-tions, ask someone. If there's no lifeguard around, local surfers are generally helpful – they'd rather give you the lowdown on water conditions than pull you out later. It's best not to swim alone in any unfamiliar place.

Shorebreaks Shorebreaks occur where waves break close to or directly on shore. They are formed when ocean swells pass abruptly from deep to shallow waters. If they are only a couple of feet high they're generally fine for novice bodysurfers to try their hand. Otherwise, they're for experi-enced bodysurfers only.

Large shorebreaks can hit hard with a slamming downward force. Broken bones, neck injuries, dislocated shoulders and loss of wind are the most common injuries, although anyone wiped out in the water is a potential drowning victim as well.

Rip Currents Rip currents, or rips, are fast flowing currents of water within the ocean, moving from shallow near-shore areas out to sea. They are most common in condi-tions of high surf, forming when water

STRONG CURRENT   MAN-OF-WAR   SHARP CORAL

HIGH SURF   DANGEROUS SHOREBREAK   WAVES ON LEDGE

Warning signs on Hawaii's beaches

from incoming waves builds up near the shore. Essentially the waves are coming in faster than they can flow back out.

The water then runs along the shoreline until it finds an escape route out to sea, usually through a channel or out along a point. Swimmers caught up in the current can be ripped out to deeper water.

Although rips can be powerful they usually dissipate 50 to 100 yards offshore. Anyone caught in one should either go with the flow until it loses power or swim parallel to shore to slip out of it. Trying to swim against a rip current can exhaust the strongest of swimmers.

Undertows Undertows are common along steeply sloped beaches when large waves backwash directly into incoming surf. The outflowing water picks up speed as it flows down the slopes. When it hits an incoming wave it pulls under it, creating an undertow. Swimmers caught up in an undertow can be pulled beneath the surface. The most important thing is not to panic. Go with the current until you get beyond the wave.

Rogue Waves Never turn your back on the ocean. Waves don't all come in with equal height or strength. An abnormally high 'rogue wave' can sweep over shoreline ledges such as those circling Hanauma Bay on Oahu or tear up onto beaches like Lumahai on Kauai. Over the years, numerous people have been swept into the ocean from both.

You need to be particularly cautious during high tide and in conditions of stormy weather or high surf.

Some people think rogue waves don't exist because they've never seen one. But that's the point – you don't always see them.

Coral Most coral cuts occur when swimmers are pushed onto the coral by rough waves and surges. It's a good idea to wear diving gloves when snorkeling over shallow reefs. Avoid walking on coral, which can not only cut your feet, but is very damaging to the coral.

Jellyfish Take a peek into the water before you plunge in to make sure it's not jellyfish territory. These gelatinous creatures, with sack-like bodies and stinging tentacles, are fairly common around Hawaii. They're most often found drifting near the shore or washed up on the beach. The sting of a jellyfish varies from mild to severe, depending on the variety. However, unless you have an allergic reaction to their venom, the stings are not generally dangerous.

In Hawaii, the Portuguese man-of-war is the worst type to encounter. Not technically a jellyfish, the man-of-war is a colonial hydrozoan, or a colony of coelenterates, rather than a solitary coelenterate like the true jellyfish. Its body consists of a translucent bluish bladder-like float, which in Hawaii generally grows to about four or five inches long. Known locally as 'bluebottles', they're most often found on the windward coasts, particularly after storms.

A man-of-war sting is very painful, similar to a bad bee sting except that you're likely to get stung more than once from clusters of incredibly long tentacles containing hundreds of stinging cells. Even touching a bluebottle a few hours after it's washed up on shore can result in burning stings.

If you do get stung, quickly remove the tentacles and apply vinegar or a meat tenderizer containing papain (derived from papaya), which acts to neutralize the toxins – in a pinch, you could use urine as well. For serious reactions, including chest pains or difficulty in breathing, seek medical attention.

Fish Stings Incidences with venomous sea creatures in Hawaiian waters are rather rare. You should, however, learn to recognize scorpionfish and lionfish, two related fish which can inject venom through their dorsal spines if touched. Both are sometimes found in quite shallow water.

The Hawaiian lionfish, which grows up to 10 inches, is a strikingly attractive fish with vertical orange and white stripes and feathery appendages that contain poisonous spines; it likes to drift along the reef, particularly at night. The scorpionfish is more drab in appearance, has shorter and less obvious spines, is about six inches in length, and tends to sit immobile on the bottom or on ledges.

The sting from either can cause a sharp burning pain, followed by numbness around the area, nausea and headaches. Immediately stick the affected area in water that is as hot as bearable (be sure not to unintentionally scald the area due to numbness) and go for medical treatment.

Cone Shells Cone shells should be left alone unless you're sure they're empty. There's no safe way of picking up a live cone shell as the animal inside has a long harpoon-like tail that can dart out and reach anywhere on its shell to deliver a painful sting. The wound should be soaked in hot water and medical attention sought.

A few species, such as the textile cone whose shell is decorated with brown diamond or triangular shapes, have a venom so toxic that in extreme cases the sting could even be fatal.

Sea Urchins *Wana*, or spiny sea urchins, have long brittle spines that can puncture the skin and break off, causing burning and possible numbness. The spines sometimes inflict a toxin and can cause an infection. You can try to remove the spines with tweezers or by soaking the area in hot water, although more serious cases may require surgical removal.

Eels *Puhi*, or moray eels, are often spotted by snorkelers around reefs and coral heads. They're constantly opening and closing their mouths to pump water across their gills, which makes them look far more menacing than they actually are.

Eels don't attack, but they will protect themselves if they feel cornered by fingers jabbing into the reef holes or crevices they occupy. Eels have sharp teeth and strong jaws and may clamp down if someone sticks a hand in their door.

Sharks More than 35 varieties of sharks are found in Hawaiian waters, including the non-aggressive whale shark and basking

Hammerhead shark

sharks, which can reach lengths of 50 feet. As Hawaiian waters are abundant with fish, sharks in Hawaii are well fed and most pose little danger to humans.

Sharks are curious and will sometimes investigate divers, although they generally just check things out and continue on their way. If they start to hang around, however, it's probably time for you to go.

Outside of the rarely encountered great white shark, the most dangerous shark in Hawaiian waters is the tiger shark, which averages about 20 feet in length and is identified by vertical bars along its side. The tiger shark is not terribly particular about what it eats and has been known to chomp down on pieces of wood (including surfboards) floating on the ocean surface.

Should you come face to face with a shark the best thing to do is move casually and quietly away. Don't panic as sharks are attracted by things that thrash around in water.

Some aquatic officials suggest thumping an attacking shark on the nose or sticking your fingers into its eyes, which may confuse it long enough to give you time to escape. Indeed, some divers who dive in shark waters carry a billy club or bang stick.

Avoid murky waters. After heavy rains sharks sometimes come in around river mouths.

Sharks are attracted by blood. Some attacks on humans are related to spearfishing; when a shark is going after a diver's bloody catch, the diver sometimes gets in the way. Sharks are also attracted by shiny things and by anything bright red or yellow, which might influence your choice of swimsuit color.

Unpleasant encounters with sharks are extremely unlikely however. According to the University of Hawaii Sea Grant College, only about 30 unprovoked shark attacks were known to have occurred in Hawaii between 1900 and 1990; about a third of these were fatal. Nevertheless, in recent years, increasing numbers of both sharks and shark attacks have been reported, with attacks now occurring on average at a rate of about two or three a year.

Theft & Violence

For the most part, Hawaii is a safe place.

However the islands do have notoriety for rip-offs from parked rental cars. The people who break into these cars are good at what they do; they can pop a trunk or pull out a lock assembly in seconds to get to loot inside. What's more, they do it not only when you've left your car in a secluded area to go for a long hike, but also in crowded parking lots where you'd expect safety in numbers.

It's best not to leave anything of value in your car any time you walk away from it. If for some reason you feel you must, at least pack things well out of sight *before* you've pulled up to the place where you're going to leave the car.

Other than rip-offs, most hassles encountered by visitors are from drunks. Be tuned in to the vibes on beaches at night and in places where young guys hang out to drink.

Overall, violent crime is lower in Hawaii than in most mainland cities. There are, however, some pockets of resentment against tourists, as well as against off-islanders moving in. Oahu tends to be worse than the other islands.

WORK

US citizens can pursue employment in Hawaii as elsewhere in the USA, while foreign visitors who are here for tourist purposes are not legally allowed to take up employment.

As Hawaii has had a relatively slow economy for the past few years, the job situation is not particularly rosy. Much of the economy is tied into the service industry, with wages hovering close to the minimum wage ($5.25 an hour). For visitors, the most common work to land is waiting on tables, and if you're young and energetic there are possibilities in restaurants and clubs.

If you're hoping to find more serious 'professional' employment, note that Hawaii is considered a tight labor market, with a lack of diversified industries and a relatively immobile labor force. Those jobs that do open up are generally filled by established Hawaiian residents.

For more information on employment in Hawaii, contact the State Department of Labor & Industrial Relations (☎ 586-8700), 830 Punchbowl St, Honolulu, HI 96813.

ACTIVITIES

Hawaii has an exhaustive variety of sports and recreational activities available to visitors. In addition to top conditions for practically all water sports, there are also fine opportunities for hiking, biking, jogging, tennis, golf, horseback riding, you name it. There's even snow skiing on the Big Island in winter.

Hawaii is a great place to learn to dive, surf or windsurf. Equipment rental is available on the main islands and most places that rent the equipment also give lessons to beginners. Hawaii has 750 miles of coastline and all of its 283 beaches are public up to the high water mark.

Except for sports competitions or specialized tours, few activities require advance planning before you get to Hawaii.

More detailed information is given in each island chapter.

Surfing

Hawaii lies smack in the path of all the major swells that race unimpeded across the Pacific, and the sport of surfing got its start in these islands hundreds of years ago with the early Hawaiians.

Hawaii has good surfing throughout the year, with the biggest waves hitting from November to February along the north shores of the islands. Summer swells, which break along the south shores, are usually not as frequent and nowhere near as large as the northside winter swells.

Oahu's north shore has Hawaii's top surf action. The winter swells at Waimea, Sunset Beach and the Banzai Pipeline can bring in 30-foot waves, creating the conditions that legends are made of. Waikiki has Oahu's top south shore surfing.

Maui and Kauai also have some excellent surfing spots. The Big Island and

Molokai are not as notable, but it is possible to surf on both islands. See individual island chapters for more details.

Windsurfing

Maui has some of the world's best windsurfing action, with Hookipa Beach near Paia hosting the top international windsurfing competitions. Tamer spots can be found on other parts of the island.

Oahu also has lots of windsurfing activity, with some spots ideal for beginners and other locales boasting advanced wave-riding conditions. Oahu's Kailua Beach attracts the biggest crowd with its excellent year-round wind.

Although Maui and Oahu are by far the top two islands for windsurfing, Kauai also has some fairly good windsurfing spots. The Big Island doesn't rate as a windsurfing destination, although if you're there and want to windsurf there are a few beaches with reasonable conditions. It's possible to rent gear and take lessons on all four islands.

Although there are good windsurfing conditions in Hawaii year round, winter can have flat periods. In general, the best winds are from June to September.

Diving

There's good year-round diving in Hawaii. Under normal conditions, the leeward shores of the islands have the best diving most months of the year. The north shores are usually best in the summer.

Hawaiian waters have excellent visibility, with water temperatures ranging from 72°F to 80°F.

The marine life around the islands is superb. Almost 700 fish species live in Hawaiian waters, with nearly one-third of those found nowhere else in the world. Hawaiian reef fish are colorful and numerous. There are more than 20 different kinds of butterfly fish, plus rainbow-colored parrotfish, wrasses, tangs, filefish and pufferfish, just to list a few. Divers often see spinner dolphins, green sea turtles, manta rays and moray eels. Although it's rare for divers to see humpback whales underwater, they do sometimes hear them singing.

Hawaii has underwater caves, canyons, lava tubes, vertical walls and sunken ships. There are all sorts of colorful sponges and corals, including the gem-like black coral.

There are numerous dive shops on the four largest islands, which all have some excellent diving opportunities. Complete gear can be rented and prices are quite competitive.

Fishing

Hawaii has some of the world's best deep-sea fishing, with Kona holding most of the world records for Pacific blue marlin. For details, see the Activities section in the Big Island chapter.

In addition to ocean fishing, the state maintains four public freshwater fishing areas: in Kokee on Kauai, in Wahiawa and Nuuanu on Oahu and at Waiakea on the Big Island. Stocked game fish include rainbow trout, largemouth and smallmouth bass, bluegill sunfish, channel catfish, tilapia and carp.

Licenses are required for freshwater fishing. A 30-day license for nonresidents costs $3.75 (free for those ages 65 and older).

No licenses are required for saltwater fishing when the catch is for private consumption. There are, however, seasons, size limits and/or other restrictions on taking *ula* (spiny lobster), crab, octopus *(hee* in Hawaiian, and also called tako or squid), *opihi* (a kind of limpet), *limu* (seaweed) and certain species of fish. Clams and oysters cannot be taken.

Also, seek local advice before eating your catch as ciguatera poisoning has become more common in recent years.

The booklets *Hawaii Fishing Regulations* and *Freshwater Fishing in Hawaii* may be obtained free from the Division of Aquatic Resources (☎ 587-0102), Department of Land & Natural Resources, 1151 Punchbowl St, Room 330, Honolulu, HI 96813.

Hiking

Hawaii has first-rate hiking opportunities. Like the islands themselves, the hiking options are incredibly varied, from desert treks to lush rainforest walks, and from beach strolls to snowline ridge trails.

The hikes range from short family-style nature walks to backpacking treks which last several days and require carrying food and gear.

Despite all the development on Hawaii, it's amazing how much of the islands are still in a natural state. There are places where you could walk for days without seeing another soul.

Hawaii's two national parks have hiking trails that have no parallels anywhere. Both have barren lunar-like landscapes as well as lush, tropical forests.

Hawaii Volcanoes National Park on the Big Island has the distinction of containing both the world's most active volcano and largest mountain mass. The park has breathtaking hikes down into steaming crater floors and up to the snowcapped summit of Mauna Loa.

At Haleakala National Park on Maui the volcano is sleepier, but equally awe-inspiring. Hikes into the caldera of the world's largest crater can take half a day while hikes across its floor can take half a week.

Still, the premier hike in all of Hawaii is on Kauai's Na Pali Coast, where the Kalalau Trail follows an ancient Hawaiian footpath along the edges of the most spectacularly fluted coastal cliffs in Hawaii. The trail winds down into lush valleys where camping is allowed and waterfalls and ruins can be explored.

There are also hiking trails into other ancient valleys, such as Waipio on the Big Island and Halawa on Molokai. On Maui and the Big Island you can follow old 'king's trails' along footpaths worn through the lava by the bare feet of travelers over hundreds of years. Every island has ridge-line trails with panoramic views, as well as trails to secluded beaches and waterfalls. On some islands there are also trails in nature preserves where you can examine native plants and birds and enjoy lots of solitude.

Safety & Tips A number of Hawaii's hiking trails take you into steep, narrow valleys with gullies that require stream crossings. The capital rule here is that if the water begins to rise it's not safe to cross, as a flash flood may be imminent. Instead, head for higher ground and wait it out.

Flash floods are the biggest dangers on trails, followed by falling rocks. Be wary of swimming under high waterfalls, as rocks can get dislodged from the top, and be careful on the edge of steep cliffs as cliffside rock in Hawaii tends to be crumbly.

Darkness sets in soon after sunset in Hawaii and ridgetop trails are not the place to be caught unprepared in the dark. It's a good idea to carry a flashlight when you're hiking, just in case.

Jeans will protect your legs from the overgrown parts of the trail and tennis shoes or sturdy walking shoes are advisable on most hikes.

Some people prefer tabis (reef walkers) for hiking, as they have good traction and also offer some protection from leptospirosis (see the Health section). Tabis can be bought around the islands at shops that sell sporting goods and fishing supplies.

Hawaii has no snakes, no poison ivy, no poison oak and few dangers from wild animals. There's a slim possibility of meeting up with a large boar in the backwoods, but they're unlikely to be a problem unless cornered.

Hiking Information You can get free recreational maps of Oahu, Kauai, Maui, Molokai and the Big Island from the Division of Forestry & Wildlife (☎ 587-0166), 1151 Punchbowl St, Room 325, Honolulu, HI 96813. If you live in the USA you can receive them in advance by sending a self-addressed 9-x-12-inch envelope with $3.00 in postage. Be sure to let them know which island or islands you'll be visiting. Although these maps are primarily geared for hunters, showing 4WD roads and trails into wilderness areas, they're useful for hikers as well.

The Oahu, Maui, Kauai and Big Island branches of the Sierra Club lead guided hikes. You can contact the central office (☎ 538-6616), 1111 Bishop St, No 511, Honolulu, HI 96803, for a schedule of upcoming hikes or simply look in the activity listings in local newspapers once you arrive.

Specific information on the various hiking trails is given in each island section.

Running

More than 100 road races, ranging from fun runs to triathlons, are held in the islands each year.

Hawaii's best known races are the Honolulu Marathon held in December and the Ironman Triathlon held in Kona on the Big Island in October. Details on those races and others are under Activities in the respective island chapters.

The Department of Parks & Recreation of the City & County of Honolulu (650 S King St, Honolulu, HI 96813) has a comprehensive schedule of annual running events that it will mail out upon request.

HIGHLIGHTS

Every island has its own unique highlights.

On **Oahu**, the standard attractions include Waikiki, Diamond Head, Pearl Harbor and the North Shore with its huge winter surf. Honolulu's historic downtown (with the only Royal Palace in the USA) and adjacent Chinatown offer a fascinating glimpse of Hawaii's multiethnic society. Other things not to be missed include the view from Tantalus, the Nuuanu Pali Lookout and Hanauma Bay.

On **Maui**, the must-do's include a trip to Haleakala summit for the sunrise, the serpentine coastal drive to Hana and a visit to historic Lahaina. Some lesser-known highlights include the Waihee Ridge Trail, the drive around the northwest end of the island and winter whale watching along the shoreline path at Wailea.

On the **Big Island** don't miss Hawaii Volcanoes National Park and its fascinating landscape of steaming craters and lava flows. Rural Waipio Valley and the cascading Akaka Falls also offer splendid natural scenery. Remnants of ancient Hawaiian culture are plentiful, including petroglyphs and heiaus (temples) at Puuhonua O Honaunau, more widely known as the Place of Refuge, and at Mookini.

Kauai is a favorite of naturalists and is known for its lush mountainous scenery, especially the Na Pali Coast and the Waimea Canyon, both of which offer excellent backcountry hiking trails. It also has fine beaches including some in remote places.

Molokai's chief attraction is its rural lifestyle and slow pace. Other highlights include Papohaku, the longest beach in Hawaii; a mule trail down to the historic leprosy colony of Kalaupapa; and a couple of scenic hikes.

Lanai offers off-the-beaten-path sights to explore, from desolate windswept beaches to the remains of an ancient Hawaiian village. Its south coast has a lovely beach, Hulopoe Bay, with fine diving and snorkeling.

ACCOMMODATIONS

Hawaii has a wide variety of accommodations in all price ranges, including B&Bs, hotels and condominiums. There are also a handful of hostels and state park cabins that are quite inexpensive.

In Waikiki there are far more hotels than condos, while in Kihei and Kona the opposite is true. In most other major tourist destinations in Hawaii the number of hotels and condos are pretty evenly divided.

There are more than 75,000 hotel and condo rooms in the state. Oahu, which once boasted all of Hawaii's visitor accommodations and until 20 years ago still had 75%, has now slipped to about 50% as development continues full speed ahead on the Neighbor Islands. The Big Island alone has nearly 35,000 new hotel and condo units on the drawing board. If it were to all go unchecked the once sleepy Kona Coast could surpass Waikiki by the year 2000.

Most places to stay in Hawaii have different rates for high season and low season (also called peak season and off season). High season most commonly applies to the winter period of December 15 to March 31. During this time many of the best-value places, particularly the smaller hotels and condos, are booked out well in advance. During the low season period of April to mid-December many places drop their rates by 10% to 30% and getting the room of your choice without advance reservations is far easier.

If you are traveling with children be aware that some smaller places in Hawaii, such as B&Bs and historic inns, prohibit children from staying, so it's important to inquire about their policies before making reservations.

Except where noted, the rates given in this book are the same for either singles or doubles. A combined room and sales tax of 10.17% is added to the price of all accommodations, including B&Bs.

Camping

Hawaii has numerous campgrounds. In general, camping in the national parks is better than in the state parks, and the state parks are better choices than the county parks.

Although local people often unofficially camp in places other than the parks, it doesn't necessarily mean that you'll be welcome to join them. They may just be out for a weekend of fishing, or they may be homeless. Either way there could be some turf issues.

Over the years there have been some assaults and numerous thefts targeted at off-island campers. The violence has decreased in most places though a few campgrounds in rough areas, including the entire Waianae Coast of Oahu, are best avoided. The biggest hassles usually come from young locals who have been drinking. People traveling alone, especially women, need to be particularly cautious.

Rip-offs still occur at some camping areas and you'll need to watch your valuables. Generally the less you look like a tourist the less likely you are to be targeted.

Pick your park carefully, especially the county parks. Some are well-established with caretakers and attract other campers, while others are pit stops along the road frequented mostly by drinkers.

For the most part the farther you are from population centers, the less likely you are to run into hassles. Thieves and drunks aren't big on hiking. Camping in the wilderness is generally safe on all the islands – a twisted ankle, a wild boar or a cross-eyed hunter are the biggest safety concerns.

More information on all the following parks can be found in the individual island chapters.

National Parks There are two national parks in Hawaii which allow camping: Haleakala National Park on Maui and Hawaii Volcanoes National Park on the Big Island. These two parks offer some of the finest camping opportunities on the islands and also provide spectacular hiking. There are no camping fees at either, getting a space is seldom a problem and both parks have drive-up and wilderness camping areas.

State Parks The five largest islands have state park campgrounds. They range from wilderness areas that you need to backpack into to developed roadside campsites. Many also have cabins that can be rented out. More information is given under 'Cabins'. State parks often have caretakers and better security than county parks.

Camping is allowed in the following places: on Kauai in Kokee, Na Pali Coast and Polihale state parks; on Oahu in Keaiwa Heiau, Malaekahana and Sand Island state recreation areas and Kahana Valley State Park; on Molokai in Palaau State Park; on Maui in Polipoli Spring State Recreation Area and Waianapanapa State Park; and on the Big Island in Kalopa State Park and MacKenzie State Recreation Area.

Camping in the state parks is free by permit and tents are required. Developed campgrounds generally have picnic tables, barbecue grills, drinking water, toilets and showers, though the maintenance of the facilities varies greatly.

The maximum length of stay allowable under a permit at any one state park is five nights. Another camping permit for the same park will not be issued until 30 days have elapsed. Campgrounds are open seven nights a week, except on Oahu where they are closed on Wednesday and Thursday nights. In addition, parks in forested areas may be closed during periods of drought due to extreme fire danger.

Camping permits can be obtained on weekdays from any of the following Division of State Parks offices, either in person, by mail or by phone:

Oahu
    Box 621, 1151 Punchbowl St, Honolulu, HI 96809 (☎ 587-0300)
Big Island
    Box 936, 75 Aupuni St, Hilo, HI 96721 (☎ 933-4200)
Maui
    54 High St, Wailuku, HI 96793 (☎ 243-5354)
Kauai
    3060 Eiwa St, Room 306, Lihue, HI 96766 (☎ 241-3444)

Note Applicants must be 18 and provide their address and phone number as well as an identification number (driver's license, passport or social security number) for each camper in the group. Applications should be received at least seven days in advance, but are not accepted earlier than 30 days before the intended camping date on Oahu or one year on the Neighbor Islands.

County Parks All the counties have parks with camping areas, although not all are of equal standard. Some county parks have wonderful white sand beaches and good facilities, while others are little more than unappealing roadside rest areas that have been turned into 'beach parks' simply by plopping down restrooms. Just because camping is allowed doesn't mean you'd want to camp there, or even use the beach.

Maui, which has the lion's share of outer island hotels and condos, seems more dedicated to getting your dollar than encouraging camping. Camping is allowed at only two county parks, each for only three nights, and neither is recommendable. The fee is $3 per person per night.

Molokai has two county parks with camping areas, one which is delightfully set on Hawaii's largest white sand beach. The fee is $3 per person per night.

The Big Island has 13 county campgrounds and a fee of only $1 per person per night.

Kauai has seven county campgrounds, including a couple of the nicest beachside camping spots in Hawaii. The fee is $3 per person per night.

Oahu has 12 county campgrounds, a couple of which are safe and recommendable. There are no fees.

Cabins

The state has housekeeping cabins on the Big Island at Kalopa State Park and at Kilauea and Mauna Kea state recreation areas, and on Maui at Polipoli Spring State Recreation Area and Waianapanapa State Park. Be sure to read the State Parks information under Camping above for addresses and phone numbers of the park offices.

The cabins are generally simple places with a kitchen, a common area, a bathroom and one to three bedrooms. They have basic furnishings, bedding, hot showers and some cooking and eating utensils. Polipoli, the most remote, has neither electricity nor refrigerators and you'll need a 4WD vehicle or hiking boots to reach it.

The housekeeping cabins are good value: $10 for one person, $14 for two, $19.50 for three, $24 for four, $27.50 for five and $30 for six. People staying in the cabins are subject to the same five-day limit as tent campers.

Reservations can be made at any of the state park offices and should be done as early as possible as the cabins are in high demand. Summer is the busiest time, but reservations often book up well in advance throughout the year. The state parks office does, however, get cancellations and if someone with a reservation doesn't pay their deposit in time the computer automatically bounces them and the site opens again.

Cabin cancellations and waiting lists are handled only on the island where the cabins are located. Even at the last moment it's worth calling to see if something has become available. If you're a little flexible you might be lucky – as we have been on occasion.

Reservations can be made in person, by phone or by mail, with 50% of the fee due within two weeks of making the reservation. Personal checks are accepted if you're paying more than 30 days in advance, but otherwise you'll need a bank check or postal money order. The remainder is due in cash when you check in. Refunds are given with notice 30 days prior to the camping date.

In addition to the state-maintained cabins, there are concession-run cabins at Malaekahana State Recreation Area on Oahu and Kokee State Park on Kauai and A-frame shelters at Hapuna Beach on the Big Island (see those sections for reservation information).

Hostels

Hawaii has two hostels associated with Hostelling International (HI), formerly known as the International Youth Hostel Federation (IYHF). Both are on Oahu; one is in Waikiki and one is in Honolulu near the University of Hawaii.

In addition, a number of private places offering inexpensive hostel-style accommodation have sprung up in the past couple of years. Private 'hostels' are located on Kauai in Kapaa and Haena; on Maui in Wailuku and Keanae; on the Big Island in Kailua-Kona and Hilo; and on Oahu in Waikiki and Waimea. Some of the places are quite nice, while others are mere crash pads. Rates for a dorm bed range from about $10 to $15, and private rooms are often available as well.

Most of these establishments are on the up and up, but we have heard complaints from people on Oahu where 'touts' are sent to the airport to round up backpackers.

Apparently some places promise more than they deliver – a $40 double room turns out to be a mattress on the floor and that sort of thing – so do your best to assess the situation before accepting a ride.

B&Bs

There are hundreds of B&Bs scattered around Hawaii. Some are modest spare bedrooms in family households, others are romantic and private hideaways, and a few are full-fledged inns. B&Bs cost as little as $35, although most average around $60 and the most exclusive properties are $100 to $150. Many require a minimum stay of two or three days, and some give discounts for stays of a week or more. B&Bs vary greatly but for the most part they represent some of the best value accommodation to be found in Hawaii.

Because Hawaii state codes place restrictions on serving home-cooked meals, most B&Bs offer a continental breakfast or provide food for guests to cook their own. Some places do provide full home-cooked breakfasts – they just don't advertise it.

Most home-based B&Bs don't handle their own reservations, but sign up with B&B reservation services. Some of these agencies can also book whole houses, condos and studio cottages as well. All require at least part of the payment in advance and have cancellation penalties. These agencies include:

Affordable Paradise Bed & Breakfast, c/o Maria Wilson, 226 Pouli Rd, Kailua, HI 96734, books reasonably priced cottages, studios and B&Bs. Maria speaks German and there's no booking fee (☎ 261-1693, (800) 925-9065; fax 261-7315).

All Islands Bed & Breakfast, 823 Kainui Dr, Kailua, HI 96734, books 475 host homes throughout Hawaii and there's no fee (☎ 263-2342, (800) 542-0344; fax 263-0308).

Babson's Reservation Service, 3371 Keka Dr, Kihei, HI 96753, is a newer service with B&Bs on all the islands (☎ 874-1166, (800) 824-6409; fax 879-7906).

Bed & Breakfast Hawaii, Box 449, Kapaa, HI 96746, is one of the larger services. For $13 they'll send you a guidebook-style directory from which you can select a B&B, or you can

Hibiscus

Anthurium

Protea

Plumeria

Heliconia

Orchid

Ilima

Ohelo Berries

Fern

Ohia Lehua

simply book by phone (☎ 822-7771, (800) 733-1632; fax 822-2723).

Bed & Breakfast Honolulu, 3242 Kaohinani Dr, Honolulu, HI 96817, despite the name, handles reservations on all the islands and can provide sample lists of B&Bs, including a list of those that welcome gay travelers. There's a $10 fee per reservation (☎ 595-7533, (800) 288-4666; fax 595-2030).

Hawaii's Best Bed & Breakfasts, c/o Barbara Campbell, Box 563, Kamuela, HI 96743, based on the Big Island, specializes in booking upscale B&Bs throughout Hawaii (☎ 885-4550, (800) 262-9912; fax 885-0550).

Hotels

Due to a slowdown in the economy and correspondingly low occupancy rates, there's a growing number of hotel discounts. Some hotels offer reduced promotional rates to pick up the slack while a few of the larger chains, such as Outrigger and Hawaiian Pacific Resorts, often throw in a free rental car. Before booking any hotel, it's worth asking if they're currently running any specials – some places actually have room/car packages for less than the 'standard' room rate!

While a good travel agent at home may know about some of these discounts, many of the best deals are advertised only in Hawaii and to find them you'll need to pick up a Honolulu newspaper. The travel section of the Sunday *Honolulu Advertiser* is best.

At most hotels the rooms are basically the same, with rates usually corresponding to two variables: the view and the floor. An ocean view often costs 50% to 100% more than a parking lot view, which is sometimes euphemistically called 'garden view'. Also the higher you go, the higher the tariff; the higher floors are generally quieter, especially on busy roads.

The toll-free numbers given in this book are for calls from the mainland and usually can't be dialed within Hawaii. However, some hotels will accept collect calls from the Neighbor Islands – it never hurts to try.

If you have a Hawaii driver's license, always ask about *kamaaina* rates. Many

middle and top-range hotels give residents big discounts.

The Hawaii Visitors Bureau (2270 Kalakaua Ave, Honolulu, HI 96815) will mail out on request a free annual accommodation guide listing member hotels with addresses and prices. It includes virtually all of Hawaii's resort hotels and most of those in the moderate range.

Condominiums

Condos are individually owned apartments that are fully furnished with everything a visitor needs from linen and towels to dishes and cutlery. Condos have more space than hotel rooms, generally with a living room and full kitchen, and many also have washer/dryers, sofa beds and a lanai (veranda). Unlike hotels, most condos don't have a daily room-cleaning service.

Condos are usually booked through rental agents, although some complexes have their own front desk. If you're staying awhile or are traveling with several people, condos almost always work out cheaper than all but the bottom-end hotels. However, most condo units booked through rental agents have a three to seven-day minimum stay, require deposits and have hefty cancellation fees.

Condos often offer weekly and monthly rates. The general rule is that the weekly rate is six times the daily rate, and the monthly is three times the weekly.

As most condo agencies deal with specific destinations, they are listed in the individual island chapters.

FOOD

Eating in Hawaii can be a real treat, as the islands' ethnic diversity has given rise to hundreds of different cuisines. You can find every kind of Japanese food, an array of regional Chinese cuisine, spicy Korean specialties, native Hawaiian dishes and excellent Thai and Vietnamese food. Even McDonald's serves up saimin and Portuguese sausage and Woolworth has sushi at the lunch counter.

Although you could spend a bundle eating out, you don't need to, as there are good, cheap neighborhood restaurants to explore on all the islands.

Hawaii also has many restaurants run by renowned chefs which feature gourmet foods of all type, including traditional continental fare. Some of the best restaurants are at the top-end hotels, although a fair number of the more successful chefs have moved on to open their own places.

Many of these 'renegade chefs' specialize in what's been dubbed 'Pacific Rim' or 'Hawaii Regional' cuisine, which incorporates fresh island ingredients and borrows liberally from the islands' various ethnic groups. It's marked by creative combinations such as kiawe-grilled freshwater shrimp with taro chips, wok-charred ahi with island greens, and Peking duck in ginger-lilikoi sauce.

Fresh fish is readily available throughout the islands. Seafood is generally expensive at places catering fancy meals to tourists, but can be quite reasonable at neighborhood restaurants.

Fish

Some of the most popular locally caught fish include:

Hawaiian Name	Common Name
mahimahi	a fish called 'dolphin', (not the mammal)
aku	skipjack tuna
ahi	yellowfin tuna
ono	wahoo
opakapaka	pink snapper
onaga	red snapper
uku	gray snapper
au	swordfish, marlin
papio or ulua	jack fish
kaku	barracuda
uhu	parrotfish
mano	shark

Fruit

Hawaii has an abundance of fruit including avocado, banana, breadfruit, star fruit, coconut, guava, lychee, mango, papaya, lilikoi (passion fruit) and pineapple. Sweet Kau oranges are grown on the Big Island.

Watermelons grown on Molokai are so famous throughout the islands that the air-lines had to create special regulations for passengers carrying them out of Molokai to prevent loose melons from bombing their way down the aisles.

Wild fruits which can be picked along trails include strawberry guava, common guava, thimbleberries, mountain apples, Methley plums and ohelo berries.

Hawaiian Food

The traditional Hawaiian feast marking special events is the luau. Local luaus are still commonplace in modern Hawaii for events such as baby christenings. In spirit, these luaus are far more authentic than anything you'll see at a hotel, but they're family affairs and the short-stay visitor would be lucky indeed to get an invitation to one.

The main dish at a luau is kalua pig, which is roasted in a pit-like earthen oven called an imu. The imu is readied for cooking by building a fire and heating rocks in the pit. When the rocks are glowing red, layers of moisture-laden banana trunks and green ti leaves are placed over the stones. A pig which has been slit open is filled with some of the hot rocks and laid on top of the bed. Other foods wrapped in ti and banana leaves are placed around it. It's all covered with more ti leaves and a layer of mats and topped off with dirt to seal in the heat which then bakes and steams the food. Anything cooked in this style is called kalua.

The process takes about four to eight hours depending on the amount of food. A few of the hotel luaus still bake the pig outdoors in this traditional manner and you can often go in the morning and watch them prepare and bury the pig.

Wetland taro is used to make poi, a paste pounded from the cooked taro corms. Water is added to make it pudding-like and its consistency is measured in one, two or three-finger poi – which indicates how many fingers are required to bring it from bowl to mouth. Poi is highly nutritious and easily digestible, but it's an acquired taste. It is sometimes fermented to give it a zingier flavor.

Tropical Fruit

Pineapple Hawaii's number one fruit crop is the pineapple. Most Hawaiian pineapples are of the smooth cayenne type and weigh a good five pounds. Pineapples are fairly unique among fruits in that they don't continue to ripen after they're picked. Although they're harvested year round, the long sunny days of summer produce the sweetest pineapples.

Papaya Papayas come in several varieties. One of the best of those found in grocery stores is the Solo, a small variety with pale strawberry-colored flesh. The flavor of papayas depends largely on where they're grown. Some of the most prized are from the Kapoho area of Puna on the Big Island and the Kahuku area of Oahu. Papayas, which are a good source of calcium and vitamins A and C, are harvested all year round.

Mango Big old mango trees are abundant in Hawaii, even in remote valleys. The juicy oblong fruits are about three inches in diameter and four to six inches long. The fruits start out green but take on deeper colors as they ripen, usually reddening to an apricot color. Mangoes are a good source of vitamins A and C. Two popular varieties, Pirie and Haden, are less stringy than those usually found in the wild. Mangoes are mainly a summer fruit.

Avocado Hawaii has three main types of avocado: the West Indian, a smooth-skinned variety which matures in summer and autumn; the rough-skinned Guatemalan which matures in winter and spring; and the Mexican variety which has a small fruit and smooth skin. Many of the avocados now in Hawaii are a hybrid of the three. Local fruit tends to be larger and more watery than the avocados grown in California.

Star fruit The carambola, or star fruit, is a translucent yellow-green fruit with five ribs like the points of a star. It has a crisp juicy pulp and can be eaten without being peeled.

Guava The common guava is a yellow, lime-shaped fruit, about two to three inches in diameter. It has a moist, pink, seedy flesh, all of which is edible. Guavas can be a little tart but tend to sweeten as they ripen. They're a good source of vitamin C and niacin and can be found along roadsides and trails.

Lilikoi Passion fruit is a vine with beautiful flowers which grow into small round fruits. The thick skin of the fruit is generally purple or yellow and wrinkles as it ripens. The pulp inside is juicy, seedy and slightly tart. The slimy texture can be a bit of a put-off the first time, but once you taste it you'll be hooked.

Mountain Apple The mountain apple is a small oval fruit a couple of inches long. The tree is related to the guava, though the fruit is completely different with a crispy white flesh and a pink skin. It fruits in the summer and is common along trails.

Ohelo These berries grow on low shrubs common in lava areas. It's a relative of the cranberry, similar in tartness and size. The fruit is red or yellow and is used in jellies and pies.

Breadfruit The Hawaiian breadfruit is a large, round, green fruit. It's comparable to potatoes in carbohydrates and is prepared much the same way. In old Hawaii, as in much of the Pacific, breadfruit was one of the traditional staples. ■

Guavas

Laulau is fish, pork and taro wrapped in a ti leaf bundle and steamed. *Lomi* salmon is made by marinating thin slices of raw salmon with diced tomatoes and green onions.

Other Hawaiian foods include baked *ulu* – breadfruit, *limu* – seaweed, *opihi* – the tiny limpet shells which fishers pick off the reef at low tide, and *pipikaula* – beef jerky. *Haupia*, the standard dessert to a Hawaiian meal, is a custard made of coconut cream thickened with cornstarch or arrowroot.

In Hawaiian food preparation, ti leaves are indispensable, functioning like a biodegradable version of both aluminum foil and paper plates: food is wrapped in it, cooked in it and served upon it.

Many visitors taste traditional Hawaiian food only at expensive luaus or by sampling a dollop of poi at one of the more adventurous hotel buffets. Although Hawaiian food is harder to find than other ethnic foods, there are a few restaurants throughout the islands that serve the real thing and it's some of the cheapest food in Hawaii.

Local Food

The distinct style of food called 'local' usually refers to a fixed plate lunch with 'two scoop rice', a scoop of macaroni salad and a serving of beef stew, mahimahi or teriyaki chicken, generally scoffed down with chopsticks. A breakfast plate might have Spam, eggs, kimchee and, always, two scoops of rice.

These plate meals are the standard fare in diners and lunch wagons. If it's full of starches, fats and gravies, you're probably eating local.

Snacks

Pupus is the word for all kinds of munchies or hors d'oeuvres. Boiled peanuts, soy-flavored rice crackers called *kaki mochi* and sashimi are common pupus.

Another local favorite is *poke*, which is raw fish marinated in soy sauce, oil, chili peppers, green onions and seaweed. It makes a nice accompaniment with beer.

Crack Seed Crack seed is a Chinese snack food which can be sweet, sour, salty or some combination of the three. It's often made from dried fruits such as plums and apricots, although more exotic ones include sweet and sour baby cherry seeds, pickled mangoes and *li hing mui*, one of the sour favorites. Crack seed shops often sell dried cuttlefish, roasted green peas, candied ginger, beef jerky and rock candy as well.

Shave Ice Shave ice is similar to mainland snow cones, only better. The ice is shaved as fine as powder snow, packed into a paper cone and drenched with sweet fruit-flavored syrups. Many islanders like the ones with ice cream and/or sweet azuki beans at the bottom, while kids usually opt for rainbow shave ice which has colorful stripes of different syrups.

DRINKS

Tap water is safe to drink but water from freshwater streams should be boiled.

Cans of Hawaiian-made fruit juices such as guava-orange or passion fruit are stocked at most stores. If you're going for a hike and want to toss a couple of drinks in your daypack, the juices make a good alternative to sodas as they don't explode when shaken and they taste good even when they're not kept cold.

Alcohol

The drinking age in Hawaii is 21. It's illegal to have open containers of alcohol in motor vehicles and drinking in public parks or on the beaches is also illegal although it's a common scene. All grocery stores sell liquor as do most of the smaller food marts. Tedeschi Vineyards, a local winery on Maui, makes a good pineapple wine, grape wine and champagne.

PAKALOLO

Hawaii's pakalolo is considered to be some of the most potent anywhere, although the scene of years past when local guys hung out in beach parking lots and whispered 'buds' to people walking by has virtually disappeared. Authorities have been so successful in rooting out marijuana crops and arresting growers that pakalolo is reportedly less common on Hawaii's streets than dangerous drugs like 'ice' and heroin. The possession of marijuana is illegal on the islands; yachties entering Hawaii should be aware that federal authorities have been known to seize boats after finding even minute quantities of marijuana on board.

ENTERTAINMENT

Hawaii has an active and varied entertainment scene and you won't suffer for want of nightlife. For detailed information, see the Entertainment sections in the island chapters.

THINGS TO BUY

Hawaii has a lot of fine craftspeople and quality handicrafts can be readily found on all the islands.

Woodworkers generally use beautifully grained native Hawaiian hardwoods, such as koa, to create calabashes and bowls. Traditionally Hawaiian bowls are not decorated or ornate, but rather are shaped to bring out the natural beauty of the wood. The thinner and lighter the bowl, the finer the artistic skill and the greater the value.

There are some excellent island potters, many influenced by Japanese styles and aesthetics. Good raku work in particular can be found throughout the islands at reasonable prices.

Lauhala, the leaves of the pandanus tree which were once woven into the mats that Hawaiians slept on, are now woven into placemats, hats and baskets.

Many music shops carry recorded traditional and contemporary Hawaiian music. Hula musical instruments such as nose flutes and gourd rattles are uniquely Hawaiian and make interesting gifts.

Niihau shell leis, made from the tiny shells which wash up on the island of Niihau, are one of the most prized Hawaiiana souvenirs. Elaborate pieces can cost thousands of dollars.

Hawaii's island-style clothing is colorful and light, often with prints of tropical flowers. The classiest aloha shirts are of lightweight cotton with subdued colors (like those of reverse fabric prints). Women might want to buy a *muu-muu*, a loose, comfortable, full-length Hawaiian-style dress.

Foods are popular purchases. The standard souvenir is macadamia nuts, either canned or covered in chocolate. Kona coffee, macadamia nut butters, lilikoi or *poha* berry preserves and mango chutney all make convenient, compact gift items.

Pineapples are not a great choice in the souvenir department. Not only are they heavy and bulky, but they're likely to be just as cheap at home.

For those who enjoy Japanese food, Hawaii is a good place to pick up ingredients that might be difficult to find back home. Most grocery stores have a wide selection of things like dried seaweed, mochi and ume plums.

Flowers such as orchids, anthuriums and proteas make good gifts if you're flying straight home. Proteas stay fresh for about 10 days and then can be dried. Foreign visitors should check with their airline in advance, however, as there are commonly restrictions against bringing agricultural products across international borders.

Facts for the International Visitor

VISAS & EMBASSIES

The conditions for entering Hawaii are the same as for entering any other state in the USA.

Canadians must have proper proof of Canadian citizenship, such as a citizenship card with photo ID or a passport. Visitors from other countries must have a valid passport and most visitors also require a US visa.

However there is a reciprocal visa-waiver program in which citizens of certain countries may enter the USA for stays of 90 days or less without first obtaining a US visa. Currently these countries are: the UK,

New Zealand, Japan, Italy, Spain, Austria, the Netherlands, Belgium, Switzerland, France, Germany, Norway, Denmark, Sweden, Finland, Iceland, San Marino, Andorra, Luxembourg, Liechtenstein and Monaco. Under this program you must have a round-trip ticket that is non-refundable in the USA and you will not be allowed to extend your stay beyond the 90 days.

Other travelers will need to obtain a visa from a US consulate or embassy. In most countries the process can be done by mail.

Your passport should be valid for at least six months longer than your intended stay in the USA and you'll need to submit a recent photo (37 x 37 mm) with the application. Documents of financial stability and/or guarantees from a US resident are sometimes required, particularly for those from Third World countries.

Visa applicants may be required to 'demonstrate binding obligations' that will insure their return back home. Because of this requirement, those planning to travel through other countries before arriving in the USA are generally better off applying for their US visa while they are still in their home country – rather than while on the road.

The validity period for US visitor visas depends on what country you're from. The length of time you'll be allowed to stay in the USA is ultimately determined by US immigration authorities at the port of entry.

Incidentally, the infamous prohibition against issuing visas to people who 'have been members of Communist organizations' has been dropped. An anachronism of the Cold War, it still appears on the unrevised visa applications although most consular offices have penned a line through the item.

Foreign Consulates in Hawaii

In Honolulu there are consulates from Australia, Austria, Belgium, Brazil, Chile, Cook Islands, Denmark, Finland, France, Germany, India, Japan, Kiribati, Korea, Malaysia, Mexico, Netherlands, Norway, Peru, Philippines, Spain, Sweden, Switzerland and Thailand.

There are also government liaison offices for Tonga, American Samoa, Palau, the Federated States of Micronesia, the Marianas and the Republic of the Marshall Islands.

Addresses and phone numbers are in the Oahu phone book under 'Consulates'.

DOCUMENTS

All foreign visitors (other than Canadians) must of course bring their passport. US citizens and Canadians may want to bring along a passport as well, in the event they get tempted to extend their travels beyond Hawaii. All visitors should bring their driver's license and any health insurance or travel insurance cards.

Members of Hostelling International (HI) or American Youth Hostels (AYH) will be able to take advantage of lower hostel rates in Oahu by bringing their membership cards. Members of the American Automobile Association (AAA) or other affiliated automobile club can get some car rental and sightseeing admission discounts with their membership cards.

CUSTOMS

US customs allows each person over the age of 21 to bring one liter of liquor and 200 cigarettes duty-free into the USA. Most fresh fruits and plants are restricted from entry into Hawaii and there's a strict quarantine on animals.

MONEY

As elsewhere in the USA, US dollars are the only accepted currency in Hawaii.

The US dollar is divided into 100 cents. Coins come in denominations of one cent (penny), five cents (nickel), 10 cents (dime), 25 cents (quarter) and 50 cents (half dollar). Notes come in one, five, 10, 20, 50 and 100-dollar denominations. There is also a one-dollar coin that the government has tried unsuccessfully to bring into mass circulation and a two-dollar note that is out of favor but still occasionally seen.

Foreign travelers will find it easier if

their traveler's checks are already in US dollars, but major currencies can be exchanged at Honolulu International Airport and larger banks.

Restaurants, hotels and most stores accept US dollar traveler's checks as if they're cash, so if you're carrying traveler's checks in US dollars, odds are you'll never have to use a bank or pay an exchange fee.

Exchange Rates
At press time, exchange rates were:

A$1	=	US$0.75
¥100	=	US$1
C$1	=	US$0.73
DM1	=	US$1.64
NZ$1	=	US$0.59
UK£1	=	US$1.52
HK$10	=	US$1.30

TOURIST OFFICES ABROAD
Hawaii Visitors Bureau (HVB) offices outside the USA include:

Australia
c/o Walshes World, 92 Pitt St, 8th Floor, Sydney, NSW 2000 (☎ (02) 235-0194; fax (02) 221-8297)

Belgium
Rue Couperin, No 87 BIS, Boncelles 4100 (☎ (41) 38-1517; fax (41) 37-7814)

Canada
205-1624 56th St, Delta, BC V4L 2B1 (☎ & fax (604) 943-8555)

Germany
c/o Hans Regh Associates, Postfach 930 247, Ginnheimer Landstrasse 1, 6000 Frankfurt/Main 90 (☎ (069) 70-4013; fax (069) 70-4043)

Hong Kong
c/o FHS Marketing Company, Penthouse, Chinese Bank Building, 61-65 Des Voeux Rd Central (☎ 868-2036; fax 869-6471)

Japan
Hibiya Kokusai Building, 11th Floor, 2-2-3 Uchisaiwai-cho, Chiyoda-ku, Tokyo 100 (☎ (03) 3580-2481; fax (03) 3580-2448)

Korea
c/o Travel Press, 10th Floor, Samwon Building, 112-5, Sokong-Dong, Chung-ku, Seoul (☎ (02) 773-6719; fax (02) 757-6783)

Malaysia
c/o Pacific World Travel, 2.5 & 2.6 Angkasa Raya Building, Jalan Ampang, Kuala Lumpur 50450 (☎ (03) 244-8449; fax (03) 242-1129)

New Zealand
c/o Walshes World, 87 Queen St, 2nd Floor, Dingwall Building, Auckland (☎ (09) 379-3708; fax (09) 309-0725)

Singapore
c/o Pacific Leisure, 11 Craig Rd, Tanjong Pagar Rd, Singapore 0208 (☎ 221-8706; fax 221-1747)

Taiwan
c/o Federal Transportation Co, 8th Floor, 61 Nanking East Rd, Section 3, Taipei (☎ (02) 506-7043; fax (02) 507-5816)

Thailand
c/o ADAT Sales, 8th Floor, Maneeya Center Building, 518/5 Ploenchit Rd, Bangkok (☎ (02) 255-6838; fax (02) 254-1271)

UK
14 The Green, Richmond, London TW9 1PX (☎ (0181) 332-6969; fax (0181) 332-7001)

TELECOMMUNICATIONS
If you're calling from abroad, the international country code for the USA is '1' and all calls to Hawaii are then followed by the area code 808 and the local number.

To make an international call direct from Hawaii, dial 011 + country code + area code + number. (An exception is to Canada, where you instead dial: 1 + area code + number.) You may need to wait as long as 45 seconds for the ringing to start. For international operator assistance dial 0.

As a general rule, it's cheaper to make international calls at night, however this varies with the country you're calling. In Hawaii pay phones are owned by a few different companies, including AT&T and MCI. The exact cost for calling overseas will depend upon which carrier you use and the country being called. Most international calls dialed direct from a pay phone cost about $5 for the first minute and about $1 for each additional minute. The operator can give more specific rate information.

Information on making phone calls within Hawaii in under the general Post & Telecommunications section near the start of this chapter.

ELECTRICITY
Electricity is 110/120 V, 60 cycles, and a flat two-pronged plug is used, the same as everywhere else in the USA.

WEIGHTS & MEASURES
Hawaii, like the rest of the USA, uses the imperial system of measurement. Distances are in feet, yards and miles; weights are in ounces, pounds and tons. For those unaccustomed to the imperial system, there is a metric conversion table at the back of this book.

Getting There & Away

AIR

Hawaii is a major Pacific hub and an intermediate stop on many flights between the US mainland and Asia, Australia, New Zealand and the South Pacific. Passengers on any of these routes can usually make a stopover in Honolulu.

With the exception of an occasional flight from the US mainland that goes directly to the Neighbor Islands, all flights to Hawaii land at Honolulu International Airport.

There are numerous airlines flying to Hawaii and a variety of fares are available. In addition to a straightforward round-trip ticket, Hawaii can also be part of a Round-the-World or Circle Pacific ticket. So rather than just walking into the nearest travel agent or airline office, it pays to do a bit of research and shopping around first.

You might want to start by perusing the travel sections of magazines and large newspapers, like the *New York Times*, the *San Francisco Chronicle-Examiner* and the *Los Angeles Times* in the USA; the *Sydney Morning Herald* or Saturday's *Age* in Australia; and *Time Out* or *TNT* in the UK.

Keeping in mind that air fares are constantly changing, the fares listed throughout this chapter should at least give you an idea of relative costs.

Round-the-World Tickets

Round-the-World (RTW) tickets, which

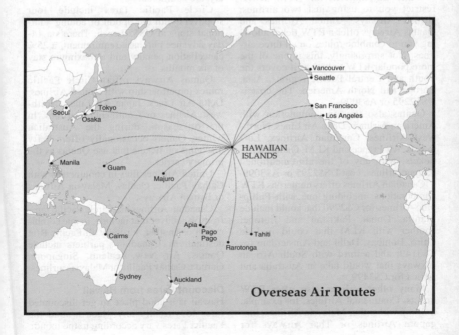

Overseas Air Routes

allow you to fly on the combined routes of two or more airlines, can be an economical way to circle the globe.

RTW tickets are valid for one year and you must travel in one general direction without backtracking. Although most airlines restrict the number of sectors that can be flown within the USA and Canada to four, and a few heavily traveled routes (such as Honolulu to Tokyo) are blacked out by some airlines, stopovers are otherwise generally unlimited.

In most cases a 14-day advance purchase is required. After the ticket is purchased, dates can be changed without penalty and tickets can be rewritten to add or delete stops for $50 each.

There's an almost endless variety of airline and destination combinations possible. Because of Honolulu's central Pacific location, Hawaii can be included on most RTW tickets.

While the majority of RTW tickets restrict you to using just two airlines, British Airways, United Airlines and Qantas Airways offer a RTW ticket allowing you to combine routes on all three airlines. Not surprisingly, this is one of the more popular RTW tickets as it covers the South and Central Pacific regions, Asia, Europe and North America. The cost is US$2295 or A$3099.

Qantas also flies in conjunction with American Airlines, Delta Air Lines, Northwest Airlines, Canadian Airlines, Lufthansa, Air France and KLM. Qantas RTW tickets, with any of the aforementioned partner airlines, cost US$2295 or A$3099.

Canadian Airlines offers numerous RTW combinations, including one with Philippine Airlines for C$2790 that could include Manila, Dubai, Pakistan and Europe; another with KLM that could include Cairo, Bombay, Delhi and Amsterdam for C$3149; and a third with South African Airways that would take in Australia and Africa for C$3499.

Many other airlines also offer RTW tickets. Continental Airlines, for example, links up with either Malaysia Airlines, Singapore Airlines or Thai Airways for US$2570, although no travel is allowed in the South Pacific. TWA's lowest priced RTW, linking up with Korean Air, costs $2087 and allows stops in Honolulu, Seoul, Tel Aviv, Amsterdam and Paris or London.

Circle Pacific Tickets

For Circle Pacific tickets, two airlines link up to allow stopovers along their combined Pacific Rim routes. Rather than simply flying from Point A to Point B, these tickets allow you to swing through much of the Pacific and eastern Asia taking in a variety of destinations – as long as you keep traveling in the same circular direction.

Circle Pacific routes essentially have the same fares: A$3149 when purchased in Australia, US$2449 when purchased in the USA and C$2899 when purchased in Canada. There are also higher business class and first-class fares. Departure and airport-use taxes, which will vary with the itinerary, are additional.

Circle Pacific fares include four stopovers with the option of adding additional stops at US$50 each. There's a 14-day advance purchase requirement, a 25% cancellation penalty and a maximum stay of six months.

Qantas Airways offers Circle Pacific routes in partnership with United Airlines, Delta Air Lines, Japan Air Lines, Northwest Airlines or Continental Airlines. In the off-season, during the Australian winter, Qantas occasionally offers hefty discounts on tickets that use Qantas as the primary carrier.

United Airlines flies in conjunction with Cathay Pacific, Qantas, Malaysia Airlines or British Airways.

Canadian Airlines has Circle Pacific fares from Vancouver that include, in one combination or another, virtually all Pacific Rim destinations. Canadian's partners include Qantas, Air New Zealand, Singapore, Garuda, Cathay Pacific or Malaysia airlines.

Discount Fares from Hawaii

Hawaii is a good place to get discounted fares to virtually any place around the Pacific. Fares vary according to the month, airline and supply and demand, but often you can find a round-trip fare to Los Angeles or San Francisco for around $250; to Tokyo for $450; to Hong Kong or Manila for $600; and to Auckland, Saigon or Singapore for $700.

If you don't have a set destination in mind you can sometimes find some great on-the-spot deals. The travel pages of the Sunday *Honolulu Advertiser* have scores of ads by travel agencies advertising discounted overseas fares.

Some agencies specializing in discount travel are:

Cheap Tickets Inc, Kapiolani at Atkinson Dr, Honolulu (☎ 947-3717, (800) 377-1000)
Hawaii Hana, 1481 S King St, Suite 125, Honolulu (☎ 951-8448)
Pali Travel, 1304 Pali Hwy, Honolulu (☎ 533-3608; fax 524-2483)
Panda Travel, 1017 Kapahulu Ave, Honolulu (☎ 734-1961; fax 732-4136)

Honolulu International Airport

Honolulu International is a modern airport that's in the process of completing a decade-long expansion. Although it's a busy place, it's not particularly difficult to get around.

The airport has all the expected services, including fast-food restaurants, lounges, newsstands, sundry shops, lei stands, gift shops, duty-free shops, a 24-hour medical clinic and a mini-hotel for naps and showers.

There's a 24-hour visitor information booth, car rental counters and hotel/condo courtesy phones in the baggage claim area. You can also pick up *This Week Oahu*, *Spotlight's Oahu Gold* and other tourist magazines from nearby racks.

If you arrive early for a flight and are looking for something to do, the new **Pacific Aerospace Museum** ($3) in the main departure lobby is open from 9 am to 10 pm daily and has multimedia displays on aviation.

Money Thomas Cook has foreign exchange booths spread around the airport, including in the international arrival area and in the central departure lobby next to the barber shop. On the opposite side of the same barber shop is a Bankoh ATM that gives cash advances on major credit cards and withdrawals using Cirrus and Plus systems ATM cards. As Thomas Cook adds on some hefty transaction fees, especially for non-Thomas Cook traveler's checks, using the ATM may be a better option.

If you're in no hurry, you can avoid needling transaction fees by going to the Bank of Hawaii on the ground level across the street from baggage claim D. It's open from 8:30 am to 3 pm Monday to Thursday and to 6 pm on Fridays.

Baggage Storage There are coin-operated computerized lockers in front of gates 13 and 24 which cost 50c per hour, up to a maximum of $3 per 24 hours; coin changing machines are located next to the lockers.

In addition, on the ground floor of the parking structure, opposite the main overseas terminal, there are older token-operated lockers that cost $1 for 24 hours and a baggage storage service that will hold items for $2 to $10 a day, depending on the size. It's open 24 hours a day; for information call 836-6547.

Airport Shuttle The free Wiki Wiki Shuttle (☎ 836-2505) connects the more distant parts of the airport, and links the main terminals with the inter-island terminals. It runs between 7 am and 10 pm and can be picked up streetside in front of the main lobby (on the second level) and in front of the inter-island gates.

Airlines Serving Honolulu

The following airlines have scheduled flights to Honolulu International Airport on Oahu. The numbers listed for each airline are the local Oahu numbers; those that begin with 800 can also be called toll free from anywhere within the state.

Air Marshall Islands	☎ 949-5522
Air Micronesia	☎ (800) 231-0856

Air Molokai	☎ 521-0090
Air New Zealand	☎ (800) 262-1234
Aloha Airlines	☎ 484-1111
American Airlines	☎ 833-7600
American Trans Air	☎ 833-0074
Asiana	☎ (800) 227-4262
Canadian Airlines	☎ (800) 426-7000
China Airlines	☎ 955-0088
Continental Airlines	☎ 523-0000
Delta Air Lines	☎ (800) 221-1212
Garuda Indonesia	☎ 947-9500
Hawaiian Airlines	☎ 838-1555
Island Air	☎ 484-2222
Japan Air Lines	☎ 521-1441
Japan Air System	☎ 924-1515
Korean Air	☎ (800) 438-5000
Mahalo	☎ 833-5555
Northwest Airlines	☎ 955-2255
Philippine Airlines	☎ (800) 435-9725
Qantas Airways	☎ (800) 227-4500
Trans Air Hawaii	☎ 836-8080
TWA	☎ (800) 221-2000
United Airlines	☎ 547-2211

To/From the US Mainland

Domestic air fares are constantly in flux. Fares vary with the season you travel, the day of the week you fly, your length of stay and the flexibility the ticket provides for flight changes and refunds. Still, nothing determines fares more than business, and when things are slow, regardless of the season, airlines will drop fares to fill the empty seats. There's a lot of competition to Honolulu from the major mainland cities and at any given time any one of the airlines could have the cheapest fare.

The airlines each have their own requirements and restrictions which also seem to be constantly changing. For the latest deals, either find a knowledgeable travel agent or just call the different airlines and compare.

When you call the airlines it's important to ask for the lowest fare, as that's not always the first one they'll quote. Each flight has only a limited number of seats available at the cheapest fares. When you make reservations the agents will generally tell you the best fare that's still available on the date you give them, which may or may not be the cheapest fare that the airline is

currently offering. If you make reservations far enough in advance and are a little flexible with dates, you'll usually do better.

Typically the lowest round-trip fares from the US mainland to Honolulu are about $600 to $800 from the east coast and $300 to $450 from the west coast. Although conditions vary, the cheapest fares are generally for midweek flights and have advance purchase requirements and other restrictions. They are usually non-refundable and non-changeable, at least on the outbound flight (although most airlines make allowances for medical emergencies).

The following airlines fly to Honolulu from both the US east and west coasts:

American	☎ (800) 433-7300
Continental	☎ (800) 525-0280
Delta	☎ (800) 221-1212
Northwest	☎ (800) 225-2525
TWA	☎ (800) 221-2000
United	☎ (800) 241-6522

In addition, Hawaiian Airlines (☎ (800) 367-5320) flies to Honolulu from Seattle, San Francisco and Los Angeles. Depending on the season and current promotional fares, a round-trip ticket from Seattle is usually around $450. Standard fares from LA and San Francisco hover around $400 round-trip, though they often offer promotional fares for under $300. Usually a Neighbor Island destination can be added on for $20 more.

Flight time to Honolulu is about 5½ hours from the west coast, 11 hours from the east coast.

To/From Canada

The cheapest standard fares (in Canadian dollars) to Honolulu with Canadian Airlines are $499 from Vancouver, $599 from Calgary or Edmonton, and $898 from Toronto. These fares require a minimum stay of seven days and allow a maximum stay of 15 days, have a 14-day advance purchase requirement and are non-refundable and non-changeable.

For $100 more ($599 from Vancouver

for instance) you can get a ticket that allows a 30-day stay and for an additional $100 ($699 from Vancouver) there's a third type of ticket that allows a maximum stay of 90 days. Both of these fares have a seven-day advance purchase requirement, a $150 cancellation penalty and a $50 fee for date changes.

Fares on all three types of tickets are for midweek travel all year round except for three weeks around the Christmas and New Year holidays.

The toll-free number for Canadian Airlines in Canada is (800) 665-1177.

To/From Central & South America

Most flights to Hawaii from Central and South America go via Houston or Los Angeles, though a few of those from the eastern cities go via New York.

Continental has flights from about 20 cities in Mexico and Central America, including San Jose, Guatemala City, Cancún and Mérida. Their lowest round-trip fare from Mexico City to Honolulu is US$900, allows a maximum stay of 60 days and has a three-day advance purchase requirement.

To/From Australia

Qantas flies to Honolulu from Sydney, Melbourne (via Sydney) and Cairns, with round-trip fares ranging from A$1160 to A$1429, depending on the season. These tickets have a 21-day advance purchase requirement, a minimum stay of seven days and a maximum stay of 60 days. For A$170 extra, you can buy a round-trip ticket to Honolulu that requires a 14-day advance purchase, allows a stay of up to 90 days and allows stopovers. At press time, no US carriers were providing service between Australia and Honolulu, though United and Continental have done so in the past.

To/From New Zealand

Air New Zealand has Auckland to Honolulu round-trip fares ranging from a low of NZ$1299 (February, October, November) to a high of NZ$1449 (December, January).

These tickets have to be purchased at least 21 days in advance and within seven days of making reservations, and allow stays of up to two months. No stopovers are permitted. The one-way fare, which allows a free stopover in Fiji, is NZ$1049 year round.

To/From Fiji

Air New Zealand has a one-way fare from Nadi to Honolulu for F$872 (US$601) and a six-month excursion ticket with no advance purchase requirement for F$1243 (US$857).

To/From other South Pacific Islands

Hawaiian Airlines flies to Honolulu from Tahiti and American Samoa. From American Samoa the fare is US$383 one way and US$540 round trip; the latter is good for one year and has no advance purchase requirement. From Tahiti the standard one-way fare is a steep US$1038 but there's a seven-day excursion ticket with no advance purchase requirement that costs just US$670. There's also a round-trip ticket that is good for one year, has a 14-day advance purchase requirement and costs US$1000.

Air New Zealand flies to Honolulu from Tonga, the Cook Islands and Western Samoa. The lowest round-trip fare from Tonga to Honolulu costs T$1125 (US$834), requires a seven-day advance purchase and allows a stay of up to 45 days. A one-way ticket costs T$647 (US$480).

From Rarotonga on the Cook Islands, Air New Zealand's cheapest round-trip fare to Honolulu is NZ$1089 (US$656) during February, October and November; NZ$1249 in December and January; and NZ$1149 in other months. The one-way fare is NZ$999 (US$602) year round.

From Apia in Western Samoa, Air New Zealand's round-trip fare to Honolulu is WS$1355 (US$540) with no advance purchase requirement and a 90-day maximum stay. The one-way fare is WS$940 (US$375).

To/From Micronesia

Continental, Northwest and United fly

from Guam to Honolulu with round-trip fares of $807 on weekdays, $859 on weekends. The Northwest and United flights are via Japan, while Continental offers direct flights. The one-way fare is $459 on weekdays and $495 on weekends. The fares jump about 10% for travel between December 15 and January 15, but are otherwise the same year round. The ticket allows a stay of up to one year and no advance purchase is required.

The more exciting way to get from Guam, however, is to take Continental Air Micronesia's island hopper which stops en route at Chuuk (Truk), Pohnpei, Kosrae and Majuro before reaching Honolulu. It costs $651 one way with no advance purchase requirement and free unlimited stopovers. If you're coming from Asia this is a good alternative to a nonstop transpacific flight and a great way to see some of the Pacific's most remote islands without having to spend a lot of money.

To/From Japan
Fares in this section are in yen; there are approximately 100 yen to one US dollar.

United Airlines has three flights a day to Honolulu from Tokyo. The one-way fare, which has no advance purchase requirement or other restrictions, costs ¥174,800. However, round-trip excursion fares are cheaper. The best published fare is ¥84,000, which has a 14-day advance purchase requirement and a two-month maximum stay. There's also an excursion ticket with the same maximum stay but no advance purchase requirement for ¥133,000.

Northwest Airlines has a three-month excursion ticket from either Tokyo or Osaka for ¥113,000 that requires purchase within three days of booking. Northwest also has an unrestricted one-way fare of ¥158,800 from Osaka, ¥144,600 from Tokyo. Flights to Honolulu are daily from both cities.

Japan Air Lines flies to Honolulu from Tokyo, Osaka, Nagoya, Fukuoka and Sapporo. Excursion fares vary a bit with the departing city and the season but, except at busier holiday periods, they're generally about ¥120,000 for a ticket valid for three months, with a three-day advance purchase requirement. The one-way fare from Tokyo is ¥168,000.

An interesting alternative if you're only going one way would be to fly from Japan to Guam (¥69,400) and then pick up a Continental Air Micronesia ticket that would allow you to island hop through much of Micronesia on your way to Honolulu – for less than the cost of a direct one-way Japan-Honolulu ticket.

To/From Southeast Asia
There are numerous airlines flying directly to Hawaii from Southeast Asia. The fares given are the standard published fares, though bucket shops in places like Bangkok and Singapore should be able to come up with much better deals. Also, if you're traveling to the USA from Southeast Asia, tickets to the US west coast are not that much more than tickets to Hawaii and many allow a free stopover in Honolulu.

Northwest Airlines flies to Honolulu from Hong Kong, Bangkok, Manila, Seoul and Singapore. From Hong Kong to Honolulu, the round-trip fare costs HK$10,150 (US$1313) from September to mid-December and from February to mid-June and HK$11,750 (US$1520) the rest of the year. From Bangkok to Honolulu, the round-trip fare is 27,640B (US$1100) from September to mid-June and about 10% higher in midsummer. From Manila to Honolulu, the round-trip fare is US$1065 from February to mid-March and from September to December and US$1142 the rest of the year. From Seoul to Honolulu, the round-trip fare is US$1120 from September to May and US$1270 the rest of the year. From Singapore to Honolulu, round-trip fares cost S$2871 (US$1930) from September to June and S$3152 (US$2120) the rest of the year. The Seoul ticket is good for a stay of up to six months, the others for a year.

Korean Air and Philippine Airlines also

have flights from a number of Southeast Asia cities to Honolulu.

To/From Europe

The most common route to Hawaii from Europe is west via New York or Los Angeles. If you're interested in heading east with stops in Asia, it may be cheaper to get a Round-the-World ticket instead of returning the same way.

American Airlines has a round-trip fare from London to Honolulu of UK£688 (US$1080), which allows a one-month maximum stay and has a 21-day advance purchase requirement. There's also an excursion ticket for UK£738 (US$1159) which requires a two-week advance purchase and allows a two-month stay.

American's cheapest round-trip fare from Paris to Honolulu is FF6160 (US$1160); it has a seven-day advance purchase requirement and is good for a stay of up to 21 days. There's also an excursion ticket for FF7350 (US$1385) that's good for a maximum stay of three months and has no advance purchase requirement.

American Airlines also flies to Honolulu from Frankfurt, Munich and Berlin. The fare is DM2130 (US$1370) with no advance purchase requirement and you can stay up to three months. All of these American Airlines' fares are for travel between Monday and Thursday.

United, Delta and Continental airlines have similarly priced service to Honolulu from a number of European cities.

You can usually beat the published airline fares at bucket shops and other travel agencies specializing in discount tickets. London is arguably the world's headquarters for bucket shops and they are well advertised. Two good, reliable agents for cheap tickets in the UK are: Trailfinders (☎ (0171) 938-3366), 46 Earls Court Rd, London W8 6EJ, and STA (☎ (0171) 937-9962), 74 Old Brompton Rd, London SW7.

SEA

Travel agents, or shops that sell discount cruise tickets, are the best sources of infor-

mation for transpacific cruises, though there are very few Hawaii-bound cruises to choose from.

Once a year, usually in January, Cunard (☎ (800) 221-4770) books the *Queen Elizabeth II* on a world cruise that stops in Hawaii. The boat can be picked up in Ensenada (Mexico) for a five-day cruise to Hawaii; the cost for just that segment starts at $2000, including one-way air fare back from Honolulu to the US west coast.

Royal Cruise Line (☎ (800) 227-4534) has a 16-day cruise to Hawaii which begins and ends in San Diego, goes via Ensenada, and includes about 11 days at sea and five days in Hawaii. The cheapest inside cabin costs about $3600, the cheapest outside cabin $4100, for early bookings. A one-way eight-day version that includes the cruise from San Diego to Honolulu and air fare from Honolulu back to the US west coast starts around $2500.

TOURS

There are a slew of package tours available to Hawaii. The basic ones just include air fare and accommodation, while others can include car rentals, sightseeing tours and all sorts of recreational activities. If you're interested, travel agents can help you sort through the various packages.

For those with limited time, package tours can be the cheapest way to go. Costs vary, but one-week tours with air fare and no-frills hotel accommodation usually start around $500 from the US west coast, $700 from the US east coast, based on double occupancy. If you want to stay somewhere fancy or island hop, the price can easily be double that.

Specialized Tours

In addition to traditional package tours, there are some study and environmental tours to Hawaii.

The University of Research Expeditions Program (☎ (510) 642-6586), University of California, Berkeley, CA 94720, runs one or two work/study tours a year assisting scholars in the field with such projects as surveying ancient petroglyphs or studying the ecology of plants that grow in lava. Most tours last two weeks. Rates range from $1300 to $1500, including food and simple accommodation but excluding air fare.

Elderhostel (☎ (617) 426-8056), 75 Federal St, Boston, MA 02110, is a nonprofit organization offering educational programs for those aged 60 or older. The organization has its origins in the youth hostels of Europe and the folk schools of Scandinavia. There's a full range of ongoing programs, some on the Big Island in conjunction with the Lyman Museum in Hilo and the Volcano Art Center, and others at the University of Hawaii. Many programs focus on Hawaii's people and culture, while some explore the natural environment. The typical fee is $440 for six nights, $880 for 13 nights, including accommodation, meals and classes.

Oceanic Society Expeditions (☎ (415) 441-1106, (800) 326-7491), Fort Mason Center, Building E, San Francisco, CA 94123, the environmental travel arm of Friends of the Earth, offers eco-tours with a noninvasive approach to viewing wildlife. Tours include a week-long expedition observing humpback whales and dolphins in the waters off Maui and a similar expedition observing Hawaiian monk seals off Kauai and Niihau. The cost is $1090 for the whale outing, $1390 for the seal outing. Air fare to Hawaii is not included, but accommodation is.

LEAVING HAWAII
Departure Tax & Fees
There's a $6 departure tax charged to all those who depart from Honolulu International Airport for a foreign destination. However, this fee, as well as a $6.50 North American Free Trade Agreement (NAFTA) tax that's charged to people entering the US from a foreign country, are hidden taxes that are added to the purchase price of your airline ticket.

Agricultural Inspection
All luggage and carry-on bags leaving Hawaii for the US mainland are checked by an agricultural inspector using an X-ray machine. You cannot take out gardenia, jade vine, mauna loa flowers or roses, even in leis, although most other fresh flowers and foliage are permitted. You can take out pineapples and coconuts, but most other fresh fruits and vegetables are banned. Other things not allowed to enter mainland states include plants in soil, fresh coffee berries, cactus and sugar cane (except 'chews'). Seeds, fruits and plants which have been certified and labeled for export aren't a problem.

Getting Around

AIR

The major airports handling inter-island traffic are at Honolulu (Oahu), Lihue (Kauai), Kahului (Maui), Kona and Hilo (both on the Big Island).

Smaller airports with scheduled commercial flights are: Molokai Airport and Kalaupapa (at the leprosy colony), both on Molokai; Lanai; Kapalua West Maui and Hana, both on Maui; Princeville, on Kauai's north shore; and Waimea-Kohala, on the Big Island.

Aloha Airlines and Hawaiian Airlines, the two major inter-island carriers, both have frequent flights in full-bodied aircraft between the five major airports.

The smaller airports are predominantly served by two commuter airlines, Island Air and Air Molokai, both of which use prop planes. However, Hawaiian Airlines also flies to Molokai and Lanai.

Air Fares

Hawaiian Airlines and Aloha Airlines both have a standard one-way fare of $74 for flights between any two airports that they serve. The only exception is the once-daily service that Aloha provides between Hilo and Kona, which costs $28.

Flights between islands on Island Air, the largest of the commuter airlines, cost from $74 to $81 one way.

Air Molokai, which services Oahu, Molokai and Maui, has fares of $42 to $74, depending upon the destination.

Round-trip fares on all the airlines are double the one-way fares.

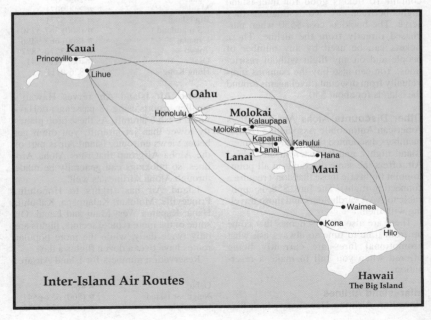

Inter-Island Air Routes

Air Passes Hawaiian Airlines offers a good-value air pass allowing unlimited air travel for a specified number of consecutive days. The cheapest pass, which is good for five days, is just a bit more than the cost of a round-trip air ticket. You can go anywhere you please as often as you want. Reservations can be made in advance or you can fly on a space-available basis, and you're free to revise your itinerary at will. Passes are non-refundable and will not be replaced if lost or stolen.

The fare is: $169 for five days, $189 for one week, $229 for 10 days and $269 for two weeks. Of note is the fact that the one-week pass is usually written to allow travel between one day of the week and the same day of the next week (ie Saturday to Saturday) so it actually allows eight days of travel. Passes are $10 cheaper for children and senior citizens.

Coupons Hawaiian Airlines sells coupon booklets at its airline counters which contain 10 tickets good for inter-island flights between any two destinations they serve. The booklets cost $550 when purchased directly from the airline. These tickets can be used by any number of people and on any flight without restrictions. You can also buy the coupons individually from discount travel agents around the islands for about $50.

Other Discounts Aloha Airlines offers American Automobile Association (AAA) members discounted tickets on all its inter-island flights, and its sister airline, Island Air, offers the same discount on all point-to-point flights (ie those that don't require a connecting flight). The fare, $58, is applicable to AAA cardholders and those traveling with them.

There are also other schemes that come up from time to time so always ask what promotional fares are currently being offered when you call to make a reservation.

Inter-island Airlines
Hawaiian Airlines Hawaiian, which flies DC-9s, has about 175 flights a day connecting Honolulu, Lihue, Kahului, Kona, Hilo, Molokai and Lanai.

Reservation numbers for Hawaiian Airlines are:

Oahu	☎ 838-1555
Big Island	☎ 326-5615
Kauai	☎ 245-1813
Maui	☎ 871-6132
Molokai	☎ 553-3644
Lanai	☎ 565-7281
US mainland & Canada	☎ (800) 367-5320
American Samoa	☎ 669-1875
Tahiti	☎ 4215-00

Aloha Airlines Aloha Airlines, which flies 737s between Honolulu, Lihue, Kahului, Kona and Hilo, has over 200 inter-island flights a day.

Reservation numbers for Aloha Airlines are:

Oahu	☎ 484-1111
Kauai	☎ 245-3691
Maui	☎ 244-9071
Big Island	☎ 935-5771
US mainland	☎ (800) 367-5250
Canada	☎ (800) 663-9396
Tokyo	☎ (03) 3216-5877
Osaka	☎ (06) 341-7241
Hong Kong	☎ 826-9111

Island Air Island Air serves Hawaii's smaller airports using 18-passenger deHavilland Dash 6 aircraft. As these prop planes fly lower than jet aircraft, you often get better views en route. Island Air is part of the Aloha Airgroup that runs Aloha Airlines, so bookings can generally be made through Aloha Airlines as well.

Island Air has flights to Honolulu, Princeville, Molokai, Kalaupapa, Kahului, Hana, Kapalua West Maui and Lanai. On some of the more remote sectors, flights are only twice daily, while the more popular routes have over a dozen flights a day.

Reservation numbers for Island Air are:

Oahu	☎ 484-2222
Neighbor Islands	☎ (800) 652-6541
US mainland	☎ (800) 323-3345

Mahalo Air Mahalo Air began flying with cut-rate fares in 1993, had a hiatus for reorganization in late 1994 and then again resumed service from Honolulu to the Neighbor Islands. It uses 42-seat Fokker F-27s to fly from Honolulu to both Kahului and Kona about eight times a day, from Honolulu to Lihue five times a day and from Honolulu to Molokai an average of three times daily. There are plans to begin service between Honolulu and Lanai, which will probably operate an average of twice daily.

Except for the flights between Honolulu and Molokai which cost $70, all regular fares are $54 one way, double that roundtrip. Unlike its competitors, Mahalo does not offer single-fare flights between Neighbor Islands. Therefore, if you're in Kona and want to go to Lihue, for example, you need to buy two tickets, one from Kona to Honolulu and another from Honolulu to Lihue.

Mahalo occasionally sells flight coupons for a one-way ticket for as little as $25 but these are restricted to residents of Hawaii.

Reservation numbers for Mahalo Air are:

Oahu	☎ 833-5555
Neighbor Islands	☎ (800) 277-8333
US Mainland	☎ (800) 462-4256

Air Molokai Air Molokai is a small commuter airline serving Molokai with nine-seater Cessna prop planes. Air Molokai has flights from Molokai to Honolulu, Kalaupapa, Kahului and Hana. Air Molokai sometimes offers special discounts, but they're mostly geared towards local residents and require proof of Hawaiian residency.

Flights on Air Molokai can be like little sightseeing tours, as the planes fly lower and offer better views than the larger airlines. Sometimes you even end up in the copilot's seat! Another advantage is that your luggage is loaded and unloaded as you get on and off the plane – so it's rarely misplaced and there's no waiting at the carousel.

Reservation numbers for Air Molokai are:

Oahu	☎ 521-0090
Maui	☎ 877-0026
Molokai	☎ 553-3636

Other Airlines Commuter airlines come and go with some frequency in Hawaii. Currently, there's a twice-daily service being provided by Trans Air between Honolulu and Waimea-Kohala, and between Honolulu and Kapalua West Maui.

BUS

Oahu's excellent all-island public bus system, called TheBus, makes that island the easiest one to get around without a car. You can get almost anywhere in Oahu on TheBus and the fare is just 85c regardless of your destination.

The Big Island has a limited public bus service between Kona and Hilo, and between Hilo and Hawaii Volcanoes National Park. There are a couple of other routes serving the Hilo area but they're geared primarily for commuters and the service is infrequent. While these buses will suffice to get you between major towns, they're not practical for short sightseeing hops back and forth in one day.

Kauai has a relatively comprehensive public bus service. However as its main funding has been post-hurricane disaster-relief money, it's expected to be scaled back substantially in the near future.

Maui has no public buses. However there's a limited bus service by a privately run company that operates between the Kihei area and the Lahaina/Kaanapali area. There are also free daily shuttles connecting Kaanapali with Lahaina and Napili.

Molokai has no buses, but there's a mule train!

TAXI

On the main islands taxis are readily available at airports and at the largest hotels in major tourist destinations. As taxis don't cruise looking for passengers, but are radio-dispatched, elsewhere you generally have to call for one, which can be done from any hotel front desk. Taxis are listed in the phone book yellow pages. Fares are based on mileage regardless of the number of passengers. Rates vary, as they're set by each county, but average about $10 per five miles.

CAR

The minimum age for driving in Hawaii is 18 years, though car rental companies usually have higher age restrictions. If you're under age 25 you should call the car rental agencies in advance to check their policies regarding restrictions and surcharges.

You can legally drive in the state as long as you have a valid driver's license issued by a country that is party to the United Nations Conference on Road & Motor Transport – which covers virtually everyone.

However, car rental companies will generally accept valid foreign driver's licenses only if they're in English. Otherwise most will require renters to show an international driver's license along with their home license.

Gasoline is about 25% more expensive in Hawaii than on the US mainland, with the price for regular unleaded gasoline averaging about $1.50 a gallon.

Road Rules

Hawaiians drive on the right-hand side of the road just like in the US mainland.

Drivers at a red light can turn right after coming to a full stop and yielding to oncoming traffic, unless there's a sign at the intersection prohibiting the turn.

Hawaii requires the use of seat belts for drivers and front-seat passengers. State law also strictly requires the use of child safety seats for children ages three and under, while four-year-olds must either be in a safety seat or secured by a seat belt. Most of the car rental companies rent child safety seats, usually from $3 to $5 a day, but they don't always have them on hand so it's advisable to reserve one in advance.

Speed limits are posted and enforced. If

you're stopped for speeding, expect to get a ticket, as the police rarely just give warnings. Cruising unmarked police cars come in the most unlikely models and colors!

Note that the word 'highway' is used very liberally in Hawaii. Just about every road of any distance gets to be called a highway, including some insignificant secondary roads and even a dirt road or two.

In this book we've given priority to using highway numbers because that's what you'll see on road signs. However, if you're asking directions keep in mind that islanders generally refer to roads by name and few pay attention to the route numbers – many wouldn't even be able to tell you the route number of the road on which they live.

Horn honking is considered very rude in Hawaii unless required for safety.

Rental

Rental cars are available on all the islands. Unfortunately the number of rental agencies has narrowed in the past few years and rates have jumped significantly.

With most companies the weekly rate works out far cheaper per day than the straight daily rate. The daily rate for a small car, with unlimited mileage, ranges from around $30 to $45, while typical weekly rates are $150 to $200. You're usually required to keep the car for a minimum of five or six days to get the weekly rate.

While bargains may be hard to find, rates vary a bit from company to company and within each company depending on season, time of booking and current promotional fares. If you belong to an automobile club, a frequent flyer program or a travel club you'll often be eligible for some sort of discount with at least one of the rental agencies.

One thing to note when renting a car is that while bottom-end rates on an economy car have jumped about 50% during the past two years, the rates for mid-size and full-size cars have risen far less, so it's now common to be able to step up to the next size car for only a few dollars more per week.

At any given time any one of the rental

companies could be offering the cheapest deal, so you can save money by taking a little time to shop around. Be sure to ask for the cheapest rate as the first quote given is not always the lowest.

It's a good idea to make reservations in advance for each destination you plan on visiting. If you don't, the cheapest category of cars might be sold out altogether. With most reservations, there's no cancellation penalty if you change your mind.

Another advantage of advance reservations is that if you have a bottom-line car reserved and there are none in the yard when you show up, the upgrade is free.

The cheapest rates, which are the ones given in this book, are for economy class, which are usually small cars like the Geo Metro, Ford Escort or Mazda 323.

For daily rentals note that most cars are rented on a 24-hour basis so you could get two days' use by renting at midday and driving around all afternoon, then heading out to explore somewhere else the next morning before the car is due back. Some companies even have an hour's grace period.

In Hawaii, rental rates generally include free unlimited mileage, though if you drop off the car at a different location from where you picked it up there's usually a fee added on and sometimes a mileage charge.

Having a major credit card greatly simplifies the rental process. Without one some agents simply will not rent vehicles, while others will require prepayment by cash or traveler's checks as well as a deposit, often around $200. Some even do an employment verification and credit check. Others don't do background checks though they reserve the right for the station manager to decide whether to rent to you or not.

Be aware that many car rental companies are loath to rent to people who list a campground as their address on the island and a few specifically add 'No Camping Permitted' to their rental contracts.

Most car rental companies officially prohibit use of their cars on dirt roads.

In addition to all rates, the state of Hawaii adds a $2-a-day tax to all car rentals.

Insurance Collision damage waivers (CDW) are the ultimate rip-off and Hawaii used to have the ultimate hard sell. It got such a bad reputation that the state finally put some controls on 'coercive sales tactics'. Still the rental agencies will try to sell you the CDW for an additional $10 to $15 a day.

The CDW is not really even insurance (the companies already insure their cars) but rather a guarantee that the rental company won't hold you liable for any damages to their car (though even here there are exclusions!). If you decline the CDW you are usually held liable for any damages up to the full value of the car. If damages do occur and you find yourself in a dispute with the rental company, you can call the state Department of Commerce & Consumer Affairs at 587-1234 and then key in 114 for recorded information on your legal rights.

If you have collision coverage on your vehicle at home it might cover damages to car rentals in Hawaii. Check with your insurance company before your trip.

A number of credit card companies now offer reimbursement coverage for collision damages if you rent the car with their credit card and decline the CDW. If yours doesn't, it may be worth changing to one that does. Be aware that most credit card coverage isn't valid for rentals of more than 15 days or for exotic models, jeeps, 4WD vehicles, vans and motorbikes.

Rental Agencies The following are international companies whose cars can be booked from offices around the world. The toll-free numbers given are valid from the US mainland.

Avis (☎ (800) 831-8000) is at the main airports on Oahu, Maui, Kauai and the Big Island as well as a half-dozen locations around Waikiki. If you're visiting at least two islands Avis has a handy multi-island deal that allows you to rent a car at the rate of $28 a day as long as you rent for a minimum of five days on the combined islands.

Budget (☎ (800) 527-7000) is at the main airports on Oahu, Kauai, Molokai, Maui and the

Big Island as well as about 35 other locations around Hawaii. All other things being equal, Budget is probably the best choice for bargain-hunters as renters are given a coupon booklet on each island that allows free admission for one person to participating tourist attractions – it's a particularly good deal on Oahu.

Dollar (☎ (800) 367-7006; in Hawaii (800) 342-7398) is at the airports on Oahu, Kauai, Molokai, Maui and the Big Island as well as numerous locations in Waikiki.

Hertz (☎ (800) 654-3131) is at the main airports on Oahu, Maui, Kauai and the Big Island as well as at Princeville and Kapalua West Maui airports.

National (☎ (800) 227-7368) is at the main airports on Oahu, Kauai, Maui and the Big Island and at a couple of locations in Waikiki.

Alamo (☎ (800) 327-9633) has locations at the Kona, Hilo, Kahului and Lihue airports and near the Honolulu and Kapalua West Maui airports.

There's a handful of smaller rental agencies in Hawaii as well, but this is one area where small is not necessarily better. For the most part the big companies offer newer, more reliable cars and fewer hassles.

BICYCLE

It's possible to cycle around all the Hawaiian Islands. However when you get away from coastal routes, there are some pretty hefty uphill climbs. Hawaii's roads also tend to be narrow, and many of the main coastal routes are rather heavily trafficked.

There are places to rent bicycles on the four largest islands (see Getting Around in each island chapter for details). If you bring your own bike to Hawaii, you can transport it on inter-island flights for $20.

HITCHHIKING

Hitchhiking is officially illegal on Maui, Molokai and Lanai, while on the other islands it's tolerated by the police. Results are mixed. We've met people who have waited on the roadside for hours with the only response from drivers being a few flipped fingers. We've also heard from

people who have hitched around the islands and claim waits of only five to 10 minutes for most rides. Generally if you look like a traveler, and are not hitching with more than one other person, you stand the best chance of getting a ride. Hitchhikers should size up each situation carefully before getting in cars and women should be especially wary of hitching alone.

Hitchhiking is never entirely safe anywhere in the world, and Lonely Planet does not recommend it. Travelers who decide to hitch should understand that they are taking a small but serious risk. You may not be able to identify the local rapist/murderer before you get into the vehicle. People who do choose to hitch will be safer if they travel in pairs and let someone know where they are planning to go.

BOAT

Inter-island Ferry There are only two inter-island passenger ferries in Hawaii. They are a good deal – about half the cost of flying – and during the winter you can often spot whales en route.

Expeditions runs a 24-passenger boat five times a day between Lahaina on Maui and Manele Boat Harbor on Lanai. The crossing, which takes an hour, costs $25.

The *Maui Princess* has twice-daily service between Kaunakakai on Molokai and Lahaina on Maui. It takes about 90 minutes and costs $25.

More details are under Getting Around in the individual island chapters.

TOURS

There are a number of companies doing half-day and full-day sightseeing bus tours on each island. There are also lots of specialized tours, such as whale watching cruises, bicycle tours down Haleakala, snorkel trips to Lanai and cruises along the Na Pali Coast, just to mention a few. All these tours can be booked after arrival on Hawaii. For details on day tours, see the individual island chapters.

Overnight Tours

If you want to visit another island but only

have a day or two to spare, it might be worth looking into 'overnighters', which are mini-packaged tours to the Neighbor Islands that include round-trip airfare, car and a hotel. Rates depend on the accommodation you select, with a one-night package typically starting around $100 per person, based on double occupancy. You can add on additional days for an additional fee, usually for about $40 per person.

If you have an air pass, the same tour companies also sell room/car packages minus the airfare (though the room/car packages offered directly by some of the hotels may work out cheaper).

The largest companies specializing in overnighters are: Island Escapes (☎ 944-8000 on Oahu, (800) 953-8889 from the Neighbor Islands), Roberts Hawaii (☎ 523-9323 on Oahu, (800) 899-9323 from the Neighbor Islands), Pleasant Island Holidays (☎ 922-1515 on Oahu, (800) 654-4386 from the Neighbor Islands) and American Express (☎ 922-0575 on Oahu).

Cruises

American Hawaii Cruises (☎ (800) 765-7000), 2 N Riverside Plaza, Chicago, IL 60606, has two cruise ships, the *Constitution* and the *Independence*, which make seven-day tours around Hawaii. One ship leaves Honolulu each Saturday, the other on Tuesday, all year round, and visits the Big Island (Kona and Hilo), Maui (Kahului Harbor) and Kauai (Nawiliwili Harbor) before returning to Honolulu.

Rates start at $995 for the cheapest inside cabin and go up to $3000, with the cheapest outside cabin priced at $1795. Fares are per person, based on double occupancy, and there's an additional $85 for port charges.

These are full-fledged cruise ships, 682 feet long, with lavish buffet meals, swimming pools and the like. Each carries a crew of 325 along with 800 passengers.

Helicopter

Helicopter tours are readily available from a number of companies on the main islands. They go to some amazing places, such as over active volcanoes, along towering coastal cliffs and above inaccessible waterfalls. Prices vary depending on the destination and the length of the flight, with a 30-minute tour averaging about $100 per passenger.

Before you book one, be ready to make some inquiries. Be aware, for instance, that not every seat in all copters is a window seat. A common configuration is two passengers up front with the pilot, and four people sitting across the back. The two back middle seats simply don't give the photo opportunities proclaimed in the brochures. It's like being a mid-seat rear passenger on a scenic drive – only there's no getting out at viewpoints! People are usually seated according to weight, so if you're dishing out a lot of money make sure it's clear where you're going to be sitting.

Oahu

The images most commonly conjured up of Hawaii are those of Oahu – places like Waikiki, Pearl Harbor and Sunset Beach.

Oahu is by far the most developed of the Hawaiian islands and, quite appropriately, has long been nicknamed 'The Gathering Place'. The island is home to 865,000 people – more than 75% of the state's population. It's an urban scene, with highways, high-rises and crowds. If you're looking for a getaway vacation you'd best continue on to one of the Neighbor Islands.

Still, despite all its development, in terms of scenic beauty Oahu holds its own. It has fluted mountains, aqua-blue bays and valleys carpeted with pineapple fields.

Oahu has excellent beaches. Hanauma Bay, southeast of Waikiki, is one of the finest, easily accessible snorkeling spots in the islands. The North Shore has Hawaii's top surfing action and windward Kailua is Hawaii's most popular windsurfing beach.

Honolulu is a modern city with an intriguing blend of Eastern and Western influences. Cultural offerings range from Chinese lantern parades and traditional hula performances to ballet and good museums. Honolulu has the only royal palace in the USA, fine city beaches and parks and some great hilltop views.

Oahu can be the cheapest Hawaiian island to visit. It's the only one you can get around easily without your own transport, thanks to the inexpensive, island-wide bus system. Oahu also has some of Hawaii's cheapest accommodations, including a couple of hostels and Ys.

Almost all of Oahu's hotels and tourist facilities are centered in Waikiki. Waikiki resembles a hybrid mix of Miami Beach and Tokyo, with a population density rivaling the latter. There's a lot happening in Waikiki, but to get a better feel for what Hawaii's all about you need to step out of it. There are plenty of places on Oahu worth exploring.

ORIENTATION

Almost all visitors to Oahu land at Honolulu International Airport, the only civilian airport on the island. It's at the western outskirts of the Honolulu district, nine miles west of Waikiki.

H-1, the main south shore freeway, is the key to getting around the island. H-1 connects with Hwy 72, which runs around the southeast coast; with the Pali (61) and Likelike (63) highways, which go to the windward coast; with Hwy 93, which leads up the leeward Waianae Coast; and with H-2, Hwy 99 and Hwy 750, which run through the center of the island on the way to the North Shore.

By the way, H-1 is a US *interstate* freeway – an amusing term to describe a road on an island state in the middle of the Pacific.

Rush-hour traffic is heavy heading towards Honolulu in the mornings and away from it in the evenings.

Directions on Oahu are often given by using landmarks, in addition to the Hawaii-wide *mauka* (inland side) and *makai* (ocean side). If someone tells you to go 'Ewa' (a land area west of Honolulu) or 'Diamond Head' (east of Honolulu) it simply means to head in that direction.

HISTORY

Oahu was the final island conquered by Kamehameha the Great in his campaign to unite all Hawaii under his sole rule.

Prior to that, however, it was not Kamehameha but Kahekili, the aging king of Maui, who seemed the most likely candidate to grasp control of the entire island chain. In the 1780s Kahekili already ruled neighboring Molokai and Lanai when he killed his own stepson to take Oahu.

After Kahekili died at Waikiki in 1794 a power struggle ensued and his lands were divided between two quarreling relatives. His son, Kalanikupule, got Oahu and his half-brother, King Kaeokulani of Kauai, got Maui, Lanai and Molokai. The two ambitious heirs immediately went to battle with each other, creating a rift that Kamehameha readily moved into.

In 1795 Kamehameha swept through Maui and Molokai, conquering those islands, before crossing the channel to Oahu. On the quiet beaches of Waikiki he landed his fleet of canoes and marched up towards Nuuanu Valley to meet Kalanikupule, the king of Oahu.

The Battle of Nuuanu

The Oahu warriors were no match for Kamehameha's troops. The first heavy fighting took place around the Punchbowl, where Kamehameha's men quickly circled the fortress-like crater and drove out the Oahuan defenders. Scattered fighting continued up Nuuanu Valley, with the last big battle taking place near the current site of Queen Emma's summer palace.

The Oahuans, prepared for the usual spear-and-stone warfare, panicked when they realized Kamehameha had brought in a handful of Western sharpshooters. The foreigners picked off the Oahuan generals and blasted into their ridge-top defenses.

What should have been the advantage of high ground turned into a death trap for the Oahuans when they found themselves wedged up into the valley, unable to redeploy. Fleeing up the cliffsides in retreat, they were forced to make their last stand at the narrow precipitous ledge along the current-day Nuuanu Pali Lookout. Hundreds of Oahuans were driven over the top of the *pali* (cliff) to their deaths.

Some Oahuan warriors, including King Kalanikupule, escaped into the upland forests. When Kalanikupule surfaced a few months later he was sacrificed by Kamehameha to his war god Ku. Kamehameha's taking of Oahu marked the last battle ever fought between Hawaiian troops.

GEOGRAPHY

Oahu, which covers 594 sq miles, is the third largest Hawaiian island. It basically has four sides, with distinct windward and leeward coasts and north and south shores. The island's extreme length is 44 miles, its width 30 miles.

Two separate volcanoes arose to form Oahu's two mountain ranges, Waianae and Koolau, which slice the island from the northwest to the southeast. Oahu's highest point, Mt Kaala at 4020 feet, is in the Waianae Range.

CLIMATE

In Honolulu the average daily maximum temperature is 84°F and the minimum is 70°F. Temperatures are a bit higher in summer and a few degrees lower in winter. The highest temperature on record is 94°F and the lowest is 53°F.

Waikiki has an average annual rainfall of only 25 inches, whereas the Lyon Arboretum in the upper Manoa Valley, north of Honolulu, averages 158 inches. Midafternoon humidity averages 56%.

Average afternoon water temperatures in Waikiki are 77°F in March, 82°F in August.

FLORA & FAUNA

Most of the islets off Oahu's windward coast are sanctuaries for seabirds, including terns, noddies, shearwaters, Laysan albatrosses, tropicbirds, boobies and frigate birds. Moku Manu ('Bird Island') off Mokapu Peninsula has the greatest variety of species.

Oahu has an endemic genus of tree snail, the achatinella. In former days the forests were loaded with these colorful snails, which clung like gems to the leaves of trees. They were too attractive for their own good, however, and hikers collected them by the handfuls around the turn of the century. Even more devastating has been the deforestation of habitat and the introduction of a cannibal snail and predatory rodents. Of 41 achatinella species, only 19 remain and all are endangered.

The *elepaio,* a brownish bird with a white rump, and the *amakihi,* a small yellow green bird, are the most common endemic forest birds on Oahu. The *apapane,* a bright red honeycreeper, and

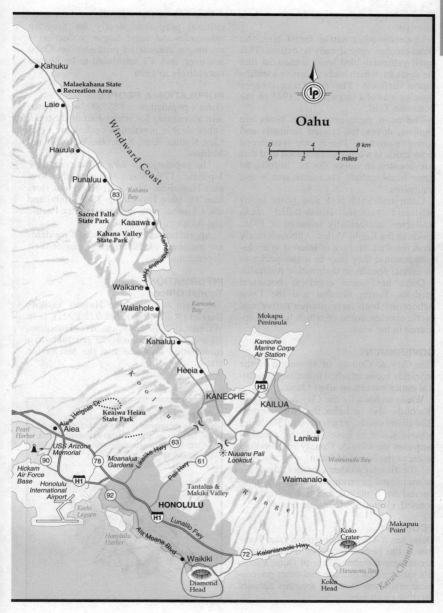

Oahu

0   4   8 km
0   2   4 miles

Kahuku

Malaekahana State
Recreation Area

Laie

Hauula

Windward Coast

Punaluu

83

Kahana
Bay

Sacred Falls
State Park

Kaaawa

Kahana Valley
State Park

Waikane

Waiahole

Kaneohe
Bay

Mokapu
Peninsula

Kahaluu

Kaneohe
Marine Corps
Air Station

Heeia

H3

KANEOHE

KAILUA

Koolau

Aiea Heights Dr

Keaiwa Heiau
State Park

Lanikai

Pearl
Harbor

Aiea

63

61

Waimanalo Bay

USS Arizona
Memorial

78

Moanalua
Gardens

Nuuanu Pali
Lookout

Waimanalo

90

Likelike Hwy

Pali Hwy

Range

Hickam
Air Force
Base

H1

92

Tantalus &
Makiki Valley

Honolulu
International
Airport

Keehi
Lagoon

HONOLULU

Makapuu
Point

H1

Lunalilo Fwy

Koko
Crater

Honolulu
Harbor

Ala Moana Blvd

Waikiki

72

Kalanianaole Hwy

Diamond
Head

Hanauma Bay

Koko
Head

Kaiwi Channel

iiwi, a bright vermillion bird, are less common.

The only other native forest bird, the Oahu creeper, may already be extinct. This small yellowish bird looks somewhat like the amakihi, which makes positive identification difficult. The last Oahu creeper sighting was of a single bird in 1985 on the Poamoho Trail.

The most prominent urban birds are pigeons, doves, red-crested cardinals and common mynas. The myna, introduced from India, is a brown, spectacled bird that congregates in noisy flocks. Introduced game birds include pheasants, quails and francolins.

Oahu has wild pigs and goats in its mountain valleys. Brush-tailed rock-wallabies, accidentally released in 1916, reside in the Kalihi Valley. Although rarely seen, the wallabies are of interest to zoologists because they may be a subspecies of an extinct species in their native Australia.

Oahu has some excellent botanical gardens. Foster Garden and the Lyon Arboretum both have unique native and exotic species, some of which have disappeared in the wild.

GOVERNMENT

The City & County of Honolulu is the unwieldy name attached to the single political entity governing all of Oahu.

While technically the City & County of Honolulu also includes the Northwestern Hawaiian Islands, which stretch 1300 miles beyond Kāuai to Kure Atoll, for practical purposes the City & County of Honolulu refers to the island of Oahu.

Like Hawaii's other counties, there are no municipal governments. Oahu is administered by a mayor and a nine-member council, elected for four-year terms.

ECONOMY

Oahu has a 4% unemployment rate. Tourism is the largest sector of the economy, accounting for about 30% of Oahu's jobs. It's followed by defense and other government employment which together account for 22% of all jobs.

One-fifth of Oahu is still used for agricultural purposes, mostly for growing pineapples and sugar. Sugar production is no longer considered profitable on Oahu however, and it's scheduled to be phased out entirely in 1996.

POPULATION & PEOPLE

Oahu's population is 865,000, with Honolulu accounting for nearly half of the total. Other sizable population centers are Pearl City, Kailua, Aiea, Kaneohe, Waipahu and Mililani.

The population is 24% Caucasian, 21% Japanese, 17% mixed ancestry other than part-Hawaiian, 16% part-Hawaiian (less than 1% pure Hawaiian), 7% Filipino and 6% Chinese, with numerous other Pacific and Asian minorities.

Approximately 14% of Oahu's residents are members of the armed forces or their dependents.

INFORMATION
Tourist Offices

The main office of the Hawaii Visitors Bureau (☎ 924-0266; fax 922-8991), is in Waikiki at 2270 Kalakaua Ave, Honolulu, HI 96815; they can mail out general tourist information on Oahu and the rest of the state.

Official Oahu
Oahu's nickname is 'The Gathering Place'. Its flower is the delicate native ilima, which is yellow-orange, the island's official color. ∎

Money

There are nine banks with nearly 150 branches on Oahu and they can easily be found in major towns. The Bank of Hawaii, Hawaii's largest bank, has a branch at the airport and at 2220 Kalakaua Ave in Waikiki.

Banks are generally open from 8:30 am to 3 pm Monday to Thursday and from 8:30 am to 6 pm on Fridays.

Automatic teller machines (ATMs), which accept major credit cards and Cirrus and Plus System ATM cards, can be found at the airport, larger shopping centers, most supermarkets and numerous other places.

Post

There are 33 post offices on Oahu. The main Honolulu post office (☎ 423-3990) is not in town, but is at the side of the airport at 3600 Aolele St, opposite the inter-island terminal. It's open from 7:30 am to 8:30 pm Monday to Friday and from 8 am to 2:30 pm on Saturdays.

All general delivery mail in the city of Honolulu must be picked up at the main Honolulu post office. Note that any mail sent general delivery to the Waikiki post office or other Honolulu branches will either go to the main post office or be returned to sender. If you're receiving mail in Honolulu, have it addressed to you c/o General Delivery, Main Post Office, 3600 Aolele St, Honolulu, HI 96820.

Media

The two English dailies are the morning *Honolulu Advertiser* and the afternoon *Honolulu Star-Bulletin*. Subscription information is under Media in the introductory Facts for the Visitor chapter. There's also one daily newspaper in Japanese/English, one in Chinese and two in Korean.

In addition, Oahu has numerous weekly or monthly newspapers, many of which can be picked up free around the island. These include the *Honolulu Weekly*, a progressive paper with an extensive entertainment section; the *Downtown Planet*, aimed at those who work in downtown Honolulu;

and regional rags such as the *Windward Oahu News* and the *North Shore News*.

Numerous free tourist magazines are available at the airport and all around Waikiki. They can be a good source of information, although most of it is paid advertising. *This Week Oahu* and *Spotlight's Oahu Gold* usually have the best discount coupons.

Honolulu has 17 commercial AM radio stations, 12 FM stations and three non-commercial stations. Radio station KCCN features slack-key Hawaiian guitar on 1420 AM and 'island music', with a blend of more contemporary Hawaiian songs and reggae, on 100.3 FM. Da KINE (105.1 FM) plays classic Hawaiian music. Hawaii Public Radio is on KHPR (88.1 FM), KKUA (90.9 FM) and KIPO (89.3 FM).

There are 10 TV stations and numerous cable stations. Cable channel 8 features continuous visitor information and ads geared to tourists.

Bookstores

Honolulu Book Shops has a good selection of general, Hawaiiana and travel books. They're on the corner of Bishop and Hotel Sts in downtown Honolulu and in the Ala Moana, Pearlridge and Kailua shopping centers.

Waldenbooks, a national chain, has shops in the Ward Warehouse, Kahala Mall, Koko Marina Shopping Center, Windward Mall, Pearlridge Center and in Waikiki at the Royal Hawaiian Shopping Center, the Waikiki Shopping Plaza and the Waikiki Trade Center. All have Hawaiiana and travel sections.

The Bishop Museum has a good selection of general Hawaiiana books as well as more esoteric works on various aspects of Hawaiian culture. The University of Hawaii at Manoa has a bookstore in its Campus Center.

Maps

There are simple island maps in the free tourist magazines, but if you're going to be renting a car and doing any exploring at all it's worth picking up a good road map, especially for navigating around Honolulu. Detailed Rand McNally and Gousha road maps are sold in stores throughout Oahu for a couple of dollars; members of the AAA or an affiliated automobile club can get a free detailed road map from the AAA office, 590 Queen St, Honolulu.

Libraries

Hawaii's statewide library system has its main library in downtown Honolulu, next to Iolani Palace. There are 21 other public libraries around Oahu, including ones in Waikiki, Kailua and Kaneohe.

Weather

The National Weather Service provides recorded weather forecasts for Honolulu (☎ 833-2849) and all Oahu (☎ 836-0121). They also have recorded tides and surf conditions (☎ 836-1952) and a marine forecast (☎ 836-3921).

Night Sky

The Hawaiian Skyguide (☎ 948-0759) is a recording with information on the current stars and planets visible in the Hawaiian sky.

Emergency

Dial 911 for all police, fire and ambulance emergencies.

Hospitals with 24-hour emergency services include the Queen's Medical Center (☎ 538-9011), 1301 Punchbowl St, Honolulu; Straub Clinic & Hospital (☎ 522-4000), 888 S King St at Ward, Honolulu; Castle Medical Center (☎ 263-5500), 640 Ulukahiki, Kailua; Kahuku Hospital (☎ 293-9221), Kahuku; and Wahiawa General Hospital (☎ 621-8411), 128 Lehua St, Wahiawa.

Divers with the bends are sent to the UH Hyperbaric Treatment Center (☎ 523-9155), 42 Ahui St, Honolulu.

A suicide and crisis line (☎ 521-4555) operates 24 hours a day.

ACTIVITIES
Beaches & Swimming

Oahu boasts 60 beach parks, most of which have restrooms and showers. Nineteen are patrolled by lifeguards. The island's four distinct coastal areas have their own peculiar seasonal water conditions. When it's rough on one side, it's generally calm on another, so you can find places to swim and surf year round.

Oahu's south shore extends from Barbers Point to Makapuu Point and includes the most popular beaches on the island, including the white sands of Waikiki and Ala Moana.

The windward coast extends from Makapuu Point to Kahuku Point. Kailua Beach Park, Oahu's busiest windsurfing spot, also has good swimming conditions and is the best all-around beach on this side. Other nice beaches are at Waimanalo, Kualoa and Malaekahana.

The North Shore extends from Kahuku Point to Kaena Point. It has spectacular waves in winter, but can be as calm as a lake in summer.

The leeward Waianae Coast extends from Kaena Point to Barbers Point. It's the driest, sunniest side of the island, with long stretches of white sands. The most popular beach on this side is Makaha, which sees big surf in the winter but has suitable swimming conditions in summer.

Swimming Pools The county maintains 17 community swimming pools, including ones in Kailua, Kaneohe, Pearl City, Wahiawa and Waipahu. Pools in the greater Honolulu area are at Palolo Recreation Center (☎ 733-7362), 2007 Palolo Ave; Manoa Valley Recreation Center (☎ 988-6868), 2721 Kaaipu Ave; Booth District Park (☎ 522-7037), 2331 Kanealii Ave; and McCully Recreation Center (☎ 973-7268), 831 Pumehana.

Surfing

Oahu has 594 defined surfing sites, nearly twice as many as any of the other Hawaiian islands. In winter, the North Shore gets some of Hawaii's most spectacular surf, with swells reaching 20 to 30 feet. This is the home of the Banzai Pipeline, Sunset

Beach and some of the world's top surfing *competitions.*

Makaha is the top winter surf spot on the Waianae Coast. The south shore gets its finest surfing waves in summer, with Waikiki and Diamond Head having some of the best breaks.

Surf News Network (☎ 596-SURF) has a recorded surf line reporting winds, wave heights and tides, updated three times a day. KPOI, an FM rock music radio station, also provides surf reports (☎ 521-SURF) as does the National Weather Service (☎ 836-1952).

The county's Haleiwa Surf Center (☎ 637-5051), at Haleiwa Alii Beach Park, holds free surfing lessons from 9 am to noon on Saturdays and Sundays between early September and late May. Surfboards are provided.

Surfing lessons can also be arranged from some of the older pros who run the Star Beach Boys concession on Waikiki Beach and from the surf shops.

H30, a monthly newspaper that interviews surfers and reports on surfing events and surf conditions, is free at surf shops around the island. For subscription information, contact H30 (☎ 685-3800), 91-1052 Pohahawai St, Ewa Beach, HI 96706.

Planet Surf (☎ 926-2060), 419 Nahua St in Waikiki, rents surfboards for $17 per 24 hours and longboard tankers for $20; it also sells used surfboards. Local Motion (☎ 955-7873), 1714 Kapiolani Blvd, rents surfboards for $20 the first 24 hours, $15 for additional days. Surfboards are also available for rent at the concession stands along Waikiki Beach.

On the North Shore, surfboards are rented by Surf-N-Sea (☎ 637-9887) in Haleiwa for $5 the first hour, $3.50 each additional hour, or $18 a day. This shop, and a few others in Haleiwa, also sells new and used boards.

Bodysurfing, Snorkeling & Boogie Boarding

The most popular boogie boarding place in Waikiki is at Kapahulu Groin.

On the windward coast, Waimanalo

Beach Park and nearby *Bellows Field Beach Park* have gentle shorebreaks good for beginning bodysurfers.

The two hottest (and most dangerous) spots for expert bodysurfers are Sandy Beach Park and Makapuu Beach Park in southeast Oahu. Other top shorebreaks are at Makaha on the Waianae Coast, Waimea Bay on the North Shore, and Kalama Beach in Kailua and Pounders in Laie on the windward coast.

For snorkeling, Hanauma Bay on the south shore is the best year-round spot. In summer, Pupukea Beach Park on the North Shore provides excellent snorkeling.

Equipment Rental If you're going to be doing much snorkeling or boogie boarding, you may be better off buying your own equipment. However, there are plenty of places to rent them.

Planet Surf (see Surfing above) rents snorkel sets for $5.50 a day, $15 a week. Boogie boards cost from $7.50 a day, $20 a week, and they also sell used boards.

Snorkel Bob's (☎ 735-7944), 700 Kapahulu Ave, about a mile out of Waikiki, rents basic snorkel sets from $15 a week and sets with silicone masks starting at $29 a week. For $3 more you can return them on one of the Neighbor Islands. It's open from 7 am (from 8 am on Wednesdays) to 5 pm daily.

Surf-N-Sea (☎ 637-9887) in Haleiwa rents boogie boards for $3 for the first hour and $2 for each additional hour, and snorkel sets for $6.50 for half a day, $9.50 for 24 hours. It's open from 9 am to 6 pm daily.

In Kailua, Naish Hawaii (☎ 262-6068), 155A Hamakua Dr, rents boogie boards for $10 a day, snorkel sets for $7.50.

Windsurfing

Kailua Bay is Oahu's number one windsurfing spot. It has good year-round trade winds, and both flat water and wave conditions in different sections of the bay. Windsurfing shops set up vans at Kailua Beach Park on weekdays and Saturday mornings, renting boards and giving lessons. It's a great place for beginners to try the sport.

Other good spots include Diamond Head for speed and jumps and Backyards for North Shore challenges. Fort DeRussy Beach is Waikiki's main windsurfing spot.

Naish Hawaii (☎ 262-6068, (800) 767-6068) – as in windsurfing champion Robbie Naish – sells and rents equipment. The shop is at 155A Hamakua Dr, Kailua, HI 96734, but they can deliver equipment to Kailua Beach. Rental rates vary with the board and rig: beginner equipment costs $15 an hour or $30 a full day; intermediate and advanced equipment is generally $25 for two hours, $40 for a full day, with harness and roof rack included. Naish gives introductory group lessons for $35 for three hours. For $55 you can get a 1½-hour private lesson that includes an additional 2½ hours of board use.

The Kailua Sailboard Company (☎ 262-2555), 130 Kailua Rd, Kailua, HI 96734, rents beginner equipment for $25 a half day, $30 a day or $99 a week; intermediate equipment costs $28/35 a half/full day, advanced equipment $35/40. Three-hour beginner's lessons are $39.

Waikiki Windsurfing (☎ 949-8952) at Fort DeRussy Beach rents windsurfing equipment for $30 for two hours, $40 with a lesson.

In Haleiwa, Surf-N-Sea (☎ 637-9887) rents windsurfing equipment for $12 for the first hour and $8 for each additional hour. Two-hour windsurfing lessons cost $38.

Diving

Top summer dive spots include the caves and ledges at Three Tables and Shark's Cove on the North Shore and the Makaha Caverns on the Waianae Coast. On the south shore, Hanauma Bay has calm diving conditions most of the year. There are a number of other popular dive spots between Hanauma and Honolulu that provide good winter diving.

Aloha Dive Shop (☎ 395-5922), Koko Marina Shopping Center, Honolulu, HI 96825, has two-tank boat dives off Koko Head for $75. Two-tank introductory dives also cost $75 and PADI certification

courses cost $375. They offer free transport from Waikiki hotels.

Ocean Concepts (☎ 677-7975, (800) 808-3483), 94-547 Ukee St, Suite 201, Waipahu, HI 96797, dives the Waianae Coast, including the WW II minesweeper *Mahi*. Two-tank boat dives cost $70 day or night, as do introductory dives.

Surf-N-Sea (☎ 637-9887), 62-595 Kamehameha Hwy, Haleiwa, HI 96712, has one-tank shore dives for $65, two-tank dives for $90. Three-day PADI certification courses cost $400 for one person, $275 each for two people.

The following are other dive shops on Oahu. All are five-star PADI operations:

Aaron's Dive Shop, 602 Kailua Rd, Kailua, HI 96734 (☎ 262-2333)
Alii Divers, 1356-B Kapiolani Blvd, Honolulu, HI 96814 (☎ 944-9762)
Beach Divers Hawaii, 4224 Waialae Ave, Honolulu, HI 96516 (☎ 737-7966)
Breeze Hawaii Diving Adventure, 3014 Kaimuki Ave, Honolulu, HI 96816 (☎ 735-1857)
Dan's Dive Shop, 660 Ala Moana Blvd, Honolulu, HI 96813 (☎ 536-6181)
Island Quest, 94-216 Farrington Hwy, Waipahu, HI 96797 (☎ 677-2399)
South Pacific Scuba, 740 Kapahulu Ave, Honolulu, HI 96816 (☎ 735-7196)
South Sea Aquatics, 870 Kapahulu Ave, No 109, Honolulu, HI 96816 (☎ 735-0437, (800) 252-6244)
Sunshine Scuba, 642 Cooke St, Honolulu, HI 96813 (☎ 593-8865)
Waikiki Diving Center, 1734 Kalakaua Ave, Honolulu, HI 96826 (☎ 955-5151)
Windward Dive Center, 789 Kailua Rd, Kailua, HI 96734 (☎ 263-2311)

Snuba Snuba (☎ 396-6163), a sort of scuba diving for snorkelers, is available at Hanauma Bay for $65 (a 3½-hour outing, including transport from Waikiki) or at Maunalua Bay in the Hawaii Kai area in conjunction with a boat cruise and lunch for $95. Snuba utilizes long air hoses attached to a tank on an inflatable raft. The diver simply wears a mask and weight belt and can dive down as far as the air hose allows.

Surfer, Oahu

Windsurfers at Kailua Beach, Oahu

Surfboards, Waikiki

Waikiki rowers

Toilet Bowl near Hanauma Bay, Oahu

Warning sign and flag at Sandy Beach, Oahu

Boogie board acrobatics, Makaha Beach, Oahu

Kayaking

Twogood Kayaks Hawaii (☎ 262-5656), at 171 Hamakua Rd in Kailua, has kayak sales, rentals and lessons. One-person kayaks rent for $20 a half day or $25 a full day, two-person kayaks cost $29/39. Kailua Sailboards (☎ 262-2555), at 130 Kailua Rd in Kailua, has one- and two-person kayaks at comparable prices.

Kayak Oahu Adventures (☎ 637-6565) rents kayaks at Waimea Falls Park and from its office in Haleiwa, south of McDonald's. Daily prices are $25/35 for a single/double kayak. In summer they also have guided kayak/snorkel tours of Three Tables that include snorkeling gear and lunch for $59.

Hiking

The trail that leads three-quarters of a mile from inside the crater of Diamond Head up to its summit is the most popular hike on Oahu. It's easy to get to from Waikiki and ends with a panoramic view of greater Honolulu.

Another nice short hike is the Manoa Falls Trail, just a few miles above Waikiki, where a quiet walk through an abandoned arboretum of huge trees leads to a waterfall.

The Tantalus and Makiki Valley area has the most extensive trail network around Honolulu, with fine views of the city and surrounding valleys. Amazingly, although it's just two miles above the city hustle and bustle, this lush forest reserve is unspoiled and offers quiet solitude.

On the western edge of Honolulu, the Moanalua Trail goes deep into the Moanalua Valley. You can hike it on your own or join a guided Sunday walk.

At Keaiwa Heiau State Park, northwest of Honolulu, the Aiea Loop Trail leads 4½ miles along a ridge that offers views of Pearl Harbor, Diamond Head and the Koolau Range.

The Kaena Point Trail is a coastal hike through a natural area reserve on the westernmost point of Oahu. There are also longer forestry trails in the same area.

On the windward side there's a pleasant hour-long hike out to Makapuu lighthouse and a longer trail at Sacred Falls State Park that follows a narrow mountain valley to a waterfall.

There are short walks from the Nuuanu Pali Lookout, along Nuuanu Pali Dr, at Hoomaluhia Botanic Garden and along many beaches.

For more details on hikes, see the respective sections of this chapter.

Guided Hikes Notices of hiking club outings are found in the *Honolulu Star-Bulletin* 'Bulletin Board' column from Monday to Saturday and in the *Honolulu Advertiser* 'Calabash' column on Sundays.

By joining one of these outings you get to meet and hike with ecology-minded islanders. It may also be a good way to get to the backwoods if you don't have a car, as they often share rides. Wear sturdy shoes and, for the longer hikes, bring lunch and water.

The Hawaiian Trail & Mountain Club has guided hikes most weekends. The hike fee is $1. Hikes generally range from three to 12 miles in length and from novice to advanced in difficulty. For a copy of the hiking schedule, send $1 and a stamped, self-addressed envelope to the club at Box 2238, Honolulu, HI 96804.

The Sierra Club (☎ 538-6616), 1111 Bishop St, No 511, Honolulu, HI 96803, leads hikes and other outings on Saturdays and Sundays. These range from an easy 1½-mile hike to Jackass Ginger to strenu-

---

Hitchhiking Weeds

Anyone who has hiked on Oahu should scrub their shoes and wash their socks and long pants before hiking on other islands to avoid transferring clinging *Clidemia hirta* seeds, which are practically invisible. This weed has infested much of Oahu, overrunning trails and choking out native plants, but it's not yet widely established on the Neighbor Islands. It's presumed that the patches of this invasive plant found along trails on Molokai and Maui hitchhiked there on an Oahuan hiker's boot. ∎

ous 10-mile treks. Most outings meet at 8 am at the Church of the Crossroads at 2510 Bingham St in Honolulu. The hike fee is $1.

The Hawaii Audubon Society (☎ 528-1432) leads bird-watching hikes once or twice a month, usually on weekends. The suggested donation is $2. Binoculars and a copy of *Hawaii's Birds* are recommended. You can also get a free brochure in advance that lists birding sites on Oahu by sending a self-addressed stamped envelope to Oahu Birding Guide, Hawaii Audubon Society, 1088 Bishop St, Suite 808, Honolulu, HI 96813.

The Hawaii Nature Center (☎ 955-0100) in Makiki leads hikes on most Saturday mornings for $5. Trails range from the easy 2½-mile Makiki Loop Trail to a strenuous six-mile hike up Mt Kaala, Oahu's highest point. Reservations are required.

Horseback Riding

The Sheraton Makaha Resort (☎ 695-9511) in Makaha has one-hour trail rides for $25 at 10 am and 1 pm Tuesday to Sunday and also at 8:30 am and 2:30 pm on weekends. The stables are closed on Mondays.

Kualoa Ranch (☎ 237-8515), 49-560 Kamehameha Hwy, Kualoa, has one-hour trail rides in Kaaawa Valley for $25 every afternoon and two-hour trail rides for $35 on weekends. There's also a weekday outing that includes pick-up at Waikiki hotels around 9:30 am, followed by a one-hour trail ride, a 2½-hour beach visit with lunch, and return to Waikiki; both Japanese and English is spoken and the cost is $66.50.

The Turtle Bay Hilton (☎ 293-8811) in Kahuku has 45-minute trail rides for $32, rides for the more experienced ($45) and sunset rides ($70).

Tennis

Oahu has 175 county tennis courts. If you're staying in Waikiki, the most convenient locations are the 10 lighted courts at Ala Moana Beach Park (☎ 522-7031), the nine unlit courts at the Diamond Head Tennis Center (☎ 971-7150) at the Dia-

mond Head end of Kapiolani Park, and the four lighted Kapiolani Park courts opposite the Waikiki Aquarium. Court time is free on a first-come, first-served basis.

With ground space at a premium, few Waikiki hotels have room for tennis courts. The Ilikai Hotel (☎ 944-6300), 1777 Ala Moana Blvd, is Waikiki's main tennis resort with six courts, rentals, lessons and a pro shop. Rates are $5 per hour per person for hotel guests, $7.50 for non-guests, plus a $2 light charge for night play. It's open daily from 7 am.

The Pacific Beach Hotel (☎ 922-1233) has two courts open from 8 am to 6 pm and charges $5 per hour per person for guests, $8 for non-guests. Racquets can be rented for $4.

Planet Surf, 419 Nahua St, rents tennis racquets for $3.50 a day, $10 a week.

Outside Waikiki, the Sheraton Makaha Resort in Makaha (☎ 695-9511) charges $12 an hour in the daytime, $14 at night, with a $2 discount for guests; racquets rent for $5 a day. The Turtle Bay Hilton in Kahuku (☎ 293-8811) charges $8 to $12 per person per day, with one hour playing time guaranteed; racquets rent for $8 a day. Both resorts also give lessons, have pro shops and rent shoes, baskets of balls and ball machines.

Golf

Oahu has four 18-hole municipal golf courses: the Ala Wai Golf Course (☎ 296-4653) on Kapahulu Ave, mauka of the Ala Wai Canal near Waikiki; the Pali Golf Course (☎ 296-7254), 45-050 Kamehameha Hwy, Kaneohe; the Ted Makalena Golf Course (☎ 296-7888), Waipio Point Access Rd, Waipahu; and the West Loch Golf Course (☎ 296-5624), 91-1126 Okupe St, Ewa Beach. Green fees are $30 per person, plus an optional $12 for a gas-powered cart. Clubless golfers can rent clubs for $15 at the driving range next door to the Ala Wai course.

The reservation system is the same at all municipal courses, with the earliest bookings taken one week in advance. Start calling at 6:30 am to book the same day of the following week, as starting times can fill by 7 am. The county also maintains the nine-hole Kahuku Golf Course (☎ 293-5842) in Kahuku.

At last count, Oahu also had 18 private (and nine military) golf courses, but the number is rising, fueling many a conflict between environmentalists and overseas developers.

For information on all Oahu golf courses, send for a copy of the *Hawaii Golf Guide*, Aloha Section PGA (☎ 593-2232), 770 Kapiolani Blvd, Suite 715, Honolulu, HI 96813.

Running
Oahu is big on jogging. In fact, it's estimated that Honolulu has more joggers per capita than any other city in the world. Kapiolani Park and Ala Moana Park are two favorite jogging spots. There's also a 4.8-mile run around Diamond Head crater that's a beaten track.

Oahu has more than 100 road races each year, from one-mile fun runs and five-mile jogs to competitive marathons, biathlons and triathlons. For an annual schedule of running events with times, dates and contact addresses, write to the Department of Parks & Recreation, City & County of Honolulu, 650 S King St, Honolulu, HI 96813.

Oahu's best-known race is the Honolulu Marathon, held in December. For information send a stamped, self-addressed envelope to Honolulu Marathon Association, 3435 Waialae Ave, No 208, Honolulu, HI 96816. Those writing from overseas are asked to include two international response postage coupons.

The Department of Parks & Recreation holds a Honolulu Marathon Clinic at 7:30 am most Sundays at the Kapiolani Park Bandstand. It's free and open to everyone from beginners to seasoned marathon runners. Runners join groups of their own speed.

Cricket
The Honolulu Cricket Club plays on Sunday afternoons at Kapiolani Park,

sometimes against visiting English teams. Visitors are welcome.

Skydiving
For $225, Skydive Hawaii (☎ 521-4404) will attach you to the hips and shoulders of a skydiver so you can jump together from a plane at 10,000 feet, freefall for a minute and finish off with 10 to 15 minutes of canopy ride. The whole process, including some basic instruction, takes about 1½ hours. Participants must be over 18 years of age and weigh less than 200 pounds. Experienced skydivers are charged $57 for jumps. They take off daily (weather permitting) from Dillingham Airfield in Mokuleia.

Organized Tours
For conventional sightseeing tours by van or bus, try TransHawaiian (☎ 735-6467), E Noa Tours (☎ 591-2561), Polynesian Adventure Tours (☎ 833-3000), Roberts Hawaii (☎ 839-4147) or Gray Line Hawaii (☎ 833-8000).

Full-day, circle-island tours usually cost about $45 to $55 and generally encompass southeast Oahu, the windward coast, the North Shore and Waimea Falls Park. There are a wide variety of other tour packages, including a few that concentrate more on Hawaiian culture.

Waikiki Trolley The Waikiki Trolley is a tourist trolley bus that runs between Waikiki and Honolulu. There are 17 stops, including the Ala Moana Center, Honolulu Academy of Arts, Iolani Palace, Hawaii Maritime Center, Bishop Museum, Chinatown and the Ward Centre. Sightseeing narration is provided en route and passengers can get off at any stop and then pick up the next trolley, which comes by every 30 minutes. It leaves from the Royal Hawaiian Shopping Center in Waikiki on the hour and half hour from 8 am to 4:30 pm. One-day passes cost $15 for adults, $5 for children ages 12 and under – a pricey alternative to the public bus.

Helicopter Papillon Hawaiian Helicopters

(☎ 836-1566) leaves from Honolulu International Airport. Its cheapest flight costs $79, lasts 20 minutes and flies over Diamond Head, Waikiki, Honolulu and Pearl Harbor. The whole-island tour takes one hour and costs $187.

Gliding Glider Rides (☎ 677-3404), an old standby, offers 20-minute flights in a glider from the west end of Dillingham Airfield in Mokuleia. Flights go daily between 10:30 am and 5:30 pm and cost $60 for one person and $90 for two.

A newer business, Soar Hawaii (☎ 637-3147), at the same location, has 20-minute glider rides for $60/70 for one/two people. For thrill seekers they also offer acrobatic rides with barrel rolls, spirals and stalls.

Cruises There are numerous sunset sails, dinner cruises and party boats leaving daily from Kewalo Basin, just Ewa (west) of Ala Moana Park. Rates range from $20 to $100, with dinner cruises averaging about $50. Many provide transport to and from Waikiki and advertise various come-ons and specials; check the free tourist magazines for the latest offers. As some of the vessels, including a few of the 'catamarans', are large impersonal operations, you may prefer to go down to the harbor where the boats are docked and check them out for yourself before buying a ticket.

The green-sailed *Leahi* catamaran (☎ 922-5665), which departs from the beach in front of the Sheraton Waikiki, has one-hour sails for $12, 1½-hour sunset sails for $22 and snorkel sails for $20. A couple of other catamarans depart from Waikiki Beach for around the same price, including the Hyatt Regency Waikiki's *Manu Kai* catamaran (☎ 923-1234).

Royal Hawaiian Cruises (☎ 848-6360) runs two-hour whale-watching cruises from January to April aboard the *Navatek I*, a sleek high-tech catamaran that's designed to minimize rolling. It leaves at noon from Pier 6, near the Aloha Tower, and costs $45 for adults and $25 for children ages five to 12, lunch included.

Atlantis Submarines (☎ 973-9811) has a 65-foot, 46-passenger sightseeing submarine that descends 100 feet about a mile off Diamond Head. The tour lasts 1¾ hours, including boat transport to and from the sub. About 45 minutes are spent cruising beneath the surface around a ship and two planes deliberately sunk to create a dive site. Tours leave from Hilton Hawaiian Village on the hour from 7 am to 5 pm daily and cost from $79 for adults, $38 for children.

ACCOMMODATIONS

All but 10% of Oahu's 40,000 visitor rooms are in Waikiki. Unlike on the Neighbor Islands, where there are multiple destinations, outside Honolulu there are only three resort hotels, one on Oahu's leeward side, another near Barbers Point and a third on the northern tip of the island.

The Waikiki/Honolulu area has a wide range of accommodations. The cheapest places to stay are the two AYH/HI-affiliated youth hostels. The one in Waikiki has dorm beds for $15, while the one by the university charges $12. In addition there are several casual hostel-type crash pads in Waikiki with tightly squeezed dorm beds for about $15. After that, there are rooms at Ys for $30 and a few bottom-end Waikiki hotels that start around $40. Waikiki has lots of middle-range hotels in the $65 to $100 range as well as high-priced luxury hotels.

B&Bs have had a hard fight in Oahu. As more and more sprung up in the 1980s, complaints from neighbors in residential areas like Kailua threatened to shut them all down. Consequently an agreement was reached that allowed those already in existence to remain open, but only if they were owner-occupied and renting out no more than two bedrooms.

Unless otherwise noted, rates given throughout this chapter are the same for either singles or doubles and don't include the 10.17% room tax. Most hotels have different rates for the high and low seasons. The high season is generally from December 15 to April 15, but it can vary by hotel a few weeks in either direction. The rest of the year is the low season, though a few hotels switch to high-season rates in midsummer.

To lure customers, some large chains like Outrigger and Hawaiian Pacific Resorts offer a free rental car if you request it at the time of booking. A few independent hotels occasionally throw in a car as well – it never hurts to ask whenever you book any hotel. If you had planned on renting a car, it can be a tidy savings.

If you're calling from outside Hawaii, add the 808 area code to all numbers. Numbers beginning with 800 are toll free from the US mainland and sometimes from Canada as well.

Camping

Camping is allowed at 12 county beach parks, one county botanic garden and four state facilities.

All county and state campgrounds on Oahu are closed on Wednesday and Thursday nights, ostensibly for maintenance, but also to prevent permanent encampments.

Although thousands of visitors use these campsites each year without incident, Oahu has more of a reputation for problems than other islands. Rip-offs, especially at roadside and beachfront campgrounds, are not uncommon.

Camping along the Waianae Coast is not recommended.

State Parks Camping is free by permit at Sand Island and Keaiwa Heiau, both in the greater Honolulu area, and at Malaekahana State Recreation Area and Kahana Valley State Park, both on the windward coast.

Keaiwa Heiau is a good choice for an inland park. A good choice for a coastal park is Malaekahana, which is also the only public park on Oahu with cabins (see the Windward Oahu section).

Camping is limited to five nights per month in each park. Permit applications must be submitted at least seven days and no more than 30 days before the first camping date. Applications may be made to the Division of State Parks by mail (Box 621, Honolulu, HI 96809), by phone

(☎ 587-0300) or in person (1151 Punchbowl St, Room 310) between 8 am and 4 pm on weekdays.

County Beach Parks Camping is free at county beach parks but permits are required. Permits are not available by mail but can be picked up between 7:45 am and 4 pm Monday to Friday at the Department of Parks & Recreation (☎ 523-4525) on the ground floor of the Municipal Office building (650 S King St, Honolulu, HI 96813), the tall grey building on the corner of King and Alapai streets.

Camping permits are also available from any satellite city hall, including the one at the Ala Moana Center (☎ 973-2600), where they are issued from 9 am to 4 pm Monday to Friday and 8 am to 4 pm on Saturdays. Other satellite city halls are in Kailua, Kaneohe and Wahiawa.

Camping is allowed at Mokuleia and Kaiaka beach parks on the North Shore; Hauula, Swanzy, Kualoa, Bellows Field, Waimanalo and Waimanalo Bay beach parks on the Windward Coast; and Kahe Point, Nanakuli, Lualualei and Keaau beach parks on the Waianae Coast.

Camping is allowed from 8 am Friday to 8 am Wednesday, except at Swanzy and Bellows Field beach parks, which are open only on weekends.

Kualoa, in one of Oahu's nicest beach settings, has a caretaker and gates that are locked at night. Bellows Field and Waimanalo Bay also have gates that are secured at night, but other beach parks don't.

County Botanic Garden Hoomaluhia is an inland park in Kaneohe at the base of the Koolau Range. It has Oahu's safest camping and is unique among the county campgrounds in that it's operated by the botanic gardens division. Reservations can be made by mail. For an application, send a legal-sized, self-addressed envelope to Hoomaluhia (☎ 233-7323), 45-680 Luluku Rd, Kaneohe, HI 96744.

Backcountry Camping The state forestry allows backcountry camping along several valley and ridge trails, including three in Hauula on the windward coast and along the Waimano Trail north of Pearl City.

All backcountry camping requires a permit from the Division of Forestry & Wildlife (☎ 587-0166), 1151 Punchbowl St, Room 325, Honolulu, HI 96813. Office hours are 7:45 am to 4:30 pm Monday to Friday. The forestry will send maps for these trails on request.

Fellow hikers on backcountry trails are likely to be pig hunters.

Camping Supplies The Bike Shop (☎ 596-0588), 1149 S King St, rents North Face internal frame backpacks and two-person lightweight tents. The rate for each is $15/35/70 a day/weekend/week.

Omar The Tent Man (☎ 836-8785), 650A Kakoi St, Honolulu, HI 96819, rents six-person canvas tents (at 55 pounds these are too heavy for backpacking!) for $57 a week, external frame backpacks or sleeping bags for $22 a week and stoves or lanterns for $17 a week. Three-day rates for those items are $52, $17 and $15 respectively.

ENTERTAINMENT

The vast majority of Oahu's entertainment takes place in Honolulu, which includes but is certainly not limited to Waikiki.

The best place to look for up-to-date entertainment information is in the free *Honolulu Weekly* newspaper. Other sources are the free tourist magazines and the daily newspapers, in particular the 'Night Life' column in the Thursday edition of the *Honolulu Star-Bulletin*.

Oahu has a lively gay scene, which is centered around the Kuhio District in Waikiki.

The island has more than 40 movie theaters, including a couple of drive-in theaters. Check the newspapers for details.

There are 13 theater companies on Oahu, performing everything from 'South Pacific' and Broadway musicals to Mamet satires and pidgin fairy tales. For recorded information on current theater productions, call 988-3255.

More detailed information is in the Entertainment sections under specific destinations. For festivals, fairs and sporting events, see the Holidays & Festivals section in the Facts about Hawaii chapter.

Luaus

Oahu's two main luaus, *Paradise Cove* (☎ 973-5828) and *Germaine's Luau* (☎ 949-6626), are both huge impersonal affairs held nightly out in the Barbers Point area. Each charges $44.50, including bus ride from Waikiki hotels (about one hour each way), a buffet dinner, drinks, a Polynesian show and related hoopla. Children pay about half price.

There are also a couple of luaus in Waikiki; for information see the Waikiki Entertainment section.

THINGS TO BUY

Honolulu is a large, cosmopolitan city with plenty of sophisticated shops selling designer clothing, jewelry and the like. For general crafts, the best deals are usually found at one of the craft shows that are periodically held in city parks (check the papers).

For kitsch souvenirs there are scores of shops selling fake Polynesian stuff, from Filipino shell hangings and carved coconuts to cheap seashell jewelry and wooden tiki statues – the largest single collection of such shops is at the International Market Place in Waikiki.

If you just want to buy a carton of macadamia nuts, Longs Drugs has better prices than places in Waikiki. There's a Longs, as well as 200 other stores at the Ala Moana Center, the 'largest open-air shopping center in the world' (see the Ala Moana section).

For local flavor, the Aloha Flea Market (☎ 486-1529), at Aloha Stadium out near Pearl Harbor, has more than 1000 vendors from 6 am to 3 pm on Wednesdays, Saturdays and Sundays. Admission is a mere 35c. A private shuttle bus (☎ 955-4050) to the flea market leaves from Waikiki at 7:30, 9 and 10:30 am at a cost of $6 round trip.

Hawaiiana Souvenirs

The Hula Supply Center (☎ 941-5379), 2346 S King St in Honolulu, sells feather leis, calabash gourds, lava rock castanets, bamboo sticks, hula skirts and the like. Although they're intended for Hawaiian musicians and dancers, some of the items would certainly make interesting souvenirs and prices are reasonable.

Quilts Hawaii (☎ 942-3195) at 2209 Young St, just a minute's walk from the Hula Supply Center, has high-quality Hawaiian quilting, including bedcovers, pillows and wall hangings. It also carries other Hawaiian crafts such as hats, koa chests and dolls. Prices are high, but reasonable for the quality.

Kamaka Hawaii (☎ 531-3165), at 550 South St in Honolulu, specializes in ukuleles.

For antique and used aloha shirts, Bailey's Antique Shop (☎ 734-7628), 758 Kapahulu Ave, near Waikiki, has the island's widest selection though prices can be high. Bargain-hunters can sometimes find used aloha shirts and muu-muus at thrift shops around the island, including the Goodwill store at 780 S Beretania St in Honolulu.

Tapes of Hawaiian music also make good souvenirs. Tower Records, which has a branch at the International Market Place in Waikiki, has an excellent collection of both classic and contemporary Hawaiian music.

GETTING THERE & AWAY
Air

Almost all flights into Hawaii land at Honolulu International Airport, the only commercial airport on Oahu. See the Getting There & Away chapter in the front of the book for information on flights to Oahu and airport facilities.

All inter-island airlines that serve the Neighbor Islands also use Honolulu International Airport. For details on flying to the Neighbor Islands, see the Getting Around chapter in the front of the book and the Getting There & Away sections of individual Neighbor Islands.

GETTING AROUND

Oahu is an easy island to get around, whether you travel by public bus, taxi or car.

Traffic in Honolulu can get quite jammed during rush hour – weekdays from 7 to 9 am and 4 to 6 pm. Expect heavy traffic in both directions on H-1 during this time, and heading towards Honolulu in the morning and away from Honolulu in the late afternoon on the Pali and Likelike highways. If you're heading to the airport during rush hour, give yourself plenty of extra time.

To/From the Airport

From the airport you can get to Waikiki by local bus (if your baggage is limited), by airport shuttle services, by taxi or by renting a car. A taxi to Waikiki from the airport will cost about $20. The main car rental agencies have booths or courtesy phones in the airport baggage claim area.

The easiest way to get to Waikiki from the airport is to take Hwy 92, which starts out as Nimitz Hwy and turns into Ala Moana Blvd, leading directly into Waikiki. Although this route hits more local traffic, it's hard to get lost on it.

If you're into life in the fast lane, connect instead with the H-1 freeway heading east.

On the return to the airport from Waikiki, take note not to miss the poorly marked interchange where H-1 splits off to the airport. It takes about 20 minutes to get from Waikiki to the airport via H-1 *if* you don't hit traffic.

Bus Travel time is about an hour between the airport and the far end of Waikiki on city buses No 19 and 20; the fare is 85c. The bus stops at the roadside median on the 2nd level, in front of the airline counters. There are two stops; it's best to wait for the bus at the first one, which is in front of Lobby 4. Luggage is limited to what you can hold on your lap or store under your seat, the latter space comparable to the space under an airline seat.

Shuttle Bus The ride between Waikiki and

the airport takes about 45 minutes by shuttle bus and there are a number of companies providing the service. These buses are picked up at the roadside median on the ground level between baggage claim areas E & F. Most companies charge $6 for adults, $3 for children, with rates including two suitcases and one carry-on bag. Generally, you don't need reservations from the airport to Waikiki, but you do need to call at least a few hours in advance for the return van to the airport.

Shuttle companies include Airport Motor Coach (☎ 839-0911), Airport Express (☎ 949-5249) and Rabi Transportation (☎ 943-7050).

Bus

Oahu's public bus system, which is called TheBus, is extensive and easy to use.

TheBus has about 60 routes, which collectively cover most of Oahu. You can take the bus to watch windsurfers at Kailua or surfers at Sunset Beach or Makaha, visit Chinatown or the Bishop Museum, snorkel at Hanauma Bay or hike Diamond Head. Some of the island's prime viewpoints are beyond reach, however; TheBus doesn't stop at the Nuuanu Pali Lookout, go up to Tantalus or out to Kaena Point.

Buses stop only at marked bus stops. Each bus route can have a few different destinations. The destination is written on the front of the bus next to the number.

Buses generally keep the same number when inbound and outbound. For instance, the No 8 bus can take you either into the heart of Waikiki or out away from it towards Ala Moana – so note both the number and the written destination before you jump on.

When in doubt ask the bus driver. They're used to disoriented visitors and most drivers are remarkably patient and helpful.

Overall, the buses are in excellent condition – if anything they're too modern. Newer buses are air-conditioned, with sealed windows and climate-control, but are sometimes so out of 'control' that drivers wear jackets to keep from freezing!

Although TheBus is convenient enough, this isn't Tokyo – if you set your watch by the bus here you'll come up with Hawaiian Time. In addition to not getting hung up on schedules, buses can sometimes bottleneck, with one packed bus after another cruising right by crowded bus stops. Saturday nights between Ala Moana and Waikiki can be a particularly memorable experience.

Still, TheBus usually gets you where you want to go and as long as you don't try to cut anything close or schedule too much in one day it's a great deal.

Bus Fares The one-way fare for all rides is 85c and bus drivers don't give change. Children under the age of six ride free.

Transfers, which have a time limit stamped on them, are given free when more than one bus is required to get to a destination. If needed, ask for one when you board.

Monthly bus passes valid for unlimited rides in a calendar month cost $20 and can be purchased at Foodland supermarkets, satellite city halls and 7-Eleven stores.

Seniors 65 years and older can buy a $15 bus pass valid for unlimited rides during a four-year period. Senior citizen passes are issued only at TheBus office (☎ 848-4444), 811 Middle St, Honolulu. The office is open from 7:30 am to 4 pm Monday to Friday.

Schedules & Information TheBus has a great telephone service. As long as you know where you are and where you want to go, you can call 848-5555 anytime between 5:30 am and 10 pm and they'll tell you not only which bus to catch but what time the next one will be there.

For 24-hour recorded information on getting to major destinations, call 296-1818 and then enter 8287.

You can get printed timetables for some routes and a handy bus route map from any satellite city hall, including the one in the Ala Moana Center.

If you're going to be using TheBus extensively it's well worth buying one of the bus guides that are sold in bookstores and convenience stores for around $3. Take time to look a few over. For instance, *Honolulu's Famous TheBus* has actual schedules, but if you're not familiar with the streets a better choice is *Honolulu & Oahu by TheBus*, a fold-out brochure which doesn't have schedules but has maps showing major visitor destinations with bus stops and numbers. Be sure to get the most up-to-date version.

Common Routes Buses No 8, 19, 20 and 58 run between Waikiki and Ala Moana Center, Honolulu's central transfer point. There's usually a bus every 10 minutes or less. From Ala Moana you can connect with a broad network of buses to points mauka and Ewa.

Buses No 2, 19 and 20 will take you between Waikiki and downtown Honolulu.

Bus No 4 runs between Waikiki and the University of Hawaii.

Circle-Island Route It's possible to circle the island by bus, beginning at the Ala Moana Center. The No 52 Wahiawa-Circle Island bus goes clockwise up Hwy 99 to Haleiwa and along the North Shore. At the Turtle Bay Hilton, on the northern tip of Oahu, it switches signs to No 55 and comes down the windward coast to Kaneohe and down the Pali Hwy back to Ala Moana. The No 55 Kaneohe-Circle Island bus does the same route in reverse. If you do it nonstop it takes about four hours.

To make the loop around southeast Oahu from Waikiki, it's bus No 58 to Sea Life Park and then No 57 up to Kailua and back into Honolulu.

Because you'll need to change buses, ask for a transfer when you first board. Transfers have time limits and aren't meant to be used as stopovers, but you can usually grab a quick break at Ala Moana. Anytime you get off to explore along the route you'll need to pay a new 85c fare when you reboard.

Taxi

Metered taxis start with a flag-down fee of $2 and then click up in 25-cent increments

at a rate of $2 per mile. There's an extra charge of 30c for each suitcase or backpack.

Taxis are readily available at the airport and larger hotels, but otherwise generally hard to find. To phone for one, try Sida (☎ 836-0011), Charley's (☎ 955-2211), Americabs (☎ 591-8830) or City Taxi (☎ 524-2121). The latter offers a 10% discount to senior citizens over the age of 55.

Car

Budget (☎ 537-3600), National (☎ 831-3800), Hertz (☎ 831-3500), Avis (☎ 834-5536) and Dollar (☎ 831-2330) all have desks at Honolulu International Airport and car lots on the airport grounds. Alamo (☎ 833-4585) has its operations about a mile outside the airport, on the corner of Nimitz Hwy and Ohohia St.

All things being equal, try to rent from a company with its lot inside the airport – not only is it more convenient but, more importantly, on the way back all the highway signs lead to the in-airport car returns.

The international companies also have numerous branch locations in Waikiki, including in the lobbies of larger hotels. General rental information and toll-free numbers are in the Getting Around chapter in the front of the book.

Budget gives renters a coupon booklet that allows one free admission to many of Oahu's more expensive tourist attractions, including Sea Life Park, Waimea Falls Park, Polynesian Cultural Center and Hawaii Maritime Center. You don't have to buy one to get one, so for a single traveler it's all free. This is a particularly good deal if you're renting a car for only a day or two and want to catch some of the sights.

In addition to the major chains, there are a few local rental companies. Some flash cheap come-on rates in their ads, but when you read the fine print you'll usually find something such as 'price applies to first day on a three-day minimum'. Bottom-end rates more typically are around $22 a day, with a three-day minimum, for cars long past their prime, and prices for new cars, when available, are generally no cheaper than the international companies. However, if you don't carry plastic, local companies are often more willing to accept cash deposits in lieu of credit cards.

Local companies in Waikiki include:

VIP, 234 Beach Walk (☎ 922-4605)
Discount Rent-A-Car, 1920 Ala Moana Blvd, Suite 105, at Inn on the Park (☎ 941-0658)
Aloha Funway Rentals, 1778 Ala Moana Blvd, at Discovery Bay (☎ 942-9696)
Paradise Car Rental, 355 Royal Hawaiian Ave (☎ 220-7777)

Moped

State law requires mopeds to be ridden by only one person and prohibits their use on sidewalks and on freeways. Renters must be 18 years or older.

Blue Sky Rentals (☎ 947-0101), on the ground floor of Inn on the Park Hotel, 1920 Ala Moana Blvd, is the best place in Waikiki to rent a moped. The bikes, including Honda Elites and Yamaha Rivas, are well maintained and the no-nonsense rates of $15 a half day, $20 a full day and $85 a week include taxes and insurance.

The biggest company is Island Scooters, which has half a dozen Waikiki locations, including ones at 234 Beach Walk (☎ 924-6743), 353 Royal Hawaiian Ave (☎ 924-9331) and 151 Uluniu Ave (☎ 924-2339). Yamaha Rivas rent for $22 a day, including mandatory CDW insurance coverage with a $250 deductible.

Bicycle

There's a lot more traffic on Oahu than on the other islands, which makes cycling seem a lot less appealing.

Blue Sky Rentals (☎ 947-0101), 1920 Ala Moana Blvd in Waikiki, has a range of bikes from $15 to $21 a day.

Planet Surf (☎ 926-2060), 419 Nahua St in Waikiki, rents mountain bikes for $20/68 a day/week and beach cruisers for $15/50.

There are also a number of other bicycle rental places in Waikiki, including one with bikes for $20 a day that's next door to Inter-Club Hostel Waikiki, 2413 Kuhio Ave.

The Hawaii Bicycling League (☎ 735-5756), Box 4403, Honolulu, HI 96812, holds bike rides around Oahu nearly every Saturday and Sunday, ranging from 10-mile jaunts to 60-mile treks. Rides are free and open to the public.

Waikiki

Waikiki was once Hawaii's only tourist destination and it still accounts for nearly half of the visitor accommodations in the state. It has an amazing density of high-rise hotels along an attractive stretch of white sand beach.

Waikiki is crowded with package tourists from both Japan and the US mainland. It has 25,000 permanent residents and some 65,000 visitors on any given day, all in an area roughly 1½ miles long and half a mile wide. Waikiki has 450 restaurants, 350 bars and clubs, and more shops than you'd want to count. Its 33,000 hotel and condo rooms have a year-round occupancy rate of 80%.

While the beaches are packed during the day, at night most of the action is along the streets, where window shoppers, cruising pedicabs, time-share touts and prostitutes all go about their business. A variety of live music, from mellow Hawaiian to rock, wafts from streetside clubs and hotel lounges.

Visitors who are into city lights or singles scenes often find what they're looking for here, while many seasoned travelers and a fair number of Oahu residents avoid Waikiki like the plague.

In an effort to upgrade Waikiki's image, the beachfront Kalakaua Ave has recently undergone an extensive beautification project, while Waikiki hotels have undertaken their own half-billion dollar face-lift.

Waikiki Beach has wonderful orange sunsets, with the sun dropping down between cruising sailboats. It's the one time of day that the area approaches the romantic image that the travel brochures like to portray.

Just beyond Waikiki is Diamond Head, a landmark so dominant that it's used as a

From Swamp to Resort

At the turn of the century Waikiki was almost entirely wetlands. It had more than 50 acres of fishponds as well as extensive taro patches and rice paddies. Fed by mountain streams from the upland Manoa and Makiki valleys, Waikiki was one of Oahu's most fertile and productive areas.

By the late 1800s Waikiki's narrow beachfront was lined with gingerbread-trimmed cottages, built by Honolulu's more well-to-do.

Robert Louis Stevenson, who frequented Waikiki in those days, wrote:

If anyone desires such old-fashioned things as lovely scenery, quiet, pure air, clear sea water, heavenly sunsets hung out before his eyes over the Pacific and the distant hills of Waianae, I recommend him to Waikiki Beach.

Tourism took root in 1901 when the Moana opened its doors as Waikiki's first real hotel. A tram line was constructed to connect Waikiki to downtown Honolulu and city folk crowded aboard for the beach. Tiring quickly of the pesky mosquitoes that thrived in the wetlands, these early beachgoers petitioned to have Waikiki's 'swamps' brought under control.

In 1922 the Ala Wai Canal was dug to divert the streams that flowed into Waikiki. Old Hawaii lost out, as farmers had the water drained out from under them. Coral rubble was used to fill the ponds, creating what was to become Hawaii's most valuable piece of real estate. Water buffalo were replaced by tourists.

Waikiki's second hotel, the Royal Hawaiian, was built in 1927 and became the crown jewel of the Matson Navigation Company.

The Royal was the land component for cruises on the *Malolo*, one of the premier luxury ships of the day. The $7.5-million ship, built while the $2-million hotel was under construction, carried 650 passengers from San Francisco to Honolulu each fortnight. The Pink Palace, as the Royal Hawaiian was nicknamed, opened with an extravagant $10-a-plate dinner.

Hotel guests ranged from the Rockefellers to Charlie Chaplin, Babe Ruth to royalty. Some of the guests brought dozens of trunks, their servants and even their Rolls Royces.

The Depression put a damper on things and WW II saw the Royal Hawaiian turned into an R&R center for servicemen.

Waikiki had 1400 hotel rooms in 1950. In those days surfers could drive their cars to the

beach and park on the sand. In the 1960s tourism took over in earnest and by 1968 Waikiki had 13,000 hotel rooms. By 1988 that number had more than doubled.

The lack of available land has finally halted the boom. In a desperate attempt to squeeze in one more high-rise, St Augustine's Catholic Church, standing on the last speck of uncommercialized property along busy Kalakaua Ave, was nearly sold in 1989 to a Tokyo developer for $45 million. It took a community uproar and a petition to the Vatican to nullify the deal. ■

directional marker – people say 'go Diamond Head' instead of 'head east'.

Orientation

Waikiki is bounded on two sides by the Ala Wai Canal and on another by the ocean. The eastern boundary varies according to who's drawing the line, but it's usually considered to be Kapahulu Ave.

There are two main roads: the beach road is Kalakaua Ave, named after King David Kalakaua; the main drag for Waikiki's buses is Kuhio Ave, named after Prince Jonah Kuhio Kalanianaole, a distinguished Hawaiian statesman.

City buses are not allowed on Kalakaua Ave and trucks are prohibited at midday. Traffic on this four-lane road is one way so it's relatively smooth for driving but pedestrians need to be cautious as cars tend to zoom by fast.

Walking along the beach is an alternative to using the crowded sidewalks. It's possible to walk the full length of Waikiki along the sand and the sea walls. Although it's rather hot and crowded at midday, it's pleasant at other times. The beach is quite romantic to stroll along at night, enhanced by both the city skyline and the surf lapping at the shore, and it's dark enough to see the stars. Police patrol the beach on dune buggies after sunset and it's generally as safe as walking the streets.

Information

Tourist Offices The Hawaii Visitors Bureau (☎ 924-0266) is at 2270 Kalakaua Ave, on the 7th floor of the Waikiki Business Plaza. It has racks of brochures and tourist magazines, including those for the Neighbor Islands, and is open from 8 am to 4:30 pm Monday to Friday.

Free tourist magazines, such as *This Week Oahu*, *Spotlight's Oahu Gold* and *Guide to Oahu*, can readily be found on street corners and in hotel lobbies throughout Waikiki.

Money There's a Bank of Hawaii at 2220 Kalakaua Ave, a Bank of America at 321 Seaside Ave and a First Hawaiian Bank at 2181 Kalakaua Ave. The latter has some interesting Hawaiiana murals by the renowned artist Jean Charlot.

Food Pantry on Kuhio Ave has an automatic teller machine that accepts major bank and credit cards, as does the nearby 24-hour 7-Eleven convenience store.

Post The main Waikiki post office, 330 Saratoga Rd, is open from 8 am to 4:30 pm on weekdays, except on Wednesdays when it's open from 8 am to 6 pm. Saturday hours are 9 am to noon.

There are branch post offices at the Royal Hawaiian Shopping Center, 2233 Kalakaua Ave, and at the Hilton Hawaiian Village, 2005 Kalia Rd.

Film & Photography Fox Photo, with Waikiki branches in the Royal Hawaiian Shopping Center and at 2301 Kuhio Ave, does good quality one-hour photo processing.

To buy film and to have slides processed, Longs Drugs is a good choice. All their stores send out to Kodak, and most also do Fuji. Slides generally take two to three days, prints a day or two, and the cost is a dollar or two cheaper than at camera shops. While there are no branches in Waikiki, there's a Longs Drugs on the upper level of the Ala Moana Center and another next to Times Supermarket at 3221 Waialae Ave.

Bookstores There are good Hawaiian and travel book sections at Waldenbooks in the Waikiki Trade Center on Kuhio Ave and the Royal Hawaiian Shopping Center on Kalakaua Ave.

Libraries The Waikiki-Kapahulu Public Library (☎ 732-2777), 400 Kapahulu Ave, is open from 10 am to 8 pm Mondays and Wednesdays and 10 am to 5 pm on Tuesdays, Thursdays, Fridays and Saturdays. It's a relatively small library, but it does have daily newspapers from the Neighbor Islands and the mainland.

Laundry There are coin laundries, open from 6:30 am to 10 pm daily, at the Outrigger West Hotel, 2330 Kuhio Ave; Outrigger Coral Seas, 250 Lewers St; and the Outrigger Waikiki, 2335 Kalakaua Ave.

Parking Parking in Waikiki is a hassle. Many of the hotels charge $6 to $10 a day at their parking garages.

At the west end of Waikiki the best bet is the free public parking lot at the Ala Wai Yacht Harbor.

On the east side, there's a small underground parking lot next to the Tradewinds Plaza on Lemon Rd, a couple of buildings down from Queen Kapiolani Hotel. It costs $3 for overnight parking and an additional $2 to park from 7 am to 5 pm.

The zoo parking lot on Kapahulu Ave has meters and costs 25c an hour with a four-hour parking limit. If you like taking chances you can try your luck parking overnight at the zoo, when the police generally don't write tickets; however if you don't move out early enough in the morning you may be greeted with the sight of an officer placing a $25 ticket on your window. Trust us.

Airline Offices Aloha Airlines (☎ 484-1111) has an office at the Royal Hawaiian Shopping Center, United Airlines (☎ 547-2211) is across the street at 2316 Kalakaua Ave, and Korean Air (☎ 923-1896) is on the same block at 2350 Kalakaua Ave.

Emergency Dial 911 for all police, fire and ambulance emergency services.

Doctors On Call has a doctor-staffed clinic open 24 hours a day in the 2nd-floor main lobby of the Outrigger Waikiki (☎ 971-6000) and from 8 am to 5 pm at Hilton Hawaiian Village (☎ 973-5252). The minimum charge for an office visit is $65. They have X-ray and lab facilities and will make house calls, though the latter will run more than twice the usual price.

Also open 24 hours is Doctors Who Care (☎ 926-7776) at the Pacific Beach Hotel, 2490 Kalakaua Ave, Ocean Tower, Suite 218. The minimum charge for an office visit is $60. A free shuttle van is available to transport patients to the clinic.

Dangers & Annoyances There's been a clampdown on the hustlers who used to push time-shares and other con deals from every other street corner in Waikiki. They're not totally gone – there are just fewer of them (and some have metamorphosed into 'activity centers'). If you see a sign touting car rentals for $5 a day, you've probably found one.

Time-share salespeople will offer you all sorts of deals, from free luaus to sunset cruises, if you'll just come to hear their 'no obligation' pitch. *Caveat emptor.*

Waikiki Beaches
The two-mile stretch of white sand that runs from the Hilton Hawaiian Village to Kapiolani Park is commonly called Waikiki Beach, although different sections along the way have their own names and characteristics.

In the early morning the beach belongs to walkers and joggers – and it's surprisingly quiet. Strolling down the beach towards Diamond Head at sunrise can actually be a meditative experience.

By mid-morning it looks like a normal resort beach, with boogie board and surfboard concessionaires setting up shop and catamarans pulling up on the beach offering $15 sails. By noon it is packed and the challenge is to walk down the beach without stepping on anyone.

Most of Waikiki's beautiful white sands are not its own. Tons of sand have been barged in over the years, much of it from Papohaku Beach on Molokai.

As the beachfront developed, landowners haphazardly constructed sea walls and offshore barriers to protect their property. In the process they blocked the natural forces of sand accretion, and erosion has long been a serious problem at Waikiki.

Sections of the beach are still being replenished with imported sand, although much of it ends up washing into the ocean, where it fills channels and depressions and alters the surf breaks.

Waikiki is good for swimming, boogie boarding, surfing, sailing and other beach activities most of the year. Between May and September, summer swells can make the water a little rough for swimming, but they also make it the best season for surfing.

As a consequence of all the activity and alterations Waikiki beaches simply aren't that good for snorkeling; the best of them is Sans Souci.

There are lifeguards and showers at many places along the beach.

Kahanamoku Beach Kahanamoku Beach, fronting the Hilton Hawaiian Village, is the westernmost section of Waikiki. It was named for Duke Kahanamoku, a surfer and swimmer who won Olympic gold in the 100-meter freestyle in 1912 and went on to become a Hawaiian celebrity.

Kahanamoku Beach is protected by a breakwater at one end and a pier at the other, with a coral reef running between the two. It's a calm swimming area with a sandy bottom that slopes gradually.

Fort DeRussy Beach Fort DeRussy Beach, one of the least crowded Waikiki beaches, borders 1800 feet of the Fort DeRussy Military Reservation. Like all beaches in Hawaii, it's public. The federal government provides lifeguards, and a grassy lawn that gets at least sparse shade from palm trees provides an alternative to frying on the sand.

The water is usually calm and good for swimming. The swimming zone is marked by buoys and you can also snorkel there, although it's nothing to rush down for. While the beach is most popular with windsurfers, it's also used by boogie boarders and board surfers. There's a beach hut, open daily, where you can rent windsurfing equipment, boogie boards and snorkel sets.

Gray's Beach Gray's Beach, the local name for the beach near the Halekulani Hotel, was named for a boarding house called Gray's-by-the-Sea that stood on the site in the 1920s. On the same stretch of beach was the original Halekulani, a lovely low-rise mansion that was converted into a hotel in the 1930s. About a decade ago, the

mansion gave way to the present high-rise hotel.

Because the sea wall in front of the Halekulani was built so close to the waterline, the part of the beach fronting the hotel is often totally submerged.

The section of beach between the Halekulani and the Royal Hawaiian Hotel varies in width from season to season. The waters off the beach are shallow and calm.

Central Waikiki Beach The area between the Royal Hawaiian Hotel and the Waikiki Beach Center is the busiest section of the whole beach.

Most of the beach has a shallow bottom with a gradual slope. There's pretty good swimming here, but there's also a lot of activity, with catamarans, surfers and plenty of other swimmers in the water. Keep your eyes open.

Offshore are Queen's Surf and Canoe's Surf, Waikiki's best-known surf breaks.

Waikiki Beach Center The area opposite the Hyatt Regency Waikiki is the site of the Waikiki Beach Center. It has restrooms, showers, a police station, surfboard lockers and rental concessions.

The **Wizard Stones of Kapaemahu** – four boulders on the Diamond Head side of the police station – are said to contain the secrets and healing powers of four sorcerers, named Kapaemahu, Kinohi, Kapuni and Kahaloa, who visited from Tahiti in ancient times. Before returning back to Tahiti, they transferred their powers to these stones.

Just west of the stones is a bronze **statue of Duke Kahanamoku** (1890-1968), Hawaii's most decorated athlete, standing with one of his longboards. Considered the 'father of modern surfing' Duke, who made his home in Waikiki, gave surfing demonstrations on beaches from Sydney, Australia, to Rockaway Beach, New York. Many local surfers took issue with the placement of the statue as Duke is standing with his back to the sea, a position they say he never would have taken in real life. In response the city moved the statue as close to the sidewalk as possible.

Star Beach Boys, a beachside concession stand, rents surfboards and boogie boards by the hour and offers inexpensive outrigger canoe rides. Private surf lessons, some by legendary beachboys like Rabbit Kekai, cost $25 an hour.

Kuhio Beach Park Kuhio Beach Park is marked on its east end by Kapahulu Groin, a walled storm drain with a walkway on top that juts out into the ocean from the end of Kapahulu Ave.

A low breakwater sea wall runs about 1300 feet out from Kapahulu Groin, paralleling the beach. It was built to control sand erosion, and in the process two nearly enclosed swimming pools were formed. Local kids walk out on the breakwater, which is called The Wall, but it can be dangerous to the uninitiated due to a slippery surface and breaking surf.

The pool closest to Kapahulu Groin is best for swimming, with the water near the breakwater reaching overhead depths. However, because circulation is limited the water gets murky with a noticeable film of suntan oil. The 'Watch Out Deep Holes' sign refers to holes in the pool's sandy bottom that can be created by swirling currents. Those who can't swim should be cautious in the deeper areas of the pool as the holes can take waders by surprise.

The park, incidentally, is named after Prince Kuhio, who maintained his residence on this beach. His house was torn down in 1936, 14 years after his death, in order to expand the beach.

Between the old-timers who gather each afternoon to play chess and cribbage at Kuhio's sidewalk pavilions and the kids boogie boarding off the Groin, this section of the beach has as much local color as tourist influence.

Kapahulu Groin Kapahulu Groin is one of Waikiki's hottest boogie boarding spots. If the surf's right you can find a few dozen boogie boarders, mostly teenage boys, riding the waves.

Duke Kahanamoku

The kids ride straight for the wall and then veer away at the last moment, drawing 'oohs' and 'ahs' from the tourists who gather to watch them. If you want to join them, boogie boards can be rented from a stand at the side of the Groin for $5 an hour.

Kapahulu Groin is also a great place to catch sunsets.

Kapiolani Beach Park Kapiolani Beach Park starts at Kapahulu Groin and runs down to the Natatorium, past Waikiki Aquarium.

Queen's Surf is the name given to the wide midsection of Kapiolani Beach. The stretch in front of the pavilion is a popular beach with the gay community. It's a pretty good area for swimming, with a sandy bottom. The section of beach between

Queen's Surf and Kapahulu Groin is shallow and has a lot of broken coral.

Kapiolani Beach Park is a relaxed place with little of the frenzy of activity found in front of the central strip of Waikiki hotels. It's a popular weekend picnicking spot for local families who unload the kids to splash in the water as they line up the barbecue grills.

There's a big grassy field to lay out on, good for spreading out a beach towel and unpacking a picnic basket. Free parking is available near the beach along Kalakaua Ave. There are restrooms and showers at the Queen's Surf pavilion.

The surfing area offshore is called Public's.

Natatorium The Natatorium, at the Diamond Head end of Kapiolani Beach, is a 100-meter-long saltwater swimming pool built after WW I as a memorial for soldiers who died in that war. There were once hopes of hosting an Olympics on Oahu, with this pool as the focal point.

The Natatorium, which is on the National Register of Historic Places, is now closed and in disrepair but the state has tentative plans to restore the facility.

Sans Souci Beach Down by the New Otani Kaimana Beach Hotel, Sans Souci is a nice, little sandy beach away from the main tourist scene. It has outdoor showers and a lifeguard station.

Many residents come to Sans Souci for daily swims. A shallow coral reef close to shore makes for calm, protected waters and provides reasonably good snorkeling. More coral can be found by following the Kapua Channel as it cuts through the reef, although beware of currents that can pick up in the channel. Check conditions with the lifeguard before venturing out.

Royal Hawaiian Hotel

The Royal Hawaiian, Hawaii's first luxury hotel, is worth a look even if you're not staying there. With its pink turrets and Moorish/Spanish architecture, it's a throwback to the era when Rudolph Valentino

was *the* romantic idol and travel to Hawaii was by luxury liner.

The hotel was originally on a 20-acre coconut grove, but over the years the grounds have been chipped away by a huge shopping center on one side and a high-rise mega-hotel on the other. The Royal Hawaiian is a survivor.

Inside, the hotel is lovely and airy with high ceilings and chandeliers and everything in rose colors. The small garden at the rear is filled with birdsong, a rare sound in most of Waikiki.

Fort DeRussy

Fort DeRussy Military Reservation is a US Army post used mainly as a recreation center for the armed forces. This large chunk of Waikiki real estate was acquired by the US Army a few years after Hawaii was annexed to the USA. Prior to that it was swampy marshland and a favorite duck hunting spot for Hawaiian royalty.

The Hale Koa Hotel on the property is open only to military personnel but there's public access to the beach and the adjacent military museum.

US Army Museum of Hawaii

Battery Randolph, a reinforced concrete building built in 1911 as a coastal artillery battery, houses the army museum at Fort DeRussy. It once held two formidable 14-inch-diameter disappearing guns with an 11-mile range that were designed to recoil down into the concrete walls for reloading after each firing. A 55-ton lead counterweight would then return the carriage to position.

The museum now houses weapons and exhibits on military history as it relates to Hawaii. There are some interesting historic displays on King Kamehameha, the 19th-century overthrow of the monarchy and Hawaii's role in WW II. It's open from 10 am to 4:30 pm daily, except Mondays, Christmas and New Year's Day, and admission is free.

Oceanarium

The Pacific Beach Hotel, at 2490 Kalakaua

Ave, houses an impressive three-story 280,000-gallon aquarium that forms the backdrop for three of the hotel restaurants. Even if you're not dining there, you can view the aquarium quite easily from the lobby. Divers enter the Oceanarium to feed the tropical fish daily at 12:30, 6, 7:15 and 8:30 pm.

St Augustine's Church

St Augustine's Church, off Kalakaua Ave and Ohua Ave, is a quiet little sanctuary in the midst of the hotel district. In the rear of the church a second building houses the **Damien Museum**, a modest museum honoring Father Damien, famed for his work at the leprosy colony on Molokai. It has a video presentation on the colony, some interesting historical photos and a few of Damien's personal possessions.

As a befitting tribute to Father Damien's life, the building also houses a lunchtime soup kitchen. Museum hours are 9 am to 3 pm Monday to Friday, until noon on Saturdays; entry is free.

Ala Wai Canal

Late in the afternoon outrigger canoe teams can be seen paddling up and down Ala Wai Canal and out to the Ala Wai Yacht Harbor.

Kapiolani Park

The nearly 200-acre Kapiolani Park, at the Diamond Head end of Waikiki, was a gift from King Kalakaua to the people of Honolulu in 1877. Hawaii's first public park, it was dedicated to Kalakaua's wife, Queen Kapiolani.

In its early days horse racing and band concerts were the park's biggest attractions. Although the race track has gone, the concerts continue and Kapiolani Park is still the venue for a wide range of community activities.

The park contains the Waikiki Aquarium, the Honolulu Zoo, Kapiolani Beach Park, the Waikiki Shell, the Kodak Hula Show grounds and Kapiolani Bandstand. It has sports fields, tennis courts, huge lawns and tall banyan trees.

The Royal Hawaiian Band presents free afternoon concerts nearly every Sunday at the Kapiolani Bandstand. Dance competitions, Hawaiian music concerts and other activities occur throughout the year.

The Waikiki Shell is an outdoor amphitheater with symphony, jazz and rock concerts. For information on performances, check the papers or call the Blaisdell Center (☎ 521-2911).

Kapiolani is one of the top-rated kite-flying parks in the USA and hosts a kite festival each March. Kite Fantasy, a kite shop at the nearby New Otani Kaimana Beach Hotel, gives kite demonstrations on the grassy lawns beyond the tennis courts.

It's a pleasant park and despite all the activities that go on, it's large enough to have a lot of quiet space.

Waikiki Aquarium

Waikiki Aquarium This interesting aquarium (☎ 923-9741), 2777 Kalakaua Ave, dates to 1904 and has recently reopened after a $3-million makeover.

The aquarium has added interactive displays, a mini-theater and an auditorium where visitors can look through a 14-foot glass window at circling sharks.

Tanks re-create various Hawaiian reef habitats, making this a great place to identify fish you've seen while snorkeling or diving. There are black-tip sharks, moray eels, flash-back cuttlefish wavering with pulses of light, and rare Hawaiian fish with names like the bearded armorhead and the sling-jawed wrasse.

There's an interesting variety of exotic marine life as well. In 1985 the aquarium was the first to breed the Palauan chambered nautilus in captivity. A couple of these sea creatures, with their unique spiral chambered shell, are on display. There are also some giant clams from Palau that were less than an inch long when acquired in 1982 and now measure over two feet, the largest in the USA.

There's also a touch tank for children, a mahimahi hatchery, green sea turtles and Hawaiian monk seals. Visitors can watch the monk seals being fed at 2:30 pm daily except on Thursdays when the pool is cleaned.

The aquarium is open from 9 am to 5 pm daily, although entry is not allowed after 4:30 pm. Admission is $6 for adults, $4 for senior citizens over 60 and students with ID, $2.50 for children ages 13 to 17, and free for children 12 and under.

Honolulu Zoo The Honolulu Zoo (☎ 971-7171) has just undergone extensive renovations that have upgraded it into a respectable city zoo. The highlight is the nicely naturalized African Savanna section which has lions, cheetahs, white rhinos, giraffes, zebras, hippos and monkeys. The zoo also has an interesting reptile section, a good selection of tropical birds and a small 'petting zoo' area.

It's open from 8:30 am to 5:30 pm (no admittance after 4:30 pm) daily except Christmas and New Year's Day. Admission is $3 (annual pass $5); children age 12 and under accompanied by an adult are admitted free.

In front of the zoo there's a large banyan tree which is home to hundreds of white pigeons – escapees from a small group brought to the zoo in the 1940s.

Art in the Park Local artists have been hanging their paintings on the fence around the zoo on weekends for more than 25 years. If you're looking for a painting, this is a good opportunity to buy directly from the artist. The artwork is on display from 9 am to 4 pm on Saturdays and Sundays.

Kodak Hula Show The Kodak Hula Show (☎ 833-1661), off Monsarrat Ave near the Waikiki Shell, is a staged photo opportunity of hula dancers, ti-leaf skirts and ukuleles. The musicians are a group of older ladies who performed at the Royal Hawaiian Hotel in days gone by.

This is the scene in postcards where dancers hold up letters forming the words 'Hawaii' and 'Aloha'. The whole thing is quite touristy, although entertaining if you're in the mood, and it's free.

Kodak has been putting on this show since 1939. The benches are set up stadium-style around a grassy stage area

with the sun at your back. The idea is for everyone to shoot a lot of film. It works. Even though Kodak doesn't monopolize the film market anymore, the tradition continues.

Shows are held from 10 to 11:15 am on Tuesdays, Wednesdays and Thursdays. Make sure you're on time because once it starts they only admit people between acts.

Dolphins
The Kahala Hilton, in the Kahala area beyond Diamond Head, has three Atlantic bottlenose dolphins in a lagoon as well as penguins, green sea turtles and tropical reef fish on display. Coached by trainers from Sea Life Park, the dolphins put on a short show for smelt and herring at 11 am and 2 and 4 pm daily. They jump and dive, stand on their tails, vocalize, hula dance, play volleyball and the like. The show is free and open to the public, but parking in the hotel garage costs $5 an hour.

Places to Stay
Waikiki's main beachfront strip, Kalakaua Ave, is largely lined with high-rise hotels and $150-plus rooms. As is the norm in resort areas, most of these hotels cater to package tourists, driving the prices up for individual travelers.

Better values are generally found at the smaller hostelries on the back streets. There are hotels in the Kuhio Ave area and up near the Ala Wai Canal that are as nice as some of the beachfront hotels but half the price. If you don't mind walking 10 minutes to the beach you can save yourself a bundle.

In many hotels the rooms themselves are the same, with only the views varying; generally the higher the floor, the higher the price. If you're paying extra for a view, you might want to ask to see the room first as Waikiki certainly doesn't have any truth-in-labeling laws governing when a hotel can call a room 'oceanview'. While some 'ocean views' are the real thing, others are merely glimpses of the water as seen through a series of high-rises.

Waikiki has many more hotel rooms than condos. Most of Waikiki's condos are filled with long-term residents and there isn't the proliferation of vacation rental agents as on the Neighbor Islands. The best way to find a condo in Waikiki is to look in the Vacation Rentals section of the daily paper, although the listings can be meager, particularly in the winter season.

Places to Stay – bottom end
Hostels In addition to the one AYH hostel, there are a number of small businesses providing hostel-like dormitory accommodation around Waikiki. Despite the 'hostel' in their names they're not members of the Hostelling International (HI) association and you shouldn't expect HI standards. While Oahu presently has few regulations regarding such businesses, that certainly could change, so it'd be a good idea to verify that the non-HI 'hostels' are still in operation before showing up at the door.

Hostelling International Waikiki (☎ 926-8313; fax 946-5904), 2417 Prince Edward St, Honolulu, HI 96815, a member of AYH and HI, is a 50-bed hostel on a back street a few short blocks from Waikiki Beach. Dorm beds cost $15. There are also four rooms for couples at $35, with small refrigerators and private bathrooms. For the private rooms, which can be booked for a maximum of five nights, paid reservations or a credit card hold are required.

Office hours are from 8 am to noon and 4 pm until midnight. There's no longer a dormitory lockout or curfew and a shared kitchen is available from 8 am to 11 pm. Four parking spaces are available at $2 a day – a bargain for Waikiki. Occasionally you can be lucky as a walk-in, but at busy times reservations are often necessary two to three weeks in advance. HI or AYH membership is required and cards can be purchased on site (AYH membership costs $25 single, $35 for a family). MasterCard and Visa are accepted.

InterClub Hostel Waikiki (☎ 924-2636), 2413 Kuhio Ave, Honolulu, HI 96815, is part of a small Australian/US chain of privately run hostels. It has about 75 bunk beds, arranged five to seven to a room. Guests are mostly backpackers. To stay at InterClub you officially need a passport and an onward ticket to a destination outside the USA; however in practice they're somewhat flexible on this. Reservations aren't taken, so if they're full, show up in the morning and hang around until someone leaves. If you call from the airport and a bed is available, they'll usually hold it long enough for you to get there by bus. There's a lounge and TV room, a washer/dryer, $1 lockers and no curfew. Try to get a bed in one of the rear units, as the rooms closest to the heavy traffic on Kuhio Ave can be very noisy. Dorm beds cost $15. The hostel also has some simple private rooms for $45 with linoleum floors, refrigerators, shared balconies and private baths.

Hawaiian Seaside Hostel (☎ 924-3306; fax 923-2110), 419-E Seaside Ave, Honolulu, HI 96815, occupies a two-story apartment building set back from the street in an alley off Seaside Ave. It's close to the main bus lines and about a 10-minute walk from Waikiki Beach. Bunk beds in dorm rooms cost $15 and have curtains that can be drawn around the bunks for a bit of privacy. Guests have use of a kitchen and a TV lounge, there's no curfew and it's open 24 hours a day.

Polynesian Beachclub (☎ 922-1340), 134 Kapahulu Ave, Room 615, Honolulu, HI 96815, has nine rooms at the Waikiki Grand Hotel that it uses to provide hostel-style beds. Each room has three to five beds, cable TV and air-conditioning and most have kitchenettes. The rate is $15 a night.

Hawaiian Style Hostel (☎ 949-3382), 1946 Ala Moana Blvd, Room 212, Honolulu, HI 96815, has eight small studio rooms in Hawaiian Colony, an unkempt apartment building. Each room has six beds squeezed in, a table, a TV, a little kitchen and a bathroom. Some units have a double bed for couples as well as beds for singles together in the same room. There's no curfew or other restrictions. The rate is $14 per person.

Waikiki

See inset map

500 m
500 yards
0　250
0　250

To Chinatown

To Downtown
Honolulu

Kapiolani Blvd

Ala Wai Yacht
Harbor

Kahanamoku
Beach

Fort
DeRussy

Fort DeRussy Beach

Ala Wai Canal

Ala Wai Blvd

McCully St

Kapahulu Ave

Leahi Ave

Paki Ave

Kapahulu Ave

Kapiolani Park

Monsarrat Ave

To Diamond
Head & Sans
Souci Beach

Honolulu Zoo

Kapiolani Beach
Park

Waikiki
Aquarium

Kuhio Beach
Park

Kapahulu Groin

Waikiki Beach

Gray's Beach

PACIFIC
OCEAN

International
Market Place

Kalakaua Ave

Kuhio Ave

■ PLACES TO STAY	60	Waikiki Resort Hotel	70	New Kapahulu Chop Suey
	61	Sheraton Princess	71	Ono Hawaiian Food
5 Hawaiian Style Hostel		Kaiulani	72	Keo's
8 Big Surf	62	Hyatt Regency Waikiki	73	Irifune's
9 Hawaii Polo Inn	63	Outrigger Waikiki	75	Rainbow Drive-In
10 Hawaii Prince Hotel	64	Sheraton Moana Surfrider		
11 Ilikai Hotel	68	Waikiki Circle Hotel		OTHER
12 Hawaii Dynasty Hotel	69	Pacific Beach Hotel		
(14) Hilton Hawaiian Village	(78)	Ocean Resort Hotel	2	Wave Waikiki
18 Hotel Honolulu		Waikiki	3	Pink Cadillac
19 Coconut Plaza Hotel	79	Hawaiian Regent	6	Blue Sky Rentals
20 Outrigger Waikiki Surf	80	Hawaiian Waikiki Beach	15	Kuhio Twins Theatre
21 Outrigger Malia		Hotel	16	Hula's Bar & Lei Stand
25 The Breakers	81	Waikiki Grand Hotel	22	Waikiki Post Office
29 Hale Pua Nui	82	Queen Kapiolani Hotel	27	First Hawaiian Bank
30 Outrigger Coral Seas			28	Urasenke Tea Ceremony
33 Outrigger Waikiki Tower	▼	PLACES TO EAT	31	Royal Hawaiian Shopping
34 Outrigger Reef Hotel				Center
35 Halekulani Hotel	1	Hard Rock Cafe	32	US Army Museum
36 Waikiki Parc Hotel	4	Eggs 'n Things	41	Planet Surf
37 Sheraton Waikiki	7	California Pizza Kitchen &	43	Waikiki Trade Center
38 Royal Hawaiian Hotel		Singha Thai	45	Scruples
39 Hawaiian Seaside Hostel	13	Saigon Cafe	46	Kuhio Mall
40 Ilima Hotel	17	Hamburger Mary's	52	Hawaii Visitors Bureau
51 Waikiki Sand Villa Hotel	23	New Tokyo Restaurant	65	Board Rentals
53 Waikiki Beachcomber	24	Moose McGillycuddy's	66	Police
54 Outrigger East Hotel	26	Camellia Yakiniku	67	Wizard Stones
55 InterClub Hostel Waikiki	42	Pizzeria Uno	74	Bailey's Antique Shop
56 Pacific Monarch	47	Jamaican Cuisine	76	Waikiki-Kapahulu Library
57 Royal Grove Hotel	47	Patisserie	77	St Augustine's Church
58 Hostelling International	48	Chili's	83	Kodak Hula Show
	Waikiki	49	Food Pantry	84	Waikiki Shell
59 Waikiki Prince Hotel	50	Perry's Smorgy		

Hotels *Waikiki Prince Hotel* (☎ 922-1544), 2431 Prince Edward St, Honolulu, HI 96815, has 30 units next door to Hostelling International Waikiki. Rooms are basic and not all that cheery, but the people working there make up for it with aloha spirit. They get an international crowd, with a lot of backpackers in the summer. Standard rooms cost $43, while rooms with kitchenettes cost $46 to $53. Rates are $5 less in summer. All rooms have cable TV and air-con. There are no room phones, but the staff are quite efficient at taking messages. Half a dozen parking spaces are available at $3 a day. The office is open from 9 am to 6 pm.

Also recommendable is *Hale Pua Nui* (☎ 923-9693), 228 Beach Walk, Honolulu, HI 96815, an older four-story building with

22 studio apartments. While the rooms are not fancy, the new manager, Hugh Cave, has spruced them up and they're well-maintained and clean. Each has the basics: two twin beds, a kitchenette, fan (no air-con), cable TV and phone, and the beach is but a five-minute walk away. Rates are $44/55 in the low/high season, and there are discounts for stays of two weeks or more. There's limited on-site parking for $5 a day.

More marginal is the *Big Surf* (☎ 946-6525), 1690 Ala Moana Blvd, Honolulu, HI 96815, on the western edge of Waikiki. It's quite run-down, the kind of place where the ceiling fans wobble and the TV picture fades to fuzz. Still, two people traveling together can have their own room with two twin beds, bathroom, fridge and small lanai for $39, which is an option to cramped $15 dorm beds elsewhere. Very small one-person studios with no lanai are a few dollars cheaper. Big Surf is not far from the YMCA (see Honolulu Places to Stay) so it gets some of its overflow, though it's certainly not on par with the Y.

So many retirees return each winter to the 85-room *Royal Grove Hotel* (☎ 923-7691; fax 922-7508), 151 Uluniu Ave, Honolulu, HI 96815, that it's difficult to get a room in high season without advance reservations. Kitchenette units cost $43 in the old wing (with no air-con) and from $57 in the new wing (with air-con). Rooms without kitchenettes, but with refrigerators, cost $38/42 in the old/new wing. This is an older, no-frills type of place, but there's a small pool.

Places to Stay – middle

The *Waikiki Sand Villa Hotel* (☎ 922-4744, (800) 247-1903; fax 923-2541) is at 2375 Ala Wai Blvd, Honolulu, HI 96815, on the Ala Wai Canal, a 10-minute walk from Waikiki Beach. The 223 rooms are rather standard tourist class with cable TV, refrigerators, central air-conditioning, room safes, bathtubs and small lanais, some with views across the golf course towards Manoa Valley. Ask for a corner unit, which has the best views. Children under 12 are free and many rooms have both a double and a twin bed. Standard rooms, which are on the lower floors, cost $62/75 in the low/high season, upper floors are a few dollars more. There are also more expensive poolside studios with kitchenettes. A simple continental breakfast is included in the rate and overall the hotel is a good value for this price range.

Waikiki Circle Hotel (☎ 923-1571, (800) 922-7866), 2464 Kalakaua Ave, Honolulu, HI 96815, booked through the Aston chain, is a small hotel with a great location. It has 104 rooms on 13 floors, all with lanais, two double beds, room safes, phones, TVs and air-con. The hotel is older, but has recently been renovated and the rooms are comfortable. This circular building has a back room on each floor that's called 'city view' and costs $79; while you can't see the

ocean, these are farther from the road and quieter. Each floor also has two rooms with partial ocean views for $99 and five rooms with unobstructed ocean views for $109 – all in all, a good deal for being right across from Waikiki Beach. Be sure to request an upper-floor room.

Waikiki Grand Hotel (☎ 923-1511, (800) 535-0085; fax 923-4708), 134 Kapahulu Ave, Honolulu, HI 96815, is a 173-room hotel opposite the zoo. Although the rooms have been renovated, they are quite small and ordinary. Still they have the standard amenities: TV, phone, air-con, mini-refrigerators, coffeemaker and a pool. Rates listed in the hotel brochure are a pricey $80 for a standard room, $95 for a room with a kitchenette, although the hotel often advertises hefty discounts in the classified section of the Honolulu paper. If you contact the front desk directly and ask for the cheapest local rate you can often get a standard room for around $45 – a good value.

Hotel Honolulu (☎ 926-2766, (800) 426-2766; fax 922-3326), 376 Kaiolu St, Honolulu, HI 96815, is Waikiki's only gay hotel. It's a quiet oasis on a side street a block from busy Kuhio Ave and the heart of the gay district. The three-story hotel has the character of an unhurried inn, with helpful management, lots of hanging ferns and potted orchids and a peach-colored cockatoo at the front desk. The 19 main units are decorated with flair, each with its own theme ('Samurai', 'Tapestry,' 'Norma Jean' etc), and these are large and comfortable, with lanais, kitchens, ceiling fans and air-con. Studios cost $79, one-bedroom units $103. There are also smaller, non-theme studios in an adjacent building for $69. Coffee is free and there's a sundeck but no pool. While the guests are predominantly gay, straights are also welcome.

The *Hawaii Polo Inn* (☎ 949-0061, (800) 669-7719; fax 949-4906), 1696 Ala Moana Blvd, Honolulu, HI 96815, is next door to the Big Surf and opposite the ritzy Hawaii Prince Hotel. The 66 motel-style rooms have cinder-block walls and are lined up in rows with their entrances off a long outdoor corridor. The rooms have been renovated but they're still straightforward. All have small refrigerators, coffeemakers and TVs; some have lanais, although generally the lanai area is at the expense of room space. Rates are $75 to $95 during the high season, $10 less during the low season.

Ocean Resort Hotel Waikiki (☎ 922-3861, (800) 367-2317; fax 924-1982), 175 Paoakalani Ave, Honolulu, HI 96815, has 451 rooms. A former Quality Inn, it's a rather ordinary place that hosts a fair number of people on low-end package tours. Still, rooms are air-conditioned and have standard amenities such as TVs, phones and room safes. Nonsmoking rooms are available on request and there's a pool. Standard rooms begin at $79, those with kitchenettes from $121. All are $10 cheaper in the low season.

Queen Kapiolani Hotel (☎ 922-1941, (800) 367-5004; fax 922-2694), 150 Kapahulu Ave, Honolulu, HI 96815, is a 313-room 19-story hotel at the quieter Diamond Head end of Waikiki. It's an older hotel with an aging regal theme: chandeliers, high ceilings and fading paintings of Hawaiian royalty. Standard rooms cost $99/110 in the low/high season. However rooms are anything but standard and vary greatly in size, with some that are very pleasant and others so small they can barely squeeze a bed in. The simplest way to avoid a closet-size space is to request a room with two twin beds instead of a single queen. Also, be sure to get a room without interconnecting doors – they act like a sound tunnel to the next room. Some of the oceanview rooms, which cost $25 more, have lanais with unobstructed views of Diamond Head. There are often special room/car packages from about $75; check for ads in the Sunday *Honolulu Advertiser.*

Ilima Hotel (☎ 923-1877, (800) 367-5172; fax 924-8371), 445 Nohonani St, Honolulu, HI 96815, is a smaller hotel in a less hurried section of Waikiki, a 10-minute walk from the beach. All 99 units are roomy and light with large lanais, two double beds, tasteful rattan furnishings, cable TV and kitchens with an oven, microwave and full-size refrigerator. Local phone calls and parking are free, a rarity in Waikiki. The staff are friendly and the lobby has interesting Hawaiiana murals. Rates vary according to the floor, although the rooms themselves are essentially the same. High-season rates start at $82/87 singles/doubles in studios on the 4th floor and rise to $97/107 for studios on the 10th to 16th floors. There are also some one and two-bedroom suites for $136 and $166 respectively. All rates are $17 less from April to mid-December.

The 200-room *Hawaii Dynasty Hotel* (☎ 955-1111, (800) 421-6662; fax 947-1799), 1830 Ala Moana Blvd, Honolulu, HI 96815, is a good-value mid-range hotel at the western end of Waikiki. Rooms are modern and comfortable with either two doubles or one king bed, a desk, remote-control TV, small refrigerator, coffeemaker and bathroom with tub and hair dryer. Some also have balconies. Rates depend on the floor, ranging from $88 to $98 in the high season, $10 less in the low season. There's a pool and sundeck and the beach is about a 10-minute walk away. Unlike most hostelries on busy Ala Moana Blvd, the Dynasty is set back from the road, so it tends to be notably quieter.

The Breakers (☎ 923-3181, (800) 426-0494; fax 923-7174), 250 Beach Walk, Honolulu, HI 96815, is a low-rise hotel with 64 units surrounding a courtyard pool. This is one of the more pleasant places at the western end of Waikiki and the staff are friendly. Regular rooms, which have one double and one single bed, as well as kitchenettes, cost $91 without a lanai or $97 for a 2nd-floor unit with a lanai. Large suites which have a separate bedroom with a queen bed, a living room that resembles a studio with two twin beds, a full kitchen and a table for four cost $130 for two people, $146 for four people. Both categories have air-con, TV, desks and phones. Avoid the rooms closest to Saratoga Rd which has lots of traffic.

The 20-story *Waikiki Resort Hotel* (☎ 922-4911, (800) 367-5116; fax 922-9468) is at 2460 Koa Ave, Honolulu, HI 96815. This Korean-owned hotel has a

Korean restaurant, the Korean Air office, Korean-language newspapers in the lobby and, not surprisingly, books heavily with Korean travelers. Its clean, modern rooms have mini-refrigerators, TVs, phones, air-con, room safes and lanais. The regular rates begin at $95/105 in the low/high season, though a better deal is the room/car special that's available for $90. Low-season rates become effective on March 1, a month before other hotels.

The *Coconut Plaza Hotel* (☎ 923-8828, (800) 882-9696; fax 923-3473), 450 Lewers St, Honolulu, HI 96815, managed by Hawaiiana Resorts, is a quiet 80-room hotel near Ala Wai Blvd. Rooms have contemporary decor and are comfortable enough, but are on the small side. Most have refrigerators, microwaves, two-burner stoves, TV, air-con and private lanais and cost $105 to $120. There are also a few rooms without cooking facilities for $95 and some larger suites for $150. Rates include continental breakfast. There's a coin laundry, a restaurant and some exercise machines on site.

Pacific Monarch (☎ 923-9805; fax 924-3220), 142 Uluniu Ave, Honolulu, HI 96815, is a high-rise condominium hotel with 216 units in 34 stories. The studios are good size, each with a table, desk, double bed, sofa bed, small refrigerator and two-burner hot plate. The one-bedroom units have a small bedroom and a roomy front room area with a full kitchen, a dining table for four, a sofa bed and a large lanai.

Colony (☎ (800) 777-1700) is the rental agent for more than half of the units, with low/high season rates at $99/109 for two people in a studio, $130/140 for up to four people in the one-bedroom units. Add $10 more for rooms above the 15th floor.

The *New Otani Kaimana Beach Hotel* (☎ 923-1555, (800) 356-8264; fax 922-9404), 2863 Kalakaua Ave, Honolulu, HI 96815, is on Sans Souci Beach on the quieter Diamond Head side of Waikiki. It's a pleasantly low-key place with 125 units. Room rates start at $99, studios with kitchenettes start at $150. All have air-con, TV, refrigerators and lanais.

Outrigger Hotels The *Outrigger*, Box 88559, Honolulu, HI 96830, has bought and renovated many of Waikiki's middle-range hotels; at last count it had 20. Overall, it's a fairly good-value chain, although there's a wide range in price and quality. At any rate, with one phone call you can check on the availability of 25% of the hotel rooms in Waikiki!

Ask about promotional deals when making reservations – currently they include 'Drive for Five' which gives you a Budget rental car for just $5 more than the regular room rate, and a 20% senior citizen discount.

To book rooms at any Outrigger in advance you can call (303) 369-7777 or fax (303) 369-9403. Outrigger also has the following toll-free numbers: (800) 688-7444 and fax (800) 622-4852 from the USA and Canada; (0014) 800-124171 from Australia; (0-800) 440852 from New Zealand; (0130) 81-8598 from Germany; (0800) 89-4015 from the UK; and (0031) 11-3479 from Japan.

The 303-room *Outrigger Waikiki Surf* (☎ 923-7671), 2200 Kuhio Ave, is one of the Outrigger's better deals. The standard hotel rooms, which cost $80, are small but sufficient, each with a TV, tiny refrigerator, coffeemaker, lanai and either one queen or two twin beds. A good value are the kitchenette units, which cost just $5 more but are roomier and have two double beds, a larger refrigerator and a either a two-burner hot plate or a microwave. There are also one-bedroom units for up to four people for $115 and two-bedroom units for $200.

If preparing your own meals is a consideration, there are two other Outriggers nearby that have kitchenettes in all the rooms. The *Outrigger Waikiki Surf West*, 412 Lewers St, and the newly renovated *Outrigger Waikiki Surf East*, 422 Royal Hawaiian Ave, are both right around the corner from the Outrigger Waikiki Surf and have rates of $75/80 low/high season for a room. Both hotels also have one-bedroom units for around $25 more.

The *Outrigger Malia* (☎ 923-7621), 2211 Kuhio Ave, is a 328-room high-rise hotel opposite the Outrigger Waikiki Surf. Rooms are comfortable, each with two double beds, remote-control TV, a room safe, mini-refrigerator, coffeemaker, phone and a tiny one-chair lanai. Nonsmoking rooms are available. Ask for an upper-floor room on the back side as they're quietest. All rooms cost the same: $90/100 in the low/high season, or $115 year round for a one-bedroom suite. The hotel has a rooftop tennis court and an inexpensive 24-hour coffee shop.

Closer to the beach, the 109-room *Outrigger Coral Seas* (☎ 923-3881), 250 Lewers St, has standard rooms for $75/85 in the low/high season, while kitchenette units are $10 more. Although the hotel is not much to look at from the outside, the rooms are rather nice.

The 439-room *Outrigger Waikiki Tower* (☎ 922-6424), 200 Lewers St, is a high-rise hotel a few minutes' walk from the beach. The rooms are comfortable with a lanai, TV, room safe, small refrigerator, phone and either two doubles or a king bed. The cheapest rates are for rooms from the 12th floor down, which cost $85/95 in the low/high season. Room on floors 14 and above are essentially the same but cost $10 more. There are also kitchenette rooms with a microwave and coffeemaker for an additional $5.

The Outrigger has two hotels right on the beach: the 885-room *Outrigger Reef Hotel*, with rooms from $145 to $250, and the 530-room *Outrigger Waikiki*, with rooms from $150 to $275. Despite the price, these are not luxury hotels – the tariff simply reflects the beachside locale.

Places to Stay – top end

The following hotels all have standard first-class amenities and in-house restaurants. All are on the beach or across the street from it and all have swimming pools.

The 298-room *Waikiki Parc Hotel* (☎ 921-7272, (800) 422-0450; fax 923-1336), 2233 Helumoa Rd, Honolulu, HI 96815, is across the street from its more upmarket sister, the Halekulani. Rooms are average in size but have nice touches like ceramic tile floors, shuttered lanai doors, remote-control TV, a room safe and two phones. The hotel has a pleasantly understated elegance. Standard rooms cost $145, while the upper-level oceanview rooms top out at $230. If you book in the mid-range request the 8th floor, which has larger lanais. The hotel occasionally runs cheaper promotional rates, including a senior citizen's rate of $95 for those over 55 years of age.

The *Hawaiian Regent* (☎ 922-6611, (800) 367-5370; fax 921-5255), 2552 Kalakaua Ave, Honolulu, HI 96815, has 1346 rooms in a huge maze-like complex. Rooms are quite ordinary for the money, with rates ranging from $150 to $260.

The 715-room *Hawaiian Waikiki Beach Hotel* (☎ 922-2511, (800) 877-7666; fax 923-3656), 2570 Kalakaua Ave, Honolulu, HI 96815, looks almost like a reflection of the bigger Hawaiian Regent across the street, and the rooms are just as nice, although cheaper. Prices start at $105/120 in the low/high season. The best value is the Mauka Tower, an annex off to the side of the main building, where the rates are at the low end and the rooms are larger, newer and quieter than in the main hotel.

The *Sheraton* pretty much owns a little stretch of the beach, boasting 4400 rooms in its four Waikiki hotels. The toll-free numbers for all of Sheraton's Hawaii hotels are (800) 325-3535 from the USA and Canada and (008) 07-3535 from Australia.

The 1150-room *Sheraton Princess Kaiulani* (☎ 922-5811; fax 923-9912), 120 Kaiulani Ave, Honolulu, HI 96815, is the Sheraton's cheapest Waikiki property. It was built in the 1950s by Matson Navigation to help develop Waikiki into a middle-class destination and from the outside looks a bit like an inner-city housing project. However, the interior is more appealing and the rooms are modern. Rooms without lanais begin at $120, those with lanais from $145. It's in the busy heart of Waikiki, across the street from the beach.

The 793-room *Sheraton Moana Surfrider* (☎ 922-3111; fax 923-0308), 2365 Kalakaua Ave, Honolulu, HI 96815, is a special place for those fond of colonial hotels. The Moana, built in 1901, was Hawaii's first beachfront hotel. It's recently undergone a $50-million historic restoration, authentic right down to the carved columns on the porte-cochère. Despite the fact that modern wings (the 'Surfrider' section) have been attached to the main hotel's flanks, the Moana has survived with much of its original character. The lobby is open and airy with high plantation-like ceilings, reading chairs and Hawaiian artwork. The rooms in the original building have been closely restored to their turn-of-the-century appearance. The furnishings are made from a different wood on each floor (koa on the 5th, cherry on the 6th), with TVs and refrigerators hidden behind armoire doors. Rates in the historic wing range from $205 for city views to $295 for ocean views.

The pink Moorish-style *Royal Hawaiian Hotel* (☎ 923-7311; fax 923-8999), 2259 Kalakaua Ave, Honolulu, HI 96815, now a Sheraton property, was Waikiki's first luxury hotel. It's a beautiful building, cool and airy and loaded with charm. The historic section maintains a classic appeal, with some of the rooms having quiet garden views. This section is easier to book too, since most guests prefer the modern high-rise wing with its ocean views. Rates

are from $245 to $350 in the historic wing, $405 in the tower.

Sheraton Waikiki (☎ 922-4422; fax 922-9567), 2255 Kalakaua Ave, Honolulu, HI 96815, is an impersonal 1850-room megahotel that looms over the Royal Hawaiian Hotel. The bustling lobby resembles an exclusive Tokyo shopping center, lined with lots of expensive jewelry stores and boutiques with French names and designer labels. The hotel has central elevators that leave guests at some of the longest corridors in Hawaii. Rates range from $185 for a city view to $365 for a luxury oceanview unit.

The *Hyatt Regency Waikiki* (☎ 923-1234, (800) 233-1234; fax 923-7839), 2424 Kalakaua Ave, Honolulu, HI 96815, has twin 40-story towers with 1230 rooms. There's a maximum of 18 rooms per floor, so it's quieter and feels more exclusive than other hotels its size. Rooms are nicely decorated in pastels with rattan furnishings and cost from $190 to $305, depending on the view. Between the towers there's a large atrium with cascading waterfalls and orchids, red torch ginger and other tropical vegetation.

Hilton Hawaiian Village (☎ 949-4321, (800) 445-8667; fax 947-7898), 2005 Kalia Rd, Honolulu, HI 96815, is Hawaii's largest hotel, with 2522 rooms. The ultimate in mass tourism, it's practically a package-tour city unto itself – all self-contained for people who never want to leave the hotel grounds. It's quite a busy place, right down to the roped-off lines at the front desk, which resembles an airline check-in counter. The Hilton is on a nice beach, has some good restaurants and offers free entertainment including Friday-night fireworks. Rates start at $155 for a garden view, $240 for an ocean view.

Halekulani Hotel (☎ 923-2311, (800) 367-2343; fax 926-8004), 2199 Kalia Rd, Honolulu, HI 96815, is considered by many to be Waikiki's premier hotel. The 412 rooms, which are pleasantly subdued rather than posh, have large balconies, marble vanities, deep soaking tubs, silent refrigerators, and little touches like bathrobes and fresh flowers. Rooms with garden views cost $265, while those fronting the ocean are $390. Suites start at $580.

The *Kahala Hilton* (☎ 734-2211, (800) 367-2525; fax 737-2478), 5000 Kahala Ave, Honolulu, HI 96816, is in the exclusive Kahala residential area on its own quiet stretch of beach. This is where the rich and famous go when they want to avoid the Waikiki scene 10 minutes away. The guest list is Hawaii's most regal: Charles and Di, King Juan Carlos and Queen Sofia, and the last six US presidents. Yet, somewhat surprisingly, the hotel has an appealing casualness. Staff who have been working there for decades and guests who return year after year know each other by name. The older two-story wing has rooms on the hotel's enclosed lagoon, with dolphins swimming just beyond the lanais. Prices range from $220 for a mountain view to $2300 for the presidential suite. (See the Southeast & Windward Oahu map.)

Places to Eat

Waikiki has no shortage of places to eat, although the vast majority of the cheaper ones are easy to pass up. Generally the best inexpensive food is found outside Waikiki, where most Honolulu residents live and eat (see Places to Eat in the Honolulu section). Waikiki's top-end restaurants, on the other hand, are some of the island's best, though they can quickly burn a hole in your wallet.

Breakfast

Signs draped from buildings advertising breakfast specials for $2 to $4 are commonplace. The *Sandwich Island Coffee Shop, Eggs 'n Things, Moose McGillycuddy's* and *Saigon Cafe* all have inexpensive breakfast specials.

Food Pantry at 2370 Kuhio Ave has a doughnut counter, while the nearby *Patisserie*, 2330 Kuhio Ave, has a full bakery serving pastries and Danish as well as a few inexpensive egg dishes. Standard fast-food places offer their quick, cheap breakfasts from just about every other corner. If you're really hungry and not too demanding on quality, the $4.95 all-you-can-eat breakfast buffet at *Perry's Smorgy* is a good deal.

For around $10 to $18 you can try one of the all-you-can-eat breakfast buffets that many of the larger hotels offer, but few are worth the money. Two noteworthy exceptions are the daily breakfast buffets at the oceanside *Shore Bird Broiler* ($7.95) in the Outrigger Reef Hotel and the *Parc Cafe* ($11.50) in the Waikiki Parc Hotel, which are both good value.

Or try one of the two romantic beachfront restaurants at Sans Souci Beach, at the Diamond Head end of Waikiki. You can get croissants and coffee at *Michel's* for as little as $5 or have a full breakfast served on fine china for less than most hotel buffets. While not as famed, an even better option is the *Hau Tree Lanai* at the New Otani Kaimana Beach Hotel, which has very pleasant courtyard dining shaded by a sprawling hau tree. The Hau Tree Lanai has a variety of breakfast combinations priced under $10 that are served from 7 to 11 am.

For more details, see the individual restaurant listings below.

Sunday Brunches

Waikiki's most renowned Sunday brunch buffet is at *Orchid's* (☎ 923-2311) at the Halekulani Hotel. The grand spread includes sashimi, sushi, baron of beef or smoked salmon, roast suckling pig, roast turkey, salads, fruits and a rich dessert bar. There's a fine ocean view, orchid sprays on the tables and a soothing flute and harp duo. The buffet costs $29.50 (more on holidays) and lasts from 9:30 am to 2:30 pm. Make advance reservations or be ready for a two-hour wait.

The Sunday brunch buffet at the *Parc Cafe* (☎ 921-7272) in the Waikiki Parc Hotel has eggs Benedict, leg of lamb, fresh catch of the day and a wonderful array of salads such as Peking duck, green papaya and mixed greens. Tempting desserts, a frozen yogurt bar and fresh fruit are also included. It's from 11 am to 2 pm. There's no ocean view and it's not as elaborate as the buffet at its sister hotel, the Halekulani, but the food is also superb and the price is just $17.50.

The Sunday brunch buffet at the *Kahala Hilton* (☎ 734-2211), out beyond Waikiki in Kahala, is generally considered on par with the buffet at Orchid's. A relaxed affair, with beachside open-air setting, brunch is served from 11:30 am to 2 pm and costs $36. The restaurant will validate your ticket for free parking in the hotel garage.

Places to Eat – budget

For inexpensive bakery items try the *Patisserie*, 2330 Kuhio Ave, at the side of the Outrigger West Hotel. It's open from 6 am to at least 8 pm daily and has reasonably good pastries, croissants, bread and coffee. If you want to eat in, there's a small sit-down area where you can get standard breakfast items, sandwiches and salads.

The *Saigon Cafe*, on the 2nd floor of 1831 Ala Moana Blvd, has good-value Vietnamese food. The summer rolls ($2.95), which come with a tasty peanut sauce, make a nice starter. A good main dish is the combination rice noodle plate, which has chopped spring rolls, barbecued pork, cucumber, mint and lettuce over a bed of noodles; it costs a reasonable $4.95 at lunch, $5.95 at dinner and is one of the higher priced dishes on the menu. Other items include green papaya salad and frosty, fresh-fruit shakes. There's also a breakfast special of pancakes and two eggs for $1.95. It's open from 6:30 am to 9:30 pm daily.

The *New Tokyo Restaurant*, 286 Beach Walk, is a popular local lunch spot with good, cheap Japanese food served in a pleasant setting. Oyako-ju, which is chicken, steamed egg and onions with a sweetened sauce over rice, costs $5, as does the yakizakana plate featuring grilled fish (often salmon!). Both are served with miso soup, pickles and rice. Other lunch specials cost from $5 to $9.50. Dinner is a far more expensive affair, with prices from $16 to $37. Lunch is served from 11:30 am to 2 pm weekdays, dinner nightly.

Pizzeria Uno, 2256 Kuhio Ave, 2nd floor, serves up Chicago-style deep-dish pizza, which has a thick pastry-like crust. One-person pizzas range from $5 for a plain cheese to $6.75 for chicken fajita toppings. The best deal is from 11 am to 3 pm weekdays, when the pizza of the day comes with a salad for $6. The restaurant also has burgers, pastas and a couple of chicken dishes. Avoid the lanai seating, as the traffic below is very noisy and you'll end up sucking in the exhaust from buses waiting at the traffic light.

Jamaican Cuisine at 2310 Kuhio Ave, a new restaurant run by a Jamaican couple, is a small place with a counter and a few tables serving authentic Jamaican food. At lunch, from 11 am to 4 pm, spicy jerk chicken or a very nicely done plum chicken costs $6 and is served with rice and peas, vegetables and plantains. At dinner the same dishes are $7.25 but include soup or a simple salad. There are also pork, beef and shrimp dishes. It's open daily until midnight.

Hamburger Mary's, 2109 Kuhio Ave, is an open-air restaurant and bar in the middle of the gay district. Burgers are good, ranging from $4.25 for a standard to $6.25 for an avocado special. A variety of salads served with multi-grain bread are about the same price and homemade soups cost $3.50 a bowl. It's open from 7 am to 11 pm daily.

Moose McGillycuddy's, 310 Lewers St, has 20 types of omelets for $6.50 each, but a better deal is the early-bird special, from 8 to 9 am, of two eggs, bacon, toast and orange juice for $3.50. The restaurant is popular with the college crowd and has an extensive menu of burgers, sandwiches, Mexican food, salads, pupus and drinks at moderate prices. It's open from 7 am to 10 pm daily, with breakfast served to 11 am. All drinks are half price from 4 to 8 pm and there's music and dancing nightly.

Spaghetti! Spaghetti!, on the 3rd floor, Building A, of the Royal Hawaiian Shopping Center, attracts a crowd with its all-you-can-eat pasta buffet and salad bar. The pasta is not memorable, and the salad bar is limited, but you can eat your fill for $6 at lunch, $7 at dinner. It's open from 11 am to 10 pm daily. The Royal Hawaiian Shopping Center has about two dozen other eateries, from Baskin-Robbins to Chinese and Japanese restaurants.

Fatty's Chinese Kitchen, 2345 Kuhio Ave, is a hole-in-the-wall eatery in an alley opposite the Baskin-Robbins ice cream shop at Kuhio Mall. It serves up some of the cheapest food to be found in these parts, with 'two scoop rice' or chow mein plus one hot entree for only $3. Add on $1 for each additional entree. The atmosphere is purely local, with a dozen stools lining a long bar and the cook on the other side chopping away. Fatty's is open from 10:30 am to 10:30 pm daily.

The two *Perry's Smorgy* restaurants, one at the Outrigger Coral Seas Hotel at 250 Lewers St and the other at 2380 Kuhio Ave on the corner of Kanekapolei St, offer cheap all-you-can-eat buffets. Breakfast, from 7 to 11 am, includes pancakes, eggs, ham, weak coffee and fresh pineapple, papaya and melon. It's a tourist crowd and the food is strictly cafeteria quality, but you can't beat the $4.95 price. Lunch, which includes a reasonable fruit and salad bar as well as simple hot dishes like fried chicken, is from 11:30 am to 2:30 pm and costs $5.95. Dinner, from 5 to 9 pm nightly, costs $7.95.

Eggs 'n Things at the Hawaiian Monarch Hotel, 1911 Kalakaua Ave, is an all-nighter, open daily from 11 pm to 2 pm. It specializes in breakfast fare, with prices starting at $2.75 for three pancakes with eggs.

Wailana Coffee House at the Outrigger Malia, 2211 Kuhio Ave, is in the midst of the entertainment district and is open 24 hours a day with inexpensive diner-style fare from an extensive menu. The food is a tad better than that at other similar low-end restaurants.

The *Sandwich Island Coffee Shop* in the Waikiki Beach Hotel on Kalakaua Ave has cafeteria-quality food and a breakfast special of French toast, an egg, bacon and a pot of coffee for $4.50. Pass up the lackadaisical $12 breakfast buffet that's geared

for Japanese pack-tourists who stay at the hotel and use breakfast coupons.

At the northwest corner of the *International Market Place* there's a food court with about two dozen stalls selling cinnamon buns, shave ice, frozen yogurt, burgers and various plate lunches – nothing distinguished, but it is cheap.

Fast-food chains are well represented in Waikiki: there are three *Burger King*, four *McDonald's* and six *Jack in the Box* restaurants, the latter open 24 hours. In addition to the usual menus, they add some island touches such as passion fruit juice, saimin and Portuguese sausage. All three chains usually have discount coupons in the free tourist magazines.

Cheap Kapahulu Restaurants There's a run of cheap neighborhood ethnic restaurants along Kapahulu Ave, the road that starts in Waikiki near the zoo and runs up to the H-1 freeway. The following restaurants are grouped together about a mile up from Kalakaua Ave.

Irifune's, 563 Kapahulu Ave, is a funky little joint complete with Japanese country kitsch and a waiting room that resembles the anteroom of a bordello. They don't use MSG in the kitchen and you can bring in beer from the nearby liquor store. The gyoza is good at $3.50, as is the garlic tofu with vegetables at $8. Combination dinners are $8.50 and include options such as tataki ahi, a delicious fresh tuna that's seared lightly on the outside, sashimi-like inside, and served with a tangy sauce. Although few tourists come up this way, the restaurant is locally popular so you might have to wait 20 or 30 minutes to be seated at dinner, but it's well worth it. Irifune's is open from 11:30 am to 1:30 pm Tuesday to Friday and from 5 to 9:30 pm Tuesday to Sunday.

Ono Hawaiian Food, 726 Kapahulu Ave, is *the* place in the greater Waikiki area to get Hawaiian food served Hawaiian-style. It's a simple diner, but people line up outside waiting to get in. A kalua pig plate costs $6.25 and a laulau plate $6.50. Both come with *pipikaula*, lomi salmon and haupia with rice or poi. It's open from 11 am to 7:30 pm Monday to Saturday.

New Kapahulu Chop Suey, 730 Kapahulu Ave, serves big plates of Chinese food. The combination special lunch plate costs $4, the special dinner $4.75, while a score of other dishes are priced under $6. It's a lot of food for the money and the restaurant is usually pretty crowded. It's open from 11 am to 9 pm daily.

KC Drive Inn at 1029 Kapahulu Ave, farther up the road near the freeway, features Ono Ono malts (a combination of chocolate and peanut butter that tastes like a liquid Reese's Cup) for $2.70 and waffle dogs (a hot dog wrapped in a waffle) for $1.75, as well as plate lunches, burgers and saimin for either eat-in or takeout. It's been a local favorite since the 1930s, complete with car-hop service until just a few years back.

If you're on foot *Rainbow Drive-In*, at the intersection of Kapahulu and Kanaina Aves, is much closer to central Waikiki, has similar food and just as much of a local following.

See also the listing for Keo's, in the same Kapahulu neighborhood but with midrange prices.

Self-Catering The best place to get groceries in Waikiki is the *Food Pantry*, 2370 Kuhio Ave, which is open 24 hours a day. Its prices are higher than those of the chain supermarkets, which are all outside Waikiki, but lower than those of the smaller convenience stores. Food Pantry, like most grocery stores, accepts credit cards.

Beyond Waikiki, the easiest supermarket to get to without a car is *Foodland* at the Ala Moana Center. There's a *Times Supermarket* at 3221 Waialae Ave, between 5th and 6th avenues, and a *Foodland* a few blocks away near the eastern intersection of King and Kapiolani Sts. There are grocery stores along Beretania St as well.

Places to Eat – middle
The very popular *Shore Bird Broiler*, at the Outrigger Reef Hotel, 2169 Kalia Rd, has a fine beachfront location and open-air

dining. At one end of the dining room there's a big common grill where you cook your own order: fish costs $8, teriyaki chicken $11 and steak $13. Meals come with all-you-can-eat chili, rice and a simple salad bar that includes slices of papaya and pineapple. The salad bar alone costs $6.95. Dinner is from 4:30 to 10 pm nightly. It's a busy place and unless you get there early expect to wait for a table – although this is scarcely a hardship, as you can hang out on the beach and watch the sun set while you wait.

Shore Bird also has a good-value buffet breakfast from 7:30 to 11 am daily, with slices off a round of ham, warm Danish pastries, granola, yogurt, fruit, eggs and homefries for $7.95. Look for coupons in the free tourist magazines that knock a dollar off meal prices.

Camellia Yakiniku (☎ 926-0443) on Beach Walk is a popular Honolulu-chain Korean restaurant with plate lunches of barbecued meats, rice, kimchee and Korean-style vegetables for $6 to $8. Lunch is served until 4 pm. At dinner the specialty is spicy meats cooked on grills at your table – dishes are priced around $15. It's open daily from 10 am to 11 pm.

In the same price range is *Chili's*, 2350 Kuhio Ave. This popular Tex-Mex chain restaurant, new to Hawaii, has soft tacos with rice and beans or burgers with fries for around $7, fajitas for $12 and baby back ribs for a couple of dollars more. It's open from 11 am to 11 pm daily.

California Pizza Kitchen, at 1910 Ala Moana Blvd on the corner of Ena Rd, serves up a good thin-crust pizza cooked in a wood-fired brick oven. One-person pizzas range from $6.50 for a traditional tomato and cheese to $9 for more intriguing creations, such as the tandoori chicken pizza which comes with mango chutney. The restaurant also has a variety of pasta dishes, both traditional and exotic, for $6.50 to $10 and good green salads, with generous half-order portions for $4.50. It's open from 11:30 am to 10 pm (to 11 pm on Fridays and Saturdays, from noon to 10 pm on Sundays).

At the same address, *Singha Thai*, 1910 Ala Moana Blvd, is the place to go on the Ewa side of Waikiki for authentic Thai food in a somewhat upmarket setting. For starters, the grilled beef salad and the hot and sour tom yum soup are tasty house specialties. Entrees, such as spicy shrimp & shiitake mushroom stir-fry and various curry and noodle dishes, average $8 at lunch, $12 at dinner. Lunch is served from 11 am to 4 pm weekdays, dinner from 4 to 11 pm nightly. A troupe of Thai dancers performs at dinner Friday to Tuesday.

Duke's Canoe Club (☎ 922-2268) at the Outrigger Waikiki on Kalakaua Ave has a nice waterfront view. The restaurant takes its name from the late Duke Kahanamoku and the outrigger canoe club that was on the beach here in earlier days. The food is a bit mass production but quite reasonable for the money. There's an acceptable breakfast buffet with granola, omelets to order and a good fresh fruit selection from 7 to 10:30 am for $10. At dinner, from 5 to 10 pm, various fresh fish dishes are priced from $17 to $20, or you can get a smaller portion of the fish-of-the-day for $14. There are a few beef dishes in the same price range and all dinners include a full salad bar. There's also a children's menu, with burgers or spaghetti and the salad bar for $5.

The Honolulu branch of the *Hard Rock Cafe* (☎ 955-7383), 1837 Kapiolani Blvd, is just over the Ala Wai Canal beyond Waikiki. It's enlivened with loud rock music and decorated with old surfboards and a 1959 Cadillac 'woody' wagon hanging precariously over the bar. They serve good burgers for around $7 and other all-American food including barbecue ribs and milkshakes, but it's the trendy ambiance as much as the food that draws the crowd. It's open daily from 11:30 am to 11 pm (to 11:30 pm on weekends).

The *Oceanarium Restaurant* in the Pacific Beach Hotel, 2490 Kalakaua Ave, has standard fare with anything but standard views. The dining room wraps around an enormous three-story aquarium filled with colorful tropical fish. At breakfast, hot cakes or oatmeal with papaya are around $5, while a full buffet is $12. Lunch and dinner are served as well. The more expensive *Neptune* (seafood) and *Shogun* (teppanyaki, sushi bar) restaurants in the same hotel also have views of the aquarium.

Keo's (☎ 737-8240), 625 Kapahulu Ave, is widely regarded as Hawaii's top Thai restaurant. It's decorated with sprays of orchids, original Thai paintings and dozens of photos of owner Keo Sananikone posing with celebrity diners, including the likes of Jimmy Carter, Stevie Wonder and Harrison Ford. Prices are surprisingly moderate considering the valet parking and the chic reputation. House specialties are the Evil Jungle Prince entree ($10.95) and spring roll appetizers and green papaya salad, the latter two each $7. The most expensive items on the menu are seafood dishes for $15, so it won't break the bank to dine with the stars here. It's open from 5 pm nightly and is about a mile up Kapahulu Ave from Waikiki.

The *Parc Cafe* (☎ 921-7272) in the Waikiki Parc Hotel has continental-style dining in a pleasant setting. There are buffets for each meal, all attractively prepared with quality food on par with Waikiki's most expensive hotels. The daily breakfast buffet, from 7 to 10 am, includes breakfast meats, eggs, French toast, fresh fruit and pastries for $11.50. The lunch buffet, from 11:30 am to 2 pm, costs $15.50 on Wednesdays when it features Hawaiian food, $18.50 on Sundays when it begins at 11 am and is called brunch, and $13.50 on other days when it's centered around a sandwich bar and taco station. All the lunch buffets include hot main dishes, salads and desserts.

The dinner buffet, from 5:30 to 9 pm, is a more elaborate event that includes catch of the day, roasted duck, leg of lamb, cote de boeuf and various tasty salads for $18.50. Parc Cafe's buffets cost $7.50 to $9.50 for children 12 and under.

The *W C Peacock & Co* (☎ 922-3111) in the Sheraton Moana Surfrider may be the only restaurant in Waikiki where you can look out across the lawn to see nothing but sailboats on the ocean and a few swaying coconut palms. If you get the right table, the only 'modern' structure in view is the 90-year-old Moana hotel, which screens out the high-rises along the beach and helps create an aura of being someplace timeless.

While the setting is a gem, the food is not as notable – but it's still good for Waikiki. The best deal is the $15.95 Sunset Special, from 5:30 to 6:30 pm daily, which consists of cajun-style mahimahi or a generous serving of chicken teriyaki, a small but select salad bar, soup and dessert. It's open for dinner only and meals other than the Sunset Special range from $17 to $35, salad bar included. Be sure to ask for a lanai table.

The *Surf Room* at the Royal Hawaiian Hotel has outdoor beachside dining, although it's rather crowded and the food tends to be pricey and undistinguished. There's an $18.50 breakfast buffet, a $20 lunch buffet and a light lunch menu that's served until 5 pm. The dinner menu changes nightly, with meat and seafood entrees averaging $29 or a fixed-price four-course option for $41.

Places to Eat – top end

The *Ilikai Yacht Club* (☎ 949-3811) in the Ilikai Hotel has open-air dining with a fine view of the yacht harbor. Dinners are served with soup or salad. Prices range from $22 for scallop and shrimp fettucine to $30 for lobster thermidor. A good deal is the Sunset Dinner menu, which includes dessert and is served from 5:30 to 6:30 pm (be seated by 6:15); it features a choice of three dishes, including cajun chicken for $16 and fresh catch of the day for $19. The food, while not outstanding, is nevertheless quite good and when there's a nice sunset it makes a very romantic scene.

For fine Chinese dining, the *Golden Dragon* (☎ 946-5336) in Hilton Hawaiian Village has both excellent food and a good ocean view. While the varied menu has some expensive specialties there are many dishes, including ginger beef, roast duck and a deliciously crispy lemon chicken,

which are reasonably priced from $12 to $14. It's open for dinner only, from 6 to 10 pm.

Michel's at the Colony Surf Hotel (☎ 923-6552), 2895 Kalakaua Ave, has been riding for years on its reputation as Oahu's most romantic restaurant. While the accolades are a bit overstated, it's certainly nice – fine dining with crystal, china and chandeliers, all fronting Sans Souci Beach. The food is largely traditional French fare and prices are steep for the offerings. One specialty is opakapaka, which is ordered a la carte for $38 at dinner, $22 at lunch. Breakfast is a far more affordable affair although the food itself is not particularly special. You can get coffee and croissants for $5 or Belgian waffles for double that. It's open daily for breakfast from 7 to 10 am, lunch from 11:30 am to 2 pm and dinner from 5:30 to 10 pm. When you make reservations be sure to ask for a window table, as it's a different experience without it.

La Mer (☎ 923-2311) in the Halekulani Hotel has a top reputation for both its creative French menu with Hawaiian influences and for its fine 2nd-floor ocean view. The dining is formal and men are required to wear jackets. There are full fixed-price meals nightly from $68. Otherwise, a la carte entrees range from $29 for lime-crusted swordfish or Waimanalo rabbit to $41 for lobster marmite. It's open nightly from 6 to 10 pm.

The *Maile Restaurant* (☎ 734-2211), at the exclusive Kahala Hilton in Kahala, is considered by many to be the best restaurant in Oahu for traditional American dishes, such as rack of lamb. The Maile sees Hawaii's greatest concentration of dignitaries and movie stars amongst its diners, although likewise prices are fit for a king! Roast duckling with Grand Marnier sauce, lychees, bananas and wild rice is a specialty and costs $33. There's a complete dinner with appetizer, salad, main course, soufflé and coffee for $64. Jackets are required, except on Sundays; however, you can borrow one at the door. It's open from 6:30 pm nightly.

to 11 am, Hawaiian guitar soloists from 2 to 4:30 pm and steel-guitar music with hula dancing from 5 to 8 pm.

Of the splashy musical revues with hula dancers, the Brothers Cazimero are the best. They perform Tuesday to Saturday at the *Royal Hawaiian Hotel* (☎ 931-7194) with dinner seating from 6:30 pm for $57 or cocktail seating from 8 pm for $32, including two drinks. There's an extra cocktail show at 10:30 pm on Fridays and Saturdays for $22.50. Or, cheaper still, have a drink at the bar and listen to them from across the lawn.

An older, genteel crowd gathers daily at the Halekulani's open-air *House Without a Key* restaurant for sunset cocktails and Hawaiian music.

The Royal Hawaiian (☎ 923-7311) has a $63 beachside luau on Mondays, beginning with an open bar at 6 pm and continuing with a buffet-style dinner and a Polynesian show. While the setting is not as interesting, there's a second and cheaper ($35) luau, Chuck Machado's Luau (☎ 836-0249), at the Waikiki Beachcomber Hotel, 2300 Kalakaua Ave, on Tuesdays, Thursdays and Saturdays.

Free hula shows are listed below under Free Entertainment.

Movie Theaters Movie theaters in Waikiki include the Waikiki Twins (☎ 971-5033), 333 Seaside Ave, near Kalakaua Ave; Waikiki 3 (☎ 971-5133), 2284 Kalakaua Ave, near Seaside; and Kuhio Twins (☎ 973-5433), 2095 Kuhio Ave. All show first-run movies.

The *IMAX Theatre Waikiki* (☎ 923-4629), 325 Seaside Ave, shows a 40-minute movie of Hawaii vistas throughout the day on a 70-foot-wide screen. It costs $7.50 for adults and $5 for children ages three to 11.

Entertainment

Waikiki has a varied entertainment scene. For updated schedule information, check the free tourist magazines and the daily newspapers.

Concerts The *Waikiki Shell* in Kapiolani Park hosts both classical and contemporary music concerts. For current schedule information, call the Blaisdell Center box office (☎ 521-2911).

Hawaiiana Waikiki has lots of Hawaiian-style entertainment, from Polynesian shows with beating drums and hula dancers to mellow duos playing ukulele or slack-key guitar.

The beachside courtyard at *Duke's Canoe Club* (☎ 922-2268) at the Outrigger Waikiki on Kalakaua Ave has become Waikiki's most popular venue for contemporary Hawaiian music. There's entertainment from 4 to 6 pm and 10 pm to midnight daily, with the biggest names – including the likes of Brother Noland, Henry Kapono and the Pahinui Brothers – appearing on weekend afternoons.

At the Sheraton Moana Surfrider's *Banyan Veranda*, you can listen to music beneath the same old banyan tree where 'Hawaii Calls' broadcast its nationwide radio show for four decades beginning in 1935. Typically there's harp music from 7

Danceclubs In addition to the following listings, a number of the larger Waikiki hotels have nightclubs, some of which double as danceclubs.

Wave Waikiki (☎ 941-0424), 1877 Kalakaua Ave, is one of Waikiki's hottest clubs with live bands playing alternative music Tuesday to Sunday and DJs between sets and on Mondays. Hours are 9 pm to 4 am nightly, the minimum age is 21 and there's no dress code. There's no cover charge before 10 pm, a $5 cover after.

The nearby *Pink Cadillac* (☎ 942-5282), 478 Ena Rd, is another popular dance spot, with a DJ playing dance music. It pulls in the early-20s crowd with music videos and dance parties, and is open from 8 pm to 2 am nightly. The cover charge is usually $5 for ages 21 and older and $10 for ages 18 to 20.

At *Moose McGillycuddy's* (☎ 923-0751), 310 Lewers St, live bands play rock 'n roll from 9 pm to 1:30 am nightly. There's a $3 cover charge on weekends (free on weekdays) and you have to be 21 to get in.

Scruples (☎ 923-9530), 2310 Kuhio Ave, is a top-40 danceclub open from 8 pm to 4 am nightly. The cover charge is $5 plus a two-drink minimum, $15 for ages 18 to 20.

Gay Scene The gay scene is centered around the Kuhio district, along Kuhio Ave from Kalaimoku to Kaiolu St.

Hula's Bar & Lei Stand (☎ 923-0669), 2103 Kuhio Ave, an open-air video dance club with tables under a big banyan tree, is a favorite place to meet, dance and have a few drinks. It's open from 10 am to 2 am daily.

Hamburger Mary's, 2109 Kuhio Ave, in the restaurant of the same name, is Honolulu's most popular gay bar. It's open from 11 am to 2 am daily.

There are numerous other gay hangouts, although many of them come and go. To find out about the most happening spots, pick up the magazine *Island Lifestyle* or the newspaper *The Gay Community News*, free at Hula's or other gay-oriented businesses.

Comedy The *Honolulu Comedy Club* (☎ WACKY-98), at the Ilikai Hotel, has stand-up comedians Tuesday to Sunday evenings. The 8 pm Sunday show is for nonsmokers. The cost is $12 plus a two-drink minimum.

Tea Ceremony The *Urasenke Foundation of Hawaii*, 245 Saratoga Rd, has tea-ceremony demonstrations on Wednesdays and Fridays, bringing a rare bit of serenity to busy Saratoga Rd. Students dressed in kimonos perform the ceremony on tatami mats in a formal tea-room.

It costs $2 to be served green tea and sweets, but you can watch the ceremony for free. Each demonstration lasts 30 to 45 minutes. The first sitting is at 10 am, the last at 11:30 am. For reservations call 923-3059. Because guests leave their shoes at the door, they are asked to wear socks. The building is across the street and makai from Waikiki's post office.

Free Entertainment A pleasant way to pass the evening is to stroll along Waikiki Beach and sample the Hawaiian shows that take place at the beachfront hotels. You can wander past the Sheraton Moana Surfrider where musicians play at the Banyan Veranda, watch bands performing beachside at Duke's Canoe Club, catch a glimpse of the Brothers Cazimero at the Royal Hawaiian Hotel, see the poolside performers at the Sheraton Waikiki and so on down the line.

Hilton Hawaiian Village (☎ 949-4321) shoots off fireworks from the beach at 8 pm on Fridays, preceded at 6:30 pm by a torch-lighting ceremony and a 'mini-Polynesian revue' at the hotel pool. The free show also takes place on Saturday minus the fireworks.

Na Mea Hula O Kahikinaokalalani, a hula troupe directed by Karla Akiona, performs a free hula show from 5 to 7 pm on Fridays on the Diamond Head Lawn of the Sheraton Waikiki.

There's also a good outdoor hula show at Kuhio Beach Park late in the afternoon Friday to Sunday.

Free hula shows are held at 7 and 8 pm nightly near the top of the escalator on the 2nd floor of the *Kuhio Mall*. Dancers from a local hula troupe take turns performing on different nights.

The *Royal Hawaiian Shopping Center* (☎ 922-0588) offers a variety of free events. A free Polynesian 'mini-show' is held at the center's Fountain Courtyard from 6:30 to 8 pm on Mondays, Wednesdays and Fridays and from 10:30 am to noon on Saturdays. On Mondays, Wednesdays and Fridays, hula lessons are given at 10 am and lei-making lessons at 11 am. On Tuesdays and Thursdays, coconut-frond weaving and Hawaiian quilting lessons are held at 9:30 am, ukulele lessons at 10 am. The shopping center's brochure shows the location of each activity.

The Royal Hawaiian Band performs from 2 to 3:15 pm most Sundays, with the exception of August, at the Kapiolani Park Bandstand. It's a quintessential Hawaiian scene that caps off with the audience joining hands and singing Queen Liliuokalani's *Aloha Oe* in Hawaiian.

At 11 am daily the *Sheraton Moana Surfrider* offers free 45-minute historical tours of the old Moana Hotel, which is on the National Register of Historic Places. Tours leave from the concierge desk and are open to the public; reservations are not necessary. You can also stroll through on your own. The 2nd floor has a display of memorabilia from the early hotel days, with scripts from 'Hawaii Calls', woolen bathing suits, period photographs and a short video.

Other free things, including the Kodak Hula Show, the Damien Museum, the Oceanarium and the US Army Museum, are detailed under Waikiki sights.

Things to Buy

Waikiki has no shortage of souvenir stalls, swimsuit and T-shirt shops, quick-stop convenience marts or fancy boutiques.

The prolific ABC discount marts (33 in Waikiki at last count) are often the cheapest places to buy more mundane items, such as macadamia nuts, beach mats, sunblock and other vacation necessities.

International Market Place, in the center of Waikiki, is a collection of ticky-tacky shops and stalls set beneath a sprawling banyan tree. Although few of the stalls carry high-quality goods, if you're looking for inexpensive jewelry or T-shirts it's

worth a stroll. The market place also has a Tower Records shop with an extensive Hawaiian music section and a set-up that allows you to listen to the CDs before you buy.

The Royal Hawaiian Shopping Center, Waikiki's biggest shopping center, spans three blocks along Kalakaua Ave. It has a few dozen clothing and jewelry shops as well as numerous gift shops, the most interesting of which is The Little Hawaiian Craft Shop with a range of Hawaii-made crafts.

Liberty House, a somewhat upmarket department store with good quality clothing, is at the Waikiki Beachcomber Hotel on Kalakaua Ave.

Still, for the best deals on most items, you'll need to leave Waikiki. Try the Ala Moana Center, the Aloha Flea Market or one of the frequent craft shows that pop up around the city.

Honolulu

In 1793 the English frigate *Butterworth* became the first foreign ship to sail into what is now called Honolulu Harbor. Its captain, William Brown, named the harbor Fair Haven. Ships that followed called it Brown's Harbor. But over time the name Honolulu, which means 'Sheltered Bay', came to be used for both the harbor and the seaside district that the Hawaiians had called Kou.

As more and more foreign ships found their way to Honolulu a harborside village of thatched houses sprouted up and the town became Hawaii's center of trade.

In 1809 Kamehameha I moved his royal court to Honolulu from Waikiki. On what today is the southern end of Bethel St, Kamehameha set up residence to keep an eye on all the trade that moved in and out of the harbor. From there sandalwood was shipped to Canton in exchange for weapons and luxury goods which Kamehameha loaded into his harborside warehouses.

In the 1820s whaling ships began pulling

into Honolulu for supplies, liquor and women. At the same time, Christian missionaries began coming ashore to save souls. The Protestant mission and Episcopal and Catholic churches all established their Hawaiian headquarters in downtown Honolulu.

Both groups have left their mark. Downtown are the offices of the 'Big Five' corporations that were in control of most of Hawaii's commerce by the turn of the century. It's no coincidence that their lists of corporate board members – Alexander, Baldwin, Cooke and Dole – read like a roster from the first mission ships.

The whalers left a different legacy. Hotel St, a line of bars and strip joints a few blocks from the harbor, remains the city's red-light district.

By the early 1900s Honolulu had expanded into a sprawling cosmopolitan city, but the downtown area up from the harbor remains the heart of Honolulu.

Honolulu Today

Honolulu is the only major city in Hawaii. It has a population of 385,000 and is the state's center of business, culture and politics. It's been the capital of Hawaii since 1845. Honolulu International Airport and Honolulu Harbor are Hawaii's busiest ports.

Honolulu is home to people from throughout the Pacific. It's a city of minorities, with no ethnic majority.

Honolulu's ethnic diversity can be seen on almost every corner – the sushi shop next door to the Vietnamese bakery, the Catholic church around the block from the Chinese Buddhist temple, and the rainbow of school children waiting for the bus.

The main federal, state and county offices and the state's highest concentration of historic buildings are found in downtown Honolulu.

DOWNTOWN HONOLULU

Downtown Honolulu is a hodgepodge of past and present, with both sleek high-rises and stately Victorian-era buildings. There's a royal palace, a modernistic state capitol, a coral-block New England missionary church and a Spanish-style city hall all within sight of one another.

The downtown area is intriguing to explore. You can take in a Friday noon band concert on the palace lawn, lounge in the open-air courtyard of Hawaii's central library, or catch a view of the city from the top of the Aloha Tower.

Information

On weekdays downtown Honolulu has a lot of traffic congestion, which, combined with its many one-way streets and confusing intersections, can make driving a bit overwhelming for visitors.

During the week the best idea is simply to take the bus. Buses No 2, 19 and 20 run between downtown and Waikiki. On weekends the traffic is light and parking isn't difficult.

Lots of city bus routes converge downtown – so many that Hotel St, which begins downtown and crosses Chinatown, is restricted to bus traffic only.

Post The downtown branch of the Honolulu post office is on the Richards St side of the Old Federal Building. It's open from 8 am to 4:30 pm weekdays except on Wednesdays when it's open until 6 pm.

Airline Offices A number of airlines have ticket offices in the downtown Honolulu area. Within a two-minute walk of the intersection of Bishop and Hotel Sts, you'll find United Airlines, American Airlines, Delta Air Lines, Hawaiian Airlines and Aloha Airlines.

Parking There's metered parking along both sides of Punchbowl St and on Halekauwila St opposite the federal building. There are also a limited number of metered spaces in the basement of the state office building on the corner of Beretania and Punchbowl Sts.

Walking Tours

Downtown Honolulu is a wonderful area to stroll and its most handsome buildings are

Downtown Honolulu

To Honolulu Academy of Arts

War Memorial

Washington Place

St Andrew's Cathedral

State Office Building

Honolulu Municipal Building

Mission Houses Museum

Kawaiahao Church

Honolulu Hale (City Hall)

State Capitol

No 1 Capitol District

Iolani Barracks

Iolani Palace

Hawaii State Library

Queen Liliuokalani Statue

Pedestrian Walkway

Territorial Building

Kamehameha Statue

Aliiolani Hale

Cathedral of Our Lady of Peace

Hawaii Pacific University

Sierra Club

Honolulu Book Shops

KFC/Jack in the Box

Panda Kitchen

McDonald's

Executive Centre Hotel

YWCA

Bandstand

Hawaiian Electric Co Building

Federal Building

Ba Le Sandwich Shop

Pauahi St

Ba Le Sandwich Shop

Pizza Hut/ Taco Bell

Longs Drugs

Woolworth

Hawaii Theatre

S Hotel St

Fort St Pedestrian Mall

King St

Prince Kuhio Federal Building

Alexander & Baldwin Building

C Brewer Building

Dillingham Building

Grosvenor Center

Seaman's Home

Honolulu Publishing

Old Honolulu Police Station

Merchant St

Queen St

CHINATOWN

Nuuanu Ave

(Nimitz Hwy)

Ala Moana Blvd

Bishop St

Alakea St

Richards St

Halekauwila St

Fort St

Aloha Tower

Falls of Clyde

Hawaii Maritime Center

Pier 8

Pier 6

(92)

Beretania St

Miller St

Kawaiahao St

Punchbowl St

Richards St

Mililani St

Alapai St

0   100   200 m
0   100   200 yards

all within walking distance. A good starting place for a self-guided walking tour is Iolani Palace.

For those who want to delve deeper into local lore, Kapiolani Community College leads downtown walking tours with varied historical themes – from ghosts of old Honolulu to the crime beat of the 1920s. Schedules are available from the Office of Community Services (☎ 734-9245), Kapiolani Community College, 4403 Diamond Head Rd, Honolulu, HI 96816. Advance registration is required. The cost is $5 for adults and $2 for children ages five to 12.

Iolani Palace

Iolani Palace is the only royal palace in the USA. It was the official residence of King Kalakaua and Queen Kapiolani from 1882 to 1891 and of Queen Liliuokalani, Kalakaua's sister and successor, for two years after that.

Following the overthrow of the Hawaiian kingdom in 1893, the palace became the capitol – first for the republic, then for the territory and later for the state of Hawaii.

It wasn't until 1969 that the current state capitol was built and the legislators moved out of their cramped quarters. The Senate had been meeting in the palace dining room and the House of Representatives in the throne room. By the time they left, the palace was in shambles, the grand koa staircase termite-ridden and the Douglas-fir floors pitted and gouged.

After extensive renovations topping $7 million, the palace was largely restored to its former glory and opened as a museum in 1978. Visitors must wear booties over their shoes to protect the highly polished wooden floors.

Iolani Palace was modern for its day. Every bedroom had its own full bath with hot and cold water running into copper-lined tubs, a flushing toilet and a bidet. According to the tour guides, electric lights replaced the palace gas lamps a full four years before the White House in Washington got electricity.

The throne room, decorated in red and gold, features the original thrones of the king and queen, and a kapu stick made of the long, spiral ivory tusk of a narwhal. In addition to celebrations full of pomp and pageantry, it was in the throne room that King Kalakaua danced his favorite Western dances – the polka, the waltz and the Virginia reel – into the wee hours of the morning.

Not all the events that took place there were joyous. Two years after she was dethroned, Queen Liliuokalani was brought back to the palace and tried for treason in the throne room. In a move calculated to humiliate the Hawaiian people she spent nine months as a prisoner in Iolani Palace, her former home.

Guided tours leave every 15 minutes from 9 am to 2:15 pm Wednesday to Saturday and are well worth the admission of $4 for adults, $1 for children ages five to 12. Children under five are not admitted. The tours last 45 minutes. Sometimes you can join up on the spot, but it's advisable to make advance reservations by phoning 522-0832. The palace is wheelchair-accessible.

Palace Grounds Before Iolani Palace was built there was a simpler house on these grounds that King Kamehameha III used when he moved the capital from Lahaina to Honolulu in 1845. In ancient times it was the site of a heiau.

The palace ticket window and gift shop are in the former **barracks** of the Royal Household Guards. The barracks look oddly like the uppermost layer of a medieval fort that's been sliced off and plopped on the ground.

The **domed pavilion** on the grounds was originally built for the coronation of King Kalakaua in 1883 and is still used for the inauguration of governors and for concerts by the Royal Hawaiian Band.

The **grassy mound** surrounded by a wrought iron fence was the site of a royal tomb until 1865 when the remains of King Kamehameha II and Queen Kamamalu (who both died of measles in England in 1824) were moved to the Royal Mausoleum in Nuuanu.

The huge **banyan tree** between the palace and the state capitol is thought to have been planted by Queen Kapiolani.

Hawaii State Library

The central branch of the state-wide library system (☎ 586-3500) is on the corner of King and Punchbowl Sts. Located in a beautifully restored historic building, its collection of over half a million titles is the state's best and includes comprehensive Hawaii and Pacific sections. The library's open-air garden courtyard is a wonderful place to sit and read.

It's open from 9 am to 5 pm on Mondays, Wednesdays, Fridays and Saturdays and from 9 am to 8 pm on Tuesdays and Thursdays.

The **Hawaii State Archives** next door holds official government documents and an extensive photo collection. It's open to the public for research.

Queen Liliuokalani Statue

The statue of Hawaii's last queen stands between the capitol and Iolani Palace. It faces Washington Place, Liliuokalani's home and place of exile for more than 20 years. The statue is holding the Hawaii constitution that Liliuokalani wrote in 1893, in fear of which US businessmen overthrew her; *Aloha Oe*, a popular hymn which she composed; and *Kumulipo*, the Hawaiian chant of creation.

State Capitol

Hawaii's state capitol is not your standard gold dome. Constructed in the late 1960s, it was a grandiose attempt at a 'theme' design.

Its two central legislative chambers are cone-shaped to represent volcanoes; the rotunda is open-air to let gentle trade winds blow through; the supporting columns represent palm trees; and the whole structure is encircled by a large pool symbolizing the ocean surrounding Hawaii.

Unfortunately, the building not only symbolizes the elements but has been quite effective in drawing them in. The pool draws brackish water; rain pouring into the rotunda has necessitated the sealing of many of the skylights; and Tadashi Sato's 'Aquarius' floor mosaic, meant to show the changing colors and patterns of Hawaii's seas, got so weathered it had to be reconstructed.

After two decades of trying unsuccessfully to deal with all the problems on a piecemeal basis, the state has closed the facility and is in the midst of a thorough renovation.

Until the work is completed, which is expected to be in late 1995, visitors will have to be content viewing the building from the outside.

In front of the capitol is a **statue of Father Damien**, the Belgian priest who volunteered to work amongst the lepers of Molokai and died of the disease 16 years later, at age 49. The stylized sculpture was created by Venezuelan artist Marisol Escubar.

War Memorial

The war memorial is a sculptured eternal torch dedicated to soldiers who died in WW II. It sits between two underground garage entrances on Beretania St, directly opposite the state capitol.

Washington Place

Washington Place, the governor's official residence, is a large colonial-style building, with stately trees, built in 1846 by US sea captain John Dominis. The captain's son John married the Hawaiian princess who later became Queen Liliuokalani. After the queen was dethroned she lived at Washington Place in exile until her death in 1917.

A plaque near the sidewalk on the left side of Washington Place is inscribed with the words to *Aloha Oe*.

The large tree in front of the house on the right side of the walkway is a pili nut tree, recognizable by the buttress-like roots extending from the base of its trunk. In Southeast Asia the nuts of these trees are used to produce oil.

St Andrew's Cathedral

King Kamehameha IV was attracted by the

royal trappings of the Church of England and decided to build his own cathedral in the capital. He and his consort Queen Emma founded the Anglican Church of Hawaii in 1858.

The cathedral's cornerstone was finally laid in 1867 by King Kamehameha V. Kamehameha IV had died four years earlier on St Andrew's Day – hence the church's name.

St Andrew's is on the corner of Alakea and Beretania Sts. The church is of French Gothic architecture, shipped in pieces from England. Its most striking feature is the impressive window of hand-blown stained glass that forms the western facade and reaches from the floor to the eaves. In the right section of the glass you can see the Reverend Thomas Staley, the first bishop sent to Hawaii by Queen Victoria, alongside Kamehameha IV and Queen Emma.

A thrift shop in the church grounds is open from 9:30 am to 4 pm on Mondays, Wednesdays and Fridays and from 9 am to 1 pm on Saturdays. If you're lucky you might find a $5 aloha shirt or muu-muu in your size. Used paperbacks are also a bargain and it appears Hawaii's Episcopalians have fairly good taste in literature, so you might spot something worth reading.

No 1 Capitol District

The elegant five-story building on Richards St opposite the state capitol temporarily houses the offices of the state legislature.

The building has something of the appearance of a Spanish mission, including courtyards and ceramic tile walls and floors. Built in 1928, it served as the YMCA Armed Services building for more than five decades.

The site is owned by the Hemmeter Corporation, which after completing a multi-million-dollar renovation used the building briefly as their corporate headquarters. Chris Hemmeter, incidentally, was the developer behind many of the extravagant 'fantasy hotels' that were constructed on the Neighbor Islands in the 1980s.

Fort Street Mall

Fort Street is a pedestrian shopping mall lined with benches and an ever-growing number of high-rise buildings. It's not interesting in itself, but if you're downtown it's a reasonable place to eat – not as good as Chinatown, but a few blocks closer. Occasionally classical music flutists, folk guitarists or other street musicians perform along the mall, although these days most of the tunes are played by jackhammers.

Cathedral of Our Lady of Peace

The oldest Catholic cathedral in the USA is the Cathedral of Our Lady of Peace, at the Beretania St end of Fort St Mall. Built of coral blocks in 1843, it's older and more ornate than St Andrew's Cathedral.

Father Damien, who later served Molokai's leprosy colony, was ordained at the cathedral in 1864.

Kawaiahao Church

Aliiolani Hale

Aliiolani Hale ('House of Heavenly Kings') was the first major government building built by the Hawaiian monarchy. It has housed the Supreme Court since its construction in 1874 and in earlier times was also home to the legislature. The building has a distinctive clock tower and was originally designed by Australian architect Thomas Rowe to be a royal palace, although it never was used as such.

It was on the steps of Aliiolani Hale, in January 1893, that Sanford Dole proclaimed the establishment of a provisional government and the overthrow of the monarchy.

Kamehameha Statue

The statue of Kamehameha the Great stands in front of Aliiolani Hale, opposite Iolani Palace. It was cast by Thomas Gould in 1880. This one is actually a recast, as the first statue was lost at sea near the Falkland Islands. The original statue, recovered after this second version was dedicated, now stands in Kohala, the Big Island birthplace of Kamehameha.

On June 11, a state holiday honoring Kamehameha, the statue is ceremoniously draped with layer upon layer of 12-foot leis.

Honolulu Hale

City Hall, also known as Honolulu Hale, is largely of Spanish mission design with a tiled roof, decorative balconies, arches and pillars. Built in 1927, it bears the initials of C W Dickey, Honolulu's most famous architect of the day. The open-air courtyard in the center of the building is sometimes used for concerts and art exhibits.

Kawaiahao Church

Oahu's oldest church, on the corner of Punchbowl and King Sts, was built on the site where the first missionaries constructed a grass thatch church shortly after their arrival in 1820. The original was an impressive structure that measured 54 by 22 feet and seated 300 people on lauhala mats.

Still, thatch wasn't quite what the missionaries had in mind so they designed a more typically New England-style Congregational church with simple Gothic influences.

Built between 1838 and 1842, the church is made of 14,000 giant coral slabs, many weighing more than 1000 pounds. Hawaiian divers chiseled the huge blocks of coral out of Honolulu's underwater reef.

The clock tower was donated by Kamehameha III and the clock, built in Boston and installed in 1850, still keeps accurate time.

Inside the church is breezy and cool. The rear seats, marked by *kahili* (feather) staffs and velvet padding, were for royalty and are still reserved for descendants of royalty today. The church is open to visitors from 8 am to 4 pm daily.

The **tomb of King Lunalilo**, the successor to Kamehameha V, is in the church grounds at the main entrance. Lunalilo ruled for only one year before his death in 1874 at the age of 39.

Around the back is a **cemetery** where many of the early missionaries are buried, including members of the Castle and Cooke families.

Mission Houses Museum

Three of the original buildings of the Sandwich Islands Mission headquarters still stand: the Frame House (built in 1821), the Chamberlain House (1831) and the Printing Office (1841).

Together they're open to the public as the Mission Houses Museum (☎ 531-0481), 553 S King St. The houses are authentically furnished with handmade quilts on the beds, settees in the parlor and iron pots in the big stone fireplaces.

The coral-block Chamberlain House was the early mission storeroom, a necessity as Honolulu had few shops in those days. Upstairs are hoop barrels, wooden crates packed with dishes and a big desk with pigeon-hole dividers and the quill pen Levi Chamberlain used to work on accounts. Levi was the person appointed by the mission to buy, store and dole out supplies to

Tomb of King Lunalilo

the missionary families who each had an allowance. Account books show that in the late 1800s, 25c would buy either one gallon of oil, one pen knife or two slates.

The first missionaries packed more than their bags when they left Boston – they actually brought a pre-fabricated wooden house around the Horn with them! Designed to withstand cold New England winter winds, the small windows instead block out Honolulu's cooling trade winds, keeping the two-story house hot and stuffy. The Frame House, as it's now called, is the oldest wooden structure in Hawaii.

The Printing Office housed the lead-type press that was used to print the Bible in the Hawaiian language.

The Mission Houses Museum is open from 9 am to 4 pm Tuesday to Saturday and from noon to 4 pm on Sundays. Admission is $5 for adults and $1 for children (under age six free). While you can explore the visitor center and the Chamberlain House on your own, the Printing Office and Frame House can only be seen with a guide. The

tours are given at 9:30, 10:30 and 11:30 am and at 1, 2 and 3 pm.

Other Historic Buildings

The **Hawaiian Electric Company's** four-story administration building, on the corner of Richards and King Sts, is of Spanish colonial architecture. It has an arched entranceway and ornate period lamps hanging from hand-painted ceilings. The entrance leads into the customer service department so it's fine to walk in and take a look.

Diagonally opposite, on Merchant St, is the **Old Federal Building**, another interesting edifice with Spanish colonial features. Completed in 1922, it holds a post office and customs house.

Also noteworthy is the three-story **YWCA** at 1040 Richards St. Built in 1927, it's a work of Julia Morgan, the renowned architect who designed William Randolph Hearst's San Simeon estate in California.

The **Old Honolulu Police Station** (1931), on the corner of Bethel and Merchant Sts, has beautiful interior ceramic tile work in earthen tones on its counters and walls. It now houses the state departments of Housing & Finance. Another building worth a look is the old Honolulu Publishing building across the street.

The four-story **Alexander & Baldwin building** on the corner of Bishop and Queen Sts was built in 1929. The columns at the Bishop St entrance are carved with tropical fruit and the Chinese characters for prosperity and long life. Inside the portico are interesting ceramic tile murals of Hawaiian fish.

Samuel Alexander and Henry Baldwin, both sons of missionaries, vaulted to prominence in the sugar industry and created one of Hawaii's 'Big Five' controlling corporations. The other four – Theo Davies, Castle & Cooke, Amfac and C Brewer – all have their headquarters within a few blocks of here.

The four-story 60-year-old **Dillingham Building** on the corner of Bishop and Queen Sts is of Italian Renaissance-style architecture with arches, marble walls, elaborate elevator doors and an arty brick floor. It's a study in contrasts, mirrored in the reflective glass of the adjacent 30-story Grosvenor Center.

Hawaii Theatre

The neo-classical Hawaii Theatre, 1130 Bethel St, with its Art Deco neon signs, first opened in 1922 with silent films playing to the tune of a pipe organ. It ran continuous shows during the war but the development of mall cinemas in the 1970s was its undoing.

After closing in 1984, the theater's future looked dim, even although it was on the Register of Historic Buildings. Theater buffs came to the rescue forming a non-profit group and purchasing the property from the Bishop Estate. They raised enough money to undertake a $10 million restoration, which is nearing completion.

Honolulu Academy of Arts

The Honolulu Academy of Arts (☎ 532-8701 for 24-hour recorded information), 900 S Beretania St, is an exceptional museum, with permanent Asian, European, American and Pacific art collections from ancient times to the present.

Just inside the door and to the right is a room with works by Matisse, Cézanne, Gauguin, Van Gogh and Picasso. There is a welcoming place to sit in the middle of the room to take it all in.

The museum is open and airy and has numerous small galleries around six garden courtyards. The Spanish Court has benches and a small fountain surrounded by Greek and Roman sculpture and Egyptian reliefs dating back to 2500 BC.

There are sculptures and miniatures from India, jades and bronzes from ancient China, Madonna and Child oils from 14th-century Italy and quality changing exhibits.

The Hawaiian section is small but choice, with feather leis, tapa beaters, poi pounders and koa calabashes. The adjacent collection from Papua New Guinea, Micronesia and the South Pacific includes ancestor figures, war clubs and masks.

The museum is open from 10 am to 4:30 pm Tuesday to Saturday and pm on Sundays. Admission is $2 for senior citizens and stud children under 12. Docent-led gallery tours are given at 11 am Tuesday to Saturday and at 1 pm on Sundays; there's no extra charge and reservations aren't necessary.

The museum is off the tourist track and seldom crowded. Bus No 2 from Waikiki stops out front; there's metered parking behind the museum.

The on-site **Academy Theatre** (☎ 532-8768) presents more than 400 programs each year, including foreign and independent films, classical music concerts and art lectures. Movies cost $4, while tickets to musical performances vary but are reasonably priced. An events calendar is available at the museum. There's also a gift shop, library and lunch cafe (by reservation).

Aloha Tower

Built in 1926, the 10-story Aloha Tower is a Honolulu landmark and for years was the city's tallest building. Back in the days when all tourists arrived by ship, the four-sided clock tower greeted incoming passengers with the word 'Aloha'. Cruise ships still pull in beneath the tower, which houses the US Customs office.

Aloha Tower is at Pier 9, off Ala Moana Blvd at the harbor end of Fort St. The tower's top-floor observation deck offers a sweeping view of Honolulu's big commercial harbor and downtown area. It's not the most scenic view of the city, but it's interesting nonetheless.

The tower reopened in late 1994 after a restoration project that included the construction of a shopping plaza on the surrounding grounds. The observation deck is open from 8 am to 9 pm daily and admission is free.

Hawaii Maritime Center

The Hawaii Maritime Center is at Honolulu Harbor's Pier 7 on the Diamond Head side of the Aloha Tower. The center has a maritime museum; the *Falls of Clyde*, said to be the world's last four-masted four-rigged ship; and the berth for the double-hulled sailing canoe *Hokulea*.

The 60-foot *Hokulea* has made a number of voyages from Hawaii to the South Pacific, retracing the routes of the early Polynesian seafarers using traditional means of navigation, including wave patterns and the stars. In its most recent voyage, which lasted for two years, it sailed from Hawaii to Tahiti, the Cook Islands, New Zealand, Tonga and Samoa and from the Tuamotus back to Hawaii. When in port it's docked beside the museum, although it's presently undergoing preparations for a journey to Rarotonga.

Permanently on display, the 266-foot iron-hulled *Falls of Clyde* was built in Glasgow, Scotland in 1878. In 1899 Matson Navigation bought the ship and added a deck house, and the *Falls* began carrying sugar and passengers between Hilo and San Francisco. It was later converted into an oil tanker and eventually stripped down to a barge.

After being abandoned in Ketchikan, Alaska, where it had been relegated to the function of a floating oil storage tank, the *Falls* was towed to Seattle, WA. A group of Hawaiians raised funds to rescue the ship in 1963, just before it was scheduled to be sunk to create a breakwater off Vancouver. With the aid of the Bishop Museum, the *Falls* was eventually brought to Honolulu and restored. Visitors can stroll the deck and walk down into the cargo holds.

The main museum has an interesting mishmash of maritime displays and artifacts, including a good whaling-era section and model replicas of ships. There's a reproduction of a Matson liner stateroom and interesting old photos of Waikiki in the days when just the Royal Hawaiian and the Moana hotels shared the horizon with Diamond Head. Both hotels belonged to Matson, who spearheaded tourism in Hawaii and ironically sold out to the Sheraton in 1959 just before the jet age and statehood launched sleepy tourism into a booming industry.

To get there, take bus No 19 or 20 from Waikiki. By car, it's off Ala Moana Blvd,

about a mile west of Ward Warehouse. There's free parking for museum visitors on Pier 6, just east of the museum.

The museum is open from 9 am to 5 pm daily and admission, which includes boarding the *Falls*, is $7 for adults, $4 for children ages six to 17 and free for kids under six.

Sand Island State Park

Sand Island is a 500-acre island on the western side of Honolulu Harbor. About a third of the island has been set aside as a state park.

The park is heavily used by locals who camp, fish and picnic there on weekends, but it has little appeal to the casual visitor and you won't find many tourists there.

Sand Island is not reached from the downtown area, but by an access road a few miles west, off the Nimitz Hwy. Sand Island Access Rd leads 2½ miles down to the park through an industrial area with a waste-water treatment plant, oil tanks, scrap metal yards and the like. The airport is directly across the lagoon and Sand Island is on the flight path.

The park has showers, restrooms and a white sand beach which, while cleaner than it's been in past years, still has sections posted as closed due to 'sharp metal objects' on the beach.

CHINATOWN

A walk through Chinatown is like a journey to Asia. Although it's predominantly Chinese, it has Vietnamese, Thai and Filipino influences as well.

Chinatown is busy and colorful. It has a lively market that could be right off a back street in Hong Kong, fire-breathing dragons curl up the red pillars outside the Bank of Hawaii, and good, cheap ethnic restaurants abound. You can get tattooed, consult with a herbalist, munch on moon cakes or slurp a steaming bowl of Vietnamese soup. There are temples, shrines, noodle factories, antique shops and art galleries to explore.

Chinatown is undergoing some urban renewal, particularly on its downtown edge. The spiffed-up image includes a new 'entranceway' to Chinatown, at the intersection of S Hotel and Bethel Sts, marked by a small park, two marble lions and a new high-rise complex. However, despite creeping gentrification, Chinatown still has its seamier side. Just a block away on S Hotel St you'll find darkened doorways advertising 'video peeps' for 25c and topless nightspots with names like Risque Theatre and Club Hubba Hubba.

Places to eat in Chinatown are listed near the end of the Honolulu section.

History

Chinese immigrants who had worked off their sugar cane plantation contracts began settling in Chinatown and opening up small businesses around 1860.

In December 1899 the bubonic plague broke out in the area. The 7000 Chinese, Hawaiians and Japanese who made the crowded neighborhood their home were cordoned off and forbidden to leave.

As more plague cases arose, the Board of Health decided to conduct controlled burns of infected homes. On January 20, 1900, the fire brigade set fire to a building on the corner of Beretania St and Nuuanu Ave. The wind suddenly picked up and the fire spread out of control, racing towards the

	PLACES TO EAT	12	Oahu Market
4	Doong Kong Lau	15	Cindy's Lei Shop
6	Buddhist Vegetarian Restaurant	16	Ramsay Galleries
		17	Nature Conservancy
7	Ha Bien	18	Bank of Hawaii
8	To Chau	19	Shung Chong Yuein
10	Ba Le Sandwich Shop	20	Pegge Hopper Gallery
13	Bakery	21	Antique Shops
14	Wo Fat	22	Lai Fong Department Store
26	Krung Thai	23	Hawaii Pacific University
	OTHER	24	Former Pantheon Bar
1	Kuan Yin Temple	25	Chinese Chamber of Commerce
2	Izumo Taisha Shrine	27	Chinatown Gateway Plaza
3	Taoist Temple	28	Police Station
5	Sun Yat-Sen Statue	29	Hawaii Theatre
9	Hale Pauahi (parking garage)	30	Cathedral of Our Lady of Peace
11	Main Bus Stop		

Foster Botanic Garden

✽ entrance

Chinatown

Chinatown Cultural Plaza

0   100   200 m
0   100   200 yards

To Royal Mausoleum State Monument, Hsu Yin Temple

To Downtown Honolulu

waterfront. To make matters worse, police guards stationed inside the plague area attempted to stop quarantined residents from fleeing. Nearly 40 acres of Chinatown burned to the ground.

Not everyone thought the fire was accidental. Just the year before, Chinese immigration into Hawaii had been halted by the US annexation of the islands, and Chinatown itself was prime real estate on the edge of the burgeoning downtown district.

Despite the adverse climate the Chinese held their own and a new Chinatown arose from the ashes.

In the 1940s, thousands of US GIs walked the streets of Chinatown before being shipped off to Iwo Jima and Guadalcanal. Many spent their last days of freedom in Chinatown's 'body houses', pool halls and tattoo parlors.

Orientation & Information

Chinatown proper is immediately north of downtown Honolulu, roughly bounded by Honolulu Harbor, Nuuanu Ave and River St. To get there by car from Waikiki, take Ala Moana Blvd and turn at Bethel St or Smith St. Or take Beretania St and head makai down Nuuanu Ave or Maunakea St. Hotel St is open to bus traffic only.

Chinatown is full of one-way streets, traffic is tight and it's difficult to find a parking space. Your best bet for metered parking (three-hour limit) is the lot off Smith St between Pauahi St and Beretania St. There are parking garages at Hale Pauahi on N Beretania St and at Chinatown Gateway Plaza on Nuuanu Ave. All three parking options cost $1 an hour.

You can avoid parking hassles by taking the bus. Buses No 2 and 20 run from Waikiki; get off on N Hotel St after Maunakea St and you'll be in the heart of Chinatown.

Walking Tours

Three organizations offer Chinatown walking tours. It should be noted, however, that Chinatown is a fun place to poke around on your own and it can feel a bit touristy being led around in a group. Still,

---

Herbs & Noodles

Chinatown herbalists are both physician and pharmacist, with a wall full of small wooden drawers each filled with a different herb. They'll size you up, feel your pulse and listen to you describe your ailments before deciding which drawers to open, mixing herbs and flowers and wrapping them for you to take home and boil up together. The object is to balance Yin and Yang forces. Viet Hoa Chinese Herb Shop, 162 N King St, is one such shop.

There are half a dozen noodle factories in Chinatown. If you look inside you'll see clouds of white flour hanging in the air and thin sheets of dough running around rollers and coming out as noodles. Yat Tung Chow Noodle Factory, 150 N King St, next to Ba Le, makes nine sizes of noodles, from skinny golden thread to fat udon. ∎

---

the guides provide a commentary with historical insights and often take you to a few places you're unlikely to walk into otherwise.

The Chinatown Historical Society (☎ 521-3045) leads walking tours of the stores and historic buildings of central Chinatown at 10 am Monday to Saturday and tours to Foster Gardens and Chinese and Japanese temples at 1 pm Monday to Friday. The cost for each is $5. Meet at the Asia Mall, an enclosed section of the Chinatown Cultural Plaza on Maunakea St.

The Hawaii Heritage Center (☎ 521-2749) leads historical walking tours of Chinatown from 9:30 am to noon on Fridays for $4. Reservations are not taken; meet in front of Ramsay Galleries at 1128 Smith St.

The Chinese Chamber of Commerce (☎ 533-3181) leads historical walking tours of Chinatown from 9:30 am to noon on Tuesdays for $5. Meet at the chamber office at 42 N King St.

Oahu Market

The heart of Chinatown is Oahu Market, on the corner of Kekaulike and King Sts.

Everything the Chinese cook needs is on display: pig heads, ginger root, fresh octopus, quail eggs, slabs of tuna, jasmine rice, long beans and salted jellyfish.

Oahu Market has been an institution since 1904. In 1984, the tenants organized and purchased the market themselves to save it from falling into the hands of developers.

Maunakea Street

Wo Fat, the distinctive pink restaurant on the corner of Hotel and Maunakea Sts, is a Chinatown landmark with a facade that somewhat resembles a Chinese temple. The oldest restaurant in Honolulu, it's been on this site since just after the Chinatown fire of 1900. However, recent renovations have stripped the interior of its once colorful Chinese decor, and now it's only the exterior that's worth a glimpse.

Shung Chong Yuein, 1027 Maunakea St, sells delicious moon cakes, almond cookies and other pastries at bargain prices. This is the place to buy dried and sugared foods – everything from candied ginger and pineapple to candied squash and lotus root. They also sell boiled peanuts, which are actually quite good if you can resist comparing them to roasted peanuts.

Across the street is **Cindy's Lei Shop**, a friendly place with leis made of maile, lantern ilima and Micronesian ginger in addition to the more common orchids and plumeria. Prices are very reasonable, starting at $3.50 for a lei of tuberose flowers. The colors and fragrances are heady.

Nuuanu Avenue

The **Chinatown Police Station**, on the corner of Hotel St and Nuuanu Ave in the Perry Block building (circa 1888), has enough 1920s atmosphere to resemble a set from 'The Untouchables'.

Just down the street is the **Pantheon Bar**, now abandoned, but noteworthy as the oldest watering hole in Honolulu and a favorite of sailors in days past.

Across the street, **Lai Fong Department Store** sells antiques, knick-knacks and old postcards of Hawaii dating back to the first half of the century. Even walking into the store itself is a bit like stepping back into the 1940s. Lai Fong's, which has been in the same family for 70 years, also

sells Chinese silks and brocades by the yard and makes silk dresses to order.

The **granite-block sidewalks** along Nuuanu Ave were made from the discarded ballast of ships that brought tea from China in the 1800s.

Antiques & Arts

Chinatown has a number of antique shops and art galleries. Pegge Hopper, whose prints of Hawaiian women adorn many a wall in the islands, has her gallery at 1164 Nuuanu Ave. Also notable is Ramsay Galleries, a block to the northwest at 1128 Smith St.

Down near the waterfront, Bushido Antiques, 936 Maunakea St, sells Japanese swords, kimonos and ukiyoe prints. Robyn Buntin, a couple of doors away, carries a good collection of Oriental antiques, largely Chinese, including porcelain vases, jade, silver, tea bowls and wooden chests.

Chinatown Cultural Plaza

This plaza covers the better part of a block along North Beretania St from Maunakea St to River St.

The modern complex doesn't have the character of Chinatown's older shops, but inside it's still Chinatown, with tailors, acupuncturists and calligraphers alongside travel agents, restaurants and a Chinese news press. One of the kiosks inside the Asia Mall section sells nuts, dried fruit and local honey at good prices. There's a post office and restrooms.

At a small courtyard statue of Kuan Yin, elderly Chinese light incense and leave mangoes.

River St Pedestrian Mall

The River St pedestrian mall has covered tables beside Nuuanu Stream, where old men play mahjong and checkers. A statue of Chinese revolutionary leader Sun Yat-Sen stands at the end of the pedestrian mall near North Beretania St.

There are eat-in and takeout restaurants along the mall, including Japanese food, Chinese food and the peculiarly named Kevin's Drive In, a hole-in-the-wall eatery serving plate lunches on a *pedestrian walkway!*

Taoist Temple

Organized in 1889, the Lum Sai Ho Tong Society was one of more than 100 societies started by Chinese immigrants in Hawaii to help preserve their cultural identity. This one was for the Lum clan, who hail from west of the Yellow River. At one time the society had more than 4000 members, and even now there are nearly a thousand Lums in the Honolulu phone book.

The society's Taoist temple on the corner of River and Kukui Sts honors the goddess Tin Hau, a Lum child who rescued her father from drowning and was later deified as a saint. Many Chinese claim to see her apparition when they travel by boat. The elaborate altar inside the temple is open for viewing when the street-level door is unlocked. The elderly caretaker is friendly, although he doesn't speak English.

Izumo Taisha Shrine

The Izumo Taisha Shrine, across the river on Kukui St, is a small wooden Shinto shrine built in 1923. During WW II the property was confiscated by the city of Honolulu and wasn't returned to its congregation until 1962.

Incidentally, the 100-pound sacks of rice that sit near the altar symbolize good health, while the ringing of the bell placed at the shrine entrance is considered an act of purification for those who come to pray.

Foster Botanic Garden

Foster Botanic Garden covers 20 acres at the northern end of Chinatown. The entrance is on Vineyard Blvd, opposite the end of River St. The garden took root in 1850 when German botanist William Hillebrand purchased five acres of land from Queen Kalama and planted the trees that now tower in the center of the property.

Captain Foster bought the property in 1867 and continued planting the grounds. In the 1930s the tropical garden was bequeathed to the city of Honolulu and it's now a city park.

The garden is laid out in groupings, including sections of palms, orchids, plumerias and poisonous plants.

If you've ever wondered how nutmeg, allspice or cinnamon grow, stroll through the Economic Garden. In this section there's also a black pepper vine that climbs 40 feet up a gold tree, a vanilla vine and other herbs and spices.

The herb garden was the site of the first Japanese language school in Oahu. Many Japanese immigrants sent their children there to learn to read Japanese, hoping to maintain their cultural identity and the option of someday returning to Japan. During the bombing of Pearl Harbor a stray artillery shell exploded into a room full of students. A memorial marks the site.

At the other end of the park the wild orchid garden can be a good place for close-up photography. Unfortunately this side of the garden is skirted by the H-1 freeway, which detracts from what would otherwise be a peaceful stroll.

The garden's East African *Gigasiphon macrosiphon*, a tree with white flowers that open in the evening, is thought to be extinct in the wild. The tree is so rare that it doesn't have a common name.

Izumo Taisha Shrine

Dr Kenneth Emory

Bishop Museum is well-respected, not only for its collections but for the ethnological research it has spearheaded. Beginning in the 1920s, supported by mainland philanthropy and Ivy League scholars, it organized teams of archaeologists and anthropologists and sent them to record the cultures of the islands in the Pacific before they were forever lost.

The most renowned of the researchers was Kenneth Emory, who was born in Boston but spent his early years in Hawaii where he became fluent in the Hawaiian language. His knowledge of Hawaiian gave him the linguistic underpinnings to understand all Polynesian dialects. For five decades he sailed schooners and mailboats to the far corners of the Pacific, cranking out film footage of native dancers, recording their songs, measuring their temples (both buildings and skulls!) and transcribing their folklore.

Emory's treatises are the most important (and sometimes the only) anthropological recordings of many Pacific island cultures, from Lanai to Tuamotu. He was affiliated with the museum until his death at age 94 in January 1992. ∎

The native Hawaiian loulu palm, taken long ago from the upper Nuuanu Valley, may also be extinct in the wild. The garden's chicle tree, New Zealand kauri tree and Egyptian doum palm are all reputed to be the largest of their kind in the USA. Oddities include the cannonball tree, the sausage tree and the double coconut palm that's capable of producing a 50-pound nut.

Foster Garden is open from 9 am to 4 pm daily. Admission costs $1 for those ages 13 and over. Trees are marked and a corresponding self-guided tour booklet is available at the entrance.

The Friends of Foster Garden provides volunteer guides who lead hour-long walking tours at 1 pm Monday to Friday. Call 522-7066 for reservations.

Kuan Yin Temple

The Kuan Yin Temple, on Vineyard Blvd near the entrance of Foster Garden, is a bright red Buddhist temple with a green ceramic-tile roof. The ornate interior is richly carved and filled with the sweet pervasive smell of burning incense.

The temple is dedicated to Kuan Yin Bodhisattva, goddess of mercy, whose statue is the largest in the prayer hall. Devotees burn paper 'money' for prosperity and good luck. Offerings of oranges, fresh flowers and vegetarian food are placed at the altar. The large citrus fruit that is sometimes stacked pyramid-style is the pomelo, considered a symbol of fertility because of its many seeds.

Hawaii's multiethnic Buddhist community worships at the temple and respectful visitors are welcome.

GREATER HONOLULU

Bishop Museum

The Bishop Museum (☎ 847-3511), 1525 Bernice St, is considered by many to be the best Polynesian anthropological museum in the world. It also has Hawaii's only planetarium.

One side of the main gallery, the Hawaiian Hall, has three floors covering the cultural history of Hawaii. The first floor, dedicated largely to pre-Western contact Hawaii, has a full-size pili-grass thatched house and numerous other displays from carved temple images to calabashes and weapons.

One of the museum's most impressive holdings is a feather cloak made for Kamehameha I and passed down to subsequent kings. It was created entirely of the yellow feathers of the now-extinct mamo, a predominately black bird with a yellow upper tail. Around 80,000 birds were caught, plucked and released to create this cloak.

The 2nd floor is dedicated to 19th-century Hawaii and the top floor to the various ethnic groups that comprise present-day Hawaii. Like Hawaii itself, the top floor has a bit of everything, including samurai armor, Portuguese festival costumes, Taoist fortune-telling sticks and Queen Liliuokalani's royal coach.

The Polynesian Hall contains masks

Greater Honolulu

from Melanesia, stick charts from Micronesia and weapons and musical instruments from Polynesia.

The Cooke Rotunda features an exhibit detailing how ancient Pacific navigators were able to journey vast distances, tuning into the seas and the skies for direction.

The museum also has a natural history section; large seashell, flora & fauna collections; and Kidspace, where children can crawl under large turtle shells, try on a hula skirt or play with Hawaiian rhythm instruments.

In the Hawaiian Hall lobby, craftspeople demonstrate Hawaiian quilting, lauhala weaving, lei making and other traditional crafts from 9 am to 3 pm Monday to Friday. A hula show is presented at 1 pm on weekdays.

The Bishop Museum is open from 9 am to 5 pm daily. Admission of $7.95 for adults, $6.95 for children ages six to 17 (under age six free) includes all exhibits, demonstrations and the planetarium.

Planetarium shows are held at 11 am and 2 pm daily. On Fridays and Saturdays there's also a show at 7 pm, which on clear nights is followed by viewing from the observatory telescope. Reservations are recommended for the evening programs. Admission to the planetarium alone costs $3.50.

The museum shop sells many books on the Pacific not easily found elsewhere as well as quality Hawaiiana gift items. There's also a snack shop that's open to 4 pm.

Getting There & Away From Waikiki or downtown Honolulu take the No 2 School St bus to Kapalama St, walk towards the ocean and turn right on Bernice St. By car, take Exit 20B off H-1, go mauka on Houghtailing St and turn left on Bernice St.

Royal Mausoleum State Monument
The Royal Mausoleum contains the remains of Kings Kamehameha II, III, IV and V as well as King David Kalakaua and Queen Liliuokalani, the last reigning monarchs.

The only one missing is Kamehameha I, the last king to be buried in secret in accordance with Hawaii's old religion.

The original mausoleum building, which is usually locked, is now a chapel; the caskets are in nearby crypts. Other gravestones honor John Young and Charles Reed Bishop, husband of Bernice Pauahi Bishop.

The mausoleum, at 2261 Nuuanu Ave (just before the avenue meets the Pali Hwy), is open from 8 am to 4:30 pm Monday to Friday.

Hsu Yin Temple

Part of the Chinese-Buddhist Association of Hawaii, the Hsu Yin Temple is on Kawananakoa Place, just across Nuuanu Ave from the Royal Mausoleum.

This temple is worth a quick look if you're visiting the mausoleum. At the altar are the standard offerings of oranges and burning incense, while prints on the walls depict Buddha's life story.

Punchbowl

Punchbowl is the bowl-shaped remains of a long-extinct volcanic crater. At an elevation of 500 feet it sits a mile above the downtown district and offers a fine view of the city out to Diamond Head and the Pacific beyond.

Early Hawaiians called the crater Puowaina, the 'hill of human sacrifices'. It's believed there was a heiau at the crater and that the slain bodies of kapu breakers were brought to Punchbowl to be cremated upon the heiau altar.

Today it's the site of the 115-acre National Memorial Cemetery of the Pacific. The remains of Hawaiians sacrificed to appease the gods now share the crater floor with the bodies of more than 25,000 soldiers, more than half of whom were killed in the Pacific during WW II.

The remains of Ernie Pyle, the distinguished war correspondent who covered both world wars and was hit by machine gun fire on Ie Shima during the final days of WW II, lies in section D, grave 109. His resting place is marked with the same style of flat granite stone that marks each of the graves.

A huge memorial at the head of the cemetery has eight marble courts representing different Pacific regions and is inscribed with the names of the 26,280 US troops missing in action from WW II and the Korean War. Two additional half courts have the names of 2503 soldiers missing from the Vietnam War.

For the best view of the city, walk to the lookout 10 minutes south of the memorial.

The cemetery is open from 8 am to 5:30 pm in winter and to 6:30 pm from early March to late September.

Getting There & Away The entrance into Punchbowl is off Puowaina Dr. There's a marked exit as you start up the Pali Hwy from H-1; watch closely as it comes up quickly! From there, drive slowly and follow the signs as you wind through a series of narrow streets on the short way up to the cemetery.

By bus, take a No 2 from Waikiki to downtown Honolulu and get off at Beretania and Alapai Sts, where you transfer to a No 15 bus (which runs hourly on the half hour). Ask the driver where to get off. It's about a 15-minute walk to Punchbowl from the bus stop.

Ala Moana

Ala Moana means 'Path to the Sea'. Ala Moana Blvd (Hwy 92) connects the Nimitz Hwy (leaving the airport) with downtown Honolulu and continues into Waikiki. Ala Moana is also the name of a land area just west of Waikiki, which includes Honolulu's largest beach park and a huge shopping center.

Ala Moana Center Ala Moana Center is Hawaii's biggest shopping center, with nearly 200 shops. When outer islanders fly to Honolulu to shop they go to Ala Moana. Tourists wanting to spend the day at a mall usually head there too. Ala Moana Center is Honolulu's major bus transfer point and tens of thousands of passengers transit through daily, so even if you weren't planning to go to the center you're likely to end up there!

Ala Moana has a Sears, Liberty House, J C Penney, Longs Drugs, Foodland supermarket and Shirokiya, an authentic Japanese department store from the chirping 'arigatos' as you walk in the door to the top-floor Japanese food market.

You'll also find local color at the Crack Seed Center, where you can scoop from jars full of pickled mangoes, rock candy, salty red ginger, cuttlefish and banzai mix.

There's a kite shop selling Molokai kites,

a shop selling old Hawaiian stamps and coins, a couple of banks, a Thomas Cook currency exchange, a travel agency and a good food court with 20 ethnic fast-food stalls.

On the mountain side of the center, near Sears, is a post office open to 5 pm on weekdays, to 4:15 pm on Saturdays. Also at the ground level, but at the opposite end of the row, is a satellite city hall where you can get bus schedules and county camping permits.

Ala Moana Beach Ala Moana Beach Park, opposite the Ala Moana Center, is a fine city park with much less hustle and bustle than Waikiki. The park is fronted by a broad golden sand beach nearly a mile long which is buffered from the traffic noise of Ala Moana Blvd by a spacious grassy area with shade trees.

This is where Honolulu residents go to jog after work, play volleyball on the beach and enjoy weekend picnics. The park has full beach facilities, several softball fields and tennis courts, and free parking. It's a very popular park yet big enough to feel uncrowded.

Ala Moana is generally a safe place to swim and popular with distance swimmers. However the deep channel that runs the length of the beach can pose a danger at low tide, particularly to poor swimmers who don't realize it's there. A former boat channel, it drops off suddenly to depths of about 30 feet.

The 43-acre peninsula jutting from the Diamond Head side of the park is the **Aina Moana Recreation Area**, otherwise known as Magic Island. There's a nice walk around the perimeter of Magic Island and sunsets can be picturesque with sailboats pulling in and out of the adjoining Ala Wai Yacht Harbor. This is also a hot summer surf spot.

University of Hawaii

The University of Hawaii (UH) at Manoa, the central campus of the statewide college system, is east of downtown Honolulu and two miles north of Waikiki.

The university has strong programs in astronomy (thanks to Mauna Kea), geophysics, marine sciences and Hawaiian and Pacific studies. The campus attracts students from islands throughout the Pacific.

Manoa Garden restaurant in Hemenway Hall is somewhat of a student hangout and occasionally has live music. Hemenway Hall and the Campus Center are behind Sinclair Library, which fronts University Ave opposite Burger King and the bus stop.

Two outside walls of the Campus Center have grand Hawaiiana murals, with scenes based on photos from a classic August 1981 *National Geographic* article on Molokai. The Campus Center courtyard usually has live music a couple of days a week from noon to 1 pm.

Information The Information Center (☎ 956-7235) in the Campus Center can provide campus maps and answer questions. Free one-hour walking tours of the campus, emphasizing art, history and architecture, leave from the Campus Center at 2 pm on Mondays, Wednesdays and Fridays; to join one simply arrive 10 minutes before the tour begins.

Ka Leo O Hawaii, the student newspaper, lists lectures, music performances and other campus happenings. It can be picked up free at the university libraries and other places around campus.

Bulletin Boards Boards in front of Sinclair Library have notices of rooms for rent, cars and surfboards for sale, concerts and campus activities. Another board with only listings of rooms for rent is at the campus post office, opposite Hemenway Theatre. Although the listings are extensive, the majority are for rooms in shared student households and most advertisers are looking for long-term roommates.

Activities Hemenway Theatre (☎ 956-6468) in Hemenway Hall shows foreign flicks, select feature films and local surf films. Admission is $3.50 for non-students, $2.50 for senior citizens and children under age 12. Printed schedules are available at the theater and posted on the bulletin boards.

Campus Leisure Programs (☎ 956-6468) in Hemenway Hall offers recreation and craft classes to the general public. Most classes, such as beginning hula, Hawaiian quilt-making, Afro-jazz dance, massage and ceramics, meet once or twice a week and cost $30 to $80 for a month-long session. More useful to short-term visitors are the outdoor programs, such as beginning sailing (four days, $81), guided hikes ($5 to $15), kayaking and windsurfing.

Attending University You can get information on undergraduate studies from the Admissions & Records Office (☎ 956-8975), Sakamaki Hall, 2530 Dole St, Honolulu, HI 96822, and on graduate studies from the Graduate Division (☎ 956-8544), Spalding Hall, 2540 Maile Way, Honolulu, HI 96822.

The summer session consists primarily of two six-week terms. Tuition is $130 per credit for nonresidents and $75 per credit for residents. For the summer catalog contact the Summer Session (☎ 956-7221), Box 11450, Honolulu, HI 96828.

Getting There & Away Parking at UH is a hassle; you're better off arriving by bus and exploring on foot. Bus No 4 runs between UH and Waikiki, bus No 6 between UH and Ala Moana.

East-West Center

Adjacent to the university is the East-West Center (☎ 944-7111), 1777 East-West Rd, Honolulu, HI 96848, a federally funded educational institution established in 1960 by the US Congress. The center's stated goal is the promotion of mutual understanding among the people of Asia, the Pacific and the USA.

Some 2000 researchers and graduate students work and study at the center, examining development policy, the environment and other Pacific issues.

Free one-hour tours of the East-West Center's facilities are sometimes given by

Friends of the East-West Center; if you're interested, call 944-7691.

Changing exhibits of Asian art and culture are displayed on the 1st floor of **Burns Hall**, which is on the corner of Dole St and East-West Rd. A single country or region is presented in each exhibit, with such themes as 'Cultural Portraits of Indonesia' and 'Silver, Silk: Khmer Artifacts'. Exhibits generally run about six weeks, with three weeks of downtime between them. There's no admission charge.

The center has other multicultural programs open to the public. They include music performances, foreign films, international culture nights and scholastic seminars. Many of the activities are free, while others have fees up to $10. For the current listing, pick up the twice-monthly *Center Events* newsletter at Burns Hall or call for the schedule.

UPPER MANOA VALLEY

The Upper Manoa Valley, mauka of the university, ends at forest reserve land in the hills above Honolulu. The road up the valley runs through a well-to-do residential neighborhood before reaching the trailhead to Manoa Falls and the Lyon Arboretum.

Manoa Falls Trail

The trail to Manoa Falls is a beautiful hike, especially for one so close to the city. The trail runs for three-quarters of a mile above a rocky streambed that leads up to the falls. It takes about 30 minutes one way.

Surrounded by lush damp vegetation and moss-covered stones and tree trunks, you get the feeling you're walking through a thick rainforest a long way from anywhere. The only sounds the birds have to compete with are the rush of the stream and waterfall.

There are all sorts of trees along the path, including tall *Eucalyptus robusta* with their soft, spongy, reddish bark, flowering orange African tulip trees and other lofty varieties that creak like wooden doors in old houses. Many of them were planted by the Lyon Arboretum, which at one time held a lease on the property.

Wild purple orchids and red ginger grow up near the falls. The area is quiet and peaceful. The falls are steep and drop about 100 feet vertically into a small shallow pool. The pool is not deep enough for swimming, and occasional falling rocks don't make it advisable anyway.

The trail is usually a bit muddy but not too bad if it hasn't been raining lately. Be careful not to catch your foot in exposed tree roots – they're potential ankle breakers, particularly if you're moving with any speed. The packed clay can be slippery in some steep places, so take your time and enjoy the trail.

Aihualama Trail About 75 feet before Manoa Falls an inconspicuous trail starts to the left of the chain-link fence. This is the Aihualama Trail, well worth a little 15-minute side trip. Just a short way up you get a broad view of Manoa Valley.

After about five minutes you'll enter a bamboo forest with some massive old banyan trees. When the wind blows the forest releases eerie crackling sounds. It's a trippy forest, enchanted or spooky depending on your mood.

You can return to the Manoa Falls Trail or go on another mile to Pauoa Flats where the trail connects with the Puu Ohia Trail in the Tantalus area.

Lyon Arboretum

The Lyon Arboretum, 3860 Manoa Rd, is a great place to go after hiking to Manoa Falls if you want to identify trees and plants you've seen along the trail.

Dr Harold Lyon, after whom the arboretum is named, is credited with introducing 10,000 exotic trees and plants to Hawaii. Approximately half of these are represented in this 124-acre arboretum, which is part of the University of Hawaii.

This is not a landscaped tropical flower garden, but a mature and largely wooded arboretum, where related species are clustered in a semi-natural state.

The Hawaiian ethnobotanical garden has mountain apple, breadfruit and taro; ko, the sugar cane brought by early Polynesian settlers; kukui, which produced lantern oil; and ti, used medicinally since ancient times and for moonshine after Westerners arrived.

The arboretum also has herbs and spices and cashew, cacao, papaya, betel nut, macadamia nut, jackfruit and calabash trees, as well as greenhouses and classrooms.

A good choice among the arboretum's many short trails is the 20-minute walk up to **Inspiration Point**, which offers a view of the hills that enclose the valley. En route you'll encounter wonderful scents, inviting stone benches and lots of birdsong. The path loops through ferns, bromeliads and magnolias and passes by tall trees, including a bo tree, a descendant of the tree Gautama Buddha sat under when he received enlightenment.

The arboretum is open from 9 am to 3 pm Monday to Saturday. A $1 donation is appreciated. Free guided tours (☎ 988-7378 for reservations) are given at 1 pm on the first Friday and third Wednesday of each month and at 10 am on the third Saturday of the month.

The reception center has a book and gift shop as well as helpful staff members who can give you a map of the garden and information on the arboretum's organized hikes, children's programs and one-day workshops.

Getting There & Away

From Ala Moana Center take the No 5 Manoa bus to the end of the line, which is at the defunct Paradise Park. From there it's a five-minute walk to the road's end, where the Manoa Falls Trail begins. Lyon Arboretum is at the end of the short drive off to the left just before the trailhead.

To get there by car, simply drive to the end of Manoa Rd. There's room to park at the trailhead, but it's not a very secure place so don't leave anything valuable in the car. Lyon Arboretum has a parking area adjacent to its gardens that's reserved for arboretum visitors.

TANTALUS & MAKIKI HEIGHTS

Just two miles from downtown Honolulu a narrow switchback road cuts its way up the lush green forest reserve land of Tantalus and the Makiki Valley. The road climbs up almost to the top of 2013-foot Mt Tantalus, with swank mountainside homes tucked in along the way.

Although it's one continuous road, the western side is called Tantalus Dr and the eastern side Round Top Dr. The 8½-mile loop is Honolulu's finest scenic drive, offering great views of the city below.

The route is winding and steep, but it's a good paved road. Amongst the profusion of

dense tropical growth, eucalyptus, bamboo, ginger and elephant-ear taro are easily identified. Vines climb to the top of telephone poles and twist their way across the wires.

A network of hiking trails runs between Tantalus and Round Top drives and throughout the forest reserve, with numerous trailheads off both roads. The trails are seldom crowded, which seems amazing considering how accessible they are. Perhaps because the drive itself is so nice, the only walking most people do is between their car and the scenic lookouts.

The Makiki Heights area below the

Tantalus,
Makiki Valley
& Manoa Falls

forest reserve is one of the most exclusive residential areas in Honolulu and the site of a museum of contemporary art. There's bus service as far as Makiki Heights, but none around the Tantalus-Round Top loop drive.

Puu Ualakaa State Park

From Puu Ualakaa State Park you can see an incredible panorama of all Honolulu. The park entrance is 2½ miles up Round Top Dr from Makiki St. It's half a mile in to the lookout; bear to the left when the road forks.

The sweeping view from the lookout extends from Kahala and Diamond Head on the far left, across Waikiki and downtown Honolulu, to the Waianae Range on the far right. To the southeast is the University of Hawaii at Manoa, easily recognized by its sports stadium; to the southwest you can see clearly into the green mound of Punchbowl Crater; the airport is visible on the edge of the coast and Pearl Harbor beyond that.

Although the best time for photos is usually during the day, this is also a fine place to watch evening settle over the city. Arrive at least 30 minutes before sunset to see the hills before they're in shadow.

The park gates are locked from 6:45 pm (7:45 pm in summer) to 7 am. For night (and anytime) views, there are a couple of scenic pull-offs before the park.

The Contemporary Museum

The Contemporary Museum (☎ 526-0232), 2411 Makiki Heights Dr, is a delightful modern art museum occupying an estate with 3½ acres of wooded gardens.

The estate house was built in 1925 for Mrs Charles Montague Cooke, whose other former home is the present site of the Honolulu Academy of Arts.

You enter the museum through a covered courtyard with bronze gates and an arrangement of parabolic mirrors reflecting the view hundreds of times over.

Inside are galleries featuring quality changing exhibits of paintings, sculpture and other contemporary artwork by both

---

Rolling Sweet Potatoes

In olden times, the slopes of Puu Ualakaa ('Rolling Sweet Potato Hill') were planted with sweet potatoes, which were said to have been dug up and rolled down the hill for easy gathering at harvest time. The hill's other name, 'Round Top', dates to more recent times. ■

---

national and international artists. A newer building on the lawn holds the museum's most prized piece, a vivid environmental installation by David Hockney based on his sets for *L'Enfant et les Sortilèges*, Ravel's 1925 opera. There's also a cafe serving lunch and afternoon desserts.

The museum is near the intersection of Mott-Smith Dr and Makiki Heights Dr. The No 15 bus from downtown Honolulu gets you there.

It's open from 10 am to 4 pm Tuesday to Saturday, from noon to 4 pm on Sundays. Admission is free on Thursdays and $4 on other days. Children ages 14 and under are admitted free.

Meditation Center

The Honolulu Siddha Meditation Center, 1925 Makiki St, Honolulu, HI 96822, operated by followers of Gurumayi Chidvilasananda, has early morning chanting sessions open to interested visitors.

There are also evening programs that include chanting, sitar playing and a video of Gurumayi from 7 to 9:30 pm on Wednesdays and Saturdays. Sometimes group meals, hatha yoga sessions and other programs are open to the public as well; for information call 942-8887.

Makiki Valley Loop Trail

Three of the Tantalus area hiking trails – Maunalaha Trail, Kanealole Trail and Makiki Valley Trail – can be combined to make the Makiki Valley Loop Trail, a popular 2½-mile hike.

The loop is through a lush and varied tropical forest that starts and ends in Hawaii's first state nursery and arboretum.

In this nursery, hundreds of thousands of trees were grown to replace the sandalwood forests that had been leveled in Makiki Valley and elsewhere in Hawaii in the 1800s.

The **Maunalaha Trail** begins at the restrooms below the parking lot of the Makiki Forest baseyard. It first crosses a bridge, passes taro patches and proceeds to climb the east ridge of Makiki Valley, passing Norfolk pine, bamboo and fragrant allspice and eucalyptus trees. There are some good views along the way.

After three-quarters of a mile you'll come to a four-way junction, where you'll take the left fork and continue on the **Makiki Valley Trail**. The trail goes through small gulches and across gentle streams with patches of ginger. Near the Moleka Stream crossing are mountain apple trees (related to allspice and guava), which flower in the spring and fruit in the summer. Edible yellow and strawberry guavas also grow along the trail. There are some fine views of the city below.

The **Kanealole Trail** begins as you cross Kanealole Stream and then follows the stream back to the baseyard, three-quarters of a mile away. The trail leads down through a field of Job's-tears; the bead-like bracts of the female flowers of this tall grass are often picked to be strung in leis.

Kanealole Trail is usually muddy, so wear shoes with good traction. Halfway down there's a grove of introduced mahogany.

Getting There & Away To get to the Makiki Forest baseyard, turn left off Makiki St and go half a mile up Makiki Heights Dr. Where the road makes a sharp bend, proceed straight ahead through a green gate into the Makiki Forest Recreation Area and continue until you reach the baseyard. There's a parking lot on the right just before the office.

You can also take the No 15 bus, which runs between downtown and Pacific Heights. Get off near the intersection of Mott-Smith Dr and Makiki Heights Dr and walk down Makiki Heights Dr to the base-yard. It's a mile-long walk between the bus stop and the trailhead.

An alternative is to hike just the Makiki Valley Trail, which you can reach by going up Tantalus Dr two miles from its intersection with Makiki Heights Dr. As you come around a sharp curve, look for the wooden post marking the trailhead on the right. You can take this route in as far as you want and backtrack out or link up with other trails along the way.

Puu Ohia Trail

The Puu Ohia Trail, in conjunction with the Pauoa Flats Trail, leads up to a lookout with a view of Nuuanu reservoir and valley. It's nearly two miles one way and makes a hardy hike.

The trailhead is at the very top of Tantalus Dr, 3.6 miles up on the left from its intersection with Makiki Heights Dr. There's a large turn-off opposite the trailhead where you can park.

The Puu Ohia Trail starts up reinforced log steps and leads past ginger, bamboo groves and lots of eucalyptus, a fast-growing tree that was planted to protect the watershed. About half a mile up, the trail reaches the top of 2013-foot Mt Tantalus (Puu Ohia).

From Mt Tantalus, the trail leads into a service road. Continue on the road to its end, where there's a Hawaiian Telephone building. The trail picks up again behind the left side of the building.

Continue down the trail until it leads into the **Manoa Cliff Trail**, which you'll go left on for a short distance until you come to another intersection where you'll turn right onto the **Pauoa Flats Trail**. The trail leads down into Pauoa Flats and on to the lookout. The flats area can be muddy; be careful not to trip on exposed tree roots.

You'll pass two trailheads before reaching the lookout. The first is **Nuuanu Trail**, on the left, which runs three-quarters of a mile along the western side of Upper Pauoa Valley and offers broad views of Honolulu and the Waianae Mountains.

The second is **Aihualama Trail**, a bit farther along on the right, which takes you

1¼ miles to Manoa Falls through bamboo groves and huge old banyan trees. If you were to follow this route you could then hike less than a mile down the Manoa Falls Trail to the end of Manoa Rd and from there catch a bus back to town (see the Upper Manoa Valley section).

MOANALUA

In olden times Moanalua was a stopover for people traveling between Honolulu and Ewa as well as a vacation spot for Hawaiian royalty. In 1884 Princess Pauahi Bishop willed the valley to Samuel M Damon and it's now privately owned by his estate.

Moanalua Gardens

Moanalua Gardens, maintained by the Damon Estate, is a large grassy park with grand shade trees. The park is the site of Kamehameha V's gingerbread-trimmed summer cottage, which overlooks a taro pond. Beyond it a Chinese-style hall is fronted by carp ponds and stands of golden-stemmed bamboo. The center of the park has a grassy stage where the Prince Lot Hula Festival is held on the third Saturday in July.

This is not a must-see spot, except during the festival, but it is a pleasant place to stroll if you happen to be passing by. To get there, take the Puuloa Rd/Tripler Hospital exit off Hwy 78 and then make an immediate right-hand turn into the gardens.

Moanalua Trail

The trail up Moanalua Valley is along a gravel and dirt road which was once a cobblestoned valley road. This is a dry area and there is only partial shade along the trail. There are both native and introduced plants, and lots of birds. Seven stone bridges remain along the path in various stages of disrepair.

The nonprofit Moanalua Gardens Foundation works to preserve Moanalua Valley in its natural state. Their efforts to raise public awareness of the valley's history and environmental uniqueness helped defeat plans that would have routed the new H-3 freeway through Moanalua Valley.

The foundation gives interpretive walks into Moanalua Valley on the second and fourth Sunday of each month. The easy five-mile walks begin at 9 am, finish around 1 pm and cost $3. Reservations can be made a week in advance (☎ 839-5334). If it's not crowded they may let you join in on the spot, but if fewer than 10 people reserve they usually cancel the hike.

If you want to hike the trail on your own, the Damon Estate requests that you first call the Moanalua Gardens Foundation for permission to enter.

If you follow the road all the way in, it's about four miles. Numbered posts along the first half of the trail correspond to a self-guided brochure available from the Moanalua Gardens Foundation office (1352 Pineapple Place, Honolulu, HI 96819) for $3, plus 75c for postage.

To get to the trailhead, take the Moanalua Valley/Red Hill exit off Hwy 78 (one exit past Moanalua Gardens). Stay to the right and then follow the Moanalua Valley sign uphill 1½ miles on Ala Aolani St to where the road ends at a parking lot. There are restrooms and drinking water in the little park at the trailhead.

PLACES TO STAY
Places to Stay – bottom end

Hostelling International Honolulu (☎ 946-0591; fax 946-5904), 2323A Seaview Ave, Honolulu, HI 96822, is in a quiet residential neighborhood near the University of Hawaii. The main house is a dormitory for students from Pacific islands attending the university. Out back, seven dorms with bunk beds can accommodate 40 travelers, with men and women in separate dorms. There are no rooms for couples. Rates are $12 for HI or AYH hostel members and $15 for nonmembers. If you're not a member there's a three-night maximum stay. AYH membership is sold on site for $25. Credit cards are accepted.

Hostel office hours are from 7 am to noon and 4 pm to midnight. Guests must be out of the dorms from noon to 4 pm, although the TV lounge and common-use kitchen are open during the day. There's a laundry room and a bulletin board that has useful information for new arrivals. From Ala Moana, catch a No 6 or No 18 (University or Woodlawn) bus, get off on the corner of University Ave and Metcalf St and walk one block uphill to Seaview Ave. By car, take Exit 24B off the H-1 freeway, go mauka on University Ave and turn left at Seaview Ave.

Fernhurst YWCA (☎ 941-2231), 1566 Wilder Ave, Honolulu, HI 96822, has rooms for women only in a three-story building about a mile from the university. There are 60 rooms, each intended for two guests, with two single beds, two lockable closets, two dressers and a desk. Two rooms share one bathroom. The cost is $25 per person. If you get a room to yourself, which is easier during the low season, it costs $5 more. Rates include buffet-style breakfasts and dinners, except on weekends and holidays. There's a small kitchen facility on each floor.

Payment is required weekly in advance and guests staying more than three days must become Y members ($30 a year). It costs an additional $20 to rent linen or you can bring your own. Reservations can be made by sending one night's rental as deposit by cashier's check or postal money order.

Fernhurst is near the intersection of Wilder and Punahou, on the No 4 (Nuuanu-Dowsett) bus line. It's a quiet community setting with an eclectic group of guests. There's a laundry room, TV room, library area, security guard and a garden courtyard with a small pool. Office hours are 8:30 am to 11:30 pm.

The *Central Branch YMCA* (☎ 941-3344; fax 941-8821), 401 Atkinson Dr, Honolulu, HI 96814, is on the Diamond Head side of the Ala Moana Center. There are 114 rooms in all. The rooms with shared bath, which are available to men only, are small and simple and resemble those in a student dorm, with an old desk, a single bed, a lamp, a chair and linoleum floors. The cost is $30 single, or for $43 they'll put in a rollaway bed and two

people can share the room. Rooms with private bath, which are a bit nicer but still small and basic, are open to both men and women and cost $36.50/51.50 for singles/doubles. Guests receive YMCA privileges including free use of the sauna, pool, gym and handball courts. There's a coin laundry, a TV lounge, a snack bar and limited free parking. Reservations can be made in advance and credit cards are accepted.

During the school year the *Atherton YMCA* (☎ 946-0253), 1810 University Ave, Honolulu, HI 96822, operates as a dorm for full-time University of Hawaii students only. During summer holidays (mid-May to mid-August) it's open on a space-available basis to non-students. Rates are $20 per day for a room with a bed, dresser, desk and chair. Reservations are made by application (available by mail) with a $150 security deposit. The Y is directly opposite the university.

Sailors between ships can try their luck getting one of the 23 rooms at the *Seaman's Home* (☎ 537-5476) at the Marine Union Hall, 707 Alakea St, near Ala Moana Blvd. Just a few minutes' walk from Honolulu Harbor, it's open to both male and female sailors. The rooms are a bit spartan and the toilets are down the hall, but at $15 a night it's one of the city's best bargains.

Places to Stay – middle

The *Pagoda Hotel* (☎ 941-6611, (800) 472-4632; fax 955-5067), 1525 Rycroft, Honolulu, HI 96814, has two sections. The cheapest rooms are $78 studios in the older apartment section, but they can feel a bit too removed from the main hotel – especially if you're checking in at night. The more standard $85 hotel rooms are nicer with the usual amenities, including air-conditioning, TV, phone, refrigerator and a central lobby. There's no extra charge for children under 18 occupying the same room as their parents. There's nothing distinguished about this hotel, other than a nice restaurant with a carp pond, but it is one way to avoid jumping into the Waikiki scene.

Places to Stay – top end

The new *Executive Centre Hotel* (☎ 539-3000, (800) 949-3932; fax 523-1088), 1088 Bishop St, Honolulu, HI 96813, is Honolulu's only downtown hotel. Geared for businesspeople, it's comprised of 114 suites, each large and comfortable with modern amenities that include phones with voice mail, two TVs, room safe and whirlpool bath. There's a heated lap pool and a fitness center. Rates range from $100 to $200.

Manoa Valley Inn (☎ 947-6019, (800) 634-5115; fax 946-6168), 2001 Vancouver Dr, Honolulu, HI 96822, on a quiet side street near the University of Hawaii, is an authentically restored Victorian inn that's on the National Register of Historic Places. All eight rooms are filled with period antiques, one with a four-poster bed, another with furnishings that belonged to silent film star Frances Beaumont. There's complimentary wine and cheese, a common parlor and a billiard room. Rates, which include continental breakfast, are $110 for rooms with a shared bathroom and from $140 to $190 for rooms with a private bathroom.

Places to Stay – near the airport

If you've got some dire need to be near Honolulu International, there are three hotels outside the airport along a busy highway and beneath flight paths. All provide free 24-hour transport to and from the airport, about 10 minutes away.

In addition, for long layovers or midnight flights there are two cheaper places where you can catnap or just take a shower.

The more attractive option is *Sleep & Shower* (☎ 836-3044; fax 834-8985), Terminal Box 42, Honolulu, HI 96819, right in the airport's main terminal between lobbies five and six. It has 17 small private rooms, each with a single bed and its own bathroom and shower. The place is clean and relatively quiet, although there is some vibration from the shuttle bus which runs overhead. Overnight (eight-hour) stays are $30, a two-hour daytime nap and shower costs $17.50, with additional hours for $5.

Only one person is allowed to stay in each room. Showers only cost $7.50, with towels, shampoo and razors provided. It's open 24 hours. Reservations are taken for the overnight stays and MasterCard and Visa are accepted.

Nimitz Shower Tree (☎ 833-1411), 3085 N Nimitz Hwy, occupies a converted warehouse in an industrial area not far from the airport hotels. The facilities are basic; the private 'roomettes' are just a line of three-walled cubicles with curtains that can be drawn across the front. The cost is $27 per person for an overnight sleep and shower, or $7.50 for a shower only. It's open 24 hours and free transport to and from the airport is available.

The recently renovated *Best Western Plaza Hotel-Honolulu Airport* (☎ 836-3636, (800) 528-1234; fax 834-7406), 3253 N Nimitz Hwy, Honolulu, HI 96819, is a comfortable, if undistinguished, mid-rise hotel with 268 rooms, each with a king or two double beds, TV and refrigerator. Rates start at $89 and nonsmoking rooms are available. There's a pool, lounge and restaurant.

Holiday Inn-Honolulu Airport (☎ 836-0661, (800) 465-4329; fax 833-1738), 3401 N Nimitz Hwy, Honolulu, HI 96819, on the corner of Rodgers Blvd and Nimitz Hwy, has 308 rooms at $115. This four-story hotel has standard Holiday Inn amenities, including a lounge, pool and restaurant. Guests have a choice of a king or two double beds; nonsmoking rooms are available. There's commonly a promotional rate that discounts the rack rate by about 20%.

The *Pacific Marina Inn* (☎ 836-1131), 2628 Waiwai Loop, Honolulu, HI 96819, is slightly farther along in an industrial area. This lackluster three-decker motel has small, straightforward single/double rooms for $70/74. The rooms do have air-con, TVs and phones and there's a pool on the grounds.

PLACES TO EAT

Honolulu has an incredible variety of good ethnic food and if you know where to look it can also be quite cheap. The key is to get out of the tourist areas and eat where the locals do.

Around the University

There are some excellent restaurants in the area around the University of Hawaii at Manoa. The following listings are all within a 10-minute walk of the three-way intersection of King St, Beretania St and University Ave.

Coffeeline (☎ 947-1615), in the YWCA on the corner of University and Seaview Aves, is run by a politically active feminist group. In addition to cheap food, there are lots of pamphlets on current progressive issues and newspapers to browse through. A bowl of homemade soup costs $2, a tofu sandwich $4 and lasagna with salad $5. They also have muffins, bagels and coffee. Although there's some creative leeway in opening times, hours are generally 7 am to 9 pm Monday to Friday, and 8 am to 8 pm on Saturdays.

Yakiniku Camellia, 2494 S Beretania St, has a tasty all-you-can-cook Korean lunch buffet for $10 from 11 am to 3 pm. It's good quality food and if you've got an appetite worked up it's a great deal. The mainstay is pieces of chicken, pork and beef that you select from a refrigerated cabinet and grill at your table. Accompanying this are 18 marinated and pickled side dishes, miso and seaweed soups, simple fresh vegetable salads and a few fresh fruits. The mung bean and watercress dishes tossed with sesame seeds are sweet and mild. As for the kimchees, generally the redder they are, the hotter they are.

Dinner, from 3 to 10 pm, costs $15.75 and is essentially the same fare with the addition of sashimi. Everything is authentic; there's even a newspaper vending machine selling the Korean-language daily.

Chan's Chinese Restaurant, 2600 S King St, is the local place to go for inexpensive lunchtime dim sum, including some delicious steamed seafood varieties. Chan's has noodles, chow mein and other Chinese dishes. Lunch specials are in the $4.75 to $6 range. It's open from 10:30 am to 10:30 pm daily.

Ezogiku Noodle Cafe, 1010 University Ave on the corner of Beretania St, dishes up miso ramen for $4.50, a gyoza, soup and rice meal for $4.75, and curries and cold noodles. While it's not gourmet quality, it is on par with similar fast-food noodle shops in Japan. It's open from 11 am to at least 11 pm daily.

Across the street at 1091 University Ave, a branch of the Vietnamese restaurant *Ba Le* sells good inexpensive French rolls, croissants and sandwiches that range from a tasty vegetarian version for $1.75 to a seafood sandwich for $3.75.

India Bazaar (☎ 949-4840), 2320 S King St, is a small cafe and food store selling inexpensive Indian food. There's a vegetarian thali that includes jasmine rice and three vegetable curries for $5.25 and chicken and shrimp thalis for $6 to $6.50. Side orders of papadams, chapatis, samosas and raita are each under $1. It's open from 11 am to 9 pm Monday to Saturday.

Maple Garden (☎ 941-6641), 909 Isenberg St, around the corner from South King St, is a popular local Sichuan restaurant with good food at reasonable prices. While chicken preparations tend to be fatty, the shrimp dishes are excellent. Vegetarian entrees, including a delicious eggplant in hot garlic sauce, cost around $6, while most other dishes are priced between $6 and $8. At lunch there are over a dozen specials for around $4.50. It's open from 11 am to 2 pm and from 5:30 to 10 pm daily.

Diem (☎ 941-8657) at 2633 S King St, near the corner of S King and University St, is a small family-run restaurant serving some of Honolulu's best Vietnamese food. The shrimp rolls ($3.95) make excellent appetizers and the spicy lemongrass chicken and the papaya salad are both very good main dishes priced at $6.50. There's a good-value lunch special served until 4 pm daily that includes an entree, salad, rice and appetizer for $7.50. The restaurant is open daily from 10 am to 10 pm.

Chiang Mai (☎ 941-1151), 2239 S King St, serves northern Thai food. Their wonderful sticky rice, which is reminiscent of Japanese omochi, is served in its own little bamboo steamer. The fresh fish green curry, which at $9 is one of the higher priced dishes, is a recommendable house specialty. There are two dozen vegetarian dishes for around $6 and a range of meat dishes for around $7. It's open from 11 am to 2 pm Monday to Friday and from 5:30 to 10 pm nightly. The menu is the same at lunch and dinner.

Down to Earth Natural Foods, 2525 S King St, is a fantastic natural foods supermarket. If it's healthy and you can eat it, you'll probably find it there. The store has everything from Indian chapattis and dahl to local organic produce; there's a dozen varieties of granola sold in bulk. It's a great place to shop and the healthier yogurts and whole-grain breads that some of Honolulu's more with-it supermarkets sell are substantially cheaper at Down to Earth. It's open from 8 am to 10 pm daily. The store also has a vegetarian deli, for either eat-in or takeout, with a salad bar ($3.75 a pound), sandwiches, soups and plate lunches.

Ala Moana Center
Ala Moana Center's central food court is a circus, with neon signs, 800 tiny tables crowded together and 20 fast-food stands circling it all. There's something for everyone, from salads to daiquiris, ice cream to pizza, and Chinese, Japanese, Korean, Hawaiian, Thai and Mexican specialties.

If you've got the munchies, this is a good place to stop when you're between buses. It's like window shopping – you can walk through, preview the food and select what you want. The food court is open from 9 am to 9 pm Monday to Saturday and from 10 am to 6 pm on Sundays.

Panda Express has good Mandarin and Sichuan food, with dishes like spicy chicken, broccoli beef and shrimp with garlic sauce. Combination plates with fried rice or chow mein and two entrees are $4.69, three entrees $5.69. The food is fresh and you can pick what looks best from the steamer trays.

Yummy Korean Bar-B-Q is a similar concept with Korean selections that include

rice and a number of tasty pickled vegies and kimchees, with plates from $5 to $6.

Patti's Chinese Kitchen, the busiest place in the food court, is a big-volume Chinese restaurant with a few dozen dishes to choose from. It costs $4.20 for two selections, $5.20 for three selections, both of which include rice or noodles. If you really want to indulge you can get a whole roast duck for $10. There's also a limited selection of dim sum and desserts, including almond cookies for 20c.

Kitchen Garden specializes in salads such as curried chicken, Thai peanut pasta, fruit, marinated vegetable and just plain greens. The salads are fresh and healthy and range in price from $3.50 to $5.

Two tasty skewers of chicken satay at *Little Cafe Siam* are $2. Big slices of acceptable pizza at *Sbarro* are $1.89, while a slice of pizza with salad costs $3.69.

Elsewhere in the Moana Center there's a *Foodland* supermarket open from 7 am to 11 pm daily and branches of *McDonald's, Dairy Queen* and *Dunkin' Donuts*.

Ward Centre
Ward Centre, a shopping complex at 1200 Ala Moana Blvd, has a bakery, a deli, a branch of *Keo's* Thai restaurant and about a dozen other dining spots.

Fresco (☎ 523-5191), on the ground level, has Italian food at moderate prices. The fresh-catch blackened ahi, which is seared on the outside and sashimi-raw on the inside, is a good choice; the 'lite diner' portion at $12 provides a reasonable serving. All dishes come in both light ($9 to $13) and regular ($13 to $18) portions. Salads, $5 to $10, include those with warm goat cheese, grilled tiger prawns or chicken with peanuts and sun-dried tomatoes. They also make brick-oven pizzas with creative toppings. It opens at 11:15 am on weekdays and 6 pm on weekends, closing at 9 pm on Sundays and 10 pm other days.

The food is a bit too Americanized at *Compadres*, but this busy Mexican restaurant still draws a crowd. Combination plates with rice and beans cost $10 to $15. It's on the center's upper level, open from

11 am to 11 pm on weekdays, until midnight on Fridays and Saturdays.

Mocha Java/Crepe Fever, on the ground level, is a popular hangout serving good coffees, crepes, croissants, sandwiches, desserts and other light eats. It's open from 8 am to 9 pm, except on Sundays when it closes at 4 pm.

Ward Warehouse

All of the following restaurants are on the upper level of Ward Warehouse, the shopping complex on the corner of Ala Moana Blvd and Ward Ave. There's free garage parking and buses No 8, 19 and 20 stop there. Each restaurant has a view of the harbor so when making reservations be sure to ask for a window table.

For cheap eats, the *Old Spaghetti Factory* is the best deal here. This family-style restaurant has an elaborate decor, filled with old antiques, heavy woods, Tiffany glass – even an old street car. At lunch, served from 11:30 am to 2 pm Monday to Saturday, you can get spaghetti with tomato sauce for $3.50, with clam sauce for $4.50 or with meatballs for $5.75. All meals

come with warm sourdough bread and a simple green salad. At dinner, served nightly from 5 pm to 10 pm (11 pm on weekends), the prices are about 50c more. Certainly not gourmet, but the price is right.

Horatio's (☎ 591-2005) has a good reputation for seafood. Dinner includes dishes such as stuffed mahimahi with brandied shrimp or mixed seafood grill for around $18, served with clam chowder or a choice of salads. At lunch, lighter versions of the same dishes are around $10. Lunch is from 11 am to 5 pm daily except Sunday, dinner from 5 to 10 pm nightly. There's live blues or jazz from 9 pm to midnight Thursday to Saturday.

Dynasty II (☎ 596-0208) is a Chinese restaurant with fine dining and good food. The a la carte menu tends to be expensive, with most entrees priced from $11 to $17. However, in recent times they've been running a good-value $12.95 dinner special that includes an appetizer, soup, entree with jasmine rice and dessert, each selected from a limited-choice menu.

Stuart Anderson's is a steak house with

Kodak Hula Show, Honolulu

DR

lunches in the $6 to $9 range and dinners about double that. *Coffee Works*, open from 9 am to 9 pm on weekdays (until 5 pm on weekends), sells coffees and pastries such as carrot cake and muffins.

Restaurant Row

Restaurant Row, a rather sterile complex on the corner of Ala Moana Blvd and Punchbowl St, caters largely to the downtown business crowd. There's a bakery with pastries and sandwiches, a wine and deli shop and about a dozen restaurants, the majority of which are quite pricey.

Among the better are *Ruth's Chris Steak House*, an upmarket mainland chain restaurant offering quality steaks for around $25; *Touch the East*, a slick Japanese bistro serving green-tea linguine and high-priced sushi; and the more relaxed and popular *Sunset Grill*, which features grilled fresh fish and meats from around $20. For something more moderate there's *Trattoria Manzo*, which has average Italian fare at average prices; pescatora at $13 is one of the better dishes on the menu.

Still, the best value at Restaurant Row is *La Salsa Rita's*, which takes its name from its salsa table where customers can select from a variety of these fresh-made sauces, ranging from the tame to the fire-eater. There's no lard or preservatives in the near-authentic Mexican fare. Burritos, either tofu or the traditional meat variety, cost $5.75, while combo plates with black beans and rice cost $9 to $12. If you're not up to a big meal there's a 'lite eaters' special of a single enchilada, rice and beans for $5. The horchata, a cinnamon-flavored rice drink, is refreshing and costs $1.50 for a huge glass.

Studebaker's, which is not a restaurant but a casual '50s-theme nightclub, offers a simple buffet from 5:30 to 7:30 pm on weekdays which is 'free' with a $1 cover charge and a one-drink minimum.

Fort St Mall

The Fort St Mall, a pedestrian street on the edge of the downtown district, has a number of cheap restaurants within walking distance of Iolani Palace. It's conve-

nient for downtown workers and sightseers, but certainly not a draw if you're elsewhere around town.

Near the intersection of Hotel St and Fort St Mall there are a number of standard fast-food places.

The best fast food in the neighborhood is at *Panda Kitchen*, 50 yards east of Fort St Mall at 116 S Hotel St. It serves good Chinese food made without MSG; the food is served from steamer trays but it's usually fresh and you can eat heartily for around $5. It's open from 10 am to 7 pm on weekdays, until 6 pm on Saturdays.

Another good local option is *Ba Le*, a branch of the Chinatown restaurant, which has inexpensive sandwiches, shrimp rolls, green papaya salads and French coffee. It's open from 7 am to 7 pm Monday to Friday and from 8:30 am to 4 pm on Saturdays. There's another Ba Le on Queen St.

Chinatown

Krung Thai (☎ 599-4803), 1028 Nuuanu Ave, is a family-run Thai restaurant on the edge of Chinatown between the business and red-light districts. Lunch, the only meal served, is geared to the business community's 30-minute lunch breaks, with dishes ready in steamer trays. There are 13 hot dishes to choose from, including chicken Panang, beef eggplant and vegetarian curry. One item costs $3.39, two items $4.29 and all are served with brown rice or noodles. It's open from 10:30 am to 2:30 pm Monday to Friday.

Ba Le Sandwich Shop, 150 N King St, bakes crispy French bread and is a good place for a quick inexpensive eat in Chinatown. Baguettes can be purchased for 40c or as sandwiches for $1.75 vegetarian style, $2.75 with meat. The vegetarian sandwich is a tangy combo of crunchy carrots, daikon and cilantro. Sweet, strong French coffee with milk costs $1.50 hot or cold. There are also good croissants, shrimp rolls, Vietnamese manapua and soursop candies. It's open from 5 am to 6 pm daily.

Our favorite Chinatown eatery is the Vietnamese restaurant *To Chau*, 1007 River St, where the specialty is pho, a delicious soup of beef broth with rice noodles and thin slices of beef garnished with cilantro and green onion. It comes with a second plate of fresh basil, mung bean sprouts and slices of hot chili pepper to add at will. The cost is $3.70 for a regular bowl and $5 for an extra-large one. The shrimp rolls with a spicy peanut sauce ($2.85) are recommendable, and the restaurant also serves rice and noodle dishes, but just about everybody comes for the soup. To Chau is open from 8 am to 2 pm daily. It's so popular that even at 10:30 am you may have to wait for one of the 16 tables. It's well worth the wait.

Ha Bien, 198 N King St, next door to To Chau, is another popular Vietnamese restaurant with good inexpensive food. Although Ha Bien specializes in noodle and long rice dishes, the menu also includes spring rolls, soups and crepes. Most dishes cost from $4 to $6. It's open from 8 am to 4 pm on weekdays, to 3:30 pm on weekends.

Doong Kong Lau, on the River St pedestrian mall, has an extensive menu that includes the expected Chinese standards as well as more exotic preparations from the mountainous Hakka region of China. Meat dishes, including the house specialty, salt-baked chicken, average about $6, while seafood plates are a few dollars higher. Generous lunch specials cost from $4 for an eggplant and rice meal to $6 for the shrimp and scallops in garlic sauce – both flavorful dishes. If you order noodles, splurge and pay the extra dollar for the cake noodles, pressed and cooked to a crisp on the edges. It's open from 9 am to 9:30 pm daily.

Just west of Doong Kong Lau on the River St mall is the *Buddhist Vegetarian Restaurant*, an upscale Chinese dining spot that uses tofu and gluten in place of meats. The menu is both creative and extensive and most dishes are priced from $7 to $10. There's also a dim sum service available at lunch. It's open from 10:30 am to 2 pm and 5:30 to 9 pm daily except on Wednesdays.

Other Places to Eat

Helena's Hawaiian Foods (☎ 845-8044),

1364 N King St, is a friendly family-run operation that's been serving excellent, inexpensive Hawaiian food since 1946. It's a totally local eatery, with 10 simple formica-top tables and a mix of vinyl chairs and stools. The restaurant makes a delicious kalua pig; also notable is the pipikaula and fried ahi. There's not a better place anywhere to sample various Hawaiian dishes. Nearly everything on the a la carte menu is under $2 and complete meals with poi (fresh, day-old or sour) or rice are $5 to $7. It's open from 11 am to 7:30 pm Tuesday to Friday only.

Thai Taste Restaurant (☎ 596-8106), 1246 S King St, is a family-run Thai restaurant with good food at honest prices. The tasty summer rolls are huge, the curry dishes quite nice and the servings generous. Service is slow. Most chicken, pork, beef and vegetarian dishes are priced around $5.50. Hours are 11 am to 2 pm on weekdays and from 5:30 to 10 pm nightly. There's free parking in the rear. Unlike some of Honolulu's better known Thai restaurants, it's not impossible to get in on a weekend night, and the food at Thai Taste is arguably the best value amongst them.

El Burrito, 550 Piikoi St (up from Ala Moana Center), could be a neighborhood restaurant on a back street in Mexico City. This hole-in-the-wall has about a dozen tightly squeezed tables and Oahu's most authentic Mexican food. The standard Mexican offerings served with rice and beans average around $8. It's a busy little place, with customers often waiting outside for tables. Inside it's noisy, crowded and alive with people chattering away in both English and Spanish. It's open from 11 am to 8 pm Monday to Thursday and to 9 pm on Fridays and Saturdays.

Mekong (☎ 521-2025), 1295 S Beretania St, is the original Keo's (now in Waikiki), and still has its original Thai cook. The menu is similar to that of Keo's, but Thai posters replace the artwork in this tiny eatery, you bring your own booze and prices are about a third less. The tasty spring rolls come with lettuce, mint leaves and peanut sauce and cost $6, while most beef, chicken and vegetarian dishes are a dollar more. Nothing on the menu is over $10. It's open from 11 am to 2 pm on weekdays and from 5 to 9:30 pm nightly. If you're driving, you may want to opt for *Mekong II* (☎ 941-6184), 1726 S King St, which has a similar menu and free parking in the rear.

For a treat, try the *Contemporary Cafe* (☎ 523-3362) at the Contemporary Museum in Makiki Valley. It has a pleasant outdoor lawn setting and suitably creative food such as Malaysian shrimp salad with a gado-gado dressing for $10.75 or New Zealand mussels in a Thai curry with ginger and lime leaves for $9.25. Grilled eggplant or tempeh sandwiches cost $8.50, each served with a side of tabouli. Lunch is from 11 am to 1:45 pm Tuesday to Saturday, from noon on Sundays. Desserts and beverages are available to 3 pm. Reservations are recommended, especially on Thursdays when admission to the museum is free.

The *Garden Cafe* (☎ 532-8734), an open-air restaurant in the Honolulu Academy of Arts, 900 S Beretania St, has seatings at 11:30 am and 1 pm Tuesday to Saturday. Salads, sandwiches, soups and hot dishes such as tamale pies and vegie casseroles cost $6 to $10. Reservations are suggested.

The Salvation Army's *Waioli Tea Room & Restaurant* (☎ 988-9488), at 2950 Manoa Rd in Manoa Valley, has a nice setting with various open-air dining rooms looking out onto gardens. In one of them is the restored grass hut that Robert Lewis Stevenson stayed in during his retreat at Waikiki Beach; the cottage was dismantled and moved to this site in 1926. Another area has a chapel that's a popular wedding spot. The food, while adequate, is less distinctive than the setting. On Sundays, from 11 am to 1:30 pm, there's a $15 brunch with half a dozen hot entrees such as eggplant parmesan, barbecue chicken and Thai curry accompanied by a simple salad and dessert bar. It's also open for lunch from Tuesday to Friday, with salads, sandwiches and a few other dishes, mostly in the $7 to

$9 range. On Thursdays there's a special Hawaiian lunch for $11 complete with a duo singing Hawaiian music. Reservations are required for all meals.

Auntie Pasto's (☎ 523-8855), 1099 S Beretania, has good Italian food, including a recommendable eggplant parmigiana, at moderate prices. Pasta costs $5.25 with tomato sauce, $7.50 with pesto or $6.50 heaped with fresh vegetables in butter and garlic. The parmesan cheese is freshly grated and the Italian bread is served warm. Dishes and prices are the same at lunch and dinner. Although it's off the tourist track, this popular high-energy spot attracts a crowd. Even at lunch you may have to wait for a table, while dinner on weekends can have lines out the door. It's open from 11 am to 10:30 pm Monday to Friday and 4 to 10:30 pm on Saturdays and Sundays.

The *Pagoda Floating Restaurant* at the Pagoda Hotel (☎ 941-6611), 1525 Rycroft, has good food and a serene setting amidst gardens and a carp pond. The breakfast menu (6:30 to 10:30 am) is extensive, with many choices for around $5. On weekdays, from 11 am to 2 pm, there's a good-value lunch buffet of Japanese and American dishes accompanied by salad and dessert bars for $10 or you can order off the lunch menu for about $6. There's also a nightly dinner buffet, available from 4:30 to 9:30 pm, which costs $17 ($15 on Mondays and Tuesdays) and features a nice array of dishes including prime rib, Alaskan snow crab, sashimi, tempura and salad and dessert bars.

The hottest new restaurant in town is *3660 On the Rise* (☎ 737-1177), 3660 Waialae Ave, which features 'Euro-Island' cuisine, blending continental and island flavors. Most lunch entrees cost around $9; one popular dish is the linguine with spicy island chicken sautéed with eggplant, shiitake mushrooms, shiso and dried tomatoes. At dinner, a la carte entrees of steak, lamb or seafood average $20. Lunch is served from 11:15 am to 2 pm Tuesday to Friday, dinner from 5:30 to 10 pm Tuesday to Saturday and until 9 pm on Sundays; reservations are often necessary for both meals.

Out of the mainstream, it's three miles northeast of Waikiki, on Waialae Ave between 12th and 13th Aves.

Two good places for sushi are *Yanagi Sushi* (☎ 537-1525), 762 Kapiolani Blvd, open 11 am to 2 pm and from 5 pm to 2 am daily except on Sundays when it's open 5 to 10 pm; and *Sada's* (☎ 949-0646), 1240 S King St, open from 11 am to 2 pm and from 5 pm to midnight Monday to Saturday, 5 to 11 pm on Sundays.

At the county-run People's Open Market program, farmers sell local produce for one hour a week at 21 locations around Oahu. Mondays and Wednesdays are set aside for the greater Honolulu area. Call 522-7088 for information or pick up a schedule at any satellite city hall.

ENTERTAINMENT
Honolulu has a lively entertainment scene. The best updated entertainment listings are in the free *Honolulu Weekly*, which is readily found around the downtown and university areas.

Classics & Concerts
Honolulu has a symphony orchestra, an opera company, ballet troupes, chamber orchestras and numerous community theater groups.

The *Blaisdell Center* (☎ 521-2911) at 777 Ward Ave presents musical concerts, Broadway shows and family events, with performers such as Depeche Mode, Sting, the Honolulu Symphony, the Ice Capades and the Brothers Cazimero.

The *Academy Theatre* of the Honolulu Academy of Arts, and to a lesser degree the *East-West Center*, present quality multicultural theater and concerts, such as performances by members of the Beijing Opera and recitals of Japanese lute music.

Music & Dancing
Anna Bannanas (☎ 946-5190), 2440 S Beretania St, not far from the university, rocks with a reggae, funk or alternative beat from 9 pm Wednesday to Sunday. It's particularly lively on Fridays and Saturdays when the house band, the Pagan Babies, plays African, reggae and soca dance music. There's usually a cover charge of $4.

Moose McGillicuddy's (☎ 944-5525), 1035 University Ave, often has contemporary Hawaiian groups on Friday nights, a DJ on Saturdays.

Cafe Sistina (☎ 526-0071), a stylish Italian restaurant at 1314 S King St, has contemporary jazz from 9:30 pm to midnight on Saturdays, with no cover charge. Wear black.

Ramsay Galleries (☎ 537-2787), 1128 Smith St, is the latest venue for top jazz musicians, such as saxophonist Gabe Baltazar. There's live music on Saturdays from 2 to 5 pm; the $10 cover charge includes two drinks.

Rumours (☎ 955-4811) at the Ala Moana Hotel, 410 Atkinson Dr, behind the Ala Moana Center, has a video disco, karaoke on Tuesdays, country & western on Wednesdays and ballroom dancing on Sundays. It's open from 5 pm (9 pm on Saturdays) to 3 am nightly except Monday. The cover is usually $5 and the age limit is 21.

For a more current scene, there's *After Dark* (☎ 533-2080), 1130 N Nimitz Hwy, which features hard rock and alternative groups such as Nine Inch Nails, Anthrax and White Zombie, usually on Saturday nights. The cover varies with the concert, but is often $15 to $20.

Movie Theaters
For progressive movies, there's the *Academy Theatre* (☎ 532-8768) at the Honolulu Academy of Arts, which showcases American independent cinema, foreign films and avant-garde shorts. Tickets are $4.

The *Hemenway Theatre* (☎ 956-6468) at the university leans towards more popular fare, including some good foreign films and select first-run offerings. General admission is $3.50.

The *Movie Museum* (☎ 735-8771), 3566 Harding Ave, shows classic oldies for film buffs. Tickets are $5.

Free Entertainment

The Ala Moana Center has a courtyard area called Centerstage that is the venue for free performances by high school choirs, gospel groups, ballet troupes, local bands and the like.

The Royal Hawaiian Band performs from 12:15 to 1:15 pm on Fridays (except August) on the lawn of the Iolani Palace.

The Celtic Pipes & Drums practice from 7 to 9 pm on Wednesdays on the mauka side of the Honolulu Municipal Building.

The Mayor's Office of Culture & Arts sponsors numerous free performances, exhibits and events, ranging from street musicians in city parks to Royal Hawaiian Band concerts in various locales around the island. Call 527-5666 for an updated listing of events.

Pearl Harbor Area

On December 7, 1941 a wave of more than 350 Japanese planes attacked Pearl Harbor, home of the US Pacific Fleet.

Some 2335 US soldiers were killed during the two-hour attack. Of those, 1177 died in the battleship USS *Arizona* as it took a direct hit and sank in less than nine minutes. Twenty other ships were sunk or seriously damaged and 188 airplanes were destroyed.

USS ARIZONA MEMORIAL

Over 1.5 million people 'remember Pearl Harbor' each year by visiting the USS Arizona Memorial run by the National Park Service. It is Hawaii's most visited attraction.

The visitor center includes a museum and theater as well as the off-shore memorial at the sunken USS *Arizona*. The park service provides a 75-minute program that includes a 23-minute documentary film on the attack followed by a boat ride out to the memorial and back. Everything is free.

The 184-foot memorial, built in 1962, sits directly over the *Arizona* without touching it. It contains the *Arizona*'s bell

and a wall inscribed with the names of those who went down with the ship. The average age of the enlisted men on the *Arizona* was 19.

From the memorial the battleship can be viewed eight feet below the surface. The ship rests in about 40 feet of water and even now oozes a gallon or two of oil each day. In the rush to recoup from the attack and prepare for war, the navy exercised its option to leave the men in the sunken ship buried at sea. They remain entombed in its hull.

The visitor center (☎ 422-2771; recorded information 422-0561) is open from 7:30 am to 5 pm daily except Thanksgiving, Christmas and New Year's Day. There's a snack bar and a souvenir/book shop.

Programs run every 15 or 20 minutes from 8 am to 3 pm (from 7:45 am in summer) on a first-come basis. As soon as you arrive, pick up a ticket at the information booth; the number on the ticket corresponds to the time the tour begins. Generally the shortest waits are in the morning; if you arrive before the first crowds you might get in within half an hour, but waits of a couple of hours are not uncommon. Summer months are busiest, with an average of 4500 people taking the tour daily, and the allotment of tickets is sometimes gone by 11 am.

Pearl Harbor survivors, who act as volunteer historians, are sometimes available to give talks about the day of the attack.

There's a little open-air museum to keep you occupied while you're waiting. It has interesting photos from both Japanese and US military archives showing Pearl Harbor before, during and after the attack. One photo is of Harvard-educated Admiral Yamamoto, the brilliant military strategist who planned the attack on Pearl Harbor even though he personally opposed going to war with the USA. Rather than relish the victory, Yamamoto stated after the attack that he feared Japan had 'awakened a sleeping giant and filled him with a terrible resolve'.

Getting There & Away The visitor center

is off Kamehameha Hwy (Hwy 90) on the Pearl Harbor Naval Base just south of Aloha Stadium. If coming from Honolulu, take H-1 west to exit 15A (Stadium/ Arizona Memorial). Make sure you follow highway signs for the Arizona Memorial, not Pearl Harbor.

The private Arizona Memorial Shuttle Bus (☎ 839-0911) picks up people from Waikiki hotels about every 90 minutes between 7 am and 1 pm. The ride takes around 40 minutes and costs $3 each way. Call to make arrangements.

By public transport, take the No 20 airport bus from Waikiki, which takes about 1¼ hours.

There are also private boat cruises to Pearl Harbor leaving from Kewalo Basin for about $20, but they should be avoided as passengers are not allowed to board the memorial.

Bowfin Park

If you have to wait an hour or two for your Arizona Memorial tour to begin, you might want to stroll over to the adjacent Bowfin Park.

The park contains a moored WW II submarine, the USS *Bowfin*, and the Pacific Submarine Museum, which traces the development of submarines from the turn of the century to the nuclear age.

The *Bowfin*, commissioned in May 1943, sank 44 ships in the Pacific before the end of the war. There is a self-guided tour with a hand-held radio receiver that picks up recorded messages as you walk through. Admission of $7 for adults, $3 for children ages seven to 12, includes entry to both the submarine and the museum.

There's no charge to enter the park and view the missiles and torpedoes spread around the grounds, look through the periscopes or inspect the Japanese *kaiten*, a suicide torpedo.

The kaiten is just what it looks like: a torpedo with a single seat. As the war was closing in on the Japanese homeland, the kaiten was developed in a last-ditch effort to ward off an invasion. It was the marine

Honolulu Star-Bulletin 1st EXTRA

HONOLULU, TERRITORY OF HAWAII, U. S. A., SUNDAY, DECEMBER 7, 1941   ★ PRICE FIVE CENTS

WAR !

(Associated Press by Transpacific Telephone)

SAN FRANCISCO, Dec. 7.—President Roosevelt announced this morning that Japanese planes had attacked Manila and Pearl Harbor.

OAHU BOMBED BY JAPANESE PLANES

SIX KNOWN DEAD, 21 INJURED, AT EMERGENCY HOSPITAL

equivalent of the kamikaze pilot and his plane. A volunteer was placed in the torpedo before it was fired. He then piloted it to its target. At least one US ship, the USS *Mississinewa*, was sunk by a kaiten. It went down off Ulithi Atoll in November 1944.

The park is open from 8 am to 5 pm daily.

PEARL CITY

Pearl City is the largest urban area in Hawaii outside Honolulu. It's home to about 45,000, including a lot of military people and civilians who work on the bases, but there's little of interest for visitors.

If you're just passing through and not going into Pearl City itself, stay on H-1 and avoid the parallel Kamehameha Hwy (Hwy 90), as it's all stop-and-go traffic, fast food and malls.

Pearlridge Shopping Center is a massive mall that runs between H-1 and Kamehameha Hwy. A swap meet is held a block west of the shopping center on weekends at the drive-in theater.

HAWAII'S PLANTATION VILLAGE

A visit to Hawaii's Plantation Village (☎ 677-0110) in Waipahu will reward you with a glimpse of plantation life and a closer look at Hawaii's multiethnic heritage.

The site encompasses 30 homes and buildings set up to replicate a plantation village of the early 1900s. The cookhouse was originally on this site and the shrine was moved here, but the other structures have been newly built to replicate the architecture of the time.

The houses are set up with period furnishings that portray the lifestyles of the eight different ethnic groups – Hawaiian, Japanese, Okinawan, Chinese, Korean, Portuguese, Puerto Rican and Filipino – that worked Hawaii's sugar plantations. One-hour guided tours of the village are given on the hour between 9 am and 3 pm.

The setting is particularly evocative as Waipahu is still largely a plantation town,

and its sugar mill, one of just two remaining on Oahu, looms on a knoll directly above this site. There's also a small museum detailing the history of the plantation workers. Artifacts, including an ofuro bath, Korean flute, straw slippers and various tools, are accompanied by insightful interpretive write-ups. All in all, it's a quality community-based production.

It's open from 8 am to 4 pm Monday to Saturday. Admission costs $5 for adults, $3 for seniors and children five to 17.

To get there, head west on H-1, take Exit 7, turn left at the end of the off ramp onto Paiwa St, then turn right onto Waipahu St, drive past the mill and turn left into the complex. The distance from H-1 is about 1½ miles.

KEAIWA HEIAU STATE PARK

This park in Aiea, north of Pearl Harbor, covers 334 acres and contains an ancient medicinal temple, campgrounds, picnic facilities and a scenic loop trail. The park is open from about 7 am to sunset for day visitors. As with all state parks there are no fees.

At the park entrance is Keaiwa Heiau, a religious site built in the 1600s and used by Hawaiian *kahuna lapaau* (herbalist healers). The kahunas used hundreds of medicinal plants and grew many on the grounds surrounding the heiau. Among those still found here are noni, whose pungent yellow fruits were used to treat heart disease; kukui, whose nuts were an effective laxative; ulu, whose sap soothed chapped skin; and ti leaves, which were wrapped around a person to break a fever.

The heiau is a 100 by 160 foot, single-terraced stone structure. Not only did the herbs have medicinal value but the heiau itself was considered to possess life-giving energy. The kahuna was able to draw forth the powers from both.

People wishing to be healed still place offerings within the heiau. The offerings reflect the multiplicity of Hawaii's cultures: rosary beads, New Age crystal pendants and sake cups sit beside flower leis and rocks wrapped in ti leaves.

Aiea Loop Trail

The 4½-mile Aiea Loop Trail begins at the top of the park's paved loop road next to the restrooms and comes back out at the campground, about a third of a mile below the start of the trail.

The trail starts off in a forest of eucalyptus and ironwood trees and runs along the ridge. Other trees along the way include Norfolk Island pines, edible guava and native ohia lehua, with its fluffy red flowers.

There are vistas of Pearl Harbor, Diamond Head and the Koolau Range. About two-thirds of the way along, the wreckage of a C-47 cargo plane that crashed in 1943 can be spotted through the foliage on the east ridge. The hike takes 2½ to three hours and is a fairly easy walk.

Camping

The camping area can accommodate 100 campers. Most sites have their own picnic table and barbecue grill. Sites are not crowded together, but because they're largely open there's not a lot of privacy either. There's a distant view of Honolulu's airport a couple of miles to the south.

If you're camping in winter make sure your gear is waterproof, as it rains a lot at this 880-foot elevation, although the temperature is usually pleasant. There are restrooms, showers, a phone and drinking water.

For Oahu, it's a good choice for a campground. There's a caretaker by the front gate, and the gate is locked at night for security.

Camping permits are limited to five nights per month and must be obtained in advance (see Camping in the Accommodations section at the start of this chapter). Like all Oahu public campgrounds it's closed on Wednesdays and Thursdays.

Getting There & Away

From Honolulu, head west on Hwy 78 and take the Aiea Stadium turn-off onto Moanalua Rd. Turn right onto Aiea Heights Dr at the first traffic light. The road winds up through a residential area 2½ miles to

the park; there are good views of the city and Pearl Harbor along the way.

Southeast Oahu

Some of Oahu's finest scenery is along the southeast coast, which curves around the tip of the Koolau Mountains. Diamond Head, Hanauma Bay and the island's most famous bodysurfing beaches are all just a 20-minute ride from Waikiki.

East of Diamond Head, H-1 turns into the Kalanianaole Hwy (Hwy 72), following the southeast coast up to Kailua. It passes the exclusive Kahala residential area, a run of shopping centers, and housing developments that creep up into the mountain valleys.

The highway rises and falls as it winds its way around the Koko Head area and Makapuu Point, with beautiful coastal views along the way. The area is geologically fascinating, with boldly stratified rock formations, volcanic craters and lava sea cliffs.

DIAMOND HEAD

Diamond Head is a tuff cone and crater that was formed by a violent steam explosion deep beneath the surface long after most of Oahu's volcanic activity had stopped.

As the backdrop to Waikiki it's one of the best-known landmarks in the Pacific. The summit is 760 feet high.

The Hawaiians called it Leahi and built a luakini heiau on the top where human sacrifices took place. But ever since 1825, when British sailors found calcite crystals sparkling in the sun and mistakenly thought they'd struck it rich, it's been called Diamond Head.

In 1909 the US Army began building Fort Ruger at the edge of the crater. They built a network of tunnels and topped the rim with cannon emplacements, bunkers and observation posts. Reinforced during WW II, it's been a silent sentinel whose guns have never fired.

Today there's a Hawaii National Guard

base inside the crater as well as Federal Aviation Administration and civil defense facilities. Diamond Head is a state monument with interpretive plaques, picnic tables, restrooms, a phone and drinking water. The best reason to visit is to hike the trail to the crater rim for the panoramic view. The gates are open daily from 6 am to 6 pm.

Hiking Diamond Head

The trail to the summit was built in 1910 to service the military observation stations along the crater rim.

It's a fairly steep hike, with a gain in elevation of 560 feet, but it's only three-quarters of a mile to the top and plenty of people of all ages hike up. It takes about 30 minutes one way. The trail is open and hot and you might want to take along something to drink.

As you start up the trail, you can see the summit ahead a bit to the left.

The crater is dry and scrubby with kiawe, koa haole, grasses and wildflowers. The little yellow-orange flowers along the way are native ilima, Oahu's official flower.

About 20 minutes up the trail you enter a long, dark tunnel. Because the tunnel curves you don't see light until you get close to the end. It's a little spooky, but the roof is high enough for you to walk through without bumping your head, there is a hand rail and your eyes should adjust enough to make out shadows in the dark. Nevertheless, to prevent accidents, the park advises hikers to tote along a flashlight.

The tunnel itself seems like it should be the climax of the long climb, but on coming out into the light you're immediately faced with a steep 99-step staircase. Persevere! After this there's a shorter tunnel, a narrow spiral staircase inside an unlit bunker and the last of the trail's 271 steps. Be careful when you reach the top – there are some steep drops.

From the top there's a fantastic 360° view taking in the southeast coast to Koko Head and Koko Crater and the leeward coast to Barbers Point and the Waianae Mountains. Below is Kapiolani Park and the orange seats of the W_____ can also see the lighth_____ sailboats and sometim_____ waiting for waves at Dia_____

Note Watch your footing at the top. There are some steep drops.

Getting There & Away From Kuhio Ave in Waikiki, buses No 22 and 58, which run about twice an hour, stop at Diamond Head. It's about a 15-minute walk from the bus stop to the trailhead above the parking lot. Once you walk through the tunnel you're in the crater.

By car, take Monsarrat Ave (which goes by the zoo) to Diamond Head Rd and then take the right turn after Kapiolani Community College into the crater.

Diamond Head Beach

Diamond Head Beach is popular with both surfers and windsurfers.

Conditions at Diamond Head are suitable for intermediate to advanced windsurfers, and when the swells are up it's a great place for wave riding. Even as a spectator sport it's exhilarating.

The beach has showers but no other facilities.

Getting There & Away To get there from Waikiki, follow Kalakaua Ave to Diamond Head Rd. There's a parking lot just beyond the lighthouse. Walk east past the end of the lot and you'll find a paved trail down to the beach.

HANAUMA BAY BEACH PARK

Hanauma is a wide, sheltered bay of sapphire and turquoise waters set in a rugged volcanic ring. Don't miss it, even if you only go to look.

Hanauma, which means 'Curved Bay', was once a popular fishing spot. It had nearly been fished out when it was designated a marine life conservation district in 1967. Now that the fish are fed instead of eaten, they swarm in by the thousands.

From the overlook you can peer into crystal waters and view the entire coral reef

■ PLACES TO STAY
1 Schrader's Windward
  Marine Resort
11 Kahala Hilton

▼ PLACES TO EAT
4 Chart House &
  Haiku Gardens
10 Roy's

OTHER
2 Valley of the Temples
  & Byodo-In
3 Windward Mall
5 Windward City
  Shopping Center
6 Ulupo Heiau
7 Sea Life Park
8 Makapuu Point
  Lighthouse
9 Koko Marina
  Shopping Center
12 Kahala Mall
13 Honolulu Zoo
14 Queen Emma
  Summer Palace

Southeast &
Windward Oahu

0   3   6 km
0   2   4 miles

that stretches across the width of the bay. You can see schools of silver fish glittering, the bright blue flash of parrotfish and perhaps a lone sea turtle. To see an even more colorful scene, put on a mask, jump in and view it from beneath the surface.

Hanauma seems to get as many people as fish. With some two million visitors a year, it's often busy and crowded.

While it's for good reason that everyone's there, the heavy use of the bay has taken its toll. The coral on the shallow reef has been damaged by all the action, and the bread and peas that snorkelers feed the fish have increased fish populations in Hanauma well beyond what it can naturally support. In fact, many of these fish are not common to Hanauma, but are more aggressive types that have been drawn in by the feeding.

A master plan is under way that aims to normalize the fish distribution and reduce the number of beachgoers from 10,000 a day to 2000. The numbers have already been nearly halved by one new restriction that prohibits tour buses from dropping off passengers to use the beach, and fish feeding will be phased out in the next few years. In the meantime snorkelers shouldn't feed the fish anything but fish food (which can be bought at the beach concession stand).

Improperly discarded plastic 'fish food' bags have been another serious problem. Sea turtles that frequent the bay confuse the plastic for jellyfish, which they love to eat, and it kills them.

Hanauma is both a county beach park and a state underwater park. It has a grassy picnic area, lifeguards, showers, restrooms, changing rooms and access for the disabled. The bay is closed on Wednesdays until noon, but is otherwise open daily from 7 am until 6 pm in winter, until 7 pm in summer. Admission is free.

The snack bar sells hamburgers, hot dogs, and soda while snorkel sets can be rented at reasonable rates at the concession stand.

Paths lead along low ledges on both sides of the bay. Be cautious when the sea is rough or the tide is high, as waves can wash over the ledges.

More people drown at Hanauma than at any other beach on Oahu. Although the figure is high largely because there are so many visitors at this beach, people drowning in the Toilet Bowl or being swept off the ledges have accounted for a fair number of deaths over the years.

Toilet Bowl

A 15-minute walk out to the point on the left side of the bay brings you to the Toilet Bowl, a small natural pool in the lava rock. The Toilet Bowl is connected to the sea by an underwater channel, which enables water to surge into the bowl and then flush out from beneath.

People going into the pool for the thrill of it can get quite a ride as it flushes down four to five feet almost instantly. However the rock around the bowl is slippery and hard to grip, and getting in is far easier than getting out. It definitely shouldn't be tried alone.

You can also get to the Toilet Bowl by walking past the overlook wall at the left side of the parking lot and continuing to the southeast for about 10 minutes. When you reach a small gulch bear left to get down to the Toilet Bowl, or bear right to view it from above.

Witches Brew

A 10-minute walk along the right side of the bay will take you to a rocky point. The cove at the southern side of the point is the treacherous Witches Brew, so named for its swirling, turbulent waters.

There's a nice view of Koko Crater from there and green sand made of olivine can be found along the way.

Snorkeling & Diving

Snorkeling is good at Hanauma Bay year round. Mornings are better than afternoons, as swimmers haven't yet stirred up the sand.

The large sandy opening in the middle of the coral, called the **Keyhole**, is an excellent place for novice snorkelers. The deepest water is 10 feet, although it's very shallow over the coral. It's well-protected and usually swimming-pool calm.

Hanauma's biggest attraction is the sheer number and variety of fish. It's got big rainbow parrotfish crunching off chunks of coral, moray eels, bright yellow butterfly fish, goatfish, Moorish idols and numerous other tropicals.

For confident snorkelers, it's better on the outside of the reef where there are larger coral heads, bigger fish and fewer people; to get there follow the directions posted on the beach signboard. Don't attempt to swim outside the reef when the water is rough or choppy. Not only will the channel current be strong, but the sand will be stirred up and visibility poor anyway.

Divers have the whole bay to play in, with clear water and coral gardens, sea turtles and lots of fish. Beware of currents when the surf is up; surges in the Witches Brew, on the right hand side; and the Molokai Express, a treacherous current that runs just outside the mouth of the bay.

Getting There & Away

Hanauma Bay is about 10 miles from Waikiki along Hwy 72. There's free parking in a large parking lot, although it sometimes fills in the middle of the day and on weekends. Parking outside a marked space will result in a parking ticket.

Bus No 22 goes to Hanauma (and on to Sea Life Park). On weekdays the first bus leaves Waikiki from the corner of Kuhio Ave and Namahana St at 8:15 am, with subsequent buses leaving at 50 minutes past the hour until 3:50 pm. Buses leave Hanauma for Waikiki every hour from 11:10 am to 5:10 pm. On weekends the buses are a little more frequent, although the times are more sporadic.

KOKO HEAD REGIONAL PARK

The entire Koko Head area is a county regional park. It includes Hanauma Bay, Koko Head, Halona Blowhole, Sandy Beach and Koko Crater.

Koko Head is backed by Hawaii Kai, an expansive development of condos, houses,

shopping centers, a marina and a golf course – all meticulously planned and quite sterile in appearance.

Koko Crater and Koko Head are both tuff cones created about 10,000 years ago in Oahu's last gasp of volcanic activity.

Koko Head

Koko Head, not to be confused with Koko Crater, overlooks and forms the southwest side of Hanauma Bay.

When it's open to the public, the one-mile walk up the road to the summit offers fine coastal views that light up nicely at sunset. The road starts near the highway at the Hanauma Bay entrance.

There are two craters atop Koko Head, as well as telecommunications facilities on the 642-foot summit. The Nature Conservancy maintains a preserve in the shallow Ihiihilauakea Crater, the larger of the two. The crater has a unique vernal pool and a rare fern, the *Marsilea villosa*. For information on work parties or weekend excursions to the preserve, call the Nature Conservancy (☎ 537-4508).

Halona Blowhole

About half a mile past Hanauma is a **lookout** with a view of striking coastal rock formations and crashing surf.

Nearly a mile farther is the parking lot for Halona Blowhole, where water surges through a submerged tunnel in the rock and spouts up through a hole in the ledge. It's usually preceded by a gushing sound, created by the air that's being forced out by the rushing water.

Down to the right of the parking lot is **Halona Cove**, the beach where the risque love scene with Burt Lancaster and Deborah Kerr in *From Here to Eternity* was filmed in the 1950s.

Immediately before the blowhole, a small **stone monument** sits atop Halona Point. It was erected by Japanese fishers to honor those lost at sea.

Sandy Beach

Sandy Beach is one of the most dangerous beaches on the island if measured in terms of lifeguard rescues and broken necks. It has a punishing shorebreak, a powerful backwash and strong rip currents.

Nevertheless, the shorebreak is extremely popular with bodysurfers who know their stuff. It's equally popular with spectators, who gather to watch the bodysurfers being tossed around in the transparent waves.

Sandy Beach is wide and very long and, yes, sandy. It's frequented by sunbathers, young surfers and their admirers. When the swells are big, board surfers hit the left side of the beach.

Red flags flown on the beach indicate hazardous water conditions. Even if you don't notice the flags, always check with the lifeguards before entering the water.

Not all the action is in the water. The grassy strip on the inland side of the parking lot is used by people looking skyward for their thrills – it's both a hang glider landing site and a popular locale for kite flying.

The park has restrooms, showers, a pay phone and lifeguards.

Koko Crater

According to Hawaiian legend, Koko Crater (Kohelepelepe) is the imprint left by the vagina of Pele's sister Kapo, which was sent here from the Big Island to lure the pig-god Kamapuaa away from Pele.

Inside the crater there's a long-neglected botanic garden of plumeria trees, cacti and other dryland plants that the county is in the process of reviving. To get there, take Kealahou St off Hwy 72 opposite the northern end of Sandy Beach. Just over half a mile in, turn left at the road to Koko Crater Stables (no trail rides) and continue a third of a mile to the garden, which is open daily from 9 am to 4 pm.

On the outside of the crater on the Hanauma side there's an unmaintained hiking trail. It follows an abandoned railroad track that once served a former army missile base on the 1208-foot summit.

Places to Eat

Koko Marina Shopping Center, on the corner of Lunalilo Home Rd and Hwy 72, has a *Sizzler* steak house, standard fast-food places and other restaurants as well as ice cream, shave ice and frozen yogurt shops.

For local flavor try *Yummy Korean Bar-B-Q*, which offers barbecued meat dishes accompanied with 'two-scoop rice' and four tasty marinated vegetable dishes or kimchees, including a terrific watercress and sesame variety, for around $6.

Roy's (☎ 396-7697), at Hawaii Kai Corporate Plaza on Hwy 72, serves some of the best food in all Oahu. Owner Roy Yamaguchi is a creative force behind the popularity of Pacific Rim cuisine, which emphasizes fresh local ingredients and blends the lighter aspects of European cooking with Japanese, Thai and Chinese influences. A large exhibition kitchen sits in the center of the dining room, where Roy orchestrates an impressive troupe of sous cooks and chefs.

Starters include spring rolls, imu-oven pizzas and a variety of salads priced around $7. The crispy lemongrass chicken, which is served on a bed of sautéed vegetables and topped with a delightful Cabernet curry sauce, costs $14 and makes a fine main dish. Most other meat dishes are priced around $17, while fresh fish specials average $23. There are more romantic settings in Oahu but in all other ways Roy's is a top choice for a night out – the food is attractively presented, the service attentive and the servings good-sized. It's open from 5:30 to 10 pm on weekdays, from 5 to 10:30 pm on weekends. Reservations are advisable.

MAKAPUU

About a mile north of Sandy Beach, the 647-foot Makapuu Point and its coastal **lighthouse** mark the easternmost point of Oahu. The mile-long service road to the lighthouse has recently been deeded by the federal government to Hawaii, thus opening this site to the public. The gate into the service road is locked to keep out private vehicles but you can park off the highway just beyond the gate and walk in from there. There are fine coastal views along the way and at the lighthouse lookout.

Back on the highway, about a third of a mile farther along, there's a scenic **roadside lookout** with a view down onto Makapuu Beach, with its aqua-blue waters outlined by white sand and black lava. It's an even more spectacular sight when hang gliders are taking off from the cliffs, Oahu's top hang-gliding spot.

From the lookout you can see two off-shore islands, the larger of which is Manana, otherwise known as **Rabbit Island**. This aging volcanic crater is populated by feral rabbits and burrowing wedge-tailed shearwaters. They coexist so closely that the birds and rabbits sometimes even share the same burrows.

The island looks vaguely like the head of a rabbit, and if you try hard you may see it, ears folded back. If that doesn't work, try to see it as a whale.

In front of it is the smaller **Kaohikaipu Island**, which won't tax the imagination – all it looks is flat.

There's a coral reef between the two islands that divers sometimes explore, but to do so generally requires a boat.

Makapuu Beach

Makapuu Beach is one of Oahu's top winter bodysurfing spots, with waves reaching 12 feet and higher. It also has the island's best shorebreak. As with Sandy Beach, Makapuu is strictly the domain of experienced bodysurfers who can handle rough water conditions and dangerous currents. Surfboards are prohibited.

In summer, when the wave action disappears, the waters can be calm and good for swimming.

The beach is opposite Sea Life Park in a pretty setting, with cliffs in the background and a glimpse of the lighthouse. Two native Hawaiian plants are plentiful – naupaka by the beach and the yellow-orange ilima by the parking lot.

Sea Life Park

Sea Life Park (☎ 259-7933) is Hawaii's only marine park. Its 300,000-gallon aquarium has sea turtles, eels, eagle rays, hammerhead sharks and thousands of reef fish. A spiral ramp circles the aquarium, which is 18 feet deep, allowing you to view the fish from different depths.

In one of two outdoor amphitheaters, jumping dolphins and waddling penguins perform the standard marine life park tricks.

In the other, the Whaler's Cove, a 1500-pound false killer whale and a group of dolphins give a choreographed performance. The dolphins tail walk, do the hula and give rides to a 'beautiful island maiden' – all bordering on kitsch!

There's a large pool of California sea lions and a smaller pool with harbor seals and a few rare Hawaiian monk seals. The turtle lagoon holds hawksbill, loggerhead and green sea turtles. Another section of the park has nesting red-footed boobies, albatrosses and great frigate birds, all seabirds indigenous to Hawaii.

Hanging from the ceiling of the park's little **Whaling Museum** is the skeleton of a 38-foot sperm whale that was washed up off Barbers Point in 1980. After the Coast Guard damaged a ship propeller unsuccessfully trying to tow the 20-ton mammal out to sea, they turned the carcass over to Sea Life Park. The park removed almost 38,000 pounds of flesh from the skeleton using many of the antique whaling tools on display in the museum. The whole process took the better part of two years.

In addition to harpoons, a trypot used to boil down whale blubber and other whaling paraphernalia, the museum has a fine collection of whaling-era scrimshaw, from toys and bird cages to suggestive 'porno' pieces.

Sea Life Park is open from 9:30 am to 5 pm, with the last series of shows beginning at 3:15 pm. On Fridays the park closes at 10 pm, with the last series of shows from 6:30 pm, followed by Hawaiian music at 8:30 pm. The Friday entertainment often features top island musicians and admission is the same as on other days – which makes it a nice time to visit.

Admission is $19.95 for adults, $8.95 for children ages six to 12, $3.95 for children ages four and five and free for children under four.

You can visit the whaling museum and the park restaurant (sandwiches, salads and other cafeteria-style food) without paying admission. You also get a free look at the seal and sea lion pools along the walk to the museum.

Public buses No 22, 57 Kailua/Sea Life Park and 58 Hawaii Kai/Sea Life Park stop at Sea Life Park. Also, a free shuttle bus (☎ 923-1531) leaves from major hotels in Waikiki six times a day.

WAIMANALO
Waimanalo Bay has the longest continuous stretch of beach in Oahu: 5½ miles of white sand running north from Makapuu Point to Wailea Point. A long coral reef about a mile out breaks up the biggest waves, protecting much of the shore.

Waimanalo has three beach parks with camping. The setting is scenic, although the area isn't highly regarded for safety.

Waimanalo Beach Park
Waimanalo Beach Park has an attractive beach of soft white sand and the water is excellent for swimming.

It's an in-town county park with a grassy picnic area, restrooms, changing rooms, showers, ball fields, basketball and volleyball courts and a playground. Camping is allowed in an open area near the road but most of the campers are homeless families and it's not a scene that invites visitors.

The park has ironwood trees, but overall it's more open than the other two parks to the north. The scalloped hills of the lower Koolau Range rise up mauka of the park and Manana Island and Makapuu Point are visible to the south.

Waimanalo Bay State Recreation Area
Waimanalo Bay Beach Park is about a mile north of the other county beach park. For board surfers and bodysurfers this area has Waimanalo Bay's biggest waves.

Locals call the park Sherwood Forest because hoods and car thieves used to hang out there in days past – it hasn't totally shaken its reputation, so watch your belongings carefully.

The park itself is quite appealing with beachside campsites shaded with ironwood trees. There are barbecue grills, drinking water, showers and restrooms.

Bus No 57 stops in front of the park and it's a third of a mile walk in from the road to the beach and campground. The gate is open from 7 am to sunset.

Bellows Field Beach Park
The beach fronting Bellows Air Force Base is open to civilian beachgoers and campers on weekends only, from noon on Friday until 8 am on Monday. This long beach has fine, hard-packed sand and a natural setting backed by ironwood trees. The small shore-break waves are good for beginner body-surfers and board surfers.

There's a lifeguard, showers, restrooms and water; the 50 campsites are set out amongst the trees. Permits are available from the county Department of Parks & Recreation.

The marked entrance is a quarter of a mile north of Waimanalo Bay Beach Park. Bus No 57 stops in front of the entrance road and from there it's 1½ miles to the beach.

Places to Eat

Bueno Nalo (☎ 259-7186) is between the two county beach parks, just north of Waimanalo's post office. Good homestyle Mexican combination plates are priced around $9, and until 2 pm there are lunch plates for $6.25. It's open from 11:30 am to 9 pm daily.

There's a grocery store and a bakery next door to Bueno Nalo and a *McDonald's* just south of Waimanalo Bay Beach Park.

Pali Highway

The Pali Highway (Hwy 61) runs between Honolulu and Kailua, cutting through the spectacular Koolau Range. It's a scenic little highway and if it's been raining heavily every fold and crevice in the mountains will have a lacy waterfall streaming down it.

Many Kailua residents commute to work over the Pali, so Honolulu-bound traffic can be heavy in the morning and outbound traffic heavy in the evening. It's less of a problem for visitors however, as most day-trippers will be traveling against the traffic. Public buses travel the Pali Hwy but none stop at the Nuuanu Pali Lookout.

Past the four-mile marker, look up and to the right to see two notches cut about 15 feet deep into the crest of the *pali* (cliff). These notches are thought to have been dug as cannon emplacements by Kamehameha I.

The original route between Honolulu and windward Oahu was via an ancient footpath that wound its way perilously over these cliffs. In 1845 the path was widened into a horse trail and later into a cobblestone carriage road.

In 1898 the Old Pali Highway (as it's now called) was built following the same route. It was abandoned in the 1950s after tunnels were blasted through the Koolau Range and the present multi-lane Pali Hwy opened.

You can still drive a loop of the Old Pali Hwy (called Nuuanu Pali Dr) and hike

another mile of it from the Nuuanu Pali Lookout.

Queen Emma Summer Palace (14)

At the Pali Hwy two-mile marker is the Queen Emma Summer Palace, which belonged to Queen Emma, the consort of Kamehameha IV.

Emma was three-quarters royal Hawaiian and a quarter English, a granddaughter of the captured sailor John Young who became a friend and adviser of Kamehameha I. The house is also known as Hanaiakamalama, the name of John Young's home in Kawaihae on the Big Island, where he served as governor.

The Youngs left the home to Queen Emma, who often slipped away from her formal downtown home to this cooler retreat. It's a bit like an old Southern plantation house, with a columned porch, high ceilings and louvered windows to catch the breeze.

The home was forgotten after Emma's death in 1885, and was scheduled to be razed in 1915, as the estate was being turned into a public park. The Daughters of Hawaii rescued it and now run it as a museum.

The house has period furniture collected from five of Emma's homes. Some of the more interesting pieces are a cathedral-shaped koa cabinet made in Berlin and filled with a set of china from Queen Victoria; feather cloaks and capes; and Emma's necklace of tiger claws, a gift from the Maharaja of India.

It's open from 9 am to 4 pm daily except holidays. Admission is $4 for adults, $1 for children ages 12 to 16 and 50c for those under 12.

Nuuanu Pali Drive

For a scenic side trip through a shady green forest, turn off the Pali Hwy onto Nuuanu Pali Dr, half a mile past the Queen Emma Summer Palace. The 2½-mile road runs parallel to the Pali Hwy and then comes back out to it before the Nuuanu Pali Lookout, so you don't miss anything by taking this side loop – in fact, quite the opposite.

The drive is through mature trees that form a canopy overhead, all draped with hanging vines and wound with philodendrons. The lush vegetation includes banyan trees with hanging aerial roots, tropical almond trees, bamboo groves, impatiens, angel trumpets and golden cup – a tall climbing vine with large golden flowers.

Judd Trail

If you want to get off the road and into the woods, you might try Judd Trail. The full trail is a 1½-mile loop, but most people just take it as far as Jackass Ginger, a little freshwater pool about 10 minutes in.

One mile up Nuuanu Pali Dr, there's a marked dirt parking lot on the right, just before a small bridge. It's best to take all valuables out of your car and leave it unlocked as thieves are fond of smashing car windows in this area.

The trail starts below the parking lot and soon makes a stream crossing. The trail then runs parallel to the stream but goes uphill a bit, so you'll need to keep an eye out for the pool. Sometimes it's a good place for a dip, other times it's muddy; and the mosquitoes are hungry!

Trees along the way include large banyans, ironwood, *Eucalyptus robusta* and Norfolk pine.

Nuuanu Pali Lookout

Whatever you do, don't miss the Nuuanu Pali Lookout (Nuuanu Pali State Wayside) with its broad view of the windward coast from a height of 1200 feet. From the lookout you can see Kaneohe straight ahead, Kailua to the right and Chinaman's Hat (Mokolii Island) and the coastal fishpond at Kualoa Park to the far left.

This is *windward* Oahu – and the winds that funnel through the pali are so strong that you can sometimes lean against them. It gets cool enough to appreciate having a jacket.

In 1795 Kamehameha I routed Oahu's warriors up the Nuuanu Trail during his invasion of the island. On these steep cliffs

Oahu's warriors made their last stand. Hundreds were thrown to their death over the pali by Kamehameha's troops. A hundred years later, during the construction of the Old Pali Hwy, more than 500 skulls were found at the base of the cliffs.

The abandoned Old Pali Hwy winds down from the right of the lookout, ending abruptly at a barrier near the current highway about a mile away. Few people realize the road is here, let alone venture down it. It makes a nice walk and takes about 20 minutes one way. There are good views looking back up at the jagged Koolau Mountains and out across the valley.

As you get back on the highway, it's easy to miss the sign leading you out of the parking lot and instinct could send you in the wrong direction. Go to the left if you're heading towards Kailua, to the right if heading towards Honolulu.

Windward Coast

Windward Oahu, the island's eastern side, follows the Koolau Range along its entire length. The mountains looming inland are lovely, with scalloped folds and deep valleys. In places they come so near to the shore that they almost seem to crowd the highway into the ocean.

The windward coast runs from Kahuku Point in the north to Makapuu Point in the south. (For the Waimanalo to Makapuu area, see the Southeast Oahu section.)

The two main towns are Kaneohe and Kailua, both largely nondescript bedroom communities for workers who commute to Honolulu, about 10 miles away.

North of Kaneohe, the windward coast is rural Hawaii, where many Hawaiians struggle along close to the earth, making a living with small papaya, banana and vegetable farms. It's generally wetter on the windward side and the vegetation is lush and green.

The windward coast is exposed to the northeast trade winds. This is a popular area for anything that requires a sail – from windsurfing to yachting.

There are some nice swimming beaches on the windward coast – notably Kailua, Kualoa and Malaekahana – although many other sections of the coast are too silted for swimming. Swimmers should keep an eye out for stinging Portuguese man-of-war that are often washed in during storms.

Most of the offshore islets that you'll see along this coast have been set aside as bird sanctuaries. These tiny islands are vital habitat for ground-nesting seabirds which have largely been driven off the populated islands by the introduction of mongoose, cats and other predators.

Two highways cut through the Koolau Range to the windward coast. The Pali Hwy (Hwy 61) goes straight into Kailua. The Likelike Hwy (Hwy 63) runs directly into Kaneohe and, although it doesn't have the scenic stops the Pali Hwy has, is in some ways more dramatic. Driving away from Kaneohe it feels as if you're heading straight into tall fairy-tale-like mountains, then you suddenly shoot through a tunnel and emerge on the Honolulu side, the drama gone.

If you're heading both to and from windward Oahu through the Koolau Range, take the Pali Hwy up from Honolulu and the Likelike Hwy back for the best of both. (See the Pali Highway section for details on that drive.)

KAILUA

In ancient times Kailua was a place of legends. It was home to a giant turned into a mountain ridge, the island's first menehunes and numerous Oahuan chiefs.

But that's all history. Kailua today is an ordinary middle-class community, with one of Oahu's finest beaches but little else of distinction to attract visitors. It's the third largest city in Oahu, with a population of 38,000.

Ulupo Heiau

Ulupo Heiau is a large open platform temple, made of stones piled 30 feet high and 140 feet long. Its construction is attrib-

uted to menehunes, the little people that legends say created much of Hawaii's stonework, finishing each project in one night. Fittingly, Ulupo means 'night inspiration'.

In front of the heiau, which is thought to have been a luakini type, is an artist's rendition of how the site probably looked in the 18th century before Westerners arrived.

If you walk out across the top of the heiau you get a view of Kawainui Swamp, one of Hawaii's largest habitats for endangered waterbirds. Legends say the swamp's ancient fishpond had edible mud at the bottom and was home to a *moo*, or lizard spirit.

Ulupo Heiau is one mile south of Kailua Rd. Coming up the Pali Hwy from Honolulu, take Uluoa St, the first left after passing the Hwy 72 junction. Then turn right on Manu Aloha St and right again onto Manuoo St. The heiau is behind the left side of the YMCA.

Kailua Beach

Kailua Beach Park is at the southeastern end of Kailua Bay. This white sand beach is long and broad with lovely turquoise waters. The park is popular for long walks, family outings and a range of water activities.

Kailua Bay is the top windsurfing spot in Oahu. Onshore trade winds are predominant and windsurfers can sail at Kailua every month of the year. In different spots around the bay there are different water conditions, some good for jumps and wave surfing, others for flatwater sails. Some windsurfing companies, including Naish Hawaii and Kailua Sailboards, give lessons and rent boards at the beach park on weekdays and Saturday mornings.

Kailua Beach has a gently sloping sandy bottom with waters that are generally flat and calm. Swimming is good year round.

The park has restrooms, showers, lifeguards, a snack shop, a volleyball court and large grassy expanses partly shaded with ironwood trees.

Kaelepulu Canal divides the park into two sections, although a sand bar usually prevents the canal waters from emptying into the bay. Windsurfing activities are on the west side of the canal; there's a small boat ramp on the east side.

Kalama Beach, an unimproved beach just north of the park, has gentle waves good for novice bodysurfers. While surfers sometimes use the beach park, they often go where the surf is bigger at the northern end of Kailua Bay at **Kapoho Point** or farther still to a break called **Zombies**.

The island offshore, **Popoia Island** (Flat Island), a bird sanctuary where landings are allowed, is a popular destination for kayakers.

To get to Kailua Beach Park, take bus No 56 or 57 from Ala Moana Center and transfer to a No 70 in Kailua. If you have your own transport, simply stay on Kailua Rd, which begins at the end of the Pali Hwy (Hwy 61) and continues as the main road through town, ending at the beach.

Lanikai

If you follow the coastal road as it continues east of Kailua Beach Park, you'll shortly come to Lanikai, a rather exclusive residential neighborhood. It's fronted by Lanikai Beach, which is an attractive stretch of powdery white sand – at least what's left of it. Much of the sand has washed away as a result of the retaining walls built to protect the homes plopped right on the shore.

The sandy bottom slopes gently and the waters are calm, offering safe swimming conditions similar to those at Kailua. The twin Mokulua islets sit directly offshore.

From Kailua Beach Park, the road turns into the one-way Aalapapa Dr, which comes back around as Mokulua Dr to make a 2½-mile loop. There are 11 narrow beach access walkways off Mokulua Dr. For the best stretches of beach, try the one opposite Kualima Dr or any of the next three.

Places to Stay

Kailua has no hotels, but there are many furnished beachfront cottages, studios and B&B-style rooms in private homes. While a few of these can be rented directly from the owners, the majority ... B&B reservation services.

Akamai Bed & Breakfas... (800) 642-5366), 172 K... Kailua, HI 96734, has two nice studio units in a private home about 10 minutes' walk from Kailua Beach. Each is modern and comfortable and has a refrigerator, microwave, coffeemaker, tiny bathroom, cable TV and private entrance. The larger room has a queen bed, the smaller has two twin beds that can be joined to make a king-size bed. Each room has a sofa bed as well. The rate of $65 includes a fruit basket and breakfast items. There's a laundry room ($1 per load) and a pleasant courtyard with a pool. The minimum stay is three days; smoking is limited to the outdoors.

Papaya Paradise Bed & Breakfast (☎ 261-0316), 395 Auwinala Rd, Kailua, HI 96734, is a 15-minute walk from Kailua Beach. Bob and Jeanette Martz, retired from the army and home most of the time, rent two rooms off the side of their home. One room has a queen bed and a trundle bed, the other two single beds, both with private entrances through the garden courtyard, which has a pool. Each room has a bathroom, air-con, ceiling fan and TV. The rate is $65 for singles or doubles with a full breakfast. There's a three-day minimum.

Most of the state-wide B&B agencies have listings of Kailua accommodation. The following are based in Kailua and each book more than 50 different Kailua-area accommodations.

Affordable Paradise Bed & Breakfast (☎ 261-1693, (800) 925-9065; fax 261-7315), Maria Wilson, 226 Pouli Rd, Kailua, HI 96734, books cottages from $65 and studios and B&Bs from $45 a double. Maria, who speaks German, can also arrange a few B&Bs for singles from $35. There's no booking fee or similar rigmarole.

All Islands Bed & Breakfast (☎ 263-2342, (800) 542-0344; fax 263-0308), 823 Kainui Dr, Kailua, HI 96734 has B&B rooms averaging $55 to $65 and studio apartments from $65 to $75.

Pacific-Hawaii Bed & Breakfast (☎ 262-

6, (800) 999-6026; fax 261-6573), c/o
Neal Realty, 602 Kailua Rd, Suite 107-C,
Kailua, HI 96734, has listings in all price
ranges. There's a $15 booking fee.

Naish Hawaii (☎ 262-6068, (800) 767-
6068; fax 263-9723), 155A Hamakua Dr,
Kailua, HI 96734, books windsurfing vacations with accommodation in Kailua.

Places to Eat

Kailua has both fast-food eateries and a
sandwich shop *Gee A Deli* near the intersection of Kailua and Kuulei Rds and some
recommendable moderately priced restaurants. Nearby is a good Mexican restaurant, *El Charro Avitia*, 14 Oneawa St,
where two-item combination plates with
rice and beans cost $9.25, three-item
combos $10.50. Both the food and atmos-
phere are authentically Mexican. On weekdays until 3 pm, menu prices are 20%
cheaper. It's open daily from 11 am to
9:30 pm.

Assaggio (☎ 261-2772), 354 Uluniu St,
serves good, moderately priced Italian food
in a somewhat upmarket setting. At lunch,
sandwiches cost $5 to $6 and hot dishes are
just a few dollars more. A good choice is
the spicy chicken Assaggio's with chunks
of white chicken meat, pepperoncini,
mushrooms and roasted bell peppers over a
bed of pasta. A generous serving costs $8 at
lunch, $13 at dinner. Other dishes include a
nice eggplant parmigiana, shrimp vegetable
linguine and filet mignon. It's open weekdays from 11:30 am to 2:30 pm and nightly
from 5 to 10 pm.

Jaron's (☎ 261-4600), 201A Hamakua
Dr, has a jazzy decor and a varied menu.
Lunch includes a nice shrimp and avocado
baguette sandwich for $7 and tasty Cajun-
style fresh fish for $11. There are also
pizzas, pastas and burgers. All dishes come
with a green salad. At dinner the menu con-
centrates on seafood and steaks priced from
$15 to $20; there's sometimes a sunset
dinner special, served until 6:30 pm, for
just $8.95. It's open from 11 am to 10 pm.

The Source, 32 Kainehe St, is a small
natural food store with bulk herbs and
spices, vitamins, general food items and a

small produce section. At lunch there's a
juice bar with smoothies, tofu burgers,
sandwiches, salads and soups – with the
exception of smoked salmon, everything
on the menu is under $5. The store is open
from 9 am to 9 pm on weekdays, 10 am to
5 pm on weekends.

Across the street from the Source is a
good little bakery selling whole-grain
breads, inexpensive pastries and Portuguese malasadas to order. The malasadas,
which are intended to be eaten hot, take
about 10 minutes to make and cost 50c
each. They also serve coffee, tea and soup
and there are a couple of small tables were
you can sit and eat. Hours are 6 am to 6 pm
daily except Mondays.

Entertainment

Fast Eddie's (☎ 261-8561), 52 Oneawa St,
is open from 9:30 pm to 4 am nightly, with
rock, Jawaiian and Hawaiian groups,
including the likes of Kapena and Willie K.
Usually there's no cover charge from
Sunday to Wednesday, while on weekends
it's from $5 to $10 plus a two-drink
minimum. No one under 21 is allowed.

Someplace Else (☎ 263-8833), 33 Aulike
St, has live rock bands from 10 pm to 2 am
Tuesday to Saturday. There's no cover
charge and no age minimum.

Jaron's (☎ 261-4600), 201A Hamakua
Dr, has live blues on Thursdays and rock or
reggae bands on Fridays and Saturdays, all
from 10:30 pm to 1:30 am. There's no
cover charge.

The *No Name Bar* (☎ 261-8725), 131
Hekili St, has reggae, rock or blues music
until 2 am nightly. There's a small dance
floor and no cover.

KANEOHE

Kaneohe, with a population of 36,000, is
Oahu's fourth largest city.

Kaneohe Bay, which stretches from
Mokapu Peninsula all the way up to Kualoa
Point, seven miles north, is the state's
largest bay and reef-sheltered lagoon.
Although inshore it's largely silted and not
good for swimming, the near-constant trade

winds that sweep across the bay are ideal for sailing.

Two highways run north to south through Kaneohe. Kamehameha Hwy is closer to the coast and goes by Heeia State Park. Kahekili Hwy runs inland from the outskirts of Kaneohe, where it intersects the Likelike Hwy and continues north past Byodo-In. The highways merge into a single route, Kamehameha Hwy (Hwy 83), a few miles north of Kaneohe.

Kaneohe Marine Corps Air Station occupies the whole of Mokapu Peninsula. H-3, the controversial cross-island freeway that's scheduled to be completed in late 1996, terminates at its gate.

H-3
Environmentalists have opposed the H-3 freeway project from the beginning, concerned not only with the degradation of the pristine valleys that the new road will slice across, but also with the probability that the freeway will open the rural areas of the windward coast to further development. Ironically, if the latter holds true, the new project is expected to *increase* traffic for Kailua-Honolulu commuters, who already contend with some of the worst traffic congestion on the island.

The H-3 freeway, which got its impetus during the Reagan era, owes its existence in no small way to the heated Cold War mania of the day. When complete, the highway will end near Pearl Harbor, connecting military bases on both sides of the island. As the post-Cold War military presence in Hawaii downsizes, the freeway's cost of $1.2 billion may well turn out to be the biggest pork barrel Hawaii will ever see. ■

Hoomaluhia Park
The county's newest and largest botanic garden is Hoomaluhia, a 400-acre park in the uplands of Kaneohe. The park is planted with groups of trees and shrubs from tropical regions around the world.

It's a peaceful, lush green setting, with a stunning pali backdrop. Hoomaluhia is not a landscaped flower garden, but more of a natural preserve. A network of trails wind through the park and up to a 32-acre lake (no swimming allowed).

The little visitor center (☎ 233-7323) has displays on flora & fauna, Hawaiian ethnobotany and on the history of the park, which was originally built by the US Army Corps of Engineers as flood protection for the valley below.

The park is at the end of Luluku Rd, which starts 2¼ miles down Kamehameha Hwy from the Pali Hwy. Buses No 55 and 56 go to Windward City Shopping Center opposite the start of Luluku Rd. It's 1½ miles up Luluku Rd from the highway to the visitor center and another 1½ miles from the visitor center to the far end of the park so, if you use the bus, expect to do some walking.

The park is open from 9 am to 4 pm daily (closed on Christmas and New Year's Day) and admission is free.

Guided two-hour nature hikes are held at 10 am on Saturdays and 1 pm on Sundays. Call the visitor center for registration. Camping is also available (see Places to Stay below).

Valley of the Temples & Byodo-In
The Valley of the Temples is an interdenominational cemetery in a beautiful setting just off the Kahekili Hwy, 1½ miles north of Haiku Rd. The main attraction is Byodo-In, the 'Temple of Equality', which is a replica of the 900-year-old temple of the same name in Uji, Japan. This one was dedicated in 1968 to commemorate the 100th anniversary of Japanese immigration to Hawaii.

Byodo-In sits against the Koolau Range. The rich red of the temple against the verdant fluted cliffs is strikingly picturesque, especially when mist settles in on the pali.

The temple is meant to symbolize the mythical phoenix. Inside the main hall is a nine-foot gold-lacquered buddha sitting on a lotus. Wild peacocks roam the grounds and hang their tail feathers over the upper temple railings.

A carp pond fronts the temple, with cruising bullfrogs and cooing doves. A three-ton brass bell beside the pond is said to bring tranquility and good fortune to those who ring it.

It's all very Japanese, right down to the gift shop selling sake cups, daruma dolls and happy buddhas. This scene is as close as you'll get to Japan without having to land at Narita.

Admission to the temple is $2 for adults, $1 for children under 12. It's open from 8:30 am to 4:30 pm daily.

On the way out, you might want to head up to the hilltop mausoleum with the cross on top and check out the view.

Heeia State Park

Heeia State Park is on Kealohi Point, just off Kamehameha Hwy. It has a good view of Heeia Fishpond on the right and Heeia-Kea Harbor on the left.

The ancient **Heeia Fishpond**, owned by the Bishop Estate, is an impressive fishpond that remains largely intact despite the invasive mangrove that grows along its walls and takes root between the rocks.

Coconut Island, just offshore to the southeast of the fishpond, was a royal playground in times past. It was named for the coconut trees planted there by Princess Bernice Pauahi Bishop. In the 1930s it was the estate of Christian Holmes, heir to the Fleischmann Yeast fortune, who dredged the island, doubling its size to 25 acres. During the war the estate served as an R&R facility and had a brief stint as a hotel. In more recent times, air-brushed shots of Coconut Island were used in opening scenes for the *Gilligan's Island* TV series. The Hawaii Institute of Marine Biology of the University of Hawaii occupies a niche

on the island, while the rest is privately owned.

You can walk around the grounds of Heeia State Park and take in the view but otherwise there's not much to do here. Friends of Heeia State Park have a little booth in the hall above the parking lot and can answer questions about the area.

Places to Stay

Camping Hoomaluhia Park has the best non-beach camping in Oahu. With a resident caretaker and gates that are locked to non-campers at 4 pm, the park is also one of the safest places to camp on Oahu. There are five camping areas, each with restrooms, cold showers and drinking water. The camping area farthest in is on an open grassy expanse with great views.

Camping is allowed from 9 am Thursday to 9 am Tuesday. Other than a few long weekends in summer the park seldom fills. There's no fee but reservations should be made two weeks (and not more than six months) in advance at the center (☎ 233-7323) or with the county Department of Parks & Recreation. It's possible to do it all by mail. For an application send a legal-size, self-addressed stamped envelope to Hoomaluhia, 45-680 Luluku Rd, Kaneohe, HI 96744.

Hotels *Alii Bluffs Windward Bed & Breakfast* (☎ & fax 235-1124, (800) 235-1151), 46-251 Ikiiki St, Kaneohe, HI 96744, has two bedrooms in a cozy home filled with Old World furnishings, oil paintings, antique toys and other collectibles. The Victorian Room has one double bed and costs $55/60 for singles/doubles, while the Circus Room has two twin beds and costs $50/55. Each room has a private bathroom. Originally from the Scottish Highlands, where his mother ran a B&B, host Don Munro gives guests the run of the house and provides beach towels and coolers. Breakfast and afternoon tea are included in the rates. There's a small pool and a view of Kaneohe Bay.

The 59-unit *Schrader's Windward Marine Resort* (☎ 239-5711, (800) 735-

5711; fax 239-6658), 47-039 Lihikai Dr, Kaneohe, HI 96744, is a spread of simple low-rise wooden buildings in a residential neighborhood. Despite the name, the ambiance is more that of a local motel than a resort. So many of the guests are military families that they offer free transport to the Kaneohe Marine Corps base. One-bedroom units range from $70 to $146, two-bedroom units from $100 to $190. All have refrigerators, microwaves, TVs and phones.

Places to Eat
Chart House (☎ 247-6671) at Haiku Gardens has a lush, open-air setting with a picturesque view of a lily pond tucked beneath the Koolau Mountains. It's open for dinner from 5 pm nightly and for Sunday brunch. The food is standard steak and seafood dishes ($16 to $27) accompanied by a nice salad bar. The real attraction is the setting; the gardens are flood-lit at night.

You can also drop by Haiku Gardens in the daytime and take a 10-minute stroll around the pond. To get there from Kamehameha Hwy turn left on Haiku Rd just past Windward Mall; after crossing Kahekili Hwy, continue on Haiku Rd a quarter of a mile farther.

Chao Phya Thai Restaurant in the Windward City Shopping Center, 45-480 Kaneohe Bay Dr, is a family-run restaurant serving good Thai food. Nearly all dishes on the extensive menu are priced between $5.25 and $6.50. It's open for lunch from 11 am to 2 pm Monday to Saturday and for dinner from 5 to 9 pm nightly.

The Windward City Shopping Center also has a 24-hour *Foodland* supermarket, fast-food restaurants and *Kozo Sushi*, part of a local chain of fast-food shops specializing in good inexpensive sushi. *Burger King* and *Pizza Hut* are on the opposite side of the Kamehameha Hwy.

The Windward Mall, on Kamehameha Hwy at its intersection with Haiku Rd, is a large two-level mall with a bank, chain department stores and numerous other shops. The mall's Food Court is sort of a mini Ala Moana with a line of food stalls selling hot cinnamon rolls, deli items, pizza by the slice and Japanese, Chinese, Mexican and Korean foods.

WAIAHOLE & WAIKANE
Waiahole and Waikane mark the beginning of rural Oahu. The area is home to family-run nurseries and small farms growing coconuts, bananas, papayas and lemons.

Large tracts of Waikane Valley were taken over by the military during WW II for training and target practice, a use that continued up until the 1960s. The government now claims the land has so much live ordnance it can't be returned to the families it was leased from. This is a source of ongoing contention with local residents who are angry that much of the inner valley remains off-limits.

KUALOA
Kualoa Regional Park
Kualoa Regional Park, a 153-acre county park on Kualoa Point, is bounded on its southern side by Molii Fishpond. From the road south of the park the fishpond is visible through the trees as a distinct green line in the bay.

Kualoa is a nice beach park in a scenic setting. The mountains looming precipitously across the road are, appropriately enough, called Pali-ku, meaning 'vertical cliff'. When the mist settles it looks like a scene from a Chinese watercolor.

The main island offshore is **Mokolii**, which in more recent times has come to be known as Chinaman's Hat. In Hawaiian legend, Mokolii is said to be the tail of a nasty lizard or a dog – depending on who's telling the story – which was slain by a god and thrown into the ocean.

Apua Pond, a three-acre brackish salt marsh on the point, is a nesting area for the endangered aeo (Hawaiian stilt). If you walk down the beach beyond the park you'll see a bit of **Molii Fishpond**, but it's hard to get a good perspective on it from there. The rock walls are covered with mangrove, milo and pickleweed.

The park is largely open lawn with a few palm trees. It has a long thin strip of beach

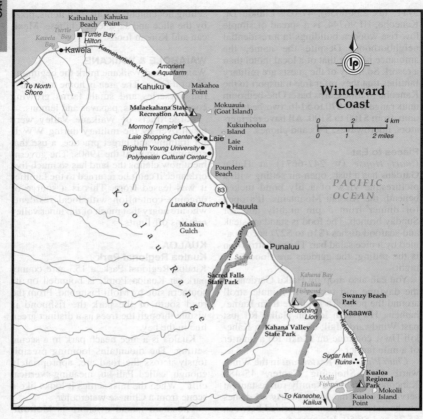

Windward Coast

0   2   4 km

0   1   2 miles

PACIFIC
OCEAN

Kaihalulu Kahuku
Beach   Point
Turtle
Bay
Kawela Bay
■ Turtle Bay
  Hilton
● Kawela

Kamehameha Hwy

To North
Shore

Amorient
Aquafarm
● Kahuku   Makahoa
                Point

Malaekahana State
Recreation Area
                Mokuauia
                (Goat Island)
Mormon Temple†
Laie Shopping Center   ● Laie
Brigham Young University ●   Kukuihoolua
Polynesian Cultural Center. Island
                Laie
                Point
                Pounders
                Beach
                83

Lanakila Church† ● Hauula

Maakua
Gulch

Koolau Range

Sacred
Falls

Sacred Falls
State Park

● Punaluu

Kahana Bay

Huliua
Fishpond

Swanzy Beach
Park

Crouching ●
Lion   ● Kaaawa

Kahana Valley
State Park

Sugar Mill
Ruins

Molii
Fishpond

Kualoa
Regional
Park
             Mokolii
             Island
Kualoa
Point

To Kaneohe,
Kailua

with shallow waters and safe swimming. There are camping areas, picnic tables, restrooms, showers, a phone and a lifeguard. It's open for day use between 7 am and 8 pm, after which the gate is locked for security.

Lots of islanders camp here on weekends – so many, in fact, that at times they open a second campground on the bay side of the point. It's more shaded than the main campground at the head of the beach. Camping is free from Friday to Tuesday nights with a permit from the county.

Kualoa used to be one of the most sacred places on Oahu. When a chief stood on the point, passing canoes lowered their sails in respect. The children of chiefs were brought here to be raised and it may also have been a place of refuge. It was at Kualoa that the double-hulled canoe *Hokulea* landed in 1987, following a two-year rediscovery voyage through Polynesia that retraced the ancient migration routes.

Kualoa Ranch
The horses grazing on the green slopes across the road from Kualoa Regional Park belong to Kualoa Ranch. The ranch offers

all sorts of activities from kayaking to target shooting but, except for horseback riding that's open to the public with reservations, everything's packaged for Japanese honeymooners who are shuttled in from Waikiki.

Back in 1850 Kamehameha III leased about 625 acres of this land for $1300 to Dr Judd, a missionary doctor who became one of the king's advisers. Judd planted the land with sugar cane, built flumes to transport it and imported Chinese laborers to work the fields. His sugar mill trudged along for a few decades but went under just before the reciprocity agreement with the USA opened up mainland sugar markets.

You can still see the remains of the mill's stone stack and a bit of the crumbling walls half a mile north of the beach park, right alongside the road.

KAAAWA

In the Kaaawa area, the road hugs the coast and the pali moves right on in, with barely enough space to squeeze a few houses between the base of the cliffs and the road.

Swanzy, a neighborhood beach park used mainly by fishers, is fronted by a shore wall. Across the road is a 7-Eleven store, a gas station and Kaaawa Country Kitchen, a takeout restaurant with a couple of tables in front.

Crouching Lion

The crouching lion is a rock formation at the back of the restaurant of the same name, which comes up shortly after the 27-mile marker.

In Hawaiian legend the rock is said to be a demigod from Tahiti who was cemented to the mountain during a jealous struggle between Pele, the volcano goddess, and her sister Hiiaka. When he tried to free himself by pulling into a crouching position, he was turned to stone.

To find him, stand at the Crouching Lion Inn sign with your back to the ocean and look straight up to the left of the coconut tree. The figure, which resembles a lion, is on a cliff in the background.

The inn itself has a tour bus ambiance.

Burgers with fries and coleslaw are around $7.50 at lunch. Dinners are $15 to $25, although there's often a cheaper early-bird special.

Continuing north, just past the inn on the right, you get a glimpse of **Huilua Fishpond**, which is currently under restoration.

KAHANA VALLEY

In old Hawaii the islands were divided into *ahupuaa* – pie-shaped land divisions reaching from the mountains to the sea that provided everything the early Hawaiians needed for subsistence. Kahana Valley, four miles long and two miles wide, is the only publicly owned ahupuaa in Hawaii.

Kahana is a wet valley. Annual rainfall ranges from about 75 inches along the coast to 300 inches in the mountains. In pre-contact times Kahana Valley was planted with wetland taro. The overgrown remnants of more than 130 terraces and irrigation canals have been uncovered in the valley.

In the early 1900s, the area was planted with sugar cane, which was hauled north to the Kahuku Mill via a small railroad. During WW II, the upper part of Kahana Valley was taken over by the military and used for training in jungle warfare.

In 1965 the state bought Kahana Valley from the Robinson family of Kauai (owners of Niihau) in order to preserve it from development.

Kahana Valley State Park

One mile north of the Crouching Lion Inn is the entrance to Kahana Valley State Park.

When the state purchased Kahana it also acquired tenants, many of whom had been living in the valley for a long time. Rather than evict a struggling rural population, the state created a plan which allows the 140 residents to stay on the land. The concept is to eventually incorporate the families into a 'living park', with the residents acting as interpretive guides. The development of the park has been a slow process but after two decades of planning and negotiating the 'living park' concept appears to be inching forward. A simple orientation center inside the park entrance has been opened although activities are still limited.

The park does have some trails, including a 1¼-mile loop trail, maintained by the Boy Scouts, that begins at the orientation center. It starts along the old railroad route, passes a fishing shrine called Kapaeleele Koa, and leads to Keaniani Kilo, a lookout that was used in ancient times for spotting schools of fish in the bay. The trail then goes down to the bay and along the highway back to the park entrance. A trail map is available at the orientation center.

The park also takes in Kahana Bay and its tree-lined beach. The bay is set deep and narrow, and the protected beach provides safe swimming, with a gently sloping sandy bottom. The 10 beachside campsites are used primarily by island families and there may be some turf issues for tourists. To camp here you must obtain a permit in person from the park orientation center (☎ 237-8858) or from the main state office in Honolulu.

PUNALUU

Punaluu is a scattered little seaside community. At Punaluu Beach Park there's a narrow beach that provides fairly good swimming. Although an offshore reef protects these shallow inshore waters in all but stormy weather, be cautious near the mouth of the Waiono Stream and in the channel leading out from it, as currents are strong when the stream is flowing quickly or the surf is high.

Places to Stay

Pat's at Punaluu (☎ 293-8111, (800) 845-8799), 53-567 Kamehameha Hwy, Box 359, Hauula, HI 96717, is a 136-room condo that has seen better days. Located half a mile north of the 24-mile marker, it has one-bedroom units from $68 with a three-day minimum. The units have cooking facilities, TV and a spare bed in the living room but no phone or air-conditioning.

Countryside Cabins (☎ 237-8169), 53-224 Kamehameha Hwy, Punaluu, HI 96717, is midway between the 25- and 24-

mile markers. Rates are $30 a day or $500 a month. It's a modest older place; don't expect anything fancy. Manager Margaret Naai keeps the gate locked to keep her dog in, so call before you get there.

Places to Eat

The *Paniolo Cafe*, 53-146 Kamehameha Hwy, north of the 25-mile marker, has chicken and fish dinners for around $10, steaks for a few dollars more; a simple salad bar is included. At lunch there are moderately priced sandwiches and burgers.

SACRED FALLS STATE PARK

Sacred Falls is a 1374-acre state park with a two-mile trail leading up the narrow Kaliuwaa Valley, which folds deeply into magical-looking mountains. The park is north of the 23-mile marker.

The trail begins across an old cane field and follows Kaluanui Stream through a narrow canyon. The upper end of the trail leads to an 80-foot waterfall beneath high, rocky cliffs. The falls are nice though not spectacular and there are lots of mosquitoes.

The hike, which is of moderate difficulty, takes about 1½ hours. The falls may be sacred, but the hike isn't blessed. Although it's generally safe to hike, and thousands do, caution is definitely warranted. There are a couple of stream crossings on the way that have slippery rocks and, more importantly, are subject to flash flooding. Even when it's sunny on the valley floor, a quick rain storm in the mountains can wash down suddenly.

In the past decade a number of hikers have been swept to their deaths in flash floods, at least one other killed by falling rocks and another by a slip over a ledge. Other hikers have been stranded during flash flooding, a few requiring rescue by helicopter.

Flash floods give little warning. Hikers caught in them here have reported hearing a sudden loud crack and then seeing a wall of water pour down the stream bed; they've had just five seconds to reach higher ground. If the water starts to rise or you hear a rumbling, get up on a bank and wait it out. Don't try to cross the stream if the water reaches above your knees.

The trail is closed when the weather is sufficiently bad or the water level is high. Decisions are made daily and posted at the park or you can call the state parks office at 587-0300 and find out the status for that day.

Thefts from rental cars left in the parking lot are notorious and you shouldn't leave anything valuable in your vehicle here (or anywhere else, for that matter).

HAUULA

Hauula is a rather tired-looking town with a fine backdrop of hills and Norfolk pines. There's a 7-Eleven store and a few small eateries.

The in-town beach looks none too appealing for swimming but it occasionally gets waves big enough for local kids to ride. The beach is actually a county park that allows camping, although it's mostly local families that camp there.

The stone ruins of **Lanakila Church** (circa 1853) sit perched on a hill opposite Hauula Beach, next to the newer Hauula Congregational Church.

Trails

The Division of Forestry & Wildlife (☎ 587-0166) maintains three trails in the forest reserve behind Hauula: **Hauula Loop Trail** (2½ miles), **Maakua Gulch Trail** (three miles) and **Maakua Ridge Trail** (2½ miles). All three trails are through a hunting area and head into some beautiful hills. Hauula Loop and Maakua Ridge trails have good views, while the Maakua Gulch Trail crosses a stream and leads to a waterfall and pool. As flash flooding is a potential problem, the Maakua Gulch Trail should not be hiked in rainy weather or when the stream is high.

The trailhead to all three is at a bend in Hauula Homestead Rd, about a quarter of a mile up from Kamehameha Hwy. Camping is allowed along the trails. Call the Division of Forestry for information, trail maps and the required camping permits.

LAIE

In ancient times Laie was thought to have been the sight of a *puuhonua* – a place where kapu breakers and fallen warriors could seek refuge. Today Laie is the center of the Mormon community in Hawaii.

The first Mormon missionaries to Hawaii arrived in 1850. After an attempt to establish a Hawaiian 'City of Joseph' on Lanai failed amidst a land scandal, the Mormons moved shop to Laie. In 1865 they purchased 6000 acres of land in the area and slowly expanded their influence.

In 1919 the Mormons constructed a **temple**, a smaller version of the one in Salt Lake City, at the foot of the Koolau Range. This stately temple, which is at the end of a wide promenade, appears like nothing else on the windward coast. Although there's a visitor center where eager guides will tell you all about Mormonism, tourists are not allowed to enter the temple itself.

Nearby is the Hawaii branch of **Brigham Young University**, with scholarship programs bringing in students from islands throughout the Pacific.

Information

Laie Shopping Center, about half a mile north of the Polynesian Cultural Center, has restaurants, a supermarket, a coin laundry and a Bank of Hawaii.

Polynesian Cultural Center

The Polynesian Cultural Center (☎ 293-3333), called PCC by locals, is a 'nonprofit' organization belonging to the Mormon Church. The center draws about 900,000 tourists a year, more than any other attraction on Oahu with the exception of the USS *Arizona* Memorial.

The park has seven theme villages representing Samoa, New Zealand, Fiji, Tahiti, Tonga, the Marquesas and Hawaii. They have authentic-looking huts and ceremonial houses, many elaborately built with twisted sennit ropes and hand-carved posts. The huts hold weavings, tapa cloth, feather work and other handicrafts.

People of Polynesian descent in native garb demonstrate poi pounding, coconut frond weaving, dances, games and the like. There's also a re-creation of an old mission house and a missionary chapel representative of those found throughout Polynesia in the mid-1800s.

Most of the people working here are Pacific Island students at the nearby Brigham Young University, who pay their college expenses by providing PCC with a source of inexpensive labor. Not all students end up at the 'village' of their home islands. Apparently there are more Samoans than Hawaiians, for instance, so you may well find a Samoan student demonstrating Hawaiian weavings. People are amiable and you could easily spend a few hours wandering around chatting or trying to become familiar with a craft or two.

The admission price includes boat rides along the waterway that winds through the park, and the Pageant of the Long Canoes, a sort of trumped-up floating talent show at 1, 2, 3 and 4 pm.

The theme park is open daily except Sundays from 12:30 to 9 pm, although most activities cease by 5:30 pm.

Although PCC can be interesting, it is also very touristy and hard to recommend at an admission price of $25 for adults and $13 for children ages five to 11.

The 'Admission-Buffet-Show' ticket, which costs $42 for adults and $25 for children, adds on a buffet dinner and evening Polynesian show. The buffet is a mass production with uninspired cafeteria food. There's also a 'luau' for an extra $12, with much the same food and the addition of an imu-baked pig.

The Polynesian song and dance show runs from 7:30 to 9 pm. It's partly authentic, partly Hollywood-style and much like an enthusiastic college production with elaborate sets and costumes.

Laie Beaches

The 1½ miles of beach fronting the town of Laie between Malaekahana State Recreation Area and Laie Point are used by surfers, bodysurfers and windsurfers.

Pounders, half a mile south of the main entrance to PCC, is an excellent bodysurf-

ing beach, but the shorebreak, as the name of the beach implies, can be brutal. There's a strong winter current. The area around the old landing is usually the calmest. Summer swimming is generally good and the beach is sandy.

From **Laie Point** there's a good view of the mountains to the south and of tiny offshore islands. The island to the left with the hole in it is Kukuihoolua, otherwise known as Puka Rock.

To get to Laie Point, head makai on Anemoku St, opposite the Laie Shopping Center, then turn right on Naupaka St and go straight to the end.

Malaekahana State Recreation Area

Malaekahana Beach stretches between Makahoa Point to the north and Kalanai Point to the south. The long narrow sandy beach is backed by ironwoods. Swimming is good year round, although there are occasionally strong currents in winter. This popular family beach is also good for many other water activities, including bodysurfing, board surfing and windsurfing.

Kalanai Point, the main section of the state park, is less than a mile north of Laie and has picnic tables, barbecue grills, camping, restrooms and showers. Papaya trees heavy with fruit grow inland of the picnic and camping areas. It may be hard to find a ripe one, however, as they're picked regularly.

Mokuauia (Goat Island), a state bird sanctuary just offshore, has a nice sandy cove with good swimming and snorkeling. It's possible to wade over to the island – best when the tide is low and the water's calm, but be sure to ask the lifeguard about water conditions and the advisability of crossing. Be careful of the shallow coral and sea urchins.

You can also snorkel across to Goat Island and off its beaches. Beware of a rip current that's sometimes present off the windward end of the island where the water is deeper.

Camping Malaekahana has the best campgrounds at this end of the windward coast.

You can camp in the park's main Kalanai Point section for free if you have a state park permit. Tent sites on this side are seldom crowded, although weekends and summer are busier.

You can also rent a cabin or camp for a fee in the Makahoa Point section of the park, which has a separate entrance off the highway three-quarters of a mile north of the main park entrance. An office at this end handles the rentals. Check-in is from 3 to 5 pm and the gates are locked to vehicles between 6 pm and 8 am.

There's a one-bedroom cabin for $40 for up to six people and five three-bedroom cabins for $50 for up to 10 people. All are old, rustic and not well maintained but they do have indoor bathrooms, refrigerators, stoves, hot water and musty mattresses. Linens and cookware are not provided.

Tent camping in this section costs $4 per person. While reservations (☎ 293-1736) are preferred, walk-in campers can usually get a tent site except during busy holiday weekends. They also rent four-person tents for $13 the first day, $10 each additional day.

Places to Stay
Rodeway Inn Hukilau Resort (☎ 293-9282, (800) 424-4777; fax 293-8115), 55-109 Laniloa St, Laie, HI 96762, is a two-story motel with 48 rooms surrounding a courtyard pool. While not special, it's comfortable enough and the management is friendly. Each room has a lanai, cable TV, air-con and mini-refrigerator. Singles/doubles cost $74/79, including a continental breakfast.

Places to Eat
Laie Chop Suey in the Laie Shopping Center is a local-style eatery with standard Chinese fare. Most main dishes cost $4 to $6, while set lunch plates cost $4.25, dinner plates $5.50. It's open from 10 am to 8:45 pm Monday to Saturday.

The shopping center also has a grocery store, *Subway Sandwiches* and *Domino's Pizza*.

Laie's *McDonald's*, on the highway at the north end of PCC, has a little more character than the usual McDonald's. Originally built as a restaurant for the hotel next door, the building resembles a Polynesian longhouse with a peaked roof and there's even a small waterfall inside.

KAHUKU
Kahuku is a former sugar town with little wooden cane houses lining the road. The mill in the center of town belonged to the Kahuku Plantation which produced sugar here from 1890 until 1971 when it closed. The mill was a relatively small concern, unable to keep up with the increasingly mechanized competition of Hawaii's bigger mills.

Kahuku Sugar Mill
A fledgling shopping center has been set up inside Kahuku's old sugar mill, with small shops ringing the old machinery. The mill's enormous gears, flywheels and pipes have been painted in bright colors to help visitors visualize how a sugar mill works. The steam systems are red, the cane juice systems light green, hydraulic systems dark blue and so forth. It looks like something out of *Modern Times* – you can almost imagine Charlie Chaplin caught up in the giant gears.

The center has not been wildly successful, but there's a restaurant, food mart, gas station, bank and a handful of gift shops in the complex.

Amorient Aquafarm
Less than a mile north of the old sugar mill is the Amorient Aquafarm. Founded in 1978, the farm has 143 one-acre ponds producing both saltwater and freshwater shrimp.

You can get a fresh shrimp cocktail at their roadside stand for $4, shrimp tempura for $7.25, or sweet steamed prawns for $12 a pound. Zoning rules restrict them to selling only what they raise but you can pick up drinks at Tanaka's store half a mile north of the farm.

Waterbirds are attracted to the ponds like kids to a candy store. They include night heron, coots, stilts, black swans, ducks and cattle egrets. If you're taking the circle-island bus and want a break, it stops right in front.

As you continue along to the North Shore there are papaya farms, a university livestock station, and some high-tech windmills on the hill.

Kuilima Cove

The shallow Kuilima Cove, which is one of the area's best swimming spots, is fronted by the Turtle Bay Hilton, the sole hotel in Kahuku. You can park at one of the 18 free spaces for beachgoers, which are just before the guard booth, and walk 10 minutes to the beach. Alternatively, there's parking inside the hotel lot for $1 for the first half hour and 50c for each additional half hour.

Kaihalulu Beach

Kaihalulu is a beautiful, curved white sand beach fronted by ironwoods. Although a shoreline lava shelf and rocky bottom make the beach poor for swimming, it's good for beachcombing and you can walk east about a mile to Kahuku Point. Local fishers cast thrownets from the shore and pole fish from the point. The dirt road just inland of the beach is also used as a horse trail.

To get there turn into the Turtle Bay Hilton and just before the guard booth turn right into an unmarked parking lot, where there are free spaces for beachgoers. It's a five-minute walk out to the beach. There are no facilities.

Places to Stay

The *Turtle Bay Hilton & Country Club* (☎ 293-8811, (800) 445-8667; fax 293-9147), Kahuku, HI 96731, is a self-contained resort and the only major hotel on the windward and north shores. The Hilton is perched on Kuilima Point, between Turtle Bay and Kuilima Cove. All 486 rooms have ocean views. Room rates range from $170 to $320, with suites up to $1350. There are two golf courses, two pools, horse stables and 10 tennis courts.

Places to Eat

The *Old Plantation Restaurant* at the Kahuku Sugar Mill has fish and prime rib dishes at moderate prices.

Ahi's Restaurant, a local eatery on a dirt road just south of the Kahuku Sugar Mill, specializes in Kahuku-raised prawns. You can order them as scampi, tempura or deep-fried for $8.25 with macaroni salad or for $10.25 with the addition of green salad, ice cream and tea. It's open from 11 am to 9 pm Monday to Saturday and has live Hawaiian entertainment on Fridays.

There are also a few restaurants at the *Turtle Bay Hilton*. The hotel's Palm Terrace has uninspired buffets ($14 to $18) for breakfast, lunch and dinner. There's a Japanese restaurant open for dinner on weekends and the Sea Tide Room has a Sunday brunch for $25.

Central Oahu

Central Oahu is the saddle between the Waianae Mountains on the west and the Koolau Mountains on the east.

Three routes lead north from Honolulu to Wahiawa, the town smack in the middle of Oahu. The freeway, H-2, is the fastest route and Hwy 750, the farthest west, is the most scenic. Hwy 99 catches local traffic as it runs through Mililani, a modern, nondescript residential community.

Most people just zoom up through central Oahu on their way to the North Shore. If your time is limited this isn't a bad idea. There are a few sights along the way and some nice scenery, but Wahiawa doesn't really warrant much more than a zip through anyway.

From Wahiawa two routes continue north to Haleiwa on the North Shore. Highways 803 and 99 both lead from Wahiawa through pineapple country and down across cane fields on the way to the North Shore.

Hwy 803 (Kaukonahua Rd) is a slightly shorter way to Mokuleia than Hwy 99 (Kamehameha Hwy) and about the same distance to Haleiwa, although it bypasses the pineapple sights, which are along Hwy 99. They are both fine scenic roads and if you're not circling the island you might as well go up one and down the other.

Highway 750

Highway 750 (Kunia Rd) adds a few miles to the drive through central Oahu but if you have the time it's worth it. Follow H-1 to the Kunia/Hwy 750 exit, three miles west of where H-1 and H-2 divide.

After you turn up Hwy 750 you enter plantation lands, with sugar cane spreading out as the road leads up hill. This route runs along the foothills of the Waianae Range and the countryside is all agricultural from here to Schofield Barracks.

Up the road 2½ miles, a narrow strip of corn fields acts as a boundary between cane to the south and pineapple to the north. In these fields the Garst Seed Co grows three generations of corn each year, which makes it possible to develop hybrids of corn seed at triple the rate it would take on the mainland. The little bags placed over each ear of corn prevent them from being cross-pollinated.

Farther north is one of the most scenic pineapple fields in Hawaii. There are no buildings and no development – just red earth carpeted with long green strips of pineapples stretching to the edge of the mountains.

From the Hawaii Country Club up the road, there's a distant view of Honolulu all the way to Diamond Head.

Kunia

Kunia, a little town in the midst of the pineapple fields, is home to the field workers employed by Del Monte. If you want to see what a plantation town looks like turn west off Hwy 750 on Kunia Dr, which makes a 1¼-mile loop through the town.

Rows of grey-green wooden houses with corrugated tin roofs stand on low stilts. People take pride in their little yards, with bougainvillea and other flowers adding a splash of brightness to an already lush green area.

Kunia Dr intersects the highway at about 5½ miles north of the intersection of Hwy 750 and H-1 (there's a store and post office near the turn-off) and again at the six-mile marker.

Kolekole Pass

Kolekole is the gap in the Waianae Mountains that Japanese fighter planes flew through on their way to bomb Pearl Harbor. The flight scene was recreated here 30 years later for the shooting of the film *Tora, Tora, Tora*.

The Kolekole Pass, at an elevation of 1724 feet, sits above Schofield Barracks on military property. It can be visited as long as the base isn't on some sort of military alert.

Access is through Foote Gate, on Hwy 750, a third of a mile south of its intersection with Hwy 99. After entering the gate, take the first left onto Road A, then the first right onto Lyman Rd. The drive is 5¼ miles up past the barracks, golf course and bayonet assault course. The parking lot is opposite the hilltop with the big white cross that's visible from miles away.

The five-minute walk to the top of the pass ends at a clearing with a view straight down to the Waianae Coast. The large, ribbed stone that sits atop the ridge here is said to be the embodiment of a woman named Kolekole who took the form of this stone so as to become the perpetual guardian of the pass.

Along the side of the stone are a series of ridges, one of them draining down from a bowl-like depression on the top. Shaped perfectly for a guillotine, the depression has given rise to a more recent 'legend' that Kolekole served as a sacrificial stone for the beheading of defeated chiefs and warriors. The fact that military bases flank both sides of the pass has no doubt had a little influence on this one.

Just west of the pass the road continues through a Navy base down to the Waianae Coast, but you can't take it. The Navy base is a stockyard for nuclear weapons and there's no public access through their side.

WAHIAWA

Wahiawa is a GI town. Just about every fast-food chain you can think of is there. Tattoo parlors and pawn shops are the town's main refinements, and if you're looking for a little excitement there are some rough and tumble bars.

To go through town and visit the botanic garden, healing stones and royal birthstones, take Kamehameha Hwy (which is Hwy 80 as it goes through town, although it's Hwy 99 before and after Wahiawa). To make the bypass around Wahiawa, stick with Hwy 99.

Wahiawa Botanic Garden

The Wahiawa Botanic Garden, 1396 California Ave, is a mile east of the Kamehameha Hwy. What started out in the 1920s as a site for forestry experiments by the Hawaii Sugar Planters' Association is now a 27-acre city park with grand old trees around a wooded ravine.

The park is a nice shady place to take a stroll. Interesting 60-year-old exotics such as cinnamon, chicle and allspice are grouped in one area. Tree ferns, loulu palms and other Hawaiian natives are in another. The trees are identified by markers and the air is thick with birdsong.

The garden is open from 9 am to 4 pm daily. Admission to the park is free, as is a brochure describing some of the trees.

Healing Stones

One of the odder sights to be labeled with an HVB marker are the 'Healing Stones' caged inside a small concrete block 'temple'. It's next to the Methodist church on California Ave, half a mile west of its intersection with Kamehameha Hwy.

The main stone is thought to have been the gravestone of a powerful Hawaiian chief. Although the chief's original burial place was in a field a mile away, the stone was moved long ago to a graveyard at this site. In the 1920s people thought the stone had healing powers and thousands made pilgrimages to it before interest

waned. The housing development and church came later, taking over the graveyard and leaving the stones sitting on the sidewalk.

There are many stories about people who built above the old graveyard being beset with bad luck, divorces and other misfortunes.

A local group with roots in India who sees a spiritual connection between Hawaiian and Indian beliefs now visits the temple, so you may see rice, flowers or little elephant statues placed around the stones. The story is actually more interesting than the sight, however.

Royal Birthstones

Kukaniloko, a group of royal birthstones where queens gave birth, is just north of Wahiawa. The stones are thought to date back to the 12th century. It was said that if a woman lay properly against the stones while giving birth, her child would be

Tattoo artist, Chinatown, Oahu

Turtle Bay, Oahu

Executive Centre Building, Honolulu, Oahu

Waikiki Beach, Oahu

Beach at Haleiwa, Oahu

Waimea Bay, Oahu

Interior of Kuan Yin Temple, Chinatown, Oahu

Byodo-In Temple, Oahu

blessed by the gods, and indeed, many of Oahu's great chiefs were born at this site.

These stones are one of only two documented birthstone sites in Hawaii (the other's in Kauai). Many of the petroglyphs on the stones are of recent origin, but the eroded circular patterns are original.

To get to them from town, go three-quarters of a mile north on Kamehameha Hwy from its intersection with California Ave. Turn left onto the red dirt road directly opposite Whitmore Ave. The stones are a quarter of a mile down through a pineapple field, amongst a stand of eucalyptus and coconut trees. If it's been raining, be aware that the red clay can cake onto your car tires, and once back on the paved road the car may slide as if it's driving on ice.

Pineapple Garden

There's a pineapple demonstration garden in a triangle at the intersection of Hwy 99 and Hwy 80.

Smooth cayenne, the commercial variety of pineapple grown in Hawaii, is shown in various growth stages. Each plant produces just two pineapples. The first takes nearly two years to reach maturity, the second about one year more. Other commercial varieties grown in Australia, the Philippines and Brazil are on display, as well as many varieties of decorative bromeliads.

You can pull off to the side of the road and walk through on your own at any time.

Dole Pineapple Pavilion

The Dole Pineapple Pavilion is a gift shop on Hwy 99 less than a mile north of the pineapple garden. Dole's processing plant is across the street and pineapple fields surround the area.

At the gift shop you can get a free cup of pineapple juice or a tasty pineapple freeze for $1.50. They also sell pineapple muffins and pastries, as well as pineapples boxed to take home. It's open from 9 am to 5:30 pm daily.

North Shore

Oahu's North Shore is synonymous with surfing and prime winter waves. Sunset Beach, the Banzai Pipeline and Waimea Bay are among the world's top surf spots and draw some of the best international surfers.

Other North Shore surf breaks may be less well known but with names like Himalayas and Avalanche, they're not exactly for neophytes.

On winter weekends convoys of cars drive up from Honolulu to watch the action from the beach. You can beat much of the traffic simply by coming up on a weekday.

It's believed that the earliest Polynesians to arrive on Oahu were drawn to the North Shore by the region's rich fishing grounds, cooling trade winds and moderate rain. The areas around Mokuleia, Haleiwa and Waimea all once had sizable Hawaiian settlements. Abandoned taro patches still remain in their upland valleys.

By the turn of the present century the Oahu Railroad & Land Company had extended the railroad around Kaena Point and along the entire North Shore, linking the area with Honolulu and bringing in the first beachgoers from the city. Hotels and private beach houses sprang up, but when the railroad stopped running in the 1940s the hotels shut down for good. Sections of track are still found along many of the beaches.

Waikiki surfers started taking on North Shore waves in the late 1950s and big-time surf competitions followed a few years later. Each December there are three major surf competitions, known as the Triple Crown, with prize purses reaching six figures.

Surf mania prevails even in the restaurants, which serve up omelets with names like 'Pumping Surf' and 'Wipe Out'. Half the North Shore population can be found on the beach when the surf's up.

North Shore Water Conditions
With the exception of Haleiwa Beach Park, North Shore beaches are notorious for treacherous winter swimming conditions. There are powerful currents along the entire shore. If it doesn't look calm as a lake, it's probably not safe for swimming or snorkeling.

During summer, waves along the whole North Shore can mellow right out. Shark's Cove is then a prime snorkeling and diving spot and Waimea Bay, famous for its winter surf, turns into a popular swimming and snorkeling beach. ■

WAIALUA

Waialua, a quiet little town about a mile west of Haleiwa, is centered around Waialua Sugar Mill, the smaller of Oahu's two remaining sugar mills.

Perhaps the most interesting building in Waialua is the town's watering hole, the Sugar Bar, which occupies the old Bank of Hawaii down by the mill.

The most scenic route between Haleiwa and Waialua is along Haleiwa Rd.

Kukui Nut Factory

The Kukui Nut Factory, 66-935 Kaukonahua Rd, sells jewelry and skin oil products made from native kukui nuts. The rock-hard nuts are polished to make necklaces and the kernels are squeezed for their oil. Visitors are given a mini-tour of the shop's tiny factory from 9 am to 5 pm daily.

Places to Stay

The *B&B Plantation House* (☎ 637-4988), Box 857, Waialua, HI 96791, near the village center, has two bedrooms in a private home. One has a queen bed, TV and private bath for $65 for a single or double. The other has a shared bath and twin beds for $45/55 a single/double. Rates include a continental breakfast served at the patio, which looks out across endless fields of sugar cane.

Owner Nattalia Richmond, who first came to Hawaii by steamer in 1929, can tell many a story of old Oahu. The minimum stay is two nights and small children are not allowed.

MOKULEIA

The Farrington Highway (Hwy 930) runs west from Thompson Corner intersection to Dillingham Airfield and Mokuleia Beach. (Both this road and the road along the Waianae Coast are called Farrington Hwy, but they don't connect, as each side reaches a dead end about 2½ miles short of Kaena Point.)

Mokuleia Beach is a six-mile stretch of white sand running from Kaiaka Bay towards Kaena Point. Although some GIs and locals come this way, the beaches don't draw much of a crowd and the area has sort of a boonies feel to it. The only visitor facilities are at Mokuleia Beach Park and the nearest store is back in Waialua.

Dillingham Airfield is the take-off site for glider rides and sky diving. For details see Activities and Organized Tours in the front of this chapter.

Mokuleia Beach Park

Mokuleia Beach Park, opposite Dillingham Airfield, has a large open grassy area with picnic tables, restrooms, showers and a phone. Camping is allowed with a county camping permit.

Mokuleia is sandy but has a lava rock shelf along much of its shoreline. It has fairly consistent winds, making it a popular spot with windsurfers, particularly in spring and autumn. In winter there are dangerous currents.

Mokuleia Army Beach

Mokuleia Army Beach, opposite the western end of Dillingham Airfield, has the widest stretch of sand on the Mokuleia shore. Once reserved exclusively for military personnel, the beach is now open to the public, although it is no longer maintained and there are no facilities.

The beach is unprotected and has very strong rip currents, especially during

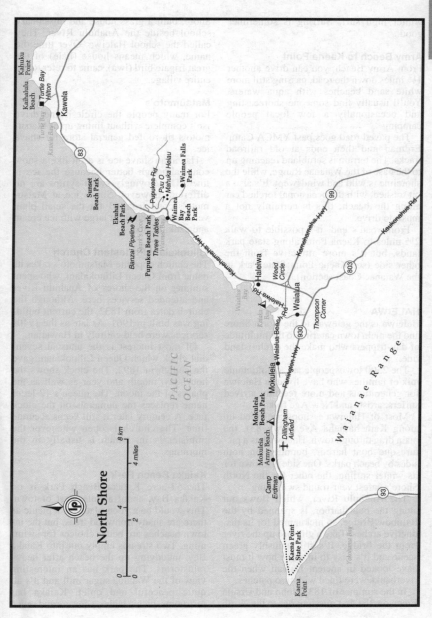

North Shore

Pacific Ocean

Kahuku Point
Kaihalulu Beach
Turtle Bay Hilton
Turtle Bay
Kawela
Kawela Bay

83

Sunset Beach Park
Ekuhai Beach Park
Banzai Pipeline
Pupukea Beach Park
Three Tables
Shark's Cove
Waimea
Pupukea Rd
Puu O
Mahuka Heiau
Waimea Falls Park
Waimea Bay Beach Park

99

Kamehameha Hwy

Haleiwa
Weed Circle
Waialua
Thompson Corner

803

930

Haleiwa Rd
Kaukonahua Rd

Kaiaka Bay
Waialua Bay

Waialua Beach Rd
Mokuleia
Farrington Hwy

Mokuleia Beach Park
Dillingham Airfield
Mokuleia Army Beach
Camp Erdman

93

Waianae Range

Kaena Point State Park

Kaena Point

Yokohama Bay

8 km
4 miles
0   2   4

winter high surf. Surfing is sometimes good.

Army Beach to Kaena Point

From Army Beach, you can drive another 1½ miles down the road, passing still more white sand beaches with aqua waters. You'll usually find someone shorecasting and occasionally a few local people camping.

The paved road goes past YMCA Camp Erdman and then ends at old railroad tracks. The terrain is scrubland reaching up to the base of the Waianae Range, while the shoreline is wild and windswept. It's also a bit trashed, with the occasional torched car along the beach; this is certainly not a must-do drive.

From road's end, it's possible to walk 2½ miles to Kaena Point along state park lands, but it's more attractive from the other side (see Kaena Point State Park in the Waianae Coast section).

HALEIWA

Haleiwa is the gateway to the North Shore and the main town catering to the multitude of day-trippers who make the circle-island ride.

The 2500 townspeople are a multiethnic mix of families who have lived in Haleiwa for generations and more recently arrived surfers, artists and New Age folks.

Most of Haleiwa's shops are lined up along Kamehameha Ave (Hwy 83), the main drag through town. Haleiwa has a picturesque boat harbor, bounded on both sides by beach parks. One side is known for its winter surfing, the other for the North Shore's safest year-round swimming.

The Anahulu River, which flows out along the boat harbor, is spanned by the Rainbow Bridge, so nicknamed for its distinctive arches. Take a glimpse up the river from the bridge. It's still a lushly green scene and it's easy to imagine how it must have looked in ancient Hawaii when the riverbanks were lined with taro patches.

In the summer of 1832, John and Ursula Emerson, the first missionaries to the North Shore, built a grass house and missionary school beside the Anahulu River. They called the school Haleiwa. Over time the name, which means house (hale) of the great frigate bird (iwa), came to refer to the entire village.

Matsumoto's

For many people the circle-island drive isn't complete without lining up at Matsumoto's tin-roofed general store for shave ice.

Hawaiian shave ice is a bit like a snow cone, although better because the ice is finer. The cloyingly sweet syrups are no different, however. Shave ice at Matsumoto's costs from $1 for the small plain version to $1.80 for a large with ice cream and azuki beans.

Liliuokalani Protestant Church

The church opposite Matsumoto's takes its name from Queen Liliuokalani, who spent summer on the shores of Anahulu River and attended services here. Although the church dates from 1832, the current building was built in 1961. As late as the 1940s services were held entirely in Hawaiian.

Of most interest is the unusual seven-dial clock which Queen Liliuokalani gave the church in 1892. The clock shows the hour, day, month and year as well as the phases of the moon. The queen's 12-letter name replaces the numerals on the clock face. A century later it still keeps accurate time. The church is open whenever the minister is in, which is usually in the mornings.

Kaiaka Beach Park

The 53-acre Kaiaka Beach Park is on Kaiaka Bay, about a mile west of town. This would be a good place for a picnic as there are shady ironwood trees, but the in-town beaches are better choices for swimming. Two streams empty out into Kaiaka Bay, muddying up the beach after heavy rainstorms. The park has an interesting view of the Waialua sugar mill and it's all quite peaceful and quiet. Kaiaka has restrooms, picnic tables, showers and seven

Haleiwa

0   400   800 m
0   400   800 yards

PACIFIC
OCEAN

Puaena
Point

Haleiwa
Beach
Park

Waialua Bay

Ukoa
Pond

Loko Ea

Haleiwa Alii
Beach Park

Boat
Harbor

Jameson's
by the Sea

Surf-N-Sea

Chart
House

Island Images

Anahulu River

Matsumoto's

Liliuokalani
Church

Wyland Gallery

Fujioka's Supermarket

Haleiwa
Shopping
Plaza

Kua Aina

Kaiaka
Point

Kaiaka
Beach Park

North Shore
Marketplace

Kaiaka
Bay

Pizza Hut

Waialua
Community
Association

Celestial
Natural Foods

McDonald's

Kaala Art

Cafe
Haleiwa

Haleiwa Rd

Paalaa Rd

Paukauila Stream

Weed
Circle

Waialua Beach Rd

To
Mokuleia

Kaukonahua Rd

To Thompson
Corner

To Wahiawa

campsites. Camping is free with a permit from the county.

Haleiwa Alii Beach Park

Surfing is king at Haleiwa Alii Beach Park. This is the site of several tournaments in the winter, when north swells can bring waves as high as 20 feet.

When waves are five feet and under, lots of younger kids bring their boards out. Any time they're six feet or better there are also strong currents and it's more suited to experienced surfers. The county (☎ 637-5051) gives free surfing lessons here on weekend mornings from September to May.

The 20-acre park has restrooms, showers, picnic tables and a lifeguard tower. The shallow areas on the southern side of the beach are generally the calmest for swimming.

Haleiwa Beach Park

Haleiwa Beach Park is on the north side of Waialua Bay. As the beach is protected by a shallow shoal and a breakwater, the waters are usually very calm and see little wave action, although north swells occasionally ripple into the bay.

While the beach isn't Haleiwa's most appealing, this 13-acre county park has full beach facilities, as well as basketball and volleyball courts, an exercise area and a softball field. It also has a good view of Kaena Point.

Places to Stay

There's no 'established' accommodation in Haleiwa, although people occasionally rent out rooms in their homes. You can usually find room-for-rent notices on the bulletin boards at the Coffee Gallery in the North Shore Marketplace and the Haleiwa Super Market in the Haleiwa Shopping Plaza.

The other option is camping, which is allowed Friday to Tuesday nights at Kaiaka Beach Park. For details on permits, see Camping in the Accommodations section at the start of this chapter.

Places to Eat

The *China Inn* in the North Shore Marketplace has filling meals at low prices. One entree is $3, two are $4 and three are $4.75, each including noodles or rice. If you select carefully the food is good for the price. Beef broccoli and dishes with lots of vegetables are a good choice, but batter-dipped dishes are heavy on the batter. It's open from 11 am to 10 pm daily, except Mondays.

Cafe Haleiwa, on the right as you come into town, is an unpretentious eatery serving good food at honest prices. An institution of sorts on the North Shore, it has long been a haunt for local surfers. A large burrito served with terrific home fries costs $4.85. You can get two large whole-wheat pancakes loaded with blueberries for $2.75 in a half order, a meal in itself. Lunch is predominantly sandwiches and Mexican fare. It's open from 6 am to 3 pm on weekdays, from 7 am to 12:30 pm on Saturdays, to 2 pm on Sundays.

Celestial Natural Foods, opposite Cafe Haleiwa, has bulk foods, trail mix, fresh produce, yogurts and just about everything else you'd expect to find in a good health food store. In the back of the store is *Paradise Cafe*, which is open from 9 am to 6 pm and has vegetable chili over brown rice for $2.50, sandwiches and salads for around $5 and a few Middle Eastern dishes for a tad more.

The popular *Kua Aina* in the center of town makes the best burgers and fish sandwiches on the North Shore. Prices range from $3.25 for a cheese sandwich to $4.70 for a mahimahi sandwich, with hamburgers in the middle range. It's open from 11 am to 8 pm daily.

The *Coffee Gallery* in the North Shore Marketplace is a fine alternative to the burger and plate-lunch scene. It has steamed coffees, scones, crepes, lox & bagels and the like at reasonable prices. At lunch, salads and sandwiches are around $6, while at dinner pasta and stir-fries are just a dollar or so more. There's open-air seating at the side of the cafe and food can be ordered for takeout. It's open daily from 8 am, with breakfast served until 11 am.

Rosie's Cantina in the Haleiwa Shopping Plaza has reasonable Mexican food, although it's best to stick with traditional dishes. Plates with rice and beans cost $8 for one item, $10.35 for two. At lunch, which is served until 4 pm, you can get a burrito or enchilada with rice and beans for $6. Rosie's is open from 7 am to about 10 pm.

Steamer's (☎ 637-5071), in the Haleiwa Shopping Plaza, has fish or chicken sandwiches for $7 at lunch. At dinner, the specialty is fresh fish prepared Thai-style, Cajun or grilled for around $18. Lunch is from 11:30 am to 4:30 pm and dinner from 5:30 to 9 pm.

On weekends, Steamer's becomes the North Shore's main dance spot. There's usually a rock or reggae band on Fridays ($2 to $5 cover) and club music on Saturdays, both from 10:30 pm to 2 am.

Chart House (☎ 637-8005), at the boat harbor, has meat and seafood dinners from $15 to $25 from 5 pm nightly. The price includes the salad bar which has hearts of palm, artichoke hearts, fresh fruit and breads in addition to the usual greens. You can get the salad bar alone for $12. Lunch, available from 11 am to 2:30 pm, includes sandwiches, salads and hot dishes in the $6 to $10 range.

Jameson's by the Sea (☎ 637-4336), north of the bridge, serves dinner, from Wednesday to Sunday, in a 2nd-floor dining room with white tablecloths and views across the boat harbor. Seafood is the specialty, with dishes starting around $19. You can also eat in a more casual pub setting downstairs, from 11 am to about 9 pm daily, with sandwiches and salads in the $8 to $10 range.

Haleiwa has two main grocery stores: *Haleiwa Super Market* in the Haleiwa Shopping Plaza and *Fujioka's Supermarket* across the street.

Things to Buy
Hawaiiana Kaala Art, next to Cafe Haleiwa, has some nice tapa handmade by a Tongan woman who lives in Kona. The shop also sells pareos from Bali and Tahiti, hand-screened T-shirts, wood sculptures and paintings.

Galleries Wyland Gallery, 66-150 Kamehameha Ave, features paintings and sculptures of whales. Marine artist Wyland is best known for his many 'Whaling Wall' murals splashed on shopping center walls around the islands.

Island Images, on the main road by the boat harbor, has prints of local scenes, such as seascapes and plantation shacks.

Boards Surf-N-Sea (☎ 637-9887), 62-595 Kamehameha Hwy, just north of the Rainbow Bridge, rents surfboards, boogie boards, windsurfing equipment, dive gear and snorkel sets. They also offer surfing and windsurfing lessons, dive trips and sport fishing and sell new and used surfboards and sailboards.

Hawaiian Surf and Strong Currents, both in the North Shore Marketplace, also sell new and used surfboards. In addition, Strong Currents has a little free 'surf museum' that's essentially a collection of old surfing photos and vintage surfboards.

WAIMEA
Waimea Valley was once heavily settled. The lowlands were terraced in taro, the valley walls dotted with house sites and the ridges topped with heiaus. Just about every crop grown in Hawaii thrived in the valley, including a rare pink taro fancied by the alii.

Waimea River, now blocked at the beach, originally opened into the bay and was a passage for canoes traveling upstream to the villages. The sport of surfing was immensely popular here centuries ago, with the early Hawaiians taking to Waimea's huge waves on their long boards.

When Captain Cook's ships sailed into Waimea to collect water in 1779, shortly after Cook's death on the Big Island, an entry in the ship's log noted that the valley was uncommonly beautiful and picturesque.

Human Sacrifices

In 1792 Captain Vancouver, who had been an officer on one of Captain Cook's vessels a decade earlier, anchored in Waimea Bay. While three of his men were collecting water on shore they were attacked and killed. It's thought that their bodies were taken up to Puu O Mahuka Heiau on the ridge above the beach and sacrificed.

When Vancouver returned a year later demanding justice, the high chief turned over three islanders. Although Vancouver doubted that these men had anything to do with the murders, he had come to set an example so he ordered their execution. ■

However, Western contact wasn't kind to the area. Deforestation above the valley, from logging and the introduction of plantations, contributed to a devastating flood in Waimea in 1894. In addition to water damage, an enormous volume of mud washed through the valley, so much so that it permanently altered the shape of Waimea's shore. After the flood, most residents abandoned the valley and resettled elsewhere.

Waimea Bay Beach Park

Waimea Bay is a very beautiful, deeply inset bay with turquoise blue waters and a wide white sand beach almost 1500 feet long. Ancient Hawaiians believed its waters were sacred.

Waimea Bay's mood changes with the seasons: it can be tranquil and as flat as a lake in summer, and savage with incredible surf and the island's meanest rip currents in winter.

Waimea has Hawaii's biggest surf and holds the record for the highest waves ever ridden in international competition. As at Sunset Beach, the huge north swells bring out crowds of spectators who throng to watch Waimea surfers perform their near-suicidal feats on waves of up to 35 feet.

On winter's calmer days the boogie boarders are out in force, but even then sets come in hard and people get pounded.

Winter water activities here are not for novices.

Usually the only time the water is calm enough for swimming and snorkeling is from June to September. The best snorkeling is around the rocks on the left of the bay.

Waimea Bay Beach Park is the most popular North Shore beach. There are showers, restrooms, picnic tables, a phone, and a lifeguard on duty daily. Parking is often tight.

Waimea Falls Park

Waimea Falls Park (☎ 638-8511), across the highway from Waimea Bay Beach Park, is a botanical garden, cultural preserve and tourist park all in one.

The main park road leads three-quarters of a mile up the Waimea Valley to a waterfall, passing extensive naturalized gardens that include sections of ginger, hibiscus, heleconia and medicinal plants. Many of the plants are labeled for identification and there are several rare species under propagation.

The park has ancient stone platforms and terraces and some replicas of thatched buildings similar to those used by early Hawaiians. Traditional hula dances, Hawaiian games and other demonstrations are given during the day. A cliff diver plunges 60 feet into the waterfall pool five times a day to thrill spectators.

The valley's natural beauty is nicely preserved and the park is pleasant to wander through, but the cost of admission is a bit steep at $19.95 for adults, $8.95 for children ages six to 12, $3.95 for ages four to five. Those under three are admitted free.

The best deal is to come at 4 pm when the rate drops to $6.50 for adults and $4 for children. Although the demonstrations stop around this time, there's still a 4:15 pm hula show and the grounds are less crowded and more pleasant for strolling. The park is open from 10 am to 5:30 pm daily and there's an in-park restaurant called the *Proud Peacock*.

A free shuttle runs from Waikiki hotels at 8 am and 11:30 am daily; call the park office for pick-up locations. Public bus No 52 stops at the highway, half a mile from the park entrance.

Kayaking Waimea River It's possible to kayak up the historic Waimea River. Kayak Oahu Adventures (☎ 637-6565), at the side of the road going into Waimea Falls Park, rents single/double kayaks for $15 for 90 minutes or $25/35 for a full day.

St Peter & Paul Church
The church of St Peter & Paul stands beneath the tall unassuming tower on the northern side of Waimea Bay. The structure was originally a rock-crushing plant built to supply gravel for the construction of the highway in the 1930s. After it was abandoned, the Catholic church converted it into Oahu's most unlikely chapel.

Puu O Mahuka Heiau State Monument
Puu O Mahuka is a long low-walled platform heiau perched on a bluff above Waimea. The largest heiau on Oahu, its construction is attributed to the legendary menehunes.

The terraced stone walls are a couple of feet high, although most of the heiau is now overgrown. This was an incredible site for a temple and it's definitely worth a ride up for the view. It can also be a fine place to watch the sunset.

Walk up above the left side of the heiau from the parking lot for a view of Waimea Valley and Waimea Bay. The plateaus rising above the southern side of the valley are covered with sugar cane. To the west, you can see all the way out along the coast to Kaena Point.

For a vitamin-C-rich treat, check out the guava trees down past the end of the parking lot.

To get to the heiau, turn up Pupukea Rd at the Foodland supermarket. The marked turn-off to the heiau is about half a mile up the road and from there it's three-quarters of a mile in. On the drive up there's a good view of Pupukea Beach Park.

Pupukea Beach Park
Pupukea Beach Park is a long beach along the highway that includes Three Tables on the left and Shark's Cove on the right. In the middle is Old Quarry, where a wonderful array of jagged rock formations and tide pools are exposed at low tide. This is a very scenic beach, with deep blue waters, a varied coast and a mix of lava and white sand. The rocks and tide pools are tempting to explore but be careful because they're razor sharp and if you slip it's easy to get a deep cut.

The waters off Pupukea Beach are a marine-life conservation district.

There are showers and restrooms in front of Old Quarry. The beach entrance is opposite the Shell gas station.

Three Tables Three Tables, at the western end of the beach, gets its name from the ledges rising above the water. In summer when the waters are calm Three Tables has good snorkeling and diving. It's possible to see some action by snorkeling around the tables, but the best coral and fish as well as some small caves, lava tubes and arches are in deeper water farther out. This is a summer-only spot, however. In winter dangerous rip currents flow between the beach and the tables. Beware of sharp rocks and coral.

Shark's Cove Shark's Cove is beautiful both above and below the water's surface. The naming of the cove was done in jest – sharks aren't a particular problem.

In the summer, when the seas are calm, Shark's Cove has good snorkeling and swimming conditions as well as Oahu's most popular cavern dive. A fair number of beginner divers take lessons here, while the underwater caves will thrill advanced divers.

To get to the caves, swim out of the cove and around to the right. Some of the caves are very deep and labyrinthine, so caution should be used exploring them. There have been a number of drownings in these caves.

The large boulders out on the end of the point to the far right of the cove are said to be followers of Pele, the volcano goddess. As an honor, she gave them immortality by turning them to stone.

Ekuhai Beach Park

The main reason people come to Ekuhai Beach Park is to watch the pros surf the world-famous **Banzai Pipeline**, a few hundred feet to the left of the park.

The Pipeline breaks over a shallow coral reef and can be a death-defying wave to ride.

At Ekuhai Beach itself, many board riders and bodysurfers brave a hazardous current and ride the waves. Water conditions mellow out in summer, when it's good for swimming.

Ekuhai Beach Park is opposite the Sunset Beach Elementary School but roadside parking isn't permitted and they do tow cars away. To get to the beach, continue past the school and turn makai opposite the

big roadside totem that marks a souvenir shop. Then turn left on the beach road which leads to the parking lot. There's a lifeguard, restrooms, showers and a phone.

Sunset Beach Park

Sunset Beach Park is near the nine-mile marker. This beach is Oahu's classic winter surf spot with incredible waves and challenging breaks. It's such a big name you expect a big beach, but it's just a little roadside attraction without even a sign. All the action is in the water.

Winter swells create powerful rips. Even when the waves have mellowed in the summer, there's still an along-shore current for swimmers to deal with. Portable toilets and a lifeguard tower are the only facilities.

Backyards, the surf break off Sunset Point at the northern end of the beach, draws a lot of top windsurfers. There's a shallow reef and strong currents to contend with, but Backyards has the island's biggest waves for sailing.

Mural of ancient Hawaiian life at the University of Hawaii

Places to Stay

Backpackers (☎ 638-7838; fax 638-7515), 59-788 Kamehameha Hwy, Haleiwa, HI 96712, opposite Three Tables at Pupukea Beach, is pretty much a surfers' hangout. It has a few different set-ups, most of it beach-house casual. The main house has four bunk beds to a room for $14 a bed, while a three-story house behind it has double rooms for $40. Both houses have shared bathrooms and kitchens. Expect clutter and aging furniture, but if you're just looking for a place to crash you can't beat the price.

A small beachfront motel across the road has eight studios with TVs, kitchens and great views. Units on the bottom floor have dorm beds for $16, while those on the top are rented out like hotel rooms for $70 to $85.

The third property, a few hundred yards away on the mauka side of the road, consists of nine cottages with either two or three bedrooms. Dorm beds are $15 while the entire cottage, which sleeps six to eight people, costs $85 to $150. They make a free pick-up at the airport early in the afternoon, and around dawn on some mornings; transport is free coming from the airport, $5 for the return ride.

Ke Iki Hale (☎ 638-8229, (800) 377-4030), 59-579 Ke Iki Rd, Haleiwa, HI 96712, has a dozen apartments fronting a beautiful white sand beach just north of Pupukea Beach Park. The rates are $125/770 by the day/week for a one-bedroom duplex and $145/945 for small two-bedroom units. There are also a couple of separate streetside units for $85.

Thomsen's Bed & Breakfast (☎ 638-7947; fax 638-7694), 59-420 Kamehameha Hwy, Haleiwa, HI 96712, is one large studio unit above the garage of Norman and Dianne Thomsen's home, near Ekuhai Beach Park. It has a king bed, queen sofa bed, bathroom, kitchen area, private entrance, phone, TV and a lanai facing the mountains. Breakfast is not included. The rate is $65.

The bulletin board at Pupukea Foodland has notices of roommates wanted as well as an occasional vacation rental listing.

Places to Eat

D'Amicos (☎ 638-9611), on the mauka side of the highway near Sunset Beach, has sandwiches, good New York-style pizza and breakfasts, all at reasonable prices. It's open from 7 am to 9 pm daily.

There's often a food van opposite Shark's Cove selling fish tacos and smoothies. You can buy groceries at *Pupukea Foodland* or at the small grocery store near Sunset Beach.

Waianae Coast

The Waianae Coast is the arid leeward side of Oahu.

In 1793 Captain Vancouver, the first Westerner to drop anchor there, found a barren wasteland with only a few scattered fishing huts. Just two years later, when Kamehameha invaded Oahu, the population jumped as many Oahuans who had been living in more desirable areas were forced to flee to the isolated Waianae Coast.

Today it still stands separate from the rest of the island. There are no gift shops or sightseeing buses on the Waianae Coast. When you get right down to it, other than watching surfers at Makaha, there aren't a whole lot of sights to see.

Although developers are beginning to grab Waianae farmland for golf courses, for the time being leeward Oahu is the island's least touristed side. The area has a history of resisting development and a reputation for not being receptive to outsiders. In the past, visitors have been the targets of assaults and muggings. There's still a major problem with thefts from cars and campsites, and although things aren't as hostile as they used to be, many locals aren't keen on sharing their space with tourists.

Overall, you need to be attuned to the mood of the people. This is the only place

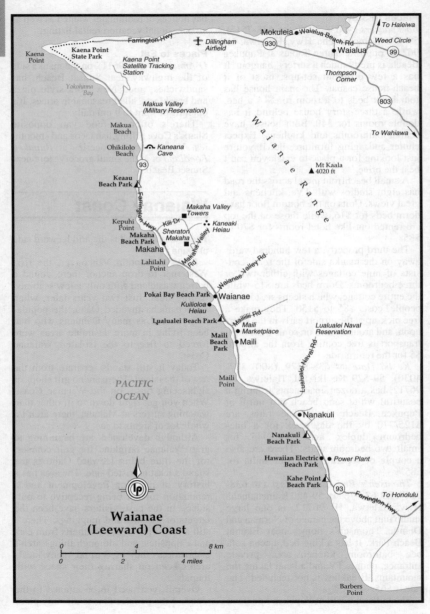

To Haleiwa

Mokuleia ● Waialua Beach Rd   Weed Circle

Farrington Hwy   ✈ Dillingham   **930**   Waialua   **99**
Airfield

Kaena   Kaena Point   Thompson   **803**
Point   State Park   Corner

Kaena Point   To Wahiawa
Satellite Tracking
Station

Yokohama   Makua Valley
Bay   (Military Reservation)

Makua   Mt Kaala   **Waianae Range**
Beach   ▲ 4020 ft

Ohikilolo   ⚬ Kaneana
Beach   Cave   **93**

Keaau
Beach Park ⌂

Kepuhi   **Makaha Valley**
Point   **Towers** ■

Kili Dr   ● Kaneaki
Sheraton   Heiau
Makaha ■
Makaha
Beach Park ●   Waianae Valley Rd
Makaha

Lahilahi   Makaha Valley Rd
Point

Pokai Bay Beach Park ●   **Waianae**
Kuilioloa ●   Maililii Rd
Heiau
Lualualei Beach Park ⌂   **Lualualei Naval**
Maili ●   **Reservation**
Marketplace
Maili
Beach   **Maili** ●
Park

Maili   Lualualei Naval Rd
Point

PACIFIC
OCEAN

● **Nanakuli**

Nanakuli ⌂
Beach Park

Hawaiian Electric ● Power Plant
Beach Park
Kahe Point ⌂
Beach Park   **93**   Farrington Hwy   To Honolulu

◆
Ⓛ Ⓟ

Waianae
(Leeward) Coast

0   4   8 km
├─────┼─────┤
0   2   4 miles

Barbers
Point

OAHU

in Hawaii where the park brochures say camping opportunities are for *local* residents.

Farrington Hwy (Hwy 93) runs the length of the leeward coast. There are long stretches of white sand beaches, some quite attractive, others a bit trashed. In winter most have treacherous swimming conditions but at that time they also have some of the island's more challenging surfing. Although the towns themselves are ordinary, the cliffs and valleys cutting into the Waianae Range form a lovely backdrop.

At road's end, there's an undeveloped mile-long beach and a fine nature hike out to scenic Kaena Point.

KAHE POINT
Kahe Point Beach Park
Despite the name, there's no beach at this park, just the rocky cliffs of Kahe Point. There are standard facilities and camping is allowed, but the park has little to recommend it.

Discarded tires, household garbage and the occasional wrecked car make it over the cliffs to the rocky coast below. The backdrop is the smokestacks of the electric power plant across the way. Along the road in front of the park a sign welcomes visitors to the Waianae Coast.

Hawaiian Electric Beach Park
This sandy beach north of Kahe Point is more commonly known as Tracks, the name given to it by beachgoers who used to go there by train before the war. In summer this is a fairly calm place to swim, while in winter it's frequented by surfers.

To get there take the first turn-off after the power plant and drive over the abandoned railroad tracks.

NANAKULI
Nanakuli, with a population of 9500, is the biggest town on the Waianae Coast. The site of a Hawaiian Homesteads settlement, Nanakuli has one of the largest native Hawaiian populations on Oahu. The town has supermarkets, the Waianae District Court, a bank and a few fast-food eateries.

Nanakuli is lined by a broad sandy beach park. There's swimming, snorkeling and scuba diving during the calmer summer season. In winter, high surf creates rip currents and dangerous shorebreaks.

To get to the beach park, turn left at the traffic lights on Nanakuli Ave. This is a community park with a playground, sports fields, full beach facilities and campsites.

MAILI
Maili has a long, grassy roadside park with an endless stretch of white sand beach. Like other places on this coast the water conditions are often treacherous in winter, but usually calm enough for swimming in summer. There's a lifeguard station, playground, beach facilities and a few castrated coconut palms to provide limited, but safe, shade.

Places to Stay
Maili Cove (☎ 696-4447), 87-561 Farrington Hwy, Waianae, HI 96792, is a crescent-shaped three-story condo right on both the highway and the beach at the south side of Maili. The large one-bedroom units have lanais with ocean views and most have cable TV and phones. There's a pool. The rentals cost about $600 a week and can be booked through McCloskey Realty (☎ 696-9606).

Places to Eat
The Anchorage (☎ 696-2869) at the Maili Marketplace serves a lunch buffet from 11 am to 2 pm weekdays for $6.95, or skip the five hot dishes and have only the soup and salad bar for $5.95. There's a $10 brunch on Sundays from 10:30 am to 3 pm. Dinner, which includes a salad bar, is priced from $8 for pasta to $16 for filet mignon or shrimp scampi.

WAIANAE
Waianae, with a population of 8800, is the second largest town on the coast. It has a beach park, protected boat harbor, satellite city hall, police station, supermarkets and plenty of fast food.

OAHU

Temple offering

Pokai Bay Beach Park

Protected by Kaneilio Point and a long breakwater, Pokai Bay Beach Park has the calmest year-round swimming on the Waianae Coast. To get there, turn makai onto Lualualei Homestead Rd at the traffic light just after the Waianae post office.

Waves seldom break inside Pokai Bay and the sea bottom slopes gently. Snorkeling is fair by the breakwater where fish gather around the rocks.

Local canoe clubs practice in the bay and you can watch them rowing if you happen by in the late afternoon. There are showers, restrooms, picnic tables, and a lifeguard on duty daily. All in all for an in-town beach it's pretty nice.

Kaneilio Point is the site of **Kuilioloa Heiau**, which was partly destroyed by the army during WW II. It's been reconstructed by a Waianae group, but because some of the point had been lost, parts of the heiau had to be moved mauka a bit and it's not exactly identical to the original.

MAKAHA

Makaha means 'ferocious' and in days past the valley was notorious for the bandits who used to hang out along the cliffs waiting for travelers to pass.

Today Makaha has world-class surfing as well as Oahu's best-restored heiau, a hotel and golf course and a few condos.

Makaha Beach Park

Makaha Beach is broad, sandy and crescent-shaped, with some of the most daunting winter surf in the islands. Experienced surfers and bodysurfers both hit the waves here.

The beach is home to some major surf competitions. The most colorful is Buffalo's Big Board Surfing Classic held in February using old-style surfboards called 'tankers' which are sometimes 15 feet long and weigh more than 80 pounds. As surfers today go for small, light boards, most competitors are of an older generation of surfers.

When the surf's not up, Makaha is a popular swimming beach. When the surf is up, swimming is hazardous because of the dangerous rip currents and a strong shorebreak.

In summer the slope of the beach is relatively flat. In winter it's fairly steep. The beach sand is slightly coarse and of calcareous origin with lots of mollusk shell fragments. As much as half of it temporarily washes away during winter erosion, but even then Makaha is still an impressive beach.

Snorkeling is good offshore during the calmer summer months. Makaha Caves, out where the waves break farthest offshore, feature underwater caverns, arches and tunnels at depths of 30 to 50 feet. It's a popular leeward diving spot.

Makaha Beach has showers, restrooms, and a lifeguard on duty daily.

Makaha Valley

For a little loop drive, turn mauka onto Kili Dr, opposite Makaha Beach Park, where the road heads into Makaha Valley skirting scalloped green cliffs.

An estimated 3000 wild peacocks live in the valley, including about two dozen white ones. They come out in the early evening, sometimes gathering at the intersection by the Makaha Valley Towers condos, a mile up from the Farrington Hwy.

At the Towers turn right onto Huipu Dr. Half a mile down on the left is Mauna Olu St, which leads a mile into Mauna Olu Estates and Kaneaki Heiau.

The Sheraton is at the intersection of Huipu Dr and Makaha Valley Rd. Most of the hotel activity is centered around its golf course.

Makaha Valley Rd completes the loop, connecting back with the Farrington Hwy.

Kaneaki Heiau Kaneaki Heiau, in the center of Makaha Valley, was originally a Lono temple, dedicated to the god of agriculture. In its final days it was rededicated by Kamehameha I as a luakini war temple. It remained in use until the time of Kamehameha's death, in 1819.

Restoration, which was done by the Bishop Museum and completed in 1970, added two prayer towers, a taboo house, drum house, altar and god images. It was reconstructed in the traditional manner using ohia logs and pili grass shipped over from the Big Island.

Supposedly, the guard at the Mauna Olu Estates gatehouse lets visitors drive through to the heiau between 10 am and 2 pm daily except Monday. However, you might want to call the gatehouse (☎ 695-8174) in advance to inquire, as they can be quite inconsistent in providing access. Admission is free.

Places to Stay

Makaha doesn't have a lot of accommodations for short-term visitors. Apart from the Sheraton, all are condos, none are terribly appealing and most require you to stay for at least a week.

Makaha Surfside (☎ 696-8282), 85-175 Farrington Hwy, Makaha, HI 96792, is a four-story cinder-block apartment complex a mile south of Makaha Beach. Although it's mostly residential, some of the 450 units are rented out on a weekly basis at $250 for studios, $400 for one-bedroom units, both with full kitchens. It's an ordi-

Making poi.

Nanaue the Shark Man

Hawaiian legend tells of a child named Nanaue who was born with an open space between his shoulders. Unknown to his mother, the child's father was the king of sharks who had taken on the guise of a man. Nanaue was born half human, half shark. He was human on land, but when he entered the ocean the opening on his back became a shark's mouth. After a nasty spell in which many villagers were ripped to shreds by a mysterious shark, Nanaue was discovered and forced to swim from island to island as he was hunted down. For a while he lived near Makua and took his victims into Kaneana Cave via an underwater tunnel. ■

nary-looking complex although there are pools and barbecue grills.

Makaha Shores (☎ 696-8415), Hawaii Hatfield Realty, 85-833 Farrington Hwy, Suite 201, Waianae, HI 96792, is a condo right on the northern end of Makaha Beach, with lanais overlooking the water. Studios cost $550 for one week, $800 for two weeks or $1050 a month, with a $45 cleaning fee tacked on. There are one-bedroom units as well. It's tough to book in the high season, as a lot of retired people winter there.

At the *Sheraton Makaha Resort & Country Club* (☎ 695-9511, (800) 325-3535; fax 695-5806), 84-626 Makaha Valley Rd, Makaha, HI 96792, the theme is country club right down to the brochure that shows a young couple practicing their putts in the bedroom. The 200 rooms have lanais and refrigerators. The hotel has an 18-hole golf course, an Olympic-size pool, lighted tennis courts, horseback riding and restaurants. Rates are from $115 to $175.

Up in Makaha Valley, there are two large condo complexes: *Makaha Valley Plantation* and *Makaha Valley Towers*. Both give the impression they're under siege, with guards and gates to keep outsiders at bay. Of the two, Makaha Valley Towers is the better value. Inga's Realty (☎ 695-9055; fax 695-8060), 84-1170 Farrington Hwy, Suite 2, Makaha, HI 96792, handles some of the 586 units as monthly vacation

rentals. In winter, studios cost $1150 a month, one-bedroom units $1350; rates are $1000/$1100 in summer.

Places to Eat

The *Sheraton* has a snack bar, open from 6:30 am to 5 pm daily, with sandwiches, saimin and other simple fare. The main restaurant, the Kaala Room, has a golf course view and serves lunch from 11 am to 2 pm daily, with salads, sandwiches and a few hot dishes averaging $10. Dinner, which includes a salad bar, ranges from teriyaki chicken for $15 to steak and lobster for $35.

Cornet Village, on the corner of Farrington Hwy and Makaha Valley Rd, has a grocery store with a mediocre deli and snack bar. There's a drive-in selling plate lunches around the side and a 7-Eleven store on the opposite corner.

NORTH OF MAKAHA

Keaau Beach Park

Keaau Beach Park is another long open grassy strip, this time bordering a rocky shore, with camping, showers, drinking water, picnic tables and restrooms. A sandy beach begins at the very northern end of the park, although a rough reef, sharp drop and high seasonal surf make swimming uninviting.

Driving north along the coast you'll see low lava sea cliffs, white sand beaches and patches of kiawe. On the mauka side you can glimpse into a run of little valleys.

Kaneana Cave

Kaneana Cave, a massive cave on the right-hand side of the road about two miles north of Keaau Beach Park, was once underwater. Its size is the result of wave action wearing away loose rock around an earthquake crack and expanding the cavern over the millennia as the ocean slowly receded.

It's a somewhat uncanny place – often a strong wind gusts near the cave while it's windless just down the road.

Hawaiian kahunas once performed rituals inside the cave's inner chamber. Older Hawaiians consider it a sacred place and won't enter for fear it's haunted by the spirits of deceased chiefs. From the collection of broken beer bottles and graffiti inside it's obvious not everyone shares their sentiments.

From Ohikilolo Beach, below the cave, you can see Kaena Point ahead. Ohikilolo Beach is sometimes called Barking Sands, as the sand is said to make a 'woofing' sound if it's walked on when very dry.

Makua

Scenic Makua Valley opens up wide and grassy, backed by a fan of sharply fluted mountains. It serves as the ammunition field of the Makua Military Reservation.

The makai road opposite the south end of the reservation leads to a little graveyard shaded by yellow-flowered be-still trees. This is all that remains of the Makua Valley community, forced to evacuate during WW II when the US military took over the entire valley for bombing practice. War games still take place in the valley, which is fenced off with barbed wire and signs that warn of stray explosives.

Makua Beach, the white sand beach opposite the reservation, was a canoe landing in days past. A movie set of Lahaina, as it was during the 1800s, was built on Makua Beach for the 1966 movie *Hawaii* which starred Julie Andrews and Max von Sydow. No trace of the set remains.

Satellite Tracking Station

Immediately before the gate to Kaena Point State Park a road leads up to Kaena Point Satellite Tracking Station, operated by the US Air Force. The tracking station's antennas and domes sit atop the mountains above the point, one of them appearing like a giant white golf ball.

There are a couple of trails above the tracking station that can be hiked, including a 2½-mile ridge trail that leads to Mokuleia Forest Reserve. You'll need to obtain a hiking permit in advance from the Division of Forestry & Wildlife (☎ 587-0166) to get past the air force's guard station.

KAENA POINT STATE PARK

Kaena Point State Park is an undeveloped 853-acre coastal strip that runs along both sides of Kaena Point, the westernmost point of Oahu.

Until the mid-1940s the Oahu Railroad ran up from Honolulu and around the point, carrying passengers on to Haleiwa on the North Shore.

The attractive mile-long sandy beach on this side of the point is Yokohama Bay, so named for the large numbers of Japanese fishers who came here during the railroad days.

Winter brings huge pounding waves, making Yokohama a popular surfing and bodysurfing spot. It is, however, best left to the experts because of the submerged rocks, strong rip currents and dangerous shorebreak.

Swimming is pretty much limited to the summer, and then only during very calm conditions. When the water's flat, it's possible to snorkel; the best spot and easiest access is at the south side of the park. There are restrooms and showers but no drinking water.

Kaena Point Legends

Early Hawaiians believed that when people went into a deep sleep or lost consciousness their souls would wander. Souls that wandered too far were drawn west to Kaena Point. If they were lucky they were met here by their *aumakua* (ancestral spirit helper) who led their soul back to their body. If unattended, their soul would be forced to leap from Kaena Point into the endless night, never to return.

On clear days Kauai can be seen from the point. According to legend, it was at Kaena Point that the demigod Maui attempted to cast a huge hook into Kauai and pull it next to Oahu to join the two islands. But the line broke and Kauai slipped away, with just a small piece of it remaining near Oahu. This is Pohaku O Kauai, a rock off the end of Kaena Point. ■

In addition to being a state park, Kaena Point has been designated a natural area reserve because of its unique ecosystem. The extensive dry, windswept coastal dunes that rise above the point are the habitat of many rare native plants. The endangered Kaena akoko that grows on the talus slopes is found nowhere else.

More common plants are the beach naupaka with white flowers which look like they've been torn in half; pau-o-Hiiaka, a vine with blue flowers; and beach morning glory, sometimes found wrapped in the parasite plant kaunaoa, which looks like orange plastic fishing line.

Seabirds common to the point include shearwaters, boobies and the common noddy, a dark-brown bird with a greyish crown. You can often see schools of spinner dolphins off the beach and in winter humpback whale sightings are not uncommon.

Dirt bikes and 4WD vehicles have, until recently, created a great deal of disturbance in the dunes. It was only after Kaena Point became a natural area reserve in 1983 that vehicle access was restricted.

Recently the reserve has again become a nesting site for the Laysan albatross, and Hawaiian monk seals now occasionally bask in the sun there.

Kaena Point Trail

A 2½-mile (one way) coastal hike runs from the end of the paved road at Yokohama Bay to Kaena Point, following the old railroad bed. Along the trail are tide pools, sea arches, fine coastal views and the lofty sea cliffs of the Waianae mountain range. The hike is unshaded (Kaena means 'the heat'). Take plenty of water and don't leave anything valuable in your car.

Hawaii – The Big Island

The island of Hawaii, commonly called the Big Island, is nearly twice the size of all the other Hawaiian islands combined. Geographically, it's so incredibly varied that it resembles a mini-continent. Climates range from tropical to subarctic. Landscapes include one of just about everything: desolate lava flows, lush coastal valleys, high sea cliffs, rolling pastures, deserts and rainforests.

Geologically, it's the youngest Hawaiian island and the only one still growing. Kilauea, the most active volcano on earth, has added 300 acres of coastal land to the island since its latest series of eruptions began in 1983.

The Big Island has Hawaii's highest mountains, which rise almost 14,000 feet above sea level. Some people liken them to icebergs, not only for their seasonal snowcaps but because their summits are merely the tips of mountain masses that rise 32,000 feet from the ocean floor.

The mountains create a huge barrier that blocks the moist northeasterly trade winds and makes the leeward western side of the Big Island the driest region in Hawaii. The Kona and Kohala coasts, on this sunny western side, have the island's best beaches and water conditions.

The windward east coast catches the rain and has a predominantly rugged coastline with pounding surf, lush tropical rainforests, deep ravines and majestic waterfalls.

Still, the island's most impressive scenery is at Hawaii Volcanoes National Park, which encompasses incredible volcanic sites. The park has excellent hiking and camping in locales that range from tropical beaches to the icy 13,679-foot summit of Mauna Loa. You can drive or cycle around the rim of Kilauea's huge caldera or walk across still-steaming crater floors.

The Big Island has many noteworthy historical sites, including Hawaii's best petroglyphs and some of its most important heiaus. It also boasts the largest privately owned cattle ranch in the USA and the world's top collection of astronomical observatories. The latter dot the summit of Mauna Kea, Hawaii's highest point at 13,796 feet.

There are two distinct centers on the Big Island. Hilo, on the lush rainy east coast, is the island's only real city. It's the oldest city in Hawaii and it shows its age with character. But it's Kona, on the dry, sunny west coast, that attracts the visitors. Kona has the lion's share of the island's accommodation and is the center of most recreational activities, including excellent diving and deep-sea fishing.

The Big Island is big on space and few places feel crowded. It attracts a lot of adventurous people. It's got cowboy country, traditional fishing villages, valleys with taro farmers and wild horses, and a fair number of alternative folks living off the land.

ORIENTATION

The Big Island has fully serviced airports in Hilo and Kona. The Hilo Airport is in town. However, most visitors land in Kona at Keahole Airport, which is between the island's main resort areas of Kailua-Kona and Waikoloa.

From the Keahole Airport you take Hwy 19, which runs along the Kona Coast, seven miles south to get to Kailua-Kona or 12 miles north to get to Waikoloa.

The Hawaii Belt Rd circles the island, taking in the main towns and many of the sights. Different segments of the road have different highway numbers and names, but it's easy to follow.

From Kona to Hilo, the northern half of the belt road is 93 miles and the journey takes about two hours nonstop. The southern Kona-Hilo route is 125 miles and takes approximately three hours.

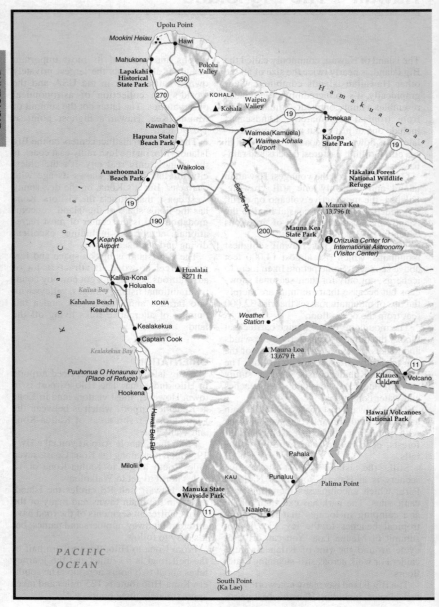

Upolu Point
Mookini Heiau
Hawi
Mahukona
KOHALA
Waipio
Valley
Lapakahi
Historical
State Park
250
270
Kawaihae
Waimea(Kamuela)
Waimea-Kohala
Airport
Hapuna State
Beach Park
Anaehoomalu
Beach Park
Waikoloa
19
190
Keahole
Airport
Hualalai
8271 ft
Kailua-Kona
Holualoa
Kailua Bay
KONA
Kahaluu Beach
Keauhou
Kealakekua
Captain Cook
Kealakekua Bay
Puuhonua O Honaunau
(Place of Refuge)
Hookena
Hawaii Belt Rd
Milolii
Manuka State
Wayside Park
11
Naalehu
PACIFIC
OCEAN

Pololu
Valley
Kohala
Waipio
Valley
Hamakua Coast
Honokaa
19
19
Kalopa
State Park
Hakalau Forest
National Wildlife
Refuge
Saddle Rd
Mauna Kea
13,796 ft
200
Mauna Kea
State Park
Onizuka Center for
International Astronomy
(Visitor Center)
Weather
Station
Mauna Loa
13,679 ft
Kilauea
Caldera
Volcano
11
Hawaii Volcanoes
National Park
Pahala
Punaluu
Palima Point
KAU
Kona Coast

South Point
(Ka Lae)

PACIFIC
OCEAN

Akaka
Falls
State
Park

Hilo Bay

HILO

Hilo
Airport

(200)

Keaau

Hawaii Belt Rd

(130)

Cape
Kumukahi

Pahoa

PUNA

(137)

Active
Lava Flow

Hawaii
The Big Island

0   15   30 km
0   10   20 miles

BIG ISLAND

HISTORY

By and large the history of the Big Island is the history of Hawaii. It's widely believed that the first Polynesian settlers landed on this island. It was on the Big Island that the first *luakini heiau* (temple of human sacrifice) and the *kapu* system of strict taboos regulating all aspects of daily life came into being. It was also here, six centuries later, that the old gods were overthrown and replaced by those of the Christians.

English explorer Captain Cook died on the Big Island in 1779, a year after 'discovering' Hawaii, and this was where Kamehameha the Great rose to power.

The Kamehameha Era

Kamehameha I Kamehameha was born on the Big Island in 1758. As a young boy he was brought to Kealakekua Bay to live at the royal court of his uncle, Kalaniopuu, high chief of the island.

Kamehameha went on to become Kalaniopuu's fiercest general. To help him amass even more strength, Kalaniopuu appointed Kamehameha guardian of the war god, Kukailimoku, the 'snatcher of land'.

The god was embodied in a coarsely carved wooden image with a bloody red mouth and a helmet of yellow feathers. Kamehameha carried it into battle with him and it was said that during the fiercest fighting the image would screech out terrifying battle cries.

Immediately after Kalaniopuu's death in 1782, Kamehameha led his warriors against Kalaniopuu's son, Kiwalao, who had taken the throne. Kiwalao was killed and Kamehameha emerged as ruler of the Kohala region and one of the three ruling chiefs of the Big Island. The other two were Kahekili of Maui and Kamehameha's cousin, Keoua.

However, Kamehameha's ambitions went beyond sharing control of the islands. In 1790, with the aid of a captured foreign schooner and two shipwrecked sailors, Isaac Davis and John Young, whom he used as gunners, Kamehameha attacked and conquered Maui.

Shortly after that, Kamehameha was in

Kamehameha the Great

Molokai preparing for the invasion of Oahu when word reached him that Keoua, chief of the Kau region, was attacking the Hamakua Coast. During the assaults Keoua had boldly pillaged Waipio Valley, which was the most sacred area on the Big Island and the site where Kamehameha had ceremoniously received his war god a decade earlier.

As an angry Kamehameha set sail for home, Keoua's soldiers retreated to Kau. When the withdrawing troops passed beneath the slopes of Kilauea Crater, the volcano suddenly erupted and many of the warriors were instantly killed as toxic fumes and ashes swept over them. It is the only known volcanic explosion in Hawaiian history to have resulted in mass fatalities. Casts of the soldiers' footprints remain on the trail today.

Around this time Kamehameha was told by a prophet from Kauai that if he built a new heiau to honor his war god, Kukailimoku, he would become ruler of all the islands.

Kamehameha did so, completing Puukohola Heiau in Kawaihae in 1791. He then sent word to Keoua that his appearance was requested at the heiau for reconciliation. Keoua, well aware that this was a luakini temple, probably knew his fate was sealed.

Upon landing at Kawaihae, Keoua and his party became the heiau's first sacrifices. With Keoua's death, Kamehameha became sole ruler of the Big Island.

Over the next few years Kamehameha conquered all the islands (except for Kauai over which he established suzerainty) and named the entire kingdom after his home island, Hawaii.

End of an Era Kamehameha the Great established the kingdom's royal court in Lahaina on Maui, but later returned to his Kamakahonu residence, on the north side of Kailua Bay, where he died in May 1819.

The crown was passed to his hesitant son, Liholiho, and Kamehameha's favorite wife, Kaahumanu, a spirited woman who wasn't content to be kept in her place by the old traditions.

In Kamakahonu, six months after Kamehameha's death, Kaahumanu sat down with Liholiho to eat a meal, something strictly forbidden under the kapu system. This breaking of the kapus by royalty marked the demise of the old religion. Almost immediately, temples throughout the islands were abandoned and their idols burned.

On April 19, 1820, the ship *Thaddeus* sailed into Kailua Bay with Hawaii's first Christian missionaries aboard. They landed beside Kamehameha's recently desecrated heiau at Kamakahonu.

Their timing was perfect as the recent abandonment of the old religion had left a vacuum into which the missionaries readily moved.

GEOGRAPHY

The Big Island has an area of 4035 sq miles (10,451 sq km) and is growing as new lava spews into the sea. It's 93 miles long and 76 miles wide. The Big Island is the youngest Hawaiian island and the farthest east. Its southern tip, called South Point or Ka Lae, is the southernmost point in the USA.

The island was formed by five large shield volcanoes: Kohala, Hualalai, Mauna Kea, Mauna Loa and Kilauea. The last two are still active, with Kilauea having the distinction of being the most active volcano on earth.

Mauna Kea ('White Mountain') at 13,796 feet (4205 meters) is the highest point in the Hawaiian Islands. It extends an additional 19,680 feet below sea level to the ocean floor and when measured from its base is the highest mountain in the world.

Mauna Loa ('Long Mountain'), just slightly lower at 13,679 feet (4169 meters) above sea level, makes up more than half the land mass of the Big Island and is the largest mountain mass in the world when measured from the ocean floor.

CLIMATE

Rainfall and temperatures vary more with location than with the seasons. The leeward northwest coast between Lapakahi and Waikoloa is the driest region in the state. Kawaihae, in the center of this strip, averages less than 10 inches of rain a year.

On the windward side of Mauna Kea, near the 2500-foot elevation, 300 inches of rain falls annually. So much rain is squeezed out of the clouds as they rise up Mauna Kea and Mauna Loa that only about

15 inches of precipitation reaches the summits, much of it as snow. Heavy subtropical winter rainstorms in Hilo occasionally bring blizzards to the mountains as low as the 9000-foot level.

Elevation makes enough of a difference that even within the city of Hilo, annual rainfall ranges from 130 inches on the shore to 200 inches on the higher slopes. Trivia buffs may be interested to know that Hilo has the world's largest measured raindrops, 4 to 8 mm in diameter!

Annual rainfall in Volcano is 101 inches. At Kailua-Kona it's 25 inches. Although winter is wetter than summer, location again is the key. In Kona seasonal rainfall variations are marginal. At Volcano it's about twofold.

The average daily high temperatures in January are 65°F at Hawaii Volcanoes National Park, 79°F in Hilo and 81°F in Kailua-Kona. In August, they are 71°F, 83°F and 85°F respectively. Nighttime lows are about 15° less.

FLORA & FAUNA

The *nene*, the endangered goose that is Hawaii's state bird, lives on the upland slopes of Mauna Kea, Mauna Loa and Hualalai. As recently as a hundred years ago there were an estimated 25,000 nene on the Big

Vog
'Vog' is a word coined on the Big Island to define the volcanic haze that has been hanging over the island since Kilauea's latest eruptive phase began in 1983. It usually blows towards Kona and conditions can resemble city smog when the trade winds falter. Vog consists of water vapor, carbon dioxide and significant amounts of sulfur dioxide.

In the early 1990s an average of 275 tons of sulfur dioxide was being emitted from Kilauea daily, causing air quality problems on the Big Island and haze throughout Hawaii. The sulfur dioxide level exceeds standards set by the US Environmental Protection Agency an average of 22 days a year. While this shouldn't present health problems for short-term visitors, scientists are currently studying the link between vog and respiratory problems for residents. ■

BIG ISLAND

Hawaii's state bird – the nene

Island. They now number just a few hundred. Still, they're a friendly species and you might come across them, particularly if you camp in the national park.

Other native birds include the endangered *palila*, a small yellow bird that survives solely on Mauna Kea's slopes, and the *io* (Hawaiian hawk), which also occupies the mountain slopes and lives only on the Big Island. Another endangered bird endemic to the Big Island is the *alala* (Hawaiian crow), which hangs on precariously with a single flock of only a dozen birds remaining.

There are wild horses in Waipio Valley and feral cattle on the slopes of Mauna Kea. The Big Island also has wild pigs, goats and sheep.

Two varieties of silversword grow on the Big Island, one on Mauna Kea and the other on Mauna Loa. Related to their better-known Maui cousin, they grow in remote areas well off the beaten path.

GOVERNMENT

The Big Island is one county unto itself with an elected mayor and a nine-member council.

Hilo is the county seat and political center. Rivalry is ongoing between old established Hilo and boomtown Kona; there's even a budding separatist movement, based in Kona, that's aimed at dividing the island into two counties. The biggest political issue on the island, as elsewhere in Hawaii, is rampant development.

ECONOMY

The Big Island's unemployment rate is nearly 8%. Employment is fairly diversified with retail trade, government, hotels and construction industries employing about half of the workforce.

Agriculture accounts for a large sector of the economy and almost 15% of the workforce. The Big Island produces the vast majority of Hawaii's macadamia nuts, coffee and tropical flowers, as well as four-fifths of its fruit, including papayas, bananas and oranges. Sugar production is in a sharp decline, with the island's main producer, Hamakua Sugar Company, having closed in 1994; the only other Big Island sugar operation, which is in Kau, is expected to be phased out in the next few years.

The Big Island has a small but up-and-coming cocoa bean industry whose early harvests have proven quite successful among chocolate connoisseurs.

There's also a sizable illicit underground agriculture in *pakalolo* (marijuana). Although it has declined greatly as the result of strict police surveillance, the vast majority of all marijuana confiscated in Hawaii still comes from the Big Island's Puna and Kau districts.

The Big Island has several sizable cattle ranches, which collectively produce the majority of the beef marketed in the state.

POPULATION & PEOPLE

The population of the Big Island is 130,500. Hilo has about a third of the island's population, but the Big Island's demographics are changing rapidly.

Between 1970 and 1980, North Kona (which includes Kailua-Kona) was the fastest growing district in the state with a growth rate of 185%. Between 1980 and 1990, neighboring South Kohala took the honors as the state's most rapidly growing district, with its population doubling.

The Big Island's ethnic breakdown is 26% part-Hawaiian, 25% Caucasian, 21% Japanese, 15% mixed non-Hawaiian and 9% Filipino. Full-blooded Hawaiians make up just 1% of the population.

INFORMATION
Tourist Offices

The Big Island has two Hawaii Visitors Bureau offices: 250 Keawe St, Hilo, HI 96720 (☎ 961-5797; fax 961-2126) and 75-5719 W Alii Dr, Kailua-Kona, HI 96740 (☎ 329-7787; fax 326-7563).

You can also receive a tourist information packet by calling (800) 648-2441 and

Official Hawaii
The island of Hawaii is nicknamed the Big Island. Its official flower is the *ohia lehua*, from a native tree that flourishes around lava flows; ceremonial leis are made from its fluffy red pompom blossoms. The island's official color is red. ■

leaving your mailing address on the answering machine.

Media

West Hawaii Today (☎ 329-9311), which is the Kona Coast newspaper, and Hilo's *Hawaii Tribune-Herald* (☎ 935-6621) are both published daily except Saturday. A single copy of *West Hawaii Today* may be obtained by sending $3 to West Hawaii Today, Box 789, Kailua-Kona, HI 96745.

Free tourist magazines such as *This Week Big Island*, *Spotlight's Big Island Gold* and *Guide to the Big Island* are readily available at the airport, in hotel lobbies and around town. They're good sources of general information and include discount coupons for activities and eateries around the island.

The island has five AM and seven FM radio stations and three cable TV stations. Commercial and public TV stations are relayed from Honolulu. Channel 6 on cable TV features visitor information programs.

Maps

The best general map of the Big Island is the one published by the University of Hawaii Press; it's sold in numerous shops around the island.

Libraries

There are public libraries in Kailua-Kona, Kealakekua, Holualoa, Hilo, Waimea, Pahoa, Pahala, Naalehu, Mountain View, Laupahoehoe, Kapaau, Honokaa and Keaau.

Weather

The National Weather Service has recorded forecasts for the Big Island (☎ 961-5582), for Hilo and vicinity (☎ 935-8555) and for water conditions (☎ 935-9883).

Hawaii Volcanoes National Park (☎ 967-7977) has recorded information on current volcano eruptions and viewing points.

Emergency

For police, ambulance or fire emergencies dial 911. The crisis & help line is 329-9111 in Kona, 969-9111 in Hilo.

The main hospitals are in Hilo (☎ 969-4111) and Kealakekua (☎ 322-9311).

ACTIVITIES

The vast majority of the Big Island's recreational activities take place on the west coast. In addition to those listed here, most of the Waikoloa-area resorts have a variety of activities, including water sports, cruises and dive trips. They generally charge higher-than-average rates and advertise mainly to their guests, but are usually open to the public as well.

Beaches & Swimming

The Big Island has 313 miles of shoreline. What it doesn't have are the expansive stretches of sandy beaches that you'll find on Maui or Oahu. Most of the Big Island's beaches are sandy pockets bordering bays and coves.

The best spots are on the west coast. Kailua-Kona has a few good beaches, although the better ones are farther up along the Kona Coast around Waikoloa and Kohala. Of these, Anaehoomalu and Hapuna are both beautiful, easily accessible public beaches. There are also a number of isolated gems dotting the coast that require a hike and are well worth the effort to reach.

Hilo is not as well endowed with beaches, although there are a few places to swim and snorkel on the east side of Hilo Bay.

The Puna and Kau districts have interesting black sand beaches although generally unfavorable swimming conditions.

Swimming Pools The county has public pools at Honokaa High School in Honokaa, Kamehameha Park in Kapaau, Konawaena High School in Kealakekua, Kau High School in Pahala, Laupahoehoe High School in Laupahoehoe and at the Hoolulu Complex in Hilo. All county pools are free to the public for both lap swims and open pool use, which are scheduled at different hours.

There's a coastal saltwater pool with public access behind the Kona by the Sea condos in Kailua.

Surfing

The Big Island is not one of the better islands for surfing, although local surfers do manage to catch waves in a number of places. Many of the island's surf spots are rocky and surfers new to the area should check out conditions thoroughly before hitting the waves.

Honolii Cove, two miles north of Hilo, is popular on the eastern side of the island. In Kona, favorite surfing locales include Kahaluu Beach in Keauhou and Banyans, which is near the banyan tree north of White Sands Beach.

White Sands Beach is also one of the best places on the Kona Coast for boogie boarding and bodysurfing.

One of the south coast's best surfing spots, Drainpipes, in the Kalapana area, was wiped out by the 1990 lava flow that engulfed Kaimu Beach.

Windsurfing

The Big Island is not a real hot spot for windsurfing. Most windsurfers head to Anaehoomalu Bay in Waikoloa, which has some of the better wind and water conditions. You can rent boards from Ocean Sports (☎ 885-5555), the beach hut in front of the Royal Waikoloan, for $20 an hour, and get a 1½-hour lesson for $35. The best winds are usually between 10 am and 2 pm.

Kawaihae Harbor and Hilo Bay are other spots that see some windsurfing activity.

Diving

The Big Island has excellent diving on the leeward Kona and Kohala coasts. Overall the best conditions are in spring and summer, although there are good, calm dive days year round.

The Kona Coast has many good shore dives, including steep near-shore drop-offs with lava tubes, caves and diverse marine life. Diving is far more limited on the Hilo side where the season is basically from April to September.

A good reference is the book *Let's Go Shore Dive'n' on the Kona Coast* by Dick Dresie.

Kona has lots of dive operations. The cost of one-tank dives averages about $60, two-tank dives about $80. Several places offer introductory dives, night dives and certification courses.

One popular dive is Red Hill, an underwater cinder cone about 10 miles south of Kona. It has beautiful lava formations, including ledges and lots of honeycombed lava tubes nicely lit by streaks of sunlight. There are also coral pinnacles and many brightly colored nudibranches.

Another good spot is off Kaiwi Point, south of Honokohau Harbor, where there are some respectable drop-offs and huge eagle rays, sea turtles and large fish.

Kealakekua Bay has good coral and marine life in a very protected cove that's calm all year round. All in all, there are

about 40 boat dives along the Kona Coast, including an airplane wreck off Keahole Point.

Jack's Diving Locker (☎ 329-7585, (800) 345-4807), 75-5819 Alii Dr, Kailua-Kona, HI 96740, at the Coconut Grove Marketplace opposite the Royal Kona Resort, is a small, friendly operation and one of the best for introductory dives.

Kona Coast Divers (☎ 329-8802), 75-5614 Palani Rd, Kailua-Kona, HI 96740, is one of the larger operations. While they're quite professional they also have a reputation for being a bit regimented.

Dive Makai (☎ 329-2025), 74-5590 Alapa, Kailua-Kona, HI 96740, is a personable little operation run by husband-and-wife team Tom Shockley and Lisa Choquette. They are very conservation oriented and have a good word-of-mouth reputation.

Sea Paradise Scuba (☎ 322-2500, (800) 322-5662), Box 580, Kailua-Kona, HI 96745, is also environmentally oriented. They're based at Keauhou Bay and tend to head south, often to Red Hill or Kealakekua Bay.

Hawaiian Divers (☎ 329-2323, (800) 356-2243), 75-5702A Alii Dr, Kailua-Kona, HI 96740, is a high-tech operation that offers mixed-gas diving in addition to standard dives.

Eco-Scapes (☎ 329-7116, (800) 949-3483), Kamehameha Square Shopping Center, 75-5626 Kuakini Hwy, Kailua-Kona, HI 96740, has an interesting night dive with the manta rays off the Kona Surf Hotel.

Kohala Divers (☎ 882-7774), Box 44940, Kawaihae, HI 96743, at the shopping center in Kawaihae, is another good operation. They organize trips up the Kohala Coast.

Live-Aboard Boat The *Kona Aggressor* (☎ 329-8182, (800) 344-5662), Live-Dive Pacific, 74-5588 Pawai Place, Building F, Kailua-Kona, HI 96740, is a 110-foot live-aboard dive boat that accommodates up to 10 guests. All-inclusive one-week trips cost $1695, starting and ending each Saturday.

BIG ISLAND

Dive Club The Kona Reefers Dive Club meets on the third Friday of the month and holds shore dives open to the public at 10 am on the third Sunday of the month. For more information, call club founder Roy Damron (☎ 325-5422).

Snorkeling

Snorkelers will find some good spots south of Kailua-Kona. The area's most popular easy-access snorkeling haunt is Kahaluu Beach in Keauhou, which is teeming with fish and is a good place for beginners. The north side of the Place of Refuge is another fine drive-up snorkeling spot. While it takes a hike, a horseback ride or a boat to reach, there's terrific snorkeling in the calm, clear 30-foot-deep waters near Captain Cook's monument at the north end of Kealakekua Bay.

Snorkeling Cruises The most common snorkeling cruise is to Kealakekua Bay. Prices include snorkeling gear, beverages and food.

Fairwind (☎ 322-2788) makes trips to Kealakekua Bay aboard a 50-foot trimaran. They leave from Keauhou Bay which allows for more snorkeling time than other boats. The 4½-hour tours depart at 9 am daily and again at 1:45 pm on Tuesdays, Thursdays and Saturdays. These trips allow 2½ hours of snorkeling and cost $59. In addition, on Sundays, Mondays, Wednesdays and Fridays there's a three-hour outing that leaves at 1:45 pm, allows one hour of snorkeling and costs $35.

Royal Hawaiian Cruises (☎ 329-6411) goes to Kealakekua from Kailua Pier and operates both a glass-bottom boat and Zodiac raft. There are two four-hour cruises a day, leaving at 8:30 am and 1:30 pm, which cost $54 for adults, $27 for children ages five to 12, free for children under five.

Captain Zodiac (☎ 329-3199, (800) 422-7824) does four-hour tours aboard bouncy Zodiac rubber rafts. Departure is from Honokohau Harbor at 8 am and 1 pm daily, with pick-up possible at Kailua and Keauhou piers. The cost of $62 includes snorkeling time at Kealakekua Bay followed by visits to sea caves.

Kamanu Charters (☎ 329-2021) takes a 36-foot catamaran out of Honokohau Harbor to snorkel at Pawai Bay, just north of the Old Kona Airport. They take a maximum of 24 people, motoring down and using the sail on the way back. The 3¼-hour trips start at 9 am and cost $39 for adults, $21 for children 12 and under. They also offer a two-hour afternoon sail during the whale-watching season for $25 for adults, $15 for children.

Snorkelers can sometimes tag along with divers on dive tours if space is available. Kohala Divers charges snorkelers just $15, while most others charge around $30.

Snuba If you haven't tried it before, Kealakekua Bay is a great place to experience snuba, which is a sort of scuba diving for snorkelers. It's a tankless operation, with an air hose attached to an air-filled raft that floats on the surface above you. Generally you get about 30 minutes underwater before you run out of air. The cost is an additional $40 with either Fairwind or Royal Hawaiian snorkeling cruises.

While the underwater scenery is certainly not on par with Kealakekua, Snuba Tours of Kona (☎ 326-7446) also offers snuba beach dives in front of King Kamehameha's Kona Beach Hotel. The cost is $49. Make arrangements at the hotel beach hut.

Snorkel Gear Rentals Snorkel Bob's (☎ 329-0770), off Alii Dr by the Royal Kona Resort, has snorkel sets starting at $15 a week. They also rent boogie boards and corrective-lens masks.

Kona Water Sports (☎ 329-1593) at Banyan Court in Kailua rents boogie boards for $4 to $7 a day or $16 to $28 a week and snorkel sets for $3/12 a day/week. They also have a few masks with corrective lenses for $5/20.

Fairwind at Keauhou Bay rents snorkel sets for $5 a day.

The beach hut at King Kamehameha's

Kona Beach Hotel in Kailua rents snorkel sets and boogie boards for $5 a day.

Kayaking

Jimbo's Kayaks (☎ 328-8448) is a small operation run by Jim Calkins who rents kayaks virtually out of his truck. Essentially, you make a reservation to meet him at a prearranged launch location and time. You can launch from Napoopoo Beach and then kayak across Kealakekua Bay to the Captain Cook Monument or depart from Kona Coast State Park and go up the coast to Makalawena and other remote beaches. The kayaks are delivered with a cooler full of ice, reef walkers, snorkel gear and a life vest and the price is a very reasonable $20 per person in either single or double kayaks. Jim will throw in a 20-minute paddling lesson to anyone unfamiliar with kayaking, and you can stay out with the kayak for five hours.

Fishing

Kona is a world-renowned deep-sea fishing spot for Pacific blue marlin, a spectacular fighting fish with a long sword. Most of the world records are held in Kona, with at least one marlin topping 1000 pounds reeled in each year. Kona is also known for its record catches of ahi (yellowfin tuna) and spearfish.

Near the Chart House restaurant at Kailua's Waterfront Row, there's an interesting 'Granders Wall' lined with photos of anglers next to their 1000-pound marlin catches.

You can watch the boats come in and see the fish weighed at Kailua Pier and Honokohau Harbor from around 11:30 am for the morning charters and from around 3:30 pm for the afternoon and full-day charters.

Kona has more than 100 charter boats. The standard cost is $80 to $100 to go out for half a day, sharing a boat with three to five other fishers. You can also charter a whole boat and take up to six people at a cost of about $400 for half a day, $575 for a full day. You might want to first take a look at the tourist magazines, which often advertise a few renegade boats at nearly half the going rate – though they'll need to be booked directly with the skippers. Prices include all fishing equipment, but not food or drink.

These centers each book numerous boats:

Kona Charter Skippers Association, 75-5663 Palani Rd, Kailua-Kona, HI 96740 (☎ 329-3600, (800) 762-7546)

Kona Activities Center, Box 70, Kailua-Kona, HI 96745 (☎ 329-3171, (800) 367-5288)

Kona Coast Activities, Box 5397, Kailua-Kona, HI 96745 (☎ 329-7529, (800) 367-5105)

There are a number of fishing tournaments held in Kona; the Super Bowl of them all is the Hawaiian International Billfish Tournament held in August and accompanied by a week of festive activities.

Hiking

There is excellent hiking all around the Big Island. Some of the best and most varied hikes are in Hawaii Volcanoes National Park, where trails lead across lava flows and steaming crater floors, through dense native forests and up to the peak of Mauna Loa.

On the northern tip of the island there are steep coastal cliffs and deep valleys reaching down from the Kohala Mountains that can be approached from either side. From the road's end on the northwest side, it's a 30-minute hike down to the beach at the bottom of Pololu Valley. On the southeast side you can take a 30-minute walk down into verdant Waipio Valley or backpack deep into remote Waimanu Valley.

North of Kona, you can hike in from the highway to secluded beaches, or explore portions of ancient footpaths and petroglyph fields. Efforts are under way by Na Ala Hele, a state-sponsored group composed mostly of volunteers, to eventually re-establish the entire 50-mile historic trail system that once ran between Kailua and Kawaihae. Mauna Lani Resort and Lapakahi State Park have easy trails, marked with interpretive plaques, around ancient fishponds and through abandoned villages.

South of Kona, a trail leads to the spot

where Captain Cook died at Kealakekua Bay. In the center of the island, a strenuous hike leads to the summit of Mauna Kea with its observatory domes. On the slopes below, Kalopa State Park has short, easy forest trails.

All hikes are detailed in their respective sections.

Guided Hikes The Kona Hiking Club has hikes open to all trekkers on the first Saturday and third Thursday of each month. They vary in both location and difficulty. Most hikes take in a beach for picnics and swimming and the majority are on the west side of the island. Car pools leave from Kailua, with passengers contributing the equivalent of about $1 an hour for gas. Announcements are usually published in *West Hawaii Today*.

Horseback Riding

Kings' Trail Rides O'Kona (☎ 323-2388) in Kealakekua takes a maximum of four riders down the Captain Cook Trail to Kealakekua Bay for lunch and snorkeling. As cowboy horses are used, riders must be experienced. The cost is $95 per person.

Kohala Naalapa (☎ 775-0330) has 2½-hour trail rides that cross the pastures of Kahua Ranch in Kohala and offer fine views of the coast. The rides depart at 9:30 am and 1 pm daily. The cost is $65.

Paniolo Riding Adventures (☎ 889-5354), off Hwy 250 in Kohala, has 2½-hour horseback rides for $70 and 3½-hour picnic rides for $100. Children must be at least eight years old, but there are also pony rides available for young children. This company also arranges mule rides.

Chalon International of Hawaii (☎ 889-6257) also has rides over green Kohala pastures. Rides leave at 11 am from the Hawi area, last two hours and cost $60. Riders must be over 12 years of age and able to ride alone unassisted.

Dahana Ranch Roughriders (☎ 885-0057), off the Old Mamalahoa Hwy between Waimea and Honokaa, is owned and operated by native Hawaiians. Horses cross the open range of a working cattle

ranch. Rides depart a few times daily, by appointment only, last 1½ hours, cost $52 and are open to both novice and experienced riders ages four and up. There's also a 'city slicker adventure' at 3 pm on Tuesdays and Thursdays in which riders can help drive 200-plus head of cattle; it takes at least 2½ hours and costs $100.

Fallbrook Trail Rides (☎ 322-1818) has one, 1½ and two-hour rides in the Kona area for $29 an hour.

For horseback rides in Waipio Valley, see the Waipio section.

Tennis

The Old Kona Airport Beach Park in Kailua-Kona has four lighted outdoor tennis courts and if you show up with racket in hand there's a fair chance you'll find a partner. Hilo's Hoolulu Complex has five outdoor courts and three lighted indoor courts.

Other county courts that are lighted for night play are at Kailua Playground in Kailua, Greenwell Park in Captain Cook, Waimea Park in Waimea, Lincoln Park and Lokahi Park in Hilo, Papaaloa Park in the North Hilo district, Honokaa Park in Honokaa, Kamehameha Park in Kapaau, and Naalehu Park and Pahala School in the Kau district. All are free to the public.

Many of the larger hotels and resorts have tennis courts for their guests. The Royal Kona Resort in Kailua-Kona opens its courts to the public for $5 per person per hour or $7 per day and rents rackets for $6 a day.

The Mauna Lani Racquet Club (☎ 885-7765), which hosts Davis Cup matches, has 10 courts and a schedule of clinics and round-robin tournaments. Court fees are $7 per person per hour but the courts are only open to club members or to guests of the Mauna Lani Resort.

Golf

The Big Island has 14 golf courses, including some world-class courses in the Waikoloa area that are laid out on top of lava flows.

The top courses are: Mauna Kea Golf Course (☎ 882-7222) near Mauna Kea Beach; Francis Ii Brown South Course and North Course at the Mauna Lani Resort (☎ 885-6655); Waikoloa Golf Club (☎ 885-6060) and Waikoloa Kings' Golf Course (☎ 885-4647) at Waikoloa Beach Resort; and Hapuna Golf Course (☎ 882-1035) at Hapuna Beach Prince Hotel.

Non-resort guests are charged $150 at each of the Francis Ii courses, $110 at Mauna Kea, $95 at the Waikoloa Beach Resort courses and $90 at Hapuna. Resort guests get discounts ranging from 20% to 50%. Green fees include carts except at Mauna Kea where carts rent for $20.

For more reasonably priced turf, the Hilo Municipal Golf Course (☎ 959-7711), at 340 Haihai St in Hilo, has 18 holes that can be played for $8, plus a rental cart fee of $15.

Other courses include the Naniloa Country Club (☎ 935-3000) in Hilo, $25 ($15 for Naniloa Hotel guests) plus a cart fee of $7; Volcano Golf and Country Club (☎ 967-7331) in Hawaii Volcanoes National Park, $50; SeaMountain Golf Course (☎ 928-6222) at Punaluu, $45; Waikoloa Village Golf Club (☎ 883-9621) in Waikoloa, $70; Kona Country Club and Alii Country Club (☎ 322-2595) in Keauhou, $100 ($60 for Kona Surf guests); and Makalei Hawaii Country Club (☎ 325-6625), off Hwy 190 northeast of Keahole Airport, $110 for out-of-state guests. All are 18-hole courses except the nine-hole Naniloa Country Club.

Golf the Big One, a brochure that lists each course's rating, slope, terrain, vegetation, hours and amenities, is available from the tourist office.

Skiing

Skiing in Hawaii is primarily a curiosity event. Snow does fall each winter on the upper slopes of Mauna Kea, although the timing is unpredictable. The ski season usually starts anywhere from early January to late February and can run for several months. There are bad years when there's virtually no skiing and good years when the season can extend through June.

Skiing Mauna Kea is not your standard sort of skiing. The altitude can be tough and the slopes can have exposed rocks. There are no ski lodges, lifts or other facilities.

When there's snow, Ski Guides Hawaii (☎ 885-4188), Box 1954, Kamuela, HI 96743, based in Waimea, can provide a full day of skiing for $180 per person. The cost includes use of ski equipment, transportation to Mauna Kea, lunch and a 4WD shuttle service up the mountain after each run.

Sporting Competitions

The Ironman triathlon, held each October, combines a 2.4-mile ocean swim, 112-mile bike race and 26.2-mile marathon into one exhaustive endurance event. It begins and ends near the Kailua Pier in Kailua-Kona.

About a thousand men and women from 50 countries compete in the Ironman each year, with worldwide media coverage. The course record, set by Mark Allen in 1993, is eight hours, seven minutes and 45 seconds. For information on the race contact Ironman Triathlon World Championship (☎ 329-0063), 75-127 Lunapule Rd, Suite 11, Kailua-Kona, HI 96740.

The Kilauea Volcano Wilderness Marathon and Rim Runs are held at Hawaii Volcanoes National Park in July. There are three separate races that include a 10-mile run around the rim of Kilauea's caldera, a 5.5-mile race that goes down into Kilauea Iki Crater and a 26.2-mile marathon through the Kau Desert. Contact the Volcano Art Center (☎ 967-8222), Box 458, Volcano, HI 96785, for information.

The Big Island has numerous other road races. An annual race schedule listing marathons, fun runs and other sporting events is available from the Ironman office or can be picked up at B & L Bike & Sports in Kailua-Kona.

Organized Tours

Grey Line Hawaii (☎ 833-8000, (800) 367-2420), Roberts Hawaii (☎ 329-1688) and Polynesian Adventure Tours (☎ 329-8008) have day-long circle-island tours that include Hawaii Volcanoes National Park for $50 to $60.

Tours down into Waipio Valley and up to Mauna Kea summit are listed in those sections.

Helicopter & Biplane

The most popular Big Island helicopter tour is a flight over Kilauea Volcano – especially when the volcano is acting up.

The cost largely depends on your departure point. Flights from the Volcano Golf Course or Hilo are about $125, from Kona about $200 and from Waikoloa about $250. However, it's a competitive market and it's worth checking the free tourist magazines

for discount coupons and calling around to compare prices.

Companies include: Volcano Heli-Tours (☎ 967-7578), which leaves from Volcano; Hawaii Helicopters (☎ (800) 994-9099); Papillon (☎ 329-0551, (800) 367-7095); Mauna Kea Helicopters (☎ 885-6400, (800) 400-4354); Io Aviation (☎ 935-3031, (800) 942-3031); Blue Hawaiian Helicopters (☎ 961-5600, (800) 247-5444); Island Helicopters (☎ 969-1172, (800) 829-5999); Safari Helicopters (☎ 969-1259, (800) 326-3356); and Kenai Helicopters (☎ 885-5833, (800) 622-3144).

Classic Aviation Corporation (☎ 329-8687, (800) 695-8100) has biplane tours over the volcano for $150 for one passenger, $99 per person for two.

Keep in mind that the volcano area is often rainy even when it's sunny in Kona. If it's raining it's not worth going up, so if you're coming from the Kona side, call first to see what the weather's like.

Dinner Cruise

Capt Beans' Cruises (☎ 329-2955), the high-profile boat with the yellow lights and orange sails, has a touristy dinner cruise in the evening for ages 21 and over. It leaves at 5:15 pm from Kailua Pier, takes two hours and costs $45, including meal, drink and a Polynesian show.

Whale Watching

While the best whale watching is off Maui, you can spot whales from the Big Island as well. The season for humpback whales, which are the biggest attraction, usually starts around January and runs through March or April. However pilot, sperm, beaked and false killer whales and five dolphin species can be found in Kona waters all year round.

Marine mammal biologist Dan McSweeney of Whale Watch (☎ 322-0028) leads three-hour whale watching cruises aboard a 31-foot boat leaving Honokohau Harbor at 9 am daily, and when business is brisk there's also a 1 pm tour. Hydrophones allow passengers to hear whale songs. The cost is $39.50 for adults, $29.50 for children ages 12 and under, including a light

Sunset at Keauhou, Big Island

Akaka Falls, Big Island

Mookini Heiau, North Kohala, Big Island

Ahuena Heiau, Big Island

Fishing Shrine, South Point, Big Island

Hawaii Volcanoes Nat'l Park, Big Island

Rainbow Falls, Big Island

Polulu Valley, Big Island

Puuhonua O Honaunau, Big Island

DR

brunch. There's a 24-hour non-refundable cancellation policy.

A couple of the snorkeling tour boats also do whale watches during humpback season, so it's worth taking a look at listings in the tourist magazines.

Submarine & Glass-bottom Boats

Atlantis Submarines (☎ 329-6626, (800) 548-6262), based at King Kamehameha's Kona Beach Hotel in Kailua, has 45-minute rides in a submarine which dives down about 100 feet in a coral crevice in front of the Royal Kona Resort. The sub has 26 portholes, carries 46 passengers and departs seven times a day. The outing lasts two hours, including the boat ride to and from the sub, and costs $59 for adults, $29 for children. There's also a longer $79 outing ($39 for children), in which scuba divers feed fish at porthole level.

A cheaper option is the *Nautilus II* (☎ 326-2003), a 34-passenger semi-submersible. Passengers sit in a glass-windowed room beneath the surface of the water and look out at the fish as the boat edges along the reef. It leaves from Kailua Pier, takes about 50 minutes and costs $35 for adults, $20 for children.

Cheaper still is Kona Reef Tour's (☎ 322-3102, 987-8588) straightforward glass-bottom boat which carries 16 passengers and leaves from Kailua Pier four times a day. The ride lasts an hour and costs $15 for adults, $7.50 for children.

ACCOMMODATIONS

The Big Island has a wide range of accommodation options. Because the island is so big, it's worth considering moving around and exploring from a couple of different bases.

Most of the island's accommodations are centered around Kailua-Kona, with the majority of the rooms in condos – although some of these are run like hotels with a front desk and daily rates. If you're staying a week or more, condos are usually a better deal than hotels.

At the bottom end, Kailua has a hostel-style place with dormitory beds. Otherwise,

the cheapest places in the Kona area are mauka of Kailua in small local hotels in the towns of Holualoa, Honalo and Captain Cook.

The Waikoloa area, north of Kona, has the island's most expensive seaside resorts. The Mauna Lani Resort attracts wealthy tourists who want an elegant hideaway and not much excitement. Kona Village is even more low-keyed, playing out the getaway fantasy in comfortable Polynesian thatched huts, while the Hilton Waikoloa Village stands in sharp contrast with splashy high-tech toys and constant titillation.

Rainy Hilo doesn't see a great many visitors and while choices aren't as numerous as you might expect for a city, there are some good bottom-end to mid-range options, including a fine hostel-like lodge.

In the uplands, Volcano and Waimea have some delightful B&Bs as well as a couple of larger hostelries. There's a scattering of other B&Bs and guesthouses around the island, including some in fine country settings. This type of accommodation is becoming more common on the island and represents some of the best mid-range values.

Unless otherwise noted, the rate given is the same for either singles or doubles, and doesn't include the 10.17% tax. If calling from outside Hawaii, add the 808 area code to phone numbers.

Camping

At first glance, the list of Big Island campgrounds seems to read like some sort of 'Camping Guide to Hell': Laupahoehoe Beach, where a village was washed away in a tidal wave; Halape Beach, where an earthquake sank the shoreline 30 feet; and Kamoamoa Beach, a once-favorite camping site that's now buried in a lava flow.

Despite all that, there's really little to worry about. Hawaii's lava isn't the rushing type which sweeps through campgrounds overnight and tsunami speakers have been set up to warn of approaching tidal waves.

Some of the best and safest camping is found in Hawaii Volcanoes National Park. Other campsites are found on beaches, in upland forests and on the floor of lush Waipio Valley. More detailed descriptions of specific sites can be found throughout the chapter.

State Parks Tent camping is allowed at Kalopa (temporarily closed; call for information), MacKenzie and Manuka state parks. There are no fees but permits are required.

There are A-frame shelters at Hapuna and self-contained housekeeping cabins at Mauna Kea, Kalopa and Kilauea.

With the exception of Hapuna, which is handled by a private concessionaire, the system is computerized and reservations can be made at state park offices on any island. The Big Island office (☎ 933-4200) is at 75 Aupuni St (Box 936), Hilo, HI 96721. The maximum length of stay at any state park is five nights a month.

The A-frame shelters at Hapuna are single rooms with screened windows, a picnic table and wooden sleeping platforms for up to four people. Shared facilities include restrooms, cold showers and a pavilion with refrigerator, electric range and sink. Although the place is a bit neglected, the cost is just $15 per shelter per night.

The Hapuna shelters must be reserved through: Hapuna Beach Services (☎ 882-1095), Box 44318, Kamuela, HI 96743.

Cabin prices at the other three parks depend on the number of people, ranging from $10/17 for singles/doubles to $30 for six people. Cabins have kitchens with limited cookware and bathrooms with hot showers.

The cabins and shelters are popular and most require booking months in advance. Cancellations do occur, however, and if you're flexible with dates and lucky, you might be able to get one without advance reservations.

County Beach Parks The county allows camping at 13 of its beach parks: James Kealoha, Kolekole, Laupahoehoe and Onekahakaha, all near Hilo; Isaac Hale in Puna; Spencer, Keokea, Kapaa, Mahukona, Hookena and Milolii, all on the western side of the island; and Whittington and Punaluu, both in Kau.

With the exception of Spencer, which is patrolled by a security guard, all the county parks can be rough and noisy areas, as they're popular among late-night drinkers.

Permits are required and are issued for specific parks and dates. You can obtain permits by mail or in person from the Department of Parks & Recreation (☎ 961-8311), 25 Aupuni St, Hilo, HI 96720. Office hours are 7:45 am to 4:15 pm Monday to Friday.

You can also make reservations by phone through the Hilo office and then pick up the permit at Park & Recreation branch offices around the island. In Kailua-Kona, the office is at Hale Halawai Park (☎ 329-5277), which is open weekdays from 7:45 am to 4:15 pm. At Captain Cook, the office is at the Yano Center (☎ 323-3060), opposite the Manago Hotel; it's generally staffed from noon, but it's best to call first. In Waimea, the office is at the community center (☎ 885-5454) at Waimea Park; it's only open a few hours in the morning and not every day, so again it's best to call ahead. In Kau, the office is at the Naalehu Community Center (☎ 929-9166), open mornings only.

Daily fees are $1 for adults and 50c for children ages 13 to 17 (free for children 12 and under). Camping is allowed for up to two weeks in each park, except in June, July and August when it's limited to one week in each park.

Only about half of the county parks, generally those near towns, have drinking water. Some of the others have catchment water that can be treated for drinking, while others have only brackish water that can be used for showers but is unsuitable for drinking.

Campers should also be aware that beach parks in the Puna and Kau areas are sometimes closed during winter storms.

Hawaii Volcanoes National Park The Hawaii Volcanoes National Park section has details on the park's two drive-up campgrounds and on trail shelters for backcountry hikers. They're all free and rarely filled.

Camping Supplies Pacific Rent-All (☎ 935-2974), 1080 Kilauea Ave, Hilo, HI 96720, rents pup tents for $3/6/12 a day/week/month, larger tents for $20/40/120 and medium-weight sleeping bags for $7/21/42. The shop also rents Coleman stoves, lanterns, water jugs and other supplies. It's open from 7 am to 5 pm on weekdays, 8 am to 5 pm on Saturdays and 9 to 11 am on Sundays.

ENTERTAINMENT

The Big Island entertainment scene is largely centered around the hotels in the Kona and Waikoloa areas. Most offer Hawaiian music of some type, often duos strumming guitars in the early evening, and a few hotels have dance bands, jazz groups and nightclubs as well.

Although it's a more local scene, Hilo also has a few places with music and dancing. In addition, each spring Hilo hosts the week-long Merrie Monarch Festival, the state's largest hula festival, which starts on Easter Sunday and features hula troupes from all the islands.

Standard Hollywood movies are shown at the Prince Kuhio Plaza and Waiakea Shopping Plaza in Hilo and at the Hualalai Theatres and Kona Marketplace Cinemas in Kailua.

For the latest entertainment listings, check *West Hawaii Today*.

Luaus

Kona Village Resort has the most authentic luau in Hawaii. It's held on Monday and Friday nights, costs $63 and sometimes books out weeks in advance.

In Kona, the most popular and scenic luau is in front of Ahuena Heiau at King Kamehameha's Kona Beach Hotel on Sundays, Tuesdays, Wednesdays and Thursdays; the cost is $49. In Waikoloa, the Royal Waikoloan has a luau on Sundays and Wednesdays for $42.

All Big Island luaus include a dinner buffet, cocktails and a Polynesian show.

THINGS TO BUY

Kona coffee and macadamia nuts are the Big Island's most common souvenir items. If you're buying coffee, note that 'Kona blend' is only 10% Kona coffee. If you want the real thing make sure it says 100%. Prices change with the market, but it is one of the more expensive gourmet coffees, priced from around $10 a pound.

Supermarkets and discount stores, such as Longs Drugs, usually have the best deals on coffee. Rooster Farms produces an organically grown coffee which is sold at Kona Healthways in Kailua and a few other places.

Shops selling local arts & crafts are plentiful. More notable ones include the Volcano Art Center in Hawaii Volcanoes National Park and the handful of galleries in the hillside village of Holualoa.

GETTING THERE & AWAY

Air

The Big Island has two main airports, in Kona and Hilo. Hawaiian Airlines (☎ 326-5615) and Aloha Airlines (☎ 935-5771) connect both airports with the other main islands. While there are frequent flights into both airports, Kona is the busier of the two and even has a few direct flights from the mainland with United Airlines. Fares on both Aloha Airlines and Hawaiian Airlines are $74 for flights between the Big Island and any other Hawaiian island.

Mahalo Air (☎ (800) 277-8333) flies between Honolulu and Kona an average of eight times a day, with a one-way fare of $54.

There's also a small airport in Waimea, with limited service by Trans Air (☎ (800) 634-2094), a little commuter airline that flies twice a day between Waimea and Honolulu. The fare is $65 one way.

More information on inter-island air travel, including discounted tickets and air passes, is in the Getting Around chapter in the front of the book.

Hilo Airport The Hilo Airport is off Hwy 11, just under a mile south of its intersection with Hwy 19. It has a visitor information booth, newsstand, lei stand, restaurant, gift shops, taxi stand and car rental booths.

Kona Airport Keahole Airport is on Hwy 19, about seven miles north of Kailua-Kona. It has a restaurant, car rental booths, visitor information booth, newsstands and a gift shop which sells the University of Hawaii map of the Big Island. For a relatively busy airport, it's surprisingly casual and all open-air (there's not enough rain to justify sealing it up!).

GETTING AROUND
To/From the Airport
Speedi Shuttle (☎ 329-5433) runs a shuttle service from Kona's Keahole Airport using seven-passenger vans. Fares from the airport for a single passenger are $12 to Kailua (up to Royal Kona Resort), $21 to Kona Surf Resort in Keauhou and $25 to Hilton Waikoloa Village. The cost for each additional passenger is $2 to $5 depending on the distance. There's no set schedule. You can call to reserve in advance or upon arrival use the courtesy phones found at the Aloha and Hawaiian airlines baggage claim areas.

Bus
Hele-On is the county public bus. Service between Kona and Hilo is along the northern route of the Hawaii Belt Rd once in each direction Monday to Saturday. The bus leaves the South Kona town of Kealia at 5:45 am. Stops along the way include the Kona Surf Resort in Keauhou at 6:25 am, Waldenbooks in Kailua at 6:45 am, Parker Ranch Shopping Center in Waimea at 8:05 am and Honokaa at 8:30 am. It arrives in Hilo at the Mooheau bus terminal at 9:45 am.

The return trip leaves Hilo at 1:30 pm and arrives in Kailua at 4:30 pm. One-way fares are $5.25 between Kailua and Hilo, $3 between Kailua and Waimea and $4.50 between Waimea and Hilo.

Drivers accept only the exact fare. Bus tickets can be bought in sheets of 10 for $6.75, which are good for $7.50 worth of

travel. Luggage and backpacks are $1 extra.

There are four other routes: Pahoa to Hilo, Honokaa to Hilo, Waiohinu to Hilo via Volcano, and Hilo to the Waikoloa hotels. Each route runs at least once a day in each direction Monday to Friday. The Waikoloa bus, which leaves Hilo early in the morning for the Waikoloa area hotels and returns in late afternoon, is mostly used by commuting hotel workers, but if you're staying in Hilo it's convenient for a day's outing at the beach.

There's limited service around the city of Hilo for 75c per ride.

You can get a schedule and more information from Mass Transportation Agency (☎ 935-8241), 25 Aupuni St, Hilo, HI 96720.

For information on shuttle service between Kailua and Keauhou, see Getting Around in the Kailua section.

Taxi
The taxi flag-down fee is $2 and it costs $1.70 a mile after that. The approximate fare from Kona's Keahole Airport is $16 to Kailua, $35 to Waikoloa.

Car
The following companies have car rental booths at Kona's Keahole Airport and the Hilo Airport:

	Keahole Airport	Hilo Airport
Budget	☎ 329-8511	☎ 935-6878
Avis	☎ 329-1745	☎ 935-1290
National	☎ 329-1674	☎ 935-0891
Hertz	☎ 329-3566	☎ 935-2896
Dollar	☎ 329-2744	☎ 961-6059
Alamo	☎ 329-8896	☎ 961-3343

Toll-free numbers and more information on car rentals are in the Getting Around chapter in the front of the book.

Harper Car & Truck Rentals (☎ 969-1478), at 1690 Kamehameha Ave in Hilo, has 4WD vehicles adjusted for use at Mauna Kea's high altitude. Unlike other rental agencies, Harper puts no restrictions

Lava Wasteland?

Flying into Keahole Airport can be a shock if you're expecting to see tropical greenery and waving palm trees. Instead the view from the airplane looks more like a black lava wasteland, as if the island had been paved over in asphalt. Don't panic! This is but one face of the Big Island – and even here, if you look closer, you can catch a glimpse of some fine secluded white sand beaches squeezed between the lava and the turquoise waters. And of course once you get on the ground there's much more to the island than lava landscapes . . . ■

on going to the summit, although Waipio Valley remains off-limits. Isuzu Troopers and Isuzu Rodeos cost $79 a day, $474 a week. Even if you purchase the optional CDW ($9), there's still a $500 deductible. Harper is open from 6:30 am to 6 pm daily.

Hilo is a good place to gas up, as gas is cheaper there than in Kona.

Bicycle & Motor Scooter

Dave's Triathlon Shop (☎ 329-4522), on Alii Dr in the center of Kailua, rents mountain and road bikes for $15 the first day, $12 the second and $10 the third.

Hawaiian Pedals (☎ 329-2294), in the Kona Inn Shopping Village in Kailua, has mountain bikes for $20/70 a day/week, performance bikes for $25 a day, tandem bikes for $35 a day and car bike racks or baby seats for $5 a day.

DJ's Rentals (☎ 329-1700), in a kiosk opposite King Kamehameha's Kona Beach Hotel in Kailua, rents mopeds for $8/30 an hour/day and two-person scooters for $15/50. A cash deposit is accepted if you don't have a credit card. Optional CDW costs $6 a day.

As Kona is the center of activity for the Ironman triathlon, there are several bike shops that sell and repair quality equipment. Dave's Triathlon Shop is one, B & L Bike & Sports (☎ 329-3309) in Kailua's industrial area and Competitive Edge (☎ 885-2115) in Waimea are others.

Kona

Kona literally means 'leeward'. The Kona Coast refers to the dry, sunny west coast of the Big Island. However, to make matters a little more confusing, the name Kona is also used to refer to Kailua, the largest town on the Kona Coast. The town's name is compounded Kailua-Kona by the post office and other officialdom to avoid confusion with Kailua on Oahu.

The weather is so consistent on this side of the island that the local paper usually just alternates two forecasts: 'Sunny morning. Afternoon clouds with upslope showers' or 'Sunny morning. Cloudy afternoon with showers over the slopes.'

The afternoon showers that hit the higher slopes rarely touch the coastline a couple of miles below. Because it sees so little rain, Kona is also dubbed the Gold Coast. It's a good bet for a sunny vacation any time of the year.

KAILUA

In the 19th century Kailua-Kona was a favorite vacation retreat for Hawaiian royalty. These days it's the largest vacation destination on the Big Island.

It's got a lot to make it a drawing card. The weather is great, the setting on the leeward side of Mt Hualalai is pretty, and it has both ancient Hawaiian and missionary-era historic sites. Even though the town's period character is a bit stifled by trinket shops and mini-malls, it's still a fun place to stroll.

There are lots of places to stay and eat, as well as plenty of activities ranging from world-class deep-sea fishing to snorkeling cruises. Kailua is centrally located and makes a good base for exploring the entire Kona coast.

Most of Kona's condos are lined up along Alii Dr, the five-mile coastal road that runs from the town center at Kailua Bay south to Keauhou. This strip sees a lot of power walkers and joggers, particularly in the early morning hours, but the hottest activity occurs here in October when it serves as the finish line of the world-famous Ironman triathlon.

Kailua has a few swimming, snorkeling and surfing spots, although the island's best beaches are up the coast to the north.

Information

Tourist Office The Hawaii Visitors Bureau (☎ 329-7787) is in the Kona Plaza. It's open from 8 am to noon and 1 to 4:30 pm Monday to Friday.

Money Both the Bank of Hawaii at the Hualalai Rd and Kuakini Hwy intersection and the First Hawaiian Bank at the Lanihau Center have full-service branches with automatic teller machines.

Post The main post office, which is open weekdays from 8 am to 4:30 pm and Saturdays until noon, is in the Lanihau Center. There's also a contract post office at the Kona Inn Shopping Village that's open weekdays from 9 am to 4:30 pm and Saturdays from 10 am to 3 pm.

Books & Newspapers Middle Earth Bookshoppe in the Kona Plaza and Waldenbooks in the Lanihau Center are both well-stocked bookstores with Hawaiiana and general travel sections.

Resort Sundries at King Kamehameha's Kona Beach Hotel sells newspapers from the mainland and a few international papers. The local daily (*West Hawaii Today*) and the Hilo and Honolulu papers are available in numerous places around town.

Travel Agents Cut Rate Tickets, in the Kona Coast Shopping Center, sells discounted tickets for inter-island travel.

Laundry There are coin laundries in the North Kona Shopping Center, on Kuakini Hwy near Eclipse restaurant, and on Pawai Place in the industrial area.

Film & Photography Longs Drugs in the Lanihau Center sells cameras and film and handles processing by major developers,

including Kodak and Fuji. They do their own same-day print processing ($8 for 24 prints). However, if you can wait two days, the send-out service costs only $5 for 24 prints.

If you can't find a specific camera accessory at Longs, try Kona Photo Center in the North Kona Shopping Center.

Parking The center of Kailua gets quite congested and finding a parking space in town can be a challenge.

There's free public parking in the lot behind Kona Seaside Hotel between Likana Lane and Kuakini Hwy. There's complimentary parking for patrons of the Kona Inn Shopping Village on Hualalai Rd behind the Kona Bay Hotel and for patrons of Kona Marketplace at the rear of that center.

King Kamehameha's Kona Beach Hotel, at the north end of Alii Dr, has a big pay-parking lot behind the hotel. The first 15 minutes is free and it's $1 per half hour after that. If you purchase something in one of the hotel shops or restaurants you can get a voucher for free parking.

Kamakahonu & Ahuena Heiau

Kamakahonu, the beach at the north end of Kailua Bay, was the site of the royal residence of Kamehameha the Great. Shortly after his death here in 1819, Kamehameha's successors came to Kamakahonu and ended the traditional kapu system, sounding a death knell for the old religion.

The ancient sites are now part of the grounds of the King Kamehameha's Kona Beach Hotel. A few thatched structures along with carved wooden kii gods have been reconstructed above the old stone temple.

Ahuena Heiau, which was a place of human sacrifice, juts out into the cove and acts as a breakwater, offering protection to swimmers. The waters at Kamakahonu, which means 'Eye of the Turtle', are the calmest in Kailua Bay.

This little beach in front of the hotel is the only downtown swimming spot. The hotel beach hut rents snorkels, kayaks and floats with windows.

King Kamehameha's Kona Beach Hotel

Be sure to take a stroll through the sprawling lobby of this hotel, which is full of museum-quality Hawaiiana displays.

One display features Hawaiian musical instruments, including a nose flute, coconut shell knee drum, shell trumpet, bamboo rattles and hula sticks. There are displays on traditional foods and fishing and others containing feather capes and leis, kapa beaters, quilts, war clubs, *pahoa* daggers, calabashes and gourd containers. The displays have interpretive plaques, but if you ask at the activity desk they'll give you a free brochure that describes them in greater depth.

Near the front desk, you'll find an interesting depiction of King Kamehameha at Kailua Bay that was painted by Hawaiian artist Herb Kane.

The hotel has guided historical and ethnobotanical tours free to the public, some which visit the indoor displays and others that take in the hotel's historic grounds. A hula show, lei-making and other activities take place a couple of times a week. Check at the hotel activity desk for the current schedule.

Kailua Pier

Although most of Kona's charter fishing boats now use the larger Honokohau Harbor north of Kailua, a few still pull in each afternoon at Kailua Pier to hoist their catch on the scales. The Kona Coast is the world's number one fishing spot for Pacific blue marlin and some catches top a thousand pounds.

Kailua Bay was once a major cattle shipping area. Cattle driven down from hillside ranches were stampeded into the water and forced to swim out to waiting steamers where they were hoisted aboard by sling and shipped to Honolulu slaughterhouses. Kailua Pier was built in 1915 and until the 1960s cattle pens were still in place.

There's a tiny patch of sandy beach on the east side of Kailua Pier that's known as **Kaiakeakua**, 'Sea of the Gods'. It once served as Kamehameha's canoe landing.

Pa O Umi Point

In the 16th century the great King Umi moved his royal court from Waipio to

Cattle drive at Kailua Pier

Kona. He is thought to have landed at a lava outcropping on the northeast side of Kailua Bay. This rocky point is called Pa O Umi, 'Umi's Enclosure'.

A sea wall has been built over it but when the tide is low you can see the tip of the lava point by looking over the wall in the area diagonally across the street from the Ocean View Inn.

Mokuaikaua Church

On April 4, 1820, Hawaii's first Christian missionaries landed at Kailua Bay, stepping out onto a rock that is now one of the footings for the Kailua Pier. When the missionaries landed they were unaware that Hawaii's old religion had been abolished on this same spot just a few months before. They established Hawaii's first Christian church on Kailua Bay, a few minutes' walk from Kamehameha's ancient heiau and house site.

The temporary church the missionaries erected was replaced in 1836 by the current Mokuaikaua Church, a handsome building with walls of lava rock held together with a mortar of sand and coral lime. The posts and beams are made from ohia wood, a strong termite-resistant wood which was hewn with stone adzes and smoothed down with chunks of coral. The pews and the pulpit are made of koa. The church steeple remains the highest structure in Kailua, at 112 feet.

There's often an interpreter around to talk about the church's history from 9 am to noon and from 1 to 4 pm Monday to Saturday. An eight-foot model of the brig *Thaddeus*, which brought those first Congregational missionaries to Hawaii, is on display in the back of the church.

Hulihee Palace

Hulihee Palace, a modest two-story house, was built in 1838 by Governor 'John Adams' Kuakini as his private residence.

Kuakini was also the Mokuaikaua Church contractor and both buildings were of the same lava rock construction. The palace got its current look in 1885 when it was plastered over inside and out by King Kalakaua, who had taken to a more polished style after his travels abroad.

The palace belonged to a succession of royal owners until the early 1900s when it was abandoned and fell into disrepair. The Daughters of Hawaii, a group founded in 1903 by daughters of missionaries, took it over and now operate the property as a museum.

Hawaiian royalty were huge people and everything inside the palace takes on those proportions, including a bed which is seven feet long.

Princess Ruth Keelikolani, who owned the palace in the mid-1800s, was indeed a lady of some presence, said to have weighed more than 400 pounds. She was an earthy woman, preferring to live in a big grass hut on the palace grounds rather than being confined within the palace. After her death the wooden posts that had supported her grass hut were carved with designs of taro, leis and pineapples and used as posts in one of the beds upstairs.

The palace is furnished with antiques, many picked up on royal jaunts to Europe. Of the more Hawaiian pieces, there's a table inlaid with 25 kinds of native Hawaiian woods, some of which are now extinct, and an armoire that was made in China of Hawaiian sandalwood and inlaid with ivory. Kamehameha the Great's personal war spears are also on display.

The palace is open from 9 am to 4 pm daily. Admission costs $4 for adults, 50c for children under 12, and includes a 40-minute tour. The last tour begins at 3 pm.

There's no charge to visit the gift shop or walk around the grounds. Take a look into the stocked **fishpond** behind the palace; it once served as a queen's bath and before that was a canoe landing.

Sea Wall Walkway

A walkway along the sea wall begins behind the Hulihee Palace and continues south to the Kona Inn Shopping Village. The short seaside stroll here offers a different angle on Kailua-Kona, one that's refreshingly free of the traffic and commercial tourism that prevails along the main road.

The sea wall is a nice place to sit and watch the surf breaking, people fishing, and boats pulling in and out of the harbor. It's typical Kona lava coastline with lots of sea urchins and scurrying black crabs camouflaged among the black rocks.

St Michael's Church

The pink church opposite Waterfront Row is St Michael's. In the cemetery next to the church, a tiny grass hut marks the spot of an earlier thatched chapel that served as the first Catholic church on the Big Island.

Kealaokamalamalama Church

The green-and-white Kealaokamalamalama ('Path of the Light') Church, is south and mauka of St Michael's Church. An independent Hawaiian Congregational church, it has an interior that's delightfully Hawaiian with tropical flowers and a big rainbow painted across the wall.

Hale Halawai Park

Hale Halawai is a quiet oceanfront park with a few shady trees. As the coast is rocky and the sand full of coral chunks, it's not a sunbathing spot, but it is a fine place to sit and read the morning paper.

A prison and courthouse once stood at the site. Now there's a pavilion used by community groups for flea markets and pancake breakfasts. There's free parking for park users.

Old Kona Airport Beach Park

The old Kona Airport, which was replaced by the current Keahole Airport in 1970, has been turned into a state recreation area and beach park. It's about a mile north of downtown Kailua, at the end of the Kuakini Hwy.

The old runway skirts a long sandy beach, but lava rocks run the length of the beach between the sand and the ocean. This makes for poor swimming conditions, but it's ideal for fishing and exploring tide pools. Some of the rocks have intriguing little aquarium-like pockets holding tiny sea urchins, crabs and bits of coral.

There are a couple of breaks in the lava that allow entry into the water, including one in front of the first picnic area.

A little cove, which can be reached by a short walk from the north end of the beach, is a good area for scuba divers and confident snorkelers. The reef fish are large and plentiful and in deeper waters there's a steep coral wall that harbors big moray eels and a wide variety of other sea creatures such as lionfish and cowries.

When the surf's up there's an offshore break that's favored by local surfers. In high surf it's too rough for other water activities.

While this local park is popular with families, picnickers and people drying reef fish, the park is much too big to ever feel crowded. There are restrooms, showers and covered picnic tables on a lawn dotted with beach heliotrope and short coconut palms.

In addition to the sanctioned recreational activities, the old runway also made a perfect drag strip and because of its rowdy nighttime reputation there's now a gate which closes off that section of the park at 8 pm.

The Kailua end of the park contains a new gym, soccer and softball fields and four outdoor lighted tennis courts.

Directly behind the tennis courts there's a break in the wall marked 'Shoreline Public Access'. This short path leads into an exclusive subdivision, but the beach fronting the subdivision, like all Hawaiian beaches, remains public. If you walk along the beach a few minutes towards downtown Kailua, you'll come to a sandy area with a big wading pool that's a few feet deep – a great spot for children.

Saltwater Pool

One of Kona's best-kept secrets is a saltwater swimming pool in a little lava outcrop so close to the ocean that waves lap in over the side. It's as large as most condo pools and it's open to the public.

The pool was originally part of a retired admiral's private estate. By the time it was

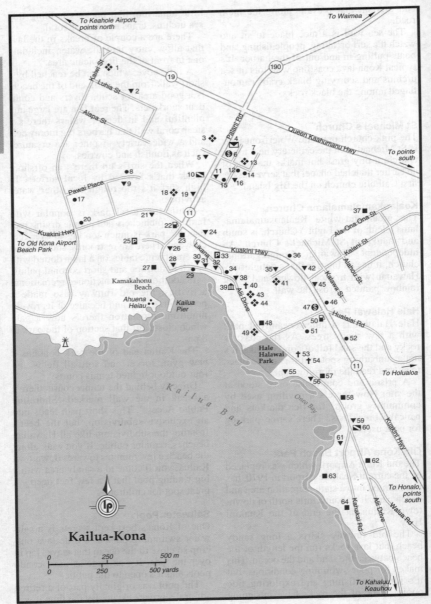

Kailua-Kona

To Keahole Airport,
points north

To Waimea

19

190

Queen Kaahumanu Hwy

To points
south

Kaiwi St

Luhia St

Alapa St

Palani Rd

Pawai Place

Kuakini Hwy

To Old Kona Airport
Beach Park

Kamakahonu
Beach

Ahuena
Heiau

Kailua
Pier

Likana Ln

Kuakini Hwy

Alii Drive

Hale
Halawai
Park

Kailua Bay

Oneo Bay

Ala-Ona-Ona St

Kalani St

Alahou St

Kalawa St

Hualalai Rd

To Holualoa

11

Kuakini Hwy

Kahakai Rd

Alii Drive

Watua Rd

To Honalo,
points
south

To Kahaluu,
Keauhou

0   250   500 m
0   250   500 yards

BIG ISLAND

■ PLACES TO STAY		31	Cafe Sibu	17	B & L Bike & Sports
		32	Marty's Steak & Seafoods	18	North Kona Shopping
23	Kona Seaside Hotel	35	Jack in the Box		Center
27	King Kamehameha's Kona	38	Basil's Pizzeria	20	Kailua Candy Co
	Beach Hotel		Restaurante	22	Gas Station (24-hour)
37	Patey's Place	42	Eclipse	25	Pay Parking
48	Kona Bay Hotel	45	McDonald's	29	Pa O Umi Point
57	Kona Islander Inn	49	Kona Inn	33	Free Parking
58	Kona Alii	55	Waterfront Row	34	Dave's Triathlon Shop
62	Kona Billfisher	56	Jolly Roger	36	Coin Laundry
63	Royal Kona Resort	59	Palm Cafe	39	Hulihee Palace
64	Hale Kona Kai	61	Huggo's	40	Mokuaikaua Church
				41	Kona Center
▼ PLACES TO EAT		OTHER		43	Kona Plaza
				44	Kona Marketplace
2	Jennifer's Korean	1	Kaahumanu Plaza	46	7-Eleven Store
	Barbecue	3	Kona Coast Shopping	47	Bank of Hawaii
5	Sizzler		Center	49	Kona Inn Shopping Village
9	Su's Thai Kitchen	4	Post Office	50	Gas Station
11	Burger King	6	First Hawaiian Bank	51	Library
16	Kona Mix Plate	7	Bowling Alley	52	Hualalai Theatres
19	Pizza Hut & Taco Bell	8	Coin Laundry	53	St Michael's Church
21	Bangkok Houses	10	Kona Coast Divers	54	Kealaokamalamalama
24	Kona Ranchhouse	12	Longs Drugs		Church
26	Quinn's	13	Lanihau Center	60	Jack's Diving Locker
28	Kona Amigos	14	Waldenbooks		
30	Ocean View Inn	15	Hilo Hattie		

sold to developers (Kona by the Sea condos are here now) all coastline had become public domain.

Kona by the Sea has put in four public beach access spaces in its parking lot. A narrow path on the north side of the complex leads from the parking lot down to the pool.

The admiral had good taste. You float above the ocean and can glance over the edge and watch surfers riding into shore. Watch it when you're getting into the pool as the steps are slippery.

White Sands Beach Park
It's called White Sands, Magic Sands and Disappearing Sands, but it's all the same beach, midway between Kailua and Keauhou. In the winter when the surf is high, the sand can disappear literally overnight, leaving only rocks on the shore. And then just as magically it returns and again becomes a fine white sand beach.

This is a very popular bodysurfing beach when the rocks aren't exposed. There's also a volleyball court, restrooms and picnic tables.

Places to Stay
In Kona, condos outnumber hotels many times over. Condos tend to be cheaper than hotels if you're staying awhile, although for advance reservations (which are recommended in the high season) there are deposits and some stiff cancellation penalties to deal with. Unlike hotels, most condos have a three-day minimum stay and during the high season some have a seven-day minimum stay.

Places to Stay – bottom end
The cheapest place to stay in town is *Patey's Place* (☎ 326-7018, (800) 972-7408 in Hawaii), 75-195 Ala-Ona Ona, Kailua-Kona, HI 96740. This hostel-style accommodation is in a rather congested residential neighborhood a 10-minute walk

from the town center. Dormitory beds cost $14, double rooms cost $35. Lockers are provided for a $2 fee. There's free pick-up from the airport and a $5 fee to get back to the airport. The operation has a reputation for being a bit loose and someone expecting the standards of an HI hostel (or Arnott's Lodge in Hilo) might not feel comfortable here. It certainly would be a good idea to look around and get your own impression before checking in.

One of the area's best deals is the *Kona Tiki Hotel* (☎ 329-1425; fax 327-9402), 75-5968 Alii Dr, Kailua-Kona, HI 96745, on Alii Dr at the 1.5-mile marker. This is an older three-story complex which has 15 pleasant, refurbished rooms, most with a queen and a twin bed and all with refrigerators and breezy oceanfront lanais. There's a friendly management, complimentary coffee and breakfast pastries, and a small seaside pool. Although it's right on the road the surf usually drowns out the sound of traffic. Rates are $54 for standard rooms, $59 for rooms with kitchenettes, plus $7 more for a third person. The hotel is very popular with return visitors and generally books up well in advance during the high season. There's a three-day minimum stay.

Kona Seaside Hotel (☎ 329-2455, (800) 367-7000; fax 922-0052, (800) 972-5164), 75-5646 Palani Rd, Kailua-Kona, HI 96740, has two sections. One's a modern six-story building with private lanais and the standard amenities, priced from $85. The older refurbished poolside wing is simpler and has walls that carry sound, making the $75 rate for those rooms a lesser value.

You can often get a cheaper local rate on both sections if you book within Hawaii. Discounted room rates, and a package that includes a free Budget rental car with the room at $98 for two nights, are perpetually advertised in the Sunday Honolulu paper. To get the best deal skip the toll-free number and call the local booking desk (☎ 922-1228). You don't have to be a Hawaii resident to qualify for the cheaper rates, but the clerk may be loath to make the reservation if you call before you arrive

in the islands and give them a non-Hawaii mailing address.

For those who want to be right in the center of town, there's Uncle Billy's *Kona Bay Hotel* (☎ 329-1393, (800) 367-5102), 75-5739 Alii Dr, Kailua-Kona, HI 96740. The older cinder-block buildings lack charm but at $64 it's relatively cheap, there's a pool and rooms have TV, air-conditioning and phones.

Three Bears' Bed & Breakfast (☎ /fax 325-7563, (800) 765-0480), 72-1001 Puukala St, Kailua-Kona, HI 96740, is a delightful cedar home seven miles north of Kailua, off Hwy 190. The home has a hillside location, sweeping views of the Kona Coast and good conditions for stargazing from the lanai, where there's also a hot tub. The two comfortable guest rooms have private baths, microwaves and cable TV. Owners Anne and Art Stockel are active in environmental issues, speak fluent German and know the island inside out. For travelers with their own transportation, Three Bears' would make a good base for exploring Kona, Waimea and the Waikoloa areas. Rates, which include a generous European-style breakfast and all the homegrown macadamia nuts you can crack, are $65 a night for one room, $75 for the other, with a two-night minimum stay. Ann also books other B&B accommodation in Hawaii.

Kiwi Gardens (☎ 326-1559; fax 329-6618), 74-4920 Kiwi St, Kailua-Kona, HI 96740, is a B&B about three miles north of Kailua center. Ron and Shirlee Freitas, former San Franciscans, rent three rooms in their contemporary home. One room has a queen-bed with a lanai and a sunset view for $60, another is a smaller room with a twin bed and a double bed for $50. These two rooms share a bathroom, although only one room is booked at a time unless there's a group traveling together. The third room is a master suite with a king-size brass bed, private bathroom and a lanai for $75. All rooms share common space with a big-screen TV, VCR, pool table and refrigerator. The house has a stylish Art-Deco theme, with antique aloha shirts on the walls, signed baseball cards and a vintage jukebox. Breakfast includes Kona coffee, fruits from the yard and pastries. If you're interested in deep-sea fishing, Ron has his own charter boat.

Hale Maluhia (☎ 329-5773, (800) 559-6627; fax 326-5487), 76-770 Hualalai Rd, Kailua-Kona, HI 96740, is a B&B on the road to Holualoa, a couple of miles southeast of downtown Kailua. The half-dozen guest rooms center around a large rambling house that's home to the family of Ken and Ann Smith. Rates range from $55 for a small room with a double bed and shared bath to $110 for a large cottage with a king bed, private bath, deck and pleasant sitting area. There are room phones with free local calls. Rates include breakfast. There's lots of common space, including a room with a pool table, TV and VCR, and guests have use of a hot tub.

Places to Stay – top-end hotels
The 460-room *King Kamehameha's Kona Beach Hotel* (☎ 329-2911, (800) 367-2111; fax 329-4602), 75-5660 Palani Rd, Kailua-Kona, HI 96740, is on Kailua Bay and the only beach in town. Located at the site of King Kamehameha's former residence, it has a sprawling koa-wood lobby full of interesting Hawaiiana displays. Rooms are comfortable with two double beds, a lanai, thermostatic air-conditioning, room safe, TV and phone. There's a pool, lit tennis courts and free guest parking. Rates range from $110 to $195, depending upon the view.

The *Royal Kona Resort* (☎ 329-3111, (800) 774-5662; fax 329-9532), 75-5852 Alii Dr, Kailua-Kona, HI 96740, formerly the Kona Hilton, has an oceanfront location on the edge of town. There's no sandy beach but there is a conventional swimming pool as well as a natural saltwater pool that's deep enough for swimming. The hotel also has tennis courts and a couple of restaurants. The 452 rooms have been going at reduced rates since Hawaiian Hotels & Resorts took over the property. While the standard rack rate begins at $150, there's currently a room and break-fast rate of $90 and a room and car package for $94; senior citizens get an additional 25% discount off all rates.

Places to Stay – condominiums
Many of Kona's condominiums can be booked through more than one rental agency, each of which handles different units within the complex. For condos with an address listed, you can write directly to the condo. Either they handle their own bookings or they'll pass correspondence on to the agents that do. For the rest, units are handled by at least one of the following agencies. They'll send their latest listings and rates upon request. It's worth comparing listings before booking.

Hawaii Resort Management, 75-5776 Kuakini Hwy, Suite 105C, Kailua-Kona, HI 96740 (☎ 329-9393, (800) 553-5035)

Kona Vacation Resorts, 77-6435 Kuakini Hwy, Kailua-Kona, HI 96740 (☎ 329-6488, (800) 367-5168 from the USA, (800) 800-5662 from Canada; fax 329-5480)

Triad Management, North Kona Shopping Center, 75-5629-M Kuakini Hwy (Box 4466), Kailua-Kona, HI 96745 (☎ 329-6402, (800) 345-2823; fax 326-2401)

Most of Kona's condos are quite nice, have complete kitchens and are fully furnished with everything from linen to cooking utensils. The general rule is that the weekly rate is six times the daily rate and the monthly rate is three times the weekly. However in the high season, if business is brisk, most places will offer only the daily rate, while in the off months of April, May and September you might be able to negotiate an even better deal.

If you wait until you arrive in Kona to look for a place, you can sometimes find a good deal in the classified ads of *West Hawaii Today*. However, this is risky during the high season as many of the better-value places are booked up well in advance.

All Kona condos listed here have swimming pools unless otherwise noted.

The *Kona Islander Inn* (☎ 329-3181, (800) 922-7866), 75-5776 Kuakini Hwy,

Kailua-Kona, HI 96740, is an older development in the town center. Some of the units can get musty, particularly those on the bottom floor. Aston handles 51 of the 144 units and maintains a front desk, running them like a hotel. Winter rates for rooms with refrigerators range from $86 to $101, depending upon the view; the rest of the year they're $10 less.

There are also a number of Kona Islander Inn units rented by Hawaii Resort Management (next door on Alii Dr), which work out to be a better deal. These cost from $50/245 a day/week in the low season, from $70/345 in the high season. The furnishings vary but most rooms have TV, aircon and phones, while some also have a VCR.

Kona White Sands is a two-story building with 10 bargain units, all with kitchenettes and lanais. One-bedroom units cost $60 for up to two people, $70 for four people, booked through Hawaii Resort Management. The minimum stay is three days. There's no pool, but it's opposite White Sands Beach.

Kona Billfisher at 75-5841 Alii Dr, on the south side of town, has 65 units that are large and quite well furnished with kitchens, lanais, sofa beds and both ceiling fans and air-con. When booked through Hawaii Resort Management, one-bedroom units cost $65/75 for the low/high season, two-bedroom units $85/95. There's a three-day minimum. It's good value for this price range.

Malia Kai Apartments, mauka of the Royal Kona Resort on Walua Rd, has 21 units, each with three levels. The bottom level has a carport and washer/dryer. The 2nd floor has a lanai, a kitchen and a living room with a sofa bed. The 3rd floor has one main bedroom with sliding shoji doors separating it from another room with a sofa bed. The complex has a nice garden courtyard with a small pool. The units aren't all that spiffy but if you're with a few people it could be economical. Rates are $480 a week in the high season, $390 in the low season, through Triad Management.

Hale Kona Kai (☎ 329-2155, (800) 421-

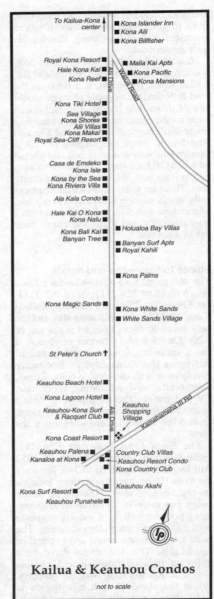

Kailua & Keauhou Condos

not to scale

3696), 75-5870 Kahakai Rd, Kailua-Kona, HI 96740, is a real find, right on the ocean in a quiet corner just beyond the Royal Kona Resort. The 39 one-bedroom units aren't brand new, but they're comfortable and have standard features like full kitchens and cable TV. All have lanais with great ocean views and the sound of the surf. Rates are $75 for up to two people. It's $10 more for a corner unit with a wrap-around lanai and $10 more per person for additional guests. There's a three-day minimum, a $150 security deposit and no Sunday or holiday check-in.

Alii Villas (☎ 329-1288), 75-6016 Alii Dr, Kailua-Kona, HI 96740, has 126 units and is a comfortable, quiet place with good ocean breezes. The units are large and each has a private lanai, cable TV and washer/dryer. Most have a phone and sofa bed. One-bedroom units average $425 to $500 a week. You can either contact Alii Villas directly or book through Kona Vacation Resorts, which has daily rates of $75 with a three-night minimum.

Sea Village (☎ 329-1000), 75-6002 Alii Dr, Kailua-Kona, HI 96740, is a condo near Alii Villas, but it's run more like a hotel. One-bedroom units start at $90/106 in the low/high season and two-bedroom units are about $25 more. The minimum stay is three nights. There are tennis courts.

Kona Makai, on the ocean side of Alii Dr next to Alii Villas, has one-bedroom units that are fully equipped with everything down to a washer/dryer, and cost from $90 a day through Kona Vacation Resorts. There's an exercise room and tennis courts.

Casa de Emdeko (☎ 329-2160), 75-6082 Alii Dr, Kailua-Kona, HI 96740, is a newer complex. The one-bedroom units are pleasant and have all the standard amenities although there's not much of an ocean view as the lanais line up at an angle facing other lanais. There are both freshwater and saltwater pools. When booked through Hawaii Resort Management the rates for one-bedroom units are $85/425 a day/week in the low season, $95/545 in the high.

Kona Bali Kai (☎ 329-9381), 76-6246 Alii Dr, Kailua-Kona, HI 96740, is a 155-unit oceanfront complex midway between Kailua and Keauhou. Colony Hotels & Resorts (☎ (800) 777-1700) maintains a front desk here and handles many of the units, which range from mountain-facing studios for $90 or one-bedroom units for $110 to two-bedroom oceanfront units for $190. If you book in advance and ask for the 'Super Saver' rate there's often a discount on these prices or a free upgrade. All units have full kitchens, TV and lanais. Units are privately owned and are decorated according to the whim of the owner – some are quite nice, while others are a bit lackluster.

Royal Sea-Cliff Resort (☎ 329-8021, (800) 922-7866; fax 922-8785), 75-6040 Alii Dr, Kailua-Kona, HI 96740, is modern and architecturally striking, with angular lines. The units are some of the nicest in Kona, with large balconies, stylish furnishings and very full kitchens. There are tennis courts, pools and a sauna. Aston runs it like a hotel with a front desk and there's no minimum stay. Studios are $125/140 in the low/high season. There are also hotel-style rooms with a refrigerator available for $95/105 and two-bedroom units from $160/180. Overall the accommodation here is ritzier than Aston's more expensive Kona by the Sea complex.

Kona Reef (☎ 329-4780, (800) 367-5004; fax 329-2762), 75-5888 Alii Dr, Kailua-Kona, HI 96740, is a 130-unit condo complex run like a hotel by Hawaiian Pacific Resorts. It's modern, with all amenities including full kitchens, washer/dryers and private lanais. Rates begin at $130 for up to four people in a one-bedroom unit, which has a sofa bed in the living room. Two-bedroom oceanfront units cost $200; rates are slightly lower in the off season.

Places to Eat – budget

For a good cheap meal on the run try the *French Bakery* at Kaahumanu Plaza in the industrial area. This is Kona's best bakery, with good French bread, tempting strudels and hearty three-seed muffins. The Tongan bread, which costs $3.25 and is filled with cheese and vegetables, makes a good meal and can be microwaved on request. There are also similarly priced quiches and sandwiches. It's open from 5:30 am to 3 pm Monday to Friday, to 2 pm on Saturday.

The unassuming *Ocean View Inn* on Alii Dr has been a central Kona landmark for generations and is the best place in town for local food. Complete breakfasts with coffee cost just $2.50 to $5. Sandwiches are $1.50 to $3, burgers with French fries $4.25. You can get inexpensive Chinese, American and Hawaiian foods and it's a good place to try lomi salmon marinated with tomatoes and green onion or a side dish of poi. Breakfast is served from 6:30 to 11 am, lunch from 11 am to 2:45 pm and dinner from 5:15 to 9 pm. It's closed on Mondays.

The *Kona Mix Plate* in Kopiko Plaza is a popular eatery with counter service and good-value local food. Cheeseburgers and mahimahi or calamari sandwiches are $4, while most plate lunches, including a nice teriyaki chicken dish, cost $5.60. It's open from 10 am to 8 pm Monday to Saturday.

For a healthy fast-food alternative *Kona Healthways*, a health food store in the Kona Coast Shopping Center, has hearty fresh green salads and sandwiches for around $4. The store sells bulk cereals, packaged goods, juices, cheese and a good variety of yogurts. Locally grown items include dried fruit, organic produce and coffee, macadamia nuts and spirulina.

The *Sizzler* in the Kona Coast Shopping Center has the best salad bar in town, with a good selection of vegies and fresh fruit plus pasta, soup and a tortilla bar for $8.95 as a meal in itself or $4 with a main course. This family-style chain restaurant, open for lunch and dinner daily, specializes in standard steak and seafood dishes with prices beginning at $9.

The Lanihau Center has a huge 24-hour *Sack & Save* supermarket, a rather simple deli and bakery, an inexpensive Korean restaurant, a pizzeria, *Baskin-Robbins* ice cream shop, *Kentucky Fried Chicken* and *Royal Jade Garden*. The latter has fair Chinese food, with combo plates served from steamer trays for around $5.

Kona also has a *McDonald's, Pizza Hut, Taco Bell, Burger King, Jack in the Box, Wendy's* and *Subway Sandwiches.*

There's a farmers' market selling fresh island fruits and vegetables in the parking lot of the Lanihau Center from 6 am to 1 pm on Sundays and opposite Waterfront Row from 6 am to 2 pm on Wednesdays and Saturdays.

Places to Eat – middle

Basil's Pizzeria Restaurante (☎ 326-7836), run by two brothers from Italy, is a hole-in-the-wall in the center of Kailua with generous servings of Italian food at honest prices. The food is good and most dishes come with a nice Caesar salad and garlic bread. Pizzas, pastas and eggplant parmigiana are priced around $7, chicken and seafood dishes a few dollars more, sandwiches a bit less. It's open from 11 am to 10 pm daily.

Bangkok Houses (☎ 329-7746), in Kamehameha Square, has good Thai food at moderate prices. At lunch there are numerous dishes, including Thai curry, fresh ginger chicken and pad Thai for $5, while at dinner the same dishes cost $8. Lunch is served from 11 am to 3 pm weekdays, dinner from 5 to 9 pm nightly. Takeout service is also available.

The *Seafood Pasta Palace* (☎ 329-4436), on the upper floor of Waterfront Row, has reasonably good Italian food, generous portions and a pleasant setting. At dinner dishes range from pastas for around $10 to steak and Hawaiian lobster for $20. All meals include a fresh salad and warm cheese bread. At lunch, served from 11 am, there are hearty thick-crust pizzas from $4 and all-you-can-eat pasta with a salad for $5. From 11 am to 7 pm there's a happy hour with $1.50 mai tais and well drinks. There are often discounted specials and two-for-one coupons that you can pick up at the door. All in all, the restaurant is one of the best food values in Kona.

Su's Thai Kitchen (☎ 326-7808), on Pawai Place in Kailua's industrial area, has good Thai food and flavorful curries. At dinner time, 5 to 9 pm daily, most standard dishes such as beef, pork or chicken curries cost $8, while the house specialty, volcano chicken with a sweet and sour sauce, is $13. At lunch, from 11 am to 2:30 pm, you can get pad Thai or the curry of the day with rice for $6. The mood, like the food, is authentically Thai – there are about a dozen tables on a small outdoor lanai, which is nicely lit by candles at night.

Cafe Sibu at Banyan Court serves delicious Indonesian food in a casual cafe setting. The combination plates at around $12 offer three dishes (with choices like Balinese chicken, spicy Indian curry and shrimp satay) over brown rice. The huge gado gado, served over rice and covered with peanut sauce, costs $9.50. There are also vegetarian dishes and a few daily specials, usually including garlic shrimp over linguine for $13. It's open from 11:30 am to 9 pm daily.

Kona Ranchhouse (☎ 329-7061), off Kuakini Hwy just south of Palani Rd, has a varied menu and straightforward food. Breakfast, served from 6:30 am to 2 pm, includes the usual standards from about $5. Lunch, served until 4:30 pm, features burgers, sandwiches and a few hot dishes, mostly in the $7 to $9 range. At dinner there are light meals for $10 and heartier plates for a few dollars more. The menu includes ribs, teriyaki chicken, a rather nice routelle and a few Mexican dishes. It's a popular place, so dinner reservations are a good idea. For a glimpse of paniolo Hawaii check out the old photos of island ranches decorating the dining room walls.

For Korean food there's *Jennifer's Korean Barbecue* (☎ 326-1155), a 2nd-floor restaurant on Luhia St in Kailua's industrial area. A dinner of yakiniku meats cooked right at your table and served with rice, soup, salad and kimchee costs $14. Kitchen-prepared lunch plates with various meat and fish combinations cost $5 to $7. The plates are essentially 'local food' with a Korean accent and include the requisite two scoops of rice and one scoop of macaroni salad. Hours are from 10:30 am to 9 pm Monday to Saturday.

Quinn's, a bar on Palani Rd opposite the

King Kamehameha's Kona Beach Hotel, serves meals in its rear courtyard from 11 am to at least midnight. The crowd is mostly long-time residents who come for the consistently good fish and steak dinners. For the setting, prices aren't cheap – $8 for fish & chips or a fresh fish sandwich with salad, $18 for an ahi dinner – but the portions are huge. There are also burgers, soups and salads.

Marty's Steak & Seafoods, an old standby on Alii Dr, is a 2nd-floor open-air restaurant with a partial harbor view. Sandwiches and burgers with salad start around $5 at lunch and mahimahi or top sirloin cost $13 at dinner. At dinner there's a rather limited salad bar that costs $3 with an entree, $8 a la carte.

Kona Amigos is a 2nd-floor open-air Mexican restaurant opposite the Kailua Pier. Between 4 and 6 pm there's a happy hour with $1.50 margaritas and draft beers and if you get a window seat you can watch the boats pull into the harbor and hoist up the day's catch of marlin and tuna. Prices are moderate with undistinguished combination dishes from around $10.

Jolly Roger, near Waterfront Row, serves rather standard fare, but you can't get any closer to the water than their oceanfront tables. Breakfast items and lunchtime sandwiches are $5 to $8 while full dinners, including pasta, meat and seafood dishes, range from $9 to $15.

The *Beach Restaurant* at the King Kamehameha's Kona Beach Hotel has a 'sunset special', a full meal that usually includes a choice of fish, chicken or beef entree for $12.95, about a third cheaper than a comparable item from the dinner menu. It's available from 5:30 to 6:30 pm.

Places to Eat – top end

Daniel Thiebaut's *Palm Cafe* (☎ 329-7765), on Alii Dr at the south end of town, is a pleasant open-air 2nd-story restaurant with a fine ocean view and superb Hawaiian regional cuisine to match. Starters include Vietnamese spring rolls, Chinese stuffed ravioli and heart of palm salad, all priced at $6. Main courses range from a vegetarian stir-fry for $15 to Hunan-style lamb chops or Hawaiian snapper in Thai salsa for $24. It's open for dinner nightly from 5:30 to 10 pm and reservations are recommended.

Kona Inn, in the center of town, opened in 1929 as the Big Island's first hotel. It's now a shopping center with a large and popular restaurant of the same name. Steak and seafood dinners are in the $15 to $30 range. Light meals, which are available from 11:30 am to midnight, include calamari sandwiches for $6 and steak sandwiches or jumbo fried shrimp for $11.

The best value at the *Chart House*, a popular chain restaurant at Waterfront Row, is the early-bird special, from 5 to 6 pm, which includes fresh catch of the day, sirloin steak or teriyaki chicken for $15. Otherwise, main dishes range from $16.50 for grilled chicken to $25 for filet mignon or fresh fish. All dinners include a reasonably good salad bar.

Jameson's by the Sea (☎ 329-3195) at Kona Magic Sands condos, 77-6452 Alii Dr, on White Sands Beach is a spin-off of the popular restaurant on Oahu's North Shore. However, while the oceanside tables are about as close as you can get to the surf without getting your feet wet, the food is not nearly as inspired as the setting. Dinner entrees typically begin at $16, fresh fish around $24, although when things are slow there's sometimes a dinner special for about $13. At lunch there are burgers and salads for $7 and a fresh fish sandwich for a few dollars more. It's open for lunch from 11 am to 5 pm Monday to Friday and for dinner from 5 to 10 pm daily.

Sam Choy's Restaurant (☎ 326-1545) is an unpretentious place on Kauhoa St in the middle of the Kaloko Industrial Area. Choy, formerly the head chef at the Hilton, is known for his expertise with Hawaiian regional cuisine and has a following among local residents and seasoned visitors. At lunch there's simple fare such as chicken teriyaki and sandwiches for around $5, while dinner features more creative dishes with lamb, duck and fresh fish priced from $17 to $20. The restaurant is open from 5

am to 2 pm Monday to Saturday and from 5 to 9 pm Wednesday to Saturday. Sam's is off Hwy 19 about four miles north of Kailua; the turn-off is just south of the 96-mile marker.

Places to Eat – buffets

For a splurge, the *Royal Kona Resort* and the *King Kamehameha's Kona Beach Hotel* put on top-notch Sunday champagne brunches. Both include an array of appetizers from Alaskan crab legs to sushi, prime rib, numerous hot dishes, salads and desserts. King Kamehameha's has more consistent quality and a richer dessert selection, while Royal Kona has a fruit smoothie bar and an unbeatable oceanfront location. Both are offered from 9 am to 1 pm and cost $20 for adults, $10 for children ages six to 12.

King Kamehameha's also does a nice breakfast buffet from 6:30 to 11 am daily that costs $9.50 with hot dishes, $5.75 if you just want the cold dishes, which include fruit, pastries and cereal.

On Friday and Saturday nights, King Kamehameha's has a very good seafood and prime rib buffet with everything from sashimi and crab legs to extensive salad and dessert bars. The price is $20 for adults, $9 for kids under 12.

Entertainment

Kona, with its restaurants and bars lined up along Alii Dr, has no shortage of sunset views and happy hours. There's also occasional live dinner music at a few of the restaurants.

The *Eclipse* (☎ 329-4686), a lunchtime restaurant and nighttime bar on Kuakini Hwy, has a dance club with rock and pop music on Fridays and Saturdays ($3 cover charge) and salsa music on Sunday ($2), both from 10 pm to 1:30 am and with an age limit of 21. On Wednesdays, the only evening the Eclipse serves dinner, it's country & western night with line dancing.

Huggo's (☎ 329-1493), a restaurant near the Royal Kona Resort, has live Hawaiian or contemporary music from 9 pm nightly, with no cover charge.

Kailua has two movie theater complexes: three screens at *Hualalai Theatres* on Kuakini Hwy and two more at the *Kona Marketplace Cinemas* in the center of town.

Luaus *King Kamehameha's Kona Beach Hotel* (☎ 329-4969) has a luau every Sunday, Tuesday, Wednesday and Thursday on its beach in front of Ahuena Heiau. It begins with a lei greeting at 5:30 pm, followed by torch lighting, an imu ceremony, a buffet dinner and a Polynesian show. The cost is $49 for adults, $18 for children ages six to 12. There's also limited seating at 7 pm, minus the dinner, which costs $25 for adults, $12 for children. If you just want to watch them bury the pig in the imu, they do that with a little commentary at 10:15 am on luau days.

Things to Buy

The center of Kailua is loaded with small shops selling trinkets, clothing and other tourist-related goods. King Kamehameha's Kona Beach Hotel has a Liberty House department store and about 20 other shops. A good place to pick up Hawaiian tapes and CDs is Mele Kai Music in the Kaahumanu Plaza in Kailua's industrial area.

The Kailua Candy Co on Kaiwi St makes wonderful homemade chocolates using island fruits and nuts. You can get a peek at their operations through picture windows and free samples at their gift shop, which is open daily until 6 pm. The candies make a nice souvenir.

Getting Around

The Alii Shuttle (☎ 329-9337) makes 45-minute runs between Kailua and Keauhou nine times daily in each direction. The bus leaves the Kona Surf Resort in Keauhou at 8:30 am and every 1½ hours thereafter, with the last run at 8:30 pm. Stops are made at Keauhou Shopping Village, Keauhou Beach Hotel, Royal Kona Resort, Kona Inn Shopping Village, King Kamehameha's Kona Beach Hotel and the Lanihau Center. Return buses leave the Lanihau Center every 1½ hours from 9:20 am to 9:20 pm.

This makes a good option for getting to Kahaluu Beach Park (next to the Keauhou Beach Hotel) if you're in Kailua without a car. Note that the schedule is subject to change, so it's a good idea to call before stepping out to wait for a bus. The fare anywhere along the route is $2 each way, or you can get a day/weekly pass for $5/20.

KEAUHOU

Keauhou is the coastal area immediately south of Kailua-Kona. It starts at Kahaluu Bay and runs south beyond Keauhou Bay and the Kona Surf Resort.

Keauhou contains a planned community of three hotels, nine condo complexes, a shopping center and a 27-hole golf course, all neatly spaced out with a country club atmosphere. Bishop Estate, Hawaii's largest private landholder, owns the land.

The area was once the site of a major Hawaiian settlement, supported by an abundance of fresh spring water. Several historical sites can still be explored, although they now share their grounds with the hotels and condos.

Information

Tourist Information Keauhou Visitors Association (☎ 322-3866), 78-6831 Alii Dr, Suite 234, Kailua-Kona, HI 96740, can mail out information and brochures on Keauhou.

Post There's a contract post office at the Keauhou Shopping Village, on the corner of Alii Dr and Kamehameha III Rd.

Pharmacy There's a Longs Drugs inside the Keauhou Shopping Village, as well as a small pharmacy inside the center's KTA Supermarket.

Other Keauhou has a free on-call shuttle service (☎ 322-3500) that runs around the resort between 8 am and 4:30 pm daily.

St Peter's Church

The little blue church on the north side of Kahaluu Bay is St Peter's Catholic Church. It dates back to 1880 although it was moved from White Sands Beach to this site in 1912. Tidal waves have since attempted to relocate it on a couple of occasions.

This is Hawaii's most photographed 'quaint church' and it's still used for weekend services and weddings.

Just north of the church is what remains of the foundation of **Kuemanu Heiau**, a surfing temple. Hawaiian royalty, who surfed the waters at the north end of Kahaluu Bay, paid their respects at this temple before hitting the waves.

Between the heiau and the church there's a spring-fed pond where the alii used to bathe after surfing.

Locals keep up the surfing tradition, although high surf usually generates dangerous northward rip currents and it's not a good spot for beginners.

Kahaluu Beach

Kahaluu, which means the 'Diving Place' in Hawaiian, is the island's best easy-access snorkeling spot. The bay is like a big natural aquarium and it's a good place to learn to snorkel. It's not even necessary to go out over your head to enjoy it.

Large rainbow parrotfish, schools of silver needlefish, brilliant yellow tangs, butterfly fish and colorful wrasses are among the numerous tropicals easily seen here.

The fish are tame enough to eat out of your hand. If you hold out some fish food the frenzied swarms can give quite a rush!

There are lots of fish in the shallows, but generally the deeper the water the better the coral and the larger the fish. Spotted moray eels are not that hard to find either. At high tide green sea turtles occasionally swim into the bay to feed.

An ancient breakwater, said to have been menehune-built, is on the reef and protects the bay. Still, when the surf is high Kahaluu can have strong currents that pull in the direction of the rocks near St Peter's Church and it's easy to drift away without realizing it. Check your bearings occasionally to make sure you're not being pulled by the current.

A plaque by the picnic pavilion has

information on the water conditions and marine life in the bay. Check it out before you go in.

A lifeguard is on duty daily. There's a snack van selling burgers, sodas and shave ice. Another van rents snorkel sets at $4 for the first hour and $1 each subsequent hour as well as 35mm underwater cameras for $12.50 an hour, plus film. Fish food can be purchased for $1.

The park has a beach of black and white sand, showers, restrooms, changing rooms, picnic tables and grills. It's a popular place and often draws a crowd.

Keauhou Beach Hotel

The grounds of Keauhou Beach Hotel, immediately south of Kahaluu Beach, contain some easily explored historical sites. A one-page brochure and map of the sites is available at the bell desk.

The ruins of Kapuanoni, a **fishing temple**, is on the north side of the hotel. The reconstructed **summer beach house** of King Kalakaua is inland, beside a spring-fed pond once used as a royal bath. You can peek into the simple three-room cottage and see a portrait of the king in his European-style royal dress, a Hawaiian quilt on the bed and lauhala mats on the floor.

Other heiau sites are on the south side of the hotel. The remains of the seaside **Keeku Heiau**, just beyond the footbridge that leads to the Kona Lagoon Hotel, is thought to have been a luakini heiau.

There are some great **tide pools** nearby, in a low shelf of smooth pahoehoe lava, which are best explored when the tide is low. The pools contain numerous sea urchins, including spiny and slate pencil types, and small tropical fish.

When the tide is at its very lowest you can walk out onto a flat lava tongue that is carved with numerous **petroglyphs**. The site is directly in front of the northern end of the Kona Lagoon Hotel, with most of the petroglyphs about 25 feet from the shore. Other than at low tide the petroglyphs are submerged and cannot be seen.

The Keauhou Beach Hotel grounds also

has a **fertility pit**, carved wooden god images, historic *kuula* stones sacred to fishers and an ancient house site or two.

Keauhou Bay

Keauhou Bay, which has a launch ramp and space for two dozen small boats, is one of the most protected bays on the west coast.

While snorkeling can be reasonably good in the bay, it's not advised because of the boat traffic. If you come by on weekdays in the late afternoon you can watch the local outrigger canoe club practicing. There are restrooms and showers.

A stone marking the site where Kamehameha III was born in 1814 is in a small clearing just south of the harborside dive shacks. The young prince was said to have been stillborn and brought back to life on this rock by a visiting kahuna.

To get to the bay turn makai off Alii Dr onto Kamehameha III Rd. Or, alternatively, drive down Kaleopapa Rd towards Kona Surf Resort. Continue to the end of the road instead of turning into the resort.

Manta Rays

If you're looking for something to do in the evening, you could go down to Kona Surf Resort and watch the manta rays that sometimes gather in the late evening at the rocky outcrop below the resort's saltwater pool. They're attracted by the spotlights that shine down onto the ocean and thus make their best showings when there's no moon.

The wing tips of these impressive creatures often measure up to 12 feet across. The manta rays cruise around in the surf, with their white underbellies flashing against the dark waters – it's hypnotic to watch.

Places to Stay

The 318-room *Keauhou Beach Hotel* (☎ 322-3441, (800) 367-6025; fax 322-6586), 78-6740 Alii Dr, Kailua-Kona, HI 96740, adjoins Kahaluu Beach Park and has interesting grounds that include historical sites and tide pools. Rooms, which have mini-refrigerators, TV, air conditioning and balconies, are good size but the

decor varies, with those in the unrenovated wing being quite lackluster. Rates range from $96 to $165, largely depending upon the view. Ask for the 'Mahalo Special' and you'll get a free rental car for the same rates.

Kona Surf Resort (☎ 322-3411, (800) 367-8011; fax 322-3245), 78-128 Ehukai St, Kailua-Kona, HI 96740, is a modern, sprawling, 553-room hotel oriented to Japanese package tourists. It has some interesting Polynesian carvings and decor, a little wedding chapel, tennis courts and both salt and freshwater pools. The hotel is rather isolated on a rugged and rocky lava point on the south side of Keauhou Bay. Rates range from $109 to $185, $10 less in the low season. There's a daytime shuttle service between the hotel and Kailua-Kona village.

The *Keauhou Resort Condominiums* (☎ 322-9122, (800) 367-5286), 78-7039 Kamehameha III Rd, Kailua-Kona, HI 96740, has 48 units with full kitchens and washer/dryers. Although the units are about 20 years old they are well maintained and are the cheapest in Keauhou. One-bedroom units are $65/75 in the low/high season with a garden view, $75/85 with an ocean view. Add $20 more for a two-bedroom unit for up to four people. The minimum stay is five days. It's near the golf course and there's a pool.

At the other end of the spectrum is *Kanaloa at Kona* (☎ 322-9625, (800) 777-1700), 78-261 Manukai St, Kailua-Kona, HI 96740, operated by Colony Hotels & Resorts. It has 114 condo units ranging from $155 for a one-bedroom apartment with a golf course view to $255 for a three-bedroom unit with an ocean view. All units have lanais with wet bars as well as the standard amenities. The oceanfront units also have spas. There are three pools and two lighted tennis courts.

Other Keauhou condos are priced between the two and are largely booked through vacation rental agents. Kona Vacation Resorts (☎ 329-6488, (800) 367-5168), 77-6435 Kuakini Hwy, Kailua-Kona, HI 96740, handles units in most of them.

Places to Eat

Rocky's Pizza (☎ 322-3223) in the Keauhou Shopping Village has good, reasonably priced pizza, pastas and sandwiches. The tasty eggplant parmesan served with a salad and garlic bread makes a nice vegetarian meal for $8. It's open from 11 am to 9 pm daily.

Drysdale's Two in the Keauhou Shopping Village specializes in sandwiches and burgers, most priced from $6 to $8, and is a hot spot for watching sports on TV. It's open from late morning to at least midnight, with the food service stopping at 11 pm.

Keauhou Shopping Village also has a supermarket, a health food store, a small coffee shop, a *Baskin-Robbins* ice cream shop and a few other fast-food eateries.

Edward's Terrace Restaurant (☎ 322-1434) at Kanaloa at Kona condos is a casual open-air spot. It has a poolside condo atmosphere but it's on the ocean and the food's good. Breakfasts and lunches cost $6 to $10 and include macnut waffles, Moroccan chicken stuffed in papaya, salads and fresh fish sandwiches. At dinner, appetizers average $6, while main dishes, many with a Mediterranean accent, are priced from $14 to $25. It's open daily except Mondays from 8 am to 2 pm and 5 to 9 pm. To get there, turn makai off Alii Dr onto Kamehameha III Rd and then right onto Manukai St. Ask the gatekeeper where to park.

Keauhou Beach Hotel (☎ 322-3441) has a decent seafood and prime rib buffet on Fridays, Saturdays and Sundays for $20 and a Sunday champagne brunch that includes fresh fruit, Belgian waffles, various egg dishes, prime rib and desserts for $17. On weekdays from 5 to 9 pm the restaurant has a Chinese buffet for $13; there's also an a la carte menu.

Entertainment

The *Keauhou Beach Hotel* has a comedy club in its open-air Makai Bar at 8 pm Wednesdays with a $8 cover charge. There's often live Hawaiian music (no cover) in the early evening, which makes it a nice spot to stop for a sunset drink.

Things to Buy

There are many shops in the Keauhou Shopping Village including Penthouse, a clearance store for Liberty House, which has good-quality clothing at discounted prices. You can sometimes find a good selection of aloha shirts and other Hawaiian print clothing. The best deals are on the first Sunday of the month when prices are slashed to make room for new stock. It's open daily.

Keauhou Village Book Shop, also in the Keauhou Shopping Village, has an excellent collection of travel guides and Hawaiiana books.

HOLUALOA

Holualoa is perched in the hills, 1400 feet above Kailua-Kona. The slopes catch afternoon showers so it's lusher and cooler than on the coast below.

Holualoa is an artist's community with craft shops, galleries and a community art center, all of which makes it a fun place to poke around.

This is pretty much a one-road village, with everything lined up along Hwy 180. There's a general store, a Japanese cemetery, an elementary school, a couple of churches and a library that opens a few days a week. Most shops are closed on Sundays and Mondays.

From Kailua-Kona, it's a scenic four miles up Hualalai Rd to Holualoa. The landscape is bright with flowers, coffee bushes, and fruit trees of all kinds.

Kona's relentless development is creeping up this way. Older homes half-hidden by jungly gardens are being joined by a jumble of new houses. It's an enviable location, with a fine view of Kona's sparkling turquoise waters below.

Kimura's Lauhala Shop
Kimura's Lauhala Shop (☎ 324-0053), at the intersection of Hualalai Rd and Hwy 180, sells items woven from lauhala, the *lau* (leaf) of the hala tree.

This was once an old plantation store which sold salt and codfish. During the Depression of the 1930s, Mrs Kimura started weaving lauhala hats and coffee baskets and taking them down to the plantations to sell.

Three generations of Kimuras still weave lauhala here. Their work is supplemented by the wives of local coffee farmers who do piecemeal work at home when it's not coffee season.

The hardest part, the Kimuras say, is preparing the lauhala, which is messy work, complicated by the sharp spines along the leaf edges. The easy part is the weaving. Once the lauhala is ready to weave, it takes a couple of hours to make a placemat which sells for around $8.

The most common items are placemats, open baskets, and hats of a finer weave. The shop is open from 9 am to 5 pm Monday to Saturday.

Kona Arts Center
The Kona Arts Center (Box 272, Holualoa, HI 96725) is in a ramshackle former coffee mill, with a tin roof and hot-pink doors.

Carol Rogers, who's been here since 1965, directs this nonprofit organization and teaches crafts, nurturing the spirit as much as the art.

This is a community scene and everyone's welcome to join; for a monthly fee of $25, you can partake in the workshops which include pottery, batik, tie-dye, basketry, weaving and painting.

Visitors are free to drop in to look around; the center is open from 10 am to 4 pm Tuesday to Saturday. There's also a small display area with items for sale including paintings, pottery and baskets made of natural fibers like sea grass, coconut palm leaves and banana poka vine.

Studio 7 Gallery
Studio 7 Gallery opened in 1980 to showcase the artwork of owner Hiroki Morinoue who works in watercolors, oils, wood block and 3D sculpture. His wife, Setsuko, is a potter and the gallery's director.

Studio 7 now exhibits some 30 top-notch artisans, about half of whom come from the Kona area. Works include ceramics, natural-dyed fabrics, sculpture, blown glass and pit-fired raku.

The gallery is like a little museum and the Zen-like setting blends both Hawaiian and Japanese influences, with wooden walkways over lava stones. It's open from 10 am to 4 pm Tuesday to Saturday.

Places to Stay
Kona Hotel (☎ 324-1155), Hwy 180, Holualoa, HI 96725, in Holualoa's town center, retains the small town character (and room rates!) of a bygone era. This old local hostelry has high ceilings and some nice views. Rooms are basic with just a bed and dresser but are clean and priced at only $15/23 for singles/doubles. Bathrooms are shared and down the hall. Rumor has it that the mattresses in the street-side rooms are the most comfortable as the burly construction workers who sometimes stay during the work-week favor the ocean side. With only 11 rooms, getting a room here is pretty

Kona Coffee

Missionaries introduced the first coffee trees to Hawaii in 1827 and by the turn of the century it was an important cash crop throughout the state. However, the erratic rise and fall of coffee prices eventually drove coffee farmers out of business on the other Hawaiian islands. Only the Big Island's Kona coffee was of high enough quality to sell at a profit during gluts in world markets.

Coffee production in Hawaii had dropped dramatically by 1980, when a rising interest in gourmet coffee sparked sales of the highly aromatic Kona beans. Today Kona coffee is the most commercially successful coffee grown in the USA. Almost the entire harvest comes from the upland towns of South Kona, from Holualoa in the north to Honaunau in the south. The coffee trees thrive in the rich volcanic soil and the cloud cover that moves in nearly every afternoon.

Coffee, a relative of the gardenia, has fragrant white blossoms in the spring. In the summer the trees have green berries, which turn red as they ripen.

Coffee trees must be hand-picked several times a year as not all the berries ripen at once. The harvesting season begins in August. Coffee farmers at the lowest elevations may finish harvesting by December, while those at the 2000-foot level might harvest into March.

During the coffee season buyers hang out signs announcing how much they'll pay for 'cherries', the name given to the red coffee berries. In a good year they may offer as much as 90c a pound. ■

much hit and miss, although it's generally easier on weekends.

Holualoa Inn (☎ 324-1121, (800) 392-1812), run by Desmond Twigg-Smith, Box 222, Holualoa, HI 96725, is a beautiful contemporary B&B atop 40 acres of sloping meadows. There are great views of the Kona Coast. The house was built as a getaway by Desmond's uncle, president of the *Honolulu Advertiser*, who at the time of construction owned a sawmill. The exterior is all western red cedar and the interior floors are red eucalyptus from Maui. Although the house has 5000 sq feet, there are only four bedrooms, each of which has a private bath. There's a large swimming pool, a billiard table, a rooftop gazebo and a TV lounge. They serve a continental breakfast which includes their own home-grown Kona coffee and fruit from the garden. There are plans to add bungalows and a restaurant in the next couple of years. As it stands now, it's one of Hawaii's better finds. Rates are $100 to $150.

Places to Eat

The *Holuakoa Cafe* (☎ 322-2233) has pastries, bagels, coffee and herbal teas. Occasionally there's entertainment, such as belly dancing with Middle Eastern music.

You can pick up groceries at *Paul's Place*, the village's general store.

South Kona

Hwy 11 heads south out of Kailua-Kona through a number of small communities: Honalo, Kainaliu, Kealakekua, Captain Cook and Honaunau. These are unhurried upland towns surrounded by coffee farms and macadamia nut groves.

Side roads off Hwy 11 lead to Kealakekua Bay, Puuhonua O Honaunau National Historical Park (better known as the Place of Refuge) and the old fishing villages of Hookena and Milolii. South Kona is short on beaches but there are a couple of excellent spots for snorkeling and diving.

HONALO

Honalo is the small village at the intersection of Hwy 11 and Hwy 180.

Daifukuji Soto Mission, in the village center on the mauka side of Hwy 11, is a big Buddhist temple with two altars, gold brocade, large drums and incense burners. Visitors are welcome to view the inside. As with all Buddhist temples, leave your shoes at the door.

Fuku-Bonsai Center

About two miles north of Honalo village, on the mauka side of Hwy 180, is the Fuku-Bonsai Center, which consists of 3½ acres of bonsai trees – Hawaii's finest collection.

It's open daily from 8 am to 5 pm and costs $5 for adults, $2.50 for children.

Places to Stay & Eat

Teshima's Inn (☎ 322-9140) on Hwy 11 has 10 rooms in a building behind Teshima's restaurant, although most are usually rented out on a monthly basis. These small rooms are very basic, each with a double bed, a private bathroom and a cabin-like ambiance. The rate is $20/30 for singles/doubles.

The unpretentious restaurant serves authentic Japanese food. The best deal is the lunch teishoku of miso soup, sashimi, sukiyaki, tsukemono (pickled cabbage) and rice, which costs $6.50 and is available only from 11 am to 1:45 pm. The same teishoku with the addition of fried fish costs $8 at dinner, which is served from 5 to 10 pm. There's a bar at the side of the restaurant.

KAINALIU

Kainaliu is a little town with positive energy. Aloha Cafe and the adjoining theater and natural food store are the focal point. Aloha Theatre, the home of the Aloha Community Players, has regular performances. Check the bulletin board in front of the theater to see what's happening

in the area; you can often find long-term room rentals posted here as well.

The town is an interesting mix of old and new influences. There are a few shops, such as the Blue Ginger Gallery, which sell quality crafts and New Age clothing, and older shops such as the Kimura Store which has been selling traditional fabrics and dry goods here for generations.

Places to Eat

The *Aloha Cafe* is the place to eat in these parts. The food includes vegetarian dishes, good salads, wonderful fresh fish specials and hearty sandwiches. A burrito or quesadilla with a side salad costs $7, while the most expensive dish, filet mignon, costs $16. There are also fruit smoothies, fresh-squeezed juices, espresso and desserts. The outside terrace has a distant ocean view. It's open from 8 am to 8 pm Monday to Saturday. If you come up for dinner in the winter bring a sweater as it can get cool in the evenings.

Next door to the cafe is the *Aloha Village Store*, a fully stocked natural foods store.

A little farther south on the makai side of Hwy 11 is *Subway Sandwiches*. Next to that is *Ohana Natural Foods*, a cooperative which sells organic produce, nuts, fruit juices, dairy products and granola at reasonable prices.

KEALAKEKUA

Kealakekua means 'Path of the Gods' and there was once a series of 40 heiaus running from Kealakekua Bay north to Kailua-Kona.

These days the town of Kealakekua is the banking center for Kona's hill towns. The Kona Coast's hospital is on the north side of town, a quarter of a mile mauka of Hwy 11. The post office is on the corner of Hwy 11 and Halekii Rd.

Kealakekua has a good library, which is open from 11 am to 8 pm on Mondays, 10 am to 5 pm Tuesday to Friday and 10 am to 1 pm on Saturdays.

Next door to the library is the coral

mortar and lava Kona Union Church, which dates back to 1854.

Flea Market
Just down Halekii Rd from the post office there's a small flea market every Tuesday, Thursday and Saturday from 8 am to 2 pm. You can buy local produce, coffee and an assortment of other typical flea market merchandise.

Kona Historical Society Museum
Kona Historical Society (☎ 323-3222) is just south of Kona Meat Company and north of the Kealakekua Grass Shack gift shop. The stone and mortar building, built in the mid-1800s, was once a general merchandise store-cum-post office.

These days it houses the society's office, archives and little museum. There are some interesting displays of the area's local history, including old photos and bottles and other memorabilia. It's open from 9 am to 3 pm Monday to Friday and admission is $1. The museum sells some nice historical post cards.

Places to Stay
Reggie's Tropical Hideaway (☎ 322-8888), Box 1107, Kealakekua, HI 96750, is in Kealakekua in an area thick with coffee and banana trees. This is a working farm and accommodation is island-style casual and not fancy, but you're free to use the family hot tub. There's a room in the main house that has a private entrance, bath and deck and costs $50 and a small room with a queen futon and shared bath for $30. There are also two separate cottages down the slope from the house that are sometimes available for short-term rental.

Merryman's Bed & Breakfast (☎ 323-2276), Box 474, Kealakekua, HI 96750, the home of Penny and Don Merryman, hospitable former Alaskans, is in a quiet residential area in Kealakekua, a quarter of a mile above Hwy 11. The house is big and airy with ample windows, a large deck and lots of natural wood and exposed-beam ceilings. There are two bedrooms with shared bath for $65/75 singles/doubles and two rooms with private bath from $75/85, breakfast included. Rooms are pleasantly furnished and there's a spacious common living area for guest use.

Places to Eat
Peacock House on Hwy 11 has inexpensive Chinese food but it's rather standard fare. You can get plate lunches from steamer trays for under $5 and a wide range of entrees for not much more.

Canaan Deli, on Hwy 11, serves omelets, pancakes and other breakfasts all day long and has ordinary sandwiches priced around $6. There's a *McDonald's* nearby on Hwy 11.

KEALAKEKUA BAY
Kealakekua Bay is a large bay, a mile wide at its mouth. Napoopoo Beach Park and Hikiau Heiau are at the south end of the bay. The north end has a protected cove with one of the best snorkeling spots on the Big Island.

Steep sea cliffs separate the two ends of the bay and there's no land passage between them. The northern end can be approached only by sea or by a hike or horseback ride along a dirt trail. (For details, see Snorkeling Cruises, Kayaking and Horseback Riding in the Activities section of this chapter.)

Kealakekua Bay is a state underwater park and marine life conservation district. Among the protected species are the spinner dolphins which frequently swim into the bay. Fishing is restricted and the removal of coral and rocks prohibited.

Captain James Cook, the first Westerner to visit Hawaii, sailed into Kealakekua Bay at dawn on January 17, 1779. The beaches were lined with 10,000 onlookers and 1000 canoes sailed out to greet him.

Cook's tall ships with high sails appeared to fulfill a prophecy of the return of the god Lono who was to arrive on a floating island covered with tall trees.

On his first evening ashore, Cook was brought to Hikiau Heiau where the high priest performed a series of ceremonies

PLACES TO STAY

2   Kona Surf Resort
5   Teshima's Restaurant/Inn
18   Manago Hotel/ Restaurant
25   Dragonfly Ranch

PLACES TO EAT

6   Aloha Cafe
7   Ohana Natural Foods/
     Subway Sandwiches
10   McDonald's
12   Canaan Deli
14   Peacock House

OTHER

1   Keauhou Shopping Village
3   Fuku-Bonsai Center
4   Daifukuji Soto Mission
8   Hospital
9   Flea Market
11   Bank of Hawaii
13   Library
15   Kona Historical Society Museum
16   Kings' Trail Rides O'Kona
17   State & County Offices
19   Kealakekua Ranch Center
20   Royal Kona Coffee Mill
21   Coffee Trees
22   Kona Country Fair & Lava Tube
23   Kona Coast Macadamia Nut
     & Candy Factory
24   Bong Brothers
26   St Benedict's Painted Church
27   Wakefield Botanical Gardens
28   Morihara Store

recognizing Cook as the incarnation of Lono.

Eleven days later at the heiau, Cook performed a burial service for sailor William Whatman who had died of a stroke. The inauspicious death of his mate raised a few questions about Cook's own mortality.

On February 14, Cook was tragically killed in a scuffle at the north end of the bay. Ironically, the world's greatest navigator was such a poor swimmer that he apparently stumbled into the direction of an angry crowd rather than swimming a few yards out to a waiting boat.

An obelisk monument on the north side of the bay marks the spot where Cook died at the water's edge.

Royal Kona Coffee Mill

On your way down to Kealakekua Bay, stop by the Royal Kona Coffee Mill to get a free cup of freshly brewed Kona coffee. You can also get a few insights into the coffee biz from the interpretive displays in the gift shop.

A separate lanai area has displays of macadamia nuts in various stages and a 1950s vintage macadamia nut husker with a car tire serving as the grinding wheel.

Coffee, macnuts and related souvenirs

are sold in the shop and both macadamia nuts and coffee are processed out back. It's open from 9 am to 5 pm daily and admission is free.

Napoopoo Beach Park

Napoopoo Beach Park is at the end of Napoopoo Rd, 4½ miles from Hwy 11.

The park's most predominant feature is **Hikiau Heiau**, the large platform heiau above the beach. The busy beach park has a boat landing, restrooms, showers and a shack near the heiau selling soft drinks and souvenirs.

The beach is rather rocky, and because it's small it often gets crowded. This is the less protected end of the bay and it can have dangerous water conditions when the surf is high and during kona storms.

There's good snorkeling at Napoopoo, but the real prize is the cove at the northern end of the bay. Some people snorkel over from Napoopoo Beach when it's calm, but it's a long haul and only strong swimmers should consider it.

From the park you can continue four miles south along a narrow road through scrub brush and lava to Puuhonua O Honaunau, the Place of Refuge. The road is bumpy, but paved and passable. Be careful if you pull over as there are roadside trenches partly concealed by grasses. Most of the stone walls that run parallel to the road were built in the early 1900s to keep cattle from straying.

Captain Cook Monument Trail

If you're up for a hike, the trail to Captain Cook Monument and the cove at the north end of Kealakekua Bay makes a good day outing. Although you can expect to work up a sweat, you'll be rewarded with fantastic snorkeling, a natural bath once reserved for royalty and some historic sites to explore.

To get to the trailhead, turn off Hwy 11 onto Napoopoo Rd and go down about 250 yards where you'll find a dirt road immediately after the second telephone pole on the right.

Start walking down the dirt road and

after 200 yards it will fork – stay to the left, which is essentially a continuation of the road you've been walking on. The route is fairly simple and in most places runs between two rock fences on an overgrown jeep road. When in doubt, stay to the left.

While in the past this has been a jungly path through tall elephant grasses, more recently the trail has been kept clear by the fellow who leads horseback rides to the monument.

Eventually the coast becomes visible, the vegetation sparser and the trail easier to walk. The trail veers to the left along a broad ledge, goes down the hill and then swings left to the beach. Once you're at the water, it's less than five minutes to the left to the monument marking Cook's death place.

The hike takes about an hour down, 1½ hours up. It's not a particularly strenuous hike, but it is hot and largely unshaded, and it's uphill all the way back. On the return, about five minutes up from the beach, there's a small fork in the trail where there are lots of air plants; bear to the right and you'll be on your way back.

There are no facilities at the bottom. Be sure to take drinking water and snorkeling gear.

Snorkeling There's fairly easy entry from the rocks on the left side of the cement dock in front of the Captain Cook Monument. The water starts out about five feet deep and slopes gradually to about 30 feet. The cove is protected and usually very calm. Both coral and fish are abundant, there's great visibility and it's a terrific place to snorkel.

Snorkeling tour boats (see the Activities section) pull into the bay in the morning, but they don't come ashore and they generally leave before lunchtime. Anyway, the cove is big enough so it doesn't feel crowded.

Exploring This area was once the Hawaiian village of Kaawaloa. Old lava stone walls still go all the way out to **Cook's Point** at the north end of the bay. There's a small light beacon on the point.

Queen's Bath, on the edge of the cove, is a small lava pool with brackish spring-fed water. It's a few minutes' walk from the monument in the direction of the cliffs. The water is cool and refreshing and this age-old equivalent of a beach shower is a great way to wash off the salt before hiking back. However, the mosquitoes can get a bit testy here.

A few minutes beyond the Queen's Bath, the path ends at the cliffs called **Pali-kapu-o-Keoua**, the 'cliffs sacred to the chief Keoua'. The cliffs contain numerous caves which were the burial places of Hawaiian royalty. It's speculated that some of Captain Cook's bones were placed here as well. As late as 1887 villagers from Kaawaloa were in the employ of King Kalakaua to maintain the burial grounds.

A few lower caves are accessible but they don't contain anything other than beer cans. The ones higher up are fortunately not as easy to get to and probably still contain bones. All are sacred and should be left undisturbed.

CAPTAIN COOK

The town named for the Pacific navigator is on Hwy 11 above the bay where he met his end. Captain Cook is a small unpretentious town with a few county and state offices, a shopping center, a hotel and a couple of restaurants. The Chevron gas station north of the Manago Hotel is open 24 hours a day.

As you continue south from town there are a handful of roadside coffee tasting rooms that sell locally grown coffee and provide free freshly brewed samples.

If you just want to examine coffee trees, there's a pull-off for that purpose midway between the 107 and 108-mile markers; look for the HVB sign. Coffee trees are planted in the front and macadamia trees beyond.

Kona Country Fair

Kona Country Fair is a large would-be flea market on a rather remote stretch of Hwy 11 between Captain Cook and Honaunau. It's been unable to fully operate because of water issues and essentially functions as another coffee shop. There's also a deli, a gift shop and a broad vista of the south Kona Coast. Just a two-minute walk behind the shop there's a walk-through **lava tube** that's worth a look.

Places to Stay

Manago Hotel (☎ 323-2642), Hwy 11, Box 145, Captain Cook, HI 96704, is a family-run hotel that started in 1917 as a restaurant serving bowls of udon to salespeople on the then-long journey between Hilo and Kona. Those wanting to stay overnight were charged $1 for a futon on tatami mats. These days the basic rooms in the original roadside building show their age without much grace but rates are just $22/25 for singles/doubles. The furniture is rickety, the walls are thin and there are shared baths down the hall.

If you want comfort over character, go for one of Manago's 42 rooms in the newer wing at the rear. These motel-style rooms are ordinary but sufficient, with private baths and radios. The highlight is the unobstructed lanai view of Kealakekua Bay a mile below. Rates are $35 to $38 for singles; $38 to $41 for doubles; the higher rates are for better views. There's a common TV room near the restaurant. Although it's pure local flavor, Manago draws a fair number of international travelers.

Doc Boone's Bed & Breakfast (☎ 323-3231), Box 666, Kealakekua, HI 96750, sits half a mile above Hwy 11 amidst a garden planted with tropical fruit trees and flaming red poinsettias. Doc is an MD who has delivered half the town's babies over the past few decades and his wife Jeannie is an artist. While the grounds have a pool, the cinder-block home is unpretentious and comfortably cluttered. The Boones are avid cyclists and snorkelers and like to show their guests around the area. They have three rooms with shared bath that rent for $65 double, however they prefer to rent only one or two units at a time so they can get to know people better.

Samurai House (☎ 328-9210), RR1, Box 359, Captain Cook, HI 96704, is a B&B in a traditional Japanese house that was brought over piece by piece from Japan and reerected in Captain Cook in the 1960s. It has shoji doors, tatami mats, exposed cypress beams, a little carp pond and distant ocean views. There are two guest rooms – a tatami room with a king bed for $65 and a westernized studio with a full kitchen for $75 – both with private baths and decks. A hot tub and TV/VCR are available. Samurai House, which is on Hwy 11 three-quarters of a mile south of the village center, caters mainly to the gay community, but is straight-friendly.

Places to Eat

The *Manago Restaurant*, in the Manago Hotel, is a Japanese version of a meat and potatoes eatery, and is known for its pork chops. It's not health food, but the portions are large. Two big chops, rice, potato salad and side dishes such as tofu curd cost $7.50. Sandwiches and burgers are around $3. Breakfast is available from 7 to 9 am, lunch from 11 am to 2 pm and dinner from 5 to 7 pm. It's closed on Mondays.

Kealakekua Ranch Center on Hwy 11 has a *Sure Save* supermarket and Mexican and Chinese restaurants.

HONAUNAU

Honaunau's main attraction is Puuhonua O Honaunau National Historical Park, commonly called the Place of Refuge, but there are other things to see in this area as well.

On Hwy 11, just south of Middle Keei Rd, Bong Brothers has a little shop where they sell their own coffee as well as organic produce, smoothies and a few deli items.

At Morihara Store, Hwy 160 connects with Hwy 11 and leads down to the Place of Refuge, passing Painted Church Rd, Wakefield Botanical Gardens and some fine rural scenery with grazing horses, stone walls and brilliant bougainvilleas.

Macadamia Nut Factory

The Kona Coast Macadamia Nut & Candy Factory, on Middle Keei Rd near Hwy 11, has a little display with a husking machine and a macadamia nut cracker. You can try it out, one nut at a time, and eat the final product.

The showroom overlooks the real operation out back, where bags of nuts are husked and sorted. The shop sells both raw and roasted macadamia nuts as well as macadamia nut honey.

St Benedict's Painted Church

This church is noted for its painted interior done by John Berchmans Velghe, a Catholic priest who came from Belgium in 1899.

He painted the walls with a series of biblical scenes as an aid in teaching the Bible to natives who couldn't read. He designed the wall behind the altar to resemble the gothic cathedral in Burgos, Spain. The ceiling is a Hawaiian sky with clouds and birds.

When Father John arrived, the church was on the coast near the Place of Refuge. One of his first moves was to bring the church two miles up the slopes to its present location. It's not clear whether he did this as protection from tsunamis or just to be on the rise – both actual and symbolic – from the old gods of 'pagan Hawaii'.

The tin-roofed church still holds Sunday services, with hymns sung in Hawaiian. The grounds are lushly tropical with two noteworthy breadfruit trees out front.

The church is on Painted Church Rd. Turn north at the one-mile marker on Hwy 160 and go a quarter of a mile – there's usually an HVB sign pointing the way.

Wakefield Botanical Gardens

Wakefield Botanical Gardens on Hwy 160 has free self-guided walks in a largely over-grown backyard. There are some interesting plants with names like snow on the mountain and Moses in the basket, as well as cactus, bonsai and more typical tropical flowers. The gardens are owned by island artist Arlene Wakefield, who also operates an informal restaurant here.

Places to Stay

Adrienne's B&B (☎ 328-9726, (800) 328-9726), RR1, Box 8E, Captain Cook, HI 96704, consists of four rooms in the home of Reginald and Adrienne Ritz-Baty, enthusiastic hosts who enjoy chatting about the island. All the rooms have private baths and a TV and VCR. There's a hot tub on the lanai with a view of the distant coast, access to the kitchen and the washer/dryer and a collection of 1200 videos. Rates range from $60 to $80 for doubles and include a breakfast of homemade bread and fresh fruit. They're on Hwy 11 about a mile south of the turn-off to the Place of Refuge.

The Dragonfly Ranch (☎ 328-9570, (800) 487-2159), Box 675, Honaunau, HI 96726, is a cosmic New Age retreat with a garden-like setting on Hwy 160 near Painted Church Rd. Accommodation options range from rather standard rooms

in the main house for $70 to a ... ... 'honeymoon suite' for $160 tha... ... waterbed on a platform deck without walls; the suite does have netting to keep out the large but harmless spiders that share the gardens. For something a bit more conventional there's a redwood cottage for $120. Rates include a breakfast of organic coffee, fruit and croissants.

Places to Eat

Wakefield Botanical Gardens has a relaxing open-air dining patio that makes for a pleasant lunch spot. A bowl of vegetarian soup with chips and homemade salsa costs $4, while sandwiches, salads and vegetarian or meat burgers are priced between $6 and $7. The macadamia nut pie should satisfy the strongest of sugar urges. The restaurant is open from 11 am to 3 pm.

PUUHONUA O HONAUNAU NATIONAL HISTORICAL PARK (PLACE OF REFUGE)

Puuhonua O Honaunau National Historical Park (☎ 328-2288) encompasses ancient temples, royal grounds and a *puuhonua*, a place of refuge or sanctuary. The park fronts Honaunau Bay.

Puuhonua O Honaunau is a tongue-twister of a name which simply means 'place of refuge at Honaunau'.

In old Hawaii, breaking any of the many kapus which strictly regulated all daily interactions was thought to anger the gods who might retaliate with a natural disaster or two. To appease the gods the offender was hunted down and killed.

Commoners who broke a kapu, as well as defeated warriors and ordinary criminals, could all have their lives spared by reaching the sacred ground of the puuhonua.

This was more of a challenge than it might appear. Since royalty and their warriors lived on the grounds immediately surrounding the refuge, kapu breakers were forced to swim through open ocean, braving currents and sharks to get to the puuhonua.

Once inside the sanctuary, priests performed ceremonies of absolution which apparently placated the gods. Kapu breakers could then return home with a clean slate.

Hale O Keawe Heiau, the temple on the point of the cove, was built around 1650. The bones of 23 chiefs were buried there. It's thought that the mana of the chiefs remained in their bones and added a spiritual power to those who came into the grounds. The heiau has been authentically reconstructed. The carved wooden statues that stand erect beside it are called kii and are said to embody the ancient gods.

The heiau is at the end of a large stone wall built around 1550. It's called the **Great Wall** and is more than 1000 feet long and 10 feet high. The west side of the wall was the puuhonua and the east side was the royal grounds.

A self-guided walk corresponding to the park brochure passes by Hale O Keawe Heiau, two older heiaus, a petroglyph, legendary stones, a fishpond, lava tree molds and a few thatched huts and shelters. The canoe on display is hand carved from koa wood.

There's also a stone board for konane, a game similar to checkers. The game pieces are small stones of black lava and white coral. Get a copy of the game rules at the park entrance and try your hand.

Medicinal plants around the grounds include the noni tree with its pear-sized warty-looking fruit. The fruit, which was eaten in times of famine, tastes as bad as it smells. More often it was used to make dyes or as a treatment for diabetes and high blood pressure.

Check out the **tide pools** in the pahoehoe lava at the south end of the park. The tiny black speckles dotting the shallow pools behind the heiau are pipipi, a kind of periwinkle. Even better are the tide pools near the picnic area farther south which harbor coral, black-shelled crabs, small fish and eels, sea hares, and sea urchins with rose-colored spines.

Twenty-minute orientation talks, largely geared to people on tour buses who don't have time to see the whole park, are given

at 10, 10:30 and 11 am and at 2:30, 3 and 3:30 pm daily.

Some of the rangers are native Hawaiians. You'll occasionally find one dressed in a malo or tapa demonstrating traditional pili grass thatching, canoe carving or kii statue making.

A program in Hawaiian studies is held monthly in the park's amphitheater, usually at 7:30 pm on the first Wednesday of the month. A festival with traditional displays and food, hukilau (net fishing) and a 'royal court' is held on the weekend closest to 1 July.

Admission is $2 per person, with a maximum of $4 per car, and is good for repeated visits over one week. Fees are generally collected between about 8:30 am and 4:45 pm but visitors are free to enter and stroll the grounds between 6 am and midnight.

Honaunau Beaches

Place of Refuge Swimming is allowed at Keoneele Cove inside the Place of Refuge. The cove was once the royal canoe landing and it's shallow with a gradual decline. Snorkeling is best when the tide is rising, as the water is a bit deeper and the tide brings in fish. Sunbathing is discouraged here.

South End of the Park Near the Place of Refuge visitor center there's a road leading a quarter of a mile south to a beach park with picnic tables and some quiet sandy patches.

Winter surf can be rough in this area. Unless the sea is flat it's best to stick to the Keoneele Cove area for swimming and snorkeling.

North End of the Park There's a terrific place to snorkel and dive just north of the Place of Refuge. From the park's parking lot, take the narrow road to the left with the 15 mph sign.

Go down about 500 feet and park just past the boat ramp. There's a little park mauka of the road, where the Keoua Canoe Club meets in the late afternoon. St Benedict's Painted Church was originally on this site.

Snorkelers step off a lava ledge immediately north of the boat ramp into about 10 feet of water. It then drops off fairly quickly to about 25 feet. There are some naturally formed lava steps that make it fairly easy to get in and out of the water.

Visibility is excellent, with good-sized reef fish and a fine variety of corals close to shore. The predatory crown of thorns starfish can be seen here feasting on live coral polyps.

For divers, there's a ledge a little way out that drops off about 100 feet.

In winter the water can get rough when the surf is high.

South on Highway 11

For about 15 miles south on Hwy 11 after the Place of Refuge turn-off, the road is winding and rather narrow with some fairly steep drops. Be careful when driving as there are sections that have no shoulder at all.

At night, sudden oncoming headlights and fog can make it particularly tricky, especially if you're tired from a long haul between Hilo and Kona.

HOOKENA BEACH

Hookena was once a bustling village with two churches, a school, courthouse and post office. King Kalakaua sent his friend Robert Louis Stevenson here in 1889 to show him a typical Hawaiian village. Stevenson stayed a week with the town's judge and wrote about Hookena in *Travels in Hawaii*.

In the 1890s Chinese immigrants began to move into Hookena setting up shops and restaurants. A tavern and a hotel opened and the town got rougher and rowdier.

In those days Big Island cattle were shipped from Hookena's landing to market in Honolulu. When the circle-island road was built, the steamers stopped coming and the townspeople moved away. By the 1920s the town was all but deserted.

These days Hookena is a tiny fishing community with a small county beach park. The storm-beaten remains of the landing are in front of the park restrooms.

Hookena is 2¼ miles down a narrow road from Hwy 11. The marked turn-off is between the 101 and 102-mile markers.

The beach has very soft black sand. The bay is backed by lava sea cliffs and there are trees for shade. When the winter surf is up, kids boogie board here.

When it's calm, you can snorkel straight out from the landing. It drops off pretty quickly, from 10 feet to about 30 feet, and there's lots of coral. Don't go too far out or you may encounter strong currents. Pygmy dolphins occasionally come into the bay, sometimes as many as a hundred at a time.

There are public toilets, a privately run shower (25c a minute) and a shack on the beach that sells shave ice and soft drinks.

Hookena is a popular weekend picnic

spot and camping is allowed with a permit from the county.

MILOLII

Milolii, while in a state of flux, remains the most traditional fishing village in Hawaii. Families who have been fishing these waters for generations still set out in outrigger canoes each morning before dawn.

Milolii means 'fine twist'. Historically the village was known for its skilled sennit twisters who used bark from the olona shrub to make fine cord and highly valued fishing nets.

Milolii sits at the edge of an expansive 1926 lava flow that covered the nearby fishing village of Hoopuloa.

The village has about 125 residents. Many of their homes are simple, shanty-like wooden structures, although the state has allocated funds to tear down the old shacks and replace them with new houses. It has also funded a solar-powered desalinization plant, providing the village with its first running water.

Milolii fishers use an age-old method resembling aqua farming in which they sail out to feed papaya and taro to opelu, a type of mackerel. After months of the fattening and taming process they return to net the fish. Folks in Milolii have long-standing complaints with some commercial fishing boats that ply their fishing grounds and scoop up the opelu they've fattened.

Along the coast, tide pools of both red and black lava provide a splashy backdrop to white coral and colorful fish. When the waters are calm the snorkeling is good.

Milolii Beach Park is past the village's little boat ramp. Camping is officially allowed but the beach park is right in the village and there's not a lot of space or privacy. This spot is also the community's playground and volleyball court. Certainly if you're thinking of camping, check it out first. Sentiments towards outsiders have not always been positive as some villagers see tourism as a threat to their privacy and lifestyle.

The turn-off to Milolii is just south of the 89-mile marker. It's five miles down a

paved but steep and winding single-lane road that cuts across the lava flow. Use low gear or your brakes will smoke on this one.

MacFarms of Hawaii

Just before entering the Kau district, Hwy 11 passes through the largest macadamia nut orchard in Hawaii, 3800 acres belonging to MacFarms of Hawaii. The orchards were started by a partnership which included Jimmy Stewart, Julie Andrews and other Hollywood stars.

MacFarms has introduced biological insect controls, composting and the use of grazing sheep for weed control in an effort to go organic. The orchards annually produce about 10 million pounds of nuts that are husked, processed and packaged on site.

North of Kona

Hwy 19 (Queen Kaahumanu Hwy) runs north 33 miles from Kailua-Kona up the Kona Coast to Kawaihae in the South Kohala district.

This is hot, arid country with a lava landscape. Along the road, clumps of brilliant pink bougainvillea look striking against the jet-black rock, but otherwise the vegetation is mainly sparse tufts of grass that survive the dry winds. On this stretch you'll also notice the Big Island's unique version of graffiti – messages spelled out in white coral against a lava background.

Honokohau Harbor and a new historical park are just a couple miles north of Kailua-Kona. Tiny fishing villages once dotted this sparsely populated coast but most were wiped out by the tsunami of 1946.

There are beautiful secluded beaches and coves on the north Kona Coast that are hidden from the road and accessible only by foot (or by boat). Once you hike in, you'll find white sand beaches tucked between a sea of hardened lava and a turquoise ocean. A few of these beaches are nesting sites of the threatened Pacific green sea turtle.

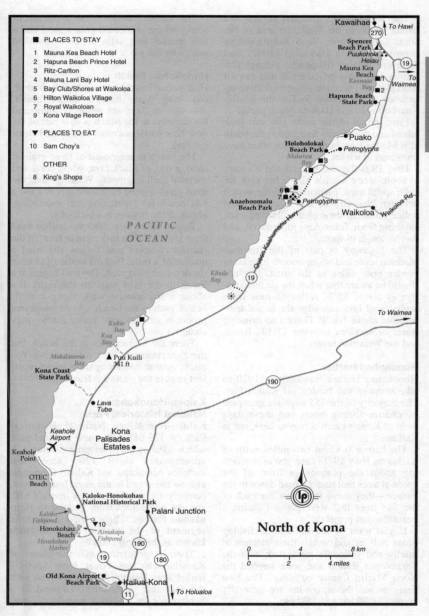

BIG ISLAND

North of Kona

PLACES TO STAY
1 Mauna Kea Beach Hotel
2 Hapuna Beach Prince Hotel
3 Ritz-Carlton
4 Mauna Lani Bay Hotel
5 Bay Club/Shores at Waikoloa
6 Hilton Waikoloa Village
7 Royal Waikoloan
9 Kona Village Resort

PLACES TO EAT
10 Sam Choy's

OTHER
8 King's Shops

Kawaihae   To Hawi
270
Spencer Beach Park
Puukohola Heiau
Mauna Kea Beach
Kaunaoa Bay
19
To Waimea
Hapuna Beach State Park
Holoholokai Beach Park   Puako
Petroglyphs
Makaiwa Bay
Anaehoomalu Beach Park
Petroglyphs
Waikoloa
Waikoloa Rd
Queen Kaahumanu Hwy

PACIFIC OCEAN

Kiholo Bay
19
To Waimea

Kukio Bay
Kua Bay
Makalawena Bay
Puu Kuili 341 ft
Kona Coast State Park
Lava Tube
Kona Palisades Estates

Keahole Airport
Keahole Point

OTEC Beach
Kaloko Fishpond
Kaloko-Honokohau National Historical Park
Honokohau Beach
Honokohau Harbor
Aimakapa Fishpond
Palani Junction
190

190
180

Old Kona Airport Beach Park   Kailua-Kona
11
To Holualoa

North of Kona

0   4   8 km
0   4   miles

The Big Island's fanciest resorts are farther north, in the Waikoloa area of the South Kohala district. South Kohala was an important area in Hawaiian history and there are heiaus, fishponds, petroglyphs and ancient stone-paved trails that can all be explored. There are wonderful drive-up beaches at the resorts and at the nearby Anaehoomalu and Hapuna beach parks.

From much of the coast you can look inland and see Mauna Kea, and to the south of it Mauna Loa, both of which often have snowcaps in winter.

Hwy 19 is flat and straight and it's easy to zoom along but it's also a hot spot for radar speed traps, particularly on the stretch between the airport and Kailua. Most police cruise in their own unmarked cars, anything from Trans-Ams to Broncos, and they're tough to spot.

The highway is part of the Ironman triathlon route and wide, smooth bike lanes border both sides of the road. Cyclists should be aware that when the air temperature is above 85°F, reflected heat from asphalt and lava can edge the actual temperature above 100°F. There's no drinking water or services between OTEC Beach and the Waikoloa hotels.

Honokohau Harbor

Honokohau Harbor was built in 1970 to take some of the burden off Kailua Pier. The majority of the 155 slips are occupied by charter fishing boats and these days most of Kona's catch comes in here, not to Kailua.

The harbor is about two miles north of Kailua on Hwy 19. In case you're wondering about the plaques in front of the coconut trees that line the road down to the harbor – they name the donor for each of the 243 trees that were planted during a beautification project!

If you want to see the charter fishing boats pull in and weigh their catches of marlin and yellowfin tuna, park near the Texaco gas station and walk beyond the Kona Marlin Center building. The best times to see the weigh-ins are generally around 11:30 am and 3:30 pm.

The harbor complex has a couple of places where you could grab a meal and a fish market that sells delicious smoked marlin by the piece.

Honokohau Beach

Honokohau Beach, just north of the harbor, has long been Kona's nudist beach, although its days are probably numbered for naturists as the beach is now part of the new Kaloko-Honokohau National Historical Park.

The beach is composed of large-grained sand, a mix of black lava, white coral and rounded shell fragments. Walking along the sand gives a good foot massage. It's not a bad beach for swimming and snorkeling, although the bottom is a bit rocky.

To get there, turn onto the harbor road from Hwy 19, then turn right in front of the marina complex and follow the road a quarter of a mile. Pull off to the right after the dry dock boat yard. The trail begins at a break in the lava wall on the right. It's about a five-minute walk along a well-beaten path to the beach. (As development proceeds on the new park, access may change.)

There are no facilities at the beach, but there are restrooms back at the marina. You might want to take along some insect repellent in case the gnats are feasting.

Kaloko-Honokohau National Historical Park

Kaloko-Honokohau National Historical Park (☎ 329-6881) is a new national park which is still in the developmental stages. It encompasses about 1200 acres and includes Aimakapa and Kaloko fishponds, ancient heiau and house sites, burial caves, petroglyphs, a holua slide, a queen's bath and the oceanfront from Kaloko to Honokohau Harbor. There's also a one-mile segment of the ancient stone footpath known as the **King's Trail**.

There's speculation that the bones of Kamehameha the Great were secretly buried near Kaloko. This, combined with the fact that Aimakapa Fishpond is a habitat for endangered waterbirds, was enough to help squeeze the national park designation through Congress in 1978.

The park entrance leads to Kaloko Fishpond, acquired in 1986 from Huehue Ranch in exchange for 300 acres of federal land on the mainland. Over the past two decades, mangrove invaded and spread rapidly throughout Kaloko Fishpond and native birds abandoned the habitat. The park service has recently finished eradicating the mangrove, a labor-intensive process that involved cutting and torching the trees, then tearing the new shoots up one by one and burning the roots. Native birds have now returned to Kaloko.

Aimakapa Fishpond, just inland from the beach, is the largest pond on the Kona Coast and an important bird habitat. Like Kaloko Fishpond, it also had to have a mangrove invasion stemmed. If you visit this brackish pond, you're likely to see *aeo* (black-necked stilts) and *alae-keokeo* (Hawaiian coots), both endangered native waterbirds. Each species now has about 20 nesting sites on the pond.

While most of the work within the park is still concentrating on natural restoration, trails are being developed and plans call for the eventual opening of a visitor center that will feature displays on Hawaiian culture and natural history. The park service is also considering a limited 'living history model' in which Hawaiian families interested in living off the land could serve as interpreters of traditional Hawaiian ways.

The park entrance is off Hwy 19, about half a mile north of the 97-mile marker. The park gates are open from 8 am to 3:30 pm daily but there's also access from the harbor (see Honokohau Beach).

Queen's Bath The queen's bath is a spring-fed pool with brackish water in the middle of a lava flow. Even though it's inland, the water level changes with the tide. At high tide more saltwater seeps in and the water rises.

You can get there by walking south for about 15 minutes from Kaloko Fishpond or inland from the north end of Honokokau

Beach. The queen's bath is marked by stone cairns as well as Christmas berries, always a dead giveaway that fresh water is nearby.

Keahole Point/OTEC Beach

The turn-off to OTEC Beach and the Natural Energy Laboratory of Hawaii (NELH), a state hydroenergy research facility, is one mile south of the Keahole Airport.

At Keahole Point the sea floor drops steeply just offshore providing a continuous supply of both cold water from 600-meter depths as well as warm surface waters. These are ideal conditions for ocean thermal energy conversion (OTEC).

The OTEC system operates like a steam turbine, with the difference in temperature between the cold and warm waters providing the energy source. Electricity has been successfully generated at the site and research continues on ways to make this an economically viable energy source.

The nutrient-rich cold waters that are pumped up are also used in spin-off aquaculture projects, such as the production of salmon, Maine lobster, abalone, oysters, seaweed and spirulina.

From the highway it's about a mile in to OTEC (Wawaloli) Beach, where there are toilets, showers and drinking water. This windswept lava coastline is rocky and not very good for swimming although there's a large naturally enclosed pool 200 yards south of the restrooms that's deep enough to wade in.

The rough dirt road that continues south from the beach leads half a mile to **Pine Trees**, one of the best surfing breaks in the Kona area. There's currently a struggle going on between Big Island residents who want Pine Trees to remain in a natural state and investors who are targeting the area for development.

Onizuka Space Center

The Astronaut Ellison S Onizuka Space Center (☎ 329-3441), at the Keahole Airport, pays tribute to the Big Island native who perished in the Challenger space shuttle disaster.

The little museum has a few exhibits about space and the role of astronauts, shows educational films and has a moon rock and one of Onizuka's space suits on display. Admission is $2 for adults, 50c for children. It's open from 8:30 am to 4:30 pm daily.

Lava Tube

There's a big open lava tube on the mauka side of Hwy 19, north of the 91-mile marker and just before a speed limit sign. It might seem rather tame if you've been to Hawaii Volcanoes National Park, but interesting if you haven't.

The tube and the expansive lava flow that surrounds the airport are all from the last eruption of Mt Hualalai, in 1801.

Kona Coast State Park

The attractive sandy beach at Mahaiula Bay has finally been opened to the public as part of the new Kona Coast State Park. The park has shaded picnic tables and portable toilets but is otherwise completely undeveloped. Most of the time there's good snorkeling and swimming but during periods of high surf, which are not infrequent in winter, there's good surfing instead, particularly at the north side of the bay.

The road into the park, which begins 2½ miles north of the airport off Hwy 19, is nearly as interesting as the beach. It runs for 1¾ miles across a seemingly endless lava flow that's totally devoid of trees and greenery before depositing you at this little oasis. The road is bumpy and only partly paved, but is easily passable in a regular car.

If you want to explore further, a trail leads north from Kona Coast State Park about 1½ miles to **Makalawena**, another beautiful stretch of beach. Makalawena is backed by sand dunes and contains some fine coves with good swimming and snorkeling.

Kua Bay

Kua Bay, also known as Maniniowali, has a beautiful secluded beach with turquoise waters and gleaming white sands. It's picture-postcard material.

It has a gentle slope and inviting waters for swimmers most of the year and for boogie boarders and bodysurfers in the winter. Although it's generally calm, winter storms can generate currents in the bay.

The turn-off to the beach is just north of both the 88-mile marker and the grassy 341-foot Puu Kuili, the highest cinder cone on the makai side of the highway. Look for the stop sign and red gate at the head of the road.

The road down is rough and over loose lava stones. Some people do drive in about half a mile and park near the roadside, but if you park near the highway it only takes about 20 minutes to walk in.

At the end of the road there's a beaten path over the rocks to the south end of the beach. There are no facilities.

Kua Bay is one of the nicest of the isolated Kona Coast beaches and you might not feel the need to go any farther. However, if you do want to explore, you could walk north from Kua Bay along the coast about a mile to **Kukio Bay**, which has a long stretch of white sand beach and an absolutely lovely cove with good swimming. You're unlikely to have the place to yourself, however, as there's a new resort under construction on the beach.

Kona Village Resort

Kona Village Resort is the most unique of Hawaii's getaway hotels. The accommodation is in thatched Polynesian-style 'hales' on stilts that are spaced around a spring-fed lagoon and along the beach. The grounds have flowering tropical plants and trees, petroglyphs and lots of birds.

The resort is on the secluded **Kahuwai Bay**, surrounded by huge expanses of barren lava. There was a fishing village on the bay years ago but it got washed away in the 1946 tidal wave. When the resort opened in 1965 it was so isolated it had its own airstrip to shuttle in guests; the highway wasn't built for another decade.

Non-guest access is limited, but guided tours are given at 11 am Monday to Friday (no reservations required), and on week-

> **Donkey Crossing**
>
> In the evenings donkeys come down from the hills to drink at the spring-fed watering holes and to eat the seed pods from the kiawe trees along the coast between Kua and Kiholo bays. The donkeys are descendants of the pack animals that were used on coffee farms until the 1950s when they were replaced by jeeps.
>
> Growers, who had become fond of these 'Kona nightingales', as the donkeys were nick-named because of their braying, released many of the creatures into the wild rather than turning them into glue. The donkeys were largely forgotten until Hwy 19 went through in 1974.
>
> The donkeys now need to cross the road for their evening feedings and it's worth keeping an eye out for them at night as they don't always pay attention to the 'Donkey Crossing' signs on the highway! ■

ends by reservation only. The turn-off is just south of the 87-mile marker.

If you don't want to visit the resort but just want to go down to the coast, tell the guard at the gatehouse you want one of the beach access parking spaces. The access is at the south side of Kahuwai Bay. Unlike the sandy beach in front of the resort, this end of the bay is rocky and is mostly used by divers going spear fishing or people hiking along the coast.

Places to Stay The 125 free-standing cottages at *Kona Village Resort* (☎ 325-5555), (800) 367-5290; fax 325-5124), Box 1299, Kaupulehu-Kona, HI 96745, look like rustic thatched huts on the outside but are modern and very comfortable inside with high ceilings, rattan furnishings, ceiling fans and louvered windows.

In keeping with the getaway concept, the units do not have phones or TVs. It's all low-key and relaxed, although there are activities available including tennis and sailing.

Daily rates range from $295 to $570 for singles, $390 to $665 for doubles, and include all meals and recreational activities. Despite the obvious irony of paying this kind of money to 'go native' there seem to be few unhappy campers here.

Places to Eat *Kona Village Resort* is open to non-guests, with advance reservations, except when the resort is at 100% occupancy. The daily outdoor lunch buffet, held from 12:30 to 2 pm, costs $28.

In addition there's expensive fine dining in the Hale Samoa, which is designed in the traditional New Hebrides style and is lined with lauhala matting. The 75-foot tapa cloth draped from the ceiling was a gift from the king of Tonga after his stay at the resort.

Kiholo Bay

Halfway up the coast, just south of the 82-mile marker, there's a lookout which commands a great view of Kiholo Bay. It appears like a little oasis in the midst of the lava, with intense blue waters and a line of coconut trees.

An inconspicuous trail down to the bay starts about 100 yards south of the 81-mile marker. It follows a 4WD road, the beginning of which has been blocked off by boulders to keep vehicles out. The hike down takes about half an hour.

Kiholo Bay is almost two miles wide and the south end of the bay has a lovely, large spring-fed pond called **Luahinewai**. It's refreshingly cold and fronted by a black sand beach. There's also good ocean swimming when it's calm.

In ancient times Kiholo provided a respite along the King's Trail, a stone footpath that ran along the coast. It was a fishing village famous for a large fishpond built by Kamehameha. The fishpond was filled in by an 1859 lava flow.

Cattle were shipped from here in the 1890s and there was once a small hotel. Now there are a few private homes on the bay, including one owned by country & western singer Loretta Lynn.

WAIKOLOA BEACH RESORT

Just after crossing into the South Kohala district, a single turn-off leads to the Royal Waikoloan and Hilton Waikoloa Village hotels and to Anaehoomalu Beach Park. The road is just south of the 76-mile marker.

Petroglyphs

As you drive into the resort there's a two-acre lava field etched with an impressive number of petroglyphs near the resort's golf course. They are off to the right, immediately before the Kings' Shops complex. If you park at the complex it's about a five-minute walk along a sign-posted path to the etchings.

Many of the petroglyphs date back to the 1500s. Some are graphic (humans, birds, canoes), others cryptic (dots and lines). Western influences show up in the form of horses and English initials.

Although the footpath that leads through the petroglyphs is called the King's Trail, this section is actually a horse and cattle trail built in the late 1800s. The trail once connected Kailua with Kawaihae. It's possible to continue on the trail to a historical preserve at the Mauna Lani Resort, about two miles away, but it's a hot unshaded walk over lava.

Anaehoomalu Beach

Anaehoomalu Beach is a long, sandy beach that curves along an attractive bay. The waters are popular for swimming and windsurfing and have a gently sloping sandy bottom. Winter weather can produce rip currents but most of the time the water is quite calm.

This is a fine beach for an outing if you're staying in Kona. The south end of the beach has public facilities, with showers, toilets, changing areas and parking. The north end of the beach fronts the Royal Waikoloan hotel.

Both ends of the bay are composed of prehistoric lava flows from Mauna Kea, with rough aa lava to the north and smooth pahoehoe to the south.

Anaehoomalu was once the site of royal fishponds and archaeologists from the Bishop Museum have found evidence of habitation dating back more than a thousand years.

There are two large fishponds just beyond the line of coconut trees on the beach. A short **trail** starts near the showers and winds by the fishponds, caves, ancient house platforms and a shrine. Interpretive plaques along the way explain the area's history.

The beach hut in front of the hotel has a good aerial photo showing the coral and rock formations in the bay and can give you the latest on water conditions. They rent windsurfing equipment for $20 an hour and give a 1½-hour lesson for $35. Snorkel sets rent for $6 an hour or $15 a day. They also have offer beginners' scuba lessons, boat dives, catamaran cruises, kayak rentals, glass-bottom boat rides and sailing.

Hilton Waikoloa Village

The 62-acre Hilton Waikoloa Village is the most extravagant resort development on the Big Island. It has the air of a sophisticated theme park and islanders have nicknamed it 'Disneyland'.

The hotel had no beach, so it built its own. There's a four-acre saltwater lagoon stocked with tropical fish, a 'river' with a current for rafting and a dolphin pool.

Canopied boats cart guests between buildings along artificial canals and there's a modernistic tram that looks like it was intended for downtown Tokyo. Because the complex is so large both actually do function as public transport and the novelty of using and waiting for them wears off quickly.

There's free parking at the hotel, but you can also walk over from the Royal Waikoloan, a quiet 15-minute stroll up the lava coast. As you climb up the back steps of the Hilton there are no clues as to what's on the other side of the fortress-like wall. Then suddenly you're in the midst of it all, crossing a rope walkway over sprawling swimming pools with cascading waterfalls and shrieking kids flying down a water-slide.

When it opened in 1988 the hotel billed itself as the world's most expensive resort at a cost of $360 million. But for all the extravagance it's surprisingly casual and anyone can cruise around in the free boats and tram.

The Hilton has a multimillion-dollar **art collection** along a mile-long walkway that runs in both directions from the front lobby. The museum-quality pieces include extensive collections from Melanesia, Polynesia and Asia.

They're particularly big on Papua New Guinea, with war clubs and spears, spirit boards, carved fighting shields and a partial replica of a ceremonial house. There's a collection of Han pottery that dates back 2000 years, antique dolls and Noh masks from Japan, 18th-century Burmese puppets and huge cloisonné vases. They've even managed to slip in a little Hawaiiana section next to the Palace Tower.

Places to Stay

The 545-room *Royal Waikoloan* (☎ 885-6789, (800) 688-7444; fax (800) 622-4852), Box 5300, Waikoloa, HI 96743, now part of the Outrigger chain, is a former Sheraton hotel. While this is the 'budget' hotel on the Waikoloa coast, with rooms beginning at $115 for a garden view, its beachside location is far superior to that of the Hilton's. The hotel also usually has a 'Drive for Five' deal that throws in a Budget rental car for $5 more – a good value for the Waikoloa area.

Hilton Waikoloa Village (☎ 885-1234, (800) 445-8667; fax 885-2902), 1 Waikoloa Beach Resort, Waikoloa, HI 96743, a mega-hotel with 1241 rooms, was developed by Chris Hemmeter and is the most indulgent of his Hawaii fantasy resorts. Rates start at $250 for garden views and $300 for ocean views and go up to $3000 for the presidential suite.

There are two upscale, fully equipped condominium complexes in the area, each with a pool but about a 15-minute walk to the beach. *The Bay Club* (☎ 885-7979, (800) 426-6367; fax 885-7780), 5525 Waikoloa Beach Dr, Waikoloa, HI 96743,

has one-bedroom units from $160/195 in the low/high season and two-bedroom units from $200/240. Complimentary continental breakfast and shuttle service to the beach is provided.

The Shores at Waikoloa (☎ 885-5001, (800) 922-7866), 5460 Waikoloa Beach Dr, Waikoloa, HI 96743, is an Aston-managed property. Rates start at $165/295 in the low/high season for a one-bedroom apartment, $210/240 for a two-bedroom apartment.

Places to Eat

The Kings' Shops has two fast-food shops, two sit-down restaurants and a small grocery store. In the food pavilion, *Subway Sandwiches* sells submarine sandwiches from 9:30 am to 9:30 pm and *Hawaiian Chili by Max* has inexpensive chili and hot dogs. *Hama Yu* has overpriced Japanese food, while the *Big Island Steak House*, open for dinner only, has steak and seafood dishes averaging $17.

The *Royal Terrace* in the Royal Waikoloan has a dinner special nightly for around $12. If you're seated between 5 and 6 pm the special includes salad and dessert, after 6 pm it's served a la carte. Otherwise most main courses are priced from $13 to $20.

Palm Terrace, in the Hilton, is open for breakfast from 6 to 11 am and for dinner from 5 to 9:30 pm. There are good quality buffets at both meals. Breakfast, which has a few Japanese touches as well as the standard American dishes and pastries, costs $16.50. Dinner, which is a different ethnic buffet (Polynesian, paniolo barbecue, Thai etc) each night, is $22. Children pay half price at both buffets. You can also order a la carte at either meal, with breakfast main courses or dinner salads and sandwiches priced around $9. It's a pleasant and somewhat casual setting overlooking a pond with exotic waterbirds. Ask for a swan-view table.

The Hilton also has fine-dining Japanese, Italian and continental restaurants. The most popular is *Donatoni's*, which has good Italian food. The cheapest pasta dish on the menu is fettucine alfredo at $19, while more exciting seafood dishes such as the cioppino cost $31. It's open from 6 to 10 pm.

Entertainment
The *Royal Waikoloan* has a luau at 6 pm on Sundays and Wednesdays. The cost of $42 for adults ($22 for children ages six to 12) includes dinner, an open bar and a Polynesian show.

The *Hilton Waikoloa Village* has a couple of bars, including the lounge at the Kamuela Provision Company where there's guitar music from 6 to 10 pm.

WAIKOLOA
Waikoloa village, about six miles inland from the beach, is a modern residential development and bedroom community for workers in the nearby resorts. Although there's not much of interest for visitors passing through, the village does have half a dozen condo complexes, a golf course, horse stables, a shopping center, a gas station and a bank.

The 12-mile Waikoloa Rd connecting Hwy 190 and Hwy 19 runs through the village.

Places to Stay
Waikoloa Villas (☎ 883-8855, (800) 998-8248; fax 883-0041), Box 38-3280, Waikoloa, HI 96738, is a quiet low-rise condo development fronting the Waikoloa Village Golf Club. One-bedroom units cost $99/115 in the low/high season, two-bedroom units cost $109/125 for up to four people and three-bedroom units cost $149/165 for up to six people. The minimum stay is two nights. Units have full kitchens and lanais, and there are two pools.

Elima Lani (☎ 883-8288, (800) 551-5264; fax 883-8170), 68-3883 Lua Kula St, Kamuela, HI 96743, is a modern 216-unit condo complex that's also on the golf course. It's not upmarket but all units have two bedrooms with queen beds, two baths and the usual amenities including kitchens with microwaves, washer/dryers etc. There are swimming pools and a spa. The daily

rate is $98, with a two-night minimum, the weekly rate $625. Up to six people are allowed in the unit for these rates, although there's just a regular sofa, not a sofa bed, in the living room.

Places to Eat
The Waikoloa Highlands Shopping Center on Waikoloa Rd has a small food court with a deli, pizzeria, yogurt shop and grocery store.

The shopping center also contains a sit-down restaurant, *Highlands Bar-B-Que & Bar*, which has burgers and fries for $6 at lunch (11 am to 2 pm) and barbecued ribs, grilled fish and chicken fried steak with gravy for under $10 at dinner (5 to 9 pm).

MAUNA LANI RESORT
After a brief encounter with coconut palms and bright bougainvilleas at the highway entrance, Mauna Lani Dr heads through a long stretch of lava with virtually no vegetation. Halfway along there's a strikingly green golf course sculptured into the black lava. Mauna Lani Bay Hotel is at the end of the road. The Ritz-Carlton Mauna Lani hotel and Holoholokai Beach Park are to the north.

Mauna Lani Bay Hotel
The hotel is ritzy but still low-key, a modern open-air structure centered around a breezy atrium which holds waterways, orchid sprays and full-grown coconut trees. A saltwater stream which runs through the hotel and outdoors into the sun holds small black-tipped sharks and a variety of colorful reef fish.

The hotel has good beaches and historical sights and there's public access to both. A free, self-guided trail map is available at the concierge desk. The hotel is welcoming and relaxed, a pleasant contrast to some of the stuffier resort hotels in the area. One-hour historical tours are given a couple of times a week and are free to the public. Call 885-6622 for the latest schedule.

Beaches The beach in front of the Mauna Lani Bay Hotel is protected but the water is rather shallow. There's a coral reef beyond the inlet that snorkelers might want to explore. Check at the hotel beach hut for water conditions.

There's also a spring-fed pool and a less-frequented cove down by the Beach Club restaurant, a 15-minute walk to the south.

An old **coastal foot trail** leads about a mile farther south to **Honokaope Bay**. It passes by a few historical sites, including a fishers' house site and other village remains. The southern end of Honokaope Bay is protected and good for swimming and snorkeling when the seas are calm.

Fishponds The ancient Kalahuipuaa fishponds are along the beach just south of the hotel in a shady grove of coconut palms and milo trees.

The ponds are stocked with awa, or milkfish. Water circulates from the ocean through traditional makaha sluice gates which allow small fish to enter but keep the older fattened ones from leaving. The fish sporadically jump into the air and slap down on the water, an exercise which knocks off parasites.

These are among the few continuously working fishponds in Hawaii and awa from here have been used to provide stock for commercial fisheries.

Historic Trail The Kalahuipuaa Trail begins at a parking area opposite the resort's little grocery store, which is mauka of the Mauna Lani Bay Hotel.

The trail meanders through a Hawaiian settlement that dates from the 1500s. There are cave shelters, a few petroglyphs and other archaeological and geological sites marked by interpretive plaques.

It's a neat little walk that ends at the fishponds and the beach. If you loop around the largest fishpond and head back the round trip is about 1½ miles.

Holoholokai Beach Park
Holoholokai Beach Park, north of the Ritz-Carlton Mauna Lani, is rocky with a mix of coral chunks and lava. It's not a great bathing beach, although when the waters are

calm there's reasonable snorkeling in the area and sometimes some good surf breaks in winter.

The park has showers, drinking water, restrooms, picnic tables and grills and is open from 6:30 am to 7 pm.

For those not picnicking, the main reason for visiting the park is to walk the trail to the Puako petroglyphs. To get there, take Mauna Lani Dr and turn right at the rotary, then right again on the beach road immediately before the grounds of the Ritz-Carlton.

Puako Petroglyphs With more than 3000 petroglyphs, the Puako petroglyph preserve has one of the largest collections of ancient lava carvings in Hawaii.

From the north end of the beach parking lot, a well-marked trail leads to the petroglyphs three-quarters of a mile away.

The human figures drawn in simple linear forms are some of Hawaii's oldest such drawings. Those with triangular shapes and curved forms are from more recent times.

The aging petroglyphs are fragile as they're carved into an ancient lava flow which is brittle and cracking. Stepping on the petroglyphs can damage them, so be careful not to. The only safe way to record them is with a camera. If you want to make rubbings there are some authentically reproduced petroglyphs just a minute's walk down the trail from the parking lot that have been made for that purpose.

Because of the sharp kiawe thorns along the trail, flip-flops (thongs) are not appropriate footwear for the walk – the thorns can easily pierce their soft soles and your feet.

Places to Stay
The *Mauna Lani Bay Hotel* (☎ 885-6622, (800) 367-2323), Box 4000, Kohala, HI 96743, is one of the finest resort hotels in the islands. Rates for the 350 rooms start at $275 for a garden view, $375 for an ocean view.

The luxury *Mauna Lani Point* condos at Mauna Lani Resort are booked through

Classic Resorts (☎ 667-1400, (800) 642-6284), 50 Nohea Kai Dr, Lahaina, HI 96761. One-bedroom units start at $210/250 in the low/high season.

The *Ritz-Carlton Mauna Lani* (☎ 885-2000, (800) 845-9905), 1 N Kaniku Dr, Kohala, HI 96743, on Pauoa Bay, has the requisite statuary on the grounds and art in the lobby. Rates for the 542 rooms start at $285 for a garden view, $400 for an ocean view.

Places to Eat

The Cafe at the Ritz-Carlton is an upscale cafe-style restaurant with an open-air setting and excellent food. Creative appetizers and salads are priced under $10, pizzas cost $12 and Asian-Hawaiian entrees average about $20. The cafe also serves breakfast and has a Sunday brunch for $25.

The best Sunday brunch in the Waikoloa area is at the Mauna Lani Bay Hotel's (☎ 885-6622) open-air *Bay Terrace*. It has a sushi and sashimi table, waffles and omelets to order, prime rib, seafood dishes and a good variety of fruits and salads. To finish it off there's a great-looking dessert table. The buffet is served from 11:30 am to 2 pm and costs $24.50.

The *Canoe House*, which has a nice al fresco setting fronting the beach at the side of the Mauna Lani Bay Hotel, is very popular, in large part due to the reputation of its former chef, Alan Wong. Wong, however, has moved to the *Le Soleil* restaurant inside the hotel, so if the food is more important than the setting, Le Soleil is the better bet. Its menu blends Mediterranean, Far East and Hawaiian influences. Both restaurants have extensive seafood offerings and are quite pricey; expect dinner for two to cost around $100 without drinks.

For someplace easier on the wallet, there's the *Beach Club*, a casual restaurant and bar at the south end of Kaniku Dr. The restaurant, which fronts a nice little swimming cove, has burgers and fries for $7.50 and Mexican dishes with rice and beans for $12. It's open Sunday to Thursday from 11 am to 8:30 pm, Friday and Saturday until 4 pm.

PUAKO

Puako is a quiet one-road coastal village where everyone either lives on the beach or across the street from it.

Puako is lined with giant **tide pools**. The sea washes in and stays in the swirls and dips of the pahoehoe lava that forms the coastline. Some of the pools are deep enough to shelter live coral and diverse marine life. Snorkeling can be excellent, although the surf is usually too rough in winter. A narrow beach of pulverized coral and lava lines much of the shoreline.

The turn-off to Puako is marked on Hwy 19 and you can also reach Puako from Hapuna Beach State Park along a passable route that's more patchwork than road.

Hoku Loa Church, which dates back to 1858, is about half a mile beyond the Puako Bay boat ramp. A plain plastered building with a few simple wooden pews, it's still used for Sunday services but at other times it's usually locked up tight.

There are several shoreline access signs, but the easiest beach access is at the end of the village where the old road meets a section of new pavement, about three miles from Hwy 19. Here a short dirt drive leads to the water. A couple of minutes' walk along the beach to the north will bring you to a few petroglyphs, a konane game board chinked into the lava and tide pools deep enough to cool off in.

HAPUNA BEACH

The long beautiful stretch of white sand along Hapuna Bay is the Big Island's most popular beach.

When it's calm, Hapuna Beach State Park has good swimming, snorkeling and diving. In the winter it's a hot bodysurfing and boogie boarding beach. The high winter surf can produce strong currents close to the shore and a pounding shorebreak. Waves over three feet should be left for the experts. Hapuna has had numerous drownings and many of the victims have been tourists unfamiliar with the water conditions.

There's a tiny cove with a small sandy beach about five minutes' walk to the north

Anti-Development Sentiments

The leeward coast of the Big Island harbors some of the finest undeveloped beaches in Hawaii. Not surprisingly these beaches are a major source of contention between islanders who want to preserve them in a natural state and overseas developers who want to wrap them in golf courses and luxury hotels.

In the late 1980s Hapuna, the most popular local beach on the island, was the focus of a major struggle between pro-development forces, who favored the construction of a resort here, and environmentalists and beachgoers who wanted to keep Hapuna free of all development. The latter initiated a 'Save Hapuna Beach' campaign that resulted in an island-wide ballot initiative on the future of the beach. Many islanders saw the issue as a choice between preservation or jobs. The initiative, which would have spared the beach from development, failed by a narrow margin and in 1994 a new resort opened at the north end of Hapuna Beach. ■

of the park. The water is a bit calmer there and in winter there's less sand kicked up by the waves.

The 61-acre state park includes the beach, A-frame cabins for overnight stays and a landscaped park with picnic facilities, showers, restrooms, drinking water and telephones.

There's a snack bar, open from 10 am to 5 pm daily, which sells burgers, beverages and ice cream. A window at the side rents boogie boards for $7 for two hours, snorkel sets for $6 a day. As part of the agreement with the state the concessionaire staffs lifeguards at the beach from 8 am to 5 pm daily.

Hapuna to Mauna Kea

An easy trail runs along the craggy coast from the north end of Hapuna Beach to the south end of Kaunaoa (Mauna Kea) Beach. As part of the trail goes through stands of kiawe, watch out for sharp thorns that can easily puncture flip-flops (thongs). The walk takes about 20 minutes.

Places to Stay & Eat

The 350-room *Hapuna Beach Prince Hotel* (☎ 882-1111, (800) 882-6060; fax 882-1174), 1 Mauna Kea Beach Dr, Waikoloa, HI 96743, opened in 1994 at the northern end of Hapuna Beach with room rates of $325 to $800. The hotel has a golf course, restaurants and cocktail lounge.

MAUNA KEA BEACH

In the early 1960s, Laurance Rockefeller obtained a 99-year lease on the land around Kaunaoa Bay from his friend Richard Smart, owner of Parker Ranch. Five years later he opened Mauna Kea Beach Hotel, the first luxury hotel on the outer islands, at the north side of this bay.

Kaunaoa Bay is a gorgeous crescent bay with a white sand beach that has since come to be known as Mauna Kea Beach. It has a gradual slope and fine swimming conditions most of the year. There's good snorkeling on the north side when it's calm.

The Mauna Kea Beach Hotel, now part of the same Prince Hotels chain that runs the new resort on Hapuna Beach, is closed for renovations until early 1996. The beach remains open to the public.

SPENCER BEACH PARK

Spencer Beach Park is a family beach park off Hwy 270, just south of Kawaihae. The shallow sandy beach is protected by a reef and by the jetty to the north. If anything, it's a bit too protected and the water tends to get silty.

The rocky south end of the beach past the pavilion is better for snorkeling, although entry is not as easy.

Spencer is a well-used beach park with a lifeguard station, picnic tables, toilets, showers, drinking water and changing rooms. Camping is allowed with a permit from the county. During the week, Hilo people who work on this side of the island sometimes camp here instead of commuting. On weekends quite a few families show up.

PUUKOHOLA HEIAU

The Puukohola Heiau National Historic Site, which is off the side of the road that leads down to Spencer Beach, contains the last major temple built in Hawaii.

In 1790, after his attempt at a sweeping conquest of the islands was thwarted, King Kamehameha sought the advice of Kapoukahi, a soothsayer from Kauai.

Kamehameha was told that if he built a temple to his war god here above Kawaihae Bay, then all of Hawaii would fall to him in battle. Kamehameha immediately began construction of Puukohola Heiau, completing it in 1791.

Kamehameha then held a dedication ceremony and invited his last rival on the Big Island, Keoua, the chief of Kau. When Keoua came ashore he was killed and brought up to the temple as the first offering to the gods. With Keoua's death Kamehameha had sole control of the Big Island, and he went on to fulfill the prophecy by conquering the other Hawaiian islands.

Puukohola Heiau, terraced in three steps, was covered with wooden idols and thatched structures, including an oracle tower, altar, drum house and the home of the high priest.

After Kamehameha's death in 1819, his son Liholiho and powerful widow Kaahumanu destroyed the heiau's wooden images and the temple was abandoned. These days only the basic rock foundation remains, but it's still an impressive site.

Puukohola means 'Hill of the Whales'. Migrating humpbacks can often be seen offshore during winter.

The visitor center (☎ 882-7218), which is open from 7:30 am to 4 pm daily, has a few simple displays and someone on duty to provide a brief introduction to the park. A free brochure describes the historic sites that are spread over the park's 77 acres. There are no entrance fees.

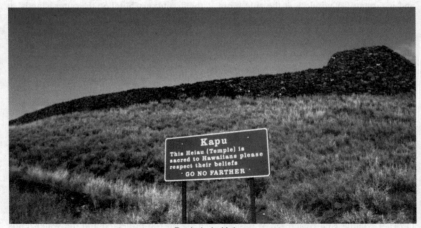

Puukohola Heiau

A trail to the heiau starts at the visitor center and takes less than 10 minutes to walk.

Just beyond Puukohola Heiau are the ruins of Mailekini Heiau, which predates Puukohola and was later turned into a fort by Kamehameha. Nearby, a heiau dedicated to shark gods lays submerged just offshore and you can still see the stone leaning post where the high chief watched sharks bolt down the offerings he made.

The path continues down by the creek to Kamehameha's former house site. Warbling silverbills, doves and mosquitoes frequent the kiawe woods, but there's not much to see.

The trail then leads across the highway to the site of John Young's homestead. Young, a shipwrecked British sailor, served Kamehameha as a military advisor and governor of the island. There's not much to see there either.

KAWAIHAE

Kawaihae has the Big Island's second largest deep-water commercial harbor. The harbor has fuel tanks and cattle pens and a little local beach park. There's not really much to attract visitors and most stop in Kawaihae just long enough to eat and fuel up on their way to somewhere else.

Kawaihae Center on Hwy 270 has two restaurants, an ice cream and shave ice shop, a 7-Eleven store and Kohala Divers.

Places to Eat

Cafe Pesto (☎ 882-1071) serves up good gourmet pizza, calzones, seafood pastas and salads. The Greek pizza is topped with feta cheese, fresh spinach, olives and peppers, while the Oriental pizza has sun-dried tomatoes, Japanese eggplant and roasted garlic. Both cost $10 for a 10-inch pizza, $15 for a 12-inch. The cafe is on the lower level of the Kawaihae Center and is open from 11 am to 9 pm on weekdays, to 10 pm on weekends. It can get pretty busy at lunchtime, as it's a favorite spot for people working in the Waikoloa area.

There's more standard fare at *Tres Hombres Beach Grill*, also in the Kawaihae

Center, which specializes in Mexican food. Sandwiches and lunch dishes are around $7, dinner plates about $10. It's open from 11:30 am to 9 pm, but closed on Tuesdays.

North Kohala

The northwest tip of the Big Island is dominated by a central ridge, the Kohala Mountains.

The leeward side of the ridge is dry and desert-like. The windward side is wet and lush with steep coastal cliffs and spectacularly cut hanging valleys.

North Kohala is often bypassed by travelers as it's off the main track, but it has a couple of impressive historical sites, a few sleepy towns to poke around in and a lovely valley lookout at the end of the road.

There are two ways to get to North Kohala, an inland road and a coastal road. You can make a nice tour by going up one and down the other.

WAIMEA TO HAWI (HWY 250)

Hwy 250 (Kohala Mountain Rd) runs north for 20 miles from Waimea to Hawi. This is a very scenic drive along the upland slopes of the Kohala Mountains. The road is lined in places with ironwood trees and goes through rolling green hills dotted with grazing cattle. At its northern end there's even a little llama farm.

As you head north, Maui rises out of the mist, with the crater of Haleakala showing up red. Mauna Kea and Mauna Loa are visible behind you. There are expansive views of the coast and Kawaihae Harbor below and a scenic pull-off where you can take it all in.

There are also a couple of new subdivisions up this way, the largest being Kohala Ranch.

Hwy 250 peaks at 3564 feet before dropping down into Hawi.

Kohala Ranch

Kohala Ranch is a residential subdivision that was once part of a real ranch. A few

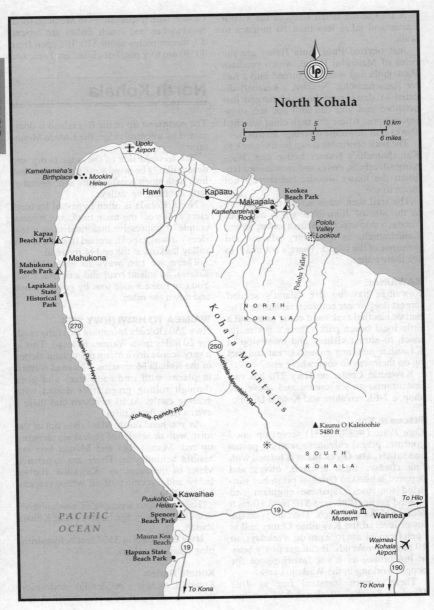

North Kohala

0   5   10 km
0   3   6 miles

Upolu
Airport

Kamehameha's
Birthplace • • Mookini
Heiau

Hawi

Kapaau

Makapala

Keokea
Beach Park

Kamehameha
Rock

Pololu
Valley
Lookout

Kapaa
Beach Park

Mahukona
Beach Park • Mahukona

Lapakahi
State
Historical
Park

Pololu Valley

N O R T H

K O H A L A

270

Kohala Mountains

250

Akoni Pule Hwy

Kohala Mountain Rd

Kohala Ranch Rd

▲ Kaunu O Kaleioohie
5480 ft

S O U T H

K O H A L A

Puukohola
Heiau

Kawaihae

PACIFIC
OCEAN

Spencer
Beach Park

Mauna Kea
Beach

Hapuna State
Beach Park

19

To Hilo

Kamuela
Museum

Waimea

Waimea-
Kohala
Airport

190

To Kona

To Kona

years back it was zoned agricultural, subdivided into lots of three to 10 acres and sold to people looking to build second homes in the country.

Despite severe water shortages, a large tract of the 'ranch' was later rezoned as urban with plans for 1500 new residential units, a shopping village and a 27-hole golf course. If allowed to go through, the project could result in a doubling of the current population of the entire North Kohala district! Disgruntled homeowners have thus far kept the development plans at bay with legal challenges.

Kohala Ranch Rd runs through the subdivision for six miles, connecting Hwy 250 and Hwy 270.

KAWAIHAE TO POLOLU VALLEY (HWY 270)

Hwy 270 (Akoni Pule Hwy), which starts in Kawaihae, takes in the coastal sights of Lapakahi State Historical Park and Mookini Heiau and ends at a lookout above Pololu Valley.

There's a trail down to the valley floor, but even if you're not up for a hike the view from the lookout is worth the drive.

Lapakahi State Historical Park

This park has the overall feel of an abandoned ghost town – which it is. Even the visitors in this desolate spot tend to be few.

This remote fishing village was settled about 600 years ago and as the terrain was rocky and dry, the villagers turned to the sea for their food. The cove provided a safe year-round canoe landing and fish were plentiful.

Eventually some of the villagers moved to the wetter uplands and began to farm, trading their crops for fish with those who had stayed on the coast. In the process, Lapakahi grew into an ahupuaa, a wedge-shaped division of land stretching down from the mountainous interior out to the sea. A stone-lined trail still leads four miles upland from the park.

In the 19th century Lapakahi's freshwater table began to drop. This, coupled with the enticement of jobs in developing towns, led to the desertion of the village.

Lapakahi was a big village and this is a good-sized park. Trails lead to the remains of stone walls, house sites and canoe sheds.

The park encourages visitors to imagine what life was like centuries ago. People worshipped at fish shrines, a few of which still remain on the grounds. Displays show how fishers used lift nets to catch opelu, a technique still practiced today, and how the salt used to preserve the fish was dried in stone salt pans.

There's a hands-on approach to Hawaiian games. Game pieces and instructions are laid out for *oo ihe* (spear throwing), *konane* (Hawaiian checkers) and *ulu maika* (stone bowling), the object of the latter being to roll a round stone between two stakes.

Most of the trees in the park were used for medicine, food or construction and many are labeled.

The park, which is just south of the 14-mile marker, is open from 8 am to 4 pm daily except on holidays. Trail brochures are available at the trailhead. Admission is free.

The park is largely unshaded so it can be hot walking around. While the park service often has a cooler of drinking water available, there's no running water in the park so it's a good idea to bring something to drink.

Lapakahi's waters are part of a marine life conservation district. The fish are so plentiful and the water so clear that you can stand above the shoreline and watch yellow tangs and other colorful fish swim around in the cove below. The coral is also good and there's excellent snorkeling inside the cove when it's calm. However, outside the cove there are dangerous currents.

Mahukona Beach Park

Mahukona Beach Park is one mile north of Lapakahi and half a mile off Hwy 270. It's the site of an abandoned landing that was once linked by railroad to the sugar mills on the north Kohala coast.

This county park has restrooms, showers, picnic tables and a grassy camping area that can get a bit buggy. If you're camping bring drinking water with you, as the water here is unfit to drink.

The area beyond the landing makes for interesting snorkeling and diving, although it's usually too rough in winter. Entry is in about five feet of water. Heading north, it's possible to follow an anchor chain out to a submerged boiler and the remains of a ship in about 25 feet of water. There's coral on the bottom and visibility is good when it's calm. There's a shower near the ladder where you can rinse off.

Kapaa Beach Park

Kapaa Beach Park is 1¼ miles north of Mahukona and nearly a mile off Hwy 270. Its biggest selling point is its view of Maui.

Camping is allowed but there's no sand beach, facilities are limited and it's rather dumpy.

MOOKINI HEIAU

Mookini is a massive heiau set atop a grassy knoll on the desolate northern tip of the Big Island. One of the oldest and most historically significant heiaus in Hawaii, it commands a clear view out across the ocean to Maui. This windswept site has a sense of timelessness and a certain eerie aura.

Chants date Mookini Heiau back to 480 AD. This is a luakini heiau, where the alii offered human sacrifices to the war god Ku.

According to legend, it was built in one night with basalt stones from Pololu Valley which were passed along a human chain stretching 14 miles.

A kapu which once prevented commoners from entering the heiau grounds was lifted only a decade ago. Not many people come this way and it will probably just be you, the wind and the spirits here.

The heiau is 250 feet long, with rock walls reaching a good 25 feet high. The entrance through the wall into the heiau itself is on the west side. The long enclosure on the right immediately before the heiau entrance was the home of the *mu*, or body catcher, who secured sacrificial victims for the heiau altar. The large

scallop-shaped altar on the north end of the heiau is thought to have been added by Paao, a Tahitian priest who arrived around the 12th century and introduced human sacrifice to Hawaiian worship.

The current kahuna nui priestess is Leimomi Mookini Lum, the most recent in a long line of Mookinis tracing their lineage back to the temple's first high priest.

To get there turn left off Hwy 270 at the 20-mile marker and go two miles down to Upolu Airport. At the airport turn left onto the road that runs parallel to the coast. Although it's usually passable, this red dirt road is rutted and bumpy and can get very muddy after heavy rains. After 1½ miles you'll come to a fork. The left road leads up to the heiau, a quarter of a mile farther.

Kamehameha's Birthplace

Kamehameha the Great was said to have been born on a stormy winter night in 1758 on this ruggedly desolate coast. If you continue straight ahead at the fork below the heiau for a third of a mile, you'll reach the stone enclosure that marks his birthsite.

According to one story, Kamehameha's mother was told by a kahuna that her son would become a destroyer of chiefs and a powerful ruler. The high chief of the island didn't take well to the prophecy and in a King Herod-like scenario he ordered the newborn killed.

Immediately after birth, the baby was taken to Mookini Heiau for his birth rituals and then into hiding in the nearby mountains.

HAWI

Hawi (pronounced Hah-vee), with a population of less than 1000, is the largest town in North Kohala. It has a post office, a couple of grocery stores and gas stations, a coin laundry, a video arcade and a few restaurants.

North Kohala used to be sugar country and Hawi was the biggest of half a dozen sugar towns. Kohala Sugar Company, which had incorporated all of the mills, closed down its operations in 1975. Hawi now has more storefronts than stores and although some people are beginning to be drawn this way by the area's lower property values it's still a very low-key place.

The park on Hwy 250 in front of the post office is cool and shady with giant banyan trees. Behind the park is the old sugar mill tower, a remnant of the town's former mainstay. You can still see the occasional strip of feral cane amongst the pastures outside town.

Places to Eat
Ohana Pizza on Hwy 270 has pizza, sandwiches, lasagna and a country & western atmosphere.

Kohala Health Food, on Hwy 270 opposite Ohana Pizza, is a small health food store that sells bulk and packaged health foods as well as a bit of organic fruit.

Bamboo, immediately north of the health food store, is the best place in town to eat. At lunch there are items such as chicken satay with rice, a vegetarian black bean tostada or burgers and fries, each for $6.50. At dinner, chicken or ribs cost around $10. It's closed on Sundays and Mondays.

KAPAAU
The statue of Kamehameha the Great on the front lawn of the North Kohala Civic Center may look familiar. Its lei-draped and much-photographed twin stands opposite the Iolani Palace in Honolulu.

The statue was made in 1880 in Florence, Italy, by American sculptor Thomas Gould. The ship delivering it sank off the Falkland Islands, so another statue was cast from the original mold. The duplicate statue arrived in the islands in 1883 and took its place in downtown Honolulu.

Later the sunken statue was recovered from the ocean floor and completed its trip to Hawaii. This original statue was then sent here, to Kamehameha's childhood home, where it stands watching the traffic trickle along in quiet Kapaau.

Kapaau has a new courthouse and police station and Kamehameha Park which includes a large, modern gymnasium and everything from a ballpark to a swimming pool. The town has a little library, a Bank of Hawaii and a couple of interesting shops.

Still, it's an aging town. The only crowd is at the senior center, which is part of the civic center. The senior citizens often staff a table on the porch with visitor information.

Kalahikiola Church
Protestant missionaries Elias and Ellen Bond, who arrived in Kohala in 1841, built Kalahikiola Church in 1855. An earthquake damaged it in 1973 but it's since been restored and the church is still in use today.

If you want to take a look, turn mauka off Hwy 270 onto a narrow road half a mile east of the Kamehameha statue, near the 24-mile marker. The church is about half a mile up from the highway.

The land and buildings on the drive in to the church are part of the Bond estate, proof enough that the missionary life wasn't one of total deprivation.

If the doors of the church seem to be locked it's because they don't push or pull, but rather slide open.

Kamehameha Rock
Kamehameha Rock is on the right-hand side of the road, about two miles east of Kapaau, on a curve just over a small bridge. It's said that Kamehameha carried this rock uphill from the beach below to demonstrate his strength.

A road crew once attempted to move the rock to a different location, but although they managed to get it up onto a wagon the rock fell off – an obvious sign it wanted to stay where it was. Not wanting to upset Kamehameha's mana, the workers left the rock in place.

Tong Wo Society
Immediately around the corner from Kamehameha Rock is the colorful building of the Kohala Tong Wo Society, founded in 1886. Hawaii once had many Chinese societies which provided immigrants with a place to preserve their cultural identity,

speak their native language and socialize. This is the last one remaining on the Big Island. The building is not open to the public.

The two-story green building next door, once the Wo On Store, now houses the Wo On Gallery, which has a nice collection of arts and crafts made solely by North Kohala residents.

Places to Stay

The *Wo On Guest House* is a simple apartment tucked behind the Wo On Gallery, east of Kapaau town. It's unpretentious but comfortable, roomy and light. There's a living room, a full kitchen and a separate bedroom looking out onto the woods. The cost is $50/250 a day/week. Smoking is not allowed indoors. The apartment is rented through gallery owner Lesley Patton (☎ 889-5002), PO Box 1065, Kapaau, HI 96755, and if her unit is full she can usually refer you to another place in the North Kohala area for about the same rate.

A much more modest possibility is at the old girls school at the Bond Estate, half a mile up the dirt road beyond the Kalahiki-ola Church. These are very simple rooms in a collection of neglected buildings; the bathroom is shared and prices are $25/35 for singles/doubles. There's limited use of a kitchen, but there's no refrigerator and you'll have to bring your own pots and pans. For information call 889-5217 or 889-5028.

Places to Eat

Don's Family Deli, in the town center on Hwy 270, is the best place to eat in Kapaau. Mahimahi sandwiches, quiche with salad or tofu burgers cost $5. They also have meat and cheese sandwiches, Portuguese bean soup, espresso and fruit smoothies. It's open from 8 am to 6 pm on weekdays, 10 am to 5 pm on weekends.

For dessert you could walk down the street to *Tropical Dreams* for a scoop of gourmet ice cream or sorbet. Tropical Dreams also makes delicious macadamia nut butters including a nice ambrosia variety with chunks of pineapple, currants and almonds. They're made and sold here, although the butters can also be bought in specialty shops around the island and make a great gift.

Mit's Drive-In, just east of Kapaau Post Office, next to H Naito general store, has inexpensive breakfasts, plate lunches and burgers.

MAKAPALA

The little village of Makapala has a few hundred residents. The last place to get anything to drink before Pololu Valley is just past the Episcopal retreat center, where there's a soda machine on the left side of the road.

Keokea Beach Park

Keokea Beach Park is on a somewhat

Kohala Ditch

Kohala Ditch is an intricate series of ditches, tunnels and flumes that were built to carry water from the rugged wet interior of the Kohala Forest Reserve out to the Hawi area. The source of the water is the Waikaloa Stream, midway between the Pololu and Waipio valleys.

The ditch was built in 1906 to irrigate Kohala sugar cane fields. The last Kohala cane was cut in the 1970s, but the ditch continues to be a source of water for Kohala ranches and farms.

It was engineered by a sugar man, John Hind, with the financial backing of Samuel Parker of Parker Ranch. Kohala Ditch runs 22½ miles and was built by Japanese immigrant laborers who were paid about $1 a day for the hazardous work. More than a dozen of those laborers died during the construction.

There were once miles of mule trails along the ditch which were used for maintenance, but the trails are now overgrown.

Much of the ditch runs through 19,000 acres of Kohala land which the agricultural giant Castle & Cooke recently sold to a Japanese developer. ■

Black sand beach fronting Pololo Valley

scenic rocky coast. There's no sandy beach and it's not great for water activities.

The park is most active on weekends and camping is allowed, with a county permit, on the grassy section below the pavilion. There are covered picnic tables, restrooms, showers, drinking water, barbecue grills and electricity.

The marked turn-off is about 1½ miles before Pololu Valley Lookout. The park is about a mile in from the highway.

There's an old Japanese cemetery on the way down to the park. Most of the gravestones are in kanji (Japanese script) and a few have filled sake cups in front of them.

POLOLU VALLEY

Hwy 270 ends at a scenic viewpoint looking down into Pololu Valley and out along the steep scalloped coastal cliffs to the east. With its high vantage the lookout has the kind of strikingly beautiful angle that's rarely experienced without a helicopter tour.

Pololu was once thickly planted with wetland taro. Pololu Stream fed the valley,

carrying heavy rainfall from the remote interior to the valley floor. When the Kohala Ditch was built, it siphoned off much of the water and put an end to the taro production. The last islanders left the valley in the 1940s and the valley slopes are now forest reserve land.

Pololu Valley Trail

The trail from the lookout down to Pololu Valley only takes about 20 minutes to walk. It's steep and can be hot walking, but it's not overly strenuous. However much of the trail is packed clay that can be slippery when wet.

Cattle and horses roam in the valley. There's a gate at the bottom of the trail which keeps them in.

The black sand beach fronting the valley stretches for about half a mile. Driftwood collects in great quantities and on rare occasions glass fishing floats get washed up as well.

Surf is usually high in winter and although it's a bit tamer in summer, there can be rip currents year round.

Waimea

Waimea has a pretty setting in the foothills of the Kohala Mountains at an elevation of 2670 feet. It's cooler than the coast, with more clouds and fog. The area has gentle rolling hills and frequent afternoon rainbows.

This is the headquarters of Parker Ranch, Hawaii's largest cattle ranch, which spreads across nearly one-ninth of the Big Island. Almost everything in Waimea is owned by, run by or leased by Parker Ranch.

Waimea has its cowboy influences, but it's rapidly growing and becoming more sophisticated. It's the main town serving the new subdivisions being developed on former ranches in the Kohala Mountains. While many of the newcomers are wealthy mainlanders, Waimea is also home to a number of the international astronomers who work on Mauna Kea.

The Keck office in the town center has a skyline display and a model of its observatory that visitors can stop by and see during business hours (8 am to 5 pm weekdays).

Waimea has a couple of good dining spots and galleries, but it's not a big tourist town with a lot of action or sightseeing attractions. The museums are nice for a short visit and the green pastures are scenic, but for most visitors Waimea is just a stopover on the drive between Kona and Hilo.

Information

Waimea is also referred to as **Kamuela**, which is the Hawaiian spelling of Samuel. Although some say the name comes from an early postmaster named Samuel Spencer, most claim it's for Samuel Parker of Parker Ranch fame. The result is the same: confusing. Address all Waimea mail to Kamuela.

The Waimea-Kohala Airport is off Hwy 190, 1¾ miles south from the intersection of Hwy 19 and is mainly used for sightseeing flights and charter purposes.

Parker Ranch

Parker Ranch claims to be the nation's largest privately owned ranch. It has 225,000 acres, 55,000 head of cattle and about 50 ranch hands. The ranch accounts for 80% of the livestock marketed in Hawaii.

The first cattle to arrive in Hawaii were a gift to Kamehameha from British captain George Vancouver in 1793. Vancouver convinced the king to place a 10-year kapu on the killing of cattle to ensure the preservation of the herd.

The kapu worked but the cattle ran wild and multiplied so quickly that they became an uncontrollable and destructive nuisance to both crops and native forests. Feral cattle still roam Mauna Kea's slopes today.

Parker Ranch owes its beginnings to John Palmer Parker, a 19-year-old from New England who arrived on the Big Island in 1809 aboard a whaler. He took one look at Hawaii and jumped ship.

Parker soon gained the favor of Kamehameha, who commissioned him to bring the cattle under control. Parker managed to domesticate some of the cattle and butchered others, cutting the herds down to size.

Later, Parker married one of Kamehameha's granddaughters and in the process landed himself a tidy bit of land. He eventually gained control of the entire Waikoloa ahupuaa clear down to the sea.

Descendants of the Mexican-Spanish cowboys brought over to help round up the cattle still work the ranches today. (The Hawaiian word for cowboy, 'paniolo', is a corruption of the Spanish word 'españoles'.)

Parker Ranch Historical Homes

Parker Ranch has two historic homes open to visitors at **Puuopelu**, a mini-estate on the ranch.

You can tour the estate's century-old manor which has an interesting collection of European art and antique Chinese vases. One room is French provincial with chandeliers, skylights and walls hung with

To Honokaa, Hilo

To Kamuela Museum,
Kawaihae, North Kohala

19

Mean
Cuisine

Kamuela
Inn

Waimea
Park

Merriman's

Edelweiss

Parker
Ranch
Lodge

Parker Ranch
Shopping Center

Bank of Hawaii

24-hr
Gas Station

Keck
Office

Imiola
Church

Waimea
Center

Parker Ranch
Historical Homes

190

Paniolo Park
(rodeo site)

Waimea-Kohala Airport

To Kona

Waimea (Kamuela)

0   .5   1 km

0   .25   .5 miles

---

paintings by French impressionists, including works by Renoir, Degas and Pissarro.

You can also visit the more modest **Mana Hale**, the original Parker home, which has been reconstructed next door to the manor. Originally built in the 1840s by John Parker in the hills seven miles outside Waimea, it's essentially of saltbox construction, a popular design in Parker's native Massachusetts where the sloping roof deflects winter's cold northeast winds. The house is simple and aesthetically striking with walls, ceilings and floors made entirely of koa. It is decorated with period

furnishings and interesting old photos of the hardy-looking Parker clan. The interior of Mana Hale was dismantled board by board and rebuilt here at Puuopelu but the exterior is a replica.

The turn-off to the homes is on Hwy 190, about three-quarters of a mile south of its intersection with Hwy 19. Hours are 10 am to 5 pm daily and admission costs $7.50 for adults, $3.75 for children.

Parker Ranch Visitor Center

Parker Ranch Visitor Center, in the Parker Ranch Shopping Center, is a little museum of the ranch's history showcasing Parker family memorabilia such as portraits, lineage charts, quilts and dishes. There's a little cowboy hut with saddles and branding irons.

There are also stone adzes, lava bowls, poi pounders, tapa bed covers and other Hawaiian artifacts, although for Hawaiiana alone other Big Island museums have more extensive collections.

Actually the museum is not terribly dynamic. Perhaps most interesting are the old photos and the 20-minute movie on Parker Ranch, including footage of cowboys rushing cattle into the sea and lifting them by slings onto the decks of waiting steamers.

The museum is open from 9 am to 5 pm daily. Admission costs $5 for adults, $3.75 for children. A ticket that includes this museum and the Parker Ranch Historical Homes costs $10/7.50 for adults/children.

At the back of the shopping center, behind the parking lot, there's a picturesque view of Mauna Kea rising above an old wooden corral and pastures.

Church Row

Waimea's churches are lined up side by side in an area called Church Row. Imiola Congregational Church is the oldest and the green steepled church next to it is Ke Ola Mau Loa Church, an all-Hawaiian church. Buddhists, Baptists and Mormons also have places of worship in the row.

Imiola Congregational Church Waimea's first Christian church was a grass hut built in 1830. It was replaced in 1838 by a wood and coral structure, built with coral stones carved out of the reef and carried inland on the backs of Hawaiian Christians. They named it Imiola, which means 'seeking salvation'.

The current building was constructed in 1857 and restored in 1976. The interior is simple and beautiful and it's built entirely of koa, most of it dating back to the original construction.

In the churchyard is the grave of missionary Lorenzo Lyons who arrived in 1832

and spent 54 years in Waimea. He wrote many of the hymns, including the popular 'Hawaii Aloha', that are still sung in Hawaiian here each Sunday. Also in the garden is the church bell, too heavy for the church roof to support.

Kamuela Museum

There's a lot of history crammed into the Kamuela Museum (☎ 885-4724) at the junction of Hwy 19 and Hwy 250. The museum contains all sorts of Hawaiiana including tapa beaters, 18th-century feather leis braided with human hair, fish hooks made of human bones, a stone knuckle duster and a dog-toothed death cup. Some items are very rare and many once belonged to royalty. The museum has Kamehameha the Great's sacred chair and tables of teak and marble from Iolani Palace.

This museum is like one of those cluttery Chinese grocery stores that has one of everything – you just have to find it. The non-Hawaiian part of the collection ranges from a Tibetan prayer horn and stuffed moose heads from Canada to a piece of rope used on the Apollo II mission.

The future of the museum is a bit uncertain as it's been up for sale. It's open from 8 am to 5 pm daily. Admission costs $5 for adults, $2 for children under 12.

Places to Stay

Waimea is upcountry and if you equate Hawaii with beach life and constant sun you may be disappointed making a base here. But if country settings and open spaces are what you're looking for, there are some fine choices.

Kamuela Inn (☎ 885-4243), Box 1994, Kamuela, HI 96743, is something in between an inn and a small hotel in both layout and atmosphere. The cheaper of its 31 rooms are rather small but comfortable. Standard rooms cost $54 to $67. Suites that have refrigerators and stoves and can sleep three cost $83. Free doughnuts and coffee are provided in the morning.

Parker Ranch Lodge (☎ 885-4100), Box 458, Kamuela, HI 96743, is a single-story motel with 20 rooms. All have full baths, phones, cable TV and good views of the Kohala hills out back. Rooms cost $78 with kitchenette, $68 without. Units numbered one to 10 are good choices as they have cathedral ceilings.

Hawaii Country Cottage (☎ 885-7441), Box 1717, Kamuela, HI 96743, is a B&B unit at the side of a contemporary home just up Hwy 250 from Hwy 19. It has double and single beds, a large living room with fireplace, Douglas fir floors and raised beam ceilings. There's a microwave, coffeepot, refrigerator and wet bar. The owner, Gale, has the 'tutu nene' business making the stuffed cotton nene found in gift shops around the island. There's a distant sunset view of the ocean and a stream running alongside the property. The rate is $65.

Waimea Gardens Cottages (☎ 885-4550, (800) 262-9912), Box 563, Kamuela, HI 96743, are a pair of charming cottages on the property of Barbara and Charlie Campbell, two miles west of town. Both have hardwood floors, French doors and a deck. The older unit has a full kitchen. While the newer one has more limited cooking facilities, it has many other pleasant touches including a working fireplace. The units come stocked with a fruit basket, banana bread and Kona coffee. The rate is $115 single or double, $15 more for a third person; there's a three-day minimum stay. Barbara also runs an upmarket B&B service called Hawaii's Best Bed & Breakfasts and can book other accommodation on the island in this price range.

If you don't mind being a few miles east of Waimea then *Mountain Meadow Ranch* (☎ 775-9376, (800) 535-9376), Michael Cowan, Box 1361, Kamuela, HI 96743, is a real find. Located in a quiet eucalyptus grove off the Old Mamalahoa Hwy, this pleasant seven-acre farm has gardens of citrus and macadamia nut trees and a splendid country setting. It would make a convenient base for exploring Waipio and the Hamakua Coast and is only about an hour's drive from Hilo.

There are two rooms with double beds and guests share a large tiled bathroom, a dry heat sauna and a lounge with a TV/VCR. There's no minimum stay, children are accepted and a rollaway bed can be added to the room. Breakfast includes homemade breads and muffins and home-grown fruits. The cost is $45 single and $55 double, credit cards are accepted and there's a 10% discount for weekly stays. There's also a two-bedroom cottage on the property that's available as a vacation rental at $600 per week for up to six people.

Places to Eat

The *Mean Cuisine* in Opelo Plaza bakes its own breads and pastries and is a popular little spot with eggplant and pasta dishes for around $6 and sandwiches and good salads at reasonable prices. It's open from 6 am to 8 pm (Sundays from 9 am to 1 pm) and you can order food for either sit-down service or takeout.

Merriman's (☎ 885-6822) in Opelo Plaza features Hawaiian regional cuisine, focusing on fresh products from Big Island farmers. Chef Peter Merriman uses Waimea-grown strawberries, goat cheese from Puna, herbs from Kealakekua and freshwater shrimp from a local aquaculturist. One of his specialties is a delicious wok-charred ahi, blackened on the outside and like sashimi inside. At dinner there are a couple of vegetarian meals, including ginger stir-fried tofu on brown rice for $15, while most seafood and meat dishes cost $22 to $25. At lunch, there's a Thai chef in the kitchen making good salads, soups and sandwiches as well as a few hot grilled dishes including a tasty coconut chicken with peanut sauce. Everything on the lunch menu is $10 or less. It's open from 11:30 am to 1:30 pm weekdays, 5:30 to 9 pm nightly. Dinner reservations are recommended.

At *Edelweiss* (☎ 885-6800) on Hwy 19 German chef Hans-Peter Hager has built a following around such German-Austrian dishes as roast pork with sauerkraut and wiener schnitzel. Dinners cost $16 to $21. Lunches are lighter with burgers, sandwiches and salads from around $6. Lunch is from 11:30 am to 1:30 pm, dinner from

5 to 9 pm. It's closed on Sundays and Mondays.

There's a branch of *Su's Thai Kitchen* in the Parker Ranch Shopping Center that's open for three meals a day and features moderately priced Thai food as well as American-style breakfasts.

The Waimea Center has a *KTA Supermarket*, a *McDonald's*, a health food store, a deli and simple Chinese and Korean restaurants. *Cattleman's Steakhouse*, at the east end of the shopping center, features steaks and a salad bar.

Entertainment

Waimea's entertainment scene is limited, perhaps because cowboys rise at dawn and astronomers work all night!

Kahilu Theatre at the Parker Ranch Shopping Center presents occasional plays, classical music concerts, dance troupes and other productions.

Getting There & Away

Waimea is 40 miles from Kailua-Kona along Hwy 190. From Kona the road climbs out of residential areas into a mix of lava flows and dry grassy rangeland studded with prickly pear cactus. There's a little one-room church, broad distant coastal views, wide-open spaces and tall roadside grasses that have an incredible golden hue in the morning light.

If you come back on this road at night the highway reflectors light up like an airport runway to guide you along.

AROUND WAIMEA
Waimea to Honokaa

Hwy 19 heads east from Waimea to Honokaa through rolling hills and cattle pastures, with views of Mauna Kea to the south.

For a peaceful, scented backroad turn right off Hwy 19 onto the Old Mamalahoa Hwy just west of the 52-mile marker. (If you're coming from Hilo, turn left at the 43-mile marker opposite Tex Drive Inn and then take the next immediate right.)

The 10-mile detour winds through hill country, with small roadside ranches, old

---

The Death of David Douglas

The circumstances of David Douglas' death are somewhat mysterious as his gored body was found trapped with an angry bull at the bottom of a pit on the slopes of Mauna Kea. Hunters commonly dug such pits and camouflaged them with underbrush as a means of trapping feral cattle, but the probability of both Douglas and a bull falling into the same hole seemed highly suspicious. Fingers were pointed at Ned Gurney, an escaped convict from Botany Bay who had been hiding out in the area and who had been the last person to see Douglas alive.

Hilo authorities, unable to solve the case, packed both Douglas' body and the bull's head in brine and shipped them to Honolulu for further investigation. By the time the body arrived in Oahu, it was so badly decomposed that they buried Douglas' remains at the missionary church and the case was closed. ∎

---

wooden fences and grazing horses. This is an untouristed Hawaii. Nobody's in a hurry on this road, if they're on it at all. It can make a great alternative route for cyclists although you'll need to be cautious as the road is narrow and winding.

Mana/Keanakolu Road

To get closer to Mauna Kea for photography or views you could drive part way down Mana Rd, the start of a road which curves around the eastern flank of Mauna Kea. It begins off Hwy 19 at the 55-mile marker on the eastern side of Waimea. After 15 miles the road becomes Keanakolu Rd and continues about 25 miles before reaching Summit Rd (the road leading up Mauna Kea) near the Humuula Sheep Station.

Only the first part of the Waimea section is paved. The entire road is passable on horseback or by 4WD vehicle but there are a couple of dozen cattle gates that must be opened and closed along the way. It's mostly ranchers and hunters that come this way and it's a long way from anywhere should you get stuck en route.

Keanakolu Rd passes along the new

Hakalau Forest National Wildlife Refuge, which protects a portion of the state's largest koa-ohia forest. The forest provides habitat for the hoary bat and four endangered bird species. Only very limited access is allowed into the refuge itself; call 969-9909 for information.

David Douglas Memorial A memorial to David Douglas, the Scottish botanist for whom the Douglas fir tree is named, is on Keanakolu Rd about halfway between Waimea and the Saddle Rd. Douglas died in 1834 at this spot.

Hamakua Coast

The Hamakua Coast, the northeastern coast of the Big Island, stretches 50 miles from Waipio Valley down to the city of Hilo.

From Waimea, it's 15 miles east on Hwy 19 to the town of Honokaa. From Honokaa, you can continue nine miles northwest on Hwy 240 to reach Waipio Valley Lookout and one of the most spectacular valley views in Hawaii.

Much of the north end of the Hamakua Coast is idle agricultural land that until recent times was planted in sugar cane. The rest of the coast is rugged with luxuriant rainforests laced with streams and waterfalls.

The Hawaii Belt Rd (Hwy 19), ·which runs along the wet windward slopes of Mauna Kea, is an impressive engineering feat that spans deep green ravines with a series of sweeping cantilevered bridges.

Hwy 19 also passes small towns and unmarked roads leading down to unfrequented beach parks. If you're just whizzing through on your way between Kona and Hilo, at the very least make time for Waipio Valley Lookout, majestic Akaka Falls and the Pepeekeo four-mile scenic drive.

HONOKAA

Honokaa's sugar mill opened in 1873 and sugar continued to be the mainstay of this town until the Hamakua Sugar Company closed down the mill in late 1994. As a result of the closing many Honokaa residents have taken up employment in new Waikoloa resorts.

Still Honokaa has its roots in sugar and most of its residents are descendants of immigrants brought here to work the plantations. The Scots and English were the first to arrive. Then came the Chinese, Portuguese, Japanese, Puerto Ricans and Filipinos in turn.

With a population of 2200, this quiet town is the biggest on the Hamakua Coast. Mamame St (Hwy 240) is the main street through town. Most of the shops lined up along it date to the 1920s and haven't changed a whole lot over the years.

The center of activity is the Honokaa Club, a hotel and restaurant built in 1908. Honokaa has a couple of antique shops, a post office, library, swimming pool, grocery stores and a few restaurants.

In ancient Hawaii, Honokaa was an overnight stop for travelers on their way to Waipio.

Macadamia Nut Factory
Hawaiian Holiday has its macadamia nut factory on Lehua St, three-quarters of a mile down the hill from the post office. For visitors, this is basically a store where nuts and cookies are sold and the 'self-guided tour' consists of watching factory workers through windows in the gift shop. A little napkin of free samples is rather cheerlessly deposited on the counter upon request.

Kamaaina Woods
Kamaaina Woods, on the road to the macadamia nut factory, makes quality bowls of koa, milo and mango woods and everything sold in the shop is made there. Prices start at around $20 with many bowls well over $100. The thinnest and lightest-weight bowls require the greatest skill to craft and command the highest prices.

Places to Stay
Honokaa Club Hotel (☎ 775-0678), on Mamane St, has 14 basic rooms that cost $32/35 for singles/doubles with a shared

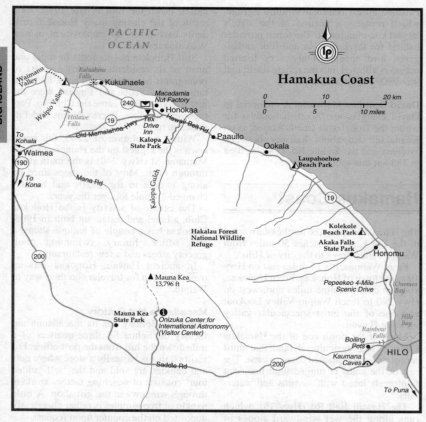

Hamakua Coast

bath, $39/44 for somewhat nicer rooms with TV and a private bath. Some of the rooms are filled with monthly lodgers, so it's hit and miss trying to get a room on a walk-in basis.

Waipio Wayside B&B (☎ 775-0275, (800) 833-8849), Box 840, Honokaa, HI 96727, between Honokaa and Waipio, is an older home in a setting of macadamia nut trees. It's pleasant and relaxed, with hammocks on the deck and a garden gazebo. There are five nicely decorated theme rooms that vary in size and price, ranging from $55/60 singles/doubles for a room with shared bath up to $85/90 for the attractive master

bedroom suite with natural wood and a private bath. Add another $10 for stays of just one night. If you book at the lower end ask for the Plantation Room, which is spacious and sunny. Owner Jackie Horne prepares a hearty breakfast that includes homegrown fruit and richly flavorful Hamakua coffee.

Paauhau Plantation House (☎ 775-7222; fax 775-7223), Box 1375, Honokaa, HI 96727, off Hwy 19 just east of the Hwy 240 turn-off into Honokaa, is a classic 70-year-old plantation manager's house with plush period furniture, a billiard room, a fireplace, and so much historic character that you might expect ghosts to come out of the walls. The bedrooms in the house are furnished with antiques, down comforters and old-fashioned bathrooms. Two of them rent for $105 a night, while a large master suite with king and double beds rents for $140.

There are also three very pleasant cottages with cooking facilities, separate bedrooms, and sofa beds in the living rooms. The smallest costs $75, the larger ones sleep four to six people and cost $90 for two, plus $15 for each additional person. Rates include a continental breakfast and there are tennis courts.

Places to Eat

Most people staying in the area pick up groceries at the supermarket opposite the post office but there are a couple of reasonable places to get a bite on Mamame St at the east side of the post office intersection. *Hilo Homemade Ice Cream* serves excellent ice cream and has a few simple items such as chili and sandwiches priced from around $3. There's a bakery next door and a pizzeria a minute's walk to the east.

The *Honokaa Club* on Mamame St is one of the more popular local places for dinner although the food's quite simple, with meals from $7 to $16.

Tex Drive Inn is up on Hwy 19 and if you're driving by in the morning, on your way from Waimea to Hilo, you might want to stop by for a couple of malasadas (55c each) and a cup of coffee. Malasadas are Portuguese pastries of sweet fried dough, rolled in sugar and served warm – like a doughnut without the hole. The diner also serves moderately priced breakfast fare, sandwiches, burgers and plate lunches. It's open from 6 am to 8:30 pm daily. There is a convenience store next door and a coin laundry across the road.

KUKUIHAELE

About seven miles beyond Honokaa heading towards Waipio Valley, there's a loop road off Hwy 240 that leads off to the right and goes down to the tiny village of Kukuihaele.

A Hard Nut to Crack

Hawaii's first macadamia trees were planted in Honokaa in 1881 by William Purvis, a sugar plantation manager who brought seedlings from Australia. For 40 years the trees were grown in Hawaii, as in Australia, mainly for ornamental purposes, as the nut shells were considered too hard to crack.

Hawaii's first large-scale commercial macadamia orchard was planted in Honokaa in 1924 and it's still producing today. Macadamia nuts have proven to be one of the most commercially viable agricultural crops in Hawaii. The nuts are high in fat, protein, and carbohydrate and make a good source of calcium, phosphorus, iron, thiamine, riboflavin and niacin. ∎

Kukuihaele means 'Traveling Light' in Hawaiian and refers to the ghostly night marchers who are said to pass through this area carrying torches on their way to Waipio. The village is less than a mile from the Waipio Lookout.

There's not much to Kukuihaele – its 'commercial center' consists mainly of the Last Chance Store and the Waipio Valley Artworks. The latter sells quality Hawaiian-made crafts, including dyed fabrics and an extensive selection of carved wooden bowls.

Places to Stay

Waipio Valley Artworks (☎ 775-0958, (800) 492-4746; fax 775-0551), Box 5070, Kukuihaele, HI 96727, has three newly constructed vacation rentals on the ridge about 200 yards before the Waipio Lookout. All are pleasant and a very good value. One of the houses has a one-bedroom apartment on the first floor that rents for $65 and a two-bedroom apartment on the second floor that rents for $90. The other rental is a two-bedroom house that goes for $80. All three places have queen-size beds, full kitchens, washer/dryers, phones, TVs and lanais with valley views. Rates are for double occupancy; add $15 for each additional guest. Visa and MasterCard are accepted.

Waipio Ridge Vacation Rental (☎ 775-0603), Roger Lasko, Box 5039, Kukuihaele, HI 96727, is a modern one-bedroom cottage perched above Waipio Valley, just below the lookout. The kitchen has a refrigerator, microwave, toaster oven and coffeepot, and a spectacular view of Waipio Valley from the dining table. There's TV, a queen-size bed in the bedroom and a queen sofa bed in the living room. The cost is $65 for two people, plus $10 more for stays of just one night and $15 more for additional guests.

Hale Kukui (☎ 775-7130, (800) 444-7130), William McCowatt, Box 5044, Kukuihaele, HI 96727, is a new contemporary vacation cottage with great views of Waipio Valley and the north coast. This is a duplex building with a studio at one side and a two-bedroom unit at the other. Both have queen beds, living room areas with a fold-out futon, lanais and kitchenettes with a hot plate, small refrigerator and microwave. Smoking is limited to the outdoors. The studio costs $75, the two-bedroom unit $95. Rates are for up to two people; add an extra $10 for each additional guest. Visa and MasterCard accepted.

On the opposite side of the gulch from Hale Kukui is the *Hamakua Hideaway* (☎ 775-7425), Box 5104, Kukuihaele, HI 96727, which has a similar view and two units, both with kitchens, phones and TV,

that rent for $65 a night. Ask for the Cliffhouse, which has a fireplace, a sunken tub and a view down the coast to Waipio Valley.

Places to Eat

Most people go into Honokaa to eat and get provisions, although there are a couple of simple options in Kukuihaele.

The village's *Last Chance Store* is just that, as there's no food or supplies in Waipio Valley. At this small grocery store you can get yogurt, crackers, canned food, beer and wine. One of the more popular items here are the hard-boiled eggs, which sell for 30c apiece.

The shop at the side of Waipio Valley Artworks sells Tropical Dreams ice cream, sandwiches and coffee during the day.

WAIPIO VALLEY

Hwy 240 ends abruptly at the edge of cliffs overlooking Waipio Valley. The view is glorious. Waipio is the largest and southernmost of the seven spectacular amphitheater valleys on the windward side of the Kohala Mountains. Waipio is a mile wide at the coast and nearly six miles deep. Some of the near-vertical pali wrapping around the valley reach heights of 2000 feet.

Everything is lushly green, a mix of tangled jungle, flowering plants, taro patches and waterfalls. The mouth of the valley is fronted by a black sand beach, which is divided in two by the Waipio Stream.

From the lookout you can see the switchback trail on the opposite cliff face which leads to Waimanu Valley and get glimpses of the rugged coastal cliffs that stretch out to the northwest.

The narrow, paved, mile-long road which leads down into Waipio Valley is so steep (25% grade) that it's restricted to all but hikers and 4WD vehicles. A couple of tour companies make the run daily, but the walk down is easier than it looks. There are restrooms and drinking water at the lookout.

History

Waipio means 'Curving Water' and is often

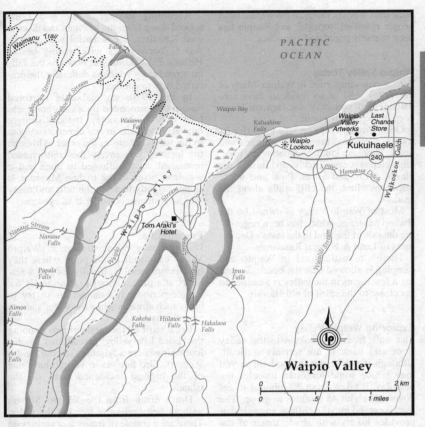

Waipio Valley

referred to as the 'Valley of the Kings'. In ancient times it was the political and religious center of Hawaii and home to the highest chiefs. Waipio was a very sacred place and the site of a number of important heiaus. The most sacred, Pakaalana, was also the site of one of the island's two major puuhonua or places of refuge.

Umi, the Big Island's ruling chief in the early 1500s, is credited with laying out Waipio's taro fields, many of which are still in production today. Waipio is also the site where Kamehameha the Great received his fearsome war god, Kukailimoku.

According to oral histories at least 10,000 people – and possibly many times more – lived in Waipio during pre-contact times. It was the most fertile and productive valley on the Big Island.

In 1823 William Ellis, the first missionary to visit the valley, guessed the population to be about 1300. Later in that century immigrants, mainly Chinese, began to settle in Waipio. At one time the valley had schools, restaurants and churches as well as a hotel, post office and jail.

In 1946 the most devastating tsunami in Hawaii's history swept great waves far back into Waipio Valley. Afterwards, most people resettled 'topside' and Waipio has been sparsely populated ever since.

Waipio Valley Today

Taro remains important in Waipio. Many of the valley's 50 or so residents have taro patches and you may see farmers knee-deep in the muddy ponds.

Other Waipio crops include lotus (for its roots), avocados, breadfruit, oranges and limes. There are kukui and mahogany trees, huge elephant ears, Turk's cap hibiscus, air plants, ferns and vines. Pink and white impatiens climb the cliff walls along the road.

Most of Waipio Valley is owned by the Bishop Museum, which has been negotiating the sale of the land to the state's Department of Land & Natural Resources.

There's a rustic hotel in Waipio and camping is allowed near the beach. Spending a few nights in the valley is a chance to get closer to the spirit of old Hawaii.

Exploring Waipio Valley

The walk from the lookout to the valley floor and back is not terribly difficult, although if you're not in good shape you may notice some forgotten muscles the next day. It takes about 30 minutes to get down and about 45 minutes to go up. The road is carved into the cliffs at an angle that provides hikers with shade much of the way.

From the bottom of the hill, if you walk to the left for about five minutes there's a fair chance you'll see wild horses grazing along the stream. It's a picturesque scene set against the steep valley cliffs.

You'll also get a distant view of **Hiilawe Falls**, which with a sheer drop of more than 1000 feet is Hawaii's highest free-fall waterfall. While hiking to Hiilawe Falls is not impossible, it is challenging as there's no real trail and it's mainly bushwhacking. There are a lot of 'Private Property' signs and generally the farther back in the valley you go, the less friendly the dogs become.

According to legend the god Lono looked down from the heavens and discovered Kaikilani, the beautiful woman who was to become his wife, sitting beside Hiilawe Falls. Lono slid down to the falls on a rainbow – which is definitely the preferred way to get there.

In the 1970s an elaborate mirrored restaurant surrounded by a carp pond was built back in the valley. It looks straight onto Hiilawe Falls in one direction and out to the valley mouth in the other. Although the location was lovely the controversial restaurant wasn't allowed to open and it was later given to the Bishop Museum. It shines brightly beneath the falls and many Waipio residents consider it an eyesore.

Precautions

During heavy rains, streams in Waipio Valley can swell to the point where they become impassable, usually for just a few hours at a time, although occasionally for longer periods. It's dangerous to try to cross such streams when the water's above your thighs.

Because of all the feral animals roaming this Eden-like valley, precautions against leptospirosis are advisable (see the Health section). Taro farmers in Waipio have one of the highest incidence rates on the islands.

Don't drink from the Waipio Stream without first boiling or treating the water. There are a couple of freshwater springs up from the beach that most people use for drinking water. You can get to one by turning left at the bottom of the hill upon entering the valley. Walk a few minutes to the first dirt path on the right, which leads down to a stream. The spring is at the bottom of the path, on the left, a few feet in.

As you walk around the valley you might come across wild horses or stray dogs along the road although both tend to veer off if you come too close.

Waipio Beach

It takes about 10 minutes to walk to the beach from the bottom of the hill. After heavy rains, the road can be like a slippery mud pie.

Waipio Beach is lined with ironwood trees that act as an effective windbreak against the strong wind that sometimes picks up here. It was an ancient surfing beach that occasionally still sees some action but there are usually rip currents and when the surf is high the waters can be outright treacherous.

Walk along the beach towards the stream mouth for a good view of **Kaluahine Falls** which cascade down the coastal cliffs to the east. They're easier to look at than to get to, however, as the coast between Waipio Beach and Kaluahine Falls is loose lava rock and rather rough walking. The surf sometimes breaks up over the uppermost rocks so it can also be dangerous.

Local lore has it that ghost marchers periodically come down from the upper valley and march down the beach where there's a hidden entrance into the netherworld, called Lua O Milu.

Waipio Tours

Waipio Valley Shuttle, which uses local drivers, first introduced tours into the valley about 25 years ago. The tour is via a 4WD vehicle, lasts about 1½ hours and is not terribly adventurous. It's more of a taxi ride for those who don't care to walk down. The driver points out waterfalls, identifies plants and throws in a bit of history. Sit as close to the driver as you can because it's hard to hear the spiel if you're bouncing around in the back. Reservations (☎ 775-7121) can be made at Waipio Valley Artworks in Kukuihaele. It costs $30 for adults, $15 for children under 11. The tours run between 8 am to 4 pm Monday to Saturday.

An alternative to the van tours is Waipio Valley Wagon Tours' 1½-hour jaunt through the valley in an open mule-drawn wagon. The tour guide usually gives an interesting commentary on the valley's history as he wheels visitors along Waipio's rutted dirt roads and fords rocky streams. Tours leave from Waipio Valley Lookout at 9 and 10:30 am and 12:30, 2

and 4 pm daily, except on Sundays. Passengers are taken to the valley floor by a 4WD vehicle where they transfer to the wagon. It costs $35 for adults, half price for children. Call 889-6850 for reservations.

The third possibility for touring the valley is on horseback. Both Waipio on Horseback (☎ 775-7291) and Waipio Naalapa Trail Rides (☎ 775-0419) offer 2½-hour trail rides in the valley, weather permitting, for $65. There are no trail rides on Sundays.

Switchback Trail to Waimanu Valley

The switchback trail leading up the northwest cliff face of Waipio Valley is an ancient Hawaiian footpath. Although it looks arduous, and is rated moderate-to-difficult, it really isn't all that bad if you're not carrying a heavy load. It's a well-beaten path, a few feet deep in places, almost like walking in a little trough. For those who are carrying a heavy backpack, once you reach the ridge the trail gets much easier.

Doing part of the trail makes a nice day hike if you're camping in Waipio. It takes about 1½ hours from the floor of Waipio Valley to the third gulch where there are little pools and a small waterfall. The trail is used by hunters as well as hikers and you might come across old-timers on donkeys heading for the backwoods to hunt wild boar.

The trail continues up and down a series of ravines to Waimanu Valley. From Waipio Valley to Waimanu it's about eight miles in all and because of the numerous climbs you should allot about seven hours. About two-thirds of the way along there's an open-sided trail shelter.

Waimanu is a smaller valley than Waipio although it's similar in appearance. It too is a beautiful deep valley with steep walls, waterfalls, a lush green valley floor and a black sand beach.

Waimanu Valley once had a sizable Hawaiian settlement and there are many ruins from pre-contact times including house and heiau terraces, stone enclosures and old taro ponds. In the early 1800s Waimanu was inhabited by an estimated 200 people, but by the turn of the 20th century only three families remained. Since the 1946 tsunami the valley has been completely abandoned.

Because it represents an unaltered Hawaiian freshwater ecosystem, Waimanu Valley has been set aside as a national estuarine sanctuary and the removal of any plant or aquatic life (except for freshwater prawns and ocean fish) is forbidden.

Water is available on this route from numerous gulches but it must be boiled or otherwise treated before drinking.

Places to Stay

Tom Araki's Hotel (☎ 775-0368), c/o Sueno Araki, 25 Malama Place, Hilo, HI 96720, is back to basics on the floor of Waipio Valley. It's about a 15-minute walk inland from the bottom of the hill, just on the other side of the stream. This unpretentious place once served Peace Corps instructors who trained new recruits in the valley before they went off on assignment to other Pacific and Asian jungles.

All quite in keeping with its surroundings, the hotel's five rooms look out onto Tom's taro patch. The rooms are rustic and simple, but comfortable enough, and blankets and linen are provided. There's a communal kitchen with a gas stove, sink, dishes and cooking utensils. Kerosene lanterns provide lighting. You'll have to carry in all your own food, and it's a custom to bring along a bottle of sake to pass the evening.

Tom gets heavily booked out and suggests making reservations well in advance, although you can also take your chances and call upon arriving on the Big Island. Rates are $15 per person.

Waipio Tree House (☎ 775-7160), Box 5086, Honokaa, HI 96727, rates as the ultimate getaway in Hawaii, as it's both a couple of miles back into Waipio Valley and 30 feet up a monkeypod tree! Owner Linda Beech, one of the more unusual hoteliers in Hawaii, is a vivacious woman who's been a journalist and a sit-com TV star in Japan and holds a doctorate in psychology. The treehouse faces a waterfall and boasts skylights, a 360° view with

screens all around and lots of Tarzan books. It has a double and single bed, a refrigerator, hot plate, electricity and running water. The cost is $175 a day, with a two-day minimum. There's also a cottage on the grounds called The Hale, which has a kitchen, living room and loft bedroom and rents for the same price. The cost includes 4WD transportation to and from the lookout. Bring your own food.

Camping Hamakua Sugar Company (☎ 776-1211) issues permits for camping on the section of Waipio Beach they control. Permits are free but must be picked up in person at their office, which is next to the post office in Paauilo, just off Hwy 19 about six miles south of Honokaa. The crux of the application is a liability release and a promise to bring a shovel to bury human waste and to carry out your trash. The office is open from 7 am to 4 pm Monday to Friday.

In Waimanu Valley, which is managed by the state, camping for up to six nights is allowed free by permit. There are fireplaces and a couple of composting outhouses. Camping reservations are taken up to one month in advance via the Division of Forestry & Wildlife (☎ 933-4221), Box 4849, Hilo, HI 96720. The actual permit can be picked up at the aforementioned forestry office, the Last Chance Store in Kukuihaele or at the state tree nursery in Waimea.

KALOPA STATE PARK

Kalopa State Park is a few miles southeast of Honokaa and about three miles inland from the marked turn-off on Hwy 19.

This unfrequented park contains 100 acres of native rainforest as well as picnic sites and some pleasant log cabins that hold up to eight people. It's at an elevation of 2000 feet and cooler than the coast. Kalopa averages about 90 inches of rain a year.

The park has a pleasant hike leading to Kalopa Gulch in the adjoining forest reserve. Begin the hike along Robusta Lane, which starts on the left after the caretaker's house. It's about a third of a mile to the edge of the gulch through a thick forest of tall eucalyptus trees with mossy bark. The deep gulch was formed by melting glaciers that originated at Mauna Kea. A trail continues along the rim of the gulch for another mile and a number of side trails branch west off it back into the park.

Kalopa Park also has a nature trail that loops for three-quarters of a mile through an ancient ohia forest where some of the trees are more than three feet in diameter.

The woods are habitat for the elepaio, an easily spotted native forest bird. It's brown with a white rump, about the size of a sparrow, and it makes a loud whistle that mimics its name.

LAUPAHOEHOE POINT

Laupahoehoe means 'leaf of pahoehoe lava'. This flat peninsula-like point jutting out from the coastal cliffs was formed by a late eruption of Mauna Kea which poured lava down a ravine and out into the sea.

Laupahoehoe Point is midway between Honokaa and Hilo. A highway sign marks the steep winding road down to the point. There are views of the coastal cliffs on the way down and after heavy rains waterfalls come to life in all directions.

Tragedy hit Laupahoehoe on April 1, 1946, when tsunami waves up to 30 feet high wiped out the schoolhouse on the point, killing 20 children and four adults. After the tsunami the whole town moved uphill, although a few families have since settled back in. A monument on a hillock above the water lists those who died.

Laupahoehoe is a rugged coastal area and is not suitable for swimming. The surf is usually rough and pounding and can sometimes crash up over the rocks and onto the lower parking lot.

Inter-island boats once landed here. Many of the immigrants who came to work the sugar cane fields along the Hamakua Coast first set foot on the Big Island at Laupahoehoe.

The county beach park on the point has restrooms, campsites, showers, drinking water, picnic pavilions and electricity, and

as it's off the highway it's relatively secluded. All this makes it convenient for camping, but makes it ideal for late-night partying too. Locals who use the park as a drinking hangout sometimes get fairly wasted and rowdy.

KOLEKOLE BEACH PARK

This grassy park, beneath a big highway bridge, is at the side of the Kolekole Stream which flows down from Akaka Falls. There are small waterfalls, picnic tables, barbecue pits, restrooms and showers, all of which make the park a popular weekend picnic spot for families. Locals sometimes surf here, but ocean swimming is dangerous. Camping is allowed with a permit from the county, although it can be busy on weekends and in summer.

To get to the park, turn mauka off Hwy 19 at the south end of the Kolekole Bridge, about three-quarters of a mile south of the 15-mile marker.

AKAKA FALLS

To get to Akaka Falls, turn mauka off Hwy 19 onto Akaka Falls Rd (Hwy 220), midway between the 13- and 14-mile markers. The good paved road passes through the town of Honomu and then climbs up through fields of sugar cane, ending at the falls 3¾ miles away.

Honomu

Honomu is an old sugar town that might have been forgotten, if not for being on the route to Akaka Falls. As it is, things are pretty slow here.

Among the village's handful of old wooden buildings you'll find a gift shop, a place to get shave ice and Ishigo's store and bakery, which sells sandwiches and a few simple pastries.

Hideo Ishigo, a spry octogenarian who still helps with the baking at Ishigo's, often sits in front of the store during the afternoon. If you happen to stop by, he loves to talk story, has an intriguing photo collection of old-time Honomu and can tell you about little-known sights in the area.

Akaka Falls State Park

Akaka Falls State Park has the Big Island's most impressive easy-to-view waterfall. It shouldn't be missed.

The waterfall lookout is along a delightful half-mile rainforest loop trail that takes about 20 minutes to walk. The paved trail passes through dense and varied vegetation including massive philodendron vines, fragrant ginger, hanging heliconia, hillsides of bright impatiens and cool bamboo groves. Look up and you might even find orchids growing wild in the trees.

If you start the loop trail by going to the right you'll first come to the 100-foot **Kahuna Falls**. It's a nice waterfall but the real treat is still to come. Up ahead is **Akaka Falls** dropping a sheer 442 feet down a fern-draped cliff. Its mood depends on the weather – sometimes it rushes with a mighty roar and other times it cascades gently. Either way it's always beautiful. With a little luck you might even catch a rainbow in the spray.

One legend says that whenever a branch of the lehua tree lands on a particular stone at the top of the falls, it will begin to rain. If so, there are apparently a lot of loose lehua branches upstream! You might want to bring an umbrella.

PEPEEKEO FOUR-MILE SCENIC DRIVE

Between Honomu and Hilo there's a delightful four-mile side loop off Hwy 19. It's a drive through lush tropical jungle. The road crosses a string of one-lane bridges over little streams. In places it's almost canopied with African tulip trees, which drop their orange flowers on the road, and with passion fruit, guava and tall mango trees. The fruit can be picked up along the roadside in season.

The road is well-marked on the highway at both ends, with the south end about seven miles north of Hilo.

Hawaii Tropical Botanical Garden

If somehow the four-mile scenic drive isn't enough, there's also the Hawaii Tropical Botanical Garden (☎ 964-5233) along the way. The garden is a rainforest nature preserve with a lily pond, 1000 species of tropical plants and a couple of streams and waterfalls.

Visitors buy tickets at the little yellow building mauka of the road and are shuttled by van down to the valley garden at nearby Onomea Bay.

This nonprofit foundation charges $12 for adults and is free for children ages 16 and under. You're given a self-guided trail map and are free to wander as long as you like. It's open daily from 8:30 am to 5:30 pm, but the last shuttle bus goes down to the valley at 4:30 pm.

Saddle Road/ Mauna Kea

The Saddle Road, true to its name, runs between the two highest points on the island, with Mauna Kea to the north and Mauna Loa to the south.

The road passes over large lava flows and climbs through a variety of terrains and climates. At sunrise and sunset there's a gentle glow on the mountains and a light show on the clouds. In the early morning it's crisp enough to see your breath and if you take the spur road up to Mauna Kea you'll reach permafrost.

Although most car rental contracts prohibit travel on the Saddle Rd, it's a paved road straight across. It's narrow and there are sections where the road's surface is a bit crumbly and potholed, but it's no big deal – particularly by island standards.

Locals looking for the rationale behind the car rental ban come up with things like military convoys or evening fog. The crux of the matter seems to be that the rental agencies just don't want to be responsible for the tow charge if your car breaks down on Hawaii's most remote road.

The Saddle Rd is 50 miles long and has no gas stations or other facilities along the way. (Neither are there any gas stations on the 33-mile stretch of Hwy 190 between the Saddle Rd and Kona.)

Crossing the island on the Saddle Rd is a bit shorter than on the northern route of the Hawaii Belt Rd, but it's also a slower road and timewise there isn't much difference either way.

To the west, the Saddle Rd starts out in cattle ranchland with rolling grassy hills and planted stands of eucalyptus trees. It's beautiful, but like the rest of the western side of the island it's changing. A new subdivision called Waikii Ranch has divided 3000 acres of the area's ranchland into million-dollar houselots and is marketing them to wealthy urban cowboys.

After about 10 miles the land starts getting rougher and the pastures and fences fewer. The military takes over where the cows leave off. Bradshaw Army Airfield comes up first, then the quonset huts of the Pohakuloa Military Camp. Most of the vehicles on the road are military jeeps and trucks, although in hunting season you'll come across a fair number of pick-up trucks as well.

MAUNA KEA

Mauna Kea is Hawaii's highest mountain and its 13,796-foot summit has a cluster of important astronomical observatory domes.

The unmarked Summit Rd which climbs up Mauna Kea is at the 28-mile marker, opposite a hunter's check station. It's a well-paved 6¼ miles to the visitor center. The road winds up a few thousand feet in elevation. If you've got a small car it's probably going to labor a bit, but it shouldn't be a problem making it up as far as the visitor center. A standard transmission is preferable.

Surprisingly, you don't really get closer views of Mauna Kea's peaks by driving up to the visitor center. The peaks actually look higher and the views are broader from Saddle Rd. But you'll find nice vistas from Summit Rd and you can often drive up above the clouds. Mauna Kea doesn't appear as a single main peak, but rather a jumble of peaks, some black, some redbrown, some seasonally snowcapped.

Summit Rd passes through open range of grazing cattle. It's easy to spot Eurasian skylarks in the grass and if you're lucky you might see the endangered io (Hawaiian hawk) hovering overhead. Both make their home on the grassy mountain slopes. The io is found only on the Big Island. Mauna Kea is also home to the nene goose, as well as the palila, a small yellow honeycreeper which lives nowhere else in the world.

One of the more predominant plants here is mullen, which has soft woolly leaves and shoots up a tall stalk. In the spring the stalks get so loaded down with flowers that they bend over from the weight of what look like big yellow helmets. Mullen was brought in by ranchers as a free-loading weed in grass seed.

Visitor Center

The visitor center (☎ 961-2180), officially the Onizuka Center for International Astronomy, was named for Ellison Onizuka, a Big Island native and one of the astronauts who died in the 1986 Challenger disaster.

The center shows an interesting short video on Mauna Kea's observatories. There are also photo displays of the observatories and information on discoveries made from the summit. Note the astronomers aren't peering through little eyepieces or looking at the sky directly but rather are watching images relayed on computer monitors.

The center also has exhibits of the mountain's history, ecology and geology.

If you're planning to go up to the summit, stop here first to check road conditions and pick up brochures.

The visitor center is currently open from 1 to 5 pm on Fridays and from 8 am to noon and again from 4 to 5 pm on Saturdays and Sundays. Hours are subject to change, so it's a good idea to call before making the trip.

In addition, the visitor center has a free astronomy program from 7 pm on Fridays and Saturdays. It starts with a presentation about Mauna Kea, followed by stargazing until 10 pm using an 11-inch telescope. Children are welcome.

For information on the tours to the summit, see Summit Tours near the end of this section.

Summit Observatories

The summit of Mauna Kea has the greatest collection of state-of-the-art telescopes on earth and superior conditions for viewing the heavens. Nearing 14,000 feet, the summit is above 40% of the earth's atmosphere and 90% of its water vapor. The air is typically clear, dry and stable.

Not only are the Hawaiian Islands isolated, but Mauna Kea is one of the most secluded places in Hawaii. The air is relatively free from dust and smog. Nights are dark and free from city light interference. To further the cause, streetlights on the island have been converted to low-impact sodium. Rather than using the full iridescent spectrum, these orange lights use only a few wavelengths which the telescopes can be adjusted to remove.

Eight out of 10 nights are good for viewing. Only the Andes Mountains match Mauna Kea for cloudless nights, although air turbulence in the Andes makes viewing more difficult there.

The University of Hawaii (UH) holds the lease on Mauna Kea from the 12,000-foot level to the summit and UH receives observing time at each telescope as one of the lease provisions. Currently nine telescopes are in operation.

UH built the first telescope in 1968 with a 24-inch mirror. In comparison, the Maxwell telescope built in 1987 by the UK, Netherlands and Canada has a 590-inch mirror.

The UK Infrared Telescope (UKIRT) with its 150-inch mirror, until recently the world's largest infrared telescope, can be operated via computers and satellite relays from the Royal Observatory in England. In 1988 UKIRT and the Canada-France-Hawaii Telescope jointly identified the most distant galaxy yet discovered at 12 billion light years.

NASA's Infrared Telescope has measured the heat of volcanoes on Io, one of Jupiter's moons. The most active of Io's volcanoes is now named after Pele.

Completed in 1992, the W M Keck Observatory, a project of Caltech and the University of California, is the world's largest and most powerful infrared and optical telescope. A price tag of $94 million makes it the world's most expensive as well.

Previously the sheer weight of the glass mirrors was a limiting factor in telescope design. The Keck telescope has a new honeycomb design with 36 hexagonal mirror segments, each six feet across, that function as a single piece of glass. Its capacity to receive light is greater than twice that of all Mauna Kea's other telescopes combined. The Keck telescope has already discovered major new evidence supporting the Big Bang theory of the creation of the universe.

A second Keck observatory, a replica of the first, is now under construction and is expected to be up and running by 1997. The telescopes will be interchangeable, and can function as one – 'like a pair of binoculars searching the sky' – allowing them to study the very cores of elliptical galaxies.

Driving to the Summit

Visitors may go up to the summit in daytime, but vehicle headlights are not allowed between sunset and sunrise because they interfere with observation. However, what you'll see in addition to the view is mainly the outside of the observatory buildings, where the scientists are at work.

The paved road ends just above the visitor center near Hale Pohaku, the stone buildings where scientists stay during the day. The road from the visitor center to the summit is accessible by 4WD vehicle only. Harper Car & Truck Rentals in Hilo is the only car rental company that allows its jeeps to be driven to the summit.

The drive takes about half an hour. You should drive in the low range and loosen the gas cap to prevent vapor lock. The upper road can get iced over during winter.

Be particularly careful on the way down and watch out for loose cinder.

About 4½ miles up is an area called **Moon Valley** where the Apollo astronauts rehearsed with their lunar rover before their journey to the real moonscape.

At 5½ miles up, look to the left for a narrow ridge with two caves and black stones. That's **Keanakakoi**, 'Cave of the Adze', an ancient adze quarry. From this spot high-quality basalt was quarried to make adzes and other tools and weapons which were traded throughout the islands. For people interested in archaeology it's an impressive site. This is a protected area and nothing should be removed.

Precautions The summit air has only about 60% of the oxygen available at sea level and altitude sickness is not uncommon. Not only is the height a problem, but also the fact that visitors often don't take the time to properly acclimatize.

Unlike Nepal, for instance, where great heights are generally reached only after days of trekking, here you can zip up from sea level to nearly 14,000 feet by car in two hours.

Scuba divers who have been diving within the past 24 hours risk getting the bends by going to the summit. It's recommended that children under 16, obese people, pregnant women and those with a respiratory condition, or even a cold for that matter, do not go beyond the visitor center.

Even the astronomers who work up here never fully acclimatize and are always working oxygen-deprived in the summit's thin air. Anyone who gets a headache or feels faint or nauseous should head back down the mountain.

Mauna Kea can have snow flurries all year round and winter storms can dump a couple of feet of snow overnight.

Lake Waiau
Lake Waiau is a unique alpine lake which, at 13,020 feet, is the third highest lake in the USA. It sits inside the Puu Waiau cinder cone in a barren and treeless setting.

Lake Waiau is rather mysterious. It's a small lake, no more than 10 feet deep and set on porous cinder in desert conditions of less than 15 inches of rainfall per year. It's fed by melting winter snows and permafrost, which elsewhere on Mauna Kea quickly evaporates. Lake Waiau has no freshwater springs and yet it's never dry.

Hawaiians used to bring the umbilical cords of their babies and throw them in the lake to give their children the strength of the mountain.

Puu Poliahu
Just below the summit is Puu Poliahu, the home of Poliahu, goddess of snow.

Poliahu is said to be more beautiful than her sister Pele. According to legend, during conflicts over men, Pele would get miffed and erupt Mauna Kea, Poliahu would cover it over with ice and snow, then Pele would erupt again. Back and forth they went. The legend is metaphorically correct. As recent as 10,000 years ago there were volcanic eruptions through glacial ice caps here.

Because of its spiritual significance, astronomical domes have not been built on Puu Poliahu.

Mauna Kea Summit Trail
There's a six-mile hiking trail to the top of Mauna Kea which starts near the end of the paved road above the visitor center. Instead of continuing on the main 4WD road, take the road to the left. The trail begins up through wooden posts and more or less parallels the summit road. It's marked with posts and stone cairns.

The trail starts at 9200 feet and climbs almost 4600 feet. Because of the altitude it's quite strenuous and it's also easy to get sunburned. Dress in layers of warm clothing and take sunscreen and plenty of water. Give yourself a full day for this hike – most people take four to five hours to get to the summit.

It's a difficult hike, as you're walking on cinders, but there are incredible vistas and strange moonlike landscapes. The trail passes through the **Mauna Kea Ice Age Natural Area Reserve**. There was once a

Pleistocene glacier here and scratchings on rocks from the glacial moraine can still be seen.

The ancient adze quarry **Keanakakoi**, at 12,400 feet, is two-thirds of the way up. **Lake Waiau** is a mile farther.

You might be tempted to hitch a ride from someone at the visitor center who's going to the summit and then walk down. But if you haven't spent the previous night in the mountains, there's a danger in doing this as you won't have as much time to acclimatize.

Summit Tours
Visitor Center Programs The visitor center (☎ 961-2180) has summit tours on Saturdays and Sundays that take in the University of Hawaii's 88-inch telescope.

The tour is free but you need to provide your own 4WD transportation to the summit. If you're lucky, you might be able to catch a ride up with someone from the visitor center, but you can't count on it. Children under 16 are not allowed because of altitude health hazards. Check in at the visitor center before 1:30 pm. The tours are subject to cancellation when there's inclement weather at the summit.

Other Tours Pat Wright of Paradise Safaris (☎ 322-2366), Box A-D, Kailua-Kona, HI 96745, conducts sunset tours of Mauna Kea summit for $105. The tour includes pick-up at West Hawaii hotels and stargazing from their own little telescope.

Waipio Valley Shuttle (☎ 775-7121), Box 5128, Kukuihaele, HI 96727, operates daytime tours that go to the summit of Mauna Kea and include an observatory visit. The tour, which costs $78 including lunch, leaves from Waimea and takes about six hours. There's a four-person minimum.

For information on snow skiing, see the Activities section at the beginning of the chapter.

Places to Stay
Mauna Kea State Park is seven miles west of Summit Rd, near the 35-mile marker. It has picnic tables, restrooms, a pay phone

and 20 acres of shrubland. At an elevation of 6500 feet, the days are commonly cool and the nights cold.

The park has seven housekeeping cabins which are mostly used by hunters who hunt pigs, goats and game birds on the slopes of Mauna Kea. The cabins have basic kitchens, electric heating, bathrooms, hot showers and beds with the standard saggy mattresses.

As most hunting is restricted to weekends, that's the most difficult time to book the cabins. Nearby military maneuvers can be noisy, but otherwise it's a good base for those planning to hike Mauna Kea or Mauna Loa.

For reservations, contact the Division of State Parks (☎ 933-4200), Box 936, Hilo, HI 96721. Rates are the same as for other park cabins: $10 for one person, $17 for two, up to $30 for six.

MAUNA LOA'S NORTHERN FLANK
The road to Mauna Loa starts just east of the Summit Rd and climbs 18 miles up the northern flank of Mauna Loa to a weather station at 11,150 feet. There are no visitor facilities at the weather station.

The narrow road is gently sloping and passable in a standard car. As it's winding, nearly one lane and has some blind spots, give yourself about 45 minutes to drive up. It might be wise to loosen your gas cap before you start in order to avoid vapor lock problems. Park in the lot below the weather station; the equipment used to measure atmospheric conditions is highly sensitive to exhaust.

The summit and domes of Mauna Kea are visible from here and when conditions are just right you can see the 'Mauna Kea shadow' at sunset. It's a curious phenomenon in which Mauna Kea sometimes casts a blue-purple shadow behind itself in the sky.

Observatory Trail
The weather station is the trailhead for the Observatory Trail which connects up with the Mauna Loa Trail after three miles. From there it's 2½ miles around the western side of Mauna Loa's caldera,

Mokuaweoweo, to the summit at 13,679 feet, or two miles along the eastern side of Mokuaweoweo Caldera to Mauna Loa cabin at 13,250 feet. The cabin marks the end of the 18-mile Mauna Loa Trail which starts down in the main section of Hawaii Volcanoes National Park.

The Observatory Trail is very steep and difficult. If you haven't been staying in the mountains, altitude sickness is very likely. The hike to the cabin takes four to six hours for strong hikers. Anyone who is not in top shape shouldn't even consider it.

Overnight hikers must register in advance with the Kilauea Visitor Center in Hawaii Volcanoes National Park. For details, see Backcountry Hiking in the Hawaii Volcanoes National Park section.

Continuing on to Hilo

Heading eastward from the hunter's check station below Mauna Kea's visitor center, the terrain along the Saddle Rd gradually becomes ohia-fern forest, shrubby at first, but getting thicker and taller as Hilo gets closer.

Red ohelo berries are fairly common in this area. These low shrubs are from the heath family, related to blueberries and cranberries. They're tart but edible.

Although most of the road is fine there's one winding stretch worthy of note as oncoming drivers often take to the center of the road to cut curves. The last part of the highway is newly paved. As the road re-enters civilization you can see Hilo Bay in the distance.

About four miles outside Hilo, Akolea Rd leads off to the left and connects in two miles to Waianuenue Ave, which passes Boiling Pots and Rainbow Falls (see the Hilo section).

Alternatively, stay on the Saddle Rd and you'll soon come to Kaumana Caves, a small county park on the left.

Hilo

Hilo, the county capital and commercial center, is along a large crescent-shaped bay and has Hawaii's second largest port. The population is 32,000, which is nearly one-third the island's total.

In terms of lush, natural beauty, Hilo beats Kona hands down any day – the only catch is in finding a sunny one. During an average year in Hilo, measurable rain falls on 278 days.

Although the rain dampens some spirits, it also feeds the waterfalls, gardens and jungle-like valleys. Consequently, cut flowers are big business in Hilo and orchids and anthuriums thrive in the area.

Many of Hilo's buildings are old and weathered and some of the small businesses within them look as if they've been there a hundred years . . . a few of them have.

Hilo is ethnically diverse, with a lot of people of Japanese and Filipino descent. There's also an alternative community that's been filtering in since the '70s, attracted by Hilo's affordability and the windward coast's scenic appeal.

Hilo is a survivor. Natural forces threaten it from both sides, tidal waves from one and lava from the other. Two devastating tsunamis have hit in this century alone and as recently as 1984 a lava flow from Mauna Loa stopped short just eight miles above town.

Hilo's reputation for wet weather has

protected it from the invasive development that has spread elsewhere on the island. In many ways Hilo is the last remaining Hawaiian city unaffected by tourism.

Not that attempts haven't been made. In the 1970s Hilo built a new airport and a few deluxe hotels and started a media blitz. The airlines began direct flights from the mainland, but the tourists never showed.

'America's rainiest city' just couldn't compete with the sunny Kona Coast. The mainland flights have all been dropped and some of the hotels have been turned into condos or cheap local housing.

Information

Tourist Information The Hawaii Visitors Bureau (☎ 961-5797), on the corner of Haili and Keawe Sts, is open from 8 am to noon and from 1 to 4:30 pm Monday to Friday.

For camping permits, the County Department of Parks & Recreation (☎ 961-8311) is at 25 Aupuni St and the Division of State Parks (☎ 933-4200) at 75 Aupuni St. Both are near Wailoa River State Park.

Money The Bank of Hawaii has branches at 117 Keawe St, 120 Pauahi and 417 E Kawili. There are numerous other banks around town.

Post Hilo has two post offices. The main one is on the road into the airport. It's open from 8:15 am to 4:45 pm Monday to Friday, 8:30 am to 12:30 pm on Saturdays.

The more convenient downtown post office is in the federal building on Waianuenue Ave. It's open from 8 am to 4 pm Monday to Friday and from 12:30 to 4 pm on Saturdays.

Bookstores Basically Books (☎ 961-0144), 46 Waianuenue Ave, is a book and map store specializing in Hawaiiana, including travel guides, diving guides, out-of-print books and Hawaiian dictionaries and literature. They also have a general travel section and USGS topographic maps of Hawaii and the Pacific.

Other bookstores include Waldenbooks

in the Prince Kuhio Plaza on Hwy 11 and Book Gallery in the Kaikoo Mall, 777 Kilauea Ave.

Coin Laundry Hilo Quality Washerette, 210 Hoku St, behind 7-Eleven, is open from 5 am to 10 pm daily.

Emergency For police, fire and ambulance, dial 911. Hilo Hospital is at 1190 Waianuenue Ave, near Rainbow Falls; dial 969-4111 for information, 969-4100 for the emergency room.

Other Aloha Airlines (☎ 935-9385) is in the Hilo Shopping Center and Hawaiian Airlines (☎ 935-0858) is at 120 Kamehameha Ave. Cut Rate Tickets, at the Puainako Town Center on Hwy 11, sells discounted air tickets.

Hilo's cheapest gas is Aloha Gas, on Hwy 11 at the start of the airport road; the station is open 24 hours.

Walking Tours

Downtown Hilo is a mishmash of classic old buildings from the early 1900s, many on the National Register of Historic Places, and aging wooden storefronts, some newly renovated, others falling apart.

One short walk that takes in historical sites and some interesting shops starts at the intersection of Kalakaua and Keawe Sts, goes northwest along Keawe, up Wailuku Dr, along Kinoole St past Kalakaua Park and back down Kalakaua St.

If you wander a little further astray you can explore the backstreets, where there are little Japanese restaurants with faded kanji signs, barber shops with hand-pumped chairs and old pool halls.

The informative brochure *Walking Tour of Historic Downtown* is available free at the HVB office, the Lyman Museum and some hotels.

Maui's Canoe

The north end of Keawe St has been spruced up, with the old welfare office being turned into a Cajun restaurant and

PLACES TO STAY

- 1 Dolphin Bay Hotel
- 2 Wild Ginger Inn
- 6 Hilo Hawaiian Hotel
- 7 Hilo Bay Hotel
- 8 Naniloa Hotel
- 10 Hilo Seaside Hotel
- 13 Arnott's Lodge

PLACES TO EAT

- 4 Nihon Restaurant
- 11 Harrington's
- 16 Pizza Hut
- 19 KK Tei
- 21 Ken's House of Pancakes
- 24 Burger King
- 29 Miyo's

OTHER

- 3 Suisan Fish Auction
- 5 Liliuokalani Gardens
- 9 Naniloa Golf Course
- 12 Big Island Candies
- 14 Hilo Tropical Gardens
- 15 Hilo Hospital
- 17 County Offices
- 18 Wailoa Center
- 20 Harper Rentals
- 23 Hilo Quality Washerette
- 25 Kaikoo Mall
- 26 State Offices
- 27 d'Angoras
- 28 Hoolulu Complex
- 30 Aloha Gas
- 31 Pacific Rent-All
- 32 Hilo Shopping Center
- 33 Prince Kuhio Plaza
- 34 Puainako Town Center

Hilo

other old shops housing trendy new businesses.

If you continue walking along Keawe St just beyond Wailuku Dr, you'll be on the Puueo St Bridge which crosses over the Wailuku River. The large rock in the river upstream on the left is called Maui's Canoe.

Legend has it that the demigod Maui paddled his canoe with such speed across the ocean that he crash-landed here and the canoe turned to stone. Ever the devoted son, Maui was rushing to save his mother, Hina, from a water monster who was trying to drown her by damming the river and flooding her cave beneath Rainbow Falls.

Kalakaua Park

In the late 1800s King David Kalakaua established Hilo as the county seat. Kalakaua Park is a quiet downtown park with a **statue** of the king sitting beneath the shade of a banyan tree, holding a taro leaf and a hula drum. The park also has a **sundial** erected by the king in 1877, a **war memorial** and a **reflecting pool** filled with carp and water lilies.

The most recent addition is a capsule containing a collection of modern-day mementos which was buried during the total solar eclipse on July 11, 1991. It's intended to be opened on May 3, 2106 at the time of the next total eclipse.

The site of the king's former summer home, Niolopa, is opposite the park at what today is the Hilo Hotel.

Around Kalakaua Park

The old **federal building** opposite the park on Waianuenue Ave was built in 1919. It's of neo-classical design with high columns and a Spanish-tile roof. It houses the post office.

On the other side of the park, on Kalakaua St, the **East Hawaii Cultural Center** has taken over the old police station (circa 1932). The center hosts quality art exhibits that change monthly. Admission is free and it's open 9 am to 4 pm Monday to Saturday. A performing arts center is upstairs.

Next door is the **Hawaiian Telephone Company building**, designed by Honolulu architect C W Dickey in the 1920s. It's of Spanish-mission influence with nice tile work.

Lyman Museum

Lyman Museum (☎ 935-5021), 276 Haili St, is a first-class museum and a great place to spend a rainy afternoon.

The ground floor features the **Island Heritage Gallery**. Displays show how adzes were made of volcanic clinker, how kukui nuts were skewered on coconut leaves to burn as candles and other aspects of life in Polynesian Hawaii. Exhibits include feather leis, tapa cloth and a house made of pili grass. Mana, kahunas and *awa* (kava) drinking are all succinctly explained.

The different lifestyles of those who came as indentured immigrants and stayed on to form Hawaii's multiethnic society are all given their due. Displays include costumes, cultural artifacts and insightful interpretive plaques. From Portugal there's a braginha, the forerunner of the ukulele. From China there's a full-size Taoist shrine that was disassembled and carried aboard a ship in the luggage of Chinese emigrating to Hilo.

Upstairs in the **Earth Heritage Gallery** is the largest mineral collection in the Pacific. There are thousands of rocks, crystals and gemstones, as well as minerals that glow in the dark.

The **lava section** explains volcanic eruptions and lava formations with samples of spatter, olivine, Pele's tears and fine strands of Pele's hair. Other exhibits include native insects, birds, seashells and land shells. Hawaii has 1000 native land shell species found nowhere else on earth.

The museum is open from 9 am to 5 pm Monday to Saturday and from 1 to 4 pm on Sundays. Admission costs $4.50 for adults, $2.50 for children.

Mission House Adjacent to the main museum is the large missionary house built by the Reverend David Lyman and his wife

Sarah in 1839. They had seven children of their own and in the attic boarded a number of island boys who attended their church school.

The mission house tour is brief and informal, led by an enthusiastic guide. You get a good feel for the people who lived in this house. Things are faded and used, such as the very old patchwork quilts. The house has many of the original furnishings including Sarah Lyman's melodeon, rocking chair and china dishes. Some of the original wavy glass windows are still in place.

The mattresses are stuffed with wood shavings, a material which provided a bed for bugs as well.

Tours of Mission House are given at 9:30, 10:30 and 11:30 am and 1, 2, 3 and 4 pm and are included in the admission price for the Lyman Museum.

Churches

Haili St was once called Church Row for the churches which lined up along it. The three that remain, one Catholic and two Congregational, are worth a look.

St Joseph's Church, on the corner of Haili and Kapiolani Sts, is an attractive pink church of Spanish-mission design that looks as if it came right out of Southern California. It was built in 1919 and has an old cracked bell, stained glass windows and a columned entrance topped with angels.

Haili Church, at 211 Haili St, was built in 1859. It has straight lines and a boxy square tower, somewhat resembling a New England barn. Services are conducted in both Hawaiian and English.

The **Central Christian Church**, on the corner of Kilauea Ave and Haili St, was built in the Victorian style in the early 1900s by Portuguese immigrants.

Hilo Library

Hilo has a good public library. It's at 300 Waianuenue Ave and is open from 9 am to 5 pm daily except Sundays, and until 8 pm on Mondays and Wednesdays.

The two large stones on the library's front lawn are the Naha and Pinao stones.

The **Pinao Stone** was an entrance pillar to an old Hawaiian heiau.

The **Naha Stone**, from the same temple

Little Tokyo & Big Tsunamis

On April 1, 1946, Hilo Bay was inundated by a tsunami which had raced its way across the Pacific from an earthquake in the Aleutian Islands. It struck at 6:54 am without warning.

Fifty-foot waves jumped the sea wall and swept into the city. They tore the first line of buildings off their foundations, carrying them inland and smashing them into the rows behind. As the waves pulled back, they sucked much of the splintered debris and a number of people out to sea.

By 7 am the town was littered with shattered buildings as far as the eye could see. The ground was not visible through the pile of rubble. Throughout Hawaii the tsunami killed 159 people and racked up $25 million in property damages. The hardest hit was Hilo, with 96 fatalities.

Hilo's bay-front 'Little Tokyo' bore the brunt of the storm. Shinmachi, which means 'New Town' in Japanese, was rebuilt on the same spot.

Fourteen years later, on May 23, 1960, an earthquake off the coast of Chile triggered a tsunami that made a beeline for Hilo at a speed of 440 miles per hour. A series of three tidal waves washed up in succession, each one sweeping farther up into the city.

Although the tsunami warning speakers roared this time, many people didn't take them seriously. The tiny tsunamis of the 1950s had been relatively harmless and some people actually went down to the beach to watch the waves.

Those along the shore were swept inland, while others farther up were dragged out into the bay. A few lucky ones who managed to grab hold of floating debris were rescued at sea. In the end there were 61 deaths and property damage of over $20 million.

Again Shinmachi was leveled, but this time instead of rebuilding, the low-lying bay-front property was turned into parks and the survivors relocated to higher ground.

All along Kamehameha Ave you can still see the curbstone cuts that once led to streets or to the driveways of businesses that made up Shinmachi. ■

BIG ISLAND

Maui's Canoe

Singing Bridge

Wailuku River

Wailuku Dr

Wailuku Dr

Shipman St

19

Kamehameha Ave

Library

Federal Building
Post Office

1 ▼

Greenpeace
Hawaii

● 2

Walanuenue Ave

200

▼ 3

Kalakaua
Park

4 ▼

5 ▼

Hawaiian
Airlines

$ ● 6

Kalakaua St

To Rainbow
Falls

Kapiolani St

Kilauea Ave

Kinoole St

Keawe St

Hilo
Hotel

East
Hawaii
Cultural
Center

Hawaiian
Telephone
Company

Lyman Museum
& Mission House 血

St Joseph's
† Church

Gas Station ⛽

Hawaii
Visitors
Bureau

▼ 7

Haili
House Inn

Haili
Church

Ululani St

▼ 8

Central †
Christian
Church

▼ ℹ
9

▼ 10
Haili St

Furneaux St

11 ▼

Downtown Hilo

Punahoa St

● 12

13 ▼

● Mooheau
Bus Terminal

14 ▼

15 ●

Mamo St

16 ▼

0   100   200 m

0   100   200 yards

---

grounds, is said to weigh 2½ tons. According to legend any person who had the strength to budge the stone would have the strength to conquer and unite all the islands. Kamehameha I reputedly met the challenge and overturned the stone in his youth.

Wailoa River State Park

Wailoa River State Park, located on the grassy expanses where Shinmachi once stood, is reached from Pauahi St. The park has two **memorials**, one dedicated to the tsunami victims and the other, an eternal flame, dedicated to the area's Vietnam War dead.

Wailoa River flows through the park and most of **Waiakea Pond** is within the park boundaries. This spring-fed estuarine pond has both saltwater and brackish water fish species, mostly mullet. There's a boat launch ramp near the mouth of the river; only non-motor boats are allowed and fishing licenses are required.

The park's **Wailoa Center**, near the memorials, is a state-run art gallery with multimedia exhibits that change monthly. Photos of the tsunami damage are on display downstairs. It's open from 8 am to

▼   PLACES TO EAT

1   Roussel's
3   Dairy Queen
4   Bears' Coffee
5   Lehua's Bar & Grill
7   Karrots
8   McDonald's
9   Andrew Oliver's
10 Pescatore
11 Abundant Life Natural Foods & Oroweat
    Bakery Thrift Store
13 Cafe Pesto
14 Royal Siam
16 Kentucky Fried Chicken

OTHER

2   Basically Books
6   Bank of Hawaii
12 KTA Supermarket
15 Farmers' Market

4:30 pm on Mondays, Tuesdays, Thursdays and Fridays; from noon to 8:30 pm on Wednesdays and from 9 am to 3 pm on Saturdays. Admission is free.

Banyan Drive

Banyan Drive goes around the edge of the Waiakea Peninsula, which juts into Hilo Bay. The road skirts the Liliuokalani Gardens, the nine-hole Naniloa Golf Course and Hilo's bayfront hotels.

Banyan Dr is lined with large, sprawling **banyan trees** that were planted in the 1930s by royalty and celebrities. If you look closely you'll find plaques beneath the trees identifying the planters – they include Babe Ruth, Amelia Earhart and Cecil B De Mille.

Suisan Fish Auction

Local fishers sell their catch every morning except Sundays at Suisan Fish Auction, near the intersection of Lihiwai and Banyan Dr, on the western side of the Waiakea Peninsula.

The auction is a lively local scene with the auctioneer running up the bids in Hilo's unique form of pidgin. It's open to the public with a roped-off sidewalk viewing area. Get there by 8 am when the auction bell rings, as the whole thing wraps up in a matter of minutes. Also note that they occasionally switch the auction time to 7 am to accommodate changes in the fishing schedules – so you might want to inquire in advance at the front desk where you're staying.

Next door there's a fish market with the freshest fish on the island and a little outdoor snack shop where the fishers talk story over coffee following the auction.

Liliuokalani Gardens

Hilo's 30-acre Japanese garden is named for Queen Liliuokalani, Hawaii's last queen. This waterfront park is filled with ponds complete with mullet that jump clear out of the water, little Japanese pagodas, stone lanterns, arched bridges and patches of bamboo.

The gardens are a monument of sorts to the Japanese presence in Hawaii. Many of the lanterns and pagodas that dot the park were donated by Japanese regional governments and sister cities in honor of the 100th anniversary of Japanese immigration to Hawaii.

It's a pleasant place to walk around, although after heavy rain you'll need to stick to high ground.

Coconut Island

Coconut Island, which is connected to land by a footbridge, sticks out into the bay opposite the Liliuokalani Gardens. The island is a county park with picnic tables and swimming but it's most popular as a recreational fishing spot. Hilo's Fourth of July fireworks display is shot off from the island.

In ancient times Coconut Island was called Moku Ola, 'Island of Life', in part due to the powers of a healing stone located there. Medical kahunas used the stone and invocations to cure the sick by ridding them of demonic spirits. Moku Ola also had pure spring water, which was said to bring good health, and a birthing stone which instilled mana to the children born there.

Beaches

Hilo is not a city for beach bums. Still, there are some decent beaches along Kalanianaole Ave, a four-mile stretch on the eastern side of Hilo. The road is basically a continuation of Kamehameha Ave, starting in front of the Hilo Seaside Hotel.

Onekahakaha Beach Park This park is a quarter of a mile off Kalanianaole Ave. The turn-off is just before the Hilo Tropical Gardens.

The park has a big sandy-bottomed pool formed by a large boulder enclosure. The water's just a foot or two deep in most places and it's popular with families with young children.

On the Hilo side of the park there's an unprotected cove that is sometimes used by snorkelers on calm days, but be careful as it has a seaward current. The park department cautions swimmers and snorkelers not to venture beyond the breakwater at any time.

There are campsites, restrooms, showers and a picnic area shaded by big tropical almond trees. Campers usually set up their tents around the edge of the lawn near the tree line at the Hilo end of the beach. But at any rate, avoid low ground because when it rains in Hilo, it pours.

James Kealoha Beach Park Kealoha is a roadside county park known locally as Four-Mile Beach because of the distance between the park and the downtown post office. It's just before the Mauna Loa Shores apartments and has camping, showers and restrooms.

For swimming and snorkeling most people go to the eastern side which is sheltered by an island and a naturally occurring rocky breakwater. It's generally calm there with clean, clear water and pockets of white sand.

The Hilo side of the park is open ocean and much rougher. You can sometimes find people net fishing there. It's also a popular winter surfing spot, although there are strong rip currents which run out to sea.

Richardson Ocean Park This park, just before the end of the road, has a small black sand beach fronting Hilo's most favored snorkeling site. The left side of the bay tends to be colder due to springs in the water. On the right side the springs are less common and the snorkeling is better.

The park has a lava shoreline at its east side that can be fun to explore. There are restrooms, showers and picnic tables, and a lifeguard is on duty daily.

Rainbow Falls

Rainbow Falls is on the western side of Hilo, off Waianuenue Ave, just below the hospital.

Waianuenue, literally 'rainbow seen in water', is the Hawaiian name for this pretty 80-foot waterfall. The huge cave beneath the falls is said to have been the home of Hina, mother of Maui. The falls are usually seen as a double drop which flows together before hitting the large pool at the bottom.

The best time to see rainbows is in the mornings, although they're by no means guaranteed, as the sun and mist need to be accommodating. You can get a straight-on look of the falls from the viewpoint in front of the parking lot.

For a little diversion take the short loop trail that begins along the steps at the left side of the falls and continues for about five minutes past a giant banyan tree and through a lush jungle-like area before leading back to the parking lot.

The site has restrooms and drinking water.

Peepee Falls & Boiling Pots

Peepee Falls and Boiling Pots are up Waianuenue Ave, about 1½ miles past Rainbow Falls.

Peepee Falls drop from a sheer rock face and as the water runs downstream over a series of basalt depressions in the river, it swirls and churns into bubbling pools which have earned it the name Boiling Pots.

Boiling Pots is most interesting after periods of heavy rain when the water runs strongest.

Kaumana Caves

The Kaumana Caves were formed by an 1881 lava flow from Mauna Loa. As the flow subsided, the outer edges of the deep lava stream cooled and crusted over in a tunnel-like effect. The hot molten lava inside then drained out, creating these caves.

The caves are wet and mossy, thickly covered with ferns and impatiens. If you have a flashlight you might want to explore them, although they tend to be drippy.

The caves, which are signposted, are on the right three miles up Kaumana Dr (Hwy 200). There's a parking area on the opposite side of the street.

Nurseries & Gardens

Most of the state's orchids are grown on the Big Island, earning it one of its nicknames, 'The Orchid Island'. Hilo is the center of activity and from here orchids, anthuriums and other tropical flowers are flown to florists around the world.

A number of Hilo's working nurseries open their greenhouses and gardens to visitors free of charge. Look for 'visitors welcome' signs along the road.

Hilo Tropical Gardens This pleasant little two-acre naturalized garden is conveniently located on the beach road at the east side of Hilo. A fading moss-covered sign here quotes Kipling, 'Gardens are not made by sitting in the shade' and this garden is obviously the result of years of labor. Paths wind around lily ponds, orchids, azaleas, hibiscus, ginger and all sorts of tropical flowers. There's a flower and gift shop in front, as well as a shop selling great homemade ice cream.

The garden is at 1477 Kalanianaole Ave, just past Onekahakaha Beach. It's open from 8:30 am to sunset daily. Admission costs $3 for adults, $1.50 for ages 13 to 18, free for children under 12.

Nani Mau Gardens Nani Mau Gardens is a large commercial garden on the tour bus route. There are over 20 acres of flowering plants, including a lovely orchid section,

and much of the flora is identified with labels. Unlike many Hawaiian gardens, it's not terribly naturalized or charmingly overgrown, but rather has sculptured plantings, wide asphalt paths, tram rides and a restaurant. Still, for those who enjoy formally manicured gardens, this ambitious project has much to offer.

Nani Mau is about three miles south of Hilo. The turn-off from Hwy 11 onto Makalika St is marked with a small HVB warrior sign. Admission is $5 and the garden has access for the disabled. It's open from 8 am to 5 pm daily.

Panaewa Rainforest Zoo

Panaewa Rainforest Zoo, the only tropical rainforest zoo in the USA, is in a forest reserve which gets 125 inches of rain annually.

It's a respectable little zoo and good for an hour of strolling. Two impressive tigers, both born here, roam a large, natural pit-style cage. There are monkeys, alligators, giant anteaters, a pygmy hippo and feral pigs and sheep. Peacocks and guinea fowl have the run of the place. You can also see some of Hawaii's endangered birds, such as the nene and the Hawaiian duck, coot, hawk, and owl.

To get there, turn off Hwy 11 onto Mamaki St (also called Kulani Hwy), a few miles south of town. The zoo is one mile west of Hwy 11. It's open from 9 am to 4 pm daily and admission is free.

Mauna Loa Macadamia Nut Visitor Center

Mauna Loa Macadamia Nut Visitor Center is on Macadamia Rd off Hwy 11, about five miles south of Hilo. The nearly three-mile road to the center cuts across row after row of macadamia trees, as far as the eye can see.

C Brewer Co, which owns Mauna Loa, produces most of the world's macadamia nuts. The large visitor center here caters to tour bus crowds and is essentially just a gift shop and snack bar.

To the side is a working factory, which has an outside walkway with windows that allows visitors to view the large, fast-paced assembly line inside.

The little planted area out behind the visitor center with its labeled fruit trees and flowering bushes is worth walking through if you've come this far. The center is open from 8:30 am to 5 pm daily.

Places to Stay

Partially due to the weather, Hilo has no self-contained resorts. People don't come to Hilo to hang around a pool, but to visit the sights and then head on. Consequently, Hilo's best values are generally its bottom-end accommodations. The 'vacation rental' condo market that's so common on the Kona Coast is virtually nonexistent here.

Places to Stay – bottom end

Arnott's Lodge (☎ 969-7097, (800) 368-8752 from the mainland, (800) 953-7773 within Hawaii; fax 961-9638), 98 Apapane Rd, Hilo, HI 96720, is a great place to connect with other travelers. This friendly and accommodating hostel-style lodge has 44 dorm beds and 10 private rooms in a converted apartment building. It costs $15 for a bunk bed in a room with two to four people, $26 for a single room and $36 for doubles, all with shared baths and kitchen facilities. Linen and towels are provided. There's a common room with a TV, a coin laundry, free airport pick-up (look for the courtesy phone at Hilo Airport) and a scheduled daily shuttle service into town.

The lodge also offers daily outings that surely rank as the best (and most adventurous!) tour values on the Big Island. The schedule includes Waipio Valley and Hiilawe Falls, Puna and Pahoa, South Point and Green Sands Beach, Hawaii Volcanoes National Park and Mauna Kea. Each outing costs $20.

To get to Arnott's Lodge, go east 1½ miles on Kalanianaole Ave from Hwy 11 and turn left onto Keokea Loop Rd. The lodge is about 100 yards down the road, on the right.

The popular *Dolphin Bay Hotel* (☎ 935-1466; fax 935-1523), 333 Iliahi St, Hilo, HI 96720, located on a hill just above down-

town, is a very friendly, family-run place. Not only is the hotel a good value but, unlike many other small inns, it welcomes travelers with children. All 18 apartment-like units have full kitchens, TVs and bathrooms, and all except the standard rooms have sunken bathtubs. Fresh-picked fruit from the backyard is available in the lobby, along with free morning coffee. There's a two-night minimum stay. Standard rooms cost $42/52 for singles/doubles, while superior rooms cost $52/62. They also have four large one-bedroom units for $72 and a two-bedroom unit for $82 for either singles or doubles. It's $10 more for each additional person. Weekly rates are available. This is one of the few hotels in Hilo with a continuously high occupancy rate and reservations are suggested.

The owners of the *Wild Ginger Inn* (☎ 935-5556, (800) 882-1887), 100 Puueo St, Hilo, HI 96720, have taken a formerly rundown motel and given it a bright face-lift in hot pink and green Caribbean colors. Rooms in this nonsmoking inn are simple but quite adequate and a good continental breakfast is included in the price. The rooms have either a double or two twin beds and private baths; most also have small refrigerators. Despite the central location, there's a wooded gulch behind the main wing that provides many of the rooms with nice views of bamboo and a little stream. The cost is $39 for singles or doubles and there's a monthly rate, without breakfast, of $350.

Hilo Hotel (☎ 961-3733), 142 Kinoole St, Box 726, Hilo, HI 96720, is an old-fashioned downtown hotel built in the 1950s on the former site of King Kalakaua's summer home. It's as much local as tourist oriented and the rooms are simple and a bit faded, but otherwise fine. There's a community lounge with a TV, and complimentary malasadas and coffee in the morning. Rooms, which have private baths, air conditioning and small refrigerators, cost $45 with TV, $39 without.

Lihi Kai (☎ 935-7865), c/o Amy Gamble Lannan, 30 Kahoa Rd, Hilo, HI 96720, is a B&B in Amy's home perched on a cliff directly above Hilo Bay, two miles north of town. There's a small solar-heated swimming pool and a large living room with a wonderful ocean view. The two bedrooms, which share a bath and a half, cost $50 for either singles/doubles with breakfast. There's a three-night minimum stay or an extra $5 charge.

Places to Stay – middle

Hilo Seaside Hotel (☎ 935-0821, (800) 367-7000), 126 Banyan Dr, Hilo, HI 96720, is a 145-unit two-story motel-style complex with a nice carp pond out front. Rooms are on the small side and rather standard, although all have TV and a small refrigerator. You might want to avoid the rooms around the swimming pool, which can get a bit noisy. Rates begin at $54 for the room only and $70 with a Budget rental car. However, if you book within Hawaii (rather than calling toll-free from the mainland) and ask for the special it's often as low as $95 for two nights with a car.

Uncle Billy's *Hilo Bay Hotel* (☎ 935-0861, (800) 367-5102; fax 935-7903), 87 Banyan Dr, Hilo, HI 96720, is a 130-room economy hotel. Rates range from $64 for a quite basic standard room to $82 for a much nicer oceanfront room in the main building. Rooms cost about $10 less in the low season.

Haili House Inn (☎ 969-7378), 239 Haili St, Hilo, HI 96720, is a new inn occupying an atmospheric 75-year-old home in downtown Hilo. There are five pleasant bedrooms with wood floors, ceiling fans, queen beds and Hawaiian-style decor. Each has a private toilet. There's a common living room with a TV and stereo. Rates, which include a continental breakfast, are $75 with shared bath, $89 with private bath, plus $10 more for stays of one night only.

Three miles north of Hilo off Hwy 19 is *Hale Kai Bjornen* (☎ 935-6330; fax 935-8439), 111 Honolii Pali, Hilo, HI 96720, a B&B in an immaculately kept contemporary home with fine views across Hilo Bay. The B&B is run by Evonne Bjornen, who comes from Norway, along with Paul, her

Hawaiian husband. The five ocean-facing rooms each have a private bath, cable TV and either a queen or king bed and range in price from $80 to $98, with breakfast included. The highest rate is for a guest cottage with kitchenette and requires a five-day minimum stay. Guests have use of a small swimming pool, a refrigerator and the living room.

Places to Stay – top end

Hilo Hawaiian Hotel (☎ 935-9361, (800) 367-5004; fax 961-9642), 71 Banyan Dr, Hilo, HI 96720, is a 285-unit high-rise hotel overlooking Coconut Island and Hilo Bay. The hotel has recently been renovated and rooms are large and comfortable. They have a pleasant though not distinguished decor, either a king or two twin beds, air conditioning, remote-control TV and phone. Most rooms have private lanais. A garden view room costs $99, an oceanview room $125. If you request it at the time of booking you can usually have a free rental car added on at no extra cost.

Naniloa Hotel (☎ 969-3333, (800) 367-5360; fax 969-6622), 93 Banyan Dr, Hilo, HI 96720, is a 325-room high-rise hotel – Hilo's largest. The rooms are quite nice, but cost $96 to $144 depending on the view and only the top-end rooms have balconies. It's popular with Japanese tour groups.

Places to Eat

Hilo has lots of hole-in-the-wall restaurants and cheap places to eat. Many places have salad-to-dessert lunch specials for around $5 and even some of the best restaurants have weekday 'business lunches' for just a bit more than that.

Places to Eat – budget

Bears' Coffee, 106 Keawe St, is a nice place for a light lunch or breakfast. They have bagels and pastries, good Belgian waffles and egg dishes (until 11:30 am) and from 10 am there are deli sandwiches, burritos and build-your-own bagels with more than a dozen fillings. Everything, except the lox and bagel, costs less than $5. It's open from 7 am to 4 pm daily except

Sundays. There are both indoor and sidewalk tables.

Miyo's (☎ 935-2273), in the Waiakea Villas complex, is a charming homestyle Japanese restaurant overlooking Waiakea Pond. The atmosphere is relaxed, the food good and the prices unbeatable. At lunch, tempura, shabu shabu, tonkatsu or sesame chicken – all served with rice and soup – cost around $6. A tempura and sashimi combination is just $7. The same meals at dinner cost a dollar more. It's open Tuesday to Saturday from 11 am to 2 pm and 5:30 to 8:30 pm.

KK Tei, 1550 Kamehameha Ave, is a family restaurant with a varied menu that includes all the Japanese standards. At lunch, oyako donburi (egg and chicken over rice) with miso soup and tea costs $4.50 and complete Japanese and American style meals are priced from $7. Dinners average a few dollars more. They're open from 11 am to 2 pm and 5 to 9 pm Monday to Saturday, but close up early on days when business is slow.

Karrots, a natural foods restaurant inside a fitness center at 197 Keawe St, is a good choice for healthy breakfasts and light lunches. Homemade granola costs $2.50, blueberry pancakes $4, sandwiches and salads under $5. They also have freshsqueezed 'karrot' juice, good 'karrot' muffins, smoothies and bagels. It's open from 7 am to 5 pm weekdays, to 2 pm on Saturdays.

Abundant Life Natural Foods, 292 Kamehameha Ave, is a health food store with a variety of products including cheeses, yogurt, juices, bulk foods and organic produce. It also has a simple deli and smoothie bar. It's open from 8:30 am to 6 pm weekdays, to 5 pm on Saturdays and from 11 am to 3 pm on Sundays. Next door, *Oroweat Bakery Thrift Store* has slightly dated breads at discounted prices.

Hilo has an abundance of fast-food restaurants spread around the town. The biggest concentration is at the Puainako Town Center on Hwy 11, which has *McDonald's, Pizza Hut, Jack in the Box, Taco Bell, Little Caesar's* and *Subway*

Sandwiches. Ken's House of Pancakes, 1730 Kamehameha Ave, is open 24 hours daily.

A convenient downtown grocery store is the *KTA Supermarket*, 323 Keawe St, which is open from 7 am to 9 pm Monday to Saturday, to 6 pm on Sundays. There's a *Safeway* supermarket at the Prince Kuhio Plaza on Hwy 11 and a 24-hour *Sack N Save* supermarket nearby in the Puainako Town Center. If you're heading for Volcano early in the morning, Sack N Save has coffee and doughnuts from 5 am.

Hilo has a great *farmers' market* on Wednesday and Saturday mornings on the corner of Mamo St and Kamehameha Ave. You can usually pick up three or four Kapoho papayas for $1, as well as Kau oranges and other island fruits, vegies and flowers direct from the growers at bargain prices.

Hilo's best ice cream can be found at *Hilo Homemade Ice Cream*, next to Hilo Tropical Gardens. Owner Fred Stoeber cheerfully scoops up his Hawaiian creations, including tasty poha berry, zesty ginger and other island flavors like lilikoi, coconut cream and macadamia nut. It costs $1.25 for a single scoop, $2 for a double. Hours are 10 am to 5 pm daily. From 11 am to 2 pm you can get a nice curry and rice plate for $4.

Places to Eat – middle

Royal Siam (☎ 961-6100), 68 Mamo St, has good authentic Thai food at reasonable prices. Spicy curry beef or chicken dishes cost $7, while most seafood dishes cost around $9. The menu is extensive, with two pages of vegetarian dishes priced from $5 to $6. It's open from 11 am to 2 pm and 5 to 9 pm Monday to Saturday.

Soontaree's (☎ 934-7426) in the Hilo Shopping Center also serves good Thai food with pad Thai, fried rice, curries and a range of other dishes priced from $5 to $9. Chef Soontaree Gervais grows many of the herbs in her own garden and uses only natural ingredients and no MSG. It's open from 7 am to 2 pm Tuesday to Friday and from 5:30 to 9 pm Tuesday to Sunday.

Cafe Pesto (☎ 969-6640), a branch of the popular Kawaihae restaurant, is on Kamehameha Ave in the newly renovated S Hata building, a classic 1912 building that once held the city's main department store. This casual restaurant serves excellent gourmet pizza, calzones and pasta dishes at moderate prices. From 11 am to 4 pm there are also a few hot sandwiches, such as a Japanese eggplant and marinated artichoke creation, for $7. It's open until 9 pm Sunday to Thursday, to 10 pm on weekends.

Lehua's Bar & Grill (☎ 935-8055), 90 Kamehameha Ave, is a trendy restaurant in the center of Hilo with a varied menu. At lunch there are moderately priced soups, salads and sandwiches as well as hot dishes including a nice charbroiled chicken with papaya salsa that's served with salad and fries for $7.25. Dinners, which come with soup or salad, begin around $10 for chicken or stir-fried vegetables over rice, and top off at $17 for Asian prawns or steak. Lunch is from 11 am to 4 pm, dinner from 5 to 9 pm.

Restaurant Miwa (☎ 961-4454) 1261 Kilauea Ave, is an authentic Japanese restaurant despite its mall location in the Hilo Shopping Center. It has a sushi bar, good sashimi and a full range of Japanese dishes at moderate prices. At lunch a full meal teishoku costs around $8, at dinner around $10, while more extensive dinner combinations cost $15. Although it's not gourmet quality the food is good, with quality, price and decor comparable to what you would find in a neighborhood restaurant in Japan. It's open from 11 am to 10 pm Monday to Saturday.

Fiascos, 200 Kanoelehua Ave (Hwy 11), is a bustling place serving sandwiches, salads, pastas, fajitas and an array of meat dishes at moderate prices. There's also a reasonably good salad bar with soup for $6.25. It's open from 11 am to 10 pm daily, to 11 pm on Fridays and Saturdays.

Nihon Restaurant at 121 Lihiwai St, next to Liliuokalani Gardens, has a fine view of Hilo Bay and a good sushi bar. At lunch there's a 'business special' for $9 which includes two entrees such as sashimi,

tonkatsu or tempura along with nigiri rice, kappamaki, miso soup and tossed salad. Dinner teishokus are a few dollars more. They also have cheaper one-bowl dishes like donburi, soba and udon. It's open from 11 am to 1:30 pm and 5 to 8 pm Monday to Saturday.

Ting-Hao Mandarin Restaurant, in Puainako Town Center on Hwy 11, is a popular Chinese restaurant. Vegetarian dishes such as broccoli with garlic and ma po tofu average $7 and Sichuan and Mandarin meat-based dishes cost $7 to $11. There's also a daily lunch special that includes a main dish, side order and rice for under $5. No MSG is used. It's open from 11 am to 2:30 pm Monday to Saturday and 4:30 to 9 pm nightly.

The Sandalwood Room at the Naniloa Hotel has a pleasant water view and a reasonably priced menu. An omelet with coffee at breakfast, or sandwiches and hot dishes at lunch, are priced around $6.50, while dinner, which includes a salad bar, features entrees that range from chicken for $13 to lamb for $25. Breakfast is from 6:30 to 10:30 am, lunch from 11 am to 2 pm and dinner from 5:30 to 9:30 pm.

Places to Eat – top end
Pescatore (☎ 969-9090), 235 Keawe St, has fine dining, attentive service and Hilo's best Italian food. Lunch is a particularly good deal, with fresh fish for $9 and an array of pasta dishes ranging from $6 for bolognese to $9 for scampi al marinara. At dinner, pasta dishes are about double the lunch prices, while meat and seafood main courses average $20. The fra diavolo is a nice, lightly spiced dinner dish combining fresh ahi, calamari and clams over pasta. Lunch is from 11 am to 2 daily; dinner is from 5:30 to 9 pm weekdays, to 10 pm weekends.

Harrington's (☎ 961-4966), perched on Reeds Bay, is a small waterfront restaurant with a fine view. Locally it's a perennial favorite for special occasions and serves good seafood, steak and chicken dishes in the $15 to $20 range. The restaurant also serves a limited menu at lunch that includes

Caesar salad or sandwiches and fries for around $6. It's open from 11 am to 2 pm Monday to Saturday and from 5:30 pm nightly for dinner. Especially on weekends, dinner reservations are advisable.

Andrew Oliver's (☎ 935-6554) at 97 Haili St, opposite the Cunningham Building, is Hilo's best fine-dining restaurant. Oliver, who formerly was the head chef at *Roussel's* (a Cajun restaurant at 60 Keawe St), has renovated one of Hilo's historic buildings into an intimate and casually elegant restaurant. At lunch, served weekdays from 11 am to 2 pm, there are creative salads and both cold and hot dishes priced around $10. Dinner, served from 6 pm Tuesday to Saturday, is a fixed-price meal that includes an appetizer, soup, salad and your choice of six main dishes. Although the menu changes nightly, there's always seafood and red meat, with main dishes such as fresh Tasmanian salmon française and filet mignon béarnaise. Dinner costs $30 except for the rack of lamb which is $37.50.

Entertainment

Periodically there are community plays, dances and concerts at the East Hawaii Cultural Center on Kalakaua St.

Lehua's Bar & Grill, 90 Kamehameha Ave, has live music with dancing from 9 pm on Fridays and Saturdays, with a cover charge of $3 to $4, and country line dancing on Wednesdays.

d'Angoras, a bar and nightclub at 101 Aupuni St, has dancing from 9 pm Thursday to Saturday and a jazz band from 3 to 6 pm on Sundays; the cover charge averages $3.

Fiascos, on Hwy 11 near Banyan Dr, has country line dancing at 8 pm on Thursdays and either a DJ or live rock, blues and country bands from 9:15 pm on Fridays and Saturdays. The cover charge is usually $3 for local groups, about $10 for big names.

Harrington's has jazz, Hawaiian or contemporary music, either guitar or keyboards, in its lounge from 5:30 pm.

Uncle Billy presents a hula show during dinner time, from 6 pm nightly, at the *Hilo Bay Hotel* restaurant.

The *Waioli Lounge* in the Hilo Hawaiian Hotel has a small dance floor and live music nightly, mostly a mix of contemporary and Hawaiian songs that attracts an older local crowd.

Movie Theaters The movie theaters at *Prince Kuhio Plaza* and at *Waiakea Shopping Plaza*, 88 Kanoelehua Ave, show standard feature films.

Things to Buy

Hilo has several shopping centers. The biggest is the Prince Kuhio Plaza, at the south side of town on Hwy 11, which has 65 stores including Liberty House, Penthouse, Hilo Hatties, Sears, Longs Drugs, Woolworth, a camera shop and a one-hour photo place.

Big Island Candies, 500 Kalanianaole Ave, sells chocolate-covered macadamia nuts, cookies and other sweet treats made on site. From the gift shop, you can sample the products and sip on a free cup of coffee while watching candy being made on the other side of plate-glass windows. It's open from 8:30 am to 5 pm daily.

A good place to look for Hawaiian-made crafts are the gift shops at the Lyman Museum on Haili St and the East Hawaii Cultural Center on Kalakaua St.

Puna

Puna is the diamond-shaped easternmost point of the Big Island. Its main attractions are in lava: vast fields of it covering former villages, an ancient forest of lava tree molds, lava tide pools and black sand beaches.

Kilauea Volcano's active east rift zone slices clear across Puna. The most recent series of eruptions has been spewing lava since 1983. These days the highway into Puna ends abruptly at the 1990 lava flow that covers the former village of Kalapana.

Not surprisingly, Puna has Hawaii's cheapest real estate. The closer to the rift, the greater the volcanic activity and the cheaper the land gets.

While a growing number of people are drawn to Puna by the idea of homesteading, many have found it tough making a living off a lava flow. For years growing pakalolo has been one alternative.

The majority of all pot confiscated by Hawaii police is still taken in Puna. However, paramilitary raids, intense herbicide sprayings and helicopters with infrared sensors that allow authorities to see into people's homes have sharply curtailed the growing.

Deserved or not, Puna has the reputation of being less than friendly. If you're traveling the main roads you probably won't pick up on those vibes at all but if you're cruising around off the beaten path you may raise a suspicious eye.

Some crops take well to lava and Puna is a major producer of anthuriums, grows the best papayas in Hawaii, and grows many of the orchids that get credited to Hilo.

Puna is not known for its beaches and for the most part waters along the coast are subject to strong currents and riptides.

Orientation

Keaau is the entrance to Puna, where Hwy 11 and Hwy 130 intersect. From there, Hwy 130 goes south 11 miles to Pahoa and then continues on to the coast.

Maps which show Hwy 130 winding down through Puna and up the Chain of Craters Road to Hawaii Volcanoes National Park were made obsolete in 1988 when a lava flow buried a large section of the road. The national park can now be entered only via the Hawaii Belt Rd (Hwy 11), which makes Puna more time consuming to visit, as you need to backtrack out the same way you go in.

Hwy 11, on the way to the national park, passes through the towns of Kurtistown, Mountain View and Glenwood.

KEAAU

Keaau is the town at the northern end of Puna. Keaau Shopping Center, at the intersection of Hwy 11 and Hwy 130, has a supermarket, post office, Dairy Queen and a couple of small local eateries.

Keaau Natural Foods, opposite the shopping center and open daily, has reasonably priced fruit and organic produce, baked goods and a full line of health foods. There's a nice little vegetarian cafe next door with inexpensive sandwiches and burritos.

PAHOA

The heart of Puna is Pahoa, a funky little town with raised wooden sidewalks, cowboy architecture and an untamed edge. There are influences from the '60s and '70s but there are other more timeless ones as well. The Akebono Theater, which was built in 1917 and is one of the oldest theaters in Hawaii, has recently been reopened to both local events and big-name concerts by the likes of Taj Mahal.

If you'd like to take a look at life on a lava flow as you're driving around, stop by Pahoa Realty on Main St and pick up their free subdivision map and listings. Prices start as low as $4500 for a small lot (no electricity, water by catchment, gravel roads) in the Black Sand Beach subdivision, on Kilauea's active east rift zone.

Wild orchids grow like weeds along the roadsides around Pahoa and throughout Puna. There are fields of cultivated orchids and lots of anthurium nurseries as well.

It may come as no surprise that the Hawaiian Hemp Company, which advocates the use of the hemp plant for a myriad of purposes, is based in Pahoa. They have a shop on Main St that sells quality hemp-fiber clothing and tote bags.

Places to Stay

The *Village Inn* (☎ 965-6444), 1 Main St, Pahoa, HI 96778, has five 2nd-story rooms in a historic wooden building adjacent to the theater. It's partly funky, slanted hardwood floors and all, and partly classy, with rooms furnished with authentic Victorian-era antiques. Rates are $40 for singles or doubles in rooms with shared bath, $60 for rooms with private baths. If you stay more than one day the rates drop to $30/40 on the second day. Credit cards are accepted.

Bamboo House (☎ 965-8322), Box 1546, Pahoa, HI 96778, a cottage rented by the owner of the natural food store, is on a side street in the center of town. One side of a duplex cottage, it's simple but clean, comfortable and pleasantly airy. There's one bedroom and a small living room with a queen-size sofa bed and cable TV. Another nearby building is also being converted into a vacation rental. Rates are $45 per night, or $35 a night for three nights or more. There's no smoking allowed; credit cards are accepted.

If you just need a cheap place to crash, you might try *Pahoa Station Rooms* (☎ 965-0077), which has a couple of upstairs rooms above the shops at the Kapoho end of the main block in the town center. The rooms are small and basic – a bed, TV and window fan – and share two toilets and a hot-water shower with a couple of permanent tenants. The cost is $20 for one person, $5 for each additional

Geothermal Energy

A few miles southeast of Pahoa is a controversial geothermal operation that's experimenting with the production of electricity from hot (675°F) subterranean water rising from deep wells.

A grand state-sponsored scheme once envisioned developing 20 geothermal plants, each with about a dozen separate wells. Collectively they'd be capable of generating up to 500 megawatts of electricity which would then be transferred by undersea cable directly to Oahu.

Although one operation, the Puna Geothermal Venture, is now supplying the Big Island's power grid with 25 megawatts of electricity, a second and more controversial enterprise, True Geothermal, ceased operations in 1994, largely as the consequence of successful challenges from environmental groups.

Greenpeace, the Rainforest Action Network and the Pele Defense Fund are three of many groups that oppose development of the new geothermal energy projects. Not only were many of the wells scheduled to be placed within Wao Kele O Puna, a rare lowland tropical rainforest, but serious concerns exist about the environmental hazards of extensive drilling into the world's most active volcano – concerns that were heightened after a major well blowout forced area residents to evacuate their homes in 1991.

Legal actions, including those which forced the developers to undertake a lengthy environmental impact study, had much to do with scaling back the project and strong opposition is expected to keep away other potential investors. The Sierra Club Legal Defense Fund has spearheaded most of the legal action with the assistance of pro bono lawyers. The state, which gave up title to 27,800 acres of the Wao Kele O Puna rainforest as part of the master plan to have it developed for geothermal energy, is now embroiled in a lawsuit intended to force it to rescind the land deal. ■

person. If you're camping elsewhere, you can also pay $2.50 here for just a shower.

Places to Eat

Luquin's on Main St in Pahoa's town center has Mexican food. A single taco or enchilada costs $2.50, while combination plates are priced from $6. Huevos rancheros with tortillas, rice and beans cost $5 and are served all day; it's open from 11 am to 9 pm daily.

Huna Ohana, on Main St near Luquin's, is an incense-scented metaphysical bookstore and espresso cafe. Eggs with potatoes and toast, a Belgian waffle with fresh fruit and whipped cream, and various vegetarian lunches average $4 to $5. They also serve organic Kona coffee and make good fruit smoothies. It's open from 8 to 11 am for breakfast and 11 am to 5 pm for lunch Monday to Saturday.

Pahoa Natural Groceries, across from the Bank of Hawaii in the center of town, is a well-stocked natural foods store with a full dairy section, bakery items, inexpensive tabouli and pasta salads and healthy sandwiches such as jack cheese and

avocado on sliced whole-wheat bread. It's open from 9 am to 9 pm daily (to 6 pm on Sundays).

Pahoa also has a ribhouse restaurant, Chinese and Thai restaurants, two competing Italian restaurants, a *Dairy Queen,* and an old grocery store where you'll find the local bulletin board.

Onward from Pahoa

The usual route after Pahoa is to make a triangle that goes down Hwy 132 past Lava Tree State Monument to Kapoho, then continues on Hwy 137 along the shore to the lava flow at Kaimu Beach and comes back to Pahoa via Hwy 130. Conveniently, highways 137 and 130 still connect, though they do so at the very edge of a lava flow.

From Pahoa, Hwy 132 passes through tropical forest reserve. The area is very lush and junglelike, with ferns growing on the bark of trees and a thick ground cover of impatiens. If you're short on time, a good alternative is Pahoa-Pohoiki Rd, which is also a nice rainforest drive along a narrow road lined by old mango trees and papaya groves.

Puna & Pele

In the Hawaiian language there are several proverbial expressions that link Puna with the volcano goddess Pele. As an example, to express anger, someone might say *Ke lauahi maila o Pele ia Puna*, 'Pele is pouring lava out on Puna'.

Equally common are both historic and modern stories of a mysterious woman traveling alone through Puna. Sometimes she's young and attractive, other times she's old and wizened, and often she's seen just before a volcanic eruption. Those who stop and pick her up hitchhiking or show some other kindness are often protected from the lava flow.

After the 1960 lava flow in Kapoho, stories circulated about how the light-keeper in the spared Kapoho lighthouse had offered a meal to an elderly homeless woman who had showed up at his door on the eve of the eruption. ∎

LAVA TREE STATE MONUMENT

The lava molds at Lava Tree State Monument were created in 1790 when this former ohia rainforest was engulfed in pahoehoe from Kilauea's east rift zone. The lava was free-flowing and moved quickly, like a river flooding its banks.

As the molten lava ran through the forest, some of it began to congeal around the moisture-laden ohia trunks while the rest of the flow moved on through and quickly receded.

Although the trees themselves burned away, the molds of lava which had formed around them remained. Now, 200 years later, there's a ghost forest of lava shells.

A 20-minute loop walk winds around the 'lava trees'. Some are a good 10 feet high, while others are short enough to look down into and shelter ferns within their hollows.

Be careful if you walk off the path as in places the ground is crossed by deep cracks, some hidden by new vegetation. It's thought one deep fracture, which may have caused an earthquake at the same time as the flow, may have drained much of the lava back into the earth.

The park is on Hwy 132, 2½ miles east from its intersection with Hwy 130. The mosquitoes can be wicked.

KAPOHO

Hwy 132 heads east through papaya orchards and long rows of vanda orchids to what was once Kapoho, a farming town of about 300 people.

On January 13, 1960, a fountain of fire half a mile long shot up in the midst of a sugar cane field just above Kapoho. The main flow of liquid pahoehoe lava ran toward the ocean. A slower moving off-shoot of aa lava crept toward the town, burying orchid farms in its path.

Earthen barricades were built and fire hoses frantically pumped water onto the lava, but none of the attempts to harden or divert the flow worked.

On January 28 the lava entered Kapoho and buried the town. A hot springs resort and nearly 100 homes and businesses disappeared.

One bizarre phenomenon occurred when the river of lava approached the sea at **Cape Kumukahi**. Within a few feet of the cape's lighthouse the lava parted into two flows and circled around it, sparing the lighthouse from destruction. If you want to take a look, the site is 1¾ miles down the dirt road which continues beyond the intersection of Hwy 132 and Hwy 137. However, the lighthouse has been replaced by a modern light beacon. Cape Kumukahi, which means 'first beginning' in Hawaiian, is the easternmost point in the state.

The most dominant landscape feature in the Kapoho area is the **Kapoho Crater**, an ancient 420-foot cinder cone. The hill is lush green with thick vegetation and has a small crater lake on top of it.

One of the earliest legends of volcanic activity in Kapoho goes back to the 1300s. It seems Kahavari, a young Puna chief, was holding a holua (sledding) contest on the slopes of Kapoho Crater. One of the spectators was an attractive woman who stepped forward and challenged the chief to a race.

Kahavari tossed the woman an inferior

sled and charged down the hill, daring her to overcome him. Halfway down he glanced over his shoulder and found her close behind, racing down atop a wave on a sea of molten lava. It was of course Pele, who chased Kahavari clear out to sea where he narrowly escaped in a canoe. Everyone and everything in Pele's path was buried in the flood of lava.

Highway 137

Hwy 137 (Kalapana-Kapoho Beach Rd) is barely above water level, bordered by invasive milo and hala trees that look as if they plan to reclaim the road. In places it's so overgrown there's almost a tunnel effect, with just a lacy bit of light filtering in through the trees. The road sometimes floods during winter storms and high surf.

Kapoho Tidepools

Kapoho Tidepools are in the Kapoho Vacationland subdivision, a mile south of the lighthouse. This network of tide pools is formed in lava basins, some of which are deep enough for swimming and snorkeling.

To get there, turn makai off Hwy 137 onto Kapoho Kai Dr and then turn left on Waiopai. There's a sign for public access, but parking can be a hassle.

PUALAA BEACH PARK

One of the few safe swimming spots on the Puna coast is Pualaa Beach Park, off Hwy 137 one mile north of Isaac Hale Beach Park. Recently turned into a park by the county, the star attraction is a lovely thermal spring-fed pool of lava rock, roughly 60 feet in diameter and deep enough for swimming. The water temperature averages about 90°F. The pool has an inlet to the ocean (which pounds upon the rocks just a few yards away) so the water is kept clean. On weekdays it's generally a quiet spot, while on weekends it's popular with families. There are picnic tables, pit toilets and usually a lifeguard on duty. The pool is directly behind a long yellow house; parking is on the opposite side of the road.

ISAAC HALE BEACH PARK

Isaac Hale Beach Park, which is on Pohoiki Bay on Hwy 137, has a shoreline of chunky lava rocks. This county park is small but on weekends there's usually a frenzy of local activity. Birthday picnics and fishing seem to be the biggest attractions.

The park has Puna's only boat ramp. Local kids like to swim near the ramp, which is somewhat protected by a breakwater, and there are sometimes surfers at the south side of the bay.

Camping is allowed, but it's not a very attractive option as the camping area is virtually in the parking lot. There's a warm freshwater spring a short walk south of the dockside house.

The park has toilets, but no drinking water or showers.

MACKENZIE STATE RECREATION AREA

There's no beach at MacKenzie State Recreation Area but rather 40-foot cliffs with a surging surf that sometimes breaks three-quarters of the way up. There's good fishing from the cliffs for ulua, a jack fish that favors turbulent waters.

This 13-acre park on Hwy 137 is quiet and secluded, in a grove of ironwood trees. There's a soft carpet of needles underfoot. Both tent and trailer camping are allowed with a permit from the state. There are picnic tables, barbecue grills and pit toilets, but no drinking water.

An old Hawaiian coastal trail, called the **King's Trail**, passes through the park. It runs parallel to the ocean about 75 yards in from the cliffs. If you take it from the parking lot for about three minutes to the northeast you'll come across the opening of a long **lava tube**, which is marked by a low thicket of ferns.

OPIHIKAO

The village of Opihikao is marked by a little Congregational church and a couple of houses.

Kalani Honua, a New Age conference and retreat center emphasizing the arts and Hawaiian culture, is 2½ miles southwest of

Opihikao village, midway between the 17 and 18-mile markers. Workshops for such things as Iyengar Yoga, tai chi, massage and dance are offered. Visitors are welcome to take a look around. There's a cafe and gift shop at the office.

Places to Stay & Eat

Kalani Honua (☎ 965-7828, (800) 800-6886), RR2 Box 4500, Pahoa, HI 96778, caters mostly to groups, but also welcomes individual travelers on a space-available basis.

There are 31 rooms, most in two-story cedar lodges which have exposed-beam ceilings, lots of wood and a screened common area with shared kitchen. Rates are $65/75 for singles/doubles with a private bath, $52/62 with a shared bath.

They also have cottages with one bedroom, bath and living room for $85. Tents can be pitched on the grounds for $15/25 singles/doubles. There's a spa, sauna, pool and tennis court for guests.

The center has a work scholar program which provides room and board in exchange for 30 hours of work per week, with a three-month commitment required. This could be an interesting budget option for a lengthy stay in Hawaii.

The dining room, which serves buffet-style vegetarian meals, is open to the public. Breakfast costs $6, lunch $8 and dinner $10. Dining room hours are short: from 7:30 to 8:30 am for breakfast, noon to 1 pm for lunch and 6 to 7 pm for dinner. The cafe at the office, open from 10 am to 5:30 pm daily, sells inexpensive snack food such as burritos, sandwiches and juices.

KEHENA BEACH

Kehena Beach, at the base of a cliff, is a black sand beach created by a 1955 lava flow. It's a nude sunbathing spot that's also occasionally used as an unofficial camping site. Coconut and ironwood trees offer shade along the beach.

When the water's calm swimming is usually safe, but during periods of heavy surf there can be powerful currents and dangerous undertows. In winter it's not un-

usual for dolphins to come close to the shore and swim with bathers.

Kehena is off Hwy 137, around the 19-mile marker. Look for cars parked at a pull-off; about 50 yards to the northeast is the start of the path down to the beach, a 10-minute walk. Don't leave valuables in your car.

End of the Road

For years, the village of Kalapana sat precariously beneath Kilauea's restless east rift. When the current series of eruptions began in 1983 the main lava flow moved down the slope to the west of Kalapana. Much of the early flow passed through a series of lava tubes which carried the molten lava down to the coast and into the sea. During pauses in the eruption in 1990, the tubes feeding lava to the ocean cooled long enough to harden and block up. When the eruption started again, the lava flow, no longer able to take its previous course, was redirected towards Kalapana. By the end of 1990 the entire village, including 100 homes, was buried.

Today the road (Hwy 137) ends abruptly at Kaimu Beach at the eastern edge of Kalapana. Kaimu, formerly the most famous black sand beach in Hawaii, is now encased under a sea of hardened lava that flowed over the sand and clear into the bay. Opposite the beach, the drive-in restaurant where the tour buses used to park, was ironically spared. The rest of the coastal village and Harry K Brown Beach Park, which lay beyond, are gone.

HIGHWAY 130

From the edge of the lava flow at Kaimu Beach, a side road leads up to Hwy 130, which goes back to Pahoa. There are a couple of sights along the way.

You can also take a short detour on the eastern stub of the old national park road, which is now cut off by a lava flow a mile west of the Painted Church. Where the road meets the lava you can often see billowing steam clouds created by molten lava pouring into the sea a few miles away.

Painted Church

The Star of the Sea is a little white Catholic church noted for its interior murals painted in trompe l'oeil style to create the effect of being in a large cathedral. The painting style is primitive but the illusion of depth is amazingly effective. The church also has a nice stained glass window of Father Damien who was with the parish before he moved to the leprosy colony on Molokai.

The church, which was in the town of Kalapana, was moved just before lava flows swept over the site. It currently sits along Hwy 130, at the 20-mile marker, waiting for a more permanent home.

Steam Vents

At the 15-mile marker, 3½ miles south of Pahoa, for some less than obvious reason a big blue highway sign marks a scenic view. While the scenery is not particularly special, if you look closely you'll notice steam rising from steam vents on the makai side of the road.

Only a few minutes' walk away there are some low spatter cones with hollowed out natural steam baths inside, perfect for a sauna. To get there, take the path leading down from the scenic lookout; when the path forks, bear right and walk to the last crater which has a little wooden bench inside.

Kau

The Kau district stretches from South Kona along the southern flanks of Mauna Loa, taking in the entire southern tip of the island all the way up to Hawaii Volcanoes National Park.

Kau is sparsely populated, with only about 5000 people and three real towns. Much of it is dry and desert-like. The highest temperature ever recorded in the state was in Kau in the town of Pahala: 100°F in April 1931. However Kau also has some lush areas in the foothills where sugar cane, macadamia nuts and most of Hawaii's oranges are grown.

Devastation Day

Kau was the center of devastation in the massive 1868 earthquake, the worst Hawaii has ever recorded. For five full days from March 27, the earth was rattled almost continuously by a series of tremors and quakes. Then in the afternoon of April 2 the earth shook violently in every direction and an inferno broke loose from beneath the surface.

Those fortunate enough to be uphill watched as a rapidly moving river of lava poured down the hillsides and swallowed up everything in its path, including people, homes and cattle. Within minutes the coast was inundated by tidal waves and villages near the shore were swept away.

This deadly triple combination of earthquakes, lava flows and tidal waves permanently changed Kau's landscape. Huge cinder cones came crashing down the slopes and there was one landslide which buried an entire village. You can see the 1868 lava flow along the highway two miles west of the South Point turn-off. The old village of Kahuku lies beneath it. ∎

MANUKA STATE WAYSIDE PARK

Manuka State Wayside Park is an eight-acre arboretum off Hwy 11 near the 81-mile marker. The trees and bushes planted here between the mid-1930s and the 1950s include 48 native Hawaiian species and 130 introduced species. Many are labeled, some with both Latin and common names.

Camping is allowed by permit in the three-sided covered shelter which has space for about five sleeping bags. It might be fine for an overnight break between Hilo and Kona, although it's quite close to the road. While camping under the trees looks tempting, it's prohibited. There are restrooms and picnic tables.

The park is in the midst of the 25,500-acre Manuka Natural Area Reserve, which reaches from the slopes of Mauna Loa down to the sea where it takes in a couple of heiaus and other ruins.

The **Manuka Nature Trail**, a two-mile interpretive loop, begins above the parking lot. The trail crosses ancient lava flows and goes through a varied mesic forest that contains both rainforest and dry lowland plants. A detailed brochure explaining the flora along the trail can be picked up from the state's Department of Land & Natural Resources offices.

HAWAIIAN OCEAN VIEW ESTATES

A few miles east of Manuka there's a grocery store, a plate lunch eatery, a pretty good pizzeria, a Texaco gas station, a post office and a hardware shop. This is the commercial center, such as it is, for Hawaiian Ocean View Estates and a couple of other isolated southside subdivisions.

This area remains one of the last sunny expanses of land in Hawaii to be totally free of resorts. A massive and controversial development that had been proposed for the barren Kahuku Coast just west of South Point has, to the relief of island environmentalists, gone belly up.

Places To Stay

South Point Bed & Breakfast (☎ 929-7466), Box 6589, Ocean View, HI 96704, is in Hawaiian Ocean View Estates, just mauka of Hwy 11. There are three comfortable units, each with a private entrance and bath. A breakfast of fresh fruit, homemade granola and baked goods is served on the lanai. Rates are $55 a double for the two smaller rooms and $10 more for the larger unit, which has a kitchenette. The rate is discounted by $5 for stays of three or more nights.

A bit more casual is *Bougainvillea Bed & Breakfast* (☎ /fax 929-7089, (800) 688-1763), Box 6045, Ocean View, HI 96704, in Hawaiian Ocean View Estates, on the makai side of Hwy 11. Martie Nitsche rents out five rooms in her home, each with private bath and entrance, for $49/59 single/double, including breakfast. There's a swimming pool and hot tub set back behind the house that makes a nice spot for stargazing. Bicycles, beach mats and coolers are available for guests to use. If you come by without a reservation, you can often find Martie at the Texaco station, which she manages.

SOUTH POINT

South Point is the southernmost spot in the USA. In Hawaiian it's called Ka Lae, which means simply 'the point'.

South Point has rocky coastal cliffs and a turbulent ocean. It was the site of one of the earliest Hawaiian settlements and may have been where the first Polynesians landed. Much of the area is now under the jurisdiction of Hawaiian Home Lands.

The turn-off to South Point is between the 69- and 70-mile markers. South Point is 11 miles south of Hwy 11, at the end of a well-paved one-lane road. There are packed shoulders most of the way allowing cross-traffic to pass without having to stop.

South Point Rd starts out in house sites and macadamia nut farms which soon give way to grassy pastures. The winds are strong here, as evidenced by the trees, some bent almost horizontal with their branches trailing along the ground.

Kamaoa Wind Farms

As you go over a hill along this country drive you suddenly come upon rows of huge high-tech windmills lined up in a pasture beside the road. With cattle grazing beneath, it's a surreal scene, and the unearthly whirring sound is what you might expect an alien invasion to sound like.

Each of these wind turbine generators can produce enough electricity for 100 families. Presently there are 37 up and running, with plans to double that number. It's thought, theoretically at least, that by using wind energy conversion the state could produce more than enough electricity to meet its needs.

Four miles south of the windmills, you'll pass a few abandoned buildings which are wasting away. Until 1965 this was a Pacific Missile Range Station that tracked missiles shot from California to the Marshall Islands.

Ka Lae

Ten miles down from the highway, South Point Rd forks and the road to the left goes to Kaulana boat ramp and a small cove.

Kau

The road to the right leads to the rugged coastal cliffs of South Point. The confluence of ocean currents just offshore makes this one of Hawaii's most bountiful fishing grounds. Locals fish from the cliffs, many precariously hanging out over the edge of steep lava ledges. Red snapper and ulua, a jack fish, are particularly plentiful.

Ruins at Ka Lae include those of a heiau and a well-preserved fishing shrine. The outcrop on the west side of the fishing shrine is a good place to find some of the numerous canoe mooring holes that have been drilled into the rock ledges. Ancient Hawaiians used to anchor one end of a rope through the holes and tie the other end to their canoes. The strong currents would pull the canoes straight out to deep turbulent waters where they could fish without getting swept out to sea.

The wooden platforms built on the edge of the cliffs have hoists and ladders which are used to get things to and from the small boats that anchor below.

There's a large unprotected and unmarked hole in the lava directly behind the platforms where you can watch water rise and fall as the waves rush in. Keep an eye out for it, particularly if you have kids with you, as it's not obvious until you're almost on top of it.

Walk down past the beacon and continue along the wall to get to the southernmost point in the USA. There are no markers here, no souvenir stands, just crashing surf and lots of wind.

Green Sands Beach

If you want to explore the area further, go back to the fork and take the road to Kaulana boat ramp. Beside the ramp you'll find pockets of green sand sparkling in the sun. These are olivine crystals worn from the lava cliffs by a relentless and pounding surf.

The highest concentration of green sand in Hawaii is at Green Sands Beach, a 2½-mile hike away. To get there take the 4WD road heading northeast from the boat ramp. The walk is not difficult, though once you reach Green Sands you'll need to scramble

down the cliffside to get to the beach. If you have a high-riding 4WD vehicle you could consider driving in but the road is rough and the drive takes about 25 minutes.

Pick a calm day to visit as during periods of high surf the entire beach can be inundated. A couple of minutes beyond Kaulana boat ramp the trail passes the site of Kapalaoa, an ancient fishing village.

WAIOHINU

After South Point, Hwy 11 winds down into a pretty valley and the sleepy village of Waiohinu, which sits nestled beneath green hills. On the right as you enter the town is the quaint little wooden Kauahaao Church, white with green trim, dating from 1841.

Shirakawa Motel is 500 feet ahead on the left and there's a monkeypod tree planted by Mark Twain in 1866 just past the hotel, on the same side of the road. The original tree fell in a typhoon in 1957 but hardy new trunks have sprung up and it's once again full grown.

In the village center is Wong Yuen's Chevron gas station, which is open from 8 am to 7 pm daily and has a small convenience store.

From Waiohinu the road runs beneath the lower slopes of Mauna Loa through sugar cane fields, cattle ranchland and macadamia groves. Inland beyond the sugar cane fields is Kau Forest Reserve, which runs all the way up to Hawaii Volcanoes National Park.

Places to Stay

Shirakawa Motel (☎ 929-7462), Box 467, Naalehu, HI 96772, is a green weatherbeaten motel with 13 basic units. The motel is plain but adequate, and the setting beneath the green hills is lovely. Rooms cost $30/35 for singles/doubles, $42 for a kitchenette unit, tax included. At dusk, flocks of myna birds fly through the area squawking.

NAALEHU

Naalehu's claim to fame is being the southernmost town in the USA. It's two miles

...hena Beach, Puna, Big Island

...ayer tower, Ahuena Heiau, Big Island

South Point, Big Island

Halemaumau Trail, Big Island

Hiilawe Waterfall, Big Island

Punaluu Beach Park, Big Island

Kiholo Bay, Big Island

east of Waiohinu and a few inches to the south.

Modest as it is, Naalehu is the region's shopping center. It has a couple of grocery stores and eateries, a gas station, a post office, an elementary school and the Kau police station. If you happen to be around between 1 and 5 pm on Tuesday or Thursday you can even catch the tiny public library while it's open.

Naalehu closes up early, so you can't count on getting food or gas here if you're driving back to Kona from Hawaii Volcanoes National Park at night.

Places to Eat

The best place to eat in town is the *Naalehu Fruit Stand* on Hwy 11, a reasonably priced produce stand, health food store, pizzeria and sandwich shop all in one. The ovens out back bake bread in the morning and pizzas to order ($8) from 11 am. The shop sells prepared sandwiches such as teri-tofu on homemade whole-wheat bread for $2.50 or you can get a sub with the works for a bit more. Macadamia nut cream cheese bars and many other pastries cost about a dollar. It's open from 9 am to 6:30 pm daily (to 5 pm on Sundays) and there are a few picnic tables near the front steps where you can eat.

WHITTINGTON BEACH PARK

Two miles beyond Naalehu there's a pull-off with a scenic lookout above Honuapo Bay. From the lookout you can see the cement pilings of the old Honuapo Pier, which was used for shipping sugar and hemp until the 1930s.

Honuapo Bay is the site of Whittington Beach Park; the turn-off is one mile from the lookout. There's really no beach at Whittington although there are tide pools to explore. The ocean is usually too rough and dangerous for swimming. Endangered green sea turtles, which can sometimes be seen offshore, apparently have been frequenting these waters for a long time, as Honuapo means 'caught turtle'.

Camping is allowed with a permit and it's far enough from the highway to offer a little privacy. Overall, it makes a pretty good choice for a county campground but avoid setting up near the street light by the parking lot. The light is on all night and illuminates much of the lawn where tenting is allowed. Whittington has pit toilets and sheltered picnic tables, but there's no running water at all.

PUNALUU

Punaluu is a small bay with a black sand beach that was once the site of a major Hawaiian settlement and in later days an important sugar port. The most visited section of the beach is the area fronting the now-closed Punaluu Black Sands Restaurant, which is lined with coconut trees and backed by a duck pond. The ruins of the Pahala Sugar Company's old warehouse and pier are a short walk away at the north end of the beach. Sitting on a rise above it is the site of Kaneeleele Heiau.

Punaluu Beach Park, a county park just to the south, has restrooms, showers, drinking water, picnic pavilions and camping. It's a flat, grassy area right on the beach and a nice place to camp although it's very open with no privacy and there can be a fair amount of activity here during the day. At night you can drift off to sleep to the sounds of crashing surf.

Be careful walking around as the area's black sands are used as nesting sites by hawksbill turtles. Swimmers should be aware that the waters along the beach can have a strong undertow and there's a particularly dangerous rip current pulling out from the boat channel near the pier.

If heading east, the first turn-off you'll reach in Punaluu is the entrance to SeaMountain, Kau's only condo complex. To get to the beach park take the turn-off marked Punaluu Park, which is less than a mile farther along Hwy 11.

Places to Stay & Eat

SeaMountain at Punaluu (☎ 928-6211, (800) 344-7675), Box 340, Pahala, HI 96777, is a small condo complex with all the amenities you'd expect to find in Kona, albeit there's much less to do in this area.

The complex has a pool, tennis courts and a golf course.

The studios are big and almost as large as one-bedroom units elsewhere, while some one-bedroom units are two-level with cathedral ceilings. Some units have phones. Rates start at $85 for studios, $110 for one-bedroom units and $140 for two-bedroom units. Ocean views cost about $10 more and all rates are $15 lower in the off season. There's a two-day minimum stay.

Currently the only place to eat is the *Golf Course Broiler* at SeaMountain, which serves lunch from 10:30 am to 2 pm. Salads, sandwiches with fries and a few hot dishes are priced around $7.

PAHALA

Pahala is really two little towns side by side. Down by the mill it's still a working sugar town with old dusty shacks, cars rusting in the yards and 'Beware of Dog' signs. This part of town has a 1920s movie theater, a little general store and big banyan trees.

The north side of town has tract homes, a hospital, bank, gas stations, a community center and a modern grocery mart.

Kau Agribusiness, which runs the mill, has 15,000 acres of sugar cane planted for about 15 miles in either direction from Pahala. The production of sugar is in a gradual decline, however, and the company is diversifying with new groves of macadamia nut trees and oranges.

WOOD VALLEY TEMPLE

About four miles up the slopes from Pahala is remote Wood Valley and the Buddhist temple and retreat center of Nechung Dorje Drayang Ling. The temple was built in the early 1900s by Japanese sugar cane laborers who lived in the valley.

In 1975 a Tibetan lama, Nechung Rinpoche, took up residence here and in 1980 the Dalai Lama visited to dedicate the temple. Since that time many Tibetan lamas have conducted programs here and the Dalai Lama himself paid a return visit in 1994. In addition to its teachings of Buddhism, the center is also used by groups conducting Vipassana and Zen meditation, yoga classes and other New Age and spiritual programs. If you're interested, the center can send you a list of upcoming workshops.

Looking over Halemaumau Crater, Hawaii Volcanoes National Park

The retreat center (☎ 928-8539), Box 250, Pahala, HI 96777, is a two-story building with a meditation hall and private rooms on the upper floor. The ground floor has two dormitories, a kitchen/dining area and a library of books and videos on Buddhist culture. Guests are free to use the library and join in the morning service.

At times when there are no programs going on, the center is open to individual guests. Room rates are $25/35 for singles/doubles and dormitory beds cost $15. There's a two-night minimum and you must bring your own food. For those seeking a peaceful retreat the temple is a special place.

TO HAWAII VOLCANOES NATIONAL PARK

Hawaii Volcanoes National Park begins 12 miles from Pahala. Hwy 11 crosses an 11-mile stretch of the park. There are no fees to drive through on the highway nor to explore the Mauna Loa side of the park.

Kilauea's southwest rift zone runs through this part of the Kau Desert, makai of the road. The rift runs for 20 miles, all the way from the summit of Kilauea down to the coast.

You'll know you're getting closer to the center of Hawaii Volcanoes National Park when the signs start reading 'Caution, Fault Zones. Watch for Cracks in Road.'

Before you reach the entrance to the park you'll pass Mauna Loa Rd. There are tree molds near the turn-off, a hiking trail through a native forest a mile farther up, and the trailhead to the Mauna Loa summit at the end of the road. All are detailed in the following Hawaii Volcanoes National Park section.

Hawaii Volcanoes National Park

Hawaii Volcanoes National Park is hands down the most unique park in the US

National Parks system. It's a which not only contains two active volcanoes but terrain ranging from tropical beaches to the subarctic summit of Mauna Loa.

The centerpiece of the park is Kilauea Caldera, the sunken center of Kilauea Volcano. This still-steaming crater, where molten lava boils just a few feet beneath the surface, is said to be the home of Madame Pele, goddess of volcanoes. Both a foot trail and a paved road circle the caldera's rim.

The park's landscape is geologically awesome with dozens of craters and cinder cones, hills piled high with pumice, and hardened rivers of lava which have frozen rock-solid on the hillsides complete with ripples and waves. There are also native bird reserves, rainforests and fern groves which have either been spared by lava flows or have grown over them.

The park is one of Hawaii's best places for camping and hiking. It has 140 miles of amazingly varied hiking trails and two free drive-up campgrounds as well as back-country camping.

The park encompasses about a quarter of a million acres of land – more than the entire island of Molokai – and it's still growing.

Kilauea's southeast rift has been actively flowing since 1983, taking everything in its path with it. The coastal road to Puna was blocked by lava in 1988. The Wahaula Visitor Center on the south coast went under the next year and the entire village of Kalapana, with more than a hundred homes, was buried in lava in 1990. By 1994 the flows had swept a couple of miles farther west, engulfing Kamoamoa Beach and campground. The current series of eruptions, which is the longest in recorded history, has spewed out two billion cubic yards of new lava.

What you'll be able to see will depend on the current volcanic activity. During the day distant steam clouds from the vents can usually be seen clearly from the end of Chain of Craters Rd. After dark, the lava tubes on the mountainside glow red in the

BIG ISLAND

night sky and lava lakes at the top of vents reflect light onto passing clouds.

Although many visitors expect to see lava fountains spurting up into the air, this is certainly the exception rather than the rule. But whenever Pele does put on one of her spectacular fireworks displays, cars stream in from all directions. In Hawaii, people generally run *to* volcanoes, not away from them.

Orientation
The park's main road is Crater Rim Rd which circles the moonscape sights of Kilauea Caldera. It's possible to take in the drive-up sites in an hour – and if that's all the time you have it's unquestionably worth it. Still, it's far better to give yourself a good three hours to allow time for a few short walks and stops at the visitor center and museum.

Volcanic Formations
Hawaii's volcanoes are shield volcanoes, formed by repeated gentle eruptions, building up over time as thin layers of lava are deposited one on top of another. As the mountains get higher and wider, long cracks break open down their gently stretched slopes. These are called fault zones, or rift zones, and lava eruptions may come from these cracks (as is currently the case with Kilauea) as well as from the summit crater.

Craters are formed when volcanic hills release their lava and collapse back into themselves.

'Pahoehoe' and 'aa' are Hawaiian words which are now used worldwide to describe the earth's two major types of lava. Pahoehoe refers to the rivers of lava which flow smooth and unbroken. When pahoehoe begins to harden it twists into rope-like coils and swirls as the outer skin cools and stiffens while the hotter lava underneath continues to move a little.

Aa is rough and jumbled lava which moves so slowly that the tip of the flow hardens. It's only the molten lava pushing from behind that keeps the flow moving, with the hard lava at the front piling up and falling over itself, slowing rolling and clunking its way along. ■

The park's other scenic drive is the Chain of Craters Rd which leads south 21 miles to the coast, ending at the site of the most recent lava activity. Allow about three hours down and back to stop at all the scenic points along the way.

While you can get a good sense of the place in one full day, it would be easy to spend days, if not weeks, exploring this vast and varied park.

Information
Hotline The park's 24-hour hotline (☎ 967-7977) has recorded information on current volcanic activity and directions to the best viewing sites.

Fees The park entrance fee of $5 per vehicle is good for multiple entries in a seven-day period. Visitors entering on foot or bicycle through the check station are charged $3 each. The check station is staffed from about 8:30 am to 4:30 pm daily, although the park is open 24 hours.

National park passes are sold here, including an annual pass for $25 which covers Haleakala on Maui and all other US National Park sites. US citizens who are disabled can get a pass allowing free entry and those age 62 or older can buy a $10 lifetime pass good for all US National Parks.

Access for the Disabled Many of the national park sites are accessible to the disabled, including Kilauea Visitor Center, Jaggar Museum, Volcano Art Center and Volcano House hotel. Many of the pull-ups along Crater Rim Dr and the Chain of Crater Rd have solid pavement free of curbstones. A few of the park's shorter trails have recently been converted to make them wheelchair accessible, including the Devastation Trail and an eastern section of the Crater Rim Trail near Waldron Ledge.

Climate The park has a wide range of climatic conditions which vary with elevation and the weather can be moody as well. Rain and fog move in quickly and on any given day it can change from hot and dry to cool and damp. Near Kilauea Crater, temperatures average about 15°F cooler than in Kona. It's a good idea to wear clothing in layers.

Road Closures During periods of prolonged drought, both Mauna Loa Rd and Hilina Pali Rd are subject to closure due to fire hazard conditions.

Precautions Hawaiian volcanoes are seldom violent and most of the lava that flows from cracks in the rift zones is slow moving. The eruptions don't spew out a lot of ash or poisonous gases either, which is what accounts for most volcano-related deaths in other parts of the world.

There have been only two known violent explosions of Hawaiian volcanoes – both from Kilauea, in 1790 and in 1924. The only direct fatality from a volcanic eruption in this century was during the 1924 explosion which tossed a boulder onto the leg of a photographer who bled to death.

The park service maintains that the presence of unhealthy gases in the volcano area is lower than in the smoggy air of many urban centers. Still, people with respiratory and heart conditions, pregnant women, infants and young children are advised to avoid the areas where sulfur fumes are most highly concentrated, including the Halemaumau Overlook.

Other potential hazards include deep cracks in the earth and thin lava crust which may mask hollows and lava tubes. If you stay on marked trails, you shouldn't have any problems. All park warning signs should be taken seriously.

Getting There & Away

The park is 29 miles from Hilo and 97 miles from Kona.

The public bus which runs between Hilo and Waiohinu stops at the visitor center (and at Volcano village) once in each direction Monday to Friday. It leaves the visitor center for Hilo at 8 am and returns from Hilo at 2:40 pm. The ride takes about one hour and costs $2.25.

Crater Rim Road

Crater Rim Rd is a field trip in vulcanology. This amazing 11-mile loop road skirts the rim of Kilauea Caldera with marked stops at steam vents and crater lookouts. From roadside parking areas, short trails lead through a lava tube, a native rainforest and a forest devastated by pumice. There are also trailheads for longer hikes into and around the caldera.

Natural forces have re-routed Crater Rim Rd on a few occasions. Earthquakes in both 1975 and 1983 rattled it hard enough to knock sections down into the caldera.

The most interesting stops are at Jaggar Museum, Halemaumau Overlook, Devastation Trail and Thurston Lava Tube. If you take Crater Rim Rd in a counter-clockwise direction you'll start off at the visitor center.

Crater Rim Rd is a good road for cyclists and unlike the Chain of Craters Rd it's relatively level.

Kilauea Visitor Center The visitor center is a good place to get oriented to the park. Rangers here have the latest information on volcanic activity, interpretive programs, guided walks, backcountry trail conditions and the like. They have free hand-outs on a few of the park trails and sell books on volcanoes, hiking and park flora.

The center contains a small **theater** where a 20-minute film on the geology of the volcano is played on the hour from 9 am to 4 pm. If you're lucky they'll show their highlights film that includes footage of rivers of lava flowing 20 miles an hour, a 13-mile-long curtain of fire and a 1900-foot fountain of lava.

In addition, commercial videos of the most recent eruptions run continuously in the center's tiny museum where you'll also find a few volcano-related exhibits. The center (☎ 967-7311) is open daily from 7:45 am to 4:45 pm and will store backpacks for park visitors.

Volcano Art Center The Volcano Art Center (☎ 967-7511), next door to the visitor center, sells island pottery, paint-

Hawaii Volcanoes
National Park

Kupaianaha Vent

Active Lava Flow

Wahaula
Heiau

East Rift Zone

Holei
Sea Arch

Puu Oo Vent

Puu Loa
Petroglyphs

Akatsuka
Orchid
Gardens

To Puna, Hilo

Chain of Craters Rd

Puu
Huluhulu

Mauna Ulu

Ke Ala Koma

Keauhou
Shelter

Volcano

Kilauea Caldera

See inset map

Halape Trail

Halape
Shelter

Hilina Pali Rd

Kipuka
Puaulu

Kipuka Nene
Campground

Kaaha
Shelter

Mauna Iki Trail

Mauna Iki

Mauna Loa Rd

Mauna Loa Trail

Kipuka
Pepeiao
Cabin

Kau
Desert

Kau Desert Trail

Footprints

PACIFIC
OCEAN

To Kona

Pahala

11

10 km
6 miles

5

3

0
0

Kilauea Iki Crater

Thurston
Lava Tube

Devastation
Trail

Park
Entrance

Kilauea
Visitor
Center

Golf Course

Crater Rim Dr

Crater Rim Trail

Lava Tree
Molds

Namakani
Paio
Campground

Kilauea
Caldera

Halemaumau
Overlook

Jagger
Museum

Halemaumau

2 km

1 miles

.5
1

ings, weavings, woodwork, sculpture and other arts & crafts. The work is high-quality, with many one-of-a-kind items.

The center is in a former Volcano House lodge, built in 1877. The nonprofit organization which runs the place offers workshops on crafts and hula dancing and sponsors concerts, plays and other activities. It's open from 9 am to 5 pm daily.

Sulphur Banks The first stop beyond the art center is the Sulphur Banks, where the day-glo colors and piles of steaming rocks look like a landscape from another planet.

This is one of many areas where Kilauea lets off steam, releasing hundreds of tons of sulfuric gases daily. As the steam reaches the surface, it deposits sulfur around the mouths of the vents, giving them a froth of fluorescent yellow crystals. The putrid smell of rotten eggs is hydrogen sulfide.

Steam Vents There are a couple of open nonsulfurous steam vents at the next pull-off, although they're nothing special to look at. Rainwater which sinks into the earth is heated by the hot rocks below and rises back up as steam.

More interesting is the two-minute walk beyond the vents out to a part of the crater rim aptly called **Steaming Bluff**. The cooler it is, the more steam there'll be. A plaque on the rim tells a legend about the struggles between Pele and the pig-god Kamapuaa.

Jaggar Museum This museum is worth stopping at both for its displays and for the fine view of Halemaumau Crater. Halemaumau sits within Kilauea Crater and is sometimes referred to as the 'crater within the crater'. Detailed interpretive plaques at the lookout explain the geological workings of volcanoes. There's also a good view of Mauna Loa to the west, 20 miles away.

The museum is named after Thomas A Jaggar, former head geologist at the Massachusetts Institute of Technology, and the first scientist to undertake in-depth studies of Kilauea. Jaggar led a group of geologists who lowered the first thermometer into

Halemaumau's lava lake in the summer of 1911. It registered 1832°F before melting. Today an observatory at this site has Kilauea completely wired and it's the most studied volcano anywhere in the world.

Jaggar Museum is open from 8:30 am to 5 pm daily. It has photo displays, a section on Pele, seismographs, tiltmeters and printed updates showing the current status of volcanic activity. The museum also sells videotapes and books.

The museum is at **Uwekahuna Bluff**, the site of an infamous hut which once sat right on the edge of the crater. Local kahunas are said to have tricked people into entering the building where they slipped through a false-bottomed floor to the crater pit below.

Drivers should be careful of the nene that congregate in the museum parking lot and at other tourist stops on the south side of the caldera. The nene move slowly and have a suicidal tendency of walking up to moving cars, looking for handouts. Feeding the nene is strictly prohibited and contributes to the road-kill of these endangered birds.

After leaving the museum you'll pass the **Southwest Rift**, where you can stop and take a look at the wide fissure slicing across the earth.

Halemaumau Overlook The next attraction is Halemaumau Overlook, where there's a five-minute walk to the crater rim. For at least a hundred years (from 1823, when missionary William Ellis first recorded the sight in writing) Halemaumau was a boiling lake of lava which alternately rose and fell, overflowing and then receding.

This fiery lake attracted people from all over the world. Some observers compared it to the fires of hell while others saw primeval creation. Mark Twain wrote about staring down at:

... circles and serpents and streaks of lightning all twined and wreathed and tied together ... I have seen Vesuvius since, but it was a mere toy, a child's volcano, a soup kettle, compared to this.

In 1924 seeping water touched off a massive steam explosion which blew up the lava lake, causing huge boulders and mud to rain down and setting off a lightning storm. When it was over, the crater had doubled in size and the lava activity ceased. The crust has since cooled, although the crater still steams. The area is pungent with the smell of sulfur.

All of the Big Island is Pele's territory, but Halemaumau is her home. During special ceremonies the hula is performed in her honor here and throughout the year those wishing to appease Pele leave flowers, coins and bottles of gin at the crater rim.

Ohelo, a bush about two feet high with clusters of bright red berries, is one of the early takers to lava and grows near the site. Before eating any of the tart berries, which are said to personify Pele's sister Hiiaka, some should first be offered to Pele.

The Halemaumau Overlook is at the start of the **Halemaumau Trail**, which runs three miles across Kilauea Caldera to the visitor center. Although few people who aren't hiking the full trail venture past the overlook, it's an easy half-mile walk to the site of a 1982 lava flow and well worth the 30 minutes it takes to walk there and back. The spewed lava along the trail has amazing textures and colors and there's an eerie sense of the earth's raw power.

Devastation Trail After the Halemaumau Overlook, Crater Rim Rd continues across the barren Kau Desert and then through the fallout area of the 1959 eruption of Kilauea Iki Crater. Ash and pumice blown southwest of the crater buried a mile of Crater Rim Rd eight feet deep. The road had to be plowed by tractors, much like clearing snow after a blizzard.

Devastation Trail is a half-mile walk across a former rainforest devastated by cinder and pumice from that eruption. Everything green was wiped out. What remains today are dead ohia trees, stripped bare and sun-bleached white, standing stark against the black landscape. It's so barren and desolate it could be the movie set for a post-nuclear scene.

The trail is paved and there are parking lots on each end. The prominent cinder cone along the way is **Puu Puai**, 'Gushing Hill', formed during the 1959 eruption. The northeast end of the trail looks down into Kilauea Iki Crater.

Chain of Craters Rd intersects Crater Rim Rd opposite the parking area for Devastation Trail.

Thurston Lava Tube On the east side of the Chain of Craters Rd intersection, Crater Rim Rd passes through the rainforest of native tree ferns and ohia which covers Kilauea's windward slope.

The Thurston Lava Tube Trail is an enjoyable 15-minute loop walk which starts out in ohia forest, goes through an impressive lava tube and then through a fern grove. The cibotium tree ferns here grow to 20 feet high.

Lava tubes are formed when the outer crust of a river of lava starts to harden but the liquid lava beneath the surface continues to flow on through. After the flow has drained out, the hard shell remains. Thurston Lava Tube is a grand example – it's tunnel-like, and almost big enough to run a train through.

You'll probably hear a lot of birdsong along this walk. The apapane, a native honeycreeper, is easy to spot at the upper end of the trail. It has a red body and silvery-white underside and flies from flower to flower drinking from the yellow blossoms of the mamane tree and the red pompom-like flowers of the ohia tree.

Kilauea Iki Crater When Kilauea Iki burst open in a fiery inferno in November 1959 the whole crater floor turned into a bubbling pool of molten lava. Its fountains reached record heights of 1900 feet, lighting the evening sky with a bright orange glow for miles around. At its peak it gushed out two million tons of lava an hour.

From Kilauea Iki Overlook there's a good view of the mile-wide crater below. Today a trail runs across the crater floor.

The hike is not dissimilar to walking on ice – here too there's a lake below the hardened surface, although in this case it's molten lava not water. For more information see Hiking Trails in this section.

Chain of Craters Road

Chain of Craters Rd winds 21 miles down the southern slopes of Kilauea Volcano, ending abruptly at a lava flow on the Puna Coast. It's a good, paved two-lane road, although there's no gas, food, water or other services along the way.

There are striking vistas of the coastline far below and for miles the predominant view is of long fingers of lava reaching down to the sea.

In some places the road slices through lava and in other places it's paved over it. You'll see both aa lava, which is crusty and rough, and pahoehoe lava, which is as shiny and black as fresh tar. You can sometimes find thin filaments of volcanic glass known as Pele's hair in the cracks and crevices.

In addition to endless lava expanses, the road takes in an impressive collection of sights, including a handful of craters that you can literally pull up to the rims of and peer into. Some of the craters are so new there's no sign of life, while others are thickly forested with ohia lehua, wild orchids and ferns.

Chain of Craters Rd once connected through to Hwy 130 and Hwy 137 allowing traffic between the volcano and Hilo via Puna. Lava flows closed the road in 1969 but by 1979 it was back in service, rerouted slightly. Flows from Kilauea's active east rift cut the link again in 1988 and have since buried an eight-mile stretch of the road.

Hilina Pali Road Hilina Pali Rd starts 2¼ miles down Chain of Craters Rd and leads five miles in to Kipuka Nene campground. It's another four miles to Hilina Pali, a lookout at 2283 feet with a view of the southeast coast. The end of the road is the trailhead for the Kau Desert Trail and for the Kaaha and Hilina Pali trails which lead down to the coast. They are all hot, dry backcountry trails.

Mauna Ulu In 1969, eruptions from Kilauea's east rift began building a new lava shield which eventually rose 400 feet above its surroundings. It was named Mauna Ulu, 'Growing Mountain'.

By the time the flow stopped in 1974 it had covered 10,000 acres of parkland and added 200 acres of new land to the coast.

It also buried a 12-mile section of Chain of Craters Rd in lava as deep as 100 yards. There's still a half-mile portion of the old road left, which you can drive to the lava flow by taking the turn-off on the left 3½ miles down Chain of Craters Rd. Just beyond this is Mauna Ulu itself.

A moderately easy three-mile round-trip hike, the **Puu Huluhulu Overlook Trail**, begins at the parking area, crosses lava flows from 1974 and goes to the top of a 150-foot cinder cone where there's a panoramic view that includes Mauna Loa, Mauna Kea, Kilauea and the east rift zone.

As you continue down Chain of Craters Rd you'll be passing over Mauna Ulu's extensive flows.

Ke Ala Koma About halfway along the road, at an elevation of 2000 feet, is Ke Ala Koma, a covered shelter with picnic tables and a superb ocean view. This would be a great place to unpack a lunch, at least on days when the wind's not whipping.

After Ke Ala Koma the road begins to descend along a series of winding switchbacks, some deeply cut through lava flows.

Puu Loa Petroglyphs The Puu Loa Trail leads to a field of petroglyphs carved into the lava by early Hawaiians. The site, about a mile in, is along an ancient trail between Kau and Puna and has one of the largest concentrations of petroglyphs in Hawaii. A boardwalk runs around a large group of them and offers some fine photo opportunities. Puu Loa ('Long Hill') was also a place where Hawaiians brought the umbilical cords of their babies in the hope that burying them there would bring their children long lives.

The marked trailhead begins on the Chain of Craters Rd midway between the 16- and 17-mile markers and makes for an interesting hour-long walk that's suitable for all ages.

Holei Sea Arch About 2½ miles after the petroglyphs and just before the 19-mile marker, look for the sign marking the Holei Sea Arch. This rugged section of the coast has sharply eroded lava cliffs, called Holei Pali, which are constantly being pounded by crashing surf.

The high rock arch carved out of one of the cliffs is impressive, although the wave action has numbered its days. The ocean here is a deep rich blue.

End of the Road Chain of Craters Rd ends near the coast at Laeapuki, where hardened lava flows seal off the road. Rangers staff a trailer here that acts as a sort of visitor information center but there are no other facilities.

In recent times most of the lava flowing from Kilauea's east rift has been coming from the Puu Oo Vent and crossing a flow field that lies between the old Kamoamoa Beach and the Wahaula Heiau; the flow enters the ocean on a jut of land just east of Laeapuki.

When this molten lava, which is carried down in lava tubes, hits the ocean, it heats the water to a boil and produces an immense acidic steam plume. Park rangers have marked a trail over the hardened lava that puts you close enough to the action to get a good view, but keeps you safe from harm. The trail is often rerouted as a consequence of the lava flows; however it always makes for an intriguing walk, generally taking about 30 minutes. The walk is over crisp, shiny lava and you need to watch your footing as there are sharp jags of lava as well as cracks and holes in the brittle surface. It's a good idea to wear sturdy shoes with good traction.

The steam plumes are impressive to see from a distance but extremely dangerous to

attempt to view up close. Not only can the explosive clash between the molten lava and the seawater shoot scalding water and debris hundreds of feet from the lava point, but the lava crust itself forms in unstable ledges, called lava benches, that eventually collapse into the ocean without warning. Many curiosity seekers have been hurt by attempting to get too close. In 1993 one of these lava benches collapsed sending an islander to his fiery death and over a dozen other people were burned by the ensuing steam explosion.

The rangers know which areas are safe and which aren't; listen to them, heed all signs and don't stray from the marked trails. If you plan to stay in the area after dark to observe the red glow, be sure to take a flashlight as there are no artificial lights in the area.

Wahaula Heiau, incidentally, is separated from the end of the road by an active lava tube and so there's currently no access to it.

Mauna Loa Road
Mauna Loa Rd leads off Hwy 11 about 2¼

miles west of the visitor center. The world's highest active volcano, Mauna Loa has erupted more than 18 times in the past century. The last eruption began in March 1984 and lasted 21 days.

The **Mauna Loa Trail**, which climbs the slopes of Mauna Loa, begins at the end of the road, 13½ miles from Hwy 11. (For more details, see the Hiking Trails section.)

Lava Tree Molds Near the start of Mauna Loa Rd there's a turn-off to some lava tree molds. These tube-like holes were formed when a lava flow engulfed the rainforest that stood here. Because the trees were so water-logged the lava hardened around them instead of burning them on contact. As the trees disintegrated, deep holes where the trunks once stood were left in the ground.

The first of the molds is very close to the parking lot, making it easy to get a quick glimpse.

Kipuka Puaulu Kipuka Puaulu, a unique sanctuary for native birds and plants, is about 1½ miles up Mauna Loa Rd. The mile-long **Kipuka Puaulu Loop Trail** runs through this 100-acre oasis of native forest.

About 400 years ago a major lava flow from Mauna Loa's northeast rift covered most of the surrounding area. Pele spared this bit of land when the flow parted, creating an island forest in a sea of lava. In Hawaiian, it's known as a *kipuka*.

Kipuka Puaulu is a tiny and unique eco-preserve of rare endemic plants, insects and birds. The lava that surrounds the kipuka has served as a protective barrier against intruding species.

Koa is the largest of the trees here. The younger trees have fern-like leaves which are replaced with flat, crescent-shaped leaf stalks as the koa matures and rises above the forest floor. The tree provides a habitat for ferns and climbing peperomia that take root in its moist bark.

Kipuka Puaulu is quiet, except for the chirpings of birds. The natives include the inquisitive elepaio and three honeycreepers – the amakihi, apapane and iiwi. The

Wahaula Heiau

Wahaula Heiau was the first luakini heiau built in Hawaii. Its construction is credited to Paao, a Tahitian high priest who migrated here in the 12th century. Paao not only introduced human sacrifice to temple ceremonies, but also the concept of mana, a divine power that could be held by the royal chiefs as well as embodied in the temple grounds themselves.

A strict social system of kapus (taboos) were enacted to protect that mana. Commoners were forbidden to eat the same foods or walk the same grounds as chiefs for fear they would absorb the chiefs' mana. Those who broke the kapus were put to death.

Mana was an elusive element that could be lost. When a temple no longer had its mana it was abandoned and a new one built elsewhere. Wahaula Heiau never lost it – it was the last luakini temple where royalty worshipped before the Hawaiian gods were abandoned.

In 1989 a lava flow buried the entire Wahaula area, including the nearby visitor center which stood just 150 feet away from the heiau. The heiau was mysteriously spared, however, when the molten lava literally parted at its walls and skirted around the main temple and the high priest's house on its way to the sea. Subsequent lava flows have continued to spare the site. Apparently it still has some mana left! ■

birds are sparrow size and brightly colored. The honeycreepers have slender curved beaks that enable them to drink nectar from the flowers of native trees.

Also along the trail is a **lava tube** in the dark depths of which a unique big-eyed spider was discovered only a few years back.

Hiking Trails

The park has an extensive network of hiking trails, spanning from sea level to over 13,000 feet. The hikes range from many short and easy ones to serious backcountry treks. Trails strike out in a number of directions – across crater floors, down to secluded beaches, across the Kau Desert, through native forests and up to snow-capped Mauna Loa.

Crater Rim Trail The Crater Rim Trail is an 11-mile hiking trail which runs roughly parallel to Crater Rim Rd. On the north side the trail is along the crater rim, while on the south side it runs outside the paved road.

Because the vehicle road is designed to take in the main sights, you'll actually miss a few of them by hiking. If you have wheels of some sort, you might want to consider riding around the crater rim and saving your hiking legs for trails into areas inaccessible by car or bike.

Halemaumau Trail Diagonally across the road from the visitor center there are signs marking the way to a number of trailheads, including the Halemaumau Trail.

The first section of the Halemaumau Trail passes briefly through a moist ohia forest, with tall ferns and flowering ginger. It then descends about 500 feet to the floor of **Kilauea Caldera** and continues for three miles across the surface of this still-active volcano.

In ancient times the caldera was much deeper, but in the past century overflows from Halemaumau Crater as well as eruptions from the caldera floor have built it up.

The process is easy to visualize as the trail crosses flow after flow, beginning with one from 1974. It continues over flows from 1885, 1894, 1954, 1971 and 1982, each distinguished by a different shade of black. The trail is marked with *ahu*, stone cairns created with piled lava rocks.

Shortly after breakfast on April 30, 1982, geologists at the Hawaiian Volcano Observatory watched as their seismographs and tiltmeters unexpectedly warned of an imminent eruption. The park service quickly closed off Halemaumau Trail and cleared hikers from the crater floor. Before noon a half-mile fissure broke open in the crater and began spewing out a million cubic meters of lava!

This 1982 flow created a landscape which is both very barren and hauntingly beautiful. Some of the spatter formed high brittle mounds, many with small hollow areas. The lava has incredible textures, unusual shapes and deep black tones accented with rich shades of orange, rust and ocher. Sunlight glitters on tiny iridescent bubbles that have cooled in the lava. Ferns have already taken hold inside the cracks of steam vents which act like little terrariums.

The trail ends about 3½ miles from the visitor center at **Halemaumau Overlook**. Needless to say there's no shade on the trail and it can be hot. Take water with you as there's none at the lookout.

Kilauea Iki Trail When Kilauea Iki Crater exploded in 1959, its lava fountains set a new height record of 1900 feet. When the ash finally settled, it covered the entire area southwest of the crater.

Kilauea Iki Trail begins near the parking lot of the Thurston Lava Tube and descends 400 feet to the crater floor. From there it goes clear across the mile-long crater, passing the main vent on the way. The crater floor is still steaming and there's molten lava beneath the hardened surface.

After you ascend the crater wall on the far side, you'll be on **Byron Ledge**, the ledge which separates Kilauea Iki from Kilauea Caldera. By looping around to the right, you can get back to the parking lot via the Crater Rim Trail which skirts the north rim of Kilauea Iki. Altogether this loop is about 3½ miles long.

If you want to check it out before hiking, there's a drive-up lookout half a mile north of the Thurston Lava Tube.

Footprints Trail The Footprints Trail is the beginning of the **Mauna Iki Trail** which leads to a network of trails through the Kau Desert. The trailhead is between the 37 and 38-mile markers on Hwy 11, nine miles southwest of park headquarters. The footprints are an easy three-quarter-mile hike in from the highway.

In 1790, a violent and massive explosion at Kilauea wiped out a regiment of soldiers retreating to Kau after attacking Kamehameha's sacred Waipio Valley. They were literally stopped in their tracks, suffocated by a rare cloud of poisonous gases. A shower of hot mud and ashes hardened around them, leaving a permanent cast of their footprints.

Two hundred years later, you can still count the toes in a few of the prints – although it takes some imagination these days as most of the trailside footprints have been seriously damaged by vandals. Still, it's a pleasant walk.

Halape Trail The 7¼-mile trail to Halape starts from Kipuka Nene campground off Hilina Pali Rd.

Halape was an idyllic beachfront campground bordered by coconut trees until November 29, 1975, when the strongest earthquake in 100 years shook the Big Island. Just before dawn, rock slides from the upper slopes sent most of the 36 campers running towards the sea, where the coastline suddenly sank. As the beach submerged beneath their feet a series of tsunamis swept the campers up, carrying them first out to sea and then tossing them back up on shore. Miraculously only two people died.

The earthquake left a fine **sandy cove** inland of the former beach. There are strong currents in the open ocean beyond the cove. Halape has catchment water, a pit toilet and a three-walled shelter. Do not set up camp in any areas that are marked as sea turtle nesting sites.

Mauna Loa Trail Mauna Loa Trail begins at the end of Mauna Loa Rd, 13½ miles north of Hwy 11. It's about an hour's drive between the trailhead and the visitor center where overnight hikers are required to register (and where you can get the latest information on trail and cabin conditions).

This is a rugged 18-mile trail that ascends 6600 feet. The ascent is gradual but the elevation makes it a serious hike and it takes a minimum of three days.

There are two simple cabins shared by hikers on a first-come first-serve basis. Red Hill cabin has eight bunks with mattresses and Mauna Loa summit cabin has 12.

The trail rises out of an ohia forest and

above the tree line seven miles to Red Hill at 10,035 feet. This leg of the hike takes four to five hours. From Red Hill there are fine views of Mauna Kea to the north and Haleakala on Maui to the northwest.

It's 11 miles and a full day's hike from Red Hill to the summit cabin at 13,250 feet. The summit has a subarctic climate and temperatures normally drop to freezing at night all year round. Winter snow storms can last a few days and bring snow packs as deep as nine feet. Occasionally snow falls as low as Red Hill and covers the upper end of the trail.

It is important to acclimatize as altitude sickness is not uncommon. Common symptoms are headache, nausea and shortness of breath. For minor symptoms, deep breathing brings some relief, as does lying down with your head lower than your feet. If the symptoms are more serious get to a lower elevation immediately.

Hypothermia from the cold and wind is another hazard. A good windproof jacket, wool sweater, winter-rated sleeping bag and rain gear are all essential.

Backcountry Hiking Hiking shelters and simple cabins are available along some of the longer backcountry trails. There's no fee to use them.

In addition to the two cabins along the Mauna Loa Trail, there's a simple cabin at Kipuka Pepeiao along the Kau Desert Trail and coastal area shelters at Keauhou, Halape and Kaaha. All have limited water catchment, which should be treated before drinking. The visitor center keeps track of current water supplies and trail conditions.

All overnight hikers are required to register and obtain a free permit at the visitor center before heading out. Permits are issued on a first-come basis, but no earlier than noon on the day before your hike. There's a three-day limit at each backcountry camping site.

Essential backpacking equipment that the park recommends for any of the backcountry trails includes a first aid kit, a flashlight with extra batteries, a minimum of two quarts of water, emergency food, a compass, a mirror (for signalling), broken-in boots, complete rain gear, cooking stove with fuel (open fires are prohibited), sunscreen and a hat.

More information on backcountry hiking, including a basic trail map, can be obtained at the visitor center or by writing to Hawaii Volcanoes National Park, HI 96718. They also sell a more detailed map of the Mauna Loa Trail for $1.50.

Volcano

The village of Volcano, about a mile east of the park, has a couple of general stores, a place to gas up, a post office, a few eateries and a growing number of B&B-type places to stay.

There's also a little **winery** at the end of the golf course road, a mile from Hwy 11, which offers samples of Volcano's first wines. Although the winery is still in its infancy, the curious may want to stop by the tasting room to try its ambitious wines, which come in flavors such as guava and passion-star chablis.

Akatsuka Orchid Gardens, between the 22- and 23-mile markers on Hwy 11, about four miles east of Volcano village, is a nursery with beautiful orchids that is worth a look, even if you're not in the market to buy anything. Women get a free orchid.

Places to Stay – Volcano Village

At *My Island B&B* (☎ 967-7216; fax 967-7719), Box 100, Volcano, HI 96785, Gordon and Joann Morse rent out three bedrooms with shared bathrooms in their home for $35/55 single/double, including breakfast. It's a quarter of a mile past Kilauea Lodge, on the left after Wright Rd. Gordon, who is very outgoing, enjoys piling guests high with information on the Big Island which he proclaims is 'the *only* Hawaiian Island worth visiting'. The living room is full of books on volcanoes, from photo essays to geological tomes, a few written by former guests.

There are also three units separate from the house, each with a private entrance and bathroom. Two units cost $45/65 while an older unit, which is not quite as spiffy but is larger and has a kitchen, TV and phone is $70. My Island also acts as a booking agent for other B&Bs around the island, most of which are in the $60 to $110 range.

Kilauea Lodge (☎ 967-7366; fax 967-7367), Box 116, Volcano, HI 96785, on the main road in Volcano village, has four delightfully renovated rooms in what was formerly a YMCA dormitory. They have the sort of country comfort you'd find in a fine inn, with working fireplaces, high ceilings, quilts and private bathrooms with tubs. The rate is $95.

A new building which has seven large cheery rooms and a common area with a large fireplace costs $80/85 for singles/doubles. Avoid rooms No 7 and 8 which are right off the common room and can get a bit noisy. There's also a two-room cottage for $105. Prices include a full breakfast from the menu in the lodge's restaurant.

Lokahi Lodge (☎ 985-8647, (800) 457-6924), Box 7, Volcano, HI 96785, is a new bed & breakfast in a contemporary house that was built specifically as a B&B. There's a spacious common area with a wood-burning stove, an upright piano and a semi-formal dining area where an ample continental breakfast is provided. Each room has its own private entrance. All four rooms are good size, have a pleasant decor that includes wallpaper and frill curtains, and are furnished with two extra-long double beds and bathrooms with tubs. Rates are $75 for singles or doubles. Visa and MasterCard are accepted.

Hale Ohia (☎ 967-7986, (800) 455-3803), Box 758, Volcano, HI 96785, is a new B&B on an old estate with pleasant grounds that include a hot tub in the backyard. Three of the four units are in a two-story building (formerly the gardener's cottage) that's located at the side of the main house. There's a three-bedroom unit on the first floor that's a bit rustic and has a full kitchen, while the second story has three contemporary suites with refrigerators and coffeemakers but no cooking facilities. There's also a separate one-bedroom cottage with a fireplace and kitchenette. All have electric space heaters. Rates, which include continental breakfast, are from $60 to $85 for doubles, $15 more for each additional person.

Kilauea Volcano Kabins (☎ 967-7773), Box 963, Volcano, HI 96785, consists of four pleasant units built by the owner, Ron Ober. Two are in a modern duplex cabin and have big picture windows looking out to a fern and ohia forest, electric heaters, queen beds, bathrooms with tubs, refrigerators and coffeemakers. They're a good value at $45/50 singles/doubles. There's also an adjacent house with two more units, each with a gas fireplace. The 1st-floor unit has a separate bedroom, a full kitchen, a living room with a sofa bed and lots of natural wood. The upstairs is a big, open studio with wood-beam ceilings, a king bed and a sofa bed. Both cost $60 for two people and $10 extra for each additional person. All units have phones with free local calls. Breakfast is not included.

The state maintains *Niaulani Cabin*, a housekeeping cabin, half a mile east of the national park. The cabin sits all by itself in the seven-acre ohia forest of Kilauea State Recreation Area, on Kalanikoa Rd near Volcano village. The cabin has two bedrooms, a living room, hot showers, a stove and refrigerator. Rates are $10/17 for singles/doubles, up to $30 for six people, but it's a long shot getting in. For reservations contact the Division of State Parks (☎ 933-4200), Box 936, 75 Aupuni St, Hilo, HI 96721, where you also pick up the key.

Places to Stay – National Park

Namakani Paio Cabins are 10 dreary, windowless plywood cabins at the national park's Namakani Paio Campground. Each has one double bed, two single bunk beds and electric lights, but there are no power outlets or heating. There are communal showers and restrooms. It can get cold at night so if you have a sleeping bag bring it along. (Or bring a tent as well and you can stay in the adjacent campground for free.)

Booking is done through Volcano House

where you pay and pick up your bag of linen. The rate is $32 for one or two people, plus $6 each for a third and fourth person, and there's a $15 deposit for keys and linen.

Volcano House (☎ 967-7321; fax 967-8429), Box 53, Hawaii Volcanoes National Park, HI 96713, is opposite the national park visitor center. Although it has an enviable location, perched right on the rim of Kilauea Caldera, most of the room views are disappointing. By and large the lower-level rooms look out onto a walkway and even some of those on the upper floor have only a partial view of the crater. The rooms are rather small and straightforward but do have some koa furnishings and a bit of character. The best (and most expensive) rooms are the 2nd-story ones in the main building. Rates are $79 to $131.

Camping The park has two drive-up campgrounds. Camping is free and the campgrounds are not usually crowded, although things can pick up in summer. There's no registration or reservation system – it's simply on a first-come, first-served basis. Camping is officially limited to seven days per campground per year. Because of the elevation, nights are crisp and cool at both Namakani Paio (4000 feet) and Kipuka Nene (3000 feet) campgrounds.

Namakani Paio Campground is the park's busiest campground as it's about three miles west of the visitor center, just off Hwy 11. If you're on your way between Hilo and Kona it's a convenient place to stop for the night. The open tent sites are in a small meadow with little privacy, although it's surrounded by fragrant eucalyptus trees. There are restrooms, water, fireplaces and picnic tables. It's about a one-mile hike to the Jaggar Museum and Crater Rim Trail.

Kipuka Nene Campground is about five miles down Hilina Pali Rd, off Chain of Craters Rd. Although it's the less developed of the two campgrounds, there's still a water catchment system, toilets and a shelter with picnic tables. The area is bushy and grassy. True to the campground's

BIG ISLAND

name, a few friendly nene often hang out here. Because of this the campground is commonly closed between November and March during the breeding season.

Information on backcountry camping in the national park is under Backcountry Hiking.

Places to Eat

If you're trying to see the park in a day, you can save time by bringing lunch and having a picnic wherever you are at noon. If you don't happen to be near the park entrance, it's a long haul from most points in the park out to a restaurant.

The only park restaurant is at *Volcano House* (☎ 967-7321), which serves up a cafeteria-quality breakfast buffet from 7 to 10:30 am for $8.75 and a lunch buffet from 11 am to 1:30 pm for $11. The quality of the food is a bit better at dinner (5:30 to 8 pm), with main courses from $15 to $25. While the dining-room view overlooking Kilauea Caldera is magnificent, it can be matched in the adjacent snack shop which serves chili and sandwiches for $3 to $4 and has yogurt, juice and coffee. The snack shop is open from 9:30 am to 5:30 pm.

The *Volcano Country Club Restaurant* at Volcano Golf Course serves inexpensive

breakfasts from 7 to 10 am and lunch from 10:30 am to 3 pm daily. The menu is simple, with light salads, Hawaiian stew and burgers and sandwiches with fries, all priced around $7. The food is straightforward, but they do make a good Portuguese bean soup. The restaurant is also open for dinner on Fridays and Saturdays.

Volcano Diner, a small local diner adjacent to the old general store in Volcano village, has breakfasts, sandwiches and plate lunches for $4 to $5. It's open from 8:30 am to 4 pm daily. There are a couple of booths where you can eat or you can order takeout and have a picnic in the national park.

The best food in Volcano is at *Kilauea Lodge* (☎ 967-7366) which is only open for dinner, from 5:30 to 9 pm daily. Reservations are recommended. Dinners of beef, seafood and chicken begin at around $18 and there's always at least one pasta dish on the menu priced around $14. The atmospheric dining room has high wooden ceilings, island artwork and window tables looking out onto a fern forest. It also has a big stone fireplace, built in 1938 when this was a YMCA camp, which is embedded with an international collection of stones and coins.

Maui

Maui has much to lure the visitor, including superb scenery and diverse landscapes. Most of the sunny west coast is lined with beautiful white sand beaches and the island has world-class windsurfing and excellent conditions for most other water sports. The shallow coastal waters around Maui are central wintering grounds for North Pacific humpback whales, making it prime whale-watching country.

In the 1960s, Hawaii's first major resort development outside Waikiki was built on Maui. Since that time, Maui has become the most visited and the most developed of the Neighbor Islands. As might be expected, the resort action all centers around the beaches of West Maui.

The main tourist destinations – Lahaina, the Kaanapali area and the Kihei strip – are urbanized experiences, complete with traffic and crowds. But Maui does have another side. It's quite easy to escape the touristed West Maui scene by heading to the east coast or the uplands. Making a base in the small towns of Haiku, Kula or Hana is a totally different experience. Those towns sit beneath Haleakala, the massive mountain that provides the scenic backdrop to all of East Maui. Its slopes hold native rainforests, eucalyptus groves and open pastures with large cattle ranches.

Haleakala Crater, with a summit of 10,023 feet, is the centerpiece of Haleakala National Park. The crater is an extraordinary landscape of spewed red cinders and grey lava hills. Haleakala is the world's largest dormant volcano, its crater so big that an entire city could fit inside. There are some incredible hiking trails across the crater floor, and sunrise at the summit is awe-inspiring.

Kula, at a cool 3000-foot elevation on Haleakala's western slopes, is Maui's gardenland. Flowers and vegetables which ordinarily don't have a chance in the tropics thrive up here. Upcountry also has the island's winery, with a tasting room in a century-old jail.

The windward side of Haleakala is lush, wet and rugged. The famed Hana Highway runs down the full length of it, winding its way above the coast through tropical jungle and past roadside waterfalls. It's the most beautiful coastal road in Hawaii.

Artists and craftspeople have long been drawn to Maui, and many of Hawaii's New Age activities are centered here.

ORIENTATION

Most visitors to Maui land at the main airport in Kahului.

From Kahului, it's five miles to Paia down Hwy 36 and another 45 miles to Hana.

Upcountry (Kula) is 15 miles from Kahului on Hwy 37. From there it's another 20 miles up to the summit of Haleakala.

It's about 10 miles to Kihei from Kahului along Hwy 350.

It's 25 miles from Kahului to Lahaina via Hwy 380 and Hwy 30, and four miles more from Lahaina to Kaanapali.

Don't read much into a name, as most main roads are called 'highways' whether they're a busy four lanes or just a country road. Islanders refer to highways by name, rarely by number. If you ask someone where Hwy 36 is, chances are they won't know – ask about the Hana Hwy instead.

HISTORY

Before Western contact, Maui had three major population centers: the southeast coast around Hana, the Wailuku area and the district of Lele (Lahaina).

In the 14th century Piilani, chief of the Hana district, conquered the entire island. During his reign Piilani accomplished some impressive engineering feats. He built the island's largest temple, Piilanihale Heiau, which remains today, as well as an extensive road system around the island.

Maui's Home
According to legend, the Polynesian demigod Maui was wandering the Pacific on a fishing expedition when his fishhook snagged the sea floor. He tugged with such a powerful force that the islands of Hawaii were yanked to the surface. He then claimed the island of Maui and made it his home. ■

Almost half of Maui's highways still bear his name.

The last of Maui's ruling chiefs was Kahekili. During the 1780s he was the most powerful chief in Hawaii, bringing both Oahu and Molokai under Maui's rule.

In 1790, while Kahekili was in Oahu, Kamehameha the Great launched a bold naval attack on Maui. Using foreign-acquired cannons and the aid of two captured foreign seamen, Isaac Davis and John Young, Kamehameha defeated Maui's warriors in a battle in Iao Valley.

An attack on his own homeland by a Big Island rival forced Kamehameha to withdraw from Maui, but the battles continued over the years. When Kahekili died on Oahu in 1794, his kingdom was divided. In 1795, Kamehameha invaded Maui again and this time he conquered the entire island and brought it under his rule.

In about 1800 Kamehameha established Lahaina as his main home and royal court. It remained the capital of Hawaii until 1845.

Whaling Days
Both the whalers and the missionaries arrived in Lahaina in the early 1820s. They were soon at odds.

Lahaina's first Protestant missionary, William Richards, converted Maui's Governor Hoapili to Christianity shortly after Richards' arrival in 1823. Under Richards' influence, Hoapili began passing laws against drunkenness and debauchery.

After months at sea, the whalers weren't looking for a prayer service when they pulled into port. Ready for grog and women, they didn't take kindly to the puritanical influences of New England missionaries. To most sailors, 'there was no God west of the Horn'.

In 1826 when the English captain William Buckle of the whaler *Daniel* pulled into port, he was outraged to discover Lahaina had a new 'missionary taboo' against womanizing. Buckle's crew came to shore seeking revenge against Richards, but a group of Hawaiian Christians came to Richards' aid and chased the whalers back to their boat.

Following Captain Buckle's purchase of a Hawaiian woman, Richards wrote to Buckle's hometown newspaper reporting the details. A libel suit followed. Richards was summoned to Honolulu to be tried but he was acquitted.

In 1827, after Governor Hoapili arrested the captain of the *John Palmer* for allowing women to board his ship, a few cannonballs were shot into Richards' yard. The captain was released, but laws restricting liaisons between seamen and native women stayed.

After Governor Hoapili's death, laws against liquor and prostitution were no longer strictly enforced and whalers began to flock to Lahaina.

By the mid-1800s two-thirds of the whalers coming into Hawaii landed in Lahaina, which had replaced Honolulu as the favored harbor. In 1846 almost 400 ships pulled into port.

By the 1860s the whaling industry started to fizzle. The depletion of the last hunting grounds in the Arctic and the emergence of the petroleum industry spelled the end of the US whaling era.

Whaling had been the base of Maui's moneyed economy. After the whalers left, Lahaina became all but a ghost town.

MAUI

MAUI

Sugar

As whaling was declining, sugar was on the rise. Two of the first planters were Samuel Alexander and Henry Baldwin, sons of prominent missionaries.

In 1870 they began growing sugar cane on 12 acres in Haiku, and the next year they added another 500 acres. It was to be the beginning of Hawaii's biggest sugar company.

In 1876 Alexander & Baldwin began construction of the Hamakua Ditch to service the Haiku plantations 17 miles away. This extensive irrigation system turned Wailuku's dry central plains into green sugar land. Sugar remained the strength of the economy until tourism took over in the 1960s.

GEOGRAPHY

Maui, the second largest Hawaiian island, arose from the ocean floor as two separate volcanoes. Eventually lava flows and soil erosion built up a valley-like isthmus between the two, linking them in their present form. The flat isthmus provides a fertile setting for fields of sugar cane and has given Maui the nickname 'The Valley Island'.

The eastern side of Maui, the larger and younger of the two, is dominated by Haleakala which has a summit elevation of 10,023 feet (3055 meters). This dormant volcano has a massive crater-like valley containing numerous cinder cones and vents. Haleakala last erupted in 1790, which on the geological clock means it could just be snoozing.

The West Maui Mountains dominate West Maui, with Puu Kukui, at 5778 feet, the highest point.

The rainy northeast sides of both mountain masses are cut with deep ravines and valleys that lead down to the coast. White sand beaches run along much of the island's western shoreline.

Maui's total land area is 728 sq miles.

Molokini

The largely submerged volcanic crater of Molokini lies midway between Maui and Kahoolawe. The crater rim has half eroded away, leaving a crescent moon shape that rises 160 feet above the ocean surface. Its land area is about 18 acres.

Molokini has transparent waters with abundant fish and coral, making it a popular snorkel and dive spot.

The US Navy used to shell Molokini for target practice and live bombs are still found on the crater floor. A few years ago demolition experts removed three which were in just 20 feet of water.

CLIMATE

Maui's west coast is largely dry and sunny. The southeast coast and the Kula uplands receive more rain and commonly have intermittent clouds.

Temperatures vary more with elevation than season. The variance between winter and summer is only about 7°F in most places. The average August temperatures (over a 24-hour period) are 77°F in Hana, 78°F in Lahaina and Kihei, 79°F in Kahului and 50°F at Haleakala summit.

The lowest temperature ever recorded at the summit of Haleakala was 14°F and temperatures hovering around freezing are common on winter nights. The mountain even gets an occasional winter snowcap.

Average annual rainfall is 69 inches in Hana, 13 in Kihei, 15 in Lahaina, 19 in Kahului and 44 at Haleakala summit.

Puu Kukui, the highest peak of the West Maui Mountains, gets 400 inches of rain a year. This is Maui's wettest spot, just five miles from the dry Wailuku plains.

FLORA & FAUNA

It's on Maui that you are most likely to see the endangered nene goose and the rare silversword plant. Haleakala is the habitat for both. Maui is also the best island for viewing humpback whales.

At least six birds native to Maui are found nowhere else in the world. They include the Maui parrotbill, Maui *nukupuu,* Maui creeper, Maui *akepa,* the crested honeycreeper and the *poouli,* all of which are endangered. The poouli, quite amazingly, wasn't discovered until 1973, when it was sighted by a group of University of Hawaii students working in a secluded area of the Hana rainforests.

Maui also has wild pigs, goats and game birds that are hunted.

Humpback Whales

After spending their summers in Alaska, more than half of all humpback whales in the North Pacific come to Hawaii for the winter. The largest numbers are found in the shallow waters between Maui, Lanai and Kahoolawe.

Humpbacks have tail flukes with distinctive individual markings, making them easy to identify. The Pacific Whale Foundation has counted over a thousand humpback whales off Maui in recent seasons.

The peak season for humpbacks in Hawaii is the same as for tourists from cold-weather climates. Some arrive as early as November and a few stay as late as May, with most in residence from January to March.

The western coastline of Maui from Olowalu to Makena (and the eastern shore of Lanai) are prime birthing and nursing grounds for mothers and newborns. Federal law protects these 'cow/calf waters', and prohibits boats and swimmers from approaching within 300 yards of the whales.

Humpbacks like to stay in shallow water when they have newborn calves, apparently as a safeguard against shark attacks. Maalaea Bay is a favorite nursing ground.

Humpbacks are highly sensitive to human disturbance and noise. Around Lahaina where the waters are buzzing with activity, they generally stay well offshore.

The best bet for whale spotting if you're in the Lahaina area is to go south at least as far as Launiupoko Wayside Park. The stretches from Olowalu to Maalaea Bay and from Keawakapu Beach to Makena Beach are prime whale-watching spots.

GOVERNMENT

Maui County consists of the islands of Maui, Molokai, Lanai and uninhabited Kahoolawe. The county seat is in Wailuku.

The county is governed by an elected mayor with a four-year term and a nine-member council with two-year terms.

ECONOMY

Maui's current unemployment rate is 4%. The major industries are tourism, sugar cane and pineapple growing, cattle grazing, and diversified agriculture, in that order.

Surprisingly, more land on Maui is used for grazing dairy and beef cattle than for any other purpose. For every acre of sugar, there are three acres of ranch land.

Kula is one of the state's major flower and vegetable producing regions, accounting for more than half of the cabbage, lettuce, onions and potatoes grown in Hawaii, and for almost all of the commercially grown proteas and carnations.

After Oahu, Maui captures the lion's share of Hawaii's tourist industry, accounting for roughly half the visitor accommodation on all the outer islands combined. Numbers, however, don't equate to bargains here. Maui has the highest room rates in Hawaii, averaging $150 a night, which is nearly 40% higher than the state average.

POPULATION & PEOPLE

Maui has a population of 99,400. The Wailuku district, which includes the sister towns of Wailuku and Kahului, is home to half of the island's residents.

Ethnically, 26% of the population is Caucasian, 16% Japanese, 15% Filipino and 2% Hawaiian. About one-third of Maui's residents consider themselves to be of 'mixed blood', with two-thirds of these having some Hawaiian ancestry.

INFORMATION
Tourist Offices

The Maui Visitors Bureau (☎ 244-3530; fax 244-1337), Box 580, Wailuku, HI, 96793, has its office at 1727 Wili Pa Loop, opposite the Wailuku post office. It's open from 8 am to 4:30 pm Monday to Friday. If you call (800) 525-MAUI before you go, the bureau will send its 'travel planner', a packet containing brochures and other promotional information.

MAUI

Other Tourist Information For information on Kaanapali, contact the Kaanapali Beach Resort Association (☎ 661-3271, (800) 245-9229), 2530 Kekaa Dr, Suite B1, Lahaina, HI 96761. For information on Wailea, contact the Wailea Destination Association (☎ 879-4258, (800) 782-5642), 3750 Wailea Alanui, Wailea, HI 96753. Both organizations will mail out brochures on accommodation at their resorts.

Media
Maui's main newspaper, the *Maui News* (☎ 244-3981), Box 550, Wailuku, HI 96793, has good coverage of local and off-island news and comes out daily except Saturday. The Friday edition can be mailed to the US mainland for $2.75 (or three months' worth for $12). It can be ordered by calling (800) 827-0347.

There are several small community newspapers that focus on local issues, including the *Maui Press*, *Lahaina News*, *South Maui Times*, *Haleakala Times* and *Maui Bulletin*.

Free tourist magazines such as *This Week Maui* and *Spotlight's Maui Gold* and pocket-sized beach guides to Lahaina and Kaanapali are full of ads, discount coupons, simple maps and general sightseeing information. They're worth picking up and are easily found at the airport and island hotels and restaurants.

All the major US mainland television networks are available on cable. Cable TV Channel 7 has ongoing programs on Hawaii geared for visitors.

Maui has 10 radio stations. Station KPOA (93.5 FM and 107.3 FM) plays Hawaiian music from 1 am to 8 pm daily, followed by tropical jazz to 1 am.

Books & Maps
The public library at Kahului is the best on Maui. There are other public libraries in Wailuku, Lahaina, Hana, Kihei and Makawao.

For books on Hawaii, try the Whalers Book Shoppe at the Wharf Cinema Center in Lahaina or Waldenbooks in Kahului, Kihei, Lahaina and Kaanapali.

The best map to buy for getting around the island is the University of Hawaii Press map of Maui. In addition to covering roads, it shows beaches and major sights.

Weather
For a recorded forecast of Maui weather call 877-5111. For a more recreational forecast, including conditions at Haleakala and the road to Hana, sunrise and sunset times, and general marine conditions call 871-5054.

For a more extensive marine forecast, including surf conditions, winds and tides call 877-3477. The park service has a recorded forecast (☎ 572-7749) for Haleakala National Park.

Emergency
Dial 911 for police, ambulance or fire emergencies. The county crisis and help line is 244-7407.

The island's largest hospital, Maui Memorial Hospital (☎ 244-9056), 221 Mahalani St, Wailuku, and the smaller Hana Medical Center (☎ 248-8294) in Hana both have 24-hour emergency service.

ACTIVITIES
Beaches & Swimming
Maui has lots of fine beaches, some of Hawaii's best windsurfing and board surfing, and plenty of good swimming, snorkeling and bodysurfing spots.

The northwest coast from Kaanapali up to Honolua Bay and the southwest coast from Maalaea down through Kihei to Makena are largely fringed with white sand beaches. This western side is dry and sunny and water conditions are generally calmer than on the windward northern and eastern coasts.

Official Maui
Maui's nickname is 'The Valley Island'. Its official color is pink; its flower is the *lokelani*, which is a type of rose; and the unofficial slogan is *Maui no ka oi* – 'Maui is the best'. ∎

Most of the west coast beaches are backed by hotel and condo developments – good if you're looking to stay right at the beach, not so good if you prefer seclusion. Some of the best undeveloped beaches are Slaughterhouse Beach and Honolua Bay in the north and Makena's Big and Little beaches in the south.

Swimming Pools The county has a couple of heated swimming pools in Wailuku that are free to the public. The pool (☎ 243-7411) on the corner of Wells and Market Sts is open from 9 am (from 10:30 am on Wednesdays and Sundays) to 11:45 am and from 1 to 4 pm daily, as well as from 6 to 8:30 pm Monday to Friday.

The pool at the War Memorial Center (☎ 243-7394) at Baldwin High School is open from 9 am to 4:30 pm daily, except on Thursdays when it opens at 10:30 am and on Sundays when it opens at 1 pm. In summer it's open evenings from 6:30 to 9 pm on Tuesdays and Thursdays as well.

Surfing
Maui has some unbeatable surfing spots, with peak surfing conditions from November to March. Hookipa Beach near Paia has surfing almost year-round, with incredible winter waves. When conditions are right, Honolua Bay on the northwest coast has the island's top action.

The Maalaea Pipeline, located at the south side of Maalaea Bay, has a very fast break, best during south swells. However the break, which *Surfer* magazine has described as one of the world's 10 best, could be seriously altered if a proposed expansion of Maalaea Harbor is allowed to go through.

A number of places give surfing lessons for beginners, including Andrea Thomas of Maui Surfing School (☎ 875-0625), Kaanapali Windsurfing School (☎ 667-1964), Hawaiian Sailboarding Techniques (☎ 871-5423), Maui Mistral (☎ 871-7753) and Windsurfing West (☎ 871-8733).

Lessons typically take 1½ to two hours and cost $50 to $60. Most places 'guaran-

tee' that students of all ages will be surfing at the end of the lesson.

The most popular beaches for body-surfing are Baldwin Beach Park, Fleming Beach Park and those in the Kihei area.

Both surfboards and boogie boards can be rented at numerous locations around Maui, including many of the windsurfing shops.

Hi-Tech Surf Sports (☎ 877-2111) rents surfboards for $18/90 a day/week at its Kahului (444 Hana Hwy) shop and boogie boards for $8/45 at its Paia (Baldwin Ave) shop.

Maui Mistral, 261 Dairy Rd, Kahului, rents boogie boards for $7.50/15 a day/week, surfboards for $20/100.

Fun Rentals (☎ 661-3053), 193 Lahainaluna Rd, Lahaina, rents standard surfboards for $20/75 a day/week, longboards for $25/85 and boogie boards for $4/20.

Reef Watchers (☎ 874-3467) at Suda's Store, 61 S Kihei Rd in Kihei, rents boogie boards for $5 a day.

Windsurfing
Maui is a mecca for windsurfers. Some of the world's best windsurfing is at Hookipa Beach in Paia, though it's suitable for experts only. Spreckelsville Beach in Paia is for intermediate and advanced windsurfers. Kanaha Beach in Kahului is good for beginners, as are parts of the Kihei coast. In Maalaea Bay, winds are usually strong and blow offshore towards Kahoolawe, good for advanced speed sailing. During the winter, on those occasions when kona winds blow, the Maalaea-Kihei area is often the only place windy enough to sail and becomes the main scene for all windsurfers.

Overall, Maui is known for its consistent winds and windsurfers can find action in any month. Although trade winds can blow at any time of the year and flat spells can also hit anytime, generally the windiest time is June to September and the flattest from December to February.

The Maui Boardsailing Association has developed a 'sail safe' program with windsurfing guidelines; brochures with the guidelines are available at the windsurf shops.

Most windsurfing shops are based in Kahului. They include:

Hawaiian Island Windsurfing, 460 Dairy Rd, Kahului, HI 96732 (☎ 871-4981, (800) 231-6958)

Hawaiian Sailboarding Techniques, 444 Hana Hwy, Kahului, HI 96732 (☎ 871-5423, (800) 736-6284)

Maui Magic Windsurfing School, 520 Keolani Place, Kahului, HI 96732 (☎ 877-4816, (800) 872-0999)

Second Wind, 111 Hana Hwy, Kahului, HI 96732 (☎ 877-7467)

Windrigger Maui/Maui Mistral, 261 Dairy Rd, Kahului, HI 96732 (☎ 871-7753, (800) 345-6284)

Windsurfing West, 397 Dairy Rd, Kahului, HI 96732 (☎ 871-8733, (800) 358-2377); lessons and lesson/equipment packages only

Shops generally rent boards and rigs for about $45/250 a day/week, which usually includes swapping privileges that let you try different equipment.

Most also give windsurfing lessons for all levels, both day classes and multi-day packages. Introductory classes for beginners are usually held at Kanaha Beach or at the north side of Kihei, last two to three hours and cost around $60, equipment included. At Kanaha there is no sailing allowed before 11 am on any day and lessons are not given on Sundays or holidays.

Most of these shops also sell windsurfing gear and book package tours that include accommodation and windsurfing gear.

A smaller operation, Kaanapali Windsurfing School (☎ 667-1964), rents windsurfing equipment and gives beginner lessons on Kaanapali Beach. The cost is $45 for a 90-minute lesson, plus $10 for an extra hour board rental. Otherwise rentals are $20 for one hour, $45 for three hours.

Diving & Snorkeling

Some dive and snorkel boat tours go along the Maui shoreline, but the main destinations are to the sunken volcanic crater of Molokini and to the island of Lanai.

Although some dive boats take snorkelers, and vice versa, in general you're better off going out on a tour that's geared for the activity you're doing.

For snorkeling from the beach, the best spots are Black Rock at the Sheraton in Kaanapali; Olowalu, south of Lahaina; around the rocky points of Wailea and Makena beaches; and, in summer only, Honolua Bay and Slaughterhouse Beach on the northwest shore. Kapalua Bay is generally calm for snorkeling year-round. Maui Dive Shops has a good free map that details the island's best diving and snorkeling spots.

Molokini Molokini is Maui's most popular snorkeling tour site. The fish are tame and numerous and the water is clear.

Morning is the best time to snorkel Molokini as winds pick up in the afternoon. The fish are given their breakfast call by boat captains who drop in loaves of bread to start the action.

For divers, Molokini has walls, ledges, white-tipped reef sharks, manta rays, turtles and a wide variety of other marine life.

Although the snorkeling and diving is good, a score of tour boats crowd the islet everyday and all of the activity has taken a toll on the reef. Some sections have been permanently damaged, largely from dropped and dragged anchors that have carved swaths in the coral.

Black coral was once prolific in Molokini's deeper waters. However most of it made its way into Lahaina jewelry stores before Molokini was declared a conservation district in 1977.

Lanai Lanai also has clear waters, but without the crowds. The most common destination is Hulopoe Bay.

Hulopoe is a big beautiful beach that was once secluded but now has a luxury hotel at its northern end. The reef at the southern end harbors large schools of fish and is good for snorkeling.

For divers, the nearby Cathedrals has intriguing geological formations, including caves, arches and connecting passageways.

Dive Shops & Boat Dives Maui has numerous dive operations. The most prolific is Maui Dive Shops, which has the following branches around the island:

Kaanapali	Whalers Village (☎ 661-5117)
Kahana	Kahana Gateway (☎ 669-3800)
Kahului	444 Hana Hwy (☎ 871-2111)
Kihei	Azeka Place II (☎ 879-3388)
	Kamaole Center (☎ 879-1533)
	Kihei Town Center (☎ 879-1919)
Lahaina	Lahaina Cannery Mall (☎ 661-5388)
	626 Front St (☎ 667-0722)
Wailea	Wailea Shopping Village (☎ 879-3166)

Maui Dive Shops offers introductory dives for beginners for $59; two-tank dives for $65 off Maui, $89 at Molokini; night dives for $89; and four-day certification courses for $235.

Lahaina Divers (☎ 667-7496, (800) 998-3483), 143 Dickenson St, Lahaina, HI 96761, has two-tank dives for $95 to either Lanai or Molokini, one-tank introductory dives for $70 and shore night dives for $55. They also offer three-day certification courses for $235, book dive vacations and lead advanced drift and deep-water dives.

Hawaiian Reef Divers (☎ 667-7647, (800) 551-6767), 156 Lahainaluna Rd, Lahaina, HI 96761, has half-day trips to either Molokini or Lanai costing $85 for two-tank dives, $79 for intro dives and $49 for snorkeling. Lanai night dives cost $65 and certification courses are $299.

Underwater photographer Ed Robinson has a dive company called Hawaiian Watercolors (☎ 879-3584), Box 616, Kihei, HI 96753. He chooses from 20 different spots, and dives are 'not prepackaged'; two dives with gear cost $95.

Snorkeling Tours & Rentals Numerous snorkeling cruises leave for Molokini daily from Maalaea Harbor. Boats are usually out from about 7 am to noon and average $35 to $50 including lunch or snacks and snorkeling gear.

Competition is heavy, so deals and discount coupons are easy to come by. Tickets are sold at activity booths around the island.

Snorkeling gear can be rented at reasonable prices from most dive and windsurfing shops and at inflated prices from hotel beach huts.

Hawaiian Reef Divers (☎ 667-7647) in Lahaina currently has the best prices, renting snorkel sets for $3.50 a day, $8 a week.

Snorkel Bob's charges $15 a week for its cheapest snorkel set, with higher prices for better versions. There are three Maui locations: 161 Lahainaluna Rd in Lahaina (☎ 661-4421), 34 Keala Place in Kihei (☎ 879-7449) and Napili Village Hotel in Napili (☎ 669-9603).

Auntie Snorkel (☎ 879-6263) at the Rainbow Mall in Kihei rents snorkel sets from $12 a week.

Kayaking

South Pacific Kayaks, at the Rainbow Mall (☎ 875-4848) in Kihei and at 505 Front St (☎ 661-8400) in Lahaina, rents single kayaks from $20 a day and doubles from $40, including car racks, paddles and life vests. Three-hour guided kayak tours (some dubbed 'whale watch') are offered in the Makena or Lahaina areas for $55. Five-hour outings from Makena by kayak to the La Perouse area cost $85, include snorkeling, short hikes and lunch.

Kelii's Kayak Tours (☎ 874-7652) also offers guided ocean kayak tours. There's a daily 2½-hour trip from Makena to the La Perouse area for $55, a Papawai Point area sunset tour on Saturday for $55 and a 4½-hour tour along Maui's north shore with lunch for $85.

Fun Rentals (☎ 661-3053), 193 Lahainaluna Rd, Lahaina, rents single kayaks for $30 a day, double kayaks for $40.

Hiking

Haleakala National Park has some extraordinary trails across the moonscape-like Haleakala Crater, varying from half-day walks to overnight treks. In the Oheo section of the park, which is south of Hana, there's a trail to two impressive waterfalls.

Polipoli Spring State Recreation Area in Maui's Upcountry has an extensive trail system in cloudforest. One of these, the Skyline Trail, leads up to (or down from) Haleakala summit.

Several pull-offs along the Hana Hwy lead to short nature walks. There's also a pleasant coastal trail between Waianapanapa State Park and Hana Bay.

A nice choice north of Wailuku is the scenic Waihee Ridge Trail, which branches off the Kahekili Hwy. From La Perouse Bay, on the other side of the island, there's a hardy hike over a lava footpath along the coastline. And, of course, Maui has many white sand beaches perfect for strolls. Hikes are detailed in their respective sections.

Sierra Club The Maui branch of the Sierra Club leads hikes or service trips once or twice a month on Saturdays or Sundays. The schedule is posted in the Datebook section of the *Maui News*. There's no fee, but a donation is appreciated.

The service trips sometimes involve helping to rid the island of invasive exotic plants, such as myconia and banana poka. The latter, a not-so-benign relative of the edible passion fruit vine, has run rampant over native forests on the Big Island and Kauai, but is kept relatively controlled on Maui thanks in large part to the Sierra Club. Eradication tactics include bagging fruit and seedlings, pulling up vines and spraying herbicide on the roots.

Cycling

Each morning before dawn, groups of cyclists gather at the top of Haleakala for the thrill of coasting 38 miles and 10,000 feet down the mountain.

Cruiser Bob's (☎ 579-8444, (800) 654-7717) was the first to start this trend, back in 1982. Other major companies include Maui Downhill (☎ 871-2155, (800) 535-2453), Maui Mountain Cruisers (☎ 871-6014, (800) 232-6284) and Mountain Riders (☎ 242-9739).

Generally it's an all-day affair (eight to 10 hours) starting with a hotel pick-up at around 3 am, a van ride up the mountain for the sunrise and about 3½ hours of biking back down. It's not a nonstop cruise as cyclists must periodically pull over for cars following behind, and the primary exercise is squeezing the brakes – it's estimated there's only 400 yards of pedaling on the entire trip! The going rate is a steep $110, which includes bikes, helmets, transportation and meals.

Bikes are generally modified with special safety brakes and each group is followed by an escort van. Pregnant women, children under 12 and those less than five feet tall are usually not allowed to ride.

A more reasonably priced alternative is offered by Makawao Mountain Bike (☎ 572-2200) at 1043 Makawao Ave in Makawao, near the post office. For $39 they'll rent you a 21-speed mountain bike and drive you from Makawao up to the 6500-foot level of Haleakala (three-quarters of a mile south of the toll booth), letting you ride back to Makawao at your own pace. Helmets, daypacks and maps are provided; there's a two-person minimum. If you prefer you can ride to Tedeshi Winery and call from there to be picked up for an additional $10 per person.

Bicycle rentals are detailed in the Getting Around section of this chapter.

Horseback Riding

Maui has lots of ranch land and opportunities for trail rides. The most unusual ride meanders down into Haleakala Crater via Sliding Sands Trail.

Pony Express (☎ 667-2200) is in a eucalyptus grove on Haleakala Crater Rd, 2½ miles up from Hwy 377. On weekdays there are rides across the rolling meadows of Haleakala Ranch, with views from 4200 feet down to the ocean which cost $35 for one hour, $60 for two hours. There's a half-day Haleakala Crater ride that leaves at 9:30 am, takes four hours and covers 7½ miles; it's open to novice riders and costs $120 including a picnic lunch on the crater floor. A full-day version covers 12 miles, goes to Kapalaoa Cabin and costs $140. There are no Sunday rides.

Charles Aki Jr (☎ 248-8209), c/o Kaupo Store, Kaupo, HI 96713, arranges overnight pack trips from his home in Kaupo into Haleakala Crater. The cost is $150 to $200 per person, depending on the number of people (two to six), and includes camping equipment or cabin fees and meals. It costs $25 less if you bring and fix your own food. As Charles is a working cowboy, trips require advance notice and a deposit.

Thompson Ranch (☎ 878-1910) in Keokea has 1½-hour trail rides for $35 and two-hour rides for $40. Six-hour trips looping through Haleakala Crater cost $150 with lunch. Overnight crater trips can be arranged if you have reserved a cabin in advance.

Rainbow Ranch (☎ 669-4991) in Napili offers one-hour introductory rides for beginners for $30, two-hour sunset rides for $55, a three-hour picnic ride for $65, and various other options. For $10 more they'll pick you up and drop you back in the Kaanapali-Kapalua area.

Hana Ranch Riding Stables (☎ 248-8211) has one-hour guided trail rides along the Hana coast at 9:30 am, 11 am, noon and 3 pm Monday to Saturday; the cost is $27.50.

Oheo Stables (☎ 667-2222), one mile southwest of Oheo Gulch, offers 2½-hour horseback rides within the Kipahulu District of Haleakala National Park. The rides depart at 11:30 am and 2:30 pm, move at a casual pace, visit waterfalls and cost $75.

Makena Stables (☎ 879-0244), on the old Makena Rd in Makena, has a variety of trail rides from Makena up the slopes to Ulupalakua Ranch.

Tennis

The county maintains tennis courts at each of these places: Lahaina Civic Center, Lahaina; Maluuluolele Park, Lahaina; Wells Park, Wailuku; War Memorial Complex, Wailuku; Kahului Community Center, Kahului; Kalama Park, Kihei; Hana Ball Park, Hana; Eddie Tam Memorial Center, Makawao; and Pukalani Community Center, Pukalani. All county courts are free to the public on a first-come first-serve basis and are lit for night play.

The Wailea Tennis Club (☎ 879-1958), Maui's largest tennis facility, has nicknamed itself 'Wimbledon West' as it has three grass courts (as well as 11 hard-surface courts) and a stadium court for exhibitions.

In addition, there are tennis courts open to the public on a fee basis at the Makena Tennis Club (☎ 879-8777) in Makena, Kapalua Tennis Garden (☎ 669-5677) in Kapalua, Village Tennis Center (☎ 665-0112) at the Ritz-Carlton in Kapalua, Maui Marriott (☎ 667-1200) in Kaanapali and Royal Lahaina Tennis Ranch (☎ 661-2092) in Kaanapali.

Rates at these resort clubs range from $8 to $20 per person. This is usually a 'per-day' fee, although in most cases only the first hour of playing time is guaranteed and the courts are subject to space availability after that. Rackets can be rented at most tennis clubs for about $5 a day.

Golf

Maui has 16 golf courses open to the public. They include, in order by listing, one municipal, five private and 10 resort courses. All are 18-hole par 71, 72 or 73 courses except Maui Country Club which is 9-hole, par 37.

Waiehu Municipal Golf Course – north of Wailuku; charges green fees of $25 on weekdays, $30 on weekends and holidays, plus $7.50 per person for a shared cart. Clubs rent for $13.50 a day. This is a busy little course and reservations for starting times are taken up to two days in advance (☎ 243-7400).

Silversword Golf Course – Kihei; charges $67 for green fees and cart, $42 after 1 pm (☎ 874-0777).

Pukalani Country Club – Pukalani; charges $62 for green fees and cart (☎ 572-1314).

Sandalwood Golf Course – in Waikapu, next to the Waikapu Valley Country Club; charges $75 for green fees and cart (☎ 242-4653).

Waikapu Valley Country Club – Waikapu; the cost of $200 covers green fees, cart and use of the spa (☎ 244-7888).

Maui Country Club – Spreckelsville; open to the public on Mondays only (reservations can be made after 8 am Sunday) and charges $45, including a cart, for either nine or 18 holes (☎ 877-0616).

Kapalua Golf Club – three courses in Kapalua; green fees and cart cost $70 for resort guests and $110 for non-guests at the Bay and Village courses, $75 for guests and $120 for non-guests at the Plantation course, with lower fees after 2 pm (☎ 669-8044). The Bay Course has extensive plantings of native flora and uses only minimal chemicals, a combination that has made it Hawaii's only course to be recognized as a 'Certified Audubon Cooperative Sanctuary'.

Kaanapali Beach Resort – two courses (North and South) in Kaanapali; green fees and cart cost $100 for resort guests, $110 for non-resort guests at either course (☎ 661-3691).

Wailea Golf Club – three courses in Wailea; green fees are $65 for Wailea guests and $115 for the general public at the Orange & Gold Courses, $10 more at the Blue Course (☎ 879-2966).

Makena Golf Course – two courses (North and South) in Makena; green fees and cart cost $110, but there's a $70 twilight rate after 2 pm (☎ 879-3344).

Organized Tours

Maui has many sightseeing tour companies. Tours to Hana and Haleakala are the most popular, followed by those to Iao Valley and Lahaina.

Grayline-Maui (☎ 877-5507, (800) 367-2420) has a $59 tour of Haleakala, Lahaina and Iao Valley aimed at day visitors to Maui. It leaves Kahului Airport daily at 8:30 am, returning at about 5:30 pm.

Polynesian Adventure Tours (☎ 877-4242) has tours of Hana for $65 and of Haleakala, central Maui and Iao Valley for $52. There's also a Haleakala sunrise tour for $49. Children under 12 are charged about 75% of the adult fare.

TransHawaiian (☎ 877-7308) has Hana tours for $74, Haleakala sunrise tours for $45 and Haleakala/Iao Valley/Lahaina tours for $51. There are discounts for senior citizens age 60 and over and for children under 12.

Helicopter & Biplane

Numerous helicopter companies fly out of the heliport at Kahului Airport for trips around the island.

Some cross the channel and tour Molokai's spectacular north shore as well.

Most companies advertise in the free tourist magazines. Prices are highly competitive, with many running perennial specials, offering free use of video cameras and the like.

Papillon (☎ 877-0022, (800) 367-7095), Hawaii's largest helicopter company, has recently lowered its prices which range from $49 for a 20-minute tour of West Maui to $149 for a 65-minute tour that includes Molokai's north shore.

The Maui-based Sunshine Helicopters (☎ 871-0722, (800) 544-2520) offers a 20-minute tour over the waterfalls of Waihee Valley for $59 and a 40-minute tour of Haleakala and Hana for $99. There are half a dozen longer tours, including one that combines a helicopter ride to Lanai with snorkeling and lunch on the beach, followed by a sailboat trip back to Maui.

Other helicopter companies operating on Maui include Blue Hawaiian (☎ 871-8844, (800) 247-5444), Hawaii Helicopters (☎ 877-3900, (800) 346-2403), Air Kauai (☎ 877-7005) and Alex Air (☎ 871-0792).

Biplane Barnstormers (☎ 878-2860) offers open-cockpit biplane rides ranging from $150 for a 30-minute tour of either the north or south shore or $450 for a 90-minute circumnavigation of the island. The cost is per plane, for either one or two passengers.

Cruises

Maui has enough dinner cruises, sunset sails, deep-sea fishing and charter sailboats to fill a book. Most leave from Lahaina or Maalaea, a few from Kihei and Kaanapali.

You can get current rates and information from activity booths all around Maui or from the tourist magazines – or just go down to Lahaina Harbor where the booths and the boats are lined up and check out the scene for yourself.

Atlantis Submarines (☎ 667-2224) has a 65-foot sub that carries 46 passengers down to a depth of 150 feet in the waters off Lahaina and Kaanapali to see coral and fish. Tours leave from Lahaina Harbor via a catamaran every hour on the hour from 9 am to 5 pm Monday to Wednesday and 8 am to 3 pm Thursday to Sunday. The cost is $79 for adults, $39 for children, including hotel pick-up.

If you want a similar effect at half the price, the semi-submersible Nautilus (☎ 667-2133) is a glass-bottom boat with a submerged lower deck that has underwater viewing windows similar to those on the sub. It leaves Lahaina Harbor five times a day and costs $40 for adults, $20 for children ages six to 12 (free for children under six), although discounted specials commonly lower the regular price to nearly half that.

Whale Watching From January to the end of March is the peak humpback whale-watching season, though there are usually whales around Maui for a month or so on either side.

In season, whale-watch cruises are heavily advertised and you'll have no trouble finding one. Whale-watch boats range from double-hulled sailboats to 92-foot cruise vessels. Most leave from Maalaea or Lahaina harbors, a few from Kihei and Kaanapali. A two to three-hour tour usually costs $20 to $40 for adults, half price for children. Some companies have hydrophones to hear whale songs, some claim to donate a portion of the ticket price to whale conservation groups, and some guarantee whale sightings or give another boat tour free.

Many of the boats that take snorkelers to Molokini in the morning go out whale watching in the afternoon. During the season there's a good chance of spotting whales on the snorkeling trip to Molokini itself.

The nonprofit Pacific Whale Foundation (☎ 879-8811, (800) 942-5311) has numerous daily cruises from both Maalaea and Lahaina, with prices beginning at $22.50 for adults, half that for children ages four to 12. They use a 50-foot sailboat and a 65-foot catamaran from Lahaina and a 53-foot motorboat from Maalaea. Whale sightings are guaranteed or you'll get a coupon good

for another free trip. A portion of the profits go to the foundation's marine conservation projects.

To Lanai Trilogy Excursions (☎ 661-4743, (800) 874-2666), at 180 Lahainaluna Rd in Lahaina, operates a day tour by catamaran from Lahaina to Lanai's Hulopoe Beach. The cost of $139 includes breakfast, a barbecue lunch, snorkeling and a land tour of Lanai.

Club Lanai (☎ 871-1144, (800) 532-5262) sails its 149-foot catamaran to secluded Kahalepalaoa Beach on Lanai's east coast. The cost of $79 includes all you can eat and drink, and a few water activities. The boat leaves Lahaina's Pier 4 at 8 am and returns at 3 pm.

ACCOMMODATIONS

Other than camping, the cheapest places to stay on Maui are the Banana Bungalow and Northshore Inn in Wailuku, both of which have dorm beds for $15.

Maui also has a number of studio-style cottages and apartments that rent from about $50. Some of the best deals for these are found in the Haiku-Paia area. There are also a number of B&Bs spread around the island, offering some very pleasant places to stay for around $75.

Kihei has the highest concentration of Maui's middle-range accommodations, most of it in condos. Other mid-range accommodations can be found in Kahului, Lahaina and Honokowai. The lower end of the mid-range is about $50 to $80, but it's easy to spend well over $100 a night and not be in anything exclusive.

Maui's two biggest resort developments are Kaanapali Beach Resort and Wailea Resort, both of which have luxury hotels and condos. Prices for the cheapest condos start around $140. The beachfront hotels start around $125 in Kaanapali and $180 in Wailea, though the more exclusive hotels have room rates that are easily double that.

Overall, rates can be substantially lower during the low season (mid-April to mid-December) and you get to pick and choose. During the high season, the better condo deals usually require reservations far in advance.

Condominiums

Maui has many more condo units than hotel rooms. Some condo complexes are booked only through rental agents. Others operate more like a hotel with a front desk, though even in those places some of their units are usually handled by rental agents.

Overall, the best rates are through the agents, but you'll have to deal with advance payments and in some cases there may be security deposits as well, although the latter have become less prevalent in recent years. Avoid any place that tries to slip in a 'cleaning fee', unless it's a condition for allowing you to stay less than the usual minimum number of days.

Most agents require deposits within one to two weeks of booking, with full payment within 30 days prior to arrival. Cancellation policies vary, but there will be a hefty charge (or no refund at all) for canceling within the last month. The minimum stay is usually four to 14 days, depending on the place and season.

Each of the agents listed here handles a number of condo complexes and will send listings with rates making it possible for you to compare values. The 800 numbers that follow can be called toll free from the continental USA and most can also be called from Canada.

AA Oceanfront Condominium Rentals, 2439 S Kihei Rd 206A, Kihei, HI 96753 (☎ 879-7288, (800) 488-6004; fax 879-7500)

Bello Realty, Box 1776, Kihei, HI 96753 (☎ 879-2598, (800) 541-3060; fax 879-3329)

Condominium Rentals Hawaii, 362 Huku Lii Place 204, Kihei, HI 96753 (☎ 879-2778; toll free: USA (800) 367-5242, Canada (800) 663-2101, Australia 0014-800-123-212)

Hawaiian Apartment Leasing Enterprises, 479 Ocean Ave No B, Laguna Beach, CA 92651 (☎ (714) 497-4253, (800) 854-8843; fax (714) 497-4183)

Kihei Maui Vacations, Box 1055, 1325 S Kihei Rd 213, Kihei, HI 96753 (☎ 879-7581, (800) 541-6284; fax 879-2000)

Klahani Resorts, Box 11108, 721 Wainee St, Lahaina, HI 96761 (☎ 667-2712, (800) 669-0795; fax 661-5875)

Kumulani Rentals, Box 1190, Kihei, HI 96753 (☎ 879-9272, (800) 367-2954; fax 874-0094)

Maui Condo & Home Realty, 2511 S Kihei Rd, Box 1840, Kihei, HI 96753 (☎ 879-5445, (800) 822-4409; fax 874-6144)

Maui Network, Box 1077, Makawao, HI 96768 (☎ 572-9555, (800) 367-5221; fax 572-8553)

Camping

Maui has fewer camping options than the other islands. Waianapanapa State Park and Haleakala National Park are good choices for places to camp.

In addition to the federal, state and county campgrounds listed here, there's also a church-sponsored campground at Olowalu, which is described in that section.

State Parks Polipoli and Waianapanapa, the only state parks on Maui with camping areas, both have tent sites and cabins. Permits are required, the maximum length of stay is five consecutive nights at each site, and tent camping is free.

Polipoli, in Upcountry, has one primitive cabin and a primitive road into it, which usually requires a 4WD vehicle. Waianapanapa, near Hana, has 12 housekeeping cabins that are very popular and must be reserved well in advance. If you can get one, the cabins are great value at $10/17 for singles/doubles.

Cabins can be reserved through the Division of State Parks (☎ 243-5354), State Office Building, 54 High St, Wailuku, HI 96793. Office hours are from 8 to 11 am and from noon to 4:15 pm weekdays.

County Parks On Maui there are only two county parks that allow camping, Baldwin and Rainbow. They're both in the Paia area and neither's a prize.

Permits cost $3 per day (50c for children), limited to three consecutive nights at each campground. Tents are required.

Permits are available by mail or in person from the Department of Parks & Recreation (☎ 243-7389), County of Maui, 1580 Kaahumanu Ave, Wailuku, HI 96793.

The office is in the Wailuku War Memorial Complex at Baldwin High School.

Haleakala National Park Tent camping is allowed at Hosmer Grove, which is at the crater section of the park, and at Oheo Gulch on the coast south of Hana. They are both fine sites, though Oheo has no drinking water. There are no fees or permits required.

Tent camping is also allowed by permit inside the crater and there are cabins as well. Full details are in the Haleakala section.

Each national park campground has a limit of three days a month.

ENTERTAINMENT

Maui's entertainment scene is second only to Oahu's, with a wide variety of music from rock, jazz and disco to mellow Hawaiian guitar.

Casanova in Makawao often brings in top-name musicians. Otherwise, most of the action is in Lahaina and at the resort hotels, especially in Kaanapali and Wailea. Hapa, Hawaii's hottest new duo, hails from Maui and shouldn't be missed if they're playing a gig.

The new Maui Arts & Cultural Center in Kahului, which has both 300- and 1200-seat indoor theaters and a large outdoor amphitheater, is the venue for performances by the Maui Philharmonic Society, the Maui Symphony Orchestra, the Maui Academy of Performing Arts and other community theater and cultural organizations.

For the best updated entertainment information, see the 'Maui Scene' in the Thursday issue of the *Maui News*.

Hawaiiana

Luaus are held regularly in Lahaina, Kaanapali, Wailea and Kihei. All include a buffet dinner with Hawaiian foods and a Polynesian show and cost from $48 to $56. The Old Lahaina Luau in Lahaina puts on one of the more authentic productions.

The Napili Kai Beach Club in Napili has a Friday dinner show that features hula dancing by local children. There are free hula shows in Lahaina, Kaanapali and Wailea shopping centers. Details on specific luaus and hula shows are given throughout the chapter.

THINGS TO BUY

For local arts & crafts, some of the best deals are at the Lahaina Arts Society's gallery in Lahaina and at the Maui Crafts Guild in Paia.

Maui Blanc, Maui's own pineapple wine, is a quality wine that makes a good gift. It sells for about $8 a bottle at liquor and grocery stores around the island.

Proteas are a Maui specialty. The best deal is to buy direct from the Upcountry farms where they are grown.

Several businesses sell food and flowers, including leis, proteas, papayas, pineapples and Maui onions, which are agriculturally pre-inspected and delivered to the airport for you to pick up on your way out. Two such places are Airport Flower & Fruit (☎ 877-6131), at 460 Dairy Rd, Kahului, near the airport, and Take Home Maui (☎ 661-8067), 121 Dickenson St, Lahaina.

GETTING THERE & AWAY
Air

The island's main airport is in Kahului. Maui also has two smaller commuter airports with scheduled air service: Kapalua West Maui Airport and Hana Airport.

Airline phone numbers and information on discounted tickets and air passes are in the Getting Around chapter in the front of the book.

Kahului Airport Hawaiian Airlines and Aloha Airlines fly directly to Kahului from Oahu, Kauai and the Big Island. Both airlines fly an average of twice hourly from Honolulu, with the last flight leaving Honolulu at 8 pm with Aloha and 9 pm with Hawaiian. From Kauai both airlines fly about once an hour, and from Kona on the Big Island they both have three direct flights a day. Hawaiian Airlines also has two direct flights a day from Hilo. One-way fares are $74 on either airline. Round-trip fares are double.

Mahalo Air (☎ (800) 277-8333) flies between Honolulu and Kahului an average of eight times a day, with a one-way fare of $54.

Island Air flies to Kahului from Honolulu, Princeville (Kauai), Molokai, Lanai and Hana. One-way fares are $74 from Honolulu or Hana and $81 from the others. Island Air also operates a daily midnight flight from Honolulu that cost $85.

Air Molokai flies three times a day between Kahului and Molokai for $53. It also has a once daily flight from Hana ($48) and three flights a day to Honolulu ($80). If you travel Monday to Thursday these flights are $5 cheaper.

From the US mainland, Kahului Airport is served by United, American and Delta.

Kahului Airport has car rental booths, a snack bar, restaurant, cocktail lounge, visitor information booth, lei stand, gift shops and newsstand.

Kapalua West Maui Airport This is a small airfield with a 3000-foot runway that's incapable of handling jet aircraft. When Hawaiian Airlines retired its fleet of propeller-driven Dash 7s in 1994, it was forced to abandon service to this airport. Island Air, which is now the main carrier flying into Kapalua West Maui, has 17 flights a day from Honolulu; the first leaves Honolulu at 6:30 am, the last at 5 pm. The fare is $74 one way. There are also four flights a day from Princeville via Honolulu that cost $81.

Trans Air (☎ (800) 634-2094) flies between Honolulu and Kapalua West Maui twice a day, with a one-way fare of $65.

The airport is located between Kapalua and Kaanapali, both of which are about two miles away.

Hana Airport Island Air flies to Hana twice daily from Honolulu, Princeville, Molokai, Lanai and Kahului. The fares range from $74 to $81 one way.

Ferry
There are ferries to Maui from both Molokai and Lanai; if you take them in winter there's a fair chance of seeing whales on either route.

The *Maui Princess* (☎ 553-5736 on Molokai, 661-8397 on Maui, (800) 833-5800 from the mainland), 113 Prison St, Lahaina, HI 96761, is a modern 118-foot boat that runs twice daily between Molokai and Maui. It leaves Kaunakakai at 5:45 am and 3:55 pm and leaves Lahaina's Pier 3 at 7 am and 5 pm. The trip takes about 1¾ hours. The one-way fare is $25 for adults, $12.50 for children ages three to 12.

Expeditions (☎ 661-3756, (800) 695-2624) runs a ferry five times daily between Maui and Lanai. The boat leaves Lahaina Harbor at 6:45 and 9:15 am and 12:45, 3:15 and 5:45 pm, arriving about an hour later. The boat leaves Manele Boat Harbor on Lanai at 8 and 10:30 am and 2, 4:30 and 6:45 pm. The one-way fare is $25 for adults and $20 for children ages two to 11. Tickets can be purchased on the boat.

GETTING AROUND
To/From the Airport
TransHawaiian has a shuttle bus that leaves Kahului Airport on the hour between 7 am and 6 pm (and at 8 pm) daily and goes to 505 Front St and Pioneer Inn in Lahaina and to the Kaanapali hotels. It costs $13. The return service to the airport is slightly less frequent and in that direction reservations (☎ 877-7308) are required.

Akina Bus Service (☎ 879-2828) serves the Kihei-Wailea area with an airport shuttle bus from Kahului Airport. The bus leaves Wailea on the hour from 8 am to 7 pm and returns from the airport at around 15 minutes to the hour, from 8:45 am to 7:45 pm. The cost is $12. Reservations are required from the Wailea direction; pick-ups can be made at Kihei hotels.

Both shuttle buses, as well as taxi dispatchers, are located outside the airport's baggage claim area.

...anae Peninsula from lookout on road to Hana, Maui

...eakala Crater, Haleakala National Park, Maui

Iao Valley State Park, Maui

Cloud forest, upcountry Maui

Oheo Gulch, Haleakala Nat'l Park, Maui

Molokini, Maui

Bus

Maui has no public bus service, but there are several private shuttles in West Maui.

The Lahaina Express makes numerous runs daily between Kaanapali and Lahaina. The Lahaina Cannery Mall operates a shuttle bus between its shopping center and the Honokowai area, with stops at Kaanapali hotels. There's a shuttle bus between Kaanapali's Whalers Village shopping center and the Napili hotels and another shuttle service around the Kaanapali Beach Resort. All four shuttles are free and are detailed under Getting Around in the Kaanapali section of this chapter. Wailea has a free shuttle service around its resort.

Akina Bus Service operates a bus from the Maui Prince Hotel in Makena to Lahaina and Kaanapali, with passenger pick-up in Wailea and Kihei en route. Although the schedule occasionally changes, the first bus generally leaves around 8 am (☎ 879-2828 for information). The one-way fare is $8.

Taxi

Taxi fares are regulated by the county. The minimum flag-down fare is $1.75; the first mile totals around $3.50 and each additional mile is about $1.75.

Approximate one-way fares from the Kahului airport are $5 to $10 to places around Kahului, $12 to Paia, $16 to $29 to Kihei, $45 to Lahaina, $49 to Kaanapali and $60 to Kapalua.

Car

Avis (☎ 871-7575), Budget (☎ 871-8811), Dollar (☎ 877-2731) and National (☎ 871-8851) have booths at Kahului Airport.

Budget has a car rental booth at the Kapalua West Maui Airport; National, Dollar, Avis and Alamo have offices on Hwy 30 in nearby Kaanapali and will pick up at that airport. Dollar is the only rental agency for Hana Airport.

More information on the national chains, including toll-free numbers, is in the Getting Around chapter in the front of the book.

In Lahaina, Wheels R Us (☎ 667-7751) at 150 Lahainaluna Rd rents older compact cars for $25/130 a day/week, jeeps for $35 a day. Cash deposits are accepted if you don't have a credit card.

Kahului also has a couple of local places renting older cars at these prices, although the better deals often sell out early, particularly in the high season. Two of these are Word of Mouth (☎ 877-2436, (800) 533-5929) and VIP (☎ 877-2054, (800) 367-6080).

Bicycle & Moped

Fun Rentals (☎ 661-3053), 193 Lahainaluna Rd, Lahaina, rents six-speed bikes for $15/45 a day/week, 21-speed mountain bikes for $20/65. The shop is open from 8:30 am to 5 pm Monday to Saturday, 8:30 am to 3 pm on Sundays.

South Maui Bicycles (☎ 874-0068) at 1913 S Kihei Rd, next to the Foodland supermarket in Kihei, rents beach bikes for $12/60 a day/week and mountain bikes for $17/79. Rentals are based on 24-hour periods. Hours are 9 am to 5 pm Monday to Saturday, 10 am to 2 pm on Sundays.

Wheels R Us (☎ 667-7751), 150 Lahainaluna Rd, Lahaina, rents Yamaha mopeds for $28/150 a day/week. Cash deposits are accepted in lieu of credit cards.

Kukui Activity Center (☎ 875-1151), at the back of the Kukui Mall in Kihei, rents mopeds for $28/125 a day/week. They provide free pick-up in the Kihei-Wailea area. Drivers must have a major credit card.

Other places renting bikes include Cruiser Bob's (☎ 579-8444) at the Chevron gas station in Paia; A&B Moped Rental (☎ 669-0027), 3481 Lower Honoapiilani Rd, Honokowai; Island Biker (☎ 877-7744), Kahului Shopping Center, Kahului; and Budget Bikes (☎ 661-7337), 126 Hinau, Lahaina.

Hitchhiking

Hitchhiking is illegal in Maui County but some people do opt to circumvent the intent, if not the letter, of the law. Essentially they stand at the side of the road and 'look' like they want a ride, without extending a thumb.

MAUI

Lahaina

In ancient times Lahaina was a royal court for Maui chiefs and the bread basket, or more accurately the breadfruit basket, of West Maui. After Kamehameha I unified the islands he set up his base in Lahaina and the capital remained there until 1845. Hawaii's first stone church, first missionary school and first printing press were all in place in Lahaina by the early 1830s.

The whaling years reached their height in Lahaina in the 1840s with hundreds of ships pulling into port each year. The town took on the whalers' boisterous nature, with dance halls, bars and brothels. Hundreds of sick or derelict sailors, who had either been abandoned or jumped ship, roamed the streets. Herman Melville, who later penned *Moby Dick*, was among the multitudes that landed there.

These days Lahaina's streets are jammed with tourists. The old wooden shops that once housed saloons and provision stores are full of boutiques and galleries.

While there are plenty of interesting historical sites to see, Lahaina is abuzz with commercial activity and if you're expecting something quaint and romantic you may well be disappointed. The coastal setting and mountain backdrop *is* pretty, however, and it's easy to see why people have been drawn here. There are soft breezes off the water and fine sunset views of Lanai.

Orientation

Lahaina's chief attractions are 18th-century historical sites. Sightseeing spots include homes of missionaries, prisons for sailors and graveyards for both.

The focal point of Lahaina is its bustling small-boat harbor, which is backed by the old Pioneer Inn and Banyan Tree Square. Half of Lahaina's sights are clustered in this area, while the other half are scattered around town.

The main drag and tourist strip is Front St, which runs along the shoreline. If Front St seems too hectic, you can stroll inland a block or two to the residential streets, where you'll find Lahaina's quieter and more Hawaiian side.

Information

Money There's a Bank of Hawaii in the Lahaina Shopping Center that's open 8:30 am to 3 pm Monday to Thursday, until 6 pm on Fridays. The First Hawaiian Bank has branches on the corner of Wainee and Papalaua Sts, and up on the Honoapiilani Hwy.

Post The post office substation in the Lahaina Shopping Center is open from 8:15 am to 4:15 pm Monday to Friday. There's often a long wait for a parking space and a long queue inside.

The main post office, where you pick up mail sent general delivery to Lahaina, is near the civic center, on Hwy 30 between Lahaina and Kaanapali. Hours are 8 am to 5 pm Monday to Friday, 10 am to noon on Saturdays.

There's also a little contract post office at the Wharf Cinema Center which opens from 10 am to 4 pm Monday to Friday and 10 am to 12:30 pm on Saturdays.

Bookstores Waldenbooks at the Lahaina Cannery Mall and Whalers Book Shoppe & Coffee House at the Wharf Cinema Center both have good selections.

Library The Lahaina public library (☎ 661-0566), 680 Wharf St, is open from 9 am to 5 pm on Mondays, Tuesdays, Wednesdays and Fridays and from noon to 8 pm on Thursdays. It carries Maui, Honolulu and a few mainland newspapers.

Laundry There's a coin laundry at Lahaina Shopping Center open from 6 am to 10 pm daily.

Pharmacy There's a large Longs Drugs at the Lahaina Cannery Mall and a small pharmacy at the Lahaina Shopping Center.

Parking Finding a space for your car in Lahaina can be a challenge. Front St has on-street parking but there's always a line of cruising cars. Your best bet is the corner of Front and Prison Sts where there's free public parking with a three-hour limit. There are also a few private parking lots, the biggest being Republic Parking on Dickenson St which charges $1.50 for up to two hours, $5 all day and $1 for overnight parking.

Pioneer Inn

The old green and white Pioneer Inn is the most prominent landmark in town. It's got a whaling-era atmosphere with swinging doors, ship figureheads and signs warning against womanizing in the rooms. The downstairs saloon is Lahaina's most popular watering hole with lively country-western bands playing all afternoon and evening.

Actually, the two-story Pioneer Inn was built in 1901, long after the whaling boom had passed, but nobody seems to notice or care.

Banyan Tree Square

The largest banyan tree in the USA covers most of the space in the park next to the Pioneer Inn. It's so sprawling that it appears to be on the verge of pushing the old courthouse, which shares the square, clear off the block.

The tree was planted in 1873 to commemorate the 50th anniversary of the first missionary arrival in Lahaina. It has 16 major trunks and scores of horizontally stretching branches reaching across the better part of an acre. Local kids like to swing between branches Tarzan-style, using the aerial roots.

There are shaded benches and walkways under the tree, which makes it a nice spot to take a break from the crowds on Front St.

Old Courthouse & Lahaina Arts Society

Beyond the banyan tree is the old courthouse, built in 1859. It once served as the government center housing customs, a post office and the governor's office.

The old jail in the basement is now used by the Lahaina Arts Society and the cells that once held drunken sailors now display artwork. The society is a nonprofit collective, with artists donating their time and paying a 30% commission to cover operating expenses. As that's roughly half of the commission charged by private galleries, you'll find some of the best prices in Lahaina here.

All the exhibits are by island artists, and include paintings, blown glass, pottery, woodcarvings and some quality basketwork. Many of the baskets are composed entirely of Maui fibers such as wattle, watsonia, philodendron, draco, ape and fishtail palm.

The society also sponsors community art classes and a number of well-known Maui artists got their start here. It's open from 10 am to 5 pm daily.

Old Fort

The Canal St corner of Banyan Tree Square has a reconstructed section of coral wall from a fort that was built in 1832 to keep rowdy whalers in line.

At one point the fort had 47 cannons, most of which had been salvaged from foreign ships which sank in Hawaiian waters.

Each day at dusk a Hawaiian sentinel beat a drum to alert sailors to return to their ships. Those that didn't make it back in time ended up imprisoned in the fort. In 1854 the fort was dismantled and its coral blocks used as building materials for the new prison.

Canal St

Canal St, bordering Banyan Tree Square, used to be part of a canal system that ran through Lahaina. An enterprising US consul officer built this section of the canal in the 1840s to allow whalers easier access to fresh water supplies – for a fee of course.

Because of problems with mosquitoes, most of the canal system was filled in long ago. Incidentally, Hawaii had no mosquitoes at all until the whalers brought them in from North America in their water barrels.

MAUI

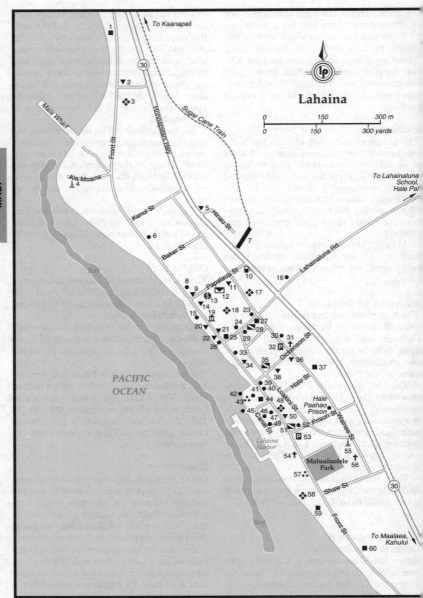

Lahaina

To Kaanapali

To Lahainaluna
School,
Hale Pai

To Maalaea,
Kahului

PACIFIC
OCEAN

Maia Wharf

Lahaina Harbor

Hale
Paahao
Prison

Maluuluolele
Park

0   150   300 m
0   150   300 yards

■ PLACES TO STAY		34	Planet Hollywood		29	Wheels R Us
		36	Kirouac's		30	Seamen's Cemetery
1	Lahaina Roads	38	Lahaina Coolers		31	Maria Lanakila Church
25	Lahaina Hotel	50	Burger King		32	Republic Parking
27	Plantation Inn				33	South Seas Trading Post
37	Maui Islander				35	Lahaina Divers
44	Pioneer Inn		OTHER		39	Masters' Reading Room
59	Lahaina Shores				40	Baldwin House
60	Tony's Place	3	Lahaina Cannery Mall		41	Library
		4	Lahaina Jodo Mission		42	Hauola Stone
▼ PLACES TO EAT		6	Seamen's Hospital		43	Brick Palace
		7	Lahaina Station		45	Carthaginian
2	Saeng's	8	Blue Tropix Nightclub		46	Old Courthouse
5	Pizza Hut	10	Chevron		47	Banyan Tree Square
9	Hard Rock Cafe	12	Post Office		48	Wharf Cinema Center
11	McDonald's	13	Bank of Hawaii		49	Old Fort
14	Longhi's	15	Lahaina Whaling Museum		51	Maui Dive Shop
20	Kimo's		(Crazy Shirts)		52	Dan's Green House
21	Moose McGillycuddy's &	16	Pioneer Sugar Mill		53	Free Parking
	Avalon	17	Lahaina Square		54	Episcopal Church
22	The Cantina	18	Lahaina Shopping Center		55	Hongwanji Mission
23	Westside Natural Foods &	19	Wo Hing Museum		56	Wainee Church
	Deli	23	Fun Rentals		57	Hale Piula
25	David Paul's Lahaina Grill	24	Snorkel Bob's		58	505 Front Street Shopping
27	Gerard's	26	Cheeseburger in Paradise			Center
		28	Hawaiian Reef Divers			

MAUI

Lahaina Harbor

The four cannons on the waterfront opposite the old courthouse were raised from the wreck of a Russian ship that went down in Honolulu Harbor in 1816.

They now point directly at Lahaina's crowded small-boat harbor which is filled with glass-bottom boats, windjammers, sport fishing boats, whale-watchers and sunset sailboats. Booths lining the edge of the harbor sell tickets for most of the cruises, as do the ubiquitous activity booths around town.

The Carthaginian

In 1972, the 960-ton *Carthaginian*, one of the last square-riggers in Hawaii, was on its way from Maui to Honolulu for repairs when it hit a reef outside Lahaina Harbor and sank. The wooden-hulled *Carthaginian* belonged to a class of swift brigantines which made freight runs between New England, Hawaii and China in the 19th century.

The *Carthaginian* that now sits in Lahaina Harbor is a replica, with a steel hull, built in Kiel, Germany in 1920. After being brought to Lahaina in 1973, the 97-foot brig had to be completely restored and all the masts and yards handcrafted – a process which took seven years.

Although the most attractive view of the ship is from the outside, you can also board the boat for $3. Below deck there's a tiny theater where films on whales are shown continuously. It's open from 9 am to 4 pm daily.

Masters' Reading Room

The Masters' Reading Room, on the corner of Front and Dickenson Sts, is the office of the Lahaina Restoration Foundation (☎ 661-3262), the group most instrumental in preserving Lahaina's historical sites. They've restored the Baldwin House, Wo Hing Temple and Hale Pai and have been involved in a number of other preservation projects.

During the whaling years the building was a reading room for sea captains. From here they could keep an eye on happenings in the harbor across the road. The original construction of coral and stone blocks has been preserved.

Baldwin House

The Baldwin House, next door to the Masters' Reading Room, is the oldest building in Lahaina, built in 1834. It was home to the Reverend Dwight Baldwin, a missionary doctor. The exterior of the coral and rock building once resembled the Reading Room but it's been plastered over. The walls beneath the plaster are a full 24 inches thick, which keeps the house cool all year round.

It took the Baldwins 161 days to get to Hawaii from their native Connecticut. These early missionaries traveled neither fast nor light and the house still holds the china and furniture they brought with them around the Horn.

The entrance fee of $3 ($5 per couple) includes a brief tour. It's open from 10 am to 4:30 pm daily, with the last tour beginning at 4:15 pm.

Library Area

The entire area surrounding the Lahaina public library was once the site of a royal taro field. It was also the location of the first Western-style building in Hawaii, the **Brick Palace**, erected by King Kamehameha I so he could keep watch on arriving ships. Despite the grand name, this 'palace' was a modest two-story structure built around 1800 by two Botany Bay convicts. All that remains today is the excavated foundation, which can be found on the ocean side of the library.

The nearby **Hauola Stone** is a waterworn lava stone on the shoreline; to spot it, look to the right as you face the ocean. The Hawaiians believed this flat seat-shaped stone emitted healing powers to those who sat on it.

If you walk north down Front St past the library there's a row of interesting **turn-of-the-century buildings** along the street, best appreciated from the sea wall sidewalk.

Wo Hing Temple

The Wo Hing Temple, on Front St, was built in 1912 by the Chinese community in Lahaina. This two-story building functioned largely as a meeting hall, though for a period after WW II it was also used as a home for elderly Chinese men.

As Lahaina's ethnic Chinese population declined, so too did the building. It was restored and turned into a museum by the Lahaina Restoration Foundation in 1983. There are cultural artifacts and period photos downstairs and a Taoist shrine upstairs.

The tin-roofed cookhouse next door (built detached because of the danger of fire) has been set up as a little theater which shows fascinating films taken in Hawaii by Thomas Edison during his visits to the islands in 1898 and 1905.

Against the wall there's a collection of little opium bottles found during the cleanup of the grounds. The museum is open from 10 am to 4:30 pm Monday to Friday and admission is free.

Lahaina Whaling Museum

Lahaina Whaling Museum is a display of whaling era artifacts along one wall of the Crazy Shirts store at 865 Front St. It's authentic and free.

The collection includes antique harpoons, harpoon guns, ship logs, scrimshaw and photos of the *Carthaginian* sinking outside Lahaina Harbor in 1972. The figurehead hanging from the ceiling in the front of the store was salvaged from the ship. It had been carved in 1965 to prepare the *Carthaginian* for its feature role in the movie *Hawaii*, the adaptation of James Michener's epic novel.

Outside on the back porch there's a rusty old cannon and anchor, and a whaler's trypot once used for boiling down blubber.

Holy Innocents' Episcopal Church

The interior of Holy Innocents' Episcopal Church, 561 Front St, is colorfully decorated with a Hawaiiana motif.

Paintings on the front of the koa altar depict a fisher in an outrigger canoe and

Hawaiian farmers harvesting taro and breadfruit. Above the altar is a Hawaiian Madonna and Child; a Lahaina mother and infant were the models for the painting.

Until the turn of the century the church property was the site of a vacation home belonging to Queen Liliuokalani, Hawaii's last reigning monarch.

Hale Piula

A couple of steps and a grassy building foundation between the Episcopal Church and the 505 Front St shopping center is all that remains of Hale Piula, Lahaina's half-hearted attempt at a royal palace.

Construction on the palace was started in the late 1830s but never completed – Kamehameha III preferred to sleep in a Hawaiian-style thatched house and at any rate decided to move the capital to Honolulu halfway through the project. The building was used for a short time as a government office, but most of the stones were later carted away and used to build the harborside courthouse.

Maluuluolele Park

Maluuluolele Park, opposite Hale Piula, was once the site of a large pond containing a legendary *moo* (water dragon). An island in the center of the pond was home to Maui chiefs and at times to King Kamehamehas I, II and III. It held an ornate burial chamber for royalty.

The park's name is literally 'the breadfruit shade of Lele' ('Lele' was the ancient name for Lahaina).

In 1918 the island was leveled and the pond filled in. Today the park has basketball courts, tennis courts, a baseball field and not a hint of its fascinating past.

Wainee Church

Wainee Church, 535 Wainee St, was built in 1832. It was the first stone church in Hawaii, but it has had problems staying standing.

The steeple and bell collapsed in 1858. In 1894 the church was torched by royalists because its minister supported the annexation of Hawaii. A second church built to replace the original burned to the ground in 1947 and the third was blown away in a storm a couple of years later. One could get the impression that the old Hawaiian gods didn't take kindly to the house of this foreign deity!

The fourth version has been standing since 1953. It's now called Waiola Congregational Church and holds regular Sunday services.

The **cemetery** next door is more interesting than the church. Here lies Governor Hoapili, who ordered the original church built; Queen Keopuolani, once the highest ranking woman in Hawaii and wife of Kamehameha I; and the Reverend William Richards, Lahaina's first missionary. Some of the old tombstones have interesting inscriptions and photo cameos.

Hongwanji Mission

The Lahaina Hongwanji Mission, 551 Wainee St, was built in 1927. It's usually locked but the front doors are glass so you can glance in. Unlike Buddhist temples in Japan, this one has rows of wooden pews. Services are held each Sunday in English and once a month in Japanese.

Hale Paahao Prison

Hale Paahao ('stuck-in-irons house'), Lahaina's old prison, was built in 1852 by convicts who dismantled the old harborside fort and carried the stone blocks here to construct these eight-foot-high prison walls.

Inside, one of the whitewashed cells has an authentic-looking 'old seadog' mannequin with a recorded story about 'life in this here calaboose'.

In another cell you'll find a list of offenses and arrests for the year 1855. The top three offenses were drunkenness (330 arrests), adultery and fornication (111) and 'furious riding' (89). Others include profanity, aiding deserting sailors, drinking awa and giving birth to bastard children. Hawaiians could collect bounties by turning in sailors that jumped ship or fooled around with local women. There's also a copy of a 16-year-old seaman's diary vividly describing his time spent in the prison. Admission is free.

Seamen's Cemetery

The Seamen's Cemetery on Wainee St is next to Maria Lanakila Church, the first Catholic church on Maui.

It's basically a local cemetery, with only one seaman's tombstone still identified. However, historical records indicate that numerous sailors from the whaling era were buried here, including a shipmate of Herman Melville's from the *Acushnet*.

Pioneer Sugar Mill

It's hard to think of tourist-jammed Lahaina as a sugar town, but it is. The Pioneer Sugar Mill has been a prominent part of Lahaina for 130 years and its cane fields still stretch for 17 miles along the coast.

The dusty mill, which sits on both sides of Lahainaluna Rd on the slopes above the town center, stands in sharp contrast to all the tourist activity below.

Lahainaluna Seminary

Lahainaluna Seminary, established by Christian missionaries in 1831, was the first US educational institution west of the Rockies.

One of the school's early graduates was David Malo, a respected Hawaiian philosopher. He became Hawaii's first native rights spokesperson, warning in his early writings in 1837 that Hawaii was about to be swallowed up by the masses of foreigners arriving on its shores. His book *Hawaiian Antiquities* is regarded as the best account of ancient Hawaiian history and culture.

Lahainaluna is now Lahaina's public high school, considered one of the finest in the state. Malo is buried on the hillside above the school.

The school is at the end of Lahainaluna Rd, 1⅓ miles above the mill. You get a nice view of Lahaina with Lanai in the background from the school's lower parking lot.

Hale Pai Hale Pai, a printing house on Lahainaluna's grounds, was the site of the first printing press in Hawaii. Although the main purpose of the press was to make the Bible available to Hawaiians, it also was used to produce other works including the first Hawaiian botany book and, in 1834, Hawaii's first newspaper.

Examples of early books are on display at Hale Pai. You can use a replica of the original Ramage press to hand print your own copy of a page from the first Hawaiian primer.

Volunteers staff the building and it's usually open from 10 am to 3 pm Monday to Friday, although when they're understaffed visits are by appointment (☎ 667-7040) only. Admission is free but donations are appreciated.

Seamen's Hospital

In 1844, the building at 1024 Front St was leased by the US government and turned into a hospital for sick and abandoned seamen.

Officials at the hospital were notorious for embezzlement. Sailors who weren't sick and others long since dead were commonly signed onto the hospital books. A US warship with a board of inquiry was sent to investigate the corruption but the ship and its findings mysteriously disappeared at sea on the return home!

The seamen's hospital has been completely restored and is now used as an office by Paradise Network, a local television station. A huge anchor on the lawn marks the site.

Lahaina Jodo Mission

A large bronze statue of Buddha overlooks the compound of Lahaina Jodo Mission, off the north end of Front St, just before the bridge. The statue was put up in 1968 in celebration of the centennial of Japanese immigration to Hawaii. With its back to the mountains, the Buddha looks out over the Pacific towards Japan.

Opposite the mission, in the sandy cemetery along the beach, the county has moved a number of graves that have been disinterred by high surf in the past few years.

Just to the north is the long **Mala Wharf**, constructed in the 1920s to allow inter-island ferries to land passengers directly ashore. It never made the grade. Rough seas prevented the ferries from pulling up alongside the pier, forcing them to continue shuttling passengers across the shallows of Lahaina Harbor in small boats.

The wharf is now crumbling and closed, though Mala does have a new launch ramp for small boats nearby.

Lahaina Beaches

Lahaina is not known for its beaches, which are largely shallow and rocky. Your best bet is to go north to Hanakaoo Beach Park or to Kaanapali. If you don't have a car use the free trolley bus (see Lahaina's Getting Around section later).

Places to Stay

You couldn't be more in the middle of the action than at the *Pioneer Inn* (☎ 661-3636, (800) 457-5457; fax 667-5708), 658 Wharf St, Lahaina, HI 96761. It can be noisy from the traffic, the throngs of tourists and the raucous bar, but this two-story, turn-of-the-century hotel has plenty of character. However, the funky old harborfront rooms for which the inn was best known are no longer available; there are plans to renovate that part of the building and it may end up becoming another dining area. Instead, there are a few dozen rooms in the newer wing facing Front St. These rooms are reasonably comfortable and have lanais, air-conditioning and private baths. Prices range from $60 to $80.

Maui Islander (☎ 667-9766, (800) 367-5226; fax 661-3733), 660 Wainee St, Lahaina, HI 96761, is a sprawling 372-unit hotel set back a few blocks from Front St. The hotel is standard middle-class fare, without a great deal of character. Rooms have cable TV, air-con, ceiling fans and safes. There's a pool, a tennis court and a barbecue area. Rates are $77 for a room with a refrigerator, $92 (for up to three people) for a studio with kitchen and $104 for a one-bedroom suite. You can add on a rental car for $15 more a day, or for only $5 a day if you stay five nights or more.

The best-value condo in the Lahaina area is *Lahaina Roads* (☎ 661-3166, (800) 624-8203), 1403 Front St, Lahaina, HI 96761. It's north of the town center, near the Lahaina Cannery Mall. All 42 of its units are oceanfront with full kitchens, lanais, TVs and phones with free local calls. There's a beachside swimming pool. Roomy one-bedroom units cost $95 for up to four people, two-bedroom units $130 for up to six people. The minimum stay is three days.

Lahaina Shores (☎ 661-4835, (800) 628-6699), 475 Front St, Lahaina, HI 96761, is a 155-room condo run like a hotel. It's on the beach next to the 505 Front St shopping center, at the south side of town. Mountainview studios cost $95/105 for up to three people in the low/high season, one-bedroom units cost $122/147 for up to four people. Add on another $20/30 low/high for an ocean view. There's a small pool.

The *Lahaina Hotel* (☎ 661-0577, (800) 669-3444; fax 667-9480), 127 Lahainaluna Rd, Lahaina, HI 96761, is a restored turn-of-the-century hotel, a project of Crazy Shirt owner Rick Ralston, who spent over $3 million restoring this 13-room hostelry. The rooms are small but delightfully atmospheric – each has hardwood floors, floral wallpaper, antique furnishings and a lanai. Modern conveniences include air-con, private bath, telephone and piped-in music, but no TV. Room rates are $89 and $99, while suites are $129. Prices, which include continental breakfast, are the same for singles and doubles. Children under the age of 15 are not allowed.

The *Plantation Inn* (☎ 667-9225, (800) 433-6815; fax 667-9293), 174 Lahainaluna Rd, Lahaina, HI 96761, is an elegant two-story Victorian-style inn with hardwood floors, antique furnishings, stained glass and a tiled pool. The 18 rooms and suites range from $99 to $179. It's classy and comfortable, and arguably the nicest place to stay in Lahaina. Prices include a continental breakfast at Gerard's, the restaurant at the front of the inn.

Tony's Place (☎ 661-8040), 13 Kauaula Rd, Box 11475, Lahaina, HI 96761, is off Front Street, a two-minute walk south of

Lahaina Shores. Owner Tony Mamo rents out three of the four bedrooms in his modest home, charging $50/60 for singles/doubles, with a two-night minimum. Breakfast is not included but guests are allowed kitchen privileges. Tony accepts MasterCard and Visa.

Old Lahaina House (☎ 667-4663, (800) 847-0761; fax 667-5615), Box 10355, Lahaina, HI 96761, is also just a few minutes south of Lahaina Shores. Owners Sherry and John Barbier have four guest rooms in their home. Two rooms have king beds, private baths and refrigerators and rent for $85/95 for singles/doubles. The other two rooms, which cost $50/60, have two twin beds and share a bath. All four rooms have TV and air-conditioning and there's a pool out back. A breakfast of fresh pastries, fruit and juice is included in the rates.

Camping The nearest campground is in Olowalu, five miles south of Lahaina. Details are in the Olowalu section.

Places to Eat – budget
The *Pikake Bakery* at 505 Front St makes good scones, pastries and hearty breads. There's also a nice focaccia – a generous slice at $2.75 would make a filling lunch. This friendly little place also has coffee, espresso and a few cafe tables. It's open on weekdays from 7:30 am to 6 pm, on Saturdays until 5 pm.

Kirouac's, a good reasonably priced deli at 180 Dickenson St, serves organic salads and smoothies for $4 and sandwiches for $4.75. It also has a varied breakfast menu that includes bagels, waffles and omelets. Hours are from 7:30 am to 9 pm (from 8 am to 8 pm on Sundays).

Westside Natural Foods & Deli, 193 Lahainaluna Rd, sells organic produce, yogurt, fresh juice and trail mix. There a salad bar and a few hot vegetarian dishes for $5 a pound. It's open from 7:30 am to 9 pm, except on Sundays when it's open from 8:30 am to 9 pm. Another deli with inexpensive vegetarian food is *Juicy's* at 505 Front St.

Lahaina has several fast-food restaurants, including *Burger King* at 632 Front St, not far from the banyan tree, and *McDonald's* on the corner of Wainee and Papalaua Sts. *Pizza Hut* on Honoapiilani Hwy has a lunchtime pizza special for $3.50.

There's a *Subway* sandwich shop, an *Orange Julius*, a *TCBY* frozen yogurt shop, a pancake restaurant and inexpensive Korean and Mexican restaurants at the Wharf Cinema Center.

Lahaina Square, off Wainee St, has a *Foodland* supermarket, a 24-hour *Denny's* restaurant, *Jack in the Box* and *Baskin-Robbins* ice cream store.

Lahaina Cannery Mall, in a former pineapple cannery on the northern side of town between Front St and Hwy 30, has a 24-hour *Safeway* supermarket and numerous restaurants, including *Marie Callender's, Burger King, Compadres, Sir Wilfred's Espresso Cafe* and an inexpensive Greek takeout restaurant.

Places to Eat – middle
Lahaina Coolers, 180 Dickenson St, has good food at reasonable prices with a varied menu that includes salads for $3 to $8 and creative pizza, pasta and Thai dishes, most priced from $10 to $12. You can also get a vegetarian burrito with rice or a burger and fries for a few dollars less. From 7 to 11:15 am daily there's an extensive breakfast menu, with egg dishes, pancakes and lox and bagels at moderate prices. It's open until midnight daily.

The atmospheric *Old Whaler's Saloon* in the Pioneer Inn has lunchtime sandwiches, salads and a few simple hot dishes priced from $7 to $10. At dinner dishes range from pad Thai for $10 to fresh ahi for $19.

Kimo's, 845 Front St, is a popular oceanfront restaurant with a sunset view. Lunch is mainly sandwiches in the $6 to $10 range, while dinner features seafood and steaks for $14 to $20, including green salad, fresh warm carrot muffins, sourdough rolls and rice.

The *Hard Rock Cafe*, 900 Front St, has good burgers and sandwiches including a vegie burger, club sandwich or a bacon-guacamole cheeseburger for $7. All come with fries and a green salad. There are also a few hot dishes such as steak, barbecued chicken and fajitas for $11 to $15. Food is served from 11:30 am to 10 pm, to 10:30 pm on Fridays and Saturdays. Expect a bit of a wait at mealtime when a line often forms outside the door.

The newest and trendiest place to be seen is *Planet Hollywood* at 744 Front St. Salads, sandwiches, pasta and pizzas average around $10, desserts and appetizers around $5. It's open from 11 am to midnight.

Moose McGillycuddy's, 844 Front St, is on the upper level in the same shopping arcade as Avalon. Breakfast is from 7:30 to 11 am with 21 different omelet plates for $6. At lunch, burgers and sandwiches cost $5 to $8. At dinner, which is served until 10 pm, dishes average $10 to $14, though from 4:30 to 5:30 pm there's an early-bird dinner with mahimahi or barbecued chicken for $8.95.

The Cantina, 839 Front St, has oceanfront dining and Tex-Mex food at moderate prices. There are numerous combination plates, such as a taco and enchilada with rice and beans, for around $10. It's open for meals straight through from 11 am to 10 pm.

There's a branch of *Saeng's* (☎ 667-0822), a good local Thai restaurant, at 1312 Front St, just north of the Lahaina Cannery Mall. Its varied menu includes pad Thai and curries for around $10, vegetarian dishes for a bit less. Lunch is served from 11 am to 2 pm, dinner from 5 to 9:30 pm.

Places to Eat – top end

David Paul's Lahaina Grill (☎ 667-5117), at 127 Lahainaluna Rd in the historic Lahaina Hotel, is a popular fine dining spot with excellent Pacific Rim cuisine and an intimate setting. A specialty here is the spicy tequila shrimp with firecracker rice for $22, but the cheapest entree on the menu, vegetarian sauté at $14, is also recommendable. Appetizers include maki sushi, pan-fried oysters and spicy crab

cakes, all priced around $10. It's open for dinner only, from 6 to 10 pm nightly.

Longhi's (☎ 667-2288), 888 Front St, is one of Lahaina's busiest upper-end restaurants. At lunch, sandwiches and pastas begin at around $8, while seafood dishes such as fresh ahi and prawns amaretto average $12. The same seafood dishes cost $20 to $24 at dinner, the pastas $13 to $21. The restaurant has a notably extensive wine list and is open from 7:30 am to 10 pm.

Avalon (☎ 667-5559), 844 Front St, is run by chef Mark Ellman, one of the island's most innovative chefs and a leading force behind the growing popularity of Hawaiian Regional Cuisine. For starters, the summer rolls in a Thai peanut sauce and the Indonesian satay are a treat at $6. There are also good salads, including gado-gado over brown rice, for around $10. Creative vegetarian dishes cost $10 to $17, while shrimp stir-fry over linguine or the signature dish, chili-seared salmon, cost $19. Avalon is open from 11:30 am to 10:30 pm daily.

Pacific'O (☎ 667-4341), 505 Front St, operated by Jean-Michel Belin, the former head chef of Chez Paul, has an ocean view and imaginative food. Appetizers include shrimp won tons in Hawaiian salsa or a Kula salad with grilled tofu and warm shiitake mushroom dressing for around $10. Main dinner dishes range from shrimp-stuffed chicken in a black bean sauce for $15 to sesame-crust lamb for $22. At lunch there are simpler offerings such as satays, fish and chips or sandwiches and fries, all for under $10. It's open from 11 am to 3 pm for lunch, from 5:30 to 10:30 pm for dinner.

Casa de Mateo (☎ 661-6700) 505 Front St, above the Pacific'O restaurant, has an excellent water view and good authentic Mexican food. Most combination dishes, such as tacos with rice and beans, are priced between $13 and $16. The menu is the same at lunch and dinner.

Gerard's (☎ 661-8939) serves traditional French country cooking in a pleasant setting at the Plantation Inn, 174 Lahainaluna Rd. The menu changes regularly but

MAUI

rack of lamb and comfit duck are house standards; a la carte entrees range from $23 to $30. Either a classical or jazz guitarist plays from 7 to 9 pm nightly. It's open for dinner only, from 6 to 9 pm.

Entertainment

Lahaina has lots of action, most of it on Front St.

The *Blue Tropix Nightclub* (☎ 667-5309) at the Lahaina Center, 900 Front St, is the hottest club in town. There's music and dancing until 2 am nightly, with a $5 cover charge after 9 pm. The type of music varies nightly, including rock, reggae, cabaret and more – call for the latest schedule.

There's a good dance floor at *Longhi's* (☎ 667-2288), 888 Front St, where rock bands play from 10:30 pm to 1 am on Fridays and Saturdays. The cover charge is usually $5.

At *Moose McGillycuddy's* (☎ 667-7758), 844 Front St, there's either a video disco with a DJ or rock, reggae or country bands nightly except Wednesdays. Entertainment is from 9:30 pm to 1:30 am and there's a $3 cover charge on live music nights.

Cheeseburger in Paradise (☎ 661-4855), 811 Front St, has two groups nightly, one from 4:30 to 7:30 pm and the other from 8 to 11 pm. Expect easy-listening sounds, Jimmy Buffett style. There's no cover charge.

The *Pioneer Inn* has live music in its Old Whaler's Saloon, often in both the afternoon and evening. The music varies from bluegrass and country to contemporary pop.

Pacific'O, 505 Front St, has live jazz from 9 pm to midnight on Thursdays, Fridays and Saturdays. There's no cover charge.

There's a Hawaiian/Tahitian dance show at 2 pm on Wednesdays and Fridays at the Lahaina Center at 900 Front St, traditional Hawaiian music at 6:30 pm on Fridays at the Wharf Cinema Center's center stage and a keiki hula show at 1 pm on Sundays at the Lahaina Cannery Mall. Admission to all are free; the shows may be canceled if it rains.

Luaus The Old Lahaina Luau (☎ 667-1998), on the beachfront at 505 Front St, has a buffet dinner with open bar, Hawaiian music and a show from 5:30 to 8:30 pm Tuesday to Saturday. The cost is $56 for adults, $35 for children ages 12 and under.

Cinemas Lahaina Cinemas (☎ 661-3347) has three screens showing first-run movies at the Wharf Cinema Center. The first show of the day costs $3.50.

The Hawaii Experience Domed Theater (☎ 661-8314), 824 Front St, shows a 40-minute film about Hawaii on a giant 180° screen on the hour from 10 am to 10 pm daily. It costs $6.95 for adults, $3.95 for children ages four to 12.

Things to Buy

Lahaina has numerous arts & crafts galleries, some with high-quality collections and others more mediocre. A good place to start is the Lahaina Arts Society, a Maui collective with an extensive gallery in the old harborside courthouse.

'Art Night', held from 6:30 to 9 pm on Fridays, is the time when Lahaina galleries schedule their openings, occasionally with entertainment and hors d'oeuvres.

Earth & Company, in the Wharf Cinema Center on Front St, has a large selection of save-the-whale paraphernalia and gives a percentage of its proceeds to Greenpeace Hawaii.

South Seas Trading Post, 780 Front St, stands apart from all the gaudy tourist shops on Front St. It sells Tongan tapa, Papua New Guinean face masks and Marshallese stick charts, as well as interesting things from Southeast Asia. The collection depends on the owner's last jaunt abroad, but is always intriguing.

Dan's Green House, at 133 Prison St, sells 'fuku-bonsai', created when the roots of the common house plant *schefflera* (octopus tree) grow around a lava rock becoming quasi-bonsai. They are treated for export and cost from $25. Dan's has live cockatoos and a couple of monkeys and is a hangout for local kids.

Getting Around

The blue double-decker Lahaina Express (☎ 661-8748) bus shuttles between the Wharf Cinema Center and the Kaanapali resort free of charge. The bus runs every 20 to 45 minutes, depending on the time of day. The first bus leaves the Wharf Cinema Center for Kaanapali at 9:25 am. The last bus leaves Kaanapali for Lahaina at 9:30 pm.

LAHAINA TO MAALAEA

The stretch between Lahaina and Maalaea has pretty mountain scenery, but during winter most people are craning their necks to look seaward as they drive along. This is a prime whale-watching road.

Launiupoko Wayside Park

Launiupoko Wayside Park, 2½ miles south of Lahaina, is most popular as a picnic spot and as a place to watch the sun set behind Lanai. There are showers, toilets, picnic tables, changing rooms and a pay phone.

Olowalu

There's little to mark Olowalu other than Olowalu General Store and a seemingly misplaced expensive French restaurant named *Chez Paul*.

When the water is calm, there's good snorkeling around the 14-mile marker, south of the general store. The coral reef here is large and shallow and there's a narrow sandy beach to lay on, though be careful of kiawe thorns.

Olowalu means 'many hills' and has a lovely setting with cane fields backed by the West Maui Mountains.

Camping *Camp Pecusa* (☎ 661-4303), 800 Olowalu Village, Lahaina, HI 96761, run by the Episcopal Church, has a low-profile 'tentground' available to individuals on a first-come, first-served basis. It's located at the side of a cane field, half a mile south of the Olowalu General Store, on the makai side of the road. Camping is on dirt, but in shade and along a beach.

The campground is very basic but it does have solar-heated showers, outhouses, water and picnic tables. A caretaker lives on the grounds, making this the most secure place in Maui to camp. No alcohol is allowed and there's a seven-night maximum stay. While they don't take advance reservations, there's usually space available. The cost is $5 per person per night.

Papawai Point

The whole area between Olowalu and Makena is humpback cow/calf waters, and in the winter whale watching can be fantastic from the shore.

There are a couple of inconspicuous roadside lookouts just south of the 10-mile marker, but they are unmarked and difficult to pull into and out of when there's heavy traffic. Your best bet is to drive a little farther to Papawai Point, which is a clearly marked scenic lookout with a big parking lot.

Because the point juts into the waters at the western edge of Maalaea Bay, a favored humpback nursing ground, it's a good whale sighting spot. Papawai Point is also good for sunsets, with Lanai, Kahoolawe and Molokini visible.

That popular bumper sticker 'I Brake For Whales' has particular significance around this stretch of road. Although they are usually spotted farther offshore, humpbacks occasionally breach as close as 100 yards from the coast. Forty tons of whale suddenly exploding straight up through the water can be a real show stopper! Unfortunately, some of the drivers whose heads are jerked oceanward by the sight slam on their brakes and others don't, with rear-ender potential.

MAUI

The Olowalu Massacre

Olowalu Beach was the site of an infamous massacre in 1790. After a skiff was stolen from the US ship *Eleanora* and burned for its iron nails and fittings, Captain Simon Metcalfe retaliated by tricking the Hawaiians into sailing out in their canoes to trade. He then gunned them down with his cannons, killing an estimated 100 people. ■

LAHAINA TO KAANAPALI

On the stretch from Lahaina to Kaanapali the driving can be aggressive and traffic often jams up, particularly during morning and late-afternoon rush hours.

Sugar Cane Train

The old train that once carried sugar cane from the fields to the mill has been restored and now takes tourists on a joy ride through the cane fields between Kaanapali and Lahaina.

At the Kaanapali end, the train can be boarded on the mauka side of Hwy 30 off Puukolii Rd. To get to the Lahaina station, turn up Hinau St off Hwy 30 at Pizza Hut.

From Banyan Square there's a free bus that connects with departures from the Lahaina station, while the free Kaanapali Trolley services the Kaanapali station.

The train (☎ 661-0089), which makes the six-mile journey six times a day, takes about half an hour each way and costs $12 round-trip or $8 one way. Children ages three to 12 are half price.

Wahikuli Wayside Beach Park

There's a wayside park on a narrow strip of beach between the highway and the ocean, two miles north of Lahaina. With a gift for prophecy, the Hawaiians aptly named this coastal stretch Wahikuli or 'noisy place'.

The beach is mostly backed by a black-rock retaining wall, though there's a small sandy area. If you don't mind the traffic noise, the swimming conditions are usually fine. There are showers, restrooms, picnic tables and a pay phone.

Across the street is Lahaina's civic center, police and fire stations and main post office.

Hanakaoo Beach Park

Hanakaoo Beach Park is a long sandy beach just south of Kaanapali Beach Resort. As with all public beach parks, the parking here is free.

The park has full facilities and a life-guard on duty daily. The beach has a sandy bottom and water conditions are usually quite safe for swimming. However, southerly swells, which sometimes develop in the summer, can create powerful waves and shorebreaks, while the occasional kona storm can kick up rough water conditions in winter.

You can snorkel down by the second clump of rocks on the south side of the beach park or walk a few minutes north to the Hyatt and snorkel out by the green buoy.

Hanakaoo Beach is also called Canoe Beach, as the Lahaina, Kahana and Napili canoe clubs all store their canoes here. You can see them paddling up and down the coast in the early mornings and late afternoons. It's a pretty scene.

Kaanapali

Kaanapali is a high-rise resort community. Despite the opulence of some of its hotels, the overall development is rather generic – the influence is as much southern Californian as Hawaiian.

In the late 1950s Amfac, owner of the Pioneer Sugar Mill, earmarked 600 acres of relatively barren sugar cane land for development as the first resort outside Waikiki. The first hotels, the Royal Lahaina and the Sheraton Maui, opened in 1962.

Now Kaanapali Beach is lined with six oceanfront hotels, each with its own shops and restaurants. The resort also includes six condominiums, two 18-hole golf courses, 40 tennis courts and the Whalers Village shopping center.

Kaanapali has three miles of sandy beach and pleasant views across the Auau Channel to Lanai and Molokai.

While Kaanapali is not a 'getaway' in the sense of avoiding the crowds, it has its quieter niches. The north side of Black Rock and the condos up around the golf course are less bustling than the central beach area.

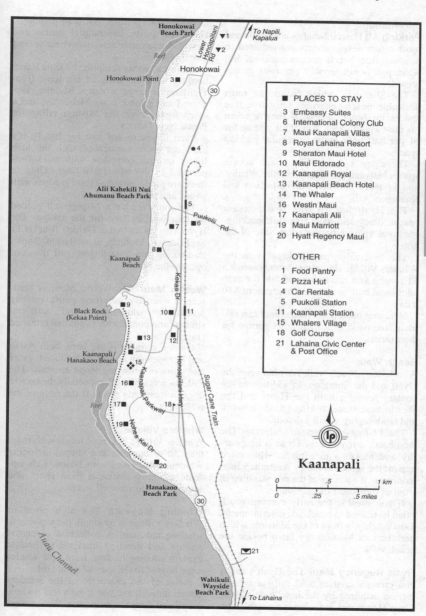

MAUI

PLACES TO STAY

3 Embassy Suites
6 International Colony Club
7 Maui Kaanapali Villas
8 Royal Lahaina Resort
9 Sheraton Maui Hotel
10 Maui Eldorado
12 Kaanapali Royal
13 Kaanapali Beach Hotel
14 The Whaler
16 Westin Maui
17 Kaanapali Alii
19 Maui Marriott
20 Hyatt Regency Maui

OTHER

1 Food Pantry
2 Pizza Hut
4 Car Rentals
5 Puukolii Station
11 Kaanapali Station
15 Whalers Village
18 Golf Course
21 Lahaina Civic Center & Post Office

Kaanapali

0   .5   1 km
0   .25   .5 miles

Information

Parking All Hawaii beaches are public and most resort developments are required to provide free beach access parking, but Kaanapali is not terribly generous in this regard.

The Sheraton, which fronts the most desirable beach, provides only five free spaces for beach access. If they're taken (as they usually are), they'll hit you up for $1 per half hour for their regular parking spaces.

There are a dozen free beach access spaces between the Westin and the Whaler, and 11 more between Maui Marriott and Kaanapali Alii.

The Hyatt has 10 free beach access spaces. They also have free 'self parking' for hotel visitors on the south side of the hotel.

The best-value pay parking is at the Whalers Village shopping center where it's $1 for the first two hours and 50c for each additional half hour, to a maximum of $10 a day.

Note that most hotel restaurants can validate free parking at their hotel garage for their diners.

Beach Walk

A mile-long beach walk runs between the Hyatt and the Sheraton. In addition to the coastal scenery, both the Hyatt and the Westin have some striking garden artwork and landscaping worth a detour.

The 17-foot-high bronze sculpture 'The Acrobats' in front of the Hyatt is noteworthy and makes a nice photo silhouetted against the sunset. Done by Australian John Robinson, it's a copy of the one standing in front of the Tower of London.

If you stroll in the early evening you'll often be treated to beachside entertainment, most notably in front of the Marriott, which performs its luau on the lawn beside the beach walk.

Hyatt Regency Maui The Hyatt's lobby and grounds contain a $2 million art collection acquired by the hotel's developer, Chris Hemmeter. It includes a notable collection of Ming vases, Balinese paintings, Hawaiian quilts, ceremonial drums and New Guinean artifacts, storyboards and war shields.

There's a bronze sculpture of King Rama battling with the King of Demons, from Thailand; a large wooden Buddha, lacquered and gilded, from Mandalay; and a spirit figure from the Misingi village in Papua New Guinea.

Even if you're not into big hotels, it's hard not to be impressed with the lush lobby atrium, complete with cockatoos perched in the tropical foliage. Outside there are pools, waterfalls and gardens with swans and flamingoes.

The concierge has a 24-page self-guided art tour booklet free for the asking. The Hyatt also has an 'Art & Garden Tour' at 11 am Friday to Monday, as well as afternoon lei-making and hula lessons, all free and open to the public.

Westin Maui The Westin Maui is landscaped with five free-form pools, rushing waterfalls, waterslides and artificial streams and ponds with swans and crowned cranes.

Garden statuary is big here, both Asian and European, with lots of Buddhas, vases and pairs of growling stone animals. The collection is a bit odd, especially the bronze dogs in menacing poses at the edge of the walkways.

Whalers Village

Whalers Village has three levels with more than 50 restaurants and shops, including Waldenbooks, Fox Photo 1-Hour Lab, upscale clothing stores, a wine shop, and scrimshaw and seashell stores.

Whaling Museum The high point of Whalers Village is its small, but top-notch, whaling museum. A collection of period photos and detailed interpretive boards explain whaling history, from how whales were hunted to the uses of whale oil.

A lot of the character of the whalers comes through and you'll get a feel for how rough and dirty the work was. Wages were so low that sailors sometimes owed the ship money by the time they got home and had to sign up for another four-year stint just to pay off the debt.

There are harpoons, logs from whaling ships, all sorts of scrimshaw, a model of a whaling barque and a film on whales that plays on the hour from 10 am to 4 pm.

A newer wing of the museum has models of various whales, as well as displays of jaw bones, teeth and baleen. It also has a small theater showing films dedicated to the current plight of whales and dolphins.

The museum is on the third level of Building G and is open from 9:30 am to 10 pm daily. Admission is free.

In addition, you can find a full skeleton of a sperm whale on display at the entrance to Whalers Village.

Kaanapali Beaches

Kaanapali can be considered two beaches, with Black Rock the dividing mark. The stretch south of Black Rock down to the Hyatt (and beyond to Hanakaoo Beach Park) is officially Hanakaoo Beach. The stretch from Black Rock north to Honokowai is Kaanapali Beach. Since the resort was built, however, the whole thing is generally called Kaanapali Beach.

Kaanapali/Hanakaoo Beach The waters in front of the Hyatt have a shallow reef that makes for poor swimming but good snorkeling. One spot where fish can be thick is the buoy where the hotel catamaran ties up. The fish come to feed on bread thrown overboard by the crew and sea turtles are occasionally spotted in the area as well.

Much of the stretch in between the Sheraton and the Hyatt can be dangerous, particularly on the point in front of the Marriott where strong currents sometimes develop. As a general rule, waters are rougher in winter, though actually the worst conditions can occur in early summer if there's a southerly swell. Be careful in rough surf as the waves can pick you up and bounce you onto the coral reef that runs from the southern end of the Westin

down to the Hyatt. Check with the hotel beach huts for the day's water conditions.

Black Rock Black Rock (Kekaa Point) is the rocky lava promontory that protects the beach in front of the Sheraton. This is Kaanapali's safest and best spot for swimming and snorkeling. According to traditional Hawaiian beliefs, Kekaa Point, the westernmost point of Maui, is a place where the spirits of the dead leap into the unknown and are carried to their ancestral home.

You can snorkel along the southern side of Black Rock where there's some pretty nice coral and schools of fish that are used to being fed. However the real prize is the horseshoe cove cut into the tip of the rock, where there's more pristine coral, abundant tropical fish and a family of eagle rays.

There's often a current to contend with off the point, which can make getting to the cove a little risky, but when it's calm you can swim right around into the horseshoe. Check with the Sheraton beach hut or snorkelers in the water regarding current conditions. Black Rock is also a popular shore dive spot. If you want to see what the horseshoe cove looks like, you can peer down into it by taking the short footpath from the Sheraton beach to the top of Black Rock.

Alii Kahekili Nui Ahumanu Beach Park

There's a new beach park at the north side of Kaanapali Beach that's dedicated to Kahekili Nui Ahumanu, the last king of Maui. The park, which is on a nice section of the beach, has free parking, showers, changing room, toilets, a covered picnic pavilion and barbecue grills.

To get there from Honoapiilani Hwy, turn left onto Kai Ala Dr (opposite Puukolii Rd) and then bear right. The waters here are open ocean, but inshore it's usually calm and good for swimming.

This is a good walking beach. If you walk north for about 15 minutes there's a reef around Honokowai Point with clear waters that are good for snorkeling when it's calm.

Places to Stay

All Kaanapali accommodations are either on the beach or within walking distance of it, and all have the expected amenities including swimming pools.

International Colony Club (☎ 661-4070, (800) 526-6284; fax 661-5856), 2750 Kalapu Dr, Lahaina, HI 96761, has 44 free-standing cottages spread over 10 acres. They are nice and spacious with big lanais and have phones (free local calls) and cable TV. The complex is about 30 years old and was one of the first in Kaanapali, back when tastes were simpler and things weren't as crowded. There are two large heated swimming pools. One-bedroom units are $120 and two-bedroom units are $130, plus $10 per person for more than two people.

Maui Kaanapali Villas (☎ 667-7791, (800) 922-7866), 45 Kai Ala Dr, Lahaina, HI 96761, is an Aston property on the edge of Kaanapali, 200 yards south of Alii Kahekili Nui Ahumanu Beach Park. As is common with Aston properties, rooms are individually owned, and overall it's of a lower standard than other Kaanapali properties. Hotel rooms with refrigerators cost $99/119 in the low/high season and studios with kitchens start at $125/155.

Maui Eldorado (☎ 661-0021, (800) 367-5004), 2661 Kekaa Dr, Lahaina, HI 96761, is a low-rise condo complex up the hill from the beach. It has a slower pace and a friendlier atmosphere than the big resort hotels. The units are individually owned so they vary, but some are quite nicely furnished with wallpapered bathrooms, wicker furniture and the like. The studios are big with kitchens completely set apart from the bedrooms and cost from $149, while one-bedroom units for four people start at $185.

The *Kaanapali Beach Hotel* (☎ 661-0011, (800) 262-8450; fax 667-5978), 2525 Kaanapali Parkway, Lahaina, HI 96761, has an enviable beachside location near Black Rock. The hotel's 430 rooms are spread across a number of three to six-story wings. While it's an older complex, it's

well maintained and is pleasantly low-key. The rooms have lanais, refrigerators, safes and remote-control TV. Prices start at $119 for a garden view, $175 for an ocean view. If you book in the $140-plus category and ask for the 'Free Ride' special, the rate includes a free rental car. For those with a Hawaiian driver's license, there's a $75 kamaaina rate.

Royal Lahaina Resort (☎ 661-3611, (800) 447-6925; fax 661-3538), 2780 Kekaa Dr, Lahaina, HI 96761, has 540 rooms on a broad stretch of beach on the north side of Black Rock. Standard rooms in the high-rise section cost from $145. Cottages, which are nicely clustered and spread out down to the beach, cost from $235. When you book ask for the 'Royal Ride' special and the rate will include a free rental car. The resort has 11 tennis courts and three pools.

The *Kaanapali Royal* (☎ 661-4804, (800) 367-7040), 2560 Kekaa Dr, Lahaina, HI 96761, is a low-rise condo complex with large, comfortable units. It has an unhurried hillside location near the golf course, a few minutes' walk from the beach. The condos are smartly designed and furnished, each with a full kitchen and a sunken living room with a sofa bed. The one-bedroom units start at $150/165 in the low/high season for up to four people, the two-bedroom units from $175/190 for up to six people.

The Whaler (☎ 661-4861, (800) 367-7052), 2481 Kaanapali Parkway, Lahaina, HI 96791, is a 360-unit high-rise condo complex that looks rather boxy from the outside but is quite pleasant inside with marble baths, private lanais and modern amenities. Studios with garden views cost $175 high season, with ocean views for $15 more. There are also one-bedroom units from $215 and two-bedroom units from $295.

The *Maui Marriott* (☎ 667-1200, (800) 228-9290; fax 667-0692), 100 Nohea Kai Dr, Lahaina, HI 96761, has 720 guest rooms in two long high-rises connected by walkways. Regular rates start at $195, though there's often a room/car package from $179. Overall, the hotel is not special for the money.

The *Sheraton Maui Hotel* (☎ 661-0031, (800) 325-3535; fax 661-0458), 2605 Kaanapali Parkway, Lahaina, HI 96761, got the prime beach spot, behind Black Rock. The 494-room hotel is large, sprawling and not distinguished. The cheapest rooms cost $129, while suites and ocean-front cottages cost $300.

The *Westin Maui* (☎ 667-2525, (800) 228-3000), 2365 Kaanapali Parkway, Lahaina, HI 96761, is a 762-room high-rise hotel. It has waterfalls flowing into free-form pools and a garden full of statues and vases. The hotel itself is not as special as the grounds, but then the Westin wasn't built from scratch – it's a remake of the old Maui Surf. Rates start at $210 for rooms in the old wing, $345 in the new.

The 815-room *Hyatt Regency Maui* (☎ 661-1234, (800) 233-1234; fax 667-4498), 200 Nohea Kai Dr, Lahaina, HI 96761, is the premier hotel on Kaanapali Beach. Not only does it have interesting artwork, but there's a massive meandering swimming pool with a swim-through grotto and a 130-foot waterslide. The rooms, which have standard Hyatt decor and amenities, begin at $240, or $330 with an ocean view.

Places to Eat

Hotels All of the Kaanapali hotels have restaurants, some formal and expensive, others more casual.

The cheapest spot to eat is the *Pizza Hut* at the Maui Marriott's poolside kiosk, open from 11 am to 7 pm daily, which has one-person pizzas for under $4.

The Marriott's *Moana Terrace* (☎ 667-1200) has a good-value soup, pasta and salad buffet Sunday to Thursday night from 5 to 9 pm. The cost is $9.95 as a meal in itself or $6.95 if you order a separate entree. On Friday nights the buffet includes prime rib at no extra cost; on Saturday nights it includes seafood dishes and costs $13.95. Dining is either indoors or on the adjacent open-air terrace.

Nikko (☎ 667-1200) is a Japanese teppa-nyaki restaurant at the Marriott, open daily for dinner only. It has a pleasant atmosphere with authentic Japanese food cooked at your table and a good ocean view from the window. Complete dinners include a ginger shrimp appetizer, miso soup, salad, rice and teppanyaki vegetables, accompanying main dishes like sesame chicken ($20) and teriyaki steak ($24). The best deal is one of the half dozen Samurai Sunset specials, which are served from 6 to 6:30 pm daily. These specials are complete dinners without the appetizer or salad, but served with green tea ice cream. They cost from $13 for chicken teriyaki to $18 for shrimp.

The *Lahaina Provision Company* at the Hyatt has a Chocoholic Bar, an all-you-can-indulge sugar rush of white and dark chocolate goodies served from 6:30 to 11:30 pm nightly. It's $4 with a meal, $8 alone. The restaurant features moderately expensive grilled meats and seafood.

Whalers Village Whalers Village has three beachfront restaurants. Top choice is the new *Hula Grill*, under the direction of Big Island chef Peter Merriman, which has outdoor dining, a kiawe grill, a wood-fired pizza oven and authentic hula shows. Hawaiian Regional Cuisine is featured. Virtually all entrees, including various grilled fish served with pineapple stir-fried brown rice, are under $20. Finger foods and pizzas start at $6.

The other two beachfront restaurants offer more standard fare. The *Rusty Harpoon* has burgers with French fries for around $7.50, chicken dinners for $17 and pricier fresh fish meals. *Leilani's*, next door, is a bit cheaper with $6 burgers from 11:30 am to 1 pm and chicken and steak dishes for around $15 at dinner. One of the two restaurants usually has some sort of early-bird dinner special for about $10.

Chico's serves American and Mexican food from 11:30 am to 2:30 pm and 5 to 10 pm daily. Combination plates, such as a taco and enchilada with rice and beans, cost $9.50, while burgers and sandwiches are a few dollars less. The bar has a happy hour from 3 to 7 pm with $1 draft beers.

Maui Yogurt is a relatively cheap place to eat for Whalers Village. Sandwiches or a large garden salad topped with a scoop of fresh avocado costs $4.75; there are also frozen yogurts, juices and fruit.

Whalers Village also has a *Haagen-Dazs* ice cream shop.

Breakfast Buffets Kaanapali has a number of breakfast buffets where you could easily whittle away the better part of a morning. The breakfast buffet at the *Sheraton Maui* has traditional fare like cereal, bacon, eggs, croissants, fruit and tempting cakes and pastries, as well as a few Japanese dishes such as musubi and miso. It's served in the 8th floor Discovery Room, which has an unbeatable view atop Black Rock – be sure to ask for a table with an ocean view. Breakfast is from 6:30 to 10:30 am and costs $14.95.

The *Maui Marriott* has a good breakfast buffet from 6:30 to 11 am daily at its Moana Terrace, including fresh fruits, juices, Belgian waffles and omelets to order, yogurt, cereals and an array of pastries. It costs $14 for a full breakfast or $10 for a continental breakfast which is everything minus the hot dishes. There's an outside patio but no ocean view.

The Westin's *Cooks on the Beach* also does a reasonably good breakfast buffet for $14.50 from 7 to 11 am daily, although there's nothing special about the setting.

The *Hyatt Regency Maui* has an average breakfast buffet in a superb setting at Swan Court. One side of the restaurant is open air and overlooks a large swan pond, artificial waterfalls and a Japanese garden. The buffet is served from 7 to 11:30 am and costs $14.95.

The bargain of the breakfast buffets is at the *Koffee Shop* off the lobby of the Kaanapali Beach Hotel. Here you can get fresh melon and pineapple, eggs, sausage, steamer trays of pancakes and French toast, cereals, Danishes, juice and coffee. While not a notable culinary experience, you can eat your fill for $6.95. Breakfast is from 6 to 10:45 am daily. There's also a reasonable lunch buffet for the same price from 11 am to 2 pm.

Entertainment

The Kaanapali hotels feature a variety of entertainment, including dance bands, pianists, Hawaiian music and Polynesian revues.

Solo guitarists play mellow contemporary music in the Hyatt's *Weeping Banyan* from 6 to 10 pm nightly.

In the courtyard of the Kaanapali Beach Hotel there's a free hula show from 6:30 to 7:30 pm nightly, and Hawaiian music from 6 to 9:30 pm nightly.

The Maui Marriott's *Makai Bar* has contemporary Hawaiian music nightly. The Marriott also has a comedy club in its *Lobby Bar* at 8:30 pm on Mondays, with a $12 cover charge.

Whalers Village has a free Hawaiian hula show on its center stage at 1 pm on Sundays and Wednesdays. There's often contemporary or Hawaiian music outdoors in the evening at one of the Whalers Village restaurants.

Luaus The Kaanapali luaus include an imu ceremony, open bar, buffet dinner and Polynesian show with music and dance. Reservations are required. Most of the shows are held outdoors so you can get a preview of them by walking along the beach.

The Hyatt Regency Maui (☎ 667-4420) has its 'Drums of the Pacific' luau from 5:30 to 8 pm on Mondays, Wednesdays, Fridays and Saturdays for $48.

The Sheraton Maui (☎ 661-3500) has a luau from 5 to 8 pm Tuesday to Sunday costing $48 for adults, $22 for kids ages six to 12.

The Royal Lahaina Resort (☎ 661-3611) has a luau from 5:30 pm nightly for $49 for adults, $25 for children ages five to 12.

The Maui Marriott (☎ 661-5828) has a luau from 5 to 8 pm nightly except Mondays for $50, $23 for children ages six to 12.

Astronomy You can look at the night sky through giant binoculars and a 16-inch telescope from the rooftop of the Hyatt Regency Maui. Its one-hour star-gazing programs (☎ 661-1234) are at 8, 9 and 10 pm Monday to Saturday and cost $10 for adults, $5 for children under 12.

Getting Around

There's a free Kaanapali Trolley running between the Kaanapali hotels, Whalers Village, the golf course and the sugar cane train's Kaanapali station about 20 times a day between 7:15 am and 10:15 pm.

There's also a free shuttle, operating a dozen times a day between Whalers Village and resorts in Kahana and Napili. Stops include the Embassy Suites in Honokowai, Sands of Kahana, Napili Shores and Napili Kai. The buses, which are scheduled to encourage dining and shopping at Whalers Village, operate from 11 am to about 9 pm.

The free Lahaina Express (☎ 661-8748) makes about 30 runs every day between Kaanapali and the Wharf Cinema Center in Lahaina. Stops in Kaanapali are at the Sheraton, Kaanapali Beach Hotel, Whalers Village, the Marriott and the Hyatt Regency. The first bus leaves Whalers Village at 9 am, the last bus at 9:45 pm.

The Lahaina Cannery Mall operates a free shuttle bus 20 times a day from 9:15 am to 9:30 pm between its shopping center in Lahaina and the Honokowai area. In Kaanapali, stops are made at the Whalers Village and most of the beachfront hotels.

For information on bus service between the Wailea and Kaanapali areas, see Getting Around in the front of this chapter.

Northwest Maui

North of Kaanapali the road forks. The main road is Honoapiilani Highway (Hwy 30) and the parallel shoreline road is Lower Honoapiilani Rd.

If you just want to zip up to the beaches, bypassing the condos and resorts, stick to Hwy 30. Cyclists may want to come this way as well, as the highway has a wide shoulder lane marked as a bike route.

Napili Bay, Kapalua Beach, Slaughterhouse Beach and Honolua Bay are all fine beaches on Maui's curving northwest coast.

HONOKOWAI

To the degree that Kaanapali is a planned community, Honokowai is an unplanned one, consisting mainly of a stretch of condos squeezed between the shoreline and Lower Honoapiilani Rd.

Many of these condos were intended to be year-round housing for island residents but the growth in tourism makes daily and weekly rentals far more profitable. Indeed, the only reason most tourists are here is because the condos are relatively cheap compared to those at the nearby resorts.

While most of the shoreline is rocky with mediocre swimming conditions, Honokowai does have fine views of Molokai and Lanai.

Honokowai Beach Park

Honokowai Beach Park is largely lined with a submerged rock shelf and has poor swimming conditions with shallow water and a rocky bottom. Most people staying here head to Kaanapali Beach for swimming. For snorkeling you can walk south to Honokowai Point (towards the pink Embassy Suites) where there's a reef, marked by buoys in front of the hotel.

Places to Stay

Honokowai Palms (☎ 669-6130, (800) 669-0795), 3666 Lower Honoapiilani Rd, Honokowai, HI 96761, is a 30-unit two-story cinder-block building on the mauka side of the road. There's a little book exchange, a ping-pong table and a pool that's seldom crowded. One-bedroom condo units cost $65 for up to four people, while two-bedroom units cost $75 for up to six people. It's not much to look at from the outside, but it's one of the cheapest places around.

Kaleialoha (☎ 669-8197, (800) 222-8688; fax 669-2502), 3785 Lower Honoa-

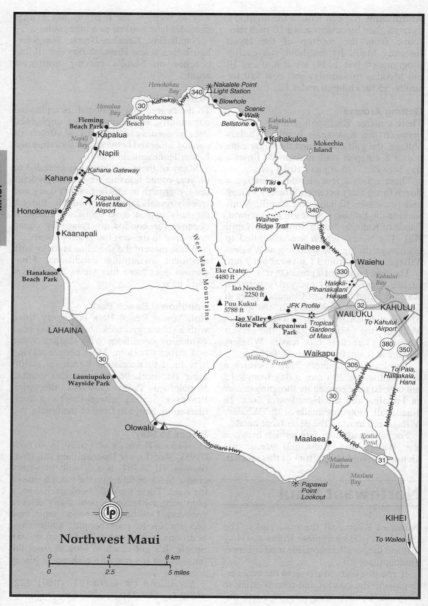

Northwest Maui

| 0 | 4 | 8 km |
| 0 | 2.5 | 5 miles |

piilani Rd, Honokowai, HI 96761, is a 67-unit condo on the beach. There's a swimming pool and barbecue area. Studios, which face the road, cost $75, while one-bedroom units with ocean views and lanais are $85 to $95. There's a three-night minimum.

Mahina Surf (☎ 669-6068, (800) 367-6086; fax 669-4534), is between Honokowai and Kahana at 4057 Lower Honoapiilani Rd, Honokowai, HI 96761. This low-rise complex is nicely set around a large grassy yard with a pool in the center. All 56 units are spacious and have lanais with ocean views. There's a three-night minimum. One-bedroom units cost $95 in the low season and $110 in the high season. It costs $15 more for a two-bedroom unit.

On the other end of the scale is *Embassy Suites* (☎ 661-2000, (800) 362-2779), at 104 Kaanapali Place, Honokowai, HI 96761, on Honokowai Point, north of the Kaanapali resorts. You can't miss this pink giant, with its blue waterfall pouring down the front. Each of the 413 units is an 820-sq-foot suite with everything down to a 35-inch TV with VCR. Rates start at $225 for up to four adults (and two children), including breakfast and evening cocktails.

Places to Eat

There aren't many choices for eating in Honokowai. Most people buy groceries at the *Food Pantry*, opposite Honokowai Beach Park, and cook in their condos. This grocery store is open from 6:30 am to 11 pm daily.

There's also a small *Pizza Hut* at the south side of the village that sells pizza for takeout only. It's open from 11 am to 11 pm, to midnight on weekends.

For fresh fruits, vegetables and fish visit the farmers' market which sets up in Honokowai on Sunday and Thursday mornings.

KAHANA

Kahana is the high-rise stretch immediately north of Honokowai. It's more upscale than Honokowai, with condo and room rates averaging well above $100. Kahana is fronted with a sandy beach that has reasonable swimming conditions; for snorkeling, a good area is along the rocky outcropping at the north side of the Kahana Sunset.

Information

The Kahana Gateway shopping center, off Hwy 30 half a mile north of the Kapalua West Maui Airport, has a Bank of Hawaii, a coin laundry open from 6 am to 10 pm daily and a Shell gas station.

Places to Stay

The following are three of Kahana's more reasonably priced condos.

Noelani (☎ 669-8374, (800) 367-6030; fax 669-7904), 4095 Lower Honoapiilani Rd, Kahana, HI 96761, has 50 nicely furnished units right on the beach. All units have lanais, phones with free local calls, sofa beds and VCRs, and all but the studios have a washer/dryer. There are two pools. Studios cost $87, one-bedroom units are $110 and two-bedroom, two-bath units for up to four people cost $140. There's a three-day minimum. It's a good deal for this area.

Kahana Reef (☎ 669-6491, (800) 253-3773), 4471 Lower Honoapiilani Rd, Kahana, HI 96761, is a four-story, 88-unit condo. All units are oceanfront and most are nicely furnished. There's a small pool on the ocean with a great view of Molokai. The studios, which cost $95/100 in the low/high season, are almost as large as one-bedroom units elsewhere and have single and double day beds as well as a tiny second room with a single bed. For another $5/10 you can get a very large one-bedroom unit. A third person costs $8 extra.

Kahana Sunset (☎ 669-8011, (800) 669-1488), 4909 Lower Honoapiilani Rd, Kahana, HI 96761, is a pleasant condominium with a good beachside location at the north end of Kahana. This quiet low-rise complex has well-groomed gardens, a pool and barbecue area. The units, which are tastefully appointed, have modern amenities and lanais and cost from $90/150 in the low/high season for one bedroom, $130/185 for two bedrooms.

Places to Eat

The best bet for places to eat is the Kahana Gateway shopping center, which has a *McDonald's*; a frozen yogurt and ice cream shop; the *Kafe Kahana* with pastries and sandwiches; and the *Whalers General Store*, a small grocery store with a few fast-food items that's open until 10 pm daily.

The Kahana Gateway also has *Roy's Kahana Bar & Grill* (☎ 669-6999), a branch of the renowned Roy's in Honolulu. Centered around a large exhibition kitchen, the restaurant features contemporary regional dishes such as lemongrass chicken in a Thai curry sauce for $14 and crispy duck in lilikoi sauce for $18. Roy's also serves superb appetizers, interesting imu-style pizzas and some of the most scrumptious desserts found on Maui.

The adjacent *Nicolina* (☎ 669-5000), a sister restaurant of Roy's, has more of a Southwest accent, with cacti on the tables and dishes like cajun shrimp and barbecued short ribs. The menu also includes Pacific Rim dishes similar to those at Roy's, which makes it a reasonable alternative should Roy's be booked solid. Salads and appetizers average $6, main courses are priced from $13 to $20. Both Nicolina and Roy's have fresh fish at market prices and are open for dinner only from 5:30 to 9:30 pm nightly.

China Boat, (☎ 669-5089), 4474 Lower Honoapiilani Rd, is open from 11:30 am to 2 pm Monday to Friday and 5 to 10 pm daily. At dinner the standard array of Chinese dishes cost from $9 to $16, while lunch plates of kung pao chicken, Sichuan spice shrimp or sweet & sour pork with soup, egg rolls, fried wonton and rice are priced from $6 to $8.

NAPILI

Napili Beach is a beautiful, curving golden sand beach, with excellent swimming and snorkeling when it's calm. Occasionally big waves make it into the bay in the winter, attracting bodysurfers but also creating strong rip currents. To get to the beach go down Hui Dr off Lower Honoapiilani Rd.

Napili Kai Beach Club, built on the bay in 1962, was the first hotel north of Kaanapali. To protect the bay, as well as their investment, Napili Kai organized area landowners and petitioned the county to create a zoning bylaw restricting all Napili Bay buildings to the height of a coconut tree.

The law was passed in 1964, long before the condo explosion took over the rest of West Maui, and consequently Napili is one of the more relaxed niches on the coast. It attracts a fair number of return visitors, the majority of them retirees escaping mainland winters.

Most of Napili's condos are on the beach and for the most part away from the road and the sound of traffic.

Places to Stay

Hale Napili (☎ 669-6184, (800) 245-2266), 65 Hui Dr, Napili, HI 96761, is an 18-unit condo on Napili Beach, with friendly Hawaiian management. The rooms have phones with free local calls, TVs, ceiling fans and lanais. Garden studios cost $75, oceanfront studios $100 and one-bedroom units $120. It has a three-day minimum and there's no pool.

Napili Sunset (☎ 669-8083, (800) 447-9229; fax 669-2730), 46 Hui Dr, Napili, HI 96761, has studios with garden views for $85 and one-bedroom beachfront units for $159. All have full kitchens, although the furnishings in some of units can be a bit worn. There's a three-day minimum.

Napili Surf (☎ 669-8002, (800) 541-0638; fax 669-8004), 50 Napili Place, Napili, HI 96761, is a motel-style, painted cinder-block place at the south end of Napili Bay. The 53 units are pleasant, the grounds well kept and there's a pool. High season rates range from $90 for studios with a garden view to $165 for one-bedroom units with ocean views; during the low season rates are about 20% cheaper. There's a five-day minimum and credit cards are not accepted.

The *Napili Kai Beach Club* (☎ 669-6271, (800) 367-5030; fax 669-5740), 5900 Honoapiilani Rd, Napili, HI 96761, is a sprawling 180-unit hotel at the northern end of Napili Bay. The staff is friendly, almost pampering. The units are tasteful, with Polynesian decor and nice touches like shoji doors. The catch here is the price: studios start at $155 without a kitchen, $175 with one.

Places to Eat
The Napili Plaza, at the junction of Napilihau St and Hwy 30, has a grocery store open from 6:30 am to 11 pm daily; a *Subway* sandwich shop; the *Coffee Store*, which has good pastries and coffees; and *Maui Tacos*, which has inexpensive Mexican food. The plaza also has *Koho Grill & Bar*, a popular local restaurant with an extensive menu including dishes such as shrimp scampi or the catch of the day for around $10 and a variety of sandwiches and burgers for $5. It's open daily to midnight.

The *Sea House Restaurant* at Napili Kai Beach Club has open-air dining with a sunset view. The usual breakfast offerings and lunchtime burgers, fish & chips, and papaya stuffed with shrimp salad are all priced from $6 to $10. Dinners, which include fish, steaks and lobster dishes, are in the $15 to $25 range, but there's often a cheaper sunset special for early diners. Spotlights on the breaking surf provide a kaleidoscopic show at night and there's live Hawaiian dinner music from Saturday to Thursday. The restaurant also has a worthwhile dinner show at 6:30 pm on Fridays for $25, which features hula dancing by area children; reservations are required (☎ 669-6271) for the show. Hours are 8 to 11 am, noon to 2 pm and 6 to 9 pm.

Whalers General Store in the Napili Village complex sells groceries, liquor, wrapped sandwiches and a few mediocre fast-food items. It's open from 7:30 am to 10 pm daily.

KAPALUA
The Kapalua resort development has the Kapalua Bay Hotel, the new Ritz-Carlton hotel, some luxury condos, a few restaurants and three golf courses. It's a small, uncrowded development – the most exclusive in northwest Maui – but truth to tell, if you're not a well-to-do golfer, there's not a lot to do here.

Kapalua Beach
Kapalua Beach, at the south side of Kapalua, is a pretty white sand crescent beach with a fine view of Molokai across the channel. The long rocky outcroppings at both ends of the beach make it the safest year-round swimming spot on this coast.

There's good snorkeling on the right side of the beach, where you'll find lots of large tangs, butterfly fish, wrasses and orange slate-pencil sea urchins.

Take the paved drive marked 'shoreline access' just north of Napili Kai Beach Club to get to a parking area with about 25 beach access spaces, restrooms and showers. A tunnel from the parking lot leads under the Bay Club restaurant to the beach.

Fleming Beach Park
D T Fleming Beach Park on Honokahua Bay, at the north side of Kapalua, is a developed county beach park with restrooms, picnic facilities, showers and a pay phone.

The long sandy beach is backed by ironwood trees. There's good surfing and bodysurfing, with winter providing the biggest waves. The shorebreaks can be tough, however, and this beach is second only to Hookipa for injuries.

Take notice of the sign warning of dangerous currents as there have been half a dozen drownings here in the last few years. The reef out on the right is good for snorkeling but only when it's very calm.

The Honokahua sand dunes just south of Fleming Beach were excavated in 1988 during the construction of the Ritz-Carlton hotel. After skeletal remains were found, construction was halted, the bodies were reinterred and the hotel was resited mauka of the seaside graves. The Honokahua burial ground is thought to contain the

MAUI

remains of over 1000 Hawaiians who were buried between 950 AD and the 1700s.

Places to Stay

The *Kapalua Bay Hotel & Villas* (☎ 669-5656, (800) 367-8000; fax 669-4690) at 1 Bay Dr, Kapalua, HI 96761, is a luxury complex with hotel rooms from $225 up as well as one-bedroom condos with modern conveniences and large lanais from $325 along the bay and from $185 on the hillside near the golf course.

One-bedroom condos in the same resort development can be rented from Ridge Rentals (☎ 669-9696, (800) 326-6284), 10 Hoohui Rd, Suite 301, Kahana, HI 96761, for $115/745 a day/week in the low season, $165/1110 in the high season. There are also two-bedroom, three-bath units for $175/1175 in the low season, $240/1500 in the high. Ridge Rentals has a five-day minimum stay and does not accept credit cards.

The *Ritz-Carlton* (☎ 669-6200, (800) 241-3333; fax 669-3908), 1 Ritz-Carlton Dr, Kapalua, HI 96761, has 550 rooms and suites with the usual Ritz standards and decor. Rates range from $285 to $2800.

Places to Eat

Honolua Store, a remnant of the area's simpler past, is an authentic general store with high ceilings, old wooden shelves and a big ice chest full of beer. It has a cafeteria-style deli with local food such as stew and fried chicken. Plate lunches are served from about 10 am to 3 pm, either 'hobo' style (a hot dish and rice for $3.50) or a full plate for $5.50. There are also sandwiches and a variety of good salads including Greek and chef's for around $4. Everything's takeout only. To get there, turn up Office Rd half a mile north of Kapalua Bay Hotel.

While the setting looks somewhat exclusive, the *Plantation House Restaurant* (☎ 669-6299), at the Plantation Course golf course, is the best place in these parts for a reasonably priced sit-down brunch. From 8 am to 3 pm three-egg omelets with toast and potatoes, or eggs Benedict, cost around

$7. Dinner is a more pricey affair with seafood and meat dishes priced from $20 to $25. There's a fine view across the fairway clear down to the ocean.

The *Bay Club* (☎ 669-8008) is perched atop a promontory at the southern end of Kapalua Bay with a beautiful view in an open-air setting. It specializes in seafood and has a good reputation. At lunch, there's a light buffet with sashimi, cheeses, fruits and green and pasta salads for $13.50 alone, or $7 with an entree. At dinner, a la carte entrees are priced from $24 for pasta to $29 for bouillabaisse. Reservations are recommended for both lunch and dinner. It's open daily from 11:30 am to 2 pm and from 6 to 9 pm.

The *Grill & Bar* (☎ 669-5653), between the tennis club and the golf club, has a predictable country club atmosphere and an ocean view across the fairway. Lunch costs from $8 to $12 and includes sandwiches, burgers, chicken satay, pizza and fresh fish dishes. Dinners range from pasta primavera for $14 to Australian rack of lamb for $24.

Pineapple Hill (☎ 669-6129), now a restaurant, is the former plantation home of David Fleming, the pineapple plantation manager after whom Fleming Beach is named. It's on a hill above a little pineapple patch and the Bay Golf Course. There's a great view down to the ocean, which is particularly pleasant at sunset. Dinners, which are served with a salad, range from baked chicken for $12 to the house specialty of prawns Tahitian for $25. The restaurant opens daily at 4:30 pm for cocktails, 5 pm for dinner. To get there go north on Kapalua Dr, a mile-long road lined with Norfolk pines.

HONOLUA & MOKULEIA BAYS

Kapalua marks the end of development on the West Maui coast. From here on it's rural Hawaii, with golf carts giving way to pick-up trucks and old cars with surfboards tied on top. The coast gets lusher, greener and more scenically rugged as you go along.

About a mile north of Fleming Beach are Mokuleia Bay (Slaughterhouse Beach) and

Honolua Bay. The two bays are separated by the narrow Kalaepiha Point and together form the Honolua-Mokuleia Bay Marine Life Conservation District. Fishing is prohibited as is collecting shells, coral, rock or sand. In the winter both bays see heavy surf and sand erosion.

In winter Honolua Bay has such perfect waves that it's made the cover of numerous surfing magazines. The bay faces northwest and when it catches the winter swells it has some of the best surfing to be found anywhere in the world.

Slaughterhouse Beach

Named for the slaughterhouse that once sat on the cliffs above, this is a hot bodysurfing spot during the summer when the rocks aren't exposed. It's also a popular nude beach.

In summer there's excellent snorkeling in both bays. Both sides of Honolua Bay have good reefs with lots of different coral formations while the mid-section of the bay has a sandy bottom. Honolua Stream empties into the bay and it can get quite murky after heavy rains.

When it's calm you can snorkel around Kalaepiha Point from one bay to the other. In addition to seeing coral and reef fish, you might get lucky and spot a sea turtle.

Access is by scrambling down the cliff. There are a few pull-offs along the road where beachgoers park their cars and where rough paths lead down to the beaches. The paths are clay and can be slick when wet, so watch your footing. Don't leave valuables in your car.

Kahekili Highway

As you continue north beyond Honolua and Mokuleia bays the road climbs, offering some nice coastal views. The beaches along this section are open ocean with rough water conditions.

It's possible to continue around on this coastal road to Wailuku (see Kahekili Highway at the end of the Kahului-Wailuku section). The last stop for gas and provisions on this side of Wailuku is at the Honolua Store in Kapalua.

Kihei

Kihei extends six miles along Maui's southwest coast, on the leeward side of Haleakala. Maalaea Bay is to the north, the more exclusive Wailea resort to the south.

Kihei is fringed with sandy beaches its entire length and has near-constant sunshine. It has long attracted sunbathers, boogie boarders, windsurfers and Kahului families on weekend picnics.

The beaches have views of Lanai and Kahoolawe as well as West Maui, which because of the deep cut of Maalaea Bay looks like a separate island from here.

Twenty years ago Kihei was a long stretch of undeveloped beach with kiawe trees, a scattering of homes and a church or two. Over the past decade it's had the dubious distinction of being Maui's fastest growing community, with development continuing nonstop.

South Kihei Rd, which runs the full length of Kihei, is lined with condos, gas stations, shopping centers and fast-food places in such congested and haphazard disarray that it's the example most often cited by anti-development forces on other Neighbor Islands. Kihei is what no town wants to become.

While Kihei's 'condoville' character doesn't win any prizes for aesthetics, it has one advantage for visitors – the sheer abundance of condos means that Kihei's rates are among the cheapest in Maui.

The Piilani Highway (Hwy 31) parallels and bypasses the start-and-stop traffic of South Kihei Rd. Several crossroads connect the two.

Information

Money The Bank of Hawaii at Azeka Place II is open from 8:30 am to 3 pm Monday to Thursday, 8:30 am to 6 pm on Fridays. In front of the bank is a 24-hour ATM that accepts MasterCard, Visa, American Express, Discover and JCB credit cards as well as Cirrus and Plus ATM cards. Similar

MAUI

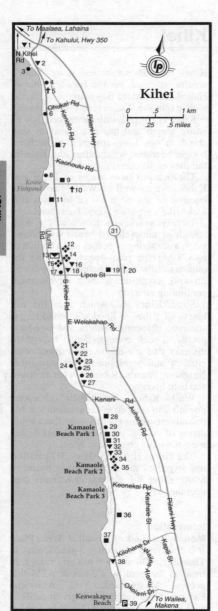

Kihei

0   .5   1 km
0   .25   .5 miles

To Maalaea, Lahaina
To Kahului, Hwy 350

■ PLACES TO STAY
7   Wailana Kai
9   Koa Resort
11   Village by the Sea
19   Maui Sun
28   Maui Coast Hotel
30   Kamaole Beach Royale
31   Kihei Alii Kai
36   Kamaole Sands
37   Mana Kai-Maui

▼ PLACES TO EAT
1   Margarita's Beach Cantina
2   Suda's Store & Surfer Joe's
16   Shaka Sandwich & Pizza
18   Jack in the Box
22   Kentucky Fried Chicken/7-Eleven
27   Kihei Caffe
32   New York Deli, Bakery & Pizza Hut
33   Wiki Wiki Pizza/
     Hawaiian Moons Natural Food
38   Carelli's on the Beach

OTHER
3   Kihei Wharf
4   Library
5   Keolahou Congregational
     Hawaiian Church
6   Maipoina Oe Iau Beach Park
8   Kalepolepo Beach Park
10   David Malo's Church
12   Longs Center
13   Post Office
14   Azeka Place II
15   Azeka Place
17   Star Market
20   Silversword Golf Course
21   Kukui Mall
23   Kihei Town Center
24   Kalama Park
25   Snorkel Bob's
26   South Maui Bicycles
29   ABC Discount Store
34   Rainbow Mall
35   Kamaole Shopping Center
39   Beach Access/Parking

ATMs can be found at Azeka's Market at Azeka Place and at the side of the American Savings Bank in Longs Center.

Post The Kihei post office, at Azeka Place, is open from 9 am to 4:30 pm weekdays, 9 to 11 am on Saturdays.

Koieie Fishpond

In a story with an unusual menehune twist, Koieie Fishpond is said to have been built by regular-sized Hawaiians. After the workers protested that the work couldn't be done properly without the help of the menehune, the chief in charge angrily ordered that when the job was finished the workers were to be cooked in an imu. The night before the last stone was to be placed, the menehune came down from the mountains and carried all the stones away. Only after the threats against the Hawaiian laborers were withdrawn did the menehune return with the stones and rebuild the fishpond. ■

Books & Library The Kihei library (☎ 879-1141), 131 S Kihei Rd, is open from 9 am to 5 pm Wednesday to Saturday and from noon to 8 pm on Tuesdays. There's a Waldenbooks bookstore in the Kukui Mall.

Laundry There's a coin laundry at the Kukui Mall open from 8 am to 9 pm daily.

Photo The Fox 1-Hour Photo Lab at Azeka Place has good quality printing. If you're not in a hurry, Longs Drugs in the Longs Center offers send-out Fuji and Kodak processing services at cheaper prices; it's also a good place to pick up film.

Maalaea Bay

Maalaea Bay runs along the south side of the isthmus between the two mountain masses of west and east Maui. Prevailing winds from the north, which funnel between the mountains straight out towards Kahoolawe, create strong midday gusts and some of the best windsurfing conditions on Maui. These are the strongest winds on the island and in winter, when the wind dies down elsewhere, windsurfers still fly along in Maalaea Bay.

The bay also has a couple of hot surfing spots. The Maalaea Pipeline, south of the boat harbor, freight-trains right and is the fastest break in Hawaii. Summer's southerly swells produce huge tubes.

Maalaea Bay is fronted by a continuous three-mile stretch of sandy beach that runs from Maalaea Small Boat Harbor south to Kihei. There's beach access at several places along North Kihei Rd (Hwy 31).

The area near Maalaea harbor has a handful of moderately priced condo complexes and would make a convenient central base if not for ongoing problems with theft and other visitor-targeted crimes.

Kealia Pond National Wildlife Refuge

Kealia Pond, on North Kihei Rd two miles south of the intersection of Hwy 31 and Hwy 30, is a saltwater marsh and bird sanctuary. From the side of the road you can usually spot Hawaiian stilts, an endangered species, wading in the water. It's also a habitat for the Hawaiian coot and herons.

Maipoina Oe Iau Beach Park

Maipoina Oe Iau Beach Park, at the northern end of Kihei, has a long sandy beach. Swimming and sunbathing is best in the morning before the wind picks up, while windsurfing is generally good in the afternoon. This is also a popular spot for windsurf shops to give lessons.

The park, whose name means 'forget me not', is dedicated to Maui's war veterans. It has full facilities.

Kalepolepo Beach Park

The waters off Kalepolepo Beach Park offer only mediocre swimming but this is one of the few places in Maui where you can see the stone wall remains of a fishpond.

Koieie Fishpond was built in the 16th century by King Umi of the Big Island. It was used to raise mullet for the alii.

David Malo's Church

Another historic site at the northern end of Kihei is the church built in 1853 by David Malo, a noted philosopher and the first Hawaiian ordained to the Christian ministry. While most of the church was

MAUI

dismantled long ago, a three-foot-high section of the church walls still stands. Eighteen pews are lined up inside the stone walls, where open-air services are held on Sunday mornings. David Malo's Church is at 100 Kulanihakoi St, at the side of the Trinity Episcopal Church.

Another notable church in the area is the little green and white **Keolahou Congregational Hawaiian Church**, next to the library at 131 S Kihei Rd, which was established in 1920. A number of the 1000 Tongans living on Maui belong to the congregation and services are held in Tongan at 5 pm on Sundays.

Kalama Park

Kalama Park, opposite the Kihei Town Center, is a local park with ball fields, tennis courts, volleyball, a playground, picnic pavilions, restrooms and showers. The park is long and grassy but the beach is shallow and unappealing for swimming.

Kamaole Beach Park

Kamaole Beach is one long beach divided into three sections by rocky points. All three are pretty golden sand beaches, though sometimes powerful kona storms temporarily wipe out much of the sand.

Each section is along the roadside opposite the condos and shopping centers. All three sections have full beach facilities and a lifeguard.

Water conditions vary greatly with the weather, but there's usually good swimming. For the most part these beaches have sandy bottoms with a fairly steep drop which tends to create good conditions for bodysurfing as well.

For snorkeling, Kamaole Beach Park 3 is the best bet, though the Wailea beaches to the south are far better.

Keawakapu Beach

Keawakapu Beach is bordered on its north end by the southernmost Kihei hotels and on its south end by Mokapu Beach and the Wailea resort area. More scenic and less crowded than the roadside Kihei beaches, Keawakapu is a sandy beach with a sandy bottom. Snorkeling is fairly good at the rocky outcrop at the southern end.

As there's no reef off Keawakapu, the state has been working to develop an artificial reef here for the past 30 years. The original drop was piles of car bodies, but a few years back about 1000 'fish shelters' made of old tires embedded in concrete, were dropped some 500 yards offshore.

There's a fine view from the beach and during the winter whales cavort in the surrounding waters, sometimes coming in quite close to shore.

To get to Keawakapu, instead of continuing along Hwy 31 as it curves up to the left to Wailea, go straight ahead on S Kihei Rd until it ends. There you'll find 25 public parking spaces and an outdoor shower.

Places to Stay

Kihei is packed with condos, but there are few hotels. In many places along South Kihei Rd the traffic will challenge you to get a good night's sleep, so when you book be sure to avoid rooms fronting the road.

In addition to the following listings, there are scores of Kihei condos that are booked through rental agents; for details see Condominiums under Accommodations in the front of this chapter.

Condos *Wailana Kai* (☎ 877-5796), 34 Wailana Place (mailing address c/o Mary Caravalho, 255-E Alamaha St, Kahului, HI 96732), is on a quiet cul de sac a block back from the beach at the one-mile marker. This newer complex has a small pool and 10 pleasant units, each with cable TV, full kitchen and everything you'd expect in a more-expensive condo except the price. One-bedroom units cost $55 in the low season and $65 in the high season. Two-bedroom units for up to four people cost $75/85 low/high. Credit cards are not accepted.

Village by the Sea, also known as *Kauhale Makai*, is a six-story concrete-block complex at 938 S Kihei Rd. Ninety of the 160 condo units are vacation rentals booked through Maui Condo & Home Realty (☎ 879-5445, (800) 822-4409; fax

874-6144), Box 1840, Kihei, HI 96753. All units have lanais and the standard amenities and while the location is not special the interiors are as nice as in more expensive condos nearby. Studios cost $60/75 in the low/high season, one-bedroom units $70/100, two-bedroom units $85/140. It has a pool and tennis court. There's a three-day minimum stay, and weekly and monthly discounts.

Kamaole Beach Royale (☎ 879-3131, (800) 421-3661), 2385 S Kihei Rd, Kihei, HI 96753, is a seven-story condo opposite Kamaole Beach Park 1, but set back from the road. It's quiet with open rangeland behind and an ocean view from the top floors. Units are spacious and well-furnished with lanais, modern kitchens, washer/dryers, TVs and phones with free local calls. It's particularly good value during the low season when one-bedroom units cost $65, two-bedroom units $75. Both are $25 more in the high season. There's a cleaning charge of $40 for stays of four nights or less, and credit cards are not accepted.

Kihei Alii Kai (☎ 879-6770, (800) 888-6284; fax 879-6221), Box 985, 2387 S Kihei Rd, Kihei, HI 96753, opposite Kamaole Beach Park 1, is a 127-unit complex with a pool, sauna and tennis courts. All units have a washer/dryer and cable TV. One-bedroom units cost $65/90 low/high for up to two people and two-bedroom units cost $80/105 for up to four people. The minimum stay is three days.

The *Koa Resort* (☎ 879-1161, (800) 877-1314), 811 S Kihei Rd, Kihei, HI 96753, has 54 very large and comfortable units spread out over 5½ acres. All are equipped with full kitchens, a washer/dryer, lanai, cable TV etc. There are two tennis courts, a putting green, a spa and a large swimming pool. The grounds are quiet and pleasantly landscaped. One-bedroom units cost $85/105 low/high and two-bedroom units are from $100/120. For this price category it's an excellent choice but because so many people return each year advance booking is usually essential. The minimum stay is five days.

Kamaole Sands (☎ 874-8700, (800) 992-7866), 2695 S Kihei Rd, Kihei, HI 96753, is its own condo city with 440 units in 10 buildings. The units are very large, quite nice and have all the modern amenities, but the complex is big and impersonal with lots of concrete and parking lots. Kamaole Sands, which is directly opposite Kamaole Beach Park 3, has a pool, spa and tennis courts. Aston, which books many of the units, charges $85/95 low/high for studio units, from $110/125 for one-bedroom units and from $155/170 for two-bedroom units.

Mana Kai-Maui (☎ 879-1561, (800) 525-2025), 2960 S Kihei Rd, Kihei, HI 96753, is a seven-story hotel/condo with a pool at the northern end of scenic Keawakapu Beach. Hotel rooms, which are small but adequate, include breakfast for $90/95 low/high. Roomier one-bedroom apartments (without breakfast but with kitchen) cost $155/175 and have lanais with fine ocean views; ask for an upper floor unit. All accommodations have TV, telephone and ceiling fans (no air-conditioning) and the rates include a rental car.

Hotels & B&Bs The *Maui Sun* (☎ 875-9000, (800) 367-5004; fax 596-0158, (800) 477-2329), 175 E Lipoa St, Kihei, HI 96753, is a modern 231-room hotel with a quiet location between Silversword Golf Course and the center of Kihei. Rooms are very comfortable, with a king bed or two double beds, a private lanai, a table and chair, remote-control TV and tasteful decor. There's a large free-form swimming pool and a whirlpool on the grounds. Rates are a reasonable $85 to $135 depending on the view, but since it's not on the ocean, the lower rates are a better value. Occasionally the hotel runs a special deal that throws in a free rental car – ask when you make reservations.

The *Maui Coast Hotel* (☎ 874-6284, (800) 426-0670, within Hawaii (800) 371-2402), 2259 S Kihei Rd, Kihei, HI 96753, is a new seven-story hotel affiliated with the Canadian Coast Hotels chain. The 264 rooms are comfortable and pleasantly decorated, all with air-con, ceiling fans, mini-refrigerators, coffeemakers, safes, remote-control TVs, phones, lanais, sofa beds and either a king or two double beds. The hotel has complimentary washers and dryers, a heated pool, tennis courts and a restaurant. As it's set back from the road the hotel is quieter than most Kihei condos. Room rates begin at $110, suites at $140.

Ann and Bob Babson (☎ 874-1166, (800) 824-6409), 3371 Keha Dr, Kihei, HI 96753, rent two upstairs bedrooms and a small apartment in their contemporary hill-side home in the Maui Meadows area, about a mile above Wailea. From the living room there's a wonderful view of Kahoolawe, Molokini and Lanai. One bedroom has a queen bed and a mini-refrigerator and costs $65. The master bedroom has a private deck, wraparound windows, a skylight and a spa and costs $80. If you want more privacy, there's a downstairs one-bedroom apartment with cooking facilities for $80 and a separate cottage adjacent to the house that rents for $95. All have TVs, phones, free laundry facilities and private baths; prices for the upstairs bedrooms include breakfast.

Places to Eat

These Kihei restaurants are listed in order from north to south.

Margarita's Beach Cantina in Kealia Beach Shopping Plaza, 101 North Kihei Rd, has average Mexican food but a nice sunset-facing deck overlooking the beach. The usual Mexican-style combination plates are priced from $9 to $14 and at lunch, which is served from 11:30 am to 5 pm, there are also a few lighter dishes, including burgers and fries, for around $8. You can sometimes find two-for-one lunch coupons in the tourist magazines.

The snack shop adjacent to *Suda's Store*, 61 South Kihei Rd, has cheeseburgers and saimin for about $2.50 as well as hot dogs, shave ice and ice cream. On the other side of the store is *Surfer Joe's*, a small, smoky bar & grill featuring pipeline burritos, hang-ten tempura fish and cowabunga burgers, each $6.50 with fries.

Stella Blues, a casual cafe and deli in the Longs Center, 1215 S Kihei Rd, opens at 8 am daily and has coffees, desserts, lox and bagels, kosher meat sandwiches and numerous vegetarian options. Full break-fasts averaging $7 are served until 11 am. Most sandwiches, salads and burgers cost between $6 and $8. At dinner, dishes such as Cajun eggplant, Alaskan crab cakes and Thai sweet chili chicken cost $12 with salad, vegetables and rice.

There's a *McDonald's* opposite the Longs Center.

Royal Thai Cuisine in Azeka Place is the best place in Kihei for Thai food. Although the servings are on the small side, the food is tasty and prices are inexpensive. The menu has pad Thai, curries and numerous other dishes priced from $6 to $8 and nearly a dozen vegetarian dishes for around $6. Lunch is served weekdays from 11 am to 3 pm, dinner nightly from 5 to 9:30 pm.

Azeka Place has a *Baskin-Robbins* ice cream shop, a *Taco Bell* and an *International House of Pancakes*. On the south side of Azeka Place is a *Star Market* with a deli and a nice salad bar.

In Azeka Place II, opposite Azeka Place, is *Panda Express*, a Mandarin restaurant with about a dozen dishes, such as broccoli beef and spicy chicken with peanuts, served from steamer trays. The food is tasty, the servings generous and the price a good value at $4.79 for any two dishes with rice or chow mein. You can also get a whole roasted duck ($16) or chicken ($9), as well as the other dishes, for takeout. It's open from 10:30 am to 9 pm daily.

Azeka Place II also has a new branch of Kauai chef Jean-Marie Josselin's *Pacific Cafe*. Despite its shopping center locale it has a stylish interior and has quickly become *the* place to eat Pacific Rim food in Kihei. Starters such as Thai seafood soup or Big Island goat cheese ravioli are priced under $10, while a variety of creative main dishes are priced from $18 to $25.

Adjacent to Azeka Place II is a *Jack in the Box* which has reasonably good fast food and is always offering some sort of discounted promotion.

Shaka Sandwich & Pizza (☎ 874-0331) at 1295 S Kihei Rd behind Jack in the Box, has the best pizza in town. An 18-inch cheese pizza costs $13, plus $1.75 for each topping, while a single slice of cheese pizza costs $1.50. There's also a variety of sandwiches on Italian bread for around $4. Shaka is open from 11 am to 9 pm and has delivery service with a $10 minimum order. It's closed on Sundays.

At the Kukui Mall, 1819 S Kihei Rd, there's a bakery and *Pair O' Dice Pizza*, with whole pizzas from $9, slices from $1.75 – soy cheese is available on request.

There's a *Kentucky Fried Chicken* and a *7-Eleven* convenience store immediately north of Kihei Town Center, where there's a 24-hour *Foodland* supermarket.

Kihei Caffe, opposite Kalama Park at 1945 S Kihei Rd, is a small cafe with cappuccino, Kona coffee and good if expensive pastries. Fresh salads and sandwiches, as well as a range of breakfast offerings, average about $6. It's open from 5 am (6 am on Sundays) to 3 pm daily.

New York Deli in the Dolphin Plaza, 2395 South Kihei Rd, has sandwiches layered with a quarter pound of meat for $5 and tortellini, Greek, fruit and other salads for about $3 a half pound. It's open from 8 am to 8 pm. Next door at the *Kihei Bakery* you can get a cup of coffee and a doughnut for $1.25. There are a couple of small tables in front of the shops where you can eat.

For American-style pizza there's a *Pizza Hut* in the Dolphin Plaza, although many people prefer the island chain *Wiki Wiki Pizza* which is a stone's throw away in the next shopping center. Wiki Wiki has pizza by the slice ($1.35) from 11 am to 5 pm, pasta, calzones and sandwiches for $6 and whole pizzas from $9. Free delivery is available in the evening from both restaurants.

Hawaiian Moons Natural Foods on S Kihei Rd, next to Wiki Wiki Pizza, has a good organic produce section, yogurts, juices, trail mix, bulk grains, granolas and a few organic wines. The food is fresh and the prices are reasonable. It also has a small deli that makes a good hearty vegetarian sandwich with goat cheddar for $5.25.

Chum's in the Rainbow Mall has fairly good local food at reasonable prices. Sandwiches and saimin are under $6, while traditional Hawaiian dishes such as laulau or kalua pig cost $6.75. It's open daily from 6:30 am to 11 pm.

Erik's Seafood Broiler (☎ 879-8400), a popular seafood restaurant at the Kamaole Shopping Center, 2653 S Kihei Rd, is open for dinner from 5 to 10 pm nightly. The restaurant features a variety of fresh Hawaiian fish dinners, as well as prawns, lobster thermidor and bouillabaisse, all priced around $20. Dinners include salad, bread and rice. From 5 to 6 pm there's a good-value early-bird special with catch of the day, steak or prawns for $12. Reservations are recommended to avoid a wait.

Also in the Kamaole Shopping Center is a *Denny's* restaurant open 24 hours; *C & R Cantina* with Mexican combination plates from $8; *Canton Chef* with a full range of moderately priced Chinese dishes; and the *Cinnamon Roll Fair* which sells goopy warm cinnamon rolls for $2.20.

Carelli's on the Beach (☎ 875-0001), 2980 S Kihei Rd, is Kihei's trendiest fine-dining restaurant, with an extensive Italian menu and a romantic waterfront setting. Main dishes range from fettuccine alfredo for $17 to zuppa di mare cioppino for $30. Appetizers are about half that. Though expensive, the food is excellent. It's open for dinner only, from 5:30 to 10 pm nightly.

Entertainment

Stella Blues cafe and deli in the Longs Center has live jazz on Wednesday, Hawaiian music on Thursdays and blues on Friday and Saturday evenings.

Chum's in the Rainbow Mall has live entertainment in its lounge some nights – occasionally you'll find top Hawaiian ukulele and slack-key guitar musicians performing here.

There's a four-screen movie theater (☎ 875-4533) at Kukui Mall.

Things to Buy

Kihei is overflowing with souvenir, gift and clothing shops of all sorts. A good place to look for good-quality inexpensive aloha shirts and other Hawaiian clothing is Penthouse, the discount outlet of the adjacent Liberty House department store at Azeka Place II.

The Maui Dive Shop in Azeka Place II has reef walkers, boogie boards, snorkels, fins, wet suits, etc. Tropics, next door, also carries boogie boards as well as a few surfboards. The ABC Discount Store, opposite Kamaole Beach Park 1, has beach mats for a dollar, suntan lotion and other practical items for visitors.

Wailea & Makena

WAILEA

As soon as you enter Wailea you'll be struck by the contrast to the cluttery commercialism of Kihei – everything is green, manicured and precise.

Wailea has a few swank hotels on the beach, a growing number of low-rise condo villas, two golf courses, a shopping center and a tennis club nicknamed 'Wimbledon West'.

Wailea's interesting lava rock coastline is broken by attractive golden sand beaches. From Wailea and neighboring Makena there are good views of Lanai, Kahoolawe and Molokini and some fantastic shoreline whale watching.

Information

If you're heading to Wailea beaches from Lahaina or Kahului, be sure to take the Piilani Hwy (Hwy 31) and not South Kihei Rd. It's less than 10 minutes' drive this way, whereas the Kihei strip can be a tedious 30 minutes through congested traffic.

Wailea's main road is Wailea Alanui which after Polo Beach changes its name to Makena Alanui as it continues south to Makena.

A free shuttle bus (☎ 879-1948) runs every 30 minutes around the Wailea resort connecting the hotels, shopping center, golf courses and tennis club. For information on bus service between the Wailea and Kaana-

pali areas, see Getting Around in the front of this chapter.

Wailea Shopping Village, in front of the Inter-Continental, has a First Hawaiian Bank (open from 8:30 am to 3 pm Monday to Thursday, to 6 pm on Fridays), two lackluster restaurants, a little grocery store and a few boutiques.

Wailea Beaches

Wailea's beaches begin with the southern end of Keawakapu Beach and continue south with Mokapu, Ulua, Wailea and Polo beaches. They are all lovely strands with free public access and parking as well as showers and toilets. Some also have picnic tables and barbecue grills.

While Wailea's beaches generally have good swimming conditions, occasional high surf and kona storms can create dangerous shorebreaks and rip currents.

Ulua Beach Ulua Beach is between Maui Inter-Continental Wailea and Stouffer Wailea Beach Resort. The first road south of the Stouffer leads to the beach parking lot.

When it's calm, Ulua Beach has the area's best snorkeling. There's coral at the rocky outcrop on the right side of the beach and you can usually spot long needlefish, schools of goatfish, unicorn tangs and other tropicals. Snorkeling is best in the morning before the winds pick up. When the surf's up, forget snorkeling – in its place there's apt to be good bodysurfing.

During WW II, US Marines trained for the invasion of Tarawa off this beach and consequently it was known locally as Tarawa Beach until the developers of Wailea resort moved in and renamed it Ulua.

Wailea Beach Wailea is the largest and widest of Wailea's beaches. The inshore waters along the sandy beach slope gradually and are good for swimming. When the water's calm, there's good snorkeling around the rocky point on the south side of the beach. Divers entering the water at

Wailea Beach can follow an offshore reef that runs down to Polo Beach. At times there's a gentle shorebreak suitable for bodysurfing.

Beach access is on the road running between the Four Seasons Resort and the Grand Wailea Resort, which both front Wailea Beach.

Polo Beach Polo is fronted by a condo development and by the Kea Lani Hotel but the south side of the beach is seldom crowded.

When there's wave action, boogie boarders and bodysurfers usually find a good shorebreak at Polo Beach. When the waters are calm, the rocks at the north end of the beach are good for snorkeling. At low tide the lava outcropping at the south end of the beach has some interesting little tide pools that harbor spiny sea urchins and a few small fish.

To get to Polo Beach, turn down Kaukahi St after the Kea Lani Hotel. There's a large beach parking lot on the right, near the end of the road.

Palauea Beach Palauea Beach is along Makena Rd, a quarter of a mile south of Polo Beach. The kiawe brushland between the beach and the road is marked private property, though there are breaks in the fence where beachgoers cross. A fair number of people use the beach for surfing and bodysurfing. It's more secluded and less frequented than Polo Beach, but otherwise much the same, sans the development. You can walk to Palauea Beach from Polo Beach in less than 10 minutes.

Places to Stay
The *Maui Inter-Continental Wailea* (☎ 879-1922, (800) 367-2960), 3700 Wailea Alanui Dr, Wailea, HI 96753, has 516 rooms spread across a number of low-rise buildings and a mid-rise tower. For Wailea, it's an unpretentious and pleasantly low-key operation. Rooms are generally comfortable with lanais, separate dressing areas and the usual resort-class amenities.

MAUI

Wailea & Makena

0 | .5 | 1 km
0 | .25 | .5 miles

Garden-view rooms cost $179, while an ocean view costs an extra $40. Sometimes there are discounted specials, although these are most common during the off-season.

The *Stouffer Wailea Beach Resort* (☎ 879-4900, (800) 992-4532), 3550 Wailea Alanui Dr, Wailea, HI 96753, is a tasteful resort hotel – upscale, but not as opulent and formal as its neighbors to the south. The grounds are lush, the 350 rooms are nicely furnished with rattan and wicker and it's on a quiet beach. Rates range from $255 for mountain views to $2000 for the Aloha Suite.

The *Grand Wailea Resort* (☎ 875-1234, (800) 888-6100), 3850 Wailea Alanui, Wailea, HI 96753, is the most extravagant resort on Maui. The lobbies are filled with sculptures and artwork and the grounds are given over to gardens, artificial waterfalls, a multimillion-dollar mosaic tile pool, fountains and the like. The 2000-foot-long system of pools, water slides and artificial grottos is the most elaborate in Hawaii. All 767 rooms have three telephones, an ocean view, marble baths, a minimum of 640 sq feet and a daily rate of at least $350.

The *Kea Lani Hotel* (☎ 875-4100, (800) 882-4100), 4100 Wailea Alanui Dr, Wailea, HI 96753, is a 450-suite resort hotel with fanciful Moorish-style architecture that resembles something out of *Arabian Nights*. Each suite has a lanai, a separate living room with a sofa bed, TV, VCR, CD player, microwave and coffeemaker. One-bedroom suites cost from $235 to $385 for up to four adults, two-bedroom suites cost $585 for up to eight people and there are

also oceanfront villas with private pools for about $1000. For the economy minded (!), a mere $10 more adds on a rental car.

The 380-room *Four Seasons Resort* (☎ 874-8000, (800) 332-3442), 3900 Wailea Alanui, Wailea, HI 96753, is relatively undistinguished and pricey with rates beginning at $340.

Destination Resorts (☎ 879-1595, (800) 367-5246), 3750 Wailea Alanui Place, Wailea, HI 96753, books about 300 units in half a dozen complexes in the Wailea and Makena area. While they aren't cheap, most of the condos are quite nice and represent far better value than Wailea's luxury hotels. Studio and one-bedroom condos in Wailea begin at $130/140 in the low/high season while the high end tops off with three-bedroom oceanfront units costing $425/525.

Places to Eat

Cafe Ciao at the Kea Lani Hotel is a great place for deli-style meals, with excellent food at affordable prices. Main dishes such as focaccia pizza, tortellini and a nice eggplant caponata cost $4 to $5. The cafe, which bakes its own breads and pastries every morning, supplies bakery goods to area resorts where they sell at inflated prices. Here these exquisite desserts, including cannolis, fruit tarts, chocolate croissants and a delicious strawberry mousse gateau, cost just $2 to $3. Caffe Ciao is open from 6:30 am to 8 pm daily; there are a few casual cafe tables on the patio where you can eat.

The Fairway, up Kaukahi St amidst the Wailea Golf Course, has a distant ocean

---

Wailea Beach Walk

For a delightful stroll, take the shoreline path that runs for 1¼ miles from the Maui Inter-Continental to the Kea Lani, connecting the Wailea beaches and the resort hotels that front them. The path winds above jagged lava points that separate the beaches and is landscaped with native Hawaiian flora, some of which is identified by plaques. In winter this is one of the best walks in all Hawaii for spotting humpback whales – on a good day you may be able to see as many as 15 or 20 frolicking in the waters offshore.

Some of the luxury hotels you'll pass along the beach walk are also worth strolling through, most notably the Grand Wailea Resort, which has $30 million of artwork and some strikingly elaborate waterways and landscaping on its grounds. ∎

view and standard breakfast offerings and lunchtime sandwiches for around $7.

Cafe Kula in the Grand Wailea Resort is an open-air cafe overlooking the hotel gardens. Lunch features a dozen salads including Kula greens for $6 and heart of palm salad for $10; soup and sandwiches cost $10. Breakfast is also served, but it's rather pricey – an omelet and coffee costs $12. It's open from 6:30 am to 3 pm daily. The hotel's *Molokini Bistro* has good, if pricey, Italian food and a setting that's enhanced at night by floodlights on the surf. Pizza and pastas begin around $15, seafood dishes $30.

The *Lanai Terrace* at the Maui Inter-Continental Wailea has dinner buffets from 5 to 9 pm Tuesday to Saturday. They include a small but fresh salad bar and feature a different cuisine each night – on Tuesday evenings it's Asian food for $17 and on Saturdays prime rib for $18.

The new *Kea Lani Restaurant* at the Kea Lani Resort is a popular fine dining spot with a nice view and good food that's a tad cheaper than other top-end Wailea restaurants. Starters range from local greens for $6 to sashimi or grilled ahi for $11, while entrees including lamb in ginger sauce and teppan-grilled scallops are mostly priced under $25.

Raffles' (☎ 879-4900), the signature restaurant at Stouffer Wailea Beach Resort, has elegant dining and good Pacific Rim cuisine. Entrees, which average about $30, include crisped whole fish in a Thai coconut curry served with nasi goreng and a Hunan-marinated rack of lamb. Starters such as duck gyoza and sugar-cured ahi with caviar cost $12. It's open from 6:30 to 10 pm nightly.

Entertainment

The Wailea hotels have a variety of Hawaiian music, dance music, pianists and guitarists in their restaurants and lounges.

The Grand Wailea Resort's high-tech *Tsunami* nightclub has a top-40 DJ from 9 pm to 2 am on Tuesdays and Thursdays with no cover charge and from 9 pm to 4 am on Fridays and Saturdays with a $10 cover.

The Wailea Shopping Village presents a free Polynesian dance show at 1:30 pm Tuesdays and offers hula classes for children and adults on Wednesdays (☎ 572-5864 for information).

The Maui Inter-Continental has a luau at 5:30 pm on Tuesdays, Thursdays and Fridays for $52 for adults, $26 for children. It's held on the lawn near the beach and you can see some of the show for free from the beach walk. The musicians are good, though they have a tendency to drift into sappy pop medleys. The Stouffer Wailea and the Grand Wailea Resort also have luaus.

MAKENA

Until recently, Makena was a sleepy and largely overlooked area at the end of the road. Its center was the abandoned Makena Landing with its small and predominately Hawaiian village.

In the 1980s the Seibu Corporation bought up 1800 acres of Makena above the landing, and a development similar to Wailea is now in the making. So far there's a golf course, a tennis center, the Maui Prince Hotel and a new bypass road to it all.

Makena's dominant shoreline feature is Puu Olai, a 360-foot cinder hill a mile south of the landing. Just beyond Puu Olai, Makena has two knockout beaches adjoining each other. They are commonly called Big and Little beaches or, together, Makena Beach.

Big Beach is a huge sweep of glistening sand and a prime sunset-viewing locale with straight-on views of Molokini and Kahoolawe. Little Beach is a secluded cove, Maui's most popular nudist beach.

In the late 1960s Makena was the site of an alternative-lifestyle camp and took on the nickname 'Hippie Beach'. The tent city lasted until 1972 when police finally evicted everyone on health code violations. More than a few of Maui's residents can trace their roots on the island to the camp at Makena Beach.

Makena Beach has recently become a

state park and long-term plans call for the addition of full beach facilities, but for now it remains in a totally natural state except for a couple of pit toilets and picnic tables.

Makena Bay

To explore the older side of Makena, turn right down Makena Rd after Makena Surf condos and go about a mile to Makena Bay.

In the 1800s Makena was the busiest landing on this side of Maui. Cattle from Ulupalakua Ranch and other Upcountry ranches were brought down the hillsides and shipped to market in Honolulu from **Makena Landing**. By the 1920s inter-island boat traffic had shifted to other ports on the island and Makena lost its economic base.

Makena Landing is now a local recreational area with boat-launching facilities, showers, toilets and picnic tables. There's good snorkeling along the rocks at the south side of the landing.

South of the landing is the **Keawalai Congregational Church**, which dates to 1832 and is one of Maui's early missionary churches. The current building was built in 1855 with three-foot-thick walls made of burnt coral rock. A small congregation still meets for Sunday services, which are held in a mix of Hawaiian and English. The church graveyard has a fine bayside view and old tombstones with very interesting cameo photographs.

The sheltered cove fronting the church is protected by two rocky outcrops and its waters are almost always calm. The showers and restrooms opposite the church are the nearest facilities to Big Beach.

Makena Rd ends shortly after the church at a cul de sac on the ocean side of Maui Prince Hotel.

Maluaka Beach

At the southern end of Makena Bay is Maluaka Beach, a beige sand beach which fronts the Maui Prince Hotel. The beach, which slopes down from an ice plant-covered sand dune, has a sandy bottom in its center and rocky formations at each end that might provide decent snorkeling.

Big Beach

Big Beach is the sort of scene that people conjure up when they dream of a Hawaiian beach. It's very big, uncrowded, and there's absolutely no development on the horizon.

The Hawaiian name for Big Beach is Oneloa, literally 'Long Sand'. This golden sand beach is well over half a mile long and as broad as they come, with clear turquoise waters.

The turn-off to the main parking area for Big Beach is about a mile past the Maui Prince Hotel. There's a second parking area a third of a mile to the south. You can also park alongside the road and walk in, but thefts and broken windshields have been commonplace in the area and the parking lot is a safer bet. Watch for kiawe thorns in the woods behind the beach.

Big Beach is open ocean and when there's heavy surf there are powerful rip currents and dangerous shorebreaks.

Little Beach

Little Beach is hidden by a rocky outcrop which juts out from Puu Olai, the cinder cone that marks the north end of Big Beach.

A trail over the rock links the two and takes just a few minutes to walk. From the top of the trail there's a splendid view of both beaches.

Little Beach fronts a sandy cove which usually has a gentle shorebreak ideal for bodysurfing and boogie boarding. Snorkeling along the rocky point is good when the water is calm.

A trail continues a few minutes beyond Little Beach to an area where lava outcrops stick out into the clear deep water like giant fingers. When it's very calm divers and confident snorkelers sometimes explore these formations, which have caves and abundant marine life.

Little Beach, also known as Puu Olai Beach, is a popular nudist beach despite posted signs to the contrary.

Beyond Makena

Makena Rd continues as a narrow paved road for 2½ miles after Big Beach. The road goes through the Ahihi-Kinau Natural Area Reserve before ending at La Perouse Bay.

Ahihi-Kinau

The Ahihi-Kinau Natural Area Reserve covers 2045 acres and includes sections of Ahihi Bay and Cape Kinau.

Maui's most recent lava flow created most of the cape on its way to the sea in 1790. The reserve has lava tide pools, coastal lava tubes and all the aa lava you could ever want to see.

It has been designated a natural area reserve because of its distinctive marine life habitat and its unique geological features, including anchialine pools and kipukas (areas of land spared when lava flows around it). The removal of any flora, fauna or lava is prohibited.

The remains of a coastal Hawaiian village sit between lava flows at Ahihi Bay, its old sites marked by walled and terraced platforms.

There's a little roadside cove with good snorkeling just one-tenth of a mile south of the first reserve sign. It's quite rocky and can be a bit challenging getting in, but the cove has lots of coral and fish.

La Perouse Bay

In 1786 the renowned French explorer Jean François de Galaup La Perouse became the first Westerner to land on Maui. As he sailed into the bay that now bears his name, scores of Hawaiian canoes came out to greet him and trade.

After leaving Hawaii, La Perouse mysteriously disappeared in the Pacific. While no one knows his fate, some historians speculate that he and his crew were eaten by cannibals in the New Hebrides.

The paved road ends just short of La Perouse Bay. Although you may be able to drive all the way in on the 4WD road, you can also park where the asphalt ends and walk down to the coast. A 10-minute foot trail leads over the lava and along the water, passing a few tiny coves with sandy patches before reaching La Perouse Bay. The bay is rather rocky and marginal for most water activities, other than advanced

diving, but there are good hiking possibilities in the area.

King's Highway Coastal Trail

From La Perouse Bay it's possible to continue on foot along the old King's Highway. This ancient trail follows the coastline across jagged barren lava flows, so hiking boots are a good idea. It's a dry area with no water and little vegetation and thus can get very hot.

The first part of the trail is along the sandy beach at La Perouse Bay. Right after the beach it's possible to take a ¾-mile spur trail down to the lighthouse at the tip of Cape Hanamanioa.

Alternatively you can continue on the King's Highway as it climbs up through rough aa lava inland for the next two miles before coming back to the coast at an older lava flow. In that area there are a number of old Hawaiian house foundations and pebble and coral beaches.

Places to Stay

The *Maui Prince Hotel* (☎ 874-1111, (800) 321-6284; fax 879-8763), 5400 Makena Alanui, Wailea, HI 96753, turns inward in typical Japanese fashion. From the outside it looks like a fortress but the interior incorporates a fine sense of Japanese aesthetics. The five-story hotel surrounds a courtyard with waterfalls and streams, carp ponds, raked rock gardens and bougainvillea draped from the balconies. All 300 rooms have at least partial ocean views, from $220.

Places to Eat

Cafe Kiowai in the Maui Prince Hotel serves very good food and is open for three meals a day. At lunch, served until 2 pm, there are moderately priced salads and sandwiches as well as a few hot dishes for under $15. Dinner entrees range from $11 for pizza to $26 for filet mignon with baked lobster tail. However the best deal is the superb salad/antipasto bar which includes soup, fresh greens, grilled vegetables, Italian antipasto, an ahi niçoise platter,

MAUI

pasta of the day, cheeses and breads; it costs $13.50 alone, $7 with an entree. Dinner is served from 5 to 9:30 pm.

Hakone (☎ 874-1111) at the Maui Prince Hotel has kimono-clad waitresses, shoji screens and authentic Japanese food, including a good sushi bar. There are a number of full meals with appetizer, rice, soup and dessert in the $25 to $30 range. It's open from 6 to 9:30 pm Monday to Saturday.

The *Prince Court* (☎ 874-1111) at the Maui Prince Hotel has Hawaiian Regional Cuisine prepared by Roger Dikon, one of the island's most creative chefs. Main dishes, which are priced from $26 to $33, include the likes of kiawe-grilled shrimp with jasmine rice or Hawaiian lobster in a Thai curry sauce. Soups and salads average $8, appetizers such as stuffed sashimi $13. It's open from 6:30 to 9:30 pm daily. There's also an indulgent Sunday champagne brunch from 10:30 am to 1 pm for $30.

Kahului-Wailuku Area

Kahului and Wailuku are Maui's two largest communities and flow together to form a single urban sprawl. This is where regular folks live, work and shop.

Kahului is the commercial center. The main road, Kaahumanu Ave, is a collection of stores, banks and office buildings and a mile-long strip of shopping centers. Kaahumanu Ave continues into Wailuku where it becomes Main St. Wailuku, the county seat, is the more distinctive and less hurried end of it all. This is an older town with back streets of curio shops, mom-and-pop stores and hole-in-the-wall ethnic restaurants.

Kahului Harbor, Maui's deep-water commercial port, services barges, cargo ships and the occasional cruise liner. This one's geared for work – there are no charming wharves or sailboats.

Maui's main airport is in Kahului. After landing, most people drive right out of

town and don't come back until they're ready to leave. And with a few exceptions, unless you're up for mall shopping, there's really not much in Kahului for visitors.

Wailuku, which you'll pass through on the way to Iao Valley State Park, has a few historic places of interest and makes for a good lunch break and stroll. Wailuku also has some of Maui's cheapest places to stay.

Information
The county and state office buildings are next to each other on High St in downtown Wailuku.

Money The Bank of Hawaii has branches at 2105 Main St in Wailuku and 27 Puunene Ave in Kahului. Both have automatic teller machines that accept major credit and ATM cards.

Post Wailuku's post office is at 250 Imi Kala St, on the north side of town. Kahului's post office is on Puunene Ave. Both post offices are open weekdays until 5 pm, to noon on Saturdays.

Bookstores & Libraries The Kahului public library at 90 School St is open from 9 am to noon on Mondays, 9 am to 8 pm on Tuesdays and Wednesdays, and from 9 am to 5 pm on Thursdays, Fridays and Saturdays.

The Wailuku library at 251 High St is open from noon to 8 pm on Mondays and Tuesdays, from 9 am to 5 pm on Wednesdays, Thursdays and Saturdays, from noon to 5 pm on Fridays.

There are Waldenbooks bookstores at both the Kaahumanu Shopping Center and the Maui Mall.

Travel Agents There are two discount travel agencies a five-minute drive from the airport. Both sell air coupons for interisland flights for $47. Maui Airport Travel (☎ 871-7666) is in the shopping complex at 395 Dairy Rd, while Cut Rate Tickets (☎ 871-7300) is just a few buildings away at 333 Dairy Rd. The latter is open seven days a week.

Emergency The Maui Memorial Hospital (☎ 244-9056) is at 221 Mahalani St in Wailuku.

KAHULUI

In the 1880s Kahului became the headquarters of Hawaii's first railroad, which was built to haul sugar from the fields to the refinery and harbor. In 1900 an outbreak of bubonic plague hit Kahului and in an attempt to wipe it out, the settlement that had grown up around Kahului Harbor was purposely burned to the ground.

The present-day Kahului is a planned community developed in 1948 by Alexander & Baldwin. It was called 'Dream City' by sugar cane workers who dreamed of moving away from the dusty mill camps to a home of their own. Their tract homes are at the southern end of town.

Kanaha Pond Wildlife Sanctuary

Kanaha Pond is a sanctuary for the endangered black-necked stilt, a wading bird that feeds along the marshy edges of the pond. It's a graceful bird in flight with long orange legs that trail behind. The total stilt population in all Hawaii is estimated at 1500.

Access to the pond is on Hwy 396, near the junction of Hwy 36. The parking lot is marked with an HVB warrior. There's an observation deck you can walk out on – a good site for spotting stilts, coots, ducks and black-crowned night herons.

Upon entering the sanctuary, if you close the gate behind you and walk in quietly you should be able to make sightings right along the shoreline. The pond is a respite in the midst of suburbia, right in the flight path for the airport and just beyond the highway where trucks go barreling along.

If you'd like to hike on the service roads in the sanctuary you can do so by obtaining a permit from the Division of Land Management (☎ 243-5352), State Office Building, 1st Floor, 54 High St, Wailuku. Office hours are 7:45 am to 4:30 pm on weekdays.

Kanaha Beach Park

If you're stuck in Kahului, Kanaha Beach Park is OK, though most locals prefer the cleaner, clearer waters of Kihei.

Kanaha has a long white sand beach and a nice view of the West Maui Mountains all the way up the coast to Hakuhee Point. There's a roped-off swimming area, restrooms, showers, phones and picnic tables under the shade of kukui, ironwood and kiawe trees. The airport noise can be annoying, however.

Kanaha is a popular windsurfing spot and when the wind is right, it can be quite crowded. It's the best place in Maui for beginners and most of the windsurfing shops give their lessons here.

The beach access sign is down by the car rental lots at the airport. Or from downtown Kahului take Amala Rd, the coastal road that runs makai of the Chevron storage tanks near the end of Kaahumanu Ave.

Maui Zoo & Botanical Garden

This is basically a little children's zoo with animals in small, confined cages. There are feral goats, pygmy donkeys, peacocks, monkeys and a flock of nene with goslings.

The 'botanical garden' part has a few labeled endemic plants, but it's a very modest little display to warrant a place on the nameplate.

Maui Zoo is between Kahului and Wailuku, a third of a mile down Kanaloa Ave off Kaahumanu Ave. It's open from 9 am to 4 pm daily and admission is free.

Places to Stay

Kahului's three hotels are all lined up on the main commercial strip in an area that hardly conjures up images of vacationing in Hawaii.

Maui Seaside Hotel (☎ 877-3311, (800) 367-7000 from the mainland, (800) 560-5552 in Hawaii), 100 Kaahumanu Ave, Kahului, HI 96732, has two wings. The older wing, which used to be called the Hukilau Hotel, has rooms for $75/87 in the low/high season. The newer wing is a modern building with larger and more com-

MAUI

Kahului & Wailuku

See Wailuku map

MAUI

fortable rooms costing $85/97. Rooms in both wings have air-conditioning, cable TV and small refrigerators. With this Hawaiian-owned chain, you'll get much better rates if you book within Hawaii – they commonly run discounted specials in the Sunday *Honolulu Advertiser* that include a room and car for less than the standard room rates.

Next door, the adjacent *Maui Beach Hotel* and *Maui Palms Hotel* are Hawaiian Pacific Resorts properties (☎ 877-0071, (800) 367-5004; fax 596-0158). Both are older and lackluster and the main attraction is the rates which have been inching down-

ward in the past few years. Prices at the 103-room Maui Palms Hotel start at $50, those at the 154-room Maui Beach Hotel are from $75. Free shuttle service is provided from the airport, but if you reserve in advance there's often a car/room package for the same price as the room only.

Places to Eat

The second level of the Kaahumanu Shopping Center has a food court with a handful of good fast-food ethnic eateries, including a *Yummy Korean BBQ*, *Panda Express* and *Aloha Mixed Plate Lunch*, all of which have plate dishes for around $5. There's also an *Edo Japan* with chicken yakisoba or ramen dishes for around the same price and a *Mama Brava* with big slices of decent pizza for $2.

The *Coffee Store*, a casual little place in the Kaahumanu Shopping Center, roasts its own coffee right in the store and serves it straight or as espresso or cappuccino. Croissant sandwiches or quiche cost $3.75, lasagna is $6.50 and there are scrumptious pastries such as baklava and white-chocolate raspberry cheesecake. The shop, which is open daily, has only a few cafe tables and gets very crowded at lunchtime.

Koho Grill & Bar (☎ 877-5588) in the Kaahumanu Shopping Center is open daily for breakfast, lunch and dinner. Despite its mall ambiance, this is one of the most popular eateries in town. The usual breakfast standards, such as omelets with potatoes and toast, are under $5. Most full meals, including shrimp scampi, primavera fettucine and catch of the day are under $10. Burgers, soups, salads and sandwiches are also available.

Mama Ding's Pasteles, in an industrial area at 255 Alamaha St, has authentic Puerto Rican food at reasonable prices. It's open from 6:30 am to 1:30 pm on weekdays, and from 9:30 am to 1:30 pm on Saturdays.

Sir Wilfred's Espresso Cafe is the best place to have lunch in the Maui Mall. Sandwiches such as vegie-tofu burger or hot pastrami are $6 or less. Breakfasts, served until 11 am, feature bagels, croissants and egg dishes. Hours are 9 am to 6 pm Monday to Friday, 9 am to 5:30 pm on Saturdays and 11 am to 5 pm on Sundays. The Maui Mall also has a few fast-food restaurants, an ice cream shop, an *International House of Pancakes* and *Maui Natural Foods*, a standard mall-style health food store.

Pinata's Mexican Food, 395 Dairy Rd, has a fast-food atmosphere but serves up Mexican fare that's good value for the price. A taco, enchilada, rice and beans plate costs $5.65, a single burrito $3 and a bottle of Dos Equis $2.50. It's open from 10:30 am to 7 pm Monday to Saturday.

Maui Coffee Roasters, 444 Hana Hwy, serves the coffee of the day at 50c a cup or $1 for a large mug. It also has good cappuccinos and scones and muffins. It's open from 7:30 am to 6 pm daily except on Sundays when it's open from 9 am to 3 pm.

Maui Bakery & Bagelry, 201 Dairy Rd, specializes in bagels but also has pastries and sandwiches. It's open Monday to Saturday from 6:30 am to 5:30 pm.

There's a *Pizza Hut*, *Taco Bell*, *Jack in the Box* and *Sizzler* steak house lined up on Kamehameha Ave between Puunene Ave and Alamaha St, and *McDonald's* is nearby on Puunene Ave.

There's a *Safeway* supermarket on Kamehameha Ave, a *Foodland* supermarket at the Kaahumanu Shopping Center and a *Star Market* at the Maui Mall.

Entertainment

There's usually some sort of local entertainment at the Kahului hotels on weekends. The *Red Dragon Room* in the Maui Beach Hotel, has a dance club from 10:30 pm to 2:30 am Fridays and Saturdays. There's a $3 cover charge.

First-run movies are shown at the *Maui Theatre* (☎ 877-3560) in the Kahului Shopping Center, 70 E Kaahumanu Ave.

For information on the new *Maui Community Arts & Cultural Center*, which is adjacent to the community college, see the Maui Entertainment section at the beginning of this chapter.

Things to Buy

Kaahumanu Shopping Center, on Kaahumanu Ave, is the area's largest mall with about 50 shops, including Liberty House (and its Penthouse discount shop) and Sears. The Maui Mall on Kaahumanu Ave has Longs Drugs, Woolworth and a one-hour photo-processing shop.

For some local flavor try the Maui Swap Meet, which is held from 7 am to noon on Saturdays on Puunene Ave, just south of the Kahului post office.

PUUNENE

Puunene is a working plantation village surrounded by sugar cane fields and centered around a mill run by the Hawaiian Commercial & Sugar Company. When the mill is in operation the air hangs heavy with the sweet smell of sugar.

The power plant next to the mill burns residue sugar cane fibers called bagasse to run the mill machinery that extracts and refines the sugar. With a capacity of 37,000 kilowatts, it's one of the world's largest biomass power plants. Excess electricity is sold to Maui Electric.

Puunene's main attraction is the sugar museum opposite the mill.

Sugar Museum

The Alexander & Baldwin Sugar Museum is a worthwhile little museum that tells the history of sugar in Hawaii. Displays explain how sugar cane grows and is harvested, complete with an elaborate working scale model of a cane-crushing plant.

What's most interesting, however, are the images of people. The museum traces how Samuel Alexander and Henry Baldwin gobbled up vast chunks of Hawaiian land and fought tooth-and-nail with an ambitious Claus Spreckels to gain access to Upcountry water. They then dug extensive irrigation systems which made large-scale sugar cane plantations a possibility.

Representing the other end of the scale is a turn-of-the-century labor contract from the Japanese Emigration Company stating that the laborer shall be paid $15 a month for working 10 hours a day in the field, 26 days a month (minus $2.50 banked for return passage to Japan). There are interesting period photos and artifacts of plantation life.

The museum (☎ 871-8058), originally the home of the mill's superintendent, is at the intersection of Puunene Ave (Hwy 350) and Hansen Rd. It's open from 9:30 am to 4:30 pm Monday to Saturday. Admission is $3 for adults, $1.50 for children ages six to 17.

WAIKAPU

The Honoapiilani Highway (Hwy 30), which runs along the east side of the West Maui Mountains, passes through the town of Waikapu a couple of miles south of Wailuku.

Although Waikapu has a new golf course sitting above its pineapple fields it remains quite rural. Its only sight is **Maui Tropical Plantation**, which features a touristy narrated tram ride past fields of sugar cane, pineapple and tropical fruit trees. The ride, which takes about 30 minutes, costs $8.

There's also a shop selling fresh fruit and a free-admission section that includes a nursery, a few taro plants and a couple of very simple exhibits on agriculture.

If you're driving by you might want to make a quick stop, but it's not worth going out of your way.

WAILUKU

Wailuku sits beneath the eastern flank of the West Maui Mountains and is an interesting juxtaposition of old and new. While the central area serves as the county capital, complete with a few mid-rise government buildings, the back streets are lined with a colorful hodgepodge of older shops and neighborhood restaurants. Wailuku is unabashedly local – there's nothing touristy in the whole town.

It's a fun town for strolling. Begin walking north from West Main St on Market St which has a handful of pawn shops, galleries and antique shops, some of them intriguingly cluttered affairs. One of the more interesting shops is Traders of the

Lost Art, which has ancestral carvings and ritual art from Papua New Guinea, Oceania and the Antipodes and some fairly inexpensive used aloha shirts. Other shops have a mishmash of goods that include Hawaiiana, Thai and Indonesian handicrafts and lots of odds and ends.

Kaahumanu Church

Kaahumanu Church, on the corner of West Main and High Sts, dates from 1837, making it the oldest Congregational church in Maui. The present building was built in 1876 by missionary Edward Bailey.

The church was named in honor of Queen Kaahumanu who cast aside the old gods and burned temple idols, allowing Christianity to flourish. She visited Wailuku in 1832 and in her ever-humble manner requested that the first church bear her name.

The old clock in the steeple was brought around the Horn in the 19th century and it still keeps accurate time. Hymns are sung in Hawaiian at Sunday morning services.

Bailey House Museum

The Bailey House, a five-minute walk up Iao Valley Rd from Kaahumanu Church, was home to the family of missionary Edward Bailey who came to Wailuku from Boston in 1837.

The building, also called Hale Hoikeike, is the headquarters of the Maui Historical Society, which has turned the former mission house into a little museum.

There's a Hawaiiana section with stone adzes, tapa, bottle gourds, calabashes and the like, as well as period furnishings from the missionary days. Bailey was a painter and engraver and many of his works are on display.

One of the most interesting sights is a surfboard used by Olympian Duke Kahanamoku; it can be seen above the parking lot at the side of the shed. Compare it to today's sleek fiberglass boards – this six-footer is made of redwood and weighs in at a hefty 150 pounds!

The museum gift shop has some good quality Hawaiiana crafts. During the day

MAUI

from Tuesday to Saturday Uncle Sol Kawaihoa teaches ukulele and slack-key guitar.

The museum is open from 10 am to 4 pm Monday to Friday. Admission is $3 for adults, $1 for children ages six to 12.

Places to Stay

Banana Bungalow (☎ 244-5090, (800) 846-7835), 310 Lower Market St, Wailuku, HI 96793, is a modest nonsmoking hostel with cheap beds, a friendly management and lots of international travelers. Private rooms are simple but clean and cost $32/39 for singles/doubles, while space in one of the dorm rooms, which have three to four beds each, costs $15. Bedding is provided. There are weekly and monthly discounts. All guests share community showers and toilets. There's a TV room, group kitchen, coin laundry, volleyball court, shed for storing windsurfing gear, free coffee and tea and a free shuttle to the airport and Kanaha Beach. Banana Bungalow organizes activities, including sunrise trips to Haleakala for $15 (breakfast and lunch included) when enough guests are interested, and rents boogie boards or snorkeling gear for $3 a day and sea kayaks for

Uncle Sol Kawaihoa

$15. If you need a car, they can arrange rusty clunkers from about $13 a day with a three-day minimum.

Located in the center of Wailuku, the *Northshore Inn* (☎ 242-8999), 2080 Vineyard St, Wailuku, HI 96793, is popular with European windsurfers, mostly from Germany. It has a few simple rooms with small refrigerators and shared baths (one also has TV and air-conditioning) for $30/40 for singles/doubles. A better deal are the community rooms, which have four to six bunks to a room and cost $15 per bunk. Add on $1 to rent a cover sheet and another dollar if you want a blanket. There's a community area with a TV near the front desk and a small group kitchen. Free shuttle pick-up is sometimes available from the airport.

Places to Eat

Wailuku has a nice range of good, reasonably priced restaurants. Within a few minutes' walk from the intersection of Vineyard and Market Sts there's Thai, Japanese, Hawaiian and just plain local food. As this is the government center, there are a lot of good weekday lunch deals, but most restaurants are closed at lunchtime on Saturdays and Sundays.

Saeng's Thai Cuisine (☎ 244-1567), 2119 Vineyard St, has excellent food and a pleasant setting with open-air dining. While it's known for its curries, other dishes such as the Thai ginger shrimp and satay tofu are also delicious. There are a dozen vegetarian dishes for around $8.50, while most meat and shrimp dishes are in the $9 to $11 range. It's open from 11 am to 2:30 pm on weekdays and from 5 to 9:30 pm nightly. The menu is the same at both lunch and dinner.

Two blocks away and run by a relative, *Siam Thai* (☎ 244-3817), 123 North Market St, also has good food. Although the atmosphere is more local in flavor, the food is nearly the same as at Saeng's and the prices are a bit cheaper. The 'Evil Prince' fish, with tender slices of fresh mahimahi, is a good choice and costs $8. The menu also includes over a dozen vegetarian

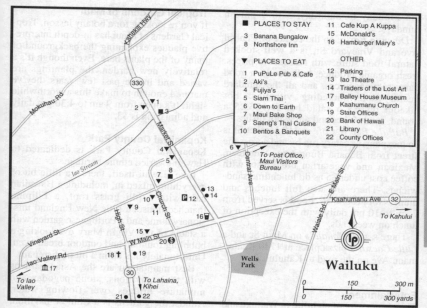

MAUI

Wailuku

To Post Office,
Maui Visitors
Bureau

To Kahului

To Iao
Valley

To Lahaina,
Kihei

Wells
Park

0   150   300 m
0   150   300 yards

dishes that average $7. The hours are identical to Saeng's.

Bentos & Banquets (☎ 244-1124), at 85 Church St, has takeout lunch specials from 10 am to 2 pm weekdays that are quite popular with local businesspeople. The menu changes daily, though a few dishes like roast pork, teriyaki steak and vegetarian tofu are standards. Most lunches cost around $6.

Cafe Kup a Kuppa, next door at 79 Church St, has quality deli food at cafeteria prices and is open from 7 am to 4:30 pm Monday to Friday and 8 am to 3 pm on weekends. A favorite is the breakfast burrito, which is filled with eggs, potatoes, cheese and homemade salsa and costs $3.50. A Belgian waffle with fresh fruit and whipped cream costs $4.50. Lunch features quesadillas, pizza and sandwiches for around $6 and a good fresh ahi plate with Caesar salad for $7. You can order takeout or eat in the upstairs dining room.

Maui Bake Shop & Deli, a small family-run operation at 2092 Vineyard St, has a wide variety of pastries as well as soups, salads and sandwiches at reasonable prices. The cinnamon-raisin rolls ($1.25) are huge and tasty and for those who like to linger the shop offers a free coffee refill. It's open from 6 am to 6:30 pm weekdays and from 7 am to 5 pm on Saturdays.

Fujiya's, 133 Market St, has a wide variety of Japanese dishes in the $5 to $8 range and some good dinner teishoku combinations for $9.50. Hours are 11 am to 2 pm Monday to Friday and 5 to 9 pm Monday to Saturday, although they commonly stop taking orders 15 minutes before closing time. No credit cards accepted.

Aki's, a five-minute walk north from Fujiya's on Market St, serves Hawaiian food. Kalua pig with cabbage and salad costs $5, a small octopus with coconut milk is $3.35 and a side of poi is $1.60. It's a local experience. Hours are 11 am to 9 pm Monday to Saturday, 5 to 9 pm on Sundays.

Down to Earth, on the corner of Central Ave and Vineyard St, is a well-stocked natural food store with reasonable prices, fresh organic produce, bulk foods, a good dairy section, juices, and all the standard health foods including vitamins. For takeout there's a salad bar for $3.25 a pound, sandwiches and a few hot dishes.

PuPuLe Pub & Cafe at 318 Market St is an inexpensive eatery run by and across the street from Banana Bungalow. American, Mexican and vegetarian breakfasts with coffee cost under $5 as do lunchtime sandwiches. There are also full lunches and dinners for around $6. Food is served from 7 am to 10 pm daily with the exception of lunch on weekends.

There's a *McDonald's* on Main St and a *Little Caesar's* pizza place at 1740 Kaahumanu Ave on the road to Kahului.

Entertainment

There's not a lot of nightlife in Wailuku and most people head off to Lahaina or to Casanova's in Makawao.

Hamburger Mary's, 2010 Main St, is a popular evening spot for the gay community.

Local theater groups sometimes present plays at the old *Iao Theatre* on Market St, which after years of neglect has recently been taken over by the county and is in the process of being restored.

IAO VALLEY ROAD

In 1790 Kamehameha I attacked Kahului by sea and quickly routed the defending Mauian warriors up into precipitous Iao Valley. Those unable to escape over the mountains were slaughtered along the stream. The waters of Iao Stream were so choked with bodies that the area was called Kepaniwai, meaning 'Dammed Waters'.

Today much of the upper valley along the stream is parkland. Iao Valley Rd leads into the scenic Iao Valley State Park, passing a few sights along the way.

Tropical Gardens of Maui

If you're looking for a botany lesson, Tropical Gardens of Maui has in-depth interpretive plaques explaining the background of many of the plants here. Even though it's a relatively new garden, the plantings are varied and in the past few years they've matured enough to make this a worthwhile sight. It's open from 9 am to 4:30 pm daily and admission is $3.

Kepaniwai County Park

Kepaniwai County Park is dedicated to Hawaii's varied ethnic heritage.

Like Hawaii itself, there's a little bit of everything mixed in, including a Hawaiian hale with a pili grass roof, a Filipino thatched house, a little New England missionary home and a Portuguese garden with a statue of the Virgin Mary overlooking a bubbling fountain and outdoor bread oven. Unfortunately it's all in a bit of disrepair.

Best maintained are the Asian gardens with their pavilions, stone pagodas and miniature bridges over flowing water. Amidst the gardens is a Chinese pavilion, red and white with a green ceramic tile roof, and the requisite statue of Sun Yatsen. Nearby a bronze statue of two Japanese sugar cane workers in traditional garb commemorates the centennial of Japanese immigration to the islands.

Iao Stream, which runs through the park, is bordered by pavilions with tables and barbecue pits that are well-used for picnics and parties.

JFK Profile

A half mile after Kepaniwai Park you'll come to a bend in the road where there are often a few cars pulled over and people staring off into Pali Eleele, a gorge on the right. One of the rock formations on the cliff face looks surprisingly like John F Kennedy's profile. There's a pipe set up as a scope to help you find the obvious.

Iao Valley State Park

Iao Valley State Park is nestled in the mountains at the 2250-foot elevation, three miles out of central Wailuku. The valley is named for Iao, the beautiful daughter of Maui and Hina.

Iao Needle, a rock pinnacle that rises 1200 feet from the valley floor, is said to be Iao's clandestine lover whom Maui captured and turned to stone.

Clouds often rise up the valley, forming a shroud around the top of Iao Needle. A stream meanders beneath the needle and the steep cliffs of the West Maui Mountains form a scenic backdrop.

A minute's walk from the parking lot, you'll reach a bridge where most people stop to photograph Iao Needle. However, just before the bridge there's a walkway looping downhill by the stream and if you take it you'll find the nicest photo angle – one that captures the stream, bridge and Iao Needle together.

Over the bridge, a short walkway leads up to a sheltered lookout with another fine view of Iao Needle. If you go a little bit farther along the trail that begins beyond the lookout you'll see Iao Needle from a closer and completely different angle.

Coming down from the lookout, those who want to explore further can turn to the right, take the steps down to the stream and then follow a well-beaten path 10 to 15 minutes upstream over rocks and tree roots and through yellow ginger. There are some pools deep enough for a dip along this path – though the mosquitoes can be thick.

HALEKII & PIHANAKALANI HEIAUS

Halekii-Pihanakalani Heiaus State Monument marks one of Maui's most important pre-contact historical sites.

Kahekili, the last ruling chief of Maui, lived here and Keopuolani, wife of Kamehameha I and mother of Kamehamehas II and III, was born at this site. After the decisive battle of Iao in 1790, Kamehameha I came to these heiaus to worship his war god Ku, offering what is thought to have been the last human sacrifice on Maui.

The two adjoining heiaus are atop a knoll and have a commanding view of the entire region, clear across the plains of central Maui and up the slopes of Haleakala. The temples were built with stones carried up from Iao Stream.

Halekii (literally 'House of the Idol'), the first heiau, has stepped stone walls and a flat grassy top. (Watch out for bullhead thorns if you're wearing flip-flops.) The pyramid-like mound of Pihanakalani Heiau is directly ahead, a five-minute walk away.

Pihanakalani, which means 'gathering place of supernatural beings', is fairly overgrown with kiawe, wildflowers and weeds. Few people come this way and as you approach doves fly up from the bushes.

Despite the heiaus' status as a state monument, the government has been somewhat negligent about the site. This is one of the fastest growing residential areas on Maui, and construction and gravel removal along both sides of the hill has been so widespread that some conservationists are fearful that the heiau site itself is being undermined.

Nevertheless, a certain spiritual essence still emanates from the site. Ignore the industrial warehouses and tract homes around the base of the hill and concentrate instead on the stacked stones of the heiau and the wide vistas to imagine it all through the eyes of the Hawaiians 200 years back. It must have been an incredible scene.

From Waiehu Beach Rd, turn mauka onto Kuhio St, which is three-quarters of a mile south of the intersection of Hwy 340 and Hwy 330. Then take the first left off Kuhio St onto Hea Place and drive up through the gates. The heiaus are less than half a mile from Hwy 340.

KAHEKILI HIGHWAY

Kahekili Highway (Hwy 340) curves around the undeveloped northeastern side of the West Maui Mountains. It's ruggedly scenic, with deep ravines, eroded red hills and rock-strewn pastures. The coastline is rocky lava sea cliffs and open ocean.

The route is pastoral and quiet with a couple of waterfalls, blowholes and one-lane bridges. It's common to spot cowhands on horseback, and egrets riding the backs of lazy cows. As a scenic coastal drive, it's second only to the road to Hana.

MAUI

MAUI

The northern end of the road is at Honokohau, the south at Wailuku, a distance of about 22 miles.

Like its counterpart to the south (the Piilani Hwy around the southern flank of Haleakala), Hwy 340 is shown either as a black hole or an unpaved road on most tourist maps. The road, however, is paved its entire length – albeit much of the drive is very winding and narrow, often just one lane, with blind curves and the occasional sign warning of falling rocks. While most of the road is posted 15 mph, there are sections where it's a mere 5 mph. But taking it slowly is the whole point anyway.

Waiehu & Waihee

Waiehu Beach Rd turns into Kahekili Hwy at the northern end of Wailuku and heads through pineapple fields and the little towns of Waiehu and Waihee. Waihee Country Store is the last store until you reach Kapalua on the other side.

Waiehu Municipal Golf Course is down near the shore, bordered by two county beach parks that have poor swimming conditions and, other than for strolling and beachcombing, little appeal.

Rock Arch

From the direction of Wailuku, the road climbs up into the mountains and the scenery just gets better.

There's a natural rock arch on the coastline that you can see by stopping at the little dirt turn-off that comes up at a bend midway between the five- and six-mile markers.

Waihee Ridge Trail

A side road up to the Boy Scouts' Camp Mahulia is a pretty winding drive through open pasture that leads to the start of the Waihee Ridge Trail. This trail is one of our favorites, a peaceful seldom-trodden route offering varied scenery and breathtaking views of the interior.

The drive up, which begins mauka just before the seven-mile marker, is a good one-lane paved road, but be prepared to stop for cattle crossing the pavement.

The trailhead is a mile up, on the left just before the camp, marked with a sign and a squeeze-through 'turnstile' through the fence. Another sign announces a $1000 reward for information leading to the arrest of cattle rustlers!

The trail is three miles one way, and takes about three hours round-trip. Consider packing a lunch, as there's a picnic table with an unbeatable view at the end. It's a well-defined trail that crosses forest reserve land and though it's a bit steep, it's a fairly steady climb and not overly strenuous.

Starting at an elevation of 1000 feet, the trail climbs a ridge, passing from pasture to cool forest, much of it through groves of rainbow eucalyptus trees. Guava are also prominent along the trail and if you look closely, you can usually find thimbleberries as well. From the three-quarter-mile post, panoramic views open up with a spectacular scene that sweeps clear down to the ocean along the Waihee Gorge and deep into the interior valleys. The ridge-top views are similar to those you'd see from a helicopter although the stillness along this route can only be appreciated by those on foot. The trail ends at the 2563-foot peak of Lanilili where there are great views in all directions, including one of the 4480-foot Eke Crater to the southwest.

Waterfalls & Tikis

Back on the highway, you'll pass a gentle waterfall on the left, rain permitting. Then at the pull-off just past the eight-mile marker a big waterfall flows into a pool in the ravine below.

Halfway between the nine- and 10-mile markers, keep an eye out for a metal gate mauka of the road, where there are two carved wooden tiki images.

Kahakuloa

The village of Kahakuloa is at the base of a small green valley. Although there are only a few dozen simple homes, Kahakuloa ('Tall Lord') has two churches. The little tin-roofed Catholic mission sits up a hill at the southern end of town, just off the road. On the valley floor is the green wooden

Protestant church with its red-tiled roof, birds of paradise by the door and shell ginger out front.

Up out of the valley at the northern edge of town there's a pull-off with a good view of the village and its boulder beach. The rise on the south side of Kahakuloa Bay is Kahakuloa Head, 636 feet high.

Bellstone

An sign marks Pohaku Kani, a large bell-stone on the side of the road just past the 16-mile marker.

If you hit the bellstone with a rock on the Kahakuloa side where the deepest indentations are you might be able to get a hollow sound. It's pretty resonant if you hit it right, but it takes some imagination to hear it ring like a bell.

Pastures & Cliffs

The wide turn-off about half a mile beyond the 16-mile marker looks down over a clifftop plateau with a rugged coast and crashing surf. The stretch of green turf practically invites you to walk from the road down to the cliffs and out along the coastline. Although it's unshaded, it would be a fine place to break out a bottle of wine and a picnic lunch.

This is hilly country, with rocky cattle pastures and tall sisal plants. There are a number of viewpoints and pull-offs where you can stop and explore.

Stone cairns are piled everywhere. They look like religious offerings, but most are just the creations of sightseers and are of no significance.

Blowhole

There's a blowhole visible from the road just past the 20-mile marker. After a sharp bend, look for a small pull-off on the mauka side of the road, opposite the area where the guardrail ends. Walk across the road and look down to the left for the blowhole. During the winter season, we've seen humpbacks breaching offshore in this area as well.

Nakalele Point Light Station

There's a walk out to the light station at the end of Nakalele Point about half a mile past the blowhole pull-off. The coastline has interesting pools, arches and other formations worn out of the rocks by the pounding of the surf. As elsewhere in Maui, don't leave valuables in your car at the parking area. The smashed glass from broken windshields is indicative of the break-ins that take place here.

As you continue north along the road, Molokai comes into view and the scenery is very lush on the way to Honokohau Bay.

Paia

Paia is an old sugar town with a fresh coat of paint.

As part of the original Alexander & Baldwin sugar plantation, Paia had a population of about 8000 in the early 1900s, more than triple its present size. In those days most Paia residents lived in plantation camps that were located on the slopes above the sugar mill.

The mill is still open though its heyday is past. During the 1950s many of the town's residents moved to Kahului, shops closed down and Paia began to collect cobwebs.

In the early 1980s windsurfers discovered nearby Hookipa Beach and Paia was dubbed the 'Windsurfing Capital of the World'.

Today Paia has as many windsurfers as sugar cane workers. They come from all over the world, including Germany, France and Australia, giving Paia more of an international flavor than any other small town in Hawaii.

Paia has small grocery stores that have been in the same families for generations and offbeat shops selling Balinese clothing and antique aloha shirts. Many of the old wooden storefronts are painted in bright tones of rose pink, sunshine yellow and sky blue, adding to the town's unique character.

The Hana Highway (Hwy 36) runs

MAUI

straight through the center of Paia – this is the last real town before Hana and the last place to gas up your car.

Paia is also a link to the Upcountry; Baldwin Ave leads from the center of town up to Makawao.

Information
Mana Foods on Baldwin Ave has a good bulletin board, with rooms for rent tacked up amid notices of such things as windsurfing lessons, Tibetan pulsing healing and tai chi classes.

Money Bank of Hawaii on Baldwin Ave is open from 8:30 am to 3 pm Monday to Thursday, 8:30 am to 6 pm on Fridays. If you want to make a credit card or ATM card withdrawal, there's a Bankoh money machine at the Minit Stop.

Post The post office, on Baldwin Ave, is open from 8 am to 4:30 pm Monday to

Friday and from 10:30 am to 12:30 pm on Saturdays.

Laundry There's a coin laundry on Baldwin Ave, just south of the Vegan Restaurant, that's open from 7:30 am to 8 pm daily.

Board Rentals Big Wave in the Paia Town Center on the Hana Hwy rents surfboards for $25 a day. Hi-Tech Surf Sports on Baldwin Ave rents boogie boards for $8/45 a day/week and also sells surfboards and accessories.

Spreckelsville Beach
Spreckelsville Beach, by the golf course between Kahului Airport and Paia, is a hot windsurfing spot. It's one of the windiest places on the north shore, with the best wind conditions occurring in summer.

Spreckelsville is a long stretch of beach composed of sandy stretches punctuated

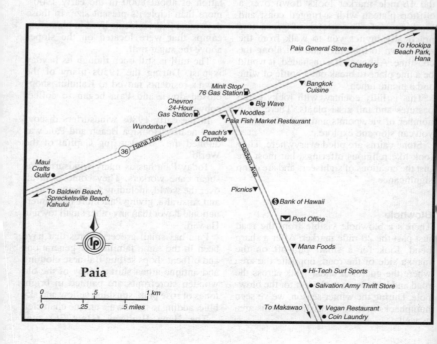

Paia

To Hookipa Beach Park, Hana

Paia General Store ●
▼ Charley's
▼ Bangkok Cuisine
Minit Stop/ 76 Gas Station
Chevron 24-Hour Gas Station
● Big Wave
▼ Noodles
Paia Fish Market Restaurant
Wunderbar ▼
Peach's & Crumble ▼
Maui Crafts Guild ●
Hana Hwy 36
To Baldwin Beach, Spreckelsville Beach, Kahului
Picnics ▼
Baldwin Ave
$ Bank of Hawaii
✉ Post Office
▼ Mana Foods
● Hi-Tech Surf Sports
● Salvation Army Thrift Store
To Makawao
▼ Vegan Restaurant
● Coin Laundry

0   .5   1 km
0   .25   .5 miles

with lava outcrops. Although much of the beach is rocky, there are a number of spots with reasonably good swimming.

To get there turn makai on Nonohe Rd, which runs along the west side of the Maui Country Club. Turn right when the road ends and look for the beach access sign.

Baldwin Beach Park

Baldwin Beach Park, a big county park about a mile west of Paia, has a long sandy beach with good bodysurfing. There are showers, restrooms, picnic tables, a phone and camping. The park also has a well-used baseball and soccer field, which tends to make it a rather congested scene.

The tent spaces are on a flat grassy spot by the road, surrounded by a chain-link fence. Even with the high visibility it's not a particularly secure place to stay and in recent years there have been some serious assaults on campers at this site.

Maui Crafts Guild

Maui Crafts Guild, on the left as you come into town from Kahului, is a collective of Maui artists and craftspeople. It is the island's best crafts shop, with dyed cloth, woodwork, pottery, baskets, beadwork, shakuhachi flutes and more. Guild members take turns staffing the store once a month and prices are much lower than in private galleries around the island.

Even if you're not looking to buy, it's worth a stop as this place is almost a crafts museum. There's also a nice view of the surrounding sugar cane fields from the top floor. It's open from 9 am to 6 pm daily.

Paia Mill

The century-old Paia Mill sits above town, less than a mile up Baldwin Ave. The power plant adjacent to the mill burns bagasse, the fiber residue of the sugar cane plant, producing steam power to run the mill.

The mill operates 24 hours a day, shutting down only four days a month. It's a whole little world of its own, and when you pass by at night it seems oddly surreal with all the lights glowing and the buzz of activity.

Rather than the more common process of squeezing sugar cane by rollers, the Paia Mill flushes juice out of shredded sugar cane in a process resembling that of a drip coffeemaker.

Mantokuji Buddhist Mission

Mantokuji, a Buddhist temple with an ocean view and a big gong in the yard, is on the Hana side of town. It's fronted with a graveyard of kanji-engraved stones, some decorated with colorful tropical flowers. During summer, the Obon holidays are observed here with religious services and Japanese dances.

Hookipa Beach Park

Hookipa, which has long been one of Maui's prime surfing spots, has more recently established itself as Hawaii's premier windsurfing spot. It has good year-round action for both – winter has the biggest waves for board surfers and summer has the most consistent winds for windsurfers.

Hookipa Beach attracts the world's top windsurfers. It is the site of several international tournaments, including the Marui/O'Neill Invitational in April and the Aloha Classic in October.

Between the strong currents, dangerous shorebreak and razor-sharp coral, this is unquestionably an area for experts. As a spectator sport, it's great – if you come by at the right time you'll be watching some of the best action to be found anywhere.

Hookipa is just before the nine-mile marker; look for the line of cars on the lookout above the beach. This county park has restrooms, showers, pay phones and picnic pavilions.

Places to Stay

While Paia has no hotels, there are a number of smaller private places to stay. Most are rented out through B&B-type services, though you can also find them by checking bulletin boards around Paia and looking through the 'Vacation Rentals' column in the *Maui News* classifieds. If you're staying any length of time, you might be able to get a room of your own in a shared house for as little as $250 to $300 a month.

The four accommodation listings that follow can be booked direct. With the exception of Hale Aloha, which is midway between Kuau and Paia, they are all near the eight-mile marker in Kuau. Kuau is about two miles west of downtown Paia and is the closest neighborhood to Hookipa.

Mike Doherty (☎ 579-9430), 4 Kaiholo Place, Paia, HI 96770, has a small apartment house with three units that he rents out as *North Shore Vacation Rental*. There's a good-sized studio that rents for $40, a one-bedroom unit for $45 and a two-bedroom unit for $65. Each has a private bath and cooking facilities. Most guests are windsurfers and the location is close enough to the beach that you can keep sails rigged in the yard, walk down the street and sail away. Guests have free use of a washer and dryer, and there's storage space for up to 30 boards.

Kuau Plaza (☎ 579-8080), 777 Hana Hwy, Paia, HI 96779, is a run-down 30-unit condo on the main road. Hotel-style rooms with TV cost $35/200 a day/week and one-bedroom units with kitchen and TV are $65/350. There's a three-day minimum.

Hale Aloha (☎ 579-9849), 16 Kulani Place, Paia, HI 96779, is a new two-story plantation-style house with large airy lanais and a nice laid-back character. It's about 500 yards mauka of the Hana Hwy in a quiet setting on the edge of cane fields. There are three studios with microwaves and small refrigerators that rent for $45, a roomier one-bedroom unit that rents for $60, a small two-bedroom unit for $75 and a large two-bedroom unit that has a full kitchen and sleeps up to six people for $125. There's free use of a washer and dryer and each room has a fan and phone.

Terry and Margit Tolman (☎ 579-9333, (800) 398-6284; fax 579-9953), Box S, Paia, HI 96779, have two units called *Hookipa Haven*. A one-bedroom apartment on the 1st floor of their home rents for $60. It has a queen bed, kitchen, bathroom,

private entrance and a hideaway bed in the living room. There's also a fully furnished two-bedroom cottage on the grounds that costs $85 for two people or $95 for four, though the walls open at the ceiling so there's no sound barrier between the rooms. There's a $150 deposit in the studio, $200 in the cottage. Margit has a small vacation rental service and books other accommodation in the Paia and Haiku areas, with daily rates starting at about $50 for studios.

Places to Eat

Picnics, 30 Baldwin Ave, is a deli with both takeout and eat-in service. Sandwiches include mahimahi and teriyaki, as well as more creative options like the vegetarian spinach nut burger with cheddar cheese for $5.50. There are excellent breakfast pastries, most priced around $1.50, including cherry Danish, large cinnamon rolls and orange pecan scones. Picnics also has both fruit and vegetable salads, cappuccino and espresso. There is a guide to the Hana Hwy on the back of the takeout menu and they prepare picnic box lunches for the road. Hours are 7:30 am to 3 pm daily. From noon to 3 pm you can get coffee and your choice of pastry for $1.75.

Peach's & Crumble Cafe & Bakery on Baldwin Ave has scones, muffins, croissants and peach crumble squares for $1 to $2.50 and sandwiches such as Mexican avocado, nutty vegie burger and smoked salmon for around $5. There are also daily specials that might include enchilada pie or lasagna, as well as picnic lunches ($7) to go. It's open from 6:30 am to at least 6 pm daily.

The *Vegan Restaurant* (☎ 579-9144), 115 Baldwin Ave, is a popular little restaurant serving tasty vegetarian food at reasonable prices. A vegan burger or one of the large salads, including guacamole, hummus and organic carrot varieties, costs $5. The menu includes a variety of imaginative dishes with Thai, Mexican and Japanese influences; a choice of two entrees with a salad costs $9. As there are only a dozen small cafe tables, it's best to arrive early for dinner to avoid a long wait. It's open from 11 am to 8:30 pm Tuesday to Sunday. Takeout is available.

Paia Fish Market Restaurant (☎ 579-8030), on the corner of Baldwin Ave and the Hana Hwy, serves burgers and Mexican food, but the specialty is fish, which is on display in a refrigerated case at the counter. The best deal is at lunch when the grilled fish sandwich on a whole-wheat bun costs $5. It's made with a slab of fresh fish of your choice – the selection usually includes ahi, marlin and mahimahi. At dinner the price jumps to $7. Another popular item, fresh fish & chips, costs $7 at lunch, $10 at dinner. It's open from 11 am to 9:30 pm daily.

Charley's on the Hana Hwy has pizza, pasta and meat dishes at moderate prices. For those who like to have a late breakfast, it's served from 7 am up until 2 pm, while lunch is from 11:30 am to 2 pm and dinner from 5 to 10 pm.

The *Wunderbar* (☎ 579-8808) on the Hana Hwy has the island's longest monkeypod bar and Paia's most upmarket food. This German-owned restaurant has a kitchen run by Swiss chef Bernard Weber, who formerly cooked for the king of Sweden. Dinner features various European foods, including pastas for around $10, wiener schnitzel for $17 and rack of lamb for $19. At lunch, there are cold plates and salads for around $10. It's all quite European – right down to the outdoor beer garden serving Warsteiner on tap.

For authentic Thai food, the family-run *Bangkok Cuisine* (☎ 579-8979), 120 Hana Hwy, has an extensive menu that includes curries, pad Thai, and various shrimp, fish and meat dishes. Most are priced from $7 to $10. It's open from 11 am to 3 pm and 5 to 9:30 pm.

Noodles (☎ 579-8383), on the corner of Baldwin Ave and the Hana Hwy, has cold noodle dishes from $3.50 and a range of hot noodle dishes such as saimin, linguine tofu and clam, chow fun, and won ton mein for $4.25 to $5.75. It's open from 10 am to 9 pm daily for sit-down dining, takeout or delivery service.

Mana Foods on Baldwin Ave is a large down-to-earth health food store with a good variety of juices, yogurts, bulk nuts, granola, cheeses and organic produce. It also has some excellent fresh baked breads, including a round loaf filled with tomatoes and feta cheese ($3.50) that makes a nice meal in itself. There's a small salad bar and a few inexpensive takeout hot dishes. Mana is open from 9 am to 7 pm on Sundays, 8 am to 8 pm other days, and like most grocery stores in Hawaii takes Visa and MasterCard.

Entertainment

The *Wunderbar* (☎ 579-8808) has live entertainment on Thursday, Friday and Saturday nights and occasionally on Tuesdays or Sundays. Saturday is blues night, while at other times it ranges from calypso to acoustic guitar. The cover charge is generally $3.

Road to Hana

The Hana Highway runs from central Maui to the village of Hana and beyond to the pools of Oheo Gulch. While all the islands have some incredible scenery, the Hana Hwy ranks as *the* most spectacular coastal drive in Hawaii. This road, which was built in 1927 using convict labor, is also very narrow; in many places it's essentially one-and-a-half lanes wide, with two-lane traffic!

The Hana Hwy is a cliff-hugger as it winds deep into lush valleys and back out above a rugged coastline, snaking around more than 600 twists and turns along the way.

One-lane bridges mark dozens of waterfalls. Some are tiny and Zen-like, others sheer and lacy. The 54 bridges to Hana have 54 poetic Hawaiian names taken from the streams and gulches they cross – names like Heavenly Mist, Prayer Blossoms and Reawakening.

The valleys drip with vegetation. There are dense rainforests, bamboo groves and

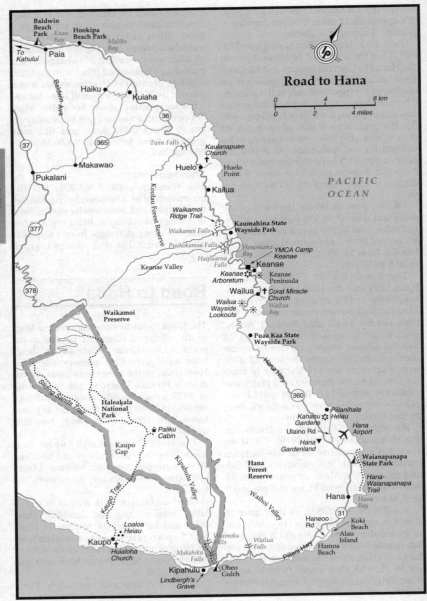

Road to Hana

fern-covered hillsides. African tulip trees add bright splashes of orange.

It would take about two hours to drive straight through from Kahului to Hana. But this is not a drive to rush. If you're not staying over in Hana, get an early start to give yourself a full day. There are short trails to hike, mountain pools to dip in and a couple of historic sites to check out, all just a few minutes beyond the road for those with time to explore.

Remember to pull over if local drivers are behind you. They have places to get to and move at a different pace.

Paia to Hwy 360

A couple of miles past Paia the road passes Hookipa Beach, where there's a clifftop vantage point of the surfing action.

After Hookipa, fields of sugar cane give way to rows of pineapples. You'll pass through Haiku, but there's not much to see as it's a spread-out little town, most of it up the slopes.

Hwy 365, which leads up to Makawao and other Upcountry towns, comes in just after the 16-mile marker. At this point the Hana Hwy changes from No 36 to No 360 and the mile markers begin again at zero.

The road then changes dramatically, slicing through cliffs and becoming more of a mountain road than a highway. Hana is 35 scenic miles away.

Huelo

Huelo Rd, half a mile past the three-mile marker, is a passable dirt road that leads down to Kaulanapueo Church, a coral and stone church built in 1853. The church is likely to be locked and if you're short on time this one can be easily bypassed.

Koolau Forest Reserve

After Huelo, the road winds and the vegetation becomes increasingly lush as the highway runs along the edge of the Koolau Forest Reserve.

Koolau, which means 'windward', is the windward side of Haleakala and catches the rain clouds. The coast in this area gets 60 to 80 inches of rain a year, while a few miles up on the slopes the annual rainfall is an impressive 200 to 300 inches.

The reserve is heavily forested and cut with numerous gulches and streams. From here there seems to be a one-lane bridge and a waterfall around every other bend.

Kailua

Kailua is home to many of the people who work for the East Maui Irrigation Company. They maintain the 75 miles of ditches and tunnels that bring water from the rainforests to the cane fields of dry central Maui. The century-old system is capable of carrying 450 million gallons of water a day.

Many of the dirt roads leading mauka from the highway are the maintenance roads for the **Koolau Ditch** which runs inland paralleling the highway.

If you want to take a closer look, stop at the small pull-off just before the bridge that comes up immediately after the eight-mile marker. Just 100 feet above the road you can see a section of the ditch, built of hand-hewn stone block, that meanders down the hillside and then tunnels into the rock face.

As you leave the village, you'll notice Norfolk pines up on the hillside, followed by a grove of painted eucalyptus trees with rainbow-colored bark, then a long stretch of bamboo and more painted eucalyptus.

Waikamoi Ridge Trail

Waikamoi Ridge Trail is a peaceful loop trail through tall trees with wonderful fresh scents. You're welcomed by a sign: 'Quiet. Trees at Work'.

Pull off at the unmarked turn-off half a mile after the nine-mile marker. The trailhead is up on the left beyond the covered picnic table.

This is an easy trail, three-quarters of a mile long. The grand reddish trees wrapped with huge climbing philodendron vines are eucalyptus *robusta*. (There couldn't be a better illustration of the etymology of philodendron, a Greek word meaning 'lover of trees'!) The trail also passes lots of hala, ferns and paper-bark eucalyptus trees.

Particularly if you're walking with children, keep an eye out for occasional metal spikes and tree roots that protrude along the path. From the ridge at the top there's a good view of the winding Hana Hwy.

Waikamoi Falls
Waikamoi Falls is at the bridge just before the 10-mile marker. There's a waterfall and pool near the road. It's possible to walk a short way up to a higher waterfall, but the rocks can be slippery and the bottom waterfall is prettier anyway.

Past Waikamoi, bamboo grows almost horizontally out from the cliff side creating a canopy effect over the road.

Puohokamoa Falls
Puohokamoa bridge and waterfall, at the 11-mile marker, is another pretty waterfall that's just a few minutes' walk from the road. Because there's more parking space and a couple of picnic tables, it's more visited than the Waikamoi or Haipuaena waterfalls.

Haipuaena Falls
Haipuaena Falls, half a mile after the 11-mile marker, is a gentle little waterfall with a wonderful pool deep enough for swimming.

Most people don't know this one's here as you can't see the pool from the road. If you want to take a dip but don't have a bathing suit, this seems like a good choice.

There's space for just one car, on the Hana side of the bridge. To reach the falls walk upstream for a couple of minutes. Wild ginger grows along the path and ferns hang from the rock wall behind the waterfall, making for a quite idyllic setting.

Kaumahina State Wayside Park
Kaumahina State Wayside Park is shortly after the 12-mile marker. A two-minute walk up the hill under the park's tall eucalyptus trees provides a broad ocean vista, with Keanae Peninsula to the southeast. The park has a large parking area, picnic tables and restrooms.

Honomanu Bay
For the next several miles, the scenery is particularly magnificent, opening up to a new vista as you round each bend. If you're on this road after heavy rains you can expect to see waterfalls galore smoking down the mountains.

Just after crossing the bridge at the 14-mile marker, an inconspicuous and very rough gravel road heads down to Honomanu Bay and a rocky black sand beach. The water's usually too turbulent for swimming and it's mostly used by surfers and fishers, though on very calm days it's possible to snorkel and dive there.

Keanae
Keanae is about halfway to Hana. The YMCA Camp Keanae is midway between the 16- and 17-mile markers. Within the next half mile the Keanae Arboretum, the road to Keanae Peninsula, and the Keanae Peninsula Lookout come up in quick succession.

Keanae Arboretum This arboretum, three-quarters of a mile past the 16-mile marker, has six acres of trees and numerous ornamental and food plants displayed along a marked nature walk. One area has introduced tropical plants, including painted eucalyptus trees and thickets of golden-stemmed bamboo with green stripes that look like the strokes of a Japanese shodo artist.

The trail leads up past sections of heliconia, ti, banana, guava, breadfruit, ginger and other fragrant plants. The higher ground has dozens of varieties of Hawaiian taro in irrigated patches, separated by earthen walls that serve as footpaths. If you have extra time, you could follow an unfrequented trail about a mile up the stream past the taro patches to a rainforest.

The Keanae Valley, which extends down from the Koolau Gap in Haleakala Crater, averages 150 inches of rain a year.

Keanae Peninsula The road down to Keanae Peninsula is just past the arboretum.

Lanakila Ihiihi O Iehova Ona Kaua (Keanae Congregational Church) is an attractive old (1860) stone church about half a mile down. This is one church made of lava rocks and coral mortar whose exterior hasn't been covered over with layers of whitewash. And rather than locked doors, there's a guest book and a 'Visitors Welcome' sign.

Keanae is a quiet little village with colts and goats roaming freely. At the end of the road there's a scenic coastline of jagged rock and pounding waves. The rock island down the coast is Mokumana Island, a seabird sanctuary.

Keanae Peninsula Lookout There's a good view of Keanae village, with its squares of planted taro fed by Keanae Stream, at an unmarked pull-off just past the 17-mile marker. Look for the mailbox under the tsunami speaker.

Keanae Peninsula was formed by a later eruption of Haleakala which flowed through Koolau Gap down Keanae Valley. Outlined with a black lava coastline, the peninsula still wears its birthmark around the edges. It's very flat, like a leaf floating on the water.

Places to Stay The *YMCA Camp Keanae*, on a knoll overlooking the coast, has three guest cabins that can sometimes fill with groups on weekends but are otherwise usually available for individual travelers as hostel-style dorms for $10 per person. The cabins have bunk beds but you have to bring your own sleeping bag, food and cookware. Cooking is on hibachi-style barbecue grills that are available from the caretaker. If you prefer to set up a tent you can do that instead of staying in the cabins. There's no pool but you can take a dip in nearby Ching's Pond. Because of space limitations, advance reservations are required and there's a three-night limit. Check-in is between 3 and 6 pm. Reserva-

tions are made through the Maui YMCA office (☎ 242-9007), 250 Kanaloa Ave, Kahului, HI 96732.

Fruit Stands
Waianu Fruit Stand, just past the Keanae Peninsula Lookout, is open from 8:30 am to 4 pm Monday to Saturday. They have fresh fruit, banana bread, coffee, ice cream and shave ice as well as a 24-hour soda machine and a pay phone.

Three quarters of a mile farther is Uncle Harry's snack shop, run by the family of the late Harry Kunihi Mitchell, a native Hawaiian rights advocate who wrote 'Mele O Kahoolawe' (Song of Kahoolawe) and represented the Hawaiian people in the Nuclear Free Pacific movement. The snack shop sells fruit, smoothies, chips and hot dogs from 9 am to 4 pm Monday to Saturday.

Wailua
Take Wailua Rd makai immediately after Uncle Harry's to get to **Our Lady of Fatima Shrine**, Wailua's main attraction.

This little white and blue chapel, built in 1860, is also known as the Coral Miracle Church. The coral used in the construction came from a freak storm which deposited coral rocks onto a nearby beach. Before this, men in the congregation had been diving quite deep but were only able to bring up a few pieces of coral at a time. After the church was completed another rogue storm hit the beach and swept all the leftover piles of coral back into the sea. Or so the story goes.

The chapel, recently renovated, has just half a dozen little pews. The current congregation now uses St Gabriel's Mission, the larger pink-shingled church out front.

From Wailua Rd you can also get a peek of the long cascade of **Waikani Falls**, which is just to the left of Wailua Lookout up on the Hana Hwy.

Wailua Rd dead ends half a mile down, though you might not want to go that far as driveways blocked off with logs and milk crates prevent cars from turning around.

MAUI

Wailua Wayside Lookout

Back on the Hana Hwy, just before the 19-mile marker, Wailua Wayside Lookout comes up on the right. It has a broad view into Keanae Valley, which appears to be a hundred shades of green. There are a couple of waterfalls in sight and if it's clear you can look up at Koolau Gap, a break in the rim of Haleakala Crater.

If you climb up the steps to the right you can get a good view of Wailua Peninsula, but there's a better view of it at a large paved turn-off a quarter of a mile down the road.

Puaa Kaa State Wayside Park

Midway between the 22- and 23-mile markers is Puaa Kaa State Wayside Park, where a tranquil waterfall empties into a pool before flowing down into a ravine.

There are shaded picnic tables along the stream, a pool that's large enough for swimming, restrooms and a pay phone. The only disadvantage to the site is the many stray cats that pester picnickers.

Hana Gardenland

Just before the 31-mile marker is Hana Gardenland, a combination landscape nursery, gift shop and cafe (see Places to Eat, Hana). There's a pleasant two-minute path shaded with exotic plants, the shop features Maui-made crafts and the nursery sells bromeliads and orchids. It's open from 9 am to 5 pm daily.

Kahanu Gardens

Kahanu Gardens (☎ 332-7361) is run by National Tropical Botanical Garden. This nonprofit foundation has been concentrating its efforts on repairing the damage caused by Hurricane Iniki to their main gardens on Kauai, and have consequently temporarily closed the Kahanu Gardens – so it's best to call ahead to see if they've reopened.

To get to Kahuna Gardens, turn makai onto Ulaino Rd just south of the 31-mile marker, it's 1½ miles to the entrance.

The 126-acre botanical garden on Kalahu Point has medicinal plants and eth-nobotanical collections of hala, breadfruit and coconut trees. On the grounds is **Piilanihale Heiau**, the largest heiau on Maui. It was built by Piilani, the 14th-century Mauian chief who is also credited with building many of the coastal fishponds and taro terraces in the Hana area.

Waianapanapa State Park

The road into Waianapanapa State Park is immediately after the 32-mile marker, half a mile south of the turn-off to Hana Airport. This 122-acre park has 12 cabins, tent camping, picnic pavilions, restrooms, showers and drinking water.

The road ends at a parking lot above Pailoa Bay, which is surrounded by a scenic coastline of low rocky cliffs. There's a natural lava arch on the right side of the bay. A short path from the parking lot leads down to the small black sand beach, which is unprotected and usually has strong rips. When it's very calm the area around the arch is said to be good for snorkeling. Check it out carefully, as people have drowned here.

Caves Two impressive lava-tube caves are just a five-minute walk from the parking lot along a loop path. On the outside the caves are covered with ferns and flowering impatiens. Inside they're dripping wet and cool on even the hottest days.

Waianapanapa means 'glistening waters' and should you be tempted to take a dip the clear mineral waters will leave you feeling squeaky clean.

On certain nights of the year, the waters in the cave turn red. Legend says it's the blood of a princess and her lover who were killed in a fit of rage by the princess's jealous husband after he found them hiding together here. Less romantic types account it to swarms of tiny bright red shrimp called *opaeula* which occasionally emerge from subterranean cracks in the lava.

Hana-Waianapanapa Trail A coastal trail that parallels the ancient 'King's Highway' leads south about two miles from the park to Kainalimu Bay, just north of Hana Bay.

Some of the original smooth lava stepping stones are still in place along the trail.

Past the cabins, the trail passes blowholes and the ruins of a heiau. There are gorgeous coastal views with cobalt blue water below craggy black lava outcrops. The most predominant vegetation is hala and beach naupaka, the latter with delicate white flowers that look as if they've been torn in half.

From the end of the trail it's about a mile farther to the center of Hana.

Camping Tent camping is free with a permit. The housekeeping cabins, which generally book out months in advance, cost $10/17 a single/double, plus about $6 for each additional person, up to a maximum of six people. Permits and reservations must be obtained in advance through one of the state park's district offices; Maui's (☎ 243-5354) is at 54 High St, Wailuku, HI 96793.

Hana

Separated from Kahului by 54 bridges and almost as many miles, Hana's isolation has thus far protected it from development and even though a line of traffic passes through each day not many visitors stay on.

Hana sits beneath the rainy slopes of Haleakala, surrounded by green pasture and a jagged black coastline. In ancient times it was the heart of one of Maui's largest population centers. The village itself was thought to have been reserved for the alii.

In the late 1800s, Chinese, Japanese and Portuguese laborers were brought in to work the newly planted sugar cane fields and Hana became a booming plantation town. A narrow-gauge railroad connected the fields to Hana Mill. In the 1940s Hana could no longer compete with larger sugar operations in central Maui and the mill shut down.

In 1943 Paul Fagan, a San Francisco businessman who owned Puu O Hoku Ranch on Molokai, purchased 14,000 acres in Hana. Starting with 300 Herefords, he converted the cane fields to ranch land.

A few years later Fagan opened a six-room hotel as a getaway resort for his well-to-do friends. Geographically and economically, Hana Ranch and the hotel became the hub of town.

Today Hana Ranch still has a few thousand head of cattle worked by Hawaiian cowhands. When the cattle are ready for Oahu stockyards, they're trucked all the way up the Hana Hwy to Kahului Harbor. The trucks leave early in the morning to avoid traffic.

Hana is not a grand finale to the magnificent Hana Hwy. People expecting great things are often disappointed. While the setting is pretty, the town is simple and sedate. What makes Hana special is more apparent to those who stay on. There's an almost timeless rural character and though 'Old Hawaii' is an oft-used cliche elsewhere, it's hard not to think of Hana in such terms.

Hana is one of the most Hawaiian communities in the state. Many of Hana's 1800 people have Hawaiian blood and a strong sense of ohana, or extended family. If you spend time around here you'll hear the words 'auntie' and 'uncle' a lot.

People in Hana hold on to their traditional ways and have largely been successful in warding off the kind of changes that have altered much of the rest of Maui. Their latest challenge has been resisting a plan to build a championship golf course on pasture lands above the Hana Ranch headquarters. The most popular bumper sticker, not just in Hana but in all of Maui, is 'Keep Hana Hawaiian – No Golf Courses'. In spite of the resistance, legal challenges have recently ruled in favor of the developers, although the county has imposed restrictions to discourage the construction of luxury homes around the course, and the project is still in limbo.

A small community of celebrities, including George Harrison and Kris Kristofferson, have long had homes in the Hana area.

MAUI

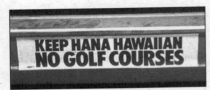

Bumper sticker politics

Information

Hana Ranch Center is the commercial center of town. It has a post office, open from 8 am to 4:30 pm weekdays; a tiny Bank of Hawaii, open Monday to Thursday from 3 to 4:30 pm and Fridays from 3 to 6 pm; and the Hana Ranch Store which sells groceries, liquor and a few odds and ends and is open from 7 am to 6:30 pm daily.

Hasegawa General Store has a Bankoh ATM that accepts MasterCard, Visa, Discover and American Express charge cards and Cirrus and Plus ATM cards. There are community bulletin boards outside of the post office and the two grocery stores.

Hana closes up early. If you're going to be heading back late, get gas in advance – the Chevron station, which has the longest hours, is open from 7:30 am to 6:30 pm daily. On most nights there's nothing open for dinner except the Hotel Hana-Maui.

Hana Airport is 3½ miles north of town. Dollar Rent-A-Car (☎ 248-8237) is at the airport.

The ball park has public tennis courts and Hana Ranch offers horseback riding.

Hasegawa General Store

The old Hasegawa General Store, Hana's best known sight, burned to the ground in 1990. After a brief hiatus, it relocated under the rusty tin roof of the old theater building in the town center. While some of its character was inevitably lost along with its eclectic inventory, it's still packed with just about everything from bags of poi and aloha dolls to fishing gear and machetes. Hasegawa also has clothing, groceries, hardware, newspapers and the record which immortalized the store in song. The business has been in the Hasegawa family since 1910. The store is open from 8 am to 5:30 pm Monday to Saturday, 9 am to 3:30 pm on Sundays.

Fagan Memorial

When Paul Fagan died in 1959 his family erected a memorial on Lyon's Hill, which was Fagan's favorite spot for watching the sunset. The huge hilltop cross is now Hana's most dominant landmark.

There's a trail up Lyon's Hill that's used by cyclists and joggers. It starts opposite the Hotel Hana-Maui and takes about 15 minutes to walk up. If you want to drive up, ask at the hotel front desk to borrow the gate key; there's a $10 deposit.

Wananalua Church

The Wananalua Congregational Church, south of the Hotel Hana-Maui, looks like an ancient Norman church. On the National Register of Historic Places, the current church was built in 1838 with thick walls of lava rock and coral mortar to replace the congregation's original grass church. There's a little cemetery at the side with graves randomly laid out rather than lined up in rows. Even at rest, Hana folks like things casual.

About 50 people still attend services each Sunday, though they're no longer conducted in Hawaiian.

Hana Cultural Center

Hana Cultural Center is a small museum with quilts, Hawaiian artifacts, woodcarvings and old photographs. It's a friendly community-run operation.

The same grounds has the old Hana district police station and three-bench courthouse which operated for over 100 years before closing in 1978. The museum is open from 10 am to 4 pm daily and a donation of $2 is suggested.

Hana Beach Park

Hana Beach Park is at the southern end of Hana Bay. It has a black sand beach, snack bar, showers, restrooms, small boat ramp and picnic tables.

Hana folks often come down here with

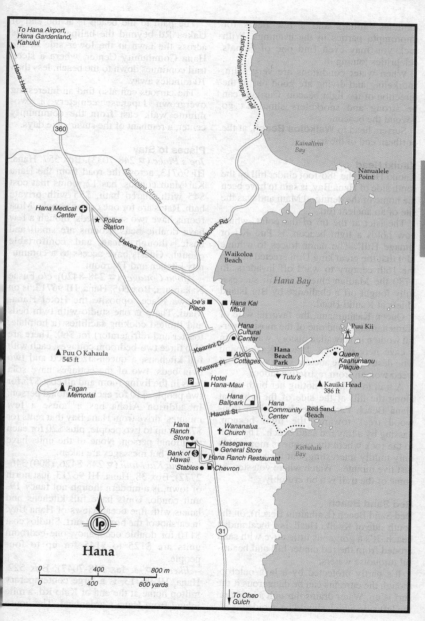

To Hana Airport,
Hana Gardenland,
Kahului

Hana Hwy

360

Kawaipapa Stream

Hana Medical
Center

Police
Station

Uakea Rd

▲ Puu O Kahaula
545 ft

Fagan
Memorial

Hana-Waianapanapa Trail

Kainalimu
Bay

Nanualele
Point

Waikoloa Rd

Waikoloa
Beach

Hana Bay

Puu Kii

Joe's
Place

Hana Kai
Maui

Hana
Cultural
Center

Keanini Dr

Aloha
Cottages

Keawa Pl

Hana
Beach Park

Queen
Kaahumanu
Plaque

▲ Kauiki Head
386 ft

Tutu's

Hotel
Hana-Maui

Hana
Ballpark

Hauoli St

Hana
Community
Center

Red Sand
Beach

Hana
Ranch
Store

Wananalua
Church

Hasegawa
General Store

Bank of
Hawaii

Hana Ranch Restaurant

Stables

Chevron

Kaihalulu
Bay

Hana

0   400   800 m
0   400   800 yards

31

To Oheo
Gulch

ukuleles, guitars and a few beers for impromptu parties in the evenings. With luck you may even find one of Hana's celebrities joining in.

When water conditions are very calm, snorkeling and diving are good out in the direction of the light beacon. Currents can be strong and snorkelers shouldn't go beyond the beacon.

Surfers head to **Waikoloa Beach**, at the northern end of the bay.

Kauiki Head

Kauiki Head, the 386-foot cinder hill on the south side of Hana Bay, is said to have been the home of the demigod Maui and was the site of an ancient fort.

The islet at the tip of the point, which now holds a light beacon, is Puu Kii or 'Image Hill'. The name traces to a huge idol that the great king Umi erected here in the 16th century to ward off invaders. In 1780 the Mauian chief Kahekili successfully fought off a challenge by Big Island chiefs at Kauiki Head.

Queen Kaahumanu, the favorite wife of Kamehameha I and one of the most powerful women in Hawaiian history, was born in a cave here in 1768. It was Kaahumanu who destroyed the ancient kapu system and freed women from restrictive taboos.

A trail to a plaque noting her birth starts along the hill at the side of the wharf at Hana Beach Park. It leads through ironwood trees towards the light beacon, passing by a tiny red sand beach. The walk to the rock where the plaque is mounted is only mildly interesting, but then again it's just five minutes. Watch where you step, as some of the trail is a bit crumbly.

Red Sand Beach

Red Sand Beach (Kaihalulu Beach), on the south side of Kauiki Head, is a local nudist beach. It's a gorgeous little cove with sand eroded from the red cinder hill and beautiful turquoise waters.

It's partly protected by a lava outcrop, though the currents can be dangerous if the surf is up. Water drains through a break on the left side which should be avoided.

The path to the beach is at the end of Uakea Rd beyond the ballpark. It starts across the lawn at the lower side of the Hana Community Center, where a steep trail continues down to the beach, less than 10 minutes away.

The curious can also find an interesting overgrown Japanese cemetery a two-minute walk east from the community center, a remnant of the sugar cane days.

Places to Stay

Joe's Place (☎ 248-7033), Box 557, Hana, HI 96713, across the road from the Hana Kai Maui condos, has 12 rooms that cost $45 with shared bath, $55 with private bath. Rates are for one or two people. Most rooms have two single beds, though a few have double beds. Rooms are small and basic, though clean and comfortable enough. Guests have access to a community kitchen and TV room.

Aloha Cottages (☎ 248-8420), c/o Fusae Nakamura, Box 205, Hana, HI 96713, is on Keawa Place, opposite the Hotel Hana-Maui. There is one studio with twin beds and limited cooking facilities (a hotplate, toaster and refrigerator) for $60. There are also three two-bedroom cottages, each with full kitchens, a queen-sized bed and two twin beds; two of the cottages have sofa beds in the living room and all cost $75 for two people, $10 for each additional person. In addition Aloha has a house a few minutes' drive from Hana Bay that rents for $75 for up to two people, plus $20 for each additional person. None of the units have phones, but messages are taken.

Hana Kai Maui (☎ 248-8426, (800) 346-2772), Box 38, Hana, HI 96713, just north of town, is a modern though not fancy 19-unit condo. Units have full kitchens and lanais with fine ocean views of Hana Bay, in earshot of the breaking surf. Studios cost $110 for double occupancy, one-bedroom units are $125 to $145 for up to four people.

Ekena (☎ & fax 248-7047), Box 522, Hana, HI 96713, is a large contemporary hilltop home at the end of Kalo Rd, a mile inland from Hana Gardenland. The house has great views, a fine setting and huge rooms with wraparound decks. It's divided into two rental units, both with kitchens, cable TV, VCR and washer and dryer. The first floor can be rented as a one-bedroom unit at $120 for up to two people or as a two-bedroom unit for $165 for up to four people, plus $10 for an extra person. The upstairs has wood-beam ceilings, two bedrooms and 2½ baths and costs $275 a day for up to four people, $300 for up to six people. There's a three-day minimum stay. Children under 14 are not allowed.

Hotel Hana-Maui (☎ 248-8211, (800) 321-4262), Hana, HI 96713, is one of Maui's more exclusive getaway hotels. On 23 acres in the center of town, the Hana-Maui is low profile, more like a plantation estate than a luxury hotel. Everything's very airy and open, with Hawaiian accents from local art to quilt bedspreads. The 61 rooms are mostly in one-story row cottages that have bleached hardwood floors, tiled baths, a view over a private garden and French doors to trellised patios. Pampering has its price – rates range from $305 to $795.

Vacation Rentals There are a few vacation rental agencies handling cottages and houses in the Hana area. As the properties can vary greatly in quality and maintenance, it's recommended that you get specific details, preferably with photos, before sending a deposit. Note that if you pay with a credit card, many of these companies tack on a 4% service charge.

Hana Alii Holidays (☎ 248-7742, (800) 548-0478), Box 536, Hana, HI 96713, manages about two dozen places, a mix of condos, private homes and cottages. They can be rented by the day, week and month. Daily rates range from a studio condo at $75 to a home for $275.

Blair's Original Hana Plantation Houses (☎ 248-7049, (800) 228-4262; fax 248-8240), Box 249, Hana, HI 96713, rents nine houses. At the low end there's a little Japanese-style studio with an efficiency kitchen and a spa on the deck for $80 and at the high end a two-bedroom home on a

black sand beach for $160. The houses are about 10 minutes outside town and all have cooking facilities. Rates are for up to two people; add $10 for each extra person.

Hana Ohana Plantation Houses (☎ 248-7248, (800) 240-7612; fax 248-7469), Box 1029, Hana, HI 96713, has a variety of rentals from around $100 a night.

Hana Bay Vacation Rentals (☎ 248-7727, (800) 657-7970), Box 318, Hana, HI 96713, also manages a handful of properties.

Camping There's tent camping and cabins at Waianapanapa State Park, just north of Hana, and tent camping at Oheo Gulch, 10 miles south of Hana. If you plan to camp at Oheo, you'll need to stock up on food and water in Hana.

Places to Eat
Tutu's, a fast-food grill at the beach park at Hana Bay, is open from 8:30 am to 4 pm daily, though the grill closes 30 minutes earlier. Hamburgers and vegie sandwiches cost $2.50, mahimahi burgers $3.75. Tutu's also has $6 plate lunches, ice cream and shave ice.

The *Cafe at Hana Gardenland* (☎ 248-7340), three miles north of town on the Hana Hwy, has a covered garden setting and is open from 9 am to 5 pm daily. Sandwiches on whole-wheat bread cost $6.75 with your choice of ahi, smoked turkey or avocado and cheese. From 9 to 11 am waffles with fresh fruit and maple syrup are available for $5. You can also get fresh-squeezed juices, bagels, granola, crisp salads, quiche, pastas and desserts. If you call ahead, food can be prepared for takeout. When Hillary Rodham Clinton visited Hana in 1993 she had lunch here two days in a row, as the photos on display attest.

The *Hana Ranch Restaurant* at the Hana Ranch Center is open for lunch from 11 am to 3 pm daily, with a simple salad bar for $8 or a buffet that includes the salad bar and a few lackluster hot dishes for $13. You can also make a one-trip takeout plate from the buffet for $8. At dinner, offered from 6 to 8 pm on Fridays and Saturdays, meals range from $15 for a smoked half chicken to $28.50 for steak and grilled prawns, salad bar included. The restaurant is also open on Wednesday nights for pizza and the salad bar only.

At the side of Hana Ranch Restaurant is a takeout counter open daily from 6:30 am to 4 pm with standard breakfast fare for under $5, plate lunches for $5.50 and saimin, burgers and sandwiches for a bit less. They also sell ice cream and there are picnic tables outside where you can chow down.

Hotel Hana-Maui (☎ 248-8211) serves three meals a day in their cheery open-air dining room. At lunch (11:30 am to 2 pm), dishes such as tropical fruit salad, a club-house sandwich or catch of the day are priced from $13 to $18. Dinner (from 6 to 9 pm) offers a small selection of main course dishes such as fresh pasta with vegetables for $21 and catch of the day for $29, with salads and appetizers for around $10. The food is good but a bit straightforward considering the price.

On Tuesday evenings the hotel offers a luau dinner on Hamoa Beach, with free punch and pleasantly low-key entertainment. Reservations are required and the cost is $50.

Hana to Kipahulu

From Hana, the road continues on to Kipahulu, passing Oheo, the southern end of Haleakala National Park. It's an incredibly lush stretch, perhaps the most beautiful part of the entire drive. As it continues south from Hana, the road changes its name to the Piilani Highway.

The road from Hana to Oheo is narrow and winding. Between the hairpin turns, one-lane bridges and drivers trying to take in all the sights, it's a slow-moving 10 miles.

You'll get extra coastal views by detouring along the 1½-mile Haneoo Rd loop, which runs past Koki and Hamoa beaches

and a couple of ancient shoreline fish-ponds. The turn-off is half a mile south of Hana Ranch headquarters.

Koki Beach is at the base of a red cinder hill less than half a mile from the start of the loop. Most of Koki's sand washes away in winter, leaving a rocky shoreline. Local surfers who know the coastline sometimes surf here, but rocks and strong currents make it hazardous for newcomers.

The offshore rock topped by a few coconut trees is Alau Island, a seabird sanctuary. The trees were planted years ago by a couple of Hana residents so they'd have coconuts to drink while fishing off the island.

A little farther is Hamoa Beach, a nice grey sand beach that's used by the Hotel Hana-Maui but is accessible to everyone. The beach has showers, restrooms and a lifeguard on duty. When the surf's up, there's good surfing and bodysurfing though be aware that rip currents can sometimes be present. When seas are calm, swimming in the cove is good. Public access is down the steps below the hotel's bus-stop sign.

As you continue south, there are water-falls down the cliffs, orchids growing out of the rocks, and lots of breadfruit and coconut trees. There's even a statue of the Virgin Mary tucked into a rock face on the side of the road.

Wailua Falls, three miles before Oheo, is particularly attractive with its 100-foot drop visible from the road. There's usually a couple of people at the waterfall pull-off selling hand-painted T-shirts and the like.

OHEO GULCH
Oheo Stream dramatically cuts its way through Oheo Gulch as a lovely series of waterfalls and wide pools, each one tumbling into the next one below. In fair weather you can swim in them. A two-mile trail runs up the stream bed.

There was once a large Hawaiian settlement spread throughout the Oheo area and the stone remains of more than 700 structures have been identified. These early villagers cultivated taro and sweet potatoes in terraced gardens.

One of the expressed purposes of the national park is to manage the Oheo area 'to perpetuate traditional Hawaiian farming and *hoonanea*' – a Hawaiian word meaning to pass the time in ease, peace and pleasure. To further this goal, the park service is in the process of developing a *kauhale* (a Hawaiian living complex) for demonstrations of Hawaiian culture.

Not so long ago Oheo Gulch was dubbed 'Seven Sacred Pools', a tourism promotion idea. There are actually 24 pools from the ocean all the way up to Waimoku Falls and they were never sacred (although it was kapu for menstruating women to bathe in them).

The park's ranger station is staffed from 9 am to 5 pm daily to answer questions. There are Hawaiian culture demonstrations occurring throughout the week and 15-minute orientation talks on the deck of the ranger station a few times a day. There's often a one-hour guided walk at 9:30 am and a four-hour guided hike to Waimoku Falls on Saturdays at 9:30 am. However, because of funding fluctuations, the ranger-led guided hikes and talks are occasionally suspended – call the park at 248-7375 for the latest.

There are restrooms near the visitors' parking lot but there's no drinking water or food at Oheo.

Lower Pools

A 20-minute path from the Oheo Gulch parking lot heads down to the lower pools and then loops back via the road, with interpretive signs along the way. The ranger station is located near the start of the trail. A few minutes down, the trail comes to a broad grassy knoll with a beautiful view of the Hana coast. On a clear day you can see the Big Island across the Alenuihaha Channel, 30 miles away. It would be a fine place to break out a picnic basket.

The large freshwater pools along the trail are almost terraced one atop the other, connected by gentle cascades. They're usually

Kipahulu Valley

In the 1960s, 11,000 acres of Kipahulu Valley was jointly purchased by the Nature Conservancy and the state of Hawaii for preservation. The valley, which borders the main body of Haleakala National Park and stretches southeast to the coast, was turned over to the US Department of the Interior and added to the national park in 1969. The coastal Oheo Gulch area is part of the Kipahulu Valley property.

The upper Kipahulu Valley is a pristine rainforest of koa and ohia trees that is refuge to endangered native plants and birds. The Maui parrotbill, whose sole population lives in this valley, has a habitat range of just over eight miles. Fewer than 500 of the birds survive. Also in Kipahulu Valley is the entire population of the Maui nuku puu, Hawaii's most endangered honeycreeper – about 30 birds in all. The last sighting of the nuku puu made outside Maui was on Kauai in 1985. The parrotbill and nuku puu are both beautiful forest birds, about five inches long, with bright yellow underbellies.

The upper part of the valley gets up to 300 inches of rain a year and is swampy with dense vegetation. In an effort to protect the habitat, no public access is allowed. ∎

calm and great for swimming, though the water's brisk. The second big pool below the bridge is a favorite.

If it's been raining heavily and the water is flowing too high and fast, the pools are closed and signs are posted. Still, at any time, heavy rains in the upper slopes can bring a sudden torrent of rising waters. If the water starts to rise, get out immediately. People have been swept from these pools out to sea by flash floods. The ocean below is not inviting at all – it's quite rough and is populated by grey sharks!

Actually, the biggest cause of injury here is from falls on slippery rocks. Another hazard is the submerged rocks and ledges in some of the pools. Check them out carefully before diving in.

Oheo is home to a rare goby fish which spends the first stages of its life in the ocean, but returns to breed in the upper stream. It works its way up the chain of pools and waterfalls by using its front fins as suction cups on the rocks.

Waterfall Trails

Opposite the parking lot is a trail leading up to Makahiku Falls (half a mile) and Waimoku Falls (two miles). The path passes large mango trees and lots of guava, forking after about 10 minutes.

Makahiku Falls, a long bridal-veil waterfall which drops into a deep gorge, is just off to the right. Thick green ferns cover the sides of 200-foot basalt cliffs where the fall cascades. The scene is quite rewarding for such a short walk.

To the left of the overlook there's a path in a ditch that goes up to the top of the waterfalls where there's a popular skinny-dipping pool. Around midday the pool is quite enjoyable but by late afternoon the sun stops hitting it and the mosquitoes move in.

Rocks above the waterfall protect the pool as long as the water level isn't high. A cut on one side lets the water fall over the cliff. Examine it carefully before getting in and if the water starts to rise once you are in, get out immediately – a drop over this sheer 184-foot falls would obviously be fatal!

Waimoku Falls is a thin, lacy 400-foot waterfall dropping down a sheer rock face. The walk to the falls is made all the more special by three thick bamboo groves. When you come out of the first grove, you'll see the waterfall in the distance. By the time you emerge from the third thicket, you're there.

It takes about 45 minutes to hike the 1½ miles to Waimoku Falls from the Makahiku Falls viewpoint. There are a couple of stream crossings on the way; don't attempt them if the water is high or rising.

The upper part of the trail is muddy with a boardwalk over sections of it. The mosquitoes which thrive along the stream bed can be pesky. There are ancient farm sites with abandoned taro patches along the way, though it takes a keen eye to recognize them.

As the pool under Waimoku Falls was partially filled in by a landslide caused by an earthquake in 1976, it's not terribly deep, but at any rate swimming is not recommended due to the danger of falling rocks. There are concerns that heavy vibrations from helicopters hovering over the waterfalls are destabilizing the rocks even more.

If you want to take a dip, there are better pools to swim in along the way. About 100 yards before Waimoku Falls you'll cross a little stream. If you go left for 10 minutes up the stream there's a beautiful waterfall and a little pool about neck deep. There's not really a trail but you can walk alongside the stream to get to it.

There's also a nice pool in the stream about halfway between Makahiku and Waimoku falls.

Places to Stay

The national park has a campground about half a mile southeast of the main Oheo Gulch visitor's area. The campground is Hawaiian style: free and undeveloped – just a huge open pasture. There are some incredible places to pitch a tent on grassy cliffs right above the coast and the pounding surf. Not only is the scenery stunning, but the camping area is set amidst the ruins of an old Hawaiian village, making this quite a powerful place to be.

In winter there are usually only a handful of tents here. It gets quite a few campers in summer but apparently never fills to the point where people are turned away. There are pit toilets and a few picnic tables but *no* water. Permits aren't required though camping is officially limited to three nights each month.

KIPAHULU

The village of Kipahulu is less than a mile south of Oheo. Around the turn of the century Kipahulu was one of several sugar plantation villages in the Hana area. It had a working mill from 1890 to 1922. Following the closure of the mill, there were unsuccessful attempts to grow pineapples before ranching took hold in the late 1920s.

Today Kipahulu has both exclusive estates and more modest homes. A scattering of impromptu fruit stands are set up along the roadside, some attended by elderly women who string leis and sell bananas and woven lauhala hats. This is the end of the line for most day visitors who have pushed beyond Hana.

Lindbergh's Grave

The Hana area was home to aviator hero Charles Lindbergh during the last years of his life. He began visiting in the 1960s, built a cliffside home in Kipahulu in 1968 and died of cancer in Maui in 1974.

Lindbergh is buried in the graveyard of Palapala Hoomau Congregational Church. His simple grave is surrounded by a chain and marked with little US flags.

Would-be visitors sometimes get the location mixed up with the peach-colored St Paul's Church, which sits on the highway three-quarters of a mile south of Oheo, but the dirt drive down to Palapala Hoomau Church is a quarter of a mile beyond that, on the makai side of the road. Turn in at the metal gate just past the wooden cistern at the end of the field. The short road in can get very rutted.

Palapala Hoomau Church, with its 26-inch-thick walls and simple wooden pews, dates from 1864. The church is known for its window painting of a Polynesian Christ dressed in the red and yellow feather capes worn only by Hawaii's highest chiefs.

The churchyard is a peaceful place, with sleepy cats lounging around, waiting for a nice warm car hood to sprawl out on.

Getting There & Away

A lot of people leave Oheo in mid-afternoon to head back up the Hana Highway. Some of them, suddenly realizing what a long trek they have ahead, become very impatient drivers.

You might want to consider leaving a little later, which would not only give you more sightseeing time, but allow you to avoid the rush. Getting caught in the dark returning north on the Hana Hwy does have certain advantages. You can see the headlights of oncoming cars around bends that would otherwise be blind and the traffic is almost nonexistent.

There are no short cuts back, but sometimes there is another option.

From Kipahulu, the Piilani Hwy (Don't be misled by the term 'highway' – there's barely a road in places!) heads west through Kaupo to Keokea in Kula. It's usually passable, but not always, and it shouldn't be done in the dark.

The ranger station in Kipahulu sometimes posts road conditions. You can also call the county public works department (☎ 248-8254) between 6:30 am and 3 pm on weekdays or, after hours, the county police department (☎ 248-8311). Another option is to drive to the far end of Kipahulu and talk to people coming from the Kaupo direction. Most likely they've either just driven down from Kula or else have started up the road from Kipahulu, found road conditions bad and turned around.

For more details on the drive, see the Piilani Hwy section of this chapter.

Upcountry

Upcountry refers to the highland area of East Maui on the western slopes of Haleakala. You have to drive through Upcountry to get to Haleakala National Park, but it's well worth visiting for its own sake. It has some of Maui's finest countryside, with rolling hills, grazing horses and green pastures.

Upcountry is uncrowded and dotted with small towns. A fair chunk of the area is occupied by ranches, with Haleakala Ranch covering vast spreads to the north, and Ulupalakua Ranch to the south.

Kula, in the center of it all, has rich farmland where most of Maui's vegetables and flowers are grown. On the mountainside above Kula are the delightful cloud-forests of Polipoli. Upcountry sightseeing spots include landscaped gardens and a winery tasting room.

From Upcountry you can look across the central plains to the West Maui Mountains and get a good view of the Maui coastline and the neighboring islands. Daytimes are cooler in Upcountry and nights can be downright brisk.

PAIA TO MAKAWAO

Baldwin Ave (Hwy 390) runs seven miles from Paia upslope to Makawao. It starts amid sugar cane, passes the Paia Mill and then runs on through pineapple fields interspersed with little open patches where cattle graze.

There are two churches up Baldwin Ave. The **Holy Rosary Church**, with its memorial statue of Father Damien, comes up first on the right and the attractive **Makawao Union Church**, a stone block building with stained-glass windows, is farther along on the left. The latter was built in 1916 and is on the National Register of Historic Places.

The roadside **Rainbow Park** is at the three-mile post. It has a covered picnic table, a portable toilet and camping, but it's in a low area that can get soggy when it rains.

On the left just after the five-mile marker is Kaluanui, the former nine-acre plantation estate of sugar magnates Harry and Ethel Baldwin, which now houses the **Hui Noeau Visual Arts Center**. The two-story pink plantation home with Spanish-style tile roof was designed by famed Honolulu architect C W Dickey in 1917. The remains of Maui's first mule-powered centrifugal sugar mill and some abandoned railroad tracks are near the entrance.

The nonprofit group Hui Noeau (☎ 572-6560) offers community classes in printmaking, weaving, batik and dozens of other visual arts at the center. The 1st floor of the house features changing exhibits and a gift shop, while the stables at the back have been turned into a ceramics studio. The gallery is open from 10 am to 4 pm Tuesday to Sunday.

Haliimaile

Haliimaile is a little pineapple town on the edge of an expansive cane and pineapple plantation. The main attraction is the old general store, circa 1918, which has been converted into one of the better upscale restaurants on this side of Maui.

Places to Eat *Haliimaile General Store* (☎ 572-2666) has high ceilings and plantation-era decor. The cooking is creative with dishes like fruit-glazed roast duck and spinach lasagna with pesto and pine nuts. At dinner, served from 6 to 10 pm, main dishes range from $16 for blackened chicken in a banana sauce to $24 for Hunan rack of lamb. Lunch, served from 11 am to 2:30 pm, features good salads, vegetarian dishes and sandwiches priced from $6 to $10.

To get there from Paia, turn right onto Haliimaile Rd, five miles up Baldwin Ave. From Kahului, turn left onto Haliimaile Rd about 4½ miles up Hwy 37.

MAKAWAO

Makawao is billed as a paniolo (cowboy) town. Despite a recent spurt of growth, it's still bordered by ranch land and the false-front wooden buildings in the town center retain an Old West look. The town's main events are a couple of big-time rodeos.

All that aside, Makawao is a town in flux. In the past decade a sizable amount of alternative culture has seeped in: the health food store has set up down the street from Makawao Feed & Garden and the gun shops have given way to boutiques and art galleries. The town's newest pharmacy is the Dragon's Den, run by herbalist Malik Cotter, who also sells crystals and Chinese teas. Next door is the Maui School of Yoga Therapy and the Grace Health Clinic which offers shiatsu massage, acupuncture and naturopathic treatment.

Makawao has some interesting upscale galleries, including those at The Courtyard at 3620 Baldwin Ave. Most notable here is Hot Island Glass, where you can watch glassblowers at work from 10 am to 5 pm daily.

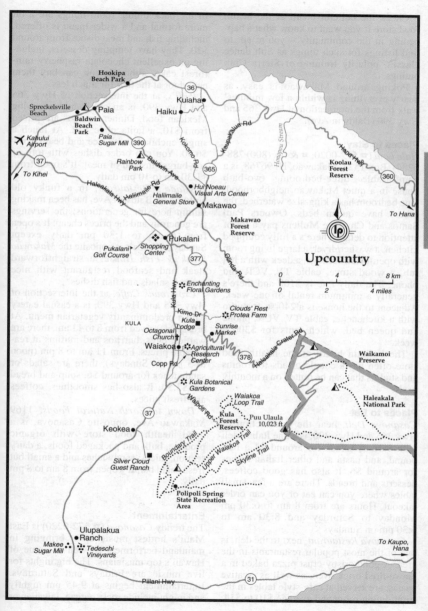

Check the bulletin board at the health food store if you want to know what's happening in the community – you're apt to find listings for such things as Sufi dance classes, polarity training or Sierra Club outings.

Poking around Makawao is easy, as nearly everything is within a few minutes' walk from the intersection of Hwy 365 and Hwy 390 (Baldwin Ave).

Places to Stay

Hale Lani (☎ 572-0020; ☎ & fax (800) 788-6284), Box 1527, Makawao, HI 96768, is a comfortable three-bedroom, two-bath house in a quiet Makawao neighborhood. One bedroom has a king-size waterbed, the others have queen beds. Owners Paul Santos and Charlene Mullens pay a lot of attention to detail. There's a fully equipped kitchen, a washer/dryer, a large living room with open-beam ceilings, a deck with a hot tub, a wood stove, cable TV, VCR and phone. The daily rate is $100 and there's generally a minimum rental of one week. Adjacent to the house is a 240-sq-ft studio with a kitchenette, cable TV, VCR, phone and queen bed, which rents for $300 a week.

The bulletin board at the health food store often has a couple of ads for rooms and studios that can be rented on a monthly basis.

Places to Eat

Casanova Deli, near the intersection of Hwy 365 and Hwy 390, is a fine Italian deli with various salads for around $4 a half pound, and pasta and other Italian dishes for around $6. It also has good coffees, desserts and breads. There are a few small tables where you can eat or you can order takeout. Hours are from 8 am to 6:30 pm Monday to Saturday and 8:30 am to 6:30 pm on Sundays.

Casanova Restaurant, next to the deli, is one of the most popular restaurants in the area. A good crispy-crust pizza baked in a kiawe-fired brick oven, as well as creative pastas, are served at cafe-style tables in the front dining room and average $10 to $14.

In the back dining room things are a bit more formal and a wider menu is offered, including fish and meat dishes from around $20. They have tempting desserts, including an excellent chocolate raspberry rainforest cake, although you can buy them next door at the deli for much less.

Polli's, at the intersection of Hwy 365 and Hwy 390, is an old stand-by serving Mexican food. Dinner combos are priced from $10, a fajita plate $12. At lunch a single enchilada with rice and beans costs $6.50. You can order dishes with tofu or soy-burger instead of meat. It's open from 11:30 am to 10 pm daily.

Kitada's Restaurant, in a funky old building on Baldwin Ave, has been making saimin here for generations; the servings are generous and the prices cheap. It's open from 6 am to 1:30 pm daily except Sundays. Kitada's is opposite the *Makawao Steak & Fish House*, a straightforward steak and seafood restaurant with nice spinach salads and fish dishes.

Crossroads Caffe, at the intersection of Hwy 365 and Hwy 390, is a casual eatery with a predominantly vegetarian menu. At breakfast, served from 8 to 11 am, there are waffles, eggs, burritos and muffins at reasonable prices. From 11 am to 8 pm (noon to 5 pm on Sundays), there are salads or sandwiches for around $6, soup and bread for $3.50. It also has smoothies, coffees and fresh juices.

Down to Earth Natural Foods, 1169 Makawao Ave, opposite Casanova, is a good health food store with organic produce, bulk and packaged foods, a dairy section, juices, sandwiches and a small but fresh salad bar. It's open from 8 am to 8 pm daily.

Entertainment

The trendy *Casanova* (☎ 572-0220) is East Maui's hottest music spot, bringing in mainland performers as well as some of Hawaii's top musicians. The big nights for live music are Fridays and Saturdays. Entertainment begins at 9:45 pm nightly and might include rock, reggae, Jawaiian or country. The cover charge is generally $3 and $5 to $20 when a live band is playing.

There's sometimes free acoustic music at the *Courtyard Deli* or *Crossroads Caffe*.

HAIKU

Scenic back roads head out in all directions from Makawao and almost any one you choose to explore will make a prime country drive.

Some of those roads lead through Haiku, a scattered community that stretches north from Makawao down the slopes to the Hana Hwy. From Makawao, take Kaupakalua Rd (Hwy 365) north. After a mile, turn left onto Kokomo Rd, which passes through pineapple fields before reaching the modest two-store village that marks the center of Haiku. Alexander & Baldwin grew their first 12 acres of sugar cane near Haiku and there was once a mill here.

Today Haiku is seeing a bit of a revival. Its rural character and its proximity to both Makawao and Hookipa have attracted a number of new residents ranging from windsurfers to artists and New Age folks. The area has some good-value places to stay and makes a fairly convenient base for exploring the whole island.

Places to Stay

Lanikai Farm (☎ 572-1111; fax 572-3498), c/o Margaret & Achim Koebke, 734 South Lanikai Place, Haiku, HI 96708, is a comfortable home on a large lot that's planted with macnut, mango and citrus trees. About 10 minutes' drive from Hookipa Beach or Makawao, this hospitable B&B has three guest rooms, each with a queen bed and a small refrigerator. The rooms share a bath and a half, and there's a common room with a TV, VCR and microwave. There's a squash court in the house that guests can use and a jeep available for rent at about $45 a day. Well-behaved children are welcome. Achim is from Germany, so both English and German are spoken. Rates, which include breakfast, are $60/65 for

singles/doubles, $10 less a night on stays of a week or more.

Pililaloha (☎ 572-1440; fax 572-4612), c/o Machiko & Bill Heyde, 2512 Kaupakalua Rd, Haiku, HI 96708, is a delightful cottage in upcountry Haiku, about two miles from the center of Makawao. Set in a eucalyptus grove, the terraced cottage has hardwood oak floors, sliding glass doors leading to a deck, a bedroom with a queen bed, and a second room with a single bed. There's a fully equipped kitchen, a washer/dryer, a phone and a living room with VCR, cable TV and a hideaway queen bed. Machiko, an artist, has quilted and painted the pillows and adds other charming touches, such as roses cut fresh daily from her garden. The cost is $85 for one or two people, $10 for each additional person. There's a two-day minimum stay and smoking is allowed outdoors only. Kona coffee, tea, fruit, cereal and homemade bread or muffins are provided for breakfast; if you don't eat sugar, Machiko will bake with honey.

Haikuleana (☎ 575-2890), 69 Haiku Rd, Haiku, HI 96708, is a pleasant B&B in an older plantation-style house that retains some graceful period touches. There's a central dining area and a sitting room with antiques and rattan and wicker furnishings. It has four guest rooms, three with queen beds, one with two twin beds, and each with a private bath. Singles/doubles cost $70/85 with a two-night minimum. A full breakfast is included, children under six are not accepted and smoking is not allowed. It's about 1⅓ miles up Haiku Rd from Hwy 36, near the Haiku Chapel.

Akahi Farm (☎ 572-8795), 915 Kaupakalua Rd, Haiku, HI 96708, is a secluded 55-acre property in Haiku. It's basically a retreat and conference center but they'll accept individual guests on a space-available basis for $30/50 for singles/doubles. The center sometimes can put together a tailored package that includes a room, vegetarian meals, hot tub, massage and other activities, with prices varying according to your interest. There are Vipassana retreats and yoga, aikido and tai chi

MAUI

workshops held here that are occasionally open to individual travelers, though for the most part those activities must be booked through the groups that sponsor them.

There's also an old plantation house, the *Bamboo Mountain Sanctuary* (☎ 572-5106), 911 Kaupakalua Rd, Haiku, 96708, adjacent to Akahi Farm. It has five rooms for $55/75 including breakfast.

Another option is *Cat Cha Rising Star* (☎ & fax 572-2117), Box 1006, Haiku, HI 96708, which has a secluded location down a dirt road. There are two separate units with high vaulted ceilings. One's a cottage with a loft sleeping area, a double bed and a greenhouse shower for $45, while the main house has a hot tub and a king bed for $75. Each has a kitchen, TV, phone and a three-day minimum stay.

PUKALANI

Pukalani, on the way to Haleakala, is the biggest Upcountry town. It's a residential community with a population of 6000.

Pukalani is two miles from Makawao along Hwy 365. Midway between the two towns is a picture-perfect ranch scene with rolling pastures, horses and cattle grazing and a mountain backdrop. Beyond this the rows of pineapple start up again.

If you're coming from Kahului, the Haleakala Highway (Hwy 37) climbs for six miles through cane fields before reaching Pukalani. If you just want to go to Haleakala or Kula there's a new bypass that skirts around Pukalani; if you want to see the town stay on Hwy 37.

Information

There are a couple of gas stations on Hwy 37 in the center of Pukalani. The Pukalani Terrace Shopping Center, south of the intersection of Hwy 365 and Hwy 37, has a coin laundry and a Bank of Hawaii. Foodland, in the same center, has a Bankoh money dispenser that accepts major credit and ATM cards.

Places to Eat

The Pukalani Terrace Shopping Center has a carry-out *Pizza Hut* open from 11 am to at least 10 pm, a 24-hour *Foodland* supermarket with a reasonable deli section and bakery, a *Subway* sandwich shop and a Chinese restaurant.

There's also a *McDonald's* a little farther up the highway, next to a convenience store that sells fried chicken and giant steak fries by the piece.

Pukalani Terrace Country Clubhouse (☎ 572-1325) is where Pukalanians head when they want to go out. It's located above the golf course, less than a mile past the shopping center on Pukalani Rd. There's a reasonably good salad bar with soup that costs $7 alone or $3 with a meal. Complete Hawaiian plates (which include kalua pig, lomi salmon, poi and haupia) cost about $8, while chicken and beef dishes are a few dollars more. Standard breakfast fare costs about $5 with coffee. The dining room has a good view down to the ocean and is open from 8 am to 2 pm and 5 to 9 pm daily. Things can be a bit hectic at lunch as the restaurant is a popular stop for Japanese tour buses.

KULA

Kula is the agricultural heartland of Maui. The average elevation is 3000 feet. Crops such as lettuce, tomatoes, carrots, cauliflower and cabbage thrive in Kula's warm days, cool nights and rich volcanic soil. No gourmet cook in Hawaii would be without sweet Kula onions.

During the California Gold Rush in the mid-1800s, Hawaiian farmers in Kula shipped so many potatoes off to the miners that the area became known as 'Nu Kaleponi', the Hawaiian pronunciation for New California. In the late 1800s, Portuguese and Chinese immigrants moved in to farm the Kula area after they had worked off their contracts on the sugar plantations.

Kula grows most of Hawaii's proteas, large bright flowers with an unusual flair. Some, like the pincushion varieties, are very delicate and others have spine-like petals.

Almost 90% of the carnations used in leis throughout Hawaii are grown in Kula, as are many of the chrysanthemums.

Hwy 377 (Haleakala Hwy) and Hwy 37 (Kula Hwy) are both scenic. Take your pick, or go up one and down the other.

Gardens

All of Kula is a garden, but if you want to take a closer look there are several established walk-through gardens that you can visit.

Clouds' Rest Protea Farm, one mile along Upper Kimo Drive off Hwy 377, has a little garden area with plants identified by plaques. You can stroll through it for free from 8 am to 4:30 pm daily. Cut protea are on sale at rock-bottom prices at the farm, and by mail order for the usual shipped cost.

Sunrise Market, on Hwy 378 on the way to Haleakala, has a free roadside garden with a small but select group of proteas.

Kula Botanical Gardens is a mature garden of tropical plants, pleasantly overgrown and shady. It's on Hwy 377, three-quarters of a mile up from the southern intersection of Hwy 377 and Hwy 37. The garden is open from 9 am to 4 pm daily and admission is $4 for adults, $1 for children ages six to 12.

The more recently established **Enchanting Floral Gardens** is sunny, open and orderly, with both tropical and coolweather flowers. It has a colorful collection with most plants labeled in both Japanese and English. It's on Hwy 37, just south of Omaopio Rd, and is open from 9 am to 5 pm daily. Admission is $3.50 for adults, $1.50 for children ages six to 12.

The University of Hawaii maintains a 20-acre **Agricultural Research Center** in Kula. It's there that Hawaii's first proteas, natives of Australia and South Africa, were established in 1965. You can walk through rows of their colorful descendants as well as dozens of new hybrids under development. The protea has more than 1400 varieties and is named after the Greek god Proteus, who was noted for his ability to change form.

There are now over 50 protea farms in Hawaii supplying fresh cut flowers to florists on the US mainland, Japan and Europe. The nearest is just across the street from the research center.

The research center can be visited until 3:30 pm, free of charge. Some sections of the garden are part of experiments in plant pathology and are thus closed to visitors. It's best to avoid Fridays, which is the day pesticides are sprayed.

The research center is about a half mile above town; to get there, take Copp Rd (between the 12- and 13-mile markers on Hwy 37) and turn left on Mauna Place.

Octagonal Church

The octagonal Holy Ghost Church is a hillside landmark in Waiakoa village. This distinctive white church has a roof that glints silver in the sun and is easily visible from the highway. Built in 1897 by Portuguese immigrants, the church's beautifully ornate interior looks like it came right out of Portugal, and much of it did. Because of termite problems, the church was dismantled and completely renovated in 1992.

Places to Stay

Kula View Bed & Breakfast (☎ 878-6736), c/o Susan Kauai, Box 322, Kula, HI 96790, in a subdivision at 140 Holopuni Rd, has a nice-sized guest room with a queen bed, mini-refrigerator, shower, deck and private entrance for $75. A good continental breakfast of muffins, fruit and coffee is included. Smoking is not allowed.

Kula Lodge (☎ 878-1535, (800) 233-1535), RR1, Box 475, Kula, HI 96790, on Hwy 377, has five cottages in the same complex as its restaurant. All have private decks and are pleasant but not notably special for the money. Cheapest is a studio without a view for $100 a night. There are two cottages for $120, each with a queen bed and a small loft with two futons, and two larger $150 cottages with a similar setup but with twin beds in the loft and the addition of gas fireplaces. It costs $30 for each person beyond two. There are no TVs or phones and breakfast is not included in the rates.

MAUI

Places to Eat

The dining room at the *Kula Lodge* is on a knoll with wraparound windows and a splendid view of central and northern Maui and the ocean beyond. Breakfast features multi-grain pancakes, tofu scramble and eggs Benedict, priced from $4 to $8. At lunch, burgers and sandwiches cost around $8, while the dinner menu includes pastas for $15, steak for around $20 and fresh catch of the day at market prices. It's on Hwy 377, less than a mile before Haleakala Crater Rd (Hwy 378) coming from Pukalani. It's open daily, for breakfast from 6 to 11:30 am, for lunch and dinner from 11:30 am to 8:30 pm.

The *Kula Sandalwoods Restaurant* (☎ 875-3523), just past Kula Lodge on the mauka side of Hwy 377, is open from 6:30 am to 1 pm daily. Breakfast, which is served until 11 am and costs from $4 to $8, includes omelets, eggs and waffles. Lunch, from $4 to $11, includes sandwiches, salads and a hot mahimahi plate. The owners are renovating half a dozen cabins on the hillside above the restaurant that they plan to use as B&B rentals.

Sunrise Market is a quarter of a mile up from the intersection of Hwy 378 and Hwy 377 on the way to Haleakala. You can pick up your morning coffee here along with bakery items, wrapped sandwiches and fresh and dried fruits. The store is open from 7.30 am to 4 pm daily.

Kula Country Store, a quarter of a mile south of the Octagonal Church in Waiakoa, is a small grocery store with a popular deli counter. Sandwiches average $4, plate lunches $5 and there are also a few bakery items. It's open from 6 am to 6 pm weekdays, shorter hours on weekends.

POLIPOLI SPRING STATE RECREATION AREA

Polipoli Spring State Recreation Area is high up in the Kula Forest Reserve on the western slope of Haleakala. The park is in a coniferous forest with picnic tables, camping and a network of trails. It's not always possible to get all the way to the park without a 4WD, but it's worth driving even part way up for the view.

Waipoli Rd, the road to the park, is off Hwy 377 just under half a mile before its southern intersection with Hwy 37.

Waipoli is a narrow switchbacking one-lane road. The drive is often through layers of clouds which drift in and out of groves of eucalyptus and past open rangeland. (Watch for cattle on the road.) When the clouds lift there are vast views across green rolling hills to the islands of Lanai and Kahoolawe.

Few people venture up this way and, except for the symphony of bird calls, everything is still.

When the clouds are heaviest, visibility is measured in feet. The road has some soft shoulders, but the first six miles are well paved. The road then enters the forest reserve and turns to dirt. When it's muddy, the next four miles up to the state park are not worth trying in a standard car.

The whole area was planted during the 1930s by the Civilian Conservation Corps (CCC), a Depression-era work program. Several of the trails pass through old CCC camps. There are stands of redwood, ash, cypress, cedar and pines. It all looks somewhat like the northern California coast.

Waiakoa Loop Trail

The trailhead to the Waiakoa Loop Trail starts at the hunter check station five miles up Waipoli Rd. Walk three-quarters of a mile down the grassy spur road on the left to a gate marking the trail which starts out in pine trees.

Since a fire a few years back, the trail has not been maintained and it's no longer possible to do the whole three-mile loop. However, you can start from the left side of the loop and walk about two miles to where it connects with Upper Waiakoa Trail.

Upper Waiakoa Trail

The Upper Waiakoa Trail is a maintained seven-mile trail that was reconstructed in 1994 by the Na Ala Hele group. The trail begins off Waiakoa Loop at an elevation of

6000 feet, climbs 1800 feet up switchbacks and then drops back down 1400 feet.

It's stony terrain, but high and open and provides good views. Bring a full canteen of water.

The trail ends on Waipoli Rd between the hunter check station and the campground. If you want to start at this end of the trail, keep an eye out for the trail marker for Waohuli Trail, as Upper Waiakoa Trail begins across the road.

Boundary Trail

The four-mile Boundary Trail is a marked and maintained trail that begins about 200 yards beyond the end of the pavement. Park to the right of the cattle grate which marks the boundary of the Kula Forest Reserve.

This is a steep downhill walk that crosses gulches and goes down deep into the woods where there's eucalyptus, pine and cedar as well as a bit of native forest. In the afternoon the fog generally rolls in and visibility fades.

Skyline Trail

It's possible to hike 8½ miles from the summit of Haleakala to Polipoli campground at 6200 feet. At Haleakala National Park, go past the summit and take the road to the left just before Science City.

The first 6½ miles is down Skyline Trail, a dirt road used to maintain the state park. It starts at the 9750-foot elevation in an open terrain of cinder and craters.

After three miles you'll reach the tree line, which is at 8500 feet and begins in a native mamane forest. In the winter mamane is heavy with clusters of delicate yellow flowers that look like sweet-pea blossoms.

Skyline Trail merges into the Haleakala Ridge Trail and then connects with the Polipoli Trail, which spurs half a mile to the campground.

There's solitude on this walk. If the clouds treat you kindly there are broad views as you pass from the barren summit into the dense cloudforest.

Places to Stay

Besides tent camping, Polipoli has one housekeeping cabin at $17 for two people, reserved through the state park system. Unlike the other state cabins, this one has gas lanterns but no electricity or refrigerator.

Come properly prepared as this is cold country and in the winter the temperature frequently drops below freezing at night. There are restrooms, but no showers. Fellow campers are likely to be pig hunters.

KEOKEA

Around the turn of the century, Keokea was home mainly to Hakka Chinese who farmed the remote Kula region.

Keokea is the last real town before Hana if you're swinging around the southern part of the island. It has two small stores with gas pumps (Fong Store/Shell and Ching Store/Chevron) and a coffee shop.

The village's green and white St John's Episcopal Church was built in 1907 to serve the Chinese community. 'St John's House of Worship' is still written in Chinese above the door.

On a clear day there are good views of West Maui and Lanai from the church and elsewhere along the roadside.

Places to Stay

Halemanu Bed & Breakfast (☎ 878-2729), c/o Carol Austin, 221 Kawehi Place, Kula, HI 96790, is in a lovely contemporary home set beneath the Kula Forest Reserve off Waipoli Rd. Accommodation is in a room with a queen bed, private bath, phone and deck. A TV and VCR are available in the loft. Carol, who writes the 'Word Has It' chat-style column in the *Maui News*, is a very outgoing person who enjoys showing her guests around, and occasionally joins them for impromptu hikes and snorkel outings. There's a two-day minimum and the cost is $75 for one or two people.

Bloom Cottage (☎ 878-1425), RR2 Box 229, Kula, HI 96790, is a two-bedroom free-standing cottage in Keokea. There's a fireplace in the living room to ward off evening chills. The cottage also has a kitchen, a TV, a VCR and a front porch. The rate is $95 for doubles, $10 for each extra person, with breakfast fixings provided. There's a two-night minimum stay. Smoking is not allowed.

Silver Cloud Guest Ranch (☎ 878-6101; fax 878-2132), RR2 Box 201, Kula, HI 96790, is a former ranch turned B&B on Thompson Rd, just over a mile from central Keokea. The atmospheric plantation home has five guest rooms, all with private baths. The cheapest room ($75) is small and simple while the most expensive ($95) is large and airy with a private porch and a wonderful ocean view. The house has a formal living room with hardwood floors, a fireplace, a piano and lots of upholstered chairs and love seats that invite lounging.

In addition, the bunkhouse out back has been converted into five small studios with kitchenettes and French doors leading to a little porch; a couple have nice ocean views. Avoid unit No 1 as the adjacent furnace is noisy. Rates are $95 to $125 but, as might be expected, the bunkhouse is not as refined as the plantation house. There's also a separate cottage with a woodburning stove and covered lanai for $135. There's no minimum stay and breakfast is included in the rates.

Places to Eat

Upcountry folks gravitate to *Grandma's Coffee House* on Hwy 37 for homemade pastries and fresh dark-roasted Maui coffee. This bright cheery place has a few small tables and also serves espresso and reasonably priced saimin and sandwiches.

Alfred Franco's family has grown coffee on the slopes of Haleakala since 1918. Alfred started selling at flea markets, packing his coffee in little brown paper bags with felt-penned labels. In 1988 he set up a 103-year-old roasting machine and opened Grandma's. Demand for Maui coffee is high and the beans command a premium price, which has drawn more Upcountry growers to coffee. If you want

to see what coffee trees look like, just walk out to the side porch.

ULUPALAKUA RANCH

From Keokea, Hwy 37 winds south through ranch country with good views of Kahoolawe and the little island of Molokini. Even on overcast days you can often see below the clouds to sunny Kihei on the coast.

Tedeschi Vineyards, in the middle of Ulupalakua Ranch, is 5½ miles south of Keokea.

In the mid-1800s, Ulupalakua Ranch was a sugar plantation owned by whaling ship captain James Makee. The 25,000-acre ranch has been owned by Pardee Erdman and family since 1963. It's a working ranch with about 6000 head of cattle, 600 Merino sheep and 150 head of Rocky Mountain elk.

Ulupalakua Ranch Store, opposite the ranch headquarters, is a small local store selling dungarees, bags of horse feed, a few groceries and Haagen-Dazs ice cream bars. It's open from 9 am to 5 pm Monday to Friday, 10 am to 5 pm on weekends.

Tedeschi Vineyards

Tedeschi Vineyards (☎ 878-6058) planted its first grapes in 1976. While waiting for the vines to mature, the vineyard began producing Maui Blanc, a pineapple wine that is surprisingly light and dry and quite reasonably priced.

Tedeschi now makes four wines from grapes, including champagne and a blush zinfandel, which you can try out in the tasting room from 9 am to 5 pm daily. The little stone building is actually Captain Makee's old jail. Winery tours are given once an hour between 9:30 am and 2:30 pm.

Opposite the winery, you can see the remains of the three stacks of the Makee Sugar Mill, built in 1878. Maui artist Reems Mitchell, who carved the three mannequin cowboys perched on the steps of the Ulupalakua Ranch Store, lives in the mill.

Piilani Highway

The Piilani Highway (Hwy 31) curves along the southern flank of Haleakala. From Tedeschi Winery it's 25 rugged miles to the town of Kipahulu, near Oheo Gulch, the southern end of Haleakala National Park.

Someday, in an asphalt future, this may well be a real highway with cars zipping along in both directions. For now, it's an unspoiled adventure. In different sections the road is of broken pavement, gravel, dirt or stones. It takes a good two hours to drive it.

Signs such as 'Motorists Assume Risk of Damage Due to Presence of Cattle' and 'Narrow Winding Road, Safe Speed 15 mph' give clues that this is not your standard highway.

Road Conditions The hardest part is finding out if the road is currently open and passable. Many tourist maps mark it as impassable and car rental agencies say just being on it is a violation of their contract.

There are a couple of possibilities for getting info on road conditions. While the best is word of mouth from other drivers, you can also call the county public works department (☎ 248-8254) between 6:30 am and 3 pm on weekdays. After hours, try the county police department (☎ 248-8311 or 244-6400).

The trickiest section of the drive is around Kaupo, where the road goes over three rocky creek beds. These are usually dry and pose little problem. But after hard rains, streams flow over the roads making passage difficult, if not dangerous. Flash floods sometimes wash away portions of the road, making it impossible to get through until it's repaired.

The best way to approach the road is with an early morning start. Take something to munch, plenty to drink and check your oil and spare tire. Go slow enough so you don't bottom out. If you break down it's a long haul to civilization and the tow

charge is said to be around $400. If all goes well it's possible to be soaking in one of Oheo's pools by early afternoon.

For the first 15 miles after the winery the road is reasonably good; some sections have been upgraded, while others are patchwork asphalt sprinkled with potholes. Around Kaupo, depending on when it was last graded, there can be some torturous climbs over rocky riverbeds. The strip between Kaupo and Kipahulu is the worst.

A 4WD is recommended, or at least a high riser with a manual transmission. Still, all said and done, we have driven this road in a low-slung compact car and, somewhat to our amazement, managed to not scrape bottom at all. There were sections where we had to take it very slow, but other than being bounced and rattled we had no problems.

Keokea is the last place on the Kula side to get gas and something to eat. In the Oheo Gulch area you might find a fruit stand, but there's no drinking water, gas stations or other services until Hana.

Tedeschi Vineyards to Kaupo

South from Tedeschi Vineyards, groves of eucalyptus trees soon give way to a drier and scrubbier terrain. It's open rangeland with cattle grazing alongside and moseying across the road.

A few miles south of the winery the road crosses an expansive lava flow dating from 1790, Haleakala's last eruption. This flow, which is part of the Kanaio Natural Area Reserve, is the same one that covers the La Perouse area of the coast south of Makena. It's still black and barren all the way down to the sea.

Just offshore is the crescent island of Molokini with Kahoolawe beyond. The large grassy hills between here and the sea are volcanic cinder cones.

Painters sometimes set up their easels along the roadside to paint scenes of the grassy rock-strewn hills and the distant ocean. There's such a wide-angle view that the ocean horizon is noticeably curved.

As the road continues it runs in and out of numerous gulches and crosses a few bridges, gradually getting closer to the coast. Around the 28-mile marker keep an eye out for a natural lava sea arch. As you continue, there are a couple of black sand beaches.

Kaupo

Kaupo Gap is a deep and rugged valley with the only lowlands on this section of the coast. The village of Kaupo is around the 35-mile marker. However, don't expect a developed village in any sense of the word as Kaupo is spread out and there's really not much to see. This is home for the scattered community of paniolos who work the Kaupo Ranch, many of them third-generation ranch hands.

Kaupo General Store, on the east side of the gap, is 'the only store for 20 miles'. Officially the hours are from 9 am to 5 pm Monday to Saturday but they can be a bit flexible so it's best not to count on it being open.

Kaupo was once heavily settled. It has three heiaus from the 1700s and two churches from the 1800s. Loaloa Heiau is the biggest and is a registered national historical monument. All three heiau sites are mauka of Huialoha Church.

Huialoha Church, which is less than a mile east of the store, is on the rocky black sand Mokulau Beach. The attractive white-washed church, built in 1859 and restored in 1978, is surrounded by a stone wall and a few windswept trees. Mokulau, which means 'many small islands', is named for the rocks just offshore. The area was an ancient surfing site.

From here the road curves in and then out at which point it's well worth stopping and looking back for a picturesque view of the church across the bay. There used to be a landing in the bay for shipping Kaupo Ranch cattle and you can still see steps leading down into the water on a rock jutting out into the ocean.

This area is cool and forested, with sisal plants on the hillsides. The road winding into Kipahulu skirts the edge of rocky cliffs and the vegetation picks up, with hala and guava trees. The road surface is like heavy

cobblestones in places and in other sections loose and sliding.

Kipahulu

The pavement begins again at Kipahulu, where the road is flat and shaded with big mango trees (which drop fruit in season), banyans, bougainvillea, and wiliwili trees with red tiger-claw blossoms.

For details on Kipahulu, see the end of the Hana to Kipahulu section.

Haleakala

Haleakala Crater is an awesome geological wonder. It resembles the surface of the moon, with a seemingly lifeless crater floor dotted with high majestic cinder cones. Haleakala is the world's largest dormant volcano, 7½ miles long and 2½ miles wide. It last erupted 200 years ago.

Haleakala National Park centers around the crater, offering impressive views from its rim and hikes across the crater floor.

Haleakala (literally 'House of the Sun') has long been considered Maui's soul. The summit is thought to be an energy vortex, a natural power point for magnetic and cosmic forces. In ancient times it was a spiritual center for Hawaiian kahunas. When the planets aligned in 1987, Haleakala drew thousands of visitors observing the harmonic convergence.

Whether it's the lingering mana of the gods who once made their home here or the geological forces of the earth which still release an occasional tremor, Haleakala does emanate a sense of some omnipresent power.

The requisite pilgrimage to witness the sunrise at the rim of the crater can be an experience that borders on the mystical. Mark Twain called it 'the sublimest spectacle' he'd ever seen.

Morning is usually the best time for viewing the crater. Later in the day warm air generally forces clouds higher and higher until they pour through the two gaps and into the crater.

Haleakala National Park

Although sunrises get top billing, sunsets can be impressive too. Sometimes there's a high thin layer of cirrus clouds and a lower layer of fluffier clouds, with the sunset reflecting colors on both levels. At other times, however, it's completely clouded over.

Haleakala National Park stretches from Haleakala Crater down to the pools of Oheo Gulch on the coast south of Hana. There are separate entrances to both sections of the park, but no passage between them. For information on the Oheo area, see the Oheo Gulch section.

Geology

In its prime, Haleakala probably reached a height of 12,000 feet before water erosion began to eke out two large river valleys. Eventually the valleys eroded into one another, forming what is known today as Haleakala Crater. The valley gaps, Koolau Gap on the northwest side and Kaupo Gap

on the southeast, are dominant features in the crater wall.

Later eruptions have added numerous cinder cones to the floor of Haleakala. The yellow colors are from sulfur, the reds from iron oxide.

Information

It's a good idea to check out the weather conditions (☎ 572-7749 for a recorded forecast, 871-5054 if it's busy) before driving up. It's not uncommon for it to be cloudy at Haleakala when it's clear on the coast. A drizzly sunrise is a particularly disappointing nonevent after getting out of bed at 4 am. The *Maui News* prints a sunrise schedule.

You can call park headquarters (☎ 572-9306) to talk to a ranger or check activity schedules.

The park never closes. The pay booth at the park entrance opens after dawn, but you can drive through before that. Entrance passes, good for seven days, cost $4 per car. National park passes are valid.

There's no food for sale in the park. Bring something to eat, particularly if you're going up for the sunrise, so that a growling stomach doesn't force you to rush all the way back down the mountain before you've had a chance to explore the sights.

Activities

Park rangers lead a guided, moderately strenuous two-hour hike that goes about a mile into the crater down Sliding Sands Trail (meet at the trailhead) from 10 am on Tuesdays and Fridays.

Guided hikes into Waikamoi Preserve leave from Hosmer Grove campground at 9 am on Mondays and Thursdays and last about three hours.

Fifteen-minute natural history talks are held at the summit building at 9:30, 10:30 and 11:30 am daily. Crater rim walks of varying lengths are held during the summer. Other walks and activities vary with the season.

Bicycle tours down Haleakala via the park road and horseback rides into the crater are detailed in the Activities section near the beginning of the Maui chapter.

Volunteer Programs

The national park service has a program allowing volunteers to work at the park. Duties may be as varied as office work, leading hikes, fence construction, trapping predatory animals, controlling invasive plants or cleaning pit toilets.

Competition is stiff; out of hundreds of applications, only a few people are selected each year. There's a preference for volunteers with a background in natural sciences and a knowledge of practicalities like first aid. A three-month (40 hours a week) commitment is required. There's no salary or help with air fare, though barracks-style housing and a daily stipend of about $12 to help pay for food are usually provided. For information write to: Volunteers in Parks, Haleakala National Park, Box 369, Makawao, HI 96768.

Another group, the Student Conservation Association (☎ 603-543-1700), Box 550C, Charlestown, NH 03603, sends five to eight people each year to work for three months as volunteers at Haleakala. There are usually a few different positions that can be applied for, with opportunities ranging from answering phones and issuing camping permits to assisting with the

---

The Sunrise Experience

Sunrise at Haleakala is unforgettable. As you drive up in the dark, the only sights are lights: a sky full of stars, scattered city lights resembling a large connect-the-dots drawing, and a distant fishing boat or two on the dark horizon.

About an hour before sunrise, the night sky begins to lighten and turn purple-blue and the stars fade away. Interesting silhouettes of the mountain ridges appear.

Plan to arrive 30 or 40 minutes before the actual sunrise. The gentlest colors show up in the moments just before dawn. The undersides of the clouds lighten up first, accenting the night sky with pale silvery slivers and streaks of pink.

About 20 minutes before sunrise, the light intensifies on the horizon in bright oranges and reds, much like a sunset. Turn around for a look at Science City, whose domes turn a surreal pink.

Temperatures hovering around freezing and a cold wind are the norm at dawn. There's often a frosty ice in the top layer of cinders which crunches underfoot.

If you don't have a winter jacket or sleeping bag to wrap yourself in, take a warm blanket from your hotel. This will give you the option of sitting outside in a peaceful spot to take it all in rather than huddling for heat inside the crowded visitor center.

Everyone comes out for the grand finale. The moment the sun appears, the earth awakens and everything glows.

Every morning is different, but once the sun is up the silvery lines and the subtleties disappear. The best photo opportunities are before the sun rises. ■

Nene

The native nene, Hawaii's state bird, is related to and resembles the Canada goose. It has been brought back from the verge of extinction (only 30 birds remained in 1951) by a captive breeding and release program.

Currently the nene population at Haleakala is holding steady at about 150. The birds generally nest in high cliffs surrounded by rugged lava flows with sparse vegetation.

Nene are rather curious. Many hang out where people do, from the crater floor cabins to park headquarters. Unfortunately they don't do well in an asphalt habitat and many have been run over by cars. ■

park's endangered species research and banding birds to study avian malaria. Round-trip airfare to Hawaii, a weekly stipend of about $75 and accommodations are provided. Anyone over 18 with a high school degree may apply.

Park Headquarters

Park headquarters, less than a mile from the park boundary, is open from 7:30 am to 4 pm daily. The office has brochures, provides camping permits and sells books on geology and flora & fauna. There are a few silverswords planted in front of the building and occasionally a pair of nene wander around the parking lot.

Hosmer Grove

Hosmer Grove, three-quarters of a mile before park headquarters, has a pleasant half-mile loop trail that begins in the campground. The trail starts in a forest of introduced trees and then passes into native Hawaiian shrubland.

The exotics in Hosmer Grove were introduced in 1910 in an effort to develop a lumber industry in Hawaii. They include incense cedar, Japanese sugi, Douglas fir, eucalyptus and various pines. Although the trees adapted well enough to grow, they didn't grow fast enough at these elevations to make tree harvesting practical. Thanks to this failure, there's a park instead.

Native plants include ohelo, pukiawe, mamane, pilo and sandalwood. There are

wonderful scents along the trail and lots of bird calls.

Walking through either Hosmer Grove or the nearby Waikamoi Preserve, you might see the native iiwi or apapane, both fairly common sparrow-size birds with bright red feathers. The iiwi has a very loud squeaking call, orange legs and a curved salmon-colored bill. The apapane is a fast-moving bird with a black bill, black legs and a white under-tail. It feeds on the nectar of ohia flowers.

You might also see the melodious laughing thrush, also called the spectacle bird for the circles around its eyes that extend back like a pair of glasses, and the greenish Japanese white-eye, also with eye circles. These two are foreign species.

Waikamoi Preserve

Waikamoi Preserve is a 5230-acre reserve adjoining Hosmer Grove. In 1983 Haleakala Ranch conveyed the management rights of the land to the Nature Conservancy.

The area contains native koa and ohia rainforest and is a habitat for Hawaiian forest birds, including a number of rare and endangered species. The yellow-green Maui creeper and the crested honeycreeper, while both endangered, are more common than some of the others. The crested honeycreeper is a beautiful but aggressive bird that often dive-bombs apapane and chases them off branches.

The conservancy has hikes on the second

Saturday of each month. Reservations are required and can be made by calling the preserve manager (☎ 572-7849). More frequent are the guided hikes led by the National Park Service, which enter the preserve from Hosmer Grove campground at 9 am on Mondays and Thursdays.

Leleiwi Overlook

Leleiwi Overlook is midway between park headquarters and the visitor center. From the parking lot it's just a few minutes' walk out to the overlook, from where you can see the West Maui Mountains and both sides of the isthmus connecting the two sides of Maui. You also get another angle on Haleakala Crater.

In the afternoon if weather conditions are right you might see the Brocken specter, an optical phenomenon that occurs at high elevations. Essentially, by standing between the sun and the clouds your image is magnified and projected onto the clouds. The light reflects off tiny droplets of water in the clouds, creating a circular rainbow around your shadow.

Kalahaku Overlook

Kalahaku Overlook is about a mile above Leleiwi Overlook. The lower section has a fenced enclosure containing lots of silversword, from seedlings to mature plants.

The upper section has an observation deck looking down into Haleakala Crater. With the help of the deck's information plaque, you can clearly identify seven cinder cones on the crater floor below.

For photography, afternoon light is best. In the early morning you can get more favorable light by walking a few minutes down an unmarked path to the left of the observation deck.

Haleakala Visitor Center

The visitor center, on the rim of the crater, is the main sunrise-viewing spot. It's open from shortly before sunrise to 3 pm daily.

The center has good displays on geological and volcanic evolution and a recording explaining what you see looking out of the window into the crater floor 3000 feet below. Books on geology, plants and the national park are for sale here and there's usually a ranger on duty.

Summit

The Puu Ulaula (Red Hill) Overlook, at 10,023 feet (3055 meters), is Maui's highest point. The octagon summit building at the overlook has wraparound windows and interpretive displays explaining the surrounding sights.

On clear days you can see the Big Island, Lanai, Molokai and even Oahu. The summit building is half a mile uphill from the visitor center.

The 37-mile drive from sea level to the summit of Haleakala is said to be the highest elevation gain in the shortest distance anywhere in the world. You can buy a certificate at the visitor center saying

Silversword

The strikingly beautiful silversword with its pointed silver leaves is a distant relative of the sunflower. The plant grows for four to 25 years before blooming just once.

In its final year, it shoots up a flowering stalk sometimes as high as nine feet. During the summer the stalk flowers with hundreds of maroon and yellow blossoms. When the flowers turn to seed in late autumn, the plant dies.

The silversword, found only in Hawaii, was nearly wiped out in the early 1900s by grazing feral goats and by people who took them for souvenirs. It's making a comeback due to efforts by the park service who have fenced in sections of the park to protect the plants. ■

you've made the trip. The dollar for the certificate goes to help exterminate pests in the park, including cats, rats and mongooses.

Science City

On the Big Island's Mauna Kea, scientists study the moon. Here at Haleakala, appropriately enough, they study the sun.

Science City, just beyond the summit, is outside park headquarters and off-limits to visitors. It's under the jurisdiction of the University of Hawaii, which owns some of the domes and leases other land for a variety of private and government research projects.

In addition to UH's solar observatory, the university's Institute of Astronomy operates a lunar ranging facility. Purdue University and the University of Wisconsin jointly operate a gamma ray telescope.

The most ominous tenant is the US Air Force, which experiments with laser technology in what's largely a remnant of the Reagan-era 'Star Wars' project. The lasers, which are beamed at a satellite orbiting in space, bounce off the satellite's mirrors and are aimed back down to an antenna farm planted above Kihei's Silversword Golf Course. Other defense-related projects at Science City include satellite tracking and identification, and a deep-space surveillance system.

Places to Stay

Camping Free tent camping is allowed at three campgrounds in the Upcountry section of the park and one on the coast at Oheo Gulch. Information on the Oheo Gulch area is in the Hana to Kipahulu section of this chapter.

Hosmer Grove is a drive-up campground immediately after the park entrance. It has a picnic shelter, toilets, water and grills. Permits are not required, though there's a three-day limit per month. It's busier in summer than in winter and is often full on holiday weekends. Located at the 6800-foot elevation, it tends to be cloudy and a bit wet.

There are two backcountry campgrounds inside Haleakala Crater. One is at Holua cabin, four miles down Halemauu Trail, and the other is at Paliku at the trail's end. Both are below steep cliffs, though Holua is dry and barren while Paliku is lush and wet.

Permits are required for backcountry camping. They are issued at park headquarters on a first-come first-served basis between 7:30 am and 4 pm on the day of the hike. Camping is limited to three nights in the crater each month, with no more than two consecutive nights at either campground.

Each campground is limited to 25 people. Permits can go quickly if large groups show up, a situation more likely to occur in summer; in winter the sites rarely fill up.

The campsites have pit toilets and water. Fires are prohibited and you'll need to carry all your trash out.

Cabins There are three primitive cabins along trails in the crater, one each at Holua, Kapalaoa and Paliku. Each has a wood-burning stove, some cooking utensils, 12 bunks with sleeping pads (but no bedding), pit toilets and a limited supply of water and firewood. Hiking distances from the crater rim range from four to 10 miles.

Cabin fees are $40 per night for a group of one to six people, $80 for seven to 12 people. There's a three-day limit, with no more than two consecutive nights in any cabin. Each cabin is rented to only one party at a time.

The problem here is the demand, which is so high the park service actually holds a lottery to award reservations! To enter, your reservation request must arrive by the last day of the month, three months prior to the proposed stay (for example, requests for cabins on any date in March must arrive by December 31).

If you have alternative dates it increases your chances. Only written reservation requests are accepted. You can get a request form from the following address: Cabin Reservation Request, Haleakala National Park, Box 369, Makawao, HI 96768.

MAUI

Don't send money with your request form. If you're selected in the lottery, you'll be notified, at which point the fees will have to be paid in full at least three weeks prior to the reservation date. They can be paid by Visa, MasterCard, check or money order.

Getting There & Away

Haleakala Crater Rd (Hwy 378) runs 11 miles from Hwy 377 up to the summit. It's a good paved road, but it's steep and winding. You don't want to rush it.

The drive to the summit takes about 1¼ hours from Paia or Kahului, two hours from Lahaina. If you need gas, fill up in Pukalani as there are no services on Haleakala Crater Rd.

On your return from the summit, much of Maui unfolds below, with fields of sugar cane and pineapple in patches on the valley floor. The highway snakes back and forth, with as many as four or five layers of switchbacks in view all at once.

HIKING THE CRATER

Hiking the crater floor offers a completely different angle on Haleakala's lunar landscape. Instead of peering down from the rim, you're looking up at the walls and towering cinder cones. It looks so much like a moonscape that US astronauts trained here before going to the moon.

The crater is a very still place to walk. Cinder crunching underfoot is often the only sound.

The trails inside the crater connect with each other and are marked at junctions.

The weather at Haleakala can change suddenly from dry hot conditions to a cold windswept rain. Although the general rule is sunny in the morning and cloudy in the afternoon, fog and clouds can blow in at any time.

No matter what the weather is like at the start of a hike, be prepared for temperatures that can drop into the 50s (F) during the day and the 30s at night, at any time of year. Hikers without proper clothing risk exposure to hypothermia.

The climate also changes radically as you walk across the crater floor. In the four miles between Kapalaoa and Paliku cabins, rainfall varies from an annual average of 12 inches to 300 inches. December to May is the wetter season.

With the average elevation on the crater floor at 6700 feet, the relatively thin air means that hiking can be quite tiring. The higher elevation also means that sunburn is more likely. Take sunscreen, rain gear, a few layers of clothing and a full canteen of water.

Sliding Sands Trail

Sliding Sands, the summit trail into the crater, starts at the south side of the visitor center parking lot. The trail leads 9¾ miles to the Paliku campground and cabin,

House of the Sun

Legend says that long ago the goddess Hina was having problems drying her tapa cloth because the days were too short. Her son Maui, the prankish demigod for whom the island is named, decided to take matters into his own hands.

One morning he went up to the mountaintop and waited for the sun. As it came up over the mountain Maui lassoed the rays one by one and held on until the sun came to a halt. When the sun begged to be let go, Maui demanded that as a condition for its release it hereafter slow its path across the sky.

The sun gave its promise, the days were lengthened and the mountain became known as House of the Sun. There are about 15 more minutes of daylight at Haleakala than on the coast below. ■

passing Kapalaoa cabin at 5¾ miles. The first six miles of the trail follow the south wall of the crater.

From Kapalaoa to Paliku there's a gentle descent and the vegetation gradually increases. Paliku (6380 feet) is beneath a sheer cliff at the eastern end of the crater. In contrast to the crater's barren western end, the heavy rainfall in this area makes for grassy campsites, with ohia forests climbing the slopes.

Sliding Sands-Halemauu Trail

One of the most popular day hikes for people in good shape is the 12-mile hike which starts down Sliding Sands Trail and returns via Halemauu Trail. It's a strenuous full-day outing.

Sliding Sands starts out at 9780 feet and descends steeply over loose cinders down to the crater floor. If you hike it after catching the sunrise you'll walk directly into a gentle warmish wind and the rays of the sun. There are great views on the way down but, except for a few shrubs, there's no vegetation in sight.

Four miles down, after an elevation drop of 2500 feet, a spur trail leads north about a mile to Halemauu Trail.

Once on Halemauu Trail it's possible to take a short loop to the **Bottomless Pit**. Legends say the pit leads down to the sea, though the park service says it's just 65 feet deep. It's basically a large hole in the ground of limited interest.

About 1½ miles up the Halemauu Trail is the short **Silversword Loop,** which passes by silversword plants in various stages of growth. If you're here in summer you should be able to see plants in bloom.

About a mile farther along Halemauu Trail is Holua cabin and campground. There's a large **lava tube** here that's worth exploring. At 6960 feet this is one of the lowest areas along this hike and there are impressive views of the crater walls rising a few thousand feet to the west. From the cabin it's four miles to the Halemauu trailhead.

Because of its steep descent, Sliding Sands Trail makes a better entry trail into the crater than a return trail. The Halemauu trailhead, at an elevation of 8000 feet, is an easier exit.

Halemauu trailhead is on Hwy 378, six miles below the visitor center (and the trailhead to Sliding Sands) and 3½ miles above park headquarters. If you haven't arranged to be picked up or left a car at the trailhead, you could try your luck hitchhiking.

Halemauu Trail

If you're not up for a long hike, you might try doing just part of the Halemauu Trail. Even hiking in the first mile to the crater rim gives a fine view of the crater with Koolau Gap to the east. It's fairly level up to this point.

If you were to continue on the trail and hike down the switchbacks to Holua cabin and back, the eight-mile round-trip would make a fine, hardy day hike. From the trailhead to the bottom of the pali the trail descends 1400 feet. Once on the floor of the crater the trail follows the west wall for about a mile to Holua cabin at 6960 feet. The trail continues another six miles to Paliku cabin.

Halemauu trailhead, 3½ miles above park headquarters, is marked. There's a fair chance you'll find nene in the parking lot.

Kalua O Ka Oo Trail

Two miles down the Sliding Sands Trail (a descent of 1600 feet), a spur trail leads up the Kalua O Ka Oo cinder cone, about half a mile to the north.

Midway along Kalua O Ka Oo Trail are some silversword plants. From the visitor center to Kalua O Ka Oo and back it's a hardy three-hour hike. Because of the uphill climb back, this is a good hike to do early in the morning to avoid the midday heat.

Kaupo Trail

From Paliku campground on the eastern edge of the crater floor, it's possible to continue another nine miles down to Kaupo on the southern coast. The first 3½ miles of the trail drops 2500 feet in elevation before reaching the park boundary. It's a rocky trail through rough lava and brushland. The last 5½ miles pass through Kaupo Ranch property on a rough jeep trail as it descends the Kaupo Gap, exiting at the east side of the Kaupo General Store. There are fine coastal views along the way.

The 'village' of Kaupo is a long way from anywhere, with very little traffic. Still, what traffic there is – largely sight-seers braving the circle-island road – moves slow enough along Kaupo's rough road to start conversation. If you have to

walk the final stretch, it's 10 miles to Oheo Gulch and what will seem like hordes of people and traffic. If you do need to spend the night in Kaupo, hikers are allowed to camp outside the walls at the Huialoha Church.

This is a strenuous hike and because of the remoteness and the ankle-twisting conditions it's not advisable to hike it alone. The National Park Service publishes a Kaupo Trail brochure that people considering the hike should pick up in advance.

Molokai

Molokai is the last stronghold of rural Hawaii. It manages to hold out in a sort of time warp: no packaged Hawaiiana, no high-rises, more farmers than tourists.

If you're looking for lots of action or anything slick, Molokai isn't the place. Instead, you can walk along Hawaii's largest beach with barely another soul in sight, or take the cliffside mule trail down to the old leprosy colony of Kalaupapa. Molokai has fine hikes, spectacular valleys, a wildlife park and a handful of historical sites.

Molokai is the most Hawaiian of the main islands, with almost 50% of its population of native Hawaiian ancestry. It's only sparsely populated, with but a handful of small towns.

According to ancient chants, Molokai is a child of Hina, goddess of the moon. This is a place to get in touch with basics.

In the morning you can sit on the edge of an 800-year-old fishpond and watch the sun rise over Haleakala on distant Maui. In the evening you can watch the sun set behind the silhouette of Molokai's royal coconut grove.

Molokai retains so much small-town character that at times it seems more like some forgotten outpost in the South Pacific than the island between the high-rises of Maui and Waikiki.

ORIENTATION

Molokai lies midway in the Hawaiian chain, 26 miles southeast of Oahu and nine miles northwest of Maui. Lanai is nine miles directly south.

The airport is on the island's flat central plains, more or less in the center of Molokai. Take a right turn when you leave the airport to get to Hwy 460. At the highway, to the left it's seven miles to Kaunakakai, the main town; to the right it's 13 miles to the Kaluakoi Resort on the west coast.

This one highway is Molokai's main road, stretching from east to west. From Kaunakakai westward it's called Hwy 460 (Maunaloa Highway). From Kaunakakai eastward it's Hwy 450 (Kamehameha V Highway).

Exploring Molokai

Molokai is not the place to explore dirt roads just to see what's there. People on Molokai spend a lot of time outdoors and their yards are extensions of their homes. Many dirt paths that seem like they could be roads are just driveways into someone's backyard. In addition, as on all the islands, there's a bit of pakalolo growing here and there. All in all, folks aren't keen on outsiders cruising their private turf.

On the other hand, if there's a fishpond you want to see and someone's house is between the road and the water, it's usually easy to stop and strike up a conversation. Molokai people are generally receptive and friendly. If you ask permission first they'll usually let you cross their property. If you appear interested they might even share a little local lore and history – the old-timers in particular can be fascinating to listen to.

HISTORY

Molokai had powerful sorcerers whose reputations were respected throughout the islands. Through carvings of poisonwood idols and other elaborate rituals, they were able to keep potential invaders at bay. For centuries, the battling armies of Maui and Oahu were careful to bypass Molokai.

By the 18th century, magic wasn't enough to protect Molokai from outside influences. Internal dissent among the alii of Molokai, largely over access to valuable fishing grounds at Moomomi, led them to align with chiefs from other islands. Oahu, Maui and the Big Island all got involved in the ensuing power struggle.

Eventually the king of Oahu, Peleio-holani, established his rule over Molokai. When the daughter he left on Molokai was

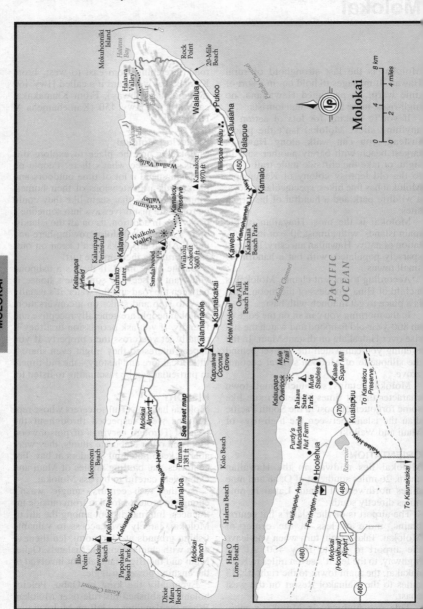

MOLOKAI

captured and killed by Molokai chiefs, Peleioholani hastily returned to the island and struck back with a vengeance. Those Molokai chiefs who were unable to flee to Maui were captured and roasted alive.

Oahu continued to rule over Molokai until 1785. Over the next decade warring Maui and the Big Island took alternate turns ruling Molokai until Kamehameha the Great finally united all the islands in 1795.

The first detailed description of the island was recorded by Captain George Vancouver, a British navigator, who anchored off Molokai in 1792. His guesstimate placed Molokai's population at around 10,000.

When the missionaries arrived in the 1830s they did a more detailed count, estimating Molokai's total population at 8700.

Molokai's largest settlements were on the rainy south coast of the eastern half of the island. The shallow waters and coastal indentations there were ideal for the construction of fishponds. In the valley wetlands, taro patches flourished.

The missionaries found the densest populations between Kamalo and Waialua and it is in this area that they established their first missions. Some of the churches still stand today.

Kalaupapa Peninsula had the island's other major settlement, with about 2500 people. The north shore valleys of Halawa, Pelekunu and Wailau were also populated. Molokai's central plains and dry western half were only lightly settled.

Ranching & Agriculture

Cattle and sheep, which were introduced in the mid-1800s, had a major impact on Molokai. Grazing resulted in widespread destruction of native vegetation, causing upland soils to wash down into the coastal fishponds, destroying the extensive centuries-old system of aquaculture.

In the 1850s Kamehameha V acquired the bulk of Molokai's arable land, forming Molokai Ranch. After his death the ranch became part of the Bishop Estate, which sold it off to a group of Honolulu businesspeople in 1897.

A year later the American Sugar Company, a division of Molokai Ranch, attempted to develop a major sugar plantation in central Molokai. They built a railroad system to haul the cane, developed harbor facilities and installed a powerful pumping system to draw up water. However, by 1900 the well-water used to irrigate the fields had become so saline that the crops failed.

The company then got into honey production on such a scale that at one point Molokai was the world's largest honey exporter. In the mid-1930s an epidemic wiped out the hives and the industry.

In the meantime, Molokai Ranch continued its efforts to find 'the crop for Molokai'. Cotton, rice and numerous grain crops all took their turn biting Molokai's red dust.

Finally pineapple took root as the crop most suitable for the island's dry, windy conditions. In 1920, plantation-scale production began in Hoolehua. Within 10 years Molokai's population tripled to over 5000 as immigrant labor was introduced to work the fields.

In the 1970s competition from overseas brought an end to pineapple's reign on Molokai. Dole closed down its operation in 1976 and the other island giant, Del Monte, later followed suit. It brought hard times and the highest unemployment levels in the state.

Then cattle raising, long a mainstay, suddenly collapsed. In a controversial decision in 1985 the state, after finding an incidence of bovine tuberculosis, ordered every head of cattle on Molokai to be destroyed. Molokai Ranch has since restocked some of its herd, but the majority of the smaller 240 former cattle owners have given up.

Molokai Ranch still owns about one-third of Molokai, which is more than half of the island's privately held lands.

GEOGRAPHY

Molokai is Hawaii's fifth largest island. It is 38 miles long, 10 miles wide and roughly rectangular in shape, with a land area of 264 sq miles.

The western half of Molokai is dry and

MOLOKAI

Taro plant

arid, with rolling hills and the gradually sloping range of Maunaloa (1381 feet). The island's highest point, Kamakou (4970 feet), is in the middle of the rugged eastern half.

Geologically Molokai is a union of two separate shield volcanoes that erupted to form two distinct islands. The rugged mountains of eastern Molokai captured the clouds. Heavy rainfall and stream erosion then cut deep valleys into its towering north face. Western Molokai formed into more modest hills and tableland. Later eruptions spilled lava into the channel that separated the two, forming the Hoolehua Plains and creating present-day Molokai.

Kalaupapa, on the north side of Molokai, seems to have been an afterthought by Madame Pele. An eruption from offshore Kauhako Crater created the flat lava peninsula long after the rest of Molokai had been formed. Kauhako Crater, at 400 feet, is Kalaupapa's highest point.

Molokai's North Shore, from Kalaupapa to Halawa, is a wilderness area of coastal mountains and deeply cut valleys. They include the world's highest sea cliffs, which reach heights of 3300 feet with an average gradient of 58°. Hawaii's highest waterfall, Kahiwa Falls (1750 feet), drops from these cliffs.

The North Shore is spectacular, but for the most part the steep slopes and rainforests are virtually impenetrable. The main way to get into the valleys is by boat, but rough winter seas restrict that to the summer season.

CLIMATE
At Kaunakakai, the average daily temperature is 70°F in winter, 78°F in summer. The average annual rainfall is 27 inches.

FLORA & FAUNA
The two most dominant forest types on Molokai are kiawe in the dryer areas and ohia lehua in the wetter. Along the banks of streams, which were once heavily cultivated with taro, forests of kukui and guava now dominate.

The axis deer that run free in Molokai are descendants of eight deer introduced from India in 1868 as a gift to King Kamehameha V. Feral pigs, introduced by the early Polynesian settlers, roam the upper wetland forests and feral goats inhabit the steep canyons and valley rims. All three wreaked havoc on the environment and are hunted game animals.

Native waterbirds include the common moorhen, Hawaiian coot and black-necked stilt, which are all endangered. Molokai has five native forest birds, mostly in the undisturbed upland forests, and the Hawaiian owl.

GOVERNMENT
Kalaupapa Peninsula is a county unto itself, called Kalawao, which is essentially administered by the State Department of Health. The rest of Molokai, along with neighboring Lanai, is swallowed up in the mire of Maui County.

In large part administrative decisions affecting Molokai are made on Maui. Since most community planning and development issues are decided at a county level, the island of Maui, with 12 times Molokai's population, has the clout.

ECONOMY
Molokai has a double-digit unemployment rate that's triple the state average. In an

effort to bring the rate down, the state charters most of the seats on the early morning and late afternoon ferry runs to Lahaina for some 200 Molokai residents who commute to jobs on Maui, primarily in Kaanapali hotels.

Homegrown Economy

After the huge pineapple plantations left Molokai in the late 1970s, islanders began to more intensely develop small-scale farming.

Molokai has rich soil and some feel the island may have the potential to be Hawaii's 'breadbasket'. Recently, watermelon growers on Molokai have not only captured the Oahu market from mainland growers, but have begun to export to Canada as well. Other crops being grown in increasing quantities include dryland taro, macadamia nuts, sweet potatoes, string beans, onions and bell peppers.

The Kaunakakai area has some of the world's best growing conditions for seed corn. Hawaii's climate makes it possible to produce three generations of hybrids each year versus only one on the mainland. Corn for seed has been raised in Hawaii since the late 1960s and about half of the corn produced in the USA can now trace its roots to Molokai. Seed production is labor intensive – each ear of corn is bagged, tagged and eventually harvested by hand. Incidentally, the paper bags that cover the ears prevent the corn from cross pollinating.

In 1991, coffee was planted on hundreds of acres of formerly fallow pineapple fields in Kualapuu.

Development

Water use is a hot issue on Molokai, with both farmers and West End developers vying for the island's limited supply. In 1994 the Sierra Club Legal Defense Fund filed a lawsuit on behalf of Molokai residents after the owners of the Kaluakoi Resort began laying a large new pipeline into the island's central aquifer for use on the dry West End. The 24-inch, nine-mile pipeline is capable of carrying 20 million gallons of water a day, half of Molokai's estimated developable water supply. Many Molokai residents see the issue as pivotal to the island's future – that if water is diverted to facilitate new development on the West End it will be at the expense of expanding native Hawaiian homestead farms in central Molokai.

POPULATION & PEOPLE

Molokai has a population of 6800. Outside of Niihau, Molokai is the most Hawaiian of the islands, with almost 50% of its people Hawaiian or part-Hawaiian. Filipino is the next largest ethnic group, followed by Japanese and Caucasian.

The large Hawaiian population is in part

MOLOKAI

Molokai Plan

In 1981 a Maui County Committee was appointed to create a community plan to address future development on Molokai. The committee conducted hearings and surveys on Molokai and much to the surprise of Molokai residents – who were used to being bullied by Maui pro-development forces – the recommendations put forth in the final plan were attuned to their own feelings on growth.

The Molokai Plan calls for the preservation of Molokai's rural lifestyle and the maintenance of agriculture as the basis of the economy. It also calls for all resort development to be limited to the West End and to be low-rise. It recommends a number of environmental protection schemes, including conservation practices to reverse erosion, the maintenance of fishponds and the creation of marine conservation areas. The Molokai Plan has been widely accepted as the guiding code for land use on Molokai and is referred to whenever there are disputes over development – which is often.

You can pick up a lot of local anti-development sentiment by walking around Kaunakakai and noticing window posters and bumper stickers, such as 'Molokai Is Too Small To Be Big' and 'Keep Molokai Molokai'. ∎

due to the Hawaiian Homes Act of 1921 that awarded 40-acre blocks of land to people with at least 50% Hawaiian ancestry. The purpose of the act was to encourage homesteading among native Hawaiians, who had become the most landless ethnic group in Hawaii. The first settlements under the act were made on Molokai.

INFORMATION
Tourist Offices
The Molokai Visitors Association (☎ 553-3876; fax 553-5288), Box 960, Kaunakakai, HI 96748, distributes tourist information about Molokai. From off the island, you can call toll free: (800) 800-6367 from the US mainland and Canada, (800) 553-0404 within Hawaii.

Money
There are half a dozen banks and credit unions on the island; the Bank of Hawaii in Kaunakakai is the largest.

Post & Telecommunications
The main post office is in downtown Kaunakakai; there are also post offices in Hoolehua, Kualapuu, Maunaloa and Kalaupapa. When phoning Molokai from out of state, add Hawaii's 808 area code in front of the local seven-digit number.

Media
Newspapers Molokai's two weekly newspapers, both distributed free around the island, provide a nice glimpse of island life. *The Dispatch* (☎ 553-3293), Box 440, Kaunakakai, HI 96748, published each Thursday, has a progressive stance on local issues; subscriptions to the mainland cost $40 a year. The more conservative *Molokai Advertiser-News* (☎ 558-8253), HC 1, Box 770, Kaunakakai, HI 96748, is published each Wednesday.

The *Maui News* and the *Honolulu Adver-tiser* are sold at the airport and at C Pascua Store in Kaunakakai.

Maps
The best map of Molokai, albeit not perfect, is the Molokai-Lanai map put out by the University of Hawaii Press and sold in shops around Kaunakakai. A free island recreation map, useful for hikers and those who want to go off on jeep roads, is available from the Department of Land & Natural Resources, Division of State Parks, Box 1049, Wailuku, HI 96793.

Film & Photography
Molokai Sight & Sound in Kaunakakai sells film and does in-house film processing; a 24-exposure roll of prints costs $9.60 for overnight service, $2 more for one-hour service. They are open from 9 am to 8:30 pm daily.

Weather
For recorded weather and marine forecasts by the National Weather Service dial 552-2477.

Emergency
Dial 911 for police, ambulance and fire emergencies. Molokai General Hospital (☎ 553-5331) in Kaunakakai has 24-hour emergency service. The Molokai Helpline (☎ 553-3311) provides crisis counseling.

ACTIVITIES
Beaches & Swimming
Papohaku Beach on the west coast is the broadest and longest sandy beach in all of Hawaii. Although it's a great walking beach, it's not safe for swimming. However, just a few miles south of Papohaku is Dixie Maru Beach, a popular family beach with a small protected bay.

For something less frequented there's Kawakiu Beach, north of Kaluakoi Golf

---

Official Molokai
Molokai's official flower is the white kukui blossom, its official color is green and its nickname is 'The Friendly Island'. ∎

Course, a beautiful crescent beach with fine coastal views and good swimming when seas are calm. Moomomi Beach, on the north coast, is another secluded coastal stretch, this one backed by expansive dunes.

In terms of swimming, the Kaunakakai area is a dud, with a coastline of silty, shallow waters. Most Kaunakakai visitors drive to the southeastern end of the island, where the beach around the 20-mile marker offers some of Molokai's best swimming and snorkeling. Rock Point, not far from there, and Halawa Bay, at the end of the road, are popular surfing spots.

There are other beaches in remote places, but Molokai is about the last place you'd need to torture yourself with washed-out roads or trips through jungles simply to get away from it all. For those who have ever fantasized about having a vast secluded beach to themselves, all that's needed is to drive up to the miles of gleaming sand at Papohaku and start walking.

Molokai Fish & Dive in Kaunakakai rents snorkel sets for $8 and boogie boards for $7 and Kaluakoi Hotel rents sports equipment at its beach hut.

Swimming Pools The Mitchell Pauole Center in Kaunakakai has a 25-meter pool open free to the public from 9 to 11:45 am daily except on Thursdays and Sundays, and from 1 to 4:30 pm daily. It's not uncommon to have the pool to yourself, particularly in winter when islanders consider the pool water to be cold.

Hiking
Molokai has a variety of hiking opportunities. The hike to Moaula Falls in Halawa Valley, on the eastern end of the island, is the most trodden.

The Nature Conservancy's Kamakou Preserve offers unique rainforest hikes in the island's rugged interior and out to scenic valley overlooks.

The Palaau State Park area has a couple of good hiking options. One, the hike down the mule trail to Kalaupapa, not only offers fine views but also provides a way to get to

the peninsula without dishing out a lot of money. A less frequented trail from the Kalaupapa Overlook provides a pleasant hour-long hike through a forest of fragrant eucalyptus and ironwood.

On the west side of the island, there's an easy hike to secluded Kawakiu Beach from the Kaluakoi Golf Course. The expansive white sands of Papohaku Beach and Moomomi Beach offer fine walks as well.

All trails are detailed in their respective sections.

Kayaking
Fun Hogs Hawaii (☎ 567-9242), in the beach hut at the Kaluakoi Hotel, rents kayaks in summer. The cost is $20/30 a half/full day for a one-person kayak, $30/45 for a two-person kayak.

From June through August they conduct guided shoreline kayak tours to Kawakiu Bay for $30, snorkeling gear included.

For experienced kayakers, they can also make arrangements for a self-guided North Shore kayak/camping trip from Halawa Valley all the way back to Kepuhi Beach, a trip of about five days.

Tennis
The Mitchell Pauole Center has two lighted tennis courts just beyond the pool. Like everywhere else in Molokai, you're not likely to find a crowd waiting.

The Kaluakoi Hotel in Kaunakakai has four lighted tennis courts open to the public on a first-come first-serve basis.

Cycling
Fun Hogs Hawaii (☎ 552-2555) at the Kaluakoi Hotel rents 21-speed mountain bikes for $6 an hour, $20 a day, including helmets and gloves.

Molokai Ranch (☎ 552-2767) rents mountain bikes for $15 a half day, $25 a day. Maps are provided that show bike trails on ranch property.

Horseback Riding
Molokai Ranch (☎ 552-2767) has 1½-hour guided horseback rides at 8:30 am on Tuesdays, Thursdays, Saturdays and Sundays

MOLOKAI

for $35. The rides cross ranch property, providing views of the ocean and Lanai. There's also a longer ride (four to five hours) offered at 11 am on Saturdays and Sundays for $75, which goes to a secluded beach for lunch (included in the price).

Molokai Horse & Wagon Ride (☎ 558-8380) offers a 1½-hour guided horseback ride for $44 with lunch or $37 without.

Golf

The Kaluakoi Golf Course (☎ 552-2739) has a fine 18-hole par 72 course open from 7 am to 6 pm, a driving range, a putting green and a pro shop. The cost for 18 holes including cart is $55 for resort guests, $75 for non-guests. Clubs can be rented for $22 per 18 holes, shoes for $10.

Although most tourists stick to the resort golf course, Ironwood Hills Golf Club (☎ 567-6000) in Kalae is the course of choice by islanders and is a real test of skill. It's open from 7 am to 6:30 pm daily. Fees are $8 for nine holes or $12 for 18, plus $2 for pull carts, $6 to $12 for gas carts.

Organized Tours

Kukui Tours & Limousines (☎ 553-5133) has three-hour island tours in seven-person vans for $24 per person which include Kaunakakai and Maunaloa towns, Kaluakoi Resort, Purdy's Macadamia Nut Farm and the Kalaupapa Overlook. Seven-hour tours, which add on the ride through eastern Molokai to Halawa Valley, cost $42. There's a three-person minimum. Kukui also has vehicles with drivers that can be chartered at an hourly rate of $54 (or $74 for a stretch limo!) with a two-hour minimum.

Friendly Isle Tours (☎ 553-9046) has similar tours at similar prices, while Molokai Off-Road Tours & Taxi (☎ 553-3369) does 4WD mountain tours as well as standard tours.

Wagon Ride

Molokai Horse & Wagon Ride (☎ 558-8380 daytime, 567-6773 in the evenings), c/o Larry Helm, Box 56, Hoolehua, HI 96729, is a small local operation that combines a horse-drawn wagon

ride from the beach at Mapulehu to Iliiliopae Heiau with coconut husking, net throwing demonstrations and hula lessons, followed by lunch. While it's touristy, most people seem to enjoy themselves. The ride leaves at 10:30 am Monday to Saturday and the cost is $37 for adults, $18.50 for children six to 12 (free for ages five and under). To get there look for a big mango grove, makai side, a quarter of a mile past the 15-mile marker on Hwy 450.

Sailing & Whale Watching

The waters between Molokai, Lanai and Maui are a frequent winter site for cavorting humpbacks.

Molokai Charters (☎ 553-5852), Box 1207, Kaunakakai, HI 96748, has a $30 two-hour sunset sail and a $40 four-hour midday sail that includes whale watching in season. There's also a full-day $75 trip to Lanai that includes snorkeling and lunch. All sailings are from Kaunakakai aboard *Satan's Doll*, a 42-foot sloop. The boat goes out with a minimum of four people.

From December through April, the *Maui Princess* (☎ 553-5736) has a two-hour whale watch cruise at 9:30 am on Wednesdays and Saturdays from Kaunakakai for $25. You can also take the boat for its regular commute from Molokai to Maui and back again, a total of about 3½ hours, leaving Molokai either at 5:45 am ('sunrise whale watch') or 3:55 pm ('sunset whale watch') for $30. In the morning, continental breakfast is included. Children pay $15 on all trips. If you're planning to travel between Maui and Molokai anyway, the best deal is obviously to take the boat as a means of transportation at $25 one way.

Joe Reich (☎ 558-8377), Box 825, Kaunakakai, HI 96748, has a 31-foot boat, the *Alyce C*, that can be chartered for fishing trips, whale-watching jaunts and interisland runs.

ACCOMMODATIONS

Molokai has a total of three hotels and five condominium complexes.

The Kaunakakai area has two hotels, Pau Hana Inn and Hotel Molokai, and one condo, Molokai Shores. All three front a beach with a good view of Lanai, but with waters unsuitable for swimming; each place does, however, have a swimming pool.

Molokai's only resort is Kaluakoi, on the west coast. It has one hotel, a golf club, three condo complexes and attractive white sand beaches.

The only other development, the Wavecrest condos, are 13 miles east of Kaunakakai, on Molokai's wetter and lusher eastern side. Molokai also has a handful of B&Bs on the southeast side of the island.

Unless otherwise specified, the rates given in this chapter are the same for both singles and doubles.

Camping

Camping is allowed at Palaau State Park, at Waikolu Lookout, at the county beach parks of Papohaku and One Alii, at the Kapuaiwa Coconut Grove and at a few remote beaches owned by Molokai Ranch.

State Parks Camping is free at Palaau State Park. Permits are required and may be picked up at the Department of Land & Natural Resources office in Hoolehua or from George, the caretaker, at the house immediately north of the mule stables. If you can't get a permit during business hours, it's OK to just set up camp and let George find you.

Free camping is also permitted at Waikolu Lookout, just outside Kamakou Preserve. For information contact the Division of Forestry & Wildlife (☎ 244-4352), Box 1015, Wailuku, HI 96793, on Maui. Otherwise, try to catch the ranger at the forestry baseyard (☎ 553-5019) on Oloolo St, which is a mile west of Kaunakakai off Hwy 460. The best bet is between 6:45 and 7 am or from 3 to 3:30 pm.

County Parks The Department of Parks & Recreation (☎ 553-3204), Box 526, Kaunakakai, HI 96748, issues camping permits for Papohaku and One Alii county parks from 8 am to 4 pm Monday to Friday at Mitchell Pauole Center in Kaunakakai.

Permits cost $3 per adult and 50c per child (age 17 and under) per day; reservations must be made in person, not by phone. Camping is limited to three consecutive days in each park and a total of 15 days a year. Both parks have restrooms, drinking water, showers and picnic areas.

Hawaiian Home Lands The Department of Hawaiian Home Lands (☎ 567-6296), Box 198, Hoolehua, HI 96729, on Puukapele Ave in Hoolehua issues permits for only one group each night for camping at Kapuaiwa Coconut Grove, on the shore just west of Kaunakakai. The cost is $5 per night for the entire site. While it's usually booked by groups for parties, reunions and the like, individual travelers can stay when it's available.

Molokai Ranch Molokai Ranch (☎ 552-2767) allows camping at Kawakiu, Moomomi, Kolo and Hale O Lono beaches. Camping is free at Kawakiu, which is the most accessible, and no permit is required.

At Moomomi, Kolo and Hale O Lono, permits are required and camping is allowed only on weekends and holidays. The camping areas are at the end of rough dirt roads (4WD vehicles are advisable) and entered via locked gates. There's a $50 refundable key deposit. These backcountry campsites are sometimes open only to Molokai residents while at other times they are available to off-islanders at a charge of $10 per person per day. There are no facilities and all supplies including water must be carried in. Camping permits, which require a week's notice, can be applied for in person from 7:30 am to 2 pm on weekdays from the Molokai Ranch office in Maunaloa, or by writing to Box 8, Maunaloa, HI 96770.

THINGS TO BUY

Craft fairs are held from 8 am to 4 pm on Saturdays at Kaluakoi Hotel. It's a good way to meet local artists who sell their own lauhala weavings, quilts, pottery, woodwork and other handcrafts.

Just about every shop in Kaunakakai

MOLOKAI

sells T-shirts proclaiming Molokai's rural pride. With slogans like 'Keep Hawaiian Lands in Hawaiian Hands' and 'Molokai Mo Bettah', they make a good souvenir.

Molokai-grown Malulani Estate Coffee can be purchased in grocery stores around the island. Or you could take back the same stash islanders do when they leave Molokai: an island-grown watermelon and some Molokai bread from Kanemitsu Bakery.

GETTING THERE & AWAY
Air
Air Molokai (☎ 553-3636) flies to Molokai about 10 times a day from Honolulu ($45), a couple of times from Kahului ($50) and once a day from Hana ($62). The round-trip fares are double.

Island Air (☎ 567-6115, (800) 652-6541 within Hawaii) flies direct to Molokai 10 times a day from Honolulu, four times from Kahului and twice from Hana. The one-way fare is $74 from Honolulu, $81 from Maui.

Hawaiian Airlines (☎ 553-3644, (800) 367-5320 from the US mainland) flies direct to Molokai twice a day from Honolulu and once daily from Kahului and Lanai. The one-way fare between Molokai

and any Hawaiian Airlines destination is $74.

Mahalo Air (☎ (800) 277-8333) flies between Honolulu and Molokai an average of three times a day, with a one-way fare of $70.

Information on flights to and from Kalaupapa is in the Kalaupapa section.

Molokai Airport Molokai Airport, sometimes called Hoolehua Airport, has car rental booths, a snack bar, a liquor lounge, restrooms, pay phones, and a visitor information booth that is rarely staffed. The Molokai newspapers can be picked up free and off-island papers are for sale.

Molokai Airport Lei Stand has attractive leis at reasonable prices. The snack bar, which is open from 6:45 am to 6 pm daily, sells breakfast and lunch plates for $5 to $6, cheeseburgers for $3 and loaves of Molokai bread.

Ferry
The *Maui Princess* (☎ 553-5736 on Molokai, 661-8397 on Maui, (800) 833-5800 from the mainland), 113 Prison St, Lahaina, HI 96761, runs between Maui and Molokai twice daily.

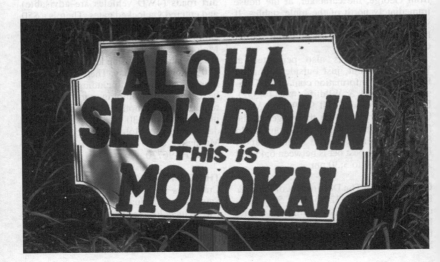

The boat leaves Kaunakakai at 5:45 am and 3:55 pm. It leaves Lahaina's Pier 3 at 7 am and 5 pm. The journey takes about 1¾ hours. The one-way fare is $25 for adults, $12.50 for children ages three to 12. This is not a leisurely ferry but rather a fast-cruising 118-foot craft with airplane-style seats, and when the seas are choppy the ride can get a bit rough. However, not only is this the cheapest way to get between Maui and Molokai, but during the season you can often spot whales en route. The boat has an air-conditioned main cabin, a snack bar and an open-air observation deck. A variety of cruise/drive and over-night packages are available through the boat company.

There are no visitor facilities where the boat pulls in at Kaunakakai Wharf and it's a three-quarter-mile walk to the center of town. All car rentals are at the airport.

GETTING AROUND
Taxi
There are no metered taxis on Molokai, but a couple of companies provide taxi services for set fees. The taxis often meet flights, but to be assured of a ride from the airport you should make advance reservations.

From the airport, Kukui Tours & Limousines (☎ 553-5133) charges $7.50 per person (minimum three people) to Kaluakoi Resort and, with a two-person minimum, $8 to Kaunakakai or $19 to Wavecrest condos.

Teem Cab Molokai (☎ 553-3633) and Friendly Isle Tours (☎ 553-9046) also offer taxi services.

Car
Renting a car on Molokai is just about essential if you intend to explore the island. However, as there are currently only two companies operating on Molokai, discounts are scarce and there are often car shortages – be sure to book far in advance, especially if you're planning on going over on a weekend.

Budget (☎ 567-6877) and Dollar (☎ 567-6156) both have booths at the airport. Dollar is open from 6:30 am to 6:30 pm, Budget until 7 pm. Dollar's regular rate for a compact car with unlimited miles begins at $42 a day, while Budget's begins at $43. Dollar rents 4WD vehicles for $60 on weekdays, $80 on weekends. Note that rental vehicles are officially not supposed to be driven on dirt roads. Dollar, for instance, makes you sign an agreement accepting a $100 addition to your bill if you drive off paved roads or even use the car for camping! See the Getting Around chapter in the front of the book for general rental info and toll-free numbers.

There are gas stations in Kaunakakai, Maunaloa and Kualapuu.

Hitchhiking
Hitchhiking is officially illegal in Maui County. It probably wouldn't be impossible to get a ride between the airport and town, but hitchhiking is fairly rare on Molokai and distant corners such as Halawa and the west coast beaches just don't get much traffic. For anyone considering hitchhiking, all the usual safety cautions apply.

Kaunakakai

Kaunakakai, Molokai's biggest town, takes much of its character from what it doesn't have. There's not a single traffic light, no shopping centers and no fast-food eateries.

Most of Molokai's businesses are lined up along Ala Malama St, the town's broad main street. The stores have old wooden false fronts that give Kaunakakai the appearance of an old Wild West town. There are a couple of restaurants, a bakery, post office, pharmacy and one of just about everything else a small town needs. The tallest point is still the church steeple.

Kaunakakai is a town that hasn't changed its face at all for tourism. It has an almost timeless quality and a nice slow pace.

Information
Since Molokai doesn't have a daily newspaper, bulletin boards around Kaunakakai are the prime source of news and

announcements. The board next to the Bank of Hawaii is the most extensive.

Tourist Office The Molokai Visitors Association (☎ 553-3876), at the corner of Hwy 450 and Hwy 460, can give you brochures and the lowdown on what's happening around the island. The office is open from 8 am to 5 pm Monday to Friday.

Money The Bank of Hawaii, on Ala Malama St, is open from 8:30 am to 3 pm Monday to Thursday, to 6 pm on Fridays.

Post The post office, on Ala Malama St, is open from 9 am to 4:30 pm Monday to Friday and 9 to 11 am on Saturdays.

Library Kaunakakai has a good public library that's open from 9 am to 5 pm on Mondays, Tuesdays, Thursdays and Fridays and noon to 8 pm on Wednesdays.

Laundry The coin laundry behind Outpost Natural Foods is open from 7 am to 9 pm. It costs 75c for a cold wash, $1 for a hot wash. There's another coin laundry opposite Molokai Drive Inn.

Kaunakakai Harbor
Gone are the days when pineapple was loaded from Kaunakakai Wharf, but a commercial inter-island barge still pulls into the harbor a couple of times a week and the commuter ferry plies between Kaunakakai and Maui each day. The harbor also has mooring facilities for small boats.

Molokai was the favorite island and playground of King Kamehameha V, who built a large vacation house of thatched grass on the shores of Kaunakakai Harbor. The house was called Malama, which today is the name of the main road leading from the harbor through town. All that remains of Kamehameha V's home is the stone foundation, now overgrown with grass. It's on the right side of the road before the wharf, mauka of the canoe shed.

Fishponds
Molokai's southeast coast is dotted with the

Walking on Water
If you're down at the beach at night you might spot what looks like ghosts walking out on the water. There's no need to be spooked – it's actually local fishers who walk far out onto the shallow coastal reef carrying lanterns. The fishing is good at night when the wind dies down and the lantern light stuns their prey. ■

largest concentration of ancient fishponds in Hawaii. Grazing by cattle and sheep introduced in the mid-1800s resulted in widespread erosion, and the clay that washed down from the mountains choked out the ponds. Over the years efforts have been made to revive a few of the fishponds, although without much commercial success.

One of the most impressive and easily visited is **Kalokoeli Fishpond**, behind Molokai Shores condos.

Kapuaiwa Coconut Grove
The coconut grove one mile west of the main part of town has 10 oceanside acres of coconut palms planted by Kamehameha V around 1860. Kapuaiwa means 'mysterious taboo'. The grove is under the management of Hawaiian Home Lands today.

Across the highway is **Church Row** where a quaint white church with green trim sits next to a quaint green church with white trim and so on down the line. Any denomination that gets a handful of Hawaiian members gets its own little tract of land to put up a church. Some of the more recent arrivals include Mormons and Jehovah's Witnesses.

Kaunakakai

	PLACES TO EAT	6	Molokai Wines & Spirits	19	Public Pool
3	Outpost Natural Foods	8	Molokai Sight & Sound	20	Public Library
5	Rabang's Restaurant	9	C Pascua Store	21	Softball Field
7	Kanemitsu Bakery	10	State Offices	22	Tennis Courts
14	Mid-Nite Inn	11	Friendly Isle Travel	23	Gas Station
26	Molokai Drive Inn	12	Misaki's	24	Bank of Hawaii
28	Molokai Pizza Cafe	13	Friendly Market	25	Baseball Field
	OTHER	15	Post Office	27	Tourist Office
1	Molokai Hospital	16	Molokai Drugs	29	Kaunakakai School
2	Coin Laundry	17	Police Station	30	Kamehameha V House Site
4	Molokai Fish & Dive	18	Mitchell Pauole Center	31	Pau Hana Inn

MOLOKAI

One Alii Beach Park

One Alii, three miles east of Kaunakakai, is the beach park nearest to town. As the water is shallow and swimming conditions are poor, the park is used mainly for picnics, parties and ball games. Two memorials erected in the park commemorate the 19th-century immigration of Japanese to Hawaii. Camping is allowed near the beach at the end of the baseball field.

Places to Stay

Pau Hana Inn (☎ 553-5342, (800) 423-6656), Box 546, Kaunakakai, HI 96748, is the closest hotel to the town center. The cheapest of its 39 rooms are those in the long house at $45, which are small and simple but sufficient, with either two twin beds or a double bed, and a toilet and shower. Try to get one of the end rooms on the ocean side, which are lighter and airier. There are five other room categories topping off with beachfront suites for $125. Pau Hana means 'work's over' and its bar is a popular drinking hole; it can get noisy on weekends when a live band plays until 1 am. Between the bar and the beach is an impressive 100-year-old Bengalese banyan tree.

Hotel Molokai (☎ 553-5347, (800) 423-6656; fax 553-5047), Box 546, Kaunakakai, HI 96748, about two miles east of town, has 55 units with a Polynesian design of sorts. While the hotel is a bit funky, the overall atmosphere is the most in keeping with the character of Molokai. The rooms, which are in clusters of two-story buildings, vary greatly. As noise from people walking on the creaky wooden floors travels down to the lower level, it's best to spend the extra money and go for one of the upper lanai units, which are also the roomiest. They cost $85 and most have a king and two twin beds as well as a large lanai. The standard rooms, priced at $55, can be noisy; for a good night's sleep, avoid the rooms next to the road where the pre-dawn ferry traffic zooms by. Rooms have small refrigerators, portable fans and louvered windows, all of which are generally quite sufficient to keep things cool at night. There's no TV, but sunsets and stargazing from the beachside hammock out back can be unbeatable.

Molokai Shores (☎ 553-5954, (800) 535-0085; fax 553-5954), Box 1037, Kaunakakai, HI 96748, about 1½ miles east of town, has 101 condo units, 40 of which are in the rental pool. Most are decorated quite nicely and each has a kitchen, sofa bed, wooden louvered windows, lanai and ceiling fans. Ask for a unit on the third floor as they are quieter and have cathedral ceilings. One-bedroom units cost $85/95 in the low/high season for up to four people, while two-bedroom units cost $115/125 for up to six people. If you stay a week or more there's a 15% discount. A rental car can be included for an additional $20 a day. There's a pool and coin-operated laundry on the premises.

Bed & Breakfast Molokai (☎ 553-5048), c/o Hannah & Will Johnstone, Box 295, 141 Kahinani St, Kaunakakai, HI 96748, is 1½ miles east of Kaunakakai, upslope from Molokai Shores. The studio unit, which is detached from the main house, has two twin beds, a small refrigerator, a two-burner hot plate, cable TV and a bath with a tub. The owners spend half the year in Scotland, so the rental is available from the beginning of November to the end of March only. The rate of $60/65 single/double includes a hearty Scottish breakfast with selections from a menu! Children are not allowed and there's a two-night minimum. Will is a retired economist and Hannah, who grew up on Molokai, is the author of a book on Moomomi Beach ecology.

Camping Camping is allowed with a county permit at *One Alii Beach Park*, a roadside park on a shallow beach three miles east of Kaunakakai. While the campsites are near the water, they have no privacy and the only shade is cast by a few coconut trees. Also, because it's close to town, the park tends to be well used and it can get a bit noisy, quite in contrast to the other county campground across the island at Papohaku Beach.

A second camping option that's sometimes available in the Kaunakakai area is at *Kapuaiwa Coconut Grove*, on Hawaiian Home Lands property, just west of town. However, this spot is often booked up far in advance as camping permits are issued to just one group at a time and priority is given to native Hawaiians. The site has electricity, water, picnic tables, barbecue grills, restrooms and showers.

For booking information for both campgrounds see Camping under Accommodations earlier in the Molokai chapter.

Places to Eat

Kanemitsu Bakery makes *the* Molokai bread that is shipped around the islands, plus other good breads, a variety of Danish pastries and doughnuts. The cinnamon apple crisp ($1) is a favorite. The restaurant in the back of the bakery serves breakfast and lunch from 5:30 am to 1:30 pm. Eggs, toast, ham and coffee or a fish sandwich and fries cost $3.50. Sandwiches and burgers average $2.25, plate lunches double that.

Outpost Natural Foods has the standard collection of natural foods and vitamins as well as fresh produce, some of it organic. *Oasis Juice Bar* inside the store makes good burritos and sandwiches for $3.50 and salads for $5. They also have a daily special, such as vegie enchilada or Korean barbecue tofu for around $6. The juice bar is open from 10 am to 3 pm Monday to Friday and there's a small picnic table out back where you can eat. The store is open from 9 am to 6 pm Sunday to Thursday and 9 am to 3:30 pm on Fridays.

The *Molokai Pizza Cafe* (☎ 553-3288), in a small complex behind the tourist office, is open daily from 11 am to 8:30 pm for sit-down dining, until 10 pm for takeout service. The pizza is very good, with single topping versions priced at $10 for a medium (12 inches) that's big enough for two – although if you're real hungry the large is only $2 more. Other items include sub sandwiches, lasagna and spaghetti and meat balls, all priced around $7. The restaurant also sells whole baked chickens and prepares Mexican food, the latter on Wednesdays only.

Pau Hana Inn serves rather standard fare at moderate prices. Breakfast, which is from 6:30 to 10:30 am, has a recommendable Molokai-bread French toast with ham and coffee for $4.75 and various egg dishes. At lunch, from 11 am to 2 pm, there's a reasonable salad bar and soup for $6.75 alone and a daily special that includes the salad bar for just half a dollar more. If you're lucky the special could be teriyaki chicken or roast pork; if you're not, it might be meatloaf. Dinner is from 6 to 9 pm and features meat and seafood dishes from $12 to $17, including the salad bar and Molokai bread. The dining room fireplace is sometimes lit on cool winter evenings, adding a nice touch.

Molokai Drive Inn has plate lunches from $4, inexpensive hamburgers, and a breakfast of two eggs, bacon, toast and coffee for $4.25 served any time of the day. The food is takeout but there are picnic tables at the side where you can chow down. This place used to be a Dairy Queen, but Molokai wasn't quite ready for a fast-food chain so the sign came down. It's open from 6 am to 10 pm daily.

Rabang's Restaurant, a simple local eatery, has Filipino lunch plates such as turkey tail adobo, tripe or pig's feet for under $5, as well as burgers, ice cream and shave ice. It's open from 6 am to 9 pm daily.

Until it burned down in 1991, the *Mid-Nite Inn* was the top eating and gathering spot on Molokai and served some of the freshest and cheapest fish in all Hawaii. Owner John Kikukawa is in the process of rebuilding and, considering the restaurant's 60-year history as Molokai's favorite eatery, when it finally reopens it'll probably once again serve Molokai's best-value food.

Misaki's and *Friendly Market* are the island's major grocery stores and are open from 8:30 am to 8:30 pm Monday to Saturday. Misaki's, which is also open from 8:30 am to noon on Sundays, has the island's cheapest wine prices although the selection is limited.

Molokai Wines & Spirits has a good assortment of imported beers and a wide selection of wine at reasonable prices. The shop, which is open from 9 am to 10 pm daily, also has Haagen-Dazs ice cream and a few food items.

Entertainment

The local band FIBRE (Friendly Isle Band Rhythmic Experience!) plays dance music including oldie standards, rock & roll and Hawaiian songs from 9 pm to midnight on Fridays and Saturdays at *Pau Hana Inn*. The cover charge is $3. The action is out on the patio, with the band setting up under the big banyan tree.

Guitarist Kimo Paleka plays mellow Hawaiian tunes from 7 to 9 pm Tuesday to Saturday at the *Pau Hana Inn* restaurant. He's accommodating with requests, the most popular being 'The Cock-Eyed Mayor of Kaunakakai'. Occasionally visiting musicians join Kimo on stage; if you're lucky, Clyde Sproat might be on the island – his salt-of-the-earth singing and ukulele playing is authentic Hawaiian folk music at its best.

Hotels aside, the baseball field in Kaunakakai is the most active spot on the island. For some local flavor, you could go down and cheer on the Molokai Farmers as they compete against their high school rivals, the Lanai Pinelads.

Things to Buy
Molokai Drugs, besides being a pharmacy, is practically a department store, selling snorkels, film, magazines and a good collection of Hawaiiana books. It's open from 8:45 am to 5:45 pm Monday to Saturday.

Molokai Sight & Sound sells Hawaiian music cassettes and is open from 9 am to 8:30 pm daily.

East Molokai

The 28-mile drive from Kaunakakai to Halawa Valley is along the Kamehameha V Highway (Hwy 450) and takes about 1½ hours one way. It's a good paved road from start to finish. Check your gas gauge before starting off as there are no gas stations after Kaunakakai.

The road edges alongside the ocean for much of the drive, with the mountains of East Molokai rising up to the north. The terrain starts out relatively dry and becomes greener and lusher as you head east. It's all quite pastoral, with small homes tucked into the valleys, horses grazing at the side of the road and silver waterfalls dropping down the mountainsides.

The beaches along this stretch are mostly shallow and silted and not good for swimming until about the 20-mile marker. The last part of the road is narrow, with lots of hairpin bends and scenic coastal views, winding up to a clifftop view of Halawa Valley. One of Molokai's best hikes starts from the valley floor, following Halawa Stream to Moaula Falls.

KAWELA
The **Kakahaia Beach Park**, a grassy roadfront park in Kawela shortly before the six-mile marker, has a couple of picnic tables but little other reason to stop. Should you

pull over, pick your spot carefully as the loaded coconut trees are like aerial bombers. This beach park is the only part of the **Kakahaia National Wildlife Refuge** open to the public. Most of the 40-acre refuge is mauka of the road. It includes marshland with a dense growth of bulrushes and an inland freshwater fishpond that has been expanded to provide a home for the endangered Hawaiian stilt and coot.

Farther inland is the **Kawela puuhonua**, a place of refuge that was used in ancient times by those running from the law or hiding from personal enemies. The stone ruins are on a high ridge separated by deep gulches and nearly impossible to get to.

In 1795 Kamehameha the Great invaded Molokai with such a large force that his war canoes were lined up for a full four miles along this coast. He quickly brought Molokai under his command and from here went on to invade Oahu, the last battle in a campaign that united all the Hawaiian islands.

KAMALO
The biggest attraction in Kamalo, a small village about 10 miles east of Kaunakakai, is the roadside St Joseph's Church.

St Joseph's Church
Two of the four churches Father Damien built outside the Kalaupapa Peninsula on Molokai are still standing, including St Joseph's in Kamalo. This simple one-room wooden church built in 1876 has a steeple and bell, five rows of pews and some of the original wavy glass panes. A statue of Damien and a little cemetery are at the side. Only the yellow tsunami-warning speaker brings the scene into the 20th century.

Across the road a minute's stroll up a driveway leads to a self-service fruit hut which usually has limes, grapefruits, coconuts and papayas for sale.

Smith-Bronte Landing
Just over three quarters of a mile after the 11-mile marker, a small wooden sign makai of the road notes the site where pilot Ernest Smith and navigator Emory Bronte safely

crash-landed their plane at the completion of the world's first civilian flight from the US mainland to Hawaii.

They left California on July 14, 1927, coming down in Molokai 25 hours and two minutes later. Oahu was the intended destination. A little memorial plaque is set amongst the kiawe trees and grasses where they landed.

Places to Stay

Kamalo Plantation Bed & Breakfast (☎ & fax 558-8236), HC 1, Box 300, Kaunakakai, HI 96748, owned and operated by Glenn & Akiko Foster, is in a small lime orchard opposite St Joseph's Church. There are two bedrooms in the main house which share a bath. The smaller bedroom has two twin waterbeds; the larger room has a TV, microwave and two twin beds that can be made up as a king. Each room has a refrigerator. Rates, which include breakfast, are $55 and $65 respectively. There's also an adjacent studio-style cottage with two twin beds, a sofa bed and a full kitchen which costs $75 and would be quite suitable for a couple with a child. A breakfast of breads and homegrown fruits is provided. The grounds, which have the stone foundation of an ancient heiau, are pleasantly quiet.

UALAPUE

The Wavecrest condo development is at the 13-mile marker in Ualapue. Wavecrest has a small grocery store that is open to 6 pm daily.

Shortly beyond Wavecrest you'll spot **Ualapue Fishpond** on the makai side of the road. Molokai once had more than 60 productive fishponds, constructed from the 13th century onward. They were built of lava rock upon the reefs. Sluice gates allowed small fish into the pond where they were fed and fattened, but did not allow the large fish to swim back out the slats in the gate. A ready supply of fish could then be easily scooped up with a net as needed.

With state aid, Ualapue Fishpond has recently been restored by a native Hawaiian group, Hui O Kuapaa, and is once again stocked with mullet and milkfish.

Beyond this, look for the defunct Ah Ping Store and its old gas pump at the roadside. This classic building, of faded green wood with red tin roof, was a Chinese-owned grocery store in the 1930s.

Places to Stay

Wavecrest Resort (☎ 558-8103, (800) 367-2980; fax 558-8206), HC 1, Box 541, Kaunakakai, HI 96748, is a 126-unit condo complex that has about 40 units in the rental pool. The condos are divided into three categories – standard, deluxe and premium – depending largely upon the decor and when they were last renovated. Rates range from $75 for a lackluster standard garden unit to $105 for a cheery premium oceanfront unit. All have separate bedrooms, a kitchen, sofa bed, TV and lanai. Even with the sofa bed open, the living room is still large enough to move around. Breezes blow right through the oceanfront units and there are great views of Maui and Lanai from the lanai. Maximum occupancy is four people, with a $5 charge for the third and fourth person. There's a $15 charge on stays less than three nights; a rental car can be included for an extra $24. The resort has a pool, tennis courts and a coin laundry.

KALUAAHA

The village of Kaluaaha is about two miles past Wavecrest. The ruins of Molokai's first church are here, a bit off the road, mauka side, but visible (barely) if you keep an eye out. **Kaluaaha Church** was built in 1844 by Molokai's first missionary, Harvey R Hitchcock. There was talk of rebuilding the church, but the rusting old steel rods in the original structure thwarted the plan.

Our Lady of Sorrows Church is a quarter of a mile past the Kaluaaha Church site. The present Our Lady of Sorrows Church is a 1966 reconstruction of the original wooden-frame building built in 1874 by Father Damien.

From the church parking lot, there's a fine view of an ancient **fishpond** with the high-rise-studded shores of West Maui providing an incongruous backdrop.

MOLOKAI

ILIILIOPAE HEIAU

Iliiliopae is the largest and best-known heiau on Molokai, and probably the oldest. Approximately 300 feet long and 100 feet wide, it is about 22 feet high on the east side and 11 feet high at the other end. It is strikingly level. It's believed the heiau may have originally been three times its current size, reaching out beyond Mapulehu Stream.

The path to the heiau is mauka of the highway, nearly half a mile past the 15-mile marker, immediately after a little bridge. It starts on a dirt drive on the east side of the creek. After a 10-minute walk a footpath leads off to the left, opposite a house. The heiau is two minutes farther.

Although once a site of human sacrifice, Iliiliopae is today silent except for the chittering of birds. African tulip trees line the trail to the site, a peaceful place with stones that still seem to emanate vibrations of a powerful past. A good place to sit and take it all in is on the north side, up the steps to the right of the heiau.

As the heiau is on private property, permission to visit should be obtained in advance; this is seldom a problem and can be done through the tourist office.

PUKOO

The village of Pukoo was once the seat of local government – complete with a courthouse, jail, wharf and post office – until the plantation folks built Kaunakakai and centered everything there. The population shifted away from Pukoo and it's been a sleepy backwater ever since. Now bit by bit islanders are beginning to move back to the Pukoo area and while it's not exactly suburbia you'll notice a handful of newer homes as the road continues.

In the village, just before the 16-mile marker, a road marked 'shoreline access' leads a few hundred yards to a sandy beach with shallow waters.

Places to Stay

Honomuni House (☎ 558-8383), HC 1, Box 700, Kaunakakai, HI 96748, is a pleas-

---

A Shrimp for their Efforts

Legend says Iliiliopae Heiau was built in one night by menehunes who brought *iliili* (stones) over the mountains from Wailau Valley. In return for their efforts each was given one *opae* (shrimp), hence the temple's name.

Lono, the god of harvest, and Ku, the war god, were both worshipped here. Human sacrifices were made at this heiau, always on the eve of a full moon. Drums were beaten to call all males to the temple where, upon the priest's direction, all fell prone and the victims to be sacrificed were brought to the platform. Amid chanting and rituals these victims, always male, were strangled to death and their bodies later burned.

One legend tells of a man, Umoekekaua, who lost nine of his 10 sons to sacrifice at Iliiliopae. He became so outraged that he went with his only remaining son to Pelekunu Valley to seek the aid of Kauhuhu, the Shark God. Kauhuhu sent a torrent of rain whose flood waters damaged the heiau and washed the priests responsible for the sacrifices into Pukoo Harbor where they were duly eaten by sharks. ∎

---

ant guest cottage just beyond the Honomuni Bridge, about a mile east of Pukoo. The cottage is studio-style with a kitchen, bath and outdoor deck and shower. The living room area has a sofa bed, a TV and a small dining table made of monkeypod wood from the grounds. Rates are $80 for two, plus $10 for each additional adult and $5 for each additional child. The weekly rate is $510. Fresh eggs, bananas and other seasonal fruits are free. Hosts Jan and Keaho Newhouse live in a large house on the same grounds.

WAIALUA

Waialua is a little roadside community around the 19-mile marker. The attractive little Waialua Congregational Church, which marks the center of the village, was built of stone in 1855. The nearby Waialua Beach is the site of Molokai's keiki surf competitions.

Sugar Mill Remains

Three quarters of a mile after the 19-mile marker begin looking for the remains of a stone chimney, a remnant of the Moanui Sugar Mill which processed sugar from a nearby plantation until it burned down in the late 1800s. The ruins are about 50 feet mauka of the road, just before a stand of tall ironwood trees.

Twenty-Mile Beach

A stretch of white sand beach pops up right along the roadside at the 20-mile marker. There are places to park just beyond that. During the winter, when other Molokai beaches are rough, this is the area everyone directs you to for swimming and snorkeling.

However, when the tide is low the water is sometimes too shallow for snorkeling inside the reef. Snorkeling is much better beyond the reef, but unless it's very calm the currents can be dangerous.

Rock Point

The point of rocks sticking out as the road swings left before the 21-mile marker is called, appropriately enough, Rock Point. This is a popular surfing spot where local competitions sometimes take place.

Onward to Halawa

After the 21-mile marker the road starts to wind upwards. Tall grasses just at the edge seem to be trying to reclaim the road, while ironwood trees and the spindly spikes of sisal plants dot the surrounding hills.

It's a good paved road – the only problem is there's not always enough of it. In places, including some cliff-hugging curves, it's really only wide enough for one car and you'll need to do some horn tooting. The road levels out just before the 24-mile marker where there's a view of the small island of Mokuhooniki, a seabird sanctuary.

The fenced grassland in this area is part of Puu O Hoku Ranch, Molokai's second largest cattle ranch. A grove of sacred kukui trees on the ranch property marks the grave of Lanikaula, a famous kahuna of the late 16th century. Over the years many islanders claim to have seen the night lanterns of ghost marchers bobbing along near the grove.

After passing the 25-mile marker, the jungle begins to close in and the smell of the soil and eucalyptus fills the air. One and a quarter miles after the 25-mile marker there's a turn-off with a great panoramic view of Halawa Valley – if the viewpoint is overgrown, just park and walk down the road a little farther to reach a clearing. In the winter, this is also a good place to watch for whales breaching off the coast.

There are lots of 'beep as you go' hairpin bends on the one-lane road that leads down to the valley, but the road is in good condition and the incline reasonably gradual.

HALAWA VALLEY

Halawa Valley once had three heiaus, two of which are thought to have been used for human sacrifice. Little remains of the sites. In the mid-1800s the fertile valley had a population of about 500 people and produced most of Molokai's taro as well as many of its melons, gourds and fruits. Taro production declined over the years, coming to an abrupt end in 1946 when a massive tsunami swept up Halawa Valley, wiping out the farms and much of the community. A second tsunami washed the valley clean in 1957. Only seven families now remain in Halawa. Sunday services are still held in Hawaiian at the valley's little church a few times a month.

Moaula Falls Trail

Access to the Moaula Falls Trail has recently been placed in dispute by a valley resident who claims that the road at the start of the trail is on private property. Na Ala Hele, in the state's Department of Land & Natural Resources, is currently undertaking an abstract of property titles to determine if there is public access. There are indications that the trailhead may be across a county road. However, as final determination hasn't been made, the trailhead should be treated as private property and the hike should not be undertaken without the owner's consent. If it's found to

MOLOKAI

be public property the trail will probably be reopened as described below. If it's not, a new trailhead may be developed. Check either with Na Ala Hele on Maui (☎ 871-2831) or with the Molokai tourist office for current access information.

The hike to the 250-foot Moaula Falls is Molokai's most-hiked trail, although it's not the easiest to follow. The one-hour walk up is neither steep nor particularly strenuous, but it is often muddy and slippery. It's more suited to old sneakers than new white Reeboks. A walking stick makes a good companion.

The trail goes through a forest of lush tropical vegetation: giant mango trees, wild taro, ti, papaya and bananas. On the ground you might see the warty yellow fruits of the noni whose pungent odor is favored by swarms of fruit flies. Stopping too long to observe this – or anything else – is a sure way to find out what the voracious mosquitoes favor.

The trail starts on a dirt road in front of the church. Go straight ahead on this road for about 10 minutes. At the last house the road becomes a footpath. About 100 yards farther the path splits. This split is easy to miss so keep an eye out for a white PVC water pipe crossing the trail here and for some rocks on either side of the trail that heads down to the right. Take this trail down to the stream.

You'll have to cross Halawa Stream, either by walking across stones that can be deceptively slippery when wet, or by stepping right into the water and walking on the streambed. If you wade across, choose your footing carefully as water depth can go from ankle-high to knee-high in one step. If it's been raining heavily, water levels can rise to the point where it's impossible to cross the stream safely.

The trail is blazed with orange markings. After crossing a narrow orange-bottomed brook (or mudflat, depending on water levels) the path will fork. Take the trail to the left which parallels the stream, usually within sound of it, although not always within sight. Along most of the trail there's a water pipe going up toward the falls, but

it does disappear in places. There are moss-covered stone walls along the way, most of which were built in the 1800s as cattle fences.

About halfway up you'll begin to hear the waterfall. Once it comes into sight there's another stream crossing, this one a little more challenging. Use the metal water pipes to help climb down to the stream and cross over the boulders to the other side. Moaula Falls is less than five minutes straight up from here. Under the waterfall is a good-sized pool, at least 40 feet wide. Partly because the pool is so deep in the center, the water is shockingly cold. Moaula translates as 'red chicken' and fittingly the water appears reddish.

If you plan on taking a dip here, it's best to first place a ti leaf in the water. Legend has it that a *moo*, a giant lizard-like creature, resides in the pool. If the ti leaf floats she welcomes company and it's OK to swim. If it sinks, it's a warning she wants no visitors.

Halawa Beach Park

Halawa Beach was a favored surfing spot for Molokai chiefs and remains so today for local kids. This beach has double coves separated by a rocky outcrop, with the north side a bit more protected than the south. When the water is calm there's good swimming, but both coves are subject to dangerous rip currents when the surf is heavy. There can also be strong currents when Halawa Stream, which empties into the north cove, is flowing heavily.

Halawa Beach Park has restrooms and running water; a sign warns that the water, which is piped down from the upper valley, does not meet health standards and needs to be treated before drinking. The old building before the park is a former village church that burned down a few decades ago.

Central Molokai

Central Molokai takes in the Hoolehua Plains, which stretch from windswept Moomomi Beach in the west to the former plantation town of Kualapuu in the east. The central part of the island also has forested interiors leading to Kamakou, the island's highest mountain and a unique rainforest preserve. On the north side of central Molokai is Kalaupapa Peninsula, the site of the leprosy colony.

The most trodden route in central Molokai is the drive up to the Kalaupapa Overlook, where you'll find one of the prettiest views on Molokai. It takes about 20 minutes to drive the 10 miles from Kaunakakai.

Turning north off Hwy 460 onto Hwy 470 (Kalae Hwy), the road starts in dry grasslands and climbs, passing the town of Kualapuu, a golf course, a restored sugar mill, a community of single-rooster dwellings, a mule stable and the trail down to the Kalaupapa Peninsula. The road ends at Palaau State Park, site of the Kalaupapa Overlook.

KUALAPUU

Kualapuu is the name of both a 1017-foot hill and the village that has grown up north of it.

At the base of the hill is the world's largest rubber-lined reservoir. It can hold up to 1.4 billion gallons of water, which is piped in from the rainforests in East Molokai and is presently the source of water for both the Hoolehua Plains and the dry West End.

Del Monte set up headquarters in this area in the 1930s and Kualapuu developed into a plantation town. The center of Del Monte's activities covered the spread between Kualapuu and the nearby Hoolehua homesteads.

In 1982 Del Monte decided to phase out its Molokai operations and the economy came tumbling down. Old harvesting equipment sat rusting in overgrown pineapple fields for a decade before a South American company leased out the abandoned fields and replanted them in long rows of coffee. The first harvests, under the brand name Malulani Estate, have just reached the market. Kualapuu is banking on this new crop to spur its revival, although much of the field work has gone to Filipino immigrants who are willing to work long hours at low wages.

Kualapuu is a friendly village with a tiny post office and beauty salon tucked beside the general store. Gas pumps are out front and a restaurant and laundromat are across the street. Up the hill there's a little church but otherwise there is not much else to see or do in this town.

Places to Eat

The *Kualapuu Cookhouse* (☎ 567-6185) is a busy little place for such a small town. The meal of the day costs $7, as do most plate lunches including a nice chicken stir-fry and rice. You can also get a cup of chili for $2.50 and burgers for around $4. Homemade pies, cooked every morning by owner Nannette Yamashita, are a specialty – for sheer indulgence try a slice of the chocolate macnut pie. The restaurant is open from 7 am to 8 pm Monday to Friday, to 4 pm on Saturdays.

KALAE
R W Meyer Sugar Mill

Four miles north of Hwy 460, in Kalae, is the sugar mill built by Rudolph W Meyer, an industrious German immigrant.

Meyer was on his way to the California gold rush when he dropped by Hawaii, married a member of Hawaiian royalty and in the process landed a tidy bit of property.

He eventually found his gold in potatoes which he grew and exported to the Californian miners. Other hats he wore were overseer of the Kalaupapa leprosy settlement and manager of King Kamehameha V's ranchlands.

In the 1850s Meyer established his own ranch and exported cattle from Palaau village. In one infamous incident, after finding his herd declining, he had all the men of Palaau charged with cattle rustling and sent off to a jailhouse in Honolulu.

In the late 1870s, when a new reciprocity treaty gave Hawaiian sugar planters the right to export sugar duty-free to the US, Meyer turned his lands over to sugar and built this mill. The sugar mill operated for about 10 years.

A lot of time and money has gone into authentically restoring the mill, including the complete rebuilding of a 100-year-old steam engine and other rusting machinery abandoned a century ago. The mill, which is on the National Register of Historic Places, is the last of its kind. If you're into sugar mills, antique steam engines and that sort of thing you'll certainly find it interesting.

The sugar mill (☎ 567-6436) is open from 10 am to 2 pm Monday to Saturday. Admission is $2.50 for adults, $1 for students.

A newly constructed building behind the sugar mill contains a small display on Molokai's history and culture. Meyer and his descendants are buried in a little family plot out back.

Ironwood Hills Golf Course

There are no polo shirts with little alligators on them here. Ironwood Hills is a delightfully casual golf course, with crabgrass growing in the sand pits and local golfers who actually look like they're having fun. The course is a third of a mile down the red dirt road at the tree-lined edge of the pasture immediately south of Meyer Sugar Mill.

Originally built by Del Monte for its employees, the course was maintained by Molokai residents after Del Monte left and is now open to all.

PALAAU STATE PARK

Palaau State Park is at the end of Hwy 470. The park's main sight, the Kalaupapa Overlook, is a few minutes' walk from the parking lot. In the opposite direction, a five-minute trail through the ironwoods leads to a phallic-shaped rock. Both trails are marked and easy to follow. The park has campsites, picnic areas and lovely stands of paperbark eucalyptus.

Kalaupapa Overlook

The Kalaupapa Overlook provides a scenic overview of the entire Kalaupapa Peninsula from the edge of a 1600-foot cliff. It's like an aerial view without the airplane.

Interpretive plaques identify the landmarks below and explain Kalaupapa's history as a leper colony. The village where all Kalaupapa's residents now live is visible, but Kalawao, the original settlement and site of Father Damien's church and grave, cannot be seen from here.

The lighthouse at the northern end of the island once had the most powerful beam in the Pacific. The 700,000-candlepower Fresnel crystal lens cast its light until 1986, when it was taken down and replaced by an electric light beacon.

Kalaupapa means 'Flat Leaf', an accurate description of the lava slab peninsula created when a low shield volcano poked up out of the sea, long after the rest of Molokai had been formed. The dormant Kauhako Crater, visible from the overlook, contains a little lake over 800 feet deep.

Kalaupapa residents use the term 'topside' to refer to all of Molokai outside their peninsula. From here it's obvious to see why.

Whether or not you get down to Kalaupapa itself, the overlook is a must. Because of the angle of the sun, the best light for photography is usually late morning to mid-afternoon.

Hiking There's an old trail that continues directly beyond the last plaque at the overlook. For one of Molokai's nicest forest walks, simply follow this trail for about 30 minutes. Few people go this way and it's very peaceful – if you're lucky you might even spot deer crossing the trail.

The path, on a carpet of soft ironwood needles, passes through a thickly planted forest of ironwood and eucalyptus, dotted here and there with Norfolk pine. These diagonal rows of trees were planted during a 1930s Civilian Conservation Corps (CCC) reforestation project. The trees create a canopy over the trail and, as is generally true under ironwood and eucalyptus trees, there's little undergrowth to obscure the way.

There's no destination – the joy here is the woods. Eventually the trail winds down into a gully and peters out a little after that.

Phallic Rock Kauleonanahoa, literally 'the penis of Nanahoa', is Hawaii's premier phallic stone, poking up in a little clearing inside an ironwood grove. Nature has endowed it well but it's obviously been touched up by human hands.

Although it's said that women who bring offerings and spend the night here will return home pregnant, there apparently is no danger in just going to have a look.

Places to Stay
Camping Camping is free at Palaau State Park. The camping area is off the road in a grove of ironwood trees which is cool and shady in the summer, but can feel a bit dark and damp when it's rainy in winter. In winter you may well have the place to yourself and even in the summer you're unlikely to find a crowd. Although you may hear a few trucks with boom boxes parked at the picnic grounds, it is generally very peaceful. The only other sounds are the roosters from the 'cock farm' and the braying of mules.

There are restrooms, cement picnic tables and fireplaces, but no showers and the tap water is not fit for drinking.

KALAUPAPA PENINSULA
Kalaupapa Peninsula appears both strikingly beautiful and strikingly lonely. Set at the base of majestic and formidable cliffs, it has been a leprosy settlement for more than a century. The trip to the peninsula – accessible only by mule, on foot or by small plane – is one of Molokai's major attractions. It's also a pilgrimage of sorts for admirers of Father Damien (Joseph de Veuster), the Belgian priest who devoted the latter part of his life to helping people with leprosy, before dying of the disease himself.

Kalaupapa Peninsula is a national historical park jointly managed by the State Department of Health and the US National Park Service. It is unique among historic parks in that many of the people whose lives are being interpreted are still living on the site.

History
Ancient Hawaiians used Kalaupapa as a refuge when caught in storms at sea. The peninsula held a large settlement at the time of early Western contact and the area is rich in archaeological sites.

The first case of leprosy in Hawaii was diagnosed in 1835, one of many diseases introduced by foreigners, this one probably by Chinese laborers. Alarmed by the spread of the disease, in 1865 King Kamehameha V signed into law an act that banished people with leprosy to Kalaupapa Peninsula.

It was a one-way trip. Kalaupapa Peninsula is surrounded on three sides by some of Hawaii's roughest and most shark-infested waters and on the fourth by the world's highest sea cliffs. Once the afflicted arrived on Kalaupapa Peninsula there was no way out, not even in a casket. Hawaiians called leprosy *mai hookaawale*, which means separating sickness, a disease all the more dreaded because it tore families apart forever.

Father Damien arrived at Kalaupapa in 1873. He wasn't the first missionary to come, but he was the first to stay.

Damien nursed the sick, wrapped bandages on oozing sores, hammered coffins and dug graves. On the average he buried one person a day. He put up more than 300 houses – each little more than four walls, a door and a roof, but still a shelter to those

MOLOKAI

cast here. He was a good carpenter. Some of the solid little churches he built earlier around the Big Island and Molokai still stand today.

The original settlement was in Kalawao, at the wetter eastern end of the peninsula. Some of the afflicted arrived in boats, whose captains were so terrified of the disease that they would not land but instead dropped patients overboard into the bay. Those who could swam to shore.

Early conditions were unspeakably horrible. Before modern medicine, leprosy manifested itself in dripping, foul-smelling sores. Eventually there was loss of sensation and tissue degeneration that could lead to fingers, toes and noses becoming hideously deformed or falling off altogether.

In 1888 Damien installed a water pipeline to the sunnier western side and the settlement moved to where it is today. Over the years, some 8000 people have come to Kalaupapa Peninsula to die. During Damien's time lifespans here were almost invariably short.

Yet even in Damien's day leprosy was one of the least contagious of all communicable diseases. All in all more than 1100 volunteers have worked with patients at Kalaupapa, but only Damien contracted leprosy. He died in 1889 at the age of 49.

Damien's work inspired others. Brother Joseph Dutton arrived in 1886 and stayed 44 years. In addition to his work with the sick, he was a prolific writer who kept the outside world informed about what was happening in Molokai. Mother Marianne Cope arrived a year before Damien died. She stayed 30 years, helping to establish a girls' home and encouraging patients to live life to the fullest. She is widely considered to be the mother of the hospice movement.

In 1909 a fancy medical facility called the US Leprosy Investigation Station opened at Kalawao. However, the hospital was so out of touch (requiring patients to sign themselves in for two years, live in seclusion and give up all Hawaiian-grown food) that even in the middle of a leprosy colony it attracted only a handful of patients. It closed four years later.

Although sulfone antibiotics have been used successfully to control leprosy since the 1940s, isolation policies in Kalaupapa weren't abandoned until 1969.

Kalaupapa Today

Today fewer than 100 patients live on Kalaupapa Peninsula. It's an old population, getting older, with only a few people younger than 50. Some of the elderly have become blind or weakened. Others fish or tend gardens, although lots of people just stay glued to their TVs.

Current residents are free to leave, but Kalaupapa is the only home most of them know. They have been given guarantees that they can stay in Kalaupapa Peninsula throughout their lifetimes. To minimize the impact on residents, the park requires all visitors to join a guided tour.

The state of Hawaii officially uses the term 'Hansen's Disease' for leprosy. Many Kalaupapa residents, who consider it a euphemism that fails to reflect the stigma they have suffered, continue to use the old term.

Things to See & Do

On typical tours the village looks nearly

Father Damien's Church

deserted. The sights are mainly cemeteries, churches and memorials. Places where residents go to talk story – the post office, store and hospital – are pointed out but no stops are made. Visitors are not allowed to photograph the residents. Kalaupapa is a tourist attraction but its people are not.

Stops are made in town at **memorials** for Father Damien and Mother Marianne and at a **mini-museum** where photographs of the original settlement are on display and books are for sale. The tours then go across the peninsula to Kalawao.

St Philomena Church (better known as 'Father Damien's Church') in Kalawao underwent a restoration for the centenary of Damien's death in 1989. You can still see where Damien cut open holes in the floor so that the sick who needed to spit could attend church and not be ashamed. The graveyard at the side contains Damien's gravestone and original burial site, although his body was exhumed in 1936 and returned to Belgium.

The view from Kalawao is one of the island's finest. It looks out on the pali of the northeast coast, each successive cliffside jutting out behind the one in front, each looking more like a shadow in the mist. The park boundaries include the Waihanau, Waialeia and Waikolu valleys, east of the peninsula.

The **rock island** just offshore is the legendary home of a giant shark. From some angles it looks like a shark's head coming straight up out of the water, while from other angles it looks like a dorsal fin.

Getting There & Around

The switchback mule trail down the pali (cliffs) is the only land route to the peninsula. No matter how you get there, you cannot wander around Kalaupapa Peninsula by yourself. You must take a guided tour.

Old state laws which require everyone who enters the settlement to have a 'permit' and which only allow entry to those 16 years of age and older are no longer required for medical reasons, but are still maintained to protect the privacy of the patients.

There's no actual paper permit. A reservation with either Damien Tours or Molokai Mule Ride is considered a permit.

Only guests of Kalaupapa residents are allowed to stay overnight. Unless you're on the mule tour, bring your own food and beverages. There are no stores or other public facilities for visitors.

Air Island Air flights to Kalaupapa leave Molokai Airport at 8:50 and 9:45 am and come back at 2:35 and 4:20 pm. The cost is $30 each way. Island Air flights leave Honolulu for Kalaupapa at 7:50 am and 3 pm and come back at 8:50 am and 4 pm. The cost is $81 each way.

Air Molokai has a daily 9:50 am flight from Molokai Airport to Kalaupapa, coming back at 2:20 pm. The cost is $26 each way. There are also flights to Kalaupapa from Kahului and Honolulu which cost $60 each way; both depart at around 9 am.

The 'airport' at Kalaupapa is just a runway on a grassy field and a covered waiting area with a few chairs, restrooms and a pay telephone.

On Foot The two-mile hike along the mule trail takes about one hour going down, a bit longer going up. It's best to begin hiking by 8:30 or 9 am, before the mules start to go down, to avoid walking in fresh dung. The narrow trail is rutted in places and can be slippery and muddy if it's been raining, but otherwise it's not terribly strenuous.

The trail starts on the right side of Hwy 470 midway between the mule stables and Kalaupapa Overlook. Don't be intimidated by the sign at the start of the path. If you have tour reservations, this is the trail in.

Tours Damien Tours (☎ 567-6171 or 567-6675), Box 1, Kalaupapa, HI 96742, does the land tours for people who come to Kalaupapa on foot or by plane. Richard Marks, who runs Damien Tours, is a wonderful storyteller, an oral historian and the third generation of his family to be banished to Kalaupapa. He leads the best tour

MOLOKAI

of Kalaupapa. Reservations must be made in advance and the cost is $25. The tours pick up visitors at both the airport and the bottom of the trail.

Mule Ride One of the best-known outings in the islands is the mule ride down the pali to Kalaupapa. While the mules move none too quickly – actually, hiking can be faster – there's a certain thrill in trusting your life to these sure-footed beasts while descending 1600 feet on 26 narrow cliffside switchbacks.

The rides have been discontinued for the past two years while the trail has been upgraded and some insurance issues worked out. However, it's expected that by the time you read this they'll be running again. The cost of the six-hour outing, which includes a van tour of Kalaupapa, will probably be between $125 and $150. For current information, contact the tourist office.

HOOLEHUA

Hoolehua is the dry plains area that separates eastern and western Molokai. Here, in the 1790s, Kamehameha the Great trained his warriors in a year-long preparation for the invasion of Oahu. Hoolehua was settled as an agricultural community in 1924 as part of the Hawaiian Homes Act, which made public lands available to native Hawaiians. The land was divided into 40-acre plots. By 1930 more than half of Molokai's ethnic Hawaiian population was living on Hawaiian homesteads.

The first homestead was attempted closer to the coast at Kalanianaole, but it failed when the well water pumped to irrigate crops turned brackish. Many of those islanders then moved up to Hoolehua where homesteaders were already planting pineapple, a crop that required little water. As the two giant pineapple companies established operations in Molokai, homesteaders found it increasingly difficult to market their own pineapples and were eventually compelled to lease their lands to the plantations.

These days there's a reliable water supply and crops that are more diversified including coffee, sweet potatoes, papaya and fresh herbs.

Orientation & Information

Three paved roads run east to west, with dirt crossroads going north to south. The post office and the Department of Land & Natural Resources office are on Puupeelua Ave (Hwy 480), just south of where it intersects with Farrington Ave.

Farrington Ave is Hoolehua's main street with a fire station, Episcopal church and Molokai's high school. The Hawaiian Home Lands office is up on Puukapele Ave.

Puukapele Ave leads westward and merges into another paved road which deceptively appears to be a find, heading beachward, but the road ends at the Western Space & Missile Center, a radio receiving station for the US Air Force. Here a

Mail Home Some Aloha
Postmaster Margaret Keahi-Leary of the Hoolehua post office stocks baskets of unhusked coconuts that you can address and mail off as a unique (and edible!) 'postcard'. These coconuts, which Margaret gathers on her own time, are free for this 'post-a-nut' purpose and she keeps a few felt pens on hand so you can jot down a message on the husk. Priority mail postage to anywhere in the USA costs $3 for an average-sized coconut. The Hoolehua post office is open from 7:30 to 11:30 am and 12:30 to 4:30 pm Monday to Friday. ■

bunch of odd metal towers and wire cables look for all the world as if grown-up kids have been playing with a giant Erector Set.

Purdy's Macadamia Nut Farm

Tuddie Purdy runs the best little macadamia nut farm tour in all of Hawaii. Everything is Molokai scale. You can crack open macadamia nuts on a stone with a hammer and sample macadamia blossom honey scooped up with slices of fresh coconut.

Unlike tours on the Big Island that focus on processing, Purdy takes you into his orchard and explains how the nuts grow. A single macadamia tree can simultaneously be in various stages of progression – with flowers in blossom, tiny nuts just beginning and clusters of mature nuts. His 1½ acres of mature trees are over 60 years old and grow naturally: no pesticides, herbicides, fertilizers or even pruning.

Purdy, a Molokai native who left a job with Aloha Airlines to work his homestead, is as interesting as the orchard and can tell you a lot about the island.

Admission is free. Macadamia nuts (roasted or raw) and honey are for sale. To get to the farm head north, turn left onto Farrington Ave from Hwy 470 and after one mile turn right onto Lihi Pali Ave, just before the high school. It's a third of a mile up, on the right.

The hours are a bit flexible but you might find Purdy there from 9:30 am to 3:30 pm Monday to Friday, until 2 pm on Saturdays.

MOOMOMI BEACH

Moomomi Beach, on the western edge of the Hoolehua Plains, is ecologically unique. It stands as one of the few undisturbed coastal sand dune areas left in Hawaii. Among its native grasses and shrubs are at least five endangered plant species that exist nowhere else on earth. It is one of the few places in the populated islands where green sea turtles still find a habitat suitable for breeding.

Evidence of an adze quarry and the fossils of a number of long-extinct Hawaiian birds have been unearthed here, pre-served over time by Moomomi's arid sands. In 1988 the Nature Conservancy purchased 920 acres of Moomomi from Molokai Ranch and established Moomomi Preserve. Moomomi is not lushly beautiful, but windswept, lonely and wild.

To get there turn off Hwy 460, east of the airport, onto Hwy 480. Then turn left onto Farrington Ave and head west. The paved road ends after about three miles. From there it's 2½ miles farther along a red dirt road that is in some areas quite smooth and in others deeply rutted. In places you may have to skirt along the edge of the road and straddle a small gully. It could be difficult going if it's muddy. Some people do make it down in standard cars, although the higher the vehicle the better.

A little over two miles after the paved road ends the road forks. Bear to the right and follow this road half a mile down to the beach. If it gets too rough there's a spot halfway down this last stretch where you can pull off to the right and park.

At the end of the road is Moomomi Bay with a little sandy beach used by sunbathers. The rocky eastern point that protects the bay provides a perch for fishers. There are no facilities here, just the foundations of a bathhouse that burned down years ago. This area is part of the Hawaiian Home Lands.

The lovely beach that people refer to as Moomomi is not here, but at Kawaaloa Bay, a 20-minute walk to the west. Kawaaloa is a broad white sand beach. The wind, which picks up steadily each afternoon, blows the sand into ripples and waves.

The high hills running inland are actually massive sand dunes. The coastal cliffs, which have been sculptured into jagged abstract designs by wind and water, are made of sand that has petrified due to the dry conditions.

The narrower right side of Kawaaloa Bay is partially sheltered, however the whole beach can be rough when the surf is up and swimming is discouraged. A tattered old changing room and pavilion belonging to Molokai Ranch are at the east end of the bay. Kawaaloa collects a lot of drifting debris, some of it driftwood and some of it less romantic. Visitors may collect human-made objects found along the coast, but should not take any natural objects including flora, rocks and coral.

There's a fair chance you'll have Kawaaloa to yourself, but if you don't you can always walk farther on to one of the other sandy coves along the shore. Most of the area west of here is open ocean with strong currents.

Because of the fragile ecology of the dunes, visitors should stay along the beach and on trails only. Foot access is allowed via the route described without a permit, although visitors can also get a gate key from the Nature Conservancy and drive directly in to Kawaaloa Bay. To do that a permit application and $25 key deposit are required. The preserve is closed on Tuesdays and Wednesdays.

The conservancy also leads monthly guided hikes of Moomomi, usually on the third or fourth Sunday of the month. The cost of $5 for conservancy members and $15 for nonmembers includes transport to and from the preserve. As it's common for hikers to fly over from other islands to join in, the pick-up run includes Molokai Airport. Reservations are required and must usually be made well in advance.

To get a hike schedule or make reservations contact The Nature Conservancy of Hawaii (☎ 553-5236), Molokai Preserves, Box 220, Kualapuu, HI 96757. If you're writing, include a stamped, self-addressed envelope.

The Nature Conservancy office is on Hwy 460 at the back of a former mortuary. The driveway is a third of a mile before Hwy 470 if you're heading west from Kaunakakai. The office hours are generally from 8 am to 3 pm Monday to Friday (closed for lunch).

KAMAKOU

The mountains that form the spine of Molokai's east side reach up to Kamakou, the island's highest peak (4970 feet). Over half of Molokai's water supply comes from the Kamakou rainforest.

Hawaiian women used to hike up to the top of Kamakou to bury the afterbirth of their babies, a process that assured their children would reach great heights in life. These days islanders come to the forest to pick foliage for leis as well as to hunt pigs, deer and goats.

The Nature Conservancy's Kamakou Preserve is a near-pristine forest that is home to more than 250 native plants and some of Hawaii's rarest birds. Just before the preserve entrance, Waikolu Lookout offers a panoramic view of remote Waikolu Valley, while a hike inside the preserve leads to another lookout, this one into the spectacular Pelekunu Valley.

Kamakou is a treasure, but it doesn't come easy. It is wilderness and is protected in that state in part because the rutted dirt road leading to it makes it challenging to get to.

To Kamakou Preserve

Coming from Kaunakakai on Hwy 460 turn right three quarters of a mile after the three-mile marker, immediately before Manawainui Bridge. The paved road ends shortly at the Kalamaula hunter check box. The 10-mile drive from the highway to Waikolu Lookout takes about 45 minutes, depending on road conditions. During the rainy season vehicles leave tracks and the road gets progressively more rutted until it's regraded in the summer.

A 4WD is recommended and may be essential. In dry weather, some people do make it as far as the lookout in a standard car but certainly if it's been raining heavily it's not advisable to try. In places where the road is narrow, if one person gets stuck the whole road is blocked.

From the Kalamaula hunter check box, the road starts out fairly smoothly, but deteriorates as it goes along. Bear left at the first fork, about five minutes' drive up the dirt road, and from there just follow the main road all the way in.

Although there's no visible evidence of it from the road, the Kalamaula area was once extensively settled. It was here that Kamehameha the Great knocked out his two front teeth while grieving the death of a female high chief that he had come to visit.

The landscape starts off shrubby, dry and dusty, later turning to woods of eucalyptus with patches of cypress and Norfolk pines. The trees were planted in the 1930s by the CCC to stem the erosion and watershed loss that the area had suffered from the free-range cattle policies of earlier times.

The Molokai Forest Reserve starts about 5½ miles in. A short loop road on the left leads to a former Boy Scout camp that's now used by the Nature Conservancy. After another 1½ miles there will be an old water tank and reservoir off to the left. Just past this a wooden sign marked 'Kakalahale' points to the right. (This is one of several 4WD roads used by hunters that lead south to the coast or to Kaunakakai. Once the roads leave forest reserve land they run across private property, often with closed gates along the way.) It's two miles more to the Sandalwood Pit and one mile past that to Waikolu Lookout and Kamakou Preserve.

Sandalwood Pit

Lua Moku Iliahi, or Sandalwood Measuring Pit, is a hull-shaped grassy depression marked with a sign on the left side of the road. It takes a little imagination to get the whole picture as over the years water erosion has rounded the sides.

The sandalwood pit was dug in the early 1800s, shortly after the lucrative sandalwood trade began. In the frenzy to make a quick buck to pay for the foreign goods they craved, the alii forced the makaainana (commoners) to abandon their crops and work the forest.

The pit was dug out to the exact measurements of a 75-foot-long ship's hold and filled with fragrant sandalwood logs cleared from the nearby forest. When the pit was full, the wood was hauled down to the harbor for shipment to China. The sea captains made off like bandits, while Hawaii lost its sandalwood forests.

After all the mature trees were taken, the makaainana pulled up virtually every new sapling in order to spare their children the misery of another generation of forced harvesting.

Waikolu Lookout

Waikolu Lookout, at 3600 feet, provides a spectacular view into Waikolu Valley and out to the ocean beyond. Even if you're not able to spend time in Kamakou Preserve, the lookout is a fine destination in itself. If it's been raining recently you'll be rewarded with numerous waterfalls streaming down the sheer cliffsides. Waikolu means 'Three Waters' – presumably named for the three drops in the main falls. Morning is the best time for views as afternoon trade winds commonly carry clouds to the upper level of the canyon.

These steep mountains effectively prevent the rain clouds from entering Molokai's dry central plains. In 1960 a 5½-mile tunnel was bored into the western side of Waikolu Valley. It now carries up to 28 million gallons of water each day down to the Kualapuu Reservoir.

A grassy picnic and camping area is directly opposite the lookout. If you can bear the mist and cold winds that sometimes blow up from the canyon, this could make a good base camp for hikes into the preserve. The site has pit toilets but no water supply. For information see the Camping section in the front of the Molokai chapter.

Kamakou Preserve

In 1982 Molokai Ranch conveyed rights to the Nature Conservancy of Hawaii to manage the Kamakou Preserve, which starts immediately beyond Waikolu Lookout. Its 2774 acres of native ecosystems include cloudforest, bogs, shrubland and habitat for many species of endangered plants and animals.

MOLOKAI

Much of the preserve is forest of ohia lehua, a native tree with fluffy red blossoms whose nectar is favored by native birds. The forest is home to two rare birds that live only on Molokai (Molokai creeper and Molokai thrush) and to the bright red apapane, the yellow-green amakihi and the pueo (Hawaiian owl). Other treasures are tree ferns, native orchids and silvery lilies.

The road deteriorates quickly from the preserve entrance. Don't even consider driving it without a 4WD vehicle. Even with a 4WD, if you're not used to driving in mud and on steep grades it can be challenging. There are a few spots where it would be easy to flip a vehicle.

The Nature Conservancy asks visitors to sign in and out at the preserve entrance. Check out the sign-up sheet: on it people write such entries as 'We've abandoned our car in the mud', 'The view into Pelekunu was breathtaking' or 'We found thimbleberries to eat along the way'.

Occasionally portions of the preserve are closed to the public. At such time notices are posted at Kaunakakai post office, Kalamaula hunter check box and the preserve entrance.

Hiking As Kamakou is a rainforest, trails in the preserve can be very muddy. Rain gear is a good idea and you should bring along an ample supply of drinking water.

The best hiking trail is the **Pepeopae Trail**, which goes east one mile to an overlook with a stunning view of Pelekunu Valley. The trail is along a raised wooden boardwalk over Pepeopae Bog. The extensive boardwalk allows hikers access to this unique area while protecting the fragile ecosystem from being trampled. Pepeopae is a nearly undisturbed Hawaiian montane bog, a mysterious miniature forest with stunted trees and dwarfed plants. The area gets about 180 inches of rain each year.

There are two ways to get to the Pepeopae Trail. The easiest is to walk from Waikolu Lookout about 2½ miles along the main jeep road to the trailhead. It's a nice forest walk that takes just over an hour. There are some side roads along the way, but they're largely overgrown and it's obvious which is the main road. You'll eventually come to the 'Pepeopae' sign marking the start of the trail, which branches to the left.

The second and far muddier way is to take the **Hanalilolilo Trail**. It begins on the left side of the road about five minutes' walk past Waikolu Lookout, shortly after entering the preserve.

The Hanalilolilo Trail climbs 500 feet through a rainforest of moss-covered ohia trees and connects up with Pepeopae Trail after 1½ miles. If you approach via the Hanalilolilo Trail, turn left when you reach the Pepeopae Trail and you'll have about a half-mile walk up to the summit overlooking Pelekunu Valley.

From the Pelekunu Valley Overlook you get a view of majestic cliffs and if it's not clouded over you can see down the valley out to the ocean.

Pelekunu Valley is also under the stewardship of the Nature Conservancy. The Pelekunu Valley Preserve covers nearly 6000 acres, extending from sea level up to a height of almost 5000 feet here at the valley's upper rim.

This inaccessible valley has one of the few remaining perennial streams in Hawaii. It's an important habitat for gobies and river shrimp that return from the ocean each year to swim up and lay their eggs in the fresh water of Pelekunu Stream.

Give yourself a good half day to do the entire hike from the Kamakou Preserve entrance and back. If you'd like to shorten the walk, consider one of the guided hikes led by the Nature Conservancy, as they enter the reserve in 4WD vehicles and start hiking from the Pepeopae trailhead. These guided hikes also give visitors insights into the history and ecology of the preserve.

The conservancy's hikes are conducted monthly, usually on the first or second Saturday. The cost and reservation information is the same as for Moomomi hikes; see the end of the earlier Moomomi Beach section for more details.

West End

The Maunaloa Highway (Hwy 460) heads west from Kaunakakai, passes Molokai Airport, and then climbs into the high grassy rangeland of Molokai's arid western side.

Hwy 460 is about 17 miles long and the drive takes about half an hour from its start in Kaunakakai to its end at Maunaloa. It's a good paved road all the way, as are the roads to and around Kaluakoi Resort and down to Papohaku and Dixie Maru beaches. Most other West End roads, however, are privately owned dirt roads that are locked off to the public.

Molokai Ranch owns most of the land on this side of the island. Access is at the whim of the ranch, but generally requires special permission.

From Molokai's West End beaches, the twinkling lights of Oahu are just 26 miles away. The view is of Diamond Head to the left, Makapuu Point to the right.

West End Development

In the 1970s Molokai Ranch joined with Louisiana Land & Exploration Co to form the Kaluakoi Corporation. They proposed developing western Molokai into a major suburb of Honolulu, complete with a ferry service. The plan called for 30,000 private homes on the heretofore uninhabited west coast. A vocal anti-growth movement boomed quicker than the buildings could, and the plan was scrapped.

In its place a somewhat more modest master plan was drawn up for the development of Kaluakoi Resort that called for 1100 hotel units, 1200 condo units, 1000 single-family homes and a 15-acre shopping center.

Only 200 of the condo units, one 18-hole golf course and one of the four planned hotels have thus far been built. The 290-room hotel never really took off and the occupancy rate has been so low that part of it has been turned into condos. The house-lots have been subdivided, but as of yet

fewer than 100 houses have been built, mostly exclusive homes scattered along the edge of the beach and up on the bluff.

The Japanese investment company that now owns Kaluakoi Resort has plans to expand the golf course in the hope it will spur more interest from Japanese tourists who have thus far largely bypassed Molokai.

MAUNALOA

The long mountain range that comes into view on the left past the 10-mile marker is Maunaloa, which means 'Long Mountain'. Its highest point is Puunana at 1381 feet. Maunaloa was the site of Hawaii's first hula school, had one of the most important adze quarries in the Hawaiian Islands and was once a center of sorcery.

The name Maunaloa not only refers to the mountain range, but also the town at the end of the road. Built in the 1920s by Libby, McNeill & Libby, this little plantation town was the center of the company's pineapple activities on Molokai. Dole, which acquired Libby, McNeill & Libby in 1972, closed down operations in Maunaloa in 1975.

Maunaloa has dusty tin-roofed houses, a cemetery, a church, a few backstreets and occasionally an unlocked road heading away from town that invites impromptu exploration, but basically that's it. These days about 400 people live in the area, most working for Molokai Ranch or at Kaluakoi Resort.

Information

Maunaloa Service, the only gas station in the West End (motto: 'Our view of Diamond Head is a gas'), is open from 7:30 am to 5:30 pm Monday to Saturday.

Maunaloa General Store, which sells groceries and a good variety of beers and liquor, is open from 9 am to 7 pm Monday to Saturday and from 10 am to 2 pm on Sundays. The little rural post office on the other side of the road is open from 8 am to 4:30 pm Monday to Friday.

The Molokai Ranch headquarters is on the right as you enter town.

Molokai Sorcery

According to legend, fire gods who roamed the heavens as shooting stars landed on Maunaloa, where they inhabited a grove of trees. Unsuspecting men who tried to cut down the possessed trees were poisoned upon touching the wood, until at last one of the gods explained to a kahuna how to cut the trees down. The kahunas were then able to carve the poisoned wood into images that harnessed the force of the gods. During the 17th century it became a powerful sorcery that could be sent off into the night to avenge enemies. It was potent stuff and none of Molokai's neighbors dared to violate Molokai's sovereignty in those days. ∎

Places to Eat

JoJo's Cafe (☎ 552-2803) with its long wooden bar, stools in front and mirrors behind, looks like an old-time saloon. In fact that's what it was, but things got so rowdy that the current owner never bothered to renew the liquor license and these days it's a quiet small town diner. If you want beer or wine with your meal, you can pick it up at the general store across the way and bring it in. At lunch there's a nice mahimahi sandwich with fries for $7 and a shrimp curry plate for $8. Dinners include fresh fish and chicken in the $12 to $15 range. The flavorings of most dishes are delicately reminiscent of Indian cuisine, adding a pleasantly exotic touch for Molokai. It's open from noon to 2 pm and from 5 to 7:45 pm daily except Wednesdays and Sundays.

Things to Buy

Big Wind Kite Factory sells designer kites of all shapes and styles. Owner Jonathan Socher's kites have a reputation throughout the islands for their creative flair. Many of the kites are made on site and if you're there at the right time you can watch the process. An extension of the kite factory is the gift shop next door which has sarongs and wood carvings from Bali, horn scrimshaw from Molokai deer, silver jewelry, books on Molokai and the like. Both are open from 8:30 am to 5 pm Monday to Saturday and from 10 am to 2 pm on Sundays.

Up the street Blue Nalu sells owner-designed Indonesian clothing, while Dolly Hale, opposite JoJo's, sells handmade coconut fiber dolls.

SOUTHWEST BEACHES

If you really want to get off the beaten track, there are a couple of remote beaches south of Maunaloa. Access is via rutted dirt roads across Molokai Ranch land and is restricted to weekends and holidays. Permits, which are required to visit these beaches, must be picked up in advance from Molokai Ranch headquarters; however the ranch has altered its policies in recent years and sometimes limits access to residents only, while at other times it allows off-islanders to use the beach for $10 per person.

The most frequented spot is **Halena Beach**, a broad white sand beach with a protective reef. About 1½ miles west of Halena is **Hale O Lono Beach**, the starting point of the Molokai-to-Oahu outrigger canoe race held each year during Aloha Week. Two miles to the east of Halena is the abandoned Kolo Wharf. Libby, McNeill & Libby shipped Maunaloa pineapples from Kolo until moving their operations to Kaunakakai Harbor in the 1950s.

MOLOKAI RANCH WILDLIFE PARK

In the late 1960s, Molokai Ranch began importing antelope in an effort to control the rapid spread of kiawe trees, which were encroaching onto their cattle pastureland. The antelope, which feed on kiawe in their native habitat, adapted so well to Molokai that the ranch later started importing other rare exotic animals to breed for game parks and zoos. When Kaluakoi Resort opened, Molokai Ranch began providing sightseeing tours for the resort's guests.

Animals native to Africa, India, Asia and South America roam the park's 350 acres. The more numerous are the eland, Indian blackbuck and oryx, all strikingly marked antelopes; Barbary sheep, with thick curved-back horns; and sika deer from Japan.

There are also a few zebras, giraffes, rheas and East African crowned cranes. Flocks of wild turkey, ring-necked pheasant, francolin, quail and other game birds have flown in on their own.

The park's grassy hillsides and scrubby kiawe trees look so convincingly like the Serengeti that both US and Japanese film companies have used it to fake African backdrops.

The presentation begins with a slide show followed by a bus tour around the park's dirt roads that lasts about 1½ hours. Stops are made for animal sightings and feedings, and for photography.

The tours leave Kaluakoi Resort at 10:10 am and 1:40 pm on Mondays, Fridays, Saturdays and Sundays – though the schedule is subject to change. It costs $35 for adults, $25 for children ages six to 17, and $10 for children under five. Reservations can be made by calling 552-2767.

KALUAKOI RESORT

Off Hwy 460 at the 15-mile marker a road leads down to Kaluakoi Resort. The 6700-acre development includes Kaluakoi Hotel & Golf Club, the condominium complexes of Kaluakoi Villas, Paniolo Hale and Ke Nani Kai, mostly undeveloped houselots and a beautiful windswept coast. Overall it's a low-keyed and unobtrusive development that's pleasantly quiet and uncrowded.

Kepuhi Beach

Kepuhi is the white sand beach in front of Kaluakoi Hotel. During the winter the surf breaks close to shore, carrying a tremendous amount of sand to and fro. Experienced surfers take to the northern end of the beach.

Swimming conditions are often dangerous here. Not only can there be a tough shorebreak, but strong currents can be present even on calm days. Check with the folks at the hotel beach hut about water conditions. The hut rents snorkel sets for $6 a day and boogie boards for $4 an hour.

Kaluakoi Resort & West End Beaches

Kaiaka Rock

A five-minute hike up to the top of this 110-foot-high promontory at the south end of Kepuhi Beach rewards strollers with a nice view of Papohaku Beach. To get there take the golf course road (Kaiaka Rd) to its end from where the trail begins. At the top you'll find the remains of a pulley that was once used to carry cattle down to waiting barges for transport to Oahu slaughterhouses. There was also a 40-foot heiau on the hilltop until 1967 when the US Army bulldozed it under. There have been on-again off-again plans to build a luxury hotel at Kaiaka Rock.

MOLOKAI

Places to Stay

Kaluakoi Hotel & Golf Club (☎ 552-2555, (800) 777-1700), Box 1977, Maunaloa, HI 96770, is run by Colony Hotels & Resorts. The rooms are fairly standard for a resort hotel but are on the small side; the cost is $90 for a garden view, $110 for an ocean view. Ask for the 'Paradise on Wheels' deal and the hotel will throw in a free Budget rental car at no extra cost. There are also condo-style units that start at $135 for a studio, $155 for a one-bedroom. The hotel has an 18-hole golf course, tennis courts, pool, restaurant, tour desk and a couple of small stores.

About 100 units of the Kaluakoi Hotel are under separate management and booked as *Kaluakoi Villas* (☎ 552-2721, (800) 525-1470), Box 200, Maunaloa, HI 96770. All the units have a private lanai, TV and kitchenette with a refrigerator, four-burner stove, coffeemaker and a basic supply of kitchenware. While the walls are on the thin side and the decor is lightly faded, they are pleasant enough and can be the island's best condo value if you get a discounted rate. Standard rates are $105 to $135 for studio units, $135 to $165 for one-bedroom units, but they commonly run promotions and advertise specials in the Honolulu Sunday papers that steeply discount those prices. Ask for a 2nd-floor unit, as they have cathedral ceilings and many have a peek of the ocean.

Paniolo Hale (☎ 552-2731, (800) 367-2984), Box 190, Maunaloa, HI 96770, is a 77-unit condominium. The units are airy and each has a kitchen, ceiling fans, TV, washer/dryer and screened lanai. Studios cost $95, single or double. One-bedroom, two-bath units cost $115 for up to four people, two-bedroom units cost $145. Units with ocean views are $40 to $50 extra. The minimum stay is three nights and there's a 10% discount for weekly stays. The complex has a pool and barbecue grills. The office is open only from 8 am to 4 pm Monday to Saturday and from 10 am to 4 pm on Sundays.

Ke Nani Kai (☎ 552-2761, (800) 888-2791; fax 552-0045) Box 126, Maunaloa,

HI 96770, is a 120-unit condominium set back from the ocean. Each unit has a kitchen, lanai, washer/dryer and TV; most have a sofa bed in the living room. Units on the 2nd floor have high exposed-beam ceilings and are among the nicest on Molokai. The rates are $105 for up to four people in a one-bedroom unit, $125 for up to six people in a two-bedroom, two-bath unit. Units with ocean views are $25 more, but it's a distant and partial view. There's a pool and two tennis courts. The minimum stay is two nights.

Places to Eat

The only restaurant at the resort is the *Ohia Lodge* (☎ 552-2555) at Kaluakoi Hotel. The dining room is pleasant, but the food is undistinguished. There's a breakfast buffet for $11, or you can order off the menu. At dinner, prices range from $10.50 for chicken stir-fry to $22 for filet mignon and shrimp. The restaurant hours are from 6:30 to 10:30 am and 6 to 9 pm.

The hotel's snack shop is open from 11 am to 5 pm. Burgers cost $3.50, a chicken plate $5, and the food's on the greasy side.

The hotel also has a sundries shop with wine, beer and some convenience foods at inflated prices.

PAPOHAKU BEACH

Papohaku Beach lays claim to being Hawaii's largest beach. It's 2½ miles long and vast enough to hold the entire population of Molokai without getting crowded, although that would be an unlikely scenario. There's seldom more than a handful of beachgoers even on sunny days and at times you can walk the shore without seeing another soul.

It's a beautiful beach and easy to get to, so why are so few people there? Well, for one, it can be windy. But the main drawback is the water itself which is usually too treacherous for swimming.

Yet for barefoot strolling it's a gorgeous stretch, with soft golden sands gleaming in the sun and wisps of rainbows tossed up in the crashing surf.

There are seven well-marked beach

access points leading off Kaluakoi Rd; all have outdoor showers and paved parking lots. The first three lead to Papohaku Beach.

The first access, the most developed of the seven, is Papohaku Beach Park, a grassy landscaped park with campsites, showers, changing rooms, restrooms, drinking water and thorny kiawe trees.

From the third access, off Papapa Place, there's a broad view of all Papohaku Beach stretching north with the sun at your back. The large concrete tunnel at this end of the beach was used to load sand onto barges for shipping to Honolulu. The sand was used in construction and to build up Waikiki beaches until environmental protection laws put a halt to the sand mining operation in the early 1970s. This beach is a good place to find small puka shells of the type used to make necklaces. It's also a great place to catch the sunset.

The next three beach accesses are of rocky coastline, more suitable for fishing than other water activities.

Places to Stay

Camping Papohaku Beach Park is a choice site for camping, beautiful and quiet, with the surf lulling you to sleep and the birds waking you up. The tent sites are grassy and level. However the wind can pick up here on occasion. The camping area has two sections and they are watered by timed sprinklers on different days of the week, so note the sign that tells which days each area is scheduled for watering – there's nothing more depressing than finding your tent and belongings soaked!

For information on permits, see Camping in the Accommodation section in the front of the Molokai chapter.

DIXIE MARU BEACH

The beach at the end of the road, which the ancient Hawaiians knew as Kapukahehu, is now called Dixie Maru after a ship that went down in the area long ago.

Dixie Maru is the most protected cove on the west shore and the most popular swimming area. Consequently, there are usually a fair number of families here. The waters are generally calm except when the surf is high enough to break over the mouth of the bay.

MAKE HORSE BEACH

Make (pronounced 'mah-kay') Horse Beach supposedly takes its name from days past when wild horses were run off the cliff north of here. *Make* means 'dead'. This pretty little white sand beach is more secluded than the one in front of Kaluakoi Hotel. It's a good place for sunbathing but it's not safe for swimming.

To get there turn off Kaluakoi Rd onto the road to Paniolo Hale condos and then turn left as if going to the condo complex. Either park just beyond the condos and walk a quarter of a mile down to the golf course or drive the rutted dirt road to the end where there's a little spot to park. From there cross a narrow stretch of fairway and you're on the beach.

KAWAKIU BEACH

Kawakiu is a special place. It's a broad crescent beach of white sand and bright turquoise waters north of the Kaluakoi Resort complex.

In 1975 Kawakiu was a focus of Molokai activists who began demanding public access to private, and heretofore forbidden, beaches. The group, Hui Alaloa, marched to Kawakiu from Moomomi in a protest that convinced Molokai Ranch to grant public access to Kawakiu Beach.

To get there, turn off Kaluakoi Rd onto the road to Paniolo Hale, but instead of turning left down to the condos continue straight towards the golf course. Where the paved road ends, there's space to pull over and park just before crossing the greens. There are restrooms and drinking water here at the 14th hole. It's the last chance to get water.

The red dirt road that continues down to the beach should be OK with a 4WD and might also be passable in a standard car. However, it's quite rocky in places and if you did bottom out or brush one of the rocks on the side it could put a dent in

MOLOKAI

things. Anyway, why bother driving when it's a pleasant half-hour hike down to the beach?

After the golf course the road passes through ranchland with kiawe trees. Trees that died during the drought of the mid-1980s now stand bleached white by the sun, making interesting silhouettes against the blue sky.

You'll come first to a rocky point at the southern end of the bay. Scramble around up here before descending to the beach and you can find old rock foundations and get a scenic view of the coast south to the sands of Papohaku Beach and north to Ilio Point.

When seas are calm, Kawakiu is gener-ally safe for swimming, though that's more common in summer than winter. When the surf is rough, there are still areas where you can at least get wet. On the southern side of the bay is a little sandy-bottomed wading pool in the rocks. The northern side has an area of flat rocks over which water slides to fill up a shallow shoreline pool. On weekends there's usually a few families picnicking under the kiawe trees.

Places to Stay

Camping Molokai Ranch allows camping at Kawakiu Beach. Unlike at its other prop-erties, permits aren't required – simply go down and camp. There's no water and no facilities.

Lanai

Until recently Lanai was a one-crop, one-company, one-town island. The latter two still hold true.

For over half a century Castle & Cooke, which owns 98% of Lanai, ran the island (through its Dole subsidiary) as its own private pineapple plantation. For a time nearly one-fifth of the world's pineapples came from Lanai, but competition from more cheaply produced Costa Rican and Philippine pineapples gradually eroded the profitability of the Lanai crop.

Now, Castle & Cooke has ceased its commercial pineapple operations completely and is turning rural Lanai into an exclusive tourist destination, under the slogan 'Hawaii's Private Island'. During the past few years they have opened two luxury resorts, both with 18-hole golf courses, and the first of the island's million-dollar vacation homes are now being built.

For sleepy Lanai, the pace of change has been dizzying. Until 1990 Lanai had only one little hotel with just 10 rooms. The few visitors who came this way were largely hunters, hikers and independent travelers trying to avoid the tourist scene on the other islands. Now, with its two new resorts, Castle & Cooke is gambling that enough wealthy visitors in search of seclusion will show up to make it all pay off.

On the surface the hotels, with 350 rooms combined, haven't altered things all that radically. The center of Lanai remains Lanai City – not a city at all, but merely a small plantation town of tin-roofed houses. It's still home to all but a few dozen of Lanai's 2800 residents, most of whom work for Castle & Cooke.

Lanai has bright red earth, dry and dusty gullies, forested ravines, white sand beaches and cool, foggy uplands. The island also has some interesting archaeological sites and petroglyphs and the last native dryland forest in Hawaii.

Although Lanai is interesting to explore, many of the sights are a good distance from town, along rutted dirt roads that require a 4WD vehicle.

Not surprisingly, Lanai can be quite expensive to visit. One of the easiest ways to get a glimpse of it is to take the boat from Maui over in the morning, snorkel at Hulopoe Bay, which has the island's finest beach, and take the boat back in the afternoon.

ORIENTATION

Lanai has only one town, Lanai City, which is smack in the center of the island. The town is laid out in a sensible grid pattern, which makes it easy to get around.

Outside Lanai City there are only three paved roads: Keomuku Rd (Hwy 44), which heads northeast towards Shipwreck Beach; Kaumalapau Hwy, which heads west to Kaumalapau Harbor; and Manele Rd, which goes south to Manele and Hulopoe bays. Both Kaumalapau Hwy and Manele Rd are marked Hwy 440, even though they are two distinct roads.

The airport is on Kaumalapau Hwy, 3½ miles from town.

Dirt Roads

Most roads on Lanai are dirt roads, many of them built to service the pineapple fields; their conditions vary from good to impassable, largely as a result of the weather.

If you rent a 4WD vehicle and plan to travel these roads, ask the car rental agency for the current best routes to out-of-the-way sights – often there are a few alternatives and they know which roads are washed out and which are passable. If you do go off the beaten path and get stuck, it can be a long walk back to the town and you can expect to get hit up for the towing and repair fees.

HISTORY

Archaeological studies indicate Lanai was never heavily settled. Villages were rela-

LANAI

tively small and scattered throughout the island.

Since ancient times, Lanai has been under the rule of Maui. In 1778, when the Big Island chief Kalaniopuu was routed in a failed attempt to invade Maui, he decided to take his revenge on tiny Lanai and sent warriors under the command of Kamehameha.

Kamehameha's troops were brutal. They killed everyone they found and virtually depopulated Lanai. In 1792 when the Western explorer Vancouver sailed by Lanai he saw no villages and noted that the

island might at best be only sparsely populated.

Due to a tough ocean swell that by the 1820s had already claimed a few foreign ships, visitors were largely dissuaded from landing on Lanai's shores. In 1823 the missionary William Ellis became the first Westerner to step ashore. He guessed the island's population to be 2000.

Although the early missionaries didn't spend much time on Lanai, they still had an influence. They introduced the heretofore unknown crime of adultery to Hawaii and in the 1830s Maui women accused of the

Spirits in the Night

According to legend, Lanai was a land of spirits, and spirits alone roamed the island until the 15th century.

It was at this time that Kaululaau, the young prince of Maui, lived in what is today the town of Lahaina. He was a troublesome kid. After he had torn out breadfruit trees that his father had just planted, it was decided to banish him to uninhabited Lanai, an almost certain death.

Not easily intimidated, Kaululaau learned to trick the evil *akua* (spirits) of Lanai. During the day the akua would see him on the beach and ask where he spent his nights, hoping to ambush him in his sleep. He convinced them he slept in the surf, though when darkness fell he slipped off to the shelter of a cave.

Night after night, the akua returned to the beach and rushed out to look for Kaululaau in the waves. The longer they searched, the more exhausted they got, until finally the pounding surf overcame them. Kaululaau continued his pranks until at last all 400 of Lanai's akua had either perished or fled to Kahoolawe.

Kaululaau's family had given him up for dead, when Mauians noticed a light from a fire across the Auau Channel, which separates Maui and Lanai. When they went over to investigate they found Kaululaau alive and well and the island rid of spirits. Kaululaau was brought back to Maui a hero. ■

offense were banished to the barren northwestern side of Lanai as punishment.

Mormons

In the 1850s the Mormons moved in and set up a community at Palawai Basin, south of present-day Lanai City. Their intention was to establish a 'City of Joseph' in Hawaii.

The community floundered until 1861 when a new charismatic elder, Walter Gibson, arrived. Mormons from around the islands poured in, as did money to buy Palawai Basin. At the height of it all, there was one Mormon for every Lanaian.

Gibson, a shrewd businessman, handled the financial matters for the community. He was more concerned with land than with preaching. Things got sticky when it was discovered that he had made the land purchases in his own name, rather than in the church's. In 1864, after refusing to turn over the title to his Lanai holdings to another church in Salt Lake City, he was excommunicated by church leader Brigham Young.

This didn't seem to faze Gibson. The Lanai congregation faded away and the 300 or so Mormons left for Laie on Oahu's north shore, where their church is centered today.

Gibson held onto the prime Lanai real estate he had cornered. In the early 1880s,

Gibson became a friend and confidant of King Kalakaua and came to hold a number of positions in Kalakaua's cabinet, including that of premier.

Sugar

Upon his death, Gibson left the land to his daughter, Talula Lucy. In 1888 she and her husband, Frederick Hayselden, established the Maunalei Sugar Company and developed a landing at Kahalepalaoa on Lanai's east coast. A water pumping station went up at nearby Keomuku, the surrounding area was planted with sugar cane and the whole shebang was connected by a little railroad. Over 400 Japanese laborers were brought in to work the fields. The sugar days were short lived, however. By 1901 the pumps were drawing saltwater, the sugar cane had died and the whole enterprise had folded.

This was not the first try at the sugar business on Lanai. In 1802 a Chinese man landed on Lanai with granite rollers to crush sugar cane and iron pots to boil down the syrup. He is credited with being the first person to attempt sugar production in Hawaii. Although this enterprise was a failure, it was Chinese know-how that became the basis for sugar mills throughout Hawaii.

LANAI

Cattle

After the dismal failure with sugar, the land was sold off to ranching interests. In 1910 the newly formed Lanai Company consolidated most of the holdings and established cattle ranching on a larger scale. The following year New Zealander George Munro was hired to manage the ranch, and a landing for shipping cattle to off-island markets was established at Manele Bay.

In 1917 the Baldwin brothers, sons of missionaries from Maui, purchased the Lanai Company. With the exception of a small haole-held ranch and about 500 acres held by Lanaians, the Baldwins owned the entire island.

Pineapples

In 1922 Jim Dole paid $1.1 million for Lanai, a mere $12 an acre. It was just enough for the Baldwins to buy the Ulupalakua Ranch that they had long coveted on Maui. Dole, who had already established pineapple production on Oahu, doubled his holdings of cultivable land by purchasing Lanai.

Dole's Hawaiian Pineapple Company poured $4 million into Lanai to turn it into a plantation island. It built the plantation town of Lanai City, dredged Kaumalapau to make it a deep-water harbor, put in roads and water systems, cleared the land and planted pineapples. By the end of the 1920s production was in full swing.

Dole had marketed his pineapples well and was producing bumper crops – the future looked rosy. Then the Great Depression hit the mainland and sales plummeted. The newly popular canned pineapples were suddenly seen as an exotic extra, one that most Americans could easily do without in hard times.

After an $8 million loss in 1932, a reorganization took place. Castle & Cooke purchased much of the stock and eventually gained a controlling interest in Dole. They've been the dominant force on Lanai ever since.

GEOGRAPHY

Lanai is the sixth largest Hawaiian island.

It's 18 miles long, 13 miles wide and shaped like a teardrop. It has an area of 140 sq miles.

Lanai lies nine miles south of Molokai and nine miles west of Maui. The name Lanai means 'hump'. When viewed from Maui it looks somewhat like the back of a whale rising out of the water.

The island was formed by a single volcano, Palawai, now long extinct. The large flat basin of Palawai crater is Lanai's main agricultural area.

Lanai's terrain and climate are dominated by a ridge running from the northwest to the southeast. It reaches a height of 3370 feet at Lanaihale. From there, a series of gulches radiate down to the east coast, ending at a strip of coastal flats.

The western side of the ridge is a cool central plateau, which includes Lanai City at 1620 feet.

The southwest coast has sheer sea cliffs, some higher than 1000 feet. Northwest Lanai is dry and barren and slopes gently down to the coast.

CLIMATE

Lanai City has a mild climate. The lowest temperature on record is 46°F, the highest 88°F. Average temperatures range from 73°F in the summer to 66°F in the winter. Evenings can be brisk, commonly dipping down to around 50°F in winter.

Lanai is rather dry. Molokai to the north and Maui to the east draw much of the rain out of the moisture-laden trade winds before they reach Lanai.

Annual rainfall averages 37 inches in Lanai City and 10 to 15 inches along most of the coast. The difference is great enough that when it's overcast in Lanai City, chances are that Shipwreck Beach or Manele Bay will be sunny.

As with the rest of Hawaii, October to April is the rainiest season. Even the island's dryer areas can get whacked with heavy rainfall during winter storms.

FLORA & FAUNA

Lanai has suffered the greatest loss of native forests, plants and birds of any of the

ghing in at fishing tournament, Molokai

Halawa Valley, Molokai

ahiki Festival, Kaunakakai, Molokai

Puu Pehe Rock, Lanai

Garden of the Gods, Lanai

main Hawaiian islands, the result of drastic overgrazing.

Lanai has about 8000 axis deer, descendants of a herd of eight brought to Molokai from India in 1868. The deer were introduced to Lanai in 1920 and are more prolific than on Molokai, the only other Hawaiian island where they roam free.

Mouflon sheep were introduced to Lanai in 1954 and inhabit the island's gullies and ridges. Both the deer and sheep are hunted.

Lanai has no mongooses, which eat the eggs of ground-nesting birds, so introduced game birds thrive. Ring-necked pheasants, francolins, chukar partridges, quails, doves and wild turkeys are all common.

However, the island has only two endemic birds remaining – the Hawaiian owl and the *apapane* (native honeycreeper) – and they are scarce.

The most noticeable types of vegetation are thorny kiawe trees and stately Norfolk Island pines. Lanai has a unique native dryland forest, under the protection of the Nature Conservancy.

GOVERNMENT

Lanai is part of Maui County. Historically Lanai has been treated as an extension of Maui, much as Niihau has been of Kauai. Lanai had only limited autonomy at most, with Maui kings maintaining suzerainty.

These days the control of the island is largely in the hands of Castle & Cooke, which owns all but 2% of Lanai. Total county and state land accounts for just over 100 acres. Beaches on Lanai, as elsewhere in Hawaii, are public domain under state jurisdiction.

ECONOMY

About 80% of Lanai's 1200 workers are employed by Castle & Cooke, mostly in its resort operations.

Although visitors will see two high-profile pineapple fields, one fronting the airport and the other on the road to Manele Bay Hotel, these small patches are only 'show fields' – the last commercial pineapple harvest was in 1992. Some of the former pineapple fields have been given

over to forage crops and cattle and hog raising, but the importance of agriculture and ranching is secondary at best.

Lanai's transition from a plantation economy to a tourism-oriented service economy is resulting in major social and economic changes for Lanaians. There is a lot of apprehension, not only among laid-off pineapple workers but also among local shop owners who worry that they may eventually be replaced by larger tourist-based off-island businesses. On the plus side, at least a few Lanaians with college degrees have returned home to find new administrative jobs at the resorts.

Although the resorts initially mounted millions of dollars in operating losses, the occupancy rates climbed with the opening of a second golf course in 1994. Castle & Cooke argues that losses can be permanently stemmed by moving on to the next stage of development – the construction of 750 luxury homes – and the government seems on the verge of granting the company approval to proceed. The homes are geared for wealthy, second-home owners who have bypassed Lanai up to now. If it all develops according to plan, Lanai's population may quadruple to 10,000 before the end of the decade.

POPULATION & PEOPLE

Lanai has seen some dramatic rises and declines in its population. It had dropped well below 200 when Dole arrived in 1922.

Lanai's current population has risen to 2800, but that's still about 500 less than it was during pineapple's heyday in the 1950s. All but a few dozen of Lanai's residents live in Lanai City. The largest ethnic group is Filipino (51%), followed by Japanese (18%), Caucasian (11%) and part-Hawaiian (9.2%).

Approximately a third of the people living on Lanai were born in the Philippines.

INFORMATION

There's no local daily newspaper, but you can buy the *Maui News* from a box in front of International Food & Clothing in Lanai

LANAI

City. Community notices, including items for sale and houses for rent, are posted on bulletin boards outside the post office and the three grocery stores.

Money

There are two banks in Lanai City, both on Lanai Ave. The First Hawaiian Bank, near 7th Street, is open Monday to Thursday from 8:30 am to 3 pm, on Fridays until 6 pm. First Federal Savings, on the opposite side of the post office, has the same Friday hours as First Hawaiian but is open to 4 pm on other days.

Post & Telecommunications

Lanai's post office, at the east side of Dole Park in Lanai City, is open from 9 am to 4:30 pm weekdays and from 10 am to noon on Saturdays. When phoning Lanai from out of state, add Hawaii's 808 area code in front of the seven-digit local number.

Library

Lanai's library is on Fraser Ave in Lanai City, adjacent to the school. It's a fairly large library with a good collection of newspapers, including *USA Today*, the *Wall Street Journal* and neighbor island papers. It's open from 8 am to 5 pm Tuesday to Friday and from 1 to 8 pm on Mondays.

Laundry

There's a coin laundry open 24 hours a day on 7th St in Lanai City.

Weather

For recorded weather forecasts and water conditions call 565-6033.

Emergency

For all emergencies call 911. Lanai Community Hospital (☎ 565-6411) on 7th St in Lanai City has 24-hour emergency service.

ACTIVITIES

There's a new $3-million public recreation center in Lanai City, next to the school, with a 75-foot-long pool, a playground, a basketball court and a couple of lit tennis courts.

Both the Manele Bay Hotel and the Lodge at Koele have 18-hole designer golf courses complete with dress codes and $100-a-day ($140 for non-guests) fees. The Cavendish Golf Course, a local nine-hole course on the north side of Lanai City, is the only free golf course in Hawaii and a popular recreation spot for islanders. Anyone can play; simply bring your clubs and begin – no dress codes, no fees.

The two resort hotels offer a variety of activities, including tennis, diving and horseback riding; however, the fees are generally quite high and many of the activities are limited to hotel guests. The Lodge at Koele does rent mountain bikes on a first-come, first-serve basis for $5 an hour or $35 a day.

Cockfighting, while not legal, takes place on Lanai. The fights are held on Sundays but they're private and you generally won't find them unless you've been around for a while and made the right friends.

GETTING THERE & AWAY

Air

Island Air (☎ 565-6744, (800) 652-6541) flies direct from Honolulu and Kahului to Lanai. From Honolulu there are seven flights a day, from Maui four. The one-way fare is $74. For $81, you can fly between Lanai and any of Aloha Airlines' other destinations, with a transfer connection in Honolulu or Maui to Island Air.

Hawaiian Airlines (☎ 565-7281) flies direct to Lanai three times a day from Honolulu, with the morning flight via Molokai. The one-way fare is $74. For the same fare, you can also fly between Lanai and any other island destination served by Hawaiian Airlines, with connections via Honolulu.

For information on discounted tickets and air passes, see the Getting Around chapter in the front of the book.

Lanai Airport lacks the navigational equipment to allow instrument landings. When it's foggy, which has been known to happen for days on end during winter storms, planes are unable to land. However, far more common is a delay of a few hours.

Airport In keeping with the island's growth, Lanai's funky old terminal has just been replaced with a new oversized complex with separate areas for arrival, departure and waiting.

Ferry

Expeditions (☎ 661-3756 on Maui, (800) 695-2624) operates a passenger ferry between Lahaina on Maui and Manele Boat Harbor on Lanai. The boat departs Lahaina at the dock in front of Pioneer Inn daily at 6:45 and 9:15 am and 12:45, 3:15 and 5:45 pm. The boat departs Manele daily at 8 and 10:30 am and 2, 4:30 and 6:45 pm. The trip takes 45 minutes to an hour. One-way fares are $25 for adults and $20 for children ages two to 11. Tickets can be purchased on the boat.

This is a great way to get to Lanai. Although the ride can be jolting when the seas are rough, it's usually quite pleasant. During the winter there's a good chance of seeing whales.

Tours

For details on diving, snorkeling and sailing tours to Lanai from Maui, see the Activities section in the Maui chapter.

GETTING AROUND

To/From the Airport

The Lodge at Koele and Manele Bay Hotel have a shuttle bus that meets hotel guests at the airport. With advance notice, Hotel Lanai will provide its guests free pickups at either the airport or the boat harbor.

Shuttle Bus

The resorts run a free shuttle bus between the Manele Bay Hotel and the Lodge at Koele for their guests, although non-guests can try their luck catching a ride. It's scheduled to run once an hour on weekdays, every half-hour on weekends.

Car

Only one car rental company, Lanai City Service, is in business on Lanai and consequently the rental rates are high. While there are currently no car rental booths at the airport, the agency provides free airport pickup to its in-town office; call from the airport when you arrive.

Lanai City Service (☎ 565-7227, (800) 342-7398 in Hawaii, (800) 367-7006 from the mainland), on Lanai Ave in Lanai City, is affiliated with Dollar Rent A Car. Unlike its other affiliates, Dollar requires a one-day deposit to make a booking on Lanai and there are no discounts available. Compact cars rent for $60 a day and 4WD vehicles for $109. Lanai City Service is open from 7 am to 6 pm daily.

While there are many dirt roads in fine condition that could easily be driven, Lanai City Service restricts all its cars to paved roads – the 4WD vehicles may be driven on most dirt roads.

Taxi

Lanai City Service provides a limited taxi service. The cost is $5 per person between the airport and town and $10 per person between Manele and town. The company sometimes books out all of its vehicles, leaving none available to use as a taxi – which means day visitors who plan on taking a taxi occasionally have to walk back to the airport!

Around the Island

LANAI CITY

Lanai City is nestled among Norfolk pines on a cool central plateau beneath the slopes of Lanaihale Mountain. For an old plantation town it's a tidy little place. Unlike Hawaii's working sugar towns, many of the homes in Lanai City are privately owned. Houses are brightly painted and many have lovely front gardens with flowering plants and trees.

The center of town is Dole Park, a large

> **Official Lanai**
> Lanai has long had the nickname 'The Pineapple Island' but Castle & Cooke's newest promotional slogan is 'Hawaii's Private Island'. Lanai's official color is yellow and its official flower is kaunaoa, a thin parasitic vine. ∎

grassy park lined with Norfolk pines. The park stretches six blocks from Fraser Ave to Lanai Ave, the two main roads in town.

Lanai's restaurants are on the north side of the park and the grocery stores are on the south side. To the east of the park are the post office, hospital and Hotel Lanai. To the west are the school and recreation center, with houses spread out for a half dozen blocks on either side – and that's about it.

At sunset, walking through the town and looking at the pines silhouetted against the crimson sky can be a delight. On Sunday mornings a stroll by the Hawaiian church on the corner of 5th and Gay Sts will treat you to fine melodies of choir music.

While the new resorts are bringing change, this is still the place to come to unwind the clock. It's hard to imagine a town less hurried than Lanai City – most shops even close for a siesta between noon and 1:30 pm.

Lanai City Shops

Richard's Shopping Center on 8th St is a fairly large grocery store for a small island. In addition to food, it also sells general merchandise, nonprescription medicines and camera film. It's open from 8:30 am to 5:30 pm Monday to Saturday, and stays open during lunch time on Fridays and Saturdays.

Pine Isle Market, also on 8th St, is the other major grocery store. It carries a bit of everything from Coleman lamps to sandals and watches. It's open from 8 am to 5:30 pm Monday to Saturday.

The only grocery store that stays open weekdays during siesta is International Food & Clothing on Ilima St. It's open from 8:30 am to 5:30 pm, until noon on Saturdays and Sundays. It has groceries

and the town's widest selection of wine and beers.

Lanai Art Studio, beside the community college, is the site of the community arts program and the place to purchase locally made arts and crafts. The works include watercolors, painted T-shirts, scarves and a few jewelry items. It's open from 9 am to 4 pm Monday to Saturday.

Walks

Strollers will find a pleasant short hike behind the Lodge at Koele. Simply take the road on the Lanai City side of the lodge to its end at the golf cart parking lot. From there take the path along the golf cart route for a 15-minute walk past stands of Norfolk pines, artificial ponds and golf course landscaping. It ends at a hilltop bench where there's a plaque with the poem 'If' by Rudyard Kipling.

It's also possible to walk from the back of the golf course up to the Munro Trail on a new trail called the Koele Nature Hike. A brochure detailing this five-mile round-trip hike is available from the Activities Desk at the Lodge at Koele.

Places to Stay

The *Hotel Lanai* (☎ 565-4700, (800) 321 4666; fax 565-4713), Box A 119, Lanai City, HI 96763, was built by Dole in 1923 to lodge plantation guests. It has a rustic mountain lodge ambiance that's a throwback to the island's plantation era. After years of neglect, the hotel has recently undergone renovations that have restored much of its original charm. The 10 rooms are pleasantly simple with hardwood floors, pedestal sinks, bleached pine furnishings, patchwork quilts and painted wooden walls that are anything but sound proof. There are various bed combinations ranging from two twins to one king-size bed. Each room has a private bathroom and costs $95. Ask for one of the four front rooms as they have porches at no extra cost. There's also a one-bedroom cottage in the rear that has a separate sitting room with sofa bed for $135 a night.

The *Lodge at Koele* (☎ 565-7300, (800

To Shipwreck Beach

Keomuku Rd

44

To Garden
of the Gods

Cavendish
Golf Course

3rd St

Fraser Ave

Gay St

Houston St

Ilima Ave

Lanai Ave

Mahana St

4th St

5th St

6th St

7th St

Nani St

Queens Ave

12

13

9 10 11

6 7 8

Dole
Park

18 19

17 23

8th St

16

20 21

22

9th St

10th St

11th St

12th St

12th St

13th St

Lanai City

0   200   400 m
0   200   400 yards

440

Kaumalapau Hwy

Manele Rd

440

To Airport,
Kaumalapau Harbor

To Hulopoe Beach,
Manele Bay

■ PLACES TO STAY
1 Lodge at Koele
2 Lanai Bed & Breakfast
22 Hotel Lanai

▼ PLACES TO EAT
9 Blue Ginger Cafe
10 ST Properties

OTHER
3 Hawaiian Church
4 Lanai Elementary
   & High School
5 Library
6 Maui Community College
7 Lanai Art Studio
8 Coin Laundry
11 Lanai Playhouse
12 First Hawaiian Bank
13 Hospital
14 Recreation Center
15 Government Offices
16 Castle & Cooke Offices
17 Police
18 Department of Land
   & Natural Resources
19 Pine Isle Market
20 Richard's Shopping Center
21 First Federal Savings
23 International Food
   & Clothing
24 Lanai City Service

LANAI

321-4666; fax 565-4561), Box 774, Lanai City, HI 96763, is a low-rise 102-room hotel with the ambiance of an overgrown plantation estate. The hotel image is genteel, complete with afternoon tea, lawn bowling and croquet. Its lobby, called the Great Hall, is stuffed with an eclectic collection of antiques, artwork and upholstered furnishings and boasts Hawaii's two largest stone fireplaces. Guest rooms, which have a plantation-era decor, are quite nicely appointed with four-poster beds, private lanais, marble bathrooms, VCRs and the like. The rooms cost from $295 to $395, while suites, which include butler service, cost from $550 to $975.

Lucille Graham rents two bedrooms with a shared bath in her home as *Lanai Bed & Breakfast* (☎ 565-6378), Box 956, 312 Mahana St, Lanai City, HI 96763. The house is below Cavendish Golf Course. One room has a double and single bed, the other a queen bed, and each costs $50/60 for singles/doubles. Rates include a full breakfast. Lucille, a spry and politically active octogenarian, can fill you in on island happenings and places to explore. Like many people on Lanai, she decorates her house with an interesting collection of glass floats picked up on Lanai's windward coast.

Sheila Black (☎ 565-6867), PO Box 765, Lanai City, HI 96763, rents out a pleasant guesthouse on Puulani Rd, a few minutes' walk upslope from the hospital. Located in a neighborhood of larger homes that once housed plantation managers, the guesthouse has two bedrooms, two baths, a full kitchen, a living room, TV and other amenities. It can sleep up to seven people and costs $163 a night. In winter, the busiest season, the guesthouse generally books up a few months in advance.

Places to Eat

The *Hotel Lanai* has good food, moderate prices and a dining room with high ceilings and hardwood floors. Breakfast costs no more here than at the simpler restaurants in town, and on cool mornings when they light the dining room fireplace there's not

another restaurant on Lanai that can match the atmosphere. Pancakes or French toast cost $4, omelets about a dollar more. At lunch stir-fried vegetables over brown rice cost $4.50, while sandwiches, cheeseburgers and fried fish or chicken – all served with French fries – are priced around $7. Dinners include burgers and sandwiches, as well as more substantial dishes like fish stir-fry or barbecued ribs priced at $15. Breakfast is available from 7:30 to 10 am, lunch from 11:30 am to 1:30 pm and dinner from 5:30 to 9 pm.

S T Properties serves 1950s-style hamburgers – big and juicy, if a bit heavy on the fat and sodium. Unquestionably the favorite burger among Lanaians, you can get one with the works for a mere $2. The restaurant, which has an old-style counter where you can sit over coffee and watch the bacon sizzle on the grill, has breakfast dishes and lunch plates for around $5. Hours are from 6:30 am to 1 pm; it's closed on Wednesdays.

The *Blue Ginger Cafe*, a combo bakery and cafe, makes doughnuts and a few sugary pastries and serves up three meals a day. It's an unassuming place with a cement floor and vinyl chairs, but if you order right the food's good. Their best dishes are the Belgian waffles at breakfast for $4.25 and the fresh fish specials at dinner. The cafe also serves inexpensive hamburgers and saimin, $6 plate lunches and pizza. It's open from 6:30 am to 9 pm daily, with breakfast served until 10:30 am.

At the *Lodge at Koele*, the lobbyside Terrace Dining Room (☎ 565-7300) overlooks the hotel gardens. A continental breakfast costs $8.50, while eggs Benedict with a cup of coffee costs $14. At lunch, omelets or sandwiches cost around $10, more elaborate dishes about $15. At dinner, main courses are priced around $20. Breakfast is served from 7 to 10 am, lunch from noon to 6 pm and dinner from 6 to 9:30 pm. The Lodge also has a formal dining room that's open for dinner only, with entrees such as smoked duck and venison from Lanai axis deer in the $30 to $35 range.

Entertainment

People go to bed early in Lanai and there's no real night life, although the *Lodge at Koele* sometimes has mellow Hawaiian music in the evening and occasionally brings in an off-island band.

The *Lanai Playhouse*, the island's new movie theater, shows standard feature movies for $5.

SHIPWRECK BEACH & KEOMUKU

Hwy 44 runs 8½ miles from town to the northeast coast. The highway is narrow but well-paved. To get there, head north on Lanai Ave and bear right on Keomuku Rd (Hwy 44).

The road heads into hills and pastures with grazing cattle. The uplands here are often cool, with fog and cloud cover drifting in and out. The Lodge at Koele is on Hwy 44, a mile above town. A mile past the lodge is a paved road on the right that leads to the Munro Trail.

The road to the trailhead is lined with Norfolk pines. It ends in half a mile at a cemetery with gravestones in Japanese and Filipino. Sake offerings are placed at some of the Japanese graves. Pinwheels, bunny rabbits and pink flamingoes adorn sites where Filipino children are buried.

Back on Hwy 44, three miles out of town, there's a pull-off to the right with a beautiful view. Straight ahead is the undeveloped southeast shore of Molokai and its tiny islet of Mokuhooniki. The view to the

right is of Maui and the Kaanapali highrises.

From the lookout, the road starts down to the coast toward Molokai. The scenery is punctuated by interesting rock formations sticking up out of the eroded red earth, similar to those at Garden of the Gods. Later a shipwreck comes into view.

The paved road ends near the coast. The dirt road to the left leads to Shipwreck Beach and a former lighthouse. Instead, if you continue on the main road, it leads down the coast to Keomuku.

Shipwreck Beach

Shipwreck Beach is the name given to nine miles of Lanai's northeast shore. It starts at Kahokunui at the end of Hwy 44 and goes up to Polihua Beach. True to its name, there are a couple of shipwrecks as well as a shore that's good for beachcombing.

The dirt road that heads left from the highway ends after 1¾ miles at the site of a former lighthouse on a lava point. Only the cement foundations of the lighthouse remain.

When it's dry the road is usually passable by car, but you'll miss the beach walk. An alternative is to hike (or drive) in about half a mile from the end of the paved road, cut down to the beach and walk to the lighthouse from there. You can walk back by the road, which is quicker.

Lots of driftwood washes up on this windswept beach. Some of the pieces are identifiable sun-bleached timbers from shipwrecks – hulls, side planks, perhaps even a gangplank if your imagination is active. There are also fishing nets, ropes and the occasional glass float.

It's likely to be just you and the driftwood, although about 20 minutes up the beach there's a cluster of small wooden beach shacks called Federation Camp, which is sometimes used by Filipino fishers. The lighthouse is 10 minutes farther.

The beach sand is a bit soft and sinks underfoot, making this a good walk for your calves. The sand gradually changes colors as you walk along. In some places it's a colorful, chunky mixture of rounded shells and bits of rock that look like some sort of beach confetti.

A low rock shelf lines much of the shore and the shallow, murky waters are not good for swimming or snorkeling.

Up on the slopes some of the beach *pohuehue* (morning glory) is entwined with an airplant that looks something like yellow-orange fishing line. This is kaunaoa, Lanai's official flower, a leafless parasitic vine.

Petroglyphs From the lighthouse, markings lead directly inland for about five minutes to some small petroglyphs. The simple figures are etched on large boulders on the right side of the path, down the slope past the 'Do Not Deface' sign.

The rocky path is through groundcover of flowering golden ilima and pink and yellow lantana. The former is native, while the latter was introduced to Hawaii just 35 years ago and has escaped from cultivation to become a major pest throughout the islands.

Keep your eyes open for animals – sightings of mouflon sheep on the inland hills are not uncommon. The males have curledback horns and the more dominate ones travel with a harem of females.

Up the Beach It's about 15 minutes farther up the beach to a rusting WW II Liberty ship that has washed up on the reef. You can see the shipwreck clearly from the lighthouse.

This is the point where most people turn around and head back but it's possible to walk another six miles down to **Awalua**, which long ago was the location of a north shore landing. There's another shipwreck at Awalua but not much else. The beach is generally windy and it's a hot dry hike, although the farther down the beach you go, the prettier it gets.

Keomuku Beach

Keomuku Beach is the stretch of shore from Kahokunui, at the end of Hwy 44, south to Kahalepalaoa Landing.

The dirt road is likely to be either dusty or muddy, with deep ruts, though if you're lucky enough to catch it after it's been graded it's not so bad. Still, it's a 4WD road. When the tide is low, locals do much of the drive down on the beach sand rather than bump along on the road. The coast is not particularly attractive and there's not much to see, although there are several historical sites and Maui is visible across the Auau Channel. There are scattered groves of coconuts along the way and lots and lots of kiawe.

Real diehards can go the full 12 miles down to **Naha**, at the end of the road. It may take as long as two hours one way, depending on road conditions.

Less than a mile down the road is **Maunalei**. An ancient heiau that once sat there was taken apart by Frederick Hayselden, who used its stones to build a cattle fence. He later lost his shirt in the ill-fated Maunalei Sugar Company. Islanders believed the temple desecration was what caused the wells to turn salty and kill off the sugar cane Hayselden had planted.

Keomuku, 5¾ miles south of Hwy 44, was the center of the short-lived sugar cane plantation. There's little left to see other than the old Ka Lanakila O Ka Malamalama Church, built in 1903 after Maunalei Sugar collapsed. The ruins of a couple of fishponds are along the coast, but not easily visible.

Another heiau at **Kahea**, 1½ miles south of Keomuku, was also dismantled by Maunalei Sugar Co, this time to build a railroad to transport the sugar to Kahalepalaoa Landing. Kahea, meaning 'red stains', was a luakini heiau where human sacrifices were made.

Kahalepalaoa Landing, just south of Kahea, has the best beach on this end of the island and is used by Club Lanai, which operates day outings from Maui. The road onward to Naha really doesn't offer much more scenery for the effort, but should you want to continue, it's about four miles farther. Naha is popular with local fishers, but is not a good place for swimming.

MANELE BAY & HULOPOE BAY

Lanai's best beach, Hulopoe, is reached by a 20-minute drive down Manele Rd, a paved road that starts just south of town. The beach is 7½ miles south of the intersection of Manele Rd and Kaumalapau Hwy.

About 1½ miles down Manele Rd, a very wide dirt road comes in diagonally to the left. This is Hoike Rd, which leads to the Munro Trail and the Luahiwa Petroglyphs.

After four miles Manele Rd veers to the left and a mile farther there's a small pull-off with a pretty coastal view of both Manele Bay to the left and Hulopoe Bay to the right. The island beyond is Kahoolawe.

Manele Boat Harbor

Manele Harbor is a scenic, crescent-shaped natural harbor backed by sheer cliffs. Lanai folks like to fish from the stone breakwater that sticks out into the mouth of the bay.

Manele is a very protected harbor and a popular sailboat anchorage. Lanai is one of the easier islands to sail to from Honolulu (although 'easy' is a relative term – the waters can be quite rough).

In the early 20th century, cattle were herded down to Manele Bay for shipment to Honolulu. The remains of a cattle chute, which was used to load them directly onto the ships, can be seen by walking around the point to the right at the end of the parking lot.

Stone ruins from a Hawaiian fishing village and concrete slabs from the days of cattle ranching are up on the hill above the parking lot. The ruins are now largely overgrown with kiawe and ilima.

Inside Manele Bay, coral is abundant near the cliffsides where the bottom quickly slopes off to about 40 feet. Beyond the western edge of the bay, near Puu Pehe Rock, is First Cathedrals, a popular dive site. Off the parking lot are restrooms, showers, drinking water, picnic tables and a little harbormaster's office. If you arrive by boat, it's a 10-minute walk from Manele Bay to Hulopoe Beach.

Hulopoe Beach

Hulopoe Beach is a gently curving white sand beach. It's long and broad and protected by a rocky point to the south. On the north side of the bay, the Manele Bay Hotel sits on a low seaside terrace.

Even with the hotel, this is a pretty quiet beach. Generally the most action occurs when the boats from Maui pull in with snorkelers.

Some of Lanai's best snorkeling is found on the left side of the bay, where there are lots of colorful coral and reef fish.

Also on that side, just beyond the sandy beach, there's a low lava shelf with tide pools worth exploring. One area has been blasted out, making a protected pool for children. Cement steps lead down to the pool from the rocks. It looks as if every kid on Lanai rushed down to scrawl their name in the cement when it was poured in August 1951.

Hulopoe Beach has a landscaped park with solar-heated showers, restrooms, picnic tables, pay phones, drinking water and campsites.

Both Manele and Hulopoe bays are part of a marine life conservation district in which the removal of coral and rocks is prohibited and many fishing activities are restricted. Water activities can be dangerous during kona storms, when strong currents and swells prevail.

Puu Pehe Cove

From Hulopoe Beach, a short path leads south to an interesting rocky point jutting out from the coast. The peninsula of land separating Hulopoe and Manele bays is a

LANAI

volcanic cone that's sharply eroded on its southerly seaward edge. Here on the point, the lava has rich rust-red colors with swirls of grey and black in fascinating patterns. The texture is bubbly and brittle – so brittle that huge chunks of the point have broken off and fallen onto the coastal shelf below. There's a small sea arch below the point.

Puu Pehe is the name of the cove to the left of the point as well as the sea stack just offshore. This islet, also called Sweetheart's Rock, has a tomb-like formation on top that figures into Hawaiian legend.

Places to Stay

The 250-room *Manele Bay Hotel* (☎ 565-7700, (800) 321-4666; fax 565-2483), Box 774, Lanai City, HI 96763, overlooking Hulopoe Beach, has spacious lobbies that are partially open-air and adorned with artwork and antiques. There's a reading room with a dark-wood decor, leather-bound books, lots of Italian marble floors and a central lounge with sofas, elegant chairs and a grand piano. Rooms are quite pleasant, all with four-poster beds, lanais and marble baths. Rates are $225 for a room without a view, $425 for an ocean-front room and from $650 for suites.

Camping Surprisingly, even with the hotel up and running, camping is still allowed at six campsites just a minute's walk from Hulopoe Beach.

As long as the Lanai Company (☎ 565-8232), Box L, Lanai City, HI 96763, continues issuing permits, here's how it goes: There's a $5 registration fee per campsite plus $5 per person per night. The maximum length of stay is seven consecutive days. Reservations can be made by mail or phone. Fees must be paid within five days of confirmation of the reservation.

Sometimes you can get permits without advance reservations if the campground's not full. The Lanai Company, in the Castle & Cooke offices opposite the post office, issues permits from 9 am to 4 pm Monday to Friday.

Places to Eat

The *Manele Bay Hotel* serves breakfast in its Hulopoe Court from 7 to 11 am. The setting has a bit of everything: high ceilings with gaudy chandeliers, ornate Chinese vases and a view of the ocean. There's a full breakfast buffet for $18, while a la carte items include croissants for $4, macnut pancakes for $9.50 and coffee for $2.50. The restaurant also serves an informal dinner with burgers, pasta, pizzas and tandoori chicken priced from $10 to $20.

Lunch is served at the poolside grill from 11 am to 5 pm, with light eats such as mahimahi sandwiches with fries and a variety of salads for around $15. The hotel's open-air Ihilani Dining Room, which is quite pleasant and somewhat elegant, serves fine French food for dinner. Appetizers include oysters mignonette and escargot priced from $15 to $20 and entrees such as Maine lobster or Lanai venison for around $40.

Puupehe
Legend says an island girl, Puupehe, was so beautiful that her lover decided that they should make their home in a secluded coastal cave, lest any other young men in the village set eyes on her. One day the lover was up in the mountains fetching water when a kona storm suddenly blew in. He rushed down the mountain, but by the time he arrived, the waves had swept into the cave, drowning Puupehe.

The islanders brought a tapa cloth and prepared to bury the girl in the village. But Puupehe's lover slipped off at night with her body and carried it out to the rock, where he built her a tomb. When he was finished, in his grief he jumped into the surging waters below and was dashed back onto the rock. The islanders recovered his body, wrapped it in the tapa they had prepared for Puupehe and buried him in the village. ∎

KAUNOLU

Kaunolu was the site of an early Hawaiian fishing village that was abandoned in the mid-1800s. It has the greatest concentration of ruins on Lanai.

Kaunolu was a vacation spot for Kamehameha the Great, who went there to fish the prolific waters of Kaunolu Bay. Kamehameha also held tournaments and sporting events at Kaunolu and had a house up on the bluff on the eastern side of the bay.

Kaunolu Gulch separates the two sides of the bay. Most of the house sites sit on the eastern side. The now-overgrown Halulu Heiau, on the western side, once dominated the whole scene. The heiau included a puuhonua, a place of refuge where renegade kapu breakers could be absolved from their death sentences. There are a number of petroglyphs, some on the southern side of the heiau.

Beyond the heiau ruins, the Palikaholo sea cliffs rise more than 1000 feet. Northwest of the heiau there's a high natural stone wall along the perimeter of the cliff. Look for a break in the wall at the cliff's edge where there's a sheer 90-foot drop. This is Kahekili's Jump, named after a Lanaian chief. There's a ledge below it that makes diving into the ocean here a bit death-defying. Apparently, Kamehameha used to amuse himself by making upstart warriors jump from this cliff.

Dr Kenneth Emory of the Bishop Museum did an extensive survey of Kaunolu in 1921 and counted 86 house sites, 35 stone shelters and a number of grave markings, pens and gardens. These days most of the sites are simply too overgrown with kiawe to even recognize.

There are a couple of ways to get to Kaunolu. The easiest is to go south from Lanai City down Manele Rd. At three quarters of a mile past the nine-mile marker, there's a sharp bend in the road. Rather than follow Manele Rd as it bears left, go straight ahead onto an old pineapple road that begins as pavement but soon turns to dirt. Just before reaching a brightly painted water pipe, a sign marks the turn-off to Kaunolu; turn left onto this dirt road which leads south in the direction of the lighthouse. If the road hasn't been washed out by rain recently, you may be able to make it most of the way down with a 4WD vehicle, but odds are you'll have to walk the last mile or so.

KAUMALAPAU HARBOR

Kaumalapau, Lanai's commercial harbor, is 6½ miles west of town, at the end of the airport road. The harbor was built for shipping pineapples and now that the industry is gone, it's a rather sleepy place. The main traffic here now is the cargo boat that comes in once a week from Oahu.

You can often find people fishing from the boulder jetty for awa (milkfish), a good-tasting fish that's a common catch in the bay. Scuba divers sometimes use the bay as well, as the deep waters at Kaumalapau are extremely clear.

As along most of the southwest coast, Kaumalapau has sheer coastal cliffs.

NORTHWEST LANAI

To get to sights in the northwest part of Lanai, go north up Fraser Ave in Lanai City and, shortly after it turns to dirt, turn right onto Polihua Rd. This dirt road passes along former pineapple fields and the Nature Conservancy's Kanepuu Preserve before reaching the Garden of the Gods after about 5½ miles.

The section leading up to Garden of the Gods is a fairly good road that usually takes about 20 minutes from town. To get from Garden of the Gods to Polihua Beach is another matter, however, as the road down to the beach is very rocky and narrow and only suitable for a 4WD. Depending on when it was last graded, it could take anywhere from 20 minutes to an hour.

Kanepuu

The Nature Conservancy manages 462 acres at Kanepuu, a diverse native dryland forest that is the last of its kind in all of Hawaii. Native plants include *iliahi* (Hawaiian sandalwood), *olopua* (an olive), *lama* (in the persimmon family), a morning

LANAI

glory, a native gardenia and fragrant vines of *maile* and *huehue*.

Native dryland forests once covered 80% of Lanai and were also common on the leeward slopes of other Hawaiian islands, but feral goats and cattle did them in. Credit for saving this one goes to the naturalist and former ranch manager, George Munro, who realized the need to protect this ecosystem and fenced hoofed animals out in the 1920s.

The Kanepuu Preserve is about six miles northwest of Lanai City. Castle & Cooke retains title to the land, but has given the Nature Conservancy an easement to the forest in perpetuity.

Garden of the Gods

There's no garden at Garden of the Gods, but rather, a dry and barren landscape of strange, wind-sculptured rocks in rich shades of ocher, pinks and browns. The colors change with the light and are much nicer and gentler in the early morning and late afternoon.

How godly they appear depends on what you're looking for. Some people just see rocks, while others find the formations hauntingly beautiful.

Polihua Beach

Polihua Beach, on the northwestern tip of the island, is a broad, 1½-mile-long white sand beach. It has a great view of the entire south coast of Molokai. Although it's a gorgeous beach, strong winds kicking up the sand often make it uncomfortable and water conditions are treacherous all year round.

Polihua means 'eggs in the bosom' and refers to the green sea turtles that used to nest there en masse. After a long hiatus, the now-endangered turtles are beginning to return.

MUNRO TRAIL

Munro Trail is an 8½-mile dirt road that can either be hiked or driven in a 4WD

vehicle. On foot, it's a full day's hike. If you're driving and the road is in good condition, it takes about 1½ hours. However, be aware that the road can get very muddy (particularly in winter and after heavy rainstorms) and jeeps occasionally get stuck. Drivers also need to watch out for sheer drops; the road can be quite dangerous when wet.

To start, head north on Hwy 44, the road to Shipwreck Beach. About a mile past the Lodge at Koele turn right onto the paved road that leads to a cemetery half a mile down.

Munro Trail starts at the left of the cemetery. It goes through sections planted with eucalyptus and up along the ridge, where it's fern-draped and studded with Norfolk pines.

The trail is named after naturalist George Munro, who planted the trees along this trail and around the island to provide a watershed. He selected species that draw moisture from the clouds and fog, both of which are fairly common in the high country (more so in the afternoon than in the morning).

Before the Munro Trail was upgraded to a dirt road it was a footpath. It's along this trail that islanders tried to hide from Kamehameha when he went on a rampage in 1778. Hookio Battleground, where Lanaians made their last stand, is just above Hookio Gulch, about 2½ miles from the start of the trail.

The Munro Trail looks down upon a series of deep ravines that cut across the eastern flank of the mountain and it passes Lanaihale, which at 3370 feet, is the highest point on Lanai. On a clear day you can see all the inhabited Hawaiian islands except Kauai and Niihau from various points along the route. The trail ends near the hog ranch on Hoike Rd.

Hoike Rd is a little more than 1½ miles south of the intersection of Manele Rd and Kaumalapau Hwy.

Luahiwa Petroglyphs

The Luahiwa Petroglyphs are carved onto

about three dozen boulders spread over three acres. This is Lanai's highest concentration of petroglyphs and includes a wide variety of forms thought to have been carved during different eras. There are lots of dogs in various poses, linear and triangular human figures and a canoe or two.

Unfortunately, many of the petroglyphs are quite weathered.

It's a little challenging to get there, but basically you turn onto Hoike Rd and then head for the water tower on the ridge. The boulders are near the head of a ravine north of the road, below the trees.

Kahoolawe

Kahoolawe, the uninhabited island seven miles off the southwest coast of Maui, was used exclusively by the US military as a bombing target from WW II until 1990. The bombing has now stopped but the island remains off limits due to the stray ammunition that peppers Kahoolawe and its surrounding waters.

The channel between Lanai and Kahoolawe, as well as the westernmost point of Kahoolawe itself, is named Kealaikahiki, meaning 'pathway to Tahiti'. When ancient voyagers made the journey between Hawaii and Tahiti they lined up their canoes at this departure point.

More than 500 archaeological sites have been identified on Kahoolawe. They include several heiaus and many koa shrines and kuula stones dedicated to the gods of fishermen. Puu Moiwi, in the center of the island, has one of Hawaii's largest ancient adze quarries.

In 1981 Kahoolawe was added to the National Register of Historic Places as a significant archaeological area. For nearly a decade the island had the distinction of being the only place of such merit that was being used as target practice.

Kahoolawe has become a symbol of the separation of Hawaiians from their land and a focal point in the growing Hawaiian rights movement.

GEOGRAPHY

Kahoolawe is 11 miles long and six miles wide, with a land area of 45 sq miles. With the help of a vivid imagination, its shape can be seen as a crouching lion facing eastward.

A ridge runs diagonally across the island and the terrain is gently sloping. The highest point is the 1477-foot Lua Makika, at the site of the caldera that formed the island. It's a dry arid island with only 10 to 20 inches of rainfall annually.

Because of the windblown red dust on the island, Kahoolawe often appears to have a pink tinge when viewed from Maui, particularly in the afternoons when the winds pick up. At night it's pitch black, devoid of any light.

HISTORY
Prisoners & Opium

Since ancient times Kahoolawe has been under the rule of Maui.

From 1830 to 1848 Kaulana Bay, on the island's northern side, was used as a place of exile for Mauian men accused of petty crimes. (Female outcasts were sent to Kaena Point on the northwestern tip of Lanai.)

Kahoolawe proved to be less of a 'prison isle' than intended. In 1841 some of the prisoners managed to swim to the Makena area of Maui where they stole food and canoes and paddled back with their booty. Later raids included one to Lanai where they picked up female prisoners and brought them back to Kahoolawe.

Kahoolawe's secluded southwestern side was used for decades by smugglers bringing in illegal Chinese opium. To avoid detection, they'd unload their caches at Hanakanaea Bay (commonly known as Smugglers Bay) on arrival from China and come back later in small fishing boats to pick them up.

In more recent times Smugglers Bay served as the site of a US military base camp.

Overgrazing

Kahoolawe was once a green and forested island. It is now largely barren and pili grass and kiawe trees are the main forces in keeping the dry red soil from blowing away completely.

The first attempt at ranching was in 1858 by R C Wyllie, the Scotsman who developed a sugar plantation at Princeville in Kauai. Wyllie leased the entire island of Kahoolawe from the Territory of Hawaii, but the sheep he brought over were dis-

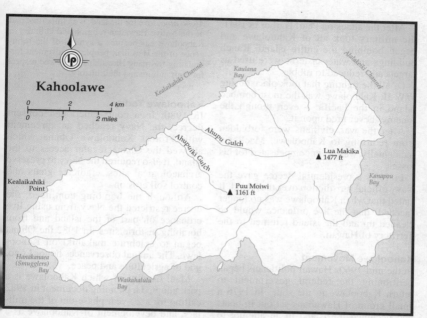

eased and the venture failed. Those sheep that survived were left to roam freely, causing serious damage to native plants.

Over the years, the territory granted a series of leases to other ranchers. Cattle were first brought over around 1880 and sheep were also tried again. Land mismanagement was the order of the day.

By the early 1900s feral goats, pigs and sheep had dug up, rooted out and chewed off so much of the vegetation that Kahoolawe was largely a dust bowl.

Kahoolawe Ranch

The most successful ranching operation on Kahoolawe was run from 1918 to 1941 by Angus MacPhee, former manager of Maui's Ulupalakua Ranch.

When MacPhee got his lease from the territorial government in 1918, Kahoolawe was overrun with goats and looked like a wasteland. MacPhee rounded up 13,000 goats which he sold on Maui and built a fence across the width of the entire island

to keep the remaining goats at one end. He then brought in large redwood tanks to store water and planted grasses and groundcover.

Once the land was again green, MacPhee created Kahoolawe Ranch Company in partnership with Harry Baldwin, a sugar plantation owner. Cattle were brought over and raised for the Honolulu market. Ranching Kahoolawe was not easy, but MacPhee, unlike his predecessors, was able to make it profitable.

Inez MacPhee Ashdown, Angus' daughter, has written her story in *Kahoolawe* (Topgallant Publishing Co, Honolulu, 1979). The book includes legends of Kahoolawe, as told to her by native Hawaiians, as well as the ranch's history.

A Bombing Target

In 1939, Kahoolawe Ranch subleased part of the island to the US Army for bombing practice and moved their cattle and ranch hands over to Maui.

KAHOOLAWE

After the attack on Pearl Harbor in 1941, the military took all of Kahoolawe and began bombing the entire island. Ranch buildings and water cisterns were used as targets and reduced to rubble.

Of all the fighting that took place during WW II, Kahoolawe was the most bombed island in the Pacific – even though the 'enemy' never fired upon it.

After the war, civilians were forbidden from returning to Kahoolawe. MacPhee, incidentally, was never compensated for his losses.

In 1953 a presidential decree gave the Navy official jurisdiction over the island. It stated that when Kahoolawe was no longer 'needed' that the live ordnance would be cleaned up and the island returned to the Territory of Hawaii.

Kahoolawe Movement

In the mid-1960s Hawaii politicians began petitioning the federal government to return Kahoolawe to the state. In 1976 a small group of Hawaiians set out in boats and occupied the island in an attempt to attract greater attention to the bombings. There were a series of occupations, some lasting more than a month.

During one of the 1977 crossings, group members George Helm and Kimo Mitchell mysteriously disappeared in the waters off Kahoolawe. Helm had been an inspirational Hawaiian-rights activist and with his death the Protect Kahoolawe Ohana movement sprang up. Helm's vision of turning Kahoolawe into a sanctuary of Hawaiian culture and identity became widespread among islanders.

In June 1977 two group members, Walter Ritte Jr and Richard Sawyer, were tried for trespassing on Kahoolawe and sentenced to six months in jail.

In a letter to President Jimmy Carter asking that the two men be pardoned, Daniel Inouye, US Senator from Hawaii, wrote:

... it was a form of protest against, what was to them, the unconscionable desecration of the land by the Navy's continued bombing of Kahoolawe.

Aloha aina, love for the land, is an important part of the Native Hawaiian religion and culture . . . Kahoolawe has become a symbol of the resurgence of the Hawaiian people, a movement formulating for many Hawaiians a renewed respect for their culture and their history.

Kahoolawe Today

In 1980, in a court-sanctioned consent decree, the Navy reached an agreement with Protect Kahoolawe Ohana which allowed the Ohana regular access to the island. It also required the Navy to preserve archaeological sites, eradicate goats and control soil erosion.

Although the bombing continued, the decree restricted the Navy from using live ordnance on part of the island and from bombing historic sites. In 1982 the Ohana began to celebrate makahiki on Kahoolawe. The annual observances honor Lono, god of agriculture and peace.

Maui County, of which Kahoolawe is a part, adopted a planning document in 1982 calling for a 20-year phase-out of the military, and development of Kahoolawe as a historical and cultural site, with Protect Kahoolawe Ohana as the stewards of the land. The Navy refused to recognize the document.

In what many Hawaiians saw as the ultimate insult to their heritage, the US military offered Kahoolawe as a bombing target to foreign nations during biennial Pacific Rim exercises. The exercises brought recognition of what was happening in Kahoolawe into a broader arena. An international movement against the bombing by environmentalist and union groups in New Zealand, Australia, Japan and the UK resulted in those countries withdrawing from the Kahoolawe exercises. With only the US and Canada willing to participate, the exercises stopped.

In the late 1980s Hawaii's first Hawaiian governor, John Waihee, and other state politicians became more outspoken in their demands that Kahoolawe be returned to Hawaiians. In October 1990, as Hawaii's two US senators, Daniel Inouye and Daniel Akaka, were preparing a congressional bill to stop the bombing, President Bush issued an order to halt military activities. The senators' bill, which became law the next month, requires the island to be cleared of munitions and restored to a pre-war condition. It also established a federally funded Kahoolawe Conveyance Commission to prepare recommendations on terms for the conveyance of the island to the state of Hawaii.

On May 7, 1994, in a ceremony marked by Hawaiian rituals, chants and prayers, the US Navy signed over control of Kahoolawe to Governor Waihee and the state of Hawaii. Following the signing, 100 native Hawaiians dressed in traditional malo and tapa cloaks went to Kahoolawe to perform sunrise rituals honoring the return of the island. Among the ceremonies was the placing of leis at memorial plaques for Helms and Mitchell.

One enormous obstacle that remains is the cleaning up of live ordnance from Kahoolawe. The federal government has established a $400 million fund for that purpose, but the clean up is estimated to take 10 years to complete. In the meantime a new state entity, the Kahoolawe Island Reserve Commission, has taken over administration of the island. Proposals for the island's future range from establishing a marine sanctuary to making the island the center for a new Hawaiian nation.

GETTING THERE & AWAY
There's no public access to the island and unless you're a member of the Ohana, or on official business, it is nearly impossible to get to Kahoolawe.

Two weekends per month, offshore waters 20 fathoms or deeper are open to the public for fishing but at all other times boats are prohibited from going within two miles of Kahoolawe. As the island and its near-shore waters are still dangerous due to the unexploded ordnance, shoreline access is expected to remain off limits to the public for the remainder of the decade.

Kauai

If you're looking for lush scenery, Kauai is a great choice – the island is so richly green that it's nicknamed 'The Garden Island'.

Kauai is the oldest of the main Hawaiian land masses and arose from the sea as a high, smooth island. Over time heavy rains have eroded deep valleys, while pounding waves and falling sea levels have cut steep cliffs.

Kauai's central volcanic peak, Mt Waialeale, is the wettest place on earth and feeds seven rivers, including Hawaii's only navigable one. A deep north-to-south rift slices the western end of the island, creating the impressive Waimea Canyon.

The North Shore is lushly mountainous, with waterfalls, beautiful beaches and stream-fed valleys. The northwest coast is lined by the steeply fluted Na Pali sea cliffs, Hawaii's main hiking destination.

Movie makers looking for scenery bordering on fantasy have often found it in Kauai. *South Pacific* and *Raiders of the Lost Ark* were both filmed on Kauai's North Shore. Honopu Valley on the Na Pali Coast was the jungle home of King Kong, and another remote valley served as the location for Steven Spielberg's *Jurassic Park*.

Kauai is the least developed of the four major islands and most of its interior is mountainous forest reserve. The Alakai Swamp is poised on a high, cliff-bound plateau, about 1000 feet below Mt Waialeale. There, clouds and mist that rarely lift support a unique ecosystem where trees grow knee high.

Kauai is dry and sunny on its southern and western sides, with long stretches of white sand beaches. Sugar cane fields cover large portions of the island just inland from the coast in a semicircle from the northeast to the west.

Kauai's main attraction is its stunning natural beauty. There are hiking trails into some incredible places.

ORIENTATION

Kauai is roughly circular. A belt road runs three-quarters of the way around the island, from Haena in the north to Polihale in the west.

Most travelers arrive at the main airport in Lihue, the county capital, on the east coast. From Lihue the road runs north past Wailua and Kapaa, continuing up to Princeville resort and Hanalei before ending at the eastern edge of the Na Pali cliffs.

South of Lihue a side road leads down to the resort beaches at Poipu while the main road continues west to Waimea. In Waimea, one road goes west to the arid Barking Sands region and another heads north along the Waimea Canyon into Kokee State Park.

HISTORY

Kauai was probably settled between 500 and 700 AD by Polynesians who migrated from the Marquesas Islands. Archaeological finds, including identical ring-shaped poi pounding stones found both in Kauai and the Marquesas, support the connection.

While in Hawaiian lore there are no direct references to the Marquesan culture, Kauai is often referred to as the home of a race of little people called menehunes. Legend after legend tells of happy Disney-like elves coming down from the mountains to produce great engineering works in stone.

It seems likely that when the first wave of Tahitians arrived in about 1000 AD they conquered and subjugated the Marquesans, forcing them into slavery to build the temples, irrigation ditches and fishponds now attributed to the menehunes.

The Tahitian term for 'outcast' is *manahune*. And the diminutive social status the Marquesans had in the eyes of their conquerors may have given rise to tales of a dwarf-size race.

The menehunes may have created the temples, but the Tahitian settlers created

Kauai

Hurricane Iniki

On September 11, 1992 Hurricane Iniki, the most powerful storm to strike Hawaii in a century, made a direct hit on Kauai. Packing gusts of 165 miles per hour, Iniki felled thousands of trees and caused serious damage to an estimated 50% of the buildings on Kauai. (To get a sense of how strong Iniki was, Hawaii's worst storm previously was Hurricane Iwa, which tore into Kauai in November 1982 with gusts of 117 miles per hour.)

While some of the structures destroyed by Iniki were aging wooden buildings, others were wings of beachfront resorts that were battered by 30-foot waves. Most homes throughout the island had windows blown out, many lost roofs and others were simply laid to waste. In all, 5000 homes were damaged and 1300 were totally destroyed. A combination of powerful gusts and abrupt changes in atmospheric pressure caused some buildings to literally shatter, as if hit by a bomb blast. Although nearly 100 people were injured by flying debris, quite amazingly only two people were killed.

Even though Kauai is small and lightly populated, the total value of the damage to the island was $1.6 billion, making Iniki the third costliest disaster in US history. Particularly hard hit were Kauai's two main resort areas – Poipu and Princeville – and many of the vacation rentals that did survive had to be turned into temporary housing for Kauai's 8000 newly homeless residents. Consequently, tourism was brought to a standstill after the storm.

The recovery has been a slow one, but by early 1995 most of the structural damage had been repaired and 75% of the island's hotels and condominiums were back on line.

As for the environment, Kauai is again lushly green and to the casual eye there's not much to indicate that the hurricane ever happened. However, while many stripped trees have sprouted new leaves, extensive sections of the Hawaiian koa forest failed to recover and opportunistic plants such as guava, banana poka and blackberry have spread through large tracts of what were predominantly native woodlands prior to Iniki.

It will take many years before the storm's impact on the island's endangered flora and fauna is fully understood, but the decline of native forest habitat will undoubtedly have detrimental effects. Four species of endangered or threatened native birds have not been spotted on Kauai since the hurricane. ■

---

the legends. Fine stonework remains, but the true identity of Kauai's 'little people' is lost.

During the second wave of Tahitian migration, around the 12th century, a high chief named Moikeha arrived at Wailua with a fleet of double-hulled canoes. There, in the royal court, Moikeha was received by Kauai's aging alii-nui (high chief), Puna.

Puna gave his daughter to Moikeha in marriage and upon Puna's death Moikeha became the alii-nui of Kauai. Moikeha introduced taro and sweet potatoes to Kauai and sent his son Kila back to Tahiti to fetch the *pahu hula*, a sharkskin drum essential for use in hula temples. This type of drum is still used in hula performances today.

Early Settlements

Kauai is the most isolated of the major islands, lying 72 miles from Oahu, its nearest neighbor. It was never conquered by another Hawaiian island and its history is one of autonomy.

Kauai was settled most intensively along river valleys near the coast, such as at Wailua, Waimea and Hanalei. Even valleys that were difficult to reach, like Kalalau and Nualolo on the Na Pali Coast, had sizable settlements. When winter seas prevented canoes from landing on the northern shore, trails down precipitous ridges and sennit-rope ladders provided access.

When Captain Cook landed on Kauai in 1778 he estimated the island had 50 villages with a total population of about 30,000. Missionaries in the 1820s estimated it to be closer to 10,000. Historians tend to side with the missionaries and discredit Cook's estimates, but considering the diseases Cook's men left behind, it's possible both were correct.

Kaumualii

Kaumualii was the last chief to reign over an independent Kauai. Though he was a shrewd leader and Kauai's warriors were fierce, it was apparently the power of Kaumualii's kahunas that protected him from the advances of Kamehameha the Great.

In 1796 Kamehameha, who had conquered all the other islands, sailed with an armada of war canoes towards Kauai. A mysterious storm suddenly kicked up at sea, forcing him to turn back to Oahu, and he never reached Kauai's shores.

During the next few years, both Kamehameha and Kaumualii continued to prepare for war by gathering foreign weaponry and trying to ally foreign ships to their cause.

In 1804 Kamehameha was once again on the shores of Oahu ready to attack Kauai. However, on the eve of the invasion, an epidemic of what was probably cholera struck the island of Oahu, decimating his warriors and forcing yet another delay.

While Kamehameha's numerically superior forces had Kaumualii unnerved, Kaumualii's uncanny luck had a similar effect on Kamehameha. In 1810 they reached an agreement that recognized Kaumualii as the alii-nui of Kauai but ceded the island of Kauai to the Kingdom of Hawaii.

It was essentially a truce, and the plotting continued, with Kaumualii never fully accepting Kamehameha's suzerainty.

Russian Presence
In January 1815 a Russian ship was wrecked off Waimea, and Kaumualii confiscated the cargo. In November, the Russian-American Company sent their agent, Georg Anton Schaeffer, to retrieve it.

When Schaeffer arrived in Hawaii he saw opportunity in the rift between Kaumualii and Kamehameha. In Kauai he exceeded his authority by entering into an agreement with Kaumualii in which he claimed the Russians would provide a ship and military assistance for the invasion of Oahu. In return Kaumualii offered the Russians half of Oahu plus all the sandalwood on Oahu and Kauai. In September 1816 Hawaiian laborers under Schaeffer's direction began to build forts in Waimea and Hanalei.

Later that year, when Russian naval explorer Otto von Kotzebue visited Hawaii, he informed Kamehameha that the Russian government did not endorse Schaeffer's alliance. Kamehameha, tired of all the scheming, ordered Kaumualii to kick the Russians out or face the consequences. In May 1817 Schaeffer was escorted to his ship and forced to leave Kauai.

The End of a Kingdom
When Kamehameha died in 1819 he was succeeded by his son Liholiho, who didn't trust Kaumualii's loyalties any more than his father had. In 1822 Liholiho set off for Kauai in an 83-foot luxury schooner he had purchased from Western traders in exchange for sandalwood.

In Kauai he tricked Kaumualii into going out for a cruise. He then kidnapped him and took him to Oahu where Kaumualii was forced to marry Kamehameha's widow, Kaahumanu. In the grand scheme of royal design this served to bring Kaumualii into the fold. When Kaumualii passed away in 1824, so too did the kingdom of Kauai.

GEOGRAPHY
Kauai is shaped like a slightly compressed ball. It is 33 miles wide and 25 miles from north to south. The highest elevation is Mt Kawaikini at 5243 feet.

The fourth largest of the Hawaiian Islands, Kauai has an area of 558 sq miles.

Kauai arose as a single volcano of which Mt Waialeale is the eastern rim. Moisture-laden trade winds blow into the deep North Shore valleys which channel the winds up to the top of Mt Waialeale. Near its 5148-foot summit cooler temperatures cause the moisture to condense, creating the heaviest rainfall on earth.

CLIMATE
Kauai's temperature varies more with location than season. Average coastal temperatures are 70°F in February and 77°F in August. At Kalalau Beach the temperature seldom drops below 60°F, while a few thousand feet above at Kokee State Park it dips into the 30s during winter nights.

Kokee averages a crisp 55°F in February and 65°F in August.

Kauai's average annual rainfall is about 40 inches but variances are extreme. Waimea in the south averages 21 inches while Princeville in the north averages 85 inches. And Mt Waialeale in the swampy interior averages a whopping 486 inches, a world record.

Summer trade winds keep the humidity from becoming oppressive and bring in showers.

Winter is far less predictable. It's quite possible to have fairly continuous downpours for a week at a time in midwinter. Then again, it might be all blue skies and calm seas. We've experienced both.

FLORA & FAUNA

Kauai has the largest number of native bird species in Hawaii. It is the only major island free of mongoose, which prey upon the eggs of ground-nesting birds.

The greatest concentration of Kauai's native forest bird species is found in the remote Alakai Swamp. Many of those species are endangered, some having fewer than 100 birds remaining.

The Kauai oo, the last of four remaining species of Hawaiian honeyeaters, was thought to be extinct until a nest with two chicks was discovered in Alakai Swamp in 1971. However, the call of the oo was last heard in 1987 – that of a single male.

Alakai Swamp is unique in that it has 10 times as many native birds as introduced. (Elsewhere in Hawaii introduced birds outnumber the natives many times over.) Not only is the swamp inhospitable to exotic bird species, but due to its high elevation it is one of the few places in Hawaii where mosquitoes that transmit avian diseases do not flourish.

The ao, or Newell's shearwater, is a threatened seabird that once nested on all the major Hawaiian islands; today it nests almost exclusively in the mountains of Kauai. The ao digs earthen burrows and lays just one egg each year. It has a call that sounds like a donkey braying.

The ao, which flies only between dusk

Honeyeater

and dawn, often fails to see utility wires strung across its path to the sea. Despite some success in a forestry program that recovers some of the many birds that crash-land, over a thousand birds still die in this way each year.

Of Hawaii's two native mammals, the hoary bat lives in Kokee State Park and the Hawaiian monk seal occasionally hauls out on Kauai beaches. Wild pigs, goats and black-tailed deer are non-native mammals that are hunted.

The most common tree in Kauai forests is the ohia lehua. Koa, guava, kiawe and kukui trees are also plentiful.

GOVERNMENT

Kauai County is composed of the islands of Kauai and Niihau. There is an elected mayor with a four-year term and a seven-member county council with two-year terms.

ECONOMY

Tourism is the leading sector of the economy and Kauai continues to experience high unemployment rates as a result of the hotel closings that followed Hurricane Iniki in 1992. In the year after the hurricane the unemployment rate jumped from 4% to 14%. In 1994, with about two-thirds of the island's hotels reopened, the unemployment rate was 8%.

Kauai's labor force is 30,900. The service industry, including hotels, accounts for 42% of all workers. It is followed by wholesale and retail trade at 21%, government at 12% and agriculture at 4%.

The sugar industry still cultivates 38,000 acres on Kauai, but mechanization has streamlined its labor force to fewer than a thousand employees. Other sizable crops grown commercially are guava, taro and papaya. Attempts to diversify as sugar production declines have resulted in the introduction of new crops including seed corn, sunflower seed and coffee.

POPULATION & PEOPLE
The population of Kauai is 55,100. People of Hawaiian and part-Hawaiian ethnicity make up 25% of Kauai's population and those of mixed ethnicity (except part-Hawaiian) 19%, followed by Japanese (18%), Caucasian (18%) and Filipino (17%).

INFORMATION
Tourist Offices
The Hawaii Visitors Bureau (☎ 245-3971) has its Kauai office at Lihue Plaza Building, Suite 207, 3016 Umi St, Lihue, HI 96766.

You can get a 'vacation planning kit' by calling (800) AH-KAUAI toll-free from the USA – but note that it can take well over a month to arrive.

Following Hurricane Iniki the tourism industry established a toll-free hotline to coordinate information about Kauai and answer questions; if you have a query about a specific activity or business, you can give them a call at (800) 262-1400.

If you have a touch-tone phone and access to a fax machine, you can also get some simple visitor information on Kauai by calling (800) 653-2963.

Money
Bank of Hawaii has branches in Lihue, Kapaa, Princeville, Hanalei, Hanapepe and Waimea. The downtown Lihue branch has an automatic teller machine. First Hawaiian Bank has automatic teller machines (Cirrus, Plus System) in its Lihue, Kapaa, Koloa and Waimea branches.

There are Western Union money transfer stations at Star Supermarket and Mail Boxes Etc, both in the Kukui Grove Center in Lihue, and at Princeville.

Books & Maps
There are public libraries in Lihue, Hanapepe, Kapaa, Koloa and Waimea.

The Waldenbooks chain, which has travel and Hawaiiana sections, has stores in the Kukui Grove Center in Lihue, the Kauai Village shopping center in Waipouli and the Coconut Marketplace in Wailua. The Kauai Museum in Lihue sells Hawaiiana books.

The University of Hawaii map of Kauai is good for general sightseeing and can be readily purchased in stores around the island. However, the best road map is the *Map of the Neighbor Islands Hawaii, Maui & Kauai* produced by Compass Maps.

For hiking, you can get a free fold-out topographical map of Kauai that shows the island's network of trails from the Division of Forestry & Wildlife office, 3060 Eiwa St, Room 306, Lihue, HI 96766. You can

---

Official Kauai
Kauai's nickname is 'The Garden Island'. Its flower is the mokihana, which blooms on a small tree of the citrus family found only on Kauai. Tiny anise-scented mokihana berries are commonly combined with twists of fragrant maile leaves as a ceremonial lei. Kauai's color is purple. ■

also request it by mail; enclose a 9-x-12-inch manila envelope with $1.01 postage.

Media

Kauai's main newspaper, the *Garden Island* (☎ 245-3681), Box 231, Lihue, HI 96766, is published Monday to Saturday.

The *Kauai Times* (☎ 245-8825), Box 3272, Lihue, HI 96766, is published on Wednesdays and Sundays. Both newspapers, as well as the Honolulu daily papers, can be purchased at food stores around Kauai.

Free tourist magazines such as *This Week Kauai*, *Spotlight's Kauai Gold* and *Kauai Beach Press* can be picked up at the airport, hotels and major shopping centers. All are loaded with ads and activity information. Also worth picking up is the free *Menu Magazine* which prints menus of many of Kauai's restaurants.

Three four-color feature magazines dedicated to Kauai are published on the island: *Sandwich Islands Magazine* and *Kauai Style*, both by Resort Publications, and *Kauai Magazine*, by H&S Publishing.

Kauai has three AM and three FM radio stations. KUAI 720 plays Hawaiian music.

Commercial and public/educational TV stations are relayed from Honolulu and cable TV is available in most communities. KVIC, on TV cable channel 3 or 18, is a visitor information channel that shows videos on Kauai sightseeing.

Weather

The National Weather Service has recorded local weather information (☎ 245-6001) and marine forecasts (☎ 245-3564).

KUAI radio (720 AM) broadcasts beach and surf reports. To find out where the surf's up, dial KUAI's surf hotline (☎ 335-3611).

Emergency

Dial 911 for police, ambulance and fire department.

The main hospital is Wilcox Memorial Hospital (☎ 245-1100), 3420 Kuhio Hwy, Lihue. Kauai Veterans Memorial Hospital (☎ 338-9431), 4643 Waimea Canyon Dr,

Waimea, is smaller but does have a hyperbaric chamber for divers who get the bends. Both hospitals have 24-hour emergency room services.

The local help-line (☎ 245-3411) provides crisis intervention services.

ACTIVITIES

Beaches & Swimming

There are respectable beaches all around Kauai. For most water activities except surfing, the North Shore is tops in summer, the South Shore in winter.

Hanalei Bay on the North Shore is the island's most popular summer beach, while Poipu, on the South Shore, has a string of beautiful white sand beaches that swimmers flock to in winter.

To the west, Salt Pond Beach Park is a popular family beach with protected swimming. Farther west, Kekaha, Barking Sands and Polihale have expansive white sand beaches, though with open ocean and often treacherous water conditions.

The beaches around Lihue and Kapaa are generally not great for swimming. The safest bet is Lydgate Beach in Wailua, a large family park with a boulder retaining wall that creates a protected year-round swimming pool.

Many of Kauai's beaches have rough water conditions at various times of the year and caution is warranted. Kauai has an average of nine drownings a year, about half of those on the North Shore between October and May.

There are year-round lifeguards at Salt Pond Beach, Poipu Beach Park, Hanalei Bay, Kee Beach and Wailua Beach.

Swimming Pools The county has swimming pools free to the public in Kapaa at Kapaa Beach Park (☎ 822-3842) and in Waimea (☎ 338-1271) next to the high school. Both are open from 10 am to 5 pm Monday to Saturday, from 1 to 5 pm on Sundays, closed on holidays.

Surfing

Kauai has 330 named surfing sites. Generally the best surfing is on the north coast in winter, the south in summer and the east during transitional swells.

Hanalei Bay is a very good spot for North Shore surfing, as well as boogie boarding and bodysurfing. Tunnels and Cannons are two other popular North Shore surf spots.

The area around the Sheraton at Poipu Beach is a top summer surf spot. Pakalas, which is near Makaweli, and Majors Bay at Barking Sands are two West Side favorites.

When the breaks are on the east coast, Kealia and the Coco Palms area can have good surf conditions.

Kayak Kauai, in Hanalei (☎ 826-9844) and Kapaa (☎ 822-9179), rents surfboards for $15 the first day and $10 each additional day, or $60 a week, and gives surfing lessons for $25 per hour ($12.50 for each additional person).

Hanalei Surf Company (☎ 826-9000), in the Hanalei Center in Hanalei, rents soft surfboards for $12/50 a day/week, fiberglass boards for $15/65, and wet suits for $4/17.

Margo Oberg, a former World Cup surfing champion, gives surfing lessons to beginners. Her 'surfing school' (☎ 742-750) is at Kiahuna Plantation Resort in Poipu.

Seasports Divers (☎ 742-9303) at Poipu Plaza in Poipu rents long, sturdy surfboards suitable for beginners for $25 a day, $75 a week.

Snorkeling & Boogie Boarding

On the North Shore, Kee Beach has good snorkeling most of the year. Nearby Tunnels Beach has excellent snorkeling in summer, but be cautious of currents.

On the South Shore, the section of Poipu Beach in front of the Stouffer Waiahai Beach Hotel is one of Kauai's best snorkeling spots for beginners. Another good snorkeling spot in Poipu is at the Koloa Landing. On the West Side, you can try Salt Pond Beach Park in Hanapepe.

For boogie boarding, Brennecke's in Poipu is Kauai's hottest spot, while on the North Shore Hanalei Bay attracts the biggest crowds.

Snorkel sets and boogie boards can be rented at lots of places. Most of the beach huts at the resort hotels charge about $5 an hour, while in-town shops are much more reasonable.

Hanalei Surf Company (☎ 826-9000), in the Hanalei Center in Hanalei, rents snorkel sets (including corrective masks) or boogie boards for $5/20 a day/week, snorkel vests for $4/17.

Pedal & Paddle in the Ching Young Village in Hanalei (☎ 826-9069) and at Kauai Village in Waipouli (☎ 822-2005) rents snorkel sets or boogie boards for $7 a day, $20 a week. Corrective masks or boogie fins are available at no extra cost.

Kayak Kauai, in Hanalei (☎ 826-9844) and Kapaa (☎ 822-9179), rents snorkel sets and boogie boards for $6 to $8 the first day, $4 each additional day, or $20 a week.

Snorkel Bob's, at 4480 Ahukini Rd in Lihue (☎ 245-9433) and Poipu Rd in Poipu (☎ 742-8322), rents snorkel sets from $15 a week. Hours are 8 am to 5 pm daily.

Seasports Divers (☎ 742-9303) at Poipu Plaza in Poipu rents snorkel gear for $4 to $8 a day, $20 a week, and boogie boards for $8/25 a day/week.

Brennecke's Beach Center (☎ 742-7505), opposite Poipu Beach Park, rents snorkel sets for $5/15 a day/week, bodyboards for $10/25, and is open daily from 8 am to 10 pm.

Kauai Snorkel Rentals (☎ 823-8300) in the Coconut Marketplace in Wailua rents boogie boards for $5/20 a day/week, snorkel sets for $4/10 (with corrective masks $8/20), and is open from 9 am to 6 pm daily.

Windsurfing

Beginner windsurfers usually start off at Anini Beach on the North Shore or at Nawiliwili Bay. Tunnels Beach in Haena, Mahaulepu Beach on the South Shore and Salt Pond Beach in Hanapepe attract more advanced windsurfers.

At Anini Beach, the main company offering beginning lessons is Windsurf Kauai (☎ 828-6838), Box 323, Hanalei, HI 96714. Anini Beach Windsurfing (☎ 826-9463), Box 1602, Hanalei, HI 96714, has lessons at all levels, but specializes in teaching those with some experience. Both rent equipment.

Diving

Popular summer diving spots on the North Shore include Kee Beach, Tunnels and Cannons, all shore dives in the Haena area. Cannons is particularly special; it's a wall dive, with crevices and lava tubes sheltering all sorts of marine life.

Koloa Landing and Poipu Beach Park in Poipu are easy beach dives. On those rare days when kona winds blow from the south, east-side diving is good and Ahukini Landing becomes a favored site. There are a number of offshore boat dives available as well, including dives around Niihau.

Dive shops sometimes give a free introductory scuba lesson at resort hotel pools; for information check at the hotel beach huts or call the dive shops.

Most dive shops offer two-tank dives with equipment for around $80 for shore dives, $90 for boat dives. Most also offer night dives for around $70, introductory dives for beginners for around $80 and certification courses for around $400.

Dive operations include:

Aquatic Adventures, 4-1380 Kuhio Hwy, Kapaa, HI 96746 (☎ 822-1434)

Bubbles Below, 6251 Hauaala Rd, Kapaa, HI 96746 (☎ 822-3483)

Dive Kauai, 976 Kuhio Hwy, Kapaa, HI 96746 (☎ 822-0452)

Fathom Five Divers, Poipu Rd, Box 907, Koloa HI 96756 (☎ 742-6991)

Ocean Odyssey, at the Outrigger Kauai Beach hotel, 4331 Kauai Beach Dr, Lihue, HI 96766 (☎ 245-8681)

Seasports Divers, 2827 Poipu Rd, Poipu (☎ 742-9303)

Sunrise Diving Adventures, Box 1255, Kapaa HI 96746 (☎ 822-7333, (800) 695-3483)

Snuba If you'd like to get underwater without loading down with dive equipment you might consider snuba, in which you breathe through an air hose attached to a tank that floats on the water surface. Snuba Tours of Kauai (☎ 823-8912) offers snuba from Lawai Beach in Poipu for $49.

Kayaking

Kauai, with all its waterways, has some of Hawaii's best kayaking.

One particularly pleasant outing is up the Hanalei River which goes through the wildlife refuge and meanders deep into Hanalei Valley. The riverfront is lushly beautiful and often canopied by overhanging trees. The journey is about nine miles round-trip, but if it's been dry recently and the water level is low you might not be able to go up that far. Another popular but quite busy route is up the Wailua River to the Fern Grotto, which is about seven miles round trip. Each outing takes three to four hours. Other popular kayaking spots include the Hanapepe, Waimea and Huleia rivers.

Kayak prices include paddles, life vest and a car rack set-up.

Pedal & Paddle in the Ching Young Village in Hanalei (☎ 826-9069) and Kauai Village in Waipouli (☎ 822-2005) rent one-person kayaks for $25 a half day or $35 a day, two-person kayaks for $35 a half day, $50 a day. It's open from 9 am to 5 pm daily, with slightly longer summer hours.

Kayak Kauai, in Hanalei (☎ 826-9844) and Kapaa (☎ 822-9179), rents two-person kayaks for $48 a day. They also have guided tours, including a three-hour one on the Hanalei River that's suitable for beginners and costs $45. In the summer full-day guided sea kayaking trips along the Na Pali Coast cost $125 and multi-day Na Pali excursions that combine kayaking, hiking and camping cost $150 to $175 per day. In the winter there's a full-day ocean kayak tour on the South Shore for $100. Both shops are open from 8 am to 5:30 pm daily.

Outfitters Kauai (☎ 742-9667) in the Poipu Plaza in Poipu rents one-person river kayaks for $30 a day, one-person ocean kayaks for $35 a day, two-person river kayaks for $45 a day and two-person ocean kayaks for $60 a day. Guided kayak trips along the South Shore are held year round, last 4½ hours, are open to all levels and cost $48. They also offer full-day $125 guided tours along the Na Pali Coast in summer. It's open from 9 am to 5 pm Monday to Saturday.

Island Adventure (☎ 245-9662) leads 2½-hour guided kayak trips up the Huleia River past the Menehune Fishpond and the Huleia National Wildlife Refuge for $39.

Fishing

For deep-sea sport fishing, Gent-Lee Charters (☎ 245-7504), True Blue Charters (☎ 246-6333) and Sea Lure Fishing Charters (☎ 822-5963) take boats out of Nawiliwili Harbor, Wayne's World (☎ 338-1312) leaves from Waimea, and Anini Fishing Charters (☎ 828-1285) and Robert McReynolds Fishing Charters (☎ 828-9379) are based at Anini Beach.

Kauai has largemouth and smallmouth bass in some of its private freshwater reservoirs. Two guide services providing half-day and full-day freshwater charters are Bass on Kauai (☎ 826-2566) and Cast & Catch (☎ 332-9707).

There's rainbow trout in several streams, reservoirs and ditches in Kokee State Park. The season begins on the first Saturday in August and runs for 16 days, usually continuing on weekends and holidays through September. A valid state freshwater fishing license is required (on Kauai call 241-3400).

Hiking

Kauai has some excellent hikes. The best known is the spectacular 11-mile Kalalau Trail which runs along the rugged Na Pali Coast.

Kokee State Park is also a hiker's paradise and has the largest concentration of trails on Kauai. Some of these trails lead to spectacular views of the Na Pali Coast. Others include short nature walks, mountain stream trails and a muddy trek through the unique Alakai Swamp.

South of Kokee, trails lead down into the scenic Waimea Canyon, forking into abandoned river valleys.

In the Kapaa-Wailua area there's a trail that goes across the chest of the Sleeping Giant mountain. A couple of ridge trails start at Keahua Arboretum in Wailua, including the Powerline Trail, which goes all the way to Princeville.

These hikes are all detailed in their respective sections.

Guided Hikes The Kauai division of the Sierra Club offers guided hikes, usually on weekends, ranging from strolls up the Sleeping Giant to overnighters in Waimea Canyon. Advance registration is required and a donation of $3 is suggested. For a hike schedule, send a stamped, self-addressed envelope to the Sierra Club, Box 3412, Lihue, HI 96766. On Kauai, updated information can be obtained by calling Micco Godinez at Kayak Kauai (☎ 826-9844).

Cycling

Kauai Downhill (☎ 245-1774, (800) 234-1774), Box 3322, Lihue, HI 96766, has a sunrise bike tour down the Waimea Canyon road. The 12-mile ride takes about 1½ hours. The entire outing lasts about four hours, depending on your pick-up point, and costs $60 including a continental breakfast.

Outfitters Kauai (☎ 742-9667) in Poipu also has bicycle tours in the Waimea/Kokee area.

Kayak Kauai has easy three-hour guided cycling tours leaving from their shop in Hanalei (☎ 826-9844) or their shop in Kapaa (☎ 822-9179). The cost is $45.

Information on bicycle rentals is in the Getting Around section of this chapter.

Horseback Riding

CJM Country Stables (☎ 742-6096) has rides in the Mahaulepu Beach area. There's a three-hour breakfast ride for $65, a two-hour morning ride for $47, a 1½-hour afternoon ride for $40 and sometimes a one-hour afternoon ride for $27. The stables are in Poipu, 1½ miles east of the Hyatt hotel.

Pooku Stables (☎ 826-6777), just past Princeville Airport, offers a four-hour ride across ranch lands to a waterfall for a picnic and swim for $90.

Both stables are closed on Sundays.

Tennis

County tennis courts are free and open to the public at the following locations: Wailua Houselots Park and Wailua Homesteads Park, both in Wailua; Hardy St, near the convention center in Lihue; opposite Kauai Community College in Puhi; Kapaa New Park in Kapaa; near the fire station in Koloa; Kalawai Park in Kalaheo; near Hanapepe Stadium in Hanapepe; at Waimea High School in Waimea; and on the corner of Hwy 550 and Hwy 50 in Kekaha.

Many resorts have tennis courts available for their guests. A few places are also open to the general public.

Kauai Lagoons Tennis (☎ 241-6000), adjacent to the Marriott in Lihue, charges $5 per person per hour; check in at the golf shop.

The Hyatt Regency Kauai in Poipu charges $20 per court hour.

The Princeville Tennis Center (☎ 826-9823) charges players staying in Princeville $9 per person, non-guests $12.

Golf

Kauai has one municipal golf course, one local course and six resort courses. Major tournaments are hosted at Princeville's Prince course and at the Poipu Bay Resort; the Kauai Lagoons' Kiele course and Princeville's Makai course are also top rated.

Wailua Golf Course (☎ 241-6666), a county-owned 18-hole par 72 course, is a highly regarded public course and very heavily played. Reservations for two people or more are taken up to a week in advance. Green fees are $18 on weekdays and $20 on weekends. Cart or club rental are $12.

Kukuiolono Golf Course (☎ 332-9151) in Kalaheo is a nine-hole par 36 course on an old estate with a grand hilltop view and an earthy appeal. Green fees are just $5 and pull carts cost $5 more.

Princeville resort has two courses: the 18-hole par 72 Prince (☎ 826-5000) and the 27-hole par 72 Makai (☎ 826-3580). Green and cart fees for the Makai course are $7 for guests staying in Princeville and $10 for non-guests. Fees for the Prince course are $85/110. Club rentals cost $25.

The Kauai Lagoons Golf Club (☎ 241-6000, (800) 634-6400) in east Lihue has two 18-hole par 72 courses. The Kiele course costs $145, the Lagoons course $100. Clubs rent for $30.

The Poipu Bay Resort Golf Course (☎ 742-9489), an 18-hole par 72 course adjacent to the Hyatt Regency Kauai, gives priority to Hyatt guests, charging $8 including a cart. Non-guests pay $120 and can use the course on a space-available basis. Club rentals cost $20.

Also in Poipu, the Kiahuna Golf Club (☎ 742-9595), an 18-hole par 70 course run by the Sports Shinko Group, charges $2 for nine holes, $45 for 18 holes, including cart. Clubs can be rented for $22.

Organized Tours

Polynesian Adventure Tours (☎ 246-012) has full-day minivan tours that include Wailua, Fern Grotto, Koloa, Poipu, Waimea, the Waimea Canyon and the Kalalau Lookout for $52.50 with pick-up in Lihue or Wailua ($57.50 from Poipu, $65 from Princeville). Half-day North Shore tours that include Hanalei, Haena and Kee Beach cost $32.50.

TransHawaiian (☎ 245-5108, (800) 25-5706) offers similar full-day tours of Kauai and half-day North Shore tours at similar prices. It also has a half-day Waimea Canyon tour, which includes most of the sights of the full-day tour except for the Fern Grotto, and costs only $34 from Lihue or Wailua.

The other major player is Grayline Kauai (☎ 245-3344, (800) 367-2420), which also has standard sightseeing tours in the same price range.

Kauai Mountain Tours (☎ 245-7224, (800) 452-1113), Box 3069, Lihue, HI 96766, tours Waimea Canyon and Kokee State Park. It uses 4WD vans capable of detouring from the beaten path to take in some of the sights along dirt roads. A five-hour tour costs $55, a seven-hour tour $78, lunch included.

All tour companies offer discounted prices for children.

Helicopter Many wilderness hikers resent the intrusion of helicopters into otherwise serene areas, and local environmentalists have successfully stopped their landings on Na Pali Coast beaches. However, these 'Kauai mosquitoes' that are an irritant to people on the ground no doubt offer some pretty spectacular views as they swoop deep into Waimea Canyon, run along the Na Pali Coast and seek out hidden waterfalls.

About a dozen helicopter companies offer flights around Kauai. The free tourist magazines advertise most of them and often have discount coupons.

The going rate is about $90 for a 45-minute tour zooming by the main sights. There's usually some sort of 'ultimate splendor' tour that can add on 20 minutes and run up another $50 to $75. Most of the helicopter offices are either in Lihue near the corner of Hwy 56 and Ahukini Rd or out past the airport.

Nuisance low buzzes are supposedly controlled. There's a helicopter hotline (☎ 826-1182) to take complaints, run by Kauai helicopter owners and operators.

Cruises Like the other islands, Kauai has its fair share of catamaran picnic sails, sunset cruises and the like. It also has

something the other islands don't: the spectacular Na Pali Coast.

Several boat companies have cruises down the Na Pali Coast. Most use small craft that can hug the coast and enter sea caves. The typical tour lasts four hours, goes down the coast as far as Nualolo, includes snorkeling when seas are calm and costs $75 to $85. If you just want a quick look at the coast without spending so much, a couple of companies also offer two-hour mini-tours for around $55.

The smoothest rides are generally in the summer. For most of the winter the seas are too rough for near-shore activities such as sea-cave exploration and on some days it's simply too rough for the boats to go out at all. A few companies then switch to the calmer southern shore for snorkeling cruises and whale-watching tours.

The following four companies are within a few minutes' walk of one near the intersection of Hwy 560 Rd in Hanalei, making it easy t compare. The boats leave from of the Hanalei River, exc uses Zodiac which leaves from 826-

Captain Zodiac (☎ 826- 826-7824), in the Ching Yo ich, while Zodiac rafts. Na Pali offer a 6804) and Catamar rafts, Sea Tours 4596) use power c2ei not as adventurou7997) has both far smoother catamarans.
(☎ 826-7254,
Zodiac rafts

ACCOMMODATIONS

Three areas in Kauai – Poipu, Princeville, and the strip from Lihue to Kapaa – have almost all the island's hotels and condos.

For the most part, Kauai's beach hotels are a bit expensive. The cheapest begin around $75, although the majority are double that. Condos have the same price range but tend to be a better deal, particularly if you're traveling in a group.

The best accommodations deals on the island are found in the scattering of B&Bs that have sprung up in the past few years. The Wailua area has the greatest concentration of B&Bs, with prices averaging about $45/55 for singles/doubles. Many are in fine homes that are very comfortable and scenically situated a few miles up the slope from the coast. Wailua also makes a good base for exploring, as it's midway between the North Shore and Kokee State Park.

Other than campgrounds, the cheapest places are the bunkhouses at the YMCA in Haena at $12 per person and the dorm beds at the Kauai International Hostel in Kapaa. For $30 there are basic cabinettes at Mountain Park near Koloa and some rundown hotels in Lihue, but they're costly options.

Kauai's camping spots. Some are driven to, forest and some camping spots. Some hikes into remote parks, some are in dense

Camping is at the end of day-long seven county pas.

trailside camps in three state parks, nearby Kokee area. forest reserve

State Parks Camping is at canyon and the Polihale and Na Pali Coast. Kokee, Permits are required and are free parks. issued from 8 am to 4 pm Mo are Friday from the Division of State to (☎ 241-3444), 3060 Eiwa St, Room 3 Lihue, HI 96766, and at state park office on other islands.

Up to 10 people may be listed on each permit, but the person applying for the

permit must show an ID (such as a driver's license or passport) for each person. Permits may be obtained by mail if a photocopy of each camper's ID (with ID number and birth date clearly readable) is sent. If you don't have time to send for an official application form, this information can be written on a regular sheet of paper; be sure to specify the exact dates and which park(s) you want to stay at (in Na Pali Coast State Park, you'll have to specify which of the three campgrounds you'll be at on which nights).

Permit applications must be received at least seven days in advance during winter and may be applied for as early as a year in advance. During the busy summer period of May to September, Na Pali Coast campsites are often booked out months ahead, so it's recommended that you apply for your permit as far in advance as possible.

Camping is allowed for up to five consecutive nights at each state park within a 30-day period.

The Milolii Valley section of Na Pali Coast State Park, accessible only by small boat, is open May to September, and has a three-day limit. Captain Zodiac (☎ 826-9371) and Hanalei Sea Tours (☎ 826-7254) can drop campers off for a round-trip fee of $165. On rare occasions when the surf gets too high, the pick-up service may be delayed, so campers should carry extra provisions.

County Beach Parks

Camping is allowed at Haena, Hanalei, Anini, Anahola, Hanamaulu, Salt Pond and Lucy Wright parks. Haena, Anini and Salt Pond are all on nice beaches and are good choices. Camping is allowed at Hanalei Beach Park on weekends and holidays only.

All county campgrounds have showers and restrooms, and most have covered picnic pavilions and barbecue grills. There's a typical Hawaiian free style to the campgrounds, so don't expect to find numbered sites or caretakers.

Permits are required and cost $3 per adult per night. Children under 18 are free. There's a limit of seven consecutive days at each campground, and a limit of 60 days of camping a year.

Permits can be applied for in advance by mail or picked up in person from 7:45 am to 4:30 pm Monday to Friday at the Division of Parks & Recreation (☎ 241-6670), 4193 Hardy St, Lihue, HI 96766, in the green row building behind the War Memorial Convention Center.

After hours and on weekends and holidays, you can get permits at the police station at 3060 Umi St in Lihue (use the yellow phone at the station entrance).

You can also just set up camp and wait for the ranger to come around and collect, but if you do this the fee jumps to $5 per person. Be aware that rangers sometimes wake up campers as early as 5 am to collect fees, and if they determine the camping area is too full, campers without permits can be asked to move.

Waimea Canyon The Division of Forestry & Wildlife allows backcountry camping at five sites along trails in Waimea Canyon and at two sites (Sugi Grove and Kawaikoi) in the Kokee State Park area. Camping is limited to four nights in the canyon and three nights in the Kokee area within a 30-day period.

Camping permits are free and can be picked up in person between 7:45 am and 4:30 pm Monday to Friday, from the forestry office at 3060 Eiwa St, Room 306, Lihue, HI 96766. You can also get the permits mailed to you in advance by writing (or by calling 241-3433); simply tell them the name and address of each camper, the camping area you want to stay at (Waimea or Kokee) and the dates you plan to camp.

Cabins Cabins run by a private concessionaire are available in Kokee State Park. There are also cabins in a mountain setting at Kahili Mountain Park, north of Koloa. See the relevant sections for more information.

Camping Supplies Pedal & Paddle (☎ 826-9069) in Ching Young Village in

Hanalei rents three-person dome tents for $8/25 a day/week, backpacks for $5/20 and light blankets, lanterns and sleeping pads each for $3/10. They sell the same supplies they rent and have a selection of hiking books, maps and backpacking items. The store is open daily from 9 am to 5 pm, a bit later in summer.

Outfitters Kauai (☎ 742-9667), in the Poipu Plaza in Poipu, rents tents for $10 a day, backpacks for $8, with discounts for rentals of more than three days. They also sell topographical maps of Kauai and other camping and hiking supplies. It's open from 9 am to 5 pm Monday to Saturday.

Kayak Kauai (☎ 826-9844) on Hwy 560 in Hanalei rents two-person tents or backpacks for $8/30 a day/week, camping stoves for $4/15 and sleeping pads for $3/15. It's open from 8 am to 5:30 pm daily.

ENTERTAINMENT

Most of the action is at the larger hotels in Poipu, Wailua and Princeville, and at the bigger resorts you can find live music and the occasional Polynesian dinner show. The Outrigger Kauai Beach hotel has a comedy club.

Kauai Coconut Beach Resort and Smith's Tropical Plantation, both in Wailua, and Tahiti Nui in Hanalei have luaus.

There are movie theaters in the Kukui Grove Center in Lihue and the Coconut Marketplace in Wailua.

Free hula shows are presented at the Coconut Marketplace in Wailua, the Outrigger Kauai Beach hotel in Lihue and the Kukui Village shopping center in Waipouli.

For more details about specific venues, see the relevant town sections in this chapter. The local papers or free tourist magazines, especially the *Kauai Beach Press*, have updated entertainment information.

THINGS TO BUY

Two good places to look for Niihau shell leis, island-made baskets, paintings and other arts and crafts are at Kilohana

Plantation in Puhi and Ching Young Village in Hanalei.

Farmers' markets (☎ 241-6390) featuring locally grown fruits, flowers and vegetables are held at the Koloa Ballpark at noon on Mondays, Kalaheo Neighborhood Center at 4:30 pm on Tuesdays, Kapaa New Town Park at 3 pm on Wednesdays, Hanapepe United Church of Christ at 3:30 pm on Thursdays, Vidinha Stadium in Lihue at 3 pm on Fridays and Kekaha Neighborhood Center at 9 am on Saturdays.

GETTING THERE & AWAY
Air
Kauai's main airport is in Lihue. Both Aloha Airlines (☎ 245-3691) and Hawaiian Airlines (☎ 245-1831) have direct flights to Lihue from Honolulu, Kahului on Maui, and Hilo and Kona on the Big Island.

The most frequent service is from Honolulu, with Hawaiian Airlines flying about once an hour and Aloha Airlines nearly twice an hour between 5:30 am and 8 pm. One-way fares from all islands are $74 on either airline. For information on discounts and air passes see the introductory Getting Around chapter in the front of the book.

Mahalo Air (☎ (800) 277-8333) flies between Honolulu and Lihue an average of five times a day, with a one-way fare of $54.

Kauai also has a smaller airport in Princeville on the North Shore. Island Air (☎ (800) 652-6541), which has the only commercial service to Princeville, flies direct from Honolulu five times a day and via Honolulu from Molokai, Lanai, Kahului, Hana and Kapalua West Maui. One-way fares are $81.

Lihue Airport Until a few years ago, inter-island flights touched down in a Lihue cane field. Now there's a big modern terminal, an airstrip that can handle direct flights from the US mainland and agricultural inspection for passengers leaving the state.

The airport has a restaurant, cocktail lounge, flower shop, newsstand and gift shop. You can find stands loaded with activity and accommodations brochures in the baggage-claim area. The car rental booths are in front of the terminal, opposite the arrival and departure gates.

Princeville Airport This little airport on the North Shore has Avis and Hertz car rental booths and a cafe/lounge.

GETTING AROUND
Kauai has a limited public bus service and renting a car is almost essential for exploring the island in depth.

Kauai's main roads are straightforward and easy to follow, but if you plan on doing a lot of exploring, consider picking up a good road map; the best is the *Hawaii, Maui & Kauai Map of the Neighbor Islands* produced by Compass Maps.

Surprisingly, Kauai has rush-hour traffic jams, especially in central Lihue and on the highway between Lihue and Kapaa. It can be an inconvenience but it's not unbearable.

Bus
One unusual benefit of Hurricane Iniki has been a Federal Emergency Management Agency (FEMA)-funded island-wide bus system. Dubbed the 'Iniki Express' this vastly extended public bus service has been making runs throughout the island from Kekaha in the west to Kee Beach in the north. Routes include Koloa, Poipu, and even the campground at Anini Beach – actually just about the only place the buses haven't gone are to Polihale and Kokee state parks.

Connections are not always frequent or convenient, but the service is daily and all runs are free. Bus stops are marked with signs along the road. Some buses are white with a green sugar cane motif and are marked 'Kauai Bus', although Polynesian Adventure Tours and TransHawaiian tour buses have also been used for the Iniki Express service. While a funding cut-off date is not yet established, the free bus will likely be phased out in the next year or so.

After that the public bus is expected to resume its more limited pre-Iniki service,

...lau, Kauai

...hale, Kauai

Wailua Falls, Kauai

...lau Trail, Kauai

Kuilau Ridge Trail, Kauai

View of Na Pali Coast from Kee Beach, Kauai

Taro Fields, Kauai

Na Pali Coast, Kauai

which consisted mainly of routes between Kapaa and Lihue and cost $1 per ride.

A bus schedule can be picked up from bus drivers or from the county Department of Transportation office, which is on Rice St next to Dairy Queen in Lihue. If you're thinking of not renting a car and relying solely on the bus, it would be a good idea to call in advance (☎ 241-6410) to make sure there's still an extensive enough service to make this a viable option.

Taxi
Taxis charge $2 at flagfall and then $2 a mile, metered in 25-cent increments. The fare from Lihue Airport is about $17 to Coconut Plantation in Wailua, $20 to Kapaa and $30 to Poipu.

Car
Budget (☎ 245-1901), Hertz (☎ 245-3356), Avis (☎ 245-3512), Alamo (☎ 246-0645), Dollar (☎ 245-3651) and National (☎ 245-5636) have car rental booths at the Lihue Airport.

More information, including toll-free numbers, is in the introductory Getting Around chapter in the front of the book.

Bicycle
Bicycles Kauai (☎ 822-3315), 1379 Kuhio Hwy, Kapaa, rents 18-speed mountain bikes for $20 for 24 hours, $15 for a partial day. It's open from 9 am to 6 pm weekdays, to 3 pm on Saturdays, and from 10 am to 3 pm on Sundays.

Kayak Kauai, in both Hanalei (☎ 826-9844) and Kapaa (☎ 822-9179), rents 21-speed mountain bikes for $20/90 a day/week, including car rack, water bottle, helmet and lock.

North Shore Bike Doktor (☎ 826-7799) on Hwy 560 in Hanalei rents 21-speed mountain bikes for $20 a day, $10 a half day.

Pedal & Paddle in the Ching Young Village in Hanalei (☎ 826-9069) and Kauai Village in Waipouli (☎ 822-2005) rents 21-speed mountain bikes for $15/80 a day/week with lock, helmet and car rack included. They also have beach cruisers for

$10/50. The stores are open from 9 am to 5 pm daily.

Bicycle John (☎ 245-7579), 3142 Kuhio Hwy, Lihue, rents 21-speed mountain bikes for as low as $10 a day, $50 a week. The shop, which also sells and repairs bikes, is open from 9 am to 5 pm Monday to Friday and from 10 am to 4 pm on Saturdays.

Outfitters Kauai (☎ 742-9667) in the Poipu Plaza in Poipu rents beach cruisers for $15 a day, mountain bikes for $20 a day and tandem bikes for $35. There are discounts for rentals of more than three days. Helmets, locks and water bottles are included in the price. The store is open from 9 am to 5 pm Monday to Saturday.

Hitchhiking
Hitchhiking is legal on Kauai as long as you're not standing on the road itself, but on the shoulder. Pick a place where there's room for a car to pull over safely.

Overall, Kauai tends to be hit and miss for hitching. Drivers on the North Shore are usually the most sympathetic, and occasionally will go out of their way to take hikers to the Kalalau trailhead. Of course hitchhiking is never entirely safe and the usual precautions apply.

East Side

LIHUE
Lihue is the county capital, the island's commercial center and the arrival point of most visitors to Kauai. Although it's the island's central town, its population is only 5500 and it's essentially a grown-up plantation town. It has inexpensive local hotels and restaurants and the island's main shopping mall. There are a few sights of interest, but Lihue itself is ordinary, with no special charm.

Information
The Hawaii Visitors Bureau (☎ 245-3971), 3016 Umi St, on the 2nd floor of the Lihue Plaza, is open from 8 am to 4:30 pm Monday to Friday.

Lihue Area

To Wailua,
Kapaa

56

Wailua
County
Golf Course

Kalepa Ridge

Kaumualii Hwy

Kauai Beach Dr

■ Aston Kauai Beach Villas
■ Outrigger Kauai Beach

Kalepa Forest Reserve

Kapule Hwy

Hanamaulu Beach Park

HANAMAULU

Hehi Rd

Hanamaulu Rd

Ahukini Landing

Hanamaulu Bay

Ahukini Rd

Hanamaulu Restaurant

To Wailua Falls

583

Maalo Rd

570

Lihue Airport

Wilcox Memorial Hospital

Ahukini Rd

Kamilo Point

Old Lutheran Church

56

LIHUE

Rice St

51

Lighthouse

Ninini Point

Hoomana Rd

See Central Lihue map

Kauai Marriott

Kalapaki Beach

50

Grove Farm Homestead

Pacific Ocean Plaza

Garden Island Inn

51

Nawiliwili Bay

Nawiliwili Beach Park

Kukui Grove Shopping Center

Nawiliwili Rd

58

Waapa Rd

Nawiliwili Harbor

Carter Point

Kilohana Plantation

Kauai Community College

PUHI

Puhi Rd

Niumalu Beach Park

Menehune Fishpond Overlook

Haupu (Hoary Head) Ridge

To Poipu,
Waimea

Hulemalu Rd

Huleia Stream

Menehune Fishpond

Kawa Point

Huleia National Wildlife Refuge

0   1   2 km
0   .5   1 miles

The government offices are centered around Rice, Umi and Hardy Sts.

Post & Money The post office is opposite the museum on Rice St, next to the Bank of Hawaii. Post office hours are from 7:30 am to 5 pm Monday to Friday, 9 am to 1 pm on Saturdays. The bank is open from 8:30 am to 3 pm Monday to Thursday, to 6 pm on Fridays.

Library The Lihue Public Library (☎ 245-3617), 4344 Hardy St, is open from 9 am to 5 pm on Mondays, Thursdays, Fridays and Saturdays and from 10 am to 8 pm on Tuesdays and Wednesdays.

Laundry There are coin laundries in the Rice Shopping Center and next to the Hanamaulu Cafe on Hwy 56 in Hanamaulu. The latter is open from 7:30 am to 10 pm daily.

Kauai Museum

A few hours at the Kauai Museum (☎ 245-6931), 4428 Rice St, will give you a good overview of the island's history.

The displays begin with Kauai's volcanic genesis from the ocean floor, then move on to describe the island's unique ecosystems. The first floor covers early Hawaii, with the likes of hula instruments, a hand-carved wooden canoe and a section on the short-lived Russian presence in Kauai.

Upstairs the sugar cane workers and missionaries arrive on the scene. A replica of a plantation worker's spartan shack sits opposite the spacious bedroom of an early missionary's house furnished with a four-poster koa bed and Hawaiian quilts. It is to these folks that Hawaii traces its multi-ethnic roots as well as its vastly unequal distribution of land and wealth. The displays are accompanied by well-written interpretive presentations of life in old Kauai.

The gift shop has a good selection of Hawaiiana books and a small collection of koa bowls and other handicrafts. If you only want to visit the gift shop, which is inside the museum lobby, you can enter without paying.

The museum is open from 9 am to 4:30 pm Monday to Friday and from 9 am to 1 pm on Saturdays. Admission is $3 for adults and free for children under age 18. If you run out of time, ask for a free re-entry pass when you leave.

Lihue Sugar Mill

The conveyer belt that crosses over Hwy 50 just south of its intersection with Hwy 56 transports crushed sugar cane to the Lihue Sugar Mill. The mill produces raw sugar crystals that are shipped to California to be refined. Molasses is also made here and if you happen by on one of those days you'll find the air laden with the sweet, thick smell of the syrup.

Old Lutheran Church

From the outside, the oldest Lutheran church in Hawaii is just one more quaint Hawaiian church. From the inside it's much more interesting.

German immigrants styled their church to resemble the boat that brought them from their homeland to Hawaii in the late 1800s. The floor has been built to slant like the deck of a ship, the balcony resembles a captain's bridge and ship lanterns hang from the ceiling. The current building was actually constructed in 1983, but it's an almost exact replica of the original 1885 church that was leveled by Hurricane Iwa in 1982.

The immigrants themselves now lie at rest in the church cemetery on a knoll overlooking the cane fields in which they toiled.

The church is a quarter of a mile up Hoomana Rd, which is just south of the intersection of Hwy 56 and Hwy 50.

Wailua Falls

Wailua Falls is a scenic 80-foot waterfall just north of Lihue. From Lihue, turn left onto Maalo Rd (Hwy 583), a narrow paved road that weaves through a sugar cane field. The road ends at the falls at precisely 3.94 miles – as the highway marker fastidiously proclaims.

Wailua, which means 'two waters', is usually seen as two falls. However, after heavy rains it becomes one wide rushing waterfall and you can watch fish being thrown out beyond the powerful waters for a flying dive into the pool below.

This is not a waterfall to explore from the top. A sign at the parking lot near a closed path reads, 'Slippery rocks at top of falls. People have been killed'. There are plenty of stories told of people sliding off the rocks, some miraculously grabbing roots and being rescued and others not so lucky.

Down the road a third of a mile, at a large dirt pull-off, there's an eroded trail that leads to the base of the falls. The steep trail down to the river can be very slippery when wet, if not outright hazardous. As the trail along the bottom follows the riverbed to the base of the falls, that part of the path commonly floods over and may be barely discernible after heavy rains. However, all said and done, local kids do manage to scramble their way through the overgrowth to the waterfall. If you decide to give it a try, expect to work up a sweat; it can be humid enough along the riverbed to steam up eyeglasses.

Back on the road, keep an eye out for wood roses, which are commonly used in dried floral arrangements. The vines, which bear bright yellow flowers shaped like morning glories, are especially thick around the bridge half a mile down the road from the waterfall.

Hanamaulu

Hanamaulu is a little village between Lihue and Wailua, along Hwy 56, that's significant in Hawaiian folklore as the birthplace of Kauai's legendary hero Kawelo. Today it's a sleepy town with just a few businesses, including an old-fashioned Japanese restaurant, a hole-in-the-wall post office and a doughnut shop that closes each day as soon as the doughnuts are gone.

Hanamaulu Beach Park Hanamaulu County Beach Park is three-quarters of a mile from the village center. From Hwy 56

turn makai onto Hanamaulu Rd and after ¼ mile turn right onto Hehi Rd. As you enter the park you'll first go under the highway bridge and then the arched trestle of an abandoned railroad bridge.

The park is at the inside of Hanamaulu Bay, a deep protected bay with a boulder breakwater part way across its mouth. It has camping with full facilities but the park is close to town and is more of a local hangout than a visitor destination, and the waters are occasionally closed due to pollution.

Ahukini Landing

If you've got some time to kill before your flight, you could drive down to the end of Hwy 570 to Ahukini Landing, 1½ miles beyond the airport. The road runs through cane fields and crosses a series of narrow-gauge railroad tracks that were once used to bring sugar cane down to the landing. Ilima and chain of love grow along the road.

Ahukini State Recreation Pier, at the end of the road, consists largely of cement pillars and the decaying framework of the old pier. A wooden walkway runs out across it, providing a prime locale for pole fishing. At the head of the bay is Hanamaulu Beach.

Ninini Point

The lighthouse on Ninini Point stands 100 feet above the shore, marking the northern entrance to Nawiliwili Bay. The road down to the lighthouse begins off Hwy 51, a little over half a mile south of its intersection with Hwy 570. Although you'll have to go through a guard gate and cross the Kauai Lagoon Golf Course property to get to the coast, access is free to visitors.

The 2½-mile drive from the gatehouse to the lighthouse skirts between the airport fence and the golf course. (If you hear popping sounds as you drive along, it's not your tires going flat but timed explosions to scare birds away from the airport runway!) After two miles the pavement ends and the road continues as dirt. This section is sometimes too rough to pass in a low-slung car and you may have to hike the last 10 minutes of it.

Not only is there a fine view from the lighthouse, but nearby is one of the few sections of accessible shore in the area where Hawaiians can still fish, pick opihi and gather limu as they've done for generations.

Kalapaki Beach

Kalapaki Beach, a white sand beach sheltered by points and breakwaters, is off Hwy 51 at Nawiliwili Harbor. Swimming is usually good, even in the winter unless storms kick the surf up.

The beach is backed by the old Westin Kauai, a luxury hotel that was heavily damaged by Hurricane Iniki and later sold to the Marriott chain, which expects to have it up and running again by 1996. The hotel grounds are quite elaborate and worth a drive through.

Nawiliwili Bay

Nawiliwili Bay is a deep-water port with a commercial harbor. The adjacent small boat harbor has a picturesque setting, backed by the edge of the Haupu (Hoary Head) Ridge which ends at Carter Point. Several deep-sea fishing boats are based at the harbor.

Waapa Rd runs past the harbor and a couple of unexciting beach parks before connecting with Hulemalu Rd, which leads up to an overview of the Menehune Fishpond.

If you continue about a mile past the fishpond and then turn right onto Puhi Rd, you'll come out to Hwy 50 opposite the community college.

Nawiliwili Beach Park Nawiliwili Beach Park is largely a parking lot facing an ocean retaining wall. From here you can look across to the light beacon on Kukui Point and at the far end of the parking lot you can also see the lighthouse on the more distant Ninini Point.

There's no beach at the beach park, but if the waters in Nawiliwili Stream are not running strongly you could cross over to Kalapaki Beach.

Right at the mouth of the stream is an old shelter under ironwood trees with a wooden sign reading 'Pine Tree Inn' – it's an impromptu neighborhood open-air bar of sorts. Old-timers gather here during the day with ice chests of beer to talk story and play music.

Menehune Fishpond Overlook

Half a mile up Hulemalu Rd there's a lookout on the left with a view of the Alakoko Fishpond, more commonly called the Menehune Fishpond. In the background is the misty Haupu Ridge.

The fishpond, created by a stone wall that runs along a bend in Huleia Stream, was said to have been built in one night by menehunes. The stone wall is now covered by a thick green line of mangrove trees. Morning is a good time for viewing as in the afternoon you look into the sun.

The waterside **Huleia National Wildlife Refuge** lies between the road and the fishpond. Once planted with taro and rice, the area now provides breeding and feeding grounds for endemic waterbirds. The refuge is not open to the public.

Grove Farm Homestead

The Grove Farm Homestead Plantation Museum, up Nawiliwili Rd (Hwy 58), 1¾ miles from Waapa Rd, is the preserved farmhouse built in 1864 by George Wilcox, son of missionaries Abner and Lucy Wilcox. It's somewhat like the house of an old aunt, bit musty and filled with memories. Rocking chairs sit on a covered porch. One room is lined with bookshelves stuffed with a home library, with koa calabashes and a model ship on top. In one corner a card table is set up, waiting for a couple of people to sit down to a wild game of cribbage.

Tours are given at 10 am and 1 pm on Mondays, Wednesdays and Thursdays. Reservations are required (☎ 245-3202) and space commonly fills up a week or two in advance. The cost is $3.

KAUAI

Kilohana Plantation

Kilohana, 1½ miles south of Lihue on Hwy 50, is the 1930s sugar plantation estate of Gaylord Parke Wilcox, once head of Grove Farm Plantation. The Tudor-style mansion built by Wilcox was the most distinguished house on Kauai in its day.

The home has been restored, with most of the rooms turned into shops that sell artwork, antiques and handicrafts. It was a nice way to preserve the old estate and you get to look around without being charged an admission fee.

Visitors are free to wander through rooms full of antiques. The hallways hold cases of stone poi pounders and other Hawaiian artifacts, and Oriental rugs litter the hardwood floors. There's also a restaurant, Gaylord's, in a U-shaped courtyard setting around the lawn.

Many island galleries rent space at Kilohana, giving it one of the widest collections of arts and crafts on Kauai. On the 1st floor, a former cloakroom is now the Hawaiian Collection Room, which sells finely strung Niihau shell leis and scrimshaw.

The upstairs bedrooms have likewise been turned into shops, with displays laid out even in the bathrooms and closets. The works include wood carvings of whales and dolphins, contemporary paintings by local artists, jewelry and dolls.

Kilohana (☎ 245-5608) is open from 9:30 am to 9:30 pm Monday to Saturday, until 5 pm on Sundays. The 35-acre grounds have gardens and a small working farm that you can explore. Turn-of-the-century carriages pulled by Clydesdale horses give 20-minute tours at $7 for adults and $4 for children.

Queen Victoria's Profile

The rock profile of Queen Victoria, part of the Haupu (Hoary Head) Ridge, can be seen from a marked 'scenic view' pull-off in front of the Kauai Community College along Hwy 50 in Puhi.

It takes some imagination, but here's how to find it. Position yourself midway in the pull-off facing the mountains to the south. Look across the highway at the phone pole, then over to the metal light pole in the background to the right. The queen's crowned head is under the arch of the lamp – the crown is the high part at the right, her chin lower and to the left.

Supposedly she's shaking her thin pointy finger at an imaginary William, saying 'Na, Willy, Willy', hence the harbor's name.

Places to Stay – bottom end

Lihue has some of Kauai's cheapest hotels. They are generally drab places and except for Motel Lani are filled mostly with local residents. You'll get a place to sleep but by no means are these vacation spots.

The family-run *Motel Lani* (☎ 245-2965), 4240 Rice St, Box 1836, Lihue, HI 96766, is the best bottom-end choice, though it's at a busy intersection. It has 10 rooms that are quite basic but are clean and have private showers, fans and mini-refrigerators. The standard rooms are $30 for singles or doubles. There are also a couple of 'deluxe' rooms for $50 that are larger and have TVs. There's a two-day minimum or a $2 surcharge.

The *Hale Lihue Hotel* (☎ 245-3151), 2931 Kalena St, Lihue, HI 96766, has 20

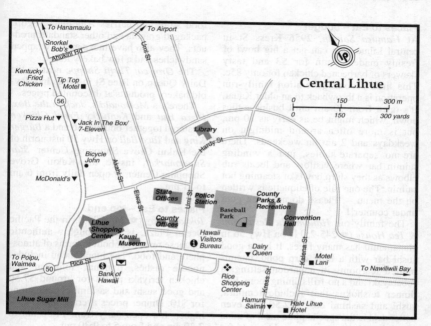

Central Lihue

rooms for $25/30/35 a single/double/triple, some with kitchenettes. Rooms have twin beds, private showers and toilets, but zilch for atmosphere.

The *Tip Top Motel* (☎ 245-2333), 3173 Akahi St, Box 1231, Lihue, HI 96766, has a couple dozen rooms in two simple two-story cinder-block buildings. Rooms are lackluster with twin beds, air-con and louvered windows. Rates are a pricey $50 for singles or doubles plus a refundable key deposit.

Places to Stay – middle & top

The *Garden Island Inn* (☎ 245-7227, (800) 648-0154), 3445 Wilcox Rd, Lihue, HI 96766, is an older three-story hotel that was extensively renovated after Hurricane Iniki. It has 21 small but tidy rooms with TVs, ceiling fans, mini-refrigerators and coffeemakers. The rate is $50 for ground floor rooms, and $60 for rooms on the 2nd floor with small private lanais. The hotel is near an industrial area and at the side of a rather

busy road, so expect to hear some traffic noise. On the plus side it's within walking distance of Kalapaki Beach and a couple of good restaurants.

A few miles north of downtown Lihue is the *Outrigger Kauai Beach* (☎ 245-1955, (800) 462-6262; fax (800) 622-4852), 4331 Kauai Beach Dr, Lihue, HI 96766, which has 346 rooms costing from $110 with a mountain view to $160 with an ocean view. The hotel was originally built as a Hilton and has the usual amenities you'd expect of that chain; the design is also standard Hilton with little Hawaiian influence. It has free-form swimming pools, tennis courts and a health club.

On the same beachfront property as the Outrigger is the *Aston Kauai Beach Villas* (☎ 245-7711, (800) 922-7866), 4330 Kauai Beach Dr, Lihue, HI 96766, which has modern studio units with kitchenettes for $99, one-bedroom condos at $145 for up to four people and two-bedroom units at $195 for up to six people.

KAUAI

Places to Eat – budget

At *Hamura Saimin*, 2956 Kress St in central Lihue, you can get a big bowl of freshly made saimin for $3 and tasty skewers of barbecued chicken for only 85c. This little second generation family-run operation is a throwback to an older Kauai. It's open from 10 am until business dies down, which might be as early as 10 pm, but is more often around midnight on weekdays and 2 am on weekends. There are no separate tables, just a winding saimin bar where visitors and locals rub elbows as they slurp bowls of steaming hot saimin. The one rule of etiquette is written on the menu – 'Please do not stick gum under counter'!

The family-run *Hanamaulu Restaurant & Tea House* (☎ 245-2511) on Hwy 56 in Hanamaulu has many faces. It has a good sushi bar with a little carp pond, tatami-matted tearooms in a garden setting, a robatayaki and a no-frills dining room. Full dinner teishokus that include tempura, sushi and sashimi cost $12.50. An even better deal is the special plate meal of miso soup, rice, shrimp tempura and teriyaki for $6.50 at lunch, $8 at dinner. Average Chinese dishes are available at similar prices. Call in advance to reserve one of the tearooms – they really set the mood. It's open from 10 am to 1 pm Tuesday to Friday and 4:30 to 9 pm daily except Mondays.

The little *Espresso Cafe*, inside the Indo-Pacific Trading Co in the Kukui Grove Shopping Center, has sandwiches, pastries, coffees and other light eats. A specialty is the Indonesian food, including gado-gado or vegetarian satay for $6.

Kauai Chop Suey, in the Pacific Ocean Plaza at 3501 Rice St, has lots of standard Cantonese dishes between $6 and $7 as well as about a dozen vegetarian dishes. Kauai is not known for its Chinese restaurants but this one has good, reasonably priced food. The menu is the same at lunch (11 am to 2 pm Tuesday to Saturday) and dinner (4:30 to 9 pm Tuesday to Sunday).

Hale O'Health in the Rice Shopping Center is a typical shopping center health food store and carries Alta-dena yogurt, packaged granola and other standard products. They also have inexpensive wrapped sandwiches and a few bakery items.

The *Oroweat Thrift Shoppe* next to the Dairy Queen on Rice St in Lihue has day-old bakery products at discounted prices.

There's a *McDonald's, Jack in the Box, Pizza Hut* and *Kentucky Fried Chicken* clustered together on Hwy 56 and a *Burger King* and *Taco Bell* on Hwy 50 just north of the Kukui Grove Shopping Center. *Star Supermarket*, inside the Kukui Grove Shopping Center, is open daily from 6 am to 11 pm.

Places to Eat – top end

Tokyo Lobby (☎ 245-8989), in the Pacific Ocean Plaza, is a thoroughly authentic Japanese restaurant both in terms of atmosphere and food. The lunch menu includes noodle dishes, donburi, tonkatsu and chicken teriyaki plates for around $7.50 and good sushi and sashimi combinations for $10. Dinner prices average about 25% higher. It's open daily from 11:30 am to 2:30 pm and from 5 to 9:30 pm.

Cafe Portofino (☎ 245-2121), in the Pacific Ocean Plaza, serves up authentic Northern Italian food. Lunch, priced from $6 to $10, features sandwiches, pastas and a few other dishes such as chicken cacciatore or calamari. At dinner, the menu is more substantial with starters such as the escargot in garlic butter or the tangy ahi carpaccio priced around $7. Main dinner courses range from $10 pasta dishes to scampi or fresh fish priced around double that. It's open from 11 am to 2 pm Monday to Friday and from 5 to 10 pm nightly.

Gaylord's (☎ 245-9593) at Kilohana Plantation has a pleasant open-air estate setting and attracts a crowd, though the food is far more ordinary than its reputation would suggest. Lunch is from 11 am to 3 pm daily except Sundays, with sandwiches and salads for $9. Dinner, from 5 pm nightly, features large servings of meat, with entrees priced from $15 for chicken or baby back ribs to $22 for steak, duck or rack of lamb. On Sundays, there's a brunch from 9:30 am to 3 pm, with dishes from $10 to $14.

Entertainment

Legends nightclub (☎ 246-0491), upstairs in the Pacific Ocean Plaza, is a trendy dance spot.

Gilligan's (☎ 245-1955), the Outrigger Kauai Beach's nightclub, has dancing from 9 pm to 2 am on Thursdays, Fridays and Saturdays, with no cover charge. The Kauai Comedy Club hosts stand-up comedians from Hawaii and the mainland at 8:30 pm Thursdays at Gilligan's.

Na Hula O Kaohikukapulani, a Kauaian halau, performs a free hula show at 5:30 pm Wednesdays at the Outrigger Kauai Beach hotel.

The *Kukui Grove Cinema* in the Kukui Grove Center shows standard Hollywood flicks.

Things to Buy

Kukui Grove Shopping Center, at the intersection of Hwy 50 and Hwy 58, is Kauai's main shopping mall. The major department stores are Liberty House and its discount Penthouse branch, J C Penney, Sears, Woolworth and Longs Drugs. The center also has Waldenbooks, J R's Music Shop, a one-hour photo shop, and several clothing and gift shops.

For Hawaiiana handicrafts, the gift shops at Kilohana and at the Kauai Museum are good places to start.

WAILUA

The three-mile stretch of Kuhio Highway (Hwy 56) from Wailua to Waipouli and on to Kapaa is largely a scattering of stores, restaurants, hotels and condos. Neither Wailua nor Waipouli have anything that resembles a town center. Most of the area's sights are clustered around the Wailua River area.

Wailua was the site of Kauai's royal court. There are 'Seven Sacred Heiaus' running from the mouth of the Wailua River up to the top of Mt Waialeale.

Six of the heiau sites are within a mile of the river mouth. Five are visible, while the

sixth is abandoned in a sugar cane field on the northern side of the Wailua River. All date back to the early period of Tahitian settlement and are considered to be typical menehune construction.

Wailua River State Park is a hodgepodge that includes most of the heiau sites, sections of the Wailua River bank, the Fern Grotto, the riverboat basin and a public boat ramp.

Wailua River, 11.8 miles long, is the only navigable river in Hawaii. Although most people travel the river on packaged riverboat tours, the more adventurous kayak or water-ski on it.

Lydgate Beach Park

Lydgate is a popular family beach with protected swimming in a large seawater pool created with stone walls. It's fun for kids but deep enough for adults to swim in too. The open ocean beyond often has strong currents and there have been many drownings on both sides of the mouth of the Wailua River, which is just north of Lydgate. The park has changing rooms, restrooms, showers, large picnic pavilions and drinking water.

Lydgate is makai of the Kauai Resort Hotel, down Leho Drive.

Hikina A Ka La Heiau

Hikina A Ka La (Rising of the Sun) Heiau is the long, narrow heiau aligned directly north to south at the far end of the Lydgate Beach parking lot.

The heiau is thought to have been built around 1200 AD. Boulders still outline the shape but most of the stones have long since been removed.

At the northern end of the heiau, a bronze plaque on a large stone reads 'Hauola, City of Refuge'. The mounded grassy area behind the plaque is all that remains of this former refuge for kapu breakers.

The stone with bowl-shaped depressions, 10 feet to the left of the plaque, is an adze grinding stone. While it's easy to recognize, the stone hasn't always been in this upright position since to grind a correct

KAUAI

■ PLACES TO STAY

2   Hotel Coral Reef
3   Kauai International Hostel
13 Pono Kai Resort
24 Kauai Kailani
26 Mokihana of Kauai
27 Kauai Coconut Beach Resort
28 Plantation Hale
30 Aston Kauai Beachboy Hotel
31 Islander on the Beach
32 Kauai Sands Hotel
35 Kapaa Sands
36 Coco Palms Resort
38 Kauai Resort Hotel

▼ PLACES TO EAT

1   Kapaa Fish & Chowder House
6   Norberto's El Cafe
8   Hana-Ya
14 Michelle's/Bubba's
14 Burger King

20 Taco Bell/
    Kentucky Fried Chicken
25 Ambrose's Natural Foods
33 Sizzler/Mema
34 Kintaro

OTHER

4   Bank of Hawaii
5   Bicycles Kauai
7   ABC Discount Store
10 Aquatic Adventures
11 First Hawaiian Bank
12 Kayak Kauai
15 Kapaa Shopping Center
16 View of Sleeping Giant
17 Waipouli Complex
18 24-hour Chevron Station
19 Dive Kauai
21 Waipouli Plaza
22 Kauai Village
23 Waipouli Town Center
29 Coconut Marketplace
37 Wailua Marina

Wailua to Kapaa

To Anahola,
North Shore

Public
Pool

Kapaa
New Park

Library

Ohana Rd

581

Kapaa Beach Park

KAPAA

Waikaea Canal

WAIPOULI

56

PACIFIC
OCEAN

To Nounou
Ridge Trail

Kuhio Hwy

COCONUT
PLANTATION

Haleilio Rd

To Opaekaa
Falls

580

WAILUA

Holoholoku
Heiau

Kuamoo Rd

Wailua River

Wailua Bay

Alakukui
Point

To Fern
Grotto

Malae
Heiau

Leho Dr

56

Hikina A Ka
La Heiau

Lydgate
Beach Park

To Lihue

0   .5   1 km
0   .25   .5 miles

edge it would have to be flat. There are also a couple of flat stone saltpans on the grounds.

If you look straight out across the bay you can see the remains of a heiau on Alakukui Point, in front of the red-roofed Lae Nani condos. Only the foundation stones are discernible, as the heiau site has been landscaped over in a carpet of condo grass. In ancient times torches were lit on the point at night to help guide outrigger canoes.

If you walk straight down to the beach while looking toward Alakukui Point you may find a few ancient stones with petroglyphs on them, though they're usually hidden under shifting sands.

Malae Heiau

Malae Heiau is in a thick clump of trees growing on the edge of a sugar cane field, a mere 40 feet mauka of the highway across from the Kauai Resort Hotel. Although this is the largest heiau on Kauai, covering two acres, it's thickly overgrown with grasses and Java plum trees and almost impossible to explore.

In the 1830s the missionaries converted Deborah Kapule, the last Kauaian queen, to Christianity and she converted the interior of Malae Heiau into a cattle pen. Except for these alterations it's relatively well-preserved, thanks largely to its impenetrable overgrowth. The stone walls, which encompass an altar, are up to 10 feet high and eight feet wide.

The whole area is state property and plans to eventually incorporate the heiau into the Wailua River State Park system are slowly moving forward.

Incidentally, the Java plums found at the site make a nice wine, but should you be tempted to try the fresh fruit you'll find they're bitter enough to dry out your mouth!

Highway 580

Highway 580, also known as Kuamoo Rd, begins at the traffic light off Hwy 56 at Coco Palms Resort. It passes heiaus, historical sites, Opaekaa Falls and Wailua

Homesteads before reaching Keahua Arboretum, the starting place for a couple of backcountry trails.

Holoholoku Heiau

Holoholoku Heiau is a quarter of a mile up Hwy 580, on the left. Like all the Wailua heiaus, this one was of enclosure-type construction, with stone walls built directly on the ground, rather than with terraced platforms. It was a luakini heiau and thus a place of human sacrifice.

This whole area used to be royal property and here on the west side of the grounds, against the flat-backed **birthstone**, queens gave birth to future kings. This stone is marked by a plaque reading 'Pohaku Hoohanu'. Another stone a few yards away, marked 'Pohaku Piko', was where the piko (umbilical cords) of the babies were left.

Above the temple where Hawaiian royalty were born, steps lead to a hilltop cemetery where later-day Japanese laborers lie at rest.

Poliahu Heiau

Poliahu Heiau, perched high on a hill overlooking the meandering Wailua River, is named after the snow goddess Poliahu, one of Pele's sisters. This relatively well-preserved heiau is thought to have been a luakini type.

Poliahu Heiau is immediately before the Opaekaa Falls lookout, on the opposite side of the road.

Bellstone

Immediately south of Poliahu Heiau, on the same side of the road, look for a 'Falling Rocks' sign that marks a short dirt drive leading to a bellstone. Because of the road angle it's easiest to approach coming downhill from Poliahu.

In old Hawaii, Wailua River was a naval entrance, and the bellstone at this lookout was thought to have been used by sentries to warn of attacks as well as to ring out announcements of royal births.

There are actually two stones at the end of the drive, one with an all-too-perfect petroglyph whose age is suspect. Archaeologists question just which stone may have been the bellstone. Although you can find depressions in the stones, they may well be the result of modern-day poundings by people trying to check out the resonance for themselves.

A short path down from these rocks leads to a vista of the river, where you can usually see cattle grazing on the banks below and hear the microphone narration from the passing riverboats.

Opaekaa Falls

Opaekaa Falls is a high, broad waterfall which, depending upon recent rainfall, usually flows as a double cascade. The peaks of the Makaleha Mountains form a scenic backdrop and white-tailed tropicbirds can often be seen soaring in the valley below the falls. The turn-off to the viewpoint is clearly marked at 1½ miles up Hwy 580. For the best angle, walk up the sidewalk past the parking lot towards the bridge. From across the highway you can look down on the winding Wailua River and the thatched huts of the abandoned Kamokila Hawaiian Village.

Wailua Homesteads

In the Wailua Homesteads area, on the west side of the Sleeping Giant mountain, the government once gave 160-acre parcels to people willing to work the land. Most early homesteaders used the land to graze cattle, though at one point Dole grew pineapples in the area. Today Wailua Homesteads is largely a mix of spacious residential lots and pastoral countryside reminiscent of Pennsylvania Dutch farmland.

The main through road is Hwy 581 (Kamalu Rd), which connects with Hwy 580.

Nounou Ridge (Sleeping Giant) Trail

The Nounou Ridge Trail goes up the Sleeping Giant to a summit on the giant's upper chest, affording views of both the east coast and the highland valleys. It's a well-maintained trail that takes 1½ to two hours round-trip.

There are two trailheads, both marked. The trail on the western side is a shaded forest trail of tall trees and moss-covered stones. The trail on the eastern side, which is more open and a bit longer, begins at a parking lot a mile up Haleilio Rd in Wailua Houselots.

The trail up the western side of the mountain starts on Hwy 581 (Kamalu Rd), near house No 1068. Walk through a metal gate marked as a forestry right of way and up along a small cattle pasture to the trailhead.

This is a wonderful trail to do early in the morning when it's relatively cool and you can watch the light slowly spread across the valley below. The eucalyptus at the trailhead soon gives way to a tall thick forest of Norfolk pines that were planted in a Civilian Conservation Corps (CCC) reforestation program during the 1930s.

A few minutes up the trail there's a fork. Veer left up the path with the large rock beside it. The packed trail can get slippery when wet so look for a walking stick. Hikers sometimes leave them near the trailhead.

The trail passes through thick strawberry guava bushes that can grow up to 15 feet high; in places the guava creates a canopied tunnel-like effect. Strawberry guava has a small red fruit that's eaten whole and is considered the sweetest of any guava.

A few minutes below the summit, the eastern and western trails merge on the ridge. Continue up to the right past some hala trees. On the summit is a picnic table shelter that offers protection from the rain. Passing showers can give some incredible valley rainbows. To the west there's a 180° view of Wailua and the Makaleha Mountains.

Below to the east you can see Kapaa, sugar cane fields, Wailua Houselots, Coco Palms and the Wailua River. To the right of the riverboat docks and mauka of the Kauai Resort Hotel there's a square dark-green area in the sugar cane field. This is Malae Heiau, now overgrown with Java plums.

If you go south across the picnic area the trail continues. About five minutes up there's a rocky area where you can sit and enjoy the view. The ridge continues up the giant's head. Should it tempt you, size it up carefully. It's sharp, and loose rocks and slides are visible.

Kuilau Ridge Trail

For the effort, the Kuilau Ridge Trail is one of the most visually rewarding trails on the island. The marked trailhead is on the right just before Hwy 580 crosses the stream at the Keahua Arboretum, 3.9 miles up from the junction of Hwy 580 and Hwy 581. Don't leave anything of value in your car.

The maintained trail starts up a wide dirt path that is also used by horses and the occasional renegade dirt bike. There's a dense growth of native plants along the way, including koa trees, ohia lehua and thickets of ti, and there's plenty of birdsong as well. In the upper reaches there are hillsides covered with lush ferns and broad vistas of the mountains. A few thimbleberries grow wild along the trail and there are many trailside guava trees.

The hike climbs up to a broad ridge that offers views into valleys on both sides and clear down to the coast. You can see Kapaa to the east and the island's uninhabited central region to the west. It takes about 35 minutes to walk the 1¼ miles up to the grassy clearing on the ridgetop where there are a couple of picnic tables and a great view of Mt Waialeale, which is due west.

Beyond the clearing, the Kuilau Ridge Trail continues as a narrow footpath offering even more spectacular views, ending in about a mile at the Moalepe Trail. If you don't want to go that far, at least walk a little of it, as some of the best vistas are along the next half mile of the trail, which continues to the right past the picnic area.

At the connection with the Moalepe Trail, if you go left you'll come to a viewpoint after about 10 minutes. If you go right on Moalepe you'll come out on Olohena Rd in Wailua Homesteads about 2¼ miles down.

Coco Palms

The Coco Palms Resort was built on the site of Kauai's ancient royal court, in the midst of a 45-acre coconut grove.

There's a Hawaiian design to it all, with thatched cottages and lagoons, and it looks a bit like a movie set. Like movie sets, the closer you get, the less authentic it appears – you begin to notice that the coconut palm pillars are made of cement and that sort of thing.

The hotel's outdoor **chapel** was originally built in 1954 for the movie *Sadie Thompson* with Rita Hayworth. The highest-profile wedding that took place at Coco Palms was that of Elvis Presley and Joan Blackman in *Blue Hawaii*. Until Hurricane Iniki struck, about 700 people a year were still coming to the little chapel in the palms to be married.

Iniki did extensive damage to the hotel, and the reconstruction plans have been slow to get off the ground.

Fern Grotto

Kauai's busiest tourist attraction is the riverboat tour up the Wailua River to the Fern Grotto, complete with corny jokes and packaged sentimentality to the tune of Elvis's 'Hawaiian Wedding Song'.

The riverboats are big with wide flat bottoms – very simple, like covered barges. Some people compare them to cattle boats even before they pack the tourists on. The grotto, a large musty cave beneath a fern-covered rock face, is pretty enough, but not a must-see sight.

Smith's Motor Boat Service (☎ 822-4111) and Waialeale Boat Tours (☎ 822-4908) both charge $10 for adults and $5 for children ages four to 13, and one or the other leaves the Wailua Marina about once an hour between 9 am and 4 pm.

Smith's Tropical Paradise

Smith's Tropical Paradise (☎ 822-4654) at Wailua Marina has a loop trail through theme gardens, open from 8:30 am to 4 pm daily. Admission is $5, with guided tram tours $4 more; it's half-price for children ages three to 12. In the evening there's a luau and Polynesian show.

Coconut Plantation

Coconut Plantation is a resort development with four hotels, a condominium and a shopping center. It fronts a half-mile-long beach partially shaded by ironwood trees.

Water activities are restricted due to the low lava shelf that runs along most of the beach and the strong currents that prevail beyond. The sand on the beach is unique, each little piece polished to a high gloss.

While water conditions are mediocre, the beach makes for good strolling. The large grassy field between the Kauai Coconut Beach Resort and the Aston Kauai Beachboy Hotel is popular with egrets and the occasional kite flyer.

Places to Stay – B&Bs & Guesthouses

If you don't need to be on the beach, the following Wailua B&Bs represent some of the best values in accommodations on Kauai. The listings in this section are all in the Wailua Homesteads area, which is about three miles from the coast in a rural country setting. All except for Kay Barker's are within a mile of the intersection of Hwy 581 and Hwy 580.

Rosewood B&B (☎ 822-5216; fax 822-5478), 872 Kamalu Rd, Kapaa, HI 96746, is in a beautifully restored 85-year-old plantation home belonging to Rosemary and Norbert Smith. Upstairs there's a master bedroom with pastel wallpaper, a king-size bed and a tiled bath with sunken tub for $60. A second room has two twin beds, a double bed and a private bathroom, also for $60. Both have a view of grazing cattle with a mountain backdrop; rates include breakfast.

There are also two new guest cottages on the grounds, both with breakfast fixings provided. The Victorian, which costs $95, is light and airy with high ceilings, natural oak floors, a master bedroom with a queen bed, an upstairs loft bedroom with two twin beds, a full kitchen, ceiling fans, TV, phone and fax machine. The second cottage, $75, is simpler and studio-style, with coconut-frond thatching on the roof and screened windows all around that open to a garden with birdsong. It has a double bed, queen-size futon, ceiling fans, indoor toilet, outdoor hot shower, microwave, refrigerator, coffeemaker and gas grill.

A third new building, the Bunkhouse, has three straightforward but comfortable rooms geared for budget travelers. Each has its own sink, coffeemaker and small refrigerator and the larger has a microwave. All share a toilet and shower. Rates are $35 to $45; breakfast is available for $5 more. Rosewood also rents a two-bedroom condo on the beach in Kapaa for $100. All accommodations are nonsmoking.

The *House of Aleva* (☎ 822-4606), Ernest & Anita Perry, 5509 Kuamoo Rd, Kapaa, HI 96746, is a B&B right on Hwy 580, two miles up from Coco Palms. Ernest is a retired merchant seaman and Anita is a retired nurse who reads palms and makes ceramic Hawaiiana sculptures. They rent out two rooms with a shared bath in their home, at $40/55 for singles/doubles. The rooms have queen beds with comfortable mattresses, telephones, TV and mini-refrigerators. The rate includes a continental breakfast. Photos of past guests, which line one wall, include a fair number of European travelers.

Lampy's Bed & Breakfast (☎ 822-0478), 6078 Kolopua St, Kapaa, HI 96746, has six rooms in a large house, from $45 for one or two people, continental breakfast included. There's an extra $5 fee if you stay just one night. Rooms have either queen beds or two twins. Four rooms have private bathrooms, while two share a bath. A couple of the units have private entrances, refrigerators and microwaves, whereas the others share a kitchen. There's a common room with TV and VCR. Lampy's is more business-like than some of the smaller B&Bs – local calls are 50c, laundry service is $5 a load, and snorkels are for rent rather than loaned free – but it's efficiently run, clean and comfortable.

Kauai's first B&B is still called *Kay Barker's B&B* (☎ 822-3073, (800) 835-2845), Box 740, Kapaa, HI 96746, though Kay has passed away and the place is now run by her son Gordon. While the house is more modest than some of the other Wailua

B&Bs, it's still quite comfortable. The backyard looks out onto a field with grazing cattle and borders the trail to the Sleeping Giant. There are four bedrooms, each with a private bathroom, which cost $35 to $50 for singles, $45 to $60 for doubles, breakfast included. Guests have use of a refrigerator; smoking and social drinking are allowed. A separate two-room cottage with a microwave, sink and refrigerator costs $60/70 for singles/doubles.

Inn Paradise (☎ 822-2542), Major & Connie Inch, 6381 Makana Rd, Kapaa, HI 96746, has three delightful units with nice touches like Persian carpets, rattan furnishings and quality Hawaiiana wall prints. Each has a cable TV, phone, refrigerator, microwave and private entrance. The three units are in a guesthouse that stands separate from the Inch's contemporary home. All share a lanai with an unspoiled view of pasture and mountains. The Prince Kuhio room, which has a king bed, is a great value at $50. The Queen Kapule suite, which costs $75 for up to two people, has a king bed and a separate living room with a Murphy bed. The King Kaumualii unit, which is equipped like a small house, has two separate bedrooms with king beds and a full kitchen and costs $100 for up to four people. Additional guests are $7 more. There's a two-night minimum; rates include breakfast provisions and use of a washer and dryer.

Royal Drive Cottages (☎ 822-2321), Bob Levine, 147 Royal Dr, Kapaa, HI 96746, consists of two studio cottages on a quiet street just off Hwy 580. The cottages are simple, but wholly adequate with two twin beds, phone, refrigerator, microwave, toaster and coffeepot. The cottages do have tin roofs and this is a wet island – some people find the sound of rain on tin romantic, while others might be kept awake by it. Rates are $60 for one person, $80 for two.

Places to Stay – Hotels & Condos

Wailua's hotels and condos all have swimming pools and the usual standard facilities, though they also tend to have an air of neglect and none are particularly special.

The *Kauai Sands Hotel* (☎ 822-4951, (800) 367-7000 from the US mainland, (800) 654-7020 from Canada), 420 Papaloa Rd, Kapaa, HI 96746, is part of the Hawaiian-owned Sand & Seaside hotel chain. The rooms, which are in a series of two-story buildings that mostly surround a lawn and pool, are a bit plainer than those in neighboring hotels but it's a good value, especially if you book at the rates commonly advertised within Hawaii: $49 for a room only, $119 for two nights with a car. Otherwise, the rate quoted to people who call from the mainland using the toll-free number is $74 for standard rooms, $100 for rooms with kitchenettes.

Kapaa Sands (☎ 822-4901, (800) 222-4901), 380 Papaloa Rd, Kapaa, HI 96746, has 24 condo units set up in either duplexes or fourplexes. All have kitchens, lanais, louvered windows to catch the breeze, and at least a partial ocean view. While the complex is an older one, the units have been thoroughly renovated since the hurricane and are relatively good value at $75 for studios for one or two people and $99 for two-bedroom units for up to four people. Oceanfront units cost $10 more. There's a three-day minimum stay in the low season, seven days in the winter.

The *Aston Kauai Beachboy Hotel* (☎ 822-3441, (800) 922-7866; fax 822-0843), 484 Kuhio Hwy, Kapaa, HI 96746, is a modern beachfront hotel with 243 standard hotel rooms in blocks of three-story buildings. Rooms have lanais, air-con, TVs, mini-refrigerators and room safes. Rates range from $88 to $118, depending on the view.

Islander on the Beach (☎ 822-7417, (800) 847-7417; fax 822-1947), 484 Kuhio Hwy, Kapaa, HI 96746, has 195 hotel rooms in half a dozen three-story buildings. The rooms are pleasant with king or double beds, refrigerators, coffeemakers, air-con, TVs, room safes and lanais. Rates range from $95 for a garden view to $125 for an oceanfront room. There's a poolside bar.

The *Kauai Resort Hotel* (☎ 245-3931, (800) 367-5004; fax 596-0158, (800) 477-2329), 3-5920 Kuhio Hwy, Kapaa, HI

KAUAI

96746, run by Hawaiian Pacific Resorts, is north of Lydgate Beach Park and next to the Wailua Golf Course. The rooms are small and the grounds are on the lackluster side. They have some basic units called economy cabanas for $75; otherwise, standard rooms begin at $99 and often include a free rental car with advance reservations.

Plantation Hale (☎ 822-4941, (800) 462-6262; fax 822-5599, (800) 622-4852), 484 Kuhio Hwy, Kapaa, HI 96746, is on the highway side of Coconut Plantation. Now part of the Outrigger chain, the complex has 160 roomy one-bedroom units with modern furnishings, two doubles or one king bed in the bedroom, a queen sofa-bed in the living room, a separate full kitchen and two TVs. The rate of $120 is the same for up to four people, which makes it a good value for small groups. Outrigger often throws in a free rental car with advance reservations.

Kauai Coconut Beach Resort (☎ 822-3455, (800) 222-5642; fax 822-1830), Box 830, Kapaa, HI 96746, a former Sheraton, is a 309-room hotel at the quieter north end of Coconut Plantation. The rooms are comfortable with either two doubles or a king-size bed, TVs, room safes, mini-refrigerators, coffeemakers and amazingly tiny lanais that barely fit two people. The 4th-floor rooms are the nicest, as they have high ceilings that make the rooms feel a bit larger. Rates, which include a full buffet breakfast, are $90 for a standard room, $135 for an ocean view and $170 for oceanfront. If you book in advance and ask for the room and car deal, you can get a free rental car at no extra cost.

Places to Eat

The *Sizzler* steak house, 4361 Kuhio Hwy, has a very good salad bar that includes greens, fresh fruit, a taco bar, pasta bar, soups and cheeses. As an all-you-can-eat meal by itself the cost is $8 at lunch, $9 at dinner; if you're ordering a separate meal it costs $4 to add on the salad bar. Chicken and burgers begin at $5 at lunch, steaks cost $7 to $12 at dinner.

Mema (☎ 823-0899), in the same com-plex as the Sizzler, has a pleasant decor and excellent Thai food. The shrimp rolls served on a bed of fresh lettuce and mint leaves make a nice appetizer, while the chicken red chili with coconut milk is a recommendable entree. Most chicken, beef and pork dishes are priced around $7, the shrimp and fish dishes around $10. There are about 40 items on the menu in all and most dishes can be ordered vegetarian. This popular little restaurant only has about a dozen tables, so at dinner it's best to arrive early or make reservations. It's open from 11 am to 2 pm weekdays and 5 to 9:30 pm daily; takeout is available.

The popular *Kintaro* (☎ 822-3341), opposite the Sizzler, has Japanese dinners in the $13 to $17 range. The sushi is good although the tempura is mediocre and some of the food is a bit salty. There's also a tep-panyaki room where the chef prepares food at your table with 'flying knives' for a few dollars more. It's open from 5:30 to 9:30 pm Monday to Saturday.

The *Voyage Room* at the Kauai Coconut Beach Resort has an open-air setting and a decent breakfast buffet with fresh fruit, eggs, breakfast meats, bread, bagels and a few pastries. It's served from 6:30 to 10 am daily and costs $9.50.

There are a handful of food kiosks in the Coconut Marketplace. Best among them are the *Fish Hut*, with fresh fish sand-wiches for $5 and fish & chips for $6, and *Paradise Chicken and Ribs*, which has a chicken-breast sandwich for $4.50 and a good Caesar salad with lemon chicken for a dollar more. Both are open from 11 am to about 7:30 pm. Coconut Marketplace also has a couple of sit-down restaurants, an average cafe/bakery and a convenience store.

Entertainment

The *Plantation Cinema* in the Coconut Marketplace is a two-screen theater show-ing first-run movies.

Free hula shows take place at the Coco-nut Marketplace at 4:30 pm on Mondays, Wednesdays, Fridays and Saturdays.

Kauai Coconut Beach Resort (☎ 822-

3455) has a luau daily except Fridays at 6:30 pm. It includes an open bar, dinner and a rather standard Polynesian revue and costs $45 for adults, $27 for children ages six to 17, free for younger children. You can catch a glimpse of it from the hotel parking lot. If you're interested in seeing the imu preparation you can watch the pig being stuffed with hot rocks and buried at 10:30 am on luau days.

Smith's Tropical Paradise (☎ 822-4654), at Wailua Marina, has a rather theatrical luau with cocktails, music and dinner from 6 pm Monday to Friday. It costs $43.75 for adults, $26 for children ages seven to 12 and $17 for children ages three to six.

Things to Buy

The Coconut Marketplace, open from 9 am to 9 pm daily, has 70 different shops, including Liberty House, a kite shop, Fox Photo one-hour processing, art galleries, clothing stores and gift shops. There's also a Waldenbooks with a good Hawaiiana section.

Portrait of Sandwich Islander wearing a gourd helmet by John Webber

WAIPOULI

Waipouli is the mile-long strip between Coconut Plantation and Kapaa. Its biggest draw is its shopping centers, which are not only the region's largest but also contain some of Kauai's best places to eat.

At Kauai Village shopping center the modest Kauai Village Museum, a Hawaiiana gift and book shop, displays a small collection of Hawaiian artifacts and a pili-grass house.

Information

Money There's a Bankoh money machine, which accepts major credit and ATM cards, inside the Foodland supermarket in the Waipouli Town Center.

Post The Kapaa post office, in the Kapaa Shopping Center, is open from 8:30 am to 5 pm Monday to Friday, from 10 am to noon on Saturdays.

Laundry There's a coin laundry in the Kapaa Shopping Center.

Sleeping Giant

There's a marked viewpoint just north of the Waipouli Complex where you can see the outline of the Sleeping Giant, who is taking his eternal rest stretched out atop Nounou Ridge with his head in Wailua and his feet in Kapaa.

Legend says a friendly giant fell asleep on the hillside after eating too much poi at a luau. When his menehune friends needed his help they tried to awaken him by throwing stones, but the stones bounced from his full belly into his open mouth. As the giant swallowed the stones, he died and turned into rock.

A hiking trail runs across the ridge connecting Wailua Houselots and Wailua Homesteads (see the Wailua section). The giant's forehead, the highest point on the ridge, is 1241 feet.

Places to Stay

Mokihana of Kauai (☎ 822-3971), 796 Kuhio Hwy, is a time-share complex that rents to nonmembers on a space available basis. It has 80 studios on the beach and while the rooms are rather plain, each has twin beds, a hot plate, a refrigerator and a lanai with an ocean view for only $55.

The front desk at Mokihana also handles the 57 two-bedroom time-share units at nearby *Kauai Kailani I & II*. These units have full kitchens and cost $65 for up to four people. Ask for Kauai Kailani I on the ocean.

You can also make advance reservations through Hawaii Kailani, (☎ (206) 676-1434; fax (206) 676-1435), 119 N Commercial, Suite 1400, Bellingham, WA 98225.

Places to Eat

The *King & I* (☎ 822-1642) in Waipouli Plaza has good Thai food at reasonable prices. The spring rolls make a nice starter while the green curry, which gets its color from fresh basil, lime leaves and lemongrass, is an excellent choice for an entree. The curries, like most other dishes on the menu, cost $6.50 for meat varieties, $9 for shrimp or fish. All can be prepared mild, medium or hot. The restaurant has both Thai and brown rice and virtually any dish can be ordered vegetarian. It's open daily from 4:30 to 9:30 pm, to 10 pm on Fridays and Saturdays.

The *Aloha Diner* in the Waipouli Complex is the place to try authentic Hawaiian food. The laulau is pretty good and the lomi salmon excellent. You can order a la carte, or get complete lunches from about $6, dinners for about $10. It's open from 10:30 am to 3 pm and from 5:30 to 9 pm; closed Sundays.

Papaya's Natural Foods (☎ 823-0191) in Kauai Village is a well-stocked health food store with a cafe serving wholesome salads, sandwiches and casserole-style warm dishes. The Garden Burger made of brown rice, sunflower seeds and cheese, served with tomato, lettuce and sprouts on a whole-wheat bun is good at $4.50. A grilled chicken burger costs a dollar more and there are healthy plate lunches priced from $6 to $8. Papaya's is open from 10 am

to 8 pm Monday to Saturday. Seating is at simple outdoor tables in front of the store.

Ambrose's Natural Foods, the island's original health food store, is opposite Waipouli Town Center. This small store carries local produce and a few health food items.

A Pacific Cafe (☎ 822-0013) in Kauai Village serves Pacific Rim cuisine at its best. French chef Jean-Marie Josselin has a creative menu with dishes like wood-grilled onaga in a hibiscus-ginger sauce, Thai coconut curried soup and Vietnamese spring rolls. The starters and soups range from $5 to $9, main dishes are $16 to $24. It's a class act, with food that is artfully presented, attentive service and generous portions. If you're saving one night for a splurge on Kauai, this is certainly a top choice. Hours are from 5:30 to 9:30 pm; reservations are usually essential, particularly on holidays and weekends.

At the opposite end of the gastronomic scale are the slew of fast-food eateries, including *Kentucky Fried Chicken* and *Taco Bell* north of Waipouli Plaza, *Subway* sandwiches in Kauai Village, *Burger King* at the Kapaa Shopping Center and *McDonald's* and *Pizza Hut* in the Waipouli Town Center.

A fine alternative to fast food is the 24-hour *Safeway* supermarket in Kauai Village which has an excellent salad bar at $3.50 a pound that includes fresh fruits, artichoke hearts, fried chicken and chili. Safeway also has a deli counter with a wide variety of pastas and salads, a bakery with crispy sourdough bread, a good produce section, and a fish counter with laulau, poi and eight kinds of poki. In addition, the store has some of the cheapest wine prices on the island.

There's a *Foodland* supermarket open 24 hours a day in the Waipouli Town Center; early birds can find hot coffee and doughnuts here from 5 am. There's a *Big Save* supermarket, open from 7 am to 11 pm daily, in the Kapaa Shopping Center.

KAPAA

Kapaa is an old plantation town with a small commercial center that is half-local, half-tourist oriented. As unimposing as it appears, Kapaa is one of Kauai's largest towns. However most of the residential area is well inland of the center and you can walk the main drag in just 10 minutes.

While many of its historic buildings were leveled by Iniki, most of the reconstruction has been in keeping with the town's original character rather than adopting the shopping mall appearance that predominates to the south of Kapaa. The town has the island's only hostel, a small hotel, a few restaurants and some water sports and clothing shops.

Information

Money There's a Bank of Hawaii and a First Hawaiian Bank on Kuhio Hwy in Kapaa center.

Library The Kapaa Public Library (☎ 822-5041), 1464 Kuhio Hwy, is open from 9 am to 5 pm on Mondays, Wednesdays and Fridays and from noon to 8 pm on Tuesdays and Thursdays.

Kapaa Beach Park

Kapaa Beach Park begins along the north side of Kapaa, where there's a ball field, picnic tables and a public swimming pool. The beach continues south for about a mile with the section fronting the Pono Kai condos having one of the nicer sandy sections. Along the length of the beach there's a shoreline foot and bicycle path that follows a former cane rail line and passes over a couple of old bridges along the way. If you're staying in the area, the path makes an appealing alternative to walking along the highway to and from town.

Places to Stay

Kauai International Hostel (☎ 823-6142, (800) 858-2295), 4532 Lehua St, Kapaa, HI 96746, is a new private hostel in the center of Kapaa. There are about 30 dorm beds, most four to a room, and five simple private rooms with double beds. The dorm beds cost $15, the private rooms $35. All rooms, including the private rooms, have shared bathrooms. The hostel has a common dining room, kitchen, TV room and coin laundry. There's a nightly barbecue dinner for $6. Bags can be stored while you're hiking and inexpensive day trips are sometimes available. German and French are spoken. Note that there's a no-refund policy, so if you're going to be paying for several days in advance it's best to make sure that this is where you want to be for that entire period.

The *Hotel Coral Reef* (☎ 822-4481, (800) 843-4659), 1516 Kuhio Hwy, Kapaa, HI 96746, is a small local hotel with two sections. The older main building, which was renovated after Iniki, has a half dozen straightforward rooms priced from $55 while the newer wing has 16 rooms with refrigerators, lanais and ocean views for $80. There's no pool.

Keapana Center (☎ 822-7968, (800) 822-7968), 5620 Keapana Rd, Kapaa, HI 96746, is a relaxing New Age B&B with a scenic hilltop location three miles above Kapaa center. There are three rooms with shared bath at $40/55 singles/doubles and two rooms with private bath at $55/70. The rooms are small and suitably simple and rates include continental breakfast and use of the hot tub. There's a common-use refrigerator and microwave, a large airy lounge and a platform for sunrise stretching that faces a splendid view of the Anahola Mountains. Metaphysical books are loaned free and massage is available for a fee. No pre-teen children are allowed.

The beachfront *Pono Kai Resort* (☎ 822-9831), 4-1250 Kuhio Hwy, Kapaa, HI 96746, is a well-maintained 219-room condominium at the south side of Kapaa. Units are roomy and well-equipped with full kitchens including dishwashers and microwaves, living rooms with queen sofa beds, air conditioning, ceiling fans, cable TV, VCR and lanais. There's a pool, spa, tennis courts and beach and it's within walking distance of the town center. Although most people book through Colony Resorts (☎ (800) 777-1700), which manages some of the units here, its rates are a steep $140 to $170 for a one-bedroom unit and $170 to $200 for a two-bedroom two-bath unit. For a much better deal contact RCIM (☎ (909) 273-7455, (800) 438-6493, ext 331), which handles the majority of Pono Kai's units as time-share properties. RCIM commonly has a few unoccupied units that it rents out to the general public at $100/125 for one/two-bedroom condos; there's a 20% discount for stays of a week or more.

Places to Eat

All of these restaurants except Kapaa Fish & Chowder House are within a two-minute walk of each other on Kuhio Hwy (Hwy 56), near its intersection with Olohena Rd.

Michelle's is a small cafe serving homemade food. Breakfast includes espresso, croissants, muesli, scrambled eggs, and papaya with yogurt. Lunch is mainly soups, salads and sandwiches from $4.50 to $6. It's open from 7:30 am to 5 pm on weekdays, 8 am to 2:30 pm on Saturdays and Sundays.

Bubba's, a hole in the wall south of Michelle's, has hot dogs, chili dogs, fish and chips and a range of burgers, all priced under $5. It's open from 10:30 am to 6 pm Monday to Saturday.

Hana-Ya is a little Japanese restaurant with a small sushi bar and a few tables. Soba costs $5, oyako donburi $6, and there's a full menu of other dishes priced from $5 to $15. It's open from 11:30 am to 2 pm and from 5:30 to 9:30 pm daily, except Sundays.

Norberto's El Cafe (☎ 822-3362), Kauai's original Mexican restaurant, has been in the neighborhood a long time and serves all the usual Mexican fare with full dinner plates priced from $12. You can wash it down with margaritas or Mexican brew. It's open from 5:30 to 9 pm daily, except Sundays.

Kapaa Fish & Chowder House (☎ 822-7488) on Kuhio Hwy, half a mile north of Kapaa center, has good fish and generous servings of sashimi at reasonable prices. Main dishes, which are served with a house salad, include calamari ($14), shrimp scampi or cioppino ($17) and fresh fish at market prices. There are also a few steak and seafood combinations for around $20. Children's portions are available for half price. It's open for dinner only from 5:30 pm daily.

KAPAA TO KILAUEA

The drive from Kapaa to Kilauea is through fields of sugar cane in varying stages of growth, from newly planted seed cane to mature stalk. Beyond the fields, the jagged edges of the Anahola mountain peaks cut their way through the clouds. In the other direction there are glimpses of bright blue ocean and distant bays.

A couple of scenic lookouts just north of Kapaa are worth pulling over for. Sunsets can be particularly nice if there's a low tide with waves breaking over the shallows and fishers out with their throw nets.

Kealia Beach

The long, pretty beach at the 10-mile marker is Kealia Beach. During transitional swells, Kealia can be a good place for surfing. There are no facilities here.

After rain storms the beach tends to be heavily littered with tree limbs that are carried down Kealia Stream, which empties at the south side of the beach.

Donkey Beach

Donkey Beach is best known as a nudist beach, though it's used by both clad and unclad sunbathers. This lovely windswept sandy beach is hidden from the road.

The trail to Donkey Beach begins about half a mile past the 11-mile marker; look for cars parked at the side of the road. It's 10 minutes down a well-worn path beside a sugar cane field and through a narrow stretch of coastal ironwoods.

Because of the strong winds along the coast here, all the ironwood trees lean away from the shore and those right at the beach are so blown over they almost look like shrubs. Naupaka and ilima grow in the sand along the shadeless beach. There are no facilities. From October to May, high surf creates dangerous rip currents and a powerful shorebreak.

Anahola

Anahola is a small, scattered village, much of it spread out along Anahola Bay. This wide bay was an ancient surfing site and has a break that's still popular with surfers today.

Anahola Beach Park, a county park on Hawaiian Home Lands, sits at the south side of the bay. To get there turn off Hwy 56 onto Kukuihale Rd at the 13-mile marker, drive a mile down and then turn onto the dirt beach road.

The beach park has been a source of contention over the last few years between county officials who want to maintain it as a public park and native Hawaiians who want to reclaim the land. So far the county has prevailed and the beach park remains open to the public. However, because of this sensitive issue, we recommend that visitors not camp here, despite the fact that it's officially allowed.

Anahola's modest commercial center consists of the Anahola post office, Duane's burger stand and a small general store grouped together at the side of Hwy 56, just south of the 14-mile marker.

Just to the north, on the mauka side of the road, is the quaint little **Anahola Baptist Church** backed by a picturesque mountain setting.

Places to Stay *Mahina Kai* (☎ 822-9451), Box 699, 4933 Aliomanu Rd, Anahola, HI 96703, is a B&B on Anahola Bay that's a popular destination for the gay community. The contemporary home has Asian-Pacific touches such as shoji doors, and a swimming pool and hot tub in a Japanese garden. It's a nice quiet place to relax. There are three rooms with private bathrooms at $95/115 singles/doubles, breakfast included, as well as a two-bedroom self-catering apartment that costs $150 for two people, $175 for four.

Places to Eat The popular *Duane's Ono Charburger* sells good burgers and teri sandwiches for $4 to $7. Best deal is the basic burger, as more expensive burgers such as the 'teri' simply add a dollop of

sauce on top. A huge order of fries costs $1.80. There are outdoor picnic tables where you can chow down. It's open from 10 am to 6 pm daily (from 11 am on Sundays).

Whaler's General Store, next door to Duane's, has hard-boiled eggs for 30c, hot dogs for a dollar and cold beer. It's open daily from 6:30 am to 9:30 pm.

Hole in the Mountain

The Hole in the Mountain can't presently be seen from the HVB marker, as the hole closed during a landslide at the time of Hurricane Iwa. But just slightly north of the 15-mile marker, look back at the mountain down to the right of the tallest pinnacle and you'll be able to see the small hole that is slowly re-opening.

Legend says the original hole was created when a giant threw his spear through the mountain causing the water stored within to gush forth as waterfalls. Incidentally, after the landslide closed the hole, Hawaii began to experience one of the worst droughts in its history.

Koolau Road

Koolau Rd is a peaceful drive through rich green pastures with white egrets and a smattering of bright wildflowers. Take it as a scenic loop off the highway or to get to Moloaa Beach or Larsens Beach. Both the road and the beaches are well off the tourist track. Neither beach has any facilities.

Koolau Rd connects with Hwy 56 half a mile north of the 16-mile marker (at Sunrise Fruit Stand) and again one-tenth of a mile south of the 20-mile marker.

Moloaa Beach To get to Moloaa Beach coming from the south, turn right onto Koolau Rd at the fruit stand and after 1¼ miles turn right onto Moloaa Rd. The road ends three-quarters of a mile down at a few beach houses. The road near the beach is narrow, finding a place to park can be quite challenging.

Moloaa is very rural, with horses grazing on the hills above the crescent-shaped bay. The northern end of the beach before the

KAUAI

rocky outcrop is somewhat protected for swimming though it's not all that deep. The whole bay can have strong currents when the surf is rough.

Larsens Beach Larsens is a long golden sand beach, good for solitary strolls and beachcombing. Although it's a bit shallow for swimming, snorkeling can be good when the waters are very calm, which is generally in the summer only. Beware of a current that runs westward along the beach and out through a channel in the reef.

Often the Holstein cattle that graze the hills above the beach are the only company you'll encounter. However, if the tide is low you may well see a few Hawaiian families on the outer edge of the reef collecting an edible seaweed called *limu kohu*. The seaweed found at Larsens is considered to be some of the finest in all Hawaii.

The turn-off to Larsens Beach is off Koolau Rd, a little more than a mile down from the north intersection of Koolau Rd and Hwy 56, or just over a mile north of the intersection of Moloaa and Koolau roads. Turn makai on the dirt road there and then take the immediate left. It's one mile to the parking area and then a five-minute walk downhill to the beach.

North Shore

Kauai's North Shore has an unhurried pace and incredible scenery. It has deep mountain valleys, rolling cattle pastures, ancient taro fields, white sand beaches and the rugged Na Pali Coast.

The North Shore is lush and often wet. In winter that can mean days of rain on end, but in summer it usually means brief showers followed by rainbows. On bright full-moon nights you might even see a moonbow – a rainbow colored with moonbeams.

Rainy days are almost dream-like. The tops of the mountains become shrouded in clouds that alternately drift and lift revealing a series of waterfalls that plunge down the face of the mountains.

The North Shore takes in the seabird sanctuary at Kilauea and a couple of small coastal villages before reaching the resort community of Princeville with its condos and golf courses.

But, it's the area beyond, from Hanalei Bridge to Kee Beach at road's end, that best embodies the North Shore spirit. This is a part of Hawaii that has resisted mass tourism and stalled development. Its appeal is not in creature comforts but in stunning natural beauty. It attracts people tuned in to the environment. Over the years musicians like Graham Nash and Buffy Sainte-Marie and numerous other alternative-minded folks have called Kauai's North Shore home.

KILAUEA

Kilauea is a former sugar plantation town whose main attraction is its picturesque lighthouse and seabird sanctuary at Kilauea Point. The sanctuary is the most visited site on the North Shore and shouldn't be missed.

Kolo Rd, the main turn-off into Kilauea, is a third of a mile beyond the 23-mile marker on Hwy 56. On Kolo Rd, you pass a gas station with a health food store at the side, a post office with a mini-mart and then an Episcopal church, all in quick succession. Kilauea Rd starts opposite the church and ends two miles later at Kilauea Point.

Episcopal Church

The little Christ Memorial Episcopal Church attracts attention because of its striking lava rock architecture. It was built in 1941 but the interesting lava rock headstones in the churchyard are much older, dating back to when the original Hawaiian Congregational Church stood on this site.

Kilauea Bay

If you're looking for someplace new to explore, you might try Rock Quarry Beach at Kilauea Bay. Also known as Kahili Beach, it's a nice, tan sand beach and the site of an abandoned rock quarry and steamer landing. This remote beach is mostly used by local fishers, but when the surf is unusually high, surfers also take to these waters. Swimmers should be aware of strong near-shore currents when the surf is up.

Public access is via Wailapa Rd, which begins midway between the 21- and 22-mile markers. Follow Wailapa Rd north for a half-mile beyond Hwy 56 and then turn left on the dirt road that begins at a yellow water valve. The dirt road, which continues for a half-mile before ending at the beach, is usually in fairly good shape and passable in a car.

Kilauea Point

Kilauea Point, a national wildlife refuge, is the northernmost point of the inhabited Hawaiian Islands. Topped by a lighthouse that was built in 1913, it's picture postcard material.

Four species of birds come to Kilauea to nest, leaving after their young have been hatched and reared. Red-footed boobies, the most visible, are abundant on the cliffs to the east of the point, where they build nests of sticks and leaves in the trees. Their peak egg laying time is March to June.

Wedge-tailed shearwaters arrive by April and stay through the summer, nesting in burrows that they dig into Kilauea Point. Another readily spotted species is the red-tailed tropicbird, which nests along the cliff edges. If you're lucky, you'll spot a pair flying in loops, performing their courtship ritual.

Laysan albatross are at Kilauea from about November to July. Some nest on Mokuaeae Rock, straight off the tip of the point. Other albatross nesting sites are on the grassy clearing to the west of Kilauea Point. If you look out beyond this clearing you can see Secret Beach, divided into three scalloped coves by lava fingers.

Great frigate birds nest on the Northwestern Hawaiian Islands, not Kauai, though these aerial pirates do visit Kilauea Point to steal food from other birds. You won't see the distinctive red throat balloon that the male puffs out to attract females though, as they're not here for courtship. Frigate birds, which have a wing span of seven feet and a distinctive forked tail, are beautiful when they soar.

While birds are certainly the main attraction at Kilauea Point, with a little luck you might also spot sea turtles swimming in the cove at the base of the cliffs. During winter it's not unusual to see whales pass by this point.

The refuge was completely closed for nearly two years after Iniki hit. The delay was largely due to lead paint that was discovered on walkway handrails during post-hurricane repairs. The paint could only be removed when there were no birds nesting at the site, as ingesting leaded paint chips could have been fatal to the birds.

The refuge is currently open from 10 am to 4 pm Monday to Friday, but will eventually reopen on weekends as well. For now, the usual entry fee of $2 per family has been waived.

Even outside opening hours it's worth driving to the end of Kilauea Rd for the picturesque view of the lighthouse and point.

Guava Plantation

The Guava Kai Plantation has 480 acres of guava trees that produce juice for Ocean Spray and a handful of other juice companies. A visitor center doles out small samples of guava juice and sells guava products. When the processing plant is in operation (mainly August to December and sporadically in the spring) you can wander around and get a glimpse of the process.

To get there, turn mauka onto Kuawa Rd from Hwy 56, just north of the 23-mile marker and a quarter of a mile south of the Kolo Rd turn-off to Kilauea. The visitor center is about a mile from the highway.

As you go up the road through endless rows of guava trees it might seem like the fruit is too big to be the same guava that grows wild elsewhere on the island – in fact these guava trees are hybrids whose fruit grows to half a pound, twice the normal size.

Places to Eat

The *Farmer's Market*, a grocery store with a good deli, is in the Kong Lung Center, half a mile up Kilauea Rd. The deli has a variety of sandwiches on whole-wheat bread, rolls with hummus, sprouts and shredded carrots, and salads sold by the pound. The store is open 8:30 am to 8:30 pm daily, the deli from 11 am to 2 pm Monday to Saturday.

Kilauea Bakery & Pau Hana Pizza, tucked in the back of the Kong Lung Center, sells a variety of hearty whole-grain breads, French breads and tempting pastries. From 11 am to 4 pm there's gourmet pizza by the slice for $2.50. Whole pizzas, available until closing, cost from $10.75 for a 12-inch cheese version. The pizza is good and the optional toppings range from pepperoni to tofurella and feta cheese. It's open from 6:30 am to 9 pm daily except Sundays. There are tables on the lawn where you can eat, weather permitting.

Casa di Amici (☎ 828-1388), also in the Kong Lung Center, has good Italian food. Main courses range from $14 for pastas to $24 for saltimbocca. The pollo al marsala, served with fresh vegetables del giorno, is a nicely prepared dish in the mid-price range. Soups or salads are priced around $6, while other starters are a few dollars more. It's open for dinner only, from 6 pm nightly. There's a classical pianist on weekends.

For a down-home treat, stop at *Banana Joe's*, the bright yellow shack on the mauka side of Hwy 56, just north of the Kolo Rd turn-off to Kilauea. Banana Joe and his sister Alex dish up a great fruit frosty, made solely of frozen fruit that is squeezed through a processor and comes out as smooth as ice cream. The papaya and pineapple flavors are the best. A bowl of this ($1.50) and a granola bar ($1.25) make a nice snack. They also dry their own banana and jackfruit strips and sell fresh fruit from their six-acre plot of bananas, citrus and guava. The stand is open from 9 am to 6 pm Monday to Saturday.

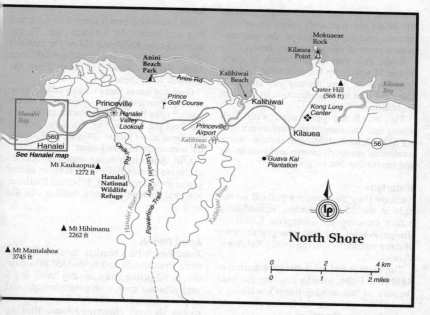

North Shore

KALIHIWAI

Kalihiwai Rd was a loop road going down past Kalihiwai Beach, connecting with the highway at two points, until the tidal wave of 1957 washed out the bridge over Kalihiwai River. The bridge was never rebuilt and now there are two Kalihiwai roads, one on each side of the river.

The Kalihiwai Rd half a mile west of Kilauea, leads down a mile to **Kalihiwai Beach**. At the very end of the road you can still see the pillars that once supported the bridge. The river empties out into a wide, deep bay. The broad sandy beach is a popular spot for all kinds of activities including picnicking, swimming, body-surfing, boogie boarding and, when the northwest swells roll in, some daredevil surfing along the cliff at the east end of the bay. The river is popular with kayakers. The beach has no facilities.

As you take Kalihiwai Rd back up to the highway, look to the left as soon as you see the 'Narrow Bridge' sign, to spot a pic-

turesque waterfall that's partially hidden in a little valley.

Secret Beach

Secret Beach is a gorgeous golden sand beach backed by sea cliffs and jungle-like woods. The beach is well off the beaten path and access to it has changed frequently over the years, so very few visitors discover it. Secret Beach is mostly frequented by Kauai's alternative community and nude sunbathers, and while tourists aren't exactly welcomed, unobtrusive visitors who can blend in are unlikely to encounter any problems.

To get there, turn down the Kalihiwai Rd half mile west of Kilauea and then turn right onto the first dirt road, which is a tenth of a mile from Hwy 56. The road ends at a parking area a third of a mile down.

The well-defined trail begins from the parking lot along a barbed wire fence that separates the woods from a horse pasture. After two minutes it leads downhill through

KAUAI

ironwood trees and mixed jungle growth. All in all the trail only takes about five minutes and deposits you at the westernmost section of this long sandy beach.

While this part of the beach is quite idyllic, if you're up for a stroll or feel the need for even more privacy you can walk along the beach in the direction of Kilauea Lighthouse.

The beach has open seas, with high winter surf and dangerous currents prevailing from October to May. In summer water conditions are much calmer and swimming and snorkeling can be good.

Waterfalls

Back on Hwy 56, there's a pull-off on the right at the 25-mile marker, immediately before crossing the sweeping Kalihiwai Bridge. A brief stop will treat you to views of three waterfalls and the lovely Kalihiwai Valley.

The highest and most distant waterfall is **Kalihiwai Falls**, seen by crossing the road (beware of fast-moving traffic), walking a third of the way onto the bridge ahead and looking up into the valley.

You can see a bit of another falls by simply walking to the side of the pull-off and looking down over the edge. For the third you must walk back along the road a minute or two toward Lihue. The falls is just above the road.

Places to Stay

At *Hale Ho'o Maha* (☎ 828-1341, (800) 851-0291), Box 422, Kilauea, HI 96754, Toby and Kirby Searles rent out three bedrooms in their contemporary home on Kalihiholo Rd at the mauka side of Hwy 56. One room has a round bed and a private bathroom and costs $70. The other two rooms cost $55 and $60 and share a bathroom. Each room has a portable fan, cable TV and phone. The house has hardwood koa floors, a fireplace and outdoor cats. Guests are free to use the washer and dryer, barbecue grill, beach equipment, lanai and kitchen. Prices include a continental breakfast and are the same single or double. Smokers and social drinkers are welcome.

ANINI

Anini has a long beach fronted by vast reef flats and backed by a beach park. To get there take the Kalihiwai Rd on the Hanalei side of the bridge and then bear left onto Anini Rd. It's about 1½ miles from the highway to the beach.

Over the years there's been talk of connecting Princeville and Anini by a direct coastal road but local resistance to the plan has kept the road at bay. For now, Anini's dead-end street means little traffic, keeping the area unhurried and quiet.

Still, Anini is growing, and a number of exclusive homes have been built in recent years, including one by Sylvester Stallone, who has sizable property holdings in the area.

Anini Beach

Anini Beach Park borders the shoreline for more than a mile and is divided into day-use, windsurfing and camping areas. It's a very pleasant spot, with gentle breezes and tropical almond shade trees. There are restrooms, showers, changing rooms, drinking water, picnic pavilions and a pay phone.

Anini has a good campground, right on the water, with the campsites shaded by trees. It's pretty spacious for a beach park although the camping area gets a little more crowded on weekends when locals, mostly families, come down.

You can swim and snorkel in the day-use area, and also in front of the camping area, though it's best when the tide is high. A pretty good spot is opposite the midpoint of Kauai Polo Club's fence.

Past the west end of the park, Anini Channel cuts across the reef. While some people use the channel for water activities when the seas are calm, waters flowing off the reef create dangerous rip currents in the channel. The protected lagoon west of the channel provides good snorkeling and safer water conditions.

At the far end of Anini you can watch people walk way out onto the shallow reef of Anini Flats, picking opihi, net fishing for bait fish and catching octopus.

PRINCEVILLE

Princeville, Kauai's biggest development, traces its haole roots to Robert Wyllie, a Scottish doctor who later became foreign minister to Kamehameha IV. In the mid-1800s Wyllie bought a large coffee plantation in Hanalei and began planting sugar.

When Queen Emma and Kamehameha IV came to visit in 1860, Wyllie named his plantation and surrounding lands Princeville in honor of their young son, Prince Albert. The plantation later became a cattle ranch and in 1968 ground was broken for the Princeville Resort.

Today, Princeville is a planned community spread over 11,000 acres on a promontory between Hanalei Bay and Anini Beach. It has 10 condo complexes, a luxury hotel, hundreds of private homes, a couple of championship golf courses, 22 tennis courts, restaurants, a shopping center and even its own little airport.

While it may seem out of place on the North Shore, and it certainly stands in sharp contrast to the free-spirited communities that lay beyond, Princeville's manicured grounds are spacious, the condos are low-rise and the development is uncrowded compared to its counterparts on other islands.

Information

Princeville Center has a gas station, supermarket, medical clinic, camera shop, Bank of Hawaii, ice cream shop and a few restaurants and boutiques.

Princeville Chevron is open from 7 am to 7 pm daily. If you're heading toward Kee Beach at the end of the road, this is the last place to buy gas.

Kuhio Hwy changes from Hwy 56 to Hwy 560 at the 28-mile marker in front of Princeville Center. The 10-mile stretch from this point to Kee Beach at the end of the road is one of the most scenic drives in all of Hawaii.

Princeville Hotel

The Princeville Hotel, at the site of an old Russian fort, offers a splendid view of Hanalei Bay and the Bali Hai mountains.

The luxury hotel was erected amidst a great deal of controversy in 1985. Locals, who were miffed at losing one of their favorite sunset spots, nicknamed the bluff-side building 'The Prison'. The hotel was indeed dark and inward-looking and it so failed to incorporate its surroundings that the owners closed it down in 1989. Over the next two years the hotel was gutted and virtually rebuilt. The newly reopened Princeville Hotel has a lobby with floor-to-ceiling windows offering 180° views of Bali Hai. It also has marble floors, posh furniture, pools of flowing water and a smattering of antiques and artwork, but the real attraction is the view.

Powerline Trail

In the 1930s electric transmission lines were run along the mountains and a 13-mile maintenance route now known as the Powerline Trail was created. There is occasional talk of turning it into a real inland road connecting Princeville to Wailua but environmental concerns make it unlikely to happen anytime soon.

To get to the trailhead take the paved road going uphill from Pooku Stables, a third of a mile after the 27-mile marker on Hwy 56. The pavement ends at a water tank 1¾ miles up and even if you don't plan to hike this makes a pretty drive, offering fine mountain views and glimpses of Hanalei Bay.

The trail continues from the end of the pavement along a rutted 4WD dirt road used mainly by hunters and the power company. It's a full day's walk to its end at the Keahua Arboretum, and is recommended only in dry weather.

Places to Stay

Sometimes you can find someone renting out a bedroom in their condo or home for about $40 a day. Most people list their rooms on the bulletin board outside the Foodland supermarket in the Princeville Center, though occasionally someone will run an ad in the newspaper.

Some of Princeville's condo complexes are perched on cliffs, others are by the golf course. While all of the complexes have some units that are vacation rentals, a fair number of the units are occupied as year-round housing.

Princeville was hit hard by Hurricane Iniki and all of its condominium complexes suffered extensive damage; many of those condos are just now coming back. As they've been extensively renovated, most places have a spiffy new appearance.

Most condo complexes are represented by a number of different rental agents. Three agents with fairly extensive Princeville rental listings are:

Blue Water Vacation Rentals, Princeville Center, Box 366, Princeville, HI 96714 (☎ 826-9229, (800) 628-5533; fax 826-9841)

Kauai Paradise Vacations, Box 1080, Hanalei, HI 96714 (☎ 826-7444, (800) 826-7782; fax 826-7673)

Oceanfront Realty, Princeville Center, Box 3570, Princeville, HI 96722 (☎ 826-6585, (800) 222-5541; fax 826-6478)

Hanalei Bay Resort (☎ 826-6522, (800) 827-4427; fax 826-6680), Box 220, Hanalei, HI 96714, recently reopened after two years of hurricane-related renovations, has both hotel-style rooms and condo units. The hotel rooms range from $130 for a mountain view to $220 for an ocean view. Studios begin at $150, one-bedroom condos at $240 and two-bedroom condos at $350. The units are pleasant, there are fine views of Hanalei Bay and the grounds include two pools and eight tennis courts.

The above rates apply to Castle Resorts, which manages the front desk and 230 of the 280 units here and offers a free rental car with advance bookings. The free car aside, you can usually find better deals through a couple of the condo rental agents listed in this section. A good one to start with is Kauai Paradise, which handles two dozen units, with rates starting from $70/90 for rooms/studios.

The *Cliffs at Princeville* is an older complex with one of the more ordinary settings, but its units have been refurbished since Iniki and it remains among the cheapest in Princeville. The units are large and

have one bedroom, front and rear lanais, two bathrooms and all the usual condo amenities. It's adjacent to the golf course and there's a pool. Village Resorts (☎ 826-6219, (800) 367-7052) maintains a front desk at the complex and handles many units, charging $120 to $195, but you should be able to get a better deal through an agent.

Sealodge is an older complex, and the quarters can be a bit cramped, but it's high on a cliff and many of the 86 units have great sunrise views across the expansive coral reef of Anini. If you leave the windows open the surf is guaranteed to give you nautical dreams. One-bedroom units generally cost from $95 to $110.

The *Princeville Hotel* (☎ 826-9644, (800) 325-3535), Box 3069, Princeville, HI 96722, a Sheraton property, has 252 luxury rooms with king beds, marble bathrooms and modern amenities that run the gamut from original oil paintings with dimmer-controlled spotlights to liquid-crystal windows between the bedroom and bath that can be turned from opaque to clear with the flick of a switch. Rates are $250 for a garden view, $380 for an ocean view and $2350 for the royal suite.

Places to Eat

Princeville is a good place to get your food from a grocery store, as restaurant prices are generally high and food at the more 'affordable' places tends to be quite ordinary.

Zelo's Cafe in the Princeville Center is open from 7:30 am to about 9:30 pm. At breakfast, which is served until 11 am, you can get a breakfast tostada or a three-egg omelet for $7. At lunch and dinner there are sandwiches and burgers from $5 to $8, specialty salads and a few hot dishes like spinach lasagna for around $10. The cafe also has espresso drinks, scones and huge muffins. From 6 pm every Sunday there's live jazz and there's usually music a couple of other evenings as well.

Chuck's Steak House in the Princeville Center has standard fare such as burgers and sandwiches for lunch and a dinner menu that ranges from $14 for ribs to $22 for steak and shrimp. Dinners include a simple salad bar. Lunch is from 11:30 am to 2:30 pm weekdays only, dinner from 6 to 10 pm nightly.

The Princeville Restaurant & Bar at the Prince golf course, half a mile west of the Princeville Airport, has a broad view, a country club setting and average food at reasonable prices. At breakfast, which is served from 7 to 11 am, granola and yogurt, a Belgian waffle or banana pancakes with an egg and bacon are all priced under $6. At lunch, served until 3 pm, there are sandwiches for around $8, salads for $10 and some good-value daily lunch specials priced from $6 to $10. It's open daily for breakfast and lunch only.

The *Bali Hai Restaurant* in the Hanalei Bay Resort has open-air dining with a wonderful view of Hanalei Bay and the Bali Hai mountains. At breakfast, from 7 to 11 am, you can get a 'taro patch breakfast' of two fried eggs, Portuguese sausage, poi pancakes and taro hash browns for $8.25 or macnut waffles for $6.75. At lunch, from 11:30 am to 2 pm, sandwiches with fries average $10. Dinner, from 5:30 to 10 pm, costs from $17 for smoked tofu stir fry to $26 for pork tenderloin. The food's good, but the view's the real attraction.

While the *Cafe Hanalei* in the Princeville Hotel has an unbeatable view of Hanalei Bay, its daily breakfast buffet is an undistinguished spread of pastries, fruit, breakfast meats and a few hot dishes at a steep $17.50. At lunch, sandwiches are priced around $10, salads a bit more. There are dinner buffets a couple of nights a week, including a popular Thai buffet on Wednesdays for $24.50 and an elaborate seafood buffet on Fridays for $36. It's open from 7 to 10:30 am, 11 am to 2 pm and 6 to 9 pm.

La Cascata, also in the Princeville Hotel, has a lovely view of Bali Hai and specializes in upscale Italian food, with seafood dishes averaging $25 and pasta dishes about $15.

Foodland supermarket in the Princeville

Center is open from 7 am to 11 pm daily except holidays.

Entertainment

At Hanalei Bay Resort there's contemporary Hawaiian music in the *Bali Hai Restaurant* on Fridays and Saturdays from about 5:30 to 8 pm and a jazz jam session on Sundays from 3 to 5 pm. There's sometimes an evening hula show at the Princeville Hotel.

HANALEI VALLEY

Just beyond Princeville, the Hanalei Valley Lookout provides you with a spectacular bird's-eye view of the valley floor with its meandering river and spread of patchwork taro fields.

The Hanalei National Wildlife Refuge encompasses 917 acres of the valley, stretching up both sides of Hanalei River. The wetland taro farms in the refuge produce two-thirds of Hawaii's commercially grown poi taro, while at the same time serving as habitat for endangered waterbirds.

In pre-contact time the valley was planted in taro but in the mid-1800s rice farming was introduced into Hanalei Valley to feed the Chinese laborers who worked the sugar cane fields. The rice grew so well that by the 1880s it became a major export crop. Now taro once again predominates.

From the lookout, to the lower right, you can glimpse the North Shore's first one-lane bridge, opened in 1912. The road leading into the valley along the western bank of the river is Ohiki Rd. From Ohiki Rd there's a trail that climbs the first ridge on the right, going up to the twin peaks of Hihimanu, which in Hawaiian means 'beautiful.'

Hanalei Bridge

The seven one-lane bridges between Hanalei River and the end of the road not only link this part of the North Shore to the rest of the island, they also protect it from runaway development.

Patchwork taro fields, Hanalei Valley

Big cement trucks and heavy construction equipment are beyond their limits. Even large package-tour buses are kept at bay.

Over the years developers have introduced numerous proposals to build a two-lane bridge over Hanalei River but North Shore residents have successfully beaten them all down.

While it's not a frequent occurrence, during unusually heavy rains the road between the taro fields and the river can flood and the Hanalei Bridge remains closed until it subsides.

After the Hanalei Bridge, the valley widens. Buffalo belonging to Hanalei Garden Farms graze in the pastures to the right. Having shed their thick woolly fur for a short tropical coat, these creatures are raised for their meat and are the source of the buffalo burgers and kebabs found on Kauai menus.

Ohiki Road

If you want to go into Hanalei Valley, turn left onto Ohiki Rd immediately after Hanalei Bridge. The drive parallels the Hanalei River, starting in taro fields and later passing banana trees, bamboo thickets, hau trees, ferns and wild ginger. It dead ends after two miles.

Snow-white egrets are common along the road. Night herons and endangered Hawaiian waterbirds live in the valley too, including coots, stilts, the Hawaiian duck and the coot-like Hawaiian gallinule with its bright red bill.

Okolehau Trail

The Okolehau Trail offers ridgetop views of Hanalei and Waioli valleys. To reach the trailhead, go down Ohiki Rd about half a mile and turn right onto the unmarked paved road.

The hike starts up the 4WD powerline maintenance road to the left of the cemetery. It goes up through fragrant eucalyptus trees and past wild orchids. When you reach the Norfolk pines you can continue up the ridge top to the 1272-foot Mt Kaukaopua. It's a little more than two miles to this point.

The trail becomes more strenuous as it rises. It's possible to continue through the Puu Ki area, following the ridge to the twin peaks of Hihimanu at 2262 feet. Give yourself an early start if you intend to go this far in and carry plenty of water.

Moonshiners who distilled a liquor called okolehao from the roots of ti plants established this trail during the Prohibition era of the 1920s. The ti they planted is still plentiful along the trail.

The literal translation of okolehao comes from *okole*, meaning 'buttocks', and *hao*, meaning 'iron', referring to the iron-bottomed still that was used. As the old-timers say, 'It'd knock you on your okole and how!'

HANALEI

After the Hanalei Bridge, Hwy 560 runs parallel to the Hanalei River. The mile before Hanalei village is a very pastoral scene of taro patches and grassland. There's no development of any kind and no buildings in sight. Take away the telephone poles and asphalt road and this is how it's looked for centuries.

Hanalei has a pleasant low-key village center. The village took a severe battering during Hurricane Iniki and many of its old wooden buildings didn't survive the storm. Most of the buildings that were downed

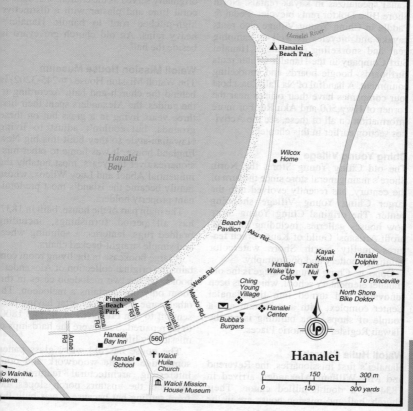

have been reconstructed in a style similar to those they replaced and the character of the town, while not quite as funky as before, remains much the same.

Hanalei is friendly, casual and slow. If you're in a hurry, you're in the wrong place.

Information

Post & Money The Hanalei post office is on Hwy 560 in the village center and there's a Bank of Hawaii in the adjacent Ching Young Village shopping center.

Activity Rentals There are several shops in Hanalei geared to outdoor sports. Kayak Kauai specializes in kayak rentals. North Shore Bike Doktor rents bicycles. Pedal & Paddle in Ching Young Village also rents kayaks and bicycles as well as camping gear and snorkeling equipment. Hanalei Surf Company in the Hanalei Center rents surfboards, boogie boards and snorkeling equipment. A handful of Na Pali Coast boat tour companies have their offices near the corner of Hwy 560 and Aku Rd. For more information on all of these, see the Activities section earlier in this chapter.

Ching Young Village

The old Ching Young Store, the North Shore's main general store since the turn of the century, has recently evolved into the larger Ching Young Village shopping center. The original Ching Young Store now houses galleries, including the non-profit Artisans' Guild of Kauai which features quality North Shore watercolor paintings, pottery and photography.

Opposite Ching Young Village is the old Hanalei elementary school, which has been renovated and turned into the Hanalei Center complex, with a restaurant and a couple of shops. The building is on the Hawaii Register of Historic Places.

Waioli Huiia Church

Hanalei's first missionaries, the Reverend and Mrs William Alexander, arrived in 1834 in a double-hulled canoe. Their church, hall and mission house are in the middle of town, set on a huge manicured lawn with a beautiful mountain backdrop. These folks knew how to pick property.

The picturesque Waioli Huiia Church is a favorite subject for watercolorists. The green wooden church retains an airy Pacific feel with large windows that open outwards and high ceilings. The doors remain open during the day and visitors are welcome to go inside. A Bible printed in Hawaiian in 1868 is on display on top of the old organ. The Waioli Church Choir, the island's best, sings hymns in Hawaiian at the 10 am Sunday service.

Waioli Mission Hall, to the right of the church, was built in 1836. The hall, which originally served as the church, was built of coral lime and plaster with a distinctive high-pitched roof to handle Hanalei's heavy rains. An old church graveyard is beside the hall.

Waioli Mission House Museum

The Waioli Mission House (☎ 245-3202) is behind the church and hall. According to the guides, the Alexanders spent their first three years living in a grass hut on these grounds, but couldn't adjust to living Hawaiian-style so they built this big New England house. It was home to other missionaries over the years, most notably the influential Abner and Lucy Wilcox, whose family became the island's most predominant property holders.

The main part of the house, built in 1837 has all period furnishings, including braided rugs, lanterns, a spinning wheel and simple straight-backed chairs.

A large bookcase in the living room contains the original collection of Alexander's books. Of the two melodeon cases in this room only one contains a melodeon. The other came back empty after having been sent off to San Francisco in the late 1800 to be repaired. Such were the hardships of missionary life.

The house has old wavy glass panes some nice simple woodwork and other interesting architectural features. For instance, the upstairs porch slopes, not from settling but because it was built that way to let water run off during the valley's frequent torrential rains.

The original cookhouse was separate so that in the event of a kitchen fire the main house would be spared. With the advent of electricity it was then linked to the main house. One corner still has iron pots hanging in the original fireplace, which was made of sandstone blocks cut in Waipa Valley, three miles away.

The museum's inconspicuous parking lot is just past the church. Turn left on the driveway before the school and then again at the second yellow hydrant. It's open from 9 am to 2:30 pm Tuesdays, Thursdays and Saturdays. Admission is free, though donations are welcomed. You're free to explore the garden area and taro patch out back.

Hanalei Bay

Hanalei means 'Crescent Bay', and that it is – a large, perfectly shaped bay, one of the most scenic in all Hawaii. Weke Rd, which runs a mile along the bay between Waioli Stream and Hanalei River, can be reached by turning off Hwy 560 at Aku Rd.

Just after turning right onto Weke from Aku there's a public beach with a picnic pavilion. The more appealing Hanalei Beach Park is about half a mile farther, at the end of Weke Rd. Pinetrees Beach Park is in the opposite direction.

All three beaches have restrooms, showers, drinking water, picnic tables and grills. Hanalei Beach Park is the best place for catching the sunset as you can see Bali Hai from there. It's a popular summer anchorage for sailboats.

The big brown house with the wraparound porch mauka of the road and midway between the pavilion and Hanalei Beach Park is the old Wilcox estate, home to descendants of early Hanalei missionaries Abner and Lucy Wilcox.

Incidentally, if the road names have a familiar sound, it means you're beginning to learn the names of Hawaiian fish – each road along the beach is named after a different one.

Hanalei Beach Park

Hanalei Beach Park, one of the North Shore's most popular beach parks, has a grassy area and a long beach shaded by ironwood trees. The beach has a sandy bottom and a gentle slope, but dangerous shorebreaks and rip currents are common during periods of high surf. While surfing is good in winter, swimming and snorkeling are good in summer when the water is calm.

The remains of a narrow-gauge railroad track, used a century ago to haul Hanalei rice, still lead up to the long pier that juts out into the bay. A lifeguard is stationed on the beach through the summer and on weekends the rest of the year.

The mouth of the Hanalei River and a small boat ramp are at the eastern end of the park. That part of the beach is called Black Pot after the big iron pot that was once hung there by local fishers for impromptu cook-outs. Camping is allowed on Fridays, Saturdays and holidays.

The bluff north of the river mouth was once the site of the old Hanalei Plantation Hotel. It was followed by Club Med which was unable to make a go of it, despite the spectacular angle on Hanalei Bay. More recently a Honolulu developer went bankrupt in the midst of building million-dollar condos and the property was sold to Princeville.

Pinetrees Beach Park

Pinetrees Beach Park, named by surfers, is actually shaded by ironwood trees.

From Weke Rd, turn either onto Hee Rd, which has the bigger parking lot, or Amaama Rd, which has the restrooms and showers. This section of the beach is also known locally as Toilet Bowls. Pinetrees has some of the bay's highest winter surf and is the site of various surfing contests. One of the most interesting is the Pinetrees Longboard Surf Classic. Held around the beginning of March, it features an aging group of surfers on the old-style 10-foot wooden boards used before the advent of fiberglass.

Places to Stay

Bed & Breakfast & Beach (☎ 826-6111), Box 748, Hanalei, HI 96714, is in a large house, a two-minute walk from the beach pavilion section of Hanalei Bay. There are four rooms, each furnished with queen beds. All have their own bath, either attached or just outside the room. The contemporary house has a wraparound 2nd-floor lanai and hardwood floors. Rates range from $65 to $90, with a two-night minimum, and include a continental breakfast.

Across the street, Mary and Dave Cunning (☎ 826-4116), Box 720, Hanalei, HI 96714, rent *Ohana Hanalei*, a pleasant studio unit attached to the side of their home. The daily rate is $50 to $60, depending on how long you stay. The unit has its own entrance and bath, a king bed, refrigerator, microwave, coffeemaker, cable TV and a phone with free local calls.

Hanalei Bay Inn (☎ 826-9333), Box 122, Hanalei, HI 96714, formerly Mahikoa's Motel, has five simple units, some with kitchens. Despite the name, this older local hostelry is not on the bay but rather located on Hwy 560, on the west side of the village. Rates are $65 to $75 a night for both singles and doubles.

Anini Beach Vacation Rentals (☎ 826-4400, (800) 448-6333; fax 826-9636), Box 1220, Hanalei, HI 96714, represents vacation rental homes in the Hanalei area, as well as in Haena, Princeville and Anini. Rates begin at around $700 a week.

Places to Eat – budget

Hanalei Gourmet in the Hanalei Center has both a deli and a restaurant with a mountain view. Breakfast includes reasonably priced muffins and pastries, as well as a couple of egg dishes or a bagel with lox and cream cheese priced around $6.50. Sandwiches cost from $5.25 for tuna or avocado to $10 for smoked salmon on a baguette. They also make fairly good deli salads and sell sandwich meats and loaves of bread over the counter. The deli hours are from 8 am to 9 pm, dinner is served until 9:30 pm.

Hanalei Wake Up Cafe on Aku Rd is a surfers' hangout that's open daily. At breakfast, from 6 to 11:30 am, you can get omelets, custard French toast or half a papaya with yogurt and granola for $4 to $6. Lunch, from noon to 3 pm, is mainly burgers with fries or plate lunches such as ahi or teriyaki chicken. Dinner, from 5 to 9 pm, is Mexican style, with burritos or tacos with rice and beans. Meals at lunch and dinner average about $7.

Pizza Hanalei (☎ 826-9494) in Ching Young Village has good pizza at reasonable prices. A 10-inch cheese pizza in either traditional white or a crisp whole-wheat crust topped with sesame seeds is $7.60, plus a dollar per topping. The spicy calzone-style pizzarittos are loaded with cheese and vegies, and make a good meal for $4.79. At lunch time you can also buy slices of pepperoni or pesto pizza for $2.50. The restaurant closes at 9 pm.

Next door, *Hanalei Natural Foods* sells juices, organic fruit and vegetables, wrapped sandwiches, a few hearty bakery products, vitamins and other health food items. It's open from 8:30 am to about 7 pm daily.

The *Village Snack & Bakery* in Ching Young Village sells breakfasts, wrapped sandwiches, $6 plate lunches, bakery goods and coffee. It's open from 6 am to 2 pm and from 3:30 to 7 pm daily.

Tropical Taco, which parks its old green van in the parking lot in front of the Hanalei Dolphin restaurant, dishes out $5 burritos and other simple Mexican fare from about 11 am to 3:30 pm daily except Mondays. For hamburgers in the same price range there's *Bubba's Burgers* at the west side of the Hanalei Center.

There's a *Big Save* supermarket open from 7 am to 9 pm daily in the Ching Young Village.

Places to Eat – top end

The *Hanalei Dolphin* (☎ 826-6113), at the east side of the village, is a steak and seafood restaurant. Entrees, which are served with a salad, range from chicken or frozen mahimahi for $14 to king crab and tenderloin for $23. It's open for dinner only, from 5:30 to 10 pm daily.

Hanalei's oldest restaurant and bar, *Tahiti Nui* (☎ 826-6277), on Hwy 560 near Aku Rd, serves straightforward meals with both porchside and indoor dining. Breakfast, served from 7 to 11:30 am, features omelets, French toast, pancakes and loco moco for around $6; add on $3.50 more for juice and coffee. Lunch, served until 4 pm, is predominantly burgers, sandwiches and plate lunches for $6 to $8. Dinner, from 5 to 10 pm, ranges from a $14 chicken teriyaki plate to fresh catch of the day, often a generous serving of ahi priced at $18.

Entertainment

Hanalei Gourmet (☎ 826-2524) has live entertainment Tuesday through Sunday evenings, with rock bands on Fridays and Saturdays and jazz or rhythm & blues on the other nights. There's also Hawaiian music from 4 to 8 pm on Sundays. Happy hour is from 3:30 to 5:30 pm.

There's live music most nights in the lounge at *Tahiti Nui*, usually country music on Mondays, blues on Wednesdays and contemporary Hawaiian music on Tuesdays, Thursdays and Fridays. On weekends there's dance music and a $3 cover charge.

Tahiti Nui also has a down-home, funky luau that can be fun, though it won't be everyone's cup of tea. This is an indoor dinner show more than a traditional luau. The show is presided over by owner Aunty Louise and is essentially a family affair, with cousins and uncles performing. There's a lot of audience participation and the whole thing has the feel of a neighborhood party. The luau is from 6 to 8:30 pm on Wednesdays and Fridays. It costs $38 for adults and $15 for children ages five to 11, including a buffet dinner and one drink.

HANALEI TO WAINIHA
Waikoko Beach

The western part of Hanalei Bay, called Waikoko Beach, has a sandy bottom, is protected by a reef and is shallower and calmer than the middle of the bay. There

are beachside places to park under ironwood trees around the four-mile marker, but no facilities.

Winter surfing is sometimes good off Makahoa Point, the western point of the bay, called Waikokos by surfers.

Lumahai Beach

Lumahai is the gorgeous mile-long stretch of beach where Mitzi Gaynor promised to wash that man right out of her hair in the 1958 musical *South Pacific*. It's a broad white sand beach with lush jungle growth on one side and tempestuous open ocean on the other.

It's a good beach for walking and exploring. Around some of the lava outcrops you can find green sand made of olivine.

There are two ways onto Lumahai. The first and most scenic is a three-minute walk that begins at a pull-off along a stone retaining wall three-quarters of a mile past the four-mile marker. Park in the direction of the traffic flow to avoid a ticket. The trail to the beach starts at a 'No Lifeguard' sign and goes down the slope to the left.

The lava point at this eastern end of the beach offers protection from the winds that often blow from the Princeville direction. These rocks are a rather popular place for sunbathing and for being photographed, but size it up carefully as people have been washed off by high surf and rogue waves. Lumahai has dangerous shorebreaks and is not a beach to turn your back on. It's particularly treacherous in winter, though there are strong currents all year round. Because of the numerous drownings that have occurred here, Lumahai has been nicknamed Luma*die* by locals.

Back on the road, there are a couple of lookouts with views down onto Lumahai. The first is at the five-mile marker, though the next one that pops up around the bend has a better angle.

The other access onto Lumahai Beach is along the road at sea level at the western end of the beach, just before crossing the Lumahai River Bridge. The beach at this end is lined with ironwood trees. Across the road is Lumahai Valley, open and flat with ranchland and grazing horses and cattle.

WAINIHA

Wainiha has the oldest general store in these parts, and it's the last place before the end of the road where you can buy groceries, wine and beer. It's open from 9:30 am to 6:30 pm daily. There's a little sandwich shop at the side that opens at lunchtime only.

Ancient house sites, heiau sites and old taro patches reach deep into the Wainiha Valley. The valley is said to have been the last hideout of the menehunes. In fact as late as the mid-1800s, 65 people in the valley were officially listed as menehune on the government census!

Wainiha Powerhouse Road

For a glimpse into an older Hawaii, take a side trip up Wainiha Powerhouse Rd, which begins off Hwy 560 shortly before the seven-mile marker. It leads up into Wainiha Valley, a narrow valley with steep green walls.

This narrow road is lined with simple tin-roofed homes, old rusting pick-up trucks and sleeping dogs. At 1½ miles up there's suddenly an incongruous manicured estate with a cool blue stream meandering through it. Shortly after this you arrive at the Wainiha hydroelectric plant, which was built in 1906 by McBryde Sugar Company and still pumps out juice today. Beyond the powerhouse the road turns to dirt and begins to feel more private.

Places to Stay

Tassa Hanalei (☎ & fax 826-7298), Box 856, Hanalei, HI 96714, at the home of Ileah and Robert Van Hubbard, is a B&B in a quiet riverside niche of Wainiha Valley. The best unit is an airy studio cottage with a queen bed, full kitchen, tables and chairs, sofa bed, deck and glass doors that look out onto a fine mountain scene; it costs $95 per couple, $125 for a family of four. Two rooms that are attached to the main house and have private entrances but share a garden (outdoor) bathroom cost $65/75 for

singles/doubles. There's a hot tub and massage is available for $50, colonic therapy for $35.

HAENA

Haena has houses on stilts, little beachfront cottages, a few vacation homes, the YMCA camp, large caves, campsites and beautiful sandy beaches. It also has the only condo complex and restaurant beyond Hanalei.

Tunnels Beach

Tunnels is a big horseshoe-shaped reef that has great diving and snorkeling when the water is calm, which is generally limited to the summer. There's a current as you head into deeper water. When conditions are right, you can start snorkeling near the east point and let the current carry you westward. It's more adventurous than Kee Beach and the coral is beautiful.

Tunnels was not named after the caves and other crevices in the underwater walls but by surfers for its tubular winter surf break at the outer corner of the reef. The beach is popular with both windsurfers and board surfers, though dangerous rip currents that prevail from October to May make it suitable for experts only.

To get there, look for cars parked at the side of the road near phone pole No 144, which is midway between the eight- and nine-mile markers, opposite the beach access road. Or you can park at Haena Beach Park and walk along the beach to Tunnels.

Haena Beach Park

Haena Beach is a beautiful curve of white sand. To the right, you can see the horseshoe shape of Tunnels outlined by breaking waves. To the far left is Cannons, another good dive spot. Haena itself is not protected by reefs and has very strong rip currents and powerful shorebreaks from October to May.

The county beach park has campsites, covered picnic tables, restrooms, showers and grills. There are usually a few hikers from the Kalalau Trail camping here. It's a bit over a mile to the trailhead and this is a safer place to park a car than the end of the road if you're going on to Kalalau.

Sometimes during the day a snack truck parks at Haena providing reasonably priced plate lunches, soft drinks and shave ice. The service is irregular, however, so you shouldn't count on it being there.

Maniniholo Dry Cave

Three large sea caves, which were part of the coast thousands of years back, are mauka of the road between Haena and Kee Beach. One is dry and two are wet.

According to legend, they were created when the goddess Pele dug into the mountains looking for a place on Kauai's North Shore to call home.

Maniniholo Dry Cave, across the road from Haena Beach Park, is a deep broad cave that you can walk into. Dry is a relative term, as the dripping water that constantly seeps from the cave walls keeps the interior of Maniniholo damp and humid.

Limahuli

Limahuli is the last valley before the start of the Na Pali Coast. Much of it is still virgin forest.

The National Tropical Botanical Garden owns 1000 acres of the valley. The garden contains collections of Hawaiian ethnobotanical and medicinal plants and other rare and endangered native species. A trail passes old stone terraces planted with taro and various fruiting trees. Endemic trees along the way include the endangered Kokio hauheleula, which has a red hibiscus-like blossom, and the equally beautiful but more common ohia lehua tree.

The garden starts at a concrete driveway on the mauka side of the highway just before the stream that marks the Haena State Park boundary. It's free to members of the NTBG for self-guided tours.

Wet Caves

Haena State Park includes the two wet caves and Kee Beach. The caves, which are near each other, less than a quarter of a mile from the end of the road, are usually marked with HVB warrior signs. The first,

Waikapalae Wet Cave, is just a few minutes' walk uphill from the road along the rutted drive with the stop sign. The second, Waikanaloa Wet Cave, is at the side of the road.

Both are big, deep, dark and dripping, with pools of very cold water. Divers sometimes explore them, but the caves can be dangerous and it's certainly best to go with an experienced local diver the first time.

Kee Beach

Kee Beach is commonly called 'the beach at the end of the road', which it is.

On the left side of the beach is the distinctive 1280-foot cliff that marks the start of the Na Pali Coast. Almost everyone calls it Bali Hai, its name in *South Pacific*. The Hawaiian name is Makana, which means 'gift'. A heiau and ancient hula school site is at its base.

Snorkeling is good at Kee Beach, which has a variety of tropical fish. A reef protects the right side of the cove and except on high surf days, it's usually calm. The left side is open and can have a powerful current, particularly in winter.

When it's really calm – generally only in summer – snorkelers cross the reef to the open ocean where there's great visibility, big fish, large coral heads and the occa-

---

Taylor Camp

If you walk down Kee Beach about 15 minutes to the northeast, you'll come to a stream and the site of the former Taylor Camp.

In the late 1960s, a little freestyle village of tents and tree houses sprang up on property owned by Elizabeth Taylor's brother. Reports of drugs, orgies and pipe organ music in the middle of the night eventually got the authorities to crack down on the camp. When the state tried to evict everyone on public health grounds, the campers challenged them in court claiming squatters' rights. The 'squatters' eventually lost and the property was condemned and incorporated into the state park system. Taylor Camp remains part of North Shore folklore, though there's nothing left to see. ■

sional sea turtle. It makes the inside of the bay look like kid's stuff, but check it out carefully because breaking surf and strong currents can create some pretty dangerous conditions.

When the tide's at its lowest you can actually walk a great distance out on the reef without getting your feet wet and peer down into tide pools.

Showers, changing rooms, drinking water, restrooms and a pay phone are tucked back in the woods behind the parking lot and a lifeguard is on duty daily.

There are several ways to get views down the Na Pali Coast from Kee Beach. One way is to walk the first 30 minutes of the Kalalau Trail. Another is to take the short walk out around the point at the left side of the beach.

Or, simply walk down the beach a few minutes to the right and look back as the cliffs unfold, one after the other.

Kaulu Paoa Heiau

To walk out to Kaulu Paoa Heiau, take the path on the western side of the beach. The walk is shaded by tropical almond trees, which drop their edible nuts along the trail. Go around the private Allerton house and then follow the stone wall as it curves uphill. You can see the heiau almost immediately.

The overgrown section at the foot of the hill is one of the more intact parts of the heiau, but don't stop there. Instead, continue walking up the terraces towards the cliff face. Surf pounding below, vertical cliffs above – what a spectacular site to worship the gods!

Beneath the cliff face, large stones retain a long flat grassy platform. A thatched-roofed halau, a longhouse used as a hula school, once ran the whole length of the terrace. Here, dances to Laka, the goddess of hula, were performed. This was Kauai's most sacred hula school and students from all the islands aspiring to learn hula came to Kaulu Paoa.

Fern wreaths, rocks wrapped in ti leaves, leis and other offerings to Laka are still placed into the crevices of the cliff face.

The site is sacred to native Hawaiians and should be treated with respect. Night hula dances are still performed on special occasions.

Lohiau's House Site

Lohiau's house site is just a minute's walk above the parking lot at Kee Beach. At the Kalalau Trail sign, go left along the barely discernible dirt path to a vine-covered rock wall. This overgrown level terrace runs back 54 feet to the bluff and is said to have been the home of Lohiau, a 16th-century prince.

Legend says that the volcano goddess Pele was napping one day under a hala tree in Puna on the Big Island when her spirit was awakened by the sound of distant drums. Her spirit rode the wind in the direction of the sound, searching each island in turn until she finally arrived at Kee Beach. Here she found Lohiau above the heiau beating a hula drum, surrounded by graceful hula dancers.

Pele took the form of a beautiful woman and captured Lohiau's heart. They became lovers and moved into this house. In time Pele had to go back to the Big Island, leaving a lovesick Lohiau behind. His longing quickly got the better of him and on this site he died from his grief.

Places to Stay

The *Kauai YMCA-Camp Naue* (☎ 826-6419 or 246-9090; fax 246-4411), Box 1786, Lihue, HI 96766, in Haena, just before the eight-mile marker on Hwy 560, has rustic co-ed bunkhouses on the beach. It costs $12 for one of the 50 bunks, which have mattresses but no linen or blankets. As there are five separate rooms (with six, eight or 14 beds), couples or groups of friends can sometimes have a room to themselves. To pitch a tent costs $10 for the first person and $7 for each extra person. There are hot showers, but the kitchen is reserved for large groups only. While there are no lockers, the camp is a safe place and theft hasn't been a problem. Guests can stay a maximum of seven nights; check-in is allowed until it gets dark. The Y doesn'

Na Pali Coast

accept reservations, but unless there's a large group staying they can usually take everyone who shows up. Call ahead, however, as in summer and some other holiday periods the camp is commonly booked by children's groups at which times it's closed to travelers. It's a 10-minute walk to Tunnels Beach.

Hanalei Colony Resort (☎ 826-6235, (800) 628-3004; fax 826-9893), Box 206, Hanalei, HI 96714, an older low-rise condo complex on the east side of Haena, has undergone a thorough Iniki-inspired renovation. Each of the 54 units has two bedrooms, a full kitchen, new furnishings and a lanai. The complex is right on the beach and there's a swimming pool, spa and barbecue area. This is a place to listen to the surf: there are no TVs, stereos or room phones. Rates range from $95 for a garden view to $170 for oceanfront in the low season, $115 to $190 in the high season. The rates are the same for up to four people

and for weekly stays the seventh night is free. There's a three-night minimum stay.

Places to Eat
Charo's restaurant is on the beach, beside Hanalei Colony Resort. At lunch, it has burgers and sandwiches for under $10; at dinner, meat and seafood dishes from $20. There's also a bar but the splashy 'Tropical Fiesta' revue of days past are gone, as Charo moved the show to Waikiki.

NA PALI COAST
In Hawaiian 'na pali' means simply 'the cliffs'. Indeed, these are Hawaii's grandest.

The Na Pali Coast is the rugged 22-mile stretch between the end of the road at Kee Beach in the north and the road's opposite end at Polihale State Park in the west. It has the most sharply fluted coastal cliffs in Hawaii.

Kalalau, Honopu, Awaawapuhi, Nualolo and Milolii are the five major valleys on the

Na Pali Coast. These deep river valleys once contained sizable settlements.

In the mid-1800s missionaries established a school in Kalalau, the largest valley, and registered the valley population at about 200. Influenced by Western ways, people gradually began moving to towns and by the end of the century the valleys were largely abandoned.

The Na Pali valleys, with limited accessibility and abundant fertility, have long served as a natural refuge for people wanting to escape one scene or another. While Koolau the Leper is the best known, there have been scores of others.

Getting There & Away

Precarious trails once led from the upland Kokee area down to the valley floors along the Na Pali Coast. In some places footholds were gouged into cliffsides and in others rope ladders were used. These trails no longer exist.

Only Hanakapiai, Hanakoa and Kalalau valleys can still be reached on foot, solely along the 11-mile Kalalau coastal trail.

The only other access is by boat. Landings are limited to the Kalalau, Nualolo and Milodii valleys and are largely restricted to summer when the seas are calm. Miloiii, part of the Na Pali Coast State Park, has primitive camping. For more information on Miloiii see the Camping section.

Captain Zodiac (☎ 826-9371) is permitted to drop off and pick up backpackers in Kalalau Valley during the summer months, which gives people the option of hiking the Kalalau Trail just one way. The Zodiac ride leaves from Tunnels Beach and costs $60. For those who prefer to hike without a backpack, Captain Zodiac will also drop off or pick up a pack in Kalalau, charging $30 each way for a 50-pound bag.

In addition to approaching the Na Pali Coast from the North Shore, you can also look down into the Na Pali valleys from Kokee State Park. The park has a drive-up lookout right on the rim of Kalalau Valley as well as hardy hikes out to clifftops that offer gorgeous views into Awaawapuhi and Nualolo valleys (for details see Kokee State

Park in the West Side section of this chapter).

Kalalau Trail

Kalalau is Hawaii's premier trail. It's common to come across hikers here who have trekked in Nepal or climbed to Machu Picchu. The Na Pali Coast is similarly spectacular, a place of singular beauty.

The Kalalau Trail is basically the same ancient route used by the Hawaiians who once lived in these remote north coast valleys. The trail runs along high sea cliffs and winds up and down across lush valleys before it finally ends below the steep fluted pali of Kalalau. The scenery is breathtaking, with sheer green cliffs dropping into brilliant turquoise waters.

While hikers in good shape can walk the 11-mile trail in about seven hours, it's less strenuous to break it up and spend a night camping in one of the two valleys along the way.

In winter there are generally only a few people at any one time hiking all the way in to Kalalau Valley, while the trail is heavily trodden in summer. As it's a popular hike for islanders as well as visitors, weekends tend to see the most use.

The hike can be divided into three parts: Kee Beach to Hanakapiai Valley (two miles); Hanakapiai to Hanakoa Valley (four miles); and Hanakoa to Kalalau Valley (five miles).

The first two miles of the hike makes a popular day trip and permits are not required for those going only as far as Hanakapiai Valley. Even if you're not planning to stay overnight, a permit is officially required (free from the state parks office in Lihue) to continue on the Kalalau Trail beyond Hanakapiai.

The trail is part of Na Pali Coast State Park. Camping is allowed in all three valleys, but is limited to five nights total, with no two consecutive nights in Hanakapiai or Hanakoa. State camping permits are required (for details see the Camping section at the start of this chapter).

Kee Beach to Hanakapiai The two-mile

Koolau the Leper

Koolau was a paniolo (cowhand) who contracted leprosy in 1893. Rather than accept separation from his family and banishment to Molokai's leper colony, as was the law at the time, Koolau hiked down into Kalalau Valley, taking along his wife and young son. Shortly after, a sheriff and deputy showed up to clear the valley of renegade lepers. Koolau was the only resister. That night, in the light of a full moon, the sheriff snuck up the valley hoping to take Koolau in his sleep. In self-defense Koolau shot the sheriff.

When word reached Honolulu, a shipload of soldiers was sent to land on Kalalau Beach. As they marched up the valley they met Koolau's gunfire. After two of the soldiers were shot off the ridge, and a third accidentally killed himself, they switched strategies. Just before dawn they blasted Koolau's hideaway with cannon fire, not knowing he had slipped through their lines the night before. From a nearby waterfall Koolau watched as the soldiers loaded up and set sail. They never returned and Koolau lived the rest of his days in the valley undisturbed.

Eventually the son, and then Koolau, died of leprosy. Both are buried on a valley hillside. When Koolau's wife, Piilani, left the valley she found Koolau had largely been forgotten. A decade later a visiting reporter, John Sheldon, recorded her story. Jack London later wrote *Koolau the Leper*, a more fictionalized account. ∎

trail to Hanakapiai is a delightfully scenic hike. Morning is a good time to be going west, and the afternoon to be going east, as you have both the sun at your back and good light for photography.

The trail weaves through kukui and ohia trees and then back out to clearings with fine coastal views. There are purple orchids, wildflowers and a couple of tiny Zen-like waterfalls. The black nuts half buried in the clay are kukui, polished smooth by the scuffing of hundreds of hiking shoes.

Just a quarter of a mile up the trail you can catch a fine view of Kee Beach and the surrounding reef. After 30 minutes you get your first view of the Na Pali Coast. Even if you weren't planning on a hike, it's well worth coming this far.

Hanakapiai has a sandy beach in the summer. In the winter the sand washes out and it becomes a beach of boulders, some of them sparkling with tiny olivine crystals. The western side of the beach has a small cave with dripping water and a miniature fern grotto.

The ocean is dangerous here, with unpredictable rip currents year round. It's particularly treacherous during winter high surf conditions, but summer trades also bring powerful currents. Hanakapiai Beach is matched only by Lumahai for the number of drownings on Kauai.

If you're just doing a day hike and want to walk farther, it makes more sense to head up the valley to Hanakapiai Falls than it does to continue another couple of miles on the coastal trail.

Hanakapiai Falls The two-mile hike from Hanakapiai Beach to Hanakapiai Falls takes about 2½ hours round-trip. Because of some tricky rock crossings, this trail is rougher than the walk from Kee Beach to Hanakapiai Beach. Due to the possibility of flash floods in the narrow valley, the Hanakapiai Falls hike should only be done in fair weather.

The trail itself is periodically washed out by floodwaters and sections occasionally get redrawn, but the path is not that difficult to follow as it basically goes up the side of Hanakapiai Stream. Since Hurricane Iniki, this trail hasn't been very well maintained and the last mile is still strewn with fallen trees, requiring scrambling over and around trunks and branches.

There are trails on both sides of the stream, but the main route heads up the stream's western side. About 50 yards up there's a picnic table, old stone walls and guava trees. If the guava is ripe it's a good place to stock up. There are also some big old mango trees along the way.

Ten minutes up from the trailhead you'll find thickets of green bamboo, interspersed with eucalyptus. Off to the left there's a picnic table shaded by horizontally leaning bamboo with wild ginger behind. It's Eden-like.

Also along the trail is the site of an old coffee mill, although all that remains to be seen is a little of the stack.

The first of four or five stream crossings is about 25 minutes up at a sign that warns: 'Hazardous. Keep away from stream during heavy rainfall. Stream floods suddenly.'

Be particularly careful of your footing on the rocky upper part of the trail. Some of the rocks are covered with a barely visible film of slick algae. It's like walking on glass.

Hanakapiai Falls is spectacular, with a wide pool gentle enough to swim in. Directly under the falls the cascading water forces you back from the rock face, a warning from nature as rocks can fall from the top.

This is a very peaceful place to spend a little time meditating. It's a beautiful lush valley, though it's not terribly sunny near the falls because of the incredible steepness.

Hanakapiai to Hanakoa Just 10 minutes up the trail from Hanakapiai to Hanakoa there's a nice view of Hanakapiai Beach, but from there the trail goes into bush and the next coastal view is not for another mile. This is the least scenic part of the trail.

The camping site at Hanakoa is tucked into the valley about half a mile inland. Of the three camping areas, Hanakoa is the wettest. It also tends to have the most mosquitoes.

The valley is lovely and Hanakoa Stream has pools perfect for swimming. There's a waterfall about a third of a mile up the valley, but it's rough getting up there as the path is overgrown. The valley was formerly settled by farmers who grew taro and coffee, both of which still grow wild.

Hanakoa to Kalalau This is the most difficult part of the trail, although without question the most beautiful. Make sure you have at least three hours of daylight left.

About a mile out of Hanakoa Valley you'll reach the coast again and begin to get fantastic views of Na Pali's jagged edges. There are some very narrow and steep stretches along this section of the trail, so make sure your gear is properly packed and be cautious of your footing. A little past the halfway mark you'll get your first view into Kalalau Valley.

The large valley has a beach, a little waterfall, a heiau site, some ancient house sites and some interesting caves that are sometimes dry enough to sleep in during the summer.

An easy two-mile trail leads back into the valley to a pool in Kalalau Stream where there's a natural water slide. If you have a quick hand, you might try your luck at catching prawns that live in the stream.

Valley terraces where Hawaiians cultivated taro until 1920 are now largely overgrown with Java plum and guava. Feral goats scurry up and down the crumbly cliffsides and drink from the stream.

Kalalau Valley has fruit trees, including mango, papaya, orange, banana, coconut, guava and mountain apple. During the 1960s and 1970s people wanting to get away from it all tried to settle in Kalalau, but forestry rangers eventually routed them out. It's still common to find a few folks hanging out in the valley, making flutes or otherwise whiling away the time.

Warnings & Information This is rugged wilderness and hikers should be well prepared. In places the trail runs along steep cliffs that can narrow to little more than a foot in width, which some people find unnerving. However, hikers accustomed to high country trails generally enjoy the hike and don't consider it unduly hazardous. The Sierra Club, which occasionally leads hikes into Kalalau, rates the trail as moderate to strenuous.

Accidents are not unknown. Most casualties along the Kalalau Trail are the result of people trying to ford swollen streams, walking after dark on cliffside trails or swimming in treacherous surf. Keep in mind that the rock that the cliffs are composed of is loose and crumbly; don't try to climb the cliffsides, and don't camp directly beneath them as goats commonly dislodge stones that tumble down the sides. For someone who's cautious and aware, it can be paradise.

There's no shortage of water sources along the trail, but all drinking water must be boiled or treated.

Bring what you need but travel light. You won't want to have extra shifting weight on stream crossings or along cliff edges. Shoes should have good traction; it's certainly not a trail for flip-flops. If you bring a sleeping bag make it a light one.

The state parks office in Lihue can provide a Kalalau Trail brochure with a basic map. There is also information posted at the Kee Beach trailhead.

Break-ins to cars left overnight at Kee Beach are very common. Some people advise leaving cars empty and unlocked to prevent smashed windows. It's generally safer to park at the campground at Haena Beach Park. Or, better yet, get a lift to the end of the road. Whatever you do, don't leave valuables in a locked car.

You can usually arrange to leave extra luggage wherever you've been staying. Another possibility is the Lihue airport, where storage can be arranged through one of the airport porters; the cost is $2/10 a day/week for an average-sized bag, $3/15 for oversized bags.

South Shore

Poipu is Kauai's main beach resort area. It's typically sunny and for the larger part of the year, including winter, it has calm waters for swimming and snorkeling. During the summer the surf kicks up and it becomes a surfers' haunt.

The village of Koloa, three miles inland from Poipu, was the site of Hawaii's first sugar plantation. This sleepy town could have doubled for Dodge City before it got caught up in Poipu's boom. Now most of its shops are geared for tourists and it catches the overflow from neighboring Poipu.

Poipu and Koloa are about 10 miles south of Lihue. To get there take Hwy 520 (Maluhia Rd) from Hwy 50 (Kaumualii Hwy).

Tree Tunnel

Immediately after turning down Maluhia Rd you enter the Tree Tunnel, a mile-long stretch of road canopied by swamp mahogany trees, a type of eucalyptus. Originally the tree tunnel was more than double this length but when Hwy 50 was re-routed south most of the tunnel was lopped off.

In 1992 Hurricane Iniki brought down many of the branches, temporarily destroying the tunnel effect, but by and large it's filling back in nicely.

The cinder hill to the right about two miles down Maluhia Rd is Puu O Hewa. From its top the ancient Hawaiians raced wooden holua sleds down paths covered with oiled pili grass. To add even more excitement to this popular spectator sport the Hawaiians crossed two sled paths near the middle of the hill. The paths were about five feet wide and if you strain your eyes you might be able to see the X on the hillside where they crossed.

Hewa means 'wrong' or 'mistake'. The hill's original name was lost when a surveyor jotted 'Puu O Hewa' (wrong hill) on a map he was making and it mistakenly went off to the printer like that.

The two grassy hills to the left of the road are Mauna Kalika, or Silk Mountain. Two American entrepreneurs introduced Chinese silkworms here in the 1830s in an attempt to develop a Hawaiian silk industry. The climate proved unsuitable for the silkworms and the hills, like the rest of the surrounding area, were eventually given over to sugar cane.

KOLOA

Hawaii's first sugar plantation was started in Koloa in 1835. The raw materials had arrived long before: sugar cane with the

Koloa

To Tree Tunnel, Hwy 50

520

0   50   100 m
0   50   100 yards

Waikomo Rd

Hongwanji ⊥ Mission

First Hawaiian Bank

⊥ Koloa Jodo Mission

Big Save ▼

Laundromat

Weliweli Rd

Matuna Rd

Sugar Exhibits ●

▼ Lappert's

● Crazy Shirts

▼ Koloa Broiler

Sueoka Store

To Lawai ←

530

Koloa Rd

● Historical Display

Chevron Gas ■

▼ Pancho & Lefty's

Poipu Rd

■ Fathom Five Divers

520

To St Raphael's Church →

↓ To Poipu

---

original Polynesian settlers and small-scale refinery know-how with the earliest Chinese immigrants. However, large scale production didn't occur until William Hooper, an enterprising 24-year-old Bostonian, arrived in Kauai and made inroads with the alii.

With financial backing from Honolulu businesspeople, he leased land in Koloa from the king and paid the alii a stipend to free commoners from their traditional work obligations. He was then free to hire the commoners as wage laborers and Koloa became Hawaii's first plantation town.

Koloa Rd (Hwy 530) runs between Koloa and Lawai and if you're heading west it's the best way out of Koloa. Koloa Rd is a rural drive through sugar cane fields, pasture and tree-covered hills.

Sugar Exhibits

Any sugarologists in the crowd? The field at the intersection of Hwy 520 and Koloa Rd is for you.

In a tiny garden a dozen varieties of sugar cane are labeled with faded interpretive markers. Some are noted for their high tonnage, others for high sucrose and some for their good ratooning abilities, though the different varieties have all grown to twist and clump together. Who knows, maybe there's a great new hybrid sprouting up amongst the tangles!

The stone stack in another corner of the field is a relic from one of Koloa's early mills and dates back to 1841.

In the center of the field, the principal ethnic groups that worked the plantations are immortalized in a sculpture. The Hawaiian wears a malo and has a poi dog by his side. The Chinese, Korean, Japanese, Portuguese, Filipino and Puerto Rican groups are likewise in native field dress. You may notice that the plaque on the wall curiously gives reference to a haole overseer – present-day islanders found the depiction of this Caucasian plantation boss seated on a high horse so unacceptable that

Statue of Filipino caneworker

at the last minute he was omitted from the sculpture.

If you want to learn more about the history of sugar, there are informative plaques at the sculpture display.

Old Koloa

Koloa looks like an Old West town of wooden buildings with false storefronts. It was a thriving plantation town and commercial center that largely went bust after WW II.

While its history is sugar, its present is unmistakably tourism. The former fish markets, tailor shops, barber shops, Japanese bathhouses and beer halls are now boutiques, galleries and restaurants.

The building that houses Crazy Shirts was until recently the Yamamoto General Store. Moviegoers would line up at Yamamoto's for crack seed and soft drinks before the movies, until the theater across the street burned down. On the sidewalk in front of the store a lifelike sculpture of a craggy mechanic stands next to an ancient Texaco gas pump. The courtyard behind the store looks onto the former town hotel,

where you'll find a little display on Koloa's history.

Although it's pretty touristy, Koloa is still a pleasant town to walk around. The 'newly quaint' shops are in stark contrast to a handful of old sugar shacks that still house cane workers farther down the street.

Koloa Jodo Mission

Koloa Jodo Mission dates back to 1910. The Buddhist temple on the left is the original, while next to it is a newer and larger temple where services are now held. During services the smell of incense and the sound of beating drums evocatively fills the air.

St Raphael's Catholic Church

St Raphael's is the oldest Catholic church on Kauai and the burial site of some of the first Portuguese immigrants to Hawaii. The original church, built in 1854, was of lava rock and coral mortar with walls three feet thick. When the church was enlarged in 1936 it was all plastered over and it now has a more typical whitewashed appearance. To get there from Koloa Rd, turn onto Weliweli Rd then right onto Hapa Rd, from where it's half a mile to the church.

Places to Stay

Kahili Mountain Park (☎ 742-9921), Box 298, Koloa, HI 96756, is a mile up a sugar cane road just beyond the seven-mile marker on Hwy 50. It is run by the Seventh Day Adventist church and has a beautiful setting beneath Mt Kahili.

There are three categories of accommodations. Cabinettes, at the bottom end, are very simple structures on cement slabs and are rather dark and dank, though they cost only $30. More appealing are the cabins which are pleasantly spread out around the grounds. There are eight older rustic cabins for $40 and five new ones for $50. The new cabins, while not as quaint in appearance, are larger, spiffier and have screened porches.

All categories have bed linens, a two-burner gas stove, pots and pans, a sink and a refrigerator, while cabins also have a

Sugar mill, Koloa

table, chairs, dresser and hot water. Cabinettes hold five people, cabins hold four to six. Rates given are for up to two people, with each additional person charged $6.50. It's an unbeatable value and only about a 20-minute ride to the beaches in Poipu. As they commonly book out solid, advance reservations are advised.

Places to Eat
Sueoka Store, *Koloa Broiler* and *Lappert's* ice-cream store are all on Koloa Rd near its intersection with Maluhia Rd.

The snack shop at the side of Sueoka Store sells burgers, cheese sandwiches and saimin for $1.50 each and plate lunches for $4. It's open from 10 am to 3 pm Monday to Saturday.

Koloa Broiler (☎ 742-9122) is in a funky old tin-roofed wooden building that used to be a soft drink bottling plant. The 'menu' is a display case of raw meat and fish. Diners get to be cooks, preparing their own orders over a communal gas grill. Dishes range from $7 for a burger to around $12 for chicken, ribs or steak and $16 for fresh fish. The portions are generous and a simple buffet of rice, beans and salad is included. It's open from 11 am to 10 pm daily.

Pancho & Lefty's (☎ 742-7377), behind the Chevron station, has standard Mexican food. Two enchiladas or tacos with rice and beans cost $8 while many other dishes, including chile rellenos, carnitas and chicken fajitas are priced around $13. Breakfast burritos and other Mexican-influenced egg dishes cost $7 to $10. Hours are from 8 am to 10 pm daily.

POIPU
Poipu is about three miles south of Koloa down Poipu Rd. Other than its lovely white sand beaches, Poipu's most popular attraction is the Spouting Horn blowhole. To get to Spouting Horn, turn right off Poipu Rd onto Lawai Rd, just past Poipu Plaza, and continue for 1¾ miles.

Prince Kuhio Park
Prince Kuhio Park is about half a mile down Lawai Rd, across from tiny Hoai Bay. Here you'll find **Hoai Heiau** and a monument honoring Jonah Kuhio Kalanianaole, the Territory of Hawaii's first delegate to the US Congress. It was Prince Kuhio who spearheaded the Hawaiian Homes Commission Act, which provided homesteads for native Hawaiians. The

KAUAI

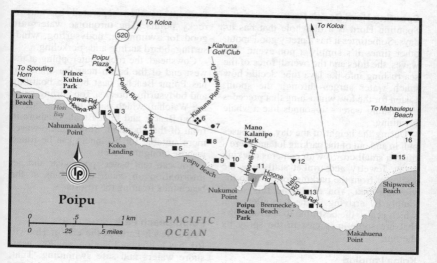

To Koloa
520
Poipu Plaza
Kiahuna Golf Club
To Koloa
To Spouting Horn
Prince Kuhio Park
Poipu Rd
Lawai Rd
Hoona Rd
Kiahuna Plantation Dr
1
To Mahaulepu Beach
Lawai Beach
Hoai Bay
2
3
Nahumaalo Point
Kapili Rd
Hoonani Rd
4
6
7
Mano Kalanipo Park
16
Koloa Landing
5
8
Poipu Beach
9
10
11
Hoowili Rd
12
Hoone Rd
15
Poipu
Nukumoi Point
Poipu Beach Park
Brennecke's Beach
Pee Rd
Lawai Rd
13
14
Shipwreck Beach
PACIFIC OCEAN
0   .5   1 km
0   .25   .5 miles
Makahuena Point

PLACES TO STAY
2   Garden Isle Cottages
3   Koloa Landing Cottages
4   Poipu Kapili
5   Sheraton Kauai Hotel
8   Kiahuna Plantation Resort
9   Stouffer Poipu Beach Hotel
10 Stouffer Waiohai Beach Hotel
13 Poipu Plantation
14 Sunset Kahili
15 Hyatt Regency Kauai

PLACES TO EAT
1   Kiahuna Golf Club Restaurant
11 Brennecke's
12 House of Seafood
16 Poipu Bay Grill & Bar

OTHER
6   Poipu Shopping Village
7   Snorkel Bob's

remains of a fishpond and an ancient Hawaiian house platform are also on the grounds.

Baby Beach

There's a protected swimming area just deep enough for children off Hoona Rd, east of Prince Kuhio Park. Look for the marked beach access post marking the pathway between the road and the beach. Adults may want to walk west down the beach where there's a sandy break with fewer rocks and deeper water.

Lawai Beach

Lawai Beach is west of Prince Kuhio Park, opposite Lawai Beach Resort House restaurant. It's a little rocky but during winter the water is usually quite clear and snorkelers can hand feed the fish. When the surf's up in summer, the beach is inundated with surfers.

Opposite the beach there's a shower and a concession stand that rents boogie boards and snorkel sets for $5 a day.

Kukuiula Bay

Kukuiula Bay, about a half mile east of Spouting Horn, is a small boat harbor maintained by the state and mostly used by fishing and diving boats. The beach is rocky and more suitable for pole fishing than other water activities. There are showers, nine mooring spaces, a launch ramp and a concrete wharf.

Spouting Horn Beach Park

Spouting Horn is a blowhole that has its days. Sometimes it has a pretty good spout, other times it's simply a non-event. The waves, the tides and the overall force of the sea rushing into the lava tube decide how much water surges through the spout. Listen for the low whooshing that precedes the rushing water – it sounds like a whale breathing.

During the height of the day, tour buses pull in and out of the parking lot and there's often a small crowd with cameras clicking away. Jewelry and trinket stalls line the walkway from the parking lot down to the viewing area. You can avoid this scene simply by arriving in the late afternoon, which is also the best time to see rainbows that are sometimes cast in the spray by the sun.

Koloa Landing

Koloa Landing, at the mouth of Waikomo Stream, was once Kauai's largest port. It not only served to ship out sugar grown on Koloa Plantation, but whalers also called at Koloa Landing to resupply provisions. In the 1850s local farmers used the landing to ship Kauai-grown oranges and sweet potatoes to California gold miners. The landing lost its importance after an island-wide road system was built, and it was abandoned in the 1920s. Other than a small county boat ramp there's nothing left to see.

Beneath the water it's another story. Koloa Landing is a popular snorkeling and diving spot. Its protected waters reach depths of about 30 feet and it's generally calm all year, although kona winds can create rough water conditions. The area has some underwater tunnels and a good variety of coral and fish. For the best sights swim out to the right after entering the water.

Poipu Beach

The long stretch of white sand fronting the Sheraton, Kiahuna Plantation and the two Stouffer hotels is generally referred to as Poipu Beach. It's actually three attractive crescent beaches separated by narrow rocky points. The turquoise waters are good for swimming, bodysurfing, windsurfing, board surfing and snorkeling.

Cowshead, the rocky outcropping at the west end of the beach near the Sheraton, has Poipu Beach's best boogie boarding and bodysurfing breaks. Top surfing spots are Waiohai, which is off the east side of Poipu Beach, and First Break, offshore in front of the Sheraton. Slow, gentle waves more suitable for beginners can be found inshore along the beach.

You can rent water sports gear and get information on water conditions at the beach huts fronting the resorts.

Poipu Beach Park

Poipu Beach Park, at the end of Hoowili Rd, has a lifeguard station, shallow nearshore waters and safe swimming. That, combined with the playground equipment at the park, makes this one of the most popular weekend destinations for families on the South Shore.

Nukumoi Point extends into the water at the western side of the park, dividing it from the beach fronting the Stouffer Waiohai hotel. At low tide you can walk out on the point and explore tide pools that shelter small fish and sea urchins. For the best snorkeling head over to the Waiohai side of the point, where there are swarms of near-tame fish.

Snorkel sets and bodyboards can be rented across the street at the Brennecke's Beach Center.

Brennecke's Beach

Brennecke's has fantastic shorebreaks that make it the South Shore's best spot for bodysurfing and boogie boarding. It breaks very close to shore and is suitable only for the experienced. While it's best when surf is highest, which is generally in the summer, there's some respectable action in winter as well. Beware of strong rips that are present with high surf. The beach is only a small pocket of sand and the waters can get crowded. For safety reasons fins are not allowed and surfboards are prohibited.

Brennecke's is off Hoone Rd, just down from Poipu Beach Park.

Shipwreck Beach

Shipwreck Beach, the sandy beach fronting the Hyatt Regency Kauai, also sees some top bodysurfing and boogie boarding conditions. There are a couple of challenging near-shore surf breaks that attract local board surfers as well. The water conditions here are not for novices, and the pounding shorebreak and high surf make for treacherous swimming conditions along the entire beach.

Mahaulepu Beach

Secluded Mahaulepu Beach, a couple of miles beyond Shipwreck Beach, has lovely white sands, sheltered coves, tide pools, lithified sand dunes and sea cliffs.

At various times of the year Mahaulepu is good for surfing, windsurfing, boogie boarding and snorkeling. In pre-contact times the area was heavily settled and many important historic sites lie buried beneath the cane fields and shifting beach sands. People still claim to see ghost marchers coming in from the sea at night along this beach.

The property is owned by Grove Farm and visitors are required to sign a waiver at the gate before being allowed to enter. The easiest way to get there is to drive past the Hyatt and continue on the cane road for 1½ miles, at which point the road will be blocked by a gate. Turn right, continue past the gravel plant and after a third of a mile you'll come to the gatehouse, which is open daily from roughly sunrise to sunset. From the gatehouse it's half a mile to the beach; bear right at the first fork and then take the middle road (which bears right) at a three-way fork near the road's end.

This will bring you to a popular windsurfing spot and a convenient place from which to explore. One striking geological feature in the area is a **cinder cone** with a cave that you can walk deep into. To get there, walk west along the beach for about

a third of a mile. After crossing a little stream, take the trail going inland which leads to the cave, a couple of minutes away. In the cave's center you'll find an opening looking straight up to the heavens – it feels like sitting in a little volcano.

Or, instead of heading to the cave, walk east along the beach for about 10 minutes and you'll reach scenic **Kawailoa Bay**, which is surrounded by sand dunes to the west and protected by jutting sea cliffs to the east. The bay has a lovely beach and it's not uncommon to find a few Hawaiians net-fishing in the waters along the shore.

It's also possible to get to Kawailoa Bay by car. Just bear left instead of right at the last turn.

Places to Stay – bottom end

Koloa Landing Cottages (☎ 742-1470), 2704B Hoonani Rd, Poipu, HI 96756, occupies five cottages across the street from Koloa Landing. All cottages have a full kitchen, TV and telephone. Studio units, which have a queen bed, cost $50. Full cottages, which have both a queen bed and two twins, cost from $70 for two people in a smaller unit to $100 for four people in the largest unit. A cleaning fee of $20 for studios, $40 to $60 for the cottages, is tagged onto the bill. Reserve as far in advance as possible, as the place is often booked solid.

Poipu Plantation (☎ 742-6757, (800) 733-1632), 1792 Pee Rd, Koloa, HI 96756, consists of nine condo-style units and a 1930s home with three B&B rooms. Best deals are the condos, which are modern and comfortable with tropical rattan furniture, air-con, TVs and full kitchens. They cost from $80 to $90 for one-bedroom units, $105 for two-bedroom units. While not as spacious, the B&B accommodations are pleasant enough, have private baths, include breakfast and costs $70 for a room in the back with either a queen or a king bed, $75 for the front room with a king bed. There's a hot tub, barbecue area and a laundry room with coin-op washers and dryers.

Garden Isle Cottages (☎ 742-6717),

2666 Puuholo Rd, Poipu, HI 96756, has seven pleasant units above Koloa Landing. The studios, which have a double and single bed, refrigerator and coffeemaker, cost $82/87 in the low/high season. One-bedroom apartments with queen beds, kitchens and roomy living rooms start at $98/109 for doubles; extra guests are $8 each. All the units have oceanview lanais, TVs, ceiling fans and abstract paintings and sculpture by owner/artist Robert Flynn. Garden Isle also rents a studio ($73/78) and a large suite ($125/135) in a separate house on a hill near Poipu Crater. Amenities at the latter include a lap swimming pool.

Sunset Kahili (☎ 742-1691, (800) 827-6478), 1763 Pee Rd, Poipu, HI 96756, is an older, well-maintained five-story condo with friendly management. Each of the 36 units has an ocean view, a washer/dryer, cable TV and lanai. Rates for the lower two floors are $90 for two people in a one-bedroom unit and $120 for up to four people in the two-bedroom units. The top floors are $10 more. The minimum stay is three nights, with prices dropping gradually the longer you stay. It can be difficult to book from January through March, particularly if you're looking for a longer stay, as a lot of retirees return here each year to spend the winter.

The newly rebuilt *Gloria's Spouting Horn Bed & Breakfast* (☎ 742-6995), 4464 Lawai Beach Rd, Poipu, HI 96756, is a lovely oceanside B&B just a few minutes' walk from the Spouting Horn. There are three comfortable bedrooms, all fronting the ocean. Each has a refrigerator, micro-wave, phone, TV, VCR, a bath with a deep soaking tub and a seaside balcony. Rates, which include a full breakfast, are $125 for singles or doubles with a three-day mini-mum, except around the Christmas holi-days when the rate is $150 and the minimum is seven days.

Places to Stay – top end

Two beachfront resorts, the *Stouffer Poipu Beach Hotel* and the adjacent *Stouffer Waiohai Beach Hotel*, remain closed with no projected opening dates.

The *Sheraton Kauai Hotel* (☎ 742-1661), 2440 Hoonani Rd, Poipu, HI 96756, had 455 rooms before Iniki hit. While the hotel's oceanfront buildings were severely damaged, 200 rooms on the inland side of the road have reopened and are being booked at $95. That price is half the normal rate and the rooms are perfectly fine, although there are no restaurants or other hotel amenities available. The grounds on the inland side have gardens and carp ponds and this side has always been the hotel's cheeriest. As for the hurricane-damaged oceanside half of the hotel, it's still roped off and tied up in litigation, and it doesn't look like reconstruction is going to begin very soon. The $95 rate is expected to hold until the oceanside is rebuilt, which might be as late as 1996. In the meantime Sheraton is not handling the bookings – they must be made directly with the hotel.

Poipu Kapili (☎ 742-6449, (800) 443-7714; fax 742-9162), 2221 Kapili Rd, Koloa, HI 96756, is a new 60-unit seaside condominium complex. All of the units are privately owned, with about 40 of them in the rental pool. They have ocean views, ceiling fans and kitchens, and in most there's a queen-size sofa bed in the living room. One-bedroom units, which have either a queen or king bed, cost from $150. The two-bedroom units typically have a king bed in the master bedroom and two twins in the second bedroom and begin at $205. There's a four-day minimum; rates drop about 10% on stays of two weeks or more. There's a tennis court and swimming pool.

The *Kiahuna Plantation Resort* (☎ 742-6411, (800) 367-7052; fax 742-1047) 2253 Poipu Rd, Koloa, HI 96756, is a 333-unit condominium managed by Village Resorts. The complex, reopened after two years of reconstruction, has pleasant units with large balconies and uncrowded grounds. Prices for a one-bedroom condo for up to four people range from $155 for a garden view to $275 for an oceanfront unit. Two-bedroom condos are $290 to $435 for up to six people. There's sometimes a free fourth night or free rental car deal available for the asking.

Poipu's most exclusive hotel is the 600-room *Hyatt Regency Kauai* (☎ 742-1234, (800) 233-1234), 1571 Poipu Rd, Poipu, HI 96756. It's quite elegant with airy lobbies adorned with antiques, and its central building nicely incorporates the ocean view into its design. There are also the prerequisite artificial lagoons and waterways spread around the resort grounds. Garden-side rooms start out at $230, while the best suites climb to $1800. There are restaurants, a health spa, tennis courts and a golf course.

Places to Stay – vacation rentals

The Poipu Beach Resort Association (☎ 742-7444; fax 742-7887), Box 730, Koloa, HI 96756, has a brochure listing most of Poipu's accommodations.

The following vacation rental companies book condos and private homes in the Poipu area:

Suite Paradise, 2827 Poipu Rd, Poipu, HI 96756 (☎ 742-7400, (800) 367-8020; fax 742-9120)
Grantham Resorts, Box 983, Koloa, HI 96756 (☎ 742-7220, (800) 325-5701; fax 742-9001)
Kauai Vacation Rentals, 3-3311 Kuhio Hwy, Lihue, HI 96766 (☎ 245-8841, (800) 367-5025; fax 246-1161)

Places to Eat – budget

Taqueria Nortenos in the Poipu Plaza has cheap Mexican food. It's essentially a takeout place with some indoor picnic tables at the side. The meatless burrito is a good value at $2.80, while two enchiladas with rice and beans cost $4.50. The food is fine for the price and it's open from 11 am to 11 pm daily except Wednesdays.

Cafe Venturi in the Poipu Shopping Village, at the corner of Poipu Rd and Kiahuna Plantation Dr, has plate lunches and good fresh fish sandwiches with fries for $5.50 from 11:30 am to 2:30 pm. At dinner, from 5:30 to 9 pm, the entree menu ranges from teriyaki chicken for $8.25 to shrimp and pasta for $12.50, while appetizers include the likes of fried zucchini and fish tempura.

The *Pizza Bella* (☎ 742-9571), also in the Poipu Shopping Village, has rather ordinary pizzas from $10 and lasagna, sandwiches and salads. Pizza is sold by the slice until 4:30 pm for $2.65. It's open from 6 am to 9 pm Monday to Saturday.

The *Kiahuna Golf Club Restaurant* has open-air dining with a view of the fairway. Until 4 pm you can choose from a handful of simple sandwiches with a soft drink for around $5.

Brennecke's is a touristy restaurant opposite Poipu Beach Park that serves good, albeit pricey, fish dishes. A fresh fish sandwich and fries costs $9 at lunch, while burgers and vegetarian sandwiches are a couple of dollars cheaper. A salad bar can be added on for an additional $4. Dinner dishes, including a salad, range from chicken stir-fry for $14 to fresh catch for $20. Lunch is from 11:30 am to 4 pm (except on Sunday when there's a brunch from 10 am to 2 pm), dinner from 4 to 10 pm daily.

Keoki's Paradise (☎ 742-7534) in the Poipu Shopping Village has an open-air Polynesian motif with artificial waterfalls, lit torches, bamboo and hanging vines. While it's a bit contrived it somehow all works quite nicely. The food is reasonably good and dishes include vegetarian lasagna for $10, teriyaki chicken or kushiyaki (a brochette) for $14 and catch of the day for around $20. Meals include fresh breads and a green salad. It's open for dinner only, from 5:30 to 10 pm daily.

Places to Eat – top end

A good choice for a not-too-expensive dinner is the *Poipu Bay Grill & Bar* (☎ 742-8888) at the Poipu Bay Resort Golf Course. It has a casual country club setting and dishes that range from $14 for grilled chicken in tomato salsa to $20 for fresh catch of the day. All dinners include a small salad bar.

A local favorite for special occasions, *The House of Seafood* (☎ 742-6433) at the side of Poipu Kai Resort, is an open-air restaurant specializing in seafood. Appetizers, including oysters on the half shell, steamed clams and sashimi, are priced from $6.50 to $10. Main dishes range from $18.50 for shrimp linguine or scallops to $34 for filet mignon and lobster. The extensive menu includes a wide variety of fresh fish at market prices. It's open nightly from 5:30 to 9:30 pm.

The *Ilima Terrace* (☎ 742-6260, ext 4244) at the Hyatt Regency Kauai offers a different buffet each night. It's not a lavish spread but it's certainly sufficient, the quality is good and there's a pleasant waterview setting. The buffets include a small salad bar, fruits, cheeses and half a dozen tempting desserts including indulgent cakes and mousses. A couple of nights a week prime rib is featured, while on other nights it's either a barbecue buffet or an island-style buffet with a few Hawaiian dishes like pipikaula salad thrown in. There's always a few main dishes to select from, including fresh fish. The buffets are served from 5 to 9 pm and cost a reasonable $17.50.

The Ilima Terrace also has a Sunday brunch from 6:30 am to 1:30 pm for $17.50, concentrating more on breakfast fare and including an omelet station.

For formal dining, the Hyatt's *Dondero's* has a good reputation for Italian food and some of the island's highest prices.

Entertainment

On most days the *Hyatt Regency Kauai* has a short but picturesque torchlighting ceremony and hula show before sunset in its open-air Seaview Terrace, which is just off the lobby.

The Hyatt's *Kuhio's Nightclub* has dancing to top-40 music from 9 pm to 2 am on Fridays and Saturdays. The cover charge is $5 and there's a bit of a dress code (no tank tops, T-shirts or short shorts).

West Side

The top destinations on Kauai's West Side are Waimea Canyon and Kokee State Park, both with ruggedly spectacular scenery.

It's 38 miles along Kaumualii Rd (Hwy 50) from Lihue to Polihale State Park, the farthest accessible point on the West Side. This is sugar country, with cane lining the roadside most of the way.

LAWAI

Lawai, a small village at the 10-mile marker on Hwy 50, is best known for the Lawai Gardens. The gardens were started in the 1870s by Queen Emma, who built a summer cottage on the site. Chicago industrialist Robert Allerton later bought the property and expanded the gardens in the 100-acre estate.

In 1971 the site became part of the **National Tropical Botanical Garden**, Box 340, Lawai, HI 96765, which propagates tropical and endangered plant species and does research in ethnobotanical and medicinal plants.

The property was heavily damaged by Iniki and the garden tours, which used to be given twice daily, have been suspended until the gardens recover. Call (☎ 332-7361) for the latest information.

To get there from Hwy 50 take Koloa Rd south three-quarters of a mile and turn right onto Hailima Rd, which ends in half a mile at the visitor center.

KALAHEO

Kalaheo is an old sleepy Portuguese community that's quintessentially local in flavor. Pig hunting is a popular pastime for people in this town, which accounts for all the hunting dogs in tiny backyard cages.

The town's main shops are clustered around the intersection of Hwy 50 and Papalina Rd. They include a couple of food marts, the post office and Kalaheo's restaurants. There's a coin laundry behind the Kalaheo Steak House on Papalina Rd.

Kukuiolono Park

Kukuiolono Park (☎ 332-9151) is a golf course with gardens and a scenic viewpoint. Kukuiolono means 'Light of Lono', referring to the torches that Hawaiians once placed on this hill to help guide canoes safely to shore.

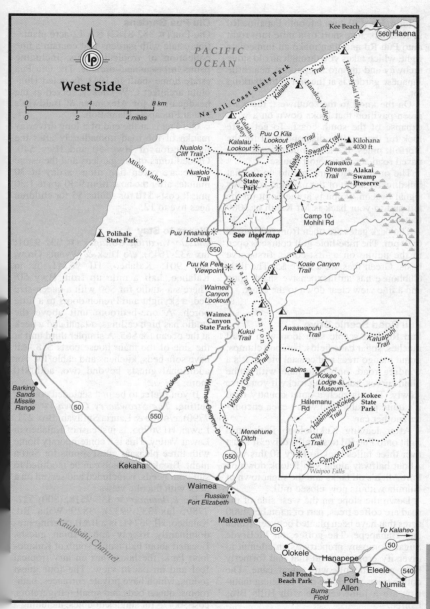

PACIFIC
OCEAN

West Side

0   4   8 km
0   2   4 miles

Kee Beach
(560) Haena

Na Pali Coast State Park

Hanakapiai Valley

Hanakoa Valley

Kalalau Trail

Kalalau Valley

Puu O Kila Lookout

Pihea Trail

Swamp Trail

Kilohana
4030 ft

Nualolo
Cliff Trail

Kalalau
Lookout

Nualolo
Trail

Kokee
State
Park

Alakai Trail

Kawaikoi
Stream Trail

Alakai
Swamp
Preserve

Miliolii Valley

Camp 10-
Mohihi Rd

Puu Hinahina
Lookout

See inset map

Polihale
State Park

(550)

Koaie Canyon
Trail

Puu Ka Pele
Viewpoint

Waimea Canyon
Lookout

Waimea Canyon

Waimea
Canyon
State Park

Kukui Trail

Awaawapuhi
Trail

Kaluapuhi
Trail

Barking
Sands
Missile
Range

(50)

Kokee Rd

Waimea Canyon Dr

Waimea Canyon Trail

Cabins

Kokee
Lodge &
Museum

Kokee
State
Park

Halemanu
Rd

Halemanu-Kokee Rd

(550)

Menehune
Ditch

Cliff
Trail

Canyon Trail

Waipoo Falls

Kekaha

Kaulakahi Channel

Waimea

Russian
Fort Elizabeth

(550)

Makaweli

(50)

Olokele

Hanapepe

To Kalaheo

(50)

Salt Pond
Beach Park

Burns
Field

Port
Allen

Eleele

(540)

Numila

KAUAI

From Hwy 50, turn left onto Papalina Rd in Kalaheo. Just short of a mile turn right onto Puu Rd and then make an immediate right, which takes you through an old stone archway and up into the park. A neat little Japanese garden is at the end of the parking lot.

On the knoll to the southwest, there's a green pavilion that looks down on a wide expanse of the south coast. To get there look for the satellite dish and head for the Norfolk pines. It's a 10-minute walk on a paved road across the golf course.

The ominous-looking gizmo on the flat hill directly south of the pavilion is a navy signal beacon. Poipu is at the point on the left and to your back is Mt Kahili at 3089 feet.

The park gates are open from 6:30 am to 6:30 pm. The nine-hole golf course is open to the public on a first-come, first-serve basis. Green fees are a mere $5. The little clubhouse has an inexpensive snack shop and a fine view clear down to the coast.

Puu Road Scenic Drive

Puu Rd is a scenic side loop with small ranches, sugar cane fields, bamboo clumps, grand mango trees and coastal views. It's a winding road, only one lane with some blind curves, but nothing tricky if you drive slowly. This is such a quiet country road it's quite possible you won't even encounter another car.

After leaving Kukuiolono Park, turn right onto Puu Rd to start the drive. It's just over three miles back to Hwy 50 this way. About halfway along you'll look down on Port Allen's oil tanks and the sugar town of Numila with its now-closed mill.

Down the slope on the west side of the road are coffee trees, part of a total of 4900 acres that have been planted between Koloa and Hanapepe. The coffee, on McBryde Sugar Company property, is an attempt to diversify crops on land that had formerly been planted only with sugar cane. The coffee trees, which are now reaching maturity, are a joint venture with Hills Bros Coffee.

Olu Pua Gardens

Olu Pua (☎ 332-8182) is a 12-acre plantation estate with gardens that contain a fine collection of tropical plants, including palms, hibiscus and orchids. The Olu Pua estate home, built in 1931 by noted Honolulu architect C W Dickey, served as the headquarters for Alexander & Baldwin's Kauai Pineapple Plantation.

Olu Pua is at the end of a long driveway mauka of the road immediately after the intersection of Hwy 50 and Hwy 540. Guided tours of the gardens and the estate house are given five times a day at 30 minutes after the hour from 9:30 am to 1:30 pm. It costs $10 for adults, $5 for children ages five to 12.

Places to Stay

Classic Vacation Cottages (☎ 332-9201; fax 332-7645), c/o Dick & Wynnis Grow, Box 901, Kalaheo, HI 96741, is in Kalaheo, half a mile up from Hwy 50. There's a studio for $60 with a queen-size bed, a skylight and French doors to a little porch. A one-bedroom unit above the studio has high ceilings, a lanai and a peek at the ocean for $65. A simpler third unit at the side of the main house costs $58. All have sofa beds, kitchens and cable TV. For additional guests beyond two, add $10 more.

If you prefer to be in a secluded country setting, *The Strawberry Guava* (☎ 332-7790), c/o Joe & Lauria Sullivan, Box 271, Lawai, HI 96765, is just east of Kalaheo in Lawai Valley. This is a contemporary home with three pleasant guest rooms for $60 a night. Breakfast, which can be modified to suit your needs, is included and served on a deck with bucolic views.

Black Bamboo (☎ 332-7518, (800) 527-7789; fax 332-9932), 3829 Waha Rd, Kalaheo, HI 96741, is a B&B catering predominantly to gay and lesbian guests. Located about half a mile south of Kukuiolono Park, the house has an airy tropical feel and an ocean view. The four guest rooms, which have private entrances, bathrooms, queen beds and small refrigerators, cost $60/75 for singles/doubles, including a

KAUAI

continental breakfast. There's a 40-foot lap pool, a hot tub and a common lounge with a fireplace and VCR. A studio with its own kitchenette and a sitting area with a TV and VCR is available for $70/85. The minimum stay is two days.

Places to Eat

Brick Oven Pizza (☎ 332-8561) on Hwy 50 is a popular place with small (10 inch) pizzas priced from $8, large ones (15 inch) from $16. The pizzas come in a choice of whole-wheat or white crust. The restaurant also has sandwiches, salads, wine and beer. Hours are from 11 am to 10:30 pm daily except Monday.

Camp House Grill on Hwy 50, opposite Menehune Food Mart, serves breakfast daily except Wednesday from 6:30 to 10:30 am with the usual standards averaging about $5. The grill also makes good burgers and chicken sandwiches for $4 to $6 and has a few hot meals, such as chicken and barbecue ribs, for a couple of dollars more. Lunch and dinner are served from 11 am to 9 pm daily.

The *Bread Box* on Papalina Rd sells good whole-grain breads, tasty macnut rolls for $1.25 and coffee for just 25c. It's open Monday to Saturday from 6 am to noon, or until the bread sells out.

For meat and potatoes, the *Kalaheo Steak House* on Papalina Rd is open from 5:30 to 9 pm nightly, with dinner offerings ranging from teriyaki chicken for $12 to filet mignon for $18.

HANAPEPE VALLEY LOOKOUT

The scenic lookout that comes up shortly after the 14-mile marker gives a view deep into Hanapepe Valley. The red clay walls of the cliffs are topped by bright green cane like a sugar frosting.

The same Robinson family that owns the island of Niihau also has substantial land holdings in these parts, including a hideaway estate deep in Hanapepe Valley.

While old king sugar may dominate the scene surrounding Hanapepe Valley, if you glance towards the opposite side of the road

from the lookout you'll see Kauai's newest commercial crop – coffee trees.

ELEELE & PORT ALLEN

Eleele is largely a residential area of limited interest to visitors. It does have a shopping center at the 16-mile marker with a doughnut shop, Dairy Queen, Big Save supermarket, bank, post office and gas station.

Hwy 540 is an alternate route that leads off Hwy 50 just after Kalaheo and connects back to Hwy 50 at Eleele. It passes a new coffee plantation and swings by Numila, a former cane town with dusty wooden houses surrounding a defunct mill.

Port Allen, immediately south of Eleele on Hanapepe Bay, is both a commercial harbor and one of Kauai's busiest recreational boat harbors. The state-run small craft harbor here is protected by breakwaters and has launch ramps, berthing and mooring spaces.

Glass Beach

Glass Beach, just east of Port Allen, is a cove piled high with colorful bits of glass that have been worn into smooth pebble-like pieces. The glass comes from a long abandoned dump site nearby and its weathering is the result of decades of wave action. At certain times of the year the glass is deep enough to scoop up by the handful, while at other times it's largely washed out to sea.

To get to the little cove, take the last left before entering the Port Allen commercial harbor, drive past the fuel storage tanks and then curve to the right down a dirt cane road that leads 100 yards to the beach.

HANAPEPE

Before Hurricane Iniki hit, Hanapepe was one of the best preserved historic towns in Hawaii. Parts of *The Thorn Birds* were filmed here because Hanapepe bore such a close resemblance to the dusty Australian outback of days past.

While the hurricane wreaked havoc on the town's old wooden buildings, claiming about half of them, Hanapepe still has lots of character and a nice unhurried pace that invites lingering.

The turn-off into Hanapepe is marked by a sign on Hwy 50.

Hanapepe Rd, the town's main street, retains a decidedly period face, with a crack seed shop, some small local stores and a few art galleries. Most interesting is Kauai Fine Arts, which occupies the former bowling alley and has a collection of antique maps and prints, including works related to Captain Cook's explorations.

For a fine little **scenic side drive** through a niche of 'old Hawaii' turn mauka onto Awawa Rd, which runs north from Hanapepe Rd at the west side of the Hanapepe River, immediately after the bridge. This narrow road is bordered by cliffs on one side and by taro patches, corn fields and grazing horses on the other. After a mile Awawa Rd forks. If you take the dead-end street to the left there's more rural scenery and lots of tall trees. After three-quarters of a mile you'll have to turn around and come back to the 'main' road, where you can turn left and loop back to town along a dirt drive. However, there's one tricky section where the road crosses a cement bridge that's really little more than a weir. As the river flows *over* rather than under this bridge, you'll need to gauge the depth of the water on top before deciding whether to continue. If it's only a couple of inches deep, you shouldn't have any problem crossing, but if it's more than that, turn around and return the way you came.

Salt Pond Beach

Kauai has long been known for its alae salt, a sea salt with a red tint that comes from adding a bit of iron-rich earth. The salt is made by letting seawater into shallow basins called salt pans and allowing it to evaporate. When dry, the salt crystals are scraped off. Native Hawaiians still make salt this way down on the coast south of Hanapepe.

Salt Pond Beach County Park is just beyond the salt ponds. It has a sandy beach, campsites, covered picnic tables, barbecue grills, a pay phone, showers and a lifeguard on duty daily. Water in the cove gets up to 10 feet deep and is good for swimming laps. Four times across equals half a mile. Both ends of the cove are shallow and good for kids.

To get to Salt Pond Beach, turn left just past the 17-mile marker onto Lele Rd, then right onto Lokokai Rd.

Places to Eat

The *Hanapepe Bookstore* (☎ 335-8544), in the town center on Hanapepe Rd, not only sells Hawaiiana gifts and books, but is also a cafe with espresso, croissants and good vegetarian meals. Breakfast, served from 8 to 11 am, includes multi-grain pancakes or waffles topped with macnuts and real maple syrup for under $5, as well as fresh croissants and pastries. Lunch, from 11 am to 2 pm, includes garden burgers, pesto pasta or baked fritatta with a Caesar salad for $6.50. Dinner is available on Fridays and Saturdays only (reservations suggested) and features creative pasta meals priced from $13 to $17. The restaurant is closed on Mondays and Tuesdays.

The *Green Garden Restaurant* just off Hwy 50 has a varied but unexciting menu and is best known as the restaurant where the tour buses stop. Sandwiches and hot plates cost $5.50 to $7, while dinners range from $6.50 for chicken chow mein to $21 for steak and lobster and include soup, salad, rice, rolls and coffee. It's open from 9 am to 2 pm and from 5 to 9 pm daily except Tuesdays. Green Garden sells Taro Ko Chips, made from Hanapepe-grown taro which is sliced thin and then fried into chips.

There's also a Mexican restaurant and a deli and bakery on the highway section of town.

OLOKELE

Olokele exists for the Olokele Sugar Company. Of the 220 employees, mostly field laborers, 200 live in Olokele.

The road to the sugar mill, immediately after the 19-mile marker, is shaded by tall trees and lined with classic turn-of-the-

KAUAI

century lampposts. Taking this short drive offers a glance at real plantation life. Everything is covered with a layer of red dust from the surrounding sugar cane fields and mill. Rather than fight it, many of the houses are painted in beige-red tones.

MAKAWELI

Makaweli is headquarters for Gay & Robinson, Niihau Ranch and Niihau Helicopters, all enterprises of the Robinson family who owns Niihau. Quite a few native Niihauans live in this area, many of them working for the Robinsons. Once or twice a week an old military landing craft makes the 17-mile trip between Niihau and Makaweli Landing.

RUSSIAN FORT ELIZABETH

The remains of Russian Fort Elizabeth stand above the east bank of the Waimea River. Hawaiian laborers started building the fort in 1816 under the direction of Georg Anton Schaeffer, an agent of the Russian-American Company. The alliance between the Russians and Kauai's King Kaumualii proved to be a short-lived one and the Russians were tossed out in 1817, the same year the fort was completed.

You can take a short walk through this curious period of Kauai's history following a self-guiding map found at the trailhead. The most intact part of the fort is the exterior lava rock wall, which is eight to 10 feet high in places and largely overgrown with scrub and colorful wildflowers. The seaward side was designed like the points of a star, but it takes some close observation to get the effect. A dozen markers point out where things used to be, such as the trading house, armory and barracks.

The fort has a good view of the western bank of the Waimea River, where Captain Cook landed. Bear right down the dirt road that continues past the parking lot and you'll find a vantage above the river mouth with a view of Waimea Pier and the island of Niihau. There are restrooms and a pay phone at the parking lot.

WAIMEA

Waimea (which means 'reddish water') was the site of an ancient Hawaiian settlement. It was at Waimea, on January 19, 1778, that Captain Cook made his first Hawaiian landing. In 1820 the first wave of missionaries to Hawaii also selected Waimea as a landing site. In 1884 Waimea Sugar moved in and Waimea developed into a plantation town.

Today Waimea remains the biggest town on this side of the island. Although Hurricane Iniki leveled many of its finer old wooden buildings, including the century-old Ako Store and the historic Waimea Hawaiian Church, the town still has some notable sites.

If you want to explore, Waimea Library, at the 23-mile marker, has a map of historical buildings that can be used for a self-guided walking tour. The library (☎ 338-1738) is open from noon to 8 pm Mondays and Wednesdays and from 9 am to 5 pm Tuesdays, Thursdays and Fridays.

Waimea has an annual Captain Cook fair around the last weekend in February with carnival games, live music, pig-on-a-spit, cotton candy and lots of beer.

Waimea Canyon Drive (Hwy 50) heads north from town to Kokee State Park.

Lucy Wright Park

The Cook landing site is noted with a simple plaque on a nondescript rock on the western side of Waimea River. The plaque is on the beach at Lucy Wright Park, on Ala Wai Rd, just over the Waimea Bridge. This county park also has a ball field, picnic tables, restrooms and showers. Camping is allowed on a flat grassy area, but it's at the side of the road in town and doesn't have much appeal.

Captain Cook Statue

The statue of Captain Cook in the center of town is a replica of the original statue by Sir John Tweed that stands in Whitby, England. The Pacific's greatest navigator, clutching his charts and decked out in his best captain finery, now watches over traffic on Hwy 50.

Waimea Pier

Until Port Allen was built, Waimea was the region's main harbor. It was a major port of call for whalers and traders during the mid-1800s and plantations started exporting sugar from here later in the century.

Waimea Pier, off Pokole Rd, is now used primarily for pole fishing, crabbing and picnicking.

Waimea Churches

The **Waimea Foreign Mission Church** was originally a thatched structure built in 1826 by the Reverend Samuel Whitney, the first missionary to Waimea. Whitney and his wife are buried in the churchyard. The present church was built of sandstone blocks and coral mortar in 1858 by the Reverend George Rowell.

In 1865 Reverend Rowell had a spat with some folks in the congregation and went off and built the **Waimea Hawaiian Church**, a wooden frame church downed in the 1992 hurricane.

It was Rowell who finished building the Gulick-Rowell House, at the end of Huakai Rd. Construction began in 1829, making it the oldest house still standing in Kauai. The two-story stone block house is now privately owned and not open to the public.

Menehune Ditch

Menehune Ditch is a stone and earthen aqueduct built prior to Western contact. Kauai's legendary little people, the mene-hunes, are said to have built the ditch in one night. The ditch was an engineering masterpiece with rocks carefully squared and jointed to create a watertight seal.

When Captain Vancouver visited Waimea at the end of the 18th century he walked up the river valley atop the wall of this ditch, which also served as a footpath. He estimated the walls to be a full 24 feet high. These days most of the ancient waterway lies buried beneath the road, but one section about two feet high can still be seen. The ditch still diverts water from the Waimea River along and through the cliff to irrigate the taro patches below.

To get there, turn at the police station onto Menehune Rd and go about 1⅓ miles up Waimea River. The ditch is along the left side of the road after a very small parking area.

On the drive up to the ditch, notice the scattered holes in the cliffs to the left. They are Hawaiian burial caves. One group of seven caves behind the Waimea Shingon Mission was explored by Wendell Bennett of the Bishop Museum in the 1920s. At that time each of the caves held a number of skeletal remains, some in canoe-shaped coffins and others in hollowed-out logs.

Places to Stay

The *Waimea Plantation Cottages* (☎ 338-1625, (800) 992-4632; fax 338-1619), 9600 Kaumualii Hwy, No 367, Waimea, HI 96796, is a collection of nearly 50 plantation workers' homes that date to the early 1900s. The wooden cottages, which are clustered in a coconut grove, are cutesy-rustic right down to their tin-roofed porches. They've been thoroughly restored and pleasantly decorated with ceiling fans and appropriately simple decor. Rates range from $110 for a smaller one-bedroom cottage that sleeps two to $225 for a three-bedroom cottage that can sleep up to eight. A three-night minimum is required for most of the year, eight nights during holiday periods. To complete the plantation facade, there's a two-story five-bedroom 'manager's estate' that rents for $2450 a week.

Places to Eat

C&K Cafe (☎ 338-0009), on the highway in Waimea, is a takeout pizza and sandwich shop that will deliver in the Waimea/Kekaha area. Pizza prices range from $8 for a small cheese to $19 for a large combination, while sandwiches average $5. It's open daily except Sundays from 11 am to 3 pm and 5 to 9 pm (10 pm on weekends).

There's a *Subway Sandwiches* near C&K Cafe and a *Dairy Queen* a few hundred yards farther west on Hwy 50. The *Kauai Kitchen*, next to Big Save supermarket, has standard plate lunches for $4.50 to $5.50.

The *Grove Dining Room* at Waimea

To Kokee State Park

Waimea

0   200   400 m
0   200   400 yards

Hospital
Gulick-Rowell House
Huakai Rd
Waimea Park
To Kekaha, Polihale State Park
Kaumualii Hwy
Waimea Plantation Cottages
Dairy Queen
Old Sugar Mill
Library
Waimea Canyon Dr
Makeke Rd
Waimea Foreign Mission Church
Waimea High School
Subway Sandwiches
C&K Cafe
Pokole Rd
Waimea Hawaiian Church
Big Save/Kauai Kitchen
Menehune Rd
To Menehune Ditch
Captain Cook Statue
First Hawaiian Bank
Waimea Pier
Ala Wai Rd
Lucy Wright Park
Waimea River
To Hanapepe
Captain Cook Landing
Russian Fort Elizabeth
Laauokala Point

PACIFIC OCEAN

Plantation Cottages serves breakfast weekdays, and lunch and dinner daily. Breakfast has the usual offerings while lunch features moderately priced sandwiches and salads. Dinners, which are served with a salad or soup, include pepper steak for $15, fresh fish for $18 and a steak and lobster combination for $29. While the food is not distinguished the setting is quite pleasant, with dining on the porch.

KEKAHA
Kekaha has great beaches, or rather it has one long glorious stretch. The road follows the beach for about two miles, with road-

side parking all along the way. This is open ocean and when the surf is high there can be dangerous currents; when there's no swell you can usually find swimmers here. Niihau and its offshore island, Lehua, are visible from the beach.

There's a very inconspicuous shower just mauka of the highway between Alae Rd and Amakihi Rd, and restrooms and picnic tables farther in.

A few blocks inland from the beach is Kekaha Rd, the main village street, which runs parallel to the highway. It has a couple of grocery stores and eateries, a post office and the last gas station before the end of the

KAUAI

Hula dancer with dog tooth leg ornaments and
feather rattle by John Webber

road. The village's most dominant feature
is its working sugar mill, which is visible
from the highway.

On its eastern end, Kekaha Rd comes out
to Hwy 50 near the Kikiaola Small Boat
Harbor. This state harbor has one launch
ramp and eight mooring spaces.

Kekaha is Kauai's westernmost town and
as you continue on towards Polihale it's a
rural scene, with the inland cliffs getting
higher and the ravines deeper. Corn and
sunflowers, which are planted for seed production, grow in farms along the road.
Cattle and cattle egrets feed in the pastures.

Places to Stay

Mindy's (☎ 337-9275), 8842 Kekaha Rd,
Box 861, Kekaha, HI 96796, is the only
accommodations alternative beyond Waimea (other than camping) and would make
a good base for exploring Kokee and the
southwest coast. Mindy and Dave Heri
have a pleasant upstairs apartment in their
house, with a large deck, a full kitchen and
a living room with a double sofa bed. The
bedroom has a double bed and a cane field
view. The place is modern and comfortable
with ceiling fans throughout, TV, radio and
a shower/tub combination in the bathroom.

The rate is $55 if there's one person, $60
for up to four people; add $10 more if
you're staying for just one night. Complimentary fruit and coffee are provided.

Places to Eat

Richie's Ono Saimin & Bento Shop, on
Kekaha Rd at the base of Hwy 550, serves
simple local food including a reasonable, if
salty, saimin for $3 a bowl. It's open from 9
am to 2 pm daily, until 10 pm on Fridays
and Saturdays.

In the same center is the *Menehune Food
Mart*, which has wrapped sandwiches and
basic salads, and a *Lappert's* ice cream
shop, which also sells sandwiches.

BARKING SANDS

Barking Sands Pacific Missile Range, a US
Navy base, usually has at least one stretch
of its beach open to the public. For a
recorded message on current access, dial
335-4229.

The road in is at the 'Pacific Missile
Range Facility' sign, less than half a mile
after the 32-mile marker. At the gate they
ask to see your driver's license and then
explain where you can go, which is usually
the beach about two miles south of the gate,
which locals call Majors Bay and the military calls RecArea No 3.

This broad curving sweep of fine golden
sand is a good sunbathing and walking
beach, though it's open and hot. The bush
behind the beach offers no shade, but it
hardly matters as the vegetation line is the
demilitarized zone line and you're forbidden to go beyond it anyway.

Majors Bay is a popular winter surfing
spot, although like all West Side beaches
the waters can be dangerous. There are no
facilities. The purple-tinged island of
Niihau can be seen on the horizon.

On very sunny days, when the wind is
blowing off the water just right, the moving
sands make sounds similar to barking dogs,
hence the area's name.

The missile range facility at Barking
Sands provides the above-ground link to a
sophisticated sonar network that tracks
more than 1000 square miles of the Pacific.

Established during WW II, it's been developed into the world's largest underwater listening device. The equipment is sensitive enough to pick up the songs of wintering humpback whales. The base has gathered the most comprehensive collection of humpback whale soundtracks recorded anywhere.

POLIHALE

Polihale is near-desert. When it's raining everywhere else, beachgoers head this way.

Polihale has a beautiful long white sand beach with aqua-colored water that often comes to shore in huge explosive waves. Expert surfers occasionally give Polihale a try, but strong rip currents make the waters treacherous for swimming.

Polihale State Park is about five miles from the Barking Sands military base. Turn left three-quarters of a mile north of the base entrance onto a wide dirt road that runs through sugar cane fields. The road is a bit bumpy but passable. Set your odometer at zero here.

At 3⅓ miles, at a large spreading tree in the middle of the road, a turn-off leads to the only safe swimming spot in the area. To get there turn left at the tree and then after a quarter of a mile follow the road up the hill to the right to the base of the dunes. Walk a couple of minutes to the north along the shore and you'll come to **Queen's Pond**, where a large semicircle of reef comes almost to shore creating a protected swimming pool. When the seas are relatively calm the reef blocks the longshore currents; however, when surf breaks over the reef and into the pool a dangerous rip current runs toward an opening at the southern end of the reef. The rest of the beach is bordered by open sea.

To get to **Polihale State Park** go back to the tree at the main cane road, turn left and continue down a mile. A turn-off on the left leads to a camping area with restrooms, outdoor showers, drinking water and a picnic pavilion. Farther down, other camping areas are in the dunes just above the beach amidst thorny kiawe trees.

At the very end of the beach is Polihale

Cliff, marking the western end of the Na Pali Coast. Combined with the untamed ocean and vast expansive beach, it's a magnificent sight. Sunsets can be a meditative experience.

There's a terraced **heiau** towards the base of the cliff. It was originally on the beach but over the years shifting sands have added a 300-foot buffer between the heiau and the sea. The heiau is so overgrown that even after you tramp into the brush and find it, it's really hard to get a perspective on it. Wasps are another obstacle – if you're allergic to stings, forget about exploring this one.

WAIMEA CANYON

Waimea Canyon is nicknamed the 'Grand Canyon of the Pacific'. This may sound like promotional hype but it's not a bad description. Although it's smaller and 200 million years younger than the famed Arizona canyon, the Waimea Canyon is certainly grand.

The canyon's colorful river-cut gorge is 2785 feet deep. The river that runs through it, the Waimea-Poomau, is 19½ miles long, Kauai's longest. All in all, it seems incredible that such an immense canyon could be tucked inside such a small island.

The view of the canyon is usually a bit hazy. The best time to be there is a sunny day after it's been raining heavily. At such times, the earth's a deeper red and waterfalls cascade throughout the canyon. You can't beat it.

Waimea Canyon Drive

Waimea Canyon Drive (Hwy 550) starts in Waimea. The road is 19 miles long, ending at lookouts with terrific views into Kalalau Valley on the Na Pali Coast.

The views start about a mile up from Waimea and get better and better as the road climbs. There are plenty of little scenic lookouts where you can stop to take it all in. The one at 1¾ miles looks down on the Waimea River and the taro patches that are irrigated by the Menehune Ditch. About 2½ miles up there are good views across cane fields to Kekaha Beach with

KAUAI

Niihau in the background. From there on it's all canyon views.

WAIMEA CANYON STATE PARK

The southern boundary of Waimea Canyon State Park is about six miles up. Waimea Canyon Drive and Kokee Road, both labeled Hwy 550, merge nearby. Kokee Rd, which climbs up from Kekaha, also has scenic views, but not of the canyon. After the two roads merge, the single road continuing north is called Kokee Rd.

Iliau Nature Loop

The marked trailhead for the Iliau Nature Loop is near the nine-mile marker. Just a hundred feet up the trail there's a bench with a scenic view, though for the best angle take a two-minute walk to the left where a cliffside bench provides a topnotch view into Waimea Canyon. After heavy rainfall waterfalls explode down the sheer rock walls across the gorge.

Iliau Loop starts at the first bench and takes about 10 minutes to walk. Iliau, a plant endemic to western Kauai, grows along the trail, with stalks up to 10 feet high. Like its cousin the silversword, iliau grows to a ripe old age. Then for a grand finale it bursts open with blossoms and dies.

Scenic Lookouts

The most scenic of the lookout points along this stretch, **Waimea Canyon Lookout** is clearly signposted a third of a mile north of the 10-mile marker. The lookout offers a sweeping view of Waimea Canyon from a perch of 3100 feet. The prominent canyon running in an easterly direction off Waimea is Koaie Canyon, which is accessible to backcountry hikers.

As you continue up the road Waipoo Falls can be seen from a couple of small unmarked lookouts before the 12-mile marker and then at the marked **Puu Ka Pele Viewpoint**. When the light is right a rainbow shows up in the spray of the 800-foot falls. Across the road from the viewpoint is a picnic area with barbecue pits,

restrooms and water, as well as Camp Hale Koa, a Seventh Day Adventist camp.

Puu Hinahina Lookout, at 3640 feet, is a major turn-off between the 13- and 14-mile markers. There are two lookouts close to the parking lot. One has a fine view down Waimea Canyon clear out to the coast, while the other has a view of Niihau.

Waimea Canyon Trails

The trailhead for the **Kukui Trail** is near the nine-mile marker. This trail continues from the Iliau Nature Loop at a sign-in box and picnic table. From there the Kukui Trail makes a steep 2000-foot descent down the western side of Waimea Canyon, 2½ miles to the Waimea River. Wiliwili Camp is at the end of the trail.

The **Koaie Canyon Trail** begins at Kaluahaulu Camp, half a mile up the Waimea River from the end of the Kukui Trail. From there it runs east for three miles along the southern side of Koaie Canyon. There are some good swimming holes in the stream along the way and at the end of the trail. This trail should be avoided during stormy weather due to the danger of flash flooding.

The canyon's fertile soil once supported an ancient Hawaiian settlement. It's long abandoned, but the remains of a heiau and some house sites are still discernible. The Koaie Canyon Trail passes Hipalau Camp and ends at Lonomea Camp.

All four camps on these trails are part of the forest reserve system. Although they have simple open-air shelters, there are no facilities and the water needs to be treated before drinking. Information on permits is given in the Camping section near the beginning of this chapter.

A third trail in this area is the eight-mile **Waimea Canyon Trail**, which runs south from Wiliwili Camp to the town of Waimea, ending on Menehune Rd. Much of the trail is along a 4WD road that leads to a hydroelectric power station. While there's public access along the route, the trail passes over private property so no camping is allowed. There are a number of river crossings, making the trail best considered only during periods of dry weather.

During weekends and holidays, all of these trails are fairly heavily used by pig hunters.

KOKEE STATE PARK

The Kokee State Park boundary starts beyond the Puu Hinahina Lookout. After the 15-mile marker, you'll pass park cabins, Kokee Lodge, a museum and a campground one after the other. Kokee Lodge is not an overnight lodge but a restaurant and the concessionaire station for the nearby cabins.

The ranger station in Kokee hasn't been staffed for years, but the people at the Kokee Museum can provide a little assistance, including basic information on current trail conditions. There's also an information board and trail map posted outside the museum.

At 7:25 and 8:25 am KUAI radio station (720 AM) announces the weather conditions at Kokee State Park.

Kokee Museum

A good place to learn about Kauai's ecology is the Kokee Museum (☎ 335-9975), which features displays of local plants, birds, climate and geology. There are also detailed topographical maps of the area and a glass case of poi pounders, stone adze heads and other historic artifacts. Koa bowls, trail maps and books are for sale. The museum is open from 10 am to 4 pm daily and admission is free.

Ask at the museum for the brochure corresponding to the short nature loop that circles in back of the museum. There are 35 numbered plants and trees, many of them native Hawaiian species, detailed in the brochure, beginning with a koa tree directly behind the museum.

By the way, the chickens that congregate in the museum parking lot are not the common garden variety, but *moa*, or jungle fowl. Early Polynesian settlers brought *moa* to Hawaii and they were once common on all the main islands. Now they remain solely on Kauai, the only island

that's free of mongooses, an introduced mammal that preys on the eggs of ground-nesting birds.

Kalalau Lookouts

The two Kalalau Valley lookouts at the end of the road are not to be missed.

The first, the **Kalalau Lookout**, is at the 18-mile marker. From a height of 4000 feet you can see deep into the green depths of the valley straight out to the sea. When the weather is cooperative, late afternoon rainbows sweep so deeply into Kalalau Valley that the bottom part of the bows curve back inward. Bright-red apapane birds feed from the flowers of the ohia lehua trees near the lookout railings.

Kalalau Valley was once the site of a large settlement and was joined to Kokee by a very steep trail that ran down the cliffside. These days the only way into the valley is along the coastal Kalalau Trail from Haena on the North Shore.

The cone-shaped pinnacles along the valley walls look rather like a row of sentinels standing at attention. One legend says that rain has sculptured the cliffsides into the shape of the proud chiefs who are buried in the mountains.

The mushroom-shaped white dome and satellite dishes visible on the hill as you walk back to the parking lot are part of the Kokee Air Force station.

The paved road continues another mile to **Puu O Kila Lookout**. This is the last leg of the aborted Kokee-Haena Hwy, which

---

Meadow Spirits

According to legend Kanalohuluhulu Meadow, opposite Kokee Museum, was once a forested hide-out for an evil akua (spirit) who enjoyed harassing people passing through on their way to Kalalau Valley. Distraught travelers appealed to the great god Kanaloa to protect them from the akua. Kanaloa responded by ripping out all the trees and declaring that they were never again to grow here, thus destroying the akua's hiding place. These days the meadow is full of good vibes and makes a nice place to throw a frisbee. ∎

would have linked Kokee with the North Shore, thus creating a circle-island road. One look at the cliffs at the end of the road and you'll understand why the scheme was scrapped.

The Pihea Trail that climbs the ridge straight ahead runs along what was to be the road.

From this lookout you get another view into Kalalau Valley and a glance inland toward the Alakai Swamp. A sign here points to Waialeale, the wettest spot on earth.

Kokee State Park Trails

Kokee State Park is the starting point for about 45 miles of trails, some maintained by the park service, others by the forestry. Pig and goat hunters use some of these trails during the hunting season, so it's a good idea for hikers to wear bright-colored clothing.

Three of the trails – Nualolo, Awaawapuhi and Pihea – offer clifftop views into valleys on the Na Pali Coast. A couple of trails go into the swampy bogs of Alakai Swamp while others are easy nature trails.

Halemanu Road Trails Halemanu Rd, the starting point for several scenic hikes, is just north of the 14-mile marker. Whether or not the road is passable in a non-4WD vehicle often depends on whether it's been raining recently. Keep in mind that the clay roads provide no traction when wet and even if you're able to drive a car in, should it begin to rain driving out can be another matter!

The first hike is **Cliff Trail**, where a short five-minute walk leads to an overlook into Waimea Canyon. From there you can continue along **Canyon Trail**, a rather strenuous 1½ miles one way that follows the canyon rim, passes Waipoo Falls and ends at Kumuwela Lookout with views down the canyon to the ocean beyond. On both trails there's a good chance of spotting feral goats scrambling along the canyon walls.

A little farther down Halemanu Rd is the start of **Halemanu-Kokee Trail**. This easy 1¼-mile (one way) nature trail passes through a native forest of koa and ohia trees that provide a habitat for native birds, including the iiwi, apapane, amakihi and elepaio. One of the common plants found on this trail is banana poka, a member of the passion fruit family and a serious invasive pest. It has pretty pink flowers but it drapes the forest with its vines and chokes out less aggressive native plants.

Nualolo & Awaawapuhi Trails The Nualolo and Awaawapuhi trails each go out to the very edge of sheer cliffs, peering down into valleys accessible only by boat. The valley views are extraordinarily beautiful.

The Nualolo and Awaawapuhi trails connect via the Nualolo Cliff Trail. You can combine the three trails to make for a hardy day hike of about 10 miles. Then you'll have to either hitch a ride or walk an additional two miles back down the road to where you started.

Bring plenty of water as there's none along the way. Edible plants along the trail include blackberries, thimbleberries, guava and passion fruit (lilikoi).

Wild goats, prolific in the North Shore valleys, are readily spotted along the cliff walls. Capable of breeding at five months of age, the goats have no natural predators in Hawaii and their unchecked numbers have caused a fair amount of ecological damage.

The 3¾-mile Nualolo Trail starts between the cabins and Kokee Lodge. The trail begins in cool upland forest and descends 1500 feet, ending with a fine view from Lolo Vista Point, a lookout on the valley rim. There's a USGS survey marker at the lookout, at an elevation of 2234 feet.

The trailhead for the Awaawapuhi Trail begins at a small parking area just after the 17-mile marker. The trail descends 1600 feet, ending after 3¼ miles at a steep and spectacular pali overlooking Awaawapuhi and Nualolo valleys. The hike starts in an ohia forest. About half a mile down the trail, the forest becomes dryer and koa begins to mix in with the ohia. Some of the trees and plants along the trail are marked a corresponding interpretive nature guide is available free from the forestry office in Lihue. Awaawapuhi means 'valley of ginger'. Kahili, a yellow ginger, is seen at marker number nine.

The two-mile Nualolo Cliff Trail is very scenic and offers numerous viewpoints into Nualolo Valley. There's even a picnic table where you can break for lunch along the way. The Nualolo Cliff Trail connects at the Nualolo Trail near the 3¼-mile mark and at the Awaawapuhi Trail a little short of the three-mile mark.

Kawaikoi Stream Trail The Kawaikoi Stream Trail begins between the Sugi Grove and Kawaikoi campgrounds, off Camp 10-Mohihi Rd. This is a scenic mountain stream trail of about three miles round-trip. It starts out following the southern side of Kawaikoi Stream, then heads away from the stream and makes a loop, coming down the northern side of the stream before reconnecting with the southern side. If the stream is running high, don't make the crossings.

Kawaikoi Stream is popular for rainbow trout fishing, which is allowed during an open season in August and September. Fishing licenses are required.

Camp 10-Mohihi Rd is up past the museum on the right. Like many of the dirt roads in Kokee, when it's dry, standard cars can usually make it in. However on those rare occasions when it's really wet and rutted, even 4WD vehicles can have difficulty.

Pihea Trail The Pihea Trail starts from the Puu O Kila Lookout and combines coastal views and an opportunity to see some of the Alakai wilderness. The beginning of the trail was graded in the 1950s, before plans to make this the last leg of the circle-island road were abandoned.

The first mile of the trail runs along the ridge, offering fine views into Kalalau Valley. The Pihea Trail eventually turns inland through wetland forest and at about 1¾ miles crosses the Alakai Swamp Trail. If you turn left here you can continue on for

about two miles through the Alakai Swamp to Kilohana Lookout. If you go straight instead, you will reach Kawaikoi camp in about two miles.

Alakai Swamp Trail Alakai Swamp is inaccessible enough that even invasive plants haven't been able to choke out the endemic swamp vegetation, and native bird species still have a stronghold.

There are parts of the swamp that receive sunlight so sparingly that the moss grows thick and fat on all sides of the trees. Most people that see this swamp see it from a helicopter but it's possible to walk through a corner of it by taking the Alakai Swamp Trail.

This rough 3½-mile trail starts off Camp 10-Mohihi Rd and goes through rainforest and bogs before reaching Kilohana Lookout on Wainiha Pali. If it's not overcast hikers will be rewarded with a sweeping view of Wainiha and Hanalei valleys. Most of the time this is an extremely wet and muddy trail, and there are plenty of stories of people slogging knee-deep in it.

If your car can't make it down Camp 10-Mohihi Rd, parking at Puu O Kila Lookout and approaching Alakai Swamp Trail via the Pihea Trail is probably your best bet.

Kaluapuhi Trail The Kaluapuhi Trail, a forest trail leading to a plum grove, is about two miles long. The trailhead starts at the highway a quarter of a mile past the 17-mile marker. This is a busy trail during midsummer when lots of islanders come up to pick the wild plums.

Places to Stay

Kokee Lodge (☎ 335-6061), Box 819, Waimea, HI 96796, manages the 12 cabins in Kokee State Park. The oldest cabins are a little tired and have just one large room with three beds for $35. Better are the two-bedroom cedar cabins at $45. The cabins have basic kitchens, linens, blankets, hot showers and wood stoves, and rates are the same for up to six people. State park rules limit stays to five days. The cabins are often booked up well in advance, although cancellations do occur and you can occasionally get a cabin at the last moment if you're flexible.

The YWCA's *Camp Sloggett* in Kokee State Park has a lodge that sleeps up to 10 people and a bunkhouse that holds 35. The place is rented to only one group at a time. The cost is $12 per person per night for Hawaiian residents, $20 per person for non-residents, and the minimum charge is for five people on weekdays and eight people on weekends. One box of wood is provided for the wood stove; additional boxes cost $5. Bookings are made through the YWCA (☎ 245-5959), 3094 Elua St, Lihue, HI 96766. The camp is about half a mile east of the park museum down a dirt road that's usually passable in an ordinary car.

Camping Kokee State Park's single campground is immediately north of the meadow at Kokee Lodge. The sites, which are in an uncrowded grassy area beside the woods, are nicely laid out, each with its own barbecue pit, picnic table and running water. There are restrooms and showers. Camping is free and allowed for up to five nights, but state camping permits must be obtained before arriving in Kokee.

If you want to get farther off the main track or extend your stay a few more days, there are also two campgrounds, Kawaikoi and Sugi Grove, off Camp 10-Mohihi Rd in the forest reserve adjacent to the state park.

The campgrounds are at an elevation of almost 4000 feet and nights are crisp and cool. This is sleeping bag and warm clothing country.

For more information on camping permits, see Camping in the Accommodations section of this chapter.

Places to Eat

Kokee Lodge (☎ 335-6061) is the only place to eat north of Waimea. Open from 9 am to 3:30 pm daily, the menu includes Portuguese bean soup, quiche, chili and sandwiches for $6 or less, and lilikoi pie for $3. The gift shop in front of the restaurant is open to 4 pm and sells candy bars and soft drinks.

If you're staying in the cabins or campgrounds be sure to bring ample provisions as the nearest stores (and gas station) are in Waimea, 15 miles away.

Niihau

Niihau has long been closed to outsiders, earning it the nickname 'The Forbidden Island'.

No other place in Hawaii has more successfully turned its back on change than Niihau, which has no paved roads, no airport, no island-wide electricity and no telephones.

Niihau is a native Hawaiian preserve and the only island in the state where Hawaiian is still the primary language. The entire island, right down to the church, belongs to the Niihau Ranch, which is privately owned by the non-Hawaiian Robinson family. They are highly protective of Niihau's isolation.

Most of Niihau's 230 residents live in **Puuwai**, a settlement on the dry western shore, and make a living working the Robinson's ranch. Each house in the village is surrounded by a stone wall to keep grazing animals out of the gardens. It's a simple life; water is collected in catchments and toilets are in outhouses.

Niihauans speak their own melodic dialect of Hawaiian. Business is conducted in Hawaiian, as are Sunday church services. Both of the Robinson brothers who manage the ranch speak Hawaiian fluently.

Children learn English as a second language when they go to school. Niihau has a two-room schoolhouse where two teachers and two educational aides teach from kindergarten through 12th grade. Courses are taught solely in Hawaiian up to the fourth grade.

The island economy is based on sheep and cattle ranching, which on windswept Niihau is a marginal operation. Niihau has been through some hard times; major droughts of the 1970s and '80s took a toll on the herds.

A secondary income comes from the production of mesquite charcoal from the kiawe that flourishes in the dry, dusty environment. The mesquite is shipped off to restaurants around Hawaii.

Niihau is 17 miles from Kauai via a weekly supply boat that plies between the two islands. The boat, an old WW II military landing craft, docks in Kauai at Makaweli, headquarters of Niihau Ranch and the Robinson family. Makaweli is also home to a settlement of Niihauans who prefer to live on Kauai, though many of them still work for the Robinsons.

Niihau is by no means a living history museum of Hawaiians stuck in time. Although it's got a foot in the past it takes what it wants from the present. The supply boat brings sodas as well as poi, and the island has more dirt bikes than outrigger canoes.

Niihau residents are free to go to Kauai to shop, have a few beers (Niihau itself is dry) or just hang out. What they are not free to do is bring friends from other islands back home with them. Those Niihauans who marry people from other islands, as well as those whom the Robinsons come to see as undesirable, are rarely allowed to return.

Still, for the most part, Niihauans seem to accept that that's the way things are. Some who leave are critical, but those who stay don't appear to be looking for any changes.

To outsiders, Niihau is an enigma. Some

Niihau Shell Leis

Niihauans create fine handcrafted necklaces made of tiny seashells painstakingly strung in spiral strands and intricate patterns. These Niihau shell leis are Hawaii's most highly prized and priced. They are sold in fine jewelry shops and craft galleries on the other islands, some for well over $1000.

The shells used in the necklaces are found mainly on Niihau beaches, where they are collected by sifting through the sand. Smaller numbers of these shells can also be found on Kauai. ■

Niihau

Lehua
Island
702 ft

Puukole
Point

Kii Landing

0   4   8 km

0   2   4 miles

Paniau
1281 ft

Puuwai

Halulu
Lake

Pueo Point

Halalii
Lake

Keamahaki
Bay

Kaulakahi Channel

Kawaihoa
Point

romanticize it as a pristine preserve of Hawaiian culture. Others liken its lifestyle to slavery.

The Robinsons see Niihau as a private sanctuary and themselves as the protectors of it all. It's that paternalism that sometimes rubs outside native Hawaiian groups the wrong way, though for the most part Niihauans don't seem to share those sentiments and they resist interference.

HISTORY

Captain Cook anchored off Niihau on January 29, 1778, two weeks after 'discovering' Hawaii. Cook noted in his log that the island was lightly populated and largely barren, a description still true today. His visit was short, but it had a lasting impact.

It was on little Niihau that Cook first introduced two things that would quickly change the face of Hawaii. He left two goats, the first of the grazing animals that would devastate the native flora and fauna. And his men introduced syphilis, the first of the Western diseases that would decimate the Hawaiian people.

In 1864 Elizabeth Sinclair, a Scottish widow who was moving from New Zea-

and to Vancouver when she got side-tracked in Hawaii, bought Niihau from King Kamehameha V for $10,000. He originally tried to sell her the 'swampland' of Waikiki, but she passed it up for the 'desert island'. Interestingly, no two places in Hawaii today could be further apart, either culturally or in land value.

Mrs Sinclair brought the first sheep to Niihau from New Zealand and started the ranching operation that her great-grandsons continue today.

GEOGRAPHY

Niihau is the smallest of the inhabited Hawaiian Islands. It is 18 miles long and six miles wide, with a total area of 70 sq miles. It has 45 miles of coast and the highest elevation is 1281 feet. The island is semi-arid, in the lee of Kauai.

Niihau's 860-acre Halalii Lake is the largest in Hawaii, though even during the rainy winter season it's only a few feet deep. In the summer it sometimes dries up to a mud pond. About 50% of Hawaii's endangered coots breed on Niihau – when there's enough water.

GETTING THERE & AWAY

The Robinsons have 'opened up' Niihau to tourism – via pricey helicopter flights.

Niihau Helicopters (☎ 335-3500), Box 370, Makaweli, HI 96769, runs tours at 9 am, noon and 3 pm, as long as they have a minimum of four passengers. The tours, which last three hours and take off from Burns Field in Kauai, cost $235 per person. The helicopter makes two stops, one at **Puukole Point** on the northern end of the island, and the other at **Keanahaki Bay**, on the southern end of the island where Captain Cook landed. They fly over much of Niihau, but avoid Puuwai village where people live.

The helicopter was purchased for emergency medical evacuations and the tours are given in an effort to defray the cost.

Northwestern Hawaiian Islands

The Northwestern Hawaiian Islands, also called the Leeward Islands, stretch from Kauai nearly 1300 miles across the Pacific in an almost straight northwesterly line.

The islands, volcanic in origin, once jutted up high above sea level as the main Hawaiian Islands do now. However, they are slowly slipping back into the sea as a result of a sagging of the ocean floor and the forces of erosion. Where the mountains once raised their heads, coral reefs now appear like flower leis left floating on the water.

There are 10 island clusters in all; together the clusters have 33 islands, all of which are small. They include atolls, each with a number of low sand islands formed on top of coral reefs, as well as some single rock islands and a reef that is mostly submerged.

Listed according to their order from Kauai, the clusters are Nihoa, Necker Island, French Frigate Shoals, Gardner Pinnacles, Maro Reef, Laysan Island, Lisianski Island, Pearl and Hermes Atoll, Midway Islands and Kure Atoll.

Excluding Midway, the total land area is just under three sq miles, though the atoll lagoon areas are a hundred times that.

All the groups except Kure Atoll (a state seabird sanctuary) and the Midway Islands are part of the Hawaiian Islands National Wildlife Refuge. The refuge, established in 1909 by US President Theodore Roosevelt, is the oldest and largest of the national wildlife refuges.

Visitors are not allowed on the islands unless they have permits, and these are granted only in the rarest of circumstances. Human activities are simply too disturbing

Northwestern
Hawaiian Islands

PACIFIC
OCEAN

to the fragile ecosystem. The only human habitation in the refuge is at Tern Island, and that is for wildlife researchers.

The Midway Islands, though geographically in the Hawaiian archipelago, are under the control of the US Navy and not part of the state of Hawaii. Midway has five islands, with a total land area of two sq miles, and a population of about 2000. Midway gained notoriety during WW II when the USA secured a major victory over Japan in a naval battle there in June 1942.

The other islands come under the political, though not the practical, jurisdiction of the City and County of Honolulu.

FAUNA

The Northwestern Hawaiian Islands are home to around 15 million seabirds, all of which find room for at least a foothold. Endangered Hawaiian monk seals, green sea turtles and four endemic land birds also live there.

Seabirds

Eighteen seabird species nest on these islands, feeding on the abundant fish that live around the submerged reefs. They include frigate birds, boobies, albatrosses, terns, shearwaters, petrels, tropicbirds and noddies.

The sooty terns are the most abundant, numbering in the several millions. These screeching black and white birds also nest on the offshore islets of Oahu's windward coast.

Shearwaters and petrels lay their eggs in burrows that they dig in the sandy soil. The roofs of the burrows can easily collapse under the feet of nonobservant walkers, which is one reason why visitors are discouraged.

Land Birds

The Laysan duck, Laysan finch, Nihoa finch and Nihoa millerbird, endemic to Laysan and Nihoa islands respectively, are all listed as endangered or threatened species.

This is not because their numbers are declining, but because these species exist in only one place on earth and are therefore susceptible to the introduction of new diseases and predators or the disruption of their habitat. One rat from a shipwrecked boat, weed seed from a hiker's boot or an oil slick washing ashore could mean the end of the species.

Monk Seals

The endangered Hawaiian monk seal, which exists only in Hawaii, uses Kure Atoll, the French Frigate Shoals and Laysan, Lisianski, Nihoa and Necker islands for pupping grounds. The seals are easily disturbed by human contact.

In the 19th century the seals were nearly hunted to extinction. Military operations in the area during and after WW II also resulted in a decline.

Fewer than 200 seal pups are born each year, many of which die from shark attacks. The total species population is around a thousand.

FRENCH FRIGATE SHOALS

The French Frigate Shoals consist of 13 sand islands and a 135-foot rock, La Perouse Pinnacle, which was named after the French explorer who was almost wrecked on the reef. One of the sand islands, 37-acre Tern Island, is the field headquarters for the Hawaiian Islands National Wildlife Refuge.

Most of Tern Island is covered by an airfield left over from the days when the US Coast Guard had a loran (radio navigation system) station there. The old Coast Guard barracks now house two refuge managers who work for the US Fish & Wildlife Service, and up to a dozen volunteers.

Tern Island is home to 17 species of seabirds and a lot of Hawaiian monk seals. Ninety percent of the green sea turtles that nest in the Hawaiian Islands nest at French Frigate Shoals.

LAYSAN ISLAND

Laysan Island is a classic example of how human interference can wreak havoc on island ecology.

Laysan is 1.45 sq miles in size, which though small is actually the largest of the Northwestern Hawaiian Islands. From 1890 to 1904 Laysan was mined for guano – the phosphate-rich bird droppings used for fertilizer. Houses were built, mules were brought ashore as pack animals and ships docked to take the guano away.

There were once millions of birds on Laysan – mostly Laysan albatrosses, otherwise known as gooney birds. In addition to guano mining, albatross eggs were collected by the hundreds of thousands to be sold for their albumen, a substance used in photo processing.

As each albatross lays just one egg a year, an 'egging' sweep could destroy an entire year's hatch. Hunters also ravaged the island. In one six-month period alone, 300,000 birds were killed for their feathers, which were used by milliners to make hats for fashionable ladies.

There are now about 160,000 pairs of Laysan albatrosses on the island, still the world's largest colony. Albatrosses sometimes court and dance for five annual mating seasons before actually mating. Once they do mate, pairs stay together for life and sometimes live for 30 years.

Rabbits, introduced to Laysan first as pets for the workers' children and later for breeding, virtually destroyed the island's vegetation, and where they left off sandstorms took over. The loss of native food plants spelled the end of the Laysan flightless rail, Laysan honeycreeper and Laysan millerbird – all endemic land birds. The rabbits were finally exterminated in 1923.

The Laysan duck reached the brink of extinction as a result of the activities of rabbits and hunters. Their numbers were reduced to just six by 1911, but they're making a modest comeback. Laysan ducks swim in the brackish lagoon in the center of the island, their only habitat. With a current population of about 300, they are one of the rarest ducks in the world.

The Laysan finch, the population of which was once as low as 100 thanks to the rabbits, is once again common on Laysan Island and has also been introduced to Pearl and Hermes Atoll. Unlike its honey-creeper cousins on the main Hawaiian islands, which feed on nectar, the Laysan finch has become carnivorous and feeds on seabird eggs as well as the carcasses of dead seabirds.

There are also more than one million sooty terns nesting on Laysan.

NECKER & NIHOA

Necker and Nihoa, the two islands closest to the main Hawaiian Islands, were probably settled more than a thousand years ago. Remains of stone temple platforms, numerous house sites, terraces and carved stone images have been found on the islands. Archaeological remains suggest that the early settlers were from the Marquesas.

Necker and Nihoa are not coral atolls but rugged rocky islands, each less than a quarter of a square mile. Nihoa is the highest of the Northwestern Hawaiian Islands, with sheer sea cliffs and a peak elevation of 910 feet.

Two land bird species live only on tiny Nihoa and nowhere else.

The Nihoa finch, which like the Laysan finch is a raider of other birds' eggs, is hanging in there with a population of a few thousand. Attempts were made in 1967 to develop a back-up colony in case something happened to the birds on Nihoa. It failed when all 42 finches sent to the French Frigate Shoals died.

The grey Nihoa millerbird, related to the old world warbler family, is rare and secretive. It wasn't even discovered until 1923 and was so named because it eats miller moths. Approximately 400 birds remain.

Glossary

aa – lava which is rough and jagged

ahi – albacore (yellowfin) tuna

ahu – stone cairns used to mark a trail; or an altar or shrine

ahupuaa – a traditional land division, usually in a wedge shape from the mountains to the sea

aikane – friend

aina – land

akamai – clever

aku – skipjack tuna

akua – god, spirit, idol

akule – bigeye mackerel

alii – chief; royalty

aloha – the traditional greeting meaning love, welcome, goodbye

amaama – mullet

amakihi – small yellow-green bird, one of the more common of the native birds

ao – Newell's shearwater (a seabird)

apapane – bright-red native Hawaiian honeycreeper

au – marlin

aumakua – ancestral spirit helper

auwe – Oh my! Alas!

awa – kava, made into an intoxicating brew; milk fish

awapuhi – wild ginger

bento – the Japanese word for a box lunch

cilantro – coriander leaves (also known as Chinese parsley)

crack seed – snack foods, usually dried fruits or seeds, either sour, salty or sweet

elepaio – a brownish forest bird with a white rump

hala – pandanus; the leaves are used in weaving mats and baskets

hale – house

hana – work; or bay, when used as a compound in place names

haole – Caucasian; literally 'without breath', it was formerly applied to any foreigner

hapa – half; person of mixed blood

hau – common indigenous lowland tree with spreading tangled branches; the flower resembles a hibiscus, the wood is often used for outrigger canoes

Hauoli Makahiki Hou – Happy New Year

haupia – coconut pudding

Hawaii nei – all the Hawaiian Islands, as distinguished from the Big Island

heiau – ancient stone temple, a place of worship in Hawaii before Western contact

Hina – Polynesian goddess (wife of Ku, one of the four main gods)

holoholo – to walk, drive or ramble around for pleasure

holoku – a long dress similar to the muu-muu, but more fitted and with a yoke

holua – sled, or sled course

honu – turtle

hoolaulea – celebration, party

huhu – angry

hui – group, organization

hukilau – net fishing, with a seine, involving a group of people; the word can also refer to the feast that follows

hula – traditional Hawaiian dance

hula halau – hula school or troupe

humuhumunukunukuapuaa – rectangular triggerfish

iiwi – a bright-vermillion forest bird with a curved salmon-colored beak

iliahi – Hawaiian sandalwood

ilili – stones

ilima – native groundcover with a delicate yellow-orange flower

imu – underground earthen oven used in traditional luau cooking

kahuna – wise person in any field, commonly a priest, healer or sorcerer

kahuna nui – high priest

kahili – a feather standard, used as a symbol of royalty

kalua – traditional method of baking in an underground oven (imu)

kamaaina – native-born Hawaiian or a long-time resident; literally 'child of the land'

Kanaloa – god of the underworld

kane – man; also the name of one of four top Hawaiian gods

kapu – taboo, part of strict ancient Hawaiian social system

kaunaoa – a thin parasitic vine

kava – a mildly narcotic drink made from the roots of *Piper methysticum*, a pepper shrub

keiki – child, children

kiawe – a relative of the mesquite tree introduced to Hawaii in the 1820s, now very common; its branches are covered with sharp thorns

kipuka – an area of land spared when lava flows around it; an oasis

ko – sugar cane

koa – native hardwood tree often used in woodworking of native crafts

kohola – whale

kokua – help, cooperation

kona – leeward, or a leeward wind

konane – ancient Hawaiian board game similar to checkers

koolau – windward side

Ku – Polynesian god of many manifestations, including god of war, farming and fishing

kukui – the candlenut tree; this is the official state tree and a native to Hawaii; the oil from the nuts was once used in lamps

kuleana – an individually held plot of land

kupuna – grandparent

kuula – fishing shrine

lanai – veranda

lauhala – leaves of the *hala* plant used in weaving

laulau – wrapped package; pork or beef with salted fish and taro leaves wrapped in leaves and steamed

lei – garland, usually of flowers, but also of leaves or shells

lilikoi – passion fruit

limu – seaweed

lio – horse

lolo – stupid, crazy

lomi – raw, diced salmon marinated with tomatoes and onions

lomilomi – massage

Lono – Polynesian god of harvest, agriculture, fertility and peace

loulu – native fan palms

luakini – a type of *heiau* dedicated to the war god Ku and used for human sacrifices

luau – traditional Hawaiian feast

mahalo – thank you

mahimahi – 'dolphin', a type of fish unrelated to the mammal

maile – native twining plant with fragrant leaves often used in leis

makaainana – common people; literally 'people who tend the land'

makaha – sluice gates

makahiki – ancient annual four-month winter harvest festival dedicated to Lono when sports and celebrations replaced all warfare

makaku – creative artistic mana

makai – towards the sea

malasada – a fried dough served warm, similar to a doughnut

malihini – newcomer, visitor

malo – loincloth

mana – spiritual power

manini – convict tang (a reef fish); also used to refer to something small or insignificant

mauka – towards the mountains; inland

mele – song, chant

menehune – 'little people' who according to legend built many of Hawaii's fishponds, heiaus and other stonework

milo – a native shade tree with beautiful hardwood

moo – water spirit, lizard spirit, water lizard or dragon

mu – a 'body catcher', who secured sacrificial victims for the heiau altar

muu-muu – a long, loose-fitting dress introduced by the missionaries

naupaka – a native shrub with delicate white flowers that look torn in half

Neighbor Islands – the term used to refer to the main Hawaiian islands outside of Oahu

nene – a native goose; Hawaii's state bird

nisei – people of Japanese descent

noni – Indian mulberry; a small tree with

yellow, warty, smelly fruit, used medicinally

nuku puu – a native honeycreeper with a bright-yellow underbelly

ohana – family, extended family

ohelo – low-growing native shrub with edible red berries related to cranberries, said to be sacred to Pele

ohia lehua – native Hawaiian tree; the flowers, most often red, are tufted feathery pompoms

okole – buttocks

olo – surfboards used by alii

ono – delicious; also the name of the wahoo fish

opae – shrimp

opakapaka – pink snapper fish

opihi – edible limpet

pahoehoe – type of lava which flows quickly and smoothly

pakalolo – marijuana; literally 'crazy smoke'

pali – cliff

palila – native honeycreeper

paniolo – a Hawaiian cowboy; the word is derived from 'espanole', as Hawaii's first cowboys were Mexican and Spanish

pau – finished, no more

Pele – goddess of fire and volcanoes, who lives in Kilauea volcano

pho – a Vietnamese soup of beef broth, noodles and fresh herbs

piko – navel, umbilical cord

pili – a bunch grass, commonly used for thatching houses

pilikia – trouble

pipikaula – a salted, dried beef served broiled

poha – gooseberry

poi – a gooey paste made from taro roots, a staple food of the Hawaiian diet

poke – chopped raw fish marinated in soy sauce, oil and chili peppers

Poliahu – goddess of snow

pua aloalo – hibiscus flower

pueo – Hawaiian owl

puka – any kind of hole or opening

pupu – snack food, hors d'oeuvres; shells

puu – hill, cinder cone

puuhonua – place of refuge

saimin – a Japanese noodle soup

tabi – Japanese reef-walking shoes

talk story – to strike up a conversation, make small talk

tapa – cloth made by pounding and mashing the bark of the paper mulberry tree; used for early Hawaiian clothing. In Hawaiian: *kapa*

taro – a plant, with green heart-shaped leaves, cultivated in Hawaii for its edible rootstock. The root is mashed to make *poi*. In Hawaiian, taro is pronounced *kalo*.

teishoku – Japanese word for fixed-plate meal

teppanyaki – Japanese style of cooking with an iron grill

ti – common native plant; its long shiny 'multi-purpose' leaves are used for a variety of things, including plates and *hula* skirts. In Hawaiian: *ki*

tutu – aunt, older woman

ukulele – a stringed musical instrument derived from the 'braginha', which was introduced to Hawaii in the 1800s by Portuguese immigrants

ulu – breadfruit

ulu maika – ancient Hawaiian game

wahine – woman

wana – sea urchin

wikiwiki – hurry, quick

Index

PLANET TALK

Lonely Planet's FREE quarterly newsletter

We love hearing from you and think you'd like to hear from us.

When... is the right time to see reindeer in Finland?
Where... can you hear the best palm-wine music in Ghana?
How... do you get from Asunción to Areguá by steam train?
What... is the best way to see India?

Every issue is packed with up-to-date travel news and advice including:

- a letter from Lonely Planet founders Tony and Maureen Wheeler
- travel diary from a Lonely Planet author – find out what it's really like out on the road
- feature article on an important and topical travel issue
- a selection of recent letters from our readers
- the latest travel news from all over the world
- details on Lonely Planet's new and forthcoming releases

To join our mailing list contact any Lonely Planet office (addresses below).

LONELY PLANET PUBLICATIONS
Australia: PO Box 617, Hawthorn 3122, Victoria (☎ 03-819-1877, fax 03-819-6459)
USA: Embarcadero West, 155 Filbert Street, Suite 251, Oakland, CA 94607
  (☎ 510-893-8555, toll-free 800-275-8555, fax 510-893-8563)
UK: 10 Barley Mow Passage, Chiswick, London W4 4PH (☎ 0181-742 3161)
France: 71 bis rue du Cardinal Lemoine, 75005 Paris (☎ 1-46 34 00 58)

Also available: Lonely Planet T-shirts. 100% heavyweight cotton (S, M, L, XL)

Guides to the Americas

Alaska – a travel survival kit
Jim DuFresne has traveled extensively through Alaska by foot, road, rail, barge and kayak, and tells how to make the most of one of the world's great wilderness areas.

Argentina, Uruguay & Paraguay – a travel survival kit
This guide gives independent travelers all the essential information on three of South America's lesser known countries. Discover some of South America's most spectacular natural attractions in Argentina; friendly people and beautiful handicrafts in Paraguay; and Uruguay's wonderful beaches.

Baja California– a travel survival kit
For centuries, Mexico's Baja peninsula – with its beautiful coastline, raucous border towns and crumbling Spanish missions – has been a land of escapes and escapades. This book describes how and where to escape in Baja.

Bolivia – a travel survival kit
From lonely villages in the Andes to ancient ruined cities and the spectacular city of La Paz, Bolivia is a magnificent blend of everything that inspires travelers. Discover safe and intriguing travel options in this comprehensive guide.

Brazil – a travel survival kit
From the mad passion of Carnival to the Amazon – home of the richest ecosystem on earth – Brazil is a country of mythical proportions. This guide has all the essential travel information.

Canada – a travel survival kit
This comprehensive guidebook has all the facts on the USA's huge neighbor – the Rocky Mountains, Niagara Falls, ultramodern Toronto, remote villages in Nova Scotia, and much more.

Central America on a shoestring
Practical information on travel in Belize, Guatemala, Costa Rica, Honduras, El Salvador, Nicaragua and Panama. A team of experienced Lonely Planet authors reveals the secrets of this culturally rich, geographically diverse and breathtakingly beautiful region.

Chile & Easter Island – a travel survival kit
Travel in Chile is easy and safe, with possibilities as varied as the countryside. This guide also gives detailed coverage of Chile's Pacific outpost, mysterious Easter Island.

Colombia – a travel survival kit
Colombia is a land of myths – from the ancient legends of El Dorado to the modern tales of Gabriel García Márquez. The reality is beauty and violence, wealth and poverty, tradition and change. This guide shows how to travel independently and safely in this exotic country.

Costa Rica – a travel survival kit

Winner of the Lowell Thomas Travel Journalism award, this best selling guidebook offers complete coverage of Costa Rica. Sun-drenched beaches, steamy jungles, smoking volcanoes, rugged mountains and dazzling birds and animals – it's all here!

Eastern Caribbean – a travel survival kit

Powdery white sands, clear turquoise waters, lush jungle rainforest, balmy weather and a laid back pace, make the islands of the Eastern Caribbean an ideal destination for divers, hikers and sun-lovers. This guide will help you to decide which islands to visit to suit your interests and includes details on inter-island travel.

Ecuador & the Galápagos Islands – a travel survival kit

Ecuador offers a wide variety of travel experiences, from the high cordilleras to the Amazon plains – and 600 miles west, the fascinating Galápagos Islands. Everything you need to know about traveling around this enchanting country.

Guatemala, Belize & Yucatán: La Ruta Maya – a travel survival kit

Climb a volcano, explore the colorful highland villages or laze your time away on coral islands and Caribbean beaches. The lands of the Maya offer a fascinating journey into the past which will enhance appreciation of their dynamic contemporary cultures. An award winning guide to this exotic region.

Mexico – a travel survival kit

A unique blend of Indian and Spanish culture, fascinating history, and hospitable people, make Mexico a travelers' paradise.

Peru – a travel survival kit

The lost city of Machu Picchu, the Andean altiplano and the magnificent Amazon rainforests are just some of Peru's many attractions. All the travel facts you'll need can be found in this comprehensive guide.

South America on a shoestring

This practical guide provides concise information for budget travelers and covers South America from the Darien Gap to Tierra del Fuego.

Trekking in the Patagonian Andes

The first detailed guide to this region gives complete information on 28 walks, and lists a number of other possibilities extending from the Araucanía and Lake District regions of Argentina and Chile to the remote icy tip of South America in Tierra del Fuego.

Venezuela – a travel survival kit

Venezuela is a curious hybrid of a Western-style civilization and a very traditional world contained with a beautiful natural setting. From the beaches along the Caribbean coast and the snow-capped peaks of the Andes to the capital, Caracas, there is much for travelers to explore. This comprehensive guide is packed with 'first-hand' tips for travel in this fascinating destination.

Also available:

Brazilian phrasebook, **Latin American Spanish** phrasebook and **Quechua** phrasebook.

Lonely Planet Guidebooks

Lonely Planet guidebooks cover every accessible part of Asia as well as Australia, the Pacific, South America, Africa, the Middle East, Europe and parts of North America. There are five series: *travel survival kits*, covering a country for a range of budgets; *shoestring guides* with compact information for low-budget travel in a major region; *walking guides; city guides* and *phrasebooks*.

Europe

Baltic States & Kaliningrad
Central Europe • Central Europe phrasebook
Czech & Slovak Republics • Dublin
Eastern Europe • Eastern
Europe phrasebook • Finland
France • Greece • Hungary
Iceland, Greenland & the Faroes
Ireland • Italy • Mediterranean Europe
Mediterranean Europe phrasebook
Poland • Prague • Russian phrasebook
Scandinavian & Baltic Europe
Scandinavian Europe phrasebook
Switzerland • Trekking in Greece
Trekking in Spain • USSR • Vienna
Western Europe • Western Europe phrase

North America

Alaska • Baja California
Canada • Hawaii • Mexico

Central America

Central America • Costa Rica
Guatemala, Yucatán & Belize: La Ruta Maya
Eastern Caribbean • Latin American
Spanish phrasebook

Africa

Africa • Arabic (Moroccan) phrasebo
Central Africa • East Africa
Kenya • Morocco • South Africa, Les
Swaziland • Swahili phrasebook
Trekking in East Africa • West Afr
Zimbabwe, Botswana & Namibia

South America

Argentina, Uruguay & Paraguay
Bolivia • Brazil • Brazilian phrasebook
Chile & Easter Island • Colombia
Ecuador & the Galápagos Islands
Peru • Quechua phrasebook
South America • Trekking in the
Patagonian Andes • Venezuela